A DEMON CALLED FIRE

A History of the

Keene, N.H. Fire Department

1745–2003

Drawing by Jaime Goldsmith.

A DEMON CALLED FIRE

A History of the
Keene, N.H. Fire Department
1745-2003

Compiled by Deputy Chief
Stevens W. Goldsmith, Retired

PETER E. RANDALL PUBLISHER
Portsmouth, New Hampshire
2012

© 2012 Stevens Goldsmith
All Rights Reserved.
First printing 2012

ISBN: 978-1-937721-04-6

Library of Congress Control Number: 2012942424

Published by
Peter E. Randall Publisher
Box 4726
Portsmouth, NH 03802

www.perpublisher.com

Book design: Grace Peirce
www.nhmuse.com

Additional copies available from:
    Stevens Goldsmith
    522 Old Walpole Rd.
    Surry NH 03431

Further Reading:

City of Keene, N.H. *Annual Report of the City of Keene containing Inaugural Ceremonies, Ordinances and Joint Resolutions Passed by the City Councils, with Reports of the Several Departments.* Sentinel Printing Company, Printers; Keene, N.H., 1874 - 1951.

Griffin, S.G. *A History of the Town of Keene: From 1732, when the Township was Granted by Massachusetts, to 1874, when it Became a City.* Sentinel Printing Company; Keene, N.H., 1904.

Keene History Committee. *Upper Ashuelot: A History of Keene, New Hampshire.* City of Keene, N.H., 1968.

Sturtevant, Isaac. *Report of the Superintending School Committee of Keene, N.H.: Also the Financial Report of the Selectmen, and the Report of the Chief Engineer, for the Year Ending March 10, 1857.* Keene, N.H., 1700(s) – 1873.

Created by Darlene Racicot Ontario, Canada

The Fire Fighter's Prayer

When I am called to duty, God
Wherever flames may rage
Give me strength to save some life
Whatever be its age.
Help me embrace a little child
Before it is too late
Or save an older person from
The horror of that fate.
Enable me to be alert
And hear the weakest shout,
And quickly and efficiently
To put the fire out.
I want to fill my calling
And to give the best in me,
To guard my friend and neighbor
And protect their property
And if, according to my fate,
I am to lose my life:
Please bless with your protecting hand
My children and my wife.

Keene Fire Department Mission Statement

*T*o protect our customers and keep them safe to provide the highest level of service to protect life, property and the environment through life safety education, prevention and inspection services, emergency planning and preparedness, efficient and effective response to all calls for assistance including fire, medical rescue and hazardous materials emergencies and other natural and man made disasters, that are delivered 24 hours a day by highly trained professionals who serve with excellence, dedication and pride.

Our Mission

The City of Keene Fire Department is a well-managed organization. Its leadership is committed to providing excellent service and has encouraged efforts to improve the service quality in all of its department related fields throughout the membership of the Keene Fire Department.

Our goal is to consistently provide and constantly, strive to improve the best possible service to the citizens of our community and to the Keene Fire Department. We are here to protect our community and to meet the ever-changing role of the Fire Service in the reduction of loss of life and property. The department exists to serve the citizens of the community and its members. Our service is not limited to traditional fire department roles, it is constantly changing to meet the needs of its customer and provide new innovative ways to accomplish our goals.

Our mission statement says that we will provide our service in the "highest level of professional trained personnel who serve with excellence, dedication and pride" It is our people that are the key to successfully fulfilling this mission; the department can be no stronger than its membership. We are proud to be a member of the Keene Fire Department. We accept the challenges of today and plan for tomorrow, which includes a commitment to our department and the customers that we serve through out the county. It is this positive commitment that has made us what we are today, and through constant assessment, will sustain us and guide us to continued excellence in the future.

Preface

ire has always been a constant threat. The need for safer community and a need to protect life and property have evolved from those with a leather bucket to the modern day firefighting equipment.

What then, was it like in the 'good old days'? In the 1700s and into the 1800s firefighting was a full community fight. It took every man, woman and even children to move buckets, the water supply, to and from the fire to protect the property. Keene as a community followed, as did the rest of the nation.

The fire service throughout our country has and still holds a noble tradition of service. In the days before motorized apparatus the power for mobility and for operation was furnished by manpower and later we moved into the horse drawn and steam age. This age was full of glamour and excitement and brought a new revelation to the fire service. In the days of the bygone era has a very noble tradition, because those firefighters were tremendously proud of their apparatus and of their ability to make best use there of.

As Keene moved from hand drawn apparatus you'll note that there were several fire companies throughout the City of Keene. When we moved into the steam era Keene began to move to it's local building at Central Fire Station on Vernon Street where we are still housed. The governing factor for locating firehouses was usually the distance a man could run. As times moved on and apparatus became better and faster the need to consolidate was completed.

The City of Keene is a well-managed community. Its leadership is committed to providing excellent service and has encouraged efforts to improve the service quality in all of its departments.

Our Fire Department is a unique organization, not just within the fire service in the State of New Hampshire, but Nationwide. One example of the is that the City of Keene was used as a national test center for the NFPA Learn Not To Burn program, quite an accomplishment for a rather small fire department organization. We are constantly being recognized for our innovations and programs that meet the need of our customer, both internal as well as external. We are frequently asked "What makes the Keene Fire Department so unique?" The answer to this question is simple: "It is our people and our philosophy to go that extra mile for our citizens, to provide a service that as members of the department we would be proud to sign our name too." As a department, we demanded excellence.

As you look ahead you will get a glimpse of how it was, and how it is today to be a Keene, New Hampshire Firefighter. This is the Creation of a Fire Fighter.

The Creation of the Fire Fighter

When the Lord was creating fire fighters, he was into his sixth day of overtime when an angel appeared and said, "You're doing a lot of fiddling around with this one."

And the Lord said, "Have you read the specification on this person? Fire fighters have to be able to go for hours fighting fires or tending to a person that the usual everyday person would never touch, while putting in the back of their minds the circumstances. They have to be able to move at a second's notice and not think twice of what they are about to do, no matter what danger. They have to be in top physical condition at all times, running on half-eaten meals, and they must have six pairs of hands."

The angel shook her head slowly and said, "Six pairs of hands….no way."

"It's not the hands that are causing me the problems," said the Lord, "it's the three pairs of eyes a fire fighter has to have."

"That's on the standard model?" asked the angel.

The Lord nodded. "One pair to see through the fire and where they and their fellow fire fighters should fight the fire next. Another pair here in the side of the head to see their fellow fire fighter and keep them safe. And another pair of eyes in the front so that they can look for the victims caught in the fire who needs their help."

"Lord" said the angel, touching his sleeve, "rest and work on this tomorrow."

"I can't" said the Lord, "I already have a model than can carry a 250-pound man down a flight of stairs to safety from a burning building, and can feed a family of five on a civil service paycheck."

The angel circled the model of the fire fighter very slowly, "Can it think?"

"You bet," said the Lord. "They can tell you the elements of a hundred fires and can recite procedures in their sleep that are needed to care for a person until they reach the hospital. And all the while they have to keep their wits about them. Fire fighters also have phenomenal personal control. They can deal with a scene full of pain and hurt, coaxing a child's mother into letting go of the child so that they can care for the child in need. And still they rarely get the recognition for a job well done from anybody, other than from fellow fire fighters."

Finally, the angel bent over and ran her finger across the cheek of the fire fighter. "There's a leak," she pronounced. "Lord, it's a tear. What's the tear for?"

"It' a tear from bottled-up emotions for fallen comrades. A tear for commitment to that funny piece of cloth called the American Flag. It's a tear for all the pain and suffering they have encountered. And it's a tear for their commitment to caring for and saving lives of their fellow man!"

"What a wonderful feature. Lord, you're a genius," said the angel.

The Lord looked somber and said, "I didn't put it there."

A fire fighter is a special breed of men and women, they look at things different than anyone else, for the men and women who wear the uniform and have the title of FIRE-FIGHTER are truly those of the Keene Fire Department.

~ *author unknown*

Contents

Downtown Keene NH, looking South from Central Square. Photo by Stevens Goldsmith, 2008

Keene Central Fire Station located at 32 Vernon St., Keene NH. Aerial view. Photo by Stevens Goldsmith, 2008

Central Fire Station, 2008, across from the fire station on Vernon Street, Keene NH. Top photo shows the ladder bay, which was added to the central station in 1971. Photos by Stevens Goldsmith

Historical Roots: The 1700s

Note: Clifford C. Wilber, writer for the **Sentinel,** *wrote a long series of articles called "The Good Old Days in the 1930s." Clifford wrote the* **Early Years of the Fire Department.** *This text is from the original book and notes. Fires were documented in the original book which is kept at the Historical Society of Cheshire County.*

*A*s the Village of Keene and surrounding areas were plagued by attacks from Native Americans (Indians) in the 1730s and through the 1740s the entire area was at their mercy. Of the 31 houses in Keene 27 were burned including the Fort on Main Street and the partly finished Meetinghouse. Fire has been as then and now a constant problem and as times changed so did the demand for fire protection.

The name Keene for which the city was named was chosen out of gratitude to and admiration for Sir Benjamin Keene who, while British Minister to Spain, had used his influence, though unsuccessfully, to help Provincial Governor Benning Wentworth obtain payment for timber delivered at Cadiz.

In the 1750s the village was rebuilt and Keene was growing. The village was relocated where the First Settlement had been planted on lower Main Street. In 1754 a new Meetinghouse was built which served as the Court House and Town Hall, and was a bit east of the present Soldiers Monument in Central Square.

Several returning settlers had replaced their crude log cabins in Keene with more substantial homes. The oldest still existing is Seth Heaton's house, now on Marlboro Street. No. 500 began in 1750. David Nims's house, formerly on Washington Street was moved in later years to 29 Page Street. Ephraim Dorman's house on Boston Street, later named Baker Street near Thomas Baker's tannery

was another early home in town and built during the resettlement of Keene or shortly thereafter. Quoting from *Upper Ashuelot, A History of Keene, N.H.* (page 19):

from Clifford C. Wilber:

As the village grew in 1760 the road known as the Old Westmoreland Road was laid out and is now called the Hurricane Road. The village began to grow and in 1762 Captain Isaac Wyman's home opened for the purpose of a tavern and is now 339 Main Street. Taverns and public houses spread throughout the village.

In 1767 the population of Keene was 427 and by 1775 it had increased to 756. In April of that year the American Revolutionary War took shape and Keene's local Commander Captain Ephraim Dorman of the local militia, along with the help of Captain Isaac Wyman set forth a list of men to go and fight the Regulars in Concord Mass. On April 22, 1775 the men met at sunrise before the tavern, drew supplies, and began the march. The war and New Hampshire Patriots endured a rough road throughout the remaining years of the war.

By the 1780s the move was for most citizens to get back to the normal routine of work and improve their standard of living. In 1786 Keene's total population was 1,122 and by 1790 it had grown to 1,314. On November 3, 1784 it was voted to build a new Meetinghouse with a belfry, which is now the First

Congregational Church at the head of the square.

On October 29, 1788 the construction of a new Meetinghouse began, with a tower at the west end in which a bell was to be hung. The bell was first hung in 1792. The town voted in March 1792 to purchase the bell for eighty pounds. In 1794 a vote was made to purchase a larger bell weighing 1,000 pounds and procured by Judge Daniel Newcomb for the town and the church. In February of 1794 another subscription was undertaken. This was to purchase a clock and keep it in repair for ten years for the sum of thirty-six pounds. The architect and master builder was Benjamin Archer. The Meetinghouse was raised in June of 1786 and its size was 70 feet by 50 feet. This created a gala event and social gathering place for the village of Keene. This building still remains in Central Square as the United Congregational Church. The new Meetinghouse was located at the common. Stores sprang up in that area and Central Square took form. This increased activity and construction is now known as Central Square.

The church bell was tolled for special events, important news, reporting of fires or calling people together for such events as when General George Washington died. Abijah Wilder Jr., then only 15 years old climbed to the church tower and tolled the bell all night.

On March 23, 1799 The *New Hampshire Sentinel* was born by John Prentiss. Within six months it had attracted 250 readers at a subscription price of $1.50 a year. This was paid for by barter in wood, butter and grain as well as cash.

By April 6, 1781 the Council and House of Representatives recognized the need for an amended fire code. It was recognized that when fires break out, "Goods inevitably are exposed to plunder, some handy and evil minded persons taking advantage of the calamity to steal such goods, whereby the loss of such sufferers is increased." Provision was made for the election of "any suitable number of free holders, persons of approved ability and fidelity, to be denominated Fire Wards." The distinguishing badge of office was a staff five feet long, painted red and headed with a bright brass spine six inches long. These Fire Wards were required, "upon a notice of the breaking out of fire, to take with them the badges of their office and immediately repair to the place where such fire may be, and vigorously exert themselves, then require and demand assistance of any inhabitants of the town, to extinguish and prevent the spreading of such fire and remove goods and effects out of any houses or places endangered thereby." The Fire Wards had power to appoint necessary guards to care for property thus removed. In 1794 "Fire Wards" were appointed as well as an "Inspector Of Measure." The principal streets in town on which the "Fire Wards" walked with their badge were Main Street, or simply "Keene" or "Town" Street; Pleasant Street, later Mill Street (West Street); Prison or sometimes Jail Street (Washington Street); School Street and later part of Court Street Packer Field Road (Water Street); Frog Lane (Church Street) and later part of Court Street.

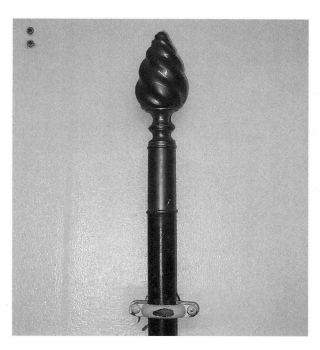

The Fire Ward Staff Presented to the Steamer Company by Mrs. Hadley P. Muchmore and Mr. H.P. Muchmore (Chief KFD 1863-1866). This badge hangs in the Keene Central Fire Station today. Photo by Steven Goldsmith.

1785 — As the village of Keene grew so did its needs. Between Gilbo Ave. where the railroad tracks were and the head of central square, there were only four buildings of importance. These being: the Meetinghouse, the third to be built in Keene, standing with its south side nearly on a line with the present northerly boundary of Roxbury street; the wooden store building of Josiah Richardson at the corner of West Street; a "ten footer" on the east side of Main Street, about midway between the present Roxbury Street and Church Street and Moses Johnson's first house and store on the northerly corner of the present Railroad Street. All of the buildings were separated by considerable distances. By 1790 the population of Keene was 1,314.

Eighty pounds was raised in 1792 for the purchase of a bell for the meetinghouse, which would be used to notify the town's people of an important event or emergency. This new bell was installed along with a clock for the belfry in the new Meetinghouse.

Village of Keene

George Sturtevant (from S. Hale: Annals of Keene, 1851)

REFERENCES.

1.—Judge Newcomb.
2.—Maj. Willard.
3.—Dorman house.
4.—Thomas Baker.
5.—Old Cemetery.
6.—School House.
7.—Blake's Tavern.
8.—Dr Adams.—Post Office.
9.—Lockhart Willard.
10.—School House.
11.—Washburn house.
12.—David Simmons.
13.—Thomas Field's house and shop.
14.—Eli Metcalf.
15.—Thomas Shapley.
16.—Widow Goodnow.
17.—Thomas Wells.
18.—Old Printing Office.
19.—Samuel Dinsmoor.
20.—Abel Blake.
21.—Alexander Ralston.
22.—Low shops.
23.—Ralston's tavern.
24.—Bemis, watch maker.
25.—Ralston's distillery.
26.—Dunbar house.
27.—Masonic Hall.
28.—Peter Wilder's house and shop.
29.—Luther Smith's shop.
30.—Dr Ziba Hall.
31.—Moses Johnson's house.
32.—Coopers' shops.
33.—Dinsmoor's office.—Store.—Printing Office.
34.—Dr Edwards's tavern.
35.—Peleg Sprague's house and office.
36.—Daniel Watson.
37.—Watson's shop.
38.—Johnson's store.
39.—Joseph Dorr's store.
40.—Lamson's Tannery.
41.—Dwelling house in rear of Johnson's store.
42.—Draper's Bake House.
43.—James Morse.
44.—Noah Cooke.
45.—Saw Mill.
46.—Grist Mill.
47.—Nathan Blake.
48.—James Wyman,
49.—John Warner.
50.—Dr Charles Blake.
51.—William Lamson.
52.—Rev. Aaron Hall.
53.—Josiah Richardson.
54.—Abijah Wilder.
55.—Moses Johnson's pot and pearlash works.
56.—Israel Houghton.
57.—Nehemiah Towns.
58.—Elias Rugg.
59.—Samuel Bassett.
60.—Asahel Blake.
61.—Court House.
62.—Meeting House.
63.—Allen & Bond's store.
64.—David Forbes's office.
65.—Blacksmith's shop.
66.—Dwelling house and shop.
67.—Dr M'Carty.
68.—Dr M'Carty's small house.
69.—Spinney house and shop.
70.—Samuel Daniels.
71.—Alpheus Nims.
72.—Eliphalet Briggs.
73.—Jeremiah Stiles.
74.—Joseph Stiles.
75.—Grout house.
76.—Jail.
77.—Abel Wilder.
78.—School House.
79.—Nathaniel Briggs.
80.—Horse sheds.
81.—Cemetery.
82.—Warner's Fulling Mill.

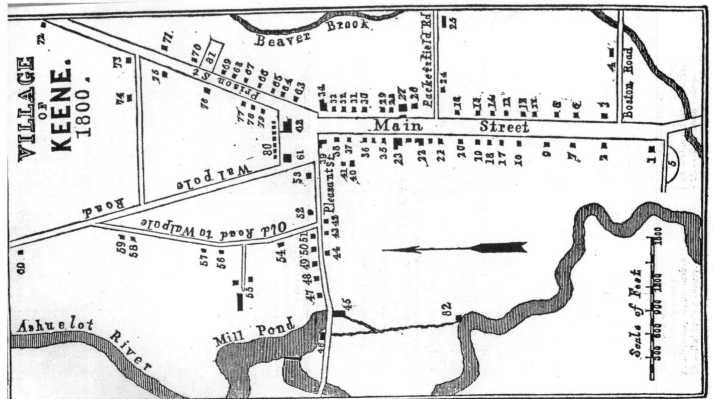

The 1800s

Note: from 1700 to 1873 all reports in this book are from Town of Keene Annual Reports. From 1874 to present, reports are from the City of Keene Annual Reports.

The population had grown to 1,645 by 1800, but brought little change to the fire community. It is noted that throughout the village there were numerous fire companies with each being said to have a few men trained and an engine housed within a structure. Examples of this were: the Neptune House and the Wyman Tavern both on Main street; Thomas Baker's Tannery off Baker Street; as well as in most of the industrial locations, such as the Faulkner and Colony Mill area and also other taverns throughout the area. In the West Keene area, at present Hurricane Road, was Jesse Clark's Mill and Tavern, which also housed a blacksmith shop. Just up the road from there was the pottery shop of Zebulon Neal & Co., which housed a small engine brigade for the area. Fire was a constant threat and as laws were passed each house and business throughout the village of Keene was required by law to have leather fire buckets in each house in case of fire. The first leather fire buckets were made by the shoemakers and hand sewn of the best tanned sole leather. The leather buckets were generally hung at the front of the house so when an alarm or cry of fire was sounded and the cry taken up, "Throw out your buckets," the residents would race to the fire with the buckets and form lines from the nearest water supply. Once the nearest source of water was located, two lines of citizens were formed in order to extinguish the fire or to supply the engine, which had been pulled by people to the fire scene. When the fire was out (more likely burned out), the buckets were loaded into a cart and carried back to the Village Meetinghouse where the Fire Wards would send out to announce that the buckets were ready to be returned to the owners by the familiar cry, "Claim your buckets!"

Leather Buckets, wood buckets, used in line passing one person to another and water thrown on the fire, then passed back for refill.

[*Compiler's note*: Fire buckets were the first means of controlling fires. Every family household hung a bucket in front of their house with the owner's name on it, like in the above picture. Buckets were also used to supply water to the hand pump engines. These buckets belonged to members of the Keene Fire Department and are displayed in the Central Fire Department Station today on Vernon Street, Keene, N.H.]

Until the 1800s private citizens furnished most of the leather fire buckets, but as time progressed it was found that this system had become unsatisfactory due to neglect of the buckets. These leather fire buckets were of

Copy of the Original Keene Fire Engine Company Records Book and the list of Original Subscribers for an Engine in 1808. From original book.

Subscribers For an Engine Or Keene Fire Engine Company Incorporated June 13th, 1808

Daniel Newcomb	Elijah Parker
Alexander Ralston	Zebadiah Kise
Daniel Watson	Wyman & Chapman
William Lamson	Thomas Edwards
Noah Cooke	William M. Bond
John G. Bond	James H. Bradford
Joseph Brown	Aron Appleton
John Prentiss	Abel Blake
Daniel Adams	Foster Alexander
Adijah Wilder	Hatch & Hall
Luther Smith	Eliphalet Briggs Jr
Able Cady	Francis Faulkner
Nathaniel Sprague	Azel Wilder
John Elliot	David Wilder
Gilbert Mellen	Josiah Willard
Justus Perry	Dan Hough
Josiah Richardson	Samuel Dinsmoor
Edward Sprague	Minoni Shutliffe
Elijah Dunbar	Ithamar Chase
Joseph Dorr	Wilder & Holbrook
Mann & Wood	Timothy Hall

various shapes and sizes. The capacity was fixed by law however, and varied between 2 ½ to 3 gallon capacities. They were usually marked with the name or initials of the owner. Many were emblazoned in paints with coat-of-arms names and even portraits or other designs. It was also required by law to have a number of buckets, being determined by the number of chimneys. One chimney required two buckets and two chimneys required three to four buckets and three chimneys required four to five buckets. Any home with four or more chimneys was required to have six buckets and a ladder.

In 1805 the number of buildings within the Main street area had grown from 4 to 16. This increase in the number of buildings created a menace of fire outbreaks throughout the village. With the enhanced danger of fire, a group of businessmen, who owned property within the Central Square and Main Street areas, felt that there was a great need for a fire engine. Hence, the first fire engine in Keene was not purchased or owned by the village of Keene, but by a company of citizens. A notice appeared in the *Keene Sentinel* that "the subscribers to the fire engine were to meet at Mr. Holbrook's tavern May 5th, 1806" in order to organize a fire engine company.

In 1808, but prior to March 22, 1808, the village used citizens to fight most of the fires. During that time 42 prominent members decided it was time to incorporate and make a Fire Department called "Proprietors of the Fire Engine." The first meeting was held on the evening of March 22nd, 1808 at the Pierce's Tavern, which was located at the present site of the Cheshire House Block at the corner of Roxbury Street and Main Street. At this meeting Noah Cooke was elected Chairman and Albe Cady was elected Secretary. Also at this meeting a committee was voted in to draw up laws, rules and regulations for governing the corporation. The committee was made up of Able Cady, Elijah Dunbar and James Mann. These regulations were drawn up and accepted on February 21st, 1809 and the society was incorporated under the name of "Keene Engine Company."

1808

A notice in the *Keene Sentinel* called for a meeting. "We the subscribers authorized and empowered by Law to call the first meeting of the Keene Engine Company, do hereby notify and warn, said Company to meet at the Dwelling-House of William Pierce, in Keene, on Monday the 6th day of February next, at 6 o'clock P.M. to act on the following articles; First - To choose a Moderator, Second - To elect officers, Third - To establish Rules and By-Laws as they may think necessary or proper, Fourth - To agree on the times and places for holding future meetings; and the method of calling the same and Fifth - To transact any other business relative to the duty of said Company, which circumstances may require. Given under our hands and seal at Keene, this 18th day of January A.D. 1809."

42 members mostly businessmen of Keene held a meeting. These members had given monies from their own pockets to form the Fire Society which had been formed under the name "Subscribers for an Engine" at the meeting on March 22, 1808, Officers voted being Noah Cooke, Chairman and Able Cady, Clerk. At this meeting it was voted that a committee be voted to draw up by-laws and a committee to find and erect a suitable building for the safe keeping of an engine which had been ordered. The committee set up to purchase land for a suitable building consisted of Samuel Dinsmoor, Aaron Hall and Mr. John Wood. They were to report back at the next meeting to be held on March 29, 1808. It was voted by the "General Court" an act to incorporate the "Proprietors for an Engine" under the name of "Keene Engine Company." This act was approved on June 13th, 1808, thus beginning the "History of the Keene Fire Department," which had been formed by 42 men. The fire engine and equipment was purchased by these members.

1809

The first meeting was held on February 6th, 1809 at William Pierce's Tavern on the present sight of the "Cheshire Block," located on the southeast corner of Roxbury Street.

Cheshire House Block picture from the Keene Fire Department scrapbook. HSCC collection.

The committee to draw up the By-Laws, Rules and Regulations necessary for governing their corporation was comprised of Able Cady, Elijah Dunbar and James Mann. The By-Laws Rules and Regulations of the society incorporated by the name of "Keene Engine Company" were accepted on February 21, 1809. The land for the first engine house was given by Noah Cooke, Esq. It was a small parcel of land south of Abijah Kingsbury's shop upon the west side of Main Street, which was a house suitable for the safe-keeping of the purchased engine. It was voted to accept the land and build the engine house immediately. It was also voted that a committee be appointed to erect an engine house 15X10 feet and 7 feet in height exclusive of the roof. Messrs, Able Wilder, John Prentiss and Aaron Hall were chosen. In addition it was voted that this committee be authorized to purchase a long hose and fire hooks.

The vote to erect an engine house on the land of Noah Cooke on the west side of the street places the first fire engine house in Keene near the present Main Street Sentinel building, perhaps slightly to the north of it. The cost of the 1st engine was $401.22

Keene Engine purchased by Keene Engine Co. between 1808 and 1810. From Fire Department records and City of Keene records.

At the meeting of March 27th, 1809 there were present, N. Cooke, D. Chapman, D. D. Hatch, A. Wilder, E. Dunbar, J. Willard, F. Alexander, Wm M. Bond, J. Wood, A. Blake, A. Hall, A. Cady, J. Mann, W. Wyman, L. Smith, J. G . Bond, J. Prentiss and D. Adams. Noah Cooke Esq. was chosen President

unanimously. Elijah Dunbar, William Wyman and John G. Bond were chosen Trustees; Albe Cady, Secretary and John Wood, Treasurer. 20 men were chosen at this meeting to constitute Keene's first fire engine company Listed below are those members: John Prentiss, Phinchas Cooke, Thomas F. Ames, Josiah Willard, James Wells, Josiah Capen, Worcester Morse, James Nutt, Jonas Royce, Zebina Billings, Joseph Davis, George W. Atwell, Enoch Bond, Ebenezer Daniels, Elisha Hunt, Amos Parmale, Daniel D. Hatch, Seth Newcomb, David Mead, Elijah Parker. Josiah Willard was chosen Captain, James Wells Assistant, and George W. Atwell Clerk. James Namm, William Lamson, William Wyman, John Bond and Daniel Adams were chosen to act as Fire Wards.

1810

On August 4th, 1810 fire broke out at the dwelling house of Abijah Foster at Ash Swamp, on the road now called "Hastings Ave." The dwelling was a tavern which was totally destroyed by the fire. Within the loss was "several hundred weight of cheese which was stored in the building." This was the fire that the engine, which had been purchased by the "Keene Engine Company," had its first use. However, the distance from the street or Central Square was so great that upon its arrival it was of little use except to prevent the spread of the fire to adjoining buildings.

1812

At a meeting held on January 12th, 1812 by the Keene Engine Company it was noted that the wells were in need of repair. It was voted to "immediately repair the pump in front of the meeting house and secure it against freezing." Also at this meeting the trustees authorized to procure one suitable fire hook and apparatus. At a meeting on January 10th, 1814 it was voted that the Trustees be authorized to "sink a well near the sign-post at the intersection of the Turnpike Road and Main Street." This well or cistern at the head of Main Street near the band stand (the use of which survived until aqueduct water was introduced) was not an enlargement of the well which had supplied the meeting-house, but was sunk in the year 1814 specifically for fire protection. The first well was believed to be just south of Central Square and had been dug in 1754 or soon after. At the meeting on January 10th, it was also voted that the Trustees procure 10 wooden and 2 leather fire buckets for the use of the engine company, and deposit them at the engine house. The first engine belonging to the company, as well as others subsequently owned would not draw water directly from a well. It had to be drawn to keep the engine filled by the use of buckets.

Two leather buckets, which used by Buckmister and Briggs of the Keene Fire Department. These 2 buckets are still in the fire department display case at the Central Fire Station, Vernon Street, Keene. Photo by Steven Goldsmith.

It was also voted at this meeting that Noah Cooke, Esq., Albe Cady and John Prentiss be appointed as a committee to petition the legislature for an act giving the Fire Wards chosen by this corporation the same authority that is given to Fire Wards chosen by towns who have adopted the act entitled "an act regulating the proceedings for extinguishing fires, etc.." As stated earlier the original act referred to was passed on April 6th, 1781. "Whereas it frequently happens where buildings contiguous take fire that the people assembled to extinguish it proceed without order or regularity, whereby the end in view is often defeated, and as goods at such times are inevitably exposed to plunder, some hardy, evil-minded persons take advantage of the calamity and steal such goods, whereby the loss of such Sufferers is increased." "Be it enacted that the freeholders, being qualified voters may at their annual or other legal town-meeting-house chose and appoint a suitable number of freeholders therein being persons of approved ability and fidelity, who shall be denominated Fire Wards, and have for a distinguishing badge of their office a staff 5 feet long, painted red, and headed with a bright brass spire 6 inches long." "The Fire Wards appointed are hereby required upon notice of the breaking out of fire to take with them the badge of their office and immediately repair to the place where such fire may be and vigorously exert themselves and require and demand assistance of any inhabitants to extinguish and prevent the spreading of such fire." The first Fire Wards were James Mann, William Wyman, John Bond and Daniel Adams. Note that the Fire Wards had power to inspect buildings and take command at fires. Additional regulations adopted in 1828, specified the number of leather buckets, ladders, and other equipment to be kept by each household (which every house with three fireplaces was to provide). While the introduction of the fire engine had been the means of saving many buildings from destruction, and had greatly reduced the fire hazard, its usefulness had been curtailed by a shortage in the water supply. The various wells, which had been sunk at this time had been done at the company's expense, and covered by assessments upon its members.

1815

At a meeting of the Keene Engine Company held at Sumner's tavern on January 2nd, 1815, it was voted that "any person living within one mile of the meeting-house in Keene who shall sink a well within the limits of the street, or within such distance as the trustees may consider convenient, and of such depth and dimensions as they may direct, and shall keep a suitable pump therein for the purpose of supplying the engine with water, shall be admitted a member of the society." It was also voted that the trustees be authorized to sink a well within 20 rods of Dr. Daniel Adams's dwelling house, which the house was then 324 Main Street.

1816

On January 1, 1816 a meeting of the Keene Engine Company was held at Chase's Inn, which was the former Ralston Tavern at this time kept by Ithamar Chase. At this meeting the Secretary was instructed to furnish the Treasurer with a list of the members absent from the meeting, and directed to collect the fines incurred as such absence agreeably to the By-Laws, which provided that: "Every member for not attending at the alarm of fire, if within a mile of the place shall be fined $1.00; for not keeping his buckets in good order or in their proper place 50 cents; for not attending the annual or any other meeting 50 cents; if an officer $1.00." At about this time, with the growing expenses of the company and the more frequent assessments upon its members, a larger membership seems to have been desired and we found many instances in the records where committees were appointed to invite certain persons who were named in the records, to become members of the organization.

1818

The Keene Engine Company failed to hold its annual meeting on January 1st, 1818 and John Wood, Aaron Hall, Timothy Hall, Elijah Parker, John Elliot and F. Alexander ("owners of more than one-sixteenth part of the property of said company") made application to Elijah Dunbar, Esq., a justice of the peace in and for the county of Cheshire to call such a meeting, which was held at Sumner's Inn, January 20th, 1818. At this meeting an assessment of $1.00 was made on each member, payable on or before April 1st next. It was voted that Samuel Dinsmoor, E. Dunbar, John Elliot, Daniel Adams and Z. Kise " are chosen a committee with full power in such way as they shall think proper to provide a supply of water for the engine, and to dispose of the pumps belonging to the company, excepting the one now standing near the meeting house."

1819

The next annual meeting of the Keene Engine Company was held at Wadley's Tavern on January 4th, 1819. Wadley's Tavern was the former Ralston Tavern, afterward kept by Ithamar Chase, who had died on August 8th, 1817 and was a member of the Keene Engine Company. He was succeeded by Jonathan E. Wadley who was the proprietor of the hotel known as the "Keene Hotel." It is also believed that Jonathan Wadley was the first in Keene to make use of the word "Hotel" in advertising a place of public entertainment. At the meeting of Jan 4th, 1819 the Trustees were authorized to sink a well in Prison Street, which is now Washington Street ("near Mr. Angier's house, if they think it expedient").

1820

The population of Keene was 1,865.
The annual meeting of January 1st, 1820 was also held at Wadley's Tavern and John Wood

was authorized to ascertain on the condition of the old engine and if it could be repaired or needed to be exchanged for a new one.

1822

On May 27th, 1822 the wooden tavern house where the first and many subsequent meetings of the Keene Engine Company was held, caught fire and burned. This was the first tavern house erected on the site of the former Cheshire House, and was opened by Mr. Lemuel Chandler, on October 27, 1788. On August 17th, 1811 an advertisement which appeared in the *Keene Sentinel* was the only known information on this tavern, which William Pierce offered for sale. The advertisement "To be sold or let, on reasonable terms, and possession given any time previous to the first of October next, that noted and it may be said with truth, the best stand for a public house in this part of the country, now improved by the subscriber, and situated near the Court House in Keene, in one of the pleasantest villages in New England, and in the most compact part, on the great and old established road from Boston to Montreal." "The premises consist of about 2 acres of land, a large and convenient house, 52x56, three stories high, with a spacious hall through the center of the third story from east to west, 56x27, handsomely arched. The outbuildings consist of 2 barns, wood and horse sheds are amply large and conveniently situated and all in good repair. The Boston & Montreal stages meet here three times a week at 7 pm., and depart the next morning at 4 am." This fire was the most destructive fire which had occurred since the purchase of the engine, but with the further assistance of a small fire engine belonging to the New Hampshire glass factory, it was confined to the building in which it originated. Note: This number of the *Keene Sentinel* is one of the 96 issues missing between 1799 and 1825 from the files of the *Keene Sentinel* in the Keene public library.

[From the original book, 1808, Records Subscribers for an engine:]

Note: In recording the story of this fire the history of Keene was such that the people were aroused to the importance of having a more efficient organization for extinguishing fires, but after mentioning the Keene Engine Company denotes the "Keene Fire Society" was also formed," making it appear that the latter named was a separate and additional organization, which in fact it was not. As a result of this fire the Keene Engine Company held a special meeting at Wadley's Tavern on June 15th, 1822. At that meeting it was "voted: that the President be requested to petition the legislature to have the name of the Keene Engine Company be altered to that of the "Keene Fire Society," and on June 28th, 1822, an Act was passed by the State Senate and House of Representatives to change the name from Keene Engine Company to the Keene Fire Society. Also at this meeting Aaron Appleton, Samuel Wood and Francis Faulkner were also directed to ascertain on what terms a new fire engine of the first class could be procured, and to report at the next meeting. The Trustees and Mr. John Wood were requested "to examine the state of the wells and see what if any new ones are necessary to be sunk, and examine the Beaver Brook and report on the expediency of turning it through the street to supply the reservoirs."

At an adjournment of the meeting, which was held August 14th, 1822 at "Wadley's Keene Hotel" which then stood on the southerly corner of the present Emerald and Main Street, Francis Faulkner, Aaron Appleton and Samuel Wood were chosen a committee "to purchase a new engine at their direction." Aaron Appleton, for the committee, reported that it was "necessary to sink the well at the crotch of the turnpike deeper." This is the cistern at the head of Main Street and this cistern was sunk in 1814." The treasurer was also instructed to collect the money subscribed for the purchase of a new engine when required. The Trustees were also empowered to "sink a well near Mr. John Prentiss's house, and what other ones they may think necessary, and deepen the old ones if necessary." It was voted to assess 50 cents on each member to defray the expense of sinking and deepening wells. The house of John Prentiss, founder of the *"Keene Sentinel,"* which is referred to, had been built by him on the west side of the Third New Hampshire turnpike in 1808. It was a large two and one-half story house, and was removed many years later for the erection of the residence now standing at 82 Court Street.

During the summer of 1822 a new hotel called the "Phoenix" had been rising from the ashes of the old tavern house that had burned in the spring of that year. It was the first brick hotel to be erected on that site, and in a sense, the last, for although the Phoenix was burned April 6th, 1836, the walls were left standing, and were made use of to a considerable extent in building the Cheshire House. The north wall for the Cheshire House was the last to be raised for the erection of the present Cheshire House Block on the Corner of Main and Roxbury Streets. This wall was undoubtedly the north wall of the former Phoenix Hotel, which was opened in December 1822 by George Sparhawk. This house was 52x56 feet, and if you look back to the description of the old tavern house that Mr. Pierce gave, you will find that the same dimensions given, so if the Phoenix was built on the same foundation.

1822 *[From Clifford C. Wilber]*

It was this fire on May 22nd, 1822 that put the village of Keene to the test and after the disaster of George Sparhawk Tavern the old Chandler House at the corner of Roxbury Street it was decided that maybe there was a need for another engine and more wells. It was at this fire the single engine aided by the Glass Factory smaller engine had all it could do but save the neighboring stores. Note: it was this fire that was the first recorded fire insurance payment in Keene. The insurance company was the Aetna Insurance Company and believed to be out of Boston Mass at the time of the fire.

————

In the *N.H. Sentinel* on August 21st, 1822 an Ad for the purchase of insurance and insurance was not new but was not to the price of everyone. This is how the Ad read:

"FIRE"

The Manufacture's Insurance Company, recently established in the City of Boston, for the express purpose of "insuring against fire," with a Capital of $300,000, now offer to manufactures throughout the United States, an opportunity of insuring their property against this destructive element, (which the greatest care and strictest attention cannot always prevent, and which, in an unfortunate moment, frequently reduces affluent and independent families to poverty and distress,) at such moderate rates, as cannot fail to induce owners of factories to secure themselves against loss.

The Company is in no manner restricted as to the description of risks, but will name premiums in all cases, however hazardous, and on the most favorable terms. Not only cotton, woolen, and other manufacturers, will be insured at this office, but also dwellings houses, stores, furniture, goods, and merchandize, with every other description of property subject to loss or injury by fire. The Company takes this opportunity to state the kind of information deemed most necessary to be made by the applicants, as the premiums, in a great measure will be graduated by their representation, to wit: The article goes on but in ending it says persons desirous of insurance who may reside out of the city, by forwarding their applications by mail or otherwise to the Secretary, may be assured the same will meet with immediate attention.

Samuel Hunt, Secretary, Office, NO.21 State Street, Boston, Mass.

———————

1823

On January 6th, 1823 the Keene Fire Society held its annual meeting at the Phoenix, on the site where they had organized as the "Keene Engine Company" about 15 years previously. At this meeting the Treasurer was again authorized to collect the money subscribed for a new engine "when required."

1824

At the annual meeting held at the Phoenix, January 5th, 1824 the trustees were requested to "remove and repair the engine house if they think expedient." This was the first engine house in town and was on Main Street just a little north of the Sentinel Building. It was about this time when Capt. John Towns built the brick store, which was torn down in 1893 for the erection of the Sentinel Building. Captain John Towns store when built most likely had an influence for the engine house to be moved elsewhere. The first firehouse was erected in 1808 and was on Main Street just slightly north of old Sentinel Building. Over the years the department headquarters moved several times and the locations; all unsatisfactory, and finally in 1884 the city purchased the property on Vernon Street the present site of the Firehouse. At this meeting the records indicate that a new fire engine had been secured, and the Trustees and Fire Wards were "requested to take charge of the old engine; to form a company of exempts to work it, and take such other measures to keep it in repair as they may deem expedient."

At the meeting of June 15th, 1822 it was also noted that the trustees and Mr. John Wood would be requested "to examine the state of the company's wells and see what if any new ones are necessary to be sunk, and examine the Beaver Brook and report on the expediency of turning it through the street to supply the reservoirs." Forty-five years later, the idea of bringing the waters of Beaver Brook into the central part of the village for the purpose of supplying the reservoirs with water was still being advocated. In 1866, before Goose Pond had been decided upon as the source of supply, the following paragraph appeared in the *N.H. Sentinel*. "We are told that in early times water in season of freshets used to flow across Main Street where the old railroad tracks crossed, and it was told that boys swim across Main Street under a bridge near that place." We find now as formerly, the water seeking this route extends from Beaver Brook through the new and ample ditches of Mr. Hutchins and others to the Cheshire Railroad woodshed. Now if we should lay down a ten inch wooden aqueduct thirty rods from the end of this shed to the reservoir in front of Dr. Twitchell's a fire engine stationed there might find a supply as long as water flowed over Beaver Brook falls." "Having once introduced the brook into this reservoir, everyone will see how for about $5 per rod, or less, this aqueduct may be continued on the same level, either south or north, perhaps as far as Central Square. A ditch of the depth required could best be dug in a dry season, for the aqueduct should be laid at low water mark, when wood will be as durable as iron. But it may be done at any time, and the great objection of expense which has defeated so many other plans does not seem to lie in the way of this."

———————

[*Compiler note*: On May 27th, 1822 the wooden tavern house burned and in the *N.H. Sentinel*, Saturday June 1st, 1822 the article appeared as follows:]

"FIRE"

The inhabitants of the village were alarmed on Monday night about 11 o'clock by the flames bursting through the roof of the large three story Stage-Tavern-House, owned by E. Parker, Esq. & Mr. Timothy Hall, and occupied by Mr. George Sparhawk. Before a sufficient number of the citizens could be collected to work the principal engine, all expectation of saving the building thus enveloped, was lost and every effort was directed to stop its further progress, and rescue from the flames as much of the furniture and other property in the house, as possible. As the fire broke out in the upper story, or garret in the S.W. corner of the house, the store of Mr. Wheelock situated only 20 feet south was at most imminently endangered providentially, the air was very still and before the heat became excessive, that part of the roof of this building which was most exposed was covered with blankets and it was kept perfectly soaked with the engine. By the time the air was in motion, and the flames had extended to the North, in the direction of the wind and the store of Mr. Laimson Mr. Clarke, (in which the Post Office was kept) with that of Col. J. Perry, adjoining, it was feared must fall a sacrifice. The small but very efficient factory engine now arrived, which was sufficient to guard effectively the store at the south, while every means was used to keep that on the north from taking fire. The water having failed in the cistern on the common, a line was promptly formed to the brook ¼ of a mile to the East. By this time the air was filled with burning cinders, which took a direction over the Meetinghouse and all the buildings to the north to a great extent, and it was soon discovered that the roof of the Meetinghouse was blazing near the ridgepole. This was quickly extinguished, by the engine on the outside and by water thrown from the upper flooring in the inside. The engine then repaired to the defense of the store, and the great and extraordinary efforts of the people, was crowned with great success. The stores on either side present the appearance of a ghost siege – that on the north, 50 feet from the burning house, having several times

caught, and was readily extinguished. No one who viewed the ruins ever thought it would be possible to save all the buildings, which were surrounded. Everything that could be done was promptly put in execution and it is a pleasing reflection that citizens yield a ready obedience to the suggestions of the Fire Wards in all cases. The importance of fire engines, and the good efforts of regulations emanating from lawful authority, were fully tested. A subscription is now rapidly filling to purchase another and more efficient engine.

Insurance, we learn, had been affected on the building, to an amount pretty near its value; so that the greatest loss fell upon Mr. Sparhawk, who had 7 or 8 beds burned, some furniture, grain and provisions, and much of the furniture saved was broken and injured. It is difficult to ascertain the origin of the fire. The most probable conjecture is that it must have caught from the chimney between the roof and the upper floor. Mr. Sparhawk has ascertained his loss to be nearly six hundred dollars.

————

[From Clifford C. Wilber]: After this report in the *Sentinel* under the same story a card of thanks, several thanks were placed in the paper. This was called "A CARD" and read as follows. G. Sparhawk, most gratefully thanks his fellow citizens for rescuing so large a proportion of his property from the late fire on Monday evening last, and particularly the ladies for their exertions to clear the house and protect the furniture, while the men were engaged in the more arduous duties of saving the adjoining buildings.

"A CARD"

Lamson & Blake, feel grateful for the providential preservation of their property, so imminently exposed by the fire on Monday night, and desire in this public manner to thank their fellow citizens for their prompt exertions in their behalf, and particularly the ladies, who were not only extremely active in assisting to clear their store of goods, but vigilant in protecting them when scattered and exposed. This is an example of several "A CARD" of thanks, which appeared in the *Sentinel*.

1825 [*from* Upper Ashuelot, A History of Keene, New Hampshire]

The Cheshire County Fire Insurance Company was established.

1826 [*from Clifford C. Wilber*]

It was a Legislative Act to form a second engine Company. It was the provisions of which "Asa L. Stone, John Hunt and Samuel Chapman and their associates and successors may hold real or personal estate not exceeding $1,000." We think that this incorporation may have been consequence of the vote at the meeting of January 5th, 1824 to form a company to work the old engine due to the purchase of a new engine. It was the legislative "Act to establish a corporation by the name of Fire Engine Company No. 2" and this was approved on June 19th, 1826 by a legislative Act.

At the meeting of the Keene Fire Society held at the Phoenix Hotel on May 28th, 1825 the sinking of a well or wells on the common at Central Square, and the provision of a suitable place for the fire apparatus was authorized.

At the meeting on January 2nd, 1826 which was held at the Phoenix Hotel, it was "Voted: That all members be excused from attending the annual meeting on arriving at the age of 65 years, if they so choose." "Voted: That Noah Cooke, Esq., is excused according to his request from attending the future meeting of the society, and that the clerk presents to him the thanks of the society for his long and faithful service as their president." Mr. Cooke had served the society

as its president for the entire period of about 17 years since its organization. He died at the well-known "Cooke house" on West Street, October 15th, 1829 at the age of 80. At his resignation as President of the society he was succeeded in that office by Samuel Dinsmoor.

1827

The business taken up at the meetings of January 1st, 1827, the meeting of January 7th, 1828 and the meeting of January 5th, 1829, all held at the Phoenix Hotel, is largely identified in a historical sense and has relation to securing a suitable place for the new fire apparatus, the examination of wells and the appointment of committees in an effort to increase the membership within the company. At the latter mentioned meeting it was voted to "see if it is necessary to furnish more ladders for the Fire Society."

1829

The First Congregational Church was moved to the head of the Square where it is today.

1830

A revised draft of the By-Laws presented at the meeting of January 4th, 1830, was adopted. Article 4 provided that "the Society may at any annual meeting assess such sum by an equal poll tax upon every member as shall be necessary to defray the expense of repairing the engines and their appurtenance; for purchasing and repairing fire hooks and ladders; for constructing wells and for discharging all other incidental expenses of the fire Society."

As the number of persons invited in the course of these meetings to have people join the society, it was greatly in excess of the number who accepted the invitation, its presumption is that the provision of article 4 quoted in the previous paragraph probably exerted a definite influence to the increase of membership or the lack thereof.

1830

Keene's population in 1830 was 2,374. This was the first time exceeding that of Walpole and Westmorland and other townships of the region.

The small fire engine owned by the glass factory, which has been mentioned in the account of the fire which destroyed the wooden tavern house on May 27th, 1822, was frequently of great assistance in bringing under control fires of a magnitude which threatened danger to a large part of the village, and due credit to its performances at various times appear in the files of the *Sentinel*, in which is invariably described as "the small engine belonging to the glass factory," which indefinite description leaves its size a matter of imagination to the reader of today, and the following quotations from a legislative act pertaining to this engine will be of assistance in clarifying that detail.

1831

On July 1st, 1831 an Act to Incorporate Fire Engine Company Number Three was passed. It was Benjamin F. Adams, Oliver Holman and Timothy Wheeler, their associates and successors, which made a body politic and corporate, etc. With further provision that "said engine company may consist of fourteen men and no more, who shall be appointed to perform the duty of "enginemen" in the same way and manner as "enginemen" are now by law appointed, and shall be exempted from the performance of military duty, provided that the number exempted shall in no case operate to reduce the number of soldiers in the first company of the twentieth regiment below forty-two rank and file."

At this time "enginemen" were exempt from the performance of military duty, and in order to avoid abuses of this exemption, laws were passed establishing the number of enginemen to each company.

Adams, Holman and Dutton were operating the New Hampshire Glass Factory at this time. While the name Ormond Dutton, of this firm, does not appear in the act of incorporation, Timothy Wheeler is listed in Keene's first directory, published in 1831, as a laborer in the glass factory.

Note [from Clifford C. Wilber]: It was the disaster in 1822 that inspired the citizens of Keene to begin subscription for a second and larger fire engine. The Engine Company was reorganized as the Keene Fire Society in 1822, and the second fire company, the "Fire Fencibles," was organized in 1825. It was at this time the foundation for the Phoenix Hotel was laid on the site of the earlier Chandler House, and the Phoenix Hotel, three stories high and made of brick with "large commodious and elegant," rose from the ashes and opened in December 1822, and was called "an ornament to our village." It contained in addition to 18 sleeping rooms and the bar, an assembly hall, a large dining room, and handsome porticoes on the west and south. There was also a horse-watering trough in front of the hotel, and almost all of the fire company meetings were held here.

1832

At the meeting of the Keene Fire Society held at the Phoenix on December 26th, 1832 it was "Voted: That the trustees be requested to take into consideration the expediency of ladders and places of deposit for the same being provided by the society, and to report as to the number required, the number of places of deposit and the expense of the arrangement. At the next annual meeting the Trustees were directed to "locate and construct one or two additional reservoirs for water."

1834

At the annual meeting held at the Phoenix December 31, 1834, the Treasurer reported in his hands $29.14 and "note against G. Brooks

$10 dollars," with the explanation that in consideration of the above named note they had allowed him to draw water in lead pipes from the well on the common for the use of one family and that they had repaired the well on West Street and sunk a new one near John C. Mason's. John C. Mason was a Gunsmith, with a shop on Winter Street. Winter Street as well as Middle Street and Summer Street, was opened in 1832 as part of a development program in that section of the village.

Note [from Clifford C. Wilber]: The Keene Fire Society, with 64 members, and the Fire Fencibles, with 45 members were the two local fire companies, still being a private organization. The third group, organized in March 1825, and was the original "Hook and Ladder Company of Keene." At the time the firemen had a long red frock, which was called their uniform.

1835

At the annual meeting of the Keene Fire Society held at the Phoenix Hotel on December 30th, 1835 the following vote was passed: "that the trustees be authorized to refund $10 dollars paid by Grosvenor Brooks for a privilege of taking water from the well at central Square on the common, which privilege has been abandoned as useless to him or the present owners of the premises to which the water was carried, as in their judgment appears, after examination, right."

The building of Grosvenor Brooks above mentioned, was the brick house built by Captain John Towns about 1825. This house stood where the present Sentinel building now stands on the corner of Gilbo Ave. and Main Street. Captain John Town's house was originally built as a store, but later was made into a dwelling. Sometime later it was acquired by the Cheshire Railroad and again converted for business purpose.

According to the writings of the late William S. Briggs, it was first occupied as a grain store by Joseph Wilson. From 1852 to 1893 when then the business carried on here was the sale of stoves and tin ware, the first occupant in this line having been the firm of J.C. &T. New and the last was Davis & Wright.

Adjoining this building on the south side where Gilbo Ave. meets Main Street stood a blacksmith shop also made of brick. The shop was removed with other buildings then standing on the present sight of the corner news shop and where the railroad tracks did cross Main Street.

Reverting to the $10 dollar refund to Mr. Brooks, as we understand the matter, he was required to tap the cistern at the head of Main Street at a considerable height, so that the supply of water should not be unduly depleted when needed for the extinguishments of fires, and unless the well was full his water privilege was of little value.

Probably Mr. Brooks, by digging a few holes along the line of the pipe and cutting it in sections could then attach horses and retrieve his pipe in pieces of various lengths without much trouble. Should it happen that in making future excavations in this locality that a small leaden aqueduct should be uncovered, those who take note of such things may feel a considerable degree of gratification should they chance to "run across" this item in what will then be "an old newspaper."

1836

At the last mentioned annual meeting the Trustees were requested "to make examination as to the state of repair of the engine house is sufficient" and to also "ascertain if the length of the engine house is sufficient, and if in their judgment more is required, procure it." This would lead to the inference that the second engine owned by the society was somewhat larger than the one for which the house was built. The Trustees are also asked "to make inquire as to the power of the present engines and to ascertain if there are any modern improvements." "Voted: That the Hook & Ladder Company be requested to report its condition to the Society."" On May 28th, 1825 the first meeting of the "Fire Fencibles" had been held at the Phoenix Hotel, which organization was the foundation of our present Hook & Ladder Company or better known as the "Washington Hook & Ladder Company."

During the year of 1836 Keene was the scene of two disastrous fires, which were called conflagrations. April 6th, 1836, Quote from the *Sentinel*: "The Phoenix Hotel kept by Mr. E. W. Boyden (formerly by Mr. Hatch) was discovered to be on fire in the garret, by the smoke, which was oozing through the roof in every part. The citizens rallied and for a time hoped to save the building, but failed, it is believed, solely from a deficiency of hose. The inside of the building was consumed. The walls, when this paper went to press, were all standing, apparently firm. Even the handsome portico on the west, erected last season, is uninjured. All the furniture was saved although some parts of it received damage."

I would like to call your to attention to that of the "portico" which, was added to the Phoenix Hotel in 1835.

Writing of the fire which destroyed the "Phoenix" by the late William S. Briggs said: "Fire was discovered in the day time under the roof, and as we had two good fire engines in town it was expected that the fire would soon be put out. But not to discourage the fire, a hole was made through the roof to give it a good draft, and then it was found that the hose was not long enough to reach the fire, so one of the engines was transported to the second story."

We would like to interrupt Mr. Briggs' story for a moment to observe that this was probably another instance in Keene's fire history where "the small engine from the glass factory" performed distinguished service. Mr. Briggs said further: "The fire was very accommodating, burnt slowly, and only one story at a time. This gave the people plenty of time to clear the house and the fire worked from the top to bottom of the house, of course going out when there was nothing more to burn; So much for the management of a fire in those days. Thanks to Goose Pond, such a farce will not be seen again at a fire in Keene. It was also told of "Uncle John" that in his excitement of the fire that he threw a looking glass out of a chamber window and carried a feather bed out into the street very carefully."

Under the caption, "Another Fire," the *Sentinel* of August 25th, 1836, says: "Yesterday morning at about a quarter of three the barns and stables connected by a shed eastwardly with the Eagle Hotel, owned by Col. S. Harrington and occupied by Alvan Merrill, were discovered to be on fire. The flames made rapid progress as there were several tons of hay, and before any efficient aid could be had the fire communicated to another large stable and sheds, south, and in the rear of the large three story brick building south of the hotel."

We pause in the relation of the story of the fire to explain that the "large three-story brick building south of the hotel" had not at that time been joined to it, but was separated by a driveway leading to the stables in the rear. Soon after this fire the buildings were connected, forming the present Eagle Hotel block, which was between Eagle Court and Cypress Street. The Eagle Hotel was on Main Street where Good Fortune and along Main Street to Eagle Court.

"The fire soon reached the barn, woodshed and back kitchen of Sumner Wheeler on the south, and a small, low house, also owned and occupied by Col. Harrington, situated on Main Street. These were all burnt, but by the aid of the engines and the most determined and efficient cooperation of the citizens, the hotel the large three-story brick building, and Mr. Wheeler's brick house were saved, the hotel and the three- story building with trifling, and Mr. Wheeler's with more damage."

Explanatory of the above paragraph, the house of Sumner Wheeler was the brick building known as the Robertson Motor Company, and was built by Captain John Towns, herein before mentioned. The "small, low house" was a wooden building then standing between the present Eagle Hotel Block and the Robertson Motor Company building at the corner of Main St. and Eagle Ct. It was also where for many years Stephen Harrington, proprietor of the Eagle Hotel since 1823 had made his residence.

Eagle Hotel. Photo by Bion Whitehouse, member of Keene Fire Department Steamer Co. No. 1. HSCC photo collection.

"The houses were all seasonally cleared of their contents. Col. Harrington lost a horse worth $200 dollars, and A. Flower & Company, proprietors of the Fitchburg Stage Lines, lost four horses, harness for a full team, 150 bushels of oats and three tons of hay. The greatest difficulty experienced was the want of water. A large reservoir should be sunk in the immediate vicinity.

"Last spring our largest hotel was burnt, and now all the barns and stables of the Eagle Hotel are swept away. Extensive improvements were about to be made to the Eagle Hotel. We hope to soon announce improvements to be made in another quarter."

The last sentence in the above paragraph refers to the project of rebuilding the Phoenix, which after a period of stagnation, was at this time being revived, resulting in the building of the "Cheshire House" by a stock company in the following year.

When the present front was added to the Eagle Hotel by Daniel E. O'Neil, a large brick cistern for the storage of water for fire purposes was uncovered between the hotel and the Old Scenic Theatre and extending under the present sidewalk which is now the Beroski Block and the cistern was located in front of the now store Good Fortune.

1836

At the annual meeting of the Fire Society held at the Eagle Hotel, on December 28th, 1836 it was "Voted: That the engines be located where they are for the present" and that a committee be appointed to "provide a better location as soon as may be and authorized to lease or purchase a lot or lots and erect such building or buildings as they may think proper." The reports of Quincey Wheeler, Captain of Engine No. 1 and Asa Maynard, Captain of Engine No. 2 were read and accepted.

For a considerable time the members of the Society had been of the opinion that the ever increasing burden of expense incident to the purchase of engines and keeping them in repair, and the building of more and more reservoirs would soon be greater than a volunteer association should be called upon to bear, and at this meeting it was "Voted: That Mr. Hall and Mr. Chamberlan be a committee to see that such articles as in their opinion are necessary be inserted in the warrant for the next town meeting as ought to be adopted in the town relating to the fire department," but the society carried on for several years before the control of its engines and property was taken over by town of Keene. We have made mention of the movement to rebuild the Phoenix Hotel, which at the time of this meeting had been standing about eight months, a hollow, blackened ruin. As the next meeting of the society was held at the "Cheshire House," we must make a digression at this point for the erection of the hotel.

A stock subscription had been inaugurated to provide funds for rebuilding the hotel on "a more extensive plan," the owners, John Wood, Aaron Hall and Timothy Hall agreeing to convey in trust for the consideration of $4500 thousand dollars to such person or persons as the subscribers should designate "the Phoenix hotel site, situated in Keene, together will all parts and portions of the house saved from the late fire, and the hay scales on the common, said site containing about two acres."

The stock subscription paper set forth the plan to rebuild the house "on its present foundation, using such portions of the late house saved from the fire and the present walls as shall be found suitable and convenient, and with such extensive additions and improvements as the amount of capital stock to be raised shall permit."

Each share was valued at $100 dollars, with a liability of assessment of the same amount, and subscriptions were taken with provision that the plan should not go into effect unless a capital stock of not less than $10,000 dollars was subscribed.

This stock subscription, dated August 31st, 1836, is recorded in the Cheshire registry of Deeds, Vol. 131, page 9, as a preamble to the deed of John Wood, et al., to Nathaniel Dana and Thomas H. Leverett, trustees, from which it appears that 151 shares were subscribed.

It was with sorrow that many viewed with sorrow the operations of the wreckers, as day by day the Old Cheshire House was erased from the picture of history. There may be some who will read with interest the names of the subscribers to the fund who paid and rose for its erection, the shares being of value of $100 dollars each:

A. & T. Hall with John Wood 46 shares Justus Perry 7 shares and William Lamson & Co. 12 shares, John Prentiss with 7 shares, Azel Wilder 5 shares, Stillman French 4 shares, John Elliot 5 shares, John H. Fuller with 5 shares, Abijah Wilder with 4 shares, Oliver Holman, 8 shares and Francis Faulkner, 2 shares S. A. Gerould, 2 shares and Sumner Wheeler, 2 shares John Elliot, with 7 shares, Abijah Wilder, 4 shares with Samuel Wood Jr.,2 shares and J. Parker 2 shares, Benj F. Adams 3 shares, T. M. Edwards 4 shares Abijah Kingsbury with 2 shares, George Tilden 2 shares, and S. Hale with 2 shares and Charles Lamson with 5 shares, Adolphus Wright 3 shares, Phineas Handerson 1 share, Francis Faulkner with 2 shares Keyes & Colony 1 share, Josiah Colony with 1 share and Sumner Wheeler 2 shares, Quincy Wheeler 3 shares, with Lewis Campbell with 1 share, and Eliphalet Briggs with 3 shares, Levi Chamberlain 1 share, and S. F. Wheelock 2 shares, W. Dinsmoor 2 shares, Henry Dorr 1 share, Samuel Wood Jr. 2 shares, Alvan Wright 1 share Jacob Haskell 1 share J. Parker 2 shares, George Kilburn 2 shares and Isaac Redington with 1 share. It was not clear but due to the fire the shareholders never saw any money from the hotel.

1837 [From Clifford C. Wilber]

The Cheshire House was opened on November 13th, 1837. According to records at a cost of nearly $25, 000 thousand dollars but they never saw their money again." When built there was a driveway on the south side from Main Street to the stables in the rear.

Next south was a wooden store building and the southerly line of the hotel property as described in the deed to the trustees as being "parallel with the north line of the stairs attached to the store owned by the heirs of Lynds Wheelock." This wooden building was soon after removed to Church Street and a brick building erected southerly of the hotel by James Raymond in 1838, which shortly afterward came into the possession of A. & T. Hall and John Wood, being known as the "Hall's building."

In 1859 Henry Pond, then owner of the Cheshire house, bought the former Hall & Wood Building then owned by Amos C. Greeley, and connected it with the hotel by building upon the driveway by which they had been separated.

The trust deed to Nathaniel Dana and Thomas H. Leverett of the Phoenix Hotel property, dated December 8th, 1836, also includes "the patent hay scales" set and fixed near the town well on the common or which is now Central Square.

1837

At the meeting of the Keene Fire Society held at the Cheshire House on December 27, 1837, reports were received and adjournment, taken for supper. Meeting according to adjournment, "James Wilson Jr., for the fire wards, made an elaborate report in which the only cause of complaint was deficiency of ladders."

1838

The population of Keene was 2,573 people

Another meeting was held at the same place on July 7th, 1838, at which the trustees were requested to erect an engine house of suitable size on the land offered for that purpose by the proprietors of the Cheshire house on the "northwest side of the garden," or procure one to be erected for the use of the society of such size and on such terms as they may think proper.

The records indicate that the matter was held up for a time, as at the meeting of December 26th, 1838, it was voted that a subscription paper for raising funds for building and engine house and contingent expenses be laid on the table, after which it was voted "to adjourn for supper and meet at this place immediately after." Returning from supper the treasure and secretary were appointed

a committee to procure subscriptions to the paper for raising money to build an engine house.

Faulkner & Colony Manufacturing Company. The Mills were originally erected in 1824 by Messrs F. & C., which were wooden buildings and were become to fire, which lead to the buildings made of brick pictured above. The nearest section of the brick factory buildings was erected in 1836. Photo by Bion H. Whitehouse. HSCC collection.

In the *N.H. Sentinel* on August 2nd, 1838 appeared the article on the fire. And it is quoted.

"FIRES"

On Monday evening last, about half past 9, our village was suddenly roused by an alarming light in the direction of Messrs FAULKNER & COLONY'S mills, on the Ashuelot, in the village. By the time the people and the engines could get there, almost the whole interior of the extensive brick edifice appeared to be in flames. No human efforts could save it. It was reduced to ashes, with the range of low buildings connected, used for dying, &c. . . These mills were erected in 1824, by Messrs F. & C., soon after the destruction of the old wooden mills, also by fire. How the fire caught is not positively known. One or two persons were in the building and the carding operation going on at the time. So no woolen waste had been burnt in the stove, and it is supposed some sparks must have lodged in the light lumber adjoining the sawmill, open on the southwest. The wind was fortunately in a northerly direction, so that by great exertions the valuable brick house, also belong to Messrs F. & C. on the east was saved, as was the manufactured stock portions of the wool &c. The piles of lumber were also saved. Still the loss is great. The main building was 73 feet by 36 feet, two stories high. The grist and flourmill had 3 runs of stones, with a corn-cracker mill. The sawmill occupied the west end, and the clothing works the east, with low buildings running some 60 or 80 feet south. The second story was occupied as a flannel factory, and the machinery for carding wool. The whole loss is estimated at not less than $12,500 dollars, of this $7,500 dollars was insured in the N. H. Mutual. The loss is not only heavy on the enterprising properties, but will be felt by the village.

1839

The December 25th, 1839 meeting held at the Cheshire House the treasure reported receipts for the year as $96.36 and expenditures of $94.17, and the trustees reported that they "had attended to the duties assigned to them so far as they had the means," which is assumed that the reference is to erecting the engine house. This engine house was sold at auction Jan 14th, 1851. This was an item in the *Sentinel* under auctions. Also at this meeting Article 4 of the by-laws of the Keene Fire Society, making members liable to assessments, were repealed, and invitations were issued to 32 persons named in the records to become members of the Fire Society.

Azel Wilder, John Elliot and E. Briggs were appointed a committee to estimate the expense of making a large and suitable reservoir on the common or which is now Central Square. This committee reported at the

meeting held on December 30th, 1840, that they had estimated the expense to be $75, or $25 dollars for every ten feet.

1840

As stated from the committee reported the estimated price of the suitable reservoir. The repeal of the provisions of the by-laws making members liable to assessment was the first step in the inauguration of a new plan for raising funds for the building of reservoirs, which had become the society's largest item of expense.

At this meeting it was voted that four persons, one from each of the principal streets, be added to the board of trustees to constitute a committee to district the village, locate reservoirs, and take a subscription for building the same, and make choice of Calvin Page for Court Street, Timothy hall for West Street, Oliver Holman for Washington Street and Thomas F. Ames for main Street.

1841

Committee appointed to district the village for the location of reservoirs, etc., reported as follows for District No. 1 Main Street "with any others within the limits of said district," the record thereof being dated April, 1841.

Keene's first directory was published in 1831, but nearly 40 years elapsed before the production of the second, therefore however incomplete the following listings may be, they have considerable historical value by showing the approximate places of residence of many citizens and the locations of various enterprises:

District No. 1 Main Street with any others within the limits of said district:

Adajah Kingsbury House
Grosvenor Brooks House and shop
J. H. Fuller House
Cheshire Bank
William Dinsmoor House
B. F. Adams House and Stable
James Wilson Tavern and Stable
James Wilson House
E. Dunbar House
Mrs. Chase House
Sumner Wheeler 2 Houses
Stephen Harrington Tavern and
    Buildings
Mrs. Carter House   Dr. Twitchel House
John Towns Jaquith House and Shop
T. F. Ames Shop
Justus Perry 2 Houses
Geo Wheelock House
& T. hall House

District No. 2 Main Street was listed as follows with "any others included within said district:"

J. Elliot House
O. Heaton House
Appleton House
Abel Blake 2 Houses
Phineas Fiske House
Mr. Simmons House
Mrs. Metcalf House
Sylvester Tilden House
Thos. F. Ames House
Nathan Bassett House and Shop
Elijah Adams House
Joseph Foster House
Mr. Buffo House

The committee for said districts was: B. F. Adams, Summer Wheeler and William Dinsmoor, and their listings were approved by the village committee "John Elliot, Timothy Hall and Azel Wilder.

District No. 3 Main Street comprised the following buildings and "any other within its limits."

Mrs. Newcomb House
Miss Withington House
Isaac Gray House
Caleb Carpenter House
Dr. Smith House
Rev. Z. S. Barstow House
Sarah Wilson House
Esq. D. Carpenter House
Dr. C. G. Adams 2 Houses
Salma Hale House
Isaac Gray Dan's house and Shop

"Dan's house and shop" refers to the shoemaker's shop of Dan Gray in which he probably lived. It was situated nearly opposite the house of Dr. Z. S. Barstow, formerly the Wyman Tavern, and it is the belief that it was the "new building opposite Col. Wyman's tavern" into which James Davenport Griffith removed the office of "*The New Hampshire Recorder* and the *Weekly Advertiser*" on November 19th, 1788.

The committee for said districts was: Salma hale, Isaac Gray and Caleb Carpenter.

At the great fire on Washington Street February 1st 1846, the furniture shops and salesroom of E. & W. S. Briggs were destroyed. The E. &. W. S. Briggs was a large cabinet shop which was located on Washington Street near Central Square, with the old two-story brick school house north of it, used for a joiner's shop and lumber room.

A carriage house belonging to French's stable, the two-story house of Joseph Willard, south of the shops, with barn, were all destroyed in this fire, with a large quantity of lumber, furniture, machinery, etc. It was Sunday morning, just at the hour for church services. Mr. Livermore dismissed his congregation and went with them and assisted vigorously at the fire; but Mr. Barstow, as tradition has it, with a different conscientiousness and a devout sense of his religious duty, although his church edifice was in great danger, continued his service as if it had been the usual quiet New England Sunday morning. Two lines were formed, as usual, to the town well on the south side of the Square, for passing buckets. The weather was intensely cold, but there was no wind and the village was saved from a further spread of the flames. The loss was about $6,500 dollars over and above a small insurance. The Dan gray shoe shop being then unoccupied, it was bought by the firm and removed to the site of the present City Hall, where it was used for about two years as a furniture store. In 1848, when the new town hall was to be built, the shop was removed to the opposite side of Washington Street. It was afterward removed again to West Street where it was occupied for many years for the sale of stoves and tin ware by the late firm of Kirk and Sewall, and was finally demolished when the present How block was built.

The division line between the second and third districts on Main Street seems to have been just south of the house of Phineas Fiske, where Samuel Dinsmoor afterward built his residence, at which time the Fiske and Newcomb houses were removed to the westerly side of Madison Street where they now stand in the same relative position.

The following buildings were listed as the "Washington Street district" by the committee appointed by the Keene Fire Society to locate and build reservoirs for fires. The committee for this district was: Eliphalet Briggs, Oliver Holman and Samuel Towns. Houses listed were

Eliphalet Briggs House
Nathaniel Dana House
Loring Frost House

County House
John Draper House & Shop
George Dort House
Amasa Brown House
Phineas Handerson House
Abel Wilder Double House
Towns & Briggs 3 Houses
& T. Hall House
John Bixby House
Lucian Page House
John Foster House
Oliver Holman House
Redington House
Thomas Leverett House
Henry Dorr House
Samuel Wilson House
Lewis Page House
Cooke House
Arba Kidder House
Jacob Esty House

While much might be written with reference to the history of some of the houses in the foregoing list, owing to space limitations it must be deferred for the present. However, we would call attention to the house of Nathaniel Dana, which formerly stood on the site of the house now numbered 64 Washington Street. On July 21st, 1835, this house was much shattered by lightning, the lightning bolt passing through rooms where members of the family were sitting, and whose escape from death was nothing short of miraculous.

The committee for the Court Street district was Abijah Metcalf, Elijah Parker and Nathan Wood, and they submitted the following list, ""including all others within said district," which was recorded by the Keene Fire Society as of September 1st, 1841:

Abijah Wilder 3 Houses & Tin Shop
Dexter Anderson 2 Houses
Abijah Metcalf House
James Perry House

Luther Smith House
Leonard   house
Adolphus Wright House
John Snow House
Elijah Parker House
Samuel Chapman House
George Tilden House
John Prentiss 2 houses
Nathan Wood House & Shop

The house of Adolphus Wright above mentioned stood on the site of the house now numbered 151 Court Street. It was first erected as a store by Captain Josiah Richardson.

At the time this list was made Luther Smith was deceased, having dropped dead on his doorstep October 21st, 1839. He had been one of Keene's enterprising men and operated the saw and gristmill on West Street before the woolen factory was established. He was also a clock maker, and made Keene's first town clock in 1794. He also built the eagle hotel in 1805-1806.

The three houses of Abijah Wilder were probably the brick house on the corner of Summer and Court Streets which had been built at about this time as a boarding house for pupils attending the Keene Academy; the small brick house which stood across from the fire station on Vernon street, which then stood on the site of the Court Street Congregational Church which has been removed, along with another wooden house in the same area.

The tin shop stood on the site of the present Barker Block. It was formerly the Courthouse and had been removed from the northwest corner of the Square in 1824 when the first brick courthouse was built, the store of Bullard & Shedd being the northerly half of the latter named courthouse. The tin shop was burned August 7th, 1861 The Barker block is the block on the corner of Court street and Center Street the present building was erected in 1870 and used through the years

for apartments and small business, each section individually owned as is today.

Dexter Anderson has been described as a "stirring business man" and was for many years the proprietor of a "hat manufactory" on the site of 15-17 Main Street. This area is the old Keene National Bank, which is Keene's Oldest and is now Citizens Bank. He died at Woodstock Vt. in 1877. Alijah Metcalf was probably keeping the "Sun tavern" at this time, and in the collections of our historical society may be seen a doorplate bearing his name.

The "Academy Square district" was recorded as follows on the book of the Keene Fire Society as of September 1st 1841 the committee having been Samuel Wood, William Marsh and Charles Kingsbury:

The Academy Square District listed as,
Samuel Wood House
William Wilson House
Mr. Shelly House
John g. Thatcher Hitchcock House
Elbridge Keyes House
Harvey Gerould House
William Marsh House
Ebenr Clarke House
John Currier House
Shubael White House
Haskell House
Charles Kingsbury House
Mrs. Breed House
Mr. Milliken House
Abijah Wilder Small House

Academy Square comprised of the territory of Winter Street School Street and Summer Street and a small part of Court Street. The name was derived from the erection of the Keene Academy in 1836 on the site of the Old Junior High School which stood in the now parking lot behind the Court house off Winter Street.

William S. Briggs, born in 1817, in one of his historical articles said that he remembered when the track of land which encompassed Winter, School, Summer and Court Streets was a vacant lot of some eight acres, and that it was a favorite resort of the boys for their ball games in the summer and for skating on the small ponds which formed upon it in the winter, and that he once saw the whole west side of this tract covered with growing corn.

The parcel was a part of the land formerly belonging to Captain Josiah Richardson, whose tavern house stood on the old site of the YMCA building, which was on West Street now where the Cheshire County offices stand. After the death of Captain Richardson in 1820 the property came into the possession of Joseph Dorr, who had married Captain Richardson's daughter, Rebecca. Dorr sold the above, described piece of land to Azel and Abijah Wilder in 1832, who caused Winter, Summer and middle streets to be laid out in November of 1832.

Six districts having been laid out for the construction of reservoirs by the committee of the Fire society appointed for that purpose, at a meeting held at the Cheshire House on December 29th, 1841, it was voted that the "trustees, together with the committee associated with the last board be requested to use their endeavors to induce the several districts established to carry out the plan devised into effect, and that a subscription paper be circulated for the purpose of raising funds to defray the necessary expenses of the Keene fire Society."

The "Center District" for the construction of reservoirs to store water for the extinguishment of fire was recorded by the committee, John Elliot, Timothy Hall and Azel Wilder, March 11th, 1842, as follows:

Cheshire house; Alvah Walker; Wm. Lamson, store; Wm. Lamson & Co., stock; Adolphus Wright, stock; Joel Parker, stock; Justus Perry, store and house; Sumner Wheeler, stock; Ichabod Ballou, stock; Thos. M. Edwards, store, stock and office; J. & R. Shelly & Co., stock; Abijah Wilder, house, shop and stock; Dexter Anderson, shop and stock; Azel Wilder, store; Carter & Wright, stock; Chas. Keyes, stock; S. F. White, stock; B. Cooke, stock B. G. Samson, stock; E. Poole, stock; S. A. Gerould, store, stock, house and gun shop; Geo. Tilden, stock; John Prentiss, store and stock; John Foster, stock; Buffum & Parker, stock; Ashuelot bank; Keyes & Colony, store and stock; john Elliot, store; B. F. Adams, stock; A. & T. Hall, store, stock, 2 shops and 2 hoses; Chas. Lamson, 2 houses, tannery and shop; Samuel Wood, bake house; Cooke house; James Raymond, store; Freeman's stock; A. & T. Hall 2 stores; Bowker stock; James White, stock; Titus house; Eliphalet Briggs, 2 houses, shop and stock; Stillman French's, house and stable; Abel Wilder, house; Nathaniel Evans, house; Estate Wheelock, house; Levi Chamberlan, house and stock.

The next meeting of the Fire Society was held at the Cheshire House on December 28th, 1842. The roll of the Fire Society recorded with this meeting shows the membership to have been 50 members. The business at this meeting was the appointment of further committees to "carry into effect the plan for building reservoirs."

The following resolution was offered by Hon. Salma Hale and unanimously adopted: "Resolved: That the members of this Fire Society, recalling to mind those respected associates, Phineas Fiske, Francis Faulkner, Justus Perry, Alvah Walker and John G. Thatcher, who have since their last meeting been summoned to leave us for their last account, desire to record the expression of their sincere grief for their bereavement and their sympathy with the families of the deceased."

"Voted: That the secretary be directed not to advertise any meeting of the Fire Society in Any Paper" (and the last two words are very heavily underscored) "except that the editor is a member of this society."

Notice of this meeting had been advertised in the *Sentinel* and the "Cheshire Republican and Farmers' Museum," the latter then published by Benaiah Cooke, whose name does not appear in the membership roll referred to, but at the next meeting this vote was rescinded.

1843

At the meeting of the Keene Fire society held at the Cheshire house on December 27th, 1843, the membership had dropped to 46. The committee appointed to carry the "Reservoir Plan" into effect was given a new lease of life.

The membership fee was reduced from $5 dollars to $2 dollars, and William S. Briggs, Adolphus Wright and Stillman French were named a committee to solicit new members.

1844

in the record of this meeting the names of 106 persons appear to whom the fire Society extends a special invitation to become associated with it, yet at the next annual meeting held December 25th, 1844 there are only 44 names on the membership roll. The same reservoir committee is reappointed with instructions to "persevere until they accomplish the objective for which they were chosen."

1845

Early in the history of the organization, the Rev. Z. S. Barstow and later, the Rev. A. A. Livermore, had been made members of the society, and at the meeting held December 31st, 1845 the Rev. H. G. Richardson was also elected to honorary membership.

During 1845, due to the "perseverance" of the committee, seven new wells had been sunk in and around Central Square, all of which were connected with the central reservoir at the head of Main Street. At this meeting it was voted to excuse the following members

for absence at the last annual meeting; Z. Keyes, John Towns, Samuel Wood Jr., Stephen Harrington, Thos. M. Edwards, James Wilson, Levi Chamberlain, Calvin Page and Nathan Wood, but Salma Hale, Geo. Tilden, Abijah Metcalf and Phinas Handerson paid fines of $1.00 dollar each for their absence.

The treasurer reporting the cash on hand to be $1.00 dollar, a subscription was taken and $19 dollars was contributed by 26 individuals to pay sundry bills against the Fire Society.

1846

at the meeting of December 30th, 1846 the treasure's report was called for "by which it appeared that there was nothing in the treasure." It was voted that J. & J. W. Prentiss' bill for advertising, $4.50, be allowed and paid from first money received, and John Wood, John Elliot and Azel Wilder were appointed a committee to negotiate with the town upon terms to take the engines. An article had been inserted in the warrant for the town meeting of 1846 relative to the purchase of a fire engine, but nothing became of it.

1847

The warrant for the town meeting of March 9th, 1847, contained the following articles:

"Art. 16. To see if the town will vote to raise a sum of money for the purpose of purchasing an efficient fire engine and apparatus for the use of the town."

"Art. 17. To see if the town will consent to take of the Keene Fire Society the apparatus for extinguishing fires, consisting of two engines, leather hose, fire buckets, etc., together with a building in which the two engines are kept, standing on land belonging to the Cheshire House, and engage to keep them in good repair."

No action was taken as to the purchase of a fire engine, but Article 17 was adopted and the engines and other apparatus of the

Keene Fire society passed to the control of the town of Keene.

From NH Sentinel, *Keene, NH:*

"FIRE"

About 6 p.m. on December 20th, 1847 fire was discovered in the woodshed of the house of Dea S. Carter, at the lower end of Main Street, and before assistance arrived the shed and barn were ablaze. The *Sentinel* said that "with anything like a respectable engine and apparatus there should not have been the least difficulty in saving the dwelling house, but with our inefficient fire apparatus and the want of fire hooks the attempt was vain, although favored by a perfectly still evening." This was one of the largest and most substantial dwellings in the village, as well as one of the oldest, called the "Maj. Willard House and built in 1775."

The *Sentinel* said further: "It is not improbable that after the village has been visited by a destructive fire, sweeping off property of ten times the cost of an efficient fire apparatus, the town will see the necessity of action. Until then we must trust to Providence and the insurance companies."

1848

At the March Meeting of 1848, the town voted to raise $800 dollars for the purchase of a fire engine and apparatus "provided individuals would subscribe $400 dollars."

According to an advertisement appearing at the town hall of "all those persons who have subscribed toward the purchase of a Fire Engine, to choose a committee to purchase an engine and the transaction of any other business as may be thought expedient for the support of an efficient fire department," which resulted in the "Deluge" engine being secured a short time afterward. This machine was of much greater efficiency that the old engines formerly belonging to the Keene Fire Society

and today may be relied upon to give a good account of it when manned by our "Fearless Fire Fighters."

In 1848 Keene purchased a new engine and it was purchased from the Hunneman Company out of Boston, Mass. and was delivered to Keene's Central Station on June 12th, 1848. This was not the last nor was it the first purchased from this company of Boston Massachusetts.

In 1848 Keene purchased this Hunneman from the Hunneman Company of Boston, Massachusetts. This engine is still owned by the Keene Fire Department and was restored in 1975 at the Keene Central Fire Station by firefighters for the bicentennial parade in 1976. Keene had purchased two "Hunnemans," but one was sold to the Winchester, New Hampshire fire department, which still has it to this day. Photos by Steve Goldsmith.

William C. Hunneman,

Charlestown, May 12, 1802.

BEGS leave to inform the public, that he has purchased the Right of making and vending the new-invented PATENT FIRE-ENGINE; which, from the simplicity of the construction and the largeness of the valves, the ease with which all the parts of the Engine can be repaired, the very great force with which it throws the water, and the great distance to which it is thrown, claims the first place in point of utility, in extinguishing Fires. Orders for the Patent Fire-Engines will be executed with the utmost dispatch, and on the most moderate terms by WM. C. HUNNEMAN, at No. 56. Fore-Street, near the Draw-Bridge. [ep3m] . June 7.

Charlestown Independent Chronicle, May 12, 1802.

William C. Hunneman,

INFORMS the public, that he is the only proprietor of the new invented

PATENT FIRE ENGINE,

invented by Mr Jacob Perkins, and Mr Allan Pollock. These Engines are warranted to be superior to any others ever made in Europe or America ; for they possess many important advantages over all other engines. The principal improvements are the following—1st, enlarging the valves ; for all the valves in these engines, are as large as the chambers. This improvement has two advantages, for it makes them work much easier, and they are not likely to freeze. The second improvement is, diminishing the diameter of the chambers, and increasing the length which together with the largeness of the valves is the cause of these Engines working much easier than any others. The third improvement is, they are not so complicated as other Engines ; for by unscrewing eight screws, you may take out all the interior parts separately, while none of the others have less than *twenty* and some *fifty* ; and every person acquainted with machinery, will pronounce that the best, which is the least complicated. These Engines are made with wood, or copper tubs, with or without a suction, and are warranted to be as strong & as durable in every part as any other Engines—to throw the water as far as any other with a less number of men ; and further than any other with an equal number of men. If these Engines do not answer the description, the purchasers shall be at liberty to return them at any time within one year and receive their money. From the following number of Engines I have made and sold in the short space of time since I purchased the patent, the public may see how highly they are approved of, viz.—1 sold for the town of Boston—1 do Nantucket—2 do. Bath—2 do Newbury—1 do Fort Independence—1 do town of Ipswich—1 do Petersburg, (Virg)—2 do Portland—2 do. Marblehead—4 do, Lynn—1 do Kennebeck—1 do Concord, (N H)—1 do Amherst, (N H)—1 do Reading—1 do Newton.   ALSO,

    1 to Brunswick, }
    1 to Topsham, } in July, 1810.

Old Engines repaired or taken in exchange for new ones.   aug 20

Charlestown Independent Chronicle, August 20, 1810.

From Keene Fire Department records and papers. Copied from Charlestown Independent Chronicle.

[*Compiler note:* Each engine had tools that were kept in the "Tool Box" at the rear of the engine, which consisted of a small hatchet to be used to chip ice that formed on the hydrants and on the engine in freezing weather.

Other tools that were kept in the "Tool Box" were hose spanners and half spanners, hydrant wrenches and engine wheel wrenches.

Pictured are assorted hatchets that were kept in the "Tool Box"

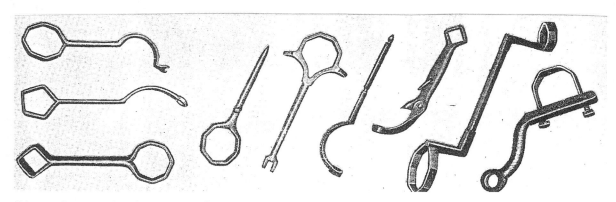

Pictured are assorted spanners that were kept in the "Tool Box"

Bed Key

Every toolbox was equipped with a "Bed Key." These were used to unbolt beds, usually considered the most valuable piece of furniture in the house, so that sections of the bed could be carried out of the burning buildings.]

Photos from Keene Fire Department Records.

Jumpers, or Tender Carts sometimes called, carried six hundred feet of hose. They were either hand drawn or could be attached to an engine by attaching it to the engines tail hook.

[Clifford C. Wilber notes]: Let's step back and give you a little history as to why Keene purchased a Hunneman style engine. In 1792 Hunneman built the first in a series of more than 700 fire engines. As the 1700s neared the 1800s it was reported that several major fires occurred and it was at this time Mr. William C. Hunneman decided to make a contribution in solving the fire problem by manufacturing a better fire engine. Mr. Hunneman purchased the patents from Jacob Perkins and he started making fire engines, which became the Hunneman Fire Engine.

There were other companies who manufactured fire engines but Hunneman design was different and the pistons were placed at a thirty-degree angle while others were at a ninety-degree angle such as the Thayer Fire Engine. The design of the Hunneman Engine was twelve inches longer and closer together at the bottom making the valve-chest shorter giving the water less distance to travel than other engines. The Hunneman was also famous for its superior drafting, never refusing, and always reliable which was an important factor in a fire engine.

The name "hand tub" or "engine" derives its origin from the fact that the body of the engine is, actually, a tub design to hold water. This tub was at first made from wood and was formed inside from sheets of cooper, such as those turned out by the canton Works of Paul Revere to sheath the bottoms of ships, fire engines was a square or oblong wooden box lined with sheets of copper to seal in the water and a pump was installed therein to force the water out. Suction hose was used to draft from the town cisterns, thus enabling the engine to discharge its own water; it was a great improvement over the buckets. Later the tub was made of steel, which gave longer life to the fire engine.

Now that the engines were able to draft and discharge its own water it created a great savings of labor. It was necessitate having something to carry hose and thus the hose reel wagon was added to the list of fire appliances which was now being built by the Hunneman fire company. The first models of the hose wagons or carts were called "jumpers," so called because they could be jumped over curbing on the sidewalks.

William C. Hunneman was a Coppersmith and learned his trade from Paul Reveres Foundry out of Boston and new the trade well. Imagine that once a month an engine was built and ready for delivery. Every bit of the engine was hand-forged and, while brass and copper parts could be roughcast in the foundry, it took hand finishing getting them ready. The engines Keene had prior were tub engines and this as mention had to have two lines of people with buckets and bucket water from the cistern or water source to fill the Hand Tub of the engine and return the empty buckets to be filled again. This all changed with the suction hose added to the fire engines and was a major step in combating fires.

The Hunneman & Company was located between Washington Street and Harrison Avenue on Hunneman Street. The Hunneman & Company partnership thrived until 1869 not only making the best hand-pumped fire engines but also hose reels, wagons and even ladder trucks as they were called.

The first delivered to Keene was called "Deluge" No. 1 and was delivered on June 12th, 1848 and the second engine was delivered to Keene on June 12th, 1855 and was called "Neptune" No. 2 The Deluge No. 1 still belongs to the Keene Fire Department and is kept at Station 2 and the Neptune No 2 was sold to Winchester, New Hampshire in 1871.

It does not appear in the records that the two fire engines owned by the Keene Fire Society had names, but after their acquisition by the town of Keene they became known as the "Lion" and the "Tiger." In his report for the year ending March 10th, 1857 Chief Engineer Daniel Buss, after mention of the "Deluge, Neptune and Hook & Ladder Companies," said: "There are also two other machines with 125 feet of hose which are apparently in good condition for service, and might be of great value at an expense of $5.75 and have at all times been in proper order for service. "In 1859 Chief Engineer Geo. W. Tilden reported these machines as capable of doing good service "providing water could be obtained."

Chief Engineer Joseph P. Wells in his report dated February 25th, 1862 recommended that "the old machines known as the "Lion and Tiger" be disposed of and the proceeds be applied to the purchase of a new hose carriage for the "Neptune" engine, as the one now used is too small." In his report dated March 1st, 1863 Mr. Wells said: "In my report last year, it was recommended that the tow old engines 'Lion and Tiger' be disposed of, they being useless. It has been done, and the proceeds, a little over $100 dollars, paid into the town treasury." We have been unable to learn the name of the purchaser of these engines, but it is lead to be that one of the larger manufacturing companies in town purchased the hand tubs to make a fire brigade for the company.

The question may arise as to which of the engines formerly owned by the Keene Fire Society came to be known as the "Lion" and which one was known as the "Tiger." In the *Sentinel* on May 6th, 1859, an item appeared relating to "Lion Engine Company No. 3," stating that the company had recently been trying out their machine. It is therefore presumed that "No 3" was the better of the two old engines, which makes it seem probable that the "Tiger" was the first engine bought by the old Keene Engine Company.

Algernon H. Hill came to Keene as a boy on July 17th, 1856, and lived at 25 Dover Street in Keene told Clifford C. Wilber a writer for the *Sentinel* that when Jim Myers circus was showing on Roxbury Street in Keene he said "that not long afterward he was a member of a juvenile company which used to work one of the old "hand tubs" occasionally for practice, it being stationed at the cistern at the head of Main Street. There seems to be little doubt of that engine having been the first small engine bought in 1808, and afterwards known as the "Tiger."

Although the Keene fire society had turned over to the town of Keene its property in March 1847, its regular annual meeting was called and it was held at the Cheshire House on December 29th, 1847. The notice of the meeting was published in the *Sentinel* and the *Cheshire Republican*.

The business transacted at this meeting does not appear, for the record of that meeting has been cut from the book. That the half page cut from the book was not blank paper is evident from the "tails and curly cues" left in the margins by the scissors.

In the last pages of the book we find the following: "We the subscribers, having associated as members of the Keene Fire Society, severally pledge ourselves to be subject to the regulations and government thereof. Witness our hands the twenty-first day of February, eighteen hundred and-nine."

The first 70 names, which follow the above heading, were written by the same hand, showing that these names were probably copied from another book when the name of the association was changed to "Keene Fire Society"

Ball Block. Photo taken by Bion Whitehouse, member of Keene Fire Department Steamer Co. #1. HSCC photo collection.

in 1822. The last 43 names are signatures, all being of the leading men of the town, and showing that in the association's life of about 40 years, 113 persons had signed its constitution and by-laws. At the last meeting of the society, the record of its transaction being missing, the membership roll numbered 42.

The record book of the Society from which the past 40+ years, contained information taken from the original book. The book was presented to the Historical Society of Cheshire County by Miss Florence G. Russell. It was soon after Mr. James W. Russell was discharged from the army in 1865 bought an interest in the firm of J. R. Beal & Co., clothiers, who then occupied the store in Balls Block, now of D.F Houran. After the Lamson's Block was built in 1877, J. R. Beal & Co. were the first to move into it. In clearing out the old store Mr. Russell found the record book of the Keene Engine Company in a closet under a stairway, and at the time was shown to many people, but as he found no one who seemed to be particularly interested as to what should be done with it, eventually it found its way to his home and later given to the Historical Society by Miss Florence G. Russell.

The last secretary of the Keene Fire Society when Its property was taken over by the town of Keene was George Hagar, of the firm of Hagar & Whitcomb, who occupied

the store in Ball's Block above mentioned, and from which we may understand why it should have been discovered in that location. Note the Ball's block 27-36 Central Square. Abijah Wilder Jr. bought his lot from Joseph Door and his wife Abigail (Rebecca) in 1821. In 1827 he conveyed a half interest to his brother, Azel Wilder, and 1828 Abijah and Azel Wilder built the brick block, which was known as Wilder's Building. When the block was first built, the upper floors were reached by exterior stairs on either end of the building. The high school was established here in December of the same year. Azel Wilder, who by this time had acquired sole title, sold in 1849 to Henry and Amos Pond, who built an additional store on the west end, extending the building to the line of Court Street. The outside stairways were removed and others built in the interior. In 1863 Henry Pond and the heirs of Amos Pond sold the building to George W. Ball. The heirs of Mrs. George Ball sold to Robert F. Carroll and Frank M. Wilder in 1927, and the building was later purchased by William Pearson, who removed the third story. The heirs of Pearson sold to Chase and Henry Shaw of the Keene Food mart in 1967. The building now houses commercial property such as the Stage Restaurant and New Hampshire Gas (Pg. 260 *Upper Ashuelot* book).

———

1840s [from Upper Ashuelot, A History of Keene, New Hampshire]

As the 1840s neared the 1850s many changes both in growth and industrial direction began to make major changes with the town of Keene. Quoting from *Upper Ashuelot, A History of Keene, N.H.*, page 86-90: One such change was the interest in railroads, when proposals from a line from Boston were advanced, and meetings were held and to arouse popular support. As Alvah Crocker of Fitchburg, the promoter largely responsible for the railroad to that town addressed a meeting in the Town Hall in December 1842. Another enthusiastic meeting was held in the First Church in December 1843, and the formation of a company to found the enterprise was begun.

Within the *N.H. Sentinel* were posted meeting of the company which was entitled Cheshire Railroad.

In June 1844 the New Hampshire Legislature granted a charter for the Fitchburg, Keene and Connecticut River Railroad, but it was rejected by the corporations. The Charter of the Cheshire Railroad Company was then granted on December 17th, 1844, and the company's first meeting was held in Keene on January 10th, 1845 Thomas M. Edwards, an active promoter of the railroad, was a strong leader of the new corporation. It was largely by his efforts that the line was completed and the railroad, introduced in to Keene. Due to the Railroad construction a large Irish influx was introduced in the area and was the first

Fitchburg Railroad Locomotive at Keene. Taken about 1900 in the west yards, the engineer in cab window is James Kellogg, fireman in gangway is William Norse, yard clerk in front of the driver is Barney Peters, conductor in short sleeves is Thomas Gorham, brakeman in light jumper is J. Edward Wood, and yardmaster leaning on engine is James Hayes. On October 1, 1890 the local Cheshire Railroad consolidated with the Fitchburg Railroad and became the Cheshire Division from South Ashburnham, Massachusetts to Bellows Falls, Vermont. The Fitchburg Railroad came under control of the Boston and Maine Railroad July 1, 1900. The building in the background, a finishing shop of the L.J. Colony Chair Co., is still standing in 1973. This picture was used on the 1956 Hampshire Press calendar. HSCC photo collection.

important influx since settlement days. This brought a new spirit to the community, a labor force for the developing industries, and a new dimension to the Yankee sense in Keene, as elsewhere throughout New England.

Railroad construction had pushed toward Keene where it was awaited with growing anticipation. The original locomotive (with one set of driving wheels), "Rough and Ready," was used during most of the construction and was the first to enter Keene, pulling work trains as the track was being laid. The line was opened to Winchester and Troy in the fall of 1847 and to Keene the next spring.

On May 16th, 1848, was a gala day in the life of the village of Keene, and historic moment no one soon forgot. The weather was showery in the morning but cleared before noon. Roads had been crowed since dawn as hundreds of people poured into the village to view the new wonder. The first train from Boston was not scheduled to arrive until 1:30, and by that time nearly 5,000 had gathered around the new railroad station inspecting everything. Most of the people had never seen a locomotive before, and excitement ran at a fever pitch. To signal the trains approach cannons were to be fired at prearranged intervals. A little before 1:30 stores closed; all business ceased while clerks and merchants joined the impatient throng. A hearty cheer was raised as the sound of the first cannon was faintly heard. Soon other shots echoed across the valley, each one louder, and all who were waiting turned their eyes eastward down the ribbons of steel. Suddenly the train, a doubleheader, came into view, a series of 15 cars drawn by two small puffing locomotives, their huge balloon stacks belching dense clouds of wood smoke. The cars were decorated with flags, banners, and evergreen. The brass works of the engines, the "Cheshire" No. 5 and the "Monadnock" No. 6 was brightly polished, and the whole spectacle were one of strength, power, and beauty. The crowd broke loose with winds hurrahs, church bells rang, artillery salutes were fired, and a band began to play as the train slowed, crossed Main Street, and entered the depot. A few of the people who arrived on the train were and addressed the crowd was Thomas M. Edwards and others leaders in the railroad enterprise, civic officials and honored guests, including Mayor Quincy of Boston. The train was turned around and left for Boston shortly after 5 p.m. as spectators applauded and cheered. This was a new beginning for Keene and a beginning of Keene's Industrial age.

1850s into 1860s [from A History of the Town of Keene, S. G. Griffin, MA]

As trains moved into Keene's industrial age so did major change to the entire village. As Per griffin's History of the town of Keene stated, "Many Irish families with children settled in temporary cabins.

In August of 1848:" That aggregation of Irishmen of different clans, particularly of Corkonians and Fardowners, produced a population of very excitable nature." The failure of one Railroad Company of contractors after another to complete their work and pay their men gave cause for complaint and, in autumn, matters culminated in a riot. Stones, bricks, bats, knives, and guns were used, and several persons were seriously injured. It would appear that riot control enforcement was handled primarily by Cheshire County Sheriff; John Foster and the Keene Light Infantry. These actions along with the trains made changes to both Police and Fire, to the way they looked at how large groups and response to emergencies would occur. The fire department now chased brush fires which occurred due to the wood and coal burning steam engines and to accidents which occurred during this the industrial age.

There were many accidents during the construction of the trains and let me move ahead and give you a quote from the December 29, 1848 *N.H. Sentinel*:

"FATAL RAILROAD ACCIDENT"

[December 29th,]: A collision occurred on the […] Cheshire Railroad, about four miles West of the village of Keene, on Wednesday afternoon of last week, causing the death of three persons and the wounding of several others. There were three trains two freight and one passenger, all moving eastward toward Keene. The first freight train was ahead of all; and had ample time to reach Keene in season but for the delay caused by the snow storm, which delay was increased by the failing of water, the locomotive tanks having been filled at the last watering place.

"As soon as the train was stopped by the failing of the water, a messenger was sent back, who signaled the next (mail and passenger) train, which came up slowly, and after sending on the same messenger to signal the rear freight train, Conductor Stone of the passenger train began to shackle on his locomotive to the forward freight train in order to push it down to Keene; but before he got under way, the rear freight train approached, not having been able to see the signal by reason of the driving snow, the difficulty being increased by the snow-plough attached and a curve in the road having prevented the conductor form seeing anything in his way on the track below him, until he was too near.

"The locomotive of the rear freight train struck the rear passenger car, the snow-plough lifting it up, and the locomotive splitting open the floor and penetrating it one-half of its length. There were some thirty passengers in the rear car that was struck, and it is wonderful that so few were hurt; a circumstance attributable to the fact, perhaps, that the train was going [sic] only some ten or twelve miles an hour when it struck; for notwithstanding the sharp curve in the road and the high banks on either side would have

prevented the men on the train from seeing what was before them, had it been a clear day, yet the men on the locomotive, as soon as they rounded the curve, saw through the driving snow, something on the track immediately before them, when they reversed the engine, giving it a full head of steam and whistling for the brakes. […] "The persons killed were Joseph Howerth (a Frenchman) and wife, of Keene, and John Moore, a lad some six years old, of Walpole. Among the bruised or injured, are Mrs. E. W. Dyer of Cambridgeport, Mass., Mrs. Elmira Cook of Westminster, Vt., P. D. Holbrook, residence unknown, and Mr. Hagar of Proctorsville, Vt. A few others were very slightly injured, but strange to say, not one except the three who were killed, had a bone broken. All but one among the wounded, were able to return home immediately. Mrs. Dyer, who was the most injured, remained at the Cheshire House here, but we learn she was to leave for home today (Wednesday.) […]"

———————

1850 *[from* A History of the Town of Keene, *S. G. Griffin, MA]*

The population of Keene was 3,392 people.

1851/1852

The Keene Fire Department made progress by moving it's companies into new uniforms, which now would be there first appearance dressed for the Centennial. It was the first time the department would appear as a uniformed department.

In June 1851 communications in Keene was about to change by the authorization for a telegraph line from Burlington through Keene to Boston was granted. The first message received by telegraph in Keene was on December 23rd, 1851

1853

The population of Keene continues to grow. This also being Keene's Centennial anniversary under its New Hampshire charter was observed on May 26th, 1853.

[*Compiler Note*: We now have a better understanding of how the Keene Fire Department became as we are today. After the Keene Fire Society turned over its engines and equipment to the town of Keene as noted in the past the fire department in 1848 made purchase of a new engine and equipment and the department started to move forward with the industrial age of steam trains and the new added telegraph.]

1854/1856

[There] was new growth for the fire department. It now had new machines and had purchased hose each year and other equipment. The village kept better reports and was now placed in booklet form. Each year the Chief Engineer would give a writing report to the selectman as to how the year went and to what expenses were paid out and to whom. In each report it was also listed the alarm of fires that the department was summoned to for that year. This writer will start with the year ending March 10, 1857.

[*from* Town of Keene Annual Report]: In March of 1856 the fire department with its Chief Engineer Daniel Buss gave his report to the selectman.

Report of the Chief Engineer:

In the discharge of my duty, as required by law, I submit the following Report of the Fire Department of the Town of Keene, for the year ending March 10, 1857.

The Board of Engineers consists of a Chief, together with seven Assistants, as appointed by the Selectmen of the Town, March, 1856, who in the discharge of their duty, organized themselves as a Board of Engineers, with proper officers, and are all provided with a badge of office, as the law requires; and the Assistants have all faithfully performed their duty during the past year. The board had provided a Constitution for the government and working of the Fire Department, that it might be more thoroughly effective in all its branches which come under the jurisdiction of the Engineers; which Constitution was adopted by the Board and accepted by both Companies, April 28, 1856.

The Deluge Company has forty-three acting members, and twenty-three honorary members. They have one Machine, with seven hundred and twenty-five feet of Hose, and other necessary apparatus for using the same, to which an addition of two hundred and fifty feet of new Hose has been added, with other necessary fixtures and repairs, during the past year, to the amount of two hundred and sixty-four dollars and fifty-three cents, all of which is in perfect order for service at a moment's notice. They have thirty-eight uniforms belong to the Town, now in the hands of members; they have also furnished themselves the past year, with firemen's hats, which have added much to the appearance of said Company, and have made other improvements on their hall, which reflect credit on themselves and the town, and yet their Treasury is in a prosperous condition. The members of said Company have all done their duty the past year, in accordance with the law and the Constitution of the Fire Department.

The Neptune Company has forty-five members; they have on machine, seven hundred and seventy-five feet of hose, and other necessary apparatus for using the same, to which an addition of two hundred and fifty feet of new hose has been added, with other necessary fixtures and repairs, during the past year to the amount of two hundred and forty-eight dollars thirty-six cents, all of which is in perfect order for services at a moment's notice: they have forty uniforms belonging to the town, now in the hands of members; they have also made improvements on their hall at their own expense, which reflects credit upon themselves, the Fire Department and the town, and yet we learn that they have surplus in their treasury, and we confidently hope that during another year, they will furnish themselves with firemen's hats, that they may be second to none, in uniform or discipline. They have all faithfully performed their duty as engine-men, during the past year, in accordance with the law and the Constitution of the Fire Department.

The Hook and Ladder Company is composed of eighteen members; they have a Hook and Ladder carriage, hooks, ladders, chains, bars, axes and other necessary apparatus for using the same, all of which is in perfect order. They have no uniform, and the members of said company have not at all times during the past year been as prompt in the discharge of their duty as might have been expected, and we would have recommend that the town provide for them a uniform, that they may not, in future, be looked upon, or found inferior, in discipline or usefulness, with the other companies.

There are also two other machines, with one hundred and twenty-five feet of hose, which are apparently in good condition for service, and might be of great value in case of a large fire. They have been repaired during the past year, at an expense of five dollars and seventy-five cents, and have been at all times in proper order for service. The reservoirs in town are many of them in a bad condition, although they have been repaired during the past year to the amount of thirty-nine dollars and sixty eight cents, yet it is not believed that they would furnish that amount of water necessary to supply our engines for any length of time in case of a large fire. But it is earnestly hoped that the time is not far distant when our village will have a full supply of water fr9m another source.

During the past year there has been but four alarms of fire in town, all of which the engineers and companies were prompt the same, with their apparatus for extinguishing the fire, and in every respect yielded entire obedience to the orders of their superiors. The first was the dwelling house Mr. Faulkner, which was extinguished with ease and but trifle of loss. The second was that of the Cheshire Railroad woodshed. Although that was extinguished with comparatively a small loss, yet at times before it was subdued, it bid fair to gain the victory, and lay a large portion of our pleasant village in ruins, and might have proved so had it not been for the promptness and energy of our efficient Fire Department. The third was that of a cooper's shop which was destroyed, but was prevented from further spreading by the promptness and energy of our fire Department in getting water to the same. The fourth was that of a sawmill, which was in flames before the alarm was given, but the engineers and two companies were prompt on the spot and ready to do everything that could be done to extinguish the same. All houses where fires are kept, also all buckets and ladders which the law requires, within the village precinct, have been inspected by the board of engineers during the past year, and many deficiencies were found in the same, which persons were duly notified thereof.

By a vote of the town, the members of the fire Department receive for their services double the sum which the law allows, and for their efficient services on the third of July last, in saving the property of the Cheshire Railroad Corporation from destruction by fire, said Corporation made a present to the Fire Department of fifty dollars, which by a vote of the board, it was divided equal between the Deluge and Neptune companies. And in relation to those two companies I here have the pleasure of saying one thing, of which the companies and the town may well be proud, that a perfect union exists between those tow companies, instead of that rivalry and strife which is so common between such companies, and such a union we hope will never maintain.

And so long as the town of Keene will maintain two such companies with such efficient officers at their head, as they at this time present to us, (and supply them with the one thing needful) we can rest assured that we have an arm on which we can rely with safety in the hour of danger and nothing will be lacking on their part to stay the devouring element, and discharge their duty with pleasure to themselves and honor to the town.

All of which is respectfully submitted, Daniel Buss Chief Engineer Keene Fire Department March 10, 1857.

———

1857 [*from* Town of Keene Annual Report]

"Trumpet Story"

An account of the Independence Day Celebration, Keene, New Hampshire and the Firemen's Muster at Bellows Falls, Vermont July 4th, 1857
The *Bellows Falls Argus* (Extra) July 4th, 1857.

At 11 o'clock the several military and fire companies formed in procession on the depot grounds under the direction of Walter Taylor, Chief Marshal, and proceeded through Canal, Westminster, Henry Atkinson and School Streets to the grove on Church Hill, in the following order:

The Green Mountain Guards, Capt. Cochran, headed by Bellows Falls Cornet Band were the advance guard and performed the duty of escort in a soldier-like manner, fully sustaining their well-earned reputation. Our band acquitted them handsomely, and did honor to the village.

The Fitchburg Fusileers, Capt. Kimball, from Fitchburg Mass., with a splendid band

The Trumpet won on Independence Day July 4, 1857. Photo by Steve Goldsmith.

made a good appearance and honorably sustained themselves as representatives of the old Bay State.

The Mazeppa Engine Company, Capt. Simons, of Brattleboro was a good looking set of boys well uniformed, with a Hunneman tub, decorated with banners, and drawn by two horses.

Claremont Engine Company No. 4, Capt. Nichols (a machine is of Button's build, drawn by a noble company of men in a neat and showy uniform), was accompanied by the Claremont Band.

Deluge Engine Company, Capt. Blanchard, of Claremont, N. H. This company drew a Hunneman machine and appeared well in an appropriate uniform.

Torrent Engine Company, (Juneville) Capt. Burrill, of Claremont, appeared in a neat uniform without their machine.

Neptune Engine Company, Capt. Davis, of Keene, N. H. This company brought a Hunneman machine and looked well in a beautiful uniform. They were accompanied by the Keene Band who played well.

At half past two the engine companies assembled near the depot to contest for the prizes, a silver trumpet and a silver goblet which were presented to the companies making the two best plays. A beautiful pole 170 feet high had been erected, having the machines play a perpendicular stream on the pole. It is estimated that there were 8,000 people on the grounds during the trial. The companies played through three hundred feet of hose in the order they are set down, the companies casting lots for their turn to play.

Deluge, Claremont, one hundred thirty one and one half feet; Mazeppa, Brattleboro, one hundred thirty feet; No. 4 Company, Claremont, one hundred nine feet, Neptune No. 2 Keene, one hundred sixty feet.

The judges were S. M. Blake, L. Amidon and S. F. Coolidge. The successful companies were then presented with the prizes by J. D. Bridgman, Esq., the trumpet to Neptune Company of Keene, and the goblet to Deluge Company of Claremont. The utmost good feeling prevailed throughout the trial.

As the *New Hampshire Sentinel* recalls on July 4th, 1857, which was printed on July 10th, 1857: "The 4th in our usually quiet village commenced on the evening of the third. A gentle rain served to keep patriotism rather cool until the small hours of the morning of the Fourth, when sleep was driven from nervous pillows. A cannonette (cannon) opened its mouth on the east side of the village and

kept up its sulphurous baying till dawn of day. The old Orthodox bell pealed dolorously upon the midnight air and a cow bell and tin band serenaded every street.

With morning came preparations for departure to different localities where the day was to be appropriately noticed. The Neptune Company was the first in motion, and attended by the Keene Brass Band, marched to the depot to receive the Fitchburg Fusileers, who came in on the 7 o'clock train, accompanied by the Fitchburg Band, and were escorted to the Eagle Hotel for breakfast, after which they paraded and passed up to the "Square," performing many evolutions with superior precision.

The Fusileers, the Neptune Company, with their machine and its appendages, the bands, and several hundred citizens of all ages left about ten A. M. in a train composed of all sorts of cars for Bellows Falls. We the senior, did not go to the Falls, but our junior donned his leather hat and marched out with those that stood by the tub and won much applause and a silver trumpet.

Three of the Sabbath schools of our village with others left in a train for Winchester soon after the delegation to the fall were fairly off. Our village wore more than Sunday quietness through the day, not even the sound of an exploding cracker breaking the tomb-like stillness, but the returning trains near the close of day brought in many smiling faces and merry hearts. The Deluge Company came out with a full company of full grown men with martial music such as makes men valorous on the tented field, prepared to give their brothers of the Neptune Company an appropriate reception.

On their arrival the Neptune Company were escorted to the engine house of the Deluge, where a cold lunch with hot coffee and lemonade had been prepared, of which all partook, and a happier set of fellows were never saw, and each looked upon the trophy of the day as though it had been won for him-self by the individual exertions of his fellows.

The band was in attendance. Afterwards both companies marched out under the command of Col. Buss, Chief Engineer, and subsequently the Neptune Company were escorted to their quarters, and all returned to the quiet of their families in due season.

We are rather proud of our fire companies. They are well organized, composed of efficient men, and act together without rivalry. The gentlemanly bearing and efficient action of the Neptune Company at Bellows Falls has secured them an enviable reputation."

The trumpet, which was presented to the Neptune Company of Keene, sits in our display case at the Central Fire Station.

1858/1859 [*from* Town of Keene Annual Report]

Report from Chief Engineer G. W. Tilden on March 7th, 1859 read as follows.

In accordance with a vote passed at the Town Meeting, I submit the following:

The Keene Fire Department consists of a Chief Engineer, with four Assistants, with two Engine Companies, about fifty men each, and a Hook and Ladder company, twenty men.

The Engine Companies have each a Machine, (which they take pride in keeping in good order for service at all times,) with about750 feet of Hose each, and other apparatus for working the same. Five hundred feet of Hose, purchased in 1856, is in good condition, and the balance, purchased in 1848, is apparently in good condition, but is so tender that it is liable to burst by any ordinary use at a fire.

I would here say that there are not uniforms enough, notwithstanding several have been furnished by individual members of the Companies.

The Hook and Ladder Company have a Carriage, with Ladders, Hooks &c., but the whole apparatus is so heavy it would be difficult to handle with expedition at a fire.

There are also two old Machines capable of doing good service in time of need, provided water could be obtained.

I would urge upon the inhabitants of the town the necessity of providing some way to obtain a supply of water, the present system of Reservoirs being inefficient. The Town Well on the south side of the Square would be exhausted by both Machines within thirty minutes, and there is not another Reservoir in town that would supply them more than five minutes.

I would suggest, that if water could be taken from some point on Beaver Brook with a pipe, and a line of Reservoirs established between Washington and Court-streets down to the Square, and thence down Main-street, (they could also branch off to School and West –streets,) and all these Reservoirs connected by a pipe, a supply of water would be obtained the expense of which would be small compared with the protection they would afford. The water could then be carried each way, as occasion might require, to Court or Washington-streets, by the Machines.

There has been only one alarm of fire the last year, W. D. Ballou's dwelling-house. The Engine Companies were promptly on the ground, but fortunately their services were not required. Damage was trifling.

G. W. Tilden, Chief Engineer Keene Fire Department March 7th, 1859 from the Village of Keene Reports.

1860/1861 [*from* Town of Keene Annual Report]

Brought trying times to Keene and the Nation, the impending conflict between the North and the South. Like most towns the citizens watched with apprehension as to what would be next.

The year was also an election year for the debate of Lincoln and Douglas. Keene cast 635 votes for Lincoln and 244 for Douglas.

The nation had a full plate and on April 12, 1861, Fort Sumter was fired upon and the news flashed through the nation. President Lincoln on April 15th, 1861 called for 75,000 volunteers, and the governor of New Hampshire issued the call for the militia. The call was answered form every corner of the state. Keene became a regional recruiting station, and as a railroad center saw many soldiers off to the field of battle. While researching this writer found on page 299 of a half filled book, in the back of the Neptune Engine Company the clerks notes to those from this department who meet their countries call to serve as a Soldier for the Union.

1861 [*from* Town of Keene Annual Report]
The Chief Engineers Report.

In 1860 the Chief Engineer Robert Wilson resigned and Joseph P. wells became the Acting Chief Engineer and later appointed to Chief Engineer. His report for the year ending in 1861.

Note: After Robert Wilson Chief Engineer resigned then Acting Chief Joseph P. Wells was appointed the acting Selectmen wrote in the Keene Records at the end of the Fire Department Report this short memo as follows:

There has been some dissatisfaction in this department the past year. The Neptune Engine Company disbanded. the Deluge Company has been well officered and manned throughout the year; also, the Hook and Ladder Company. Sometime last July, the Chief Engineer requested us to buy new hose for the Department, but we did not feel fully authorized to run the town into debt for hose, when at the last Annual Meeting there was an article in the warrant to instruct the Selectmen to buy hose, and to raise money for the same; and the town voted to pass over the article.

Under the circumstances we did not buy the hose, and the Chief Engineer and one Assistant Engineer, felt grieved and resigned their appointments, and the Neptune Engine Company disbanded. Immediately after the Company disbanded, the First Assistant Engineer, (acting as Chief) organized, a volunteer Company, and the Neptune is now well manned by our citizens, volunteering to run with the machine in case of fire. The Acting Chief has full charge of the machine. Too much praise cannot be bestowed on our acting Chief in the prompt manner in which he organized a volunteer company immediately after the Neptune Company disbanded. After the Company was organized, the machine was found to be in bad condition, and he felt it his duty to put it into good order, and he sent for one of Messrs. Hunneman & Co.'s mechanics, who came and put it in good repair and working order. There has been two Reservoirs built the past year, one near Mechanic street, and one on Summer street, near Middle street they are each ten feet in diameter, and about twelve feet deep. There is most of the year a small stream of water running through the one near Mechanic Street.

In accordance with a vote passed at the last Town Meeting, I submit the following:

The Keene Fire Department, at the commencement of the year, consisted of a Chief engineer, with four Assistants, two Engine companies, about fifty men each, and a Hook and Ladder company, twenty men.

About the first of August the Chief resigned: soon after, one of the Assistants resigned; immediately following which, the Neptune Engine Company, through their officers, requested to be discharged from further service, as Firemen; their request was complied with, which left the Neptune Engine without men to work her. To obviate this difficulty, a call for volunteers, to answer an alarm of fire, was responded to by forty-five of our citizens, most of them old firemen. They have been called out once, and did the Department much honor.

The Deluge Company is in good condition, well officered and manned, and maintains their old reputation.

Both Companies need more Hose, and I would recommend the earliest attention of the incoming Board of Selectmen to the fact.

The supply of Water I consider inadequate to the wants of a village as large as Keene.

The Chief Engineer, before he left the Department, put the apparatus pertaining to the Hook and Ladder Company in good repair. It has a Company of good men, and is all right. There have been two alarms of fire this past year: the first originated in a lumber room over Jacob Green's Drug Store, which was subdued without damage to the building. The second alarm was from the premises of Mr. Greenwood, on Court Street. The Engines were on hand promptly, but the fire had made such progress that it was impossible to save the house. The barn was saved, through the exertions of both citizens and firemen.

Joseph P. Wells, Acting Chief Engineer, Keene Fire Department, from the Village of Keene Reports 1861.

[*Compiler Note*: As each year moved on the village kept a record of each expense. The period ending for this report is March 1st, 1862. See Report below:]

1862 [*from* Town of Keene Annual Report]

Report of the Chief Engineer

To the Honorable Board of Selectmen of the Town of Keene:

Gentlemen: I would respectfully submit the following Report:

The two Engines Deluge and Neptune are in good and effective condition; a good and full Company is attached to each, under the foremanships respectively of Samuel Frank and Col. G. D. Dort. The Engines have both been somewhat improved the past year

by enlarging the outlet for leading hose; the hose purchased last year being larger, rendered the alteration necessary. It is a decided improvement.

The Hook and Ladder Company is in good condition and all right, under the orders of David H. Parker, Esq.

I would recommend that the old Engines known as the Lion and Tiger be disposed of and the proceeds be applied to the purchase of a new hose carriage for the Neptune Engine; the one used now is too small. It will be necessary to purchase at least five hundred additional feet of hose the ensuring year, as some of the hose now on hand is becoming unfit for use. We have had an unusual number of fires the past year.

March 10th, the Shook Shop occupied by Porter & Willard and owned by Chase & Fairbanks, was entirely consumed. The Department was able to save surrounding property. Loss, about $500; insurance, $250.

April 22nd, The Coal House attached to the Gas Works was burned. The Department was promptly on hand, and by their exertions saved the coal. Loss, $300; no insurance.

July 4th, Esty's barn burned; no alarm given; the Department no out. Loss, $200.

July 28th, the wood shed connected with No. 10 School House was discovered on fire and an alarm given. The Department was prompt, and prevented the fire from extending to the House. Loss, about $150.

August 7th, Woodward's Stove and Foster's Organ Shops were burned. The Department was promptly on hand and saved the adjoining buildings. The Deluge Engine House was slightly damaged. Woodward's loss, $2,500; insurance $1,000. Foster's loss, $1,200; insurance, $1,000. Wilder's loss on Building, $2,000.

October 19th, Oscar Burritt's House and outbuildings (known as the Hastings Place) were burned. The Department was called out, but the fire had made such progress while the

Engines were being drawn some three miles through the mud and rain, that it was impossible to save the buildings, with the exception of a small House in the rear yard. The contents of the House were saved. Loss, about $1,600; insurance, $1,600.

February 4th, Richards' wooden Building, between the Town Hall and shelly & Sawyer's Block, was discovered to be on fire about 10 o'clock in the evening. The Department was promptly on the ground and did all that men could do, but the fire made such rapid progress that their efforts were only crowned with success in saving the adjoining property. The Building was occupied by Stephen Barker, Grocer, H. D. Randall, Shoe Shop, and Samuel Woodward, Tin Shop. G. H. Richards' loss on Building, $2,500; insurance, $1,600. Samuel Woodward & Co., Goods, $1,200; insurance, *00. H. D. Randall Goods, $1,500; insurance, $1,500. Shelly & Sawyer's loss on Building, $130.

It will be seen by the above Report that we have had warnings enough of affording the Firemen a better supply of water. We have as good Engines and as good men to man those as anyone could desire, but the all-important article we are shore of, and I do hope that something can be done the ensuing season to obviate the present difficulty.

I would here express the deep sense of obligation I feel toward the Assistant Engineers of the Board and to every man connected with the Department, and to that portion of citizens (who always do as they would be done by) for their cheerful co-operation in the affairs of the past year.

Joseph P. Wells Chief Engineer February 25th, 1862 City Report

----

1863 [*from* Town of Keene Annual Report]

Report of the Chief Engineer

To the Honorable Board of Selectmen of the Town of Keene:

Gentlemen: I would respectfully submit the following report: The two Engines Deluge and Neptune are in good working order; good and effective companies (although not full) are attached to them, under the Foremanship, respectively, of Augustus T. Wilder, Esq., and Col. G. D. Dort.

The Hook and Ladder Company is in good condition, with a full complement of men. It sustains its ancient reputation under the lead of K. H. Parker, Esq.

We have had ten fires the past year, three of which were subdued without a general alarm. The Department has been called out seven times, as follows:

March 21st, 1863 Alarm, from the burning of Kate Tylor's house. Through the exertions of the Department, saved the Ell and Out-Buildings. No Insurance.

June 4th, the Paint Shop, in the three-story building in the rear of the steam shop known as Buss & Woodward's, was discovered to be on fire. The Department was prompt in their response and saved the building. Damages about $200. Insured.

August 5th, Edward Joslyn's Barn, on West Street, was set on fire by lighting. Although the fire spread very rapidly, yet the Department, by their efficiency and prompt action, saved most of the lower story of the building and a part of the hay, in a damaged condition. Damage $700. Insured.

October 28th: Alarm, caused by burning a bed and wearing apparel in an upper room in the Cheshire House. Department promptly on hand; fire subdued without working the Engines. Damage about $50.

November 26th, Alarm, caused by the burning of a shed attached to house of Eli Reynolds, on Roxbury Street. Department were on hand, and with the aid of Citizens saved the house. Damages about $125.

December 1st, Dr. Thomas E. Hatch's barn and shed were discovered to be on fire. It being one of those places not adjacent to our bountiful supply of water, the barn and shed, with their valuable contents, were entirely consumed. Damages about $1000. Insured for $300.

Alarm, caused by the burning of pail staves in the Dry House belonging to Chase & Fairbanks' Steam Mill. The Building being brick, the fire was kept within the walls. Damage about $75.

In my report last year, it was recommended that the two old engines, Lion and Tiger, be disposed of, they being useless. It has been done, and the proceeds, a little over $100, paid into the Town treasury.

We have had much inconvenience in times past, in getting the requisite quantity of hose to fires, as our Hose Carriages belonging to the Engines, are not large enough to carry more than half it is necessary to use in most cases. There was an old Carriage belonging to the Department, but time that causes iron to rust and wood to decay, has been too much for it, and it has gone down under its burdens, leaving us in the lurch. Upon consulting with the Selectmen, it was deemed best to appoint a committee to investigate the subject. The result was an order to build a good, substantial, for wheeled Hose Carriage. The order was given to George Holmes & Brother, who in doing justice to the order have done much credit to themselves in the workmanship. The Carriage will add much to the efficiency of the Department.

I may be allowed here to congratulate the citizens of Keene that they have been spared so long by the Fire King. I do not believe he knows the condition of our water works. I would again express the deep sense of obligation I feel toward the Assistant Engineers of the Board, and to every man connected with

The New Niagara Hose Reel purchased in 1863. Picture taken at head of Central Square with Ball Block and UCC Church in foreground. The photo came from the fire department scrapbook. HSCC collection.

The above is a hand blown glass replica of the Niagara Hose Reel. It is unsure as to the creator of the above replica. It could have possible been made by a member of the Niagara Hose Company and donated to the department. It sits in a glass case on the piano in the big hall of the Central Fire Station. This replica has sat within the fire station for more than 100 years. Photo by Steve Goldsmith.

the Department. I would also impress it upon the citizens that we always need their help. For their cheerful co-operation in times past, I thank them.

Joseph P. Wells, Chief Engineer, Keene
March 1st, 1863 Town Records

1863 [*from* Town of Keene Annual Report]

[*Compiler note*: On March 1st, 1863 Francis A. Perry became the Chief Engineer and submitted his report on October 1st, 1863 as follows.]

Report of the Chief Engineer to the Board of Selectmen.

Gentlemen: I respectfully submit the following report:

When entering upon the duties of Chief Engineer I found the Department in good condition, and on retiring am happy to report to you that the interest in the Department is unabated.

We have had five fires, one of which was subdued without a general alarm.

March 23rd, 1863 Fire at the Passenger Depot of Cheshire Railroad. Extinguished without an alarm.

March 24th, 1863 Alarm caused by Erastus Chase's house being on fire. Department all out engines not worked.

April 22nd, 1863 Alarm caused by the burning of pail staves in the dry house of Chase & Fairbanks. The building being of brick the fire was kept within the walls. Department all out. Damage about $100. No insurance.

May 11th, 1863 Alarm caused by the roof of George Hamlet's house being on fire. Department all out extinguished without working the machines. Damage trifling.

August 10th, 1863 Alarm caused by Charles Greenwood's house being on fire. Department all out extinguished without working the machines. Damage about $100. Fully insured.

On the first of October 1863, I found myself in possession of more business than I could properly attend to, in consequence of which I resigned my position as Chief Engineer of the Keene Fire Department, said resignation taking effect on the above date.

Francis A. Perry, Chief Engineer. Keene, October 1st, 1863.

Central Square 1863 – Photo from Fire Department scrapbook. HSCC collection.

[*Compiler note*: In 1863 a New Chief had taken the rains of the department due to the resignation of Chief Perry; his report is as follows:]

1864 [*from* Town of Keene Annual Report]

The Chief Engineer's Report

To the Board of Selectmen:

Gentlemen: I respectfully submit the following report:

When entering upon the duties of Chief Engineer I found the Department in a flourishing condition, and now, at the end of the year, am able to report to you that the interest in all of the companies has not in the least diminished, but rather increased, Niagara Hose

Company having been added to the Department during the year which has just closed. I am happy to be able to say that upon all occasions they have performed their part nobly and manfully, and the officers of the Department consider them of indispensable value as a branch of the Fire Department. During the time I have filled the office of Chief Engineer we have had two fires, viz:

December 15th, 1863 Alarm caused by the burning of a small building near the railroad Machine Shop. Department out Neptune No. 2 worked. Damage about $25.00. Insured.

CONSTITUTION

OF THE

KEENE FIRE DEPARTMENT,

ADOPTED FEBRUARY 1, 1864.

KEENE:
PRINTED AT THE N. H. SENTINEL OFFICE.
1864.

CONSTITUTION.

The following Constitution was adopted by the Engineers of the "KEENE FIRE DEPARTMENT," from a conviction of its necessity in making the work of the Department thoroughly effective. Its design is to furnish some general rules which shall apply, under all circumstances, to the operations of all Fire Companies under the jurisdiction of the Engineers.

ARTICLE I.

This organization shall be known as the "KEENE FIRE DEPARTMENT," which shall consist of the Chief Engineer, and seven Assistants, the Deluge, Neptune, Niagara Hose, and Hook and Ladder Companies, to be appointed and hold their office as provided by law.

4

ARTICLE II.

The Board of Engineers shall be provided with a badge of office; shall choose a Clerk, who shall also be a member of the Board, whose duty it shall be to keep a record of all the doings of the Board when called together by the Chief Engineer, and shall notify all members of such meeting when directed by the Chief Engineer.

ARTICLE III.

Every member of the Board, who shall be absent from any Fire, shall be fined fifty cents; or from any meeting, as provided by article second, shall be fined twenty-five cents, to be collected by the Clerk, and disposed of as a majority of the Board may direct. Absence from town, or sickness, shall be considered a sufficient excuse.

ARTICLE IV.

It shall be the duty of the Engineers to inspect all houses and fire apparatus within the village precinct at least once in each year, and note all deficiencies, and report the same to the Chief Engineer.

5

ARTICLE V.

The Deluge and Neptune Companies shall be furnished with Engine and Hose; Niagara Hose Company with Carriage, Hose, and other apparatus; Hook and Ladder Company with Hooks and Ladders, and all other things belonging to the same.

ARTICLE VI.

Each Company shall be officered by a Foreman, First and Second Assistant, Clerk, and Treasurer, who shall hold their office for one year, or until others are chosen or appointed and qualified in their stead.

ARTICLE VII.

The Deluge and Neptune Companies shall have a regular meeting, at their Engine Houses, on the last Saturday of each month, commencing in April and ending in September, at 7 o'clock, P. M., and the remainder of the year at 7 1-2 o'clock. The Annual Meeting for choice of officers shall be holden on the first Saturday of April, at the same time and place.

ARTICLE VIII.

It shall be the duty of each Foreman, together with his Assistants, at each regular meeting, to instruct and discipline his men in the use of their implements for extinguishing or quelling fire.

6

ARTICLE IX.

Each Engine, Hose, Hook and Ladder man at the alarm of Fire, shall immediately repair to his respective Company, of which he is a member, and endeavor to get the same to the Fire as soon as possible.

ARTICLE X.

It shall be the duty of each Foreman, (subject to the order of the Chief Engineer,) to see that his Engine, Uniforms, Hooks, and Ladders, and all the apparatus belonging to his Company, be kept in proper and effective order, at all times; to observe that every member does his duty, and in case of Fire to obtain a release of his Company as soon as found practicable.

ARTICLE XI.

It shall be the duty of the Assistant to assist the Foreman, and in his absence to perform the duties of that office.

ARTICLE XII.

It shall be the duty of the Clerk of each Company to call the roll at the precise time stated for meeting, and at the close of the same, and immediately after the return of the Company to the Engine House after any Fire.

7

ARTICLE XIII.

It shall be the duty of the Foreman of each Company to render to the Chief Engineer, when required, an account of the members of his Company who have violated this Constitution, together with a statement of the times and character of such violations.

ARTICLE XIV.

Every absentee from a Fire shall be fined not less than twenty-five cents; from a regular meeting, twelve and one-half cents; unless he shall give satisfactory excuse to the Foreman or Standing Committee. Any member leaving his Company, when on duty, without permission of the Foreman, shall be fined not less than twenty-five cents. All fines shall be settled monthly.

ARTICLE XV.

Any candidate to be admitted into either of said Companies must receive the appointment of the Board of Engineers, and upon his admission shall be entitled to all the privileges of said Company.

ARTICLE XVI.

It shall be the duty of the Foreman of each Company to see that the Uniforms belonging to the Company are kept in good order; and that each member be required to return his Uniform before he can obtain a discharge from the Company.

ARTICLE XVII.

This Constitution may be altered or amended at any meeting of the Board of Engineers, by a major vote, the same having been proposed in writing at some previous meeting.

February 12th, 1864 Alarm caused by Messrs. Faulkner & Colony's Dry House being on fire. Department promptly on duty, all working their machines. Damage about $100. No insurance.

As you have read over the reports of the fires during the year, you have doubtless arrived at the same conclusion that the members of the Department have that we have highly favored during the year, inasmuch as the number of fires have diminished from ten to seven. The damage has been comparatively small when we refer to former years, the damage not exceeding $350.00.

I find Neptune Engine House, No. 2 too small for the accommodation of the machines and equipment belonging to the Department since the addition of Niagara Hose Company, and would beg leave to recommend the enlargement of the present building or the sale of the same and building a larger one.

In order to the maintenance of a good and efficient Fire Department in any place it is necessary that the citizens feel something of an interest for its members, and as some of the uniforms of some of the companies are mush worn and soiled, (while others have none) we would therefore recommend that a sufficient sum of money be raised to replenish those who have been uniformed, and to furnish new to Niagara Hose and Hook and Ladder Companies.

In Closing my report I should fail to do justice to the Assistant Engineers and the whole Department, did I not tender them our thanks for the promptness and efficiency with which they performed every duty assigned them maintaining an abiding confidence in the citizens of our town that we shall still in the coming future, as we have had in the past, their hearty co-operation.

H. P. Muchmore, Chief Engineer Keene Fire Department Keene, March 1st, 1864 Town Records

Osborn and Hale Fire, Mechanic Street – March 25, 1864

1865 [*from* Town of Keene Annual Report]

The Chief Engineer's Report to the Board of Selectmen:

Gentlemen: I respectfully submit the following report.

At the close of another year, I am happy to report that the department is still in a prosperous condition, the companies having been kept full; and the friendliest feeling prevails throughout the whole department. I am pleased to be able to say that upon all occasions they have performed their duties faithfully. During the year just past I report the following fires, viz:

March 24th, 1864 The fire department called out about 2 o'clock, P.M.; caused by the grass taking fire from a locomotive on the R. R. south of Metcalf's Crossing; department all out; extinguished without working the machines; damage trifling.

March 25th, 1864 The Department called out about 8 o'clock, A. M., caused by the boiler explosion at Osborne & Hale's Steam Shop, on Mechanic St.; No fire, No. 1 playing upon the ruins awhile; Hook and Ladder Co. also worked; the whole department promptly out.

May 7th, 1864 Alarm given about 4 o'clock P. M., caused by the roof of the Revere House taking fire; department all our; No. 1 working its machine; damage $15.00; insured.

September 12th, 1864 A partial alarm of fire, caused by benzene taking fire in the evening, while drawing at J. B. Knowlton's store; Hook and Ladder Co. out only; no damage,

January 10th, 1865 Alarm of fire, caused by the burning of pail staves in the dry house of Chase & Fairbanks' Steam Mill; whole department out and worked; damage about $75.00; no insurance.

The Department and Town may consider themselves highly favored, as the fires have been diminished from 7 to 5, and the damage comparatively small, not exceeding $90.00. At the last annual town meeting an appropriation of $300.00 was made for the enlargement of Neptune Engine House, for the accommodation of Niagara Hose Company, but upon examination and consultation it was thought best to build a new house instead of enlarging the old one. The appropriation not being sufficient to complete the building, I would recommend that a sufficient sum be raised to complete the same. By a vote of the town one new reservoir has been made, which I consider of indispensable value to the north part of the village, as 50 families or more can be benefited therefore, and the Engineers consider it a valuable reservoir with its abundant supply of water. In closing my report the assistant engineers and the whole department will receive my thanks for the promptness and efficiency with which they have performed their duty assigned them on each and every occasion.

H. P. Muchmore, Chief Engineer Keene Fire Department. Keene March 1st, 1865 Town Records.

BY-LAWS

OF

Neptune Engine Company,

No. 2,

ADOPTED JUNE 24, 1865.

KEENE:
PRINTED BY T. C. RAND & CO.
1865.

BY-LAWS.

PREAMBLE.

The undersigned, members of " NEPTUNE EN-GINE COMPANY No. 2," do mutually agree to support the Rules and Regulations of the Fire Department of the Town of Keene, and adopt the following code of By-Laws for the government of this Company :

ARTICLE I.

This Company shall be known as " *Neptune Engine Company No. 2.*"

ARTICLE II.

The officers shall consist of a Foreman, First and Second Assistants, a Clerk, a Treasurer, a Steward, and a Standing Committee of three, who shall be chosen by ballot.

ARTICLE III.

The Regular Meetings of this Company shall be holden at their Engine House, on the last Saturday of each month, commencing in April and ending in September, at 7 o'clock, P. M., and the remainder of the year at 7½ o'clock, P. M. The Annual Meeting for the choice of Officers shall be held on the first Saturday in April, at the place of the regular meetings, at 7 o'clock, P. M.

4

ARTICLE IV.

The Foreman shall have command of the Company at all times, preside at all meetings, and call special meetings of the Company, on application of five members or the Standing Committee ; it shall also be his duty to see that the uniforms belonging to the Town are kept in the Engine House, except when in use. In his absence these duties shall be performed by the senior officer present.

ARTICLE V.

The First Assistant shall aid the Foreman in the discharge of his respective duties. The Suction Hose shall be under his control, and he shall appoint three Suction Hosemen, subject to the approval of the Company.

ARTICLE VI.

The Second Assistant shall have charge of the Leading Hose, causing it to be placed in such situation as his superior may direct. He shall appoint six members as Leading Hosemen, subject to the approval of the Company.

ARTICLE VII.

It shall be the duty of the Clerk to keep a true record of all proceedings of the Company ; notify members of their being appointed on Committees, and also of all meetings of the Company, with printed, written or verbal notifications, giving at least six hours' notice before the time of meeting ; he shall have charge of all records and papers belonging to the Company ; read the record of the last meeting ; shall call the roll at the hours stated for all meetings of the Company ; he shall also call the roll after all alarms of fires, as soon as the Engine is housed ; he shall keep a copy of the roll in some conspicuous place in the Engine

---

5

House ; he shall give to the Treasurer a statement of the fines incurred as soon as practicable after each meeting ; shall exhibit his books to the Standing Committee whenever called upon so to do, and on leaving the office he shall deliver to his successor all books and papers belonging to the Company.

ARTICLE VIII.

It shall be the duty of the Treasurer to collect all fines ; receive all moneys due to the Company; keep regular entries of the same as the Company may direct ; keep correct accounts between the Company and the members ; pay all demands against the Company, approved by the Standing Committee, if he has funds sufficient in his hands belonging to the Company ; give a statement of his account once a quarter, and oftener if the Company require him so to do. He shall deliver to his successor in office all moneys and records belonging to the Company.

ARTICLE IX.

The Steward shall keep the Uniforms, House, Engine and apparatus in good condition ; report to the Foreman all repairs that are necessary ; remove all obstructions from before the House ; provide all refreshments for the Company when on duty, under the direction of the commanding officer, and attend to lighting and warming the House for all meetings of the Company, and hoist the flag on day of meeting.

ARTICLE X.

It shall be the duty of the Standing Committee to receive all applications for membership and report the same to the Company for their action if on investigation approved by them, and all motions for a discharge from the same, unless made

---

from Keene Fire Department records.

"The Civil War"

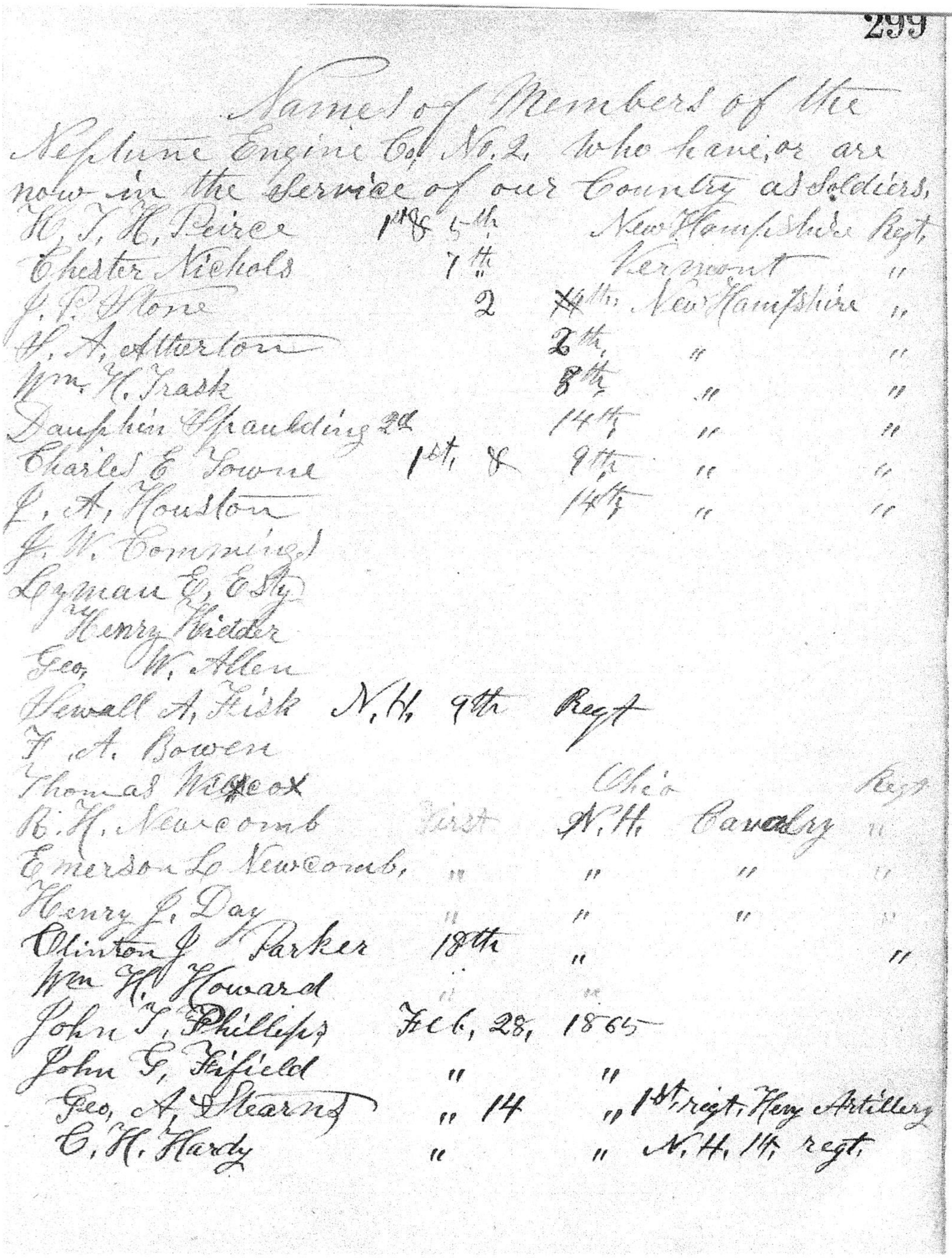

Names of Members of the Neptune Engine Co. No. 2. who have, or are now in the service of our Country as Soldiers.

H. J. H. Peirce	1st & 5th	New Hampshire Regt.
Chester Nichols	7th	Vermont "
J. P. Stone	2 #4th	New Hampshire "
H. A. Atherton	2th "	"
Wm H. Trask	8th "	"
Dauphin Spaulding 2d	14th "	"
Charles E Towne	1st & 9th "	"
J. A. Houston	14th "	"
J. W. Cummings		
Lyman E. Esty		
Henry Kidder		
Geo. W. Allen		
Sewall A. Fisk	N.H. 9th	Regt
J. A. Bowen		
Thomas Wilcox	Ohio	Regt
R. H. Newcomb	First	N.H. Cavalry "
Emerson L. Newcomb,	"	" " "
Henry J. Day	"	" " "
Clinton J. Parker	18th	" "
Wm H. Howard	"	"
John J. Phillips	Feb, 28, 1865	
John G. Fifield	" "	
Geo. A. Stearns	" 14	" 1st regt, Heavy Artillery
C. H. Hardy	"	" N.H. 14, regt,

From Keene Fire Department Records. [Compiler Note: While researching names in the Neptune Engine Company book, there were about 100 pages that were blank. I had the book in my hand when a fire call came in and I responded with the on duty shift. I picked the book back up and it opened to the page pictured above. The page listed the Neptune Engine Company No. 2 whose members served in the service of their country.]

☙ *A Demon Called Fire*

PARADE AND REVIEW.

THE KEENE FIRE DEPARTMENT

WILL HOLD THEIR ANNUAL PARADE AND REVIEW

On Friday, October 13, 1865.

ORDER OF EXERCISES.

Companies to form in line on Depot Grounds at 11 o'clock A. M.,—the right to rest near the Warehouse of J. B. Elliot & Co. Immediately after the line is formed the Companies will be reviewed by the Engineers. After the Review the line of march will be as follows :

Chief Engineer ;

Ashburnham Brass Band ;

Engineers ;

Neptune Engine Co. No. 2 ;
Foreman, GEO. D. DORT.

Hook and Ladder Co. ;
Foreman, JOHN PROCTOR.

Deluge Engine Co. No. 1 ;
Foreman, WM. H. BABBITT.

Niagara Hose Co. No. 1.
Foreman, C. F. HOLTON.

Leaving the Depot Grounds the march will be up Main St.—around Centr   —out Roxbury St.—up Church St.— down Main St. to Capt. Robinson's—up Main St.—ou   to Faulkner & Colony's Factory—up School St.—out Winter St.—up Middle St.—out Summer St. up Court St. —out Mechanic St.—up Washington St.—out Union St.—up Court St.—out Cross St up Washington St.—out High St.—up Court St. to Bancroft & Lyman's Factory—out High St down Elm St.—out Union St.—out Beaver St.—up Spring St.—down Washington St., and form   of Companies on North side of Central Square ;—after which the Companies will be escorted to ir respective Houses by the Engineers and Band. The Department will then be dismissed for Di r.

AN ALARM BELL

Will be rung at 3 1-4 o'clock, when the whole Department will be exercised under their respective Engineers.

Music by the Ashburnham Brass Band, - - 16 Pieces.

FIREMEN WILL APPEAR IN UNIFORM.

H. P. MUCHMORE, Chief,				ASA FAIRBANKS,
GEO. A. BALCH,	}	ENGINEERS.	{	JOSEPH P. WELLS,
D. H. PARKER, Clerk,				WARREN W. STONE.

From Keene Fire Department Records. October is the annual fire department parade and musters. All Company's participated in this event. This poster was in the fire department scrapbook. In October of each year the fire department continues to have its fire prevention parade.

1866 [*from* Town of Keene Annual Report]

Chief Engineers Report to the Board of Selectmen:

Gentlemen: I respectfully submit the following report:

At the close of another year I am happy to report that the Department is in good condition, all Engines, Carriages and Apparatus in good repair, with the exception of a portion of the Hose, which is old and much worn. I would recommend the purchasing of 1000 feet of new hose. A general good feeling prevails throughout the whole Department. During the past year I report the following fires, viz:

August 30th, 1865 The Fire Department called out at 3 o'clock, P. M., caused by burning of a dry-house in Swanzey Factory Village. The Department all out, but owing to the high wind and dry weather it was not considered prudent for the Department to go outside the limits of the Town.

Block by City Hall Burned on October 19th, 1865. Buildings from L to R from City Hall to Roxbury Street, T.M. Edwards, which was the Post Office then a vacant lot due to a fire in 1863 and then Shelly & Sawyer and Colony, which was a single store and G.H. Richard, which was on the corner of Roxbury Street. On February 4th, 1863 Richard's wooden building between the Town Hall and Shelby & Sawyers Block was discovered to be on fire. About 10 o'clock in the evening the department was promptly on the grounds. HSCC photo collection.

October 19th, 1865 The Fire Department Called out at 11 ¾ o'clock, P. M., caused by fire in Block owned by G. H. Richards, which was consumed, together with the Blocks owned by T. Colony and H. & A. Colony. The Estimated loss on building and contents, $46,500. Insurance, $25,510. The above fire proved the most disastrous of any fire our citizens had ever been called to witness in the town.

The building destroyed.

November 12th, 1865 The Department called out at 91/2 o'clock, A. M., caused by fire in the Dwelling House of W. D. Ballou, on Church Street. The Department promptly out, but their services were not required. Damage $100. Insured.

The Department has not been called out as often the past year as in former years, but owing to the destructive fire of October 19th, the loss has been far greater than in any former year. The Town will readily see that it is discouraging to the Department to be defeated where success is apparent wholly for the want of water. The past season has been an unusually dry one, and for the past six months there has been little or no water in our reservoirs. With the exception of the Cummings reservoir, which is of little use to the business part of the Town, there is not one other reservoir that will supply our engines thirty minutes.

In closing my report I tender my sincere thanks to the Assistant Engineers, and to the officers and members of the different fire companies, for the prompt and efficient manner in which they have performed their duties; also to those citizens who have often rendered us valuable services, and have so ably assisted in sustaining the Fire Department.

H. P. Muchmore, Chief Engineer of Keene Fire Department Keene, March 1st, 1866 Town Records

1867 [*from* Town of Keene Annual Report]

The Chief Engineer's Report to the Board of Selectmen of Keene.

Gentlemen: I have the honor to submit the following report: When I entered upon my duties as Chief Engineer, I found the Fire Department in a very disaffected condition, but with the help of the Assistant Engineers and the Foremen of the several companies, I am happy to report the department in a good condition and that they have sustained their reputation as firemen, by cheerfully attending to their duty. Deluge Engine and apparatus are in good order, with 700 feet of leading hose, and a good company, under the direction of W. H. Babbitt, Foreman. Neptune Engine and apparatus are also in a good working condition, with 400 feet leading hose with a good company under the direction of V. A. Wright, Foreman. The Hook & Ladder Company, is full, and is an excellent company, under the orders of Henry N. Stone, Forman, but is in great need of a new Hook & Ladder Carriage, or through repairs upon the old one and I would recommend that the town take some action to secure a better carriage for this company. The Niagara Hose Co., under the command of Charles F. Holton, foreman, is also full, and has 1600 feet of leading hose which with the other apparatus, is in good condition.

The past year we had four fires as follows: July 6th, 1866, partial alarm of Fire, caused

By some canvass taking fire in the Railroad Shop. Damage about 50 dollars; extinguished without the aid of the Fire Department.

October 25th, the Fire Department called out at 7 o'clock, A M., caused by the burning of the Cheshire R. R. Bridge over the Ashuelot River. Damage: $3500. Insured $200. The whole Fire Department was on hand promptly, and through their exertions the abutments of the bridge were kept from heating and thus saved.

November 3rd, brought another alarm of fire, which sent a thrill to all, as soon as the place of the fire was discovered, since it was one of the most difficult of access in town. This fire was caused by what is called "Union Oil" taking fire while drawing the same, in the cellar of the store of Messrs. Gerould, Richardson & Skinner.

The firemen were immediately on the spot, and worked with a good will, and soon had the flames under their control, with the water pouring in at the rear and front. The fire was soon subdued, and thus the buildings on the west side of the square were saved. The firemen were called out about twenty minutes past five o'clock p. m., and dismissed about 9 o'clock.

By this fire we have it demonstrated what a prompt organization and efficient companies will do; for had the firemen been a few minutes later it is impossible to tell where the ravages of the fire would have been stayed. It was fortunate for the town that we had good organized companies who are always prompt to respond to the alarm of fire. The following losses are nearly correct. Gerould, Richardson, & Skinner, on goods, $850; Insured. Gerould & Son, on building, $650; Insured. O. G. Dort, on goods $100; Hills & Chase, on goods, $50; Insured. O. D. Pratt, on furniture, $50; not insured. S. C. Dustin and others sustained more or less loss. January 28th, 1867, the Fire Department called out at 8 o'clock p. m., caused by the partial burning of Mr. Fairbank's Dry House, near his steam mill. The fire was kept under control, through the supply of water was short. But only a portion of the Dry House was destroyed. Damage about $400. The Firemen were all out and worked well. I would further recommend the purchase of another Hand Engine, similar to those we have now, and in closing my report I tender my sincere thanks to the Assistant

Engineers and to the officers and members of the different companies for the prompt manner in which they have performed their duties as Firemen, also to the citizens.

All of which I respectfully submit.

G. D. Dort, Chief Engineer Keene, February 11th, 1867

1868 [*from* Town of Keene Annual Report]

1868 was a busy year for the Fire Department and Keene.

On the 20th, day of March 1868 at nine o'clock in the forenoon at the Town Hall a vote would be taken for the town affairs:

The 13th, article to be voted on was to see if the town will pay members of the Fire Department a sum in addition to that allowed by law.

The 14th, was to see what sum of money the town will raise to defray the expenses of the Fire Department.

The 17th, was to see if the town will vote to purchase uniforms for the members of Engine Co. No. 3 and appropriate money therefore.

The 27th, was to see if the town will vote to purchase a new Hook and Ladder Carriage and additional number of ladders, or repair the old Carriage and raise money therefore.

The Chief Engineer's Report 1868

To the Selectmen of Keene, I respectfully submit the following report:

At the close of another year I am happy to report that the department is in good condition, the companies having been kept full, and the friendliest feeling prevails throughout the whole department.

By vote of the Town the Committee purchased a second-hand Fire Engine, Hunneman's make, the same capacity as the Deluge and Neptune which proves to be a good machine, which makes the Department Larger and more efficient.

Deluge Engine and apparatus are in good working order, company not quite full, at this time; under the direction of J. E. Sandall, Foreman.

Neptune Engine and apparatus are in good order, with a full company, under the direction of S. E. Hall, Foreman.

Niagara Engine and Hose Company are in good order with a full roll of men under the direction of A. O. Fisk, Foreman. I would recommend that the town take some action to secure an additional number of uniforms for the Niagara Company.

Hook and Ladder Company is a good company under the order of C. Mason, foreman, but are in great need of a better Carriage and Ladders.

We have had eleven fires the past year, three of which were subdued without a general alarm. The Department has been called out eight times, as follows:

June 26th, 1867 Alarm of fire about 5 o'clock, P. M., caused by the burning of Cheshire Railroad wood shed below depot. Damage to Railroad $3500; J. & F. French $1000; C. S. Coburn, $50; all insured. This was a very hard fire lasting all night. Firemen promptly on hand and worked with a will and thus prevented a large fire.

August 3rd, alarm of fire about 6 1-2 o'clock, P. M., caused by a defect in the chimney of Bancroft's' slaughter house damage small. Firemen all started promptly and would soon have been on the spot for action. Extinguished without their aid

August 9th, the house of John Lahiff burnt. Being the last one in Keene on the Swanzey Road, therefore no alarm reached us till too late. Damage $600. Insured $400.

August 12th, alarm of fire about 4 1-2 o'clock, P. M., caused by the burning of Nims & Crossfield's Steam Shop together with other shops and houses near the same. Total loss $44,500. Insured $13,075. This was the most disastrous fire that the town has hand for many a year. Firemen all out promptly. No. 1 and 2 dismissed about 12 o'clock at night. No. 3 was not dismissed till 2 o'clock next morning. Engineers out all night.

September 23rd, alarm of fire about 9 o'clock, A. M., caused by the partial burning of M. Fairbank's Dry House. Department all out promptly and soon deluged it. Damage $50.

October 10th, fire about 5 o'clock P. M., caused by the burning of James Birne's barn. Department out promptly. House saved without much damage. Insured. No insurance on Barn. Damage $500.

November 15th, fire about 4 1-2 o'clock A. M., caused by the floor taking fire from the chimney in Grimes' Store. Damage small. Extinguished without working the Engines. November 16th, fire at 6 o'clock, P. M., caused by M. Fairbanks' Dry House taking fire. Companies all out.

Worked 3 1-2 hours before being relieved. Damage $200. No insurance.

It will be seen by the above report that we have had warning enough the past year to rouse up the citizens of Keene to the importance of affording a better supply of water. I do hope that something will be done the ensuing Town Meeting that will give us more water.

In closing my report I tender my sincere thanks to the Assistant Engineers, Officers and members of the different companies for the prompt manner in which they have performed their duties as Firemen.

George D. Dort, Chief Engineer Keene February 20th, 1868

1869

In 1869 Uniforms for the Niagara Engine Company was appropriated a total of $551.75 and also appropriated was the Carriage for the Hook and Ladder. The Chief Engineer's Report of 1869 will explain.

1869 Chief Engineer's Report to the Town:

To the Selectmen, Gentlemen I beg to submit the following report of the condition of the fire apparatus of the town, and such matters as pertain to the Fire Department:

There have been four fires only in this town during the past years, as follows:

March 14th, 1868, alarm of fire about 6 o'clock, A. M., caused by a defect in the chimney of Col. N. Hart's house on Pearl Street. Damage $50. Insured. Firemen out promptly.

July 29th, alarm of fire about 8 o'clock, A. M., caused by a pipe bursting in the Gas house. Damage small. Firemen out promptly.

January 15th, 1869, Fairbanks's Steam Mill was discovered to be on fire about 11 o'clock in the evening. The Department was promptly on the ground and did all that men could do, but the fire made such rapid progress that their efforts were only crowned with success in saving the Engine and surrounding buildings. M. Fairbanks loss the building, saw mill, grist mill and sash and blind machinery, in all about $40,000, insured $22,675. E. Kendall loses in pails and boxes $3000. Insured for $2000. E. Murdock, manufacturer of sash and blinds, loss $2000, insured for $1000. D. Buss loses in machinery $300, no insurance. J. & A. H. Grimes and A. H. Freeman lose in grain and meal $50.

February 21st, D. W. Buckminster's house was discovered to be on fire about noon and an alarm was given; the Department were prompt, and prevented the fire from burning the building; damage large Insured.

The Deluge, Neptune, Niagara Engines and Hose Carriages and entire equipment are in excellent condition.

The committee has bought a new Hook and Ladder Carriage named Washington, when the new ladders are done it will be a splendid carriage and will add greatly to the Department. It will be necessary to purchase at least two thousand feet of leading Hose the ensuing year; it may be necessary to change the size of Hose to fit the Hydrants which will be the fire steamer size two and a half inch. Our Hose being smaller than is in general use.

Detailed statements of the expenses of the Fire Department are given elsewhere by the selectmen and it is not necessary to report it here.

I cannot close this report without acknowledging my deep obligation to the Assistant Engineers, officers and men, of the Department, and bear testimony to their efficiency upon all occasions connected with their duty as firemen.

Geo. D. Dort, Chief Engineer. Keene, February 22nd, 1869

1870 [*from* Town of Keene Annual Report]

Report of the Chief Engineer.

To the Selectmen, Gentlemen: In accordance with the law of the State I present the following report of the Keene Fire Department for the past official year, respectfully submitting a brief statement of its operations, present condition, and a few suggestions respecting its prospective requirements.

Comparatively little active duty had been required of this Department in the suppression of fires; although the "destroyer" made us quite frequent visits during the first quarter of the year, the reception he received from our firemen so effectually dampened his and or that his stay was in no case protracted, and by the commendable vigilance and care of our citizens we have not been called upon to meet him during the last mine months. This immunity from his appearance may perhaps in part be accredited to the through examinations which have been made annually by the Board of Engineers, to ascertain in regard to the safety of buildings, &c., in the compact portion of the town; and I may say in this connection that the reports of the examinations made by my Assistants during the past year show a marked improvement in the condition of places and things heretofore reported

as unsafe or hazardous; and our citizens have in most instances complied with the recommendations or requirements of the Engineers in regard to the removal of causes from which danger might be apprehended; but too many cases may yet be found where proper care is not exercised, particularly in the storage of ashes and the keeping of combustible materials in exposed places; we would therefore urge the importance of increased care in these matters.

Since the last annual report we have had fires and alarms as follows, viz:

March 29th, 1869, the department was called out about 3 o'clock, A. M., by the burning of the dwelling house of Cyrus Hurd, near the upper end of Washington Street. Although a prompt response was made to the call, the flames had made such rapid progress before the alarm was given that nothing could be done to save the building and no other property being endangered the engines were not worked. Fire supposed to have been set by occupant, causing about $1000 loss to his creditors. No insurance.

March 30th, about 6 P. M., a small barn belonging to Mr. John Lahiff near Swanzey line was burned down. No alarm given; loss $200. Supposed to have been set by children playing with matches.

April 12, alarm about 8 o'clock, P. M., caused by breakage of a gas pipe and ignition of escaping gas in basement of Clark's Block. Department on hand immediately and just ready to apply water when the cause of the alarm was suppressed in a novel manner by one of our citizens who had presence of mind to apply a piece of bar soap to the broken pipe, making an effectual stopper for the orifice and preventing further escape of gas.

April 15th, 10 o'clock, A. M., an alarm caused by a defective flue in the house of W. D. Ballou, on Church Street, the attic of ell part being well on fire when discovered; but the flames were quickly subdued by the firemen who were on hand early and had a convenient supply of water. Damage $375; insured.

May 25th, about 2 o'clock, P. M. fire discovered in ell part of the dwelling house of Zebina Knight, Main Street, by one of the occupants of the house. Alarm given, which brought the firemen out promptly, and the fire was extinguished before it had made great progress. Damage about $300; no insurance; origin unknown.

June 6th, 3 o'clock, P. M., Bancroft & Greeley's slaughter barn discovered on fire and alarm given. Department promptly represented, but the combustible nature of the building and its contents, with a limited supply of water, made it impossible for the engines to do any service except in protecting the adjoining property. Loss about $1000; insurance $500; Origin of fire attributed to carelessness of tobacco smokers.

June 16th, an alarm on account of the burning out of a chimney in the Cheshire House called out the department, but without cause. Making in all five fires and two alarms, with total loss of about $300.00, during the year.

The condition of the apparatus for extinguishing fires, belonging to the town, never was better than at present. That which was on hand at the commencement of the year consisted of three hand engines, all good machines, No. 1 and 2 having hose carriages attached, and No. 3 having an independent four-wheeled hose carriage. Also, one hook and ladder carriage with a very good and serviceable supply of ladders and fire hooks; these with the tools and fixtures, uniforms, &c, have all been kept in good repair and are now in good order for use. The hose then on hand comprised about 2000 ft. leather hose and 500 ft. linen hose, mostly two inch, all of which had been considerably worn, although most of it will yet be serviceable for occasional use.

The addition of 2000 ft. best oak tanned leather two and one half inch hose, with couplings, goosenecks and fittings for using the same either with the engines or with hydrants, and other articles provided during the year, makes our equipment more complete than ever before; and with 43 hydrants connected with the water works recently completed which afford a supply of water that can be applied to fires within the compact part of the town without the aid of engines, we think our citizens may enjoy a sense of security which they have never known before; and with a few changes that may be necessary for the proper use of the hydrants, we trust their property may be saved from any very destructive conflagration.

We have now four well organized fire companies, to wit: Deluge Engine Co. No. 1, with 40 men; Neptune Engine Co. No. 2, with 40 men; Niagara Engine and Hose Co. No. 3, with 60 men; and Washington Hook and Ladder Co. No. 1 with 20 men.

These have all been well filled with efficient men, who have been ready and willing to do the duties required of them, and they have on every occasion since my connection with this department been entitled to great credit for their promptness in responding to alarms and in getting their apparatus ready for use at fires. In this respect I think I may safely say that our department cannot be excelled, and I believe it is seldom equaled, y any other similar organization. This affords us the advantages of coping with a fire in its earlier stages, which is an important element of success, especially in localities where the supply of water is limited, as it has formerly been with us.

And unless an ample supply of water is to be had, I think our hand engines well manned have many advantages over the steam fire engine, as ordinarily managed in our smaller cities, and towns like ours; as being more readily transported, they can in many cases be put to work and a small fire subdued in less time than would be required to get a steamer into position and easy for use. But for a more extensive conflagration wherever a supply of water is attainable we should certainly prefer the more powerful and untiring services of the latter. Yet we consider the ever-ready, constant and powerful jets thrown by the hydrants of our new water works, better than either as a protector to all property within their reach, and unless the increasing boundaries of our village exceed a proper extension of the water pipes and hydrants, which they should not be allowed to do, we shall probably have little use for engines of either description.

As the use of the hydrants will effect quite a change in the modus operandi of extinguishing fires, it is necessary that some changes should be made in the organization and equipment of the fire department; therefore I would recommend that the town take such action at its annual meeting as may be required for a proper reorganization of the department, and for the procurement of such additional apparatus as may be needed; also to authorize the sale of any property which it may be expedient to dispose of.

I would also recommend that the laws "in relation to the extinguishment of fires," now in force by former votes of the town be repealed and superceded by Chapter 96 of Compiled Statutes, which combines all the essentials features of several former enactments in a simpler and more concise form.

In relation to what changes it may be advisable to make in order to enable the department to operate in the most successful and economical manner, I would say that our present experience may not warrant any definite recommendations. But as increased facilities for supplying hose are required, I will suggest that additional hose carriages should be provided so that we may be able to carry at least 2000 feet of hose. For this purpose I think light two-wheeled carriages, carrying about 300 feet each, are better than

Larger ones. These may be used in connection with our present engine companies, or by independent hose companies of ten or twelve men each.

As the territorial limits of our village are constantly enlarging, I would suggest the expediency of having hose companies located at different points in the vicinities of the more hazardous places; as for instance one such company might be advantageously located on or near Mechanic Street, and another in the vicinity of the rail-road shops, foundry and steam mills on Ralston Street, provided proper accommodation for houses for same could be obtained without great expense to the town. This would afford a more immediate protection to a larger amount of property of a class which suffers more by delays in case of fire than other kinds and these companies in most cases would be just as serviceable for fires in other localities as though they were located in the vicinity of Central Square.

Better facilities are needed for washing and cleaning hose, which can now be easily furnished from our water works at a small outlay. I think however that it one place was fitted up for that purpose, and one or two suitable men put in charge of same, the hose could all be taken care of in a much better manner and at less expense than by the stewards of the several companies, each carriage being taken there for a relay of dry hose whenever necessary. This would cause but little trouble and would save the expense of maintaining the appurtenances for washing and drying at so many places, and it would require a less quantity of hose for supplying several carriages than if each kept a relay; and in case the whole should ever be required for use at one time, it could be obtained more readily than if kept at several different places.

Perhaps some of the old two inch hose now on hand might be sold with advantage to the town, as it will do but little further service to the town; yet it might answer well for the occasional requirements of private parties. As we anticipate but little use for our engines except in localities were the hydrants are not available, (which places are not so generally subject to fires) it will probably be unnecessary to maintain more than one or two of the engine companies as at present organized; and it may be advisable to dispose of one of the machines should a favorable opportunity occur, yet it is better to be prepared in case of any accidents to the hydrants with proper facilities for subduing fires which may happen at such times, and I would not advise the sale of apparatus that shall make us deficient in such cases; and it is also necessary that our reservoirs be kept in proper condition for use at such times.

In closing this report I desire to acknowledge my obligations to the Assistant Engineers for their efficient aid, and for the kindness and courtesy which they have ever manifested in our official intercourse; and to express our thanks to the officers and members of the several companies for their gentlemanly conduct and faithful discharge of duty whenever their services have been required; and we congratulate them that harmonious action amicable feelings have so generally prevailed. Our citizens are also entitled to much credit for their interest in our welfare, and as their cooperation is always needed we ask a continuance of their aid by their influence and services-that our companies may at all times be supplied with reliable men whose only aim shall be to maintain the efficiency of the department and to promote the public good.

Respectfully submitted.

John Humphrey, Chief Engineer. Keene, February 22, 1870

Note: August 4th, 1870 was the first real test of the new hydrant system in Keene. A fire on Court Street, the Metcalf's had two barns catch fire and the hydrant system proved to be very satisfactory to all who witnessed its operation.

Report of the Chief Engineer March 1st, 1870

To the Selectmen of Keene, gentlemen: I have the pleasure to report to the town that the Fire Department is in excellent condition; its apparatus now more complete than ever before, and the companies well organized and filled with efficient and reliable men, who have at all times responded promptly to the calls for their services which have been made as follows, wiz.:

1st. June 25, 1870, about 8 o'clock, P. M. the buildings of Ashley Mason were struck by lightning. Their distance from the engine houses and from any accessible supply of water, and the rapid progress of the flames, made it impracticable for the department to render any service after its arrival. Loss $3,000; insurance $1,400. This was the first alarm for more than a year, the last previous fire having occurred June 6th, 1869.

2nd. July 10, about 9 o'clock, P. M., an alarm was given during the burning of the buildings of Franklin D. Reed, about four miles north-west of the village; but it was evidently useless for the department to attempt to reach it and the apparatus was returned to the houses. Loss about $4,000; not insured.

3rd. August 4, about noon, during a very heavy thunder shower, two barns belonging to E. A. & A. E. Metcalf on Court Street were fired by the lighting and speedily enveloped in flames; but the application of Spring Lake water from the hydrants nearby soon extinguished the fire, and saved the adjacent buildings, making the first practical test of the Keene Water Works in subduing fire, which was very satisfactory to all who witnessed it. Damage to house and contents $500.

4th. August 26, about 11 o'clock, A. M., a fire in the fuel room of the steam mill on Mechanic

St., was extinguished by the use of hydrants, with slight damage.

5th. December 29, about 4 o'clock, P. M., at the residence of Rev. G. W. Browne, on School St.; the lathing being left in too close proximity with a stove pipe or thimble at the entrance to a chimney became ignited, and was discovered in time to extinguish with only slight damage.

6th. the next day, **December 30**, about 11 o'clock, A. M., a similar occurrence happened at the dwelling of Samuel Gordon, on Elm St.

7th. January 29, 1871, about 7 o'clock, P. M., fire was discovered in a wood room in Clark's block, but causing no material damage. The last three fires, and two or three others of a similar character for which no alarm was given, were extinguished without the use of hose.

8th. February 15, about 9 o'clock, P. M., the department were called out by a fire in the work room of Messrs. Buffum's clothing establishment, which was extinguished with but slight damage from the fire, but the location of the fire, which was in the partitions contiguous to a chimney near the center of the upper story of the building, was not at first apparent; and the rooms were so completely filled with smoke and heat that no entrance could be made without the use of considerable water, which occasioned some damage to the goods in the stores below, which was adjusted and paid by the insurers as follows; Messrs. Buffum, damage to building and stock $1,050; Messrs. Joslin & Gay, damage to stock by water $175.00. Making the total damage by fires in the town during the past year about $9,000, and that coming within the limits of the fire district only about $2,000.

The annual examination of the fire district for the past year was delayed until winter as more appropriate season for that purpose, being when the largest number of stoves, &c., are in use. Particular attention was given to the examination of partitions around chimneys and stove pipe thimbles, and several cases similar to those causing the alarms No. 5 and 6 were reported as unsafe; other defects and delinquencies in the safe keeping of ashes. &c., were much less numerous that those reported in former years. This we believe accounts in part for the comparative immunity from accidental fires which we have enjoyed. Several buildings are in need of ladders, which owners should not neglect to provide, as those belonging to the department cannot always be transported to a fire as soon as the application of water can be made either with buckets, or with hose if suitable ladders were at hand; a small expense in precautionary measures may save much loss.

The annual parade and review of the Fire Department was held September 24th, and was made the occasion for a series of experiments for testing the capacity of the Water Works, which showed the practicability of carrying water through hose to protect buildings situated one-fourth or even one-half mile distant from a hydrant; and, in cases where several hydrants can be used, it was found that twelve or more streams of water could be used at one time with good effect.

The fine appearance of the firemen with their apparatus, their gentlemanly conduct and the skill displayed in making these and other experiments during the day, was highly creditable to them, and, we believe satisfactory to the citizens present on the occasion; and the exhibition of our present ability to resist the fiery element (which we believe is not exceeded by any town or city in the country) should give our citizens the advantages of a material reduction in the rates of insurance for their property.

The number of firemen belonging to the several companies of the Department has, in accordance with the vote of the town, been reduced to 120, and a further reduction of 20 men, as thereby authorized, has been contemplated and perhaps may be advisable, although that would dispense with one hose carriage attached to the engine they now operate. It has been the rule to have two engines taken out in readiness for use if required at any alarm of fire, but they have not been used on any occasion during the past year, and if our water works were provided with an additional reservoir or other means to afford a supply in case of repairs of the main line to the pond, the engines would be seldom, if ever required for use.

Four new hose carriages have been procured and put into use. They are light and convenient to handle, and make a valuable accession to the equipment of the department. They are at present kept in the engine houses of the town as no other accommodations have been provided although the subject has frequently been brought to the attention of those most interested in the matter. A new tower for drying hose has been erected at engine house No. 1. This was decided to be preferable to the alteration and enlargement of the old towers as at first designed. This involved a larger expenditure than was first contemplated and makes some changes in the previous practices of the companies, but the plan, if properly carried out, will save the town considerable expense in the future purchase and care of hose.

Manual containing useful information in relation to the appliances for the extinguishment of fires, with instructions in regard to the duties of the firemen in the use and care of same, has been published during the year, which we believe is a judicious expenditure to promote the efficiency of the department.

The tower was added to the Town Hall in 1864 for the purpose of adding a fire bell to notify the public of a fire or other notices that the public should know. In 1955 the tower was removed and the bell in the tower was donated to the Cathedral of the Pines in Rindge, NH, where it still rings.

GENERAL BY-LAWS
OF THE KEENE FIRE DEPARTMENT

Adopted by the Board of Engineers.

ARTICLE I.

ENGINEERS' BADGE OF OFFICE.

Each Engineer of the Keene Fire Department when on duty at any fire shall be known by a badge worn on his hat having thereon the word "Engineer."

ARTICLE II.

MEETINGS OF THE BOARD OF ENGINEERS.

The regular meetings of the Board of Engineers shall be holden on the Tuesday next following the last Saturday of each month; and special meetings may be called by the Chief when he may deem it necessary, or at the request of two members of the Board, the hour of meeting to be 7 1-2 o'clock, P. M., unless otherwise designated.

ARTICLE III.

DUTIES OF THE CLERK.

The Clerk shall record the doings of the Board, notify meetings as directed by the Chief, and serve such notices of the ordinances of the Board as he may be required.

ARTICLE IV.

INSPECTION OF THE FIRE DISTRICT.

It shall be the duty of the Assistant Engineers to visit and inspect all buildings within the village precinct at least once in each year; to examine in regard to the safety of stoves, fire-places, flues, &c., and to ascertain respecting the supply of ladders, and the proper removal, care or storage of ashes, shavings and other combustible materials; noting and reporting all deficient and unsafe places, and any violations of the rules of the Board, of which parties concerned should be notified, and informed of any changes which may be deemed necessary.

ARTICLE V.

CARE OF THE FIRE APPARATUS, &C.

It is the duty of the Engineers to acquaint themselves properly with all the apparatus, hydrants and reservoirs used for fire purposes, and to keep proper watch in regard to the condition and care of same, reporting any deficiency or needed repairs which may appear. Also, to note the requirements of the fire companies, and to take into consideration and to act in relation to any matters which may be necessary in order to make the Department more thoroughly effective; endeavoring at all times to promote the permanent good of the organization.

ARTICLE VI.

APPOINTMENT OF FIREMEN.

In the appointment of firemen to any Company the Engineers will receive and consider any nominations of the Company, with such information as may be furnished respecting the residence and location of the business of the proposed member; his age, character and ability to perform the duties which may be required of him; but it is the duty of the Board to reject all candidates which from want of proper information or otherwise, they may not regard as suitable or for the best interest of the Department to have appointed. Due notice of the decision of the Board relative to the appointment of any person nominated by any Company shall be given to the clerk of such Company; and any person having received an appointment may in acceptance thereof sign the By-Laws of the Company and of this Department (in the Company's book) and he shall be entitled to all the privileges of the Company; and be bound to perform all the duties incumbent on him as a fireman, in accordance with the laws of the State and rules of this Department, until legally discharged.

ARTICLE VII.

DISCHARGES AND EXPULSIONS.

Any member of this Department having complied with its rules and those of his Company, and having returned all company and town property entrusted to his care, shall be entitled to an honorable discharge at his own request.

And any member who by removal from town or otherwise, shall in the opinion of the Board of Engineers neglect or become incapable of attending to and performing the duties appertaining to his appointment, may be discharged by a vote of the Board and their record of same shall terminate his membership, and his name shall be stricken from the roll of his Company.

Any member who wilfully neglects or refuses to perform his duty as a member of any Company, or to pay the fines imposed for such neglect, for the space of three months, or any member guilty of insubordination, disorderly conduct, drunkenness or indecent behavior when on duty, may be expelled by a vote of the Company, (subject to the approval of the Board of Engineers); and any member so expelled shall be held liable for all fines and demands of the Company against him.

ARTICLE VIII.

COMPANY ORGANIZATIONS AND DUTIES OF MEMBERS.

It shall be the duty of each Fire Company organized in accordance with the laws of the State and votes of the town, and all volunteer companies who shall have charge of any engines, hose, fire hooks, ladders or other apparatus or property provided by the town, and of each member thereof, to exercise proper care and diligence to prevent unnecessary waste or injury of such apparatus or

From Fire Department records. General by Laws adopted by the Board of Engineer's for the entire Keene Fire Department

☙ *A Demon Called Fire*

property, and to have the same kept at all times in proper order and readiness for service ; and to meet at proper times for discipline and practice, also for the transaction of the business of the company. And at any time upon hearing an alarm of fire to repair without delay to get the apparatus of the company into position and readiness for use ; and in accordance with the directions of the Engineers or other proper authority to exert themselves to extinguish and prevent the spreading of such fire ; and after the release of the company by the Engineers to assist in taking care of the apparatus and returning same to its proper place.

ARTICLE IX.

COMPANY MEETINGS.

The annual meeting for the choice of officers of the several fire companies shall be holden on the first Saturday of April in each year.

Regular meetings for the transaction of the business of any company may be holden not more than once in each month, at such times as the company may provide in their by-laws ; and special meetings whenever necessary or proper for business of the company or for their instruction and discipline.

ARTICLE X.

OFFICERS OF COMPANIES.

Each company shall have a foreman, and two or more assistants, a clerk, and such other officers as may be necessary for their proper organization and the transaction of their business ; to be chosen (subject to approval of the Engineers) for the term of one year from the annual meeting of the company, or until others are chosen and qualified in their stead. Vacancies may be filled whenever they occur, but in case of the neglect or failure of the company to elect suitable officers the Board of Engineers may appoint.

ARTICLE XI.

DUTIES OF FOREMAN.

It shall be the duty of the Foreman of each company to take command of same and to have (subject to the direction of the Engineers) the general supervision of the affairs of the company; to see that the house and all apparatus assigned to them is properly used and cared for, and kept in proper condition for use at all times ; and to keep a correct account of all uniforms or other articles entrusted to the use or care of individual members, and to report to the Chief Engineer any repairs that should be made. To assist him in these duties he shall be entitled to the services of a steward who shall receive a reasonable compensation for such service, on approval of the Chief Engineer. It is also the duty of the foreman to instruct and discipline his men in the use of their implements for extinguishing or quelling fire, to observe that each member discharges his duty faithfully, and in case of a fire to obtain a release

of his company as soon as it may be found practicable.

ARTICLE XII.

DUTIES OF ASSISTANTS.

The Assistants shall assist the Foreman and perform such duties as may be assigned them ; and in his absence they shall (in the order of their rank) take command of the company and perform the duties of Foreman.

ARTICLE XIII.

DUTIES OF CLERK.

It shall be the duty of the Clerk to keep a record of the doings of the company, to call the roll of its members at their meetings and before dismissal of the company after an alarm of fire ; keeping a fair and impartial register of all members present and absent at each regular meeting of the company and at each alarm of fire, which he shall present to the Board of Engineers at such times as they shall require. Also, he shall report to the Clerk of the Board of Engineers at the end of each month all vacancies occurring in the offices or membership of the company by resignation or otherwise, and all nominations for appointment or discharge by the Board ; and he shall perform the duties of his superior officers in their absence.

ARTICLE XIV.

HYDRANT AND PIPE MEN.

Each engine and hose company shall have two or more pipemen to each hose carriage, who shall assist at the pipe or butt. Also, two or more hydrant men to operate the hydrant valves ; who shall be appointed by the Engineers or approved by them.

ARTICLE XV.

FINES AND EXCUSES.

Each company may impose proper fines for the neglect of duty by any of its members, and all moneys accruing therefrom shall be for the benefit and use of the company as they may direct. And it is understood that each member by signing the by-laws agrees to conform thereto, and pay such fine as they may legally impose, and shall thereby make all moneys which he may receive from the town for his services as a fireman holden to the company for such payment. Provided however that no fine shall be required of any member who shall furnish a valid excuse for his neglect of duty, as personal sickness, necessary attendance upon the sick, absence from the town and having no knowledge of an alarm, or any other reason which the company may decide as proper to be

ARTICLE XVI.

AMENDMENTS AND ALTERATIONS OF BY-LAWS.

These by-laws may be altered or amended at any meeting of the Board of Engineers by a major vote, the same having been proposed in writing at some previous meeting and due notice having been given of the time when such amendment would be acted upon.

The expenses of the fire department for the current year will be found in the financial report of the town.

A small amount of old two inch hose has been sold and efforts made, with some prospect of success to dispose of an engine; but such property does not sell readily, as the demand is less than the supply.

Before closing my term of office I desire to express my thanks to the citizens of the town for the encouragement they have given the department since my connection with it, by the purchase of apparatus; also to those who have so liberally extended their aid at the annual parade and social levees of the firemen, and we trust the department will ever merit and receive the encouragement and respect so much needed to induce reliable and efficient men to identify themselves in its organization and to maintain its efficiency.

To my associate engineers, and the officers and members of the several companies, I have to acknowledge the kindness and respect you have shown me, and to congratulate you on the unanimity of feeling, which pervades the entire department.

Respectfully submitted, John Humphrey, Chief Engineer Keene Fire Department. Keene, March 1st, 1870

1870 [*from* Town of Keene Annual Report]

Population is now 5,971, and the Soldier Monument is erected in Central Square.

1871/1872 [*from* Town of Keene Annual Report]

Fire Department Report of the Chief Engineer.

To the Selectmen of Keene: I have the pleasure to report to the town that all the apparatus belonging to the Fire Department is in good condition and the several companies are prompt at all calls for duty.

"FIRE"

1st. April 26, 1871 about 2 o'clock a. m., the building used as a storehouse and work shop, and occupied by the Keene Furniture Co., and the Cheshire Chair Co., in rear of their shop Mechanic street, was discovered to be on fire, and was nearly destroyed, together with its contents. The abundance of water saved the town from a large fire, and perhaps saved property enough to pay for the construction of our Water Works. Loss, $15,000; no insurance.

2nd. October 22, about 1 o'clock a. m., the Pottery of J. S. Taft & Co., at the lower end of Main street, was entirely consumed. Loss, $2,000; insured for $1,000.

3rd. October 22, about 2 o'clock p. m., fire was discovered in the woods of Lucian Page at the upper part of the town, causing an alarm. No material damage.

4th. January 22, 1872, at 9 o'clock a. m., fire was discovered in a bin of fine dust and shavings at the steam shop on Mechanic Street. It was extinguished by use of the hydrants. Damage small.

6th. February 9th, about 1 o'clock p. m., J. S. Taft & Co's Pottery was again on fire, burning the roof of the kiln house. Damage $125; fully insured.

April 17th, 1872, the Neptune engine was sold to the town of Winchester for the sum of $650. Everything considered this was a fair price for the machine. Five hundred feet of new hose have been purchased and the couplings so arranged that they are uniform on the entire lot of 3000 feet of 2 ½ inch hose. There are also 500 feet of good tow inch linen hose.

The statement of expenses of this department will be found in the financial report of the town.

My brother engineers and the officers and members of the several companies have rendered me valuable aid in discharging my

A Demon Called Fire

duty for the past year, for which they have my thanks.

Respectfully submitted, John Proctor Chief Engineer Keene Fire Department. Keene, March 1, 1872.

1872/1873 [*from* Town of Keene Annual Report]

Report of the Chief Engineer.

To the Honorable Board of Selectmen of the Town of Keene:

Gentlemen I respectfully submit the following report:

When first entering upon the duties of Chief Engineer I found dissatisfaction in one company. The Deluge Engine and Hose Company through bad counsel among its members; Some members desired to break up, and divide Company property, but they were successfully defeated in their designs by discharging a portion, and immediately reorganizing without any sacrifice of Company property.

This was the first of June, and, with this exception, there has been the best of harmony throughout the department. And allow me, in this connection, to tender my thanks to the officers and members of the several companies for the many tokens of respect and their ready acquiescence to fulfill every duty that belongs to good citizens and firemen. Also, I tender to all friends who take and manifest a vigilant interest in the welfare of the Fire Department, my best wishes, hoping always to merit their approbation.

There has been a very thorough examination made by my Assistant Engineers with regard to the general dangers incident to fire, with urgent requests, wherever thought advisable, to make changes and improvements, which have very generally been acceptable to owners of property. Yet, occasionally, some citizens feel somewhat indignant to be advised upon this point, which is to be regretted by all who are thoughtful upon this subject, as no Engineer would wish to impose upon any property owner needless improvements. And allow me here to say upon this point that I believe that it is greatly attributable to "the eternal vigilance" of our citizens and firemen that our beautiful village has thus far been spared so remarkably from the terrors of fire.

Out of the four fire alarms for the past year, three have been caused by imperfections about the chimney or funnel. At the house of Orlando Seward, on Court street, a funnel burned out and filled the wood work and damaged the house about $20. No alarm. Owners and builders can note the above statement. We all ought to feel an awful and earnest interest in this subject of cause and prevention of fire, and thus we may defy in a great degree its ravages. We have always been pleased to note the alacrity of our Firemen at an alarm, and we trust they will ever guard this honor. And here allow me to tender my thanks to my Assistant Engineers for the very cordial aid rendered me in the general management of the Department.

Fires and Alarms

May 15th, an alarm was caused by shavings and sawdust taking fire about the large chimney of Crossfield, Scott & Co's Shop on Mechanic Street. Damage slight.

July 21st, at 3 o'clock in the morning, an alarm was given, which proved to be a house on the side of Beech Hill, owned by Benj. Nichols was entirely consumed. It being at a very unfavorable hour for getting an alarm the building was entirely burned down before the firemen arrived. Damage about $1,500; insured for $2,000; supposed to be incendiary.

December 10th, there was an alarm at 2 p.m., caused by a chimney burning out which caused the wood surrounding to take fire, but was soon stopped. This house was Mrs. Emmon, on School Street.

February 2nd, There was an alarm on Water Street at the house of J. S. Towne, at 11 o'clock a. m., caused by a funnel burning out and firing wood surroundings, but was soon put out. Damage slight about $15. Moral see to your chimneys and stovepipes.

To all the above alarms the Department was promptly on hand and rendered all the assistance that could be required or expected.

Our attention was called, not long since to a large building where the wood work about the stove pipe was fired in two or three places caused by the funnel burning out. Another warning to all.

Total number of hydrants 93; all but one being in good working condition and it is expected that will be put in working order another summer.

The Fire Department consists of four companies, viz.: Deluge engine and hose company, 40 men; Phoenix hose company, 20 men; Neptune hose company, 20 men; Hook and Ladder company, 20 men; Board of Engineers, 6; total, 106

Recommendations

1st. I would recommend that the Niagara engine be stationed at South Keene, as our town has considerable property in this vicinity; together with 500 feet of hose and one hose carriage; providing that it can be housed and manned by the Chair company free of expense to the town. If this should be agreed to, it would be proper to appoint one engineer in that village.

2nd. I would recommend, if the above be accepted, that there be one more small hose carriage build; estimated cost, $150.00.

3rd. I would recommend that a suitable uniform be procured for the Deluge engine company; estimated cost, $300.00.

4th. I would recommend an appropriation for the coming year, to meet current expenses, of $1,500.

For expenditure the past year, see financial report. Virgil A. Wright, Chief Engineer. February 20th, 1873. Town Report.

1874 [*from* Town of Keene Annual Report]
Report of the Chief Engineer.

To the Board of Selectmen of the Town of Keene:

Gentlemen: It is with pleasure that I submit the following Report: and allow me here, to congratulate the citizens of Keene upon their remarkable preservation from the ravages of fire for the past year, and we might add, years. Our Fire Department is in a good and prosperous condition, with the best of harmony; the only thing complained of is the great dearth of fires to show their skill; consequently the duties of our firemen for the past year have been very light; yet there are numerous cares and responsibilities which firemen are obliged to go through, whether on duty at a fire, or at regular or special meetings, which take his time. We think our firemen are poorly paid. We believe that in a place as our village, where so much property is at stake, we should pay our firemen enough so that each man could afford to lose about three days in a year for especial drill and practice in familiarizing themselves with the various lessons of firemen. Those who think the firemen well paid should join our department, and submit himself to its duties, and they will soon learn that no one is a fireman for the pay he gets, but from pure patriotism. Give us more pay, and in return we can give you better firemen, because this will be an incentive to instruction, and our ranks will be more regularly filled. As it is, it is with a good deal of exertion that we can keep our companies full.

Allow me here to tender my highest regards to officers and men of the department, for the faithful discharge of their several duties, and the uniform courtesy, which I have received from them. I also wish to thank my board of Assistants for the aid which each has manifested in promoting the welfare of the Department.

In the annual examination of the village for carelessness of protection against fires, we find much improvement. Very generally, our citizens appreciate this annual visit, and we certainly believe it to be of the greatest importance, in many instances removing the cause of fire.

We regret that there was not an appropriation last year for more Hose; yet as there was quite a balance left over from the previous year's appropriation, we supposed this might be applied for this emergency. But it has been found necessary to use this balance to meet other financial obligations, and it will become necessary to appropriate a larger sum that usual to provide means for paying for Hose which I have purchased by the advice and consent of your Board, during the past winter, viz: five hundred and nineteen feet of the best 2 ½ Leather Hose, and five hundred and nineteen feet of 2 ½ inch best Linen Hose. The reason of this extra purchase of Hose was this. We had a lot of poor 2 inch Hose which I was obligated to condemn for various reasons, but chiefly on account of size and age. The indiscriminate mixing of two sizes of Hose and couplings, is very liable to cause great confusion at fires, and might be of far greater damage than to cast it aside from the Department. Yet, this Hose might be of great service to private parties having hydrants of their own, who wish for more immediate protection than the Department can give. Any Parties wishing to avail themselves of this opportunity to purchase this Hose, can do so by applying for the same to the Engineers. We have already sold some, and rendered an account for the same to the Town treasurer.

There is need of another four-wheeled Hose Carriage; and it is hoped that with the appropriation called for the present year, it may be granted, as there will be a suitable article in the warrant to cover this point. We would here add that a good four-wheeled Carriage, such as are built at Manchester, N. H., costs six hundred dollars.

With the present supply of good Hose, another good four-wheeled Hose carriage, a Department well paid and the abundant supply of force water which we have, we feel that it will be a long time before Keene will need a Steam Fire Engine. When that time does come, there must necessarily be many other expenses accompanying the Steamer.

Fires and Alarms

There were seven Fires and Six alarms during the past year Viz:

March 6th. Fire corner of Washington and Cottage Streets, caused by lathing too near a flue. Damage was $10.

August 26th, dwelling hose on 'Winchester St., owned by Geo. Porter, partially burned. Damage $900, fully insured. Cause unknown.

October 11th, this was an old house owned by Thomas Lahiff. No alarm loss small. Cause, supposed incendiary.

October 24th, fire at West Keene Cheshire Railroad Wood shed. Loss $1,500. Cause accidental. Fully insured.

November 17th. Building owned by N. G. Gurnsey. Fire originated in shoe store occupied by S. W. Howard and was stopped there. Cause, funnel too near the ceiling and not protected. Loss, $487 fully insured.

November 22nd. Fire at Lavery Brothers' Shoe Store in the American House Block. Cause funnel too near woodwork and not protected. Loss, $500. Insured $480.17.

December 6th. Fire at 3 ¼ o'clock A. M. at Faulkner & Colony's Wood shed and Storehouse adjoining Factory on West St. Cause unknown. Loss, $22,000. Insured $10,000.

Total Loss by Fire for the Past Year, $25,397.00. Total Insurance Paid $12,030.00 and Total Net Loss $13,367.00.

Valuation of Property in the Fire Department:

Deluge Engine & House, located in rear of Town Hall, $1,200.00

Neptune Hose & Hook & Ladder House, Depot Land, $800.00.

Phoenix Hose House, Depot Land, $800.00

Deluge Engine and Fixtures at Deluge House, $700.00

Niagara Engine and Fixtures Phoenix House Depot Land $600.00

Phoenix Four-wheeled Hose Carriage, Phoenix House, $300.00

Four Two-wheeled Hose Carriages, $500.00

Fire Alarm, Town Hall, $100.00

Washington Hook & Ladder Carriage & Fixtures, $300.00

3,000 feet 2 ½ Inch Very Good leather Hose, $3,000.00

519 Feet 2 1/2 Inch New, Best leather Hose 856.35

500 Feet 2 1/2 Inch New Best Linen Hose $458.00

Total Valuation, $9,614.35.

Total Valuation

Total length of good Hose in the Department, 4,019 feet. There are also, about 1,200 or 1,500 feet of condemned Hose.

There is one thing which ought to be improved upon. By some means, we ought to have access to the church bells in case of fires in the night, as it is quite difficult sometimes to give a sufficient alarm to bring out a full force of the department.

We deem it unnecessary to publish the list of Hydrants again this year, as we put them in our last year's report, but would add that there are in all 101 Hydrants in good order. There have been nine new ones put in during the last year; besides these, there are some 10 or 12 at the different mills and factories, which can be of great use if needed.

Number of Men in the Department, and their pay.

Deluge Engine & Hose Co., 40 Men, $320.00

Neptune Engine & Hose Co., 20 Men $130.00

Phoenix Engine & Hose Co., 20 Men $130.00

Washington Hook & Ladder Co., 20 Men $130.00

Board of Engineers, 7 Men, $165.00

Total for the year $875.00

There have been considerable repairs made to the Neptune Hose House, and the bills have not all come in, but will be reported in due time.

For receipts and expenditures, see Financial Report.

Having endeavored to discharge my duties faithfully for the past year, I return my sincere thanks for the confidence you have reposed in me, and

The ready co-operation we have received at your hands all of which is respectfully submitted.

Virgil A. Wright, Chief Engineer. February 12th, 1874.

Quoting from *Upper Ashuelot, A History of Keene, N.H.,* (page 126, by David R. Proper):

Keene Becomes a City.

Agitation to make Keene a city was begun early in 1865 with action by the New Hampshire legislature to permit such a change in government, but voters turned down the proposal and did likewise in 1866. In 1867 a similar measure by progressives was voted down 460 to 430, and a protest was lodged which resulted in the whole issue being dropped. In 1868 city status was defeated 700 to 378, and in 1869 it lost by a vote of 784 to 177. The issue again failed in 1870. Those in favor of city government formed a committee in June 1872 to draft a charter, which was approved by the legislature on July 3rd, 1873. On March 10th, 1874, Keene adopted the new municipal status by a vote of 783 to 589 and thus became a city. The New Hampshire town charter of 1753 was surrendered to a new city government headed by Horatio Colony as first Mayor. The municipal government was organized on May 5th, when, somewhat to the dismay of many, Democrats took control in what had traditionally been considered a Republican town. A city seal was adopted which showed the figure of Justice surrounded by symbols of Commerce, Industry, and Agriculture. The change from government by a board of three selectmen to that of a mayor, aldermen representing each of the nearly-created five city wards, and a common council of 15 began a new era for Keene as a municipality.

1874 [*from* Town of Keene Annual Report]

Made changes to our way of government from a Town to a City. Chapter VIII. States for the Fire Engineers as follows:

Section 1. That in the month of May, A. D. 1874, and thereafter in the month of January, annually, there shall be appointed by the board of Mayor and Aldermen, a Chief Engineer and six Assistants Engineers, to hold their offices one year, or until others are appointed and qualified to fill their places; and they shall constitute the Board of Engineers, and perform all the duties, and exercise all the powers of Fire-wards, provided, however, that they shall be subject to removal at any time by the Mayor and Aldermen, who shall have power to fill vacancies.

Section 2. The By-Laws adopted by the Board of Engineers of the Keene Fire Department, April 25th, 1870 and all rules and regulations they have since adopted and that are now in force, shall be considered as continuing in force, and the Board appointed under this ordinance shall have power to make such other rules and By-Laws as may be deemed necessary, provided they shall not be repugnant to, or inconsistent with the laws of the State or the ordinances of the City.

Report of the Chief Engineer March 1st, 1874 to December 1st, 1874. To His Honor the Mayor and Board of Aldermen of the City of Keene:

Gentlemen: In obedience to your request we herewith submit the following report of the condition and doings of the Fire Department from March 1, 1874 to December 1, 1874, making a term of nine months.

Changes

Since our last annual report the Town voted to purchase a four-wheeled hose-carriage. That vote has been carried out by the purchase of a very substantial carriage of the Amoskeag Manufacturing Company.

It was further voted that the Board of Engineers station the hand engine known as Niagara Engine at South Keene, which vote has been carried out; also, to station a hose-carriage near Blodgett's corner, on West Street, which has been fulfilled.

The new four-wheeled hose-carriage is manned by the Deluge Engine Company. This has been reduced to a company of twenty men, which makes a reduction of twenty men in the Department, and yet we think the Department more efficient with this change than before. The old Deluge Engine is kept in perfect working order, and its services are in all probability so very seldom needed that it was deemed expedient to make this change of companies; and should the emergency come when the services of a hand engine could be of use, it necessarily could happen when the hose-men could be put to work upon the engine without detriment to the interest of the City, also making a financial saving of the pay of twenty men.

The following is a list of the Companies and payroll, and Board of Engineers.

This writer elects not to list the names of the members of the company and payroll. The companies will be listed:

Deluge Hose Co. No. 1   23 Men

The above company is to have but twenty men, when by natural causes it arrives at this number, which, without doubt, will be before another year. The Board deemed this a better way to reduce its numbers, as many of its members had served the greater part of a year before this change in the company was determined.

Neptune Hose Co., No. 2.   19 Men
Phoenix Hose Co., No. 4.   20 Men
Washington Hook and Ladder   20 Men
Engineers   6 Men

This made a total of 88 men, who are paid.

At South Keene we have stationed the Niagara Engine, manned by a company of 40 men, not paid; West Street, No. 7 Hose Station, 10 men, not paid; Hope Mill, No 5, Hose Station.

The following is a list of apparatus and location and appraised value of the same:

Deluge Hose Co., No. 1 rear of City Hall, $600

Phoenix Hose Co., No. 4. Depot Grounds, $500.

Neptune Hose Co., No 2, Two Jumpers, Depot Grounds $250.

No. 5 Hose Station, Hope Mills ground, $125.

No. 7 Hose Station West Street, near Blodgett's Corner, $125.

Washington Hook and Ladder, No. 1 Depot Grounds, $300.

Niagara Engine, South Keene, $600.

Deluge Engine, Station rear of City Hall, $700.

Deluge Engine and Hose House, $1200.

Neptune Hook & Ladder & Hose House, Depot Grounds, $800.

Phoenix Hose House, Depot Grounds, $800.

Fire Alarm City Hall, $100.

519 feet 2 ½ inch New Leather Hose, $850.

500 feet 2 ½ inch Linen Hose $458.

8,000 Feet 2 ½ Old Leather Hose very good, $3,000.

275 feet 2 inch Old Leather Hose, at South Keene, $137.50

Total Valuation, 10,545.50

Distribution of Hose nearly as follows:
At Deluge Hose, 2 ½ Inch Hose 1,369 Ft.
At Phoenix House 2 ½ Inch Hose 800 Ft.
At Neptune House 2 ½ Inch Hose 1,300 Ft.
At No. 5 Station 2 ½ Inch Hose 250 ft.
At No. 7 Station West Street 2 ½ Inch Hose 300 Ft.
At South Keene Chair Shop, 2 Inch Hose 275 Ft.
Total Length of Hose
4,294 Feet.
Number of fires for the year; none
Number of Alarms; Two

The first fire was caused by, your humble servant for the double purpose of testing the Fire Alarm and response of the Department, both of which were entirely satisfactory. The second alarm rang, caused by a chimney burning out. The firemen were very promptly on the ground, but as their services were not needed, they soon returned to quiet homes. Such has been the active duty performed the past year; but should the services of our firemen be required, I have the greatest confidence in their ability to command the admiration, respect and esteem of our citizens by the faithful discharge of their duties.

The Department was called out in the month of June for parade and inspection, which was well attended, showing much true discipline in behavior, and manner in which the apparatus appeared. The Department is in the best condition; officers and men are in the best of humor, ready and willing to do service when called.

Allow me here to tender my thanks to both officers and men for their courtesy to me since I Have been connected with them in the Fire Department; also to my brother Assistant Engineers I wish to return my sincere thanks for their cheerful support in all my duties as the executive officer of the Department.

The Increase of Pay: Its Influence, &c.

At our last annual town meeting the town voted to increase the firemen's pay to eight dollars in addition to the sum allowed by law (which is one dollar and fifty cents.) This was a just and generous consideration, and, I believe, one of the best moves that had been made for the Department. For instance, it has a tendency to keep our companies full; and our records will show that not more than one quarter as many men have been appointed during the past year as were the previous year, and men are standing ready to join at a moment's notice as I am told by officers of companies. This gives more reliable men, which is just what we want: So much for the increase of pay.

Recommendations

It is becoming more apparent every day that our city needs a Steam Fire Engine that shall be kept in readiness so that in case of any trouble with the water works either being out of order or their power being diminished from its greatest head to that of the reservoir on Beech Hill, or a fire in some building outside the limits of the hydrants, as the Pottery establishments, it could be used. It will be in some unforeseen manner that we shall see the need for a Steamer. I trust you will give due consideration to this subject.

I would recommend that our City Authorities provide, annually, a supper for the Fire Department, and furnish music for a Fall Parade to be holding every year in the month of October. It would cost but a small amount in all, and I think it would have good effect. I could give many reasons for this, which perhaps is not necessary here. The sum required for this object would not exceed one hundred dollars. I would also recommend all persons who are using water in greater or less

quantities, in case of a fire, to stop its use, as it diminishes the power of the hydrants.

The necessary appropriations for the coming year for ordinary expenses, need be no more than for the past year.

For the Expenses and Financial Report of the Department see elsewhere in City Report, under expenditures.

All of which is respectfully submitted, Virgil A. Wright Chief Engineer. City Report.

1875

...made a few changes. (Compiler's notes:) The changes made were now the Board of Engineers was back to 7 and the names of all the members were listed with their occupation outside the fire department along with their residences address. Also the number of paid men dropped from 88 to 37. The Deluge Hose Co. No. 1 is to be increased to forty men, as the Deluge Engine is to be run by them in connection with the Hose Carriage. The additional men will be appointed fast as suitable ones can be found.

Note: The Niagara Engine is stationed at South-Keene, and run by workmen in the chair shop, not paid; Hose Carriage No. 5 is stationed near Hope Mills, and run by the workmen in the mills, not paid; Hose Carriage No. 7 is stationed on West Street, near the Tannery, and run by the workmen in the Tannery, not paid.

This is the change from 88 paid men to 37 paid men.

Fire Department [*from* Town of Keene Annual Report]

Report of the Chief Engineer:

To his Honor the Mayor and Board of Aldermen of the City of Keene:

Gentlemen: In compliance with the General Statutes of New Hampshire, I hereby submit the following report of the conditions and doings of the Fire Department, for the year ending November 30th, 1875.

No important changes have occurred in the Department the past year. The members composing the different companies I believe to be men who can be relied upon for promptness and efficiency in the discharge of their duties.

The apparatus is in good condition, and most of it is well adapted to the needs of the Department.

The houses are in good condition and sufficient for the accommodation of the companies.

List of fires and alarms that have occurred the past year:

1st. April 12th, 11 o'clock, A. M. J. S. Taft & Co.'s Pottery, near Water street, was discovered to be on fire. The firemen were on the ground as soon as possible; but the flames had made such progress before the alarm was given, that they arrived too late to save anything but the surrounding buildings. Loss $10,000, insurance $4,000.

2nd. May 28th, 8 o'clock, P. M. Alarm, caused by the explosion of a lamp at City Hotel. Loss trifling.

3rd. June 4th, 3 ½ o'clock, P. M. Peter Bouvier's dwelling house, on Howard Street, was discovered to be on fire. The firemen were on the ground promptly, and the flames were extinguished before they had made much progress. Children playing with matches in a room upstairs caused this fire. Two unfortunate children were injured so badly by smoke and heat before they could be rescued, that they died soon after. Loss, on house and furniture, $76.00, fully insured.

4th. July 2nd, 6 ¼ o'clock, P. M. The roof of the Kimball house, on Roxbury Street, was discovered to be on fire, caused by sparks from the chimney. Extinguished without much loss.

5th. November 20th, 5 o'clock, A. M. The furniture shop owned and occupied by N. G. Woodbury, on Washington Street, was discovered to be on fire. The firemen were on the ground as soon as possible; but the flames had made such progress when it was discovered, and the distance was so great, that they arrived too late to save the buildings. Loss $10,000; no insurance.

Total amount of loss by fires this year $20,076.00

Total amount of insurance, $4,076.00

Making a loss, above insurance, of $16,000.00

On the 24th of July last the Department was called out for the annual parade and inspection and trial of skill, and most of the men responded cheerfully. The appearance and behavior of the men on that occasion, and the condition of the apparatus, was eminently satisfactory.

Recommendations

I would join with my predecessor in recommending a Steam Fire Engine as soon as the City authorities shall feel warranted in making the outlay. Until that time I believe we ought to have at least one Hand Engine manned. It would be well to procure, say 500 feet of hose next year, and an extension ladder or two.

In conclusion, I would tender my thanks to the members of the City Councils for their general interest, courtesy and esteem evinced towards the Department at all times. To the Mayor, the Finance and Fire Committees I am especially grateful, for their disposition and efforts to answer all requirements; to the City Marshal and his assistants, for aid rendered in our behalf; to the Superintendent of Water Works, for valuable suggestions; and finally, to my assistants and to all the members of the Department, for their cordial support and prompt and united exertions in the discharge of their duties, for which much praise is due.

Respectfully submitted, L. J. Tuttle, Chief Engineer.

🔱 *A Demon Called Fire*

A JOINT RESOLUTION in relation to rent of ground occupied by the Neptune and Phoenix Engine and Hose Carriage Houses.

Resolved, by the City Councils of the City of Keene, as follows:

That the Cheshire Railroad Company be paid thirty dollars a year rent for the grounds now occupied by the Neptune and Phoenix Engine and Hose Carriage Houses, until otherwise ordered by the City Councils. The Depot Grounds were behind St. James Church area, which is now a parking lot off Gilbo Ave.

1874 was a very significant year. Town of Keene becomes a City with a population exceeding 6,000. The figure of justice surrounding by symbols of industry, commerce and agriculture was adopted as the City of Keene Seal. City Seal: The Seal of the City of Keene shall be as follows: A circle one inch and five-eighths in diameter; around the border in the capital letters the words "City of Keene" in the upper portion, and the words "New Hampshire" in the lower portion; on the disk a figure of Justice seated, with her right arm resting on a circular shield having represented upon it an arm in the act of striking with a hammer; on the right an inverted horn with coins issuing there from; on the left a toothed-wheel and sheaves of wheat; a railroad train in the background; the figures 1874 underneath within the border. Photo courtesy of Keene Records clerk's office.

1876 [*from* Town of Keene Annual Report]
Report of the Chief Engineer

Chief Engineer's Office, December 1st, 1876. To His Honor the Mayor, and the City Councils:

Gentlemen: Herewith, in accordance with the laws of New Hampshire, the Board of Engineers has the honor to submit for the consideration, the report of this Department for the fiscal year ending November 30th, 1876, showing the condition of the Department under our charge. Annexed thereto will be found a list of the officers and members of the Department; also the number of fires that have occurred during the year, with losses and insurance on same; together with the condition of the engine houses and apparatus belonging to the city, with such suggestions as would, in our opinion, tend to improve and render more efficient the working of the same. And in this connection the Board is happy to state that upon proper representation, your assistance and co-operation have always been promptly and cheerfully rendered in aiding them in the discharge of their duties; for which the Board desire to tender their sincere thanks.

Manual Force

The Manual force of the Department consists of a Chief and six Assistants Engineers, sixty members of Hose Company, twenty members of Engine Company, and twenty members of Hook & Ladder Company, making a total of one hundred and seven men. In addition to the regular force of the Department there is a volunteer Engine Company at south Keene, and a volunteer Hose Company at Symonds' Tannery, who would render efficient services in case of fire in their vicinity. It would be difficult for the Board to speak too highly of the zeal and efficiency displayed by the officers and members of the Department as a body.

We are pleased to note a constant improvement in the matter of discipline, without which no organization of this character can be perfect. The firemen of this city are justly entitled to the highest praise for their efficiency, their

Cheerful compliance with all orders and their prompt response to the call of duty. It is gratifying to report that between the several companies comprising this Department a general good feeling exists; a healthy enthusiasm being developed into a generous rivalry, which only needs to be led in the right channel, to make them fully equal to any similar body of men in any organization.

The Board desire to call your attention to the necessity of procuring another four-wheeled hose carriage for Neptune Hose Company No. 2, to take the places of the two jumpers they now run, which are not fit for any company. They are regular " man-killers," as the boys call them. A four-wheeled carriage would put this company on an equal footing with the rest of the Department.

Condition of Engine Hoses

The engine houses generally, are in good order, although in some of them much remains to be done to make them more comfortable for the members. The headquarters of the Department, under City Hall, with a few alterations and improvements, will answer admirably the purpose intended; they are now occupied by the Board of Engineers, and night-watchmen.

The house of Deluge Engine and Hose Company No. 1, in the rear of City Hall, is good order, with the exception of the floor of the hose tower, which is about rotted out; the

Board would suggest that a good plank floor be substituted. The house of Neptune Hose Company No. 2, on Railroad Square is in good condition, but the Board would recommend that a partition be run across the back end of the house to aid in drying hose. The house of Phoenix Hose company No. 4, on Railroad Square has been newly painted outside, and a new sign added; it is in as good condition as any hose house in the State. For some time past this house has been used for a ward room at State and municipal elections, for

Ward 5, and if a fire should occur at the time it would seriously interfere with the duties of the company; we would call your attention to this matter.

The house of Washington Hook and Ladder Company No. 1, is in very good repair. A new extension ladder has been procured for the Company, which was given a very thorough trial at the annual parade last summer, and all were convinced that it was just what the Department needed to reach the top of any block in the city.

Hose

There is now in the Department 4,969 feet of hose, divided as follows: 3,069 feet of 2 ½ inch leather hose in good condition, 500 feet of which was procured the past year; 500 feet of 2 ½ inch linen hose, in fair condition, and 400 feet of 2 inch hose, nearly useless.

Water

During the past year a branch pipe had been laid, and thirteen hydrants set, greatly relieving the fire risk on Pearl Street, Winchester Court and Winchester Street. The Board would recommend that a branch pipe be extended up Washington Street beyond Woodbury's mills.

We would call your attention also to the large number of hydrants that are situated in the middle of sidewalks, some of which cannot therefore be covered up in Winter, and which, when covered with ice and snow it is almost impossible to get at. If we keep them cleaned off it leaves large holes in the sidewalks for people to break their legs in; and when it thaws they fill with water, and, freezing they are rendered useless. We earnestly hope that they may be removed to the edge of sidewalks another season. The whole number of hydrants now, with the thirteen new ones, is 114. The average water pressure is between sixty-five and seventy pounds. The Board of Engineers desire to express their thanks to Mr. Daniel Holbrook, water Commissioner, and to Mr. Lewis Holmes, Superintendent, for the valuable and rendered at all fires, and the careful attention given to the wants of this Department.

Horses

We would also recommend that the city procure a span of horses, which could be worked on the highways in the day-time, and be kept at the engine house at night, always ready to draw the machines to a fire. In our opinion his would be true economy for the city.

Fire Alarm

The Board would call your attention to the necessity of having reliable fire alarm, as there is nothing sure about the one we have now. When there is no fire it is apt to go off, but when there is a fire it is almost always sure not to go off. We have arranged to have the Unitarian Church Bell rung for the present.

We hope that the Councils will take immediate action in regard to this matter.

Conclusion

In conclusion the Board will avail themselves of this opportunity to express their sincere thanks to the officers and members of the entire Department for the prompt and efficient manner in which they have, on every occasion, responded to the call of duty. We also return thanks to the Joint Standing Committee on Fire Department, for their cordial support in all matters tending to promote the best interest of the Department. Finally, the Board desire to acknowledge their gratitude to His Honor the Mayor, the Board of Aldermen and gentlemen of the City Council, for their continued liberality shown for the promotion of this Department.

Alarms of Fire

1st. December 16th, 1875 J. W. Buckminster's house, Valley Street. Loss $2,000: Insured $3,000.

2nd. January 21st, 1876. Bancroft & Griswold's slaughter house, Court Street. Loss $2,000; insured $1,000.

3rd. January 26th, False alarm.

4th. March 27th, House of Hollis Prush, Elm Street. Damage slight.

5th. April 21st, Moses Ellis foundry. Damage slight.

6th. July 29th, House of Maria Ruffle, Elm Street. Loss $300; not insured.

7th. August 5th, False Alarm.

8th. August 26th, Mrs. Driscoll's house, emerald Street. Loss $300; not insured

9th. October 8th, Faulkner & Colony's house, West Street. Loss $400; insured $150.

10th. November 29th, False Alarm.

Total amount of loss by fires this year $5,000.00

Total amount of insurance, $4,150.00

Making a loss above insurance, of $850.00

Roll of the Department

Recapitulation
Board of Engineers 7 men
Deluge Engine and Hose Co. No. 1, 39 men
Neptune Engine and Hose Co., No. 2, 20 men
Phoenix Hose Co., No. 4, 20 men
Washington Hook and Ladder, No. 1, 20 men.

Making a total of 106 men who are paid. Their pay $1,120.50

Inventory of property in possession of the Department.

Deluge, No 1, Engine and hose carriage, $1,300. Neptune, No. 2, two hose carts, $250. Phoenix, No. 4, hose carriage, $250. No. 5, hose station, near Hope Mills, $125. No. 7, hose station, West Street near tannery, $125. Washington No. 1, hook and ladder carriage. $350. Niagara engine and hose cart, South Keene. $600. Deluge engine house, $1,200.

Neptune hose and hook & ladder house, $800. Phoenix hose house, $800. Fire Alarm at City Hall $50.

519 feet 2 ½ inch leather hose $850. 500 feet linen hose, $458. 500 feet old leather hose, $625. 3,000 feet old leather hose, very good, $3,000

450 feet 2 inch old leather hose, $180.

100 Uniforms, 40 at Deluge, and 20 each at Neptune, Phoenix and Hook & Ladder houses, $300.

Total Valuation, $11,463.50

Respectfully submitted, William H. Babbitt, Chief Engineer.

1877 [*from* Town of Keene Annual Report]

Report of the Chief Engine.

Office of Board of Engineers, December 1st, 1877

To His Honor the Mayor, and Gentlemen of the City Councils:

Gentlemen: In compliance with the city ordinances for the government of the Keene Fire Department, I have the honor to submit the following annual report of the affairs of the Department for the year ending December 1st, 1877, with a statement of its labors during the year, and such other matters pertaining to its general management as occur to me. This has been a most fortunate year in the small number of fires that have occurred. Seldom, if ever, in the history of the city, have the losses caused thereby been so small. This is mainly accounted for by the efficiency of the Department, and our ample water supply. The entire force of the Department at present is as follows: One Chief Engineer and six Assistants; one hand fire engine, 20 men; one hook and ladder truck, 20 men; three four-wheeled hand hose carriages, each 20 men; also one hand engine at South Keene, and two two-wheeled hose carriages, one of which is located at Symonds' Tannery and the other at Beaver Mills. The engine and carriages are manned by men employed at the works where they are located. Some changes have taken place in the membership of the Department during the year, but the full complement of members has been maintained throughout. The Department has been called out six times to fires and alarms during the year. I am glad to state that no very destructive fire is to be reported in this number. Annexed herewith is a list of alarms, fires, losses, &c.

Apparatus

The apparatus is in perfect working order. During the year a new four-wheeled hose carriage has been procured for Neptune Hose Company, No. 2, to take the place of the jumpers. The Engine hoses are also in good condition.

Hose

There is now in the Department 5019 feet of hose, of the following descriptions: 3069 feet of leather hose, 2 ½ inch, is good condition; 450 feet of linen hose, nearly worn out; 100 feet of 2 ½ inch rubber lined hose. Procured the past year, and 400 feet of 2 inch hose, about played out. One 50 feet length of the linen hose has been condemned after another year's service. I would recommend that there be 500 feet more of rubber lined hose procured, so that all three companies can have a relay of good 2 ½ inch hose, which would make 1200 feet for each company, and they generally carry 600 feet on each carriage.

1878 - Members of the Deluge Hose Company. Photo was taken at Central Square with their new uniforms and helmets. HSCC photo collection.

Steamer

I would also recommend that the Hand Engines and two Jumpers be sold, and that a light Steamer be procured; the water pressure is getting so low that it is almost impossible to get any force of stream half a mile away from the main pipe. With a Steamer, the Department might be reduced to one third the numbers of men, and the expense is no greater than at present.

I would again call attention to the larger number of hydrants in the sidewalks, and urgently request that they be removed to the outside of the walks nest season.

Conclusion

In conclusion I would return my thanks to His Honor, the Mayor, for the many courtesies shown me during the year; to the several gentlemen of the City Government with whom my official relations brought me in contact, particularly the Committee on Fire Department, and the Superintendent of Water Works; also, to the Police Department, for promptness and efficiency at all times, and to the citizens generally for the kindly interest they have always manifested in the welfare of the Department. I can heartily commend the discipline of the Department, which I think was never better than at the present time, and for which I return thanks to my Assistant–Engineers, to the Foremen of the several companies, and to each member of the same, almost all of whom were prompt to obey orders, to each and all of whom, in a measure, is due the useful management of the department during the year, and of which the citizens of Keene Have just cause to be proud.

Alarms of Fire

1st. April 7th. House of Mrs. James Mahar, Elm Street Saved ell and barn. Loss $1,00, insurance $700.

2nd. June 10th. House of A. Stiles, Pearl Street. Loss slight.

3rd. August 10th. Faulkner & Colony's house and barn West Street. Loss $1,200, insurance $600

4th. September 20th. House of B. F. Nichols, Beech Hill. Loss $4,000, insurance $3,400.

5th. October 10th. Cheshire Railroad dry house. Damage slight.

6th. October 13th. House of Faulkner & Colony, Ashuelot Street; Chimney burnt out; damage slight.

Total amount of loss by fires this year $6,200 Total amount of insurance $4,700 making a loss above insurance of $1,500.

Men from last year was up 1 which makes a total of 107 men paid and the expenses of the Department remained the same $2,000 and the Inventory of property in possession of the Department was up by $634.50 which of made up the difference in uniforms, 100 ft. rubber lined hose new and an additional $100 dollars for valuation in the Fire Alarm at City Hall.

Submitted, William H. Babbitt, Chief Engineer Keene Fire Department.

Joint Resolution relating to Fire Department. Resolved, by the City Councils of the City of Keene, as follows:

That the Joint Standing Committee on Fire Department be authorized to take down the old fire alarm, and attach Steam fire alarm apparatus to the bell on city hall, after said committee are satisfied it will prove satisfactory.

That the committee is authorized to purchase one four-wheeled hose carriage, on the best terms possible, and that an additional appropriation of five hundred dollars to made for that purchase.

1878 [*from* Town of Keene Annual Report]
Report of the Chief Engineer.

Chief Engineer's Office December 1st, 1878.

To the Honorable Mayor and City Councils:

In presenting my first annual report of the operations of the Department which have come under my supervision for the year ending December 1st, 1878, I shall endeavor in this report to embody all matters of interest with the working of the Department which I judge to be for the best interest of the City and the Department. I have been connected in one way or another with the Department for a good many years, which leads me to ask some questions concerning the reasons why Department is not up to the letter of the law. Do we, as citizens, take that interest in the Fire Department which we ought? Do we pay our firemen compensation enough, so that we can get the best men? I would recommend for your consideration the sum of $12 per year, which seems to me small compensation enough for our firemen.

Apparatus.

The apparatus is in good working order. Nothing new has been ordered for the Department during the year. The engine houses are in very fair condition, having been moved the past season to more suitable grounds. The grounds in front of the houses should be put in more passable condition: there should be a covering over the course gravel, so as to make good wheeling for the hose carriages.

A Demon Called Fire

Manual Force.

The manual force of this Department consists of a Chief Engineer and six Assistants, twenty members of the Engine Company, sixty members of the hose company, and twenty members of the hook and ladder company. In addition to the paid Department there are: one engine and hose carriage at South Keene, one two-wheeled jumper at Symonds' Tannery and one at Hope Steam Mills. The Engine and hose company are manned by men employed at the works where they are located.

We have been called out eight times this year, the fire at Taft & Co.'s pottery resulting in the heaviest loss.

Hose.

There are now in the Department 4519 feet of hose, of the following descriptions: 3069 feet of 2 ½ inch leather hose, in good condition; 500 feet of linen hose, worn out and condemned; 100 feet of 2 ½ inch rubber lined hose, in good condition; and 400 feet of 2 inch hose, good as long as it lasts. We have gone through the year without any addition of hose to the Department; and it seems to me that with care we can get through another year without any addition to the above.

Fire Alarms.

This is one of the most important branches of the Fire Department. We have what purports to be an alarm, and it seems to be anything but what it should be. It is almost impossible to hear it outside of the Square, and can scarcely be designated from the city clocks. I hope that our city fathers will give this their most earnest attention. It is almost at any time liable to operate disastrously to us. Everybody knows it is necessary for firemen to hear an alarm before its call can be answered.

Steamer.

I would recommend that if the two engines and jumpers can be sold, a steamer should be procured. Everybody is aware that by the extension of our water works among the water-tankers, the pressure is thereby reduced. With a steamer we might add more efficiency to the Department without costing any more than it does at present. There should be one jumper located in the vicinity of High Street, which can be done without any additional expense to the city except the cost of new hose. There are citizens enough who will volunteer to take it out in case of fire.

Fire Patrol.

This is a most important branch of the service, which should be added to every well-organized Fire Department. It is for the purpose of looking after property at fires, and protecting the same. My thanks are especially due to the City Marshal and his assistants for their services in this direction for the past year. There should be three or four of our policemen appointed, in connection with their other duties, to look after goods and chattels which have to be moved more or less at fires, as a great savings thereby might be made.

Conclusion.

In conclusion I extend my thanks to His Honor the Mayor, and also to the various members of the different boards with whom I have had official relations; also to the Assistant Engineers who have helped me so faithfully during the year; and last, though not least, to the Fire Department, who have responded so cheerfully to the feeble calls made upon them from our alarm. It is a gratification to me to know that we have men in our Department that can be trusted in any emergency that may arise.

Alarms of Fires.

January 5th. Taft & Co.'s pottery. Loss $20,000, insurance $16,000.

March 24th. Barn on the Mahar place, Elm Street. Loss trifling.

March 30th. Spencer's house, on Dunbar Street; was burning out of chimney. Loss Small

April 23rd. Watchman's shanty burnt near Cheshire railroad bridge; used as a shelter for bridge boy.

May 1st. Fire at Jason French's, on Franklin Street. Insurance covered loss.

June 6th. Fire caused by spark from chimney, carpenter's house, on Water Street. Loss small.

July 7th. Fire at Robert Doyle's house, on Marlboro Street. Insured for $2,000, loss $600.

July 30th. Fire at the old bakery on Washington Street. Insured for $600 on stock and building. Total loss.

Note: This writer elected not to list all the assets for the year ending which was a small amount or change. Men from last year remained the same in number a total of 107 men paid. The expenses of the Department remained the same $2,000 and the Inventory of property in possession of the Department was up $383.00 which made up the difference for the year.

Submitted, William H. Babbitt Chief Engineer Keene Fire Department.

1878 [*from* Town of Keene Annual Report]
Report of the Chief Engineer.

Chief Engineer's Office Keene, December 1st, 1878. To the Honorable Mayor and City Councils:

In presenting my first annual report of the operation of the Department which has come under my supervision for the year ending December 1st, 1878, I shall endeavor in this report to embody all matters of interest with the working of the Department which I judge to be for the best interest of the City Department.

This complier makes Note that 1878 was the same as 1877. The City Reports were word for word except for the Chief Engineer's Inventory of property in possession of

the Department total. The total for the year ending was down by $383.00.

Respectfully yours, Albert O. Fiske, Chief Engineer. 1878

[*Compiler Note*: Compilers notes, each year the Honorable Mayor and Council would summarize the year and I think this is a good time to put in year ending 1878/1879 before moving onto 1879.]

Fire Department [*fromChief Engineer Albert O. Fiske*]

I think our Fire Department is in good working order, and well manned. I refer you to the details of the report of the Chief Engineer. His remarks in regard to the insufficiency of the fire alarm and pertinent, and I hope a better one will be provided without further delay. He does not, in my judgment, overestimate the importance of the matter. A committee was appointed in regard to this mater, but they have not yet remedied the evil. You will also notice his suggestions as to an increase of the amount paid the firemen, and for improvements in the grounds in front of the engine houses on the Cheshire railroad land, and in regard to purchasing a steamer; and take such action as seems advisable. While I always wish to enjoin economy, I think it important to supply everything needful for a good and efficient fire department; I also concur in his recommendation relating to a fire patrol.

Each and every year the Chiefs Report was summarized and in most cases the city supported the Chief recommendations. But as like today money has always been an issue. The Council would put off what it could and hoped for the next year.

1879 [*from* Town of Keene Annual Report]
Report of the Chief Engineer.

Chief Engineer's Office, Keene December 1st, 1879 to His Honor the Mayor and City Councils:

It is with pleasure that I now have an opportunity of reporting to you the general working of this small though very important part of our institutions; and in accordance with the usages of the branch I herewith present my annual report for the year ending December 1st, 1879

In the first place I have endeavored to keep everything connected with the working of the Department in complete order; also made some needed repairs to the several houses belonging to the Department, where the outlay was small. Two of the halls have been improved by plaster, whitewash, paint and paper, and we should be glad to have the fathers of our city government examine the several houses and hall accommodations for the firemen, and see if it is not worthwhile to make a little more improvement in this direction. If we want men to act like men they must be treated like men. Put men into dirty, unsightly places and they partake of the surroundings, and vice versa: a word to the wise is sufficient, &c., &c.

We have made a reduction in the Department of twenty men, and in our opinion without impairing the efficiency of the Department. These twenty were dropped from the Deluge Engine & Hose co., which was composed of forty men, but now a hose company only, which gives us three good hose companies upon equal footing. If the case should happen where there was a possible chance to need the engine, I have made arrangements with Mr. P. Howland to take out the engine, and under such circumstances we should have a plenty of hose men to man the engine; therefore I think it is self-evident that we are just as well off without these extra twenty men, and make a savings of $190.00 besides the wear and tear of that number.

Number of Men

The manual force of the Department is eighty-seven men, and organized as follows: Seven engineers, three hose companies, twenty men each, viz Deluge, Neptune and Phoenix, and Washington Hook and Ladder, of twenty men. We have a two-wheeled jumper stationed near Hope

Steam Mills and one at Symonds' tannery, also a very good engine and hose carriage at South Keene Chair Shop, and manned by volunteer men of the shop, and the old Deluge, which is kept in readiness at the Deluge Hose Station No. 1.

Hose.

There are now in the Department about 4000 feet of hose of all descriptions: 3000 feet of 2 ½ inch good leather hose 100 feet of 2 ½ inch hose, rubber lined, good and 400 feet of two-inch hose.

The Fire Alarm.

There was great need of an improvement in the fire alarm, and the past Summer the Humphrey Machine Co. has made us one for the small sum of one hundred dollars, which works very satisfactorily.

Discipline.

It gives me great pleasure to state that the discipline never was better than at the present time, and I feel that it is no flattery to say that Keene Fire Department are keen, and cannot be beat. When on duty each company, and we might add each man, does his best and what more can be required of firemen? As far as my observation goes, there is the best of harmony throughout the Department. This accounts in no small degree for the discipline. As an act of appreciation on the part of the citizens, I think our authorities ought to give the Department a good supper annually, and there meet the men who are ready to risk their lives for your pleasant homes and places of business.

Alarms of Fires.

The two first alarms mentioned below were not reported last year, but handed to me by my predecessor to report:

December 11th, 1878. At Woodbury's mills, Washington Street; dry house. Loss $100.

December 27th, 1878. Cottage house on Valley Street, owned by the Bank. Loss $1,300; fully insured.

January 14th, 1879, at 11 o'clock P. M. Sash and blind shop on Mechanic Street. Loss $500; no insurance.

February 10th, House on Maple Avenue; the Department no called. Loss $1,000; insurance $800.

February 22nd. School house on Lincoln Street. Loss $10.

April. Alarm caused by chimney burning out in Clarke's block.

May 18th. Alarm caused by a small shanty burning near gas house. Loss small.

June 27th. Taft & Co.'s storehouse was struck by lighting and burned. Estimated loss $10,000; insurance $6,000.

September 4th. Caused by a fire starting at the gas house. Damage small.

September 12th, Alarm caused by a chimney burning out on Gerould's block.

September 20th. A small house on Howard Street, owned by Mrs. Mitchell; burned to the ground. Loss $300; insurance, $200.

October 3rd. Alarm caused by a carload of coal burning; loss not learned.

October 4th. Alarm caused by roof taking fire from chimney, on house east of cemetery. Damage slight.

October 9th. J. M. Farnum's grain mill on Emerald Street was badly damaged. Loss $1,500; fully insured.

Total Loss for 1879 $12,928.00 and total Insurance, $9,326.00 and that which was not insured, $3,326.00

Total number of men paid 100 making a drop of 7. Total of property in possession of the Department valuation is $10,8880 for the year 1879.

Conclusion.

In conclusion allow me to make a few suggestions. When our company uniforms get so poor that the men are ashamed to appear out in them, it is about time to make an appropriation in this direction. This was the case with the Neptune Hose Company, and it is with credit to the Foreman, William C. Cleary, and company, that they contributed each their mite that they might make a decent appearance at our annual inspection, and they made it; therefore the city are debtors to that company, certainly to the amount of twenty pairs of pants. Let it be cancelled as soon as convenient. When we see men contributing to improve their surroundings it speaks well; and here let me express my sympathy and best regards personally, to my Assistant Engineers, Foremen and men of the Fire Department, also the members of City

Government for the seemingly unmerited confidence placed in me. Thanking all, I remain your most obedient servant, Virgil A. Wright, Chief Engineer 1879.

Note: When a horse was needed for the ladder carriage or the steamer at first it was noted that one was rented, Example as just a few listed in the Report L. E. Joslin was paid $2.00 dollars for use of horse and the next year L. Martin was paid $24.00 and S. P. Bowker for use of horse at fire. Later on you will see that the Department purchased their own horses.

1880 [*from* Town of Keene Annual Report]

1880 proved to be a big year for the fire department. The city Council acted and passed several ordinances in moving the Fire Department forward. Ordinances as follows for 1880:

An Ordinance relating to pay of Firemen, &c.

Be it ordained by the City Councils of the City of Keene, as follows.

Section 1. The foremen of the several fire companies of the city of Keene, shall at the expiration of each quarter, report to the City Clerk the number of men who have been active members of their companies for the quarter preceding the date of their report, and if any men have joined the companies or been discharged during the quarter, the foremen shall report the date of their election as members, or discharge, and shall make oath before the City Clerk to the correctness of their report.

Section 2. The members of the fire companies shall receive for their services the sum of twelve dollars per year in addition to the amount allowed by law; but no member shall receive pay unless he shall perform his duties in a manner satisfactory to the officers of his company, and respond to all calls that are made upon him, or give satisfactory excuse for absence.

Section 3. In computing the pay of members, the foremen of the several companies shall report the number of months that the men have been active members of their companies. A half month shall entitle the member to a full month's pay. For less than half a month the member shall not be entitled to pay, and each member shall draw pay only for the actual time he had been a member of a company, computed as above.

Section 4. The City Clerk shall have printed, and furnish to the foreman of each company, proper blanks for their quarterly reports and pay rolls.

Section 5. All ordinances, or parts of ordinances, or joint resolutions inconsistent with the provisions of this ordinance are hereby repealed.

Section 6. This ordinance to take effect from April 1st, 1880.

Passed May 20th, 1880.

A Joint Resolution relating to Steam Fire Engine.

Resolved by the City Councils of the City of Keene, as follows:

That a committee of three be appointed by his Honor the Mayor and the President of the Council, to consider the matter of the purchase of a steam fire engine with the necessary appurtenances; to ascertain, as far as they may be able, the comparative merits and cost of those made by the most reliable manufactures, together with such other information as may be desirable, and report to the Councils at as early a date as practicable.

Passed April 1, 1880.

A Joint Resolution of Thanks to the Keene Fire Department. Etc.

Resolved by the City councils of the City of Keene, as follows:

That the thanks of the city of Keene are tendered the fire department of the city for their able and judicious management during the recent fire, whereby almost the entire business part of the city, as well as much valuable private property, was saved from destruction. Also that the thanks of the city are tendered City Marshal Babbitt and officers Kellogg, Roach and Staples of the police force for their efficient services during the fire.

Passed April 1st, 1880.

Also on May 13th, 1880 An Ordinance relating to Building a Fire Precinct was passed by the City Council. In general this stated that No person shall erect or cause to be erected, move or cause to be moved, enlarge or cause to be enlarged, any wooden building, or set up a steam engine in any building within the city limits, without the consent of the Board of Mayor and Alderman. A license is asked under this chapter.

1880 [*from* Town of Keene Annual Report]

Report of the Chief Engineer.

Again it gives me pleasure to report to you the condition of the Fire Department for the year ending December 1, 1880.

It certainly cause for gratitude that we have been so wonderfully preserved from fires the past year; and we doubt whether another place in New England has been so highly favored as Keene in this respect. But this is no reason for relaxing our vigilance; and I trust that our citizens appreciate the necessity of a through, live and active Department.

I have endeavored, with the aid of my assistants, to keep the Department in complete working order; and I believe that when occasion calls for their services, our firemen will acquit themselves worthily as firemen and citizens.

There have been some changes made in the Department during the past year. An ordinance increasing the firemen's pay from nine and one-half dollars annually to fifteen dollars, too affect the first of last April. I believe it to be a great improvement over the old way, as it guarantees pay to everyone in proportion to the time he serves faithfully, and a little more, as will be seen by reading the ordinance. The old way was very unfair, as a member might serve faithfully ten months, and then through some unavoidable cause the obliged to leave the department, when the new member succeeding him would draw a year's pay after two months' service. I think the new ordinance will have the effect of keeping the companies full during the whole year; while heretofore they have been full only on or near pay-day. It was quite a change for the foremen to make their quarterly reports of the number of men on duty appointed and discharged, yet I think they have done remarkably well and that all are satisfied that the change is for the better.

By the advice and consent of the Committee on Fire Department, I have purchased six hydrant gates and five hundred feet of good oak-tanned leather hose. The foregoing purchase was received in August last, in complete order, from Hunneman & Co., Boston. A quantity of old hose at South Keene, belonging with the Niagara engine, was sold, and 300 feet of good hose put in its place.

Another change in the Department was in moving the Deluge engine and hose house from the rear of City Hall to Vernon Street. This was a necessity, on account of the improvements about to be made on City Hall building; and upon the whole the change is a good one in my opinion. The house is well situated, and well repaired and fitted up.

The ordinary running expenses of the Department have been very light the past year, which is no doubt an agreeable feature to all; and I see no reason why we may not anticipate as little or even less expense another year.

The number of fires has been very small, and the damage slight, with one exception the burning of Elbridge Clarke's block in March last. This occurred at a very unfavorable time, on account of the severity of the wind and weather; and it seemed almost a miracle that it was checked where it was. I think the firemen well deserved praise for their perseverance and success on that eventful night. The pleasant recognition of their services by the First Congregational Society; was an event to be long remembered by our firemen.

Alarms of Fires.

The following are the alarms and fires for the past year:

January 19th, 1880. Alarm at Wm. P. Chamberlain's house; caused by throwing ashes into the barn cellar, making considerable smoke. Damage slight; scare a good deal.

February 19th. Alarm on Island Street; cause, chimney burning out.

Clark Block – Corner of Washington Street and Central Square before the fire. HSCC collection.

Clark Block – Corner of Washington Street and Central Square after the fire. Photo taken March 25, 1880 by J.A. French, Keene NH. HSCC collection.

March 24th. Alarm on Square, caused by fire breaking out near or over apothecary store. Damage $50,000; insurance $16,100.

Clark Block Fire

1880 Clark Block Burned as reported by the *Keene Evening Sentinel*. On March 25th, 1880. A Destructive Fire in Central Square.

Fire was discovered in the Northeast portion of Clarke's block at 10.45 last Wednesday night and an alarm immediately sounded by Officer Kellogg. Probably twenty-five or thirty men were in city hall at the time attending the Universalist festival. By the assistance of some of these persons the Deluge hose cart was quickly got out, hose attached to the hydrant on the corner and a stream brought to bear on the flames through a rear window in Appleton's drug store. There is a considerable diversity of opinion as to the location and extent of the fire at this time, but we think without doubt, it must have started in the partition between Appleton's and the express office, or in the floor above, as we do not see how it could otherwise have been seen coming through the second floor by Mrs. Chase as soon as she got up. Had it been burning only on the lower floor we should think the large stream from the hydrant would have extinguished it at once. Mr. Appleton closed his store only about twenty minutes before the alarm, and several gentlemen saw him extinguish the kerosene lamp in the back room, leaving them in the dark. The origin of the fire will probably always remain a mystery.

It may be well to give a short description of the buildings injured and a list of the occupants. Clark's block was built entirely out of wood and was composed of a two-story building of about forty feet front with gable roof; a narrow addition of one story on the extreme South eastern corner running up to two stories on the North eastern corner and a three story building on the West of the first named portion, measuring about forty five feet in front and covered with a flat tinned roof. These buildings are joined together forming a continuous block. Directly west of this block and joined to it by a shortway is the First

Congregational Church, which is also built of wood. The two-story portion of the block, is which the fire caught, was occupied on the lower floor by Mr. Appleton's drug store and Sprague Bros. Bakery and Dining room. On the upper floor lived Mr. Ira M. Sprague and wife and brother, Mr. Arobbani Chase and wife and a boarder named Marston. The addition on the East was occupied by W. F. Whitcomb and James Johnson, who kept paper hangings groceries confectionery, &c., Morrill & Co's express office, John Gauthier shoe maker, and Norman Denio, harness maker. Bancroft & Roby (basement) provision dealers occupied the three-story building. Elbridge Clarke variety store, Edward Harlow, eating house, John Carpenter, harness maker and W. H. Battrick, billiard hall.

To return to the fire. A sharp Northwest gale was blowing at the time of the alarm, which continued all night and it was so cold that ice immediately formed whenever the water struck, unless the fire prevented. Before the alarm on city hall had run down, dense volumes of smoke poured out of the building causing those who lived there no time to secure any of their household goods. It became evident that a serious fire was started and the city marshal ordered the bells on the Episcopal, Unitarian and Congregational churches to be rung. A large crowd of people soon collected, and assisted in removing goods from the stores. About everything was taken out of Clarke's, Bancroft & Roby's, Sprague's, Johnson's and the express office, and much out of Appleton's. It was impossible to get into the upper stores except in the Western portion however, on account of the smoke and fire. The wind drove the flames through the upper portion of the two story building very fast in spite of the six streams of water that had long since been turned onto the fire, and before the stores were cleared the whole upper portion of the building was in flames.

Dense volumes of smoke rolled down Main Street and over the blocks on the Eastside of the square, and a perfect shower of cinders filled the air and settled on roofs and among the buildings and sheds on Roxbury and Church streets. It seemed almost impossible to escape another fire in this direction as a quantity of barns, sheds and old wooden buildings filled with or surrounded by boards, hay, straw and rubbish were known to be thickly packed together in that direction, as far South as the railroad track. A large force of men kept vigilant watch through the district, however, and by the aid of a lot of small hose and pails, kept everything as wet as possible, and extinguished several small fires that caught in various places. The grass as far off as B. D. Hutchins on Church Street was twice set on fire, a pile of straw in rear of the Cheshire House was ignited and several other small fires are reported to have caught.

In the meantime the fire gained rapidly on the firemen, and by 12 o'clock all the lower portion of the block was in flames and the fire began to appear in the top of the three-story portion. The Washington Street side of the block was all in flames and burned fiercely and with great heat. The canvas message board caught fire and was torn off, and the wooden awing on city hall caught twice. About 12.20 the roof on the lower building all fell in and the flames rolled up against the high portion of the block working rapidly into the second and third stories. There had seemed for some time to be no possible hopes of saving the rest of the buildings and as this was so much higher and deeper and would burn so much hotter, no one doubted that the old church and probable Ball's brick block beyond must go, indeed it seemed highly probable that a large portion of our city would be laid in ashes before morning. The wind blew as violently as over though it seemed to be swinging more toward the East; the firemen and the ladders on which they worked were covered with ice. Mayor Kimball telegraphed to Fitchburg for aid, where a steamer and two hose carriages were loaded with all possible dispatch ready to start at once.

By this time, however our firemen had got over their first excitement and had gone earnestly and systematically to work responding quickly to all orders of their officers. They had attacked the fire in two vital points and were holding their ground in front and rear, if they could only reach the center of the building perhaps they could hold the flames in check. A steam fire engine was greatly needed to give a sufficient force to the water to put it where it was wanted, and to knock the fire well out of everything it struck. Had it not been for the hard wind, which carried the smoke and heat directly away from the building and the firemen, they could not have got near enough to reach the most dangerous part of the fire. The flames had crept into the center of the third story as far as the partition that separated the billiard room from Harlow's chambers, and at the same time had worked under the whole of the tin roof, which, being nearly flat, was only raised above the upper plastering from one to three feet leaving excellent place for the fire to burn in.

A portion of the rear of the block was two stories high with a flat roof, here the firemen worked bravely for a long time, benumbed with cold and covered with ice regardless of the fire which was working under the tin roof on which they stood. From this point the water could be thrown over into the hottest part of the fire and up into the center of the high portions of the block. The wind aided in keeping back the firemen in that direction. In front of the building the wooden awnings and the front wall of the two-story portion were torn away by the hook and Ladder Company. The extension ladder was placed to roof of the intact portion and ladders put into the upper windows from the roof top of the awing on

the Western portion of the block, two good streams could be thrown well into the center of the second and third stories where the fire was fast gaining a foothold and its advance in this direction checked. The firemen attacked the high tin roof with their axes and made several holes through which the water was poured. Advancement was made into a room where a large hole was cut through into one of Harlow's chambers, which had got well on fire. A stream of water was at hand to throw into the room, and here again the progress of the fire was checked.

It was now after 1 o'clock and it was evident that the fire was under control unless it broke out in some new spot. The floods of water poured into the front center and rear of the building were fast doing their work and the portion of the building already laid flat was nearly continued so that the heat was not very great. Word was sent to Engineer Reed at Fitchburg that the fire was under control, and a dispatch received from him stating that he had immediately got ready to come to our assistance as before stated, and congratulating our home department on being able to control a dangerous fire on such an awful night. Mayor Kimball returned the thanks of our citizens and offered the services of our department should they ever be needed by the city of Fitchburg. By two o'clock the fire in the three-story portion was nearly all extinguished and the crowed had dispersed. The firemen kept at work until everything was out, the different companies going home at intervals between four and seven o'clock.

The losses and insurance's are about as follows E. Clarke, on block, $25,000, insured $8,500; on stock in store loss $1,000, insured $1,800; Sprague Bros., loss on dining rooms and household furniture, $1,500, insured $500; G. J. Appletons & Co. drug store, loss $5,000, insured $3,000, insured $1,200; James Johnson groceries, &c., loss $500, insured $300, insured $250, Norman Denio, harness maker loss

$1,000 insured $500; John Carpenter, harness maker, loss $200, no insurance. W. H. Battrick, billiard hall, loss $800, no insurance: Bancroft & Roby's meat market loss $1,000, insured; Archibald Chase household furniture, loss $300 no insurance.

We are sorry to learn that a large quantity of goods removed from the burning building were stolen during the fight by some miner able scamps, and hope our citizens will take measure to protect themselves from such thieves in the future.

South Keene – Keene Chair Company Storehouse Fire

1880 The Fire at South Keene as reported by the *Keene Evening Sentinel*. On March 25th, 1880.

A fire broke out in the paint shop of the Keene Chair Company at South Keene shortly after 12 o'clock noon last Thursday. This shop was a three story wooden building 115 x 30 feet, and was filled with chairs, which were being painted and finished. The fire caught in some unknown way in a roof where benzene was used, while the workmen were at dinner, and spread very rapidly, soon the whole building was in flames. The hose kept by the company at their shops were attached to the hydrants from their force pump and the hand engine kept their got out. As is frequently the case on such occasions the hose were old and burst and the hand engine would not work. Word was sent to Keene that assistance was needed and one department called out at about 12.20. The boys had a hard run, and could do no good when they got there, as their hose would fit the company's hydrants. The hand engine was started up however. Had the wind been Southeast the main brick shop and out buildings would have been in great danger, and a steamer would have been the only thing that could have saved these buildings.

The paint shop was entirely destroyed before help arrived from Keene and a storehouse and barn adjoining it on the South side of the road, both of which were filled with chairs. Were nearly burned. Quite a lot of chairs were got out of the latter buildings. The wind blew the fire into the woods and brush south of the buildings, and houses on the hill to the Southeast were in danger, the fire catching around them. The loss on the buildings was $5,000, insured $2,000 and losses on chairs $3,000, insured.

What Our Fire Department Needs
[Clifford C. Wilber]

The fire of Wednesday night was the first large blaze that has occurred in our city for several years; yet it was no more serious, nor no more difficult to control than almost any fire must be that gets well started in any thickly built portion of the city. Indeed we doubt if our firemen could do as well with their present facilities, if a fire should get in to the top of any of the higher buildings on Central Square. Every one admits that we have been remarkably fortunate in regard to fires, in our large blocks especially, and at the same time have we not been remarkable in different in regard to our fire department. True, we have good hose carriages and hose, and excellent water works, on which we chiefly rely, and a good department, which our citizens have been, more inclined to laugh at and find fault with than to assist and encourage. It is nevertheless a fact that where fire have occurred well off the line of the main water pipes it has been impossible to get more than one or two streams to reach the ridgepole of an ordinary two-story building. This was the case when Ellis's foundry caught on fire, when Buckminster's house on Valley Street burned when Farnum's gristmill caught fire, when the pottery burned, and on numerous other occasions we remember. Everyone who was present must have seen how little force the water had when all the streams were playing on Clarke's block the other night, though the hydrants were most favorably situated. The firemen had to almost get into the fire in order to get the water where it was wanted. Had the block been three or four stories high they could not have reached a large part of it.

A good steam fire engine is what is needed to obviate this difficulty, and one should be procured without delay. The Amoskeag and the Silsby steamers stand at the head, and by a little inquiry we can easily find out which is best. One of our prominent businessmen informs us that he has assisted in the manufacture of the Amoskeag steamers and has had considerable experience in working them. He pronounces them perfect machines, and generously offers his service as engineer in case the city government decides to purchase one for us in our fire department. A steamer can be handled on the same principal that our apparatus now is and without greater expense than a hand engine.

In the second place a protective police force of thirty or forty of our businessmen should be organized, provided with suitable badges and placed under control of Chief Engineer and such officers' as they may elect, to serve at all times when a fire is in progress. These police should be regularly qualified as policemen though only subject to duty at times of fires, when they should see to moving and guarding property and do whatever might be required of them. Such an organization would be for mutual protection and need not cost the city anything except the expense of badges, clubs and belts.

The engine houses in rear of the Episcopal Church should be more favorably located if possible. They should be near Main Street, so that the apparatus could be easily got at and drawn out where people are and where assistance can be obtained. These companies are no obliged to make good while for men or horses before they can get their carriages out of sight of the engine houses, and they cannot be expected to arrive at a fire as promptly as the companies more favorably located.

A more rigid system of discipline should be enforced in the department, and all cases of disobedience, rowdies or anything of the kind investigated and punished by prompt dismissal or otherwise, as circumstances may require.

In this way our fire department can be made fully equal to that of other cities and towns of our size, and the expense of main training it need not be increased but a slight amount.

The Firemen's Supper

[from Fire Department records]

The First Congregations Society gave our firemen a supper Friday evening at the church vestry, as a token of their thanks for appreciation of the gallant service rendered by the department at the fire Wednesday night. We need not waste words in attempting to convince our readers that the supper was bountiful, excellent and well served, as the fact the ladies of the society managed this part of the entertainment is a sufficient guarantee of its character. It is the practical assurance of the appreciation of their services, and the manifestation of an interest in their organization by our best citizens, that the firemen have for a long time felt the need of, and for which they are most thankful. The several companies of the department marched to the church in good order, and were received and conducted to their seats by the committee of reception. Their appetites were doubtless sharpened by the severe work of Wednesday and Thursday, so that they were anxious to enjoy the supper before them. After every one was conformable seated at the tables, Mr. Skinner introduced the pastor of the society, who welcomed the guests of the evening in a few well-chosen words. He tendered to the firemen the heartfelt thanks of the people of Keene, and especially of his society, for the noble work done by them Wednesday night, and for saving the old church in which many of our citizens and their fathers had worshipped so many years, and which is so dear to them. He asked the firemen to partake of this supper as the best token the society could give of their appreciation and thanks. Rev. Wm. Eakins asked the Divine blessing, and then everyone went to work with a good will to supply the wants of the dinner. An orchestra furnished entertainment in attendance. The ladies took good care that no one would have to wait long for a full supply of everything the night ordered. The firemen worked valiantly, as they did Wednesday night but could not make any very apparent introduction on the bountiful supply provided.

After supper various gentlemen present very pleasantly spent a couple of hours in listening to remarks. The pastors of all the churches except the Episcopal and Catholic were in attendance, (those would doubtless have been there had it not been Good Friday) and all of them spoke during the evening. Chief Engineer Wright, Mr. John Humphrey, Mr. Tuttle of Haverhill Mass., formerly chief of the fire department there, E. F. Lane, Elbridge Clarke and Engineer Batchelder also spoke. An exceedingly good feeling was manifested, everyone who spoke had something good to say, and the audience frequently applauded loudly. Chief Engineer Wright said that this was the first token of the kind the department had ever received, that he knew of, and assured the donors that words could hardly express the thanks for the firemen felt for the interest manifested in the words of thanks. He definitely could only speak words of praise for the faithful, obedient and cheerful manner in which the men had performed their duties at the fire. Mr. Turner of Haverhill stated that he

had served as a fireman, from private to Chief Engineer. His experience had taught him that the way to have a good department was for the citizens to see the firemen well provided with tools and well paid for their services. The citizens must also take an interest in the department and encourage good men to join it. He gave some figures showing how well this had paid in his city. The firemen must also respect themselves, and every man must conduct himself in such a manner as to merit the confidence of the citizens. He had found it of vital importance for the firemen to obtain from all use of intoxicating liquors, to obey all orders promptly, and to refrain from acts of cowards at all times. He believed the position of a fireman to be as honorable as that of a soldier; and their success depended as much on their discipline and co-operation as that of any army. His motto for firemen was "Deeds, not words." Mr. Walkley said he was sorry to see any man's buildings burn but he thought it a good thing for the city to have these old tinderboxes destroyed. He thought it would be better if the whole block had gone. He hoped our citizens would see to it that a fire proof, brick building be erected where the ruins now are. He related the experience of Chicago, which should be a warning to everyone as well as our own narrow escape. Mr. Clarke said it made a man rather nervous to see his property being crumbled, but he had endeavored to keep as cool as he could. He thought wooden buildings better than none, and presumed the earlier settlers of Chicago had done as people had done here put up the best buildings they could at the time. He reminded his hearers that the building in which they were then assembled was a wooden building, and said he for one, could not rejoice to see his flatten curling round its graceful spire. Fifteen years ago he had all his goods stored in a fireproof block and lost everything by fire. He had furnished as good buildings as he could, but believed in

☙ *A Demon Called Fire*

evolution and improvement, and could only say if our citizens demanded a brick block, let them put their hands in their pockets, buy the land and build one. He certainly should not object. He thanked the firemen for their services, and adjured them never to use intoxicants at a fire. The other gentlemen mentioned spoke very happily on various subjects, each receiving a good clap as he was called upon by Mr. Skinner and as we have stated, the occasion was very social and enjoyable. Rev. Mr. Richardson, after which the assembly dispersed, having had a good supper and a good time, so, prayer offered when everyone had spoken who desired to do.

1880 [*from* Town of Keene Annual Report]

Report of the Chief Engineer [*continued*]

March 25th. Alarm at South Keene, caused by Keene Chair Co.'s store-house burning. Loss $8,000; insurance $5,000.

April 5th. Alarm caused by J. M. Farnum's grist mill taking fire. Damage slight.

April 10th. Alarm caused by grass taking fire from passing engines. Damage not ascertained.

April 25th. Alarm on Washington Street caused by chimney burning out at the house of J. N. Morse, by which he was reminded that they had better slate, and did so.

May 13th, Alarm at Cheshire Railroad wood-shed, caused by sparks setting fire to the shingles. Damage small $25.

June 8th. Alarm on Washington Street, caused by Allen Griffin's house taking fire, which was badly damaged. Loss $2,000.

October 29th. There was a slight alarm on Franklin Street, which came near disturbing a torch-light procession.

Number of Men.

The manual working force of the Department is 87 men, organized as follows: seven engineers, three hose companies, 20 men each, viz: Deluge, Neptune and Phoenix hose, also a Hook and Ladder Company of 20 men.

Hose.

There are now in the Department 4200 feet of good hose, located as follows: 1200 at Phoenix hose house on Depot ground, in rear of the Episcopal church, 1200 at Neptune hose house, 1250 at Deluge hose house on Vernon Street, 100 at Hope Mills, 150 at Symonds' tannery, and 300 at South Keene-making a total of 4200 feet.

Discipline.

It gives me the greatest pleasure to state that there has been manifested a general acquiescence in every rule and regulation of the Department. I think all have endeavored to do their duty, and although some may have fallen short, yet we take the will for the deed, in part.

In my last report I suggested, as an act of appreciation and for the good of the Department, that our city authorities give annually a supper to the firemen. It would cost but little compared with the good effect it would have upon the men. It would be to the firemen like Thanks giving to the home circle.

Our Fire Department is just what we make it. If every man who thinks himself capable of doing better than our firemen, would take hold and try his hand at it, no doubt there might be some improvement in our Department. Good example is better than street lectures. Let our citizens take hold and make our Department what they would have it. We are all aware of our many shortcomings, for which we sincerely desire as lenient judgment as possible.

Appropriation for the Department $2,500.
Expenses, for the Department $2,200.

The large expenditure and appropriation was caused by the necessity of purchasing new hose and moving and repairing Deluge hose house.

Total valuation of inventory property of the Department for 1880 $9,775.00+

In conclusion, allow me to thank the City Government for their kindness to us and the Department. And I would here tender my personal thanks to my Assistant Engineers for the aid and counsel they have given me; and I would most cordially thank both officers and men of the several companies who have always been ready and willing to do their duty, and for the many tokens of respect given me, which I fear have been but poorly merited.

Virgil A. Wright, Chief Engineer 1880

1881

Report of the Chief Engineer.

Chief Engineer's Office, Keene, December 1st, 1881

To His Honor the Mayor and City councils:

In accordance with the usages of the past, I herewith report to you the condition of the Fire Department for the year ending December 1st, 1881. In my opinion we have cause for gratitude for the remarkable preservation from heavy losses from fire the past year, which I think is partially owing to the vigilance of our citizens, and hope they will continue to be on the alert in the future.

I have endeavored, with the aid of my assistants, to keep the Department in complete working order; and I believe that when occasion calls for their services, our firemen will acquit themselves worthily both as firemen and citizens. At the present time the two hose companies Phoenix and Neptune and the Hook and Ladder company are working under protest, and the Hook and Ladder company have lost a part of their men on account of the location of their houses on the depot grounds rear of Episcopal church; and it seems to me our poor policy to delay the bettering of the location of these houses any longer than is actually necessary, for we cannot afford to let the value of a few hundred

KEENE FIRE DEPARTMENT.

TO THE BOARD OF ENGINEERS:

GENTLEMEN: At a Meeting of the _Neptune Hose_ Company No. _2_, holden _Dec. 27_ 188_1_, NOMINATIONS FOR APPOINTMENT AND DISCHARGE OF MEMBERS WERE MADE AS FOLLOWS, VIZ:

Assignment.	Names for Appointment.	Age.	Residence.	Location of Business.	Remarks.
	Fred Woods		Church St	Beaver Mills	
					Frank E. Shely
	Members Discharged.				Clerk

When a potential member of one of the Keene Fire Department Companies was nominated for appointment, or a member was discharged the above form was completed. The member nominated on the above form on December 27, 1881 was Fred Woods, he lived on Church Street in Keene and worked at Beaver Mills. He was appointed to Neptune Hose Co. #2. From Fire Department records.

A Demon Called Fire

dollars cripple a well drilled and efficient portion of our Fire Department.

The Deluge Company is suited with their location, and we see the interest they feel in fixing up their hall and keeping things in good shape: and if these other companies (Phoenix, Neptune and Hook and Ladder) were suitably located, their interest would soon be manifest in the same way. It is hoped the city fathers will see to this immediately. In my opinion the old Baptist church is the best location, all things considered.

Early last summer the Deluge engine was taken to a house near Woodbury's mill, built by Mr. Woodbury; and the engine is to be kept in working order by him, and to be used by the city when occasion requires.

The ordinary running expenses of the Department have been small the past year, which will be an agreeable feature to all, and I see no reason why it should be any more another year; although I would suggest that the Deluge hose carriage should be repainted the present winter, as it has not been painted since bought.

The number of fires has been small, and the damage slight, with the exception of the Ashuelot shoe shop, which was burned February 22nd. The firemen were on the ground very promptly, but owing to the long distance of small water pipes in that locality and the very combustible nature of the building, which was high with very few partitions, the fire spread rapidly, and little could be done to check the flames.

The fire alarm apparatus broke at this alarm on account of a key getting loose: but it is so repaired that it will not break again in the same place.

The following are the alarms of fire the past year:

January 1st, 1881. Alarm at house on Beaver Street; cause burning out chimney: no damage.

January 12th. Alarm at R. P. Leonard's house on Douglas Street; cause, the carpenter put the door causing too near the stove. On account of the peculiar construction of the house fire burned slowly, and was put out without using the hose. Loss estimated at $50; claimed to be $130 on account of interruption of business. No insurance.

February 12th. Alarm at house of John Buckley, on Myrtle Street; cause, burning out chimney. No damage; big scare.

February 22nd. Alarm at Ashuelot shoe shop, on Leverett Street. Loss $40,000 to $50,000; insurance $25,000, probably incendiary.

March 4th. Alarm at house on Carroll Street; burning out chimney; no damage.

April 25th. Alarm at house owned by Cheshire Railroad, occupied by Dennis Callahan. Loss on house $650; insured for $350; loss to Mr. Callahan $360. Caused by sparks form locomotive.

July 6th. Alarm at house of Patrick Mahar, probably caused by ashes in a barrel close to corner of barn.

July 26th. Alarm at house of Edward Joslin, on West Street; cause burning out chimney, the heat from which set the adjoining wood work on fire. Loss $125, fully insured.

November 6th. Alarm at house of Marcus M. Smith, on Butler Court; caused, defective chimney, probably. Loss $1500 to $1800; insured for $1800. Ryan's loss on house hold goods, $300; no insurance.

Number of Men.

The manual working force of the Department is 87 men, as follows: seven Engineers, three hose companies of 20 men each viz: Deluge, Neptune and Phoenix, also a hook and ladder company of 20 men.

Hose.

There are now in the Department 4200 feet of good hose, located as follows: 1200 feet at Phoenix house, 1200 at Neptune house

Ashuelot Boot & Shoe Shop was located on Leverett Street in Keene. This photo was taken around 1878 by J. A. French of Keene. On February 22, 1881 the building was destroyed by fire. HSCC collection.

on depot grounds, 1200 at Deluge house on Vernon Street, 50 feet at N. G. Woodbury's with engine, 100 at Beaver mills, 150 at Symonds' tannery and 300 at South Keene making a total of 4200 feet, as good as last year with the exception of ordinary wear.

Discipline.

It gives me great pleasure to state that there had been manifested a disposition to obey all rules and regulations of the Department. I think all have intended to do their duty, and although some have erred and come short, we take the will for the deed and let it pass.

I am confident our firemen will compare favorably with the firemen of any

place, taking into account all circumstances, and I sincerely hope our City Councils will encourage the members of the companies situated on depot grounds by speedily giving them a better location, and I think they will see a keen interest manifested as a result.

Total valuation for the Department property 1881 is $10,127.00.

There are also, belonging to the Department, the uniforms of the members, the value of which is difficult to estimate, as some of them are well worn; also rubber coats, badges of engineers, &c.

In conclusion, allow me to thank the City Government for their kindness to us and the Department. And I would here tender my

A Demon Called Fire

MANUAL

OF THE

KEENE FIRE DEPARTMENT,

ADOPTED JUNE, 1881.

REVISED MAY, 1884.

2

PREAMBLE.

It being the desire of the Board of Engineers to do everything consistent with right and justice to promote the general welfare and the efficiency of our Fire Department, and the best interests of our city with regard to protection against fire, and to promote harmony and concert of action of both Engineers and Firemen, we have thought it best to present the following revision of rules and general instructions for the above purpose, and we would recommend that they be read in open meeting at least once in three months.

Adopted June, 1881.

EXTRACTS

FROM THE LAWS OF NEW HAMPSHIRE IN RELATION TO FIREMEN.

In accordance with a law of the State (enacted in 1844) adopted by the City of Keene, the Board of Mayor and Aldermen appoint a Chief Engineer and Assistant Engineers of the Fire Department, who have the powers and perform the duties of a Board of Firewards.

36

some previous meeting, and due notice having been given of the time such amendment would be acted upon.

ARTICLE XVIII.

INSTRUCTIONS AND SUGGESTIONS TO THE FIREMEN.

It is important that the several Fire Companies be filled with active and reliable men who shall be ready, able and willing to render such service as may be required of them, therefore, men whose residence or business is too distant from the company house, and those who cannot usually be relied upon in case of fire, should not be admitted or retained as members, and no person should have his name enrolled upon the company's books as a member until appointed by the Engineers.

Each member is expected to meet at suitable times for discipline and practice, so that he may be properly skilled and expert in the use of the apparatus used by the company, also to inform himself in regard to his duties as a fireman, and he should in case of fire endeavor to act with coolness and discretion in the discharge of the duties assigned him.

Each hydrant man, pipe man and officer in

37

charge of any line of hose connected with a hydrant should ascertain the number of such hydrant that it may be designated thereby in giving orders for operating the same.

Great care should be used in opening and closing the hydrants, and all hydrant men should be instructed in this point.

In laying hose two lines may be attached to a hydrant if a sufficient quantity is at hand for that purpose, but in all cases it is better to make use of a single line from each hydrant near any fire before double lines are laid.

Believing that the observance of the foregoing rules and the By-Laws adopted by the Board of Engineers will tend to make the Fire Department more efficient and worthy of confidence, we trust they will receive the approval and support of each member and our citizens.

(Signed.)

GEO. D. WHEELOCK, Chief.
J. A. BATCHELDER, Assistant.
H. H. BARKER, "
C. L. KINGSBURY, "
W. H. REYOUM, "
H. W. HARVEY, "
C. L. KINGSBURY, Clerk of Board.

Adopted June of 1881 and revised in 1884 was the Manual for the Keene Fire Department, the actual manual consisted of more than 37 pages in accordance with the laws of New Hampshire in relation to Firemen. From Fire Department records.

personal thanks to my Assistant Engineers for the aid and counsel they have given me; and I would most cordially thank both the officers and men of the several companies for their promptness to duty as well as obedience to orders, and for the many tokens of respect given me which I feel have been poorly merited. We all feel our many shortcomings, for which we sincerely desire as lenient judgment as possible.

Freeman A. White, Chief Engineer Fire Department 1881

In 1881 A Joint Resolution, relating to Deluge Hose Co., is given the sum of twenty dollars for the purpose of purchasing chairs for their hall. Passed Nov. 2nd, 1881.

The City of Keene used the above form for City Officers, which the board of engineers of the Fire Department were appointed officers and took their oath and this commission form was completed and signed by city officials and the individuals taking the oath The above is one was Henry H. Parker appointed second assistant Engineer on January 16th. From Fire Department records.

A Demon Called Fire

MANUAL

OF THE

KEENE FIRE DEPARTMENT,

ADOPTED JUNE, 1881.

REVISED MAY, 1884.

WITH

LIST OF HYDRANTS.

KEENE:

SENTINEL PRINTING COMPANY, BOOK AND JOB PRINTERS.
1884.

LIST OF HYDRANTS.

Adams Street.
No. 21, West corner of Emerald street.

Ashuelot Street.
No. 32, opposite South end on West street.
" 101, East side, 800 feet north of West street.

Baldwin Street.
No. 37, South corner of Elm street.

Beach Street.
No. 64, East corner of Roxbury street.
" 52, East side, 600 feet from Roxbury street.

Beaver Street.
No. 48, North side, 150 feet West from tannery.
" 49, opposite East corner of Franklin street.
" 51, Southeast corner of Cemetery.
" 50, Northwest corner of Lincoln street.

Beaver Mills.
No. 88, fifty feet Northwest of machine shop.
Private, North side, in sprinkler box.
" 89, fifty feet North of saw mill.
" 90, Southwest corner of chair shop.
Private, Southwest corner furniture shop.

26

Franklin Street.
No. 63, West corner of Roxbury street.
" 49, opposite East corner on Beaver street.

George Street.
No. 126, North side, 300 ft. from Washington st.
" 127, North side, 550 ft. beyond the brook.

Gilsum Street.
No. 99, West side, 300 ft. South Joslin's house.

Grant Street.
No. 56, East side, 350 ft. North of Roxbury st.

Grove Street.
No. 94, West corner of Water street.
" 123, West side, opposite Myrtle street.

Hart Street.
No. 104, South corner of Pearl street.

High Street.
No. 36, Northwest corner of Elm street.
" 18, Southwest corner of Howard street.
" 23, South corner of Washington street.

Howard Street.
No. 17, West corner of Cross street.
" 18, Southwest corner of High street.
" 57, East side, 400 feet North of Maple st.

Island Street.
No. 75, West corner of West street.

Leverett Street.
No. 86, Southest corner of River street.

Lincoln Street.
No. 60, East corner of Water street.

27

No. 59, East side, midway between Water and Church street.
" 58, East side, opposite North corner of Church street.
" 65, Northwest corner of Roxbury sreet.
" 50, Northwest corner of Beaver street.

Madison Street.
No. 91, opposite North end on Winchester st.

Main Street.
No. 1, Central Park.
" 2, South corner of West street.
" 3, South corner of Roxbury street.
" 4, Southeast corner of Davis & Wright's.
" 5, Southwest corner of Eagle Hotel.
" 6, North corner of Davis street.
" 7, North corner of Marlboro street.
" 8, West side, near school house.
" 9, East side, 100 ft. North of Gates street.
" 10, West side, 75 ft. North of Appleton st.
" 109, West side, opposite pottery.

Maple Street.
No. 22, North corner of Washington street.

Marlboro Street.
No. 7, North corner of Main street.
" 11, front of E. E. Lyman's.
" 61, South side, 150 ft. East of Grove street.
" 62, North side, 70 ft. East of Kelleher st.
" 117, South side, 100 ft. beyond the brook.

The above manual was adopted and issued in June 1881 to each member of the Fire Department for the purpose of knowing the location of hydrants in the City. From Fire Department records.

1882 [*from* City of Keene Annual Report]

Report of the Chief Engineer.

Office of Chief Engineer, Keene December 1st, 1882

To His Honor the Mayor and city Councils:

Gentleman: I herewith submit the following report of the Fire Department for the year ending December 1st, 1882

The year just has been a very fortunate one., we have had but few fires, and the losses have been small.

I have endeavored, with the valuable aid of my assistant, to keep the department in good working order at all times; and I must say that Keene may well be proud of her fire department.

The condition of the apparatus at the present time is good. But little has been expended this year except for the painting of the 'deluge hose carriage. The Deluge Hose Company has a very good house. They have refitted and refurnished their hall in a very neat and appropriate manner, nearly the whole being done at their own expense. They have also procured, at their own expense, a very neat uniform. I think these things speak well for the interest they take in their work. The Neptune Hose Co., while in every way the equal of the other companies, labors under the disadvantage of poor quarters; and certainly before another year passes some change will have to be made here. The Phoenix Hose Co. is in good working condition, and though comparatively a new company, has proved itself to be one of the best. The Hook and Ladder Company is in as good condition as it is possible to make it under the disadvantage of poor quarters, which are even worse than those of the Neptune Hose Co. A good hook and ladder company is just as essential as a good hose company, and I trust that something will be done toward giving this company better quarters another

year. Here let me say, also, that the uniforms of the Neptune and phoenix hose companies, and of the Hook and Ladder Company, is very poor, and I would recommend that they be provided with suitable uniform.

The locations of the hand engines and extra hose carts are the same as in years past, with no material change in their condition.

In regard to the fire alarm, I would say that the experience of the year just past is such that I am confident that it is for the interest of the city to make some arrangement with the Telephone Company so that the alarm can be struck from their general office. There is now a telephone in nearly every part of the city, and an alarm can be given through that office much quicker than in any other way. The following are the alarms of fire the past year:

January 23rd, 6.35 A. M. Fire at F. A. Barker's, Main Street; cause, sparks from locomotive. Loss $50; insured.

February 7th, 5 P. M. Chimney burnt out at Richards' house, High Street. No loss.

February 20th. Fire at Dort & Farrar's drug store. No loss.

August 21st. Fire at G. M. Gowen's, Madison Court; cause defective chimney. Loss $2,000; insured.

November 13th. 9:15 A. M. Fire at S. W. Hale's furniture shop, Ralston Street. No loss.

Number of Men.

The working force of the department consists of three hose companies of twenty men each, one hook and ladder company of twenty men, and seven engineers.

Discipline.

It gives me pleasure to say that there has been a general disposition shown to obey the rules and regulations of the department.

Inventory of property belonging to the department, a total of $10,792.00

In conclusion allow me to thank the City Councils for the many favors received; and to my assistants and to the several companies I return my most sincere thanks for the courtesy received and their obedience to all orders and promptness to duty.

Geo. D. Wheelock, Chief Engineer. City Report Dec. 1st, 1882

1883 [*from* City of Keene Annual Report]

The City of Keene paid to the Manchester Locomotive Works $3,600.00 for a Fire Steamer. Keene's AMOSKEAG STEAMER. Paid out also was a total of $26.27 for members to examine the Steamer prior to its acceptance.

1883 Report of the Chief Engineer.

To His Honor the Mayor and City Councils: Gentlemen: I respectfully submit the following report of the fire department for the year ending Dec. 1st, 1883.

In the year just passed, we have had an unusual amount of fires, and of course have sustained greater losses than usual, but the companies have been very prompt in the discharge of their duties. The department is in fine working order, which is greatly done to the value of my assistants. The condition of the apparatus is good.

The Deluge Hose Company has made some more improvements in their already handsome hall; their hall is now one of the best , as it should be, for it is the headquarters of one of the best hose companies in the state.

Picture of new Amoskeag Steamer in front of the Old Fire Station, located behind St. James Church at Railroad Square. At one time Saturday on the site of the Abbot Grocery Building, which was moved to St. James Street about 1875. Hook & Ladder, Neptune Hose and Engine Company, Niagara Hose and Engine Company and Phoenix Hose Company were stationed there at times. Picture given by C.L. Barrett. Phoenix House at left was partly destroyed by fire. Was sold at auction and bought by John E. Wyman and was moved to his farm in West Keene about 1893 or 1894. From Fire Department Records scrapbook.

Additional fire house locations were N.G. Woodbury's, which was upper Washington Street, Beaver Mills on Railroad Street, Symonds Tannery, which was in South Keene where Cheshire Oil is today, even at a time there was a fire house behind City Hall and of course Vernon Street and.

Amoskeag Contract Cover

MEMORANDUM OF AGREEMENT

Made this *Eleventh* day of *August* 1883, by and between the Manchester Locomotive Works, of Manchester, N. H., the party of the first part, and *a committee* representing for this purpose the *City of Keene N.H.* the party of the second part: Whereby it is agreed as follows, to wit:

That the said Manchester Locomotive Works, the party of the first part, will build and finish in accordance with the following specifications, for said *City of Keene N.H.*, the party of the second part, a *second* class (in size) Steam Fire Engine, and will also deliver the same to said party of the second part in *about two weeks from date* Said Manchester Locomotive Works are to deliver said Engine *in the City of Keene N.H.* in complete running order, and to warrant its material and workmanship to be of the best quality, and to replace at their own expense such parts, if any, as may fail within *ten years* if such failure is properly attributable to defective material or inferior workmanship.

Said party of the second part hereby agree, that, as soon as practicable after the delivery of said Steam Fire Engine, as above provided, it shall have a full and complete trial of its working powers, under the superintendence of the Engineer in charge; and if said Engine shall then prove in accordance with the specification, it shall be accepted by the party of the second part; and they hereby agree to pay to said Manchester Locomotive Works for the same the sum of *three thousand, six hundred* Dollars, (*$3600.00*) payment to be made *in cash within thirty days after the delivery of the engine –*

SPECIFICATION.

The Engine to be of the *second* class (in size), and to weigh, exclusive of supplies, about *6000* pounds. *Double* steam and water cylinders, — *Crane necked Frame Improved Platform Springs*

BOILER.—To be vertical *30½* inches diameter, and *64* inches long, and is to contain *187 Seamless steel* tubes, each *24* inches long and *1½* inches diameter. The boiler to be made of the best steel plate double riveted and well stayed. It is to be cased in wood and covered with *nickel plated jacket* with *red metal* bands, and to be surmounted with a *red metal and german silver* dome and chimney casing. The boiler is to be completely supplied with a safety valve, a set of gauge cocks, a glass water gauge, a pressure gauge, a whistle, plugs for cleaning out, and a blow-off cock.

STEAM CYLINDERS.—To be *6 7/8* inches diameter, *8* inches stroke. *Each* cylinder to exhaust into the chimney of boiler through an independent exhaust pipe and tip. Body of cylinder to be covered with *nickel plated jacket* heads to be covered with *red metal*, and steam chest sides to be covered with *red metal* *Valve Rods to have Guides at their lower ends*

Amoskeag Contract

1883 The Steam Fire Engine as reported by the Keene Evening Sentinel *on August 22nd, 1883.*

The new Amoskeag Steamer "Keene No. 1," manufactured by the Manchester Locomotive, Works arrived here on a late train Thursday night, and according to the programs which had been announced, an exhibition, was given upon the Square Saturday afternoon. As had been before stated, the steamer is a second sized (or "second class" as it is termed) crane-neck Amoskeag engine. The machine weighs when ready for use, about 6000 pounds. She has a steel boiler 31 inches in diameter, with a firebox 20 inches high and containing 192 half-inch steel flues, 2½ inches long. The boiler is of the "cone top" pattern as it is termed, giving ample steam and water space above the flues. There are two double acting pump 41/2 inches in diameter by 8-inch stroke. The steam cylinders, two in number, are situated upon the same piston rods as the pump cylinders, their diameter being 77/8 inches. The capacity of the pumps is about 650 gallons per-minute. The engine is furnished with double exhaust pipes and all the very latest improvements. In point of finish she is one of the finest engines ever made at the Amoskeag Works, nearly all the metallic parts being nickel-plated. We have no doubt that the workmanship upon the machine is as fine as the finish, as Mr. Blood intended this engine both for exhibition at Boston and the trial at the Portsmouth muster. We think the committee on fire department is to be commended for and congratulated upon the purchase, which they have made.

The engine was drawn to the Square about eleven Saturday morning, that people might have a chance to look it over. About noon it was placed in position at the hydrant near Davis & Wright's. As the boiler had not been used except to test it, no attempt was made to fire the engine quickly, it always being advisable to work an engine and get the grease, &c., out of a boiler, so that it will not foam before this is done. Mr. John F. Wilson of the Amoskeag Works, who was in town with Superintendent Blood to give the engine such trial, as was desired, started the fire at 1,10 smoke appearing at the tip of the stack at 1.11. In 2 ¾ minutes the gauge indicated 3lbs. of steam. People then crowded round the engine so that the fire got scarcely any draft for two minutes or so, the gauge standing perfectly still. Five pounds of steam was indicated in 6 minutes, 10 lbs. In 8 ¾ minutes, 15 lbs. In 9 ¼ minutes, 20 lbs. In 9 ½ minutes, 30 lbs. in 10 minutes, and 40 lbs. In 10 ½ minutes when the engine was started. In 11 minutes she had 50 lbs. of steam and 70 lbs. of water pressure and in 13 minutes she was playing with 125 lbs. of water pressure through 150 feet of hose with an inch and a quarter nozzle. This stream was thrown horizontally 209 ½ feet when the hose burst. Other plays were made with a 1 ¼ inch nozzle, the hose bursting at from 140 to 170 lbs. A 1 1/8-inch stream was then thrown over the top of the Unitarian spire. Two lines of hose were then attached to the steamer and two 1 1/8-inch streams were thrown 184 feet, the hose bursting when the water pressure revealed 140 lbs. Two lines of hose from the engine, 50 feet each, were then Siamesed into one 50-foot length and a 1 ¾ inch stream from an open pipe was thrown 170 feet horizontally, the hose bursting at this point. This was a remarkably strong and powerful stream. Its execution if at a fire could not be doubted. With the same arrangement a 1 ¼ inch stream was thrown 20 to 30 feet over the Unitarian spire. The steamer it should be stated, was taking her water through a brass pipe, 2 3/8 inches in diameter, which was attached to one opening of the hydrant and to the suction hose of the steamer by means of a reducer. In order to test the question of the capacity of the hydrant to supply the steamer, fifty feet of ordinary hose was attached to the other opening of the hydrant and an inch and an eighth stream allowed to play there from. The steamer was then started up as fast as she could work without bursting the hose, the result being that the stream from the other side of the hydrant continued to play some 70 feet, showing that the pressure of water in the hydrant was not reduced over 15 lbs. Experiments were then made with the relieve valve upon the steamer, which regulators the water pressure. This was set at about 100 lbs. The engine was then worked rapidly and the steamer shut off by a right angle cock in the hose-nozzle, the water pressure in the pumps not ringing higher that the point at which the relief valve was set.

The steamer was run during the exhibition by Mr. Geo. H Piper of this city, who is thoroughly acquainted with the building and working of these engines, and by Mr. Wilson, W. B. Hastings of the Cheshire road doing the firing and keeping a steady, even fire. The engine made steam in abundance, all the time the top valve opening constantly when she was working her hardest. It was of course impossible to make any kind of lost of the power of the machine, as there was no hose in the department which would hold over half the water pressure used at steamer trials. There is some question whether the hose, which the Neptune Company furnished for this trial, were the best in the department but at any rate, it is evident that some new hose should be bought at once for use with the steamer. At the same time there is no reason why the engine should be allowed to carry sufficient water pressure to burst fairly good hose at a fire, as some people seem to anticipate who will do. A pressure of 110 lbs. Will give a very good fire stream or streams and if necessary the relief valve upon the pump can be set at this point so that the pressure cannot exceed that amount.

In order that the organization of the old companies of the fire department might not be disturbed an independent company has been organized to man the steamer. The first meeting of this company was held Thursday evening of last week. The following are the officers and members: E. S. Foster, Captain; Henry H. Hains, Lieutenant; Frank E. Foster, Foreman of hose; Geo. H. Piper , engineer, D. E. Ladd, assistant engineer; J. H. Howes, Fireman; C. F. Metcalf, Driver; Geo. G. Dort, Clerk; M. V. B. Clark, Treasurer. The other members of the company are C. E. Joslin, J. F Emmons, C. W. Cummings, J. Q. Jones, Jas W. Russell, A. W. Dickinson, J. P. Wellman, C. W. Penslec, F. A. Shaw, F. M. Davis and Chas H. Clark. The company will serve without pay. The steamer is housed for the present in the Neptune engine house. The building is old and not suitable for permanent use for this purpose. The Steamer Company now has no hall in which to hold meetings but we presume suitable quarters will be soon provided.

Members of the Deluge Hose Company August 25, 1883. Sitting L to R, E.H Holbrook, Joseph Burnes, C.H. Spofford, G.L. Starkey and Firefighter Reed. Standing L to R, E.H. Stone, F.W. Towne, F.O. Quinn, Pat O'Leary Foreman, Billy Richards and C.G. Gilmore. From Keene Fire Department scrapbook.

A Demon Called Fire

The Hook & Ladder Company has greatly improved, and is a far better company than I should suppose we could have in the miserable quarters they occupy. We have this year added 2 twenty-foot ladders, 2 forty-foot ladders and I sixty-five foot Bangor extension ladder to their carriage: and I recommend that they be provided with better quarters as soon as possible.

It has been found expedient and necessary by the Board of Engineers to discharge from service the Neptune Hose Company, and there is now no such company in the department.

There has been a very valuable addition made to the department this year by the purchase of a very fine Amoskeag Steamer, and 850 feet of steamer hose; the machine is a very fine one, and the city might well be proud of it. We have formed a Steamer Company that runs the steamer, and hose cart formerly used by the Neptune Company. The Steamer Company consists of 20 volunteers who serve without pay. Great credit is due to Capt. E. S. Foster and Engineer Piper of the Steamer Company for their energy and perseverance in forming so fine a company in so short a time. The steamer is now located at the Old Neptune House, and I would recommend an early removal to more suitable quarters.

Uniforms.

The whole department is well uniformed.

The Fire Alarm.

Are the same as last year, and I will again recommend that some arrangement be made for a telephone alarm.

The following are the alarms for the past year:

March 30th, 1.15 P.M., N.G. Woodbury, pail shop. Loss $2,500; insured $1,500.

April 11th, 3 P.M., A.S. Whitcomb, dry house, Loss $200; not insured.

June 5th, 6.30 A.M., Bancroft & Roby, ice house. Loss $100; not insured.

June 11th, 4 P.M., Beaver Mills. Loss $4,000; insured $3,500

June 23rd, 4 P.M., Butler's Court, Chimney burnt.

July 21st, 1.30 P.M., O'Conner house, Kelleher Street. Loss small.

July 29th, 4.15 P.M., George E. Holbrook & Co., oil house. Loss $175.

August 19th, 3.05 A.M., Cheshire House Block. Loss $12,000; insured $8,900.

Cheshire House Block on the corner of Roxbury Street burned on August 20th, 1883. The rear of this building at one time housed one of the hand engines. HSCC photo collection.

Disastrous Fire in Keene

As reported by the Keene Evening Sentinel. *On August 20th, 1883 in the Rear of the Cheshire House a Fire was discovered.*

At about five minutes past three o'clock, Monday morning, Night watchman Staples noticed a bright light down Roxbury Street, in rear of the Cheshire House, which he at once saw to be the reflection of a fire. At the same time Engineer Underwood of the Cheshire road who was just running into Keene upon his locomotive, saw the fire from his engine and at once blew his whistle as a signal of alarm. Officer Staples pulled the fire alarm off a few seconds after. The telephone promptly informed inquirers in various parts of the city that the Cheshire House was on fire. The firemen were out with commendable promptness, the Deluge boys getting the first stream, and the Hook & Ladder cart being the second piece of apparatus to arrive, we are told. It seemed to be a good while, however, before a large force of firemen or citizens was on the ground, the city hall bell failing to arouse many people even within a quarter of a mile of the Square. As we have before suggested arrangements should be made for the blowing of a steam whistle or the ringing of more bells in cases of fire in the nighttime.

Upon the arrival of the firemen, and others, upon the ground soon after three, the fire was burning fiercely in the East end of the wooden block in rear of the Cheshire house upon the second and third floor occupied by A. D. Cook, furniture dealer. Just where or how it started is a mystery, but it must have been near the stairways and elevator, which ran upon in this part of the building probably upon the second floor. This whole floor was occupied as a furniture show room and it was the full size of the block. On the third floor was first the undertaking room at the head of the stairway, the upholstery room in the North most corner and the painting and finishing rooms in the West end of the building next to the Cheshire House. On the first floor was A. D. Cook's furniture and at the East end of the building, a store occupied by G. W. Foster, dealer in musical instruments and W. F. Whitcomb, dealer in wall papers and M. V. B. Clark & Co's grocery store. H. P. Muchmore's coal office was upon the East End of the building. The fire ran rapidly through the upper floor of the block where there were light partitions and much combustible material. On the second floor it progress was not as rapid. It dropped down into the furniture store at once, however, preventing the removal of nearly everything, which was in it. Nothing whatever was taken out of the upper floors of the block. All the goods in the other two stores were removed.

The elements seem to be always favorable in Keene, of late, when we have a dangerous fire. When Clark's block burned, a fierce wind drove the flames out of the line of buildings through which the fire was creeping. Again at the Beaver Mills fire the wind was favorable. On Monday morning, when a burst in almost any direction would have been dangerous not a breath of air stirred. The roofs and yards of neighboring buildings were still wet from Sunday's showers and heavy dew and fog added to the accumulation of moisture. Profiting by his recent experience at Beaver Mills Engineer Wheelock has wisely obtained a number of new ladders of suitable length and construction for use at fires, and these the Hook & Ladder boys handled to great advantage, enabling the hose men to bring their streams to bear upon the fire at the proper points. The department is improving in this respect, in our judgment, and is there by strengthening itself where it was weakest. The long struggle, which ensured before a line of hose could be carried to the top of the brick ell South of the burning building, showed the need of the other extension ladder, which the

Councils have ordered. There is no danger of having too many ladders yet.

At 3.30 nearly the whole block was in flames and the firemen were being driven steadily back. At 3.45 the fire was found to have reached the attic of the brick ell of the hotel adjoining the block a window in the gable, which was not bricked up when the wooden block was built up serving as an entrance for the flames. The fire was so hot at this time that surrounding buildings were greatly on danged and word was sent to Winchendon for a steamer. Two or three streams were brought to bear upon the fire in the attic of the brick part through holes in the roof and a scuttle, and here a determined fight was made which proved successful, the advances of the fire being stopped at this point. At 4.15 most of the wooden building fell in. The heat was intense at this time. Blistering point upon the buildings on either side or cracking the glass in several windows. Soon after this the streams began to tell upon the fire and the heat diminished perceptibly. It was evident that the fire was under control. The wooden block was nearly consumed and there was no further danger. Word had been sent to Winchendon that the steamer would not be needed. Before five o'clock the excitement was over and people began to pick up their goods or go home as the case might be.

The block, which was burned, was part of the Cheshire House property, M. J. Sherman proprietor. It cost about $10,000 and was insured for $6,800. A. D. Cook values his furniture, &c., at about $5,000 insured for $3,500. G. W. Foster's stock and fixtures in store, valued at $3,000 to $4,000 was nearly all removed. Insurance $1,800, which will cover loss. W. F. Whitcomb had ^600 to $700 worth of wallpaper, which was removed, loss covered by insurance. M. V. B. Clark & Co. was insured for $2,500. Their stock was mostly removed-loss on same estimated at from $1,000 to $1,500. The Cheshire House

ell was thoroughly water soaked and the roof destroyed. Loss $2,000 to $3,000, insured. Mr. Sherman's loss on his furniture, &c., is doubtless over $1,000 insured. Alfred Spaulding's goods were removed at a loss of perhaps $500 not insured. C. W. Shedd lost all his tools, value at over $200. H. P. Muchmore loss on office, &c. $500 uninsured. Lucins Thatcher lost over $200 worth of furniture, which was stored in the building: uninsured. The Telephone Company sustained a slight loss upon wires and poles broken or destroyed.

———————

1883 Report of the Chief Engineer
[continued]

August 28th, 11.45 A.M., Cheshire R. R. Co., car shop. No loss.

September 5th, 11.15 A.M., Ashuelot Mills. No loss.

September 16th, 9 A.M., gas house. Loss $400; not insured.

September 19th, 1 A.M., I Cheni's barn, Douglas Street. Loss $400; insured.

October 23rd, 3 P.M., Beaver Mills dry house. Loss $200; insured.

December 22, 8 A.M., Butler's Court. No loss.

December 23rd, 5.40 A.M., Faulkner & Colony's boarding house, on Ashuelot Street. Loss $2000; insured $2900

Number of Men.

The working force consists of two hose companies of 20 men each, one hook and ladder company of 20 men, one steamer company of 20 men, and seven engineers. I would recommend that the number be cut down to six.

Discipline.

It gives me pleasure to say that there has been a general disposition shown to obey orders, and the rules and regulations of the department.

Inventory total of property belong to the fire Department for year ending $11,747.00

In conclusion, allow me to thank the City Councils for the many favors received; and to my assistants and the several companies, I return my most sincere thanks for the courtesy received, and their obedience to orders and promptness to duty.

G. D. Wheelock, Chief Engineer, Keene, December 1st, 1883

Joint Resolution for 1883: Repairs to Engine House and Purchase of Sled for Hose. Passed Jan. 18th, 1883

For purchase of Supplies, one extension Ladder and ten rubber coats. Also 20 chairs for Phoenix Hose Company Also authorizing the Payment to purchase Uniforms a total of $150 for Washington Hook and Ladder company No. 1 and the sum of $150 for the purchase of uniforms for the Phoenix Hose Company, No. 4 Passed July 5th, 1883

A Joint Resolution for the purchase of 1000 feet of fire hose. Passed Sept. 4th, 1883

STEAM FIRE ENGINE AND HOSE COMPANY---"KEENE NO. 1,"
KEENE, N. H.

Keene Fire Engine and Hose Company No. 1, 1883. Front Row seated L to R: Herbert W. Keyes, Dewey Ladd (Asst. Engineman), M.V.B. Clark, Lt., H.H. Haines, Capt. E.S. Foster, Lt. J.P. Wellman, G.H. Piper (Engineman), C.M. Cummings. Back Row Standing L to R: Frank M. Davis, C.E. Joslin, A.W. Dickenson, A.W. Green, C.H. Clark, Ed Crown, George G. Dort, Mr. Hulett, J.Q. Jones, W. Ellery Wright, E.A. Shaw, G.O. Wardwell and John H. Howe (fireman). From Keene Fire Department records.

A Joint Resolution of the Steam Fire Engine which makes the re-organization of the Fire Department by reducing the force by either dismissing one of the old hose companies, or dispensing with the hose men now on the steamer. This was to be done as brief time as possible. Passed September 20th, 1883.

A Joint Resolution relating to Engine House to fit up temporary the Neptune Engine House for the steamer, not to exceed $200 dollars, passed October 8th, 1883

Note: A Joint Resolution relating to Purchase of Horses for the use of Fire Department be authorized for service on steamer and highways a span of horses, a pair of harnesses and all other necessary outfit for working the horses on the streamer, and the same be paid for from any funds in treasury not otherwise appropriated. Passed November 15th, 1883

Quoting from the *Keene Evening Sentinel*:

An Elegant Hose Wagon for the Use of the City.

At the coming inspection of the Fire Department, which is to take place on the afternoon of October 22nd, the Keene Steam Fire Engine and Hose Company will parade and exhibit for the first time, an elegant new hose wagon of the most modern construction which has been manufactured to order expressly for this company by the Abbot-Downing Company of Concord, N. H. This hose wagon will be used by the Steamer Company, in the future, in place of the four wheeled hose cart owned by the city, with which they are no equipped; and while it will be much more modern and convenient piece of apparatus to handle, it will also be much safer, more serviceable and considerably more useful in actual service than any form of hose cart which has ever been invented.

Purchased on October 23rd, 1883 Steamer Hose Wagon No.1 Picture taken on West side of Central Station Vernon Street, Keene. From Fire Department scrapbook.

The history of the purchase of this wagon by the Steamer Company may be briefly summed up as follows: At the time of the purchase the steamer and the formation of the present engine and hose company, in 1883, or soon after the city equipped the new company with the old Neptune hose cart. This cart was of a light pattern, intended to carry some four or five hundred feet of hose only, and had seen pretty hard service. The Steamer Company took the cart, fitted it with a pair of shafts, a driver's seat, &c., at their own expense, and put it into use. They were required to carry from 600 to 1000 feet of hose upon it, and although the cart was strengthened, it has been considered dangerous and unfit for the heavy service required of it ever since. Last Spring the members of the company began to seriously consider what means could best be adopted to give them a more safe and useful piece of apparatus. They saw that the city had recently expended a large sum upon its new fire station and that it had upon its hands important public improvements which had already been too long deferred, and which must at once involve a large outlay of money. It was therefore unreasonable to

suppose that any new apparatus would be purchased by the Councils during the present year. After making careful investigations and enquiries into the subject among the engineers of several cities, it was decided that a hose wagon was the most useful and serviceable form of carriage yet made, and after negotiations with various builders, the Steamer Company, which has from the first had more at heart the improvement and advancement of the service of the department than the personal or pecuniary gain of its own organization or members, voted to purchase a hose wagon out of its own treasure and from the salaries of its members, at a cost of five hundred dollars.

A contact was therefore made with the famous Abbott-Downing Company, in July for a wagon with all the latest improvements, to be completed in the time for the October inspection-the earliest date at which they could fill an order even thus early in the season.

The body of the new wagon will be 9 feet long by 3 feet 8 inches in wide and 13 inches high. The wheels 3 feet and 4 and 4 feet 6 inches in diameter with 1 ½ and 1 5/8, inch axles with solid collar and tires 2 by ½ inch steel. The springs will be of the "table" pattern. The hub bands and side rails will be nickel plated, also lanterns, ornaments, gong, &c. A crow bar, axe and plaster hook will be furnished and properly mounted. The running part and body will be painted carmine striped with gold and lettered. The wagon will easily carry 1000 feet of hose and a number of men. The canvas, which is stretched over the hose as it lays in the wagon, is supported by a framework, and is used for carrying home wet or soiled hose or as an ambulance stretcher in case of an accident, and the wagon will be useful for getting fuel, hose, or whatever is wanted at a fire after its load of hose is unreeled, instead of being useless as is an ordinary hose cart.

It is to aid the company as much as possible in this liberal expenditure by which the public are to be so largely benefited, that the grand musical entertainment at city hall, is to be given on the night of the inspection. The Steamer company was organized in August, 1883. Its members served until Sept 1st, 1884, without any pay from the city. They have never asked any pecuniary assistance from the public except the fund which they obtained from their honorary members soon after their organization. With this they purchased uniforms and fitted up their house, apparatus, &c. For their uniforms and money expended for articles furnished the other fire companies of the city they have been reimbursed from the public treasury since they ceased to be a voluntary organization. They have always turned their whole annual salary as firemen $15 to each member into their treasury and although they have funds sufficient to meet their bills treasury will of course be much depleted by the large outlay which they are now making. Our people will doubtless be glad to assist them and to patronize them liberally.

1884 [*from* City of Keene Annual Report]
Report of the Chief Engineer.
To His Honor the Mayor and the City Councils:

Gentlemen: In compliance with the requirements of the city ordinances, I would respectfully submit the following statements relative to the condition of the fire department:

Membership.
The department is composed of one Chief and five Assistants Engineers, two Hose Companies of 20 men each, one Hook & Ladder Company of 20 men, one Steamer and Hose Company of 20 men.

Houses
The condition of the houses is the same as last year with the usual amount of repairs added.

Apparatus
The apparatus is in very good condition considering the time it has been in use, and I would recommend the exchange of one of our hose carriages for a hose wagon. The Steamer as well as the hose company's apparatus is kept in the very best manner possible under the circumstances. The Hook & Ladder truck has been supplied with new running gear this season.

Supplies
We have in the department 2500 feet of leather hose, a portion of which will have to be replaced with new very soon, and I would recommend that as fast as practicable it be replaced with cotton fabric hose; we also have 1500 feet of very nice steamer hose.

Uniforms.
The department is well uniformed.

Fire Alarm
The fire alarm remains the same. We are greatly in need of some change in our alarm system; I think there is nothing so badly needed in the department as a new system of fire alarm, and I would recommend again that some arrangement be made for a telephone alarm.

The following are the alarms for the past year:

Jan. 6th, 3.15 A.M., A.R. & E.S. Foster's shop. Loss $200; insured $100.

Jan. 10th, 2.30 A.M., Lewis Broulett's house, Marlboro' Street Loss $800; insured.

Feb. 23rd, 10.30 P.M., Ashuelot Mills, S.W. Hale's. Loss $65,000; insured $42,000.

1884 Ashuelot Mills Burned

As reported by the Keene Evening Sentinel.

On February 23rd 1884. 75,000 worth of property destroyed.

Nearly one hundred men thrown out of employment,

It was a severe blow to the business interests of Keene.

The total destruction of Ashuelot Mills so called by fire, which took place between the hours of eleven and two o'clock on the night of Saturday the 23rd, inst. not only throw's heavy pecuniary loss upon the owners of the property which was burned, but strikes a serious in not irreparable blow at the business interests of Keene. The life and prosperity of our city depends almost wholly upon the effort and success of her manufactures. There is neither a merchant a trader nor a property owner in town who will not feel the loss of the business, many of them seriously, if it not replaced. It is a fact probably beyond dispute that Gov. Hale has done more to build up Keene and make her prosperous than any one or perhaps any half dozen of her most wealthy citizens. He is a man so constituted that he can create and successfully prosecute business upon a large scale, a man of nerve and energy and good judgment, who makes up his mind that, he is right and then goes ahead paying little regard to the gloomy foreboding of croakers or busy bodies or those who are jealous of his success. In fact he is about the kind of man that we want here in Keene, it wouldn't hurt us if we had a dozen of them and what we were about to say is this. That we hope he will be urged and encourage in every reasonable way by his fellow citizens, to replace this business which has been so suddenly destroyed, and still to contribute, so far as he is able, to the success and prosperity of his adopted city. Let us how a little public spirit about this thing and see to it that the hundred people are not allowed to go elsewhere to seek homes and employment. But to return to the fire. It was discovered by the watchman in the fuel room about half past ten and doubtless enough, maybe a spark from the boilers which was probably drawn unseen, into the fuel rooms by the draft while the door was opened to get fuel to fill the fire boxes a short time before. The whistle was blown and the alarm on the city hall at once sounded. The fireman was out respectfully, the Phoenix hose getting first stream. It had been ordered that in case of fire here, the steamer should be sent upon the Winchester Street, Main, leaving the Davis and Emerald Street hydrants where there would be most force, for the hose companies. The steamer was therefore set at the nearest hydrant on Winchester Street, but this was over eight hundred feet from the north end of the shops and there was not enough steamer hose for but one steamer from the engine. It was a great mistake that the city government did not put in a hydrant on Ralston Street, from the Winchester Street main, as they were asked by Mr. Hale to do last fall. Here was where the engine ought to have been located.

To those who first arrived at the fire, it seemed probable that the steam blast and the sprinklers, both of which were at work inside the fuel room, would subdue the flames. The trouble seemed to be that there was no way to close the two huge ventilators upon the roof of this room, thus making it air ready steam tight. Huge tongues of flame would burst out of these ventilators for a moment and then the fire within would seem to be suffered and it would be dark. Smoke and steam poured out increasingly, however, showing a pretty current of air and soon the wood on building in which were the fuel room, boiler room &c. burst into a mass of flames. The fire was then very hot and the wind blew a gale from the North throwing the flames directly into and against the brick shop, a building 50x250 feet; three stories high and the wooden store house and the old saw mill upon the opposite end of the fuel room. For some time the steamer stream was kept playing into the fuel room and against the brick shop from the South side, the pipe men maintaining their position upon the roof of the boiler house with great difficulty and being slowly driven back by the flames. The fire was fast spreading through the wooden buildings in front of them and upon their left, and the smoke was getting unbearable. The fire was also making its appearance upon the two upper floors of the brick shop at the North end, when the stream from the engine was ordered into the second floor at the brick shop at this point where the fire was burning briskly.

If the steamer had been too near the mill so that two of three streams could have been thrown in upon the two upper floors through the window upon the North, at this time, we think the fire might have been put out at this joint, but it would doubtless have caught beyond as the wooden buildings, the lumber in the yard and the dry houses, could not have been protected at the same time and they burned with a tremendous heat as soon as the flames began with the wind. Although the fire in the brick shop noticeably checked by the steamer streams upon the second floor, the third floor was soon a mass of flames and while the stream was being changed to this floor, the fire got beyond all control and started the long building to the South, regardless of the brick partition walls. At the same time about 200,000 feet of lumber piled in the yard and in the dry houses behind the mill began to burn fiercely, the wind carrying the flames almost horizontally through it.

At 12.15 the whole brick shop, the wooden buildings on the West and most of the lumber piles were masses of flames. The Deluge boys who had been pluckily fighting whenever they were wanted had a struggle to save the house on the corner of Davis Street about this time, but they kept their position

between the hose and the mill in spite of the heat, and saved the building. The Phoenix hose men were also in a number of hot and dangerous places, holding their positions until ordered elsewhere or driven back. After it became evident that the mill must burn the steamer hose was carried round into the North West corner of the mill yard a steamer carriage put into the main line some 600 feet from the engine, and two streams from the steamer brought to bear upon the lumber piles and sheds in order that the flames might be stopped and the house just south of the mill yard saved. After a long and at times a very hot fight here the fire among the lumber was checked and the house saved. The barn belonging to this house, owned by Messrs, Spaulding, Doane and Seward, were entirely destroyed together with some tools. Loss about $500. Not insured.

A number of the men who worked in the shops, many of whom have been in Mr. Hale's employ ever since the business was started, lost quite valuable chests of tools, while others lost similar sets which they used about their work. Frank Labron lost carpenters and machinists tools worth $200. Mr. Winchester, Mr. Thurston and Mr. Fish lost iron seventy five to a hundred dollars.

The buildings, upholstery and furniture burned and the lumber destroyed cannot be valued at less than $75,000. The insurance upon the same omitting the lumber, which was not insured was about $45,000. Some goods were saved, but probable $20,000 worth of manufactured goods was stored in the burned building.

———

1884 Report of the Chief Engineer
[continued]

March 22nd, 4.00 A.M., Daniel Murphy's house, Marlboro Street Loss $1,000; insured.
April 10th, 1.30 A.M., Patterson Brothers rag shop, Elm Street. Loss $1700; insured.

May 2nd, 8.30 A.M., A. Plastridge's house, West Keene. Loss $2,500; insured.

May 29th, 8.30 A.M., C.R.R. woodshed. Loss $800; insured.

August 4th, 3.00 A.M., Sweeny's house, Island Street. No loss.

August 17th, 11.30 A.M., A. Beauregard's house, Elm Street. Loss $600; insured.

August 25th, 3.45 P.M., Cheshire House Boiler room. No loss.

Sept. 3rd, 3.40 P.M., H.P. Muchmore's coal shed, Railroad Street. No Loss.

Sept. 24th, 3.30 P.M., P. Pender's house, Carroll Street. No Loss.

Nov. 3rd, 11 P.M., S. W. Hale's Limber shed. Loss small.

Nov. 8th, 6.30 A.M., Kelleher & Holt's stable. Loss $1,800; insured.

Nov. 20th, 10 P.M., Spaulding's harness shop; Mechanic Street. Loss $300; no insurance.

Nov. 25th, 12.30 P.M., Anthony Gero's house, Howard Street. No loss.

Nov. 25th, 7 P.M., Faulkner & Colony's tenement house, West Street. Loss $500; insured.

Nov. 29th, 7 P.M., Bartlett's house, Court Street. Loss $700; insured.

Dec. 4th, 11 A.M., Russell's shop, Eagle Hotel. No loss.

Discipline

It gives me pleasure to say that the discipline of the department is good.

Inventory of Department property value for year ending.

$12,236.00

An in conclusion, would most heartily acknowledge the co-operation of my assistant engineers and the constant interest manifested by the city government, and the energetic manner in which the firemen have performed their duty.

Respectfully submitted, G. D. Wheelock, Chief Engineer. December 1st, 1884.

1884 Was an important year for Joint Resolutions'. The big ticket item was the Resolution for the new Central Fire Station. That a joint special committee, consisting of one Alderman and two Councilmen, be appointed by nomination, with instruction as follows:

To procure general plans and estimates for the construction of a suitable building for a central fire station, in Keene, to accommodate three companies, including a steamer, hose and hook and ladder companies; with suitable stables for horses, rooms for drivers and for the use of companies and the storage and care of their fire apparatus.

That said committee also report whether the lot offered for sale in rear of city hall would be suitable for such purpose, and how a proper way of access to the same can best be secured; also whether, in their opinion, any better lot can be secured for said purpose, and if so where and at what cost.

Any necessary expenses which said committee may incur in procuring said plans shall be paid out of money in the treasury no otherwise appropriated.

Passed June 5th, 1884

Also A Joint Resolution relating to a Local Fire Station Resolved by the City Council of the City of Keene, as follows:

That the Joint Special Committee on Fire Station, consisting of Alderman Howard, Councilmen Abbott and Ward, be authorized and directed to purchase for the city of Keene the land on Vernon Street owned by David M. Nichols and the Baptist society, for a sum not exceeding $1500; the same to be paid for fro9m any money in the treasure not otherwise appropriated.

Passed June 28th, 1884

A Joint Resolution relating to a Location and Building for the Fire Department was Passed March 21st, 1884 On June 28th, 1884 the committee had the a Joint Resolution to purchase the land where the Central Fire Station now sits, Vernon Street. Also a Joint

Resolution relating to a Special Committee on the Engine House was passed to receive proposals for building the same, and to engage a superintendent to see that the work is properly done; that said committee are instructed to take as a model for size, and shape and expense of building the steamer house at Winchendon, Mass., and cause the plans to follow that model as nearly as practicable with our wants here, with the addition of apparatus for heating by steam and washing hose in the basement; providing, however, that the terms of the contract for building are not to be accepted until submitted to and approved by City Councils and the necessary amount of money appropriated. All bills contracted for the foregoing work must be approved by said building committee. Passed August 9th, 1884

List of expenses for the Engine House paid out

Baptist Society, Land on Vernon Street $500

To D.M. Nichols, Land on Vernon Street $1000 for a total for land $1,500. Paid out to W.P. Wentworth, plans, etc., $200

A.P. French, Surveying, $12.50 to J.R. Livermore, labor of men grading, $67.00 and to Geo. E. Forbes, Moving Deluge House, $90.00 and Sawyer & Burnham, work on Engine-house, in part, $1,200 for a total to date $2,069.50

A joint Resolution was passed on December 18th, 1884 for the salary of the engineers, engineer, assistant engineer, fireman and steward of the Steamer company for the year commencing October 1st, 1884, be as follows in addition to their regular pay as firemen: Engineer $60.; assistant engineer, $25; fireman, $10; steward $25; as recommended by the committee to whom the same was referred.

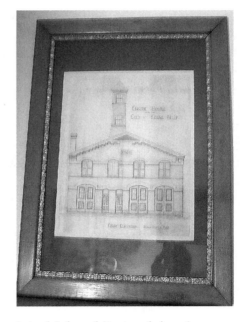

The original ink architectural drawing on Parchment paper of the new proposed engine house. This paper was found in a pile of old papers to be thrown out. It was set aside and sent out by Deputy Fire Chief Steven Goldsmith to be preserved and framed. The frame was restored by Deputy Chief Goldsmith and was presented to the Keene Fire Department. Photo by Steven Goldsmith

A Demon Called Fire

1883/1884

1883/1884 Picture of new Steamer Wagon, see story (An Elegant Hose Wagon for the use of the City) Pictured in front of the New Fire Station, Vernon Street right side of Central Fire Station, standing on ramp. Note the difference between proposed engine house and completed engine house due to budget. From Fire Department records.

Quoting from the *Keene Evening Sentinel*:

A Pleasant Affair

1884 New Engine House contract 1884 for a cost of $5,400 dollars. New Steamer Wagon in front of new Steamer House and Steamer Hose No. 1

The members of the Keene Steam Fire Engine and Hose Company No. 1 Gave a "house warming" and reception at their new engine house, last Thursday evening, which was a very pleasant and sociable affair and served a good pleasant and sociable affair and served a good purpose in bringing together the members of various companies of the fire department, the city government and quite a large number of citizens-honorary members of the Steamer Company. The guests began to assemble early in the evening and the Steamer boys were kept busy in entertaining successive arrivals until a late hour. An excellent lunch,

consisting of scalloped oysters, coffee, fruit, &c., was served by Messrs. Ladd & Nims and was partaken of with evident relish by those present. An examination of the new engine house was if interest to many. The company has just got its rooms furnished and they are very neatly and appropriately fitted up. On entering the main room it is found to be well lighted and pleasant. The Steamer, as it stood in its place, looked as if it had just been taken out of a band box, and was designed for an ornamental, rather than a useful affair. The exquisite condition in which this machine is kept is a credit to Engineer Piper and his assistants. Passing on to the stable everything was found "in apple pie order." In the two outer stalls stood the pair of bays owned by the city, looking in good spirits and flesh, while in the center stall stood Capt. Foster's gray mare "Kate," 17 ½ hands high weighing 1575 lbs. Easy-making the city horses look like a pair of light driving ponies, so great was the contrast between them. Kate was put in the stall for use in case of a fire during the evening. It was general remarked that the city ought to own a pair of horses of her size for use upon the steamer, and when we take into consideration the fact that an actual savings of from $150 to $200 a year can be made by the city in owning horses rather than in hiring them, we see no reason why another pair should not be purchased in the interests of economy. But to return to our subject. Passing up stairs, upon the left is the driver's room, comfortably furnished, but occupied on this occasion by members of the band orchestra instead of the driver. Turning to the right we come to the property room for storing uniforms, &c., the Engineers room where, judging from the number of official's present, important business was then being discussed, and thence to the company's hall, extending across the building in front. This hall has just been fitted up and looks very neatly. A modern paper with heavy border, dado, &c., covers the walls, while a handsome mahogany set, corresponding with the finish, comprises the furniture, On the whole, the company has very comfortable quarters, although the internal arrangement of the building might have been made much more convenient.

Members of other companies of the department were entertained early in the evening and later the city government came up in a body and were received and entertained. After the company had largely dispersed, Capt. Shedd announced the results of a little subscription which he had been taking up during the evening, with the proceeds of

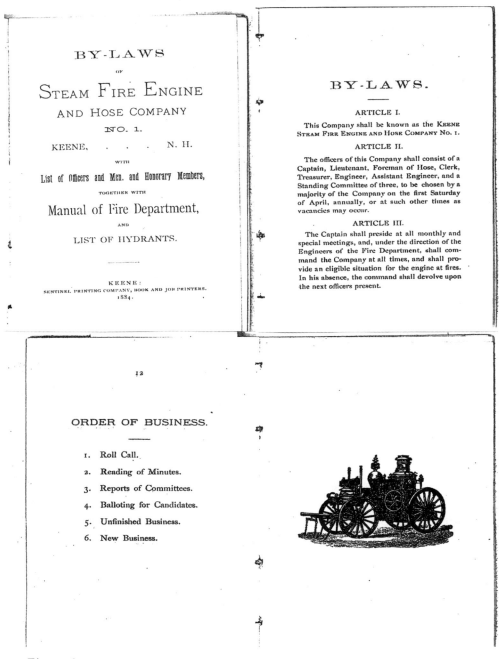

Figure 1

A Demon Called Fire

which a handsome steel engraving now on exhibition at Dunn's entitled "An August Morning with Farragut," is to be purchased and presented to the Steamer Company.

———————

Each Company within the Keene Fire Department had their own set of Bi-Laws. Each Bi-Law listed

articles and consisted of how each Company would operate. Figure 1 is the Bi-Laws of the Steam Fire and Hose Company No.1. Figure 2 is the Bi-Laws of the Board of Engineers, Keene Fire Department.

BY-LAWS

Adopted by the Board of Engineers

OF THE

KEENE FIRE DEPARTMENT.

REVISED MAY 1, 1884.

———

ARTICLE I.

ENGINEERS' BADGE OF OFFICE.

Each Engineer of the Keene Fire Department, when on duty at any fire, shall be known by a badge worn on the left breast with the word "Engineer" thereon, also the Chief by a red and the assistants by a green lantern by night.

ARTICLE II.

TIME OF HOLDING MEETINGS.

The Board of Engineers shall meet on the first Saturday of each month, at 7.30 o'clock p. m., and at such other times as may be thought necessary by the Chief or a majority of the board.

20

some previous meeting, and due notice having been given of the time such amendment would be acted upon.

ARTICLE XVIII.

INSTRUCTIONS AND SUGGESTIONS TO THE FIREMEN.

It is important that the several Fire Companies be filled with active and reliable men who shall be ready, able and willing to render such service as may be required of them, therefore, men whose residence or business is too distant from the company house, and those who cannot usually be relied upon in case of fire, should not be admitted or retained as members, and no person should have his name enrolled upon the company's books as a member until appointed by the Engineers.

Each member is expected to meet at suitable times for discipline and practice, so that he may be properly skilled and expert in the use of the apparatus used by the company, also to inform himself in regard to his duties as a fireman, and he should in case of fire endeavor to act with coolness and discretion in the discharge of the duties assigned him.

Each hydrant man, pipe man and officer in

21

charge of any line of hose connected with a hydrant should ascertain the number of such hydrant that it may be designated thereby in giving orders for operating the same.

Great care should be used in opening and closing the hydrants, and all hydrant men should be instructed in this point.

In laying hose two lines may be attached to a hydrant if a sufficient quantity is at hand for that purpose, but in all cases it is better to make use of a single line from each hydrant near any fire before double lines are laid.

Believing that the observance of the foregoing rules and the By-Laws adopted by the Board of Engineers will tend to make the Fire Department more efficient and worthy of confidence, we trust they will receive the approval and support of each member and our citizens.

(Signed.)

GEO. D. WHEELOCK, Chief.
J. A. BATCHELDER, Assistant.
H. H. BARKER, "
C. L. KINGSBURY, "
W. H. REYOUM, "
H. W. HARVEY, "
C. L. KINGSBURY, Clerk of Board.

Figure 2

The Amoskeag Steamer pictured outside the new Steamer House, which as of 2003 is still part of the Keene Central Fire Station, located on Vernon Street, Keene, NH. From Fire Department scrapbook.

1885 [*from* City of Keene Annual Report]

Report of the Chief Engineer.

To his Honor the Mayor and City councils:

Gentlemen: In compliance with the requirements of the city ordinances, I would respectfully submit the following statements relative to the condition of the fire department.

Membership

The department consists of six engineers and eighty firemen.

Houses

The houses remain the same as last year, with the addition of a very fine brick house, barn and shed for the accommodation of the Steamer and Hose Company, and the horses and tools belonging to the city.

Apparatus

The condition of the apparatus remains the same as last year with the addition of a new hook and ladder truck for the use of the poles in the Phoenix and Deluge hose carts with shafts and whiffletrees.

Supplies

We have this year purchased 500 feet of cotton fabric hose for the use of the hose companies, and I would again recommend that all our leather hose be replaced by cotton fabric hose as fast as practicable.

Uniforms

The department is well uniformed.

Fire Alarm

We have this year added to our system the Stevens electric fire alarm telegraph, with five boxes, one striker, three gongs, and I would recommend that a striker be put on City Hall bell, and a gong be placed in the Deluge hose house as soon as possible, and I would also recommend that more boxes be added to the system.

The following are the alarms for the past year:

January 13th, 4.45 P.M., alarm at Keene steamer house. No fire; no loss.

March 3rd, 3, P.M., George. Wood's house, Taylor Street. Loss estimated at $800; insurance received, $480.

March 24th, 1 P.M., James Donahue's house, Grove Street, chimney. No Loss.

June 12th, 1 A.M., E.A. Renouf's house, Roxbury Street. Loss $1200; insurance received, $1200.

July 3rd, 1.30 P.M., Mr. Calef's barn, Washington Street. No loss.

August 5th, 7.30 P.M. chimney on Grove Street. No Loss.

August 22nd, 3.50 P.M., Can Company, Mechanic Street, dry house. Loss $200; insurance received $200.

November 3rd, 10.30 P.M., False Alarm, Marlboro Street.

Total amount of loss from January1st, 1885 to December 17th, $2200. Insurance received for losses, $1880.

Discipline

The discipline of the department is good.

Inventory of Property.

Steamer and hose Carriage, $4,600
Hand engine at Woodbury's $500
Hand engine at South Keene, $500
Deluge hose carriage, $800
Phoenix hose carriage, $650 with 4 jumpers, at $300 and 2 Hook and ladder trucks, etc., $1,100
3 hose sleighs, $75.00
Cotton hose, $1,725
Leather hose, $1,000
Fire alarms, $700
Engineers' Lanterns. $21.00 and six hydrant gates, $45.00 with one Y coupling, $65.00 bring a total of property $12,081.00

And in conclusion allow me to thank his Honor the Mayor and the Committee on Fire Department, and in fact the whole city government, for the many favors received, and I heartily acknowledge the co-operation of my Assistant Engineers and the cordial and energetic manner in which the firemen have performed their duties.

Fire Alarm Telegraph

Location of boxes and instructions to firemen and officers. Approved Nov. 10th, 1885

Location of Boxes

Box 9, Central Square, corner Roxbury Street.
Box 16, Main Street, Cor. Marlboro Street Box 23, Roxbury Street corner Beech Street.
Box 32, Elm Street, corner High Street.
Box 42, School Street, corner West Street.

Each box when pulled strikes its number on all the bells on the circuit and repeats five rounds if properly pulled in. Whenever a box alarm is sounded, firemen will proceed directly to the box pulled in, unless sooner ascertaining the exact location of the fire.

Signals

One-The Engineers reserve the right to the Superintendent to strike one blow upon the bells at any time, to test the circuit; also to ring in one round from any box, preceded by a single blow, exactly five minutes after the noon strike, on Mondays, for the purpose of testing the boxes.

Two-Two blows struck upon the bells after a fire alarm is a signal to "limber up," and recalls all firemen and apparatus to the engine houses unless specially detailed for duty.

Three-In case of a serious fire the Engineers may cause a second or third alarm to be sounded from the nearest box, said alarm to be followed by three blows to distinguish it from a first alarm.

Picture of New Fire Alarm Box. Photo by David Wagstaff

Telephone Signals.

An adjustable alarm box has been provided in the central telephone office, by which alarms sent in by telephone may be immediately sounded on the fire alarm bells.

All telephone alarms will begin with the number six (I-I-I-I-I), followed by the number of the ward from which the alarm comes, thus:
61 signals a Telephone alarm from Ward 1.

62 signals a Telephone alarm from Ward 2.
63 signals a Telephone alarm from Ward 3.
64 signals a Telephone
Alarm from Ward 4.
65 signals a Telephone
Alarm from Ward 5.
67 signals a Telephone
Alarm from South Keene.
68 signals a Telephone
Alarm from West Keene.

Firemen should endeavor to ascertain the location of the fire upon leaving their Engine houses, or soon after, when a telephone alarm is sounded.

A telephone alarm cannot, like a box alarm, show the exact point to which the firemen should proceed, and judgment must therefore be sued to ascertain where the fire is.

General Rules

Firemen, as well as citizens, should familiarize themselves with the following rules for giving alarms of fire:

One-Never pull a box for a fire seen at a distance.

Two-Never pull a box while the alarm bells are ringing, nor until a box has completed its five (5) rounds. Two boxes cannot operate together and neither will work if two are pulled at the same time. Never pull two alarms or two boxes for the same fire. The engineers will sound second alarms if necessary

Three-To ring in an alarm, break the glass in the key box and open the alarm box door with the key. Pull down the brass crank seen inside till it stops, then let go. Then let the box alone. The clock work will be seen or heard to be running, and the alarm will follow in half a minute or so. Close the box and remove the key.

Four-Remember that the firemen will come directly to the box which has been pulled. See that they are directed to the fire, if necessary.

Telephone Alarms.

Do not send a telephone alarm if there is any alarm box within reasonable distance. Box alarms are always the surest and best. Telephones can seldom be used during thunder showers; the boxes can always be used.

To send in a telephone alarm, call the central office. Tell the operator slowly first the ward, then the street and house where the fire is situated. The operator will repeat, "Fire, Ward so and so, such street or house." Answer, "All Right," if you are correctly understood. If the fire is in South Keene or West Keene, give the fact instead of the ward number. The operator will than leave the telephone and sound the alarm.

Respectfully submitted,

George D. Wheelock, Chief Engineer, Keene, December 1st, 1885.

Note: I think this is a good time to make comet on Resolutions.

Each year salary was made a Resolution to improve pay and other small odds and end etc. Therefore if not there was no important move than it will not be written down in the years forth coming.

Resolutions for 1885 and 1886 consisted in purchasing Rubber hose and coats. Passed March 5th, 1885.

Resolution for uniforms for Steamer Company. Also for repairing hook and ladder carriage. Passed March 20th, 1885.

A Joint Resolution for the purchase of a pair of horses and a pair of harnesses for the Dept. Passed May 21st, 1885.

A Demon Called Fire

In 1885 the Fire Department purchased three bells and additional equipment for the horses and the Amoskeag Steamer. Pictured is one of the bells and one of each side button used for the bridle. One on the left is made of brass with a red star and the other one is brass with a black star. There would have been four, two each, and it is believed that the black one was used for funerals and the red one was used for daily runs. The bell was attached to the girth or belly strap of each horse and one was attached to the steamers tree. It must have been quite something to not only hear, but see responding to a fire call. These items are courtesy of the Bohannon family of Keene. Photo by Steve Goldsmith.

A Joint Resolution for four shut-off nozzles, and a pair of shafts and seats for each hose companies.

A Joint Resolution pass the same day was to change the fire striker location from the bell on St. James church, as specified in the contract between said city and the New England Telegraph and Telephone Company, to the bell on the Second Congregational church. Passed September 15th, 1885.

A Resolution passed on September 23rd, 1885 relating to extension of steamer house on Vernon Street. Price $2,200.

A Resolution passed relating to keys for fire alarm boxes. Passed October 1, 1885

Work completed on the New Steamer house is itemized on page 59 and page 60 of the City Reports of 1885/1886 which was a total of $4,829.95 and $942.40 for steamer house extension. The purchase of the steamer horses from D.C. Howard, a gray mare at a cost of $277.65 and one from S. Spaulding, a gray horse at a cost of $235.00.

When the new engine house was built in 1884 it was Keene's Pride and Joy. This is a look inside the new Steamer House as the horses are being led to the front of the station.

The electric Fire alarm for key boxes NET&TC. Materials and batteries for the amount voted as per joint resolution. $620.83

1886 [*from* City of Keene Annual Report]

Report of the Chief Engineer.

To His Honor the Mayor and City Councils:

Gentlemen: In compliance with the ordinances of the city I respectfully present my report as Chief Engineer of Keene fire department.

Membership

The fire department consists of six engineers and four companies of firemen, Steamer and hose, Washington Hook and Ladder, Deluge and Phoenix hose companies, each company containing twenty men.

Houses

The Steamer house needs a larger steam heater, as the one used is not sufficient to warm the house. The Deluge house needs painting on the outside. And the Phoenix and Hook and Ladder companies, houses in a better location should be provided.

Apparatus

With one exception the apparatus remains as last year. The Steamer Company bought a fine hose wagon and requested the engineers to permit them to use it in place of the hose carriage. The request was granted and I would recommend that the carriage be sold.

Hydrants

We have now 132 hydrants. As all the hydrants about the square, except the one in the park, and near the buildings, they could not be used in case of a large fire, therefore I would recommend that one with four or more gates be put in at the south end of the park.

Supplies

The Committee on Fire Department have purchased 1000 feet of cotton fabric hose and have sold 1000feet of old leather hose. The leather hose now in use must soon be replaced by new.

Uniforms

The Deluge uniforms belong to the company. The engineers have provided themselves with new. All are in good condition.

Fire Alarm

Our electric fire alarm gives general satisfaction. There have been two new boxes added this year, one at Cheshire RR. Shop and one at Beaver Mills. I would recommend that at least six more boxes be added. One at the corner of Water and Grove Streets should be put in as soon as possible, because if the box at Beaver mills should be rung in for a fire at the shop, or on Grove Street, the department would go to box 13 and cause much delay, as there is no place to cross the railroad except at main Street.

Condition of the department

The department was never in better working order than at present. I think the annual inspection on the 22nd of last October showed to our citizens that we have one of the finest departments, of its size, in the State.

Fire Alarms

January 15th, 1.30 P.M., Gerould's block. Loss $225; insurance received, $225.

February 4th, 11.57 A.M., box 32 house on Forest Street, Owned by Keene Five Cents Savings bank. No loss.

March 7th, 11.20 P.M., box 23 False alarm.

March 12th, 1.05 A.M. box 23 house on Beech Street, owed by Edwin H. Clark, occupied by W. Page. Loss on house $525; insurance, $525, not accepted. Furniture well insured; insurance company refused to pay it.

March 21st, 3.15 A.M., Cheshire R.R. Depot, chimney burnt. No loss.

March 25th, 12.05 A.M. box 16, T. O'Connor's house, Kelleher Street. Loss$37.

May 23rd, 7.20 P.M., box 2-2, brush fire, west hill.

May 30th, 1.20 A.M., Baker's Block, Main Street Loss $175; insurance received, $175.

June 28th, 1.15 P.M. Green's dry house, Washington Street. Loss $65; no insurance.

June 28th, 5.30 P.M., accidental alarm caused by telephone men.

July 7th, 12.45 P.M. box 16, tar barrels, Main Street. No loss.

July 9th, 7.45 P.M., box 42, Pratt's ice house, West Street. No loss.

September 21st, 2.45 P.M., telephone alarm, gas house. Loss $300; not insured.

A Demon Called Fire

October 21st, 1.15 P.M., box 42, H. Aldrich's house, School Street, chimney burnt. No loss.
October 23rd, 10.14 A.M., call alarm, 2-2, brush fire. West hill.
October 24th, 11.59, A.M., call alarm, 2-2 brush fire, old Gilsum Road.
December 10th, 6.03 P.M. box 9, Impervious Package Co., Mechanic Street, Chimney burnt. No Loss.

Total amount of loss during year 1886 to December 16th, $1,327.00. Insurance received for losses, $400.00.

Inventory of property is almost the same as last year except for Uniforms of Steamer Co., and Uniforms of Phoenix Hose Co., and Uniforms of Washington Hook and Ladder Co. and Rubber Coats. The total for the year is $13,305 a difference of $1,224.00.

Conclusion

In conclusion I wish to extend my sincere thanks to his Honor the Mayor and the City Councils; also to express my gratitude to my assistants and to the companies who have always so promptly and cheerfully responded to all calls to duty. It is highly gratifying to note the interest which the men take in their work and their hearty co-operation in its performance.

Mr. Pratt also deserves commendation for his efficient service in the care of the fire alarm telegraph.

Fire Alarm Telegraph added two new boxes Box # 6, Central Telephone office, general telephone alarm, and Box 52, Cheshire R. R. Shops.

Signals

One-The Engineers reserve the right to the Superintendent to strike one blow upon the bells at any time, to test the circuit; also to ring in one round from any box, preceded by a single blow, exactly five minutes after the noon stroke, on Saturdays, for the purpose of testing the boxes.

Two-The signal 22 repeated on the bells is to call the firemen to their houses for further orders.

Three-Two blows struck upon the bells after a fire alarm is a signal to "limber up," and recalls all firemen and apparatus to the engine houses unless specially detailed for duty.

Four-In case of a serious fire the Engineers may cause a second alarm to be sounded from the nearest box. A second alarm is given by striking ten blows, followed by the box number.

Five-As box 9, which is located on city hall, is still likely to be used for a general alarm, and to be pulled for a fire which is not in or near the Square, the Engineers will ring in a second alarm of four full rounds from this box, if there is a fire of any magnitude near the Square.

Six-The old alarm on city hall will only be rung in case of serious fire.

Seven-Arrangements have been made with the Beaver Mills Co., and alarms of fire will be given on their whistle same as by the bells.

General Rules same

Telephone Alarms

Box 6, which is located in the central telephone office, is the box which will be pulled to sound all alarms of fire sent in by telephone. When this box is pulled, firemen and others can ascertain the location of the fire from the telephone office.

Do not send a telephone alarm if there is an alarm box within reasonable distance. Box alarms are always the surest and best. Telephones can seldom be used during thunder showers; the boxes can always be used.

To send in a telephone alarm, call the central office. Tell the operator slowly first the ward, then repeat, "Fire, Ward so and so, such street or house." Answer, "All right," if you are correctly understood. If the fire is in South Keene or West Keene, give that fact instead of the ward number. The operator will then leave the telephone and sound the alarm.

Respectfully submitted, J. A. Batchelder, Chief engineer Keene, December 16th, 1886 City Records.

Resolutions for 1886 relating to purchasing 1000 feet of hose for fire department. Passed March 18th, 1886

Resolution relating to the extension of fire alarm which was authorized to purchase a suitable electric striker and move the gong from the telephone office to the Deluge engine house and the purchase of two additional fire alarm boxes and to have the steam whistles sounded in case of fire. Passed April 1st, 1886.

In addition a Resolution was passed November 4th, 1886 to make improvements at steamer house on Vernon Street. This was to add a bulk-head and cement the cellar. And on November 18th, a resolution to pay firemen and other work at brush fires.

1887 [*from* City of Keene Annual Report]
Report of the Chief Engineer.

To His Honor the Mayor and City Councils:

Gentlemen, In compliance with the ordinances of the city I herewith submit the annual report of the Keene Fire Department for the year 1887; also an inventory of the property of the department and statement of alarms, fires, losses, etc.

There have been nine box alarms during the year, viz: four from box 32, and one each from boxes 16,33,9 and 53; also one caused by the breaking of one of the battery jars. The aggregate loss at the fires two which the department had been called is $2,675.00 on which insurance has been allowed to the amount of $1,750.00 making the net loss over insurance allowed $925.00.

Striker Machine and Bell

The striker machine and the bell with the striker. The striker system worked by winding the machine with a weight, which would drop and the hammer would strike the bell. The hammer would tap out the box that was being pulled. The striker bell was used in the City Hall and the Court Street Congregational Church and one was also believed to be used in the St. James Church on West Street in Keene. The new, self-acting fire alarm, which was attached to the bell on the Town Hall about a year since, greatly facilitates giving alarms, but we regret that the unfavorable situation of the bell prevents its sound from reaching as far as it should.

List of Fires and Alarms.

February 1st, 7.19 P.M., box 32 Woodbury's mills, Spruce Street. Loss $50.00; insured.
February 9th, 3.45 P.M., box 32 house on Cottage Street, owned by F. A. Perry, occupied by Fred Perry. Loss $700.00; insurance, $500.00.

GEO. M. STEVENS,

MANUFACTURER OF

FIRE ✦ ALARM ✦ TELEGRAPHS,

TOWER STRIKERS, GONGS, SIGNAL BOXES, &c.,

15 Chardon St., Boston, *April 8* 1886

Agreement Between City of Keene and Geo M Stevens, of Boston

Mr Stevens hereby agrees to furnish to said city one medium Bell Striker; one non=interference pull box and one 10 inch mechanical gong, all new and first class in all respects Also to take the present box 32 owned by the city and exchange the same for a non=interference pull box .. He will send a man to put up the striker, the city to pay the expenses of said man while doing said work He will warrant said apparatus to be all right in every respect.. The price for furnishing the above to be Three Hundred Seventy=five Dollars =

Edward Gustine. Chum. com

Geo. M. Stevens.

Contract for new signal box and striker 1886.

February 9th, 7.49 P.M., box 32, Woodbury's dry house on Spruce Street. Loss $1,000.00 insurance $700.00.

February 11th, 11.48 P.M., box 16 chimney burnt out on Water Street. No loss.

May 21st, 11.50 A.M. box 33 house North End of Washington Street, owned by N. G. Woodbury. Loss $100.00; no insurance.

July 4th, 10 A.M. box 32, house on prospect Street, owned by N.G. Woodbury. Loss $100; No insurance.

August 21st, 10 A.M., box 9, Gerould's block, in room occupied by Mrs. E.H, White. Loss $25.00; no insurance.

August 21st, 12.09 P.M., box 53 house on Winchester Street. Owned by Joseph Carpenter. Loss $700.00; insurance $500.00.

October 27th, 8.20 P.M., General alarm, caused by breaking of a battery jar.

Membership

The fire department consists of six engineers and four companies of firemen, Steamer and Hose, Washington Hook and Ladder, Deluge and Phoenix Hose companies, each company containing twenty men.

Houses

The Steamer house has been supplied with a larger heater, and is now in good condition. The Deluge house has been repaired and painted, and a coal stove for drying hose, etc., has been put in. These improvements were much needed. The houses of the Phoenix and Hook and Ladder remain as last year. The city can hardly afford to let another year pass without providing better quarters for these companies.

Apparatus

There have been no changes since last year. I would recommend that the steamer hose carriage be sold. A sled of some kind should be provided at once for the Hook and Ladder, as it is very difficult to draw the truck through deep snow.

Hose

We have in the department 3,550 feet of cotton fabric hose in good condition, 100 feet of rubber hose, 1,700 feet of leather hose in fair condition, and about 500 feet of condemned leather hose.

Horses

The city now owns six horses, having purchased two during the present year. This is sufficient to take all the apparatus to a fire. Heretofore we have been obliged to depend upon the livery stables for horses, which often caused much delay.

Hydrants

We now have 138 hydrants. Six were put in this year, but none near the park. One should be put in as recommended last year.

Supplies

The committee of Fire Department has purchased 600 feet of rubber lined cotton fabric hose, seven ladders from 16 to 22 feet long, and two plaster hooks.

Uniforms

The Hook and Ladder Co. have recently bought new uniforms. All others remain as last year.

Fire Alarm

Our electric fire alarm has proved a success. Six new boxes have been added this year.

Condition of the Department:

The department is in good working order and always responds promptly and cheerfully to all calls to duty. Just now there is a little trouble in the Phoenix, caused by some disturbing element in the company. Two men have been discharged and no doubt the usual good order will soon be restored. The discipline of the department is good.

Expenses

The increase from 1886 is $665.00 and is due to 3 hose sleighs and fire alarms and equipment.

Fire Alarm has added 6 new boxes and Signals remain the same and General Rules remain the same as did the Telephone Alarms.

Conclusion

I desire to extend my thanks to the Mayor and City Councils for their kindness. I wish also to thank the Assistant Engineers for the aid and council they have given me. The officers and members of the companies deserve commendation for their ready response to all calls to duty, prompt attention to orders and gentlemanly conduct.

Respectfully submitted, J. A. Batchelder, Chief Engineer. Keene, December 15th, 1887.

1888 [*from* City of Keene Annual Report]

Report of the Chief Engineer. To his Honor the Mayor and City Councils:

Gentlemen: In compliance with city ordinances, I present the following report of the Keene Fire Department for the year ending December 1st, 1888.

The Department has been calling out by alarms as follows, viz: Three from box 52, 2 from box 9, 1 each from boxes 6, 14 and 23, and one false alarm.

The aggregate loss at the fires which the Department has been called is $5,865.00, on which insurance has been allowed to the amount of $1,450.00 making a net loss over insurance of $4,415.00

January 11th, box 23, Mount Huggins Hotel.

January 30th, box 52, C.R.R. Lobby. Loss $200.00; insured.

March 10th, box 9, Duffy's block. Loss $3,4000.00; no insurance.

March 12th, box 14, George Buckminster's house on Water Street. Loss $50.00; insured.

August 29th, box 52, C.R.R. shop. Loss $5.00; insured.

September 6th, box 52, C.R.R. shop. Loss $10.00; insured.

September 17th, box 9, C.R.R. baggage room. Loss $200; insured.

November 18th, box 6, Heald ice house. Loss $2,000; insurance $1,000.

The Department as heretofore consists of six engineers; Steamers and Hose Co., 20 men; Deluge Hose Co., 20 men; Phoenix, Hose Co., 20 men Washington Hook and Ladder Co., 20 men. Total 86 men.

There has been no important change in the apparatus during the year, with the exception of the addition of 1,000 feet of cotton fabric hose.

The original Steamer Hose carriage and one of the hand engines, which has been kept at the north part of the city might be sold, without detriment to the Department, and a set of runners for the Hook and Ladder truck would be worth much more than their cost during the winter season.

Although greatly needed, nothing has been done to improve the condition of the houses occupied by the Phoenix and Hook and Ladder Companies, which is a matter that hardly seems profitable for the city to neglect.

Four horsed, owned by the city, and are present kept for the use of the Fire Department. Two more are needed to supply the ordinary requirements, and probably could be owned by the city quite as well as to hire.

The hydrant service has been improved by the enlargement of the main from the new reservoir and the putting in of several post hydrants in place of the old flush hydrants on Roxbury Street, the former avoiding much trouble from being covered with ice and snow; also, by the addition of a large hydrant near the park in Central Square, which will be very useful in case of fire in that vicinity.

The Department now has 140 hydrants attached to the city water mains, all in good condition, and an ample water supply, largely decreasing the risk of any disastrous conflagration.

The system of electric alarm recently introduced, has worked very satisfactorily, and is a great improvement to save time and to prevent loss, and a liberal extension of the system would add much to the efficiency of the Fire Department.

Seventeen signal boxes are at present in use.

The organization and membership of the Department is in the main quite as good as at the last annual report, excellent discipline and order, has in general been maintained, except in one instance of which we are sorry to say, a little disturbing element caused some contention in one company in relation to the selection of certain important officers, which the Board of Engineers could not consistently approve. This led to the unpleasant manifestation of a spirit of insubordination on the part of a few members of the company, being undoubtedly influenced thereto by a leader having less regard for the propriety of his position than for the gratification of personal ends. Such occurrences notwithstanding success in the subversion of right are neither creditable nor conducive to the good of the Department.

The expenses for the year will be found in the report of the Committee on Finance. Inventory of Property total is $13,402.00.

Fire Alarm

Telegraph with the addition of new boxes remains the same as does Signals, General Rules and Telephone alarms. Most new item or information is noted in the Chief Engineers Report.

Conclusion

In conclusion, I tender my sincere thanks for the aid and encouragement of my assistant engineers, and the ever ready response and efficient action of the officers and members of the several companies in all call to duty.

Respectfully submitted, J.A. Batchelder, Chief Engineer. Keene December 3rd, 1888

Joint Resolution relating to the Fireman's Relief Fund.

This is the start of this Fund.

THE FIREMAN'S RELIEF FUND passed February 16th, 1888.

Also a Resolution was passed to place a gong in the sleeping room of the Superintendent of Fire Alarm. Passed March 1st, 1888

Also a Resolution was passed to place a 2nd circuit to the fire alarm telegraph. Passed October 18th, 1888.

1889 [*from* City of Keene Annual Report]
Report of the Chief Engineer December 1st, 1889

To His Honor the Mayor and City Councils:

Gentlemen: In compliance with the city ordinance and in behalf of the Board of Engineers I present the following report of the Fire Department for the year ending December 1st, 1889.

The Department has responded to ten alarms the past year subjoined and the details.

Total Value of property destroyed, $17,612.00 and Insurance paid on same, $7,086.50 which leaves Loss over insurance, $10,525.50.

Fires and Alarms 1889.

February 23rd, box 23, Mechanic Street, brick building occupied by the Impervious Package Co. Loss on building and stock, $76.52; insurance paid $76.52. Cause of fire, explosion of gas from furnace.

March 11th, box 9, head of Central Square, wood frame building owned by Elbridge Clarke, occupied by John Carpenter, harness maker; C.W. Wilber, meat and provision dealer; O.P. Murdick, confectionery; M.J. Auger, billiard parlor. Loss on building, $212.00; insurance $212.00. John Carpenter, Loss on stock. $106.00; insurance paid, $106.00. C.W. Wilber, loss on stock, $300.00; insurance paid, $225.00. O.P. Murdick, loss on stock, $60.00; insurance paid $60.00. M.J. Auger, Loss $100.00; no insurance. Cause of fire careless use of matches.

March 26th, box 13, Railroad Street, Beaver Mills building owned by Beaver Mills Co., occupied by the Keene Furniture Co., and the Cheshire Chair Co. Loss on building, $4,500.00 ; insurance paid, $1,800.00. Keene Furniture Co., loss $7,000.00 insurance paid, $2,000.00 Cheshire Chair Co., loss $5,000.00;

insurance paid, $2,475.00. Cause of fire sparks from boiler room.

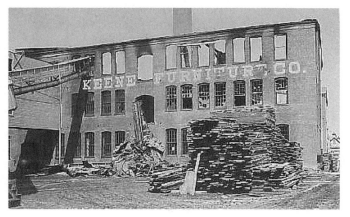

On March 26, 1889, the Keene Furniture Company and the Cheshire Chair Company located on Rail Road Street, owned by Beaver Mills burned. Above photo is the front side of the building. Pictured below is the rear of the building. HSCC photo collection.

15,000 FIRE AT BEAVER MILLS.

As reported by the *Keene Evening Sentinel*. On March 26th, 1889 The Keene Furniture Company and the Cheshire Chair Company Patricianly Burned Out. Bad Failure of the Water Supply at a Critical Moment

At 7:15 Tuesday evening a bright light from the cupola on the south brick shop at Beaver Mills gave notice of a dangerous fire which was burning in the building below. The origin of the fire is unknown but the theory that it ran up the fuel spout from the engine room does not seem feasible. Watchman John King was just starting his rounds from the engine room through the North building. He saw the fire when he got up stairs and ran to the fire alarm box and in pulling it off broke the dog on the lever by pulling too hard so the box could not be worked. He then sounded the whistle and an alarm soon followed. The hose companies had steam on in three or four minutes and the sprinklers the Beaver Mills steam pump, the steamer and hydrant streams were soon working.

The fire burned rapidly through the upper story of the Furniture Companies shop, which was soon a mass of flames. The firemen were just getting into position for good work, about 7:40 when the water supply from the brook conduit gave out rendering the steam pump, three streams and the steamer almost useless. The steamer moved to the brook and water was finally got to work, two fair streams from the steam pump. The hydrant streams were useless above the second story.

In the meantime the fire got very hot and worked into the Chair Companies upper story, burning $3,000 worth of cane and finished chairs. Finally by hard and persistent work the advance of the fire was checked and by nine o'clock was under control. It destroyed everything on the third floor of the Furniture Company's shop. Including the tools of the workmen worth $800, a wood saw and lath and a few other machines along with stock, benches etc. The roof is all burned off and the floor pretty much destroyed.

On the second floor the machinery is not much injured. In the Chair Companies shop the paint room is gutted, some fire worked down in to the second floor and there is a considerable loss on stock and chair and damage by water throughout the shop.

The losses are estimated as follows: Beaver Mills Company on building $5,000 not insured. Keene Furniture Company $1,000 to $5,000 partly insured. Cheshire Chair Company $1,000 to $5,000 partly insured.

———

Fires and Alarms 1889 [*continued*]

April 10th, box 23, brush fire in rear of Mrs. Edward Farrar's house on Beaver Street. No loss. Cause of fire children playing with matches.

April 21st, box 23, brush heap East of Woodland cemetery. No loss. Cause of fire incendiary.

April 24th, box 52, Emerald Street. Caused by the burning of a lot of old railroad ties belonging to the Cheshire Railroad Co. Loss $50.00; no insurance. Cause of fire sparks from a locomotive.

April 26th, box 46, false alarm.

June 21st, box 37. Elm Street, wood frame tenement house owned by George occupied by the families of J.J. Crowley and C.E. Jackson. Loss on building, $132.50; insurance paid, $132.50. J.J. Crowley, loss $25.00; no insurance. C.E. Jackson, loss $50.00; no insurance. Cause of fire defective flue.

August 28th, box 33, Washington Street, brush fire near N. G. Woodbury's dry house. No loss.

November 15th, box 46, false alarm.

The Department at the present time consists of five engineers; Steamer and Hose Co., 20 men; Deluge Hose Co., 20 men; Washington Hook and Ladder Co., 20 men Total 65 men.

There has been no important change of the apparatus during the past year, but I regret very much to say that the Phoenix Hose Co. resigned and went out of service October 1st, 1889 because they were dissatisfied with their quarters; and I think they had the sympathy of the entire Department and the citizens in general, for it was a lamentable fact that their quarters were very poor as well as no credit to the city; and I would earnestly recommend

their improvement of the quarters of the Hook and Ladder Co., also, the Deluge Hose Co., by building for them suitable quarters on Vernon Street East of the Steamer building. It seems to me to be the proper place for our Department, location and all being taken into consideration. The city at the present time owns six good horses, and if the Department is located here all together, I think it is all they will require for the fire purpose for years to come.

I am glad to report that our hydrant service has been improved in the past year by increasing the size of our water mains, and discarding the old flush hydrants for post hydrants of an improved pattern; and gentlemen, I wish to call your attention to the need of a better water supply for the protection of Dunn & Salisbury's chair shop, the Cheshire Railroad shops, also N.G. Woodbury's pail shops, for I think our past experience has taught us that it is our duty as well as to our interest that we should give our manufacturing interests suitable protection against fire.

We have at the present in the vicinity of about 150 hydrants, and I would recommend that in the future they be set nearer to each other, as a plenty of them does away with using so much hose and also aids the firemen in getting water to the fire quicker.

The electric alarm system has given general satisfaction in the past year, and the great amount of time it saves in locating the fires becomes more apparent each year; and I would recommend a further extension of the system by the addition of more boxes.

I am very much pleased with the action taken by your Honorable body at your last meeting in regard to purchasing another steamer. It will be a great addition to the strength of our Department. And I think we are very much in need of a first class modern Hook and Ladder Truck, as this is a very important piece of apparatus, at a large fire, especially.

Inventory of Property

Remains the same except for lack of men who belonged to the Phoenix Hose Co. The total $13,665.00

Fire Alarm Telegraph

Remains the same with no addition of new boxes, The signal for the boxes remain the same as do the General Rules. The Telephone alarms also remain the same for the year 1889.

Conclusion

In closing my report of the year I will take this opportunity, in behalf of the Board of Engineers and myself, to extend our thanks to all members of the City Government, who have in any way rendered the Department assistance during the past year.

To Superintendent Babbidge and the Commissioners of the Water Board, our sincere thanks are due for prompt information of changes in system and for the many courtesies other ways rendered.

To my Assistant Engineers, and to all the officers and members of the Fire Department, my sincere and heartfelt thanks are due for their unselfish support, excellent deportment, devotion to duty and for their gentlemanly zeal and efficiency, as manifested on all occasions; and may a good feeling of harmony be maintained and strengthened for years to come, and may they never forget that a good, true firemen is always a gentleman.

Respectfully submitted, Henry H. Haines, Chief Engineer, Keene December 5th, 1889.

Note: This year 1889 was the 1st, year in which G.M Rossman, Superintendent of Fire Alarm gave a full report to the Mayor and City Councils: His Report follows the Chiefs and even though short I elect not to write it down as the Chief Engineers Report covers it.

Ordinances and Joint Resolutions.

Passed February 21st, 1889 the sale of a single bay horse owned by the city Fire Department and to purchase a pair of horses. The Washington Hook and Ladder Co for uniforms passed February 21st. Deluge Hose Co. to purchase uniforms passed September 5th, and also by resolution the sum of $60.00 dollars of annual inspection of the Fire Department. Under the same Resolution the Council gave by said committee to investigate the purchase of another steam fire engine. Passed September 19th.

1890 [*from* City of Keene Annual Report]

The Report of the Chief Engineer

To His Honor the Mayor and City Councils: Gentlemen. In compliance with the city ordinance and in behalf of the Board of Engineers I present the following report of the Fire Department for the year ending December 1st, 1890.

The Department has responded to fourteen alarms in the city and one at Swanzey Factory in the past year-subjoined are the details.

Total value of property destroyed, $8,539.39 and Insurance paid on the same, $7,484.39 with a loss over insurance of, $1,055.00.

Fires and Alarms 1890

December 18th, box 9, 12.30 A.M., head of Central Square, wood frame building owned by Elbridge Clarke, occupied by John Carpenter, harness maker; O.P. Murdick, confectionery; C.W. Wilber, meat and provision dealer. Loss on building, $100.00; insured. John Carpenter, loss on stock. $239.39; insurance paid, $239.39. O.P. Murdick, loss on stock, $65.00; insurance paid, $65.00. C.W. Wilber, loss on stock, $225.00; insurance paid, $175.00. Cause of fire unknown.

December 22nd, box 9 9 A.M, dwelling, wood frame, 54 Washington Street, Owned by Mrs. J.H. Wellington, occupied by Geo. M. Rossman. Loss on building and stock, $25.00; insured. Rossman, loss on furniture, $125.00; insured. Caused of fire, careless way of setting an iron fire place.

January 21st, box 46, 10.41 P.M., ice house owned and occupied by J.E. Heald. Loss on building and stock, $175; insurance paid, $175. Cause of fire, boys smoking.

January 25th, box 43, 3.45 P.M., saw mill owned and occupied by Faulkner & Colony, on West Street. Loss on building and contents, $60.00; no insurance. Cause of fire, caught by sparks from a locomotive on Cheshire R.R.

July 10th, box 16, 11 A.M., wood dwelling house, corner of Marlboro and Grove Streets, owned and occupied by Patrick Ryan. Loss on building and furniture, $400.00; insured. Cause of fire, defective chimney flue.

July 22nd, box 17, 5.02 P.M., barn corner of Kelleher and Barker Streets, owned by Mrs. Timothy O'Connor. Loss $50.00; no insurance. Cause of fire, supposed to have been set by children playing with matches.

July 24, box 53, 7.35 P.M., foundry owned and occupied BY Humphrey Machine Co. Loss on building, $3,000.00 insurance paid, $2,130.00. Loss on contents, $3,000.00; insurance paid, $3,000.00. fire caught in the boiler room.

August 3rd, box 13, 1.30 P.M., wood frame tenement house on Harrison Street, owned by Gleason and Sawyer, occupied by Fred H. Hill. Loss on building, $25.00; insurance paid, $25.00. Fire caught under the attic floor in the L, it was thought that rats must have got some matches in there.

August 10th, box 14, 2.30 A.M., false alarm.

September 27th, box 32, 7.10 A.M., chimney burning out in a building known as the Sun Tavern, up Court Street. No loss.

October 7th, box 32, 9.45 A.M., wood frame tenement house, corner of Elm and High Streets, occupied by E.H. Stone. Loss on building $25.00; insured. Loss on contents, $25.00; no insurance. Fire caused by using liquid stove blacking.

November 8th, box 13, 7.35 P.M, dry house at Beaver Mills, owned and occupied by Beaver Mills Co. No loss of any account, thanks to a good live watchman. It was supposed that some of the help dropped some matches in the house while getting out stock that day.

November 12th, box 14, 6.50 P.M., shoe shop on Dunbar Street, owned and occupied by C.B. Lancaster & Co. Loss on building, none. Loss on stock by water from sprinklers, $1,000.00; insurance paid, $1,000.00. Cause of fire, a pot of cement ignited while warming it over a gas jet.

November 22nd, box 17, 4.15 P.M., pottery on Main Street, owned by J.S. Taft & Co. Fire caught in the fire room, no loss, workmen put it out, a needless alarm.

The Department at the present time consists of five engineers; Steamer and Hose Co., 25 men; Deluge Hose Co., 20 men Washington Hook and Ladder Co., 20 men. Total 70 men. During the past year our Department has been greatly strengthened by the addition of another Steamer and five more men to the Steamer Co.

We have at the present time one of the best Departments of its size to be found in New England. It is composed of good men, men that you can depend on in time of need.

I would earnestly recommend the improvement of the quarters of the Hook and Ladder Co., also the Deluge Hose Co., by building for them suitable quarters on Vernon Street east of the Steamer Building. It seems to me is the proper place for our Department, location and all being taken into consideration. The city at present time owns six good horses, and if the Department is located here all together, I think it is all they will require for fire purposes for years to come.

I am glad to report that our hydrants service has been improved in the past year by increasing the size of our water mains, and discarding the old flush hydrants for post hydrants of an improved pattern; and, gentlemen, I wish to call your attention to the need of a better water supply for the protection of Dunn & Salisbury's chair shop, the Fitchburg Railroad shops, also N.G. Woodbury's pail shops, for I think our past experience has taught us that it is our duty as well as to our interests that we should give our manufacturing interests suitable protection against fire.

We have at the present in the vicinity of about 165 hydrants, and I would recommend that in the future they be set nearer to each other, as a plenty of them does away with using so much hose and also aids the firemen in getting water to the fire quicker.

The electric alarm system has given general satisfaction in the past year, and the great amount of time it saves in locating the fires becomes more apparent each year; and I would recommend a further extension of the system by the addition of more boxes this year.

I think we are very much in need of a first class modern Hook and Ladder truck, as this is very important piece of apparatus, at a large fire, especially.

Inventory of Property

Added to the inventory was a new Steamer, Button No. 2 at a Cost of $3,500 so now the Amoskeag No. 2 has a sister. This has increased the value of property for the Department.

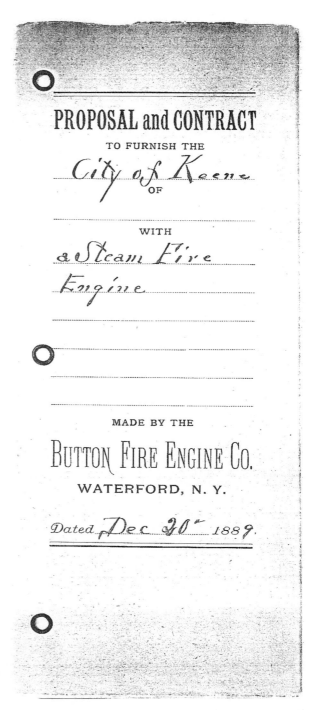

Button Steam Fire Engine Contract. From Fire Department records.

PROPOSAL

3rd size

FOR ONE, DOUBLE PUMP CRANE NECK STEAM FIRE ENGINE

MADE BY THE

BUTTON FIRE ENGINE COMPANY.

Waterford, N. Y., Decem 28th 1889.

To the Hon. *City Government*

of the *City of Keene N.H.*

GENTLEMEN :—We propose to manufacture and furnish the *City of Keene N.H.* *one* double pump, crane neck, steam fire engine, to be finished in accordance with the following specifications, and we will, unforeseen delays excepted, ship the same within *30 to 40* days of the acceptance of this proposal.

SPECIFICATIONS.

The Engine is to weigh without fuel and water about *5800* pounds.

Boiler to be of best steel boiler plate of suitable thickness in all its parts.

To be vertical, with copper flues securely held at both ends, and protected from external injury.

To be well cased in wood and covered with *nickled brass* properly banded with ~~Prince's~~ *nickled* metal bands, and to be surmounted with a ~~Prince's~~ *nickled* metal dome having an ornamental ~~German silver~~ band at the centre.

To be furnished with dumping grate.

To generate all the steam necessary to run the engine to its full capacity.

Engine. To consist of two double-acting horizontal steam cylinders with balanced piston valves, neatly cased with *nickled brass* and having a proportion to the pumps of more than two to one, steam chest and ports to be under cylinders, so as to completely drain them of the water of condensation.

Each Steam Valve to be moved by the opposite piston by means of a direct lever, without the intervention of crank shaft, link blocks, connecting rods, eccentrics, or any revolving parts, and the motion to be controlled smoothly and without concussion.

Pumps. To be two double acting horizontal plunger pumps in one bronze casting without packed partitions, having a capacity of *six hundred* gallons per minute. Valve seats of hard brass. Valves of vulcanized rubber, bushed and backed with hard brass. Valve springs of brass. The pumps to be fitted with a relief valve by means of which engine can be operated and boiler fed without discharging water.

Air Chamber. To be pear shaped, of *nickled* copper, *36* inches high, *20* inches diameter.

The Steam Pistons and Water Plungers to be connected by straight phosphor bronze rods.

. . . . . . can be "set up" or tightened when worn.

Running Gear. Forward wheels four feet in diameter. Rear wheels five feet in diameter, to be *Best* . . . . tires capped with *nickled brass* Tires of wrought iron, *5/8* inches thick. The rear hung upon *half elliptic* . . . . oil tempered steel springs. The front upon *Platform* oil tempered steel springs.

The Axles to be of best steel.

SUPPLIES AND FIXTURES.

. . . . . feet long . . . . inches inside diameter.

DISCHARGE PIPES and full assortment of *flexible hose with connections 15 ft.*

In 1889 Chief Engineer Henry H. Haines proposed to the Council that another steam engine should be purchased. On September 19th 1889 the Council passed the Resolution and a proposal and contract to furnish the City of Keene with a Steam Fire Engine (see facing page), which was made by the Button Fire Engine Company of Waterford, N.Y. for a cost of $3,500 dollars. Button Fire Engine No. 216

Button Fire Engine No. 216. Photos from Keene Fire Department Scrapbook and HSCC photo collection.

Fire Alarm Telegraph remains the same as do the Signals and the General Rules. The Telephone Alarms also remain the same.

Conclusion

In closing my report of the year I will take this opportunity, in behalf of the Board of Engineers and myself, to extend our thanks to all members of the City Government, who have in any way rendered the Department assistance during the past year.

To Superintendent Babbidge and the Commissioners of the Water Board, our sincere thanks are due for prompt information of changes in system and for the many courtesies other ways rendered.

To my Assistant Engineers, and to all the officers and members of the Fire Department, my sincere and heartfelt thanks are due for their unselfish support, excellent deportment, devotion to duty and for their gentlemanly zeal and efficiency, as manifested on all occasions; and may a good feeling of harmony be maintained and strengthened for years to come, and may they never forget that a good, true fireman is always a gentleman.

Respectfully submitted Henry H. Haines Chief Engineer, Keene, December 16th, 1890.

Resolutions for 1890 was $150 for uniforms for Steamer Co. passed April 2nd, 1890 Pay for Firemen passed Sept. 17th, 1890 and $60.00 for the Annual Inspection of the fire Department.

A report was also given by the Superintendent of Fire Alarm for 1890.

1891 [*from* City of Keene Annual Report]

Report of the Chief Engineer.

To His Honor the Mayor and City Councils:

Gentlemen. In compliance with the ordinance and in behalf of the board of engineers, I present the following report of the fire department for the year ending December 1st, 1891.

The department has responded to eleven alarms in the city and one at South Keene during the year-subjoined is the total value of property and insurance paid on same.

Total value of property destroyed, $24,353.00, on which insurance has been allowed to the amount of $14,400.00, making the net loss over insurance allowed, $9,953.00. **March 27th**, House Stone, Patterson Bros. Loss $750.00 Insurance Paid $500.00 Building Totaled and Cause was Furnace Boiler. **April 11th**, Dry House Beaver Mills Loss $150.00 No Insurance. Cause Furnace Problem. **June 9th**, House G. J. Landers House Total Insurance Paid $3,000. Cause Children playing with Matches. **June 15th**, Mowing Machines, Clipper Machine Co. Loss $3,000 Insurance Paid $3,000 Cause by Spark from Train. July 7th, House Faulkner & Colony Loss $8.00 Insurance Paid $8.00 Cause Lamp Exploded.

The department at the present time consists of four engineers; Steamer and Hose Co., 25 men; Deluge Hose Co., 20 men; Washington Hook and Ladder Co., 20 men. Total, 69 men.

We have at the present time one of the best departments of its size to be found in New England. It is composed of good men, men that you can depend upon in time of need. I would earnestly recommend that more suitable quarters be provided for the Hook and Ladder co., and the Deluge Hose Co. I would also recommend that more fire alarm boxes be put in the present year and it seems to me that our fire alarm system would be more efficient if it were more properly cared for.

I am glad to report that our hydrant service has been improved by the addition of twenty-five post hydrants the past year, in all about 180.

Inventory of Property

The total inventory value for the year 1891 totals $16,685.

Fire Alarm Telegraph

The fire alarm boxes remained the same as did the Signals and General Rules. The Telephone Alarms also remained the same as well.

Superintendent of fire alarm report was submitted by G.M. Rossman and a new addition was the addition of a bell line connecting the stable driver's residence and Chief Engineer's residence, which should prove a great savings of time at night.

Conclusion

In closing my report, I will take this opportunity in behalf of the board of engineers to extend our thanks to all members of the city government who have in any way rendered the department assistance during the past year.

Compiler's note: Line of Duty – Death

In conclusion, we wish to express the sorrow of the department that this report will not receive the signature of our late chief engineer, Henry H. Haines, who was called form active and useful career while in the performance of his duty. By a sad fatality he lost his life after the fire in the rear of St. John's block, on Saturday, December 12th, 1891.

Respectfully submitted, Joseph E. Griffith, Acting Chief Engineer, Keene, December 18th, 1891

RESOLUTIONS

ON THE DEATH OF

Chief Engineer Henry H. Haines.

At a special meeting of the Board of Assistant Engineers held at their room on Saturday evening, Dec. 12, to take action relative to the death of Chief Engineer Henry H. Haines, the following resolutions were offered and unanimously adopted, and were subsequently adopted by each company of the Fire Department:—

Whereas, It has seemed good to the Almighty disposer of events to remove from our midst our late worthy and esteemed Chief, Henry H. Haines; and

Whereas, The intimate relations long held by the deceased with the members of the Board of Engineers and the Fire Department, render it proper that we should place upon record our appreciation of his services as a fireman and his merits as a man; therefore, be it

Resolved, That we deplore the loss of our Chief Engineer with feelings of regret, softened only by the confident hope that his spirit is with those who, having fought a good fight here, are enjoying a perfect happiness in a better world.

Resolved, That we tender to his afflicted wife and relatives our sincere condolence and our earnest sympathy in their affliction at the loss of one who was a kind and affectionate husband and father, a good citizen, a devoted fireman and an upright man.

Resolved, That the members of the Board of Assistant Engineers and the Fire Department will attend our deceased Chief to the grave in a body, and that the Engineers' room be draped with black for thirty days.

Resolved, That a copy of these resolutions, signed by the Assistant Engineers, and committee on resolutions, be presented to the relatives of the deceased.

J. E. GRIFFITH,
O. P. APPLIN,
REUBEN RAY,
W. H. WILLETT,
Assistant Engineers.
D. FOLEY, JR., Captain of Hook and Ladder Co.
E. S. FOSTER, Captain of Steamer and Hose Co.
W. F. TOWNE, Captain of Deluge Hose Co.

A Resolution of the Death of Chief Engineer Henry H. Haines. From Fire Department records.

1892 [*from* City of Keene Annual Report]
Report of the Chief Engineer

To His Honor the Mayor and City councils: Gentlemen, In compliance with the ordinance and in behalf of the board of engineers, I present the following report of the fire department for the year ending December 1st, 1892.

The department has responded to ten alarms, two false alarms, and nine brush fires.

Loss to property, $9,750.00; insurance, $7,675.00; total loss, $2,075.00.

November 8th, House. John Kimball, Loss $200 and Insurance Paid $200 Cause was Incendiary.

November 30th, House J. H. Hamblett, Loss $9,000 Insurance Paid $7,435. Cause was Defective Chimney.

December 15th, House, W. U. Elliot. Loss $135.00 Insurance Paid $135.00 Caused by oily rags.

The department at the present time consists of three engineers; Steamer and Hose Co., 25 men; Deluge Hose Co., 20 men; Washington Hook and Ladder Co., 20 men. Total, 68 men.

We have at the present time one of the best departments of its size in New England. There is the best of feeling between all the members of the department. I am also glad to report that our new quarters will soon be ready to occupy, which will add very much to the efficiency of the department.

I would recommend the purchasing of a pair of horses for the Hook and Ladder Co., at

Amoskeag Steamer: picture taken on Vernon St., Keene across from Central Fire Station. 1893 Chief Oscar P. Applin, Chief Engineer hired Keene's first permanent driver for the Steam Engine. He was housed at the fire station 7 days per week until another part time driver was hired so time off could happen. The above photo, driver Fay, and from right FF. Sterns, FF. Smith and FF. Morse. From Fire Department scrapbook.

once , as they will be much needed when they are located in the new house.

Our hydrant and fire alarm service are both in the best condition they ever were.

Inventory of Property for 1992 is a total of $15,280.00 down from 1891. by $1,405.00

Fire Alarm Telegraph remains the same as do the Signals, along with the General Rules remaining the same. The Telephone Alarm remains the same as well.

Conclusion

In closing my report, I will take this opportunity in behalf of the board of engineers to extend our thanks to all members of the city government who have in any way rendered the department assistance during the past year.

Respectfully submitted, Oscar P. Applin Chief Engineer, 1892.

Note: In 1892 Superintendent of Fire Alarm G.M. Rossman gave his report to the Mayor and City Councils: and due to his retirement to this position and taken over by Fred F. Page, now became the new Superintendent of Fire Alarms and also gave his report for the year 1892. Fred F. Page was appointed to this position on July 1st, 1892 and made the recommendation that on each Saturday the Fire Alarm Circuits be tested due to the little interruption on that day.

[*Compilers note*: Recommendation that on each Saturday the Fire Alarm circuits be tested, this continues to the present time.]

1893 [*from* City of Keene Annual Report]

Report of the Chief Engineer.

To His Honor the Mayor and City Councils: Gentlemen, In compliance with the ordinance and in behalf of the board of engineers, I present the following report of the fire department for the year ending December 1st, 1893.

The department has responded to sixteen alarms and two false alarms.

Loss to property, $29,200; insurance paid, $13,430; total loss, $15,770.

The department at the present time consists of two engineers, Deluge Hose Co., twenty men; Steamer and Hose Co., twenty-five men; Washington Hook and Ladder Co., twenty men. Total sixty-seven men.

Our department still maintains its high standard which it has held for so long a time, and we feel, with our new hook and ladder truck and horses, and a permanent driver, that Keene is a well-equipped as any city of its size, in New England.

I would recommend that we have more fire alarm boxes put in the coming year, which would aid very much in location a fire.

Inventory of Property

Steamer, Button No, 3; Steamer, Amoskeag No. 2; hand engine at Woodbury's mills, hand engine at South Keene, Deluge hose carriage , Phoenix hose carriage, three jumpers, three Hook and Ladder trucks, steamer hose carriage, three hose sleighs, 4,100 feet of cotton hose, fire alarm, engineers lanterns, six hydrant gates, one Y coupling, rubber coats, uniforms of Steamer Co., uniforms of Washington Hook and Ladder Co., uniforms of Deluge Co., one Siamese.

Fire Alarm Telegraph.

The city still has 17 Fire Boxes, and when pulled, a box alarm will repeat on the circuit 4 rounds of that box if properly pulled which leads the firemen to the exact location of the box or fire.

The Signals remain the same as adopted by the board of engineers, December 2nd, 1887. General Rules and Telephone Alarms remain the same as well.

Conclusion

In closing my report, will say, that we deplore the loss of our Assistant Engineer, Charles H. Spofford, with feeling of regret. I will take this opportunity in behalf of the board of engineers, to extend our thanks to all members of the city government, who have so promptly responded to all requests made them by the department during the past year.

Respectfully submitted, Oscar P. Applin, Chief Engineer. Keene, 1893

Superintend of Fire Alarm.

This position was held by Fred F. Page, and was held for a short time for the year 1893. On March 1st, J. F. Emmons, was appointed Superintendent of Electric Fire Alarm and both Superintendents gave report to the Mayor and City Councils for the year 1893.

Resolutions passed by the City Councils in 1893 related to the Fire Department.

Resolution for purchasing fire hose. Passed, 1893

Resolution authorizing the sale of Phoenix hose house, which was on St. James Street and was damaged by fire. Passed March 16th, 1893.

First
Annual Banquet
of
Keene Fire Department.

Friday, October 6,
1893.

Menu.

Tomato Soup, aux Croutons.

———

Escalloped Oysters, a l'Americaine.

French Fried Potatoes.

Celery Salad.

———

Chicken Croquettes, aux Petits Pois.

Queen Fritters, Glace au Sabayon.

Mashed Browned Potatoes.

———

Cold Roast Beef.

Cold Boiled Tongue.

Cold Boiled Ham.

Lobster Salad, Mayonnaise Dressing.

———

French Rolls.

———

Vanilla Ice Cream.

Orange Cake.   Angel Cake.

Rose Cake.

———

Lemon Jelly.   Wine Jelly.

———

Crackers and Cheese.

———

Fruit.   Coffee.

The first annual banquet of Keene Fire Department was held on October 6th 1893. Above is the invitation by the Steamer Co. From Fire Department records.

"FIRE"

1893 THREE MEN KILLED, TERRIBLE BOILER EXPLOSION AT BEAVER MILLS. As reported by the *Keene Evening Sentinel.* On Monday May 22nd, 1893 The Boiler House Blown Down and Wall of Mill Falls. Five Men Injured Besides the Three Who Died.

A terrible explosion occurred at Beaver Mills about twenty three minutes past twelve o'clock Monday by which two and perhaps three men lost their lives and five or more men were badly injured.

The boiler house was completely demolished by the explosion and a large section forty feet long was torn out of the brick wall of the main brick building on the north occupied by the Beaver Mills Company.

Herbert G. Holton, a son of Obed M. Holton of this city, a pail Hooper who boarded at 44 Madison Street is dead. He was unmarried and about 30 years of age.

His body was found buried among the rubbish just north of the boiler room and was among the first to be taken from the ruins.

Frank Drollett, the fireman on duty at the time, was taken from the ruins at 1:115. He was terribly burned but was still alive and able to lift his hands. He was put into one of the teams standing near and started for the hospital. But he was too badly injured to last long and his death occurred at 4 o'clock in the afternoon. He was about thirty years old was married and a year or so ago and leaves a widow and a young child about three weeks old. He lived upon Marlboro Street about halfway to South Keene.

Lewis W. Starkey, a pail turner, was known to have been in the crowd of injured men but his body was not recovered until 3:15 o'clock. Mr. Starkey was forty-five years old, lived at 115 Wilber Street and leaves a widow and one child.

Geo. W. Piper, a pail turner, living at 107 Wilber Street, was taken out after some hard work by the rescuers. He was unable to walk, being cut about the head and jammed by the timbers and brick.

George H. Carpenter, a sawyer, was sitting in the passage way between the buildings, and was injured, although not fatally. He was taken away soon after the explosion.

Gregory Carpenter, a sawyer, was cut about the head with a brick but was able to get out without aid.

Michael Roach was eating dinner with George Carpenter and was cut about the head and injured in one leg. He was taken away for treatment.

William Clark, a pail tuner living on Grant Street was cut about the head with falling bricks, but was not seriously hurt.

The boiler which exploded was one of a pair of 120 horse power each which supplied power for the engine. It was new only a few years ago. The boilers were all examined regularly by the Hartford Steam Boiler Insurance Co.'s inspectors and were supposed to be in first class condition. No cause for the explosion can avert be assigned.

Besides the two large boilers there were three or four smaller ones in the boiler house. These were thrown up from their setting by the terrific force of the explosion and lay disconnected among the bricks and broken timbers. The boiler house is demolished to the line of the chimney, which bordered the area in front of the boiler where the fuel was kept and the firemen worked. Beyond this is the engine room separated by a brick wall, which did not fail.

The boiler house and main building on the north were separated by a passage way wide enough for a railroad track. Into this space fell the north wall of the boiler room and the section of the wall of the main building, which was blown out. In the mass of debris in this passage way the men who were killed or injured were buried.

Every square of glass in the Keene Furniture Company's shop south of the boiler house was blown out by the force of the explosion, and the entire wall was blackened as if scorched by fire. Bricks were blown into this building in large numbers, and had the men been at work there would have been other casualties. Some of the bricks were blown south as far as the shoe factory on Dunbar Street.

Immediately after the explosion an attempt was made to pull in an alarm from box 13 at the mills, but the box would not work, the wires probably being tangled up by the explosion. One or two blows only were struck on the bells.

The news of the explosion was brought to the Square by two men, who rushed up in Dr. Hyland's team, the doctor having seen the explosion from Valley Street, and hastened to the mills.

The concussion and jar of the explosion was felt in various parts of the city, especially to the south and east of the mills. People sitting at dinner rushed from their houses many of them in time to see the column of bricks and dirt still in the air.

Patrick Cashill, one of the firemen at the mills, went home to dinner at 11:45. He says at the time he left there was plenty of water in the boiler and the pump was working.

The debris caught fire but the flames were promptly extinguished by the department. The work of hunting for bodies was ten prosecuted with less difficulty. Axes and crowbars were used and heavy timbers and pieces of machinery were drawn away by the crowd with the aid of ropes.

The injured men were most of them eating dinner, either in the pail shop or between that shop and the boiler room.

There was boiler insurance to the amount of $20,000 on the property, in the Hartford steam Boiler Insurance Co.

A number of express teams were early on the ground and their services were offered in taking the dead and wounded from the scene.

The physicians were on hand at once. Every doctor in town aided in caring for the wounded, either at the mills or at the hospital.

The hospital was filled with the wounded, the doctors and the nurses. Everyone who was brought in was treated as soon as possible and ten released if the injuries would permit of it.

After the Smoke Cleared Away

Hundreds of people have visited Beaver Mills since Monday to view the wreck caused by the explosion. No such violent explosion ever occurred in this vicinity, and the destruction is by far greater than one could well believe.

The great gap fifty feet long and three stories high torn in the wall of the main shop and the large boiler house, which is entirely demolished, tell only part of the story. For rods to the east and south everything is covered with bricks and black soot and dust blown from the boiler house.

A large force of men is busy clearing away the debris and the broken pipes and timers from the main building and the engine room. The Beaver Mills Company will doubtless rebuild at once. A meeting of the directors will be held at once to take definite action. The following additional particulars regarding the explosion have been gleaned.

Michael Roach was perhaps the most fortunate of all the dead and injured men who were in the very midst of the explosion. His injuries, although bad enough to use up some men, are fortunately not painful. He did not for a moment lose consciousness at the time of the explosion and his strong nerves and quick realization of what to do in an emergency rendered him a most valuable man during the few moments after the catastrophe before assistance arrived.

A Demon Called Fire

When others came Mr. Roach told them who the men were who lay in the ruins and he knew where all of them were except Mr. Starkey, who had made no sound and could not be seen. Monday while standing for a few moments in the north shop waiting for some conveyance to take him home Mr. Roach gave a *Sentinel* reporter correct information regarding those who were in the ruins and the next morning he was glad to give a representative of this paper many other interesting facts.

Mr. Roach's injuries consist of a sprained ankle, which is quite painful, and wounds upon his face and scalp. Dr. Hyland, who dressed his wounds Monday at the hospital, found two deep gashes near the left eye and a burse covering the temple, eye and side of the face which this morning is badly swollen although the eye is not closed. Then there is another bad gash in the scalp on the top of the head which required a number of stitches; a gash on the back of the head and another near the ear. There are smaller bruises and burns on his hands and body which Mr. Roach does not mind much about.

Our reporter called at Mr. Roach's home on Baker Street yesterday and found him dressed and upon the sofa talking to several shop mates who had called to see him. Mr. Roach whose morning's work had evidently been finished early was neatly dressed ready to receive those who called or to wait upon her husband. Mr. Roach's story of the explosion is as follows:

I finished my dinner a few minutes before the accident occurred. I had eaten it in the carpenter's shop, which is the wooden building east of the boiler house and just south of the large new dry house in rear of the sawmill. I left the carpenter's shop and started to inspect the main belts and shafting in the mill, which it is my duty to look after every noon.

I crossed over toward the furniture shop and went through the boiler room, passing in front of all the boilers. I noticed as I went across that the big boilers were blowing off, as they usually do at noontime. As I passed the boilers I looked at the gauges as I always do. There were almost three gauges of water in the big boilers. The injectors were not running. Possibly the boilers might blow off on gauge of water during the noon hour. They had been filled as usual before the engine and pump were shut down and I know the water was all right.

I passed through to the north doorway of the boiler room and sad down against the east side or casing. George Carpenter sat beside me. Frank Drollett sat just behind us in the boiler room upon a barrel. Lewis W. Starkey stood in front of me in the middle of the doorway. He had just asked me for a match and I had taken out my matchbox and was handing him one when the explosion came. Herbert Holton and George Piper sat on the opposite side of the passage way between the boiler house and the north brick shop facing toward the boiler room door. They were smoking.

When the explosion came I heard no noise and had no warning. It felt as if a mighty gust of wind took me and hurled me across the passageway against the brick wall of the north shop, right where Holton and Starkey were sitting. We all went together, of course, and the brick wall of the boiler house went with us. The door casing against which I was leaning went with me and rested over me against the wall of the north shop, forming a protection to keep bricks and timbers from falling on my head. This causing doubtless saved my life. My head and shoulders struck against the building cutting my head as you see. The wall and timbers fell over around and upon us but the steam did not reach us. Many of the bricks were very hot.

I pulled the bricks off my head and got a place to breathe, burning my hand some in getting down the bricks and rubbish, which were just over me lodging on the door causing mostly. I got my body loose but found one ankle fast under a timber. Geo. Carpenter was partly over me, his legs touching mine and I felt him pull himself up and thought he must have got hold of something above to lift on.

Holton lay just east of me. His head was beyond the piece of door casing which, protected me but his legs were under mine. I heard others crying for help and as soon as I could get free began pulling the bricks off them. I uncovered Holton's face and found at once that he was dead. Then I went for Piper, who lay beside Holton. I uncovered his face, saw he was alive and did what I could to help him. Heard Drollett crying for help but he was further in under the fallen wall and timbers and I could not reach him. I know he was being burned by bricks or steam. I told those who came to help Piper and Drollett, as Holton was dead. Then they helped me get out, as you know, and I saw no more of the boys till they were brought to the hospital. I would not care for anything if those poor fellows had not been killed.

What the Carpenters Say

George H. Carpenter, one of the sawyers who were hurt, is in the worst condition of any of the injured men who have survived. He is scalded on his back right cheek, right arm and shoulder and theirs is a long cut from his lip into the left check and another cut over the right eye. He is confined to the bed and passed an uneasy sight. Dr. Maloney, who attends him, thinks the wounds are not serious and that the only danger is that erysipelas may set in.

Mr. Carpenter is able to talk and when visited by a reporter yesterday said that he was sitting in the doorway of the boiler house with Michael Roach. Back of them was Drollett. They were sitting on kegs. On the other side of the railroad track sat Starkey. Holton and Piper with their backs against the pail shop and facing the boiler house. They had all eaten dinner and had come out into the passage way to smoke and talk. The next thing Carpenter remembers is recovering consciousness at the hospital. He then asked, "What has happened?"

Mr. Carpenter lives in a two-story house on the Winchester road about a quarter of a mile below the Pearl Street schoolhouse. George Carpenter's farther, Gregory Carpenter, who was slightly injured by the explosion, was also at home when the reporter called. Gregory Carpenter says he was going from the saw mill to the dry house when the accident happened. He was in the road between the two buildings and had nearly reached the dry house. The explosion came with a terrible wind and noise bricks were flying about and the buildings near him he thought were surely falling. One of the bricks hit him upon the head, producing a scalp wound which, however, he said was not painful and didn't amount to much.

Another Experience

Wallace Dodge, formerly of Stoddard who lives at 77 North Street and worked for Walter D. Lovering, one of the turners in the pail shop, was sitting on his lathe eating dinner when the explosion came. William Clark was standing near the next lathe. Dodge felt the blast of the explosion, which lifted him up. Then he went down with the wreck losing conciseness for a time. He found himself buried in dirt and debris and saw the fire, which was then beginning to burn. Finding himself free, he crawled up to the pail shop floor again. Clark, who went down with him, as he supposes, got out some other way. Dodge escaped with a lame arm.

George W. Piper's Condition

George W. Piper was taken to his home Monday and passed rather a restless night. The injuries upon his head including a number of bad cuts are doing well. Yesterday he complained of much pain in his back and hip resulting, evidently, from the debris which fell upon him. William Clark is doing nicely.

Investigating the Cause

F. B. Allen second vice president of the Hartford Steam Boiler Insurance company, and J. B. Dumond, consulting engineer of the company, are both in town and have looked over the wreck at beaver Mills as it lies.

Mr. Allen was seen by a *Sentinel* reporter and asked if anything had as yet been ascertained which would throw light upon the cause of the explosion.

He relied that as yet it is impossible to make an examination of the ruptured boiler. The very parts which must be most carefully scrutinized are buried, as yet in the ruins. He could give no intelligent opinion at this time regarding the cause of the accident and probably would be unable to make a through and sufficient examination of all parts of the ruptured boiler for some days. Defects may be found which have escaped detection so long as the boiler was whole. If the steel of the boiler has been burned that fact will be apparent on examination.

Regarding the force of the explosion and the wreck which followed, Mr. Allen says he sees no indication of violence greater that usually follows the explosion of a large boiler. It has been demonstrated that the explosive force of one cubic foot of water under a steam pressure of 90 lbs. to the square inch is equal to that of one pound of gun powder. This boiler was 72 inches in diameter and 16 feet long, and contained a great many cubic feet of water. Hence its enormous explosive power when set free.

Had the boiler been filed with steam alone, no such violence could have resulted. There must have been a power and explosive element in the boiler and the water continued under pressure and at a high temperature was that element. A cylinder of that size filled steam, as the boiler might have been if the water was nearly all out, would doubtless have escaped from a rupture with very much less violence something as it does from a locomotive escape pipe.

The Mechanic Street Explosion

The older inhabitants of Keene in talking about the fearful explosion at Beaver Mills frequently refer to a previous explosion, which took place in the Mechanic street Mills in 1864. The more recent residents of the city do not remember this accident.

By reference to the files of the *Sentinel* of that year it appears that the catastrophe occurred at 8 o'clock Friday morning, March 25th,. The boiler at the mill of Osborne and Hale exploded, injuring about a dozen men, two of whom died from the effects.

The fire box was thrown into the air from seventy five to one hundred feet and deposited in a yard across the street. The boiler, weighing eight or ten tons was thrown back its whole length (over thirty feet) plowing into the solid frozen earth. The engine house, 20 x 40 feet and two stories high, was blown into fragments and the large building connected with it a good deal shattered.

The killed were William Lang, age 20, and Salmon G. Metcalf, age 32, both of whom were at work in the main building. The injured were roger S. Derby, the only person in the engine room at the time of the explosion. George W. Briggs, Henry Reason, Samuel H. Woods, Chas. H. Briggs and John E. Jones. The loss to property was estimated from $10,000 to $15,000. The cause is stated to have been unknown.

Boiler Room Explosion at Beaver Mills taken from right.
Photo by T.A. French, Keene NH. HSCC photo collection.

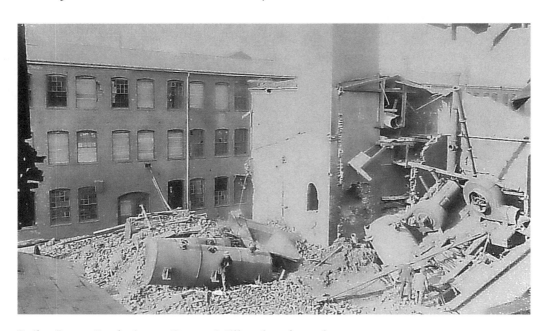

Boiler Room Explosion at Beaver Mills taken from the center.
Photos by T. A. French, Keene NH. HSCC photo collection.

View of the Beaver Mills after the fire.

The [three] pictures shown here were taken by J.A. French photographer of the City. Soon after the great boiler explosion on Monday May 22nd 1893. The boiler house was blown to pieces, was situated on this side of the big chimney as you look at the picture, were the ends of the boilers did not explode may be seen protruding from the debris. The engine house is beyond the chimney and was not thrown down. The large building at the left was occupied by Keene Furniture Company and that on the right by the Beaver Mills Company. The hole in the wall of the latter building is about 50 feet in width. Between that building and the boiler house was a passageway, it was in that the passageway that the killed and injured were taken out. The bodies lay near the wall of the Beaver Mills building at the farther edge of the whole in the wall as you look at the picture. The boiler, which exploded was of the size of the large on shown above which, is picture 2 and was

set to the right of it. The main parts of the exploded boiler lies at the foot of the chimney and the smaller part of one sheet lies under the debris of the Beaver Mills wall.

Beaver Mills was on Rail Road Street and the building still exists on RR Street and is now elderly apartments along with Whitney Brother's, a manufacturer of children's wooden toys.

From Fire Department records:

"FIRE"

1893 PHOENIX HOSE HOUSE AFIRE

One end of the building damaged and 150 feet of hose ruined

At 11:11 last night box 9 was run in. This meant a fire in the square or near it. Before the alarm stopped ringing the blaze was plainly visible in back of St. James Church. It was the old Phoenix Hose House that was burning. The flames were seen at the same time by Officer Chapman, who was at the lower end of the square, and by F.F. Page, night telegraph operator at the depot. They rushed to the city hall box, reaching it at about the same time, and pulled in both alarms.

The fire department made an unusually quick response. Officer Chapman says the steamer hose passed through the square in two minutes and forty seconds after the bell struck. The steamer was close behind in the Deluge came as soon as possible considering the difficulty, which it had to overcome. The Hooks, however were first on the ground as they occupied the building adjoining the one on fire. Their cart was drawn out before the old Phoenix Hose Wagon, which was in the burning house was rescued.

When the firemen arrived on the scene they found the East end of the structure in the flames. The fire was in the second story, hose tower and roof. It was blazing fiercely and the building was filled with smoke. It was not easy to approach from the sides, the hook and ladder house being on one side and the marble shop of George's & Chilton on the other. The firemen therefore worked from the ends. In a short time they were in control of the situation and by midnight the last tongue of flame had disappeared.

There were in the house the Phoenix Hose Cart, some 600 feet of hose and furniture belonging to the Deluge Company, which uses the house for drying hose. The doors were burst opened and the cart dragged out. The hose was in the East end and could not be reached. About 150 feet of it were spoiled.

It is not known how the fire caught. Firemen and been drying hose there during the day, but the stove and chimney are at the other end of the house. It originated some way in the second story tower or roof. When first seen it was bursting from the tower. Part of the roof has fallen in, but with that exception the building stands.

With a stiff breeze from the northwest there might have been quite a conflagration, as the structures in that vicinity are built of wood and near together. The storehouses on the Railroad Square, Wilkinson & McGregor's harness manufactory and Chase's livery stable are not far away and would carry the fire to Lamson Block, Davis & Wright's and other places on the Square. As it was, there was scarcely any wind and the roofs of the buildings were covered with snow. The loss is therefore comparatively small.

Resolution relating to the purchase of a hook and ladder truck was passed June 15th, 1893.

————

1893 On October 3rd, 1893 False Alarm Last Night

as reported by the *Keene Evening Sentinel*.

Even in the early days the fire department had to deal with False Alarms. On to the call. The fire department was called out to another false alarm at ten minutes before 1 o'clock last night, when box 46 was pulled in. Some miscreant took out the glass and removed the key from the box and afterwards opened and pulled in box 46. The firemen were out in quick time, but soon found the alarm was a false one. The horses for the hook and ladder wagon did not get to the station until the rest of the apparatus had been gone some time, and word had arrived that the alarm was a false one. The new horses on the horse wagon behaved well. There is neither meaner trick nor one, which requires less brain than to pull a fire alarm and turn out the department in the middle of the night. Nevertheless there is some rogue town who is mean enough to do this to the firemen should happen to get hold of him he would not feel like pulling another box, for a few days at least.

————

"FIRE"

1893 On November 18th, 1893 An Overturned Lantern Sets the Quick Destruction of Farm

Buildings as reported by the *Keene Evening Sentinel*.

The Buke E. Joslin's Barn Burned With Its Contents Including Three Horses, Two Cows, and Several Pigs. The Firemen Unusually Delayed in Their work.

Just before six o'clock Saturday evening Buke E. Joslin, who lives at No. 81 Backer Street, was in his barn with Leon Whipple, a young man who has worked for him the past week or two, doing the usual work required to feed and prepare the horses, cows, etc., for the night.

Hay had been thrown down from the hayloft to give the animals their supper. Whipple was in the barn floor and Mr. Joslin was in the stable just to the left. Whipple was working by the light of ordinary kerosene Lantern, which stood upon a barrel. In some way he hit the lantern and knocked it over upon the barn floor near the hay which he thrown down. The oil that ran out of the lantern when it went over quickly ignited and set the hay on fire. In a moment the flames leaped to the loft of the barn upon the hay and in no time, almost the whole barn was a seething cauldron of fire and smoke.

Mr. Joslin says that if there had been a large blanket at hand, or if he had worn a heavy coat, he thinks he could have smothered the fire. But there was nothing within reach but some grain sacks, which were too small. Realizing quickly that the barn must burn he ran to the house, which was but a step, to tell his wife and to let her know that he was safe. Mr. Whipple ran to give the alarm.

Mr. Joslin is now of the opinion that Mr. Whipple or he himself had instantly untied the horses, they might have been led out through a door near their stalls. But his cows, he says, could not have been saved. When he returned to the barn it was impossible to go into it.

That is not surprising that Mr. Joslin's first thought was for his wife, as she was sick and in an extremely nervous condition. He doubtless feared the effect which so great a calamity and danger as she must in a moment see would produce upon her and felt it his immediate duty to look to her safety.

Help was summoned by the cries of those near at hand and by an alarm from Box 17, at the corner of Main and Baker Streets, at 5.57. The firemen were out in remarkably quick time. All the apparatus had passed down through the Square in two or three minutes. Several people remarked that they thought the men must have been at the fire station, because they were off for the fire so quickly.

The steamer hose wagon was well in the lead upon the run for Baker Street. It arrived at the hydrant, corner Baker and Adams Streets, at 6.03 ½, and at once laid a line of hose into Mr. Joslin's yard, three or four hundred feet distance. The Deluge hose arrived at the same hydrant at 6.05 and the Hook and Ladder truck and the steamer followed about one minute later.

The steamer hose line was attached to the hydrant and the hydrant gate was opened, it is said, before the engine got there. But certainly there was no water thrown upon the fire until 6.10 When the steamer arrived at the hydrant at 6.06 the hose, if already connected to the hydrant had to be disconnected and the connections with the engine had to be made. While this was being done the hydrant had to be shut off.

The Deluge Hose Company, on their arrival at 6.06 asked permission to connect their hose to the hydrant already taken by the Steamer Company. But the steamer hose men objected, saying their engine was close at hand and would use all the water the hydrant could furnish. They said also that the Deluge Company was not entitled to the hydrant that they had secured, but offered to allow the

Deluge hose men to attach their line to the steamer.

It was currently reported at the fire that the hose men were quarreling as to who should have this hydrant and hence no water was thrown. But it does not appear that any time was lost unless it is claimed that the engine should not have been attached to the hydrant at all, and that said hydrant should have been given up to the first two lines of hose laid, the lines being used with hydrant pressure only.

It was 6.12 before the engine had steam enough to faintly sound her whistle and start her pumps. At 6.14 the engine was beginning to develop some power when orders were received to attach the third line of hose, which had been laid by the Deluge hose men, but had not been used. It took 2 ½ minutes to do this, so that it was 6.16 ½ before the engine fairly began work.

At this time the barn was half burned. A shed, a story and a half high, connected the barn and the ell. The fire was burning in this shed and was working into the ell, the upper story of which was on fire. But the firemen had not got a position where they could get at the fire or drive it back at that time.

All the furniture was cleared out of the hose before the firemen fairly began work. Things were handled pretty roughly more so than would be permitted if Keene had an organized protective police department whose duty it would be come to immediately take charge of the moving and protection of goods at every fire. The businessmen of Keene should have such an organization.

Before the fire was brought under control it had burned through the attic of the house and consumed so much of the roof that a large portion of the slates dropped off and the roof was destroyed. The ell of the house was wrecked and the main part thoroughly soaked with water.

There were in the barn when the fire caught, three horses, one of which belonged to Mrs. R. S. Perkins, of Main Street, and was an old family pet. Mr. Joslin owned the others. There were also two extra fine cows, two shoats a sow and five pigs. These animals all perished, with the exception of one pig or shoat.

The barn was about 40x40 feet in size and was well filled with hay, grain etc., Mr. Joslin loses twenty tons of hay, a lot of oats, rye, shorts, straw, etc., and nearly all his farming tools, including a mowing machine, wagons, plows, horse rakes, etc., etc. His loss is probably between three and four thousand dollars.

The property was insured $1,000 through G. H. Aldrich & Son's agency there being $1,000 on the house, $200 on the furniture, $200 on the barn and $200 on hay, grain and farming tools.

The big ticket and I quote from the Annual Report. " In May last the councils undertook the work of providing new and better quarters for the Hook and Ladder Company and Deluge Hose Company, and appropriated therefore the sum of $9,000. Proposals were received by the special committee having the matter in charge, and the contact awarded to Mather & Whiting of Holyoke, Mass., for $8,220. But the condition of the ground necessitated the driving of piles for a condition, and that and other extra work brought the total expenditure up to the appropriation.

The building thus provided is substantial and convenient. All the fire companies and their apparatus are now amply accommodated in one place, on Vernon Street.

———

This picture was taken in 1893 just before the move to the new Central Station on Vernon Street. This Station on Railroad Square was behind the St. James Church. The Hook and Ladder Companies along with the Neptune Companies and Phoenix Hose Companies. From Fire Department scrapbook.

New Central Fire Station, Vernon Street Keene. In 1892 The Fire Station was contracted to be enlarged by Mather & Whiting of Holyoke, Mass., for $8,220 dollars. The station was enlarged from 2 bays, 2 deep, which housed Steamer No. 1 and the Steamer hose. This new station would house the Deluge Companies and the Washington Hook & Ladder Company. All the Fire Company's moved into their new quarters in 1893. The Fire Station is still located at 32 Vernon Street and has been a strong steadfast building with changes over the years. HSCC photo collection.

1894 [*from* City of Keene Annual Report]

Report of the Chief Engineer.

To His Honor the Mayor and City Councils: Gentlemen, In compliance with the ordinance and in behalf of the board of engineers, I present the following report of the fire department for the year ending December 1st, 1894:

The department has responded to seventeen alarms. Damage to buildings, $3,281; insurance paid, $2,097; total loss, $6,817.

The department consists of three engineers; Deluge Hose Co., twenty men; Washington Hook and Ladder Co., twenty men; Keene Steamer and Hose Co., twenty-five men; total, sixty-eight men.

Our department at the present time is in excellent condition; the city has purchased in the last year a new hose wagon for the Deluge Co., and the department has equipped themselves with three pairs of swinging harnesses, which adds very much to the efficiency of the department, and that we now have one pair of horses and a driver at the fire station all the time, is still another improvement.

I would recommend that the stables in the steamer barn be turned around, so that the horses will not have to back out of their stalls and turn around to go and take their places on the engine and hose wagon, as they now do.

I would also recommend that we have more fire alarm boxes put in as early as possible.

Inventory of Property

Steamer, Button No. 3; Steamer, Amoskeag No. 2; hand engine at Woodbury's mills, hand engine at South Keene, Deluge hose carriage, Phoenix hose carriage, two jumpers, three hook and ladder trucks, steamer hose carriage, 4,100 feet of cotton hose, fire alarm, engineers' lanterns, six hydrant gates, one Y coupling, rubber coats, uniforms of Steamer Co., uniforms of Washington Hook & Ladder Co., uniforms of Deluge Hose Co., one Siamese.

Fire Alarm Telegraph

A new box has been added Box 35, and Box 52 & 53 have been changed covering more territory. The Signal 12, which is the Military call.

Signals

The following signals were adopted by the board of engineers, December 2nd, 1887 and remain the same.

General Rules remain the same as do Telephone Alarms.

Conclusion

In closing my report, will take the opportunity in behalf of the board of engineers, to extend our thanks to all members of the city government, who have so promptly responded to all requests made them by the department during the past year.

Respectfully submitted, Oscar P. Applin, Chief Engineer 1894

Superintendent of Fire Alarm Report

[*Note*: This Compiler thinks this is a good time to place into the Report of the Fire Alarm Superintendent. This year was a step forward in Fire Alarms.]

The City of Keene signed a contract with New England Telephone and Telegraph Company for poles to house the fire alarm telegraph system wire and street boxes throughout the city.

FIRE ALARM TELEGRAPH.

LOCATION OF BOXES.

Box 6. Central telephone office.
Box 9. Central Sq.,on city hall.
Box 13. Beaver Mills.
Box 14. Water st., cor. Grove.
Box 16. Main st., cor. Marlboro.
Box 17. Main st., cor. Baker.
Box 23. Roxbury st., cor. Beech.
Box 24. Beaver st., cor. Dover.
Box 32. Elm st., cor. High.
Box 33. Wash. st., cor. Gilsum.

Box 35. Court st., cor Prospect.
Box 37. Mechanic st., cor Pleasant.
Box 42. West st., cor. School.
Box 43. West st., cor. Ashuelot.
Box 46. Court st., cor. School.
Box 52. Emerald st., cor. Ralston.
Box 53. Winchester st.,cor.Island.
Box 72. West Keene.
Box 12. Military Call.

SIGNALS :—The Superintendent has the right to strike one blow upon the bells at any time, to test the circuits ; also to ring in one round from any box, preceded by a single blow, exactly five minutes after the noon stroke, on Saturdays, for the purpose of testing the boxes. The signal 22 repeated on the bells is to call the firemen to their houses for further orders. In case of a serious fire the engineers may cause a second alarm to be sounded from the nearest box. A second alarm is given by striking ten blows followed by the box number.

Listed are the locations of street boxes and the signals. The superintendent has the right to test the fire alarm circuits, which is repeated today. Since then hundreds of fire alarm boxes have been added throughout the City. From Fire Department records.

Report: To His Honor the Mayor and Gentlemen of the City Councils:

I herewith present this report as superintendent of fire alarm, from December 1st, 1893, to December 1st, 1894.

As the present fire alarm system will in a few weeks be a thing of the past, and a new and improved system supersedes it, there is no need of extended criticism.

The boxes are in good condition; one box (35,) has been added during the year; the location of boxes 52 and 53 have been changed, covering more territory. Several bells have been placed on the lines, and about three miles of wire put into the system, causing the addition of a twenty-cell battery.

The committee on fire department, has my sincere thanks for their cordial co-operation in rectifying troubles during the last few months.

J. F. Emmons, Superintendent Fire Alarm Telegraph.

Box 35 was placed on Court Street, corner Prospect Street. Box 52 was moved to Emerald Street, corner Ralston Street and Box 53 moved to Winchester Street and Corner Island Streets.

Box 72 West Keene.

Resolutions for the Fire Department year of 1894.

Resolution related to the purchase of a hose wagon for the Deluge Hose Co. For the Sum of $500.00. Passed September 6th, 1894.

A Resolution relating to pay firemen and others for work at brush fires for the fires on Beech Hill in August. Passed Sept 6th, 1894. Also another Resolution was passed to pay Firemen for Brush fires on September 7th, 8th, and the 10th, of September 1894 and this was passed on September 20th, 1894.

Resolution relating as in the past for the Annual Inspection of the Keene Fire Department $60.00 Passed September 6th, 1894.

As companies moved into the newly built station on Vernon Street it was evident that during winter months it was easier to travel with runners attached to the wheels of the engines. The new station was fitted with rollers in the flooring to ensure the movement of fire equipment out of the station on snow covered streets. Two engines are pictured in front of the Cheshire House with the fire horses covered in blankets to protect them against the cold. Picture by Bion H. Whitehouse. HSCC photo collection.

Resolution passed on October 18th, for the purchase of a sled for the Steamer Co.

A Resolution relating to changes improvements in the fire alarm system $1,235.12.

The Fire Department also purchased a Horse, Harnesses and Cart Etc. for the price of $611.29

Note: Horse $350.00 and blankets, $6.50 Freight, $11.00 and expenses of committee $13,79 Harnesses, $80.00 and cart $150.00 for a total of $611.29

The Resolution passed June 15th, 1894 for the purchase of a Hook and Ladder Truck with a total purchase cost of $1,432.32.

Hook and Ladder.

1894 on June 15th, a Resolution passed for the purchase of a Hook and Ladder Truck with a total purchase cost of $1, 432.32. Pictured is Ladder wagon returning and looking at the ladder truck from the rear (below) at the Impervious Package Company, Mechanic Street. From Fire Department records.

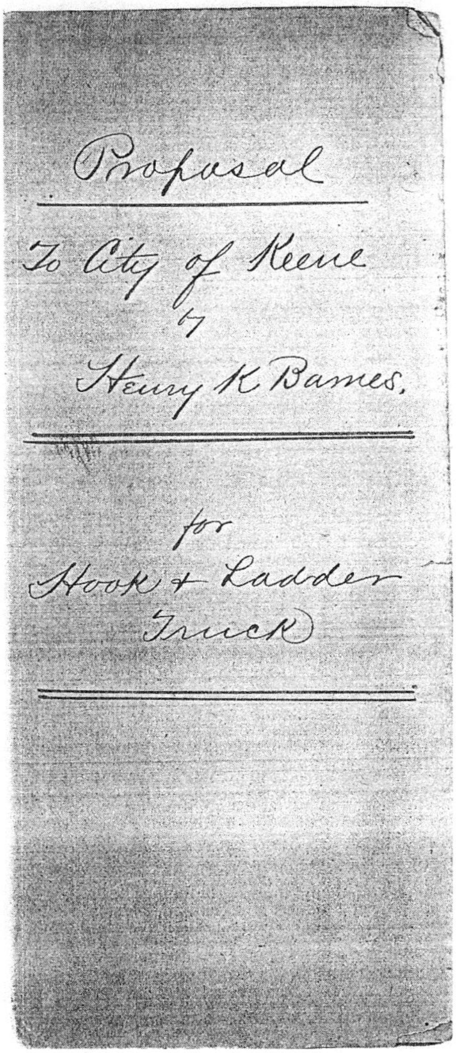

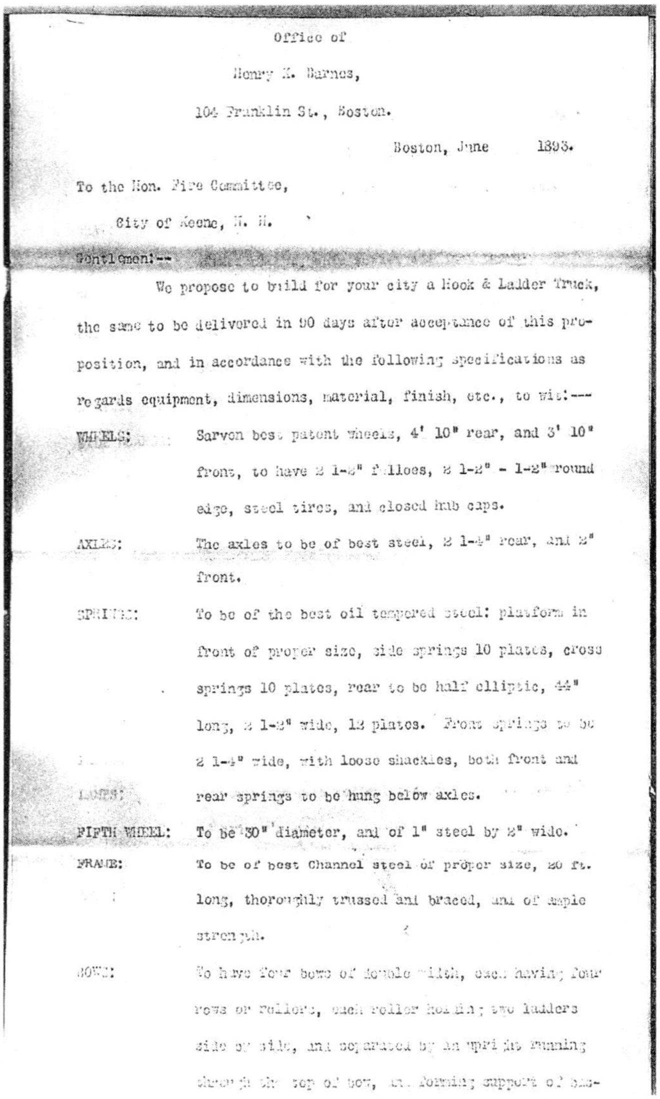

Office of

Henry K. Barnes,

104 Franklin St., Boston.

Boston, June   1893.

To the Hon. Fire Committee,

City of Keene, N. H.

Gentlemen:--

We propose to build for your city a Hook & Ladder Truck, the same to be delivered in 90 days after acceptance of this proposition, and in accordance with the following specifications as regards equipment, dimensions, material, finish, etc., to wit:---

WHEELS: Sarven best patent wheels, 4' 10" rear, and 3' 10" front, to have 2 1-2" felloes, 2 1-2" - 1-2" round edge, steel tires, and closed hub caps.

AXLES: The axles to be of best steel, 2 1-4" rear, and 2" front.

SPRINGS: To be of the best oil tempered steel: platform in front of proper size, side springs 10 plates, cross springs 10 plates, rear to be half elliptic, 44" long, 2 1-2" wide, 12 plates. Front springs to be 2 1-4" wide, with loose shackles, both front and rear springs to be hung below axles.

FIFTH WHEEL: To be 30" diameter, and of 1" steel by 2" wide.

FRAME: To be of best Channel steel of proper size, 20 ft. long, thoroughly trussed and braced, and of ample strength.

BOWS: To have four bows of double width, each having four rows of rollers, each roller holding two ladders side by side, and separated by an upright running through the top of bow, and forming support of bus-

Pictured here are the contracts for the new Hook and Ladder Truck. From Keene Fire Department scrapbook and HSCC photo collection.

FIRE PRACTICE SEPTEMBER 14TH, 1894

AT THE ANNUAL INSPECTION OF THE KEENE DEPARTMENT

Results of the Trials by the several Companies—A Test of the Time Saved by the Use of Spring Harnesses. Reported by the *Keene Sentinel*.

The exhibition, of skill in handling the apparatus given by the firemen yesterday afternoon, beginning at 4 o'clock, were equal to the displays of former years, but by reason of the new elements which entered into the trials, close comparisons with other records cannot be made.

One of the principal object of the practice was to test the new spring harnesses which the Deluge and Hook and Ladder Companies have become proficient in using. For this reason all horses stood in their stalls unharnessed when the signals were struck, while here to fore they have been harnessed to the apparatus.

The first exhibition was given by the Washington Hook and Ladder Company. This company has patient spring fire harnesses and their horses stand in their stall facing the ladder truck. Their heads are free, the only fastening required being a rope behind them. There is a door which forms the front of each stall and when an alarm strikes both doors are opened simultaneously, and the horses are trained to rush forward and take their places on either side of the pole of the ladder truck directly under the spring harnesses, which are suspended above, the tugs and pole straps being fastened to the pole and whiffletrees. It is only necessary to snap the collars together, place the bit which hangs behind the horse's jaw, in his mouth, catching one side in place with a snap, and snap on the reins—and the apparatus is ready to go.

The time required for this company to get out of the house was:

	seconds
Horses' necks in door,	21
Rear wheel in door,	24 ½

The companies were to run to Lane's new building, erect their new extension ladder and send a man to the roof. Their time was as Follows:

	hrs.	min.	sec.
Time of signal,	4	00	00
Arrived at block		1	15
Ladder dismounted,		1	20
" raised,		1	48
" extended,		1	58
Man on roof,		2	08

The ladder went up quickly and smoothly and E. J. Carr made the ascent to the roof in good time.

The Deluge Hose Company has stalls and spring harnesses similar to those of the Hook and Ladder Company. Their horses have been in training longer than those of the other company. The time which it required for this company to get out of the house was:

	sec.
Horses' neck in door,	13
Rear wheel in door,	14 ½

The company was ordered to turn to the hydrant at the corner of Lane's new building, lay two lengths of hose of 50 feet each, break couplings and get water through both. The time clocked was as follows:

	hrs.	min.	sec.
Time of signal,	4	10	00
Arrived at hydrant,		1	06
First stream,		1	16
Second stream,		1	33

The signal blow for the practice of the Steamer Company was struck at 4.20. The horses for the steamer and hose wagon stood in their stalls, which are in the barn in rear of the engine house, and are so arranged that the horses have to be backed out to be harnessed. The steamer horses were harnessed with ordinary harnesses. The hose wagon horses were harnessed with the new spring harnesses hung up that morning, but the horses were not trained for the work nor did the harnesses hang high enough for them to run underneath, so no time was probable saved. The time of harnessing the steamer horses with ordinary harnesses, was

	min.	sec.
Horses' neck in door,	1	57
Rear wheel in door,	2	00

The following is the record of the Amoskeag Steamer, the time of arrival at the hydrant being taken by stopwatch, as well as the steam indications. In recording steam pressures 2 minutes is subtracted from the actual time to allow for harnessing, before fire was lighted:

	hrs.	min.	sec.
Signal struck,	4	20	00
Arrived at hydrant,	4	22	54
Time of harnessing,	1	57	
" of run,		53	

	min.	sec.
Steam, hydrant pressure:		
From signal blow	3	20
After leaving station,	1	23
From lighting of fire:		
5 lbs. of steam,	2	05
10 lbs. of steam,	3	45
15 lbs. of steam,	5	00
20 lbs. of steam,	5	21
25 lbs. of steam,	5	40
Engine started.		

The Button Steamer was drawn to the Square by the horses which took down the Amoskeag steamer, the team returning at once to the station for this machine. The engine arrived at the hydrant 5 minutes and 50 seconds after the first engine left quarters. The fire in the Button was lightened as the engine left the engine house. Allowing 50 seconds as the time consumed going from the station to the hydrant we have the following time recorded:

	hrs.	min.	sec.
Signal struck,	4	20	00
Left station,*	4	25	00
Arrived at hydrant,	4	25	50
Time of run,		50	

	min.	sec.
Steam, hydrant pressure:		
After leaving station,	1	30
From lighting of fire:		
5 lbs. of steam,	5	30
10 lbs. of steam,	6	00
15 lbs. of steam,	7	34
20 lbs. of steam,	8	10
25 lbs. of steam,	9	00
Engine started.		
*Estimated.		

The two engines were each of them worked a short time, playing one stream only on account of the scarcity of water. One hundred feet of hose was laid from each engine. The practice then ceased.

"Ready for Inspection" Picture taken in front of the new Central Station on Vernon Street when all the Companies were in the new Station and the Niagara hose wagon on the left with Deluge Hose Company members on the right.

1895 [*from* City of Keene Annual Report]

Report of the Chief Engineer

To His Honor the Mayor and Gentlemen of the City Councils:

I herewith present the following report of the fire department for the year ending December 1st, 1895:

The department has responded to twenty alarms during the year, eight of which were false ones, or the fire was put out before the apparatus arrived. The amount of insurance paid upon buildings and contents during the past year has been $3,482.84; $3,230.02 on buildings and $252.82 on contents. The value of buildings in which the fires originated was given as $53,350.00, which does not include contents or surrounding property. I think this an exceedingly good showing for the work of our department, and I can safely say that a much larger amount of damage would have been done had it not been for the prompt action of the department.

All the companies are now in very comfortable quarters, and all pieces of apparatus are in good repair. The recommendations of Chief Applin in his last report regarding changing the horse's stalls in the steamer house are now being carried out, and will be completed before January 1st.

The companies are all full, and the total number of men connected with the department is sixty-nine. I think you will agree with me when I say that a better body of men cannot be found connected with any fire department, and certainly, the losses of the past year will support me in saying that a smarter or more efficient one is not known. The secret of preventing large fires and corresponding losses is in having men at the fire before it can gain much headway.

The expenses of the department for the past year have been light, the cost of keeping one pair of horses and one man in service all the time making quite a share of it. The plan of having one pair of horses in the barn all the time had proved a success in every instance, and I hope it will be continued.

The experience of the past few fires have shown us that more extinguishers should be in the department, and I recommend that four more be purchased and placed on the two hose wagons.

The fire alarm has been in excellent condition since it was changed over last January, one new box having been added at the corner of Water and South Lincoln Streets. I recommend that at least three more be purchased and put up at an early date. False alarms have been sent in a few times during the year by some malicious persons, and every possible means should be taken to detect those who are thus meddling with so efficient an agent as this.

The experience of the last trial of the Amoskeag Steamer shows us that the flues of the boiler may give out at any time, in fact they have already done longer service than is usual with steel flues, and we therefore recommend that the matter be given your attention at once.

Inventory of Property

Steamer Button No. 3, Steamer Amoskeag No. 2, hand engine at Woodbury's mills, hand engine at South Keene, Deluge hose carriage, Phoenix hose carriage, two jumpers, three hook and ladder trucks, steamer hose carriage, 4,600 feet of cotton hose, fire alarm, engineers' lanterns, six hydrant gates, one Y coupling, rubber coats, uniforms of Steamer Co., uniforms of Washington Hook and Ladder Co., uniforms of Deluge Hose Co., one Siamese.

Fire Alarm Telegraph, Signals and General Rules as well as Telephone Alarms remain the same with little changes except for the addition of Box 15 at Water Street, corner South Lincoln Street.

Conclusion

In conclusion, I wish to thank the assistant engineers for their hearty support and valued suggestions, the officers and men of the department for the promptness with which they have responded to all calls, and the city government for the readiness they have shown to grant us all requests.

Very respectfully, J. P. Wellman Chief Engineer. Keene, December 2nd, 1895.

Resolution for the year 1895 as follows, the purchase of 800 feet of fire hose for the department $445.00. Passed April 18th, 1895.

Purchase of Hose wagon $375.00 Sled $66.80 and Annual Inspection $60.00

BY-LAWS

ADOPTED BY THE BOARD OF ENGINEERS

OF THE

KEENE FIRE DEPARTMENT.

REVISED DEC. 2, 1895.

ARTICLE I.

ENGINEERS' BADGE OF OFFICE.

Each Engineer of the Keene Fire Department, when on duty at any fire, shall be known by a badge worn on the left breast with the word "Engineer" thereon; also the Chief by a red and the assistants by a green lantern by night.

ARTICLE II.

TIME OF HOLDING MEETINGS.

The Board of Engineers shall meet on the first Friday of each month, at 8 o'clock p. m., and at such other times as may be thought necessary by the Chief or a majority of the Board.

Pictured above is the Chief Engineer's lantern with red glass, the assistant Chief Engineer's had a lantern with green glass, also this style lantern was used on fire apparatus to designate a piece of fire apparatus while responding at night. Photo by Steven Goldsmith. From Keene Fire Department records.

FIRE ALARM AND TELEPRAPH EQUIPMENT USED BY KEENE FIRE DEPARTMENT

by Steven Goldsmith

Displayed is a 10" House Gong, which was placed on the wall of each company. These bells or gongs are electromechanical, tripped by interruptions in the closed electrical alarm circuit, with powerful stokes, which are spring-assisted. The glass window was placed over the mechanism as proof of its reliability. This equipment was like a clock with a key to keep the spring wound. The alarm was tripped by the street pull box. The system worked on batteries which were stored at the fire station, the box would be pulled and ring the bells or gongs and at the same time could ring the alarm taper, which would alert the watch desk or the Chief in his home as well as those fast asleep at the fire station.

Pictured here are Keene's first desk alarm tapper and house bell. The following tapper was manufactured by the J.H. Bunnell & Company of NY or the Western Electric Company and varied from 20 OHMS to 300 OHMS. Photos by Steven Goldsmith.

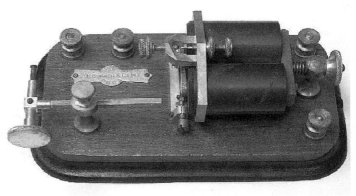

Each fire company had a bell and a tapper in their quarters on Vernon Street. The following bell was manufactured by the Electric Light Company of Boston, Mass. The bell was patented on 29 December 1887.

1895 Board of Chief Engineers. L to R: Jerry Wellman, Chief John Jones, Paul B. Babbuke, Oscar Fay. From Fire Department scrapbook.

Keene Fire Department Memorial Services

[*from Keene Fire Department records*]

1895, as recorded the earliest date for which a Firefighters Memorial Service was held dates back to May 26th, 1895. The members of the Keene Fire Department were invited by the Pastor of the 2nd Congregational Church, which was on Court Street. The invitation by the Pastor was to have the full body of the fire department to a special service to honor their deceased members. This practice continued and was carried throughout the local churches in Keene.

On April 28th, 1902 a Permanent firemen's Memorial Association was organized with the Fire Chief as president. The 2nd Sunday of June was adopted as Memorial Sunday for the deceased members of the fire department. The services were held at a different church each year, after which members of the fire department would visit the local cemeteries and place Fire Department markers and flags on their department brother's graves.

On May 28th, 1923, this changed; it was voted to hold the Memorial Sunday at the Keene Fire Station assembly hall, with an invitation to one of the local Pastors from one of the churches to conduct the Memorial Service.

On May 13th, 1948 the Keene Fire Department chose its first Chaplin and it was Rev. Norman James. He was succeeded in 1951 by Rev. Muery who was Chaplin until 1953, at which time Rev. Charles Austin replaced him.

On April 2nd, 1955 Rev. Roland Montplasair of St. Bernard's Parish was chosen as the Catholic Chaplin to serve alongside Rev. Austin at these services. Rev. Montplasair was transferred to another church and was replaced by Rev. Leo Declos of St. Bernard's Parish, was appointed June of 1958. Captain Millie of the Salvation Army was named Chaplin at this time, replacing Rev. Austin. On May 25th, 1960 Rev. Fay Gemmell replaced Captain Millie who was transferred to Augusta, Maine. Rev. Francis Curran, Pastor of St Margaret's Parish in West Keene was named to replace Rev. Declos in 1963 but transferred before he was able to attend his first service at the Keene Fire Department. Rev. James

Moran of St. Bernard's Parish served faithfully for the year of 1964 and was succeeded by Rev. Quirk of the same parish who served as Chaplin in 1965 and was then replaced by Rev. Valley of the same parish who was also Chaplin of the Keene State College Newman Club. Rev. Ken Batchelor of the Sturtevant Chapel was appointed by Chief Robert N. Guyette to replace Rev. Valley.

Rev. Andre Bedard of the St. Margaret Mary's Church on Arch Street was appointed and today the Fire Department Chaplin we have is Rev. Robert Hamm of the United Church Of Christ, which is on Central Square Keene just behind the Central Fire Station.

———————

Standing in front of Engine House, which is now Central Fire Station on Vernon Street around 1895 with Button Steamer in rear showing through the glass. From L to R: E.T. Woodward, Joel Ford, Arthur Thomas, C.U. Briggs, Milan Jones, Raymond Bert, E.P. Carrigan, and G.C. Symonds. From Keene Fire Department scrapbook.

1896 [*from* City of Keene Annual Report]

Report of the Chief Engineer

To His Honor the Mayor and Gentlemen of the City Councils:

I herewith present the following report of the fire department for the year ending November 30th, 1896.

During the year the department has responded to seventeen calls to fires, nine of which were false alarms, or where for chimneys burning out, or slight fires which were put out before the department arrived.

The losses paid by the insurance companies during the year upon buildings and their contents has been $37,848.50, $34,925.00 of which was paid the Keene Furniture Co. on their loss by fire of June 10th, 1896. In all the other fires the loss was small, amounting to only about $2,923.00, owing to promptness of the whole department in responding to the calls.

"FIRE"
Keene Furniture fire of 1896

1896 On June 10th, 1896 SHEETS OF FLAME as reported by the *Keene Evening Sentinel* Staff. Sheets of Flame Burst from the Keene Furniture Company's Finishing Shop.

$50,000 Worth of Furniture and Property Destroyed. Firemen Subdue the Flames in a Big Wooden Building (Keene Furniture Company. An alarm was sounded from box 14 at 9.05 last night for a fire in the Keene Furniture company's finishing shop and storehouse. The fire was breaking out of the windows when discovered and was seen from Water Street by the family living in the house near the railroad crossing, one of whom pulled in the box.

The firemen were out very quickly, the hose companies passing through the Square in about two minutes, the Deluge Company ahead. The hook and ladder wagon followed

closely and the steamer were down by the railroads in less than five minutes.

The firemen were placed at some disadvantage by being called to box 14, Water street, instead of the beaver mills Box, but it is a question if much time would have saw the fire had stopped to run over to box 13. He did well to get out the department at the earliest possible moment.

The Deluge hose men laid a line of hose from a hydrant on Water Street, and were quickly at work. The Steamer hose men, knowing where their engine would be stationed, at once went through to the hydrant near the bridge on Harrison Street. One line was extended from that point to the east side of the burning building and a line was started between the brick shops to reach the west side. There was not enough hose on the wagon to complete the latter. Two streams from the Beaver mills pump were started through the bridge connecting the finishing shop with the brick manufactory, one on the second and one on the third floor, under the direction of Engineer Jones. The Beaver Mills employees also laid hose lines from the fireplug and hydrant on the south side of the brick shop.

When the firemen arrived the flames, which had apparently started in or near the room on the East Side of the finishing shop where oils and varnishes were stored had gained great headway in the lower and second story finishing rooms. The flames had broken out both on the east and west sides of the shop and storehouse. This was a wooden frame building about 150x40 feet in size and three stories high, with a dry house on the East Side separated by a brick wall. There were finishing rooms on the different floors, cut off by light board partitions only, while the greater part of the building was simply a big store room packed full of furniture, the floors being connected by stairways and two elevator shafts. The largest finishing room was in the lower story and the floors were, of course, well covered with shellac, varnish, etc., making them very flammable.

The first attack of the Deluge and Steamer hose men upon the flames from the east side was determined and well directed. It looked for some time as if they would extinguish the fire. Access to the store-room was gained and Captain Towne's men, who knew their ground perfectly, were fast getting into the main building, driving the fire before them.

During the interval, however, and for a long time afterwards, no corresponding attack could be made on the West Side of the shop owing, apparently, to a lack of hose. Both wagons had exhausted their supply, probably. The fire was also deceptive, and was doubtless burning among the furniture on two if not three of the floors. The flames would be entirely inaccessible among the long rows of headboards, footboards, bureaus and commodes closely packed together.

There was a serious delay in getting the second steamer to the fire. It was 9.45 before that engine arrived at the mill and it was not doing a particle of good till 10 o'clock or after. Engineer Fay called for the second steamer immediately after the first apparatus arrived. He gave directions to set the engine at the hydrant opposite 93rd Street and ordered the hose wagon to return to the station, get hose and supply the engine. It is said that the driver of the steamer walked his horsed back after the second engine. However this may be, thirty minutes should be an ample allowance of time to get two engines to the mills, one going by way of Water Street.

The hose for the second engine had to be taken from the hose tower, largely. The hose men did not lay a line for the second steamer from the 93rd Street hydrant, but first finished out the west line, which had been started from the Amoskeag engine. Then there was not hose enough to lay from 93rd Street. Where

the Deluge hose wagon was during this half hour no one appeared to know, but finally the Button engine was moved to a hydrant close to the fire in the mill yard, hose was procured and the engine gave three very effective streams thereafter.

At 10.15 the department was fairly at work. The south end of the big shop had then fallen in and the building was a mass of flames to the center. The fire was fast working north toward the main brick shops. But the firemen, shone from the roof, some from the dry house on the east and some from the west side, were directing many powerful streams into the steelhing furnace, while the mill's employees under Michael Roach, who knows every nook and corner at the mills, were holding their own and keeping the fire back from the north end of the building.

At one time, when it looked as if the entire finishing shop would burn, Engineer Jones gave orders to the Hook and Ladder Company to tear away the sides of the double deck in closed bridge or passage connecting the wooden and brick shops. A most serious weakness of the department was divulged in attempting to execute this order. Had the safety of the mills depended upon quick and thorough work against the flimsy sides of this bridge, which only required the ripping off of clapboards to thoroughly open the enclosure, the result would have been disastrous. The ladder men were not on hand in any organized force. They had no hooks on poles suitable to use on a burning building, and there were no men with ladders and hand hooks to mount the bridge and quickly tear it to pieces, which could easily have been done by one or two men. The truck having upon it the large pole hooks, etc., belonging to the department was at the fire station. It should have been at the fire as quickly as the second steamer. After much delay a hole was torn in the side of the bridge by a hook with rope attached, which had to be hooked into place

A Demon Called Fire

from a ladder every time it was used-a most worthless tool in a hot, burning building.

The connection between the finishing shop and the brick shop through the enclosed bridge, carried so much heat into the upper stories of the brick shop that the automatic sprinklers went off early in the evening and the entire manufactory of the furniture company was drenched with water. The shops were filled with goods in process of manufacture, including much veneered work, which the water has ruined. The machinery is covered with rust and the belts are soaked out and separated in many cases. Some of the stock in process was so piled that only the outer pieces, probably, are injured. It was estimated that the loss in this part of the shops alone would be $3,000.

The fire was getting under control about 11.30, when it became evident that the flames were not advancing toward the main brick shops. By midnight the firemen were in possession of the burning building, which was consumed and had fallen in nearly to the line of the stairway and elevator, not far from the center of the structure. At 2 a.m. the Amoskeag steamer and the Deluge hose men were relieved. The Button engine remained till morning, and the Steamer hose men had streams going until 8 o'clock this morning.

The loss is estimated at $50,000, divided about as follows; furniture, finished and in process, $40,000; stock, etc., $5,000; building $5,000. The burned building was owned by the Keene Furniture Company, the Beaver Mills Company owning the brick shops only.

The insurance held by the company on the stock in the burned building, the burned building itself, the stock in the brick building in process of manufacture, and the machinery in the brick building foots up at $37,975. It is proportioned as follows: Machinery, $5,149.96; storehouse stock, $27,500; the burned building, $3,450; stock in main brick shop, $1,875.04. In addition, sawyer & Mason

had placed $500 on the stock in the veneer shop, and $500 on the shop itself, on neither of which there was any damage. Of this sum, $24,975 was placed by Sawyer & Mason and $17,000 by G. H. Aldrich & Son. The former firm placed $3,000, through Calvin B. Perry and $3,000, through George F. Ball.

The insurance is divided as follows between the several companies represented: granite State, $1,5000; Connecticut, $1,750; Manchester, $1,000; Phoenix, of New York, $1,500; Manufacturers and Merchants, $1,000; Queen, $1,000; concord Mutual, $750; Lancashire, $2,000; Springfield, $1,000; New Hampshire, $1,000; Phoenix, of Hartford, $1,000; Portsmouth Fire Association, $500; Commercial Union, $1,500; Niagara, $3,000; Etna, $2,034.38; Hartford, $2034.34; North British, $1,034.38; Sun $1,534,38; Caledonian, $2,034.38; Palatine, $1,034.38; Imperial, $1,700; Capital, $1,034.38; Underwriters, $1,000; Norwich Union, $1,034.38; Mutual Fire Insurance Co., $500; Continental, $1,500; National, $1,500; Liverpool, London & Globe, $3,000.

The cause of the fire was spontaneous combustion or incendiaries. The proprietors are fully of the opinion that the building was set on fire. Mr. Champion says there was nothing upon the premises, which could have ignited spontaneously. Furthermore, foreman O. I. Applin of the finishing department, and a man with him, who were among the first to reach the fire, say they found the lower half of a window raised, which was never opened. This window leads into a room or corner used for storage. It was near the shipping door on the east side. Access could have been had through this window to the finishing rooms, or to the stock room further south.

————

June 10, 1896 – The aftermath of the fire at Keene Furniture. Pictures from Keene Fire Department scrapbook and HSCC collection.

1896 Report of the Chief Engineer
[continued]

The apparatus is now all in excellent condition, new flues having been put in the boiler of the Amoskeag engine during the year, and new wheels placed on the steamer hose carriage, and two Babcock extinguishers put on each hose carriage.

The department consists of four engineers, Steamer and Hose Co., twenty-five men, Washington Hook and Ladder Co., twenty-five men, and Deluge Hose Co., twenty men.

The uniforms of the men are getting badly worn in some cases, and the caps of some of the men must be replaced by new ones before long.

The general appearance of the men and apparatus, as well as the uniforms, I presume you noticed at the last inspection. You saw at the same time the quarters occupied by the different companies, and the neat and orderly manner in which they are kept.

All the companies have been very careful in asking for expenditures on their rooms or furnishings. A good many of the men spend most of their leisure time in their quarters, and anything reasonable, which they ask should be granted. You have seen at several times during the past year that the service of a fireman is not all fun, especially when they are called out in the evening and are obligated to work all night. They all do more for the city every year than the small sum of fifteen dollars can pay them for, so do not grant their requests grudgingly.

I think you will agree with me that we have one of the best volunteer fire departments that can be found, and their quickness in responding to alarms surprises everyone, even old firemen who are used to the service. Twice during the past year have they been highly complimented for the efficiency by good judges.

The plan of keeping one pair of horses in the barn all the time has proved such a success that no one thinks of going back to the old way.

The fire alarm service is in excellent condition, owing to the watchful care taken of it by Superintendent Emmons. Accidents to it, like the breaking of a wire etc., are liable to occur at any time, but after comparing it with the electric alarms in other places, I am satisfied that we are getting the best service. I would suggest that at least three new boxes be added during the coming year.

We have only hose enough for a relay for each company, and I would suggest that a thousand feet be purchased as soon as may be.

A Demon Called Fire

Inventory of Property

Steamer Button No. 3, Steamer Amoskeag No. 2, hand engine at Woodbury's mills, hand engine at South Keene, Deluge hose carriage, two jumpers, three hook and ladder trucks, steamer hose carriage, 4,000 feet of cotton hose, fire alarm, engineers' lanterns, six hydrant gates, one Y coupling, rubber coats, uniforms of Steamer Co., uniforms of Deluge Hose Co., one Siamese.

Fire Alarm Telegraph remains the same except of the addition of one new bell and J. F. Emmons remains the Fire Alarm Superintendent of Fire Alarm Telegraph for the year 1896. Signals and General Rules remain the same, as do the Telephone Alarms.

Conclusion

In conclusion, I wish to thank the assistant engineers for the hearty support they have always given me, and the officers and men of the department for the manner in which they have responded to all calls and discharged all the duties of a fireman.

Very respectfully, J. P. Wellman, Chief Engineer. Keene, December 1st, 1896.
Resolution passed June 4th, 1896 relating to pay of firemen for work at brush fires on May 19th, 1896 along with the work of a team of Horses from the fire department to carry the men back and forth.

FIREMEN'S QUARTERS INSPECTED YESTERDAY BY MANY CITIZENS

Reported by the *Keene Evening Sentinel*
September 26th, 1896
How Many Companies have fitted up they're Rooms and what they have done to Increase Their Efficiency-Some Ingenious Automatic Devices.

A very considerable number of citizens, including many ladies, availed themselves of the opportunity presented at the close of the firemen's parade yesterday afternoon to inspect the quarters at the fire station. Members of the city government and friends who comprised the inspecting party went through the quarters at the close of the parade, first visiting the fire alarm battery and repeater rooms in the basement of city hall.

Superintendent Emmons explained to the party the general plan of the three circuits in the city, showing the batteries required for each circuit, the operation of the five-circuit repeater which is used, three circuits being in service, the operation of the ground testing switches and galvanometer and the instruments used to measure the current upon the lines. The ground switch showed the effect of a wire, which cuts through the bark of a tree just above city hall. A second ground as sharp as this one would throw the boxes on this circuit out of service. This ground is now constant, and in wet weather it endangers the efficiency of the apparatus. It should be remedied by setting an extra pole between city hall and Spring Street, where the stretches are too long, and attaching all the fire alarm wires to long cross arms extending out beyond the trees. This will entirely avoid the removal of large tree limbs.

At the fire station on Vernon Street the inspecting party visited the engine houses, stables and company rooms. Exhibitions were also given in the Deluge, Hook and Ladder and Steamer houses, of the celerity with which the horses are hitched up with the spring harnesses, from 7 to 12 seconds elapsing from the time a gong blow is given and the stall doors opened to the time when the apparatus is ready to leave the station.

There are now at the station stalls for eight horses equipped with doors in front, opening into the engine houses, and the horses on the Deluge and Steamer hose wagons and the ladder truck are trained to run out and take their places on the apparatus when the doors are opened and the bell sounded, these companies having spring harnesses purchased by their own members, which are always attached to the apparatus. Ordinary harnesses are used upon the steamers.

The company rooms have all been furnished and equipped by the members. They are models of neatness and well-appointed in every instance.

The Deluge Company has a hall of moderate size, neatly carpeted and equipped with handsome desks, chairs, tables and numerous pictures and trophies, which the company has accumulated. They have also a smoking room and a well-furnished bed room in which one the members always sleeps. This company consists of 20 men; Fred W. Towne Captain, Chas. A. Balch and Edwin H. Stone, Lieutenants.

The Hook & Ladder Company has a large hall, probably 35 feet in length. This they have recently papered very tastefully, adding a frieze and picture molding. The hall is carpeted and provided with chairs, tables, etc., and pictures and other furniture will be added. This company also has a sleeping room furnished for one of the members, who is always on hand for night calls. The company consists of 20 men; Elwin H. Johnson, Captain; W. A. Byam, M. A. Holleren, Lieutenants.

The Steam Fire Engine and Hose Company's quarters have been materially improved the past year. The chimney and stairway in the center of their house were removed, the stalls altered and fitted with doors opening into the apparatus room and the rooms upstairs changed. The company has two good rooms, the smallest some 22x13 feet in size for the use of the members, besides a well-furnished sleeping room where one or two men are always ready for night calls. This company's hall is furnished with mahogany tables, chairs and desks and numerous steel engravings and other pictures. The other room is not carpeted, but is provided with pictures and with tables and chairs for everyday use.

This company consists of 25 men; C. M. Cummings, Captain; H. W. Keyes, Lieutenant; L. K. Stiles and W. K. Church, foremen of hose.

The boards of engineers of the department have a good-sized room carpeted and well furnished, adjacent to the hall of the hook and ladder company. The board consists of Jerry P. Wellman, Chief, John Q. Jones, Oscar H. Fay, Frank M. Davis, Assistants.

The interest which the men of the different companies take in increasing the efficiency of their organizations, and which has resulted in making the standard of much of their work equal to that expected in the salaried departments of larger cities, is seen in numerous appliances which the companies themselves have from time to time procured such, as regulations, uniforms and caps, hose wagons, spring harnesses, etc. All the above but the latter are now supplied by the city. But the men keep adding new things, like the voluntary night service, now maintained by members sleeping in the station.

In the Deluge house there are also some electrical and mechanical appliances worthy of note, the inventions of Mr. Jean P. Howes, and in the Steamer house appliances by Mr. Frank F. Stearns. The Deluge Company has in the first place an Electro-mechanical register, which clearly records on a strip of paper every blow or box number struck at any time upon the fire alarm circuit. This register was invented and made by Mr. Howes and works perfectly. It prints a distinct record of all calls upon a tape in characters which can be read twenty feet or more from the machine and the firemen always refer to the register to get correctly the box number before leaving the engine house on a fire call.

Connected with the house apparatus is also a mechanical gas lighter which lights two gaslights up stairs and two down stairs when an alarm comes in. Another Electro-mechanical arrangement of Mr. Howes' opens the doors of the stalls in from of the horses when a push button is pressed, or when an alarm comes in. This is done by an Electro-magnet which releases a metal ball which in turn falls several feet striking a collar on a rod, the impact of the blow lifting the latches of the doors upon the stalls.

A convenient device used in cold weather is an arrangement of Mr. Howe's that closes the engine house, doors after the hose wagon leaves the house. A lever pivoted in the floor of the engine house, under the hose wagon, and which lies flat when the wagon is out, strikes the rear axle of the wagon and releases a clock work in the basement. Ten seconds later this clock releases a lever and throws a weight, which shuts one of the double doors, and four seconds after that a second lever is released which closes the second door.

Mr. Howes has also arranged a chime of two bells upon the hose wagon to be rung by a chord pulled by one of the men on the cart, to warn people of the approach of the wagon. A similar arrangement is used in some of the large cities. These bells do not excite the horses on the wagon as the drivers' gong does

In the steamer house is a neat Electro-mechanical device for opening the doors of the stalls, which is operated. either by a push button or by connection with the fire alarm apparatus. This device is enclosed in a nickel cylinder, the Electro-magnet releasing a hammer, which falls and trips a weight, which opens the bolts. Mr. Stearns has also arranged a device for lightening the gas in this house.

In the hook and ladder house the levers for opening the doors is operated by a mechanical arrangement, a cord being pulled to release them.

———

BY=LAWS

OF

Washington Hook and Ladder Co. No. 1,

AND

MANUAL

OF THE

KEENE FIRE DEPARTMENT.

KEENE,
SENTINEL PRINTING CO., PRINTERS.
1896.

INDEX.

BY-LAWS.

PREAMBLE.

The undersigned, members of WASHINGTON HOOK AND LADDER COMPANY No. 1, do mutually agree to support the Rules and Regulations of the Fire Department of Keene, and adopt the following code of By-Laws for the government of this Company.

ARTICLE I.

This Company shall be known as WASHINGTON HOOK AND LADDER COMPANY No. 1.

ARTICLE II.

The officers shall consist of Captain, First and Second Lieutenants, Clerk, Treasurer, and a Standing Committee of three, who shall be elected by ballot, subject to the approval of the Engineers.

ARTICLE III.

The Regular Meetings of this Company shall be at their House on the last Monday of each

22

ARTICLE XXIV.

Any company attaching a second line to a gate already attached to a hydrant, shall have control of the gate attached to, but it is advisable to attach to another hydrant rather than to lay a second line from the first hydrant, if within convenient distance.

ARTICLE XXV.

AMENDMENTS AND ALTERATIONS OF BY-LAWS.

These By-Laws may be altered or amended at any meeting of the Board of Engineers by a major vote, the same having been proposed at some previous meeting, and due notice having been given of the time such amendment would be acted upon.

ARTICLE XXVI.

INSTRUCTIONS AND SUGGESTIONS TO THE FIRE-MEN.

It is important that the several Fire Companies be filled with active and reliable men who shall be ready, able and willing to render such service as may be required of them, therefore, men whose residence or business is too distant from the company house, and those who cannot usually be relied upon in case of fire, should not

From City Reports, 1896.

be admitted or retained as members, and no person should have his name enrolled upon the company's books as a member until appointed by the Engineers.

Each member is expected to meet at suitable times for discipline and practice, so that he may be properly skilled and expert in the use of the apparatus used by the company, also to inform himself in regard to his duties as a fireman, and he should in case of fire endeavor to act with coolness and discretion in the discharge of the duties assigned him.

Each hydrant man, pipe man and officer in charge of any line of hose connected with a hydrant should ascertain the number of such hydrant that it may be designated thereby in giving orders for operating the same.

Great care should be used in opening and closing the hydrants, and all hydrant men should be instructed in this point.

In laying hose, two lines may be attached to a hydrant if a sufficient quantity is at hand for that purpose, but in all cases it is better to make use of a single line from each hydrant near any fire before double lines are laid.

Believing that the observance of the foregoing rules and the By-Laws adopted by the Board of Engineers will tend to make the Fire Department more efficient and worthy of confidence,

we trust they will receive the approval and support of each member and our citizens.

(Signed.)

J. P. WELLMAN, Chief.
P. F. BABBIDGE, Assistant,
JOHN Q. JONES,   "
OSCAR H. FAY,   "

The Washington Hook and Ladder Co. #1 Bi-Laws were adopted by the members and approved by the Keene Fire Department board of Engineers. As years go by each company's Bi-Laws are revised and amended to meet the ever-changing fire service world.

1897 [*from* City of Keene Annual Report]

Report of the Chief Engineer.

To His Honor the Mayor and Gentlemen of the City Councils:

I herewith present the following report of the fire department, for the year ending November 30th, 1897.

During the year the department has been called out fourteen times. Five of these alarms were false, or for chimneys burning out.

The losses paid by the insurance companies during the year, upon buildings and their contents have been $2,720. Making the total loss small in comparison with that of some other years.

The apparatus is now in good condition. New brakes have been added to the Hook and Ladder Truck, and the Deluge Hose Wagon, and three fire extinguishers and a pair of spring harnesses have been purchased. The department consists of sixty-nine men. Four engineers, Steamer and Hose Co., twenty-five men, Washington Hook and Ladder Co., twenty men, and Deluge Hose Co., twenty men.

The uniforms of the men have been repaired, and the Hook and Ladder Co., furnished with new caps.

The fire alarm service is in good condition, owing to the excellent care taken of it by Superintendent Emmons. I would suggest that three new boxes be added during the coming year. One to be reserved to replace one that may at any time needs repairs.

One thousand feet of hose has been purchased this last year, and I recommend that one thousand more be added the coming year.

Inventory of Property

Steamer Button No.2, Steamer Amoskeag No. 2, hand engine at hospital, hand engine at South Keene, Deluge hose carriage, two jumpers, three hook and ladder trucks, steamer hose carriage, 4,6000 feet of cotton hose, nine fire extinguishers, six for the department and three at city hall; fire alarm, engineers' lanterns, six hydrant gates, one Y coupling, rubber coats, uniforms of Steamer Co., uniforms of Washington Hook and Ladder Co., uniforms of Deluge Hose Co., one Siamese.

Fire Alarm Telegraph

Fire Alarm Superintendent J. F. Emmons has added a new box to the circuit, Box 8, Main Street, corner Railroad Street.

Signals and General Rules along with Telephone Alarms remain the same.

Conclusion

In conclusion, I take this opportunity in behalf of the board of engineers, to extend our thanks to all members of the city government who have in any way rendered assistance to the department who have in any way rendered assistance to the department the past year.

I wish to extend my sincere and heartfelt thanks to my assistant engineers, to all officers and members of the fire department, for their efficient work, excellent deportment, unselfish support and devotion to duty as manifested on all occasions.

I also desire to thank all citizens who have aided the department in any way whatever, and for all words of encouragement and praise bestowed on the men, never forgotten and always appreciated by them.

Very respectfully,

John Q. Jones, Chief Engineer. Keene December 1st, 1897

Joint Resolutions passed by the City Councils in 1887.

Passed December 17th, 1896 Swing harnesses and hangers for the Deluge Hose Co., horses and for the Steam Fire Engine and Hose hoses for a price of$288.50 The swing harnesses and hangers for the Steamers was passed October 21st, 1897 for $150.00 and the Deluge Hose was $138.50 to make the total of $288.50.

1896 Swing harnesses were purchased for Deluge Hose Company and the Steam Fire Engine Company. These harnesses expedited the placing of the harnesses on the horses that created a quicker response for the engine to leave the station. As shown in the picture in the steamer house over the Amoskeag Steamer you can see the swing harnesses without the leather harnesses on the swing harness bracket. From Keene Fire Department scrapbook.

Resolution relating to the purchase of fire hose. Passed April 1st, 1897

Passed November 4th, 1897 pay for brush fire near Albert Pond's property and for the team of horses to bring them to and from. Note: A Resolution was passed on May 6th, 1897 to place the two cannons in the Central Park or Central Square surrounding the soldier's monument.

"FIRE"

1897 BARN AND ELL BURNED. As reported by the *Keene Evening Sentinel*. On April 20th, 1897 A Fire at the Home of Albert L. Harkness South Lincoln Street.

Fire alarm box No. 15 corner Water and South Lincoln Street, was rung in at 2:51 Tuesday afternoon for a fire in the cottage house and barn of Albert L. Harkness. The Hook and Ladder Company's wagon and the Steamer hose wagon were first on the scene, and soon two hydrant steamers were playing on the flames. The fire was subdued quickly, but not before the almost complete destruction of the barn and ell. The main part of the house was not seriously damaged, excepting the attic and roof. Most of the furniture and personal effects were saved.

The Deluge hose wagon arrived on the scene when the fire was well under control, followed by the Button engine. Two pairs of horses were at the North End when the fire broke out, and the drivers evidently did not hear the alarm. Three alarms were sounded to hurry them in.

The fire caught in the barn, where one of Mr. Harkness's little boys had been playing. He ran into the house suddenly and alarmed his sister, Miss Una, by the statement that there was a bonfire in the haymow. She ran to the barn and found it full of flames and immediately turned in the alarm. The loss will be several hundred dollars. The insurance aggregates $1,800 on the buildings and $400 on the house.

The aftermath of the Harkness Fire, South Lincoln Street. From Keene Fire Department scrapbook.

On July 17, 1897 shown above is the wreck of the Fitchburg 246, which derailed in West Keene. The two locomotives and 5 freight cars of hogs were damaged as a result of the derailment. Engineer Milan Curtis and many of the hogs from the freight cars lost their lives. The Amoskeag Steamer and the Steamer Hose Wagon and the Deluge Hose Company responded, but no action was taken by the department. HSCC photo collection.

1898 [*from* City of Keene Annual Report]

Report of the Chief Engineer.

To His Honor the Mayor and gentlemen of the City Councils:

I herewith present the following report of the fire department, for the year ending November 30th, 1898.

During the year the department has been called out seventeen times. Once for a brush fire, three times for chimneys burning out, and one false alarm.

The losses paid by the insurance companies during the year, upon buildings and their contents, amount to $26,391.15. Of this sum, $21,950.60 was for one fire alone.

The apparatus is in good condition. $1,500 feet of hose and one cellar pipe have been purchased during the year. 850 feet of hose have been turned over to the sewer and water department.

One telephone has been put in at the fire station. In case the department is needed outside the city limits, if people would telephone direct to the station instead of going some distance to pull in the nearest box, better results would follow. The men would then know just where to go, and if the fire was some distance away they could start prepared for the long run.

The department consists of sixty-nine men. Four engineers, Steamer and Hose Co., twenty men, and Deluge Hose Co., twenty men.

Some uniforms for the men have been repaired, and the Deluge Hose Co., furnished with new caps.

The fire alarm service, under the care of Superintendent Emmons, is good condition. I would suggest that three new boxes be added this coming year. One to be put on Marlboro' Street, somewhere at the lower end of the Street, one near Giffin's mill, and one to be reserved to replace one that may need repairs.

Inventory of Property

Steamer Button No. 2 Steamer Amoskeag No. 2, hand engine at hospital, hand engine South Keene, Deluge hose carriage, two jumpers, three hook and ladder trucks, steamer hose carriage, 5,050 feet of hose, nine fire extinguishers, six for the department ant three at city hall, fire alarm, engineers' lanterns, six hydrant gates, one Y coupling, rubber coats, uniforms of Steamer Co., uniforms of Deluge Hose Co., one Siamese and one cellar pipe.

Fire Alarm Telegraph remains the same as do the signals as adopted by the board of engineers December 2nd, 1887. The signals remain the same as do the General Rules. Telephone Alarms also remain the same.

Conclusion

In conclusion, I take this opportunity in behalf of the board of engineers, to extend our thanks to all members of the city government, and to all citizens who have in any way whatever rendered the department assistance during the past year.

I wish to extend my sincere thanks to my assistant engineers, to all officers and members of the department for their suggestions, assistance, hearty support, and their readiness to respond to all calls of duty.

Very respectfully,

John Q. Jones, Chief Engineer. Keene December 1st, 1898

Board of Chief Engineers. L to R: Chief John Jones, Oscar Fay, Fran Davis, Fred Townes. From Fire Department records.

Resolutions for year 1898. Purchase of fire hose 1,000 feet. Passed May 5th, 1898

Resolution relating to a substitute driver. The Chief Engineer of the fire department is hereby authorized to hire a substitute, for the drivers employed by the department, four evenings per week at an expense not to exceed fifty cents per night, so that each driver may be granted one evening off duty in every week. Passed May 19th, 1898.

Also a Resolution was passed to purchase an additional 500 feet of fire hose. Passed September 15th, 1898

A Resolution was passed to widen the doorways at the fire station, and not exceed $140.00 Passed November 17th, 1898

1898 Hook and Ladder Company Officers. L to R: F.H. Tenney, W.A. Byam, A.T. Chilton. From Keene Fire Department scrapbook.

The above picture is the Washington Hook and Ladder Members of 1898. This picture, when taken, hung in the Washington Hook and Ladder's engine house. After the fire, which destroyed the Keene Central Fire Station, pictures were placed in storage. The start of the oldest scrapbook of the Keene Fire Department used this picture as its first 3 pages, the picture was torn into 3 sections, and therefore it was placed in the scrapbook to preserve it, which was the start of one of the Keene Fire Department Scrapbooks. The scrapbook became so brittle and the above picture was so deteriorated that the paper would break to the touch. In 2001, Chief Bradley Payne and the City Clerk's office, Deputy City Clerk , William Dow proposed to restore the scrapbook by a professional company. At the direction of Deputy Chief Steven Goldsmith this picture was removed from the scrapbook, pieced together as it originally was and sealed in plastic so that if the City desired the could frame and display it as it originally was

1899 [*from* City of Keene Annual Report]

Report of the Chief Engineer.

To His Honor the Mayor and Gentlemen of the City Councils:

I herewith present the following report of the fire department, for the year ending November 30th, 1899.

There have been forty-two alarms during the year. Of these fourteen were telephone calls and two were false.

The losses paid by the insurance companies the past year, upon buildings and their contents, amount to $21,461.99. Estimated losses not covered by insurance, $9,425.00. The apparatus is in good condition with the exception of the Button Engine. 1,000 feet of hose and one extension ladder have been purchased. I would recommend the painting of the steamer hose wagon, also the Amoskeag engine.

One telephone has been put in at the house of the chief engineer. Good use has been made of the telephone at the station in sending in calls where the whole department was not needed. If people outside the city limits would telephone direct to the station, quicker time and better results would follow than can be secured by running some distance to pull in the nearest box.

The department consists of sixty-nine men. Four engineers, Steamer & Hose Co., twenty-five men, Washington Hook and Ladder Co., twenty men, and Deluge Hose Co., twenty men.

Some new uniforms have been bought and some have been repaired. I would recommend the purchase of some rubber coats and rubber boots for the use of the men.

The fire alarm service, under the care of Superintendent Emmons , is in good condition. Three new boxes have been added and three have been repaired. I would suggest that a box be placed at the lower end of Marlboro Street near the residence of Mr. Taft. Another on Spring Street corner of Brook Street.

Inventory of Property

Steamer Button No. 2, Steamer Amoskeag No. 2, hand engine at hospital, hand engine at South Keene, Deluge hose carriage, two jumpers, three hook and ladders trucks, steamer hose carriage, 6,050 feet of hose, about 500 feet of this condemned, nine fire extinguishers, six for the department, and three at city hall, fire alarm, engineers lanterns, six hydrant gates, one Y coupling, rubber coats, uniforms of Steamer Co., uniforms of Washington Hook and Ladder Co., uniforms of Deluge Hose Co., one Siamese and one cellar pipe.

Fire Alarm Telegraph three new boxes have been added and three repaired as mentioned in the Chiefs Report. Signals remain the same as adopted as do the General Rules and Telephone Alarms remain the same as well.

Conclusion

In conclusion, the engineers extend thanks to all members of the city government, and to all citizens who have by word or deed given the department assistance and support during the past year.

I desire to extend my thanks to my assistant engineers for their efficient help, and to all officers and members of the department for their prompt and energetic response to all calls of duty.

Very respectfully,

John Q. Jones, Chief Engineer. Keene December 1st, 1899.

Superintendent of Fire Alarms Report given by J. F. Emmons for the year 1899 advised that three new United States Company's boxes have been added. Boxes 18 and 25, and the other to take place of box 9, on city hall building. Three of the Stevens old style boxes have been thoroughly renovated, modern works being supplied. We now have three circuits and four hundred feet of insulated wire has been purchased to be placed in the underground conduits furnished the city by the New England Telephone and Telegraph Company.

Resolutions for 1899

A Resolution was passed on December 15th, 1898 to heating appliances for the fire station.

Resolution to purchase three fire alarm boxes and locate two of them in connection with the present system of fire alarm telegraph.

A Resolution relating to the purchase of fire hose 1,000 feet passed October 19th, 1899.

A resolution relating to the purchase of horse blankets. Three pairs of horse blankets for the fire horses. Passed November 2nd, 1899

Front Cover of Scrapbook. In 1974, the front cover of the scrapbook was designed by Emile Desrosier. The cover of the scrapbook was sent out to be painted; as shown above. Over the years the scrapbook became so brittle that the cover was preserved separately, when in 2001 Chief Bradley Pane and the City Clerk's office, Deputy City Clerk William Dow had the scrapbook professionally preserved. It is now kept in the vault at the City Clerk's Office. This scrap book was begun in 1899 and has continued from one to several scrap books with pictures and newspaper clippings.

An Era of Unforgettable Images

Once the fire equipment was on the scene of the fire the horses would be unhooked and led to a safe place or returned to the station to pull another piece of equipment. Keene had its ups and downs with horses. They were shared at one point with public works but a fire horse was always a fire horse first, as some found out over the years. Pictured is the Button Steamer being hooked up after a call by Roxbury Street to return the steamer back to the fire station.

Tom and Jack pose for pictures on the east side of the central fire station The era of horse and steam moved to motorized fire apparatus but the horses and fire equipment drawn by these special animals have left an unforgettable image of a bygone era. The fire horses stand so proud and trained so well to pull the fire apparatus to the scene of a fire. The clamour of the engine going through central square with the bell ringing and the horses hoofs against the cobblestone was a sight to see. Over the year the department kept as many as 8 horses to pull the fire equipment.

Each piece of equipment had a kick bell and the horses had belly bells that rang to alert the citizens of a fire apparatus approaching. Pictured is the Amoskeag steamer racing through central square by Roxbury Street. Adults and children stopped and watched as they passed by. Central square was always a busy place in Keene.

1900–1949

From Horsepower to Motorpower

1900 [from *City of Keene Annual Report*]

Report of the Chief Engineer of the Fire Department.

To His Honor the Mayor and City Councils:

I hereby tender for your perusal my report of the fire department, for the year, ending December 1st, 1900.

During the year, the department has responded to twenty-one bell alarms and nine still alarms, the losses resulting thereby aggregating $18,365.80, with insurance of $10,671.43.

(See detailed report at end of report).

I find it is not universally known, that there is a telephone at the fire station, and that assistance can be had at any time, during the day or night, by sending in a call, and I wish to impress upon the public, the advisability of taking advantage of this service, in cases where a general alarm is not needed, but where some protection is required such as the burning out of chimneys, etc.

The yearly inspection of property by the engineers, which has been in vogue the past few years, has been conducive to excellent results. Property owners and tenants have interested themselves very much in this work, and the willingness to cooperate with the board of engineers in accepting their suggestions to guard against fires, has been greatly in evidence, which fact makes the labor of inspections very much easier.

You will observe by the inventory that there are only 4,200 feet of hose in the department, none having been purchased during the year. In addition to this amount there is some which can perhaps be repaired. For some reason a large amount of hose has given out in the past few months, and the number of feet now in service is inadequate to the demands which are frequently made upon the department. A careful investigation demonstrates that much of the hose purchased has not seemingly given as much service as could reasonably be expected. The bursting of hose when the efforts of the department are taxed to the utmost, is a serious and costly hindrance, and I believe the adoption of a better quality of hose will prove more economical and at the same time tend to lessen the losses.

The efficiency of the department can be materially increased by the purchasing of more rubber coats, the present supply being insufficient to protect the entire fireman from exposure in the discharge of their duties.

With the exception of the Amoskeag engine which needs repainting, and the relief ladder truck, which needs repainting, the apparatus and its appendages are in excellent condition. The Steamer hose wagon has been repainted and greatly improved by the addition of fenders and guard rails.

The cost of keeping in order the uniforms has always been an item of considerable expense, and in anticipation of lessening this

REGULATIONS

BY THE ENGINEERS OF

KEENE FIRE DEPARTMENT.

JANUARY, 1900.

1st. No person shall make any public exhibition of Fireworks without the consent of a majority of the Engineers.

2d. No person shall kindle, or allow any fire in the open air, near any building or other property liable to be endangered thereby, unless the same be under the immediate and constant watch and care of some competent person.

3d. No person shall smoke any pipe or cigar nor carry or use any unenclosed lighted candle or lamp or fire in any Barn, Stable or Shed, or in any Planing Mill or other Shop, or place containing combustible matter liable to be fired thereby. And all stoves used in a hazardous place shall be underlaid with sheet metal or brick hearths, or furnished with proper safeguards against fire.

4th. No person shall deposit or keep any ashes in any combustible vessel or place, nor keep any 'Friction Matches except in places properly secured against taking fire from their ignition, nor any Benzole, Camphene, Gunpowder or other highly inflammable or explosive articles, except in places remote from and not exposed to fire, and no large quantity shall in any case be kept where other valuable property will be endangered thereby. Great care must also be exercised in handling the same.

5th. Shavings, waste and combustible material, from which fire is to be apprehended, shall be seasonably removed from buildings and properly disposed of.

6th. Wooden fireboards are unsafe and must not be used. All ovens, ash ovens and other like places shall be provided with proper metallic doors or lids, and all woodwork which may be unsafe from its proximity to any stove or pipe, shall be properly protected by sheet metal or otherwise.

All chimneys should be properly built, and of suitable height to render the same secure against communicating fire, and no uncovered pipe-holes or openings shall be allowed in them; and it is recommended that when building chimneys they be thoroughly plastered or coated with mortar inside.

A proper observance of these rules will do much to prevent accidental fires, and it is the duty of all persons owning, occupying or having the care of any buildings to see that they are carried into effect for the safety of their own and their neighbors' property. And any person who shall violate or neglect to comply with the provisions and requirements of either of them shall be liable to a penalty of five dollars for each offense, or after a special notification by the Engineers in regard to any improper neglect, the penalty for a further violation shall be fifteen dollars for each offense, to be recovered in the manner provided by law.

The law provides that the Board of Engineers may at any time order such repairs and alterations to be made on any buildings which they may deem to be dangerous to the property of others, as may be required to render them safe, which if not made within thirty days after due notice is given, makes the owner or occupant liable to a penalty of ten dollars for every month's neglect, also to the owner of any buildings or property consumed by fire communicated from such dangerous building, for the damage suffered by him.

[See Public Statutes, Chap. 115, Sec. 14 and 15.]

It is also the duty of all citizens present at a fire to render such assistance as the Engineers may require to extinguish and prevent the spreading of such fire, and to remove property endangered, etc.

[See Public Statutes, Chap. 115, Sec. 8 and 9.]

And it is hoped that our citizens will cheerfully comply whenever necessity may demand; also at all times to encourage the observance and execution of all proper precautionary measures for the prevention and suppression of fires, and to save property from destruction thereby.

The foregoing Rules and Regulations were made and established by the Board of Engineers for the city of Keene, on the 16th day of January, A. D. 1900, and were duly posted and recorded in accordance with the laws of the State of New Hampshire.

Fred W. Towne Chief
Edward P. Carrigan
Louis C. Nims
Denis Foley

} Engineers
for the
City of Keene.

Regulations by the Engineers of the Keene Fire Department were posted though out the City of Keene, dating back to the late 1800s, the one shown above was posted for the year 1900 and was displayed in all places of business within the City. This document was found in the basement of the Colonial Theatre.

outlay, wardrobes have been supplied to the several companies so that proper care can be given them.

While rendering efficient service at the disastrous fire, which visited the town of Winchester on July 4th, 1900, the Button steamer met with an accident while attempting to life water to greater height than the pumps were capable of, in the probable somewhat worn condition of the pistons, and to the unfortunate loosening of a forking gland at that time. This injury to the pumps necessitated immediate repairs of quite an extensive nature and at the same time the removal of the boiler which had for some time been in bad condition. I am glad to report that the whole matter was promptly taken in hand by the councils through the committee on fire department and a contract made with the Amoskeag Manufacturing Co. to place a new tubular boiler of their standard make in the engine, and to thoroughly overhaul and repair the machine in every particular. The engine was returned in a few weeks, and afterwards, a few preliminary trials were made and alterations in the artificial draft mechanism, at a slight expense. Since this change the machine has been given several severe service trials with most satisfactory results, and I believe I am warranted in starting that the city now has in the Button Engine, repaired at a cost of about $1,700, as reliable and efficient piece of apparatus as it would have possessed had an engine been purchase at a cost of perhaps three times as much.

The discipline of the department has been, and is most excellent, and the interest the members display in improving the efficiency has been very marked.

I take this opportunity to express to my assistants and the members of the department, my thanks for the many favors received at their hands and for the enthusiasm exhibited in entering upon their work and in promoting good fellow ship among the members.

In conclusion I beg to tender my thanks to His Honor the Mayor and members of the city government for their thoughtful consideration in responding to the needs of the department.

Very respectfully,
FRED W. TOWNE
Chief Engineer. Keene December 1st, 1900.

Inventory of Property

Steamer Button No. 2,

Steamer Amoskeag No. 1, one hand engine, Deluge hose wagon, steamer hoe wagon, two hook and ladder trucks, two jumpers, 4,200 feet hose, six Babcock fire extinguishers, four engineers' lanterns, four hydrant gates one Y couplings, one Siamese, one cellar pipe, rubber coats, uniforms for Steamer Co., uniforms of Washington Hook and Ladder Co., uniforms of Deluge Hose Co., and rubber coats.

Number of Alarms for the Year Ending 1900

December 7th, 1899 to the G. W. Porter house for a Chimney fire with no damage reported.

December 9th, 1899 to the Aldrich & Dutton. Property for an unknown type fire. Damage $694.88 and Insurance paid $694.88.

January 5th, 1900 to the Shoe shop for a Chimney fire with no reported damage.

January 23rd, 1900 to the Bullard & shed for an unknown type fire. Damage $25.00 and Insurance paid $25.00.

January 25th, 1900 to the Albert Hubbard House for an unknown type fire. Damage $105.00 and Insurance paid $105.00.

March 7th, 1900 to the Rodney Giffith House for a Chimney fire with no reported damage.

March 13th, 1900 to the Cheshire House Block for a Chimney fire with no reported damage.

March 13th, 1900 to the Patrick Mulvey house for an unknown type fire. Damage $200.00 with no Insurance.

March 24th, 1900 to the J. H. Spencer House for a Chimney fire. Damage $10.00 with no Insurance.

April 15th, 1900 for a Brush fire.

April 15th, 1900 to the Hyland Estate for a Stove pipe problem. Damage $5.00 and Insurance paid $5.00.

April 26th, 1900 to the D. A. Brown property for a brush fire which caught the house on fire with $300.00 damage and no Insurance?

April 27th, 1900 for a brush fire. May 7th, 1900 to the James Strong for a chimney fire with no damage reported.

May 12th, 1900 to the Edward Hartnett House for an unknown type fire with $400.00 damage. Insurance paid $400.00.

June 12th, 1900 to the J. B. Edwards for a Chimney fire with no reported damage.

June 20th, 1900 to the Wm. Brown House for a chimney fire with no damage reported.

July 4th, 1900 to a brush fire caused by fireworks.

July 4th, 1900 to Winchester, N. H. for a fire.

July 12th, 1900 to the Mrs. Henry Chapman for a Chimney fire. Damage $4.10 and Insurance paid $4.10.

July 16th, 1900 to the Impervious Pkg. Co. for an Unknown type fire. Damage $328.82 and Insurance paid $328.82.

July 20th, 1900 to the Cheshire Chair Co., for an unknown type fire. Damage $12,000.00 and Insurance paid $6,715.63.

September 1st, 1900 for a Brush fire.

September 8th, 1900 for a Brush fire.

September 13th, 1900 for a Brush fire.

September 14th, 1900 for a Brush fire.

September 20th, 1900 to the Wilkins Toy Co., for an unknown type fire with no reported damage.

September 24th, 1900 to the S. Bradley House for a Chimney fire with no reported damage.

September 27th, 1900 to the Geo. Wiggett for an unknown type fire with Damage of $135.00 and Insurance paid $135.00.

November 8th, 1900 to the A. J. Williams estate, for an unknown type fire with unreported damage.

November 10th, 1900 to the A. H. Hamblett for a reported House fire with Damage of $4,150.00 and Insurance paid $2,250.00.

November 28th, 1900 to the Mrs. H. H. Tenney House for a Chimney fire with Damage of $8.00 and Insurance paid $8.00.

Total loss $18,365.80 and Insurance paid $10,671.43.

Joint Resolutions for the Year ending 1900.

A Joint Resolution was passed on January 11th, 1900 that the Button steam fire engine is used for the purpose of pumping water from the Ashuelot River in to the water mains, so long as the mayor shall deem it necessary.

A Joint Resolution was passed on July 9th, 1900 relating to the Button Steamer fire engine for repairs not to exceed $1,700.

A Joint Resolution was passed on September 6th, 1900 relating to the pay of firemen and others for work at brush fires.

On September 20th, 1900 a Resolution was passed relating to the expenses for attending the annual inspection of the Keene Fire Department. The sum to be $60.00.

Note: 1900 the department paid $5.00 per week for the keeping of 1 pair of horses for 52 weeks. A total of $260.00. The department also paid for the use of addition horses from the Highway Department a sum of $10.50 for 19 alarms for a total of $199.50.

Also 3 pair of horses were used and paid for at a cost of $3.50 for the annual inspection for a total of $10.50.

Reported by the *Keene Evening Sentinel*. July 20th, 1900:

"FIRE"

1900 TWICE IN SIXTEEN MONTHS. As reported by the *Keene Evening Sentinel*. July 20th, 1900 A Fire at the Cheshire Chair Company's Storehouse Again Burned.

Indications That Fire Was Set Intentionally or by Marauders-Large building and a Heavy Stock of Goods Consumed-Loss, Probably $10,000.

A second bad fire, thought to be of incendiary origin, occurred about 1 a. m. Saturday in the large storehouse of the Cheshire Chair Company, at Beaver Mills. The fire was almost identical in its place of belonging, apparent cause and general progress and extent with that of March 19, 1899, which occurred in the same building, and broke out within fifteen minutes of the same hour in the night. The building was largely destroyed with its contents, involving a loss of $8,000 to $10,000, covered in part by insurance amounting to $7,197. The fire of 99 was preceded by the taking of a horse from the barn, while this time no animals was kept there.

Watchman James T. Cone made his usual rounds through the shops of the chair company about midnight. Everything then appeared to be in its normal conditions. It was not part of his duty to go into the chair company's stable at the southern extremity of the storehouse. This stable had not been used for a month or more and had been locked up since July 1, the key being in the office. In making his external examination of the buildings, Mr. Cone either on his last round before the fire or previously, heard voices near the railroad tracks, and on investigation found thee were persons talking over near the shoe factory, but as there is much passing along the tracks this was not a circumstance to arouse suspicion.

After making his tour of the shops Mr. Cone went to the engine room to eat his luncheon. While there he detected the odor of smoke, and starting out soon found that the stable at the end of the storehouse was on fire. He ran to the Beaver Mills office and pulled in box 13 about 12:45. The alarm for the fire of March 1899 was at 12:30. About the time Mr. Cone pulled the box the fire broke

out and was seen by Mark Barron, telegraph operator at the depot, and others someone on Main Street pulled in box 8, on Railroad Street corner while box 13 was ringing, or just before it was pulled, thus causing the box numbers to be mixed up, but the department was not delayed on this account.

The firemen got out very quickly and were on the ground and at work in two or three minutes. Beaver ills employees, who are always ready for such emergencies, also gathered quickly and had two lines of hose that were speedily connected with the big steam pump in the engine room, which was handled by Engineer Wilson. Later mill hose was used to complete a line from the second steamer, the mill company having 1000 feet in use.

The fire department first laid several hydrant streams and connected No. 1 steamer at the hydrant near the office of the mills, where it did very effective work through the night. The other Amoskeag steamer was set at the hydrant near the bridge across Beaver brook at Harrison Street. There was some delay in getting hose for the engine all of that first brought on the hose wagons being in service before this engine arrived. A line was at length made up, however, as before stated, and the engine worked finely, giving 140 pounds of water pressure. Before the engine went home she was tried with two short lines of hose and worked very satisfactorily. Engineer Green is confident that with a good hydrant supply this engine will carry two or three strong fire streams through lines of hose of the average lengths.

For about two hours a larger volume of water was poured upon the fire, apparently, than was ever delivered at any fire in Keene. Eight or ten streams were in use, certainly, and it is said there were twelve lines in use at one time.

The building was a three-story wooden structure, 60x100 feet in size. At the south end was a small stable and hayloft. This was where the fire originated. The greater part of the building was used as a storehouse and was filled with chairs knocked down and ready for shipment, and with stock. At the north end was the office, a bending room and a brick dry house. The fire did no great damage in the dry house or bending room, the result being similar to that of the fire of 1899.

The first work of the firemen checked and beat down the flames, but the fire had worked into the storehouse and was too hot and among too much inflammable material to be held back. There was quite a lot of hay in the barn loft, which was all afire, and those who got there early found the sheathing and walls of the stable already consumed so that they were dropping to pieces. The whole south end of the building was soon ablaze and the fire gained headway in spite of all efforts until 2 o'clock, occasionally blazing up very brightly. About 2, a slight east wind arouses. This quickly ended the fire and for ten minutes the flames rolled up in huge masses almost the entire length of the building. Fifteen minutes later, however, the firemen had gained the upper hand and for that time on it was merely a question of time the fire being evidently under control.

When the breeze sprung up about 2 o'clock, great quantity of burning embers and cinders were carried over up the piles of lumber and stock in the yard westerly of the burning building, and in the Cheshire Company's lumber and stock shed. It was fortunate that no other fires were set in this way. Very like the rain, which fell during the event and until after 1 o'clock prevented this.

The work of the firemen was commended by nearly everyone present apparently. Their work was done systematically and quietly, and there appeared to be no confusion or clash, among the officers in charge. Chief Towne and the officers and men of his department are entitled to praise and credit for the way the fire was fought. The wind was less in their favor than in 1899, which was from the northwest instead of the southeast, but in spirit of the dusting gain was made in controlling the fire.

While the chair company will be disconnected by their misfortune the factory was in operation as usual Monday. The dry houses in the brick side are not disturbed and those in the store house can be put in operation again once, probably. The manufactured and other stock in the burned building will be a total loss. Much of this was sold and held awaiting delivery orders. It has not been determined what repairs if any, will be made on that part of the building left standing.

A feature of the fire was the dense and blinding smoke, which continually beat down and hugged close to the ground for a considerable distance west of the fire. This made it difficult for the firemen to maintain their positions. No smoke or cinders were carried toward the building on the east however.

The automatic sprinklers in the two stories in closed bridge connecting the storehouse with the brick manufacture were open early and kept this bridge drenched with water. The water than ran from the bridge was burning not showing how great the heat must have been through the bridge. Some of the water from the sprinklers ran in under the upper floors of the brick shop, and the doors, but no especial damage was thus done, the sprinklers being shut by order of Superintendent Norwood early, as it was safe to do so.

A report that tar was found smeared through the building and upon the main floor appears to have arisen from the tar that the roofing on the storehouse was material resembling paper and having black substance like tar between the ladders. Evidently this melted out and ran down. It was thrown on the walls, etc., by the fire streams and was floated

A Demon Called Fire

in the brick mill by the water from the bridge. The roofing remains in large quantities where the roof fell in, showing that it is practically incombustible.

1901 [from *City of Keene Annual Report*]

Report of Chief Engineer of the Fire Department

To His Honor the Mayor and City Councils:

It is my pleasure to render herewith the report of the fire department, for the year ending December 1st, 1901.

Forty-eight alarms have been answered, an increase of more than fifty percent over the number of the year preceding. Fifteen were bell alarms and thirty-three still alarms. No doubt this increase is in a measure due to the system of telephoning for assistance in the case of overheated chimneys, etc., where bell alarms, locations, damage, insurance, etc., see following table.

During the year there have been added to the department one 58-foot extension ladder, six ladder dogs, one Y coupling. Rubber coats, hats and boots have also been purchased which have greatly added to the efficiency of work during fire duty.

A new traverse hose sled to replace the old one of the Deluge Hose Co., was put in service last winter, the old one, which was unsafe, being discarded.

One thousand feet of new hose has been bought, and the same amount of old hose has been repaired, making 5,600 feet now on hand.

There have been instances during the past year when fires occurred with such frequency that nearly all the hose in the department was wet, and not enough dry hose was left to reload the wagon. To load wet hose on a wagon is destructive, as it invariably causes it to mildew. In view of this fact, I believe that more hose is necessary if we are to get all the wear possible out of it. Partition hose racks could be bought for a nominal consideration, this would insure reserve hose being free

from attacks of dampness which is prevalent during the summer months.

Since the ladder truck, which is now in use, was purchased, many large buildings have been erected, and the number of ladders, particularly long ones, are inadequate to the demands which are sure to be made upon them in the event of fires in these sections. The shortage of ladders at the fire in the warehouse of the Holbrook Grocery Co., made it apparent that the department is weak in this respect. It is also evident that steps should be taken with a view to affording better protection to property should a fire occur, while another is in progress.

I would recommend that a new truck be built and equipped with a sufficient number of ladders to reach our tallest buildings, and a good number of others of medium lengths. This piece of apparatus to respond to alarms in sections where long ladders would likely be needed, the old one for reserve in case of an alarm of fire when both trucks would be needed.

This arrangement would serve in having the truck now in use, answer calls from the residential and suburban districts, leaving the other to respond to calls as stated. The members of the Hook and Ladder Co. are qualified, I am sure, to take charge and man both trucks in case it should be deemed desirable to adopt my recommendation.

I would call your attention to the Amoskeag engine, which is very much in need of painting.

Two horses have grown unfit for service, and have been disposed of, theirs having been procured to replace them.

Most excellent discipline prevails among the men, who have shown much pride in keeping the service up to the highest standard, and who are constantly endeavoring to better it in every way.

I wish to extend my thanks to the members of this department, for the many favors which have been extended to me, and for their hearty cooperation.

Finally, I beg to tender my thanks to His Honor, the Mayor, and to the members of the city government, for the many courtesies received at their hands, and for their prompt response in attending to the needs of the department.

Very respectfully, FRED W. TOWNE, Chief Engineer, December 1st, 1901.

Inventory of Property

Steamer Button No. 2, Steamer Amoskeag No. 1, one hand engine, Deluge hose wagon, steamer hose wagon, one hook and ladder truck, one relief truck, poor, two jumpers, 5,600 feet hose, six Babcock extinguishers, four engineers' lanterns, two hydrant gates, two Y couplings, one Siamese couplings, one cellar pipe, six ladder dogs, uniforms, rubber coats and rubber boots for Steamer Co., uniforms, rubber coats and rubber boots for Hook and Ladder Co., uniforms, rubber coats and rubber boots for Deluge Hose Co., one sled for Hook and Ladder Co., one sled for Steamer Hose Co., one sled for Deluge Hose Co., new, four set swing harnesses.

Signals and General Rules remain the same as adopted by the board of Engineers, December 2nd, 1887 and are still in force.

The telephone alarm Box 22 which is located in the central telephone office is still pulled to sound all alarms of fire by phone.

Report of the Superintendent of Fire Alarm

The condition of the fire alarm system, which was defective last year by reason of frequent contacts with the wires of the Keene Gas Light Power Company, has been improved by placing the fire alarm wires above those attached to the light and power poles, wherever it was necessary to cross them.

The fire alarm line was extended to the house of 'engineer Louis A. Nims, at West Keene, requiring about a mile of wire, and also to the village of South Keene, requiring about three miles of additional wire. New Fire alarm Boxes have been added box number 19, on Lower Marlboro Street, and alarm box number 65 near the Keene Electric Railway Company's power station, the mills of D. R. & F. A. Cole, affording greater protection to those commercial plants, and the numerous dwellings in the village.

The present system comprises seventeen miles of wire, twenty-seven pairs of magnets, a battery of one hundred and fifty cells, twenty-four alarm boxes, two public alarm bells and numerous private call bells for firemen.

Respectfully,

J. F. EMMONS, Superintendent of Fire Alarm.

Fires and Losses for Year ending November 30th, 1901.

December 6th, 1900 at 8.42 p.m. a Still to Church Street the W. H. Brooks house for a Chimney fire.

December 11th, 1900 at 1.23 p.m. Box 13 for Beaver Mills for a Lamp explosion.

December 27th, 1900 at 4.45 p.m. a still alarm to Pearl Street for Sparks from a Locomotive.

January 5th, 1901 at 6.50 a.m. a Still alarm to the Ball's Block for a Chimney fire with damage of $12.00 and Insurance paid $12.00.

January 13th, 1901 at 5.40 p.m. a Still alarm to the F. E. Keyes Hayward Est. Store for a Chimney fire. Damage $50.00 and Insurance paid $50.00.

January 15th, 1901 at 8.23 p. m. Box 22 Winchester Street to the F. A. Hopkins for a house and barn fire. Damage $1,200 and Insurance paid $1,075.

February 1st, 1901 at 6.00 p.m. on a still for Page Street the W. H. Hill for a Chimney fire. No damage reported.

February 3rd, 1901 at 10.20 p.m. on a Still alarm to the Y.M.C.A. block on West Street for an overheated boiler. No reported damage.

February 7th, 1901 at 3.15 p.m. on a still alarm to Ashuelot Street the Faulkner & Colony House for a chimney fire with no reported damage.

February 14th, 1901 at 12.55 p.m. on a Still alarm to the Abbott Lane House on Court Street for a chimney fire with no damage.

March 10th, 1901 at 10.15 on a still alarm to Mrs. Hubbard House Court Street for an ash pile fire. No damage.

March 28th, 1901 at 11.25 p.m. to the I. Longiver House and barn on Sullivan Street for unknown fire. Unknown damage reported and Insurance paid $35.00.

April 1st, 1901 at 11.35 p.m. Box 52 for the B.& M.R.R. Repair Shop for Lime Dust.

April 5th, 1901 at 11.42 Box 9 West Street the Y.M.C.A. Block for an unknown fire. Damage $125.00 and Insurance paid $125.00.

April 10th, 1901 at 8.12 p.m. a Still alarm to Central Square the George H. Colony block for Lace curtains on fire. Damage $40.00 and Insurance paid $40.00.

April 20th, 1901 at 8.45 a.m. on a Still alarm to the Brown House on Sullivan Street for a Chimney fire with no damage.

April 29th, 1901 9.00 a.m. on a Still alarm to the Chas Reid House on Franklin Street for a Furnace problem, no damage reported.

May 3rd, 1901 at 1.15 p.m. on a Still alarm to the Jordan House on Butler Court for a Chimney fire with no damage reported.

May 15th, 1901 at 4.17 p.m. Box 22 for the J. W. Buckminster Wood lot for a Brush fire.

May 19th, 1901 at 8.00 a.m. on a Still alarm Main Street to the E. F. Lane Block for a Furnace problem. No damage reported.

May 26th, 1901 at 6.00 a.m. for a Still alarm at the C. G. Sheed House on Marlboro Street for a Defective fire place fire. Damage $65.00 and Insurance paid $65.00.

June 17th, 1901 at 4.32 p.m. for Box 8 Railroad Street the C. A. Jones Factory for a gasoline fire. No damage reported.

June 17th, and 18th, 1901 both still alarms to Robin Hood Park for Brush fires. The 17th, at 8.30 p.m. and the 18th, at 7.45 p.m.

June 26th, 1901 for a Still alarm at 7.10 p.m. to the City High School on Middle Street for Burning paper in boiler no reported damage.

July 2nd, 1901 at 7.05 p.m. on a Still alarm to Robin Hood Park for a Brush fire.

July 13th, 1901 for a Still alarm at 1.00 a.m. at the Impervious Pkg. Co. on Mechanic Street for Sparks from the boiler. No reported damage.

July 17th, 1901 at 5.44 p.m. Box 8 for C. A. Jones Factory on Railroad Street for a gasoline fire. Damage $155.00 and Insurance paid $155.00.

July 22nd, 1901 at 2.15 p.m. on a Still Alarm to the City High School on Middle Street for an unknown fire. Damage $100 and Insurance paid $100.00.

July 23rd, 1901 at 3.50 p.m. to Box 37 the Keene Steam Power Co. factory off Mechanic Street for Dust on top of boilers. Damage $176.00 and Insurance paid $176.00.

July 28th, 1901 at 2.50 a.m. Box 8 for Holbrook Grocery Co. Store. Also a 2nd call to the Holbrook Grocery Co. at 9.45 p.m. on St. James Street for a probable Incendiary fire. Damage was $59,000 and Insurance paid $44,000.

September 15th, 1901 at 5.40 a.m. on a Still alarm to Mechanic Street the Keene Steam Power Co. Factory for a fire caused by Ashes from the fire box. No damage reported.

September 17th, 1901 at 6.30 p.m. Box 13 Beaver Mills boiler room for a boiler room fire. Unknown damage.

September 27th, 1901 at 3.35 p.m. to Box 13 the Colburn House on 93rd. Street for wood ashes on fire. Also at 6.45 p.m. on a still and also at 8.26 p.m. for a 2nd call to the same Box. Damage reported was $1,285.00 and Insurance paid $1,285.00.

September 30th, 1901 at 8.00 p.m. on a Still alarm to Central Square the Gerould Block for a fire caused by Spontaneous combustion. No damage reported.

October 12th, 1901 at 10.00 p.m. on a Still alarm the F. Pett's House on Washington Street for a Chimney fire with no damage reported.

October 21st, 1901 at 7.55 p.m. on a Still alarm to the Horatio Colony House on West Street for a chimney fire with no damage reported.

November 14th, 1901 at 7.30 p.m. on a Still alarm to Davis Street the A. W. Eastman House for a chimney fire with no reported damage.

November 17th, 1901 at 8.05 a.m. on a Still alarm to the D. H. Woodward House on Court street for a Chimney fire with no reported damage.

November 18th, 1901 at 4.00 p.m. on a Still alarm to the L. J. Brooks House on West Street for a chimney fire with no reported damage.

November 28th, 1901 at 8.00 p.m. on a Still alarm to the H. E. White House on Lincoln Street for a chimney fire with no damage reported.

November 28th, 1901 at 11.40 a.m. on a Still alarm to the Faulkner & Colony House for a chimney fire off Ashuelot Street. No reported damage.

November 29th, 1901 at 12.43 a.m. Box 22 for the Chesterfield Road the H. R. Parker Mill for an unknown type fire. Damage $700.00 and no Insurance reported.

November 30th, 1901 at 4.35 p.m. on a Still alarm the Mrs. Gould House on Beaver Street for a chimney fire.

Note: There were 48 calls in all and 15 calls from boxes and 33 were still alarms.

Ordinances and Joint Resolutions ending for the year 1901

On January 17th, 1901 a Joint Resolution was passed relating to the purchase of fire hose and a suitable Siamese coupling, not to exceed seven hundred dollars.

On March 21st, 1901 a Joint Resolution was passed to purchase a sufficient number of rubber coats, hats and boots for the use of the fire department not to exceed $125.00.

A Joint Resolution was passed on September 5th, 1901 relating to the extension of fire alarm telegraph to the village of South Keene. The sum of $185.00 to constructing a line of fire alarm telegraph wire from the present terminus on Marlboro Street near Kelleher Street to a convenient point between the power house of the Keene Electric Railway Company and F. B. Pierce's mills for the purchase of a Stevens fire alarm box and the incidental changes required at the battery room.

A Resolution passed September 20th, 1901 for $60.00 for the annual inspection of Keene Fire Department.

A Joint Resolution was passed on October 3rd, 1901 to purchase a fire alarm box number 511 to be placed on Marlboro Street for the sum of $50.00.

[*Compiler's Note*: Horses were shared throughout the city and Resolution at times is unclear if it was one of the fire department fire horses or other department horses to be replaced.]

Reported in the *New Hampshire Sentinel* Keene, N.H. Wednesday, July 31, 1901:

"FIRE"

FIRE LOSS OF $70,000 At Holbrook Grocery Co.'s. Wholesale Warehouse.

On July 28th, 1901 a Dangerous Fire Breaks Out at 250 Sunday Morning.

Flames Controlled after an Hour and a half of Lively Work.

The most dangerous fire that Keene has had near its mercantile center for a number of years broke out at 250 Sunday morning in the large wholesale warehouse of the Holbrook Grocery Company on St. James Street. The flames burst out with much fury from the second and third stories, the entire building being well heated and filled with dense smoke. It looked as if the whole structure was doomed. The proximity of so many wooden buildings on three sides, the Abbot Grocery Company's large wholesale warehouse and the large buildings on the Lamson estate caused much anxiety. Fortunately there was no wind. The firemen attacked the flames repeatedly within three or four minutes and fought with system, coolness and persistency, and in an hour and a half had won a single victory. Subduing the fire in the lower stories very soon, they afterwards conquered the flames to the upper or third floor. The building contained a large stock of groceries of all kinds valued at $75,000 or more on which there will be but a small salvage it is claimed. The insurance is $13,500. The loss upon the building is estimated at $3,000. The probable loss, not reckoning insurance is about $70,000.

The fire broke out with a noise like an explosion, it is said, which was heard by several persons, among them Dr. J. B. Duffy, who was at his office in the Gurnsey building. Night yardmaster Barron said his men of the Boston & Main road also saw the flames at once and hastened to give an alarm, but Dr. Duffy reached box 8 first and pulled it in. The railroad men had been in the yard near the building shortly before and had seen nothing said Officer Sweeney had been through that section on his regular beat not long before. Mr. Barron says he had just noticed the odor of wood smoke, and was about to investigate.

Officer Sweeney, who came down with the first hose wagon, says the bulk of the fire appeared to be in the third story, and broke out on the west side near the center some way toward the north of the side doors and others to the south. It was soon seen that there was fire on first and second floors also near the south end. Those approaching from the East Side also saw the fire through the windows.

The men at the fire station made quick hitches and hose lines were laid in from three to five minutes, and the attack begun. The Button was the first call engine. It was station at the hydrant at the foot of St. James Street on Railroad Square. Hose lines were laid from the hydrant, the hydrant at the depot and the West street hydrant near Kirk & Seawall's. The Button was ready to play at 3 o'clock.

Driver Fay returned at once with the steamer horses to get the Amoskeag engine. In spite of the pauses for hitching and unhitching the broken winded horses on his team was hard pressed for breath, and before reaching the hydrant with the second engine the animals began to stagger and would have fallen had not the team been stopped short. The men on the Amoskeag started to set the engine at the Sentinel building but Chief Towne ordered them to the hydrant at Kirk & Seawall's, where hose lines were ready.

When the Button began playing Byron E. Robertson and another man, whom he says was not a fireman, had one of the lines of hose on a ladder on the west side of the building, playing into a second story window. The man left the ladder about the time the engine began to increase the previous pressure and the reaction of the stream threw the ladder sideways, precipitating Mr. Robertson to the ground with a good deal of violence. He struck on his shoulder and hip. Although much bruised and shaken up he went to work again after a few moments, but had to give up in half an hour and go home. After the hose got loose some men caught it and tried to hold it and play a stream, again the hose got away from them. More regular pipe men had arrived by that time and there was no further trouble in holding the hose lines.

The falling ladder above referred to struck William Winn of the Ladder Company, His left foot and ankle and his right foot was both severely bruised and his leg, shoulder and wrist hurt. He was taken home and probably will not be able to work for several days.

An unsteadiness at times in directing the streams so that they were ineffective was noticed, but this was largely due to the interference of the different hose lines while some of them were being moved by order of the engineers. It was noted that during the fight, the men held their positions as directed by Chief Towne and his assistants, and did not move them with orders.

There were from eight to ten streams brought to bear on the burning building. Of these the Button steamer supplied 4 and the Amoskeag 2, being farther away. This engine could have carried a third stream through a Y coupling but it was not well to shut off a line to make the change. The hydrant streams did very good work.

The ladder service was more speedy and efficient than usual and Capt. Tenney and his men are entitled to commendation therefor. All company's ladders were used and it was apparent that more of them would have been badly needed had the fire been in a longer or taller building or had it spread.

There were windows at the top of the elevator well, above the roof, and the fire broke out there by the time the firemen got to work. The blaze in the second story was soon checked and what fire there was on the lower floor gave no trouble. The fire at the north end of the building was very hot when opened indicating that the fire had been burning some time. The entire building was filled with dense smoke.

The upper story was the main seat of the fire by 3:20 and was a mass of flames suppressed for want of air. At 3:30 the firemen appeared to be checking the blaze, but in 10 minutes angry toughens of flame appeared above the roof and through the windows all over the upper story. The flames were also approaching under the eves all along the north end and in spots on the south, east and west sides. The fire was very hot and it looked too many as if the entire building would be speedily consumed.

Chief Towne and his assistants thought differently, however, and the chief said to Mayor Perry, when questioned, that if nothing gave out he should hold the fire. Engineer Carrigan was emphatically of the same opinion. This did not look possible on the north and east side where the whole upper floor was blazing brightly, but the four big streams projected through the doors and windows from well station ladders on the west were doing their work and two or more lines on both the south and west ends from roofs and ladders effective. Evidently the heavy plank floor of the third story was not burning through, but was holding water. This was of the greatest advantage. At 1 o'clock the firemen were advancing into the upper story on the West Side. The attention then begun to change rapidly, and at 1:30 the fire was well out on the upper floor and entirely under control.

Before the building could be inspected, the men of the proprietors and others were that the fire probably caught among a quantity of matches on the upper floor, being set, perhaps by rats. On entering the building, however, it was apparent that it had burned earlier on the lower floor. The timbers being deeply charred and the sheathing of a partition burned off. The fire on this floor was a pretty hot and extensive one, and was not extinguished till the firemen put it out. From this point the flames mounted the elevator well and the blaze or the intense heat that went up the shaft like a chimney, ignited cases near the shaft on the upper floor. There was a large quantity of ignitable material, which sprung into flame, that may have caused the fire to break out and caused the explosion.

Further investigation Monday morning pointed to the basement as the origin of the fire. In the basement ten or fifteen feet from the elevator and stairway near the doors on the west side was a barrel of rubbish. Cases of goods were stacked all around it. A glass kerosene can was kept on a shelf near there. Officers Lawrence says he found this can on the floor near the waste barrel. The entire top of this barrel and whatever was in it is consumed to within 6 or 8 inches of the bottom. The plank floor timbers and tiers of boxes show a well-defined path where the fire worked to the stairway near the elevator well. Thence up to the first floor and then along the sheathing partition above mentioned and into the room where the cases of goods were much burned. The elevator car was down, closing the well hole through the first floor.

Another peculiar thing in the basement near a doorway leading north at the foot of the stairway was large timber virtually a part of the door casing is well charred near the tip where there may have been a picky spot. Against this timber is built a sheathing partition for a coal bin running north. In the middle of this partition some 5 feet from the doorway, a hole some 8 inches deep and 6 inches wide is completely burned out of the sheathing. On the inside is a mark indicating that some very flammable article that was so completely burned that no trace of it could be found, what ever hung over the side of the bin, where it had left a well scorched outline below the hole burned in the sheathing. This must have been the cause or the spot must have been saturated with oil. There is also another slightly scorched place just beyond.

The latter fire and the fire in and around the rubbish barrel, both went out of themselves evidently, but not until the rubbish barrel fire had started the fire around the stairway on the first floor which became much hotter and did not go out of itself. No water was thrown onto the basement to put out the fire and not could have run down so as to do it. The proprietors are of opinion that the fire surely caught in this basement rubbish barrel, and others, who have examined it, agree with them. They know of no way it

could have caught there unless it was set. If this is so it is a question whether the coal bin fire was also set, or whether it caught from the barrel fire, Spontaneous combustion or something having fire in it accidentally put into the barrel are of course also suggested.

The warehouse was a three-story structure 88 to 98 feet in size, built in 1891 especially for the business. It was heavily timbered and had tight plank floors. It contained the company's office, a coffee roasting and milling plant and a large stock of groceries mainly in cases and boxes, and including canned and bottled goods, coffee, teas, spices, and the like, and some flour and sugar. The stock was valued at from $75,000 to $80,000. It is claimed that there can be but a small salvage on the goods, all of which are injured by smoke or water. The labels on canned goods and the like will come off, and it is said the goods in tins must be quickly sold to prevent routing. The company carried an insurance of $10,000, of which $4,000 was on the building. The company has other storehouses and buildings here and elsewhere, and will continue business as usual. The building will be repaired as soon as possible. A temporary office has been opened in the St. James parish home basement.

Holbrook Grocery Wholesale Warehouse fire broke out in the front of the building pictured above on St. James Street, Keene. Photo by Bion H. Whitehouse. HSCC collection.

The story of this fire should not omit a word of commendation for the excellent work of the firemen. Officers and men are both to be commended on their good and systematic work. Chief Towne had one thing done as a time, as a rule, saw that each thing was well done and kept his force steadily advancing. Engineers, officers and men carried out their orders quick and with out confusion. The building shows the excellence of their work. The entire lack of wind sided with the department.

The firemen were called back by the building by a still alarm about 8 o'clock Sunday evening, the fire having burned up cases of goods. About 9 PM they were again called. The number of men available was found insufficient and box 8 was pulled at 9:13, the steamer having ordered not to respond. The fires that had broken out were quickly put out after handling over some of the goods. Police officers and other watchmen were kept on the premises Sunday and Monday. It is expected to be three or four days before the underwriters adjust the insurance, a large number of companies being involved that will probably want to have representatives here.

STEAM FIRE ENGINE AND HOSE CO.
1883-OF KEENE, N.H.-1901
B.F. Robertson H.N. Aldrich F.N. Shaw F.J. Bennett D.W. Mitchell
P. Langdon H.G Cram Lt. W.H Hill G.F Stone M.V.B Clark J.A Denison J.E Wyman F.W Wellington
Foreman of Hose   Treas.   Asst. Foreman of Hose
E. O. Rice A.W. Green Capt. W. K. Church Sam Whitney G. B.Robertson J.P.Morse
H. L. Barrett C. S. Aldrich F.F. Stearns J. H. Simpson G. C. Buckminster

1902 [from *City of Keene Annual Report*]
Report of the Chief Engineer of the Fire Department
To His Honor the Mayor and City Councils:

Herewith please find the report for fire department for the year ending December 1st, 1902.

During the year forty-nine alarms have been responded to, twenty-two of which were bell calls and twenty-seven were still alarms.

Eight hundred feet of hose has been bought, and seven hundred feet given out entirely which cannot be replaced. Several times during the year we have had temporal an insufficient amount of dry hose being added, which will be little more than make up for constant depreciation. Moor tower attachments are needed to facilitate the drying hose.

The efficiency of the department has been materially increased by the addition of a new ladder truck with the equipment of long ladders. For a long time the department had felt the need of more long ladders, but with the new piece of apparatus we are well supplied with ladders in the event of fires in our tallest buildings. Under the present condition truck No. 1 responds to all first alarms leaving truck No. 2 in reserve. This arrangement allowed for protection while truck No. 1 is out on duty, and in case of a large fire both can be called into service if the occasion requires.

Two extension ladders have been bought, one for each hose wagon, for use at chimney fires, etc., and the Amoskeag engine has been repainted. Ladder truck No 1, needs repainting, and if in your judgment it is deemed wise to have done, it would seem that the most favorable time for it would be while the ladders are on runners. The new reservoir in Roxbury has added considerably to the hydrant pressure, besides giving protection at South Keene.

Very frequently we are called to fires when extinguishers are inadequate to the occasion, and hydrant steams tend to cause more or less water damage. This weakness could be remedied by procuring a combination chemical engine. It is very apparent that losses could in many instances be lessened with an engine of this kind, and I assure that a full investigation by you would warrant the purchase of one of these machines.

The chief has been approached several times as to the advisability of placing a fire alarm box on the fire station. There seems to be much in favor of this suggestion and I would call your attention to the matter. One of the most suitable acquisitions to the department is the cellar pipe, the one is hardly sufficient for the present needs. With one or two exceptions, which I have alluded to, the apparatus and appendages are in excellent condition. I desire to express my thanks to my assistants and the members of the department; also to the city government, for their attention and courtesies and for caring for the wants of the department.

Very respectfully,
FRED W. TOWNE, Chief Engineer Keene December 12th, 1902.

Inventory of Property

Steamer Button No. 2, Steamer Amoskeag No. 1, one hand engine, Deluge hose wagon, steamer hose wagon, two hook and ladder trucks, two jumpers, 5,7000 feet hose, six Babcock extinguishers, four engineers' lanterns, two hydrant gates, two Y couplings, one Siamese coupling, one cellar pipe, six ladder dogs, uniforms, rubber coats and rubber boots for Hook and Ladder Co., uniforms, rubber coats and rubber boots for Deluge Hose Co., one sled for Hook and Ladder Co., one sled for Steamer Hose Co., one sled for Deluge Hose Co., new, four sets swing harnesses.

Signals and General Rules

The signals that were adopted December 2nd, 1887 remain in force as do the General Rules for giving alarms of fire.

Report of Superintendent of Fire Alarm

The general condition of the fire alarm telegraph system in the city is good. The fire alarm was extended to the house of Engineer Foley requiring about 600 feet of wire. A new Fire alarm box number 26 was added to the corner of Spring and Brook Street.

On September 4th, 1902 the councils accepted, free of expense, the fire alarm wire and other property of the Keene Private Line Association, for the use of firemen and others. All applications for connections with the private line shall be made to the joint standing committee on fire department and all connections shall be made by the superintendent of the fire alarm telegraph. The Rental for such line shall be $3.00 for fireman and for all other others $5.00 and this will be an annual fee.

Respectfully,
J.F. EMMONS, Superintendent of Fire Alarm Keene, December 12th, 1902.
[*Note*: The fire alarm report was reduced by this writer.]

The above horse, named Jack was purchased to pull fire apparatus for the Keene Fire Department in 1901. Jack was a member of the Keene Fire Department until 1912.

"FIRE"

RUST'S FACTORY BURNED.
THE LARGEST PAIL MAKING
ESTABLISHMENT IN KEENE

On February 10th, 1902 A Fire Was Hot and Lively One for About an Hour-Wooden Buildings Went up like tinder –Loss Estimated at $35,000, Largely Insured.

John P. Rust's large pail manufacturing establishment on Water Street was destroyed by a fire, which caught about 10:50 o'clock Monday morning around the fuel collectors over the engine room. By noon the entire plant was a mass of ruins. The loss is estimated at $35,000; insurance $25,000. About 80 hands are thrown out of employment.

The fire was first seen by some of the employees in the mill yard and was then burning on the roof of the engine room, which was really a part of the main building. It probably ignited around the cyclone fuel collector pipes from a spark from the chimney. The men hustled out with the pails and other apparatus provided for quick work, and succeeded in putting out the fire outside of the roof. But there was some dust filled crack or crevice, through which the fire crept inside, where it could not be reached.

The mill whistle was sounded as soon as the fire was discovered and a locomotive near by aided in giving the alarm. It was some moments before an alarm was rung in from box 14, which was the nearest to the shops. A shoe factory employee named Ernest Fletcher saw the fire it is said, jumped out of a window and pulled the box. The Deluge hose horses were at the station and Driver Rice was near at hand with the grays. Driver Dean made a quick start with the hose sled and Rice followed soon with the hook and ladder wagon. There was a short delay in waiting for the steamer horses and also for Driver Reid, who was away with his team, and it was also necessary to drive cautiously on the icy streets. The response of the department was about an average day response.

By the time the firemen reached the mill a large section of the upper part of the main building had a floor area of about 133x50 feet in the main part, with various wings and additions. A good portion of it was two stories high. There were numerous dry houses, storage buildings, etc., near it, the whole plant being of wood, except the engine and boiler house, and this was not fire proof. The building was coated, inside with the dry powder-like dust, which accumulates in such shops, and there was no possibility of saving it after the fire got fairly started. There was a paint shop in the second story containing much in flammable materials.

There were three alarms rung in from box 14 after the fire began and all the apparatus was got down there as soon as possible. The steamers were set on the Beaver Brook Bridge, leaving a full aqueduct pressure for the hydrant streams. The firemen got lines of hose laid so as to attack the main building, but as this was doomed it was soon seen that the danger lay to the south, west and east, where the saw mill is situated and where there were huge piles of pine planks estimated to contain from 500,000 to 800,000 feet of lumber. The wind was blowing quite freshly from the northwest and with the numerous small buildings near the piles of lumber and the main building it looked at one time as if the lumber and the sawmill, some distance south of the main shop and it annexes, would go.

The firemen had considerable difficulty in getting through the mill yard to extend their hose lines, owing to the burning debris and the heat and smoke from the buildings. Lines were finally run through, however, and the flames checked in their southerly course so that most of the lumber and the sawmill was saved.

Early in the fire agent Parkman of the Boston & Main road got out two locomotives and pulled several cars out of the mill yard. Later cars were provided on which to load and remove some of the lumber.

Mr. Rust is out of town, being away on a western trip, it is understood.

It is impossible to obtain a reliable estimate of the value of the property burned, but $35,000 is considered by many a conservative figure. The insurance on the buildings and their contents was about $25,000, besides which, there was insurance on the lumber. There were several hundred cords of pile logs in the mill yard, but they are green and were not injured. There were also large quantities of staves in racks, which were saved. Mr. Rust lost a large amount of special machinery.

Fires and Losses for the Year Ending November 30th, 1902.

December 6th, 1901 at 4.05 p.m. Box 13 for the Coburn House on 93rd Street for a chimney fire with no reported damage.

December 21st, 1901 at 4.02 a.m. for Box 8 Main Street the Mrs. Doolittle House for a house fire. Cause was Cigarette or cigar stub. Damage was $577.00 and Insurance paid $577.00.

December 23rd, 1901 at 8.15 a.m. for Box 18 Kelleher Street for the Phillips House for a fire caused by Spontaneous combustion. Damage $130.00 and Insurance paid $130.00

January 7th, 1902 at 5.10 a.m. for Box 24 Oak Street the J. W. Buckminster House for a chimney fire with $140.00 dollars' worth of damage and Insurance paid $140.00.

January 8th, 1902 at 12.40 p.m. on a Still alarm to the F. O. Nims House on Green Street for a chimney fire with no reported damage.

January 11th, 1902 at 12.10 p.m. on a Still alarm to the Mrs. Asa Smith on Washington Street for a chimney fire with no reported damage.

January 12th, 1902 at 4.00 p.m. on a Still alarm to Central Square the Gerould Block for a chimney fire with $35.00 dollars damage. Insurance paid $35.00.

January 15th, 1902 at 7.35 p.m. on a Still alarm the Mrs. Osborne on Court Street for an over-filled Kerosene stove. No damage reported.

January 25th, 1902 at 12.07 p.m. for Box 13 Church Street the Charles Putney House for an overheated stove pipe with $25.00 dollars damage and Insurance paid $25.00.

January 27th, 1902 at 6.20 p.m. on a Still alarm to the John Cullinance House on Island Street for a chimney fire. No reported damage.

January 31st, 1902 at 8.00 a.m. on a Still alarm to the C. B Lancaster Co. Shoe factory on Dunbar Street for sparks in a heater. No reported damage.

February 2nd, 1902 at 4.50 p.m. on a Still alarm to the A. S. Bruder House on Main Street for a Chimney fire. No reported damage.

February 8th, 1902 at 11.00 p.m. A Still alarm for Cheshire National Bank and the alarm was a police call. Honest mistake.

February 10th, 1902 at 10.50 a.m. Box 14 to Water Street the J. P. Rust Pail Factory for a fire caused by sparks from the furnace. Damage $35,000 and insurance paid $23,400.

February 24th, 1902 at 7.45 a.m. on a Still alarm to the P. O'Leary House on Beaver Street for a Chimney fire with no reported damage.

March 1st, 1902 at 6.35 p.m. for Box 25 for Washington Street for a false alarm.

March 15th, 1902 at 3.00 p.m. on a Still alarm to the A. B. Peters House on High Street for a Chimney fire. No reported damage.

March 19th, 1902 at 6.20 a.m. for Box 18 Foster Street the Mrs. Parker House for a Chimney fire with no reported damage.

March 26th, 1902 at 9.30 p.m. the F. Ellis House on George Street for a Chimney fire. No reported damage.

March 28th, 1902 at 3.15 a.m. for Box 37 Impervious Pkg. Factory on Mechanic Street for an unknown type fire. Damage $3,355.54 and Insurance paid $2,354.54.

March 28th, 1902 at 1.00 p.m. on a Still alarm to Park Ave. the Wellman property for a brush fire.

March 31st, 1902 at 12:00 noon for Box 18 South Street the W. Hannon House for a chimney fire with no reported damage.

April 1st, 1902 at 8.00 a.m. on a Still alarm to the Hopkins House on Winchester Street for a chimney fire with no reported damage.

April 19th, 1902 at 1.05 p.m. Box 22 the Arba Stearns property on West Street for a brush fire.

April 24th, 1902 at 1.15 p.m. on a Still alarm to Taylor Street the Wilbur Knight House for a Chimney fire with no reported damage.

April 27th, 1902 at 2.40 p.m. on a Still alarm to Pearl Street the Don Staples House for a Chimney fire with no reported damage.

April 29th, 1902 at 3.45 p.m. on a Still alarm to Island Street the John Sweeney House for a chimney fire with no reported damage.

April 30th, 1902 at 8.40 a.m. on a Still alarm to Willow Street the Levi Randall House for a Chimney fire with no reported damage.

May 9th, 1902 at 10.40 a.m. on a Still alarm to Myrtle Street the J. S. Taft House for a Chimney fire with no reported damage.

May 15th, 1902 at 7.15 p.m. on a Still alarm to Carroll Street the John Fitzgerald House for a Chimney fire with no reported damage.

May 18th, 1902 at 2.15 p.m. on a Still alarm to Spruce Street the L. Martell for the remains of the mill which was a bonfire.

May 23rd, 1902 at 1.30 p.m. on a Still alarm to Dunbar Street the C. H. Ellis House for a furnace problem with no reported damage.

May 28th, 1902 at 6.25 a.m. on a Still alarm to 10 Dunbar Street the C. Putney House for a Chimney fire.

June 8th, 1902 at 5.50 p.m. on a Still alarm to Ashuelot Ct. the Faulkner & Colony House for a Chimney fire with no reported damage.

June 16th, 1902 at 11.20 p.m. for Box 13 the Beaver Mill Dry House on Railroad Street for an unknown fire. Damage $3,500 and Insurance paid $2,050.

June 18th, 1902 at 9.00 a.m. for Box 23 Spring Street the Mrs. Tiffin House for a Spontaneous combustion fire. Damage $125.00 and Insurance paid $110.00.

June 21st, 1902 at 3.10 a.m. for Box 8 the G. E. Holbrook & Co. Store House on railroad Street for an Incendiary fire. Damage $2,600 and Insurance paid $2,211.00.

July 2nd, 1902 at 2.00 a.m. on a Still alarm to the Dunn & Salisbury Chair Factory on Emerald Street for an Incendiary Extinguished fire. No reported damage.

July 12th, 1902 at 10.45 p.m. for Box 25 Washington Street the Charles Giffin Pail Factory for Sparks from a locomotive by B.&M. Damage $10,000 and No insurance reported possible B. & M. paid.

July 16th, 1902 at 9.30 a.m. on a Still alarm to High Street the P. H. McCushing House for a Chimney fire. No reported damage.

September 14th, 1902 at 11.15 p.m. for Box 9 Central Square the G. H. Colony Block. Fire caused by Spontaneous combustion. No reported damage.

September 18th, 1902 at 4.30 a.m. for Box 24 Page Street the Francis Truth House for a Chimney fire with damage of $100.00 and Insurance paid $100.00.

September 25th, 1902 at 9.30 p.m. on a Still alarm for Roxbury Street the Hayward Block for smoke in the building with no reported damage.

September 26th, 1902 at 10.00 p.m. for a Still alarm on Dunbar Street the C. B. Lancaster Co. Shoe Factory for an Incendiary extinguished fire. No reported damage.

October 23rd, 1902 at 1.15 a.m. for Box 13 on Railroad Street the Mrs. Hattie Hill Store house for a fire caused by the B. & M. Engine. Damage $2,650.00 and Insurance paid $2,100.00.

October 31st, 1902 at 3.50 p.m. for Box 43 the Faulkner & Colony House on Ashuelot Ct. for an unknown fire, Damage $176.65 and Insurance paid $76.65.

November 1st, 1902 at 6.30 p.m. on a Still alarm to Wyman Way the Joseph Bolster House for a Chimney fire with no reported damage.

November 7th, 1902 at 3.00 p.m. on a Still alarm to Roxbury Street the E. C. Tolman House for a fire place problem. No reported damage.

November 20th, 1902 at 9.00 a.m. for Box 8 Main Street the Mrs. L. Martin Livery stable for an overheated stove pipe with no reported damage.

November 29th, at 8.15 p.m. on a Still alarm to Washington Street the D. L. Hill Factory for a Chimney fire with no reported damage.

November 29th, 1902 at 10.35 p.m. for Box 8 on Church Street the F. Pete's Store for an unknown type fire. Damage $605.00 and Insurance paid $555.00.

Note for the year 51 call in all and 21 call from boxes and 30 still alarms.

Ordinances and Joint Resolutions for the year ending 1902.

On December 19th, the city council passed the purchased a resolution relating to wardrobes for the fire station. The sum of seventeen dollars.

A Joint Resolution was passed on February 6th, 1902 for a special committee for the matter of procuring a suitable ladder truck and a sufficient number of ladders to equip the same.

A Resolution was passed on February 6th, 1902 for the sum of $75.00 for the painting of the Amoskeag fire steamer.

On March 6th, 1902 a Joint Resolution was passed that the superintendent of streets be and hereby is instructed to furnish the said committee with two pair of city's horses and drivers there for, for the purposes aforesaid; but such horses hall always be at the absolute disposal of the proper authorities whenever required for the use of the fire department.

A Joint Resolution was passed relating to the hook and ladder truck, etc. That the sum of $1,273.08 be hereby appropriated for the purchase of the said ladder truck.

A Joint Resolution was passed to the purchase of fire hose and ladders. The ladders were two twenty-foot extension ladders, suitable for use in answering still alarms. Passed May 1st, 1902.

A Joint Resolution was passed on September 4th, relating to private fire alarm system, and how the applications and connections and other related fees will work.

1903 [from *City of Keene Annual Report*]

Report of the Chief Engineer of the Fire Department.

To His Honor the Mayor and City Councils:

During the fiscal year which closed December 1st, 1903, there have been seventy-nine fire calls; fifty four of them being still alarms and twenty-five calls; bell alarms. Sixteen calls, which proved to be the worst fires, occurred in the night. No doubt the extensive use of wood, owning to the coal famine, was in a great measure accountable for the large number of chimney fires, nearly all of which came under the head of still alarms.

There have been more firemen sleeping at headquarters during the past year than in previous years, which has resulted in far better and quicker night service. I think it is safe to say that this feature had tended to lessen the losses. For detailed list of fires, etc. see appended list.

Eleven hundred (1100) feet of new hose has been purchased, making the total amount now on had 6,300 feet. Attention has been called in my previous reports to better ways for caring for hose with a view to increasing its duration of wear. If we are to get all there is out of hose, it must have proper care and this we are, at times, unable to give it, as the present facilities are entirely in sufficient to dry wet hose. At a comparatively small outlay, the towers can be so arranged as to accommodate nearly double the amount of hose they do at present. Several times during the past years, a number of days have elapsed before wet hose could be strung up and we have had also to resort to drying in the open air, which has not proved very successful.

There is no doubt but what hose can be made to last longer than it does, if we have the facilities to care for it as it should be. I wish to lay especial stress upon this issue as it is very doubtful economy to allow property to go to ruin from lack of care. Two (2) new pipes, fitted with shut-off nozzles, have been added to the equipment, also, rubber coats, hats, and boots. Ladder truck No. 1 has been newly painted and alterations made on the running board. Both hose wagons need touching up and re-varnishing.

I would call your attention to the advisability of a fire alarm box being placed on outside of fire station. This subject has been brought to my notice many times, both as to occasions when we have needed it, and by citizens expressing themselves as believing it would be a wise thing to do. The five gallon extinguishers now in use are very difficult to use in many instances, and I would ask that you consider the advisability of procuring some smaller ones, also a cellar pipe. The cellar pipe has been demonstrated to be one of the most useful pieces of apparatus in the department. We have only one, but with the liability of it being crippled, together with the probability of an occasion arising, when we may need more than one leads me to feel that another should be bought. There is a strong feeling in the department, as well as outside, that the merits of a combination chemical and hose wagon should be investigated. I am free to say that there is much in favor of these machines, and am sure if the matter was thoroughly looked into you would find much to warrant the purchasing of one for the department.

In concluding my report, I take this opportunity to thank my assistants and the member of this department for their support and faithfulness; also to extend to your body, my assurance of my fullest appreciation of your interest in the department's welfare, which has been so manifest.

Yours respectfully,
F. W. TOWNE,
Chief Keene Fire Department.
December 1st, 1903.

Inventory of Property

Steamer Button No. 2, Steamer Amoskeag No. 1, one hand engine, Deluge hose wagon, steamer hose wagon, two hook and ladder trucks, two jumpers, 6,300 feet hose, six Babcock extinguishers, four engineers' lanterns, two hydrant gates, two Y couplings, one Siamese coupling, one cellar pipe, six ladder dogs, uniforms, rubber coats and rubber boots for Steamer Co., uniforms, rubber coats and rubber boots for Hook and Ladder Co., uniforms, rubber coats and rubber boots for Deluge Hose Co., one sled for Hook and Ladder Co., one sled for Steamer Hose Co., one sled for Deluge Hose Co., new, four sets swing harnesses.

Signals and General Rules remain as adopted December 2nd, 1887.

Report of the Superintendent of Fire Alarms.

The general condition of the fire alarm telegraph system is good. A new Box has been placed at the corner of Spring and Brook Streets and numbered 26. The system comprises 20 miles of wire, 29 pairs of magnets, a battery of 150 cells, 26 fire alarm boxes, 2 public alarm bells, and numerous private call bells for firemen.

A Demon Called Fire

JOSEPH F. EMMONS, Superintendent Fire Alarm Telegraph. Keene, December 7th, 1903.

Fires and Losses for Year Ending November 30th, 1903

December 9th, 1902 at 3.30 p.m. Box 25 The Castor House on Sullivan Street for a chimney fire with $10.00 dollars damage and Insurance paid $10.00.

December 27th, 1902 at 5.00 p.m. for Box 52 Imperial Package Co. Dry House on Emerald Street for an overheated stove. Damage $300.00 and Insurance paid $100.00.

January 8th, 1903 at 6.40 a.m. for Box 22. The A. A. Morse Barn on Winchester Street for an unknown type fire. Damage $1,600 and Insurance paid $1,600.

January 26th, 1903 at 7.10 p.m. Box 8 the Lamson Stores Main Street for an unknown type fire. Damage $585.00 and Insurance paid $585.00.

February 7th, 1903 3.15 p.m. Box 24 the Wm. Gilbo House on Douglas street for Coal gas explosion. Damage $675.00 and Insurance paid $475.00.

February 10th, 1903 at 6.05 a.m. Box 72 the Frank Russell House on Russell Street for a Chimney fire with no reported damage.

February 26th, 1903 at 3.00 a.m. Box 8 the J. Tierney Block on Main Street for a rats nest fire. Damage $859.79 and Insurance paid $707.79.

February 28th, 1903 at 12.00 Noon for Box 16 the Chas Giffin Tenements on Marlboro Street for a Chimney fire with no reported damage.

April 7th, 1903 at 12.30 a.m. for Box 8 the E. F. Lane Block on Main Street for a Spontaneous combustion type fire. Damage $771.00 and Insurance paid $771.00.

April 25th, 1903 at 12.08 a.m. Box 32 the Mike Paterson Junk Shop on North Street for a Defective stove pipe. Damage $10.00 No Insurance paid.

May 2nd, 1903 at 7.00 p.m. Box 22 the B. & M. R. R. for Brush fire on the Branch Road.

May 10th, 1903 at 9.00 p.m. for Box 22 the John Barry on Woodbury Street for a Brush fire.

May 12th, 1903 at 2.30 p.m. the C. W. Wyman off West Street for a Brush fire caused from Sparks from locomotive.

May 26th, 1903 at 4.45 p.m. Box 22 the J. G Perry property off the Old Walpole Road for a Brush fire.

May 31st, 1903 at 11.30 p.m. Box 22 to a Call to West Swanzey.

July 3rd, 1903 at 5.40 p.m. Box 9 the Hayward Hotel on Main Street for a fire caused by fireworks. Damage $35.00 and Insurance paid $35.00.

July 8th, 1903 at 11.20 p.m. Box 53 the C. M Trescott House on Madison Ct. for a Chimney fire. Damage 850.00 and Insurance paid 680.00.

July 25th, 1903 at 11.15 p.m. Box 9 Keene City Hall Central Square for a Spontaneous combustion type fire. Damage $215.00 and Insurance paid $200.00

July 26th, 1903 at 8.20 p.m. Box 9 the E. Clark Stores on Central Square for Chimney fire. Damage $2,878 and Insurance paid $2,878.00

August 1st, 1903 at 8.52 p.m. Box 13 the C. H. Bridgman Store House on Railroad Street for an Incendiary type fire. Damage $25.00 and Insurance paid $25.00.

August 26th, 1903 at 4.40 p.m. the Mrs. Drummer House on Elm Street for a Chimney fire with no reported damage.

October 14th, 1903 at 40.40 p.m. Box 16 the Thayer & Collins Manufactory on Appian Way for a Chimney fire. Damage $1,150 and Insurance paid $1,150.

October 24th, 1903 at 11.55 p.m. Box 9 the E. Clark Stores on Central Square for an unknown type fire. Damage 20.00 and Insurance paid $20.00.

October 31st, 10.20 a.m. Box 42 the G. H. Colony House on Park Street for a Chimney fire. Damage $20.00 and Insurance paid $20.00.

Picture taken by Bion H. Whitehouse with Keene Fire Department equipment lined up ready for the parade of the 1903 Centennial from L to R: Chiefs Wagon, Deluge Hose Wagon, Washington Hook & Ladder Hose Wagon, Steamer Hose Wagon, Button Steamer, Amoskeag Steamer and Chemical Wagon.

November 20th, 1903 at 4.15 a.m. Box 8 the B. & M. R. R. Main Street for a Defective Stove pipe. Damage $300.00 and Insurance paid $300.00.

Note: Total estimated value of above property $227,250.00. Total loss, $10,103.79.

Insurance paid $9,317.79.

Total Number of alarms 79.

Total Number of still alarms 54 Total number of bell alarms 25.

Ordinances and Joint Resolutions Ending for the year 1903.

A Joint Resolution was passed on January 15th, 1903 relating to painting the old hook and ladder truck for a sum of $100.00.

A Joint Resolution was passed on April 16th, 1903 relating to the 150th, anniversary of the founding of the town of Keene.

A Joint Resolution relating to the inspection day of Keene Fire Department. A sum of $60.00.

Purchase of fire hose for the year $345.00

Monies paid out for brush fires for the year $74.25

'FIRE'

THREE FIRES IN ONE NIGHT

The year of 1903 and 1904 proved to be a year for many fires. Many of them were the work of arsonists. In one evening, on December 19, 1903, there were three fires all within five

Keene Fire Department's Washington Hook & Ladder members and ladder wagon on parade. 1903 Centennial Parade at head of Central Square. Photo by Bion H. Whitehouse. HSCC collection.

hours. The first fire was in the cellar of the City Hall, in the Water Works Department. This fire occurred at 11:12pm while a dance was in progress in the hall above. The fire was the work of an arsonist, who had set a mop afire on the cellar stairs. The fire was discovered by a passerby who notified the fire department. Frank Stearns, a fireman; first on the scene, extinguished the blaze before any amount of damage was done.

At 3:15 the following morning, Driver Frank Reid of the fire department discovered a fire in the Chase's Stables, located in the rooming house, located in the rear of the fire station, awoke with a pain in his leg from a recent sprain. As he rolled over in bed he noticed a glow of fire, from the south side of the Chase's Stables. A call was quickly made to the Steamer house at the fire station and also the Hook and Ladder house. Scripture of the Steamer Company and Milan Jones of the Hook and Ladder, who was on duty in place of Frank Reid, quickly put out the blaze with an extinguisher. They did not take the time to awaken the mend sleeping in the Deluge House.

The third fire was at 4:21 on the same morning. This was at the firehouse. It was started in the hayloft over the stables of the Steamer House. This fire was a hot one. There was extensive damage to the hayloft and the roof in the rear of the fire station.

1904 [from *City of Keene Annual Report*]

Report of Chief Engineer of the Fire Department.

To His Honor the Mayor and City Councils:

In rendering my report of the Keene Fire Department for the year ending November 30th, 1904, would state that there have been fourteen bell calls and forty-two "stills." For data see detail list attached.

There have been purchased and added to the equipment, two three gallon extinguishers, one set harness hangers and one hose sled. Both hose wagons have been re-varnished. Two new rooms have been finished off in the steamer house and the towers have been re-arranged to admit the drying of larger quantities of hose.

In my last report (December 1st, 1903), I called attention to the need of more hose to make up for the depreciation which is constantly going on. During the year we have lost 800 feet of hose and none has been bought to keep the supply up to the point it should be. In the event of a big fire in the business section of the city we would be greatly handicapped in this direction, and I feel it my duty to you and to the taxpayers and citizens of Keene who have so much property at stake to lay especial stress upon the fact that no time should be lost in procuring more hose if the department is to be expected to meet the demands made on it in such an emergency.

It is with much regret that I can only report on hand 5,500 feet of hose, of which but 4,000 feet can be considered good, the poor hose is old and liable to burst at any time and if our full resources are called upon as would be the case at a large fire in or near the Square, it would not be surprising if the department came in for a great deal of unjust criticism. Hose is not guaranteed for over four and sometimes not over three years, and allowing six years as being its average life you can readily see that it would be a wise practice to purchase each year 1,100 feet to keep up with the depreciation.

To put the hose question on an equal basis with a year ago not less than 2,000 feet would be required during the coming year, and I cannot but urge the necessity of procuring at least half this amount as speedily as possible. The Deluge horses are utterly unfit for fire purposes.

The above horse, named Tom was purchased to pull fire apparatus for the Keene Fire Department in 1901. Tom was a member of the Keene Fire Department until 1912.

I would also call your attention to the need of a fire alarm box on Vernon Street station, more rubber coats and boots and another cellar pipe.

Duly mindful of the many favors and appreciating the numerous courtesies received at your hands, I beg to remain.

Respectfully yours,

F. W. TOWNE, Chief Keene Fire Department.

December 1st, 1904

Inventory of Property

Steamer Button No. 2, Steamer Amoskeag No. 1, one hand engine, Deluge hose wagon, steamer hose wagon, two hook and ladder trucks, two jumpers, 5,500 feet hose, eight extinguishers, four engineers' lanterns, two hydrant gates, two Y couplings, one Siamese coupling, one cellar pipe, six ladder dogs, uniforms, rubber coats and rubber boots for Steamer Co., uniforms, rubber coats and rubber boots for Hook and Ladder Co., uniforms, rubber coats and rubber boots for Deluge Hose Co., one sled for Hook and Ladder Co., one sled for Steamer Hose Co., one sled for Deluge Co., new, four sets swing harnesses.

Signals and Telephone alarms remain the same as adopted by the board of engineers, December 2nd, 1887.

Fires and Losses for the Year ending November 30th, 1904.

December 19th, 1903 at 11.12 p.m. for Box 9 City Hall for an unknown type fire. Damage $100,000, unknown on Insurance not reported.

December 20th, 1903 at 4.20 a.m. for Box 22 Vernon Street the Central Fire Station for an Incendiary fire. Damage $175.00 and Insurance paid $175.00.

December 28th, 1904 at 8.30 a.m. for a Still alarm on Main Street the O. J. Howard House for a house fire. Damage $30.00 and Insurance paid $30.00.

January 4th, 1904 at 3.00 p.m. on a still alarm to School Street the Mrs. F. A. Faulkner House for a fire place problem. Damage $16.00 and Insurance paid $16.00.

January 5th, 1904 at 5.00 a.m. for Box 22 the Mrs. J. A. French House on Summer Street for a fire place problem. Damage $55.00 and Insurance paid $55.00.

January 19th, 1904 at 3.45 a.m. for Box 9 the Kirk & Sewall Stores on West Street for a chimney fire. Damage $882.50 and Insurance paid $882.50.

January 29th, 1904 at 1.15 p.m. on a Still alarm to the Hayward Hotel on Main Street for a fireplace fire. Damage $75.20 and Insurance paid $75.20.

January 30th, 1904 at 11.00 p.m. for Box 8 Main Street the Boston & Main R. R. Stable for an Incendiary fire. Damage $875.00 and Insurance paid $825.00.

February 20th, 1904 at 11.20 a.m. for Box 26 Taylor Street the F. H. Fay House for a chimney fire. Damage $560.00 and Insurance paid $560.00.

May 9th, 1904 at 10.00 a.m. for Box 25 Washington Street the M. D. Carpenter property for a brush fire.

May 30th, 1904 at 2.10 p.m. for Box 19 Marlboro Street the G. F. C. Eaton House for a chimney explosion. Damage $750.00 and Insurance paid $750.00.

June 25th, 1904 at 4.20 p.m. for Box 9 West Street the F. E. Kingsbury auto and barn. Cause gasoline explosion with Damage of $1,325.00 and Insurance paid $25.00.

July 4th, 1904 at 2.05 a.m. on a Still alarm to the H. M. Nims Barn on West Street. Damage $800.00 and no Insurance, fire caused by Incendiary.

September 21st, 1904 at 1.30 p.m. on a Still alarm to the Wm. C. Hall House on Prospect Street for a chimney fire. Damage $4.57 and Insurance paid $4.57.

September 24th, 1904 at 9.15 p.m. on a Still alarm to the A. E. Bennett House on Prospect Street for a fire place problem. Damage $30.92 and Insurance paid $30.92.

October 19th, 1904 at 5.15 a.m. for Box 46 Leverett Street the S. K. Stone Barn. Unknown cause and Damage was $3,350.00 and Insurance paid $1,650.00

October 24th, 1904 at 9.05 p.m. for Box 8 the Beaver Mills Manufactory Co. on Railroad Street for a dust explosion. No damage reported.

October 25th, 1904 at 5.15 p.m. Box 17 for Appleton Street the E. P. Hardy House and Barn. Damage $1,175.00 and Insurance paid $1,140.00. Caused by smoking in barn.

October 29th, 1904 at 9.20 p.m. for Box 22 the Milton Blake wood lot on Gilsum Street for a brush fire.

November 11th, 1904 at 6.20 p.m. for Box 8 Main Street the E. F. Lane Block for a fire caused by Spontaneous Combustion. Damage $5,650.00 and Insurance paid $3,820.00.

There were a total of fourteen bell alarms and forty still alarms. For 1904.

Superintendent of Fire Alarm Telegraph.

Joseph F. Emmons

The system remains in good condition and two boxes were recommended for remodeling within the coming year.

December 8th, 1904

Joint Resolutions for the Year ending 1904

A Resolution was passed on April 7th, 1904 relating to the purchase of fire extinguishers. A sum of $45.00.

A Joint Resolution relating to the state convention Firemen's Relief Association was passed on June 16th, 1904, The sum of $125.00.

A Resolution was passed on September 15th, 1904 relating to the annual inspection of the Keene Fire Department a sum of $60.00.

A Resolution was passed on October 6th, 1904 for the purchase of a sled for the Steam Fire Engine Company not to exceed the sum of $125.00.

"FIRE"

1904 FIRE AND FATALITY. James Beaman Victim of His Own Indiscretion. On October 25th, 1904 a Loses his Life in Fire in Barns on E. P. Hardy Farm-Last seen alive Husking Corn and Smoking-Barns Soon After Discovered to Be All on Fire.

A man whose name is said to have been James Beaman, aged about 60 and employed by E. P. hardy on the farm on Appleton street where he had for a log time lived lost his life Tuesday afternoon, Oct. 25, in a fire which he doubtless started himself while smoking and husking corn in the barn. The remains were found by Engineer Nims and others of the fire department about 6.45, after the fire, which had been burning an hour and a half, had been sufficiently extinguished to allow the firemen to go upon the remains of the barn floor. The body was burned beyond recognition, the legs and arms being almost wholly consumed.

Mr. Hardy was in nelson and the only persons at the far were Beaman and the housekeeper, Mrs. Ida S. Reed. Mrs. Reed says Beaman had some liquor and refused to stop smoking in the barn when she asked him to. She went up stairs in the house and on coming down discovered the barn a mass of flames. She went out and called to Beaman, whom she could not find, and than ran for help.

An alarm was sent in from box 17 at 5.15, and on arriving the firemen found two of three barns at the farm a mass of flames and the ell and roof of the house on fire. The steamer was sent in the river and streams brought to bear by which they saved the house and one barn, doing excellent work.

There were probably 30 or more tons of hay, a lot of corn and some pigs and calves burned, together with a horse belonging to Fred Ellis. Most of the cattle were in the pasture when the fire broke out and a bull and some calves that were in the barn were let out and thereby saved. The loss is estimated at $2500. There was an insurance of $1,000 on the contents of the buildings. The household articles were mostly removed.

[Printed in the *New Hampshire Sentinel* Keene, N.H.]

————

"FIRE"

1904 A SMOKE LOSS On November 11th, 1904 A Smoke Loss And Some Other Damage Caused by Hot Basement Fire.

A fire which made its presence known by quantities of smoke which suddenly began to pour from the rear basement openings of the E. F. lane block about 6.20 Friday evening, caused a smoke loss estimated at several thousand dollars in the large stock of goods in the new department store of Alfred E. Yeates, besides damaging a section of the timbers and planking of the first floor of the block considerably.

The escape from a very serious fire was a narrow one, as a delay of five or ten minutes in its discovery, which would have been probable

Members of the Keene Fire Department, picture donated by Ralph Hayward. Front Row L to R: Dan Gilbo, Oscar Applin, Arthur Dean, Ike Applin, Chief Fred Towne, Carl Roche, Oscar Nims, Tim O'Connell, Shorty Foster. Back Row L to R: Ralph Hayward, Bill Morrison, Jerry Power, Warren Howe, Tom Roche, Tom Walbank, Kid Irwin, Albion Howland, Milon Jones, Louis Dean. 1904.

had it occurred a few hours later, would have resulted in the firing of the upper floors of the building, probably, through shafts in which sewer stream and water pipes are carried. An alarm from box 8 about 6.20 quickly brought the firemen to the block.

Among the first to reach the fire was Engineer Carrigan, who was eating supper in Gurnsey's restaurant at the time. Superintendent Jennings of the electric railway and sever citizens whose places of business are in that immediate vicinity were also on the ground before the firemen got there. It then appeared that an area ten or fifteen feet in length and two or three feet wide, some twenty feet inside the basement, was all ablaze. On opening the door the smoke was found to be stifling and the heat too intense to use extinguishers effectively. Hose streams were therefore turned in through the basement door as soon as the firemen arrived. The fire was fortunately so located

that those streams at once reached the greater part of the burning area. In a short time the firemen forced an entrance to the basement and quickly put out the blazing floorboards and timbers. Fortunately a large bin of coal adjacent to the fire had not become ignited.

The Keene National bank and the Yeates department store, just opened with a fresh stock of goods, where filled with smoke and even the banking rooms, which contain almost nothing to retain the odor, smelled strongly of smoke Saturday. In the Yeates store all the textile goods are of course affected and the delicate fabrics and white goods show visibly the smoke traces. It will probably take a number of days to adjust the loss. It is hoped that the loss will be adjusted in a day or two. Mr. Yeates carried an insurance of $14,750 on his stock and it is thought that the stock in the store would invoice from $20,000 to $25,000 before the fire.

An examination made after the fire had been subdued indicated that it had caught in some unknown way in a small sack of rubbish that was in the passageway leading to the boilers and probably ten feet from them. There were two sacks they're containing papers and waste collected in the block by the janitor. It has been the custom to remove those sacks from the block every day or two and whatever rubbish that was there was removed Wednesday. The janitor says he finds almost everything including partly burned matches and those that have been lighted in the rubbish he gathers. If this is the cause in this building it is probably so in other block in town indicating the dangerous character of such rubbish.

The fire burned off boards over an inch think that had been nailed across the basement timbers and burned into the floor timbers and planking more that half an inch over a considerable area. It also burned the planking of the coal bin against which the rubbish sacks were leaning. The fire was working up into a shaft containing sewer and water pipes when it was put out and would soon have reached the Yeates store. Two firemen and Arthur Morrison, one of the clerks in the Yeates store, watched the basement and store all night. The telephone company suffered a small loss to materials and supplies in their basement storeroom, but the telephone cables, bringing in all the wires for the exchange, were uninjured.

[Printed in the *New Hampshire Sentinel* Keene, N.H.]

———

1905 [from *City of Keene Annual Report*]

Report of Chief Engineer of the Fire Department

To His Honor the Mayor and City Councils:

Gentlemen. I have to report that the department has responded to sixty-two calls during the past year, sixteen bell and forty-six still alarms.

As per list appended, of fires' origin, losses, etc., you will find that the city has been unusually fortunate as regards losses the net loss being but $720-over one-half of which was from brush fires.

There has been added to the department as follows:

One pair horses for Deluge hose, fifteen hundred feet of rubber lined hose, one hose sled for Steamer Company, uniforms to the extent of $125.00, three dozen mittens.

There is on hand at this date, 7,000 feet of hose, 1,000 of which has given out and has been repaired.

Among the needs of the department I make the following memoranda: Five hundred feet of new hose to keep up with the depreciation, new horses for steamer, new body for sled of ladder truck, fire alarm box on station, rubber coats and boots, painting of station inside and out.

I have watched with much interest the plan adopted this year by the city of collecting rubbish, etc., weekly. I think there can be no doubt that this custom has diminished fires also to quite an extent, and an extension of the system would still further tend to lessen the fire losses.

Extending thanks to your honorable body and to my assistants and members of this department for their cooperation, I remain,

Yours respectfully,

FRED W. TOWNE,

Chief Engineer. Keene, December 11th, 1905.

Inventory of Property

Steamer Button No. 2, Steamer Amoskeag No. 1, one hand engine, Deluge Hose Wagon, steamer hose wagon, two hook and ladder trucks, two jumpers, 7,000 feet hose, eight extinguishers, four engineers' lanterns, two hydrant gates, two Y couplings, one Siamese coupling, one cellar pipe, six ladder dogs, uniforms, rubber coats and rubber boots for Steamer Co., uniforms rubber coats and rubber boots for Hook and Ladder Co., uniforms, rubber coats and rubber boots for Deluge Hose Co., one sled for Hook and Ladder Co., one sled for Steamer Hose co., one sled for Deluge., new, four sets swing harnesses.

Signals and General Rules and Telephone alarms remain the same.

Fires and Losses for Year Ending November 30th, 1905

January 11th, 1905 at 8.30 a.m. for Box 16 Winchester Street the L. P. Butler Office for an unknown type fire. Damage $87.80 and Insurance paid $87.80.

January 13th, 1905 at 5.30 a.m. for Box 46 Castle Street the H. H. Barker House for a Furnace fire. Damage $150.00 and Insurance paid $150.00.

February 28th, 1905 at 6.40 p.m. for Box 14 Water Street the J. P. Rust Manufactory for a chimney fire with damage of $10.00 and Insurance paid $10.00.

March 14th, 1905 at 5.50 p.m. for Box 18 off Marlboro Street the A. C. Hemmingway House for a chimney fire. Damage $80.00 and Insurance paid $80.00.

April 15th, 1905 at 3.00 p.m. for Box 22. Help to the Town of Surry.

April 19th, 1905 at 3.52 p.m. Box 22 for the Electric Railway on Main Street for a brush fire. Damage $400.00 and Insurance paid $50.00.

April 24th, 1905 at 2.35 p.m. for Box 22 Goose Pond Wood Lot for a brush fire.

April 27th, 1905 at 11.30 a.m. for Box 22 Winchester Street the Antoine Lower property for a brush fire. Damage $25.00 unknown Insurance.

May 12th, 1905 at 6.20 p.m. for Box 22 the Giffin, Carroll & Mun property for a brush fire. Damage $75.00, unknown Insurance.

May 28th, 1905 at 12.04 p.m. for Box 14 Grove Street the Levi Fuller House for a Cushion in chair on fire. No reported damage or Insurance.

July 4th, 1905 at 12.45 a.m. Box 22 for Main Street a City owned Storage Barn on fire. Cause was Incendiary. Unknown insurance or damage.

July 4th, 1905 at 1.40 p.m. for box 9 Roxbury Street the Hayward House for an unknown type fire. Damage $550.00 and Insurance paid $300.00.

August 10th, 1905 at 10.20 p.m. for Box 8 Main Street the Boston & Main R. R. Restaurant. Damage $510.00 and Insurance paid $510.00.

August 22nd, 1905 at 12.45 p.m. for Box 22 Branch Road the H. W. Nims Wood lot for a Brush fire.

August 26th, 1905 at 11.30 a.m. for Box 14 Water Street the L. J. Martell Shop for a Kerosene Engine fire. Damage $40.00 and Insurance paid $20.00.

November 1st, 1905 at 6.50 p.m. for Box 52 Foundry Street the Humphrey Mach Co. Foundry for a Hot Stack. Damage $100.00 and Insurance paid $100.00.

Total number of alarms Sixty-two. sixteen bell alarms and forty-six still alarms.

Report of Superintendent of Fire alarm Telegraph

JOSEPH F. EMMONS, superintendent of fire alarm, December 11th, 1905

A new Box has been added Box 5 to Elliot City Hospital building.

It is recommended that four old boxes Box 52,53,72, and 1`3 be remodeled the coming year.

[*Compiler's Note*: Box 5 which was placed on Elliot City Hospital building in 1905 when on Main Street was removed and placed on the new Cheshire Hospital on Court Street and has remained the Hospital box today.]

Joint Resolutions Ending the Year 1905

A Resolution was passed February 2nd, 1905 for the purchase of horses for the fire department. One pair not to exceed $500.00.

A Resolution was passed on February 16th, 1905 for the purchase of fire hose not to exceed $1,000.00.

On April 6th, 1905 a Joint resolution was passed relating to a special driver for the fire department.

That the joint resolution relating to a substitute driver, adopted May 19th, 1898, is hereby replaced and the following substituted in place thereof:

That the drivers employed by the fire department shall each be entitled to a vacation in each year of two consecutive weeks without loss of pay, at such time as the chief engineer of the fire department may determine, but no driver shall have his vacation during any part of the time of the vacation of any of the other drivers; and the chief engineer of the department is hereby authorized and directed to employ a substitute for the drivers so

In 1905 Tom and Jack were teamed together, they pulled Amoskeag steamer and the Button steamer to most fires from 1905 to 1912. Photo from Fire Department Scrapbook.

Fire at the restaurant of F.O. Quinn, in the building, which formerly occupied the site of 25 Roxbury Street. The steam fire engine is Button Steamer #216 and was the City's second steamer. Photo from Fire Department Scrapbook.

absent on their vacations at any expense not to exceed thirteen dollars per week.

On June 15th, 1905 a Resolution was passed by the committee on lands and buildings to be laid in three apartments of the fire station, at an expense not exceeding $235.00.

1906 [from *City of Keene Annual Report*]

Report of Chief Engineer of the Fire Department

To His Honor the Mayor and gentlemen of City Councils:

The closing of the fiscal year ending November 30th, 1906 finds the department fully up to the standard as regards apparatus and equipment, and with a full quota of men in each company.

You will note from the following tables of fires and losses that the department has responded to fifty-six alarms, thirteen bell alarms and forty-three still alarms. The net loss of $355.00 is much smaller than the preceding year, representing less than one-half of one percent of the estimated value involved, and only a trifle more than ten percent of the actual loss. These figures emphasize the fact that the firemen of Keene handle fires most admirably and are not only entitled to merited praise from the engineers and officers; but also, it seems to me from the citizens in general.

The city has appropriated the sum of $125.00 to provide hot water for the accommodation of the men at the fire station, which will be greatly appreciated when it is installed. One pair of horses has been purchased for the steamer to replace a pair considered unfit for the work.

The inventory of the property of the department is as follows:

Amoskeag Steamer No. 1, Button Steamer No. 2, one hand engine, Deluge hose wagon, Steamer hose wagon, two hook and ladder trucks, two jumpers, 5,500 feet No. 1 hose, 1,000 feet No. 2 hose, 350 feet hose loaned to water department, eight extinguishers, four engineers' lanterns, two hydrant gates, two Y couplings, one Siamese coupling, one cellar pipe, six ladder dogs, uniforms, rubber coats and rubber boots for the department, suitably marked with the names of the several companies, one sled for the Hook and Ladder Co., one sled for Steamer hose Co., one sled for the Deluge Co., and four sets of swing harness.

I make the following recommendations:

Hose.—The purchase of 1,000 feet of hose to keep up with the depreciation. The best quality of hose should always be purchased, experience in the past having demonstrated that it was the cheapest in the end.

Repairs.—The purchase of a new body for the sled of the hook and ladder truck and needed repairs to the steamer hose wagon. The painting of the rest of the fire station, part of which has been done the past year.

Fire Alarm Telegraph.—The purchase of four new boxes to be located as follows: Fire Station, George Street, corner of Sullivan Street, upper Elm Street and upper Court Street at or near the plant of the Keene Glue Company. The unreliability at times of our fire alarm system, together with its high cost of maintenance, strongly urges that improvements in this important branch of the fire service be effected in the near future. I would especially call attention of the committee on fire alarm to these matters and ask their careful consideration.

New Apparatus.—The purchase of a combination chemical and hose wagon. I do not wish to convey the idea that the department is lacking in present equipment or unable to meet any emergencies which may arise; but there are many occasions when such a piece of apparatus would answer all purposes, prevent loss by water, promptly reach a fire outside of our hydrant service and do effective work or hold the fire in check until the arrival of the steamer, it being equally serviceable as a chemical or hose wagon. It is in my opinion far better that the department be at all times, a little ahead in matters of apparatus and equipment.

The complaints heretofore received by the department from the district in which the city collects garbage, seem to have been materially lessened by this scheme since its adoption.

I take pleasure in further reporting that harmony prevails between the officer and men of the several companies, that they appreciate their quarters and the liberal spirit manifested by the city councils in promptly providing for the needs of the department. It also gives me pleasure to speak of the cordial relations which exist among the members associated with me on the board of engineers who, with the officers and members of the department have efficiently supported me during this term, returned.

LOUIS A. NIMS, Chief Engineer. Keene, N. H., December 10th, 1906

Fires and Losses for Year Ending November 30th, 1906

December 3rd, 1905 at 12.30 p.m. for Box 9 Roxbury Street the Odd Fellows Livery Stable. Cause was an overheated stove and Damage was $180.00 and Insurance paid $130.00.

December 18th, 1905 at 10.15 p.m. for Box 9 rear of City Hall the F. L. Carey Store House. Fire caused by matches and Damage was $2,784.00 and Insurance paid $1,000.00.

February 6th, 1906 at 12.40 p.m. for Box 22 Court Street the F. & C. Mfg. Co. House for a Chimney fire with Damage of $111.32 and Insurance paid $111.32.

February 28th, 1906 at 11.00 a.m. for Box 14 Grove Street the L. A. Fuller House for a Chimney fire. Damage $10.00 and no Insurance.

March 29th, 1906 at 12.45 p.m. for Box 16 Davis street the Russell Hill House for a Chimney fire. Damage $45.00 and Insurance paid $45.00.

April 1st, 1906 at 6.45 p.m. for Box 18 Marlboro Street for a False call.

August 14th, 1906 at 1.10 a.m. for Box 22 Elm Street the Lewis Nalibo House for an unknown type fire. Damage $1,500.00 and Insurance paid $1,500.00.

August 27th, 1906 at 7.47 p.m. for Box 17 Appleton Street the G. F. Ball Brick kiln for an unknown type fire. Damage $150.00 unknown insurance.

September 2nd at 12.31 p.m. for Box 8 Main Street the N. G. Gurnsey Block for a Lace curtain fire. Damage $65.40 and Insurance paid $65.40.

September 7th, 1906 at 11.50 a.m. for Box 13 Church Street the C. Putney House for a Chimney fire. Damage $5.60 and Insurance paid $5.60.

October 4th, 1906 at 4.15 a.m. for Box 37 Mechanic Street the Imperial Package Co Manufactory for a Dust on boilers. No reported damage.

November 2nd, 1906 at 12.20 p.m. for Box 52 the B. & M. yard N. E. Telephone Co. poles. Damage $25.00 and no insurance paid reported.

November 12th, 1906 at 5.20 p.m. for Box 18 Dartmouth Street the Harry Pierce House for a Kerosene lamp fire. Damage $50.00. Insurance paid $30.00.

For the year there were Forty-three still alarms; and thirteen bell alarms.

Signals

The following signals were adopted by the board of engineers, January, 1906 and are as follows:

1. The Superintendent has the right to strike one blow upon the bells at any time, to test the circuit; also to ring in one round from any box, preceded by a single blow exactly five minutes after the noon stroke, on Saturdays, for the purpose of testing the boxes.

2. The signal 22 repeated on the bells is to call the firemen to their houses for further orders.

3. Two blows struck upon the bells signify a still alarm.

4. In case of a serious fire the engineers may cause a second alarm to be sounded from the nearest box. A second alarm is given by striking ten blows, followed by the box number.

5. As box 9, which is located on city hall, is still likely to be used for a general alarm, and to be pulled for a fire which is not in or near the square, the engineers will ring in a second alarm or four full rounds form this box, if there is fire of any magnitude near the square.

6. The old alarm on city hall will only be rung between 9 p.m. and 6 a.m., except in case of serious fire.

7. Arrangements have been made with the Beaver Mills Co., and alarms of fire will be given on their whistle same as by the bells.

Report of the Superintendent of Fire Alarm Telegraph

The fire alarm telegraph system comprises twenty-five miles of wire, twenty-eight fire alarm boxes, two tower strikers, attached to the city hall bell and the Court Street Congregational church bell, respectively, a battery of one hundred and forty cells, a relay battery of fifty dry cells, open circuit, furnishing power for a number of private call bells for firemen.

Box numbered 54 located at Fowler's box shop, on Island Street, and box numbered 57 on Pearl Street, at third pole south of the Boston & Main railroad crossing, are new boxes which the committee on fire department have purchased and located this year.

Two alarm boxes, numbered 52 and 72 have been built over and are as good as new.

ALBERT W. GREEN,
Superintendent of Fire Alarm Telegraph

Joint Resolutions Ending for the year 1906

A Resolution was passed on December 21st, 1905 relating to an installation of a fire alarm box at Fowler's box factory on Island Street.

A Resolution was passed on January 18th, 1906 relating to a fire alarm box on Pearl Street near the railroad crossing.

An Ordinance was passed on January 18th, 1906 defining the use of the city's horses and duties of drivers.

That Chapter VIII of the City Ordinances be amended by adding the following section.

Section 8. The chief engineer shall have control of the horses and drivers at fires and until they are dismissed, and may require their services whenever he may consider it necessary for drill or parade; the drivers shall also perform such services as the chief engineer may assign to them while they are on fire patrol duty at the fire station.

LOUIS A. NIMS, Chief Engineer. Keene, N. H., December 10th, 1906.

During inspection day the Amoskeag steamer is shown making an exhibition run to the hydrant near the sentinel building on Main Street in 1906. The Amoskeag steam fire engine is being driven by Fred H. Fay.

A Resolution was passed relating to the purchase of coats and boots for the use by the fire department. 18 rubber coats and twelve pairs of rubber boots for the sum of $100.00.

A Resolution was passed on April 5th, 1906 for the purpose of disposing of the pair of city horses used by Driver Fay as they deem best and purchase one pair of horses in place of the pair so disposed of; a total of $345.00 is hereby appropriated for this purpose.

A Resolution was passed on June 7th, 1906 for notices against setting fires.

That the Chief of the fire department be, and he hereby is, directed to cause to be posted in such places in the city as shall seem proper for the purpose, extracts from the fire laws of the state and such other notices as may seem proper to him in connection therewith, for the purpose of giving notice and warning in respect to the setting of forest and brush fires.

"FIRE"

1906 HOUSE AND BARN BURNED. On August 14th, 1906 the Home of Louis B. Nalibow Destroyed and Family Nearly Suffocated.

The home of Louis B. Nalibow at 387 Elm Street was badly damaged by fire early Tuesday morning, the barn being burned flat to the ground and the rear part of the house so badly burned that it is not worth repairing.

The fire was discovered about 1.15 o'clock by Mrs. Robert Carroll, who lives in the next house. The barking of her dog, in the kitchen awakened her. She awoke Mr. Carroll, fearing that some one was trying to break into the house, but on going to a window she saw the cause of the dog's anxiety, for the Nalibow barn was a mass of flames while from the roof of the house small flames were shooting forth.

Mr. Carroll, who has a telephone, at once called central and gave notice of the fire, and the night operator pulled the telephone office box No. 22. The alarm came in all right on circuit No. 2, on which the telephone office box is situated, and the Beaver mills watchman, whose gong is on the same line, picked up the call and sounded the whistle. On the other two fire alarm circuits only tow blows were struck, however, owing to failure on the part of the repeater, apparently. The big bells and many of the firemen's call bells and gongs therefore only struck two blows and the signal not being well understood, there was some delay in getting the firemen together and in responding to the call.

After Mr. Carroll had telephoned for the fire department he went to the Nalibow house, and seeing no one about broke open one of the windows and entered the building. In the front part of the house he found Mrs. Nalibow's two children nearly suffocated by smoke. He led the women to the window and had to use considerable force to get them out of the house. He then carried the children out. By this time the room was so full of smoke that it was impossible to breath and if the minutes had been allowed to stay there a few minutes longer the chances are that they would have been found dead from suffocation. Mr. Nalibow was not at home, being away on business.

The firemen on arriving on the scene directed their efforts to saving as much as possible of the house for the barn was to far gone to need attention. The flames illuminated the sky brightly and the light could be seen for miles around. There was very little in the house that could be saved by the time the firemen got there and nearly everything was burned including quite a large amount of furniture. The loss is estimated at not less than $1,000 and the property was insured for $1,200. The fire evidently caught in the barn but the cause is not known.

[Printed in the *New Hampshire Sentinel* Keene, N.H.]

———

"FIRE"

1906 BAD FIRE IN DWELLING On December 2nd, 1906 Home of Alfred E. Gates wrecked by Fire, Smoke and Water.

A still alarm soon followed by a general alarm from box 5, at Elliot City Hospital, was sent in shortly before 8 Sunday evening for a bad fire in the home of Alfred E. Gates, who has occupied the Samuel O. Gates house on Main Street for some time. Mrs. Gates reserved several rooms there, also and although in Worcester herself this winter

had her household goods much damaged. The loss is probably not less than $3,000. Mr. Gates carried an insurance of $1,000 on his household goods and Mrs. Gates had $500 on her furniture and $4,700 on the house so that her loss should be made good, so far as insurance can do while that of Mr. Gates, he thinks, will not be.

No one was at home when the fire broke out, Mr. and Mrs. Gates and their son having gone to church about 7. Just before 8 some of the nurses came out of the nurses' home, heard the crackling of the fire and plainly saw it in the northwest chamber of the house. They quickly sent word to the matron in charge to telephone for the firemen and themselves ran to the house, smashing in the front door, going through the rooms down stairs as far as they could and calling loudly to arouse if possible anyone who might be in the house. Miss Twitchell whose house is next one to the north was quickly at work and helped to call the neighbors, sending a nurse ringing in box 5. Thus everything possible was soon being done. But the fire when discovered had burned a large hole in the second floor and followed along the timbers to the north wall, where it was just breaking through the clapboards. There was therefore, no chance of preventing serious damage to the building and its contents.

A delay occurred after the first hose wagon arrived and hose had been laid, it being impossible to open the hydrant for quite a number of minutes. The nut on which a hydrant wrench must be placed to open the hydrant was somewhat but not badly worn and the hydrant wrench carried on the hose wagon, which was perhaps also worn, was too large for the nut and persisted in slipping around without turning it. The hydrant was not opened until another wrench was procured. But the condition of the fire was such at the time that the delay made practically no difference with the result.

Those who arrived and went into the house before the firemen began work, found the rug and floor in the northwest sitting room just getting on fire from coats that were dropping from the ceiling above where a large hole had been burned out and the laths and plastering had falling from the chimney back to the second floor timber and for several feet between the floor timbers which ran north and south. There was a coal grate in this room suitable for either coal or a wood fire. The same chimney was used for the furnace. Mrs. Gates states that there was a wood fire in the grate in the forenoon, but the family was away in the afternoon, excepting a short time at supper hour, when nothing wrong was noticed.

The rooms of the second floor, especially on the north side of the main house, got very hot and were filled with dense smoke and more or less fire. The flames worked across the second floor to the south side of the house and up and own the north wall from the foundation to the roof plate. Some fire got into the attic, where the firemen used their cellar or roof pipe, which is made to be thrust through an aperture in a floor or roof and thus to throw water into the apartment be low in all directions. Various holes had to be cut in the walls and floors also to reach the fire in the wall and floor spaces, the entire house being deluged with water including the ell, which was pretty well soaked.

Quite a lot of the goods and furniture of Mr. Gates was taken out and moved to the hose and barn of C. J. George, on the south, but a large amount was spoiled or badly damaged. Clothing, bedding, rugs, draperies and ornaments of all kinds were burned or badly damaged. So far as Mr. Gates knew Monday morning his clothing and that of his wife and boy was substantially all gone including Mrs. Gates jewelry, but the firemen say a good deal of this is at Mr. George's house. The loss on Mrs. Gates effects was mainly from smoke and water.

[Printed in the *New Hampshire Sentinel* Keene, N.H.]

1907 [from *City of Keene Annual Report*]
Report of Chief Engineer of Fire Department

To His Honor the Mayor and gentlemen of the City Councils:

The closing of the fiscal year ending November 30th, 1907 finds the department fully up to the standard as regards apparatus and equipment, and with a full quota of men in each company.

You note from the following table of fire and losses that the department has responded to eighty-three alarms, nineteen bell alarms and sixty-four still alarms, two being out of town, one at Swanzey and one at Surry.

The net loss at these fires was $224.00. These figures emphasize the fact that the firemen of Keene handle fires most admirably and are not only entitled to merited praise from the engineers and officers, but also, it seems to me from the citizens in general.

Improvements and new apparatus added to the department:

The hot water system ordered by the councils of 1906 has been installed and gives perfect satisfaction and is much appreciated by the department. There has been one combination chemical and hose wagon purchased which carries two thirty-gallon tanks, two three-gallon tanks, a thousand feet of hose, two hundred feet of chemical hose, two ladders, and is in very respect a fully equipped first-class hose wagon. Hobbs' runners have been purchased for this wagon. Money has been appropriated to buy one pair of horses to take the place of the horses used on the Hook and Ladder truck which are getting unfit for fire service.

The station has been painted outside, and put in good condition inside. A new floor has been laid in the hall of the Hook and

Ladder house, and new chairs purchased for the same.

The inventory of the property of the department is as follows:

Amoskeag steamer No. 1, Button steamer No. 2, one hand engine, one combination chemical and hose wagon, Deluge hose wagon, Relief hose wagon, two hook and ladder trucks, 5,000 feet No. 1 hose, 1,000 feet No. 2 hose, (about 500 feet condemned), 200 feet chemical hose, ten extinguishers, four engineer's lanterns, two hydrant gates, two Y couplings, one Siamese coupling, one cellar pipe, six ladder dogs, uniforms, rubber coats and rubber boots for the department, suitably marked with names of the several companies, one sled for Hook and Ladder company, one sled for Steamer Hose company, one sled for Deluge company, four sets of swing harnesses, and two extra Barry collars.

I make the following recommendations:

As you will note by the inventory that we have only 5,000 feet of No. 1 hose, none having been purchased for two years, I would advise purchasing 1,000 feet early in the year, also repairing Deluge hose wagon, adding new wheels, one thirty-gallon chemical tank, thus converting this into a combination wagon; also installing electric lights in barn, at the fire station, as we consider it unsafe for drivers to use lanterns in hay lofts.

Fire Alarm Telegraph:

The purchase of four new boxes to be located as follows: Fire station; George Street, corner of Sullivan Street; upper Elm Street; in vicinity of High School building; West Keene near corner of Russell and Wheelock streets.

I take pleasure in further reporting that harmony prevails between the offices and men of the several companies, that they appreciate their quarters and the liberal spirit manifested by the city councils in promptly providing for the needs of the department. It also gives me pleasure to speak of the valuable aid afforded by the chairman and members of the joint standing committee on fire department and the cordial relation which exist among the members associated with me on the board of engineers who, with the officers and members of the department have efficiently supported me during this term, and to them and the city councils my thanks are hereby returned.

LOUIS A. NIMS, Chief Engineer. Keene, N. H., December 10th, 1907

Fires and Losses for the Year Ending November 30th, 1907

December 1st, 1906 at 8.30 p.m. for Box 52 Emerald Street the Keene Gas Light Co. (Gas Plant) for a Gas Explosion. No claim made.

December 2nd, 1906 at 8.20 p.m. for Box 5 Main Street the Mrs. S. O. Gates House for a fireplace fire. Damage $2,576.75 and Insurance paid $2,576.75.

December 5th, 1906 at 5.30 a.m. for Box 42 Winter Street the H. T. Kingsbury House for a furnace problem. Damage $2,053.50 and Insurance paid $2,053.50.

January 28th, 1907 at 9.15 a.m. for Box 46 Court Street the William Foster House for a Furnace problem. Damage $60.00 and Insurance paid $60.00.

January 29th, 1907 at 8.00 a.m. for Box 43 Ashuelot Street the Faulkner & Colony House for a Chimney fire with no damage reported.

February 2nd, 1907 at 8.56 a.m. for Box 16 Main Street the Milton Blake house for smoke from the furnace. No reported damage.

February 8th, 1907 at 6.35 a.m. for Box 46 Portland Street the A. S. Mason House for a Chimney fire. Damage $175.00 and Insurance paid $175.00.

February 14th, 1907 at 7.05 a.m. for Box 24 Douglas Street the Mrs. Isaac Cheney House for a Chimney fire. Damage $8.00 and Insurance paid $8.00.

April 10th, 1907 at 7.53 p.m. for Box 15 Water Street the Warren Bissell Poultry house for a

Kerosene lamp fire. Damage $50.00 with no insurance.

May 2nd, 1907 at 2.30 p.m. for Box 22 George Street the Frank Cota property for a Brush fire.

May 11th, 1907 at 8.20 p.m. for Box 43 Island Street the Boston & Main R. R. Rubbish pile. No damage.

May 12th, 1907 at 4.40 p.m. for Box 14 Water Street the J. P. Rust Hall. Hake pine wood which was caused by sparks from a R. R. Engine. Damage $69.00 and was not insured.

May 16th, 1907 at 4.50 p.m. for the Knights of Columbus on Main Street. Unknown cause and Damage $194.65 and Insurance paid $194.65.

June 23rd, 1907 at 11.55 a.m. for Box 52 Emerald Street the Fred Desrosier House for Children playing with matches. Damage $75.00 and no Insurance.

August 26th, 1907 at 10.30 a.m. for Box 16 Main Street the W. J. Lovejoy Automobile for a gasoline fire. No damage reported.

August 30th, 1907 at 12.00 p.m. for Box 32 High Street the E. H. Bartlett House for a Chimney fire. Damage $55.00 and Insurance paid $55.00.

October 5th, 1907 at 6.50 p.m. for Box 53 Winchester Street the M. Keirce House and Barn fire. Unknown cause and Damage $235.00 and Insurance paid $205.00.

November 2nd, 1907 at 6.00 a.m. for Box 32 Carroll Street the John Pender House. Fire caused by Carelessness and Damage was $50.00 and Insurance paid $50.00.

November 2nd, 1907 at 2.00 p.m. for Box 8 Main Street the Elm. I. Blake Hotel & Barn. Children playing with matches. Damage $105.00 and Insurance paid $105.00.

November 15th, 1907 at 11.20 a.m. for Box 22 Probate Street the F. C. Pilke House for a Chimney fire with no damage reported.

Note: Causes of still alarms Chimney fires thirty nine; plumber's torch, two; smoke from furnace, one carelessness, one lumber piles two; brush, two; grass, three; vent pipes, two; hay stack, one; waste wood, one; gasoline, one; kerosene, one; gas jet, one; dust in heater, one and false alarms, five.

A total of Nineteen bell alarms; and sixty four still alarms

Signals remain the same.

Report of the Superintendent of Fire Alarm Telegraph

Very little work has been done during the term in extending the system, but a new box numbered 7, has been located at the corner of St. James Street and Railroad Square.

New Boxes West Keene corner of Russell and Wheelock streets, on upper Elm Street, on the corner of George and Sullivan Streets, near John P. Rust's mill, near the High school building, and at the fire station.

Respectfully,

ALBERT W. GREEN,

Superintendent of Fire Alarm telegraph.

Keene, December 5th, 1907

[*Compiler's Note*: Box 22 was moved from the phone co. to the Central fire station which is still on the building today.]

Joint Resolutions for the Year Ending 1907

A Joint Resolution was passed on December 20th, 1906 relating to the purchase of a combination hose carriage and chemical engine for the fire department. Not to exceed $2,300.00.

A Resolution was passed on February 21st, 1907 for making repairs at the Fire Engine House as follows: Deluge Co., painting large room down stairs, $35.00

Hook and Ladder Co., painting large room down stairs, $40.00.

Hook and Ladder Co., painting assembly room and hall upstairs, $40.00

Steamer Co., painting large room down stairs, $40.00

Painting windows outside, $$35.00.

Hook and Ladder Co., hard pine floor in assembly room, $40.00.

Combination number one was first of its kind in Keene. The wagon was a chemical firefighting engine, which combined soda water and acid to produce foam, which smothered fires. The picture was taken on Vernon Street across from the fire station. Photo by Bion H. Whitehouse. HSCC collection.

Also building a roof over the opening between engine house and shed to the south, $150.00 for a total of $380.00.

A Resolution was passed on May 16th, 1907 relating to a fire alarm box on St. James Street.

On October 17th, 1907 a Resolution was passed relating to runners for the chemical wagon not to exceed $175.00.

1908 [from *City of Keene Annual Report*]

Report of Chief Engineer of the Fire Department

To His Honor the Mayor and Gentlemen of the City Councils:

The closing of the fiscal year ending November 30th, 1908, finds the department fully up to standard as regards apparatus and equipment with the exception of the Deluge hose wagon and Hook and Ladder sled that need repairing, and with a full quota of men in each company.

You will note from the following table of fires and losses that the department has responded to sixty-six alarms, sixteen bell alarms and fifty still alarms, one being out of town, at Gilsum. The net loss at these fires was $12,885.32. Most of this loss was the result of

the fire at Pierce's brush handle shop, at South Keene, which carried very little insurance, only $9,948.00 on a $30,000.00 plant, there being a $20,000.00 loss and $9,948.00 paid makes the net loss of $10,052.00.

Improvements and new apparatus added to the department:

There has been 1,000 feet of cotton, double jacket, rubber lined hose purchased for the department, a new hose rack has been built in the steamer house, rubber coats and boots have been purchased. A new hose house has been built at South Keene, one reel repaired and put in good condition, 1,500 feet of linen hose and two pipes purchased, and everything that is needed for a hose house of this kind supplied. There has been one new pair of horses purchased for the Hook and Ladder company to take the place of the pair that was unfit for service.

Apparatus and force:

The apparatus and force of the department, under a chief and three assistant engineers, located at central fire station Vernon Street, is as follows:

Steamer company (25 men) with Amoskeag steamer No. 1, Button steamer

No. 2, one combination chemical and hose wagon, one Relief hose wagon. Washington Hook and Ladder company (20 men) has one service truck, and one relief truck. Deluge Hose company (20 men) has one hose wagon.

There are 7,000 feet rubber lined fire hose, 200 feet chemical hose, ten extinguishers, one cellar pipe, uniforms, rubber boots, and rubber hats for the department; four sets of swing harnesses, and two extra Barry collars, and three sleds one for each company.

There will be located at South Keene, one hose reel, and 1,500 feet of linen hose.

I make the following recommendations:

The Deluge hose wagon needs repairing, there should be new wheels and axles placed under it, one 30 gallon chemical tank added, and painted. This should be done as soon as possible as it is very inconvenient and we lose much valuable time in answering still alarms especially in the night, as the horses have to be led from one barn to another while we have one chemical wagon at the present time.

On account of the crowded floor apace in the steamer room there should be additional room, in convenient quarters, for the relief hose wagon, as has been demonstrated twice in the past year when extra hose was wanted quickly. A new body for the Hook and Ladder sled is also needed.

The Fire Alarm Telegraph: Box 22 has been taken from the telephone office and placed on the fire station, which proves to be a very satisfactory change. There should be four new boxes to be located as follows: George Street, corner of Sullivan Street; upper Elm Street; in vicinity of the high school building; West Keene.

The fire alarm system is in very good condition, but I would recommend that our present gravity system be changed to storage battery as I think, on investigation it would be proved that storage battery would be more efficient and less expensive.

I take pleasure in further reporting that harmony prevails between the officers and men of the several companies, that they appreciate their quarters and the liberal spirit manifested by the city councils in promptly providing for the needs of the department. It also gives me pleasure to speak of the valuable aid afforded by the chairman and members of the joint standing committee on fire department, and the superintendent of streets, who has done all in his power to further the efficiency of the department. A most cordial relation exists among the members associated with me on the board of engineers, who with the officers and members of the department have efficiently supported me during this term, and to them and the city councils my thanks are hereby returned.

LOUIS A NIMS.

Chief Engineer. Keene, N. H., December 10th, 1908

Fires and Losses for the Year Ending November 30th, 1908

December 24th, 1907 at 1.15 p.m. for Box 54 Island Street the B. & M. R. R. Workman's car, for an overheated stove. Damage $300.00 and no Insurance reported.

February 11th, 1908 at 3.30 a.m. for Box 22 Roxbury Street the Keene Gas Light Co. Work room. Gas radiator problem. Damage $2,480.00 and Insurance paid $2,480.00.

April 24th, 1908 at 10.15 a.m. for Box 52 Emerald Street the Keene Gas Light Co. Dwelling for sparks from the mill on Emerald Street. Damage $45.00 and Insurance paid $45.00.

May 16th, 1908 at 3.24 p.m. for Box 53 Winchester Street the F. O. Hamblett Barn. Unknown cause and livestock was also lost. Damage $1,150.00 and Insurance paid $1,150.00.

May 17th, 1908 at 11.25 a.m. for Box 14 Water Street the C. L. Russell & Chair manufacturing.

Fire caused by rats and damage $12.00 and Insurance paid $12.00.

June 11th, 1908 at 4.15 p.m. for Box 53 Winchester street for a false alarm

June 12th, 1908 at 11.00 p.m. for Box 5 Appian Way the Thayer & Coll's Lumber dealer. The fire was an Incendiary fire and Damage was $200.00 and Insurance paid $200.00.

June 18th, 1908 at 11.20 p.m. for Box 65 South Keene the F. B. Pierce Brush handle factory. Fire caused from the Cyclone machine and damage $161.00 and Insurance paid $161.00.

June 28th, 1908 at 5.35 p.m. for Box 17 Main Street the E. F. Lane Barn for a Lightning strike. Damage $6,000.00 and Insurance paid $4,353.00.

July 8th, 1908 at 4.00 p.m. for Box 22 and July 9th, at 6.50 a.m. for Box 22 and July 12th, 1908 at 1.30 p.m. and for July 16th, 1908 at 10.15 a.m. all for Brush with no reported damage.

August 6th, 1908 at 11.50 p.m. for Box 9, Middle Street the J.B. Hyland House for Electric wires on fire. Damage $2,750.00 and Insurance paid $2,750.00.

September 19th, 1908 at 12.35 a.m. for Box 65 South Keene the F. B Pierce Brush Handle Factory for a fire caused by sparks from the boiler. Damage $9,948.00 and Insurance paid $9,948.00.

November 14th, 1908 at 7.00 a.m. for Aid sent to Gilsum for a fire.

November 22nd, 1908 at 5.10 p.m. for Box 13 Railroad Street the Beaver Mills Factory for an unknown type fire. No damage reported.

Report of the Superintendent of Fire Alarm Telegraph

During the year Box 22 was removed from the telephone office to the outside of the fire station building. A new still alarm call box, was installed in the new telephone exchange which gives the operators the opportunity to respond immediately to telephone calls.

For the most part the Fire alarm system is in good condition.

ALBERT W. GREEN,
Supt. Fire Alarm Telegraph. Keene December 7th, 1908

Resolutions for the Year Ending 1908

A Resolution was passed on February 6th, 1908 relating to electric lights for barn and hay-loft at the fire station. Not to exceed $50.00.

A Resolution was passed on February 20th, 1908 for the purchase of hose and rubber clothing not to exceed $785.00.

A Resolution was passed on May 7th, 1908 for the sale of a hose reel belonging to the city fire department.

A Resolution was passed on September 3rd, 1908 for the purchase of uniforms for firemen. To procure parts of uniforms or alterations and repairs to be made not to exceed $75.00.

A Resolution was passed on October 15th, 1908 in relation to fire house and fire hose in South Keene.

The sum of $550.00 dollars be appropriated for the construction of a suitable house for holding a hose wagon or hose reel in South Keene. Also 850 feet of fire hose will be housed in this house along with the necessary appurtenances.

"FIRE"

1908 LIKE A CANNON SHOT. On June 28th, 1908 Lightning from Sunny Skies Strikes E. F. Lane Barn.

Which Bursts Into Flame Almost instantaneously. No One Hurt by Shock-Barn Destroyed With Loss of $6,000.

A thunderbolt of unusual violence came down from a sky largely cloudless, from which the sun was shining brightly, about twenty minutes before 6 o'clock Sunday afternoon, striking the large barn 75 feet in rear of Elisha F. Lane's Main Street residence and instantly setting fire to the hay in numerous places so that the whole upper part of the building burst into flames. The barn was destroyed with most of its contents, four horses and a pig, the only animals it contained, is estimated at $6,000, insurance on building, $3,000 and on contents about$1,400.

There were several persons near the barn and in full sight of it when the lightening struck F. C. Tilton and wife and W. H. Britton and wife were among those driving by George A. Keith was sitting on his piazza on the opposite side of the street and Supt. Wallace was talking with him. Robert H. Henry, Mr. Lane's hired man, had just come into the yard on his bicycle and was close to the barn and about to enter it when the bolt came down. The lightning appeared to explode in the barn, scattering in all directions. It certainly blew out the windows, some of the glass from overhead striking Henry as he stood near the front door. At the same time the hay in the barn was ignited from one end to the other. Mr. Keith; who sat on the opposite side of the street saw the fire bursting out at once and several people who had but a few steps to walk to get in sight of the barn saw the flames bursting out as soon as they got in sight of it. Mr. Henry did not appear to feel the effects of the lightning, but rushed into the barn which was then in flames overhead and began liberating the four horses that were in there. As fast as he could unfasten them the animals ran out, apparently much frightened and glad to get free. Henry W. Lane, who was on or near his piazza on the opposite side of the street, ran over in time to liberate the last horse. Loads of hay on the barn floor were then burning and the fire was so hot that Mr. Lane said it felt as if his hair was being singed as he followed the horses out. E. H. Fletcher, who lives directly opposite the Lane house, says the barn was all on fire as soon as he was able to get out upon his piazza. There is thus ample testimony that the bolt resulted in an electric or atmosphere explosion in the barn, which thoroughly ignited the hay and dust all through the upper portions of the building.

Mr. Wallace was hurrying to box 17, at the corner of Baker Street, a few seconds after the lightning struck and the alarm was turned in within a minute or two. It seemed to those waiting that the firemen were slow in responding, but others say the apparatus was on the ground in five minutes. People who were up street were impressed with the quick procession of the fire apparatus down through the Square followed each other.

The barn was a mass of flames when the firemen reached it and there was little if any hope of saving much of value. Still they made a vigorous attack and were not long in checking the flames. Gradually the fire was subdued but the roof was substantially all burned off and the rear end and sides consumed half was to the front. The portion that remains will probably be all taken down as the timbers are burned badly nearly all the way through. There was a hot fire in the basement at the rear end, but the foundation walls are probably not injured. The main floor did not all fall in, but it is more or less burned.

The barn was large well lightened and well arraigned being about100 feet long, 75 feet wide and beam posted. There were a number of wagons and carriages in it besides the farm and driving harnesses, farming tools, etc. Several wagons and carriages etc., were got out and quite a lot of the tools. The rest including a covered carriage and Concord Coach wagon nearly new were burned. There were fifteen tons of new hay and about ten tons of old hay in the barn. The barn was built with a good deal of care from first class pine lumber, and cost over $5,000. The fire was the first of any account, which Mr. Lane has had in his experience of over 60 years, during a good portion of which he has been a large property owner. The barn will be rebuilt.

[Printed in the *New Hampshire Sentinel* Keene, N. H.]

———

A Demon Called Fire

"FIRE"

1908 LARGE FACTORY BURNED On September 19th, 1908 the Brick Mill of F. B. Pierce Co., at South Keene was Destroyed Together With all Its Contents-Loss Estimated at $40,000, Partly Insured-About Seventy Hands Thrown Out of Employment.

The worst fire that Keene has experienced for a number of years broke out about 12:30 Friday night in the fuel room at the F. B. Pierce company's brush handle and chair manufactory at South Keene, destroying the brick shop, a finely constructed mill 145x45 feet in size and two and a half stories high with a connecting boiler house, engine room, etc. The loss is estimated at from $40,000 to $50,000. The insurance on the property is $9500. The indications at this writing are that the mill will be rebuilt, although the proprietors have reached no definite conclusion as yet. About seventy hands are thrown out of employment, the number working there being nearly one hundred when business is good.

The fire evidently started in the boiler and fuel room, where a fire that was fortunately discovered early and controlled, started last June. The boiler room is brick and one story, but was nearly high enough for two stories. It was a number of feet easterly of the main brick shop and next to it, in the direction of the shop, was a brick engine room over it. A brick wall cut off the boiler and fuel room, but there were the customary cyclone fuel and dust collector spouts running into both the brick ship and large three story wooden shop some fifty fee further north used for the manufacture of chairs. The chair shop was not injured. It was through the large galvanized iron pipe or spout for conducting the fuel that the fire got into the main brick shop very soon after it was discovered.

An electric car from Marlboro, where there had been a dance, passed the mill about 12:15 and no sign of fire was then seen. This car had just returned to the car barn when the fire broke out. Mrs. Fitch, who lives in the house easterly of the mill, was probably aroused first by the noise of the fire, which she thought at first was a wagon going by. She awoke her husband who worked at the mill. A cry of fire was raised and in a very short time an alarm was rung in from box 65, near the mill.

Rubert H. Abbott, who lives at South Keene, was one of those who got out early and he says that soon after he reached the shop the fire broke out in the main part. He says it traveled through the shop as fast apparently, as a person could go at a brisk walk, being held back for a time by a brick division wall some fifty feet from the south end. This wall, manager Hopkins states, was provided with iron doors, which should have been closed. The firemen however, are confident that they were not closed and such appears to be the case because the fire had got clear through the upper room and the attic of the shop before the firemen got to work.

The hose wagons and Ladder Company responded to the first call, leaving one pair of horses and the relief wagon to protect the city proper. Chief Nims went down in Dr. Spaulding's automobile and firemen who did not reach the station quickly enough to catch the apparatus came down on an electric car, which manager Jennings had run up immediately and placed at their disposal. Streams from the Pierce Company's mill pump and from the big steam pump at the electric railway power station were soon brought to bear on the fire, but it was altogether beyond control by that time so far as the main shop was concerned. The hose wagons on their arrival laid more lines from the electric road's steam pump, which at length supplied five or six powerful streams that were carried to the rear of the mill. Two or three lines were also laid in front of the mill, but the engineers at once saw that more hose would be needed and telephoned for the relief hose wagon, which had been-loaded with an extra supply6. This wagon was started quickly and the empty chemical wagon was sent back later to reload and cover the city. The aqueduct water pressure at south Keene is 80 lbs. Or more, which gives very efficient fire streams and additional hose, was considered more important than a steamer. The engineers state that the hydrant lines from the water works all did good service.

At the north end of the shop there were dry houses and storage buildings beyond the boiler room, in an easterly direction to be covered, also the engine room and the room over it, the overhead bridge leading to the large wooden shop and the shop itself. Fortunately there was no wind, so that the latter was not endangered except by flying sparks. The firemen succeeded in protecting the engine, so that it was not heated enough to break the glass oil cups or interfere with the bearings. It was turned easily by hand after the fire. The boiler was not hurt, probably, the fire in the fuel room being kept down most of the time.

The firemen made a firm stand and had the liveliest fight at the East End of the brick factory, where the fire was kept from spreading through openings on three floors into the wooden office and factory building next to the highway. Engineer Towne was in charge at this end and he has reason to feel more than satisfied with the persistent and plucky work his men did, the fire in that end of the brick building being distinctly beaten back with the roof and attic floors burned off and the wooden building saved, The most valuable machinery in the factory was in this end of the brick shop.

The wooden building is of two stores with a low attic and there were large doorways opening into each story and the attic from the burning factory. The firemen made a stand at these openings as well as on the front of the brick shop. It took a pretty good man to stand

his ground in that attic, against the smoke and heat, and with the knowledge that the fire was likely to work under him in the other stories and cut off the stairways at any time. Once it did this a mass of smoke and flame poured into the lower floor of the wooden section. Engineer Towne call to his men to come down at once and leave their hose. This was done, and a determined attack made from the lower floors. Soon the firemen drove back the flames in the brick building and determined to retake their position in the attic. They found the roof well on fire when they got there, but soon put this out and again reached the doorway of the brick shop, from which they were not again driven. At 2:30 the fire was under control, and then it was easy work until morning, when most of the men and apparatus were sent home.

The brick mill at South Keene was built about 1850 by the late J. A. Fay and Edward Joslin, manufactures of wood working machinery, later the well known J. A. Fay company of Ohio. It was built on honor and well planned, being high posted and remarkably well lighted throughout. It was a waterpower mill, and the wheels and jackshaft are still in a brick head house and are unharmed by the fire. The walls of the mill were build with pilasters between the broad window openings, to reinforce them, and the walls have been hardly warped at all by the fire, the floors which cell in not being trussed or bolted in such a manner as to pull in the walls. The indications are that the walls can be used almost as they remain in rebuilding the mill. The water wheels and engine and boiler, which remain, are of each of 125-horse power. The fire was a spectacular one to witness, the flames shooting high into the air, with little smoke. By the time the firemen got there the whole valley was as light as day as far away as the stone arch railway bridge.

About the time the fire was being under control there was some trouble with the electric road's steam pump, owing to the clogging of the strainer by the coals and charred embers which dropped into the flume when the lower floor of the mill burned from above it, and floated down in great quantities. Superintendent Jennings, who kept careful watch of the lines from the pump and aided the firemen in many ways, quickly set men at work to clear the strainer and maintained his streams nearly intack, starting his auxiliary pump. The power thus produced, giving a heavy pressure and large streams on the pump lines, was a great aid to the department. Engineer Foley handled the fire at the north end of the shop.

When the gable of the wall at the south end of the factory fell, about 1:30, it broke a trolley feed wire and the fire alarm wire causing blows on the bells in Keene. The loss of the special machinery and patterns in the brush handle shop is especially felt, as it will take a good deal of time and money to renew them, but the Pierce company is an old concern of years standing, having been in business in Chesterfield before coming to Keene, and it will doubtless arrange at an early date to supply its customers.

AT SOUTH KEENE F. B. Pierce Company Preparing to Quickly fill General Orders.

There has been little change since Saturday in the situation at the F. B. Pierce Company's brush handle factory, which was destroyed by fire that morning. The brick walls of the factory are found to have been very little injured by the fire.

The insurance men have not been here yet to adjust the loss and nothing has been done toward cleaning up or rebuilding.

Manager Harry D. Hopkins of the company stated Monday that he would be able to make arrangements at once to start up for or five moldings machines on brush handle work and would thus be able to fill promptly almost any order he was likely to receive, provided he is able to secure the

molding machines. And he is quite hopeful of being able to do this.

The water wheel at the mill is uninjured and with a temporary shaft it will not be difficult to provide power enough to run the uninjured chair shop at the mills, and some brush handle machinery as well.

Another solution of the power problem may be found through the Electric railway or the Keene Gas and Electric Company. The latter would only have to run a set of feeders from Swanzey Factory to South Keene to supply all the power required at the Pierce mills.

While Mr. Hopkins has perfected a way to put machines back milling he says that he hopes to be able to find work in a short time for nearly all the hands that were thrown out of employment by the fire.

The latter appears to have come at rather a fortunate time in one respect. It has been reported recently that Mr. Pierce was contemplating the erection of another large building to permit on a decided increase of the chair business at the plant. Had this been completed before the fire came, the results might have been more serious. As it is now there is opportunity for the powerhouse and mills that are entirely separate, and of almost any capacity.

[Printed in the *New Hampshire Sentinel* Keene, N.H.]

1909 [from *City of Keene Annual Report*]

Report of Chief Engineer of the Fire Department

To His Honor the Mayor and Gentlemen of the City Councils:

The closing of the fiscal year ending November 30th, 1909 finds the department fully up to the standard as regards apparatus and equipment, with the exception of the hook and ladder truck and sled, which need repairing, and with a full quota of men in each company.

You will note from the following table of fires and losses that the department has responded to sixty-four alarms, twenty bell alarms and forty-four still alarms. The loss at these fires was $2,467.53 and the insurance paid was $2,417.53, leaving

The net loss of these fires $50.00, the smallest total loss for many years. Much of this is due to the use of chemical wagons and prompt response of the drivers and men in answering the alarms, for which there cannot be too much praise given them. We have responded to three alarms from out of town, one from Winchester, and one from Swanzey and one from Roxbury.

Improvements and new apparatus added to the department:

The Deluge hose wagon has been thoroughly repaired with new wheels and axles, also Hobbs runners, one 30 gallon chemical tank, two 3 gallon chemicals, 100 feet chemical hose, basket, and all other necessary supplies to make it a first-class hose wagon in every respect. The Amoskeag engine is now at Providence, R. I., being thoroughly overhauled and will be put in first-class condition, the company furnishing us with an engine while this is being repaired. There have been new stall doors put in at the Deluge stables, equipped with Clay springs, and new stall doors have been ordered for the Hook and Ladder stables, which will be hung as soon as finished.

All necessary repairs have been made in the house. The fire district has been thoroughly inspected five times in the past year by the board of engineers. I consider this a very important matter as with-out doubt it prevents many fires from being started in dangerous places.

Apparatus and force:

The apparatus and force of the department, under a chief and three assistant engineers, located at central fire station, Vernon Street, is as follows:

Steamer company (25 men) with Amoskeag steamer No. 1, Button steamer No. 2, one combination chemical and hose wagon, one Relief hose wagon. Washington Hook and Ladder company (20 men) has one service has one combination chemical and hose wagon.

There are 6200 feet hose, 300 feet chemical hose, and 1500 feet linen hose a South Keene, six 6-gallon extinguishers, one cellar pipe, uniforms, rubber boots and hats for the department, four sets of swing harnesses, two extra Barry collars, and three sleds. As Hobbs runners take the place of two sleds I would suggest that the city dispose of one sled, as the department has use for but two.

I make the following recommendations:

That the city purchase 1000 feet of cotton rubber lined 2 ½ inch fire hose, as none has been purchased this year; that the Hook and Ladder truck be repaired and Hobbs runners purchased for same as the sled is in bad condition; and that new Clay springs be placed on the stall doors in front of the horses in the Steamer house as these springs are more reliable and give better satisfaction than those now in use.

The Fire Alarm Telegraph:

There has been a great improvement made in the fire alarm telegraph in the past year for which I wish to thank the board of aldermen, the committee of fire department and the superintendent of fire alarm for providing. The iron wire has been replaced with covered copper wire which has proved to be a most satisfactory change; two boxes have been added to the system, one at the corner of Main and Emerald Streets, and one at the Keene Glue factory, the Keene Glue Co. paying for the latter. I think for better protection of property there should be four new boxes added to the system, located as follows: George Street, corner of Sullivan; upper Elm

Street; in vicinity of high school building; West Keene.

I take pleasure in further reporting that harmony prevails between officers and men of the several companies, that they appreciate their quarters and the liberal spirit manifested by the city councils in promptly providing for the needs of the department. It also gives me pleasure to speak of the valuable aid afforded by the chairman and members of the joint standing committee on fire department, the lands and buildings committee, and the superintendent of streets. A most cordial relation exists among the members associated with me on the board of engineers, who, with the officers, members of the department, and public have assisted me in making this one of the most successful years in the history of the department, and to them and the city councils may thanks are hereby returned.

> LOUIS A. NIMS,
> Chief Engineer.
> Keene, December 8th, 1909

Fires and Losses for the Year Ending November 30th, 1909

December 7th, 1908 at 6.05 a.m. for Box 8 the B. & M paint shops for an overheated light. No reported damage.

December 17th, 1908 at 7.20 p. m. for Box 8 Main Street the B. & W. Hotel, C. H. Ellis owner for a gasoline ignition type fire with no reported damage.

December 24th, 1908 at 9.50 p.m. for Box 16 Marlboro Street the G. C. Shedd House for a plumber thawing frozen pipes. Damage $160.00 and Insurance paid $160.00.

January 16th, 1909 at 11.25 a.m. for Box 18 Marlboro Street the J. E. Sevigny House for a Chimney fire with no reported damage.

February 3rd, 1909 at 1.05 a.m. for Box 37 Mechanic Street the S. W. Dart Fish market for a steam pipe which set wood on fire. Damage $50.00 and no insurance reported.

February 10th, 1909 at 7.50 a.m. Box 52 the B. & M. Carpenter Shop for a spontaneous type fire. No reported damage.

February 16th, 1909 at 6.30 a.m. to Spruce Street the M. A. Sterling House for a Chimney fire with Damage of $15.00 and Insurance paid $15.00.

March 21st, 1909 aid sent to the town of Winchester.

March 22nd, 1909 at 11.45 p.m. for Box 9 Washington street the City Store F. L Carey for an unknown type fire. Damage $1,051.47 and insurance paid $1,051.47.

April 19th, 1909 at 3.30 p.m. for Box 54 Island Street the J. A. Cullane House for a Chimney fire with no reported damage.

April 24th, 1909 at 4.12 p.m. for Box 33 Maple Street the A. H. Fisk House for a grass fire which started the house on fire as well. Damage $407.50 and Insurance paid $407.50.

May 13th, 1909 at 7.39 a.m. for Box 22 for West Hill the Mrs. G. W. Stratton property for a brush fire. The same day at 11.50 a.m. also the department responded for a brush fire same address.

May 18th, 1909 at 10.13 a.m. for Box 19 Marlboro Street the Mary Davis House for an unknown type fire. Damage $5.00 and Insurance paid $5.00.

June 28th, 1909 aid sent Roxbury for a fire.

June 29th, 1909 at 9.15 a.m. to Wheelock Park City of Keene for a brush fire. No reported damage.

August 2nd, 1909 at 2.28 p.m. for box 22 Brush fire at the Sidney Ellis property. No reported damage.

August 4th, 1909 at 5.40 p.m. aid sent to Swanzey for a fire.

August 15th, 1909 at 12.30 p.m. the F. D. Colony property for a brush fire with no reported damage.

September 27th, 1909 at 3.00 p.m. to South Keene for a Train Wreck of the B. & M. R. R.

November 7th, 1909 at 11.30 a.m. for Box 23 Church Street the F. Pett's House for a Hot stove pipe with no reported damage.

November 20th, 1909 at 9.25 p.m. for Box 8 Main Street the Miss L. J. Brown House for a Kerosene heater. Fire was upgraded with addition equipment. For smoke in the house of G. H. Jackson as well. Damage was $45.00 and Insurance paid $45.00.

Note: 20 bell alarms 44 still alarms for the year.

Report of Superintendent of Fire Alarm Telegraph

During the year of 1909 the joint standing committee on fire department secured the services of Engineer George F. Atwood of New York city, for a survey of the fire alarm system.

The report advised that repairs to be made to the system and install appliances and also to release on the repeater, bells, and strikers in the towers of city hall and the Court Street Church.

The committee also purchased two boxes for the corner of Main and Emerald Streets, numbered 6, and one for the corner of High and Elm Streets, numbered 32 and caused three of the old Stevens boxes to be rebuilt over. The Glue Factory on Court Street added a new box numbered 47 and may be used by the public.

ALBERT W. GREEN, Superintendent of Fire Alarm Telegraph Keene, December 8th, 1909.

Joint Resolutions ending for the year 1909

On January 21st, 1909 a Resolution was passed relating to the Deluge hose wagon. The hose wagon to be repaired including new axle-tree, a new pole, a thirty gallon chemical tank and the varnishing and lettering of said wagon and the sum not exceed $700.00.

A Letter was written to the Chairman of the Fire Department Committee for the purpose of a fire alarm box be placed at 480 Court Street. This site is the site of the Keene Glue Company. The Box would be paid for by the Keene Glue Company and would be available to the public as the letter read.

A Resolution relating to this fire alarm Box was passed on September 16th, 1909 for the purpose of placing a Fire Alarm Box at the Keene Glue Company not to exceed $100.00.

A Resolution was passed on September 16th, 1909 for the purpose of uniforms and repairs on clothing for the fire department. Not to exceed $75.00.

A Resolution was passed relating to the purchase of runners for the Deluge hose wagon not to exceed $150.00.

1909 UPBOUND FLYER WRECKED

An Interesting Story, which involved a response by the Keene Fire Department. On September 27th, 1909 an Engine and Tender Derailed

Train Had Taken Siding to Wait for Down Train Derailing.

Switch Was Open and Engine and Crew Did Not See it

Crew Jumped No One Hurt.

The flyer from Boston, due to arrive in this city at 1:49 Monday afternoon, was saved from a sad fate by a very narrow chance when the engine and tender left the track just this side of the stone arch a few rods west of the South Keene Station. The engine and tender were overturned upon their sides on the steep bank, but not a car of the heavily laden passenger train left the iron. Engineer Phalen and his fireman jumped and were not hurt.

The train had orders to wait at South Keene for the 2:17 train from Keene to Boston, the up train being nearly an hour late. It pulled out on the siding at the South Keene Station and had proceeded far enough so that the engine and tender were across the bridge part of the arch.

There is in this siding, just at the west end of the abutment, a derailing switch intended to derail freight cars which are sent onto the siding, instead of allowing them to go past the switch and onto the main line track. This derailing switch was open and was not seen by the engineer or fireman on the flyer or by the man who went ahead, after the train stopped to throw the main line switch as soon as the down train passed. It is said that the derailing switch was partly concealed by the engine while it stood on the siding.

When the front wheels of the engine struck this switch they were at once sent to the left off the rail and the engine and tender were derailed, toppling over on their left sides on the bank. The train was going so slow that there was not power enough to send the baggage cars and the passenger coached behind off the iron after the engine and tender and they remained on the rail, the wheels of the baggage car within a few inches of the derailing switch.

The engine lay upon its side with the front truck off the frame. It had plowed into the dirt and the tender had flowed it. When the engine left the rail the engineer and firemen jumped, although the engineer did not get off until the engine was tipping over.

A telephone message was sent to this city saying that the flyer was wrecked and this was somehow construed to mean that there was a fire. The chemical was therefore sent out, without knowing where the fire was. A few minutes later an alarm was rung in from box 22, at the Vernon Street Station, and the fire department was sent down to the wreck. It was not needed however, as nothing was burning.

A large number of people from Keene some of whom expected friends or relatives on the train went to South Keene to see the wreck, not whether or not anyone had been hurt. The accident took placer at the same point where a big freight engine was similarly derailed a year or so ago. The engine was picked up Tuesday morning by the steam derrick car and wrecking crew from Deerfield.

The flyer was delayed by the accident nearly two hours.

1910 [from *City of Keene Annual Report*]

Report of Chief Engineer of the Fire Department

To His Honor the Mayor and Gentlemen of the City Councils:

I herewith submit for your consideration the following report of the fire department for the fiscal year ending November 30th, 1910, which finds the department fully up to the standard as regards apparatus and equipment and with a full quota of men in each company.

You will note from the following table of fire and losses that the department has responded to sixty-nine alarms, sixteen bell alarms, fifty still alarms and three calls from out of town. The loss at these fires was $5,650.00. The insurance paid was $5,650.00. The estimated valuation of the buildings that the fires were in was $76,650.00. Much of this small loss is due to the use of chemical wagons, and prompt response of the drivers and men in answering the alarms, for which there cannot be too much credit given, and to the aid given by the citizens in keeping their cellars and alley ways free from rubbish and other combustible matter. We have responded to three alarms out of town, all in Swanzey, two brush fires and one at the hotel at Swanzey Center, Swanzey, having paid the city for the entire expense of these fires.

Improvements and new apparatus added to the department:

The Hook and Ladder truck has been painted and Hobbs runners ordered for the same; 1,100 feet of 2 ½-inch rubber –lined fire hose have been purchased. The Amoskeag engine, reported last year as being taken away for repairs has been returned and works to our entire satisfaction. The fire district has been kept thoroughly inspected from time to time by the board of engineers. This I consider a very important matter as without doubt it prevents many fires from being started in dangerous places. With the aid and advice of the county solicitor we had fire escapes placed on eleven buildings including all coming within the law passed at the last legislature.

Apparatus and force:

The apparatus and force of the department, under a chief and three assistant engineers, located at central fire station, Vernon Street, is as follows:

Steamer company (25 men) with Amoskeag steamer No. 1, Button steamer No. 2, one combination chemical and hose wagon, one Relief hose wagon. Washington Hook and Ladder company (20 Men) has one service truck and one Relief truck. Deluge Hose company (20 men) has one combination chemical and hose wagon.

There are 6,800 feet of fire hose, 300 feet of chemical hose, 1,500 feet of linen hose at south Keene, six 6-gallon and four 3-gallon extinguishers. One cellar pipe, uniforms, rubber boots and hats for the department, four sets of swing harnesses, two extra Barry collars and three sleds. As Hobbs runners take the place of the three sleds I would recommend that the city dispose of two of these as the department has use for but one.

I make the following recommendations:

That the city purchase 1,000 feet of 2 ½-inch cotton rubber lined hose to replace hose that has given out in the past year, as hose is only warranted for four years and some of ours is much older than that and liable to give out at any time; that the city purchase a Deluge set which would be a great convenience in case of fire in large blocks where a heavy steam is required, and in a measure take the place of a water tower and be of much less expense to the city; that new stall doors with Clay springs and hinges attached, these being more reliable and giving better satisfaction than those now in use, be placed in front of the horses at the steamer house; that the city purchase rubber coats for the department to replenish as well as to replace those that are now giving out; that there be three new fire alarm boxes installed, one at West Keene, one at upper Elm Street, and one on George street at the corner of Sullivan Street. As these are places situated at some distance from the fire station these boxes would insure a more prompt response to an alarm. I also deem it necessary to have at our disposal from December 1st, to April, during the season of high winds and heavy snow, two pair of horses at the station. Under the existing condition this is impossible without infringing upon the rights of the superintendent of highways, as the fire department pays for but one regular team, and for the other three for answering alarms only, I think that the fire department should bear the expense of the extra team. This would provide for emergencies during this time of the year when the drivers are apt to be plowing out sidewalks, where it is impossible for them to hear the alarm.

The Fire Alarm Telegraph

Since the fire alarm telegraph was repaired and improved last year it has given good satisfaction and very little trouble for which I extend my thanks to the superintendent. There has been one new box authorized to be located on Middle street in the vicinity of the high school building, the number to be 41.

I take pleasure in further reporting that harmony prevails between officers and men of the several companies, that they appreciate their quarters and the liberal spirit manifested by the city councils in promptly providing for the needs of the department. It also gives me pleasure to speak of the valuable aid afforded by the chairman and members of the joint standing committee on fire department, the lands and buildings committee and the superintendent of the streets. A most cordial relation exists among the members associated with me on the board of engineers, who with the officers, members of the department, and public have assisted me during the past year

and to them and the city councils I extend my thanks and hearty appreciation.

LOUIS A. NIMS,

Chief Engineer, Keene, N. H., December 10th, 1910

Fires and Losses for the Year Ending November 30th, 1910

January 11th, 1910 for Box 18 Jennison Street the George S. Dodge House for a chimney fire with no reported damage.

January 31st, 1910 at 7.00 a.m. for Box 13 Beaver Mills Co. Railroad Street for friction from a belt on a machine. Damage $13.75 and Insurance paid $13.75.

February 5th, 1910 for Box 32 Elm Street the Mr. Doody House for a Chimney fire with no reported damage.

February 14th, 1910 at 7.10 p.m. for Box 53 Winchester Ct. the George W. Porter House for a Lamp fire. Damage $7.00 and Insurance paid $7.00.

March 8th, 1910 at 4.25 p.m. for Box 25 Sullivan Street the J. Boyea House for a Defective Chimney. Damage $691,50 and Insurance paid $691.50.

April 5th, 1910 at 5.30 a.m. for Box 33 Washington Ave. the Ellen A. Ellis Barn. Unknown cause and damage was $475.00 and Insurance paid $475.00.

May 14th, 1910 at 9.15 p.m. for Box 22 West Street the Carl Johnson House for an Unknown type fire. Damage $3,050.00 and Insurance paid $3,050.00.

July 4th, 1910 at 1.20 p.m. for Box 22 the Driving park, Keene Electric R. R. for a Brush fire. No reported damage.

July 4th, 1910 at 8.15 p.m. for Box 24 Douglas Street the Mrs. Clara S. Fay House for Firecrackers. Damage $10.00 and Insurance paid $10.00.

August 15th, 1910 at 12.40 p.m. for Box 52 Emerald Street the Boston & Main R. R. Carpenter Shop. Sparks on the roof from an engine. No reported damage.

October 2nd, 1910 at 3.00 a.m. for Box 52 Emerald Street the Impervious Pkg. Co. Saw mill for sparks from an engine.

October 13th, 1910 at 5.18 p.m. for Box 42 School Street the Dr. E. A. Tracey Barn for an unknown cause for the fire. Damage $1,104.95 and Insurance paid $1,104.95.

October 14th, 1910 at 4.53 for Box 46 Forest Street the W. S. Garfield House for an over turned lamp fire. Damage $183.50 and Insurance paid $183.50.

October 15th, 1910 for Box 22 Winchester Street the Hiram Blake property for a brush fire. No reported damage.

November 27th, 1910 at 12.03 p.m. for Box 18 Dartmouth Street the Harry Levine House for a Chimney fire with damage of $50.00 and Insurance paid $50.00.

November 28th, 1910 at 3.30 a.m., for box 18 Marlboro Street the George W. Porte House for a Chimney fire with damage of $65.00 and Insurance paid $65.00.

Report of Superintendent of Fire Alarm Telegraph.

Few changes have been made on the circuits of the fire alarm lines during the present year.

Box 53 has been moved to a new location from the corner of Island and Winchester streets to the corner of Winchester Street and Winchester Court, opposite the Marcus Ellis place. This move was made on the account of the habit of some very young children of using the box for a plaything.

A new fire alarm box numbered 41 has been ordered and placed in Middle Street.

ALBERT W. GREEN, Superintendent Fire Alarm Telegraph.

Joint Resolutions Ending for the Year 1910.

A Joint Resolution was passed February 3rd, 1910 relating to the purchase of fire hose. Not to exceed $750.00.

Two Joint Resolutions was passed on October 6th, 1910. One for the free use of city hall by the Steam Fire Engine & Hose Co. for the purpose of holding a social gathering, on the night of the annual inspection of the fire department October 13th, 1901. 2nd, Resolution relating to the repairs on uniforms and or purchase parts of uniforms not to exceed $75.00.

On November 3rd 1910 a Resolution was passed to purchase runners for the hook and ladder wagon not to exceed $150.00.

On November 17th a Resolution was passed to purchase a new fire box to be placed on Middle Street not to exceed $75.00.

1911 [from *City of Keene Annual Report*]

Report of Chief Engineer of the Fire Department

To His Honor the Mayor and Gentlemen of the City Councils:

I herewith submit for your consideration the following report of the fire department for the fiscal year ending November 30th, 1911, which finds the department fully up to the standard as regards apparatus and equipment and with a full quota of men in each company.

You will note from the following table of fires and losses that the department has responded to one hundred and five calls, divided as follows:

Twenty bell alarms, seventy-two still alarms, and thirteen brush fire calls. Five of these were calls for help from out of town. This is much the largest number of call we have had in the history of the department. The loss at these fires was $23,203.38. The insurance paid was $9,861.16. The estimated valuation of the buildings that the fires were in was $107.800. Much of this loss was due to the fire on Emerald Street July 6th, to the property owned by the Impervious Package Co., there being no insurance on this stock.

Improvements and new apparatus added to the department:

There have been purchased 1000 feet of 2 ½ inch rubber-lined hose, one Eastman Deluge set, rubber coats and boots, and all necessary repairs have been made in fire station. The buildings are now in good condition with the exception of the tin roof on the fire station. There have been three new fire alarm boxes installed, number 41, located on Middle Street near high school building, number 31 on Washington Street opposite Pine Street, and number 73 at corner of Arch Street and Park Avenue.

Apparatus and force:

The apparatus and force of the department, under a chief and three assistant engineers, located at central fire station, Vernon Street, is as follows:

Steamer Company (25 men) with Amoskeag Steamer No. 1, Button Steamer No. 2, one combination chemical and hose wagon, one Relief hose wagon, Washington Hook and Ladder Company (20 men) has one service truck and one Relief truck. Deluge Hose Company (20 men) has one combination chemical and hose wagon.

There are 8,500 feet of fire hose, 300 feet of chemical hose, 1,500 feet of linen hose at South Keene, six 6-gallon and four 3-gallon extinguishers, one cellar pipe, uniforms, rubber boots and hats for the department, four sets of swing harnesses, two extra Barry collars, three sleds, one three-way Eastman Deluge set, and three sets of Hobbs runners.

I make the following recommendations:

That the city purchase a triple combination automobile fire truck. This piece of apparatus was thoroughly demonstrated at the recent National Convention of Fire Chiefs and unanimously acknowledged by the fire chiefs as being the most complete, practical and satisfactory piece of fire apparatus ever exhibited; that the city purchase 1000 feet of fire hose; that the department be allowed two pairs of horses to be kept at fire station, and available at all times. As I recommended last year, that our fire alarm telegraph system be changed from gravity to a storage battery. This change will necessitate the expenditure of several hundred dollars, but can be operated at much less expense and give better satisfaction than the system now in use.

Report of the National convention of Fire Chiefs held at Milwaukee on Sept. 19th, 1911, which I was delegated by the city to attend:

The convention lasted four days and was attended by about seven hundred fire chiefs representing all sections of the United States and Canada.

The greatest interest was manifested throughout all the meetings and much valuable information was obtained. The discussion in regard to the prevention and extinguishing of fires, the exhibition of all kinds of modern fire apparatus and everything manufactured for the use of fire departments, the automobile manufacturers' exhibit of pumping engines were most instructive and valuable to all in attendance.

It was the unanimous opinion of the delegates that more attention should be given to the prevention of fires, and that the fire districts should be most rigidly guarded, and that the automobile fire trucks were the only kind of fire apparatus to be purchased at the present time. I made special effort to investigate the different kinds of these machines, there being several kinds manufactured, as without doubt the city will be called upon in the near future to purchase an additional fire truck.

We received a most cordial welcome from the mayor and firemen of Milwaukee, who did all in their power to make our visit to their city an agreeable and pleasant one.

The convention will be held next year in Denver, Colorado, and I trust that every city in our state will be represented by its fire chief.

It is gratifying to note that through the efforts of the mayor, the committee on fire department, and local firemen the State Firemen's Relief Association held its annual convention in this city in September, which event proved a pleasant feature of the year's work.

I take pleasure in further reporting that harmony prevails between officers and men of the several companies, that they appreciate their quarters and the liberal spirit manifested by the city councils in promptly providing for the needs of the department. It also gives me pleasure to speak of the valuable aid afforded by the chairmen and members of the joint standing committee on fire department, the lands and buildings committee and the superintendent of the streets. A most cordial relation exists among the members associated with me on the board of engineers who with the officers, members of the department, and public have assisted me during the past year and to them and the city councils I extend my thanks and hearty appreciation.

LOUIS A. NIMS,

Chief Engineer. Keene, N. H., December 6th, 1911

Fires and Losses for the Year Ending November 30th, 1911

[*Compiler's Note*: For the date December 1910 and on, the times were not placed on the fire losses in the city's annual reports.]

December 12th, 1910 to the Dan'l W. Clark house for an unknown fire. Damage $80.00 no insurance.

December 14th, 1910 to the Mrs. Chas E. Keith house for an unknown fire. Damage $572.56 and Insurance paid $572.56.

December 25th, 1910 to the Anna M. Richards house for an oil stove problem. Damage $190.54.

January 4th, 1911 to the Nellie E. Warren house for an overturned lamp. Damage $50.00 and Insurance paid $50.00.

January 17th, 1911 to the Lizzie C. Chase house for a defective flue. Damage $50.00 and Insurance paid $50.00.

January 18th, 1911 to the H. A Lesure house for a plumber thawing out pipes. Damage $13.40 and Insurance paid $13.40.

January 22nd, 1911 to the Annie M. Maloney house for a plumber thawing out pipes. Damage $7.50 and Insurance paid $7.50.

February 23rd, 1911 to the Putney and Buckminster Apt. house for a chimney fire. Damage $74.35 and Insurance paid $74.35.

February 8th, 1911 to the Chas. Crain house for a chimney fire. Damage $10.00 and Insurance paid $10.00.

February 24th, 1911 to the Boston & Main Hotel and Stores for a chimney fire. Damage $600.00 and Insurance paid $600.00.

February 24th, 1911 to the Wright & Moore Barn for unknown fire cause. Damage $1,130.15 and Insurance paid $1,130.15.

February 25th, 1911 to the Henry Ellis house for a chimney fire. Damage $40.00 and Insurance paid $40.00.

March 9th, 1911 to the Harry Levine house for a chimney fire. Damage $50.00 and Insurance paid $50.00.

March 29th, 1911 to the Chas A. Jones N.E. Machine Met Co. Rag Shop for a Chimney fire. Damage $1,775.00 and Insurance paid $1,775.00.

April 2nd, 1911 to the Herbert M. Brown house for a chimney fire. Damage $20.70 and insurance paid $20.70.

April 11th, 1911 to the Mrs. Anne Maloney for a Chimney fire. Damage $10.00 and Insurance paid $10.00.

April 11th, 1911 to the John L. Perry house for a chimney fire. Damage $17.69 and Insurance paid $17.69.

May 4th, 1911 to the Wm. Brown Stores for an unknown fire. Damage $146.41 and Insurance paid $146.41.

June 6th, 1911 to the Wm. Brown house for a combustion type fire with Damage of $100.00 and Insurance paid $100.00.

June 22nd, 1911 to the E. M. Bullard house for an overheated stove. Damage $31.42 and Insurance paid $31.42.

July 6th, 1911 to the Impervious Pkg. Co. Storage building in the mill yard for an unknown type fire. Damage $12,000 and Insurance paid, building totaled.

'FIRE'

PATCH FIRE OF IMPERVIOUS PACKAGE COMPANY

One of Keene's most spectacular fires for many years was known as the Patch Fire located at the lower end of Emerald Street. It extended from the Gas House to Ellis Bros. Florist and from Ralston St. to the Canal. In this area was a saw mill and storage area owned by the Impervious Package Co. The entire contents, 6,000 cords of staves, 300,000 feet of headings and a large supply of logs, were destroyed in this $30,000 fire which swept the entire area of the patch. This was one of the hottest and most dangerous fired Keene had witnessed for many years. The temperature on this day, July 6, 1911 was 106 degrees, and this head had been hovering over the city for the past few days. This fire was under the direction of chief Louis Nims of the Keene Fire Department, who had requested help from Marlboro and West Swanzey fire departments for their steamers along with men and hose. Water was pumped from all the hydrants in the area and drafted as far away as the Faulkner and Colony dam on West Street.

Many homes in the area were threatened by this blazing fire, which took its toll when it burnt the home of Mr. Charles Burns on the south side of Emerald St. and a three story storage building, owned by Humphrey's Foundry, that was used for patterns and many two and three story wooden buildings belonging to the Impervious Packaging Co. Ellis Bros., to the south of the Patch suffered a great loss in flowers.

Sparks from the fire had set fire to the awnings of the Cheshire House Block, Which was located on the corner of Main and Roxbury Streets. There were many firemen overcome by the intense heat along with Engineer Fred Towne who was placed under doctor's care and ordered to remain home for several days.

The fire had burned for several days and left only the remains of ashes. In recapping the history of this great fire many firemen of today have told this writer the part that they had played. Earl Smith and Fred Sharkey, who only ten years old, worked very hard at this fire carrying water for the tired firemen. Today they are both members of the Hook and Ladder Co. Chief Walter R. Messer, who was only five years old, at the time of this fire, says he remembers going to the fire in a baby carriage accompanied by his mother. Little did he realize that someday he would become Chief of a fire department. Walter Barnard, a member of the Steamer Co. was employed by Beaver Mills Co. when the alarm was run in. He immediately ran to the Main St. just in time to catch a ride on the horse drawn Hook and Ladder wagon. As he jumped for the wagon he slipped and almost fell beneath the wheels of the fire apparatus but was grabbed by the belt and saved by Fordyce Thomas.

"written by Emile Desrosier"

————

July 6th, 1911 to the Fred Desrosier house for an overheated stove. Damage $44.65 and Insurance paid $44.65.

July 6th, 1911 to the N. Hart house for an unknown type fire. Damage $60.00 and Insurance paid $60.00.

July 6th, 1911 to the Humphrey Machine Co. Foundry & Store for an unknown type fire. Damage $3,803.00 and Insurance paid $3,803.00.

July 6th, 1911 to the W. D. Britton House for fire damage of $13.75 and Insurance paid $13.75.

July 6th, 1911 for the Mrs. Chas Burns House for fire damage of $200.00 and Insurance paid $200.00.

July 6th, 1911 to the P. B. Heywood Hotel for Starks on the awnings. Damage $44.00 and Insurance paid $44.00.

July 6th, 1911 to the N. G. Gurnsey & Co. store for Sparks on the awnings. Damage $5.00 and Insurance paid $2.50.

July 6th, 1911 to the Bertram Ellis House for fire damage. Damage $14.89 and Insurance paid $14.89.

August 12th, 1911 to the George W. Porter House for a defective chimney. Damage $50.00 and Insurance paid $50.00.

September 30th, 1911 to the George O. Hayward House for a fire caused by Sparks from a bonfire. Damage $30.98 and Insurance paid $30.98.

October 11th, 1911 to the Fowler, Norwood Box Co. for an overheated tar kettle on the roof. Damage $25.00 and Insurance paid $25.00.

October 29th, 1911 to the Leonard O. Boyce House for a defective chimney. Damage $15.00 and Insurance paid $15.00.

November 3rd, 1911 to the Lucius Allen House for a chimney fire. Damage 10.00 and Insurance paid $10.00.

November 16th, 1911 to the Boston & main R. R. Junk shop for Combustion in rags. Damage $300.00 and Insurance paid $300.00.

November 16th, 1911 to the Horace W. Bond House for a chimney fire. Damage $55.00 and Insurance paid $55.00.

Report of Superintendent of Fire Alarm Telegraph.

Three new alarm boxes have been purchased and installed this year: No. 73 at the junction of Park Ave. and opposite Pine Street; and No. 13 at the Beaver Mills, the old box to be rebuilt over with new appliances and to be numbered 1-4-2, and to be installed on Willow Street. Attention is particularly called to this new ring. Commencing as usual, with the ward number, it is followed by 4-2.

Respectfully,
ALBERT W. GREEN, Superintendent Fire Alarm Telegraph.
December 7th, 1911.

Joint Resolutions for the year Ending 1911.

Passed on September 7th, 1911 the sum of $130.00 for the purchase of uniforms or parts of uniforms for the fire department.

A Joint Resolution was passed on September 7th, 1911 to install new fire alarm box on Park Ave. opposite the residence of Louis A. Nims and to have the old box at the Beaver Mills Mill be rebuilt with modern improvements and latter to be located on Willow Street.

1912 [from *City of Keene Annual Report*]

Report of the Chief Engineer of the Fire Department and the Superintendent of Fire alarm Telegraph

To His Honor the Mayor and Gentlemen of the City Councils:

In accordance with the requirements of the city ordinance, I herewith submit for your consideration the following report of the fire department for the fiscal year ending November 30th, 1912, which finds the department fully up to the standard as regards apparatus and equipment, and with a full quota of men in each company.

You will note from the following table of fires and losses that the department has responded to ninety –two calls, divided as follows: fifteen bell alarms, seventy still alarms, and seven brush fire calls. This number is thirteen less than the number of calls in 1911. The loss at these fires was $14,941.92. The insurance paid was $13,202.85. The estimated valuation of the buildings, where the fires occurred, is $113,493.97.

Improvements and new apparatus added to the department:

With the exception of the expense of, and what pertains to the new fire alarm system, there has been very little purchased for the fire department. A much needed new roof has been put on the fire station and other necessary purchases made to keep the department up to its usual standard.

Apparatus and Force:

The apparatus and force of the department, under a chief and three assistant engineers, located on Vernon Street, is as follows: The Keene Steam Fire Engine Hose Company (25 men) has Steamer No. 1, Amoskeag, Button Steamer No. 2, one combination chemical and hose wagon, one Relief hose wagon; Washington Hook & Ladder Company (20 men) has one service truck and one Relief truck, Deluge Hose Company (20 men) has one combination chemical and hose wagon.

There are 7,450 feet of fire hose. About 2000 feet of this hose is old and unreliable. There are 300 feet of chemical hose, 1,5000 feet of linen hose at South Keene, six 6-gallon and four 3-gallon extinguishers, one cellar pipe, one three-way Eastman Deluge set, uniforms, rubber coats, hats and boots for the department, four sets of swing harnesses, two extra Barry collars, three sleds and three sets of Hobbs runners.

I respectfully make the following recommendations: That the city purchase a triple combination automobile fire truck, as the city is constantly extending its water mains, in some cases two or more miles from the fire station, making it almost impossible for us to answer alarms at so great a distance, in time to render much, if any, service without injury to the horses; also in case of fire in sets of farm buildings located in the suburbs of the city the automobile fire truck would spare the horses the long hard runs and do quicker and better service; that until the city provides the automobile fire truck the department be allowed two pair of horses to be kept in the fire station available at all times; that the city purchase 1000 feet of new fire hose, not having been purchase the past year and much of that now in use being very unreliable.

In accordance with my recommendation of last year, the city has purchase and caused to be installed new up-to-date fire alarm equipment from the Star Electric Company of Binghamton, N.Y., at an expense of $1,895.00; it has also purchased a whistle blowing machine at a cost of $350.00. The fire alarm apparatus has been installed in a room adequately fitted up for it, at the fire station. The new fire alarm system which replaces the old consists of a repeater, storage battery, automatic switchboard, whistle blowing machine, and a manual transmitter.

The board of engineers has caused certain numbers to be known as transmitter calls. These calls are to be given for fire in location where there are no fire alarm boxes and assistance is called in by telephone. This

System, which is in charge of Mr. E. B. Riley, a very efficient operator, has worked to our entire satisfaction since the date of installation, October 11, 1912. Too much credit cannot be given Mr. Riley for the efficient care that he has given the new fire alarm system since it was installed. As all of the wire used in the system is copper-covered, with the exception of five miles which is iron, I would recommend that this wire be replaced with copper-covered wire.

There has been one new fire alarm box, number 141, installed on Willow Street, and two more boxes have been ordered and will be installed in the near future, one on Railroad Street, number 113, and one, number 27, on Washington Street, opposite the Burdett chair shop.

I take pleasure in further reporting that harmony prevails between officers and men of the several companies, that they appreciate their quarters and the liberal spirit manifested by the city councils in promptly providing for the needs of the department. It also gives me pleasure to speak of the valuable aid afforded by the chairmen and members of the joint standing committee on fire department, the lands and buildings committee and the superintendent of the streets. A most cordial relation exists among the members associated with me on the board of engineers, who with the officers, members of the department. And public, have assisted me during the past year, and to them and the city councils I extend my thanks and hearty appreciation.

LOUIS A. NIMS.

Chief Engineer and Superintendent of Fire alarm Telegraph. Keene, December 6th, 1912.

Fires and Losses for the Year Ending November 30th, 1912.

December 2nd, 1911 to the A. Amidon Greenhouse for an oil stove problem. Damage $200.00 no Insurance.

December 20th, 1911 to the Mrs. Forman house for a Chimney fire. No damage reported.

December 28th, 1911 to the Mr. Dow House for a false call.

December 30th, 1911 to the Nan Hard Est. for a Burning Grass. Fire caused damage to Barn and house Damage $150.00 and Insurance paid $50.00.

December 30th, 1911 to the Mr. Bushy house and Barn and to the W. L Goodnow House and Barn for children playing with matches. Damage $1,012.00 with Insurance paying only $12.00.

December 30th, 1911 to the Dr. Chas. Walker House for a Chimney fire with no reported damage.

January 6th, 1912 to the Hiram Houghton House for a Chimney fire. Damage $3.79 and Insurance paid $3.79.

January 7th, 1912 to the Mr. Vigneau House for a Chimney fire with no damage reported.

January 11th, 1912 to the Mr. Rivers for a Chimney fire with no reported damage.

January 13th, 1912 to the Mrs. Deyo House for a Chimney fire with no reported damage.

January 18th, 1912 to the B. & M. R. R., the Mrs. Chas Hunter House for an overheated oven with no reported damage.

January 27th, 1912 to the Chas. G. Putney House for a Chimney fire with damage of $135.00 and Insurance paid $67.50.

February 3rd, 1912 to the Clark Knapp House for a Chimney fire with no reported damage.

February 4th, 1912 to the W. T. Winn House for a Chimney fire with no reported damage.

February 4th, 1912 to the Chas. G. Wyer for a Chimney fire with damage of $13.00 and Insurance paid $13.00.

February 9th, 1912 to a reported Chimney fire the Chas G. Wyer with no damage reported.

February 10th, 1912 to the F. I Wetmore House for a Chimney fire with Damage of $12.00 and Insurance paid $12.00.

February 12th, 1912 to the Anna W. Hyland House for an overheated furnace. Damage $97.04 and Insurance paid $97.04.

February 12th, 1912 to the Geo. S. Dodge House for a Chimney fire. No damage reported.

February 12th, 1912 to the Mr. Lovely House for a Chimney fire with no reported damage.

February 12th, 1912 to the Impervious Pkg. Co. for a Chimney fire with no reported damage.

February 12th, 1912 to the Hober White House for a Chimney fire with no reported damage.

A Demon Called Fire

February 12th, 1912 to the Robinson & Brett Manufactory for an unknown fire. Damage $1,867.85 and Insurance paid $1,867.85.

February 18th, 1912 to the Keene Steam Power Co. Nims, Whitney & Co. for a Chimney fire with no reported damage.

February 18th, 1912 to the C. H. Barnard House for an unknown fire. Damage $4.00 and Insurance paid $4.00.

February 18th, 1912 to the Rev. M. Miller House of the Methodist Church for a Chimney fire with no damage reported.

February 19th, and February 22nd, 1912 to the Keene Realty Co. for a Chimney fire with no reported damage either time.

February 24th, 1912 to the Geo. Whitney House for a Chimney fire with no reported damage.

March 20th, 1912 to the Mrs. Ellen A. Ellis for a Chimney fire with damage of $40.00 and Insurance paid $40.00.

March 21st, 1912 to the Ellis Bros. Boiler Houser for Sparks from the boiler. Damage $50.00 and Insurance paid $30.00.

March 26th, 1912 to Bellows Falls Vt. for a fire.

March 26th, 1912 to the Dr. Brown House for a Chimney fire with no reported damage.

February 26th, 1912 to the Chas. Holt House for a Chimney fire with no reported damage.

February 30th, 1912 to the Chas. Beauregard for a Chimney fire with no reported damage.

March 30th, 1912 to the B. & M. R. R. Spring Shop for an unknown type fire. Damage $2,802.65 and Insurance paid $2,408.58.

April 10th, 1912 to the Robert Leveroni House for a False call.

April 16th, 1912 to the Elbridge Kingsbury House for an unknown type fire. No reported damage.

April 23rd, 1912 to the Julia O'Mara House for a Chimney fire with no reported damage.

April 23rd, 1912 to the Harry Levine House for a Chimney fire with no reported damage.

April 25th, 1912 to the Frank Griswold House for a Chimney fire with no reported damage.

April 26th, 1912 to the Fred Page property for a Brush fire.

April 25th, 1912 to the Emily I. Stearns Barn caused by sparks from a chimney fire. Damage $65.00 and Insurance paid $65.00.

April 26th, 1912 to the Mr. Heywood House for a Closet fire with no reported damage.

April 26th, 1912 to the Fred H. Locke House for sparks from the chimney. Damage $1,800.00 and Insurance paid $1,800.00.

April 28th, 1912 to the Mr. Pond property for a brush fire.

April 28th, 1912 to the Mr. Kingsbury House for a Chimney fire with no reported damage.

May 1st, 1912 to the Burdett Chair Co. for sparks from the chimney. No reported damage.

May 3rd, 1912 to the Mr. Woodward property for a brush fire.

May 4th, 1912 to the Harvey Patterson House for a chimney fire with no reported damage.

May 5th, 1912 to the Cota & Seaver property for a brush fire. which was set.

May 6th, 1912 to the Robert Leveroni property for a brush fire caused by burning out moth nests.

May 6th, 1912 to the Fred Leonard House for a Chimney fire no reported damage.

May 7thg, 1912 to the Lucius Ellis House for an unknown type fire. Damage $242.50 and Insurance paid $242.50.

May 22nd, 1912 to the Mrs. J. B. Edwards for a Chimney fire with no reported damage.

June 2nd, 1912 to the George Ball Stores for smoke in the building. No reported damage.

June 10th, 1912 to the Mrs. Gunnell House for a Chimney fire. No reported damage.

June 10th, 1912 to the L. W. Spafford property for a brush fire.

June 12th, 1912 to the R. C. Jones Carriage Shop for sparks from a chimney with no reported damage.

June 23rd, 1912 to the Geo. H. Colony Stores for smoke from the chimney back up. Damage $345.35 and Insurance paid $270.75

July 7th, 1912 to the E. F. Lane Stores & Offices for combustion type fire. No reported damage.

July 10th, 1912 to the Lane Bld. the Bullard & Shedd Co. for smoke in the building. No reported damage.

July 28th, 1912 to the Mrs. Geo. E. Holbrook House for sparks from the chimney. No reported damage.

August 1st, 1912 to the Misses Tuttle House for a Hot stove pipe with no reported damage.

August 26th, 1912 to the James White House for a Chimney fire with no reported damage.

September 7th, 1912 to the Mr. Barcomb House in the town of Swanzey for an Incendiary type fire. House totaled.

September 8th, 1912 to the Timothy O'Brian House for kids playing with matches. Damage $15.00 and Insurance paid $15.00.

September 8th, 1912 to the Leander Page for an Auto fire. Caused From a gasoline explosion with little damage.

November 3rd, 1912 to the Austin Ellis House for children playing with matches. Damage to cloths and cost $38.42 and Insurance paid $38.42.

November 4th, 1912 to the Keene Steam Power Co. for an overheated boiler with Damage of $78.42 and Insurance paid $78.42.

November 10th, 1912 to the 2nd Congregational Church for an overheated furnace. Damage $8,000.00 and Insurance paid $6,000.00.

'FIRE'

SECOND CONGREGATIONAL CHURCH

A fire in the Court Street Congregational Church was discovered by a ten year old girl, Dorothy Foley on Sunday afternoon, November 10, 1912, as she was returning home from Sunday School at St. Bernard's Church. She ran to the fire station, across the street, to notify her uncle Engineer Foley. The firemen were hampered by the dense black smoke as they tried to enter the building. The fire burned along the inside of the partition on the east wall to the attic and burned a hole in the roof. There was extensive fire and water damage to the complete building and was estimated between $6,000 and $10,000. This Church was razed in 1965 and a vacant lot remains on the corner of Court and Vernon St.

———

November 11th, 1912 to the Henry S. Stevens House for a Chimney fire. No reported damage.

November 16th, 1912 to the Henry Derby House for a Chimney fire with no reported damage.

November 17th, 192 to the Leroy Blood Hose for a Chimney fire with no reported damage.

November 20th, 1912 to the Wm. Rivers House for a Chimney fire with no reported damage.

November 24th, 1912 to the following houses for chimney fires with no reported damages. 1. Marcus Damon House. 2. the Laurel Street House. 3. to the Young Jones House. 4. to the Patrick O'Leary and 5. to the Harry Buckminster House all for chimney fires.

November 25th, 1912 to the Mrs. Washburn House for a Chimney fire with no reported damage.

November 28th, 1912 to the Mrs. Polland House for a Chimney fire with no reported damage.

November 29th, 1912 to the Elmer S. Ware House for Hot ashes left in the shed. Damage $10.00 and Insurance paid $10.00.

November 29th, 1912 to the Mrs. Wm. Tucker for a Chimney fire with no reported damage.

Signals:

Transmitter Calls for Boxes on notification
    Box 117 Edgewood
    Box 124 North Lincoln Street.
    Box 125 George Street
    Box 132 Upper Elm Street
    Box 172 Colony Farm, West Keene

Box 173 Arch Street
Box 153 Lower Winchester Street
Box 174 Maple Street
Box 12 Military Call
Box 2 Still Alarm
Box 122 Brush Fire Call.

Joint Resolutions for the Year Ending 1912

On January 4th, 1912 a Joint Resolution was passed relating to the fire alarm telegraph. A committee may employ an expert electrical engineer to investigate the needs of the department and to aid them in the preparation of specifications for said apparatus relating to the fire alarm telegraph.

Resolution passed on July 12th, 1912 relating to a storage battery system for the fire alarm telegraph. The committee is hereby instructed to close a contract with the Star Electric Co. of Binghamton, New York for a storage battery system for the fire alarm telegraph, accordance with the id of said company for the automatic switch board, amounting to the sum of $1,895, and not to exceed $2,500.

A Joint Resolution relating to a whistle blowing machine was passed on July 12th, 1912. The whistle blowing machine was purchased from the Star Electric Co. at a cost of $350 and additional sum of $50.00 for incidental expenses.

A Resolution was passed on September 19th, 1912 in reference an agreement between the City and Beaver Mills reads as follows.

To the City Councils of the City of Keene dated September 17th, 1912:

Gentlemen: In order to perfect an arrangement for better fire protection both for the city and for ourselves, we hereby make the offer that the city may install a whistle blowing machine to be connected with the city fire alarm telegraph system and also to be connected with our steam power plant on our premises, without charge therefore from us for such installation, or for supplying steam for blowing said whistle, subject to the condition that we may have the exclusive use of fire alarm box 13 for our property and that a new public fire alarm box be installed in the neighborhood to protect such other property as said box No.13 no serves.

Under this arrangement it is understood that box No. 13 is to be moved and set up on our premises at the city's expense, and that we shall be under no obligation to furnish steam during such time as our boilers may be under inspection or repair. It is also understood that this arrangement is to be a mutual one and is indefinite as to the time for which it shall remain in force. So long as we continue to own our property and to maintain the present situation, we should expect to make no changes in this arrangement.

Yours truly
BEAVER MILLS
R. P. Hayward
Note: A Joint Resolution was passed on October 7th, 1912 relating to the visit of President Taft.

Whereas, William Howard Taft, President of the United States, is to make a short stop in Keene, on Thursday, October 10th, therefore be it resolved by the city councils of the city of Keene, that an invitation be extended to the president to be the guest of the city at that time, and that a committee consisting of the mayor, one alderman and two councilmen be appointed by the mayor to carry out all necessary arrangements for the reception and entertainment of the presidential party.

FRED C. NIMS.
President Common Council.
CHARLES GALE SHEDD, Mayor. 1912.

A Resolution relating to purchase of fire alarm boxes was passed on October 17th, 1912. To purchase two non-interfering fire alarm boxes from Star Electric Co. not to exceed $180.00.

A Resolution was passed on November 12th, 1912 relating to the sale of old apparatus belonging to the former fire alarm system, which is no longer of use to the city.

1913 [from *City of Keene Annual Report*]

Report of the Chief Engineer of the Fire Department and Superintendent of Fire Alarm

To His Honor the Mayor and Gentlemen of the City Councils:

As required by the city ordinance of governing the fire department, I have the honor to submit my eighth annual report for the fiscal year ending November 30th, 1913.

You will note from the following tables of fires and losses that the department has responded to 16 bell alarms, 80 still alarms, and 5 brush fire calls. This is an increase of 1 bell alarm and 10 still alarms over the calls of 1912. The estimated value of the buildings damaged by fire was $165,200.00. The damage to said buildings was $3,702.21. The insurance paid was $3,702,21. The value of the contents of these buildings was $61,857.00. The damage to said contents was $7,994.15, and the insurance paid was $4,119.02. The actual loss on buildings and contents in excess of insurance was $3,875.13.

Improvements and new apparatus added to the department:

There have been purchased 1,000 feet of 2 ½ inch double jacket rubber lined fire hose, rubber coats and boots, and general supplies required to keep the department up to its usual standard. New quarters are being provided for the relief hook and ladder truck and when ready will greatly relieve the crowded quarters at the fire station, besides providing room for the new auto truck when purchased (the purchase of the same now being considered by the city). During the past year there has been an increase in the firemen's pay for which I wish to extend to the city councils the thanks and appreciation of the department (or firemen).

Apparatus and Force:

The apparatus and force of the department, under a chief and three assistant engineers, located on Vernon Street, is as follows:

The Keene Steam Fire Engine and Hose Company, J. H. Simpson, Captain (25 men), has Steamer No. 1, Button Steamer No. 2, one combination chemical and hose wagon, one Relief hose wagon; Washington Hook and Ladder Company, G. C. Simonds, Captain (20 men), has one service truck and one Relief truck; Deluge Hose Company, E. H Applin, Captain (20 men), has one combination chemical and hose wagon.

There are now 7,300 feet of fire hose of which 2,500 feet are old and unreliable, 300 feet of chemical hose, 1,500 feet of linen hose at South Keene, six 6-gallon and four 3-gallon extinguishers, one cellar pipe, one 3 way Eastman Deluge set, uniforms, rubber coats, hats and boots for the department, four sets swing harnesses, two extra Barry collars, three sleds, and three sets Hobbs runners.

There has been 400 feet of hose not fit for fire service turned over to the water works department and 300 feet to the highway department.

I respectfully make the following Recommendations:

That the city purchase a triple combination automobile truck, and as the past city government has provided quarters for this much needed apparatus I sincerely trust the present city government will purchase the same without delay; that until the city does purchase the auto fire truck the department be allowed two pair of horses to be kept in the fire station available at all times.

The new fire alarm telegraph system which has been operated in a most careful and efficient manner by Mr. E. B. Riley, has given excellent satisfaction. The expense of maintaining the system the past year has been very slight outside of the line work which has been more that in the past year on account of the telephone company resetting may of their poles, this change necessitating our putting on new arms. This work was done by Mr. Riley, the fire alarm electrician. I would recommend that all of the iron wire now in use which is about five miles be replaced by insulated copper wire, also that one new fire alarm box be installed on upper Elm Street and that all fire alarm boxes purchased in the future be of the non-interfering type.

Three new fire alarm boxes have been installed during the past year, one on Railroad Street No. 113, one on Washington Street opposite the Burdett Chair Shop No. 27, and one on the corner of Beaver and North Lincoln Streets No. 28.

I take the pleasure in further reporting that harmony prevails between officers and men of the several companies, that they appreciate their quarters and the liberal spirit manifested by the city councils in promptly providing for the needs of the department. It also gives me pleasure to speak of the valuable aid afforded by the chairman and members of the joint standing committee on fire department, and the superintendent of the streets. A most cordial relation exists among the members associated with me on the board of engineers, who with the officers, members of the department, and public, have assisted me during the past year, and to them and the city councils I extend my thanks.

LOUIS A. NIMS, Chief Engineer and Superintendent of Fire Alarm Telegraph. Keene, December 6th, 1913.

Picture taken in 1911 of Tom and Jack on the East Side rear of the Central Fire Station on Vernon Street. This was Tom and Jack's last appearance for Inspection Day. They were known as "THE DOUBLE GRAYS." Fire Dept. collection.

Statement of Fires Occurring in The City of Keene, From December 1st, 1912 to November 30th, 1913, Inclusive.

December 8th, 1912 to the J. H. Pender House and Barn for an unknown type fire. Damage $1,328.58 and Insurance paid $1,328.58.

December 16th, 1912 to the H. E. Swan & Co. Store for a combustion fire in a waste can. Damage $100.00 and Insurance paid $100.00.

December 24th, 1912 to the Chas. Putney House for a defective chimney. Damage $15.00 and Insurance paid $15.00.

January 23rd, 1913 to the William C. Hall House for a defective chimney. Damage $15.00 and Insurance paid $15.00.

January 26th, 1913 to the Impervious Package Co. for sparks from a blower. Damage $3,582.68. Insurance paid $3,127.64.

Reported by the *New Hampshire Sentinel* on January 26th, 1913:

"FIRE"
IMPERVIOUS PACKAGE COMPANY

Visited by fire in Dry Houses, Which is Stubborn

Breaks Out in blower Room and Spreads to dry houses Over Boiler Room. Breaks Out Later in Other Dry houses to the North.

Fire broke out in the blower room at the factory of the impervious Package co. on Mechanic Street about 1.30 this afternoon and spread to the dry houses over the engine and boiler room, which were filled with heading, etc., causing a difficult blaze to handle and a considerable loss, largely from smoke and water.

An alarm was sent in from box 37, corner of Mechanic and Pleasant Streets, but the department for lack of horses and other reasons was rather slow in responding. The Deluge Hose co. wagon was started out of the house when it was found that the harness was not fastened. Men of the department drew up one of the engines.

Engineer Russell of the mill had his hair burned considerably and was nearly laid out by the burns and the smoke while trying to fight back the fire at first, but was unable to after a few minutes.

The blower house where the fire apparently started is at the rear of the brick mill building and brick engine house. It has a blower, which sends heat to the dryhouses. From this wooden building the fire spread to the engine house and a dry house for heading above the engine room. This room, which was in the neighborhood of 20 by 40 feet was almost completely filled with fairly dry stock and burned like tinder.

The pine stock gave out a great amount of smoke, which filled the entire plant. It gave rise to the belief that the fire was much worse than it was, for the big brick mill was so full of smoke on the upper floors that it was impossible for firemen to stay there. They put several streams of water into this building, though windows to keep the fire from coming through the doors which separated this building from the others in the rear.

So thick was the smoke that it impeded the fire department greatly and it was a difficult jot job to put out the fire in the staves and heading. The work had to be done from the outside of the building and the piles of staves kept the water from circulating as freely as was necessary to touch all parts of the room and stock.

Streams of water were put in from Pleasant Street and from the West Side of the mill and in through windows on the Mechanic Street side. These were kept going until late in the afternoon, the fire was reported under control. The fire also spread into another dry house north of the mill, which is quite large, and the firemen had a hard fight there. The loss, which is difficult to estimate at this time, is doubtless covered by insurance.

February 4th, 1913 to the Emily I. Sterns House for a defective chimney. Damage $12.00 and Insurance paid $12.00.

February 14th, 1912 to the Patrick Donohue House for a Defective chimney with Damage $13.00 and Insurance paid $13.00.

March 3rd, 1913 to the J. G. Warren House for a Defective Chimney, which caused damage to other tenants. Damage to Henry V. Foster $13.25 and Insurance paid $13.25. Damage to J. G. Warren $12.40 and Insurance paid $12.40, and to Wm. B Chandler, damage $10.00 and Insurance paid $10.00.

April 2nd, 1913 to the C. J. & S. M. Driscoll for a defective Chimney with damage of $475.50 and Insurance paid $475.50.

April 4th, 1913 to the Peter Cota House for a Defective Chimney with damage of $15.00 and Insurance paid $15.00.

The aftermath of the Impervious Package Company Fire. The building is covered in ice due to the cold temperatures during the fire. The picture was taken 2 days after the fire and there is still steam coming from the building due to the tremendous heat. The building stands today as 35-37 Mechanic Street, which is now the Community Kitchen. After the fire the building was rebuilt with the removal of the roof and 3rd floor. HSCC collection.

The Amoskeag Steamer, just disconnected getting ready to pump at the Impervious Package Company fire on January 26, 1913. HSCC collection.

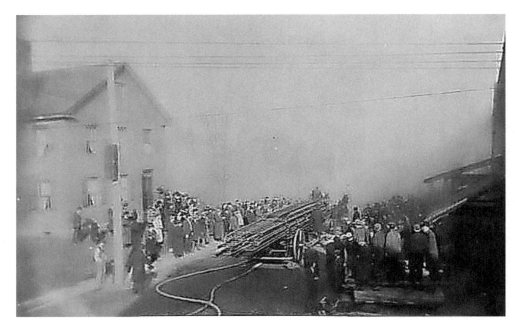

Ladder Wagon making headway to the fire at Impervious Package Company to set ladders up to advance hose lines to upper stories.

Once equipment was positioned at a fire, such as the Impervious Package Company fire. The horses were disconnected and moved to a safe place or returned to the central fire station to respond with additional equipment.

May 1st, 1913 to the Keene Gas & Elec. Co. Stores & Office for a rubbish fire in the basement. Damage $367.50 and Insurance paid $367.50. Other business were effected with damage Perkins & Griffin for $505.00 damage and Insurance paid $505.00. The Geo. M. Rossman with $50.00 damage and Insurance paid $37.50. The Walter A. Sawyer Office with $275.00 damage and Insurance paid $275.00.

May 3rd, 1913 to the Keene Wooden Ware Co. for an unknown type fire with damage of $142.83 and Insurance paid $142.83.

May 6th, 1913 to the Clarence A. Wright House for an unknown type fire with damage of $105.00 and Insurance paid $105.00.

May 14th, 1906 to the Helen L. Wright House for an unknown type fire. Damage $100.00 and Insurance paid $100.00.

June 9th, 1913 to the Ella L. Damon House for an unknown type fire. Damage $15.00 and Insurance paid $15.00.

June 12th, 1913 to the Beaver Mills Co. for an unknown type fire and damage to the Sprague & Carleton Furniture Mfg. Damage $3,500.00 with no Insurance reported. Also damaged was the Norwood Calef. Co Mfg. Damage $15.00 and Insurance paid $15.00. Also damage from sparks from this fire was Mary E. Halpine house with damage of $106.03 and Insurance paid $106.03.

[From *New Hampshire Sentinel*, Keene, N.H.:]

'FIRE'

1913 DANGEROUS FIRE AT BEAVER MILLS.

On June 12th, 1913 around 2:30 Thursday afternoon sparks Set Fire in Mill Building and at Other Places on Streets to the North-One at F. A. Carpenter's Barn Was Quite Hot. Yards, Sheds and Contents Blaze Fiercely.

A dangerous fire broke out about 2:30 Thursday afternoon at the Beaver Mills in the mill yard debris, or the lumber, staves, heading, etc., stored not far from a big stave and limber shed, just southeast of the main brick building furthest south and within a few feet of a connecting wooden building two stories high put up for the purpose of storing shavings and sawdust for loading into teams.

When the fire was first seen it appeared to be a small blaze on the ground, but before an alarm could be sounded had spread into the shed, as high as a two-story building and about 170-50 feet in size. This she was filled with lumber and stretchers for chairs belonging to Sprague & Carleton and contained three bins of heading belonging to the Beaver Mills Company. This was all destroyed, besides more or less heading, staves and boards in the mill yards.

There was a fresh south wind blowing when the fire broke out, and as the flames spread in the lumber piles and the big shed the fire became very hot, and like the fire at the Impervious package company's yards on Emerald Street two years ago, sent showers of sparks to leeward. The sparks not only endangered the large dry house to the north, at Beaver Mills, and other structures in the mill yard, but were also a menace to houses to the north as far as Beaver Street. Two more fires were set in that direction, and at 2:55, when all the apparatus was busy at the mills, box 22 was pulled for two fires near Roxbury Court, and a hose wagon, ladder wagon and several men under Engineer Towne, were dispatched to attend to them.

One of these fires had caught among the shingles on the roof of Fred A. Carpenter's barn and was getting quite hot when the firemen arrived, in spite of the efforts of neighbors to extinguish it. It burned through the roof somewhat and took off the shingles up and down the roof for a width of two feet or more.

Another fire caught in the roof of Mrs. Mary Halpine's house on Spring Street. A hose line was laid there by the firemen and the blaze extinguished.

The main fire at Beaver mills burned fiercely and gained rapidly in intensity in spite of several streams from the mill pump, and the arrival of the firemen was none too quick. As soon as they got a sufficient number of hose lines in operation they made a stand at the West End of the burning shed. At that time it was difficult to stand at the East End of the south brick shop because of the intense heat and it looked dubious for adjoining buildings. Powerful streams sent in to the flames had their effect, however and at 2:35 it was evident that the fire was considerably checked. At 2:50 it was well under control in the big shed and had not spread to adjacent buildings.

The firemen and mill men were then able to give their attention to stopping the spread of the fire among piles of staves, heading and lumber in the mill yard. Several of these caught and some were consumed before the big shed fire was under control. With this practically off their hands the firemen were not long in extinguishing adjacent fires.

A large number of citizens helped the firemen innumerous ways and Mayor Shedd was on the ground early, directing men with a hose line to wet down the roofs and exteriors of buildings in the mill yard likely to catch fire at any moment. In fact, everything was so dry that the chips and bark refuse on the ground in the mill yard were set on fire in many places and were a considerable menace. Men in the employ of the Mill Company and citizens did efficient work in watching inside the buildings for incipient fires. It was very fortunate that the results were not more serious.

The escape, for instance, from what might be termed a secondary fire in a large, two-story building, and one in which firefighting has proved most difficult, was most fortunate, as were several other critical issues during the progress of the general scorching which the mill yard and its contents received. During the first 10 or 15 minutes the fire burned it spread with alarming rapidity in all directions, both on the ground of the mill yard, among chips and dry debris, and in piles of staves, heading and planks and in the limber shed. Then came the first effective check at the West End of the lumber shed, within a few feet of the south brick section of the main mill. Following this, while nearly all the energies of the department and the mill force with hose lines hand to be centered on this fiercely burning shed of lumber, 170 feet in length and substantially two stories high, came another period where the danger to adjacent buildings and to barns and houses for half a mile to the north was a serious one, as shown by several incipient fires set by sparks in the mill buildings and on roofs as far north as Spring street.

Before the call for the fires set on Roxbury Court and Spring street came in at 2:55, a number of onlookers were watching puffs of smoke that continued to come from beneath the northwest corner of the roof of the large two-story dry house and storehouse which was burned in November, 1899 and again received a scorching in June, 1902. Evidently something was wrong inside this building. Mill employees and others went in and reported a good deal of smoke inside, apparently from the other fire, but no fire in the building. For some little time exterior conditions remained substantially the same, but about 3 o'clock the smoke from the interior increased and the firemen were ordered to the building. A fire under the roof at the West End was fortunately located with accuracy on cutting a hole into a blind attic under the roof and over the dry house in the second story. To put this out holes were cut in the roof at either end of the building and a good deal of water put under the roof at the West End. This caused a considerable water loss on finished pails in the large storeroom under the dry house. Two or three fires caught in the brick pail shop and the passageway connecting with the

A Demon Called Fire

dry house during the afternoon, which were promptly extinguished by mill employees on duty inside. The services of these men were important, as in the dry and dust rooms of the pail shop a few moments would be sufficient for a small blaze to spread all through a room.

It was found on investigation, later, that the fire in the dry house caught from a spark entering around a window facing east in the deck at the West End of the building. This blazed up and set off an automatic sprinkler nearby. The sprinkler put out the original inside fire, but in the meantime a train of dry wood dust, such as settles through pail shop rooms led the fire through the adjacent sheathing partition supposed to cut off the blind attic over the dry house. This was beyond the reach of the water from the sprinkler, which had been set off. Hence the final blaze in the blind attic.

The cause of the original fire in the mill yard is not likely to become known. Milan F. Jones, an employee in the yard, came through the yard near where the fire started not long before it broke out, and saw no fire or smoke and no one in the yard. Within a short time George H. MacKenzie, foreman of the saw mill, and his assistant, Axel Johnson, smelled the pungent odor of burning pine, and looking over through a bent of the lumber shed that soon burned, saw a fire south of it among staves or rubbish in the mill yard. They ran out there, calling to others. Mr. Mackenzie though that if he had a horse blanket could have put the blaze out. An extinguisher at that time would have done the business, but before one could be brought the fire was many times larger and beyond control.

The Beaver Mills loss is estimated, roughly, at from $4,000 to $5,000, and Sprague & Carleton's at $3,000 or $4,000. The loss of the Mills Company will depend largely on the condition of pails and packages that were injured by water. The insurance was practically all on property inside the storehouse, it not being customary to carry mill yard insurance.

Printed in the *New Hampshire Sentinel* Keene, N.H

————

September 8th, 1913 to the J. G Perry House for a defective chimney. Damage $$1,000.00 and Insurance paid $700.00.
September 24th, 1913 to the Peter Heffron House for Old Rags with Damage of $15.00 and Insurance paid $15.00.

Note: 16 Bell alarms and 80 Still alarms and 5 Brush fires.

Ordinances and Joint Resolutions for the Year Ending 1913.

A Resolution was passed on February 13th, 1913 to purchase 1000 feet of 2 ½ inch cotton rubber lined hose and twenty (20) rubber coats. Not to exceed $850.00.

A Resolution was passed February 21st, 1913 relating to the purchase of a fire alarm box. One non-interfering fire alarm box be purchased from the Star Electric Co. said box numbered 28 and to be installed on the northeast corner of the intersection of North Lincoln Street and Beaver Streets. Not to exceed $90.00.

On March 24th, 1913 a Resolution was passed to the purchase and sale of 3 city owned fire department horses. These horses were jointly used by the highway department as well.

Ordinance relating to the setting of fires

Section 1: The board of engineers may prohibit smoking, the use of matches or other inflammable articles and the building and setting of fires in any building or portion there of or upon any land or premises within the limits of the fire precinct as constituted by Chapter VIII of City Ordinances, when requested by the owner of such building, land or premises.

Section 2: When any rule or order is made by the board of engineers in pursuance of Section 1 the owner or occupant of the building, land or premises to which the rule or order applies shall post in a conspicuous place a printed notice of such rule or order.

Section 3: Any person violating such rule or order after notice has been posted as provided by Section 2 shall be fined not exceeding twenty dollars.

Passed June 19th, 1913.

1914 [from *City of Keene Annual Report*]

Report of Chief Engineer of Fire Department and Superintendent of Fire Alarm Telegraph

To His Honor the Mayor and Gentlemen of the City Councils:

I herewith submit my annual report for the fiscal year ending December 1st, 1914.

You will note from the following tables of fires and losses that the department has responded to 14 bell alarms, 78 still alarms, 5 brush fire calls from out of town. This is a decrease of 2 bell alarms and 2 still alarms from the calls of 1913. The estimated value of the buildings damaged by fire was $147.700.00. The damage to said buildings was $13,765.81. The insurance paid was $11,252.59. The value of the contents of these buildings was $269.500.00. The damage to said contents was $20,247.19 and the insurance paid was $15,547.12. The actual loss on buildings and contents in excess of insurance was $7,213.29.

Improvements added to the department:

The fire of May 29th, damage the second floor of the fire station to such extent that it necessitated the remodeling of the building, which, when the repairs are completed, will give more sleeping rooms, which are much needed by the department. There has also been a new fireproof building annexed to the fire station for the fire alarm system, thus eliminating all danger from fire that might occur in the main building.

Apparatus and Force:

The apparatus and force of the department, under a chief and three assistant engineers, located on Vernon Street, is as follows: The Keene Steam Fire Engine and Hose Company, J. H. Simpson, Captain, 25 men, has Steamer No. 1, Button Steamer No. 2, one combination chemical and hose wagon, one relief hose wagon; Washington Hook & Ladder Company, G. C. Simonds, Captain, 20 men, has one service truck and one relief truck; Deluge Hose Company, E. H. Applin, Captain, 20 men, has combination chemical and hose wagon.

There are now 6,500 feet of fire hose, much of which is old and very unreliable, 300 feet of chemical hose, 1,500 feet of linen hose at South Keene, six 6-gallon and four 3-gallon extinguishers, one cellar pipe, one 3-way Eastman Deluge set, uniforms, rubber coats, hats and boots for the department four sets swing harnesses, two extra Barry collars, three sleds and three sets Hobbs runners.

All hose unfit for fire service has been turned over to the water works department.

A recommendation was made last year I would repeat: That the city purchase a triple combination automobile truck, a piece of apparatus which is especially needed for the protection of property situated outside the city limits; that the city; purchase 2,000 feet of fire hose at once, none having been purchase the past year, and I consider the amount now available inadequate for use in case of serious fire. I trust the city councils will give this matter their immediate attention that the fire department be allowed two pair of horses to be kept at the fire station available at all times.

The fire alarm telegraph system in care of Mr. E. B. Riley, the fire alarm electrician, continues to give excellent satisfaction. I would recommend that all of the iron wire now in

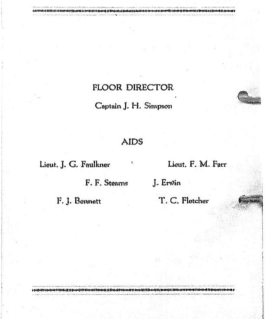

INSPECTION

Concert and Dance

Keene Steam Fire Engine & Hose
Co. City Hall, Keene. Thursday
Evening, October 16th, 1913

Music by
Maynard's Orchestra
Eight Pieces

FLOOR DIRECTOR

Captain J. H. Simpson

AIDS

Lieut. J. G. Faulkner   Lieut. F. M. Farr

F. F. Stearns   J. Erwin

F. J. Bennett   T. C. Fletcher

Each year the Fire Department Company's held fundraisers for equipment. This concert and dance held by the Keene Steam Fire Engine and Hose Company on October 16, 1913 is an example of the invitations that were assigned to those special events. From Keene Fire Department Records.

use which is about five miles, be replaced by insulated copper wire, also that one new fire alarm box be installed on upper Elm Street, and that all fire alarm boxes purchased in the future be of the non-interfering type.

There have been two new private boxes added to the system, No. 114, at the Keene Wooden Ware Company on Water Street, and No. 152 at the Railroad Shops, Emerald Street.

I would further report that harmony and good will prevail among officers and men of the several companies, and the members of the board of engineers with whom I am associated.

I also wish to extend my appreciation of valuable aid rendered us by the superintendent of streets, superintendent of water works, and citizens during the past year, and to them and the city clerk and city councils I extend my thanks.

LOUIS A. NIMS, Chief Engineer and Superintendent of Fire Alarm Telegraph. Keene, December 7th, 1914.

Statement of Fires Occurring in the City of Keene, From November 30th, 1913, to December 1st, 1914, Inclusive.

December 10th, 1913 to the Humphrey Machine Co. Foundry for a Hot Stack. Damage $250.00 and Insurance paid $250.00.

December 12th, 1913 to the Newbury Silver Co. for a Gas Generator fire. Damage $256.83 and Insurance paid $243.60.

December 14th, 1913 to the C. M. Brooks House for a Chimney fire. Damage $5.00 and Insurance paid $5.00.

December 19th, 1913 to the Silas Hardy Est. House for a chimney fire. Damage $15.00 and Insurance paid $15.00.

December 20th, 1913 to the Charles Griffin House for a Chimney fire. Damage $15.00 and Insurance paid $15.00.

December 24th, 1913 to the Hattie K. Flagg House for a Chimney fire. Damage $12.00 and Insurance paid $12.00.

December 26th, 1913 to the William P. Carr House for a Lamp fire. Damage $5.00 and Insurance paid $5.00.

December 30th, 1913 to the R. C. Jones Carriage Shop for an Unknown type fire. Damage $8,000.00 and Insurance paid $800.00.

January 5th, 1914 to the John F. Gallagher House for an unknown type fire. Damage $1,400.00 and Insurance paid $1,400.00.

January 13th, 1914 to the George H, Nims House for a chimney fire. Damage $15.00 and Insurance paid $15.00.

January 19th, 1914 to the Henry W. Lane House for an unknown type fire. Damage $18.67 and insurance paid $18.67.

February 3rd, 1914 to the Newell Pair House for an unknown type fire. Damage $66.28 and Insurance paid $66.28.

February 5th, 1914 to the Keene Development Co. for a building. Fire. Damage $19,233.42 and Insurance paid $19,233.42.

[from *New Hampshire Sentinel*, Keene, N.H.:]

'FIRE'
1914 NEW GRANITE SHEDS BURN; LOSS $20,000.

On February 5th, 1914 A Fire Consumes Two-Thirds of Long Building—Lack of Water Hinders Firemen.

The new building of the Keene Development Co. on Victoria Street, off Water, occupied by the Victoria White granite Co. for cutting sheds, was two thirds gutted by fire Thursday forenoon and a loss estimated between $20,000 and $25,000 caused.

The blaze started around the 100 horsepower motor and air compressor, located in the northeast corner of the big shed. Had there been anyone in this part of the shop at the time the fire could probably have been easily extinguished, but as it happened there was no one there and the fire gained a good headway before being discovered.

A door leading from the compressor room into the sheds was kept closed usually, but was evidently left open by someone who went through after the fire started. This gave a draft, which fanned the flames, and allowed the blaze to spread into the big shed where it ate along the roof to the big doors through which the side racks from the railroad enters. Smoke was to be seen coming from the roof and eaves of the entire building, but the fire only went to the big doors and was held there.

A transmitter call gave an alarm from box 15 about 10:45, after an attempt had been made to extinguish the blaze which pails of water. When the fire department reached the scene, after a long run and a hard one, the north end of the shed for some seventy or eighty feet southward was all ablaze. The fire was hottest in the location on the East Side where the motor compressor was located and the blaze started.

There was considerable difficulty in getting a sufficient amount of water for there is only one hydrant near the shop, put in by the city at the corner of Victoria Street nearest the shop, the company having no large main to its sheds. The Victoria Street pipe is 6 inches in size and 900 feet long. The hydrant is some 300 feet from the shed. The relief steamer was set on Eastern Avenue and lines of hose laid from it across lots to the blaze. The steamers through the six or seven lines of hose were not strong most of the time. At times they would not reach the peak of the roof. At other times they seemed strong enough.

Ordinarily with plenty of water, the fire would have been held within one hundred feet of the north end of the building, but as it was, it ate along quite rapidly for some two hundred and fifty feet being held at the big doors, where a couple of streams of water were placed and played from inside of the building. Had the firemen had water and been able to get inside the building near the north end when they reached the place, which was

not a difficult matter, they could have held the flames in check far short of the doors.

The two-thirds of the shop north of the big doors is practically a total loss, the walls being left in some places, but well charred. The roof all fell in, little and the walls on both sides and the north end were badly burned so that what did not fall was pulled down. The office building was untouched.

Besides the motor and compressor around which the blaze centered at first much other machinery, including pneumatic tools owned by the company and many tools owned by the employees were burned, while there was probably $10,000 worth of granite finished and in process of construction, which was ruined. There was a good deal of nice work finished, for a large shipment to Brooklyn was about to be made.

The compressor can probably, be repaired at a reasonable expense, but the motor is a loss, while the tools are much injured. The company has two large travelling cranes, valued at $2,500 each, but these were in the section of the shed near the big doors. One was burned some and the other was not apparently harmed, but it was later found that both the crane motors would have to be replaced and the cranes sent away for repairs.

The Keene Development Co., divided among the Palmer, Mason and Aldrich agencies insured the building, cranes, compressors, etc., for $1,500. The Granite Company had within a few days put on $15,000 of insurance through the Mason agency on the stock and tools, etc. There was also $1,000 on the office building which was not burned. The total cost of the buildings, equipment with compressor, crane, and heating plant, was about $19,500. The Granite Company began Work at the shops early last spring.

The granite shed was 468 feet long and was 56 feet wide at the north end where there was a lean-to on the East Side. Where the lean-to ended the shed was some 16 feet less in width. The big doors for the siding were nearly two-thirds of the way down from the north end. The roof at the Southland of the shed will have to be repaired considerably.

There have been 133 men at work in the sheds recently and the company has much work to get out, including a contract for $117.000 worth of work for the Brooklyn bridge approaches, besides several large mausoleum contracts. A new 100 horsepower motor has already been telegraphed for to come by express and the electrical equipment will be put into shape as soon as possible. With this going the south end of the shed can be used and a good deal of work gotten going within a few days. The sheds were run entirely by electricity, and compressed air from the electrically driven compressor and there was no fire used except in the boiler room, which was about in the center of the shed, below the level of the inside of the sheds.

A report was given out from Milford Mass. Wednesday that the Victoria company had acquired full title to some 300 acres of quarry in Milford, formerly owned by the Milford Pink Granite Co. superintendent Robertson understands that this is correct. The Victoria Company intends to build new sheds near the track in Milford.

Superintendent Robertson of the local plant at once sent for Contractor Churchill, who built the shop, to come here and begin the work rebuilding.

Mr. Churchill is here and has ordered lumber and supplies for the workmen. Men have also been busy since the fire clearing away the debris.

Printed in the *New Hampshire Sentinel* Keene, N. H.

————

February 6th, 1914 to the Chas H. Vigneau House for a Lamp fire. Damage $25.00 and Insurance paid $25.00.

February 13th, 1914 to the Alice H. Ellis Hotel and Stores for a Fire place problem. Damage to stores of J. A. Reynolds, Damage $52.50 and Insurance paid $52.50 and to the F. Morris Wheeler Store Damage of $71.05 and Insurance paid $71.05 and to the some tenants property with no report of damage.

February 14th, 1914 to the W. J. Malloy House for a Chimney fire. Damage $14.74 and Insurance paid $14.74.

May 29th, 1914 to the Fire Department Vernon Street for a fire in the back shed. Damage $4,000.00 and Insurance paid $4,000.00.

August 12th, 1914 to the Robert F. Carroll House for a Chimney fire with Damage of $20.00 and Insurance paid $20.00.

November 8th, 1914 to the Spencer Hardware Co. for Children playing with matches. Damage $54.74 and Insurance paid $54.74.

November 8th, 1914 to the Pearson Bros. Store for Children playing with matches. Damage $15.00 and Insurance paid $15.00.

November 12th, 1914 to the Mrs. K. Cunningham House, two Tenants for a chimney fire with damage of $307.77 and Insurance paid $307.77.

November 29th, 1914 to the H. J Fowler House for an unknown type fire. Damage $50.00 and Insurance paid $50.00.

Joint Resolutions for the year ending 1914

A Resolution was passed on September 9th, 1914 relating to an addition to the fire station. The committee on lands and buildings and the committee on fire department acting jointly authorized to erect a suitable fireproof structure at the fire station and install the fire alarm apparatus therein; and that the sum not exceed twelve hundred Dollars.

[*Compiler's Note*: This addition today houses the Fire Alarms Office and a section of Dispatch, SWMA.]

On May 29th, 1914 the Fire Station on Vernon Street sustained a fire. As Recorded June 1st, 1914 by the *New Hampshire Sentinel*, Keene, N.H.:

'FIRE'

A HOT FIRE AT VERNON STREET STATION.

Keene Department Conquers Stubborn Blaze in Its Own Quarters.

A fire which attacked the fire department of Keene in a most vital point, and which for a time seriously threatened its temporary demoralization, even though confined within a small area broke out about 7:15 Friday evening in the rear portion of central fire station. This consists of a covered passageway and shed for carts and highway tools, over which there is a store room and directly connecting with which, under the same roof, are doors and windows entering the fire station stables and the lofts for hay overhead.

A large doorway for backing in wagons opens from this wagon shed to the passageway on the westerly side of the station, and the shed also opens to the north at the opposite end, there connecting with a passageway on the east side of the station leading to Vernon Street. The latte is the main driveway used by horses and teams going to or from the fire station stables. But as the doors to the passageway

White Granite Companies stone cutting sheds off of Victoria Street, burned February 5th, 1914. Photo by Bion H. Whitehouse.

between the Square and Vernon Street, on the west side of the station have been left open much of the time especially in warm weather, the shed itself has formed a convenient short cut for persons on foot going to and from the Square via the alleyway westerly of the First Church, to Vernon and Elm Streets and points beyond.

The door was open Friday night and anyone could have gone through there, lighting a match and throwing it down carelessly of dropping a lighted cigar or cigarette. This, very likely accounts for the fire which might have been so kindled. But no one has as yet been able to account, so far as is known, for the immense volume of flame and smoke which poured out of there, certainly within a minute of the time when the fire was first seen and did not appear to be dangerous one.

The entire shed, the whole width of the city lot in the rear, was filled with a hot fire, as the charred timbers over it plainly show, and the side of the paint shop on the Warren property to the east was blackened. The paint was thoroughly blistered and burned on two or three carts in the shed of the kind used every day by the department teams. Ana a sheet of flame rolled up and into the loft over the Hook and Ladder and Deluge houses igniting the hay that was in the lofts which caused a lot of trouble subsequently in controlling the fire. Nevertheless the fire under the shed and around the carts very quickly burned itself out, having all the characteristic of a flash fire started with a volatile spirit or oil like naphtha. There was no persistency to this part of the fire such as would characterize one traveling along on cart bodies and along floor timbers ten or twelve feet overhead, and there appears to have but little chaff and litter on the dirt floor of that shed over which horses and wagons were moving every day. No one remembers that this floor looked dirty or appeared covered with anything flammable.

There is a story that a barrel of asphalt was broken and spilled in this shed at one time Superintendent Wallace says this occurred a year or two ago near the west door. That door would not slid freely afterwards, and last year the asphalt was dug out and removed so that there could have been but little if any asphalt on the shed bottom. No oils or naphtha were handled or used in the shed. Asphalt will not burn till heated to 300 degrees or more and wherever it has been used it has been found that it takes time to do this. When it does burn it makes a hot fire, however. The men who first attacked the fire do not appear to have got the impression that there was any hot fire on the floor of the shed where the asphalt must have been, if anywhere. In fact, they easily and quickly put out the shed fire, only to find the hay lofts over the Ladder and Deluge houses a mass of flames.

There were several firemen in and about the station at the time that the fire broke out. Two or three among them Oscar P. Applin and Ben Symonds, were out in front of the station and Symonds started for the Square, going down the west side of the building, he discovered a fire in the shed. There was a bin for shavings for bedding near the west door and the fire was near it. It did not look very badly and he ran for an extinguisher and notified others. In a few seconds the fire could be seen through the engine house and a hose wagon was hustled out and a still rung in. Engineer Aldrich, who was in front of his store, ran at once for the station. He found the shed a mass of flames and ordered box 22 pulled in. The horses in the stables were all out quickly, but by the time this was done it was difficult to get in and run out the second steamer and the relief hose wagon on account of the dense smoke which poured in from the rear.

The first streams reaching the fire in the shed were sufficient to extinguish it quickly so far as could be seen. The shavings were put out and also the carts, if they were still burning and the floor timbers overhead. A wooden partition around the shavings bin and a stairway that was burning yielded quickly.

Thinking the fire practically out, the firemen went further into the shed only to find the hay all ablaze in the lofts upstairs. This fire spread rapidly as it always does in hay and poured out clouds of blinding smoke. There were few if any fire proof partitions in the lofts and the flames were soon eating their way into the firemen's rooms the hose tower on the west side and other parts of the building.

Over the Hook and Ladder Company's quarters, in the center of the building, is a large attic. A stairway connected this with the haylofts, and at the floor line of the attic the spaces between the rafters of the roof were open into the hayloft. The fire quickly worked its way into the attic and until much of the hay could be thoroughly soaked and streams worked along so they would reach the attic the whole building was in great danger.

A ladder was raided in front of the building to the gable windows none too soon. It would have been well if there had been two ladders put up there earlier and hose lines taken up. As it was the flames burst through the attic windows by the time water was ready there, and for five or ten minutes there was a hard fight from the first ladder, a second one following, Streams reaching the attic from the rear about this time, also had their effect and about 8 o'clock it was evident the fire was under control.

Especially anxiety was felt for the fire alarm switchboard, battery room and repeater, which are in the middle of the building, where it seemed that the heat must be great. A shaft for a light well and make of sheathing, extended from the top of the fire alarm room above the roof directly through the attic where the fire was the hottest. The flames broke into this shaft and out through the top of it,

where they quickly made an open chimney of the light shaft. This created so strong an upward draft that the heat of the fire did not work down into the apparatus room, and after the fire was sufficiently under control, it was found that the glass case over the six circuit repeater had not even been broken and that the switchboard was all right, although soaked considerably with water. The wires from the pole lines outdoors, which came into the building through one of the hay lofts, in an iron pipe, had been heated so that their insulation was destroyed so that the wires were virtually crossed and all the boxes and bells temporarily put out of commission.

As it was at first impossible to tell the extent to which the alarm might be demoralized by the water or whether any of the delicate coils of the switch board and repeater had been injured by the heat, Chief Nims the mayor and others decided to get in touch at once with the Star Fire Alarm Company of Binghamton, N. Y., makers of the apparatus. The Company started a man for Keene during the night and he reached here at 5:30 Saturday. He found the apparatus uninjured except by water, the effects of which can be quickly eliminated.

As soon as the fire was under control L. M. Willard, who is familiar with the apparatus was engaged to assist Electrician Riley in providing an alarm service from the city boxes. Superintendent Smith of the gas and electric company offered to cooperate and enough men were soon secured. Tests showed the storage batteries and inner circuits to be all right and before midnight temporary wires had been run from the apparatus room to the pole cable outside the station and all the circuits were in working order.

During Friday night the fire apparatus and horses were now housed in the Cheshire House sheds and stables. The telephone company connected an emergency telephone line to Perry' carriage shop where a man was

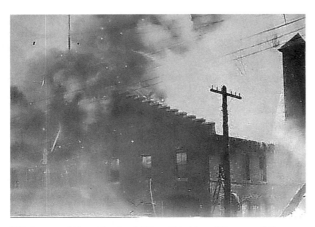

Picture of the Central Fire Station Fire on May 29, 1914 with heavy smoke pushing throughout the station, building was located on Vernon Street. Fire Dept. photo.

kept on duty and men were stationed at the Beaver Mills office to give whistle calls if necessary, and at Mins's stable. By Saturday noon steam having been put on and the floors swept it was dry enough to return horses and apparatus to the station.

The loss to the city is difficult to estimate, but it probable over $2,500 owing to injury to the station roof, lofts etc. The building was insured for $5,000 through the Aldrich and Palmer agencies.

The firemen, themselves, made quite heavy losses on the furniture and equipment for their rooms, which they owned. The Steamer Company had just expended $30. for new bedding and furniture. All the companies lost carpets, pictures and various conveniences ruined by water.

The men who slept in the station were Elmer Woodward, Lewis Dean and Herbert Warner. The latter lost a new suit of clothing or at least it was badly injured and all of them met with more or less loss. It is expected that the insurance adjusters will be here tomorrow to adjust the loss on the building. No personal property or apparatus was insured.

1915 [from *City of Keene Annual Report*]

Report of Chief Engineer of Fire Department and Superintendent of Fire Alarm Telegraph.

To His Honor the Mayor and Gentlemen of the City Councils:

As required by the city ordinance governing the fire department, I have the horror to submit my tenth annual report for the fiscal year ending November 30th, 1915.

You will note from the following statement of fires and losses that the department has responded to 14 bell alarms and 96 still alarms, including brush fire calls. We have also responded to 1 call at Surry and 1 at Swanzey. This is an increase of 11 still alarms over the calls of 1914.

The estimated value of buildings damaged by fire was $84,200.00.

Damaged to buildings was $4,616.53.

Insurance on said buildings, $52,900.00.

Insurance paid was $4,310.53.

The value of contents of said buildings was $18,600.00.

Damage to said contents, $2,722.60.

Insurance upon said property was $20,400.00.

Insurance paid, $2,681.80.

The losses on buildings and contents in excess of the insurance paid was $346.80, which is 3 2-10 cents per capita, according to census of 1910, as compared with 65 cents for the previous year. This is the smallest loss per capita for several years.

New Equipment added to the department during the year consists of 2,000 feet of 2 ½ inch rubber lined fire hose. The remodeling of the fire station necessitated by the fire of May 29th, 1915, has been completed, providing seven good sleeping rooms and two large halls. The fire alarm equipment has been transferred to the new fire proof building adjoining the fire station.

Apparatus and Force:

The apparatus and force of the department under a chief and three assistant engineers, located on Vernon Street, is as follows: Keene Steam Fire Engine & Hose Company, J. H. Simpson, Captain. 25 men, has Steamer No. 1, Button Steamer No. 2, one combination chemical and hose wagon, one relief hose wagon. Washington Hook & Ladder Company, G. C. Symonds, Captain 20 men has one service truck and one relief truck. Deluge Hose Company, E. H. Applin, Captain 20 men has one combination chemical and hose wagon.

There is now on had about 6,000 feet of No. 1 hose, and 2,300 feet of No. 2 hose, which is old and unreliable, 300 feet of chemical hose, 1,500 feet of linen hose at South Keene, six 6-gallon and four 3-gallon extinguishers, one cellar pipe, one 3-way Eastman Deluge set, uniforms, rubber coats, hats and boots for the department, four sets swing harnesses, two extra Barry collars, two sleds and three sets Hobbs runners.

There was 650 feet hose unfit for fire service, which was turned over to the water works department.

Recommendations:

The board of engineers after a thorough and painstaking investigation in regard to the proper type of motor fire apparatus is of the unanimous opinion that a triple combination motor truck will best meet the present needs of the city as a whole. Such a truck would be a valuable protection to the many outlaying buildings where water is available, as well as effecting a material reduction in the present rates of insurance. In recommending this type of fire truck I wish to call your attention to the fact that the Amoskeag steam fire engine has been in active service for thirty-two years and we do not consider it any too reliable for hard usage. The board also recommends that the city purchase 1,000 feet of fire hose; a hose testing apparatus and a fire net; that the city pass an ordinance establishing building laws to reduce the fire hazard and furnish definite information by which the inspector would be governed.

The fire alarm telegraph system in care of Mr. E. B. Riley, the fire alarm electrician, continues to give excellent satisfaction. I would recommend that there be four new fire alarm boxes installed, one at Edgewood and one at George Street, one at Upper Elm, Street and one on congress Street near the Martell factory.

I would further report that harmony and good will prevail among officers and men of the several companies and the members of the board of engineers with whom I am associated. I also wish to extend my appreciation of the valuable aid rendered us by the committee on fire department, superintendent of streets, superintendent of water works, and the citizens during the past year, and to them and the city clerk and city councils I extend my thanks.

LOUIS A. NIMS,

Chief Engineer and Superintendent of Fire Alarm Telegraph. Keene, December 6th, 1915.

Statement of Fires Occurring in the City of Keene, From November 30th, 1914 to December 1st, 1915 Inclusive.

December 20th, 1914 to the Lars J. House for an overheated stove with Damage of $460.50. Insurance paid $460.50.

January 15th, 1915 to the Geo E. Nichols for an overheated Stove with damage of $630.97 and Insurance paid $590.17.

January 16th, 1915 to the Impervious Pkg. Co. Blacksmith Shop for an overheated stove. Damage $556.00 and Insurance paid $250.50.

January 18th, 1915 to the Mrs. Frank O. Nims for an unknown type fire. Damage $819.32 and Insurance paid $819.32.

STAR

FIRE ALARM TELEGRAPH APPARATUS

POLICE TELEGRAPH APPARATUS AND SUPPLIES

ELECTRIC COMPANY

686 FRELINGHUYSEN AVE.

NEWARK, N.J.   March 10th, 1915.

Mr. William H. Ryder, Chairman,
Joint Committee Lands & Bldgs. Fire Dept.,
Keene, N. H.

Dear Sir:—

      We have your letter of March 6th, addressed to our Mr.
C. E. Beach, and hasten to advise you that we will be willing
when you are ready, to send one of our engineers to overhaul
your repeater and inspect your fire alarm apparatus, after same
has been removed to new building. This we will do according to
the terms of our letter of July 14th, 1914, which are $10.00 per
day, including engineer's expenses, except railroad fare, which
will be charged at cost, and we will furnish any material necessary at cost, plus fifteen per cent.

      We would ask you to advise us, as far in advance as pos-
sible as to when you will want this engineer, for the reason that
we will have to lay our plans accordingly, and by having this
information promptly we can arrange to send a man to your city
with as little delay as possible.

      You state in your letter that you hoped to have a reply by
Tuesday, but this is to advise you that your letter did not reach
this office until Tuesday afternoon. Rest assured that if it had
reached us in time, we would have carried out your request.

      Expecting to hear from you further in this matter, we re-
main,

        Yours very truly,

        STAR ELECTRIC COMPANY.

RDS-GRS.   By

*Contract to overhaul fire alarm repeater and inspect alarm apparatus due to the fire at Central Fire
Station on May 29, 1914.*

January 20th, 1915 to the Fred H. Towne house for an open Gas Cock. Damage $3.34 and Insurance paid $3.34.

February 19th, 1915 to the Ella L. Damon Block for an unknown type fire. Damage 37.00 and Insurance paid $37.00.

February 27th, 1915 to the Fred A. Carpenter House for a furnace problem. Damage $676.10 and Insurance paid $676.10. Also damaged was E. P. Carrigan with damage of $150.00 and Don Williams with Damage of 9.80. Insurance paid both the same amount.

March 17th, 1915 to the Louis J. Carpenter House for paper under the stove. Damage $30.00 and Insurance paid $30.00.

March 27th, 1915 to the W. H. Ellis house for a chimney fire. Damage $18.13 and Insurance paid $18.13.

March 31st, 1915 to the Tenants of C. G. Putney for an unknown fire. Damage $69.00 and Insurance paid $69.00.

April 21st, 1915 to the Carey Chair Mfg. Co. for dust on the boiler. Damage $1,542.43 and Insurance paid $1,542.43.

April 27th, 1915 to the N. G. Gurnsey & Co. Bottling Works for an unknown type fire. Damage $96.34 and Insurance paid $96.34.

May 11th, 1915 to the S. A. Morse house for a Chimney fire. Damage $91.14 and Insurance paid $91.14.

May 12th, 1915 to the H. W. Bond House for a Chimney fire. Damage $56.50 and Insurance paid $56.50.

May 25th, 1915 to the Chas. W. Russell for a chimney fire. Damage $569.00 and Insurance paid $569.00.

June 15th, 1915 to the Catherine Jordan Tenant house for a combustion type fire. Damage $1,085.00 and Insurance paid $1,085.00.

July 1st, 1915 to the Keene Police Dept. for an explosion. Damage $39.89 and Insurance paid $39.89.

September 26th, 1915 to the J. N. Hevey house for a chimney fire. Damage $50.10 and Insurance paid $50.10.

September 27th, 1915 to the Mary C. Ramsey house for a chimney fire. Damage $18.17 and Insurance paid $18.17.

October 13th, 1915 to the Mary C. Eno house and Barn for an unknown type fire. Damage $97.00 and Insurance paid $97.50.

October 29th, 1915 to the Jas. W. Hartnett est. for an unknown type fire. Damage $140.00 and Insurance paid $140.00.

November 6th, 1915 to the Stephen Loveland House and store. Cause was matches with damage of $60.40 and Insurance paid $60.40.

November 13th, 1915 to the Elisha Munsell house for a chimney fire with Damage of $30.00 and Insurance paid $30.00.

[*Compiler's Note*: The Annual City Report Book for the year 1915 has the copy of the City Charter April 11th, 1753 pg. 24 front and back.]

Ordinances and Resolutions for the year ending 1915

On April 1st, 1915 an Ordinance amending Sect. 7, Chapter VIII, was passed.

That Sect. 7, Chapter VIII, City Ordinances, be and hereby is amended by adding at the end of said section the following:

Regulation Governing the Storage of Gasoline, Naphtha and other Combustible Oils

No person shall locate any tank or other receptacle of greater capacity that ten gallons for the storage of gasoline, naphtha or any combustible oils without the consent of the board of engineers of the Keene Fire department being first obtained in writing thereto.

Any person violating the provision of the foregoing regulation shall be punished by a fine not exceeding twenty dollars.

A Resolution was passed on May 6th, 1915 relating to the purchase of horses for the fire department. Not to exceed $650.00.

Impervious Package Company sawmill fire, which was January 16th, 1915 located off Emerald Street, Keene. HSCC collection.

1916 [from *City of Keene Annual Report*]

Report of Chief Engineer of Fire Department and Superintendent of Fire Alarm Telegraph.

To His Honor the Mayor and Gentlemen of the City Councils:

As required by the city ordinance governing the fire department, I herewith submit my report for the fiscal year ending November 30th, 1916.

You will note from the following statement of fire and losses that the department has responded to 13 bell alarms and 83 still alarms, including brush fire calls. We have also responded to one call from Marlow. This is a decrease of one bell and 13 still alarms from the calls of last year.

The estimated value of buildings damaged by fire was $136.000.00.

Damaged to buildings was $7,617.21.
Insurance of said buildings, $2,900.00.
Insurance paid was $7,617.21.
Value of contents of said buildings was $34,497.34.

Damage to said contents, $5,033.41.
Insurance upon said property was $52,050.00.
Insurance paid, $5,033.41.

You will note from these figures that there was no loss above the insurance that was paid which is an unusual circumstance.

There has been very little equipment purchased for the department the past year, other than the general supplies required to keep the department up to its usual standard of efficiency, thus enabling us to keep our expenses within the appropriation for 1916. All of the property including furniture, etc., in and about the fire station formerly belonging to the several companies, has been purchased by the city, making it the direct owner which seems a judicious change.

Apparatus and Force:

The apparatus and force of the department under a chief and three assistant engineers, located on Vernon Street, is as follows: The Keene Steam Fire Engine & Hose Company, J. H. Simpson, Captain 25 men, has Steamer

No. 1, Button Steamer No. 2, one combination chemical and hose wagon, one relief hose wagon; Washington Hook $ Ladder Company. G. C. Symonds Captain 20 men, has one service truck and relief truck; Deluge Hose Company, E. H. Applin Captain 20 men, has one combination chemical and hose wagon.

We now have on hand about 6,500 feet of No. 1 hose, 1,400 feet of No, 2 hose, 300 feet of chemical hose and 1,500 feet of linen hose at South Keene, six 6-gallon and four 3-gallon extinguishers, one cellar pipe, one 3-way Eastman Deluge set, uniforms, rubber coats, hats and boots for the department, four sets of swing harnesses, two extra Barry collars, two sleds and three sets Hobbs runners.

There were 500 feet of hose being unfit for the fire service turned over to the water works department. Our entire supply of rubber-lined hose consisting of 8,450 feet has been tested out with the Nims hydraulic tester purchased by the city and found that 1,700 feet would not stand a pressure of 200 pounds. This has been laid aside for emergency use.

Recommendations:

The board of engineers at the present time do not think that the city is giving the suburban districts of Keene the fire protection that they have right to demand. In our judgment the only remedy for this is the purchasing of a triple combination motor driven fire truck. We therefore strongly recommend that the city purchase at its earliest convenience such a piece of apparatus. Through the courtesy of Acting Mayor Eames not long since, I had the pleasure of visiting with him the convention of the International Association of Chiefs Engineers held in Providence, R. I., where we saw many kinds of motor driven apparatus. It was the unanimous opinion of the engineers present that the triple combination motor driven truck was the most desirable and efficient piece of apparatus for a city to own that had a limited supply of motor driven apparatus. I would also recommend that the city purchase 1,000 feet of 2 ½ in. rubber-lined hose and a rescue life net. In case of serious fire in high buildings a life net might be in dispensable in saving life. I would also recommend that the old flush hydrants be replaced by post hydrants. The flush hydrants are an annual expense to the department it being necessary to re-box and pack with hay each winter.

The fire alarm telegraph system in care of Mr. E. B. Riley the fire alarm electrician continues to give excellent satisfaction. The batteries which should

Have lasted two years longer are to be renewed, the material being already ordered for the same, on account of the injury caused by the fire at the station two years ago. I would recommend that Mr. Riley's salary be increased tow dollars per week making it $17 per week.

I would further report that harmony and good will prevail among the officers and men of the several companies and the members of the board of engineers with whom I am associated. I also wish to extend my appreciation of the valuable aid rendered us by the committee on fire department, superintendent of street, superintendent of water works, and the citizens during the past year, and to them and the city clerk and city councils I extend my thanks.

LOUIS A. NIMS

Chief Engineer and Superintendent of Fire Alarm Telegraph. Keene, December 7th, 1916.

Statement of Fires Occurring in the City of Keene, From December 1st, 1915 to November 30th, 1916, Inclusive.

December 7th, 1915 to the Carl Adams for a chimney fire. Damage $15.00 and Insurance paid $15.00.

December 22nd, 1915 to the A. S. Bruder Stores & Rooms for an overheated gas iron.

Damage $25.00 and Insurance paid $25.00. Also Damage to J. Klapholtz of $150.00 and Insurance paid $150.00.

December 26th, 1915 to the R. M. Barry house for a Chimney fire with Damage of $71.00 and Insurance paid $71.00.

January 17th, 1916 to the Henkle & Sam Manufactory for a fire caused by smoking materials. Damage $13.25 and Insurance paid $13.25.

January 30th, 1916 to the Grant W. Hall house for a Chimney fire with Damage of $32.60 and Insurance paid $32.60.

February 4th, 1916 to the John N. Reed house for a Chimney fire. Damage $64.00 and Insurance paid $64.00.

February 7th, 1916 to the Boston & Main R. R. for an unknown fire with in the Stores and houses. Damage $2,128.81 and Insurance paid $2,128.81.

March 18th, 1916 to the Beaver Mills Co (Sprague & Carleton for an unknown type fire. Damage $513.11 and Insurance paid $513.11.

May 10th, 1916 to the Henry Paterson House for an unknown torch. Damage $1,139.00 and Insurance paid $1,139.00.

May 27th, 1916 to the Gertrude E. Spaulding House for an explosion caused by a plumber. Damage $1,843.13 and Insurance paid $1,843.13.

June 11th, 1916 to the George O. Hayward House for a Chimney fire with Damage of $25.00 and Insurance paid $25.00.

July 22nd, 1916 to the Mrs. F. O. Nims House For the Tenant Arthur Mayo for a child playing with a lantern. Damage $4.00 and Insurance paid $4.00.

August 5th, 1916 to the Peter Bergeron House for a Chimney fire. Damage $16.50 and Insurance paid $16.50.

August 23rd, 1916 to the J.F. & F.H. Whitcomb Farm & Buildings for a Lighting strike. Damage also to Della N. Pickett Farm & Buildings and to Chas L. Smith's. Damage totaling $6,376.15 and Insurance paid $6,376.15.

Reported in the *New Hampshire Sentinel:*

'FIRE'
1916 WHITCOMB FARM BARNS DESTROYED

On August 23rd, 1916 The Whitcomb Farm Barns Destroyed Struck by Lightning Late Wednesday Afternoon.

After a succession of electric storms in Keene and to the south of Keene, continuing most of Wednesday afternoon and putting electric power lines out of commission, a still more severe storm came up about 6 o'clock and appeared to be met by a storm that had been violent in Walpole, Alstead, Acworth, etc., and was there accompanied by a hail storm or renewal of the storm with considerable lightening and a down-pour, occurred about 7:30 in the evening.

The 6 o'clock storm did not appear to be more violent than its predecessor until a few minutes before 6, when a very heavy discharge of lightning came down in Keene, making electric wires of all kinds snap like pistols, instantly putting out all the electric lights and shutting off the electric power circuits. The bulk of this discharge came down at the Whitcomb farm on Winchester Street just below the bridge across the Ashuelot river, where the large barns filled with 75-tons of hay were struck and in a moment sprang into flames.

This farm, which has for a long time been one of the largest producers of pure milk for Keene, is owned by J. Fred and Frank H. Whitcomb and was occupied by Charles L. Smith the milk dealer, whose family lived in the house and who kept about 30 head of stock, nine horses and three pig on the farm. Of these all were saved except one horse, a registered bull and three hogs. It was a matter of good luck, almost that the twenty odd milk cows were saved. The milkers had finished but a short time before and Thaddeus Smith, who help take care of them, had come into the house, where Mrs. Smith and John Ramsdell were a short time before, and remarked that he believed he would not turn the cows out till the shower that was coming up was over. Mr. Ramsdell told him to go back and turn the cattle right out, as they would be just as well off outdoors as in the barn. Smith had just finished doing this, and was still in the cattle barn, when the lightning struck.

Mr. Ramsdell and Mrs. Smith were still in the house at that time. They thought it had struck close to them, but did not think the barns had been hit. Mrs. Smith went to the door at once, however, and even then the barn was in flames. Ramsdell rushed out and got seven horses out of one barn, but could not get a driving horse out of the other barn. Thaddeus Smith came out of the main apparently more or less dazed by the lightning and before anyone could get back into this barn, it was too late to save the bull and the driving horse. Mr. Ramsdell and others got out quite a few wagons, farming tools, etc. Charles Smith was not at home at the time, but was up near School Street with his other horse, delivering milk.

The first call for help was about 8 minutes of 6, from box 53. This was followed several minutes later by a call from box 57, which should not have been pulled in. There was no excuse for doing this. It is hardly probable that anyone could have failed to have heard the four rounds of the first call, and people should understand that pulling more than one box calls the firemen away from the box first sounded, often mixes up the alarm and always makes confusion and adds a lot to the general fire risk and danger.

The firemen got away for box 53 as quickly as possible, but the barns were entirely beyond saving long before their arrival. Hose lines were laid from a hydrant near the schoolhouse and from one or perhaps two hydrants below the Whitcomb farm. The first steamer to arrive was set at a hydrant opposite the farm but could not get enough water to work with the suction hose used and other hydrants open and had to move to the river.

As has always been the case with fires on Winchester Street, of which there have been half a dozen since 1890, there was a very inadequate water supply for hydrant streams or for an engine. This is because the Winchester Street main is a 4-inch main, a size of pipe entirely inadequate for fire service. The firemen might well make a series of tests down this street and find out how to best utilizes the water from this main. Possibly if both plugs of a hydrant nearest a fire could be connected to a steamer the engine could get water enough to play two 5/8-fire streams of considerable value. But probably this would be the limit and not more than one hydrant should be opened on the main. If more are opened none of them will be any good. Additional water on this street mush now is got from some other source.

A wood shed connected the barns at the farm with the ell of the hose and Chief Nims decided that the place to stop the progress of the fire was at this shed. Streams and ladder were therefore brought up on either side and a stand made. The streams were so poor; however, that it was difficult to cut the fire off and Mr. Nims said afterwards that had it not been for the streams from the chemical wagons and tanks, which the firemen had, he doubted if the house could have been saved.

When box 57 was pulled in the relief hose wagon was manned and sent there and an outside team was secured to take down the second steamer which was set on Pearl Street but was not used, probably for lack of hose to reach so far and to the other engine at the river as well.

Before it was sure that the firemen were going to be able to save the farm house it had been stripped and emptied, many things being insured or broken, of course, in so doing, and afterwards injured by the rain.

Here is a place where the Keene department has long been weak. There are no officer charged with the job of looking after and protecting goods in such cases, and there is no responsible officer to give this attention to this and to say whether or not it should be allowed and when removal should begin.

All the farm buildings except the house and ell, a shed for wood and hen house were burned together with 75 tons of hay, a load of grain, the animals mentioned, quite a number of tools, etc. The value of the barn destroyed is estimated at $5,000 to $7,000.

The Messrs, Whitcomb were insured for $1,750 on the house, $2,750 on the barns and $500 on the content of the barns.

Mr. Smith, who owned the hay livestock and most of the personal property was insured for $3,000 on his stock, $1,000 on his hay, $300 on his farming tools and $600 on his furniture.

The insurance was placed through the Aldrich and Palmer agencies.

Neighbors and friends saw to that Mr. Smith and his family were cared for that night, and next morning the cows were cared for and milked at Mr. Safford's farm, which is just opposite the Whitcomb farm.

Thursday Mr. Smith erected a temporary shed in the field east of the barn to provide a place to tie up and care for his cattle. Some old lumber he had was used for this and a lot of men helped him.

The Messrs, Whitcomb, will as soon as plans can be perfected, erect new barns upon the premises. The barns burned were very conveniently arranged and equipped for the milk business and a good deal of money, outside of their original cost had been expanded in making them sanitary and convenient.

The easterly side of Winchester Street below the bridge, has been the scene of not a few fires since 1890, three of which have been caused by lightning, while upon the adjacent meadows fires by lightening are recalled at the Hampshire pottery Main Street the Thompson or Clark Farm, on the silent way, West of main street and the large barn at E. F. Lane's residence.

In November 1892, the A. H. Hamblett place on lower Winchester Street was burned because of a defective chimney, and 1898 the A. Williams barns on the lower farm were struck by lightning and burned. In 1900 the barns on the upper Williams farm, next north were struck and the barns burned and a horse barn on the latter was struck about 1897 or 1898 and the cupola torn off another barn on the original Hamblett farm, owned by Fred Hamblett was burned, but was not struck and the barn on the Fred Hamblett place on the corner of the Matthew's road was set on fire by a defective chimney it was thought, and burned.

Printed in the *New Hampshire Sentinel* Keene, N. H.

————

September 10th, 1916 to the C. A. Robinson House for a Chimney fire with Damage of $2.75 and Insurance paid $2.75.

September 12th, 1916 to the F. H Wilkins (Cheshire Laundry) for sparks on the roof. Damage $40.00 and Insurance paid $40.00.

October 29th, 1916 to the Stores & Offices of Hiram Blake, Bullard & Shedd Co. and Fred E. Howe Store and Harry Watson Office for a Gasoline Explosion with Damage totaling $734.07 and Insurance paid $734.07.

November 3rd, 1916 to the Tim'y O'Brian Store and House for a Chimney fire with a stove problem. No damage reported.

November 8th, 1916 to the Mrs. George Dodge House for clothing falling on the stove. Damage $1.25 and Insurance paid $1.25.

November 21st, 1916 to the Boston & Main R. R. Blacksmith Shop for a Hot Bearing. Damage $300.00 and Insurance paid $300.00.

November 29th, 1916 to the Beaver Mills Manufactory for a Hot bearing with damage of $85.00 and Insurance paid $85.00

Note: 13 Bell alarms 1 Bell Alarm Military Call not counted and 81 Still Alarms and 1 Still for a Brush fire and 1 Still Alarm for out of town.

There were no Resolutions per say for the year of 1916. Repairs at the fire station were carried over and Furniture for fire station from Burdett Chair Manufacturing Co. was carried over.

During the annual inspection of each year, demonstrations were performed at Central Square of the Keene Fire Companies throwing a stream of water to the top of the First Church Spire. This was stopped after water damaged wooden ornaments on the steeple and penetrated the building. Photo by Bion H. Whitehouse. HSCC collection.

1917 [from *City of Keene Annual Report*]

Report of Chief Engineer of Fire Department and Superintendent of Fire Alarm Telegraph

To His Honor the Mayor and gentlemen of the City Councils.

As required by the city ordinance governing the fire department, I herewith submit my report for the fiscal year ending November 30th, 1917.

You will note from the following table of fires and losses that the department has responded to 13 bell alarms and 78 still alarms, including brush fire calls. This is decrease of five still alarms from the calls of last year.

The estimated value of buildings damaged by fire was $323,550.00.

Damage to buildings was $10,372.05.

Insurance on said buildings was $107,350.00.

Insurance paid was $9,537.30.

Value of contents of said buildings was $116,823.77.

Damage to said contents $20,125.52.

Insurance upon property was $54,750.00.

Insurance paid $17,178.09.

While several fire have occurred in dangerous places there has been but one very serious fire, that in Buffum Block. The fire occurred on one of the coldest days of the season and the department was handicapped by a hydrant being out of commission, an unusual occurrence for this city.

Apparatus and Force:

The apparatus and force of the department under a chief and three assistant engineers, located on Vernon Street, is as follows:

The Keene Steamer Fire Engine & Hose Company, J. H. Simpson, Captain, 25 men has Steamer No. 1, Button Steamer No. 2, one combination chemical and hose wagon, one relief hose wagon; Washington Hook & Ladder Company, M. J. Carey, Captain, 20 men, has one service truck and one relief truck; Deluge Hose Company, E. H. Applin, Captain, 20 men has one combination chemical and hose wagon; the motor combination truck with equipment comprises two 40 gal. Chemical tanks, two 3 gal. Extinguishers and carries 900 feet of fire hose, 250 feet chemical hose, 2 ladders and other necessary equipment. This motor truck was purchased of the Kissel Kar Co. and gives perfect satisfaction. The City is most fortunate in securing the services of Mr. Fred A. Johnson, an efficient operator of the car, and he also has charge of it. We have on hand about 5,500 feet of No. 1 hose. 1,500 feet of linen hose at South Keene, 1,500 feet of No. 2 hose much of which is unfit for fire service; 300 feet have been turned over to the highway department and 200 feet to the water works department.

Recommendations:

The board of Engineers recommend that the city purchase 1,500 feet of fire hose at its earliest convenience.

The fire alarm telegraph system in care of Mr. E. B. Riley the fire alarm electrician, continues to give excellent satisfaction. The batteries having been renewed should prove good for at least five years. The City Councils have ordered Box No. 5 now installed on the outside and used by the public, to be placed at the inside Elliott City Hospital. This will be a private box, rung only for a fire at the hospital. One new box will be placed at the corner of Winchester and Blake Streets.

The 20th annual convention of the New Hampshire State Firemen's Association held in Keene, September 26th, proved a success in every way, and I wish to extend my thanks to all who helped make it successful.

To the Mayor, and members of the joint standing committee on fire department, the members associated with me on the board of engineers, officer and members of the department, and to the public, I cordially extend my sincere thanks and appreciation for the liberal aid and generous support rendered me during the past year.

LOUIS A. NIMS,

Chief Engineer and Superintendent of Fire Alarm Telegraph. Keene, December 7th, 1917.

[*Compiler's Note:* 1917 was a big change for the Keene Fire Department, moving into the motor driven age of gas powered.]

Statement of Fires Occurring in the City of Keene, From December 1st, 1916 to November 30th, 1917, Inclusive.

January 6th, 1917 to the Roman C. Bishop House for an overheated Ash Flue. Damage $10.00 and Insurance paid $10.00.

January 16th, 1917 to the Louis Papile House for a Chimney fire with Damage of $80.00 and Insurance paid $80.00.

February 5th, 1917 to the Chas. S. Bergeron House for an Accidental fire. Damage $60.35 and Insurance paid $60.35.

February 5th, 1917 to the Frank Blake House for an unknown type fire. Damage $1,082.75 and Insurance paid $1,082.75.

February 12th, 1917 to the Store & Offices of Sarah A. Buffum for an overheated gas plate. Damage $5,461.38 and Insurance paid $5,435.00. Also damage was the Geo. E. Holbrook & Co. from the above fire. Damage $3,587.27 and Insurance paid $2,835.43. Also Damage was the Harry H Burley Store. Damage $4,730.00 and Insurance paid $3,680.79. Also the John J. Landers Office was Damage $70.00 and Insurance paid $70.00. The W. H. & J. W. Elliot Store & Office was damaged by exposure. Damage $154.55 and Insurance paid $154.55. The Keene Masonic Assn. Hall was damaged by the fire due to exposure. Damage $6.00 and Insurance paid $6.00. Also the Cheshire National Bank and Offices were damage by exposure as well. Damage $16.50 and Insurance paid $16.50.

[From *New Hampshire Sentinel:*]

'FIRE'

Buffum Block – Building on left. Photo by: Bion H. Whitehouse. HSCC collection.

1917 A BLIND ATTIC AND EXTREME COLD On February 12th, 1917 Firemen were Handicapped Seriously at Fire in Buffum Block.

Worst Blaze Near Central Square Since Clark's Block Burned in 1880 Firemen Worked Over Four Hours In Nearly Zero Temperature Excepting the Roof the Main Damage Is From Water.

Starting from a lighted gas plate need to heat a small amount of water, which was left forgotten for a time by men who were cleaning in the block until it set fire to something which happened to be near, the worst fire which Keene has seen in a good many years in its mercantile section got its origin in a closed in Tiffin's Business institute on the third floor of Buffum's block about 4 o'clock Monday afternoon. It raged unchecked over the top floor, particularly in a blind attic several feet high between the ceiling and the roof above until it caused a damage to the block of probably 48,000 to $10,000 and the fire, water and smoke damage the property of the occupants of the block to a further amount of probably $10,000.

The fire was discovered before it had made much headway and one man who went upstairs early declared he was very sure he could have checked it with an extinguisher. There were extinguishers on that floor and in the building, it is stated, but it is asserted that they failed to work for some reason. The fire swiftly crept up the walls and partitions of the small room to the ceiling where there was a skylight and scuttle hole, and hence through the whole space between it and the roof. Fire also burned in two or three rooms of the Tiffin school, dropping embers and setting the furniture, floor, etc., going.

It was practically impossible for the firemen to get at the blaze between the ceiling and roof for a long time. A trap door by which entrance to the space might have been secured was directly above the spot where the fire started, being thus cut off entirely by the fire and smoke. Numerous streams of water were put into the block from the front, up the stairs and through windows from the top of St. John's block on the north, the Cheshire bank block on the south and up ladders in the rear. There must have been ten streams going part of the time but until holes were cut or burned into the blind attic they were of little avail. Eventually they put the fire out, but it was four hours after the alarm before the steamers were replaced. Meanwhile a stream several inches deep ran down the front stairs of the block and into the street. Besides saturating everything in the officers on the second floor and the stores beneath to a considerable extent, so that next morning a thick covering of dirty ice was over everything above the first floor.

One steamer was set at the hydrant in front of the Keene national bank and the other at the foot of the Common, while line upon line of hose was laid by the hose companies from the engines and from every available hydrant on Main Street and in other locations nearby. Ladders were raised to permit of throwing streams of water into windows and from other blocks and the firemen worked, as they have not for a long time. The fire was soon well covered with streams and ladders but it was simply a case where it was found impossible to get at the flames.

Added to everything else with which the men contended there was an enormous amount of thick smoke to start with and this caused several men to collapse. Among them was Engineer D. J. Foley, who answered the still alarm first, sent in for the blaze. The men were gotten out and recovered shortly. Then after work had been going on but a short time, the extreme cold of the day began to make itself felt. It was only a few degrees above zero when the fire started and it fell much lower before the men were through with their work. They were coated with ice from head to foot and many that were not suitable clothed to begin with, suffered greatly until they secured warm clothes.

There was for a time a pond of water several inches deep over the ice and snow in Main Street, but the water from the block finally wore a channel some two feet wide and nearly a foot deep from the block to the surface drains openings further south. These were at first open, but ice and debris from the block soon closed them tight and sent the water down to railroad square where it flowed to a drain near J. Cushing & Co.'s stopped this up and would have run into the Sentinel basement if it had not been dammed off and the drain opened. Superintendent Chaplin got men with hoes and shovels soon after to open the drains on Main street, and by keeping busily at work as long as the fire streams were in use the drains were kept clear so they carried off the water easily.

The roof upon the main part of the block was of the valley type so called, that is it sloped toward the center where the roof-water conductors led down through the building. The outside of the roof was thus higher by a foot or more than the center and there was no opening into the blind attic resulting except by the scuttle hole just about where the fire started. It is said that there was a second blind space in the roof some of the way owing to changes made after it was first built, and that the first covering was of tin the roof being difficult to cut through from the top. However this may be the entire roof over the main part of the block was destroyed before the fire could be put out, the third floor ceiling supporting was is left of it. This roof will all have to be rebuilt and new timbers will very likely be required to a greater or less extent for the third floor ceiling. A section of the rear of the building was only two stories high. This section has a tin roof, which was not injured.

On the top floor of the block all the rooms were occupied by the Tiffin business institute and were mostly filled with school desks and seats, tables, etc. These were not badly burned, but were hurt by water and the ice, which formed. There were also some typewriters, books, paper, supplies, office furniture clothing, etc., which were much damaged.

On the second floor front were the offices of Dr. Murray V. Wright dentist, and that of the late Hiram Blake Esq., and R. J. Wolfe. Dr. Wright got out some of his most valuable possessions, but his chair; smoke, water and ice damaged office furniture, etc. The law books in the law office of Mr. Blake, Mr. Wolfe and John J. Landers on the south side were taken out together with some other property, but many papers, books, some furniture, etc. were covered with water and ice and hurt by smoke. Miss Myrtle Safford whose music room was in the rear under another roof had

A Demon Called Fire

her piano and furniture taken out. The fire did not damage to her room however.

Before the fire had burned long help was secured by Mr. Burley and the Holbrook Co., and a considerable quantity of clothing was removed from the front store of Mr. Burley to a connecting rear store, in the Elliot block, under another roof, and groceries were taken out of the Holbrook store and piled up near the rear of the Federal Street block. Goods remaining in Burley's was largely protected with rubber blankets and canvas coverings he owns. Canvas heavy paper, etc., were also used to protect the Holbrook goods.

he Burley store Tuesday did not present a very bad appearance, but nearly everything in it was somewhat damaged, presumably, by smoke if not by water. The Holbrook store was not in bad shape considering the quantities of water poured into the building. Then, too, everything over head was frozen up Tuesday morning, and there will be more water to come down for some days when the ice on the floors above begins to melt, even if it is found possible to get a new roof built quickly over the block.

The walls of the building, the wires nearby, the hose and everything about the block were quickly crusted with ice during the fire and the place looked like an ice palace in the evening. There was a band of Boy Scouts and others out passing hot coffee and sandwiches and doughnuts around among the firemen and helping to gather up the wet and frozen hose later. A large crowd of people stood in the cold until dark and some remained into the evening.

It is difficult to estimate the loss of the different owners as yet, but it is thought the entire loss will exceed $20,000. The block was insured for $14,000 through the Mason agency and $5,000 through the Aldrich agency, with $5000 on the fixtures with the Mason agency and $1,500 on furniture with Aldrich. Mr. Burley had $5,000 insurance with

A. B. Palmer, $4,000 with Aldrich and $2,000 with mason. Holbrook & Co. carried $3,000 with A. B. Palmer, $2,000 with Aldrich and $1,300 with mason. J. J. Landers had $200 with Aldrich. Some of the other tenants may have insurance.

Fred E. Howe, who has charge of the Buffum block, was able to have a fire started in the heating boiler that might, after the firemen were substantially through work, and steam was turned on to all the radiators possible, thus warming the stores down stairs and preventing the freezing of other pipes, to a greater or less extent.

Tuesday it has been possible to close up the windows in the second floor and put on the heat. Just what can be done with the third floor and roof remains to be seen.

Monday evening Manager Slade hired two empty stores, No. 15 and 19 Church Street, and got carpenters from M.O. Spaulding to put up temporary shelving, tables, etc. Telephones were installed there next morning and business will be done there as well as possible for the present. The goods handled will be new goods, no adjustment of the insurance of goods that were in the Buffum block being possible for some days probably.

Besides a failure to get fire extinguishers enough in the block to stop the fire when it was first discovered there was trouble with the first hose lines laid by the department. The first line was from the hydrant in front of Person's store. This line was carried upstairs and the firemen expected water quickly. But when John Dennison of the waterworks department turned the hydrant valve, the gate would not work. The gate mechanism made a noise as if something was broken, and Mr. Dennison did not dare to try to open it any more for fear the gate would break and the water get loose, thus crippling the service by reducing the pressure everywhere. Valuable time was lost while this hose line was being charged. The water came up around the hydrant when it was turned. Showing that the gage began to open. The gate pushes down into the pipe, so it is difficult to see how ice could have stopped it. The hydrant had been tested that morning and appeared to be free from ice.

The Button engine first came to this hydrant. It had to be sent to the larger hydrant south of the common where it might better have gone to begin with. The Amoskeag engine worked at the Church Street Hydrant. Both engines were used till 8 o'clock or after.

The second, or at least one of the first hose lines was laid from the hydrant at the Sentinel building. When the water was turned on this time the hose burst near the Sentinel building causing another delay in the use of streams. Whether either of the two streams mentioned would have been available before the fire reached the blind attic had there been no mishaps is all open questions.

Walter Potter, who was in the block at the time of the fire, had his hands and face quite badly burned. It is said that no attempt was made to use the large chemical tank on the first hose wagon reaching the fire. If this is so a most important and efficient implement provided for just such emergencies was left untried at a critical moment.

Chief Nims and his men were driving back by smoke several times while endeavoring to break into the blind attic from the rear. They worked hard to do this both from the lower roof through the wall and on the main roof.

Printed in the *New Hampshire Sentinel* Keene, N.H.

———

May 28th, 1917 to the Gertrude M. Pike House for an unknown fire. Damage $25.00 and Insurance paid $25.00.

May 30th, 1917 to the Keene Screen & Ladder Co. for a Chimney fire. Damage $7.00 and Insurance paid $5.25.

April 6th, 1917 to the Nellie Ahern House for a Chimney fire. Damage $7.51 and Insurance paid $7.51.

May 15th, 1917 to the Sumner W. Parker House for a Chimney fire with Damage of $76.50 and Insurance paid $76.50.

May 16th, 1917 to the Chas C. Buffum House for a Chimney fire. Damage $7.00 and Insurance paid $7.00.

May 27th, 1917 to the Alice H. Ellis Hotel & Stores for a chimney fire. Damage $686.69 and Insurance paid $686.69. Also to the Judson A. Reynolds from the above fire with Damage of $291.41 and Insurance paid $291.41. Also to the Law Office of Roy M. Pickard with damage of $5.00 and Insurance paid $5.00. and also the Clarence A. More Candy & Cream Shop with Damage of $10.00 and Insurance paid $10.00.

July 18th, 1917 to the Louis J. Martell Carpenter Shop for Child playing with Matches. Damage $3,000.00 and Insurance paid $1,500.00. Also 3 other were damaged by the fire. The House & Garage of Louis Martell with Damage of $105.00 and Insurance paid $105.00 and the House of C. R. Partridge with Damage of $299.40. and Insurance paid $299.40.

July 27th, 1917 to the Robertson & Bennett Garage & Mfg. For an unknown type fire. Damage was $98.50 and Insurance paid $98.50. Also damaged was the Int'l Narrow Fabric Co. with damage of $8,260.29 and Insurance paid $8,260.29.

August 17th, 1917 to the Mrs. D. E. Hawthorn House for a fire caused by painters, Damage $200.00 and Insurance paid $200.00.

September 23rd, 1917 to the Mrs. E. Thibadeau House for a Chimney fire. Damage $25.00 and Insurance paid $25.00.

October 14th, 1917 to the Omer L. Buxton House for an unknown type fire with Damage of $375.00 and Insurance paid $375.00.

October 24th, 1917 to the O. H. Thayer House for a Chimney fire with Damage of $8.00 and Insurance paid $8.00.

November 16th, 1917 to the Beaver Mills Co. Sprague & Carleton for an unknown type fire. Damage $563.02 and Insurance paid $563.02.

November 29th, 1917 to the Alice H. Ellis Hotel & Stores for an overheated furnace. Damage $200.00 and Insurance paid $80.00.

Ordinance and Resolutions for the Year Ending 1917.

On February 15th, 1917 an Ordinance amending Section 11, Chapter VIII, city Ordinance was passed. It read Section 11, Chapter VIII, City Ordinances, be so far modified that the same shall read when amended, as follows:

Section 11. The chief engineer shall inspect or cause to be inspected as often as once in four months all hotels and buildings used partly or wholly for business purpose within the limits of the fire precinct, and shall see that all regulations established by the engineers of the fire department respecting the prevention of fires and otherwise are enforced.

He shall keep in detail a record of such inspection. Compensation for such inspection service at the rate of thirty-five cents for each hour given for the purpose shall be allowed and made in the manner provided for special service in Section 3 of this chapter.

Keene, N. H., February 12th, 1917 To the City Councils of Keene:

Your committee, appointed for the purpose of looking into the advisability of motorizing the Keene Fire department, finds that it would, in their opinion, be wise to start upon motorization, this year.

The committee as a whole visited several cities which have been more or less motorized for some time. Some have large pumping engines, others have the lighter combination chemical and hose apparatus.

Pumping engines of suitable size range in price from $8,600 to $9,000. Combination chemical and hose apparatus range in price from $3,500 to $5,000. The cheaper kind being

bodies built on standard chassis such as are used in other lines of business. These bodies are built on order and are built as you might wish them.

The committee had before it all the time the recommendations of the Board of Engineers of Keene as to a Triple Combination Pumping Engine and agree with the board that the City will probably require the services of one of these engines later. The companies are now working on and will later put out a pumping engine with four wheel drive, giving it more traction in snow road. This in itself would be a great improvement for cities situated in our climate. This machine is no yet on the market.

It seems to the members of the committee who sign this report that the citizens would get better protection from the prevailing percentage of fires which we call "stills," by the use of a light type of motor apparatus which carries chemical tanks and also about 1,500 feet of hose.

It also appears to the committee that the future motorization of the department depends upon the performance and cost of maintenance of this first piece of apparatus.

Geo. H. Eames, Jr.
H. C. Tiffin
Earle W. Capron
L. P. Butler
Ora C. Mason
Louis A. Nims
Charles A. Robinson

A Resolution relating to Motor Fire Truck was passed on February 15th, 1917 from the special committee on Motor Fire Apparatus (above names) hereby authorized to purchase a Combination Chemical & Hose motor fire truck, not to exceed five thousand dollars in value.

KEENE'S FIRST MOTOR FIRE WAGON

Sixty Horse Power Kissel Combination Purchased

To give Quick Service with Chemical and Hydrant Streams Reached Here Sunday and is being tested Out.

Keene's first piece of motor driven fire apparatus, a Kissel combination hose and chemical wagon ordered in march last, came to Keene from Boston by its own power Sunday afternoon reaching the fire station soon after 4 o'clock.

The Wagon made the run up from Boston easily and without incident and the motor, although new, was running nicely on its arrival here and showed no signs of heating. Monday afternoon the wagon was tested over Beech hill roads with a load of eighteen men, and operated perfectly and it was given another tryout Tuesday. It was to be accepted and put in service Tuesday night. The contract price of the apparatus was $3750, or six or seven hundred less, it is said, than such a wagon could be bought for today.

The new wagon has been delivered here by W. D. Foskett, of Trefry & Foskett, New England agents for the Kissel fire apparatus. He brought with him Chauffeur Kersten, who handled the wagon at the demonstration. Guy F. Fairfield, who introduced Mr. Trefry, when he was here in March, and who knew Mr. Foskett, was at the fire station with quite a number of the firemen when the wagon arrived.

The new motor has a business-like rather than a flashy appearance, although it is painted a bright fire department red with gold stripes and letters and black shading and has nickel trimmings. The steering wheel control, levers, etc., are all conveniently arranged at the driver's seat and there is a search light, a siren and an engine bell which he or the man riding with him can handle easily. Underneath the driver's seat are two 35-gallon chemical tanks with a special connection for 2 ½ inch hose so that the chemical stream may be charged to a hydrant stream if desired. The basket carrying 200 feet of chemical hose is just behind the driver's seat and beyond this is the hose wagon proper having a flaring steel body with lockers in each side opening on top, the body being capable of carrying 1200 to 1500 feet of 2 ½ inch fire hose. The tool box equipment is under the wagon body and is reached from the rear. There are running boards with nickel hand rails in the rear and on the sides and seats for additional men if necessary, the tops of the lockers on the sides provide seats for additional men if necessary.

The equipment of the wagon comprises, besides the chemical outfit already mentioned, two 3-gallon chemical tanks; four Deitz fire department lanterns, two pick head axes; a Detroit door opener; crow bars, two extra acid receptacles; one 30-foot extension ladder; one 15-foot roof ladder and a plaster hook.

The motor is a 60 horse power Kissel engine and is geared to give a speed of 35 miles an hour. It has a Westinghouse self-starter and a 4-cylinder tire pump. The electric lights are of the octagonal type. The wheels are of wood and are strongly built carrying 38x5 ½ inch non-skid Goodyear tires. The motor

Keene's first motorized fire apparatus – 1917 Kissel. Fire Dept. Scrapbook.

and chassis were built at the Kissel factory in Wisconsin and assembled and finished at the Boston factory, where this work is done and repairs for the Kissel apparatus are kept.

Fred A. Johnson, whose experience as an automobile driver and mechanic covers a number of years and includes service on the difficult Benguet road from Manila to Baguio, has been engaged to drive and look after the wagon for the city. Electrician Eugene Riley will also learn to run the wagon, and the two men, together, with probably a third man later to fall back on in case of sickness, vacations, etc., should provide a person at the station competent to handle the wagon at all times.

Hereafter, when motorists in Keene hear the somewhat doubtful and unusual sound of a horn or siren such as fire wagons use, it will be up to them to clear the road speedily and wait for fire apparatus. There has been complaint already that motorists keep in the road and obstruct horse drawn fire apparatus when there are alarms in Keene, besides kicking up a cloud of dust sometimes that adds to the discomfort of the horses and the danger of all upon the road. With the coming of motor apparatus and higher speeds, greater care and more stringent rules for a clear right of way for the firemen are likely to be essential.

_____

1918 [from *City of Keene Annual Report*]

Report of Chief Engineer of Fire Department and Superintendent of Fire Alarm Telegraph.

To His Honor the Mayor and Gentlemen of the City Councils:

As required by the city ordinance governing the fire department, I herewith submit my report for the fiscal year ending November 30th, 1918.

The department has responded to the following alarms: 19 bell alarms and 98 still alarms, 2 brush fire calls, 2 calls for searching parties, 2 false alarms, November 11th, and 1 call to County Farm at Westmoreland.

The estimated value of buildings damaged by fire was $99,250.00.

Damage to buildings was $5,552.32.

Insurance on said buildings was $52,700.00.

Insurance paid was $5,052.32.

Value of contents of said buildings was $64,800.00.

Damage to said contents $10,752.02.

Insurance upon property was $36,425.00.

Insurance paid $9,385.24.

Apparatus and Force:

The apparatus and force of the department under a chief and three assistant engineers, located on Vernon Street, I as follows: The Ke3ene steam Fire Engine & Hose Company, J. H. Simpson, Captain, 25 men, has Steamer No. 1, Button No. 2, one combination chemical and hose wagon, one relief hose wagon, the motor combination truck with equipment comprising two 40-gal. Chemical tanks, two 3- gal. Extinguishers and carrying 900 feet of fire hose, 250 feet chemical hose, 2 ladders and other necessary equipment; Washington Hook & Ladder Company, M. J. Carey, Captain. 20 men has one service truck and one relief truck; Deluge Hose Company, E. H. Applin, Captain, 20 men, has one combination chemical and hose wagon. Our Motor truck continues to give excellent service. We have on hand about 7500 feet of No. 1 hose, 1500 feet linen hose at South Keene, and 1000 feet of No. 2 hose, which is unfit for fire service: 100 feet have been turned over to the Highway Department and 300 feet to the water works department.

Recommendations:

The Board of Engineers recommend that the city purchase 1000 feet of fire hose; also a much needed life net.

The fire alarm telegraph system, in care of Mr. E. B. Riley, the fire alarm electrician continues to give excellent satisfaction. A new box, No. 151, has been installed at the corner of Winchester and Blake Streets, and a new box No. 119 on Congress Street, opposite the A. E. Martell Co. factory. At the present time we have three paid men in charge of the motor truck and fire alarm. I would recommend that this force be increased to four men.

To the Mayor, and members of the joint standing committee on fire department, the members associated with me on the board of engineers, officers and members of the department, and to the public, I cordially extend my sincere thanks and appreciation for the liberal aid and generous support rendered me during the past year.

LOUIS A. NIMS. Chief Engineer and Superintendent of Fire Alarm Telegraph. Keene, December 6th, 1918.

Statement of Fires Occurring in the City of Keene, From November 30th, 1917 to November 30th, 1918.

November 16th, 1917 to the Beaver Mills Co. Sprague & Carleton Co. for an unknown type fire. Damage $563.02 and Insurance paid $$563.02.

November 29th, 1917 to the Alice H. Ellis Hotel & Stores for smoke from a heater. Damage $200.00 and Insurance paid $80.00.

December 2nd, 1917 to the Bessie M. Dee Tenant house for a Chimney fire with Damage of $12.00 and Insurance paid $12.00.

December 2nd, 1917 to the Henry Ellis House & Barn for an oil stove fire with Damage of $2,222.66 and Insurance paid $2,222.66.

December 20th, 1917 to the Henry Swan House & Tenants for smoke from the chimney with damage of $30.00 and Insurance paid $30.00.

December 24th, 1917 to the Cheshire Beef Co. for an unknown type fire. Damage $322.00 and Insurance paid $322.00.

December 30th, 1917 to the Wyman Lawrence House for an overheated stove pipe with Damage of $45.00 and Insurance Paid $45.00.

December 31st, 1917 to the Store of Sewell & Co. for a plumber thawing pipes. Damage $88.00 and Insurance paid $88.00.

January 18th, 1918 to the Carpenter shop and House as well as the garage of Louis J. Martell for a fire caused by children playing with matches. Damage $3,105.00 and Insurance paid $1,605.00.

August 3rd, 1918 to the Est. of Jas. Boyce House for an unknown type fire. Damage $10.00 and Insurance paid $10.00.

August 7th, 1918 to the Barn of Nunzie Diluzia for children playing with matches. Damage $35.00 and Insurance paid $35.00.

November 29th, 1918 to the mercantile building of R. F. Gurnsey. This was a large property loss fire and was an unknown cause. The Gurnsey building, Damage of $6,515.10 and Insurance paid $2,668.32. The R. F. Gurnsey Damage of $168.00 and Insurance paid $168.00. The J. B. Duffy property Damage of $21.43 and Insurance paid $21.43. The S. Finklestein property with Damage of $500.00 and Insurance paid $500.00. The F. L. Allen property with Damage of $1,801.16 and Insurance paid $1,801.16. The C. C. Wilber property with Damage of $50.91 and Insurance paid $50.91. The James H. Goodhue property with Damage of $158.00 and Insurance paid $158.00. The Herbert A. Putney property with Damage of $15.00 and Insurance paid $15.00. The Wilfred J. Dubois property with Damage of $397.06 and Insurance paid $397.06. The Robert A. Ray property with Damage of $50.00 and Insurance paid $50.00.

[From *New Hampshire Sentinel:*]

'FIRE'

1918 A HOT FIRE THAT WAS WELL HANDLED, November 29th, 1918 A Hot Fire That Was Well Handled with Many Lives Endangered and Good Rescue Work Done. The

Kitchen of Georgian Cafe in Gurnsey Building Bursts Suddenly Into Flames-Excessive heat Quickly Generated, Fire Bursting Out and Into neighboring Store-Block Filled with Smoke and Fire Escape Cut Off

A fire of unknown origin and evidently of unusually violence with an explosive element in it suggesting a benzene compound, broke out suddenly about 1:15 Friday morning in the kitchen of the Georgian café in the Gurnsey building. It is understood that at the time there were some twenty or thirty people in the block nearly all of them asleep. Those who were awake however appear to have known nothing of the fire until Officer Buckminster, who was on his rounds on Church Street saw a suspicious light and hurrying round to main Street could see the flames in rear of the Dubois barber shop. He quickly pulled box 8 at 1:20 summoning the firefighters who were there in short notice and did excellent work.

With the help of Officer Swanstrom, who soon arrived and H. A. Putney, L. S. Upton and perhaps others who were in the block and had partly dressed, the inmates of the building were awakened just as rapidly as possible, the officers and other going through the halls to the fourth floor and bringing down at least two women, it is understood who were overcome.

At this time the halls were densely filled with smoke while the fire escapes and the piazzas in rear of the block were cut off by a column of smoke and flames pouring up from the café kitchen on the lower floor. Some of the women remained at the windows in front shouting for ladders and in carrying one of them down through the halls. Officer Swanstrom was so much overcome by smoke that he nearly fainted on getting down stairs while others who were assisting were almost exhausted. Proprietor F. L. Allen of the café, who rooms on the fourth floor and had not gone to bed, said he had all he could do to get down stairs with his wife although familiar

with the way. The halls were so filled with smoke that he could not see the lights in them.

To return to the fire. How it caught is a mystery or perhaps a surprise it apparently did not catch from fat on the rang as was reported for the kettle for doughnuts was there on Saturday with its fat in fact and nothing remained on the range but a kettle of water and some cooking utensils. Next to the range was a gas pie oven full of cooked pies put in for the night and beyond a big pie oven with nothing burnable about it. A large dish rack through the middle of the room gave no clue nor did the refrigerator, flour barrel, cooking table etc., on the opposite side of the room.

It appears that Mr. and Mrs. Allen did not leave the restaurant until nearly 1 o'clock a friend being there with whom they talked for some time after closing about midnight. Previously a man and been there with a spray pump with liquids such as had for some time been used for waterbeds or cockroaches. The kitchen ceiling which is of sheathing and the walls tables dish rack floor etc. had been drenched with this. The range was quite hot business having been lively all day and the pipe ran up near the sheathed ceiling.

Perhaps the best suggestion of the origin of the fire lies in the theory that after the Allen's left the restaurant something set fire to the ceiling or to condensed spray that dropped upon the stovepipe. There is every indication that an explosive fire resulted. It is reported that an explosion was heard and something broke out the rear windows of the kitchen speedily and also broke the windows near the ceiling lighting part of the Gurnsey harness department just in the rear of the kitchen.

It is difficult to otherwise explain what occurred in the big Gurnsey store with nothing more inflammable in it that harness blankets, tobacco etc., both largely in boxes or containers. The fact remains that this entire store got so hot that the paint was blistered so it is peeling clear to the front door and down nearly to the floor while of the plastic glass windows in front only two out of nine remained unbroken.

The fire likewise tore its way across the room in rear of the kitchen into the Dubois barber shop where there were also windows near the ceiling to light the rear room of the harness shop behind the barbershop and the kitchen. The smoke and fire rushed through the barbershop blistered the paint and broke the front windows.

On arrival of the fire department the restaurant kitchen was a roaring furnace and the flames in rear were shooting up lighting the sky over the block. The chemical motor made a quick response attacking at once with chemical lines and laying a hydrant line. Other apparatus soon followed including the chemical wagon. Hose lines were run through the Dubois shop and to the rear of the building. There was some criticism that water was turned on through these lines but it evidently seemed necessary and it should be said that there are no signs of the use of water above the first floor while little was used beyond the restaurant kitchen.

The losses of the fire cannot be estimated with any assurance at this time. Mr. Allen's loss has been adjusted at $1,801 but at last accounts the other losses had not been adjusted.

The loss on the Gurnsey store stock is said to be quite number of thousand dollars and the smoke went up into the Finkelstein store where it is claimed that a lot of goods are smoked and damaged. Tenants in the block got their things smoked up pretty well, some of the officers estimating a damage of $50. But the basement tenements largely escaped. Roomers must have lost in proportion. On the block itself there must be a loss of $5,000 or more and Mr. Dubois claimed about $500. It is understood that practically all the losses are covered by insurance.

Printed in the *New Hampshire Sentinel* Keene, N. H.

Joint Resolutions for the Year ending 1918

On January 3rd, 1918 a Resolution was passed relating to fire hose. The sum of $1,400 dollars was appropriated for the purchase of 2,000 feet of fire hose.

On May 16th, 1918 the Chief of the fire department along with the superintendent of streets were authorized to sell a pair of horses and purchase a pair of horses not to exceed $650.00.

A resolution was passed on September 19th, 1918 That, whereas, the Board of Engineers and the foremen of the fire department companies have deemed it expedient not to hold an inspection of the Keene Fire Department this year, their action in the matter be ratified, confirmed and commended.

1919 [from *City of Keene Annual Report*]
Report of Chief Engineer of Fire Department and City Electrician.

To His Honor the Mayor and Gentlemen of the City Councils:

As required by the city ordinance governing the fire department, I herewith submit my report for the fiscal year ending November 30th, 1919.

The department has responded to the following alarms, 10 bell alarms, 108 still alarms, 1 brush fire call and one false alarm from box 51 on September 7th, 1919.

The estimated value of buildings damaged by fire was, $187,600.00.

Damage to buildings was $4,883.46.

Insurance on said buildings was $121,300.00.

Insurance paid was $4,883.46.

Value of contents of said buildings was $57,700.00.

Damage to said contents, $5,055.22.

Insurance upon property was $39,950.00.

Insurance paid $5,055.22.

Apparatus and Force:

The apparatus and force of the department under a chief and three assistant chiefs, located on Vernon Street, is as follows: The Keene Steam Fire Engine & Hose Co., H. E. Raymond, Captain, 25 men, has Steamer No. 1, Button Steamer No. 2, one combination chemical and hose wagon, one relief hose wagon and one motor chemical with two 40-gallon chemical tanks and other necessary equipment; Washington Hook & Ladder Company, M. J. Carey, Captain, 20 men, has one service truck and one relief truck; Deluge Hose Company, E. H. Applin, Captain, 20 men, has one combination chemical and hose wagon. Our motor truck continues to give excellent service. We have on hand about 7,000 feet of No. 1 hose, 1,500 feet of linen hose at South Keene, 1,000 feet of No. 2 hose which is unfit for fire service; 200 feet have been turned over to the water works department during the year. During the year the Chief and his assistant chiefs have inspected the buildings in the fire precinct several times.

Recommendations:

The Board of Engineers recommend that the City motorize all its fire apparatus as soon as possible. But especially we would recommend the motorizing of the service ladder truck this year, as the ladders and truck itself is getting unserviceable.

The fire alarm telegraph system in care of Mr. E. B. Riley, the fire alarm electrician, continues to give excellent satisfaction.

There is about 25 miles of wire in the six fire alarm circuits of which 20 miles of it is copper wire, and the other five miles is of No. 12 galv. Iron of the taper circuits, which is very rusty and unserviceable and will have to be replaced the coming year. I recommend that it be replaced with copper instead of iron wire which will then make it a permanent job.

To the Mayor, and members of the joint standing committee on fire department, the members associated with me on the board of engineers, officers and members of the department, and to the public, I extend my sincere thanks and appreciation for the liberal aid and generous support rendered me during the past year.

F. W. TOWNE, Chief Engineer Keene, December 4th, 1919

[*Compiler's Note*: A law was passed in 1919 relating to the investigation of the causes of fires. Public Statutes, Chapter 115 reads as follows:

Penalty for not making return as required by law, $200.00.

The law related to the investigation of the causes of fires.]

Public Statutes, Chapter 115

Sec. 21. When property is destroyed by fire, it shall be the duty of the board of fire wards or engineers of towns having such officers, and of selectmen in other towns, to make investigation of the cause, circumstances, and origin thereof, and especially to examine whether it was the result of carelessness or of design. The investigation shall be commenced within two days of the occurrence of the fire, not including the Lord's day. They shall have the powers vested in justices of the peace to compel the attendance of witnesses to testify before them upon such inquest.

Sect. 22. They shall present to the city or town clerk, for record by him in a book provided by the insurance commissioner, a written statement of all the facts relating to the cause of such fires, the kind, value, and ownership of property destroyed, and of such other particulars as may be called for in the form provided, and of any other facts which to them seem pertinent; and such record shall be make within two weeks of the occurrence of the fire.

Sect. 23. The clerk shall make a transcript of such fire record upon a blank form provided by the insurance commissioner, for each six months preceding, and forward the same to the insurance commissioner within fifteen days from the first of July and the first day of January in each year. He shall also transmit to the insurance commissioner at any time upon his request, a copy of the record as to any particular fire, or any facts concerning it.

Sect. 24. Any officer neglecting or refusing to perform any duty required of him by any of the provisions of the three sections next preceding, shall be fined not exceeding two hundred dollars.

[*Compiler's Note*: Logs and Books were kept both by the fire department and the City Clerk's office which are kept still by the fire department today.]

Statement of Fires Occurring in the City of Keene, From December 1st, 1918 to November 30th, 1919, Inclusive.

[*Compiler's Note*: In the Chief Towne's Annual Report covering the fire loss the damage loss and contents loss are listed separate.]

January 7th, 1919 to the G. H. Colony Estate for a Gas Leak in the stove. Damage to building $14.43 and to Furniture $8.00 with insurance paying both.

February 28th, 1919 to the Junk Shop of Louis Tatleman for a fire caused by items to close to the stove. Damage to building $175.00 and to contents to building $300.00 and Insurance paid both.

March 7th, 1919 to the house of George Conway for a Chimney fire and stove fire with damage of $15.24 and to Furniture of $20.00 and Insurance paid both.

May 14th, 1919 to the Meat Market of Louis Tatleman for items too close to the stove. Damage to store of $50.00 and contents inside of $75.50 and Insurance paid both.

May 30th, 1919 to the Mrs. B. Ellis Hotel for a chimney fire with damage to furniture of $40.00 and Insurance paid.

April 23rd, 1919 to the House of W. H. Spalter for a chimney fire. Damage to house $20.00, and Insurance paid $20.00.

May 2nd, 1919 to the house of C. W. Wilber Estate Tenement for children playing with matches. Damage to house $894.00 and Insurance paid.

June 6th, 1919 to the house of E. J. Carr for a closet fire with damage to the hose of $125.00 and Insurance paid.

June 12th, 1919 to the house of Ike Goldsmith for a closet fire with damage of $372.25 and for damage to furniture of $250.00 and Insurance paid both.

June 22nd, 1919 to the Joseph Gorman house for a Chimney fire with damage of $190.00 and Insurance paid.

July 4th, 1919 to the Corrin Hall House for a fire caused by fireworks. Damage of $15.00 and Insurance paid.

July 8th, 1919 to the Restaurant of Warren French and owner Boston & Main for an unknown type fire with damage of $1,224.00 and contents of furniture $2,000.00 and Insurance paid.

July 15th, 1919 to the Mercantile property of G. J. B. McCushing for a fire caused by Cigar or Cigarette. Damage to Furniture $100.00 and insurance paid.

July 19th, 1919 to the E. F. Lane Building Keene National Bank for an unknown type fire. Damage to building $44.67 and damage to Furniture of $125.00 and Insurance paid.

September 3rd, 1919 to the Hotel & Stores of Mrs. Alice H. Ellis for a fire in the store- room. Damage $ 1,706.87 and damage to contents $2,096.72 and Insurance paid.

[from *New Hampshire Sentinel:*]

'FIRE'

1919 A DANGEROUS FIRE WELL HANDLED. September 3rd, 1919 A Blaze Starts In Storeroom in Cheshire House Block and Fills Part of Hotel With smoke.

From some unknown cause which so far as-present knowledge and investigation goes, might as well be attributed to rats and matches, a dangerous fire in a storeroom on the ground floor of the Cheshire House block was started early Wednesday and when discovered kept the firemen busy for nearly an hour in locating it and putting it out. They did their work effectively and although the flames worked into the hotel walls and under a broad stairway, very little water damage resulted. The loss, which will be largely from smoke and water, is covered by insurance and cannot be estimated with any accuracy because good many rooms may be involved. There will be some loss upon carpets, rugs and furniture.

One of the maids in the hotel smelled the smoke and called Landlord Reynolds who started through the house to find where the smoke came from. Mrs. Reynolds at the same time called the fire station, resulting in a still alarm shortly before 4 o'clock. Officer Perry who was down on Railroad Street and Officer Wheelock, who was on the other side of main street smelled smoke, but on coming up main street could not tell at first where it came from. Officer Buckminster joined in the search and it soon appeared that the Cheshire House was the seat of the trouble. Landlord Reynolds having ascertained about where the trouble was, he and Engineer Foley who responded to the still alarm, and Officer Perry broke into Leveroni's fruit store, finding the fire beyond that store in a good sized storeroom used by M. E. Daniels the druggist and filled with his goods. The fire was hot and rapidly becoming dangerous, requiring soon more help and a general alarm was sounded from box 9.

Officer Perry kept the storeroom door closed until the chemical line was ready to begin work and a hose line was also brought in. In the meantime all the people in the hotel were aroused and were getting up. It got so Smokey on the third floor that four or five women employed in the house who were sleeping in the south ell came down the rear fire escape, with blankets and the like wrapped around them. The ladder truck men first arriving put up a short ladder and helped them off the fire escape and into the carriage house. Later an automobile was procured and Treasurer E. L. Gay saw that they were made comfortable at the office of the Keene Gas and Electric Company. Guests of the hotel came down into the lobby some very lightly clad and some with all their belongings, but before very long they were assured that there was no immediate danger and some of them went back to their rooms. There were about 100 guests sleeping in the hotel.

The firemen laid a hose line through the Cheshire House office and up the stairs opening from the dining room to the hallways on the second floor. Lines were also carried to the rear of the hotel and others were laid in front, a steamer being set at Pearson's corner on account of trouble with the four way hydrant at the common from which the first hose line through the Leveroni store was laid. Had it been possible to open this hydrant giving water on this hose line as planned no general alarm would have been sounded. But Engineer Foley was already using his last chemical tank and had no auxiliary stream when the whole line failed with which to drive the fire back and help the men on the chemical line to get control. Of course this was remedied later, but it was not deemed safe to take any risk at the time, so the bell alarm was ordered.

Following the general alarm access was gained to the storeroom through a door opening out doors on the south side of the ell. The flames in the storeroom were thus rapidly overcome excepting among the druggist supplies of all kinds piled upon shelves extending to the ceiling on each side. These goods had to be largely thrown out and a good deal of the shelving demolished before all the fire could bereted. One set of shelves toppled over being burned at the foot and hit Engineer Foley an ugly blow upon which the fire was burning were cleared d out. There had been no fire in the paper-bailing machine that stood in the room.

The line of hose laid through the Cheshire House office and dining room stairway proved essential, barring a second chemical line, for the fire had worked from the storeroom along some steam pipes that were red hot when the storeroom door was first opened and into the wall and floor overhead. Luckily the brick wall at this point came over under the entry floor to the dining room stairway and the second floor of the ell being two or three steps higher than the floor of the main part, the fire was thus prevented from running under the main part floors and to the inner walls where it must have got a strong upward draft and spread almost instantly. As it was it burned and charred the wood thoroughly underneath the steps leading to the ell hallway close to those coming up from the dining room. The firemen cut holes and put this blaze out before it could get away under the ell floor. Another fortunate thing was that the wall through which the fire came up into the ell from the store room underneath, also in the ell part was cut off close above the second floor by an unusually broad window provided to light the halls. This kept the fire in the ell wall from running up long enough for the firemen to open into the wall in two or three places and get into the floor, thus putting out all the fire above the storeroom, the ceiling of which did not burn through.

M. E. Daniels had perhaps $1,200 to $1,400 worth of goods in the storeroom, which were virtually all ruined. They were insured through the Mason agency, which also carries insurance for Mr. Reynolds. The Aldrich and Palmer agencies have insurance on the Cheshire House.

Printed in the *New Hampshire Sentinel* Keene, N. H.

October 4th, 1919 to the House of Mosher for a chimney fire with damage of $10.00 and insurance paid.
October 17th, 1919 to the Mercantile building of Sewall & Shepardson for a chimney fire. Damage $10.00 and Insurance paid.
October 25th, 1919 to the house of Grace S. Upton for a chimney fire. Damage $10.00 and Insurance paid.
October 28th, 1919 to the house of Johanna Ellis for a chimney fire with damage of $16.50 and also Furniture damage of $30.00 which Insurance paid.

Resolutions for the year Ending 1919

On February 6th, 1919 a Resolution was passed for the purchase of coats and boots for the fire department not to exceed $293.01. Also for the sum was passed for $250.00 for doors at the fire station.

A Resolution was passed on September 4th, 1919 for the sum of $700.00 for a new heating apparatus for the fire station.

1920 [from *City of Keene Annual Report*]
Report of the Chief Engineer of the Fire Department and City Electrician.

To His Honor the Mayor and Gentlemen Of the City Councils:

As required by the City ordinance governing the fire department, I herewith submit my report for the year ending November 30th, 1920.

The department has responded to the following alarms, 17 bell alarms, 132 still alarms and 3 out of town calls making a total of 152 alarms. The department has responded to more fire calls this year than in any other year in the history of the city. A great number of these still alarms would have been bell alarms but for the quick response of our Motor Combination Chemical.

On October 4th, 1920, the new Motor Ladder Truck arrived at the fire station and on October 9th, was accepted by the Fire

Department Committee. On October 11th, the new truck was placed in service at 7:30 p.m. taken to Beaver Mills where the ladder and chemical tanks were tried out. The new truck which is a Mack Motor Ladder Truck of 40 horse power carries 240 ft. of ladders, 600 ft. of 2 ½ in. fire hose, one 40 gal. Chemical tank with 200 ft. of chemical hose, two 3 gal. Chemical tanks, one door opener, 2 axes, 2 bars, 2 hay forks, 2 shovels, 1 tin roof cutter and 2 plaster hooks. This new piece of fire apparatus in great addition to the department as it will be able to respond to alarms more quickly than horse drawn apparatus.

The estimated value of buildings damaged for fire was: $194,100.00.

Damage to buildings was, $15,352.33.

Insurance on said buildings was $113,000.00.

Insurance paid was $15,352.33.

Value of contents of said buildings was $279,900.00.

Damage to said contents, $23,350.98.

Insurance upon property was, $246,575.00.

Insurance paid $23,350.98.

Apparatus and Force:

The apparatus and force of the department under a Chief and three assistants chiefs, located on Vernon Street, is as follows:

The Keene Steam Fire Engine and Hose Company, H. E. Raymond, Captain, 25 men, has Amoskeag Steamer No. 1, Button Steamer No. 2, one Combination Chemical and Hose Wagon, 1 relief Hose Wagon and 1 Motor Chemical with two 40 gallon chemical tanks and other necessary equipment. Washington Hook and Ladder Company, M. J. Carey, Captain, 20 men, has one Auto Ladder Truck and two relief Trucks. Deluge Hose Company, E. H. Applin, Captain, 20 men, has one combination Chemical and Hose Wagon. We have on hand about 7,000 feet of No. 1 hose, 1,500 feet of linen hose at South Keene, 1,000 feet of No. 2 hose which is unfit for fire service. During the year the Chief and his assistants Chiefs have inspected the buildings in the fire precinct several times.

Recommendations:

The Board of Engineers recommend the purchase of 1,000 feet of hose this year. We also recommend further motorizing the department by the addition of a motor pumping engine. Also we recommend that the City place another permanent man in the department to drive the new Motor Ladder Truck, so as to give the city better and more efficient service. The fire alarm telegraph system in care of Assistant Chief E. B. Riley, the fire alarm electrician, continues to give excellent satisfaction.

There is about 25 miles of wire in the six fire alarm circuits of which 20 miles of it is copper wire, and the other five miles is of No. 12 galvanized iron wire of the tapper circuits, which is very rusty and nearly unserviceable and will have to be replaced the coming year. I recommend that this be replaced with copper instead of iron wire which will then make it a permanent job.

To the Mayor, and members of the joint standing committee on fire department, the members associated with me on the board of engineers, officers and members of the department and to the public, I extend my sincere thanks and appreciation for the liberal aid and generous support rendered me during the past year.

F. W. TOWNE,
Chief Engineer

'FIRE HORSES, THE LAST OF AN ERA'

by Steven Goldsmith

A Genuine Fire Horse.

A short story of one of the Fire Department horses sold to a Mr. Fish who was in the business of delivering milk and firewood etc. For the sake of the story we'll say that the horse was "Old Tom," which was one of the last fire horses sold.

The horses that pulled the horse-drawn firefighting equipment in those days were young horses with speed, strength, stamina and intelligence, and Old Tom had apparently gotten too old for the job as a fire horse and also motorized fire equipment was making a play into the fire service.

Old Tom was about 14 or 15 years old when sold to Mr. Fish. Old Tom also had a teammate, "Jack," which was also sold to another person somewhere in the North Walpole area.

The fire horses had been special horses and had been through training for "fire horses." Like most fire stations they housed fire wagons, steamers, hose carts, and all other types of firefighting equipment.

When the fire bell sounded, the firefighters would hastily don their boots and bunker gear and slide down the pole to the horse drawn steamer or hose wagon or ladder cart.

Horses were stationed in front of the wagon with their harnesses suspended overhead.

A pull of the harness lever dropped the harnesses in place on the horses, which were usually dancing with excitement and eager to hit the run for the fire call. It must have been fun and thrilling to see the fire steamer speeding down Main Street to a fire with the horses snorting and tugging at their bits, and "Pep Little" stomping on the pedal that activated the bell to warn wagons and pedestrians to stay out of the way.

Well, back to Old Tom. He was a proud horse and quick to learn. All Mr. Fish had to do to hitch him to one of his wagons was lift the shafts, and Old Tom just backed into place on his own so the tugs could be fastened to the single tree.

Mr. Fish was hooked up one morning in November delivering firewood to North Swanzey. At the intersection of Main Streets and Marlboro and/Winchester Street the fire whistle began to blow for a box alarm at the Central Fire Station on Vernon Street. It was loud and piercing; due to the cold morning and it could be heard for many blocks.

The moment the whistle sounded, Old Tom took off, broke into a full gallop and headed for the fire station. As Old Tom pounded up Main Street to the Central Fire Station a wood trail was left from the intersection at Main and Winchester all the way to Vernon Street. Where the Fire Station was. Once at the station Old Tom tried to back into the bay where he had responded from so many times before.

This story like so many others was told to me a long time ago when I was just a young firefighter by then Deputy Chief Lawrence Thompson a long time member of the Keene Fire Department. As a boy he had visited the

A Demon Called Fire

fire station and had seen the fire horses and remembered stories about them. He stated, "It truly was a sight to see."

————

[from 1920 *City of Keene Annual Report:*]

Statement of Fires Occurring in the City of Keene from December 19th, 1919 to November 30th, 1920, Inclusive.

December 6th, 1919 to the Manufactory of New Brat'o Ov'all Co. for paper bales on fire. Damage to building and stock. Insurance paid $376.65.

December 7th, 1919 to the Y. Jones Dwelling for an oil stove fire. Damage to building and Furniture. Insurance paid $140.00.

December 10th, 1919 to the Chas Russell Dwelling for a Chimney fire. Damage to building and Insurance paid $10.00.

December 13th, 1919 to the M. O'Leary Dwelling for a Chimney fire. Damage to building and Insurance paid $13.01.

December 18th, 1919 to the H. S. Pollard Dwelling for a Chimney fire. Damage to building and Insurance paid $12.00.

December 18th, 1919 to the Mrs. M. Northway Greenhouse for a defective flue. Damage to building and stock and Insurance paid $887.50.

December 19th, 1919 to the M. A. Ball Mercantile building for a furnace pipe fire. Damage to building and stock. Insurance paid $1,699.62.

December 24th, 1919 to the Clarence A. Wright Dwelling for a Chimney fire. Damage to dwelling. Insurance paid $193.50.

December 25th, 1919 to the W. F. Burpee Dwelling for an unknown type fire. Damage to building and Insurance paid $510.00.

December 25th, 1919 to the C. A. Dee Dwelling for an overheated boiler. Damage to building and Insurance paid $10.00.

December 27th, 1919 to the City of Keene for an Incinerator fire of waste material. Damage was to Incinerator and Insurance paid $125.00.

December 29th, 1919 to the F. Petts Mer'le & Dwelling for an unknown fire. Damage to building and stock and Furniture. Insurance paid $3,404.60.

[from *New Hampshire Sentinel:*]

'FIRE'

1919 SERIOUS FIRE CAUSED BY EXPLOSION DRIVES TENANTS FROM PETTS BLOCK. On December 29th, 1919 a Fire Damage of $12,000 to Building and Contents. Children Carried from Second Floor-Firemen Do Good Work.

Fire in the three-story wooden Petts building on the south side of Church Street near Main Monday night at 8:25 o'clock, which started by an explosion in the dry goods store of Economy Brothers, resulted in a loss estimated at $12,000 and forced several persons to flee for safety from the burning structure. The cause of the explosion is unknown. The blaze, which caused greater loss that any the local department had had to combat in several years, was confined mostly to the rear of the building. Only the timely arrival of the apparatus and the energetic work of the fire fighters saved the building.

Following the discovery of the fire the four children of Mr. and Mrs. D. W. Buckley, who occupied apartments on the floor directly above the dry goods store, were carried to safety and were taken to the residence of Miss Mari Leonard in West street, where they were provided accommodations for the night.

Miss Laura Fenton, who has been ill for some time, was escorted to safety and was sent to the Elliot City hospital in an automobile. She occupied an apartment in the rear of the building on the second floor. Others who resided in the block are Fred Simeneau, Fred Sharkey and Chester Brown. The latter went to his room after the arrival of the department and succeeded in saving money and belongs.

John H. Parker, who occupies the store adjoining Economu Brothers, was in the rear of his store last evening. He heard an explosion, felt the shaking of the building and saw flames pouring from the rear of the store. He ran to the corner of main and Railroad Streets and pulled in box 8, returning to his store to save what musical instruments and supplies he could.

The motor truck was the first to leave the station and went to the box, being delayed shortly until the driver was told the location of the fire. The truck went down Railroad Street and up Wells Street to Church Street. Hose was laid from the hydrant at the corner of Wells Street and lines of chemical were used. While the motor truck was making the circuit to reach the scene of the blaze the Deluge Hose Company wagon arrived laying a line of hose from the corner of Main and church Streets and another from the hydrant farther down Church Street. Some time was lost in getting a stream of water as the lines of hose when first laid were not long enough to reach and additional lengths were put on.

The fire was mostly confined to the store of Econumu Brothers but broke through into the Parker store. Firemen used lines of hose at either end of the former store and soon had things pretty thoroughly wet down. A line of hose was used in the tenement on the second floor of the building as the flames had worked their way up through the rear of the building to the piazzas overhead. The roof in the rear of the building, which is over the one-story section of the stores, was ablaze underneath and firemen were forced to cut holes through the tin roofing and timbers to extinguish that fire. Smoke and water went through the partitions into O'Connor & Goode's restaurant, which adjoins Economu Brothers store on the east, also into Parker's store on the other side and Shea & Culliton's grocery store in the west end of the building.

Economu brothers carried insurance amounting to $3,500 on stock and fixtures through the Nilsen and Palmer agencies. The loss in this store has not been determined. Stephen Economu, manager of the store was in Manchester purchasing stock for the store. He was expected to return today. O'Connor & Goode carried $1,500 insurance through the mason insurance agency. Their loss may reach $500. John H. Parker carried $1,100 insurance through the agency of G. H. Aldrich & Sons. He will sustain a loss of about $1,000. Some of his stock was carried into the office of the N.G. Gurnsey Co. bakery, across the street, as were a few articles from Shea & Culliton's grocery store. The loss in this store may reach $2,000, which is equal to the amount, which they carried through the mason insurance agency. The insurance on the block, amounting to $3,500, was carried through the Aldrich agency. The loss is estimated at $3,000. Mr. Buckley was insured through the Cheshire insurance agency for $500.

The furniture of the occupants of the block was badly smoked and some was wet down. Work was commenced at once to put the apartments in condition for the families to live in. The restaurant of O'Connor & Goode was put in shape so that it opened for business Tuesday morning. The store of Shea & Culliton is being fixed up to open for business.

Printed in the *New Hampshire Sentinel* Keene, N.H.

———

January 3rd, 1920 to the F. W. Carey Chair Shop for an unknown type fire. Damage to several buildings as follows: F. W. Carey Damage to building and stock. Insurance paid $16,500.00. John Powers Dwelling caught fire from the above fire and damage to dwelling and auto. Insurance paid $10.00. The H. Crocker Storage building with damage to building. Insurance paid $50.00. The Wastow Sobolsiski Dwelling caught fire from the above fire (Carey) with damage to building and Insurance paid $30.00. The A. Reyor dwelling also sustained damage from the above fire which Insurance paid $$64.00. The Alex Pananitis Dwelling for damage of dwelling and Insurance paid $22.76. The Omer Buxton Dwelling for building damage caused by the above fire and Insurance paid $20.00.

January 3rd, 1920 to the C. J. Ware dwelling for a chimney fire, which set the roof on fire with damage to building. Insurance paid $36.51.

January 5th, 1920 to the R. M. Barry dwelling for a Chimney fire with damage to the roof. Insurance paid $35.00.

January 14th, 1920 to the Humphrey Mach Co. which was a Foundry for an unknown fire. Damage to building and machines. Insurance paid $128.60.

January 16th, 1920 to the A. Henderson Dwelling for a Chimney fire which set the house on fire. Damage to house and Furniture. Insurance paid $108.25.

January 31st, 1920 to the M. Dubois Grocery Store for an oil stove fire. Damage to building and stock. Insurance paid $199.93.

February 27th, 1920 to the Boston & Maine R. R. Hotel the room of Dan O'Neil for a closet fire. Damage to clothing and room. Insurance paid $725.28.

February 27th, 1920 to the E. J. Bahan Dwelling for Hot ashes in the shed. Damage to Dwelling and Furniture. Insurance paid $468.75.

February 28th, 1920 to the N. G. Gurnsey Est. which is a Mercantile building for an overheated furnace pipe. Damage to stock. Insurance paid $ 55.00.

February 28th, 1920 to the S. A. Burnap Dwelling for a chimney fire. Damage to building and Insurance paid $6.00.

March 11th, 1920 to the Lynn Wood Heel Co. which is a Manufacturing building and the fire was unknown cause and damage to building and stock. Insurance paid $10,025.45.

[from *New Hampshire Sentinel:*]

'FIRE'

1920 WATER CAUSES LOSS AT HEEL SHOP FIRE. On March 20th, 1920 Sprinklers Wet Down Finished Goods, Stock and Machinery.

Workmen employed on the second floor of the Lynn Wood Heel Company's factory on Emerald Street discovered a fire on the third floor about 7 o'clock Thursday evening. The fire department was called by a general alarm from box 6, following the still alarm sent in a few minutes earlier. The loss, mostly by water, will probably not exceed $10,000; Damage to the building will be small and will not prevent the progress of any of the work.

The cause of the fire is not known. It had not gained a great deal of headway when it was discovered. It set off the automatic sprinklers, and a large amount of smoke was pouring out of the windows on the tip floor of the building when the firemen arrived, The department laid three lines of hose but did not use any. Chemicals were used on the flames and the automatic sprinklers kept the wood-work, boxes and heels in the room well wet down, preventing the spread of the flames.

The water, which came from the sprinklers, ran down into the two rooms below, wetting most of the finished heels in the building and much of the machinery. The machinery is being cleaned up to prevent parts from being damaged by rust. The employees are all working at the factory, as the fire did not put any of the machines out of commission.

Printed in the *New Hampshire Sentinel* Keene, N.H.

————

April 6th, 1920 to the Luigi Ricci Dwelling for a Chimney fire with damage to dwelling. Insurance paid $15.00.

April 11th, 1920 to the M. A. Duffy Dwelling for children playing with matches and set the closet on fire. Damage to building and clothing. Insurance paid $514.00.

April 18th, 1920 to the E. M. Spencer dwelling for a chimney fire. Damage to dwelling and Insurance paid $22.50.

April 24th, 1920 to the George Hayward Dwelling for a chimney fire with damage to building. Insurance paid 35.00.

May 26th, 1920 to the E. J. Barry Dwelling for a chimney fire with damage to building. Insurance paid $12.50.

September 25th, 1920 to the Dwelling and Barn of E. Kingsbury. Damage to building and barn. Insurance paid $1,274.90.

[from *New Hampshire Sentinel:*]

'FIRE'

1920 BIG BARN BURNED; HOUSE THREATENED. On September 25th, 1920 the Kingsbury Place Is Scene of Hot Blaze Saturday Night.

A fire which practically destroyed the large barn connected with the house at 257 Roxbury Street, owned by Mrs. Kingsbury, broke out about 11 o'clock Saturday night from unknown causes. An automobile owned by Arthur A. Hunt was destroyed, also some tools. The firemen succeeded in checking the flames before they reached the ell, which connected the barn and the house. The loss is estimated at from $3,000 to $4,000.

The motor chemical was the first to arrive at the scene of the fire and laid a line of hose from the hydrant at the corner of Roxbury and Beech Streets. The other pieces of apparatus followed soon after. It was the belief of some that the horse drawn apparatus did not get out as soon as usual. The first streams which were played upon the flames lacked force, but after the engine was connected there was sufficient force to subdue the flames, which were fast eating their way toward the ell of the house. Firemen were station on either side of the house with lines of hose and one line was carried into the ell.

Much smoke worked its way through the rooms in the house which is occupied by Mrs. Elbridge Kingsbury on the lower floor and Ernest E. Holton and family in the upper tenement. Volunteer workers commenced to remove furniture and valuables from the house to safety across the street. It was soon seen that the fire was under control and this work was stopped.

While the cause of the fire is unknown, there are two versions of the origin. Some claim that the fire caught from the automobile which was stored in the barn, and which had been left there a short time previously. Another version is that it caught near the chute which had been used for conveying the hay from the loft to the basement. It was at this place that the most of the fire seemed to be when the blaze was discovered. Mr. Hunt, who went to the barn to get out his machine, said that after he opened the large door most of the fire seemed to be near the hay shut. At that time the top of his car was ablaze and no other part, as far as he could see. The flames burst out of the door, preventing him from getting the automobile out.

The fire was first discovered by George Warner, who resides in the house nearly opposite. He sent his wife to notify Mr. Hunt, called the fire station and told the location of the fire and then pulled in box 23 at the corner of Roxbury and beech Streets. The same box number had already been pulled in by other persons, which was the reason for the two alarms in such quick succession.

There was $500 insurance on the barn, but none was carried on the automobile, it is understood.

Mrs. Kingsbury started that the barn will not be rebuilt. The shell of the structure which is left standing will be torn down and the debris cleared away. The barn had not been used since the death of Mr. Kingsbury for anything except storage purposes.

Suggestions From The Fire

It was noticed at Saturday evening's fire that the hydrant streams first put on were of hardly sufficient force to reach the ridgepole, and would have been of small service to "knock out" fire under the barn roof, which was finally handled with streams from the steamer. The first hydrant lines from Beech and Lincoln Street corners or from Douglas Street were the hydrant is well up the street required some 600 feet of hose each. The loss in pressure due to friction is estimated to be as much as six pounds on such a line.

If the hydrant pressure was 65 pounds to begin with, it is declared there would be at least a 5 pound drop for each hydrant opened of which there were two at first and four later, the engineers report. This, it is believed, would account for ineffective streams, even, even if only two hydrants were opened and similar results it is said will follow at almost any fire in Keene. The way to remember the loss by friction through the hose, which always occurs, is said to be to lay two hose lines from the hydrant to the fire, siamesing them together close to the blaze. A larger and much more effective stream according to the experience where this I habitually done, is said to follow.

It is stated that the motor chemical in responding to the telephone alarm first received, cut in to the left on the Roxbury Street corner and barely escaped collision with a motor going towards the Square. It has before been noticed the fire motor often disregards rules of the road, and much complaint has been heard of this because people say they cannot plan to get out of the way if the motor goes on the wrong side of a street. In case of still alarms, at least they say, it is unsafe for the firemen to assume that everyone knows there has been an alarm or that anyone can tell where the call comes form.

On the other hand the practice of motorists to crowd into and stop upon a street, from whence a box alarm comes, which they did Saturday night on Roxbury Street, bothering the firemen to considerable extent

is declared most reprehensible by the fire department officials. In many cities the rule that all traffic shall stop and clear a road for the firemen is strictly enforced. Keene is soon to have a second motor and it is suggested by those interested in safety that more strict rules to govern traffic, especially after box alarms, will be needed.

————

October 24th, 1920 to the Boston & Maine R. R. Hotel the room of D. E. O'Neil for a chimney fire. Damage to room and Insurance paid $95.00.

October 30th, 1920 to the W. J. Foley Garage for a fire set by children. Damage to building and Furniture. Insurance paid $153.00.

November 4th, 1920 to the Woodshed of W. C. Rivers for an Automobile fire. Damage to auto and Insurance paid $200.00.

November 25th, 1920 to the Dwelling of J. H. Carter for an oil stove fire. Damage to building and Furniture. Insurance paid $100.00.

Joint Resolutions and Ordinances ending for the year 1920.

Ordinance passed February 19th, 1920 to take effect April 1st, 1920 related to pay for the fire department reads as follows.

That section 3, Chapter 8 of the City Ordinances be amended by striking out the words "Forty seven" on the second line of said section, and substituting therefore, the words "Seventy two" and be further amended by striking out the words "Thirty five" in the twelfth line of said section, and substituting therefore the word "Fifty" so that said section shall read, when amended, as follows:

Each member of every company in the fire department shall receive for his services at the rate of seventy-two dollars per year in addition to the sum allowed by law; but no member shall be paid for less than three months' service, unless sooner discharged from his company by the proper authority, for cause other than his own request, nor unless he shall have performed his duties in a manner satisfactory to the company officer, and responded to all calls made upon him, or given satisfactory excuse for any failure to do so. In addition to the foregoing compensation, each fireman, or other person, who, under the direction of the board of engineers, answers a telephone or still alarm, not exceeding four persons, or performs service at a brush fire, shall receive fifty cents per hour in full payment for such service. The names of such persons as may perform the foregoing services, with the place visited, time employed, and compensation due, set opposite their respective names, shall be certified within fifteen days from the end of the month, as a pay-roll by the clerk of the board of engineers to the city clerk, who shall certify the same to the auditor and disburse the amount specified to the employees, taking their receipt therefore.

Also the Ordinance change on the same day February 19th, 1920 to the Ordinance section 13, of Chapter 23, of the City Ordinance be also amended by striking out the words "Two hundred" in the second line, and substituting therefore, the words "Three hundred" and be it further amended by striking out the words "One hundred and twenty five" in the third line, and substituting therefore, the words "One hundred and seventy five," and be it further amended by striking out the words "One hundred" and substituting the words " One hundred and fifty," so that said section when amended, shall read as follows:

The chief engineer of the fire department shall receive the sum of three hundred dollars, the clerk of the board of engineers the sum of one hundred and seventy five dollars, and each of the other assistant engineers the sum of one hundred and fifty dollars per year in full for their services, and for all duties appertaining to their respective offices, to be

paid at the expiration of their official year. Effective April 1st, 1920.

[from *New Hampshire Sentinel:*]

'1920 DEFEATS BILL FOR MOTORIZATION OF FIRE DEPARTMENT'

[*Compiler's Note: Clear and reasonable justification for cost expenditure was just as important in earlier times as it is today. Council Not Satisfied With Proposed Measure. Proposed March 20th, 1920 and appeared in the* New Hampshire Sentinel, *Wednesday, March 25, 1920.*]

Against Appropriating $10,000 Before Details of Plan Are Worked Out a Bill introduced by the committee on fire department to provide for the appointment of a joint special committee to look into the subject of further motorization of the fire apparatus and appropriating for that purpose the sum of $10,000 to be expended at the direction of the committee, was defeated in the common council Thursday evening by a vote of 7 to 5, after considerable debate. The form of action proposed that is, the appropriating of such much money for a project that had not yet been worked out in detail prevented voters for the measure, it is said, which it might very probably have had if the bill had provided for the appointment of the special committee and the working out of details before an appropriation was asked.

The resolution to appropriate $10,000 to motorize more of the fire apparatus and to be expended by a special committee should be councils so direct, was the outcome of investigations by the fire department committee as to how to best provide for the future needs of the department. These plans contemplated a hook and ladder motor truck with chemical tanks and hose carrying facilities. This it is believed, would be an excellent apparatus to supplement the present motor truck taking its place for still alarms when necessary providing quick ladder service on a general alarm and conveying hose for additional fire streams from hydrants on its arrival.

It seems to be generally conceded that whatever may be done for protection from fires, there must be a larger water supply available from the hydrants in all parts of the city, with perhaps a somewhat higher pressure. The proposed dam in the Fairfield pasture on Beech Hill, which Engineer Wadsworth plans show will impounds over a million gallons of water, at a suitable head, practically as close to the city as the old octagon reservoir, and higher up the hill will provide what is believed to be an ideal supply, allowing twice as many strong hydrant streams as at present and permanently adding an always-ready supply at every hydrant in the city. The two motors would thus constitute efficient firefighting equipment except in deep snow, when sleds must be used in any event.

Another plan, in addition to the special truck, or in place of it if too expensive for now, would be to purchase a four wheeled tractor or truck that will draw a ladder wagon or a steamer anywhere in place of horses. This sort of a motor is easily obtainable and, it is said, could not fall to give the city its money's worth. It could be used to haul one or more pieces of apparatus more quickly than horses. Probably, although one of the present horses apparatus can be drawn very fast because of large wheels and iron tires, not built for high speed. The committee had investigated the motor proposition and the combination truck, more or less, and desired the councils to appoint a special committee to decide what to buy. The first vote on the resolution was a tie, and it was lost, but a standing vote being called for as there were five in the affirmative and seven in the negative. As before stated, some members declined to vote for so large an appropriation without a definite statement as to how the money was to be used.

It should be added that the committee felt positive that the city will have to buy at least four new horses if it decides not to use motors for its fire apparatus.

————

A Joint Resolution was passed on April 15th, 1920 relating to an appropriation of the MACK LADDER TRUCK. That the sum of ten thousand dollars ($10,000) in addition to the sum already appropriated, for the Keene Fire department, is hereby appropriated, from any money in treasure not otherwise appropriated, for the purchase of a combination hook and ladder, chemical and hose truck of standard make; and that the Joint Standing Committee on Fire Department and such other members of the city government as the Mayor may appoint, constitute a committee to purchase said truck, but in no event shall the amount to be expended for said truck exceed the sum mentioned in the appropriation.

[from *New Hampshire Sentinel:*]

'1920 MACK FIRE TRUCK HERE FOR INSPECTION DAY'

New Apparatus Appears to Be Well Designed, Built and Equipped

The Mack combination hose and ladder truck purchased last May be a committee appointed by the city council and consisting of Mayer E. H. Watson, Chief F. W. Towne, Aldermen Ingalls and Russell and Councilmen Buckminster, Trask and Howes reached Keene between 5 and 6 o'clock Monday afternoon under its own power. It was in charge of Demonstrator William McDonough, who has had much experience in handling and delivering this type of apparatus. The truck has attracted considerable attention since its arrival, both at the fire station and on short runs made by it thorough some of the streets, including a trip over lower Beech Hill. It is stated that the makers have delivered this truck more nearly on time than any which they have made for a number of months, recent delays having been from 60 to 90 days in getting materials to make such apparatus E. H. Applin and Joseph Beals local agents for the Mack Trucks and the city committee both made every effort to have the apparatus here for inspection day.

The truck is a strong and well-proportioned piece of apparatus and the weight is so distributed as to control, put a short distance above the axles so that the truck is not top heavy as was the case with some of the earlier built motors. It is painted a fire truck red with ornamental striping and is finished in nickel plate for the rails and accessories. The weight of the apparatus is about 7,200 pounds. The wheel base is 24 feet, so that the truck could not be weighed on any local scales.

The equipment carried consists of 100 to 600 feet of 21/2 inch fire hose, 200 feet of ¾ inch chemical hose up in a reel, a 40 gallon chemical tank extension ladders 50 feet long, 40 feet long and 35 feet long and two 25 feet long also a 16 foot extension ladder for inside work. These ladders are all made of the truss plan, of Oregon fir, and are lighter and more convenient to handle than ladders with solid sides, and the same time being more rigid. Four fire extinguishers are carried on the truck. The total length of the ladders provided is about 275 feet. There is also a tool box underneath with axes, bars, pole hooks, door openers, fire cutters, forks, shovels and equipment of hand lanterns, the truck lamps proper being electric. Metal baskets on top of the truck, only one of which provides a place for carrying firemen's coats, hats, boots, etc. There are also containers on the running board carrying extra chemical or the extinguisher tank, a battery box and small toll boxes. A new piece of equipment is a very strong hook with a heavy chain to be used in pulling down portions of buildings. There are hooks on the rear of the chassis to which this chair can be

attached and the truck thus used as positive power for this work.

The total length of the chassis 40 feet and, with its load, the length of the truck is about 50 feet. The engine is rated at 72.6 brake horse power and the motor is of the 6 cylinder type with both magneto and battery ignition. It has three speeds ahead and one reverse and is equipped with a self-starter. There are strong brakes, both on the rear wheels and on the jack shaft. The connection between the rear wheels and the jackshaft is of the chain drive type. The truck is equipped with Kelley, Springfield tires for the present, but the makers will furnish "caterpillar" tire later, when they can be obtained. There are ample running boards the whole length of each side of the truck which are capable of carrying some 20 men. A hand siren and a search light are provided and there is also a 12 inch locomotive engine bell to use as a warning signal. The tank for gasoline holds 25 gallons and the oil case carries sufficient oil to run the engine 100 miles. The truck will make about five miles to each gallon of gasoline on fairly good going.

Special equipment is a small electric connector to be used in the engine house in very cold weather, keeping the water in the radiator at suitable temperature for the immediate use of the engine. The speed of the truck is said to be about 35 miles an hour.

The truck was brought on by Mr. McDonough from the factory at Allentown, Penn., where it was built. On the way here it was demonstrated at Providence, R.I. Putnam Conn., Worcester, Leominster, and Fitchburg, Mass. The run to Keene was made through Rindge, Jaffrey and Dublin.

Printed in the *New Hampshire Sentinel.*

[*Compiler's Note*: When the Mack Ladder was replaced with the Segrave Ladder, the Mack was purchased by the Bellows Falls Vermont Fire Department, and was in service

On October 4, 1920, the new Mac Motor Ladder truck arrived at the Central Fire Station. On October 9th 1920, it was accepted by the Fire Department committee.

until they replaced it with the ladder that they have today.]

A Joint Resolution relating to a Fire Alarm Box being placed at the corner of Marlboro and Martin Streets was passed on November 18th, 1920.

Department Turns out With Full Ranks For Inspection as reported by the *New Hampshire Sentinel* October 6th, 1920:

FIREMEN'S PARADE AND PRACTICE RUNS

The Inspection day exercises of the Keene Fire department, which it has been customary to observe in October of each year, with few exceptions, took place Tuesday, beginning at 1.30 with a parade and review of the men and apparatus, and followed later by practice runs and a demonstration of skill in handling the apparatus. At 5 o'clock the annual banquet at the fire station occurred and in the men's dance was held under the auspices of Washington hook & Ladder Company.

The display of apparatus and equipment in Tuesday's parade was augmented by the new combination chemical, fire hose and ladder wagon that had just arrived and which appeared large in size as well as in opportunities for quick and efficient service when ladders of good length are needed speedily, together with more chemical or hydrant streams than the motor hose wagon can provide. In a city like Keene, where the hydrant service is quite widespread but the number of efficient streams the hydrants can provide is found to be restricted by the limited volume of water available, safety is believed to lie in quick service which will enable the men to control a fire before it has time to spread much. It was with this idea in view; it is understood that the new motor was bought.

The parade in the afternoon was headed by Chapman's drum corps, four fifers and three drums, with Oscar P. Applin as drum major. The board of fire engineers, Chief Fred W. Towne, followed. Washington Hook & Ladder Company, Capt. M. J. Carey, and 16 men was next in line. The new motor wagon headed the apparatus of this company which also had in line the two horse-drawn ladder trucks used up to this time.

The Deluge Hose Company, Capt. E. H. Applin, had its hose and chemical wagons.

The Steam Fire Engine and Hose Company Capt. H. E. Raymond, turned out with 20 men, the two steam fire engines and the relief hose wagon. The parade was to the foot of Main Street and return and the mayor and menders of the city government reviewed the department at city hall. The apparatus and teams were all found to be in excellent condition and the men, with their neat blue uniforms, marched well.

The usual practice runs in connection with the inspection started at 3 o'clock. On the first stroke of the bell, Washington Hook & Ladder Company truck went by the way of Washington Street to the Bridgman block, making the run in 1 minute and 25 seconds, and in 2 minutes and 23 seconds had a ladder raised to the top of the block.

On the second stroke of the bell the button Steamer went by the way of Washington Street and connected with the hydrant at the south side of the park. The run and connection was made in 1 minute and 22 seconds. At the third stroke of the bell the Amoskeag Steamer went by the way of Court Street to the hydrant in front of the Sentinel building. The run and connection was made in 2 minutes and 1 second.

On the next stroke of the bell the Deluge hose wagon, going by the way of Washington Street, connected with the Button Steamer and had a stream of water in 1 minute and 35 seconds. On the last stroke of the bell the motor chemical went by the way of Court Street and connected with the Amoskeag Steamer, getting the first stream in 1 minute and 3 seconds.

1921 [from *City of Keene Annual Report*]

Report of Chief Engineer of the Fire Department and City Electrician

To His Honor the Mayor and Gentlemen of the City Councils:

As required by the City Ordinance governing the fire department, I herewith submit my report for the year ending November 30th, 1921.

The department has responded to the following alarms, 12 bell alarms, 155 still alarms and 5 out of town calls making a total of 172 alarms. This being the largest number of fire calls the department has ever answered in any one year in the history of the city.

The estimated value of buildings damaged by fire was $155,400.00.

Damage to buildings, $7,989.60.

Insurance on said buildings, $98,050.00.

Insurance paid, $7,989.60.

Value of contents of said buildings, $33,300.00.

Damage to said contents, $4,422.56.

Insurance upon property, $22,100.00.

Insurance paid, $4,422.56.

Apparatus and Force:

The apparatus and force of the department under a Chief and three assistant chiefs, located on Vernon Street, is as follows:

The Keene Steam Fire Engine and Hose company, H. E. Raymond Captain, 25 men has Amoskeag Steamer, No. 1, Button Steamer No. 2, one Combination Chemical and Hose Wagon, one Relief Hose Wagon, and one Motor Chemical with two 40 gallon chemical tanks and other necessary equipment. Washington Hook and Ladder Company, M. J. Carey, Captain, 20 men, has one Motor Combination Chemical and Ladder Truck and two Relief Trucks. Deluge Hose Company, E. H. Applin, Captain, 20 men, has one Combination Chemical and Hose Wagon. We have on hand about 7,500 feet of No. 1 hose, 1,500 feet of linen hose, at South Keene,

500 feet of No. 2 hose, which is unfit for fire service. During the year 500 feet of No. 2 hose was sold to the Water Works Department. As usual the buildings in the fire precinct have been inspected by the Chief and his assistants.

Recommendations:

The Board of Engineers recommend the purchase of 1,000 feet of hose; Pumping Engine Extra Driver for Motor Ladder Truck, also that the old flush hydrants be replaced by post hydrants. The Fire alarm Telegraph system in care of Assistant Chief E. B. Riley, the fire alarm electrician continues to give excellent satisfaction.

The cell plates in the batteries of which there are 152 on the fire alarm circuit, have about reached their limit of usefulness and these will have to be replaced this year. During the year 2 new fire alarm boxes of the latest type have been installed, also 5 miles of new copper wire for the fire alarm system, which was purchased this past year, has been installed.

To the Mayor, and members of the joint standing committee

On fire department, the members associated with me on the board of engineers, officers and members of the department and to the public, I extend my sincere thanks and appreciation for the liberal aid and generous support rendered me during the past year.

F. W. Towne, Chief Engineer December 1st, 1921

Statement of Fires Occurring in the City of Keene From December 1st, to November 30th, 1921, Inclusive.

December 26th, 1920 to the F. O. Whitcomb Dwelling for a Chimney fire. Damage $95.00 and Insurance paid $95.00.

January 17th, 1921 to the Gurnsey Estate, Dwelling and Stores for an unknown type fire. Damage $1,989.51 and Insurance paid $1,989.51.

January 18th, 1921 to the L. M. Barrett Dwelling for a chimney fire. Damage $90.48 and Insurance paid $90.48.

February 7th, 1921 to the John W. Goode Dwelling for a chimney fire which set the roof on fire. Damage $245.20 and Insurance paid $245.20.

February 9th, 1921 to the Alesio Papile Dwelling for a chimney fire. Damage $35.01 and Insurance paid $35.01.

February 13th, 1921 to the B. E. Jenkins Dwelling for a chimney fire. Damage $30.00 and Insurance paid $30.00.

February 16th, 1921 to the A. Vigneault for a chimney fire. Damage $30.00 and Insurance paid $30.00.

February 19th, 1921 to the H. W. Brown Dwelling for a Chimney fire. Damage $54.44 and Insurance paid $54.44.

February 25th, 1921 to the K. C. Robertson Dwelling for a Chimney fire which set the roof on fire. Damage $130.00 and Insurance paid $130.00.

March 29th, 1921 to the Nils Johnson Dwelling for an unknown type fire. Damage $5,200 and Insurance paid $1,300.00.

March 30th, 1921 to the O. Auburn Dwelling for a chimney fire. Damage $20.00 and Insurance paid $20.00.

March 31st, 1921 to the Dr. Helf Dwelling whose owner was B & M for a defective chimney. Damage $15.00 and Insurance paid $15.00.

April 4th, 1921 to the George Avery Dwelling for a chimney fire. Damage $115.00 and Insurance paid $115.00.

April 11th, 1921 to the Y. Jones Dwelling for a chimney fire. Damage $125.00 and Insurance paid $125.00.

April 12th, 1921 to the S. Morse Dwelling for a Chimney fire which set the house on fire. Damage $358.27 and Insurance paid $358.27.

May 17th, 1921 to the M. E. Daniels dwelling for a chimney fire. Damage $10.50 and Insurance paid $10.50.

June 17th, 1921 to the W. Soboliske Dwelling for a chimney fire. Damage $25.00 and Insurance paid $25.00.

June 20th, 1921 to the F. Petts Dwelling for a chimney fire which set the roof on fire. Damage $180.00 and Insurance paid $180.00.

July 6th, 1921 to the Mrs. Lela Young Dwelling for an oil stove fire. Damage $59.00 and Insurance paid $59.00.

August 27th, 1921 to the J. C. Faulkner Hen house for an unknown fire. Damage $250.00 and Insurance paid $250.00.

August 30th, 1921 to the Samuel Croteau Dwelling for children playing with matches. Damage $1,000.00 and Insurance paid $1,000.00.

August 30th, 1921 the house caught fire from the above Dwelling which was Louis Robbins Dwelling and caused $25.00 dollars damage and Insurance paid $25.00.

August 30th, 1921 to the Alexander Mosher Dwelling for a house fire caused by the Croteau fire. Damage $1,400.00 and Insurance paid $1,400.00.

September 28th, 1921 to the George H. Eames & Son Store House for an unknown type fire. Damage $1,686.75 and Insurance paid $1,686.75.

[from *New Hampshire Sentinel:*]

'FIRE'

1921 STOREHOUSES BURN IN OLD FREIGHT YARD. On Wednesday September 28th, 1921 A Hot Blaze Does Damage Estimated at More Than $4,000.

Fire destroyed two old buildings used as storehouses, with their contents and the portion of another, Wednesday September 28th, in the old freight yard off Cypress Street. The loss is estimated at more than $4,000, partly covered by insurance. Robertson & Bennett and George H. Eames & Son were the heaviest losers. The origin of the fire is unknown.

The blaze was first seen between the end storehouses, used by Louis Tatelman for bailed paper and Robertson & Bennett for oil storage. These buildings were leveled and everything in them destroyed. The garage owners had 50 barrels of oil in their building. The third structure, owned by George H. Eames & Son, was burned on the side. This concern lost heavily by water damage to many bags of grain.

Joseph Myers, who was supervising the unloading of some coal cars had his attention attracted to the fire by a man walking up the tracks, who shouted at him. He ran to a telephone and called fire headquarters and a general alarm was sounded. Before the arrival of the apparatus both end buildings were ablaze and clouds of dense black smoke poured skyward from the oil storehouse.

The firemen worked quickly and within a short time had five streams playing on the buildings. The water had little effect in quenching the flames and the end buildings soon collapsed. Fire in the Eames building, which had caught was put under control, but not before much water was poured into it.

A big crowd watched the fire while it was in progress. Owing to the heat of the flames they were forced to keep some distance away and the firemen were unhampered in their work. The police were on hand early and did good work directing the traffic. It is believed that the fire may have been started by either a cigarette or lighted match thrown on the oil soaked ground near the automobile dealer's storehouse. It is said that many noontime "jakey" parties have been held there. Various kinds of bottles strewn about the ground were noticed.

Printed in the *New Hampshire Sentinel* Keene, N. H.

———————

October 9th, 1921 to the George B. Robertson Dwelling for a defective fire- place. Damage $45.00 and Insurance paid $45.00.

October 18th, 1921 to the Mrs. E. Kinison Dwelling for a Chimney fire. Damage $10.00 and Insurance paid $10.00.

October 22nd, 1921 to the T. Baldwin dwelling for a chimney fire. Damage $38.00 and Insurance paid $38.00.

November 10th, 1921 to the S. L. White Dwelling for a chimney fire. Damage $50.00 and Insurance paid $50.00.

Joint Resolutions for the Year Ending 1921:

On March 17th, 1921 a Resolution was passed for the appropriation for $1,000.00 for the purchase of fire hose.

Also the City received one criticism, as follows, "without reflecting in anyway upon the department, may be made. The Chemical truck is almost habitually driven at an unreasonable speed, particularly in returning to the station. To any one at all familiar with motor vehicles, it is only too apparent that such practice can only result in reducing the life of the truck without accomplishing any beneficial result." The Mayor recommend that the subject or driver to the consideration of the committee on Fire Department and of the Engineers for appropriate action and regulation.

1922 [from *City of Keene Annual Report*]

Report of Chief Engineer of the Fire Department and City Electrician

To His Honor the Mayor and Gentlemen of the City Councils:

As required by the City ordinance governing the fire department, I herewith submit my report for the year ending November 30th, 1922.

The department has responded to the following alarms, 20 bell alarms, 120 still alarms and 5 out of town calls, making a total of 145 alarms.

The estimated value of buildings damaged by fire was, $70,100.00.

Damage to buildings, $6,029.26.

Insurance on said buildings, $46,600.00.

Insurance paid, $6,029.26.

Value of contents of said buildings, $63,600.00.

Damage to said contents, $10,428.67.

Insurance upon property, $48,700.00.

Insurance paid, $10,428.67.

Apparatus and Force:

The apparatus and force of the department under a Chief and three assistant chiefs, located on Vernon Street, is as follows: The Keene Steam Fire Engine & Hose Company, J. A. Denison Captain, 25 men has Amoskeag Steamer, No. 1, Button Steamer No. 2, one Combination Chemical & Hose Wagon, one Relief Hose Wagon, and one Motor Chemical with two 40-gallon chemical tanks and other necessary equipment. Washington Hook & Ladder Company, M. J. Carey, Captain, 20 men, has one Motor Combination Chemical and Ladder Truck and two Relief Trucks. Deluge Hose Company, E. H. Applin, Captain 20 men has one Combination Chemical and Hose Wagon. We have on hand about 8,000 feet of No. 1 hose, 1,500 feet of linen hose, at South Keene, 500 feet of No. 2 hose, which is unfit for fire service. During the year 250 feet of No. 2 hose was sold to the Water Works Department. 150 feet of No. 2 hose has been left with the Pittsburg Glass Company, South Keene, for fire service.

Recommendations:

The Board of Engineers recommend the purchase of 1,000 feet of hose; Pumping Engine and Wagon Gun. We also recommend that the City Councils give their earliest attention to the report of the hydraulic Engineer on more water for fire protection, as water is the most essential thing in fighting fires.

The fire alarm telegraph system has had new cell plates in the batteries this past year, and is now in excellent condition.

Recommendations:

We recommend that $200 be appropriated this year for the installation of one new fire alarm box and to make repairs on several of the boxes which are now in service.

During the term of my office as Building Inspector, I have given 38 permits for the erection of new buildings, and 9 permits for repairs on old buildings.

To the Mayor, and members of the joint standing committee on fire department, the members associated with me on the board of engineers, officers and members of the department and to the public, I extend my sincere thanks and appreciation for the liberal aid and generous support rendered me during the past year.

EUGENE B. RILEY, Chief Engineer

Statement of Fires Occurring in the City of Keene From December 1st, 1921 to November 30th, 1922, Inclusive.

December 5th, 1921 to the T. R. Lee House for an oil stove in the attic. Damage $4,207.50 and Insurance paid $4,207.50.

[from *New Hampshire Sentinel*:]

'FIRE'

1921 FIRE CAUSES LOSS OF $4,000 AT LEE HOUSE. On December 5th, 1921 a Kerosene Stove in Billiard Room Is Responsible for Blaze.

Fire in the billiard room at the residence of Thomas R. Lee, 284 Court Street, Monday night gave local firemen a stubborn fight for more than an hour before the blaze was extinguished. Loss of approximately $4,000, which is covered by insurance, was caused largely by water.

A still alarm was sounded at about 7 o'clock and box 35 was soon rung in. The firemen were handicapped at first by the amount of smoke in the billiard room, which made entrance almost impossible. The fire was confined to that room, which has been finished off in beaverboard and it, was necessary to cut much of this away before chemicals could be put on the flames.

A ladder was raised to the front window and chemical and water was soon pouring into the room. Soon afterward water began to pour down through the ceilings of the rooms below and a force of volunteers carried much of the house furnishings out of the building and covered other pieces with rugs and carpets.

The top part of the residence was completely ruined by the fire, the beams and flooring on the third story being demolished by the flames. On the lower floors much plastering and woodwork were ruined by water.

The fire originated in a kerosene stove, which had been lighted by a member of the family, who was to play a game of billiards. When Mr. Lee's son went into the room he found it ablaze and a telephone call was sent in to the fire department. Mr. Lee, the owner of the residence was away at the time of the fire and could not be located until later in the night.

Much praise was given the firemen for the efficient way in which they handled the blaze and for their prompt arrival in spite of the icy roads. Four horses were hitched to the steamer, which arrived in much better time that if the customary pair of horses had been used. It was suggested by insurance men who watched the fire that if the city had rubber blankets to cover the furniture, much of the loss could have been prevented. This has seemed to be the case; it is started, at numerous store block and dwelling house fires in former years.

Printed in the *New Hampshire Sentinel* Keene, N. H.

December 21st, 1921 to the E. Coppo House for a Chimney fire with Damage of $15.00 and Insurance paid $15.00.

December 25th, 1921 to the E. E. Mansfield House for a Chimney fire with damage of $12.00 and Insurance paid $12.00. The Tenant from above fire W. J. Cahill also received Damage of $12.00 and Insurance paid $12.00 from that chimney fire.

January 14th, 1922 to the John H. Fitzgerald House for a Defective Chimney with damage of $74.52 and Insurance paid $74.52.

January 14th, 1922 to the Mercantile building of Frank Hopkins for an unknown type fire. Damage $3,429.22 and Insurance paid $3,429.22.

January 16th, 1922 to the House of Chas Philips for a Chimney fire with Damage of $40.00 and Insurance paid $40.00.

February 13th, 1922 to the House of E. V. Aldrich for a Chimney fire. Damage of $73.25 and Insurance paid $73.25.

March 2nd, 1922 to the House of J. F Whitcomb for a Chimney fire. Damage $450.00 and Insurance paid $450.00.

March 10th, 1922 to the K. Normal School of Mary Brown for a Chimney fire with Damage of $40.00 and Insurance paid $40.00.

March 16th, 1922 to the Hotel & Stores of B. & M. R. R. for smoking in a room. Damage $47.20 and Insurance paid $47.20.

March 18th, 1922 to the Screen Shop Co. for a chimney fire which set fire to the roof. Damage $239.12 and Insurance paid $234.12.

April 15th, 1922 to an unknown type fire at the W. C. Smith House with Damage of $1,200.00 and Insurance paid $800.00.

May 2nd, 1922 to the Store House of Keene Chair Co. for an unknown type fire. Damage $5,409.96 and Insurance paid $5,409.06.

[from *New Hampshire Sentinel*:]

'FIRE'

1922 STOREHOUSE AT SOUTH KEENE IS DESTROYED

On May 2nd, 1922 A storehouse owned by the Keene Chair Company caught fire.

A storehouse owned by the Keene Chair Company at South Keene, together with contents, was destroyed by fire Tuesday afternoon and sparks set fire to grass nearby and also to the wooded section on the hill several hundred feet distance which burned until evening. The cause is unknown.

Volunteers from the shop connected two lines of hose to a hydrant in the mill yard and played upon the shed, while the firemen had two streams on the south side of the storehouse. The building was filled with rattan and chair stock and the interior were like a roaring furnace. Men with pails of water were stationed on the tips of several of the nearby buildings.

One line of hose laid, from the south side of Marlboro Street, ran across the electric car track preventing one car from going to Marlboro.

Printed in the *New Hampshire Sentinel* Keene, N. H.

May 5th, 1922 to the House of Russell Ellis for an overheated stove. Damage $60.00 and Insurance paid $60.00.

August 17th, 1922 to the House of George W. Sargent for a closet fire. Damage $150.00 and Insurance paid $150.00.

August 27th, 1922 to the Mercantile Building of E. J. Barry for sparks from a chimney fire, which started the awning on fire. Damage $106.00 and Insurance paid $106.00.

October 20th, 1922 to the House of A. B. Blake for a gas leak with fire. Damage $50.00 and Insurance paid $50.00.

October 20th, 1922 to the Garage of Wassookeag Woolent Co. for an unknown type fire. Damage $211.00 and Insurance paid $211.00.

October 26th, 1922 to the Keene Gas & Electric Co. for a fire in a wood box. Damage $62.41 and Insurance paid $62.41.

November 11th, 1922 to the I. O. O. F. Hall for Fat on fire in the gas stove. Damage $8.00 and Insurance paid $8.00.

November 13th, 1922 to the E. F. Lane Estate for a chimney fire which set house on fire. Damage $25.00 and Insurance paid $25.00.

November 30th, 1922 to the John Gallaher House for an unknown type fire. Damage $535.75 and Insurance paid $535.75.

[from *New Hampshire Sentinel:*]

'FIRE'

'BELL ALARM FOR FIRE AT I.L. KIBBEE HOUSE"

On May 8th, 1922 A Fire was Reported at the I. L. Kibbee Home.

Fred A. Johnson, driver of the motor chemical who fell 15 feet to the ground from a ladder at the fire at I. L. Kibbee's home, 26 Forest Street, May 8, received only an injury to his back which although not serious will lay him up for several days. The fire was on the roof and burned over a considerable area. It did not get into the interior of the house, but much water went inside.

The firemen were first called by still alarm, which was answered by the motor chemical, driven by Fred Johnson. Shortly after Don Hayward, who was coming down Court Street saw the roof a blaze. He reported to the fire station and the bell alarm was sounded. Several lines of hose were laid and the chemicals from the tanks on both motor trucks were used.

Printed in the *New Hampshire Sentinel* Keene, N. H.

Resolutions for the year ending 1922.

An Ordinance change was made on March 16th, 1922 to Section 13. Chapter XXXIII.

The Chief Engineer of the fire department shall receive the sum of two thousand dollars per year, payable in equal monthly, the clerk of the board of engineers the sum of one hundred seventy-five

Dollars and the other assistant engineer and the associate engineer the sum of one hundred fifty dollars each. Per year in full for their services, and for all duties appertaining to their respective officers, clerk and assistant and associate engineer to be paid at the expiration of their official year.

A Resolution was passed on May 18th, 1922 for the purchase of 1,000 feet of fire hose not to exceed $900.00.

NOTE: 1922 was an important time and movement forward for the Keene Fire Department. The Mayor Orville E. Cain gave recommendation to the Committee for careful study that the Chief Engineer should be employed full time and the department look at its present apparatus in part and purchase motorized equipment. It was also noted that the city purchase an automobile chassis to which the present horse-drawn apparatus can be attached. The injury to horses in answering an alarm at any considerable distance and the improvement in motor-driven apparatus are such that the Mayor believed a combination of this kind may prove of advantages. The department in 1922 was confronted with the necessity of purchasing more horses and was a matter of early determination.

Last year A contract was entered by the city by which the city is supplied with as good a pair of horses as it owns, driven by a capable driver who owns them, who supplies his own harness, etc. and also the feed for the horses, for $35 per week.

It's also noted that most of the fire alarms are answered by a few men of the department with a motorized peace of apparatus.

[from *New Hampshire Sentinel:*]

FIRST PERMANENT CHIEF ENGINEER EUGENE B. RILEY

1922 - 1926

Eugene B. Riley, the Keene fire department's first permanent chief, who retired on pension January 3rd, was guest of honor at a surprise testimonial dinner Wednesday night in the assembly hall of the Central fire station. About 65 present former members of the fire department, members of the city government and other friends were present. Speakers paid him many tributes for his 45 years of service with the department and present him a number of gifts in token of friendship and admiration.

Former Chief Riley was invited to the fire station by Chief Walter R. Messer who went to the Riley home and told him there were a "couple of old friends" at the fire station who wanted to see him. He found the fire station filled with friends ready for a gull-scale party for the retired chief.

Among former firemen present were Frank J. Bennett, John A. Dennison, Cleon Symonds, Fred S. Morse, C. Elliot Witham and Frank Streeter.

William F. Abbott of Springfield Mass, salesman for the Eureka Hose Co. and longtime friend of Mr. Riley, motored to Keene for the affair. Fred J. Baker, deputy forest fire warden, also attended.

Alderman Don W. Cook and Councilmen Walter Royle and Arthur Kingsbury, members of the fire department committee, former Alderman Harold T. Packard and former Council Herbert H. Sanderson were among the guests.

Companies Work as Unit:

After the dinner, Chief Messer turned the meeting over to John H. Simpson, for about 45 years an active fireman and now clerk of the board of engineers. Mr. Simpson called on Alderman Cook, chairman of the fire department committee, who praised Mr. Riley and also congratulated the city on its new chief. Former Councilman Sanderson a former member of the Lancaster fire department and an auxiliary fireman in Keene, complimented Mr. Riley on his accomplishments and said that he knew the three companies in the department worked as a unit.

Louis Pierre, a representative of the Mason Insurance agency, said that Mr. Riley had always been very cooperative. Due to the efficiency of the department, he said, Keene has one of the lowest fire rates in the state. He said that the department continues to be fortunate in having a chief of the alert competence of Walter Messer.

Frank J. Bennett remarked that members of the department, who had cooperated 100 percent with Mr. Riley would unquestionably do the same for Chief Messer.

Low Losses No Luck:

Harold T. Packard, Chairman of the fire department committee for the past two years, emphasized the point that maintaining a low fire loss is not all luck, but is brought about by the work of efficiently trained men with such training as Chief Riley had given. Riley's reputation he said, is high throughout the state because there is no large city near enough to aid Keene in the event of a serious conflagration, Mr. Packard said that Mr. Riley had demonstrated wise foresight in seeing to it that the department should have a new aerial ladder, which will soon be delivered.

Others who paid tribute to Chief riley were Dr. Harvey Grimes of Sullivan, Fred J. Baker, Norman O. Trask, William P. Abbott and Robert M. Clark.

Lawrence M. Pickett, a member of the Washington Hook & Ladder Co., on behalf of the company presented Mr. Riley a gold badge with the inscription "Retired Chief, K.F.D. 1901-1946." Mr. Pickett recalled that the company had previously made Mr. Riley an honorary member.

Recalls Horse-Drawn Engines:

Chief Riley thanked the members of the department for their cooperation during his term of service and said he knew they would give his successor the same cooperation. He said he enjoyed working with the department members and is ready at any time to assist Chief Messer in any way possible. Mr. Riley recalled that when he first became a member of the department it as all horse-drawn and he had seen it grow to its present condition of modern motorization.

Chief Messer praised his predecessor and said that he knew the department members were ready to give him the same cooperation they had extended Mr. Riley.

The regular drivers and Fred S. Morse, a retired driver, presented Mr. Riley an electric hand drill. The call men and representatives of insurance agencies presented him a portable typewriter. Members of the department gave him a smoking stand and a supply of tobacco. Department members did not forget Mrs. Riley. Although she was not present, she was remembered with a sewing cabinet fully equipped.

Mr. Riley became a member of the department kin 1901 as a call fireman. In 1912, when the Stark fire alarm telegraph system was installed, he became city electrician in charge of the system and so became the first regular member of the fire department. In 1919 he was named deputy chief and in 1922 became the first permanent chief of the department. Louis A. Nims and Fred W. Towne were call chiefs.

He is a member of the New England Fire Chiefs Association; charter member and former president of the New Hampshire Chiefs club former president of the New Hampshire Fireman's relief Association; member of the International Fire Chief Association; former president of the Cheshire County Forest Fire Wardens Association and a member of the Masonic fraternity.

While reminiscing on the old days, Chief Riley recalled some of the more important fires in Keene, the Carey Chair Co. on Willow street, the "Patch" fire on Emerald Street; W. L. Goodnow Co. block, the Burdette Chair Co. and the Robertson Motor Co. building.

Walter R. Messer, the present chief, first became interested in the fire department as a lad when his stepfather, the late Fred W. Towne, was a call chief.

Members of the board of engineers, Walter R. Messer, Elwin H. Applin, Thomas Wallbank and John H. Simpson, were in charge of the Wednesday night's special tribute to Chief Riley.

————

1923 [from *City of Keene Annual Report*]

Report of Chief Engineer of the Fire Department and City Electrician.

To His Honor the Mayor and City Councils:

As required by the City Ordinance governing the Fire department, I herewith submit my report for the year ending November 30th, 1923.

The department has responded to more alarms this year than in any other year in the history of the city; the property valuation to which they have been called to is far in excess of a million dollars; in some cases the loss was small and not insurance was collected.

The following alarms were answered by the department: 2 false alarms; 22 bell alarms; 234 still alarms; 10 out-of-town calls; making a total of 268 alarms.

The estimated value of buildings damaged by fire was, $358,400.00.

Damage to buildings, $16,486.26.

Insurance on said buildings, $181,300.00.

Insurance paid, $15,417.61.

Value of contents of said buildings, $284,950.00.

Damage to said contents, $7,605.24.

Insurance upon property, $208,150.00.

Insurance paid, $7,205.24.

Apparatus and Force:

The apparatus and force of the department, under a Chief and three Assistants Chiefs, located on Vernon Street, is as follows:

The Keene Steam Fire Engine & Hose Co.-J. A. Denison, Captain; 25 men has Amoskeag Steamer No. 1, Button Engine No. 2, and one Motor Chemical with two 40-gallon chemical tanks and other necessary equipment; also one Cadillac tractor.

Washington Hook & Ladder Co.-F. W. Streeter, Captain; 20 men; has one Motor Combination, chemical and ladder truck, one relief truck.

Deluge Hose Co.-E. H. Applin, Captain; 20 men has one Combination Chemical and Hose Wagon and one Motor Chemical with two 30-gallon tanks.

We have on hand 8,500 feet of No. 1 hose, 1,500 feet of linen hose at South Keene, 500 feet of No. 2 hose which is unfit for fire service.

During the year 550 feet of No. 2 hose was sold to the Water Works Department.

There has been additional motor apparatus added to the department this year as follows: The Combination Chemical and Hose Wagon body of the Steamer Company has been mounted on a Reo Speed Automobile chassis. This apparatus had two 30-gallon tanks and carries 800 feet of 2 ½ inch fire hose, and has been assigned to the Deluge Hose Co.; also a 1913 Cadillac tractor, which is in very fair condition had been attached to one of the steam fire engines. This will drive the same at a rate of speed better than horses, as about twelve miles an hour is a maximum speed for a steamer. This tractor was purchased for a small amount of money and will give good service for this kind of equipment, as the horses are not in the best of condition for fire service and are at times too far from the Fire station to answer alarms promptly.

There has also been installed a new sliding pole in the Hook and Ladder house, which helps to make a quicker start on a fire call at night.

The Fire Alarm telegraph system is in No. 1 shape. There has been an addition of three new fire alarms boxes to the system this year. Box 143, private box at Kingsbury Manufacturing Co., Myrtle Street; Box 115, at Church and Valley Streets; and Box 36 at Elm corner North Streets. Box 119 has been changed to 182 and Box 152 has been changed to 521.

There has been an exceptional large amount of line work on the fire alarm circuits this year, owing to the setting of new poles, or joint poles, so-called, where the Electric Light Company, Telephone Company and Fire Alarm use the same set of poles, thereby doing away with one line of poles on a street.

During this year as Building Inspector, I have given 48 permits for the erection of new buildings, also 19 permits for repairs and alterations on old buildings.

Recommendations:

The board of Engineers recommend the purchase of 1,000 feet of hose, one Invincible nozzle, one fire alarm box, also that eh

1923 Reo Speedwagon, purchased for the City of Keene. Note: The hosebody of the 1923 Reo, was removed from the Steamer Wagon and placed on the Reo in 1923 when purchased.

remaining flush hydrants be replaced by post hydrants.

To the Mayor and members of the Joint Standing Committee on Fire Department, the members associated with me on the Board of Engineers, officers and members of the department and to the public, I extend my sincere thanks and appreciation for the liberal aid and generous support rendered me during the past year.

EUGENE B. RILEY,
Chief Engineer

Resolutions for the Year Ending 1923.

On February 1st, 1923 a Resolution was passed for the purchase of a Fire Alarm Box. The box to be installed at or near the corner of Church & South Lincoln Streets not to exceed $150.

On March 1st, 1923 a Resolution was passed to purchase 1,000 feet of fire hose and certain coats and boots for the fire department. Not to exceed $1,065.

On May 17th, 1923 a Resolution was passed relating to Motor Fire Apparatus. The sum of $2000. dollars be appropriated for changes to be made in the Motor Chemical Apparatus

In the year 1923 the City passed an ordinance Enacting Rules for driving and Traffic Regulations. This writer to conserve space writes only that pertains to the fire department. Under Article VI Traffic Regulations Section 3. No person shall hitch any horse to any tree or shrub, fire alarm support or hydrant, nor shall any vehicle be left within ten feet of any fire hydrant. Section 5. In case of fire, all vehicles shall, on approach of fire apparatus, immediately drawn up as near as practicable to the right-hand curb and parallel thereto, and remain there until the fire apparatus has passed. "Fire Apparatus" in this section may include vehicles used to convey members of the Fire department to the fire.

Section 6. Except in main thoroughfares, no vehicles shall enter any section of a street where a fire is in progress without permission of the police, nor shall any vehicle approach within fifty feet of the farthest hydrant in use at such fire.

[*Compilers Note*: This writer, due to the length of fire calls and Growth of the City, elects from this point on to select fires of importance for the upcoming years. The increase for fire calls is due to both population growth and the motorization of the fire department from horse drawn to motor driven. This moved the department forward and provided a greater protection throughout the city.]

1924 [from *City of Keene Annual Report*]

Report of Chief Engineer of the Fire Department and City Electrician.

To His Honor the Mayor and City Councils.

As required by the City Ordinance governing the Fire Department, I herewith submit my report for the year ending November 30th, 1924.

The following alarms were answered by the department: 11 bell alarms; 197 still alarms, 12 out-of-town calls; making a total of 220 alarms.

The estimated value of buildings damaged by fire was, $521,667.00.

Damage to buildings, $16,345.12.

Insurance on said buildings, $288,675.00.

Insurance paid, $15,106.99.

Value of contents of said buildings, $550,945.75.

Damage to said contents, $50,380.41.

Insurance upon property, $451,031.41.

Insurance paid, $50,361.19.

Apparatus and Force

The apparatus and force of the department, under a Chief and three Assistant Chiefs, located on Vernon Street is as follows:

The Keene Steam Fire Engine & Hose Co. J. A. Denison, Captain; 25 men; has Amoskeag Steamer No. 1, Button Engine No. 2, and one Motor Chemical with two 40-gallon tanks and equipment; also one Cadillac tractor.

Washington Hook & Ladder Co. F. W. Streeter, Captain; 20 men; has one Motor Combination, chemical and ladder truck, and one relief truck.

Deluge Hose Co. E. H. Applin, Captain; 20 men; has one Combination Chemical & Hose Wagon and one Motor Chemical with two 30-gallon tanks.

We have on hand 7,000 feet of No. 1 hose, 1,500 feet of linen hose at South Keene, 2,750 feet of No. 2 hose which is unfit for fire service.

During the year 500 feet of No. 2 hose was sold to the Water works Department.

During the year an Overland automobile with a truck body on it, was purchased for the department to be used as a Chiefs Car and all other necessary work of the Department.

The Fire alarm telegraph is in No. 1 shape. During this year as Building Inspector, I have given 67 permits for the erection of new buildings, also 3 permits for additions and 12 for remodeling.

Recommendations:

The Board of Engineers unanimously recommend the purchase of a modern pumping engine to give the outside district as well as the Central district better protection; we are also taking into consideration that these steamers are better than 30-years old, one being purchased in or about the year 1883 and the other in 1890. We also recommend 1,000 ft. of hose and one new fire alarm box.

To the Mayor and members of the Joint Standing Committee on Fire Department, the members associated with me on the Board of Engineers, officer and members of the department, and to the public, I extend my sincere thanks and appreciation for the liberal aid and generous support rendered me during the past year.

EUGENE B. RILEY, Chief Engineer

The largest dollar amount fire in 1924 was the Holbrook Grocery Co. On February 9th, 1924 which possible started in a closet. Damage was $26,792.68 and Insurance paid $26,792.68.

As Reported by the *New Hampshire Sentinel* on February 11th, 1924:

Holbrook Grocery Company, ST. James Street. Photo by Bion. H. Whitehouse. HSCC collection.

'FIRE'
HOLBROOK GROCERY CO. SUSTAINS FIRE LOSS

Flames Threaten Wholesale Establishment In Heart of the Business Section.

Intense excitement prevailed in Keene for a time Saturday night when fire broke out in the office and warehouse of the Holbrook Grocery Company's wholesale plant on Lamson Street. Being in the heart of the business district a large crowd of Saturday night shoppers were attracted to the scene. The flames were shooting out through the roof when the firemen first arrived, about 7:15 o'clock, in response to Box 7 on St. James Street. It was the first bell alarm since Oct. 31st.

It was only by diligent effort that the firemen were able to keep the flames confined to the east end of the building. Four hydrant streams were poured into the heart of the fire which was in the seed room at the top of the building. After the first ladder was raised on of the firemen climbed up with a hose line but before the water was turned on the top of the ladder caught fire from the amount of flame which darted through the open window. The fire started in the office behind a radiator which was enclosed in a ventilator shaft and

is believed to have been caused by rats and matches. The flames licked their way up the ventilator shaft to the roof and broke out through a small opening in the shaft in the office but were easily extinguished at this point.

The loss is entirely covered by insurance. The company was unwilling to give an estimate of the loss this morning. Employees were at work to day figuring out the inventories to determine the exact loss. The water and smoke damage will be greater than the fire.

The blaze was discovered by George Rix, a freshman at high school, who sounded the alarm. If it had been any other night but Saturday when people were around or had it been early in the morning the building would probably have been reduced to ashes.

The seed room on the third floor is an entire loft as what products were not damaged by the blaze were spoiled by the heat and water which will spoil germination. Rolls of paper were burned on the second floor. The flames had an outlet through a cupola air space and thus saved them from spreading into the center of the building.

Tons of water were poured into the blaze and men were kept busy for a considerable time afterward wetting it down, the elevator shaft to the basement is in order to keep it from destroying goods as much as possible. A gasoline engine was put at work to pump it out from the cellar. Employees responded in good season and worked with the owners, Edward F. and William E. Holbrook, in clearing out the office. A good many clothes of employees and firemen were destroyed. The men in the office had to wade through a foot or more of water. The firemen had considerable difficulty in battling the smoke. One hose line was carried up the fire escape on the west side of the building from a hydrant connection at the B. & M. depot. Two lines were laid from Federal Street and one from St. James Street and these were sent in from the front of the building. One man was knocked off the ladder when the house got away from him and crashed through the plate glass window into the office.

––––––––

[from *New Hampshire Sentinel:*]

KEENE FIREMEN PREPARE FOR ANNUAL INSPECTION

Event Thursday to Close With Banquet and Dance as Reported by the *New Hampshire Sentinel* October 3rd, 1923.

Thursday is the day for the annual inspection and practice runs of the Keene Fire Department companies. At 5 o'clock there is to be a banquet at the fire station and in the evening the department will conduct a dance in city hall. The proceeds will go toward the benefit of the Firemen's Relief Association. The mayor and members of the city government will inspect the various companies as they pass in review in front of city hall and also inspect the quarters on Vernon Street.

The several companies with apparatus will move from the fire station at 1.20, in the following order. Motor Chemical, Keene Steam Fire Engine & Hose Company, Motor Ladder Truck, Washington Hook & Ladder Company, service steamer, Deluge Hose Company relief steamer. On a single stroke of the fire alarm the department in line will march down Court Street, through Central Square, and Main Street as far as Appian way, and there countermarch to Central Square and pass in review of the city fathers at city hall. The members of the department are to be in full uniform and wear white gloves.

––––––––

[from *New Hampshire Sentinel:*]

MAYOR KINGSBURY LAUDS KEENE FIRE DEPARTMENT

Annual Inspection, Banquet and Dance Successful Affair as Reported by the *New Hampshire Sentinel* October 10th, 1923.

Highest praise for members of the Keene Fire department was given by Mayor Robert T. Kingsbury and other speakers, at the annual banquet of the firemen, city government and invited quests, at the fire station Thursday. This was one of the events in connection with the annual inspection. In the afternoon there was the parade followed by practice runs. The affair was brought to a successful close by a dance in city hall at night.

Chief Eugene Riley presided at the postprandial exercises and called upon Mayor Kingsbury. He stated that the city government and citizens of Keene feel proud of the fire department and the excellent record of the companies. "I want you men to know that the city government feels proud of its fire department," he said. The mayor said the large number of still and bell alarms, which total about 250 since December 1st, and the comparatively small loss of $20,000, is not a coincidence, but shows ability on the part of the members of the department. The mayor said he is pleased with the nearness of completion of motorization of the department. One truck was added this year and with one of the steamers connected with a motor truck, which is not under way, the motorization will be about complete. He said that as long as the present committee from the city government represents the fire department, the members need not feel that anything will be put over on them.

Mayor Kingsbury in closing spoke of "Fire Prevention Week which starts October 8th, The Chamber of Commerce and the engineers of the department are to cooperate. It is the duty of each fireman to work for the prevention of fires as well as infighting them, by reporting fire hazards to the department in order they may be cleaned up. Mayor Kingsbury said there was an increased fire hazard from soft coal and that the engineers will warn users of the necessity of watching the coal in the bins.

Rev. Joseph Simpson of Grace Methodist Church, who offered prayer at the banquet, was called upon. He started that he could say amen to all the complimentary remarks handed to the department by the mayor. He said he rarely ever went to a fire because it was quite certain that it would be out before he could get there. He related a number of amusing stories.

———

[*Compiler's Note:* 1924 was an important year for Keene. The new War Memorial was dedicated which still stands today at the head of the square. Dedication of the Keene Soldier's War Memorial on Central Square took place on Sunday, November 9th, 1924 at 2:30 P.M. This memorial is important not only to those who served but because each company of the fire department donated monies for its construction.]

1925 [from *City of Keene Annual Report*]

Report of Chief Engineer of the Fire Department and City Electrician.

To His Honor the Mayor and Gentlemen of the City Councils:

I hereby submit my annual report for the year ending November 30th, 1925.

The following alarms were answered by the department: 22 bell alarms; 168 still alarms; 6 out-of-town calls, making a total of 196 alarms.

The estimated value of buildings damaged by fire, $457,236.18.

Damage to buildings, $31,693.60.
Insurance on said buildings, $229,273.20.
Insurance paid, $25,205.82.
Value of contents of said buildings, $185,437.41.

Damage to said contents, $42,996.56.
Insurance upon property, $149,350.00.
Insurance paid, $40,142.02.

Apparatus and Force

The apparatus and force of the department, under a Chief and three Assistants Chiefs, located on Vernon Street, is as follows:

Keene Steam Fire Engine & Hose Co. John A. Denison, Captain, & 24 men.

Washington Hook & Ladder Co. Frank W. Streeter, Captain, & 19 men.

Deluge Hose Co. Elwin H. Applin, Captain, and 19 men.

Ahrens Fox, 750 gallon pumping engine, hose and booster.

New 1925 Ahrens Fox, 750 Gallon pumping engine. Driver: Fred Morse.

Kissel Combination, chemical and hose.
Reo Combination, Chemical and hose.
Mack, Ladder truck and chemical. Amoskeag Steamer, Tractor drawn.

Button Steamer, Horse drawn. Deluge Combination. Horse drawn. Relief Ladder Truck. Horse drawn.

We have on hand 8,000 feet No. 1 hose, 1,500 feet of linen hose at South Keene and 1,300 feet of No. 2 hose. Old hose sold during the year, 1,400 feet.

During the year there has been placed in service the following:

A Fire Alarm Box No. 174 has been installed on lower Main Street at Edgewood.

A Traffic siren has been installed at the south end of Central Park, which is used on all alarms going into the square except the hours between 11:00 p.m. and 6:00 a.m. this siren is valuable to the department as it gives the warning that the apparatus is coming and ample time for all traffic to pull in towards the curb and stop as per Ordinance.

A Triple Combination, Pump, Hose and Booster system has been placed in service. This pumping engine is an Ahrens Fox make and piston pump type and 750 gallons capacity. It also has a thawing device if in any case that we may connect to a hydrant that may be frozen it can be thawed out quickly. On May 19th, it was given the Underwriters test as to capacity and pressure. This test requires two hours pumping at capacity at 120 lbs. And one half hour at one-half capacity at 200 lbs. And one-half hour at one-third capacity at 250 lbs. The Pumper made the test easily and exceeded the capacities required. And also with the increase in the water pressure form the new reservoir on Beech Hill, giving an increase of about 25 pounds and its storage capacity of 1,500,000 gallons makes a valuable factor in fire protection.

An Invincible Nozzle of the A. J. Morse type has been purchased and will be mounted on Chemical No. 1 by the time this report goes to press. This is a nozzle of the 1,100 gallon size for use on large fires as it has a three-way automatic Siamese connection for 2 ½ inch hose.

The apparatus quarters at the Station have been painted during the year.

The Fire Alarm System is in A No. 1 condition. We now have 48 fire alarm boxes on the system which is divided into six circuits, two of which are taper circuits, and about 27 miles of wire in the alarm circuits.

During the year as Building Inspector I have given 68 permits for the erection of new buildings, 13 for additions, 9 remodeling .

Recommendations:

The Board of Engineers recommend the purchase of 1,000 feet of fire hose. The standardizing of the fire hose thread to the National standard which is 7 ½ threads to the inch.

To replace the 4 inch water main on Vernon Street with an 8 inch pipe. Also another permanent man.

To the Mayor and Members of the Joint Standing Committee on Fire Department, the members associated with me on the Board of engineers, Officers and members of the department, and to the public, I extend my sincere thanks and appreciation for the liberal aid and generous support rendered me during the year.

Respectfully submitted,
EUGENE B. RILEY, Chief Engineer

[from *New Hampshire Sentinel:*]

'FIRE'

1925 Firemen Respond To 16 Alarms Since April 1St.

Fires During Past Ten Days Cause Loss Was Approximating $100,000.

Firemen answered the 16th alarm since April 1st, when the motor chemical responded to a call for a grass fire near the old Country club Friday morning about 9:40.

Five of the 16 calls to the department have been box alarms and have been within the past six days. Box eight was pulled in Sunday night and Monday morning early for fires in the blocks on Main Street and box 16 came in Wednesday morning for the Duffy house fire. Box 13, the same afternoon called the firemen to the Beaver mills property and a double alarm was sounded on box 27 this morning.

Fire losses suffered in the five box alarm fires aggregate very close to $100,000 and if the Ridge fire were included the figures would reach nearly $170,000.

Printed in the *New Hampshire Sentinel* Keene, N. H.

———

[from *New Hampshire Sentinel:*]

1925 Two Fires Cause Heavy Damage In Business Section.

April 4th, 1925 Flames That Originated In Tierney Block Basement Reach Wright Building. F. A Carpenter and Morin Shoe Concern Chief Victims of Blazes.

Discovery of two fires in adjoining buildings in the heart of the city's business section, soon after their origin, coupled with quick and efficient response by the fire department last night doubtless prevented extremely disastrous results through the damage is estimated as well towards $10,000.

The first fire was discovered about 10:30 Sunday night, in the basement of the Tierney block and the second two hours later, in the Wright block, owned by Roy V. Whitney, with a lively blaze near the rear of the Morin System Shoe Company's store. The loss, which affected all of the occupants of the two blocks, may reach $10,000. Hundreds of people crowed Main Street and watched the fires.

Three water lines and two chemical lines of hose were laid to each fire, one from Central square, one from the corner of Main and Lamson Streets and the third from Federal Street. The firemen tried to use as little water as possible in order to keep down the water damage. The only water used in the Tierney block was in the basement, but a stream had to be used in the Whitney block from the rear door as the flames and smoke filled the store and firemen were unable to get near the fire with chemicals.

The fire in the basement of the Tierney block is believed to have originated around some rubbish in the basement of the block used by Mr. Tierney. Some worked its way up through the building and into the Whitney block. Miss Bertha Wright, who has a piano studio on the Whitney block, discovered this blaze and she called Frank B. Forbes, who lives on the third floor of the Whitney block. He called the fire department and a still alarm was sounded. Soon after the chemical arrived, the alarm from box 8 was sounded as it was seen that the chemical apparatus was not able to cope with the blaze. Occupants of the Tierney block, on the second and third floors, some 15 in number, were awakened and left the building. They had plenty of time to dress.

The front of the basement of the Tierney block is occupied by Fred J. Field's barbershop and the first floor by the pool and tobacco store of Fred A. Carpenter, the second and third floors by John C. Tierney and lodgers. Mr. Carpenter lost considerable quantity of goods in the humidor in the basement of the building and the stock on the main floor was smoked. The entire building was badly smoked, as was field's barbershop, although the blaze did not get into his place of business. The fire worked its way into partitions on both sides of the block and holes were cut in the walls and chemicals poured in to check the blaze. Two water lines were used in the basement from the rear of the building.

The fire was checked within 30 minutes and the "all out" was sounded about 11:15. Most of the firemen had answered roll call and gone home, a few remaining at the station to discuss the fire, when the second call came in from box 8. Louis Eno, night officer, who was making his rounds in the rear of the block, discovered this fire. He was conversing with John Driscoll, who was in charge of the apparatus being used to pump the water from the Tierney clock basement. The fire appeared to burst out suddenly, but from appearances it had been in progress for a considerable time as more that 100 pairs of shoes in boxes on the north wall of the store, were burned. When the firemen arrived they had to force the rear door and smoke and flames drove them back. They had to use water to check the fire, and were then able to get in and use chemical lines.

There will be considerable damage to the Morin System Shoe Company's store due to fire, smoke and water. Smoke and water as well as fire also damage the block. Firemen had to go to the second floor in the part occupied by Miss Bertha Wright on the second floor and cut holes in the wall to check the fire from creeping up the partition. Many pairs of shoes piled in boxes on shelves on the north side of the store were damaged and the shelves burned. Considerable woodwork had to be chopped away to get at the fire in the partitions.

The block is occupied by the Morin System Shoe store on the first floor, by Miss bertha Wright's music studio and Dr. Clarence A. Wright's dental office on the second floor and the third floor by Frank B. Forbes and family. Mr. Forbes was unaware of the second fire being in progress until a policeman notified him. Although he smelled smoke he believed it was the result of the first blaze as the Whitney block was considerably smoked. Mrs. Forbes and her niece, who were aroused for the second time and forced to leave the block, went to the Cheshire House.

At first firemen believed that the fire in the Whitney block was in no way the outcome of the blaze in the blaze in the Tierney block, but it was later discovered that it was the direct cause. The fire worked its way along beams into the Whitney block, the construction being of such type that the beams in the two blocks nearly met. Employees of the Morin Shoe store were in the store during the first fire and kept them from and rear doors open to allow the smoke to clear and when they locked up to go home, they did not notice any indication of fire in the store.

Most of the occupants of the two blocks carry insurance through the local agencies. The firemen, by their efficient manner in handling the fire, were able to keep the water loss down.

Printed in the *New Hampshire Sentinel* Keene, N. H.

————

[from *New Hampshire Sentinel:*]

FLAMES DRIVE 13 GIRL STUDENTS INTO STREET

On April 10th, 1925 An Early Morning Fire Does Considerable Damage to Mary Duffy House.

Thirteen normal school girls rooming in the Mary Duffy house at 284 Main Street were driven into the Streets at 6:20 Wednesday morning and Elton Winch and family, 11 Elliot Street, were also forced out by smoke from a fire which started in the shed connecting the two houses, the Winch home being in rear of the main house which is on the corner of main and Elliot Streets. The damage may reach $500. Bernard McCabe, janitor, who was in the building to attend the furnace, discovered the fire. The loss is covered by insurance. Mrs. Della Davis, is matron of the building.

The fire started in some barrels of rubbish in the shed in the rear of the house, according to the engineers, of the fire department. The blaze worked its way up through the roof of the shed connecting the two houses. A portion of the roof of the house occupied by Mr. Winch was damaged and the ell part of the Main Street house was somewhat burned. Smoke entered the rooms occupied by the normal school girls and only for timely discovery of the blaze more serious results might have followed.

The girls, terrified by the smoke pouring into the rooms but unaware that the flames were at a considerable distance, dressed hurriedly and grabbed some of their books and personal effects and rushed into the street. The blaze was controlled in a short time. One Motor Chemical being sent to the scene of the fire on a still alarm and when the firemen arrived it was evident that more help might be needed and a general alarm was sounded. The men who manned the chemical had the blaze practically controlled when the department arrived and the reinforcements soon extinguished the last trace of fire.

Smoke entered the tenement occupied by Mr. Winch but the furnishings of his house were not removed.

Printed in the *New Hampshire Sentinel* Keene, N. H.

————

The largest dollar amount fire for 1925 was the Burdett Chair Plant. As Reported by the *New Hampshire Sentinel* on April 10th, 1925:

"FIRE"
BURDETT CHAIR PLANT SWEPT BY FIRE AND MAIN UNIT IN ASHES

Three-Story Structure destroyed By Blaze Originating In Center of Building—Estimated Loss $75,000---Marlboro Sends Aid To Keene Department.

The main unit of the Burdett Chair and Handle Manufacturing Company's plant on Washington Street is in Keene and tons of twisted machinery lie in the ruins of the three-story factory which was flame swept shortly after 6 o'clock this morning by most disastrous and spectacular fire Keene firemen have had to battle with in many years. The property loss, estimated in the neighborhood of $75,000 to $100,000, is partially covered by insurance. The George Street Chapel and the reel-dense of Fred H. Fay, Washington Street were threatened. Firefighting apparatus summoned from Marlboro, aided in subduing the blaze which at time for more than an hour threatened to assume the properties of a conflagration.

Keene's entire firefighting equipment was called out to combat the blaze and practically all of the department's hose was used from hydrants and Beaver Brook, as more than 10 lines were laid besides the chemical lines. Help was asked of Marlboro and its new motor pumping engine, manned by 10 men, made the run to the scene of the fire in less than nine minutes.

The Marlboro pumping engine was not needed, but the chemical lines were used to protect the George Street Chapel. The pumping apparatus would have been needed had any other buildings caught fire.

All the firemen and volunteers did extremely commendable work in fighting the fire, considering the adverse conditions, a low water pressure and flames of such proportion that much were unable to get very close to the blaze. Several firemen were temporarily overcome by the intense heat but soon recovered and returned to their posts.

Mrs. Domina Discovered Fire.

The fire was discovered by Mrs. Cleon Domina, who lives on Wilford Street southeast of the factory, and Walter Bixby ran in the alarm from box 27, on the opposite side of the street from the factory. Albert Calkins, an employee at the factory arrived at the building soon after 6 o'clock and when he found the door on the Washington Street entrance locked he went around to the rear and saw the flames burning forth near the dry houses.

The men in charge of the motor chemical apparatus laid several lines of hose from nearby hydrants and two lines of hose were laid from the factory hydrant on the area of the burning building. Low water pressure prevented a stream of sufficient force to be of much effect in checking the flames and soon the entire structure was a roaring furnace and the firemen were forced to retreat. The Amoskeag Steamer was connected with the hydrant at the corner of Wilford and Washington Streets but again the firemen found insufficient water pressure. When the Button Steamer arrived it first went to the pond on the jail lot, the department depending to take water through a suction hose but it was not deemed advisable and the apparatus went to the hydrant on Washington Avenue. After a few minutes the steamer was transferred to Beaver Brook, several hundred feet in the rear of the factory. There was sufficient water in the brook and two substantial streams wee soon playing upon the flames.

Steamer Becomes Mired

The steamer had considerable difficulty in locating at the brook, owing to the soft ground. The apparatus had to go over a small bank to reach the brook and when within a few feet of where it was to stand one of the rear wheels sank into the mud to the hub. Volunteers had to practically lift the apparatus and roll it along to a place where the suction hose could reach the water.

The fire started in the center of the main building and worked either way. A brick wall at the south end of the building withstood the flames and heat and this probably saved the house 30 feet to the south from destruction. The north wall was wood and covered with metal and several firemen were between this wall and the large storehouse 30 feet to the north with a line of hose checking the flames from reaching the store house. The north end wall collapsed without warning and buckled in the center, the top falling into the fire. Had the wall toppled toward the storehouse several firemen would have been endangered.

Many Spectators

Throngs watched the fire while it was at its height and the intense heat drove spectators away from the building. The heat scorched the paint on the east side of the George Street Chapel, which is on the opposite side of the street from the factory, and cracked the glass in nearly every window on the side near the fire.

Several lines of hose from chemical apparatus and a garden hose line from the chapel were used to wet down the east side of the chapel. The slate roof was so hot that when the line of hose was played upon it, volumes of steam arose giving the appearance that the roof was on fire.

Insulation on the electric light wires in front of the factory on the opposite side of the street was burned off. Wires which ran into the factory had to be cut to prevent danger from electric current.

The Police established a fire line and put up ropers to keep the spectators away from the building. This was necessary at first but when the flames broke through the structure the people retreated.

Flying embers set fire to Fred H. Fay's house but the Marlboro firemen, who were giving their attention to protecting the George Street Chapel, put a ladder on the roof and extinguished the fire. Burning brands landed on dry grass in the lot north of the chapel building and started fires, but these were stamped out by onlookers before they had gained much headway. Owners of houses and buildings near the fire kept roots and sides of their property wet down as much as possible to prevent them from catching fire. All of the property in the neighborhood was closely watched. The lack of any wind was a great asset to the firemen in holding the fire to the building in which it started, and they deserve much credit for the manner in which they handled the fire handicapped as they were by low pressure of water.

Storehouse Largest in City

The main building was about 150 feet long three stories high and more than 70 feet in width. There were several wings on the south and east side of the building. The first floor of the building was used for the manufacture of chairs and equipped with modern machinery. There was considerable chair stock at the various machines and a large amount of stock ready to be distributed to the machines.

The second floor had machines and stock for the manufacture of brush handles, while the third floor was used for a finishing room. The storehouse north of the factory is the largest wooden building in the city and will hold from 75,000 to 100,000 chairs. This building was connected with the main factory by two runways used to convey chairs to the warehouse.

Valuable Papers Burned

The safe which was in the office on the second floor of the building at the northwest corner was hauled out after the blaze had died down. It was too hot to handle and was not to be handled until this afternoon. Most of the correspondence and some records which were not in the safe were destroyed Frank F. Hapgood bookkeeper at the factory, was quickly on the scene this morning and he and several firemen made an attempt to enter the building and reached the office but they were driven back smoke. The machines and steam pipes were a mass of twisted metal, which could be seen among the charred timer and ashes.

At the present time there were about 50 employed at the factory which was not running to its full capacity. A number of employees had been laid off during the past two weeks.

Incidents of the Fire

About 3,000 feet of hose which is nearly half of the department's supply was used during the fire, some of this was damaged.

Some of the new hose recently purchased by the department was used to refill the trucks this morning on their return to the fire station.

The paint on one side of the Reo chemical truck was scorched when it was driven in front of the George Street Chapel to apply chemical to the side of that building.

Sandwiches and coffee were made and furnished by the Salvation Army and taken to the firemen by Capt. J. J. Sweet. Doughnuts were obtained from Callahan's bakery and taken to the firemen.

During the progress of the fire several small boys arrived with baskets and began

carrying off waste wood at the rear of the factory.

————

[from *New Hampshire Sentinel:*]

"STORY"
1925 FIRE WARDENS OF COUNTY ASSEMBLE

In Month of April 1925 Over 35 Men Gather In Keene to Discuss Fire Prevention Methods.

Current problems in the prevention and fighting of fires as they particularly affect the wardens and deputy wardens in Cheshire county towns were discussed Tuesday morning in annual spring conference at the fire station. More than 35 fire wardens from nearly every town in the county and some outside were present and took part in the discussion. The conference was continued this afternoon after lunch.

The meeting and discussion of problems was led by Charles F. Young, district chief of the three southern counties, and Warren Tripp of Epson, chief of the central district, who was here as a substitute for State Forester John Foster, unable to be present.

Already this year 74 fires outside of those that have been set by railroad locomotives, have been reported to Mr. Young, who said that of this number 16 were roadside fires. The season has opened much earlier than usual and in expectation of this all of the fire look stations in the southern district, which includes Cheshire County, have been opened by the men at the stations. Thirteen fires have been reported from the Monadnock station to date.

Roadside fires came in for considerable discussion and suggestions as to how the menace could be stopped where asked for. One warden suggested that a right of way along the state highways be burned as is done by the railroads. It was agreed that the number of fires starting from the roadside would probably increase instead of decrease because of tourists.

Brush Beside Roads

This subject brought up the problem of roadside brush and slash since the two are closely connected. It was the opinion of the wardens that there was a considerable amount of brush along the highways in this county.

Mr. Tripp talked on the problem of roadside slash and said that he thought it a question of education, town and civic pride and that it was the duty of each town to see that such slash was cleaned up as fast as possible. He urged the fire wardens to "get after" the selectmen and see if something could be done to alleviate the present hazard and stated that it was one of the problems to be "tackled" this year.

Changes in the lumber mill slash law, made at this session of the legislature were explained. Portable mills, including tractor mills are to be required to register in Concord the same as automobiles. A fee of $2 is to be charged and a number will be attached to each mill. This will enable all fire wardens, the district chiefs and the Concord office to know the exact location and the number of mills operating in the state. The new operation permits will throw the responsibility of cleaning up slash around mills onto the stumpage owner. It is the policy of the state forestry department to hold the stumpage owner responsible although the land owner, operator or agent may be held. Whenever a mill moves its location on the lot or to other lots the operator must notify Concord under the provisional of the new legislation.

Another change that has been made in the law is distance slash must be removed from the edge of the highway. Instead of 25 feet from the "traveled part of the highway" the new reading is 25 feet from the "nearest edge" this is merely a clarification of the old law, however.

Outlines for discussion made by Mr. Young and State Forester Foster were distributed. The major topics listed included: prevention of forest fires, method of handling fires, fire reports and bills and permits for brush burning.

Those Attending:

Those in attendance at this morning's session included: Charles A. Sheldon, W. D. Crowell, Hancock; Ralph L. Hoyt, Rindge; John B. Crosly, West Rindge; Mark H. Carlton, Swanzey; George L. Porter, George Benware, Mark W. Baldwin, Henry J. Ormsby, B. E. Durlong, Langdon; A. M. Worcester, West Swanzey; John E. Wyman, West Keene; Eugene B. Riley, Keene; C. Hart, Walpole; George A. Alibay, Dublin; William F. Lane, Stoddard; Roger A. Haskins, Troy; Clifford D. Stearns, Hinsdale; S. A. Bullock, Richmond; Albert Georgina, Nelson John P. Kemp, East Alstead; C. J. Newell, Alstead; G. F. Amidon, West Chesterfield; B. A. Hastings, E. F. Nims, Edward L. Jewett, Sullivan; Henry E. Spaulding, Stoddard; Edward C. Greene, Westmorland Depot; Charles A. Gilchrist, Harrisville Depot; Edward l. Leighton, Jaffrey; George G. Mason, Bernard F. Bemis, Harrisville; Clarence M. Damon, Fitzwilliam C. H. Kinsman, Marlboro and A. H Post, Chesterfield.

———————

Resolutions for the year ending 1925

A Joint Resolution was passed on March 5th, 1925 for the sum of $13,000.00 for the purchase of a motor pumping apparatus.(1924 Ahrens Fox)

A Joint Resolution was passed on May 7th, 1925 relating to a Fire Alarm Box being installed at Edgewood Ave.

CHAPTER VIII.

Fire Department

The City Ordinance relating to the Fire Department is as follows:

Section 1. There shall be appointed by the bard of mayor and aldermen, in the month of January, annually, a chief engineer, who shall give his entire time to the fire department, and two assistant engineers, who shall be call men, to hold their officers one year, or until others are appointed and qualified to fill their places; and they may appoint an associate engineer; and they shall constitute the board of engineers, and perform all duties, and exercise all the powers of Fire Wards; provided, however, that they shall be subject to removal at any time by the mayor and aldermen, who shall have the power to fill vacancies.

Sect. 2. The by-laws adopted by the board of engineers and all rules and regulations that are now in force shall be considered as continuing in force, and the board shall have the power to make such other rules and by-laws as may be deemed necessary, provided they shall not be repugnant to, or inconsistent with, the laws of the state or the ordinances of the city.

Sect. 3. Each member of every company in the fire department shall receive for his services at the rate of seventy-two dollars per year, in addition to the sum allowed by law; but no member shall be paid for less than three months' service, unless sooner discharged from his company by the proper authority, for cause other than his own request, nor unless he shall have performed his duties in a manner satisfactory excuse for any failure to do so. In addition to the foregoing compensation, each fireman, or other person, who, under the direction of the board of engineers, answers a telephone or still alarm, not exceeding four people, or performs service at a brush fire, shall receive fifty cents per hour in full payment for such service. The names of such person as may perform the foregoing services, with the place visited, time employed, and compensation due, set opposite their respective names, shall be certified, within fifteen days from the end of the month, as a pay-roll by the clerk of the

board of engineers to the city clerk, who shall certify the same to the auditor and disburse the amount specified to the employees, taking their receipt therefore.

Sect. 4. The foreman of each company in the fire department shall report to the city clerk at the expiration of each quarter, the names of all men who have been active members of his company during the quarter, or any part thereof, giving date of all discharges, and of all elections of new members; and he shall, annually, in September, compute the pay of each member according to the preceding section, and make oath to the correctness of said reports and pay-rolls thereon.

Sect. 5. The city clerk shall furnish to each foreman proper blanks for his reports and pay-rolls.

Sect. 6. The chief engineer shall have control of the horses and drivers at fires and until they are dismissed, and may require their service whenever he may consider it necessary for drill or parade; the drivers shall also perform such services as the chief engineer may assign to them while they are on fore patrol duty at the fire station.

Sect. 7. No building shall hereafter be erected, moved, enlarged, remodeled or dismantled, nor shall any steam, gasoline or kerosene engine be set up in any building within the limits of the city, mentioned in section 9 of this chapter without consent of the board of mayor and aldermen, to be duly notified by public notice posted at the door of the city hall building, at least fourteen days before the day of hearing, and further notice given to or left at the last and usual place of adobe of the owner or occupants of the land adjoining the premises, where license is asked under this chapter. Each person asking the consent of the mayor and alderman shall file at least fourteen days before the day of hearing, and further notice given to or left at the land adjoining the premises, where license is asked under this chapter. Each person asking the consent of the mayor and aldermen shall file at least fourteen days before the hearing provided for above, a plan and detailed specifications of the building proposed to be erected. No person shall, in repairing or re-shingling the roof of any building in the limits of said city described in section 9 of this chapter use any material other than fireproof material.

No person shall locate any tank or other receptacle of greater capacity than ten gallons for the storage of gasoline, naphtha or any combustible oil, without the consent of the board of engineers of the Keene fire department being first obtained in writing thereto.

Sect. 8 Any person violating the provisions of section 7 shall be fined not exceeding twenty dollars, and any person maintaining a building erected or enlarged in violation of said section, or using an engine set up in violation of said section, shall be subject to fine not exceeding ten dollars for each day of such maintenance or use.

Sect. 9 The limits of the fire precinct hereby constituted shall be as follows: Beginning at the corner of Main and Dunbar Streets; thence on Dunbar Street to Crossfield Street; thence southerly thereon to Water Street; thence easterly thereon to Beaver Brook; thence northerly up Beaver Brook to Roxbury Street; thence westerly thereon to the west line of Roxbury Court; thence northerly on west line of said Court and continuation thereof to Spring Street; thence westerly thereon to Washington Street; thence northerly thereon to Mechanic Street; thence westerly thereon to Pleasant Street; thence northerly thereon to the northeast corner of land of the Impervious Package Company; thence westerly thereon to Elm Street; thence southerly thereon to Mechanic Street; thence westerly thereon to Court Street; thence southerly thereon to Summer Street; thence westerly thereon to Middle Street; thence southerly thereon

and on the east line of land of Keene Public Library to West Street; thence southerly from a stone post about 80 feet westerly of the west line of St. James Street to the north line of the right of way of the Boston & Main Railroad; thence westerly thereon to the canal; thence southerly thereon to Winchester Street; thence easterly thereon to Ralston Street; thence northerly thereon to Davis Street; thence easterly thereon to Main Street and to the point of beginning.

Sect. 10 No person shall kindle or light a fire within the limits of the fire precinct, except inside a house or other building, without first obtaining written permission from the chief engineer of the fire department. Any person violating the provision of section 10 shall be fined not exceeding twenty dollars.

Sect. 11. The chief engineer shall inspect or cause to be inspected as often as once in two months all hotels and buildings used partly or wholly for business purpose, within the limits of the fire precinct and shall see that all regulations established by the engineers of the fire department respecting the prevention of fires and otherwise are enforced. He shall keep in detail a record of such inspections.

Sect. 12. The chief engineer shall have the care and general supervision of all lines and apparatus connected with the electric fire alarm circuits and all apparatus used for extinguishing fires belonging to the city.

Sect. 13. The chief engineer shall keep the circuits and apparatus in good working order, at all times, and shall promptly repair or renew all work or interruptions to the circuits or the apparatus connected therewith. He shall see that all electric or other wires are kept at a safe distance from the fire alarm circuits. In cutting or removing such wires or other obstructions, he shall act under the direction of the mayor and aldermen. All materials and supplies and assistance needed for making repairs and maintaining the fire alarm he shall procure with the approval of the mayor and board of aldermen, who shall see that proper supplies for ordinary repairs and maintenance are kept on hand by the city. He shall carefully inspect or cause to be properly inspected all portions of the fire alarm circuits and apparatus each month and report all repairs or changes needed to the committee on fire department.

Sect. 14. He shall carefully inspect or cause to be properly inspected each fire alarm box and test the same as often as once in every month, keeping a record of all such tests with the date and number of the box tested. He shall cause one circuit to be used on Saturday of each week as provided by the regulations. The boxes shall be pulled alternately, and a record kept of the same.

Sect. 15. Whoever shall maliciously interfere or tamper with any of the boxes or wires connected with the fire alarm, or shall intentionally ring in any false alarm, shall be punished by a fine of not more than twenty dollars and the cost of prosecution.

Sect. 16. Any person or persons giving information which shall lead to the detection and conviction of any person or persons violating the provisions of the preceding section, shall be entitled to one-half of the fine imposed.

Sect. 17. The chief engineer shall also be inspected of buildings of the city. All plans for buildings proposed to be erected or altered in the city, shall, before any work is done upon such buildings, be submitted to said chief engineer for his approval or disapproval. In accordance with Chapter 40, section 3, Session Laws of 1893, as amended, any person violating any of the provisions of the section, shall be fined not exceeding One Thousand Dollars.

Sect. 18. Buildings or shelters housing more than three automobiles containing live tanks of gasoline, naphtha, or volatile and combustible oil, used for public livery, repair or temporary shelter purposes, shall be deemed public garages.

Sect. 19. No building hereafter erected shall be used as a public garage, nor shall any existing building be converted to such use without first filing plans. Specifications, and a statement of all facts as to location and proposed use with the board of mayor and aldermen, and obtaining from them a permit to so erect, use or convert.

Sect. 20. No permit shall be issued for a public garage within two hundred feet of any building uses as and or a hospital, church, public or parochial school, or other state or city public school, or the grounds thereof, or on any site where two-thirds of the buildings within a radius of two hundred and fifty feet are used exclusively for residential purposes and fifty or more per centum of said buildings so used are of wooden or chiefly wooden construction.

CHAPTER IX.

Relating to the setting of fires.

Section 1. The board of engineers may prohibit smoking, the use of matches or other inflammable articles, and the building and setting of fires in any building or portion thereof, or upon any land or premises within the limits of the fire precinct as constituted by chapter VIII of City Ordinances, when requested by the owner of such building, land or premises.

Sect. 2 When any rule or order is made by the board of engineers in pursuance of section 1, the owner or occupant of the buildings, land or premises to which the rule of order applies shall post in a conspicuous place a printed notice of such rule or order.

Sect. 3. Any person violating such rule or order after notice has been posted as provided in section 2 shall be fined not exceeding twenty dollars.

1926 [from *City of Keene Annual Report*]

Report of Chief Engineer of Fire Department and City Electrician.

To His Honor the Mayor and Board of Aldermen:

I hereby submit my annual report for the year ending November 30th, 1926. The following alarms were answered by the department:

17 bell alarms; 234 still alarms; 11 out-of-town calls, making a total of 262 alarms.

The estimated value of buildings damaged by fire, $206,300.00.

Damage to buildings, $16,877.50.

Insurance on said buildings, $112,200.00.

Insurance paid, $11.577.69.

Value of co9ntents of said buildings. $59,650.00.

Damage to said contents, $4,282.25.

Insurance on property, $17,450.00.

Insurance paid, $3,882.25.

Apparatus and Force

The apparatus and force of the department under a Chief and three Assistants Chiefs, located on Vernon Street is as follows:

Keene Steam Fire Engine & Co. John A. Dennison, Captain and 24 men.

Washington Hook & Ladder Co. Frank W. Streeter, Captain and 19 men.

Deluge Hose Company Edwin H. Applin, Captain and 19 men.

Ahrens Fox 750 gallon pumping engine hose and booster.

Kissell Combination chemical and hose. Reo Combination chemical and hose. Mack ladder truck and chemical.

Amoskeag Steamer, tractor drawn.

Deluge Combination, horse drawn.

Relief Ladder Truck, horse drawn.

We have on hand 9,000 feet No. 1 hose, 1,500 feet of linen hose at South Keene, and 500 feet of No. 2 hose. Old hose sold during year 800 feet.

During the year there has been another permanent man added to the force. The permanent force now consists of four men and a Chief.

Also another siren has been installed at the corner of Washington and Vernon Streets which was a very bad corner for traffic. This siren is used on alarms going up or down Washington Street.

On March 14th, 1926 the Fire Station had a fire of unknown origin and damage to the upper part of the building of about $10,000. His Honor the Mayor, members of the Fire Department, Land and Buildings Committee and Board of Engineers in taking the matter up decided not only to repair the damage done by fire but to modernize the building.

This included a new front to the building with a granite stone marked Central Station set in the front, larger door openings, steel and cement floors and steel ceilings, automatic door openers on first floor, a modern bath room with showers, social room, also a larger meeting and banquet hall. All walls are finished with steel lath and cement plaster on second floor.

The stables and hay mows have been removed to the so called steamer barn with a solid wall between this barn and the station also extending three feet above the roof. This makes a first class fire proof construction.

The reconstruction is very nearly complete and on completion will be open to the public for inspection. The Fire Alarm System is in good condition. In the coming year the battery needs to be removed as five years is about the life of this type of a battery.

During the year as building inspector I have given 100 permits for new houses, 83 for garages, 22 for other buildings, 36 for additions, 65 for alterations and remodeling, 9 for moving and dismantling.

Recommendations:

The Board of Engineers recommends the purchase of 1,000 feet of fire hose and a new fire alarm box.

To the Mayor and Members of the Joint Standing Committee on Fire Department, The members associated with me on the Board of Engineers, Officers and members of the department, and to the public, I extend my sincere thanks and appreciation for the liberal aid and generous support rendered me during the year.

Respectfully submitted,
EUGENE B. RILEY,
Chief Engineer

The fire noted for the year 1926 is the fire at Central Fire Station on March 14th, 1926. As the *New Hampshire Sentinel* reported the fire on March 15th, 1926 reads as follows:

"FIRE"

CENTRAL FIRE STATION SUFFERS LOSS ESTIMATED AT $20,000 FROM FLAMES ORIGINATING IN ADJOINT HAY LOFT

Fire Breaks Out In Department Headquarters While Firemen Fighting Blaze In Ralph Lane House On Grant Street-Services Suspended In Five Churches During Progress Of Fire

While Keene firemen were battling Sunday morning with a blaze in a house owned and occupied by Ralph Lane at 75 Grant Street a was gaining headway in their own quarters at the fire station on Vernon Street and after nearly two hours work they extinguished the flames. Services in five churches within 200 feet of the burning structure were suspended. The damage at the fire station may reach $20,000 and the loss at the Lane Home about $1,500. There was $5,000 insurance on the building, the amount being increased by $1,000 after the last fire at the fire station.

The blaze at the fire station is believed to have started in the hay loft over the Deluge Hose Company's part of the building and in all probability was in progress when the firemen were called to the Lane fire on Grant Street about 10.25 o'clock. Before the Lane fire was under control the alarm for the fire station blaze was sounded. Some of the firemen and apparatus returned to combat the blaze while others remained and extinguished the Lane house fire.

Just what started the fire at the station will probably never be known but it had gained headway when discovered by a passerby who rushed into the station and notified the firemen who remained at headquarters to" cover" any other blaze. Brands of fire were dropping into the horses mangers as the animals were released from their quarters and taken to Fish's stable on Roxbury Street. John Sewall and others released the horses, which are stabled in the rear of the station. The animals are used by the highway department. Every piece of apparatus available at the station was pressed into service and 12 lines of water were poured into the building. The motor pumper was at the corner of Washington and Vernon Streets and the Amoskeag steamer was on duty in front of the Methodist church. Other lines of hose were attached nearby hydrants. Firemen had to combat the blaze from all sides of the structure. The firemen were assisted by volunteers. During the progress of the fire a considerable quantity of the station furnishings was removed to safety. While the fire was at its height members of the Boy Scouts under Scout Master Fred Mitchell and several citizens went about among the firemen serving coffee and doughnuts. Hot coffee and doughnuts were also served from the basement of the parish house of the First Congregational church to the firemen.

After a considerable time in combating the blaze firemen were able to enter the burning building with lines of hose. While several were in the building a section of the ceiling in the social room fell and inflicted slight injuries to Timothy O'Connell and Cleon Symonds, but they remained on duty in spite of their injuries. The roof of the building is totally destroyed and the drying tower on the west side of the building was rendered useless. The seven rooms for the firemen, Chief Engineer E. B. Riley's room, the meeting and social rooms were also destroyed. Fire did not descend to the first floor but this portion of the building was damaged by water. The cellar of the building was flooded by water and did not rise high enough to put out the fire in the heating apparatus in the basement and this was forced to its limit after the fire in order to dry out the building as much as possible. The lighting system was temporarily put out of commission but repaired during the afternoon.

The fire alarm telegraph system which is in a fire proof room in the northeast corner of the building was disabled only for a short time. The alarm system is now in perfect condition and three still alarms have been answered by the department since the big blaze.

As Church services were about to begin there were many persons on the streets and the two alarms brought out a large number of spectators who were crowded in Vernon Street and other available positions watching the progress of the fire. Some of those who had entered the churches watched the fire from open windows. Services in the Baptist, the Church of the Nazarene, Court Street Congregational, First Congregational and Methodist churches were suspended. All of these buildings are within 200 hundred feet of the fire station. Some of the churches held adjourned services and the Sunday school sessions.

The fire apparatus was temporarily housed in Frank J. Bennett's garage which is within 25 feet of the fire station. This morning the lower portion of the fire station was dried out sufficiently for the apparatus to be returned to its quarters. Several firemen remained on duty at the station all night, but were unable to go to bed however.

Philip Barrett, one of the drivers of the motor apparatus left his room about 10 minutes before the fire was discovered and he had not detected the odor of smoke at that time. Several persons at the Gasco Inn detected the odor of smoke several minutes before the station blaze was discovered. Shortly after the alarm was sounded a great volume of smoke settled over 'Central square and for a time it looked as though Keene was to experience a conflagration.

Proof that the fire must have been raging at the time the firemen answered the other call is found in the fact that several of the firemen answering the first box alarm saw the smoke coming out from the rear of the station and went directly to the station instead of the Lane fire.

The firemen were somewhat hampered by lack of hose as a large amount of it had been used at the Lane house fire. Most of the hose used at the fire station had to be taken from the racks and coupled.

The fire in the Lane house evidently originated in a chimney extended to the roof and burned down into the attic rooms. Most of the rafters of the roof in the main part of the house were burned or weakened by the blaze. The firemen succeeded in extinguishing the fire without pouring much water into the house to damage the furniture and the lower rooms. Some of the furniture was removed from the hose by volunteers. A temporary roof was put on the house Sunday afternoon.

Hold Special Meeting

Mayor Arthur R. Jones, Chief Eugene B. Riley, members of the fire department board of engineers joint standing committee on fire department and Alderman Frank R. Bennett, chairman of the lands and buildings committee met at the city clerk's office Sunday afternoon at 2.30 for the purpose of discussing problems facing the city as a result of the disastrous blaze. Following the meeting the officials went to the fire station and s spent considerable time viewing the damaged building. Chairman Bennett of the lands and buildings committee announced at the meeting that carpenters were already at work putting a temporary roof of heavy tarred paper over the second story ceiling which would keep out rain and snow and would keep the heat in so as to allow the rooms to dry out. This construction is merely temporary but will serve until a definite building plan has been settled upon.

There was a frank expression from all attending the meeting that the time had come when the stables with the hay and horses must be divorced from the Central fire station, and two suggestions advanced by Chief Riley were talked over.

Two Propositions

The first suggestions was that the stables, hay and horses be separated from the main part of the station by a brick firewall. In case this was done it would mean that the part of the building used by the highway department would be entirely shut off so far as entrances are concerned, from the main part of the station and that the entrance and exit for the teams and men would be so located that it would be impossible to reach the stables through the fire station proper.

Another suggestion was that the stables be located in a building entirely separated from the fire station. It was pointed out, however that a solid brick firewall between

Central Fire Station fire 1926—Fire shows heavy smoke in rear and middle of building by hose tower.

Central Fire Station fire 1926—Picture shows at the height of the fire attack on the fire changing the heat to steam during its extinguishing phase. Photos from Fire Dept. Scrapbook.

the main part of the station and the stables would give the same safety results.

Will Eliminate Attic

It was the consensus of those at the meeting that the "blind attic" over the second story of the fire station should be eliminated and that a flat roof be put on the building.

The fire department and lands and building committees with Mayor Jones and the board of fire engineers will make a careful study of the situation plans and suggestions before advancing a program for rebuilding.

———————

[*Compiler's Note*: The fire station was rebuilt after the fire of 1926 and has remained the same until present day except for the addition in 1963 of the Southwestern Mutual Aid area, the addition in 1971 for the new ladder and the changing of the engine bay doors in 1994.]

Chief Riley's rolltop desk. Chief Riley purchased this desk when he became chief. It remained in his office until the early 1960s, when Chief Messer upgraded the office. The desk was purchased by Tal Hood and is in use at Millbrook Farm Woodwork in Westmoreland, NH. Photo by Steve Goldsmith.

When permanent drivers were added to the department, each member was issued a wooden locker with shelves and a drawer to keep their uniforms and personal equipment. Each bedroom had two bunks and each locker had two doors and drawers. On the front of each door was a plate with the firefighter's name, which have long been removed. After the fire in 1926 only a few remain. The ones that remain are still used by firefighters in the bedrooms. Photo by Steve Goldsmith.

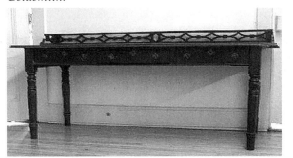

Left: Before the 1926 fire at the Central Fire Station each company had its own set of quarters. Each company had its own desk in which was housed, their specific area that was used by the company's officers. Pictured is one of the desks, which is in the main hall at the Keene Central Fire Station.

Resolutions for the year ending 1926

That the Mayor and Joint Standing Committees on Lands and Buildings and Fire Department advertise for bids for the work of reconstruction the fire station in accordance with plans and specifications made therefore; and perform all other acts necessary in their discretion, to carry into effect the plans for such alterations and repairs of said station. Passed June 3rd, 1926.

A Resolution was passed relating to the remodeling and reconstruction of the Fire Station. On July 1st, 1926 for the sum of Twenty-Five Thousand Dollars.

1927 [from *City of Keene Annual Report*]

Report of Chief Engineer of Fire Department and City Electrician

To His Honor the mayor and Board of Aldermen:

Keene, N. H., Nov. 30th, 1927.

I hereby submit my annual report for the year ending November 30th, 1927. The following alarms were answered by the Department:

16 bell alarms; 228 still alarms; 9 out-of-Town calls, making a total of 253 alarms.

The estimated value of buildings damaged by fire, $270,800.00.

Damage to buildings, $5,244.80.
Insurance on said buildings, $205,550.00.
Insurance paid, $5,244.80.
Value of contents of said buildings, $26,370.68.
Damage to said contents, $10,438.74.
Insurance on property, $20,400.00.
Insurance paid, $10,438.74.

Apparatus and Force

The apparatus and force of the d Chief and three Assistants Chiefs, located on Vernon Street is as follows:

Keene Steam Fire Engine & Co. John A. Dennison, Captain and 24 men.

Washington Hook & Ladder Co. Frank W. Streeter, Captain and 19 men.

Deluge Hose Company Edwin H. Applin, Captain and 19 men.

Ahrens Fox 750 gallon pumping engine hose and booster.

Kissell Combination chemical and hose. Reo Combination chemical and hose. Mack ladder truck and chemical.

Amoskeag Steamer, tractor drawn.
Deluge Combination, horse drawn.
Relief Ladder Truck, horse drawn.

The department has on hand 9,400 feet of serviceable hose, 1,500 feet of linen hose at South Keene. 150 feet of unserviceable hose.

About 600 feet discarded during the year. The old hose has been turned over to Water Department. The fire hose thread of the department has been standardized by cutting it to 7 ½ threads to the inch which is now the National Standard thread.

As the life of fire hose is about ten years, a thousand feet should be purchased the coming year to offset the amount discarded each year.

During the year a new Chief's car has been purchased, an Oldsmobile Six Coupe to replace the overland, which has been in service about four years.

The motor apparatus and its equipment, including tools are in very good condition.

The Fire Alarm System and its equipment is also in very good condition. There has been quite a lot of work done on the system during the year. Some of its work is changing over on joint-line construction also where new poles are set, also we had a cross with the Electric Light Co. high voltage circuit which caused damage to the underground wires and the Fire Alarm Repeater.

Box 47 has been placed on a pole near Keene Glue Co's Office, this box was down on the side of the office, and its present location is more convenient for the public.

Chief Eugene Riley standing in front of his 1926 Oldsmobile along with Jack Simpson and Dennis Foley. Photo from Fire Department scrapbook.

During the year as Building Inspector I have issued:

57 permits for new houses.
70 permits for new garages.
45 permits for other buildings.
41 permits for additions.
31 permits for alterations and remodeling.
8 permits for moving and dismantling.

Recommendations:

The board of Engineers recommend the purchase of 1,000 feet of fire hose.

Also a Fire Alarm Box Pedestal for the corner of Main and Railroad Streets, and the removal of the pole where Box 8 is now located.

The replacement of the old flush hydrants by post hydrants on lower Winchester Street and Roxbury Street.

In the near future a Foam Generator should be purchased as this is the only equipment to subdue large gasoline and oil fires, as the City has a large amount of gasoline in storage and quite a number of oil burners.

To His Honor the Mayor and Members of the Joint Standing Committee on Fire Department, Members of the Board of Engineers, Officers and members of the

Chief Eugene Riley showing off the Gold Leaf on the side of his new Oldsmobile. Photo from Fire Department scrapbook.

department, and to the public, I extend my sincere thanks and appreciation for the aid and support rendered me during the year.

EUGENE B. RILEY, Chief Engineer.

Fire April 17th, 1927 for the Pike & Whipple Building, along with a 2nd, fire Theatre & Fur, due to exposure from 1st fire. Reported by the *Keene Evening Sentinel* on Monday April 18th, 1927:

'FIRE'
FIRE WRECKS STORE OF PIKE & WHIPPLE AND SCENIC THEATRE

First blaze discovered about 9:30 Sunday night and second alarm sounded at 1:30 this morning. Origin of fire not determined. Damage heavy as stock of Merriam building tenants practically ruined either by flames or water.

Two spectacular and stubborn fires Sunday night and early this morning destroyed two storehouses and gutted the Merriam building on Main Street occupied by Pike & Whipple, furniture dealers, and wrecked the Scenic theatre building which is owned by Pike & Whipple and leased to Fred P. Sharby, manager of the theatre. The loss had not been estimated today but will run into many thousands of dollars. The origin of the first fire is unknown but the second is attributed to the first outbreak. Two alarms were sounded for each fire.

Property owned by J. Hubert Wright the Eagle Hotel building owned by the Boston and Main railroad, the manufacturing plant owned by the Robinson & Brett Lumber company, and the building occupied by the Keene Oil company were threatened. The wall of the Eagle hotel caught fire twice but the flames were quickly extinguished.

The first fire was confined to the storehouse owned by the Boston & Main railroad and occupied by Pike & Whipple. This blaze was discovered about 9:30 and the firemen did quick and excellent work in controlling this fire and preventing it from extending into other buildings which were within 30 feet, and some within 15 feet of the burning buildings. Eight lines of hose were laid by the firemen, two from the motor pumper which was set at the corner of Main and Emerald Streets, two from the old steamer which was set in front of the Sentinel building, and two lines each from the hydrants which are located in front of the Colonial building and the Robertson Motor Company's garage. With these eight lines of hose, the firemen were able to surround the burning structure and keep the flames from nearby buildings.

The fire in the storehouse had a big start when discovered and Box 6, which is at the corner of Main and Emerald Streets, was sounded. Following the arrival of the firemen and engineers it was apparent that the fire might get beyond control and more help was summoned by the sounding of the second alarm from Box 6.

Train Held Up

The alley between Scenic theatre and the Eagle Hotel property and the driveway between the Merriam block, which is occupied by Pike & Whipple, and the J. Hubert Wright house, gave the firemen room to lay lines of hose and fight the blaze from the west and south sides. Lines of hose were extended down Cypress Street and Water Street from these were played on the fire from the north and east sides. Two lines of hose which were laid from the old steamer in front of the Sentinel building crossed the railroad tracks in main Street, and necessitated the holdup of the "sleeper" from Boston to Montreal in the east yard until the fire was under control. The hose was uncoupled to allow the train to pass.

One of the largest crowds to witness a fire in Keene is believed to have been present at the first blaze. About one-third as many were at the second blaze. Many in the city did not hear the whistles for the second alarm, although four rounds from boxes 6 and 8 were sounded.

Practically the same hook-up of hose was used at the second fire as at the first, with the exception that three lines were used from the motor pumper instead of two. Only a few ladders were used during the first blaze, while practically every ladder was brought into play during the early morning fire. The old horse-drawn hook and ladder truck was taken to the scene of the fire and the ladders from it used.

The two storehouses and the Merriam building which are occupied by Pike & Whipple are owned by the Boston & Main railroad. The show room in front of the Merriam building and the Scenic Theatre building is owned by the Pike & Whipple Company and built on land leased from the railroad company.

The Merriam building besides being occupied by Pike & Whipple Company has as tenants the Shoe Shining Establishment of Nicholas Anastaslom, and Clarence W. Brooks, who conducts a sales room of automobile tires. The greatest damage to the two latter tenants was from smoke and water as the blaze did not reach the lower front part of the building. There was more than two feet of water in the basement occupied by Mr. Brooks.

Following the first blaze for firemen were detailed by Chief Eugene B. Riley to watch the property as a prevention of any further out break. The firemen made rounds of the Pike & Whipple sales building about five minutes before the fire broke out and they did not see indications of any fire. While they were in the rear, one of the firemen noticed a red light in the upper part on the east end of the Merriam building and it suddenly appeared to sweep through the upper section of the building.

Fire Seen Miles Away

Several thousand citizens turned out for the first fire being attracted by the reflection in the sky caused by the great mass of flames, which leaped high into the air. Huge billows of thick yellow smoke rolled heavenward and made a sight, which was seen for miles.

Main Street was jammed with people as was Cypress Street and the yards in the rear of the burning Robertson –Brett Lumber Company buildings. Freight cars were lined with spectators who climbed to the tops to gain a better vantage point.

There were comparatively few persons at the second fire although it was a much more stubborn blasé than the first.

Chief of Police William H. Philbrick distributed his men at the first blaze to keep the firefighters from being troubled by traffic and spectators.

Officer Carl Swanstrom was in command of the police squad at the second fire Special officers were pressed into service. By soon curious kind of fate the film advertised for today's show at the Scenic was entitled "Burning Gold".

Practically all of the available ladders on the motor trucks and two or more from one horse drawn truck were used on the front north and south sides of the buildings. Firemen fought the blaze from the roofs of the two structures as well as from the sides and rear.

The roof of the ell of the Merriam building and a part of the roof on the main section were damaged. The ell roof collapsed. Practically all of the stock of furniture in the building was either burned, soaked with water or smoked.

The fire worked its way into the Scenic theater building and the larger part of the roof of this building was burned. The stage scenery and curtains in the theater were destroyed or heavily damaged, as were many of the seats near the stage. Mr. Sharby the manager had installed 430 new seats in the theatre within a week.

The fire was under control shortly before 3 o'clock and before 3:30 the firemen had the blaze extinguished.

An automobile delivery truck owned by Pike & Whipple was destroyed during the fire. The truck was in the barn at the rear of the furniture store.

Firemen were called to the scene again this afternoon when remnants of a mattress began to smolder. The motor chemical responded.

———

Resolutions for the year ending 1927

A Joint Resolution was passed on March 17th, 1927 for monies received for insurance for the sum of $2,657.76 for the New Fire Station.

[from *Keene Evening Sentinel:*]

Fire equipment parked on the Keene Central Fire Station ramp being prepared for open house after the newly remodeled station, which will be open to the public for inspection today. Equipment Fire apparatus from L to R 1923 Reo-Driver - Timothy O'Connell, 1917 Kissell – Driver- Frank Reid, 1925 Ahrens Fox – Driver-Fred Morse, 1919 Mack Ladder-Driver Lyman Cass.

'FIRE'
FIRE DAMAGES PLANT OF ASHUELOT SHOE CO

Flames Originating In Stock Room Cause Loss Of Several Thousand Dollars

A fire which at first appeared to be of considerable proportions was discovered shortly before 6 o'clock Saturday afternoon on the top floor of the Jones Building on Church Street which was recently purchased by the Fitch Motor Company, Inc., and occupied by that concern and the Ashuelot Shoe Company. A still alarm and, two general alarms were sounded for the fire, which brought out all of the apparatus. The loss which resulted from water and smoke is estimated at from $6,000 to $10,000 and is covered by insurance.

The fire originated in the stock room of the shoe company located on the top floor of the building, where lasts and sole leather is stored. The heat started the automatic sprinklers and thus kept the flames down until the firemen arrived.

Smoke was pouring from the upper windows of the building when the firemen arrived. One line of hose was taken up the front stairway and water from this line was used to extinguish the flames. A considerable amount of sole leather and lasts which were stored in the room where the fire broke out were burned or damaged by water. A stock of top leather nearby was also damaged by water and smoke, although the exact extent cannot be determined until an expert on leather from the insurance company arrives.

Water poured into the second floor, the part occupied by the shoe company, damaged shoes which were in the process of manufacture and found its way into the part occupied by the Fitch Motor Company, wetting down the stock room of that concern.

There were 26 automobiles and trucks on the floor of the garage during the fire but the machines were not damaged.

The motor pumping engine was set at the corner of Main and Church Streets and the steam pumping engine on Railroad Street, south of the building, a precaution taken by Chief Engineer Eugene B. Riley to prevent a conflagration. One of the long ladders from the Mack truck was raised in front of the building that it might be in readiness. The firemen were handicapped in raising this ladder owing to the small space available.

Some trouble resulted in sounding the first general alarm as only one blow was recorded. There were seven or eight rounds of the second general alarm, however and this brought a large number of people to the neighborhood of the fire.

The shoe company has been doing a large volume of business recently and adding experienced help from time to time. The fire will not prevent the company from resuming manufacturing business today.

1928 [from *City of Keene Annual Report*]
Report of the Chief Engineer of The Fire Department
Personnel Of Fire Department For 1928
Board of Engineers

Eugene B. Riley, Chief;
Fred W. Towne, Associate;
John H. Simpson, Assistant & Clerk;
Dennis J. Foley, Assistant

Captains

John a. Dennison, Keene Steam Fire Engine and Hose Co.; Elwin H. Applin, Deluge Hose Company; Frank W. Streeter, Washington Hook and Ladder Co.

Permanent Drivers

Lyman O. Cass. Ladder Truck; Fred S. Morse, Pumping Engine; Philip A. Barrett, Combination No. 2; Frank M. Reid, Combination No. 1
Substitute Melvin I. Pishon

Keene Steam Fire Engine & Hose Co.

Lieut. H. W. Mason, Lieut. G. S. Raymond, Clerk C. F. Russell, F. J. Bennett, H. L. Barrett, R. E. Bridge, W. H. Beauregard, F. R. Austin, G. C. Erwin, F. A. Johnson, E. W. Little, R. O. Mitchell, B. G. Harvey, W. R. Messer, J. F. Piper, F. A. Russell, F. F. Stearns, J. M. Sewell, F. J. Thomas, R. H. Turner, C. E. Witham.

Deluge Hose Company

Lieut. L.H. Dean, Lieut. A. D. Irwin, Clerk W. C. Howes, C. M. Ballou, E J. Bahan, Wm. David, C. S. Dean, E. R. Damon, L. M. Fitch, Frank Foley, T. J. O'Connell, E. T. Keating, J. J. Keating, Wm. Morrison, S. W. Pollock, T. E. Roache, H. V. Roache, V. E. Swan, H. H. Spaulding.

Washington Hook & Ladder Company

Lieut. T. B. Wallbank, Lieut. W. B. Stickles, Clerk C. H. Symonds, E. J. Auger, D. P. Driscoll, S. F. Guyette, M. A. Holleren, Sidney Higgins, A. D. Mason, M. I. Pishon, T. R. Pickett, E. L. Reason, C. E. Symonds, G. C. Symonds, S. F. Thompson, and W. T. Winn.

Apparatus And Equipment

Kissel Combination Chemical and Hose: 1,000 feet fire hose, 200 feet chemical hose, one 26 foot extension ladder, one 14 foot roof ladder, two 40 gallon chemical tanks, two 3 gallon extinguishers, one foamite extinguisher, four shut-off nozzles, one Siamese for two streams into one, one hydrant gate, one set reversible couplings, two hydrant wrenches, two axes, one crow bar, one plaster hook, one adjustable door opener, two electric lanterns, two kerosene lanterns, one smoke helmet, one first aid kit, hose spanners, ladder straps, rubber coats, boots, hats, and mittens.

Mack Ladder Truck and Chemical: 239 feet of ladders, one 40 gallon chemical tank, two 3 gallon extinguishers, one Eastman deluge set, one Baker Cellar pipe, one combination door opener and hose shut- off clamp, two axes, two hammer picks, two crow bars, one time roof cutter, six ladder dogs, two plaster hooks, four pike poles, one pull down hook, one Cooper hose jacket, one pair 24 inch wire cutters, six hay forks, two hay knives, four kerosene lanterns, chains, ropes, Rubber coats, boots, hats and mittens.

Ahrens Fox Triple Combination Hose, Pump and Booster: A 750 gallon pump, 1,200 feet of fire hose, a 60 gallon booster tank, 200 feet chemical hose, two 3 gallon extinguishers, two shut-off nozzles, one Siamese for one stream into two, one hydrant gate, two hydrant wrenches, one set of reversible couplings, two axes, one crow bar, one plaster hook, one hydraulic jack, one 20 foot extension ladder, one 12 foot roof ladder, one pair 24 inch wire cutters, two electric lanterns, two kerosene lanterns, spanners, ladder straps, rubber coats, boots, hats and mittens.

Reo Combination Chemical and Hose: 800 feet fire hose, 200 feet chemical hose, one 20 foot extension ladder, one 12 foot roof ladder, two 30 gallon chemical tanks, two 3 gallon extinguishers, one foam extinguisher, one Morse three-way turret nozzle, one set reversible couplings, three shut-off nozzles, two axes, two plaster hooks, one crow bar, one hydrant gate, two hydrant wrenches, two electric lanterns, two kerosene lanterns, spanners, ladder straps, rubber coats, boots, hats and mittens.

Amoskeag 500 gallon steam fire engine tractor drawn

Chief's Car Oldsmobile Coupe

One Horse Drawn Hose Wagon

Relief Ladder Truck: Horse drawn 357 feet of ladders

Forest Fire Equipment

17 3-gallon extinguishers, one 5-gallon pump tank, 57 shovels, 24 hoes, 22 14-quart water pails.

Resolutions for the year ending 1928

A Resolution was passed on April 19th, 1928 for the purchase of a clock for the sum of $300.00 from the Standard Electric Time Company shown in their catalogue on page No. 7 and Fig. No 104, list No. 12. This was installed for the fire alarm system, master clock.

Pictured is the clock that was purchased in 1928. The purpose of this clock was to keep the master time for the fire alarm system and to look quickly to document the time of the fire call or box. Once the air tanks were installed a 24 hour tape was installed to blow the whistle automatically. The whistle is no longer used, but the clock is still used today and hangs in the Central Fire Station by the Watch Desk. Photo by Steve Goldsmith.

1929 [from *City of Keene Annual Report*]

Report of Chief Engineer Fire Department

To His Honor the Mayor and Board of Aldermen:

I hereby submit my report for the year ending December 1st, 1929.

The alert system works great, even today, to notify the deaprtment of a fire. The boxes on a pole or building can be pulled or tripped by an internal device such as a sprinkler, smoke or heat detector. The box sends an electric pulse by opening and closing the circuit and ringing a bell on the wall according to the box number. As the bell taps out on the ticker tape machine it punches holes in the paper displaying the box number. The fire department then knows the street address in which to respond. Photo by Steve Goldsmith.

There were 26 bell alarms, 239 still alarms, and 12 out of town calls, making a total of 277 alarms.

The estimated value of buildings damaged by fire, $782,350.00

Damage to buildings, $19,575.47

Insurance on said buildings, $555,400.00

Insurance paid $18,844.47.

Value of contents of said buildings, $794,816.89

Damage to the contents, $67,452.25

Insurance on said property, $755,750.00

Insurance paid, $67,452.25.

This is the largest fire loss that the City has had in many years. A large part of this loss was due to water damage at the Crescent Shoe Co. fire on April 24th.

This water damage was not the fault of the Fire Department. The fireman at the shop shutting off the sprinklers when he saw water leaking through the floor, then investigating the trouble, and then turning the sprinklers back on again, caused thus wetting stock, machines and supplies in the whole shop.

The Department has on hand 8,450 feet of double jacket rubber lined fire hose, and 1,500 feet of linen hose on hose reel in house at South Keene.

During the year there has been turned over to the Water department 450 feet of hose, also 650 feet to Highway Department for their road work.

The Motor Fire Apparatus and its equipment including tools are in very good condition, except the steam Fire Engine which is 46 years old. This piece should be replaced by a modern Pumping Engine.

There has been added to the equipment a Foam Generator for oil fires, also two Electric Sirens to replace the hand ones, one on the Kissell Combination and Reo Combination, also two gas and smoke masks.

The Fire alarm System and its circuits are in very good condition. The system has been extended from Arch Street to Arlington Avenue and Box 49 added to the circuit. This makes 49 boxes on the system.

There were two of the old fire alarm boxes replaced this year with the latest Peerless type, Box 22 and 52.

There should be purchased each year three or four new fire alarm boxes to replace the old ones, until they are all replaced. These new boxes give protection from lightning and high voltage. A modern punch register has been installed at Fire Station for recording fire alarm signals.

Recommendations:

The Board of Engineers recommends the purchase of 1,000 feet of fire hose.

A triple Combination, Pump, Hose and Booster, to replace the Steamer

Also the purchase of three fire alarm boxes to make a start on the replacing of old boxes that were installed in 1885

That a hydrant be installed on Proctor Court for protection of the two Laundry and Dry Cleaning plants.

To His Honor the Mayor and members of the Joint Standing Committee on Fire Department, Members of the Board of Engineers, Officers and members of the department, and to the public, I extend my sincere thanks and appreciation for the aid and support rendered me during the year.

EUGENE B. RILEY,
Chief Engineer Fire Department

Fire for the year 1929 was Crescent Shoe Factory, April 24th, 1929. As reported by the *Keene Evening Sentinel* on April 24th, 1929:

'FIRE'

Crescent Shoe Factory Suffers Heavy Damage Be Early Morning Fire

Two Alarms Sounded for Blaze That Causes Loss Estimated in Excess of $20,000 and Throws More than 200 Workers Out of Employment. Insurance on Building and Contents

A two-alarm fire in the shoe factory of the Crescent Company of Keene, Inc. on Water Street, shortly after 3 o'clock this morning resulted in a loss estimated in excess of $20,000 and threw more than 200 workmen out of employment. The damage by flames will not be large but the loss by water and smoke will mount to thousands of dollars. The building is owned by E. F Lane estate. There is insurance carried on the building and contents.

A Demon Called Fire

The fire was discovered by Mrs. George O'Neil of 91 Water Street, who lives directly across the street from the factory. Mrs. O'Neil telephoned the fire station and the alarm was sounded from the station. About the same time Mrs. O'Neil was awakened by the light of the flames, Edward Casavant, fireman at the shoe factory, who had arrived at the building about an hour previous to attend to the boiler, discovered the blaze and started for the fire alarm box which is directly in front of the building, when he heard the alarm being sounded.

Flames Had Good Start.

When the firemen arrived the entire front and west side of the second floor of the building appeared to be ablaze. Engineer John H. Simpson, who was one of the first to arrive there, gave orders for sounding the second alarm.

The fire was confined to the cutting room which is on the second floor of the building and at the front. The blaze extended across the front of the building a distance of about 60 feet and to the rear a distance of about 40 feet. The heat blackened the walls of the upper story and put into operation the automatic sprinkling system. Water kept the fire from spreading throughout the building. The heat however caused the leather belts to crumple although they were 50 feet or more from the flames. Water from the sprinklers soaked the leather in the stock room and shoes in the process of manufacture and the machines on the top and first stories. There was about three inches of water on the first floor after the fire was extinguished.

Heavy Water Damage.

There were several hundred cases of shoes in the shipping room ready to be sent out and also several hundred cases in the process of manufacture in the factory. Everything was thoroughly soaked with water largely from the sprinkler system. It is reported that several weeks will be required to clean the machines and make the necessary repairs for resumption of business. For several weeks past the employees had been working overtime due to the large number of orders.

Two lines of hose were laid from a hydrant in front of the building, two from a hydrant on Dunbar Street, one from the corner of Water and Grove Streets and another from a hydrant near the Russell Chair Company's factory. The Ahrens-Fox pumper was stationed on Dunbar Street and the Amoskeag Steamer went to the hydrant at the corner of Water and Grove Street on the second alarm. Neither pumper was used as the water pressure was sufficient.

Another Factory Endangered.

One line of hose was carried to the roof of the Daly Shoe Company Factory which is east of burning building and afforded the firemen an opportunity to send a stream in the east windows of the Crescent Company's building and keep the fire from spreading toward the Daly Factory. Two lines were used in the windows on the west side of the Crescent factory building and these halted the blaze from extending north toward Dunbar Street. Another line of hose was carried in a front window of the factory.

Chief of Police Harry F. Buckminster answered the alarm in plain clothes and finding that his men had things well in hand upon his arrival at the scene of the fire he went to the station and donned his uniform and patrolled one of the business sections beats, taking no chances of anyone putting anything over while the fire was in progress. It was the first time he has covered a regular beat since he was appointed chief.

———————

Personnel Of Fire Department

For 1929

Board of Engineers remains the same as last year.

Captains

Captains remain the same as last year.

Permanent Drivers

Frank M. Reid moved to Combination No. 2 and Samuel J. Guyette became Driver of Combination No. 1. Other driver remains the same.

Keene Steam Fire Engine & Hose Co.

Remain the same:

Deluge Hose Company

Remain the same:

Washington Hook & Ladder

Remain the same:

NOTE: The Firefighters that have moved on have not been listed, and only new members are listed, and the companies remain the same as 1927.

Apparatus And Equipment:

Kissell Combination Chemical & Hose remain the same:

Mack Ladder Truck & Chemical remain the same.

Ahrens Fox Triple Combination Hose Pump & Booster remain the same.

Reo Combination Chemical & Hose remains the same.

Chief's Car Oldsmobile Coupe remains the same.

Amoskeag 5,000 Gallon Steam Fire Engine Tractor Drawn remains the same.

Relief Ladder Truck Horse drawn. 357 feet of ladders remain the same.

Forest Fire Equipment remains the same.

Resolutions for the year ending 1929

A Joint Resolution relating to Foamite Generator was purchased for a price of $500.00.

1930 [from *City of Keene Annual Report*]

Report of Chief Engineer Fire Department

Keene, N. H., December 1st, 1930.

To His Honor the Mayor and Board of Aldermen:

I hereby submit my report for the year ending November 30th, 1930.

There were 24 bell alarms, 311 still alarms, making a total of 335 alarms, 14 of these calls were out of town.

The estimated value of buildings damaged by fire, $647,900.00

Damage to buildings, $11,762.41

Insurance on said buildings, $383,350.00

Insurance paid $11,762.41.

Value of contents of said buildings, $33,500.00.

Damage to contents, $14,712.94

Insurance on said contents, $29,100.00

Insurance paid $14,712.94.

The Department has on hand 9,200 feet of double jacket rubber lined fire hose and 1,500 feet of linen hose on hose reel at South Keene hose house.

During the year there has been turned over to the Highway Department 200 feet of hose for its road work.

The motor fire apparatus and its equipment including tools are in first class condition.

There has been added to the department a 750 gallon pumping engine. This pump is of the high pressure type, and will deliver its capacity at 150 pounds pump pressure instead of 120 pounds as is the minimum for capacity. This pump will also on long lines of hose build up a pressure at the pump of more than 400 lbs., an important factor in overcoming the friction of fire hose, which is 21 lbs. to the 100 feet of hose when delivering at the nozzle 300 gallons per minute.

This pump was given the Underwriters test on August 20th, at the Faulkner and Colony mill pond on West Street by F. S.

Birtwhistle of the State Board of Underwriters and was pronounced O.K. in every way.

This test consists of two hours at capacity or 750 gallons at 120 pounds pressure, 30 minutes at half capacity or 375 gallons at 200 pounds pump pressure and 30 minutes at one third capacity of 250 gallons at 250 pounds pump pressure.

There has been installed on the Ladder Truck a new Three-Way Deluge Gun and an electric Siren. This makes all the apparatus equipped with electric Sirens.

The Fire Alarm System is in very good condition.

The circuits have been trimmed out this autumn from twigs and small limbs which cause the circuits a certain amount of grounding. Also some labor has been done in replacing cross arms and pulling up slack wire to keep the system in proper shape.

The under-ground wire on No. 4 Circuit has been extended on West and St. James Street where the poles are to be removed.

There have been two new fire alarm boxes purchased and installed to replace two of the old boxes. They are Box 14 on Water Street corner Grove, and Box 16 on Main Street corner Marlboro.

The replacement of the old boxes should be continued until all of the old boxes are changed.

Recommendations:

The Board of Engineers recommends the purchase of 1,000 feet of fire hose.

Two fire alarm boxes for replacement of the old type.

Also that a fire alarm box be installed at the corner of West Street as there is no box on the west side of Square.

And that the 4 inch connected hydrant at the corner of the old Sentinel Building be replaced with at least a 6 inch connected hydrant.

To His Honor the Mayor, and members of the Joint Standing Committee on Fire Department, Members of the Board of Engineers, Officers and Members of the Department, and to the Public, I extend my sincere thanks and appreciation for the aid and support rendered me during the year.

EUGENE B. RILEY,
Chief Engineer Fire Department

Fire on November 18th, 1930 in the E. F. Lane Block. As Reported by the *Keene Evening Sentinel* on November 19th, 1930:

'FIRE'

Flames And Smoke Cause Heavy Loss In E. F. L. Block

Fire in Woolworth Store Basement Results in $20,000 Damage

Damage approximating $20,000 was caused by fire which drove between 50 and 60 person from their beds in the E. F. L. block on Main Street shortly before midnight Tuesday and which, combined with smoke and water ruined the greater part of the new Christmas stock of the F. W. Woolworth company store in the basement of the building.

Trustees of the E. F. Lane estate owners of the block estimated damage to the building at $2,000. Charles M. LaCourse, Manager of the Woolworth store, said this morning that losses from stock stored in the basement would total between $15,000 and $20,000.

During the excitement from the fire and the scramble to get out of the smoke choked building, one woman fainted and a man near suffocation was carried down three flights of stairs to safety. The smoke victim, William Henderson, was asleep on the top floor of the four story brick apartment and business building.

Being deaf, the man was not awakened by the clamor and confusion. After everyone was outside Robert Henry Jr. who lives in the building remembered Mr. Henderson and rushed upstairs to his room. He found the man asleep in the smoke filled quarters and nearly overcome by the fumes.

Several women were partly overcome by smoke and excitement while they carried to snatch valuables without waiting to learn the extent of the fire, which was confined to the Woolworth storage room beneath the sidewalk. Children were rushed outside of the building in short order and some were taken by their parents to the police station where they waited with them until other provisions were made.

Some children and women spent the night at homes of relatives and friends and others returned to their home several hours later when the sleeping quarters had been ventilated.

Despite the lateness of the hour, several hundred people left their homes and crowed at the front and rear of the building where the fire hose were laid.

The fire started in a waste paper pile in the Woolworth store basement and was discovered almost simultaneously by several persons.

Lewis Finestone, manager of the M. F. L. block adjoining the Woolworth store was checking inventories. Going to the basement of his store to look at room stock he saw flames through a glass partition in the Woolworth stockroom. He rushed upstairs and telephoned to the fire department.

Almost at the same time Miss Doris Darling, who lives in the block with her mother, Mrs. Flora Darling, became alarmed at the smell of some and call the janitor Robert Henry. Mr. Henry quickly discovered the fire and sent a still alarm to the fire station.

Officer Griffin Rings Alarm

The apparatus had not arrived before Patrolman Michael Griffin saw smoke coming through the front door of the store and rang Box 8 at Main and Railroad Streets.

The men with the chemical apparatus which responded to the still alarm had deadened the blaze by the time the hose outfit arrived. A door at the rear of the building near the origin of the fire was broken in and the hose dragged in side. When the water struck the blaze dense columns of smoke poured out of the opening making entrance impossible.

At the same time smoke billowed out of the front of the store where other hose had been dragged through to a stairway leading to the rear of the store to the basement. A thick door at the foot of the stairway closed the passage and helped to box the flames in the storage room.

Flames Reach Store

Had the door not been closed to retard the spread of the flames the fire would have quickly found its way to the light, flammable articles on the counters of the store and would have greatly endangered the entire building. As it was the fire had crept through paneling along the stairway and was burning cloth articles on one of the counters when firemen entered. A couple of pails of water extinguished the flames which were then henceforth confined to the basement.

A gas pipe which sprang a leak in the basement was a menace to firemen until the supply could be shut off.

The fire burned in places throughout more than half the area of the stockroom. Water poured on the flames stood several inches deep on the floor before the fire was extinguished.

Electric and gas connections in the basement were cut off. This morning Mr. LaCourse with one or two stockmen carrying flashlights splashed about with rubber boots endeavoring to determine the extent of the damage.

Half of Stock Ruined

Until lights are restored it will be difficult to tell to what extent the store floor has been burned, but Mr. LaCourse said that at least half of his stock was ruined. The loss is especially heavy at this time because of extra holiday goods on hand.

Trustees of the Lane estate, Roy M. Pickard, James T. Melvin and Ferdinand D. Rodenbush, went over the building this morning and said damages to the building would be about $2,000. Besides damaged in the basement and stairway, the ceiling and walls of the stove were discolored by smoke and will have to be repainted, they said. They could not tell whether the store floor would have to be relayed. There was no material damage to the rooms above the store they said.

Mr. Finestone said that goods in the Fishman store had been saturated with smoke and that he had notified the firm headquarters and that a representative would be at the store today to decide about damages. Only a small quantity of water seeped into the Fishman storeroom.

Upstairs in the apartments, which this morning still smelled of smoke, women were hanging clothing out to air on improvised clothes lines stretched in front of windows.

Business places on the second floor of the building include the dentist office of Dr. R. J. Parker, a beauty shop and a cloths cleaning establishment.

An incomplete list of occupants of rooms and apartments in the building includes Mr. And Mrs. Robert Henry and family, William Henderson, Maude L. Marshall, Mrs. Vera D. Wilmont and two children, Mr. And Mrs. Otto B. Hausbandt, Edward F. Sevigney, and daughter, Mrs. Elizabeth Beaudoin and two daughters, Mr. And Mrs. William G. Dewya and two children, William LaBarre, Henry Naylor, Denis B. Kearney. Miss Edith Matthews, Mrs. Flora Darling and daughter, Mr. And Mrs. Warren H. Jennison and two children and Miss Frances Congdon, a quest of Mrs. Darling. The names of others with rooms in the building could not be learned.

Personnel Of Fire Department For 1930

Board of Engineers remains the same as last year.

Captains

Captains remain the same as last year.

Permanent Drivers

Permanent Drivers remain the same as last year.

Keene Steam Fire Engine & Hose Co.

Remain the same:

Deluge Hose Company

Remain the same:

Hook And Ladder Company

Remain the same:

Apparatus And Equipment:

Kissell Combination Chemical & Hose remain the same:

Mack Ladder Truck & Chemical remain the same.

Ahrens Fox Triple Combination Hose Pump & Booster No. 1 remains the same.

Ahrens Fox Triple Combination Hose Pump & Booster No. 2

A 750 gallon pump, 1,300 feet of fire hose, 80 gallon booster tank, 200 feet chemical hose, one soda-acid extinguisher, one Foamite extinguisher, two shut-off nozzles, one Siamese for one stream into two, one hydrant gate, two hydrant wrenches, one set of reversible couplings, two axes, one crow bar, one plaster hook, one hydraulic jack, one 20 foot extension ladder, one 12 foot roof ladder, two electric lanterns, spanners, ladder straps, rubber coats, boots, hats and mittens.

[*Compiler's Note*: This pumper is known as "OLD ROSIE." This 1930 Ahrens Fox is still a member of the Keene Fire Department and is used for funerals and parades.]

Keene's new Ahrens Fox, triple combination hose pump and booster #2. Keene now has 2 Ahrens Fox Pumpers. The 2 pumpers are positive pressure piston pumps and pump 750 gallons per minute. Photo by Ronald Amadon.

Reo Combination Chemical & Hose remains the same.

Chief's Car Oldsmobile Coupe remains the same.

Amoskeag 500 Gallon Steam Fire Engine Tractor Drawn remains the same.

Relief Ladder Truck Horse drawn. 357 feet of ladders remain the same.

500 Gallon Steam Fire Engine Button Horse Drawn

Forest Fire Equipment remains the same.

Resolutions for the year ending 1930

A Joint Resolution was passed on June 19th, 1930 for the Fire Department to contract for the purchase of one 750 gallon Ahrens Fox Triple Combination Piston Pump at a cost not to exceed $13,000.

A Resolution was passed on October 16th, 1930 for the old Amoskeag Steamer belong to the Fire Department be sold and the Chief Engineer and Standing Committee on Fire Department be hereby empowered to dispose of same at their discretion to the best advantage of the City.

[*Compiler's Note*: Chief Eugene B. Riley was empowered to dispose of the Amoskeag Steamer and he elected to dispose of the Button Steamer instead. No notes were found as to why but it was believed that the Amoskeag had been rebuilt and seemed to be a better save for the City Fire Department.]

Steamer Company in front of Keene Central Fire Station Standing 1st to R F. Russell, C. Russell, F. Stearns, J. Dennison, G. Raymond, J. Sewall, R. Turner, B. Harvey, G. Irwin, E. Little, F. Thomas, R. Bridge, A. Little, F. Bennett. Driver of the Kissell is Mel Pishon and Driver of the new 1930 Ahrens Fox is Frank Reid. Driver of 1917 Kissel: Mel Pishon. Fire Dept. photo.

After "ROSIE" was delivered, a full complement of motorized equipment was taken in front of the Central Fire Station on Vernon Street from L to R 1919 Mack Ladder – Driver Lyman Cass, 1923 Reo – Driver Sam Guyette, 1925 Ahrens Fox – Driver Fred Morse, 1917 Kissel – Driver Mel Pishon and the new 1930 Ahrens Fox "ROSIE" and Driver Frank Reid. Fire Dept. photo.

1931 [from *City of Keene Annual Report*]

Report of the Chief Engineer of Fire Department

To His Honor the Mayor and Board of Aldermen:

I hereby submit my report for the year ending November 30th, 1931.

There were 23 bell alarms, 255 still alarms, making a total of 278 alarms, 11 of these calls were out of town.

The estimated value of buildings damaged by fire, $541,877.00

Damage to buildings, $23,590.35
Insurance on said buildings, $344,540.00
Insurance paid $20,430.48.
Value of contents of buildings, $250,932.07
Damage to contents, $26,026.83
Insurance on said property, $257,200.00
Insurance paid $26,026.83.

The number of alarms for the year are 57 less than that of last year, but the losses as you will note are some larger. The forest fires for the past year have been less in number than for several years.

There has been added to the department for new equipment three Salvages covers, these covers are 12X18 feet in size and will cover up a whole room of furniture, also one smoke and gas mask, this makes the department three of these masks. There has been installed on the apparatus three Cambridge wind-shields, as follows: Engine No. 1, Engine No. 2, and Ladder No. 1.

The Motor Fire Apparatus and its equipment including tools are in very good condition, the ladders have all been refinished during the year. The Chief's car has been repainted. The tires on Engine No. 1 have been renewed; also the rear tires on the Kissell Combination, these tires were all six years old.

The department has on hand 9,000 feet of double jacket rubber lined 2 ½ inch fire hose, and 1,500 feet of unlined linen hose on reel and in hose-house at South Keene. There has

been turned over to the Water Department 200 feet of unserviceable hose.

The Fire Alarm System and its circuits are also in very good condition. Quite a large amount of damage was done to the fire alarm system on March 8th, and April 7th, also July 21st, caused from limbs falling on wires and breaking them, and this crossing them up with the high voltage wires, damaging alarm boxes, under-ground wires, and equipment at the station. There has been installed on the fire alarm circuits a complete set of vacumn lighting arresters on poles where the over-head wires enter the underground, also a set at the station to work in connection with the present Protector Board. This will give better protection to the circuits and boxes and also the equipment at the station.

There has been one new fire alarm box and pedestal installed during the year at the corner of Main and West streets, and numbered box 7 and the old box 7 at the Holbrook wholesale grocery on St. James Street has been changed to 512. The underground wire on No. 4 circuit, West Street has been extended from St. James Street to the Turner Inn.

There has been a new fire alarm battery installed of 160 cells to replace the old one, as the life of these batteries are four to five years.

Recommendations:

The Board of Engineers recommend the purchase of 1,000 feet of fire hose, also another permanent man be added to the force at the station, making five men in all. A compressed air whistle was also to be installed at the station.

The permanent man and the compressed air whistle are recommended by the State Board of Underwriters.

To His Honor the Mayor, and members of the Joint Standing Committee on Fire Department, members of the Board of Engineers, Officers and members of the department, and to the Public, I extend my sincere thanks and appreciation for the aid and support rendered m during the year.

Respectfully submitted,

EUGENE B. RILEY, Chief Fire Department.

Fire for 1931 was on March 6th, 1931 Box 182 at 4.50 a. m. for the Keene Development Co. Building, Occupied by A. Henkel & Son on Congress Street for a fire with damage of $24,727.00. As Reported by the *Keene Evening Sentinel* on March 6th, 1931:

'FIRE'

The Plant of Henkel & Son, Manicure Device Makers, Is Destroyed By Flames

Fire which was discovered before 5 o'clock this morning in the plant of Henkel and Son manufactures of manicure implements on Congress Street destroyed the main building and damaged much of the machinery and stock. Loss which may reach $20.000 is partially covered by insurance. The origin of the fire has not been determined. Two alarms from Box 182 were sounded.

The fire was discovered at 4:50 by employees in the Congress Street factory of the International Narrow Fabric company and they telephoned the fire station.

While the first round of the alarm was sounding the roof of the building tumbled in which determined that the fire had been in progress considerable time before it was seen. Fire was in every part of the main structure when the firemen arrived. Two small buildings east of the main structure which houses some heavy and valuable machinery were saved.

Owned by-Development Company

The building is owned by the Keene Development Company and is part of the buildings formerly occupied by the Morgan Manufacturing Company. The main plant of what was formerly the Morgan Manufacturing

Company was threatened but firemen kept water on the building. The new Ahrens Fox pumper balked near the Hotel Ellis on the way to the fire. It is believed that gears on the drive shift broke a mechanic from the factory of the fire apparatus was in Keene today making repairs on the apparatus.

The fact that the pumper did not reach the fire did not apparently cripple the department, as the pumper which was on duty pulled all at the water from one of the hydrants near the fire so the second piece of apparatus would not have had any water.

There were two good streams flowing from the pumper and these were used to advantage in extinguishing the blaze.

The loss is hard to estimate as it is not known how bad the machines in the plant were damaged. The factory employees had been working overtime recently; some of the employees had been working nights and Thursday night there were men working in the plant until

9 o'clock. About 30 men were employed in the factory.

August Henkel, senior member of the firm stated this afternoon that he expected operations would not be interrupted very long, as arrangements had been made with the Keene Development Company to use the west portion of the brick factory formerly occupied by the Morgan Manufacturing Company, which is but a short distance from the burned structure.

Work began immediately after the factory cleaning up the debris and salvaging the machinery which can be transferred to the new location. New machinery will be purchased at once so that operations can be continued and the large number of orders, which the firm had, can be filled without much loss of time.

———————

Personnel Of Fire Department For 1931

Board of Engineers

Board of Engineers remained the same as last year.

Captains

The Steamer Hose Company and the Deluge Hose Company remain the same. The Hook and Ladder Company has a new Captain Thomas B. Wallbank.

Permanent Drivers

Permanent Drivers remained the same as last year.

Keene Steam Fire Engine & Hose Company

Remained the same except for the addition of A. I. Little

Deluge Hose Company

Remained the same:

Hook & Ladder Company

Remained the same except for the addition of F. W. Streeter

Apparatus And Equipment

Ahrens Fox Triple Combination No. 1
  Ahrens Fox Triple Combination No. 2
  Mack Ladder truck and Chemical
  Reo Combination Chemical and Hose
  Kissel Combination Chemical and Hose
  Relief Ladder Truck Horse Drawn
  500 Gallon Steam Fire Engine Horse Drawn
  Forest Fire Equipment

Resolutions and Ordinances for the year ending 1931

On March 19th, 1931 an Ordinance relating to the construction, alteration, maintenance and use of buildings was passed.

Amend section 9 of the General Provisions of the Ordinance relative to the Construction Alteration, Maintenance and Use of Buildings in the City of Keene passed December 15th, 1927, by inserting in place there of the following new section:

Section 9: No wooden addition or alteration to any building now existing within such fire district shall be made except on license thereof first obtained from the Mayor and Board of Aldermen upon recommendation of the Inspector of Buildings who may prescribe such terms, conditions, limitations, and restrictions as he deems wise; provided, however, that any alterations which, in the opinion of the Building Inspector, do not materially affect the strength of the building or which, in the opinion of the Fire Chief, do not increase the fire risk in said building, may be made without such license.

Before such license is granted a notice of application thereof shall be published three days successively in some one daily newspaper printed in the City of Keene. Such wooden structure or addition shall be made in accordance with the requirements of this chapter.

1932 [from *City of Keene Annual Report*]

Report of the Chief Engineer of Fire Department

To His Honor the Mayor and Board of Aldermen:

I hereby submit my report for the year ending November 30th, 1932.

There were 25 bell alarms. 324 still alarms, making a total of 349 alarms. 23 of these calls were out of town.

The estimated value of buildings damaged by fire, $712,643.00
  Damage to buildings, $38,854.55
  Insurance on said buildings, $535,360.00
  Insurance paid $38,854.55.
  Value of contents of buildings, $407,444.58
  Damage to contents, $67,894.76
  Insurance on said contents, $404.543.18
  Insurance paid $67,894.76.

The number of alarms for the year will be the largest the department has ever answered.

Also the fire loss will be the largest, for the reasons that a large percent of the fires for the year have been in the high valued sections. But taking in consideration the value of buildings and their contents, where the fires have occurred, compared with the loss will give the department some credit for their efforts.

There has been another man added to the permanent force of the department. This makes five permanent men and a Chief in the permanent force.

There has also been added to the department for new equipment, a compressed air outfit for the outside alarms.

Alert Whistle

Figure 1. Whistle. Photo by Steven Goldsmith.

Figure 2. Airtank. Photo by Steven Goldsmith.

[from the compiler, Steven Goldsmith:]

In 1932 three large 4 foot steel riveted air tanks were placed in the basement of the fire station. These air tanks were than piped to the hose tower roof some 65 feet tall to the whistle shown in *Figure 1*. A 10-horse air electric compressor supplies the tanks shown in *Figure 2*. The whistle was blown for fires and at noon and at 9'oclock when curfew was put into effect for World War II. The whistle is still used for fires in the Keene Fire Department to sound 2nd alarm and for Mutual Aid calls to other towns for fires.

This equipment consists of three large air tanks 4x10 feet and carry a pressure of 120 pounds, these tanks are all equipped with safety valves, also an air-compressor with a ten horse-power motor, a switch-board with automatic switches and pressure regulators, and an 8-inch three-chime whistle. This outfit has a storage of air that will give the department two full alarms in succession. This equipment was installed by all local men and by doing this the city saved from $300 to $500 on the installation.

_____

The Motor Fire Apparatus and its equipment are in very good condition. There has been a new engine installed in the Kissel

Combination truck, as the old one was beyond repairing. This truck is used for forest fires to carry men and equipment in the forest fire season, also to truck hose to and from fires, and in the winter months is loaded with fire hose.

The Fire Station has been painted on the outside by the permanent men at the station. New lead flashing has been put on the barn roof and the tin roofs have been painted and patched.

The department has on hand 9,450 feet of double jacket rubber lined hose and 1,200 feet of linen unlined hose at South Keene in their house. There has been 350 feet of unserviceable hose turned over to the Water Department, also sold to them 200 feet of new and serviceable hose.

The Fire Alarm System and its circuits are in very good condition. There have been purchased two fire alarm boxes to replace old ones; these are Box 27 at the corner of Washington Street and Washington Ave., also Box 43 West Street at Faulkner and Colony mill opp. Ashuelot Street. Fire alarm wires changed over to north side of Vernon Street and poles on south side removed.

Also fire alarm wires on Ralston Street have been changed to the West side of the street and the poles on the east side of the street have been removed.

Box 47 which was at the old Glue Company's plant on Court Street has been changed to the junction of Court Street and Allen Court.

Recommendations

The Board of Engineers recommend the purchase of 1,000 feet of fire hose, also that two new fire alarm boxes be purchased to replace old ones now in service.

To His Honor the Mayor, and the Joint Standing Committee on Fire department, also to the Police Department, and the board of Engineers. Officers and members of the Fire department, I extend my sincere thanks and appreciation for the aid and support rendered me during the year.

Respectfully submitted,
EUGENE B. RILEY, Chief Fire department.

Fire on Sunday February 28th, 1932 in the business area of Keene, Spencer Hardware Company and W. L Goodnow Company. Reported by the *Keene Evening Sentinel* on February 29th, 1932:

'FIRE'

FIRE IN LANE BLOCK CAUSES LOSS ESTIMATED IN EXCESS OF $40,000. STARTS IN SPENCER STORE CELLAR

Spencer Hardware Company and W. L. Goodnow Company Stores Heaviest Losers in Sunday Morning Blaze, Dense Smoke Overcomes Several Firemen

Fire which threatened a section of the business area of the city about noon Sunday caused a loss in the Lane block, at the corner of Main and Church Streets, of more than $40,000. Several firemen were temporarily overcome by some, several were cut and bruised, and Elmer Damon a hoseman, was hurled across Church Street by an explosion of gases which accumulated in the cellar of the Spencer Hardware Company, where the fire originated. Extra police were called to duty and fire lines were established because of the large number of people attracted to the scene.

The heaviest loss will be on the stock of the Spencer Hardware Company. There was about $20,000 worth of merchandise in the basement and this is probably a total loss, according to one of the members of the company. Stock in the store and in the storerooms on the second and third floors was also damaged. The W. L. Goodnow Company also suffered a loss from smoke which may be more than $15,000. Damage to the building will probably be between $5,000 and $6,000. Tenants in the block were driven out during the fire. There will be several hundred dollars damage to property of tenants.

The fire was probably the most stubborn which firemen have had to combat in many years due to the fact that the streams of water did not reach the blaze on the north side of the basement. The firemen combated the blaze from the Church Street side of the building, which was the only access to the fire. A hole was cut in the floor of the main store near the north side and a cellar pipe set was used in this opening and in a short time this stream of water checked the blaze.

After the fire was checked there was a stream of flame protruding from a gas pipe where the connection had been melted. A gasman was called to shut off the gas in order to prevent the flame from stating another fire.

Robert Henry Discovers Blaze

The fire was discovered by Robert Henry, janitor of the building, as he entered the store to attend the fire in the basement. He summoned the motor chemical apparatus by still alarm. When firemen arrived they realized that the fire was of larger proportions than could be handled by one piece of apparatus and a few firemen and orders were given for sounding a general alarm and Francis Callahan, who was on the scene, ran to the corner of Main and Railroad Streets and sounded Box 8. Many of the firemen left church services to answer the call.

———

[from *Keene Evening Sentinel:*]

'FIRE'

FIRE IN LANE BLOCK CAUSES HEAVY LOSS

Smoke in dense clouds, which filled Church Street, poured out the basement windows and at times tongues of flames shout out the windows driving the fire men back. During the progress of the fire an explosion of gases at one of the windows blew Elmer Damon across Church Street and he landed up against the curb, but he clung to the nozzle of the hose which he was holding at the window. He sustained an injury to his right leg but remained on duty.

The fire had not progressed long before the smoke began to work its way up through the store into the apartments and stock rooms on the third and fourth floors of the building. Occupants of the block were forced to leave the building owing to the dense smoke.

On Lookers Get Ducking

Men on duty on the hose lines had to be relieved from time to time because the smoke which poured from the windows. At one time a line of hose "got away" from the firemen and a number of people who were watching the blaze from Church Street received a ducking and a small boy was knocked down by the nozzle which was flopping about in the street.

Samuel Guyette smallest firemen in the department was one of the men overcome by some and cut by glass. He had entered the store wearing a gas mask and was partially overcome when he reached the side door on Church Street. He succeeded in breaking the glass in the door, but was unable to crawl out through the opening. Several firemen and volunteers succeeding in pulling Mr. Guyette through the opening and to safety. Among the other firemen overcome by smoke where Bertram G. Harvey, Samuel Thompson and Ralph Turner.

Nine firemen were treated for cuts and bruises having sustained injuries during the progress of the fire.

When the fire was extinguished there was nearly two feet of water in the basement of the store of the Spencer Hardware company and a large amount of stock was afloat. The basement was used by the company for storage of a large amount of stock, immediately after the fire a city pump was used to pump water from the basement.

Extra Policemen Called

Officer Walter A. Perry, who was on duty at the police station realized the seriousness of the fire and summoned the night officers and several special policemen for duty. Chief of Police Harry W. Buckminster, who was having a day off from duty went to the police station and remained on duty there and sent Officer Perry to the scene of the fire. The police summoned M. Edward Kepple to shut off the gas main.

The police established fire lines and ordered automobiles parked in front of the Goodnow store to be moved. The night officers called for duty were Carl B. Swanstrom, Clifton A. Smith and Michael F. Griffin and the special officers on duty were Fred J. Bergeron, William Cotter and Harry N. Aldrich. The officers on duty at the station, who went to the fire besides Officer Perry, were William J. Wheelock and William C. Hardley.

Much credit is due the firemen for the manner in which they handled the fire and checked it before it burned through the floor of the store.

———

As Reported by the *Keene Evening Sentinel* on September 22nd, 1932:

TO IMPROVE EQUIPMENT OF FIRE DEPARTMENT

City Government Committee Will Expend About $500 in Making Changes

Improvements and necessary changes, which the city government joint standing committee on fire department is planning to carry out a cost of approximately $500, were discussion at a meeting Thursday afternoon in the fire station.

The changes contemplated include the moving of fire alarm box 47, near the site of

Spencer Hardware Store in Sunday morning blaze, picture taken after the fire. Photo by Granite State Studio.

the old glue shop on Court Street, to Allen Court and Court Street. This will provide better protection for the property owners in that section. The change will require the purchase of about a mile of cooper wire.

The committee favors the purchase of a few modern alarm boxes to replace the old type, which have been in use since the alarm circuit was installed. It has been the policy of the department in recent years to replace the old type boxes as fast as possible.

Attention was called to the committee by Chief Eugene B. Riley, of the discovery of the theft of about 60 feet of lead flashing from the roof of the station buildings. This damage will have to be replaced.

Those at the meeting included Alderman Claude A. Putnam, Councilman Reginald F. Howe and Earl W. Little, Chief Riley and Engineers John Simpson and Dennis J. Foley.

———

As Reported by the *Keene Evening Sentinel* on September 23rd, 1932:

'FIRE'

FARM BUILDINGS BURN ON OLD WALPOLE ROAD

Home of Mr. and Mrs. C. G. Crain Destroyed With Livestock; Loss $5,000 to $7,000

Farm buildings owned by Charles G. Crain on the Old Walpole Road, were destroyed by fire this afternoon. The loss is estimated at about $5,000 to $7,000. The fire started in the barn. Mr. Crain had insurance on his buildings but none on hay and other articles. Volunteers saved some of the furniture on the first floor of the house.

Soon after the fire was discovered in the barn the flames spread rapidly and within a short time the house, which was about 25 feet distant, caught fire from the intense heat.

The Keene fire department was called and a motor pumper responded with several firemen. No water was available and the firemen were unable too safe the house, as they could have done had there been a supply of water in the vicinity of the buildings.

Besides the buildings, Mr. and Mrs. Crain lost between 40 and 50 tons of hay, two horses, about 40 hens, two dogs, farming implements and tools, wagons, harnesses, furniture, potatoes and nearly 500 cans of fruits, vegetables and berries which Mrs. Crain had canned during the summer. The barn was 40 by 60 feet in size and the house was a two and a half story structure.

Mr. Crain is undecided as to whether he will rebuild.

This fire was in Surry but the picture was in the Keene Fire Department Scrapbook.

———

Personnel Of Fire Department

Board of Engineers

Eugene B. Riley, Chief
John H. Simpson Assistant and Clerk
Dennis J. Foley, Assistant Fred W. Towne, Associate

Captains

John A Dennison, Steamer Hose Co.
Elwin H. Applin, Deluge Hose Co.
Thomas B. Wallbank, Hook & Ladder Co.

Permanent Drivers

Lyman O. Cass, Ladder Truck Fred S. Morse, Engine No. 1 Frank M. Read, Engine No. 2 Samuel J. Guyette, Combination No. 1 Charles M. Ballou Combination No. 2

Fire September 23rd, 1932 Old Walpole Road the Charles Crane residence. L to R - Paul Symonds Sr., Chief Riley, Frank Read in seat and Charles Ballow. Rosie 1930 Ahrens Fox and the house burnt to the ground, property inside was saved to a degree.

Keene Steamer Hose Company in front of the 1917 Kissel and the 1930 Ahrens Fox at the Central Fire Station on Vernon Street in 1932. As members listed from L to R: Fred Russell, Charles Russell "clerk," Frank Sters, Capt., John Dennison, George Raymond, John Sewall, Ralph Turner, Bert Harvey, George Irwin, Earl Little, Fordyce Thomas, Roy Bridge, Albert Little, Frank Bennett, Driver Mel Pisham "Kissel" and Driver Frank Read "Ahrens Fox, "Old Rosie".

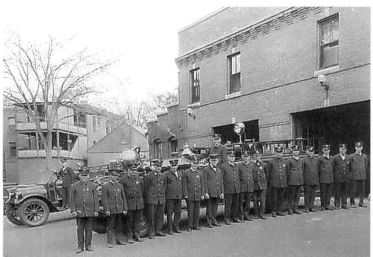

Keene Deluge Hose Company in front of the 1923 Reo and the 1924 Ahrens Fox at the Central Fire Station on Vernon Street in 1932. Pictured L to R: Timothy O'Connell, Clarence Dean, Verne Swan, Lewis Dean, Edward Keating, Jeremiah J. Keating, Steve Pollock, Harry Spaulding, Charles Ballou, Capt. Ike Applin, Elmer Damon, Gardner Davis, Harry Roche, "Kid" Irwin, Frank Reid, Tom E. Roche, Driver 1923 Reo Sam Guyette and Driver 1924 Ahrens Fox Fred Morse.

Steamer Hose Company

Lieut. H. W. Mason, Lieut. G. C. Raymond Clerk, C. F. Russell, F. J. Bennett, R. E. Bridge, G. C. Erwin, B. G. Harvey, R. H. Turner, J. F. Piper, F. A. Russell, E. W. Little, J. M. Sewell, F. J. Thomas, A. I. Little, C. E. Witham, F. F. Stearns.

Deluge Hose Company

Lieut. L. H. Dean, Lieut. A. D. Irwin, Clerk, W. C. Howes, T. E. Roach, Wm. David, C. S. Dean, E. R. Damon, Frank Foley, T. J. O'Connell, E. T. Keating, J. J. Keating, Wm. Morrison, S. W. Pollock, H. V. Roache, P. E. Symonds, V. E. Swan.

Hook & Ladder Company

Lieut. W. B. Stickles, Lieut. E. L. Reason, Clerk, C. H. Symonds, E. J Auger, D. P. Driscoll, Sidney Higgins, A. D Mason, M. I. Pishon, T. R. Pickett, C. E. Symonds, G. H. Symonds, S. F. Thompson, W. T. Winn, F. W. Streeter, and F. J. Driscoll.

Apparatus And Equipment

Ahrens-Fox Triple Combination No. 1,
    Ahrens-Fox Triple Combination No. 2
    Mack Ladder Truck and Chemical
    Reo Combination Chemical and Hose
    Kissell Combination Chemical and Hose
    Chief's Car Oldsmobile Coupe

Washington Hook and Ladder Company *in front of the 1919 Mack Ladder at the Central Fire Station on Vernon Street in 1932. Members listed from L to R: Buckley Redson, Dennis Driscoll, Tom Pickett, Bill Winn, Mel Pisham, Cleon Symonds, Frank Streeter, Ed Avger, Clare Symonds, Sam Thompson, Bill Stickles, George Symonds, Capt. Tom Wallbank, and Driver Lyman Cass 1919 Mack Ladder.*

Relief Ladder Truck 357 Horse drawn
500 Gallon Steam Fire Engine Horse drawn (Amoskeag)
Forest Fire Equipment

1933 [from *City of Keene Annual Report*]

Report of the Chief Engineer of Fire Department

To His Honor the Mayor and Board of Aldermen:

I hereby submit my report for the year ending November 30th, 1933.

There were 15 bell alarms, 330 still alarms, making a total of 345 alarms. 12 of these calls were out of town.

The estimated value of buildings damaged by fire, $300,600.00

Damage to buildings, $5,237.67
Insurance on said buildings, $208,585.00
Insurance paid $5,237.67.
Value of contents of buildings, $155,200.00
Damage to contents $2,739.09
Insurance on said contents, $167,600.00
Insurance paid $2,739.09.

The number of alarms the department has answered for the year is four less than that of last year, but the fire loss is only about one-tenth of that of last year. It is the smallest fire loss for 18 years. Last year the largest loss that could be traced on record.

The Motor Fire Apparatus and its equipment are in very good condition except the Reo Combination Chemical and hose, which is too light for its load and service required of it, and should be replaced in the near future with a modern piece of apparatus.

The Mack Ladder Truck has been changed over to steel disk wheels and pneumatic tires. This piece of apparatus was purchased thirteen years ago with solid tires which was being used on heavy equipment at that time and has continued on them until this time. The new tires are 38x7 on the front and 40x8 on the rear. This makes a more modern piece of apparatus, as it will carry its load easier and a big advantage as to its safety, as solid tires are very slippery on snow and ice.

The department has on had 9,500 feet of double jacket rubber lined fire hose and about 1,200 feet of linen unlined hose at South Keene in hose house. There has been 200 feet of unserviceable hose, and 150 feet of new hose sold to the Water Department. Also sold was 300 feet of unserviceable hose to the Highway Department.

The Fire Alarm System is in very good condition. There have been purchased two fire alarm boxes for replacement. They are box 6 Main Street corner Emerald, and Box 42 West Street corner School. There were also seven new outside box doors with quick pull attachments, making these boxes up to date. They are Boxes 9, 45, 118, 143, 174, 182, and 512. The system now has nineteen of the latest type of non-interfering boxes and thirty-one of the old type. There are 50 boxes on the system. The Fire Alarm boxes have been painted during the year. The compressed air whistle outfit which was installed last year has given very good service.

Recommendations

The Board of Engineers recommend the purchase of 1,000 feet of fire hose; also that two new fire alarm boxes be purchased so as to continue to dispose of the old boxes now in service.

To His Honor the Mayor and Joint Standing Committee on Fire Department, Board of Engineers, Officers and members of the Fire Department, and to the Police Department, I extend my sincere thanks and appreciation for the aid and support rendered me during the year.

Respectfully submitted,
EUGENE B. RILEY, Chief Fire Department

NOTE: No large loss was reported in 1933. It was the smallest Fire Loss in 18 years for the City of Keene.

Personnel Of Fire Department

Board of Engineers

Remain the same as 1932

Captains

Remain the same as 1932

Permanent Drivers

Remain the same as 1932

Steamer Hose Company

Remain the same as 1932

Deluge Hose Company

Remain the same as 1932

Hook & Ladder Company

Remain the same as 1932

Apparatus And Equipment

Ahrens-Fox Triple Combination No. 1
Ahrens-Fox Triple Combination No. 2
Mack Ladder Truck and Chemical
Reo Combination Chemical & Hose
Kissel Combination Chemical & Hose
Chief's Car
Relief Ladder Truck
500 Gallon Steamer Fire Engine Horse drawn
Forest Fire Equipment

A Demon Called Fire

1934 [from *City of Keene Annual Report*]

Report of the Chief Engineer of Fire Department

To His Honor the Mayor and Board of Aldermen:

I hereby submit my report for the year ending November 30th, 1934.

There were 24 bell alarms. 455 still alarms, making a total of 479 alarms. 25 of these calls were out of town.

The estimated value of buildings damaged by fire, $892,200.00

Damage to buildings, $80,752.98
Insurance on said buildings, $647,750.00
Insurance paid $80,752.98.
Value of contents of buildings, $374,967.25
Damage to contents $147,704.18
Insurance on said contents, $295,400.00
Insurance paid $138,085.68.

The number of alarms the department has answered for the year is the largest number on record of the department. The increase in alarms is mostly chimney fires, owing to more people burning wood, also to chimneys not being properly taken care of.

The fire loss for the year will be the largest the department has had in a good many years in valuation, but not the largest in business blocks consumed by fire. In 1865 the business blocks from Roxbury Street to City Hall were burned, the valuation of property at that time was far below the present value.

The fire in the Lane Block on August 17 was not only one of the largest fires the department has had to extinguish but was a different type of a fire. This fire which started in the basement of the W. L. Goodnow Co. had reached such a high temperature of hear that it had melted the connections of the gas meters, also the ammonia tank of the refrigerating plant. Thus retarding the progress of the firemen in reaching the seat of the fire, than as the fire men started to ventilate the second floor a hot air explosion took place and then through the large light shaft in the center of the building

The fire immediately spread to all parts of the block. All the department's apparatus and equipment was in service at this fire.

The Motor Fire Apparatus and its equipment are in very good condition. There has been purchased for the department a 600 gallon triple combination pump, hose and booster, carries 1,200 feet of 2 ½ " hose and a 100 gallon booster tank.

This pump was given the Underwriters test at the swimming pole on Beech Hill and passed the requirements with extra capacity. With this piece of apparatus the city is as well equipped for the apparatus as any city of its size. This piece of equipment will save the city nearly the interest on its purchase price, as it uses clear water instead of soda and acid.

The State of New Hampshire Forestry Department has placed in Keene a 40 Gallon portable forest fire pump and 2,000 feet 1 ½" hose for same. The state maintains and services the pump and hose. This pump is for the use of any town in the county, the costs to the towns will be to pay the operator and mileage on the truck. The Kissel Combination is used to transport this equipment.

The department has on hand 10,200 feet of double jacket rubber lined fire hose, and about 1,200 feet of linen unlined hose at South Keene. There has been 300 feet of unserviceable hose turned over to the Water Department.

The Fire Alarm system is in very good condition. All the circuits have been trimmed out from branches and limbs, also wires and cross arms have been put in good shape. There have been two fire alarm boxes purchased for replacement; these are Box 51, Winchester Street corner Blake; and Winchester Street corner Winchester Court.

There has been installed on fire alarm battery four copper-oxide rectifiers. These rectifiers give the batteries a continuous charge or are floating on the line, supply the line current and giving the battery a slow rate of charge at all times. This does away with half of the regular battery and nearly doubles the life of same at less cost of charging.

The Board of Engineers recommends the purchase of 1,000 feet of fire hose, two fire alarm boxes, also rubber coats, boots and mittens.

To His Honor the Mayor, and Joint Standing Committee on Fire Department, Board of Engineers, officers and members of the fire department, and to the Police Department, I extend my sincere thanks and appreciation for the aid and support rendered me during the year.

> Respectfully submitted,
> EUGENE B. RILEY,
> Chief Fire Department

Fire on Friday August 17th, 1934 in the Lane Block. As Reported by the *Keene Evening Sentinel* on August 18th, 1934:

'FIRE'

Lane Block Gutted By Most Disastrous And Spectacular Fire Keene Has Had For Years With Loss Estimated Over $400,000.

Flames Destroy Goodnow Store and Part of Building Occupied by Spencer Hardware is Ruined.

Many Families Driven To Street While Tenants Are Rescued; Several Firemen Overcome By Gas Fumes and Smoke and Others Are Treated For Minor Injuries.

Fire, Which Started in Basement of Block Late Friday Night, Difficult to Reach and Thousands of Gallons of Water Are Poured Into Building From All Sides to Bring the Flames Under Control.

The most devastating and spectacular fire which the city has experienced in modern times and which gave the fire department a stubborn battle lasting for many hours, destroyed the E. F. Lane block on the east side of Main Street late Friday night and early this morning, and resulted in a loss which will run close to a half million dollars. The fire was not brought under control until about 3 o'clock this morning.

Only the walls remain standing of that part of the building which was occupied by the W. L. Goodnow Company and the entire upper part of the building in which the Spencer Hardware company store is located is badly gutted. Other property in the business district was threatened by the fire.

Every available piece of firefighting equipment owned by the local department was pressed into use and the tow alarms, which were sounded, brought every fireman in the city to the scene. Several firemen were overcome with ammonia gas fumes and smoke and many were treated for minor injuries and cuts. Firemen, police and others affected rescues of tenants in the upper stories of the block. Many families were driven to the street.

Started in Basement

The fire, which started in the basement, was difficult to get at in its early stages. Hundreds of thousands of gallons of water were poured into the blazing four-story brick building from all four sides by the firemen in an effort to confine the flames to the section of the building where the fire started by the valiant efforts of the fire fighters were in vain. Roofs of nearby and abutting structures were used as points of vantage by the firemen in combating the fire.

Firemen were still pouring water on to the ruins this morning and the section of the street in front of the block was roped off to prevent the crowd from getting too close. Hundreds of persons congregated at the scene this morning and police were stationed at various points. Tourists traveling through the city were attracted to the scene and many stopped their cars and looked over the ruins.

Favored by Lack of Wind

Firemen and city officials were thankful that the old Cheshire House was not standing for the fire would have swept through the old hostelry and a general conflagration would probably have resulted.

The fire department was favored in one respect and that was that there was no wind to spread the blaze to other sections of the business district, and small wooden buildings on Church Street. Sparks and burning embers soared high into the sky but ascended almost vertically.

Insurance Coverage

The Lan Estate Trustees announced this morning that the block is insured for $89,000. It is estimated by the trustees that the cost of rebuilding will exceed this figure.

The W. L. Goodnow Company's stock in trade and fixture were well covered with insurance and the same is true of the Spencer Hardware Company.

Employees Lose Work

About 40 persons employed by the W. L. Goodnow Company are thrown out of work at least for a time, as a result of the fire. The Spencer Hardware Company has about 20 employees, store officials stated this morning.

Assessed Valuation

The assessed valuation of the E. F. Lane block for purposes of taxation this year is $170,000. Stock in trade of the W. L. Goodnow Company is listed at $45,000, while the stock in trade valuation of the Spencer Company is given as $75,000 making a total of $290,000.

Several thousand dollars damage was done to the electrical and other equipment in the dental office in the block on the second floor. Some equipment and supplies can be salvaged according to Dr. Robert R. King, who this morning made arrangements for an expert to look over the equipment.

Much of the loss in the dental office was in the form of finished plate and bridge work much of which was ready to be shipped out. This means a loss of time as well as money. Losses sustained by other tenants will bring the total well over $400,00.

Discovery of Fire

The fire was first discovered by "Joe" Leveroni about the time he was closing his fruit store in the new block next door. He called the fire station and a still alarm was sounded. Smoke was belching forth from the basement both in the front and the rear and as a big fire was imminent an alarm was sounded from Box 8, corner Main and Railroad Streets. Mr. Leveroni after calling the fire station also notified officials of the Goodnow Company who made a hurried response. Atty. Roy M. Pickard and Jaime T. Melvin, trustees of the E. F. Lane estate owners of the block, were also early on the scene.

Tenants Carried Out

Police Officers Fred J. Bergeron and Walter M. Barnard on duty on Main Street and other police officers were among the first arrivals at the blaze and went in from the front of the blocks and aroused the residents on the upper floors.

Robert H. Henry, janitor of the E. F. Lane block on the opposite corner of Church Street, and his son Robert H. Jr., made their entrance from the fire escape in the rear and over the back roof and the younger Henry had to carry Mrs. Ernest C. Allen out of a window and down a narrow wall ladder.

Chauffeur "Sam" Guyette of the fire department rescue John Holman from the top floor of the Spencer Hardware Company section of the block. Holman is deaf and while he smelled the smoke he did not dare to move from his room as all corridors lead in the center of the building where the heart of the fire was. He was a friend of Guyette and other firemen and they thought of him and went in after him fearing he might not hear any call.

Not knowing that Guyette had gone into the block for Holman other firemen raised a long ladder in front and smashed in the screen and window.

Firemen Partially Overcome

While heavy black smoke was rolling out from the front basement the fire seemed to be more in the rear and Fire Chief Eugene B. Riley and John H. Simpson and Dennis J. Foley centered their first attack in the rear from the Goodnow cooling system. Due to ammonia fumes and the intense smoke the exact location of the fire could not be immediately determined, seemingly being in the center of the store basement. Firemen Frank W. Streeter was overcome as he forced his way in and Frederick M. Crosby and "Chick" Nims had to drag him out and they were nearly overcome a number of firemen having to assist all three of them into the open. George C. Erwin was also "out" for a time and others had chocking spells. There were only a few fire masks and these did not seem to be in good working order.

Maintains Emergency Station

Dr. Walter F. Taylor, 226 Main Street, maintained an emergency dressing station in the middle of the street near one of the fire trucks, bandaging cuts which several firemen received. Most of the cuts were from glass. There were no serious injuries resulting from cuts or falls.

As soon as the injured firemen had their injuries treated they went back into action. One fireman overcome with gas and smoke was hustled into a taxi and sent home by orders of the local physician. Contrary to reports which were circulated during the progress of the fire two firemen were admitted to the Elliot Community Hospital.

Three Pumpers Used

Practically every available line of hose was brought into use and lines were laid from all hydrants within a reasonable distance. All three of the department's pumping engines were used in combating the blaze and they rendered excellent service, pumping a t capacity.

Engine No. 1 was stationed at a hydrant on Railroad Street near Wells Street and Engine No. 2 was at the corner of Church Street and the department's latest acquisition in firefighting equipment. Engine No. 3, was stationed at the hydrant near the Roxbury Street corner.

Although all pumpers were kept running practically continuously there were a few shutdowns in order to allow the firemen to change their positions as the course of the fire shifted.

The water gun which is mounted on one of the smaller trucks was used for the first time since its installation, several hose lines feeding water into the large single nozzle. The truck with the water gun was stationed on Church Street and used when the fire gained its big headway in the part of the building occupied by the Spencer Hardware Company. Its use was very effective.

The old hood and ladder piece which carries the longest ladders of the department was brought to the scene of the fire when extra ladders were needed. One of the motorized pieces towed the ladder truck from the fire station.

Additional firefighting apparatus from surrounding towns was not called although many persons thought that help had been sent from Marlboro.

Cause Unknown

While the exact cause of the fire is not known it is believed to have started from some form of combustion so quickly did it spread. The block had only recently been stocked with nearly 70 tons of pea coal and it may have started from that, or from the refrigeration plant. Company officials and employees of Goodnow aided the firemen in giving directions as to how to open doors and windows to make necessary entrances.

Quick Blaze

The flames seemed to break out all at once and the firemen then commenced to throw streams onto the block from all sides but the blaze had evidently worked its way up through the partitions and an air shaft and within a short time had broken through the roof and the firemen were almost powerless. It was then that a general alarm was sounded about 11:30. Within a few minutes the whole interior was gathering mass of flames and the building was doomed. Firemen had to content themselves with keeping the walls from falling.

Firemen Change Attack

The roof of the new one story building proved a good point of approach and three hose lines were poured in from that side. This drove the fire into the Spencer Hardware section of the block and quickly enveloped the upper stories and the flames were fanned into renewed fury when large pile of baskets proved good tinder. The hose lines were then shifted to Church Street to prevent the flames from jumping across the street to the group of wooden buildings. The firemen also made an effort to stop the fire from reaching stored explosives in the upper part of the Spencer Hardware Company. They also worked to keep the blaze from spreading to the Gurnsey Bros. Company block. There was considerable water damage in the Gurnsey Bros. Building.

Over a Million Shells

"Pop, Pop" went hundreds of rounds of ammunition, many of the shells going turn a skyward spray as the flames reached some of the boxes of cartridges and other ammunition.

Block Built In 1890

The E. F. Lane block was built in 1890 and the Goodnow Company, largest and oldest department store in Keene. A part of the Goodnow chain was established in the Lane block Jan 1, 1893. The stone block with the date on it and other parts of the top frame work fell to the sidewalk with a striking thud as the onlookers thought of the extensive damage to one of Keene's oldest business blocks.

Windsor H. Goodnow, Ronald P. Bach, Herbert D. Chandler and Waldo W. Buckminster, Goodnow Company officials were early on the scene but were helpless as it was impossible to get into any part of the store. Many of the office records were lost and it was daybreak before they could determine any salvage from the safe which fell into the basement and also to get into the vaults. One of the department heads from Greenfield, Mass., who was notified of the fire hurried to Keene and remained over for conferences today.

Mr. Buckminster, manager of the men's department was in the store during the mid-evening but did not notice any smell of smoke or other signs of fire, and the manager in Rice's kitchen shop in the basement also visited his store during the evening and did not recall anything which would lead him to believe there was any fire.

Dentists, lawyers, insurance men, and others of all trades and professions who have offices in the block could not make any saving of equipment of any kind.

Spencer Records Saved

Employees of the Spencer Hardware Company sensed the possible. Danger to their store early during the fire and moved the officer records to an automobile across the street.

The Spencer section of the block was built after the original building but all upper story entrances were from the middle section of the old building, one stairway leading to all parts. There was a "bad" fire in the Spencer Company store two years ago last March John M. Duffy, who has conducted a shoe store on Church Street for over half a century, near the scene of the fire recalled that his place was wiped out by fire when he was 21 years old and he had no insurance.

Blueprints and a transit were taken from the office of the W. J. Hadley Company of Fitchburg, Mass., the contractor who is erecting a new store building for the S. S. Kresce Company.

Police Detail

Chief of Police Harold M. Tibits moved to different vantages points and Police Commissioner Wells R. Sargent was also on duty. All of the reserve policemen responded without any special call from the chief.

Legion Med Report

Members of Gordon Bissell Post American Legion responded and did emergency duty assisting in policing of the crowd and traffic. The war veterans, reporting to Charles Leahy and Guy Bailey for their assignments roped off the entire east side of Main Street to keep the crowd back and give the firemen plenty of room to work.

The rope is kept on hand at the Legion headquarters for just such emergencies Frederick L. Gober was in charge of relieving the 23 Legionnaires who reported for emergency duty.

Church Street was also roped off and only firemen and persons who had special business were allowed inside of the fire lines. With the fire raging in that section of the Spencer Hardware Company store room where the ammunition was kept police and firemen feared for safety of spectators.

All possible precautions were taken to safeguard the firemen who entered the building, especially during the early stages of the fire when dense black smoke filled the building. All available smoke masks were used and ropes were tied about the waists of the men who went into the basement so that if they were overcome they could be hauled out to safety.

Thousands Witness Fire

Thousands of citizens from every section of the city and many surrounding towns jammed all points of vantage on all four sides of the fire. Officers in many blocks were used as lookout points and many ventured onto the roofs of blocks up and down the street.

Outside of Main Street the largest crowd assembled in the area back of the Cheshire House Block and in the driveway to Fairfield's garage. The excited though orderly throng was moving one going from place to place as to view the blaze from all angles.

It was not until about 3 o'clock this morning that the crowd began to disperse in noticeable numbers most of the spectators evidently wishing to remain until it was evidently wishing to remain until it was evident that the fire was well under control.

Practically all parking spaces in the square and on radiating streets were filled with automobiles and cars were placed on Roxbury, West Main, St. James Federal Church and other streets in numbers approaching that of a busy Saturday night.

Restaurants Busy

The "eating places" of all kinds were filled to capacity and many volunteers filled in behind the counter and as cashiers to relieve the pressure on the regular force and to help speed up service. There was an unusually large crowd of women both young and old among the restaurant crowd. Many of these persons went in to get the chill out of their systems after standing around for an hour or more many of them having been near enough to catch some of the spray from the hose lines.

Doughnuts and Coffee

The bakery department of Goodnow's functioned as usual and Herbert D. Chandler had the men take time off to make an added supply of doughnuts for the firemen, policemen and others in the line of duty. Shea and Culliton, Church Street grocery opposite the site of the fire furnished the supplies for coffee which was made in the Goodnow bakery. There were plenty of volunteers who did service in the distribution of the "coffee and" Capt. William J. Cashman new commander of the Salvation Army assisted in manning the rope line on Church Street in banning the curious. Patrolmen William C. Hadley helped to drive the crowd outside the ropes.

Take Fire Pictures

The Granite State Studio Photographers were busy taking both motion and still pictures of the fire. As fast as the pictures were taken they were rushed to the studio and developed in order that newspaper men might have them for papers outside the city. Reginald F. Howe proprietor of the photographic establishment is a member of the joint standing committee on fire department.

Alderman Paul D. Minnick, chairman of the fire department committee was present at the fire throughout.

One Less Tennis Prize

Keene Tennis players felt a severe personal loss today in the Lane Block when they learned that a scheduled Goodnow Company prize will not be given the winner of the city tournament. Waldo W. Buckminster, head of the men's clothing department at Goodnow's offered to donate a prize and asked a committeeman to call at the store Friday or today to collect the prize. The committeeman decided on today to make his visit and thus no prize.

Clothing Gone

An undetermined number of spare trousers were mourned by their owners today when they called at the tailor shop of Walter S. Herdman, only to find that his entire establishment had gone up in smoke. Many suits were also demolished and any decrease in attendance at tonight's dances and Sunday's church services will be directly attributed to this cause. What is one man's loss is another's gain as other clothiers did on extra week-end business.

Comment of Engineers

Fire Chief Eugene B. Riley, and Engineers John H. Simpson and Dennis J. Foley who have seen nearly two score years of fire fighting in Keene declare the Lane Block blaze the most disastrous fire to their knowledge. Simpson ordered the box alarm shortly after his arrival when he was among the first to encounter the ammonia fumes. While many of the fire companies gradually withdrew as daybreak broke, Chief Riley and Assistant Chief Simpson remained on duty until way past breakfast time conducting a detailed investigation as soon as they could get into the charred ruins.

Mrs. Urusula Lombard was carried from her sick bed out a window and down the fire escape by Robert Henry Jr. and taken to the home of her son Guy Lombard, 412 Washington Street.

Contrary to report no persons were taken to the hospital. Doctors and others advised many persons to go there but they all went homeward bound instead.

The Goodnow company bakery in a wooden building across the alley from the main block was untouched by the flames. The Holbrook Grocery company store was secured as a sales outlet so that Saturday customers could be taken care of as usual.

A few employees of Goodnow's and Spencers wee able to work today but the majority will be out of employment for some time until adjustments can be made.

The telephone switchboard was one mass of lights for several hours during the night and early morning. Extra girls responded to assist the regulars preference was given to local calls over toll service.

The fire demonstrated to many persons the need of an aerial ladder in the department for such equipment could have been used to the advantage as a hose tower.

————

Walls are but a mere shell of the E.F. Lane Block, damage to Spencer Hardware Co., largely on Church St side, where roof and floors of the Goodnow store collapsed. Photo taken by Granite State Studio.

[from *Keene Evening Sentinel:*]

VALUABLE RINGS AND MONEY ARE RECOVERED BY TENANT OF BURNED BLOCK

One of the "luckiest" of the tenants in the Lane block, which was destroyed by this morning's fire if any tenant can be termed "lucky," is Miss Elizabeth Gorman a nurse who lived on the third floor.

Mrs. Gorman had several valuable rings and money in a common steamer trunk which she fully believed had been destroyed. This morning Herbert L. Beverstock local insurance man who employs Mrs. Gorman as a nurse for his mother went into the room in which the trunk was located and after considerable digging through the accumulated debris with a board found the trunk.

The trunk had been burned through in places but the treasured valuables were found to be safe.

Lane Block gutted by most disastrous and spectacular fire Keene has had for years. Flames during the night, destroying the Goodnow Store and part of the building occupied by Spencer Hardware. Photos taken by Granite State Studio.

[from *Keene Evening Sentinel:*]

SIDELIGHTS ON THE FIRE

Poor old tabby came near losing two of her fabled nine lives. A black cat was retrieved form the basement of the Lane block in the early part of the fire last night and deposited on the sidewalk a lifeless shadow of her former self. After some time kitty's ears and legs emitted a flutter, after which she raised her head to view the situation. Simultaneously a fireman's axe came skidding across the sidewalk missing the cat's head by inches. Noticing the danger kitty was in and the fact that she came close to losing two of those lives a little girl rescued the feline from its dangerous position.

Whether or not Friday night is the proper time to take a bath seems to remain a matter of personal opinion. Several spectators were served unceremoniously with a generous shower bath when one of the hose lines got away from the firemen and lashed itself up and down the street like a mad monster venting its fury on all that came near. Finally the hose became lodged in a pile of lumber at the edge of the sidewalk.

Probably the largest crowed to ever be congregated in one place in Keene viewed the fire from the sidewalks, top of buildings top of cars and every other vantage spot. The crowd which was estimated to be around ten thousand in number came flocking to the fire in the widest range of dress, which ran from the sheer gowns to overcoats.

A chorus of mournful sights went up from a group of feminine firefans in the rear of the Lane block as the flames came lapping up around the latest fall fashions. The dresses and all the poetry flurries of the ladies could be seen burning from the rear of the building, where the flames came belching out of holes that were once windows.

___

[from *Keene Evening Sentinel:*]

NASHUA FIRE CHIEF OFFERS HIS ASSISTANCE TO LOCAL DEPARTMENT

One of the chiefs of the Nashua Fire Department came to Keene early this morning to offer any assistance, which he might be able to render the local department. The Gate City fire chief wore his uniform and was "all set" to go to work if the occasion demanded.

___

Personnel Of Fire Department

Board of Engineers

Remain the same as 1933

Captains

Remain the same as 1933

Permanent Drivers

Remain the same as 1933

Steamer Hose Company

Remain the same as 1933

Deluge Hose Company

Remain the same as 1933 except with the addition of R. C. Swan.

Hook & Ladder Company

Remain the same as 1933 except for the addition of T. C. Auger.

Apparatus And Equipment

In 1934 Keene purchased a new pumper Engine 3. As reported by the *Keene Evening Sentinel* on May 22nd, 1934.

[from *Keene Evening Sentinel:*]

KEENE'S NEW PIECE OF FIRE FIGHTING APPARATUS IS HERE

Firemen, city government, Committeemen and others look over Aherns-Fox Rotary Pump

New Fire Truck, a 1934 Ahrens Fox, as pictured above. From L to R: Fred Morse, Charlie Ballou, Lyman Cass, Chief Eugene B. Riley, Sam Guyette Driver, Dennis Foley Asst. Chief and Bud Dee, Grandson to D. Foley.

Keene's new piece of fire-fighting apparatus, an Ahrens-Fox 600 gallon rotary pump, arrived in Keene about 8:30 Monday night. A number of firemen and interested citizens, including one member of the fire department committee form the city government. Reginald F. Howe, were present when the apparatus arrived.

Two members of the city government, members of the fire department committee which purchased the first Ahrens-Fox pumper, former Alderman Charles F. Robbins and former Councilman Ralph W. Newell were also among the first to "inspect" the new pumper.

The pumper was delayed in arriving here as several stops were made along the way to show the apparatus to fire department members in Massachusetts cities.

Members of the fire department committee with Chief Engineer Eugene B. Riley and Engineers and firemen will look over the machine before the tryout. Thursday morning at 9 o'clock at the Faulkner & Colony Mill pond on West Street members of the board of fire underwriters of New Hampshire will attend the tryout and if approved by the board members the apparatus will probably be accepted by the city government members.

Earl G. Moulton of Worcester Mass., salesman and George Wheeler of Taunton, Mass., mechanic came to Keene with the machine. Mechanic Wheeler will instruct local firemen in the "ins and outs" of the apparatus to familiarize them with its use.

The apparatus is a 600 gallon rotary type pump. The other two previously purchased by the city for the same company are the 1,200 gallon piston type.

The new pump has a 100 gallon booster tank with 150 feet of booster hose and a place for 1,200 feet of regular hose. There are three lengths of hard suction hose and one length of soft suction hose with reducers. There is a ladder on one side, equipped with hooks for roof use. There is a foam tank and soda acid extinguisher on the truck. There are three auxiliary lights over the rear of the apparatus. These are used to aid firemen in picking up hose after a fire. The truck equipped with booster vacuum brakes.

The word "Keene" is painted either side of the hood of the pump also "No. 3."

Ahrens-Fox Triple Combination No. 1
Ahrens-Fox Triple Combination No. 2
Ahrens-Fox Triple Combination No. 3
A 600 Gallon pump, 1,200 feet of 2 ½ inch fire hose, 100 gallon booster tank, 150 feet chemical hose and one soda-acid and one Foamite extinguisher, one 20 foot extension and one 12 foot roof ladder, two shut-off nozzles, and other necessary equipment.
Mack Ladder Truck and Chemical
Reo Combination Chemical & Hose
Kissel Combination Chemical and Hose
Chief's Car Oldsmobile Coupe.
Relief Ladder Truck Horse drawn
500 Gallon Steam Fire Engine Horse drawn, "Amoskeag"
Forest Fire Equipment

[*Compiler's Note*: In 1934 Keene had a rough year. This writer feels that this fire even though the large dollar loss was picked and written for the year, this fire is important to mention. As reported by the *Keene Evening Sentinel* on April 13th, 1934. Headlines Read:]

'FIRE'
WRIGHT CARTER PROBABLY SAVES SISTER ADDIE FROM DEATH IN FALL OF 4 STORIES FROM BURNING BLOCK

Scores See 22 yr.-old Woman Drop from Window of Bank Building Menaced by Flames; Brother, Athlete, Catches Sister.

The heroism and physical strength of Wright Carter, former Keene High School and Austin Cate Academy athlete, probably saved his sister Miss. Addie Carter, 22 from the fourth-story window of her room in the Bank Block onto the sidewalk in Central Square a few minutes after she discovered the building was on fire early this forenoon. Young Carter caught his sister frenzied by burns. In his arms and partially broke the impact of her fall. Brother and sister the latter suffering from burns were rushed to the Elliot Community Hospital. Two elderly women were removed from the fire-menaced building. The young man was uninjured but his sister is suffering from first and second degree burns. The damage to the bank building will amount to a number of thousand dollars.

Scores of persons called to the woman not to jump or fall as she crawled onto the window ledge but apparently she was suffering intense pain from her burns and could not control herself as she frantically called for help.

Smoke Awakens Miss Carter.

Miss Carter was awakened by the smell of smoke about 8:20 o'clock. She ran into the hallway, which was filled with fire and smoke, in an attempt to alarm other tenants but found the stairway ablaze. Before she could retreat into her room she sustained burns upon her back and arms and her hair was also burned. Frenzied with pain the woman managed to crawl onto the ledge of the four-story window from which she dropped into the arms of her brother as a horrified throng shuddered.

Calls Frantically for Help

Miss Carter's frantic calls for help as she was leaning out of the window for air attracted many persons to the scene, including her brother. Persons called to Miss carter to remain where she was but suffering as she was from the burns she had received in her attempt to notify others of the fire and almost suffocated by the dense smoke pouring out of the window, she crawled onto the window ledge and hung for a moment and then dropped. The force of her falling body dropped her brother to the sidewalk, but he doubtless saved the life of his sister.

Persons that watched the woman fall quickly picked up Miss Carter and her brother and they were rushed to the hospital. The young man was not admitted to the institution as he recovered from the shock he received before arriving at the hospital.

Elderly Woman Rescued

Mrs. Emma Lockwood, 84 one of the two elderly women occupying the top floor of the block, who was rescued, was taken to the hospital suffering from a shock. It is expected that the she will be discharged from the hospital this afternoon or tomorrow. Mrs. Nettle Bardwell who is over 70, was the other woman rescued.

Others who occupied rooms on the top floor of the block were Byron Lockwood, Thomas Monahan, Mr. And Mrs. Joseph Joubert and Miss Annie Jardine.

Tenants of Building

Those occupying rooms or apartments on the third floor were; Robert Bowker and daughter, Mrs. Elwin Bailey and grandchild, Miss Edith Gourely, Mrs. O. R. Cheney, Harry Sargent, John H. Lovering, Alfred Estey, Herbert Raymond and Frank Crossman.

The second floor is occupied by offices of the Mason Insurance Agency, the Employees' Insurance Agency, the Travelers' Insurance Agency, Dr. Thomas M. Pendexter, Dr. Roy Pratt and William B. Jones. Mrs. Agnes Locke and Margaret Sadoques have rooms on this floor.

The ground floor is occupied by the Cheshire County Savings Bank, the Granite State Dry Cleaners, Inc., and Harry Grower, shoe store. The block is owned by the Cheshire County Savings Bank.

Thinks of Other Tenants

While being taken to the automobile Miss Carter managed to gasp that there was an elderly lady still in the burning building. Firemen raised a ladder on the Roxbury Street side of the block and the first man entering the building reported three women there. By that time firemen had succeeded in subduing the blaze enough to permit these women being carried down the main stairs.

Cause of Fire Not Known

The Fire department officials were unable to learn the cause of the fire but are conducting a further investigation in view of two other "smudges" on the same floor with in 10 days which prompted still alarms. One of the occupants of the lower floor ran to grab a key, but before he could get up the stairs the entire stair casing and hall were ablaze. The fire and police officials are unable to account for the rapid spread of the blaze. The fire spread quickly to the roof and clouds of smoke poured through the building indicating a more widespread fire.

Extensive water damage was caused throughout the building. Generous use was made of blankets and other protection for the stores on the first floor. The clothing in the Granite Stare Dry Cleaners' Inc. was quickly removed.

All hydrants on Central Square were pressed into service, one on Roxbury Street and several others.

No Life Net Available

Scores of persons were attracted to the square not only by the fire alarm but by the piercing shrieks of Miss Carter who made a hysterical plea for rescue before she finally dragged herself to the outer edge of the window.

The onlookers were helpless to do anything for Miss Carter as the fire department has no life net and it was as impossible for anyone to reach her by the blazing stairway as it was for her to make her escape.

She evidently could not stand the pain of her burns and started to drop but had presence of mind to grab the ledge and break her fall a bit. Many persons turned their heads as she hurled downward and the majority of people expected to see her picked up dead or badly injured.

Parked cars blocked the rescue act from the majority of people and only a few knew about it until Carter and his sister were picked up and carried to an automobile to be taken to the hospital.

The two district nurses, Miss Anna M. Savage and Miss Shirley I. Grout, were on the scene and used the District Nursing Automobile to take the two Carters to the hospital. The nurses gave them first aid treatment on the way. The taxicab at the head of the square and the District Nursing cars were also used for taking the other three women to the hospital.

Carter's Second Heroic Act

The miraculous life-saving feat accomplished by Wright Carter is not the first heroic act that his young man performed.

While a student at Austin Cate Academy, Wright, familiarly known as "Bull," saved the life of Ex-Mayor Arthur R. Jones when an automobile in which he was riding as a passenger with Mr. Jones tipped over in a water-filled ditch on the Concord road near Munsonville on November 7th, 1932.

Mr. Jones was pinned under the car and after he was extricated Carter used his knowledge of artificial respiration to bring Mr. Jones back to consciousness. It was said at the time that Carter's aid saved Mr. Jones.

Is Very Modest

Carter passed off his act this morning lightly and did not care to discuss it with persons who quickly gathered about him when he returned to the scene of the fire after going to the hospital with his sister. He seemed to be more concerned with finding a tip coat which he had lost than talking about his act.

Carter ran all the way from a point near the old Sentinel building to make the rescue and arrived in front of the block only seconds before his sister dropped. His experience in catching football punts is believed to have assisted him in catching his sister and thereby breaking her fall.

The only outward sign that Carter was hurt was a limp and he complained about one of his knees being hurt. After inspecting the fire damage in the block he said that he was going to visit a doctor.

Officer William C. Hadley, who was on the west side of Central Square saw some issuing from the upper floor of the block and while on his way to City hall to sound Box 9, the alarm began sounding and he went directly to the burning building. He made an investigation to see that everyone on the third floor was out of the building and to aid them in case of necessity.

The officer was not able to ascend to the fourth floor, as the stairway between the third and fourth stories of the building was ablaze, when he arrived.

Does Daring Act

Reginald Swan, a fireman, did the "human fly"-act during the height of the fire by crawling out of one of the windows on the fourth floor and working his way along the narrow ledge to open windows in the other rooms and allow smoke to escape. His act was daring one.

———

Shortly after the curtains caught fire, Miss Addie Carter appeared in one of the front windows of her 4th floor apartment in an endeavor to escape the flames and smoke. She seemed to hesitate for a few seconds and crawled outside the window and hung and then suddenly released her hands from the windows ledge where she hung where her brother Wright Carter caught her. Photo by Granite State Studios.

1935 [from *City of Keene Annual Report*]

Report of the Chief Engineer of Fire Department

To His Honor the Mayor and Board of Aldermen:

I hereby submit my report for the year ending November 30th, 1935.

There were 34 bell alarms. 414 still alarms, making a total of 448 alarms. 16 of these calls were out of town.

The estimated value of buildings damaged by fire, $527,100.00

Damage to buildings, $16,757.19

Insurance on said buildings, $432,000.00

Insurance paid $16,757.19.

Value of contents of buildings, $60,290.77

Damage to contents $6,073.06

Insurance on said contents, $46,427.88

Insurance paid $6,073.06.

The number of alarms the department has answered for the year is 448; this is 31 less than that of last year. Chimney fires are the largest part of the alarms the department answers.

The fire loss for the year is what would be called a fair average, as there were no large fires during the year. There were a number

that the loss would exceed $1,000, and with number of alarms the loss was reasonable.

The building inspections carried on during the year show that the business men in their Stores, Office rooms, Garages, Hotels and shops, keep their places in very good condition.

The Motor Fire Apparatus and its equipment are in very good condition. Most of the apparatus in the department has been painted or re-finished. Engine No. 1 painted, Engine No. 2 varnished, Ladder No. 1, painted, Combination No. 1 and 2 painted, also Chief's car varnished. The department was lucky to get a painter to do the work here at the station; also his price for labor was very reasonable. There was no time that the apparatus being painted was out of commission, but that it could be used if necessary. The permanent men at the station painted Combination No. 2. This makes the apparatus look as good as new also it is much easier to take care of.

There has been added to the equipment, during the necessary attachments for the use of 1 ½ inch hose, via: Nozzle tips so that the small hose can be connected to the end of the large stream, also a two-way Siamese so that one 2 ½ inch hose line will supply tow 1 ½ inch hose lines, also reducers from 2 ½ inch to 1 ½ inch for hydrant connections direct to 1 ½ inch hose, 1,000 feet of 1 ½ inch hose was purchased for this purpose, 100 feet is carried on each pumping engine to be used a leader lines.

A good many fire departments throughout the country are placing this small hose equipment in their departments, as the water loss is much smaller and it is very much easier to handle, and also a good number of fires in the residential sections can be handled with these small lines of hose

The department has on hand 9,900 feet of 2 ½ inch double jacket rubber lined hose, and 200 feet of unserviceable hose, also about 1,200 feet of linen unlined hose in hose house at South Keene, and 1,000 feet of 1 ½ inch single jacket rubber hose.

There has been turned over to the Water Department 100 feet of unserviceable hose.

The Fire Alarm System is in very good condition.

There has been purchased this year a new set of battery for the fire alarm, this purchase did not require only half as many cells of battery as before on account of the rectifiers which were installed last year and takes the place of one set of batteries.

There have also been purchased two fire alarm boxes for replacement, No. 41 Middle Street cor. Center, and 113 Railroad Street cor. 93rd.

Three deaths occurred in the department during the year. Associate Engineer Fred W. Towne died January 1, 1935.

Private Harry V. Roache, Deluge Hose Company, died April 17th, 1935

Assistant Engineer Dennis J. Foley, died August 10, 1935.

The Board of Engineers recommend the purchase of 1,000 feet of fire hose, two fire alarm boxes, and a booster pump for Combination No. 2. There will also have to be purchased some new tires for some of the apparatus during the year.

To His Honor the Mayor, Members of the City Government, Joint Standing Committee on Fire Department, Officers and members of the Fire Department, and to the Police Department, I extend my sincere thanks and appreciation for the aid and support rendered me during the year.

Respectfully submitted,

EUGENE B. RILEY Chief Fire Department

The fire noted for year 1935 is the fire at the home of Charles Chakalos, as told by the *Keene Evening Sentinel* on April 17th, 1935:

'FIRE'
Fire Alarm System Goes Wrong And Firemen Delayed In Reaching Fire That Gutted Baker St. House

Confusion Arises Over Receipt of Still Alarm and Box Signal for Blaze in Home of Charles Chakalos; Auto Operators Create Traffic Jam; Telephone Company Besieged With Calls Following Report Children Were Endangered

A fire chief facing a blazing house, without any firemen, was the predicament which faces Chief Eugene B. Riley for a few minutes shortly before 9 o'clock Thursday night when, due to confusion in receiving a telephone call and mechanical trouble at the station in sounding the bell and whistle of the fire alarm system, the apparatus went in several directions before it arrived at the blaze.

The house of Charles Chakalos at 225 Baker Street, corner of Congress Street, was gutted and practically all the furniture was ruined.

Crowd Gets Panicky

The fire was not the chief concern of the crowd, however, as almost immediately upon the arrival of the firemen there went up a cry from somewhere that there were children in the upper smoke –filled rooms. Fireman Paul E. Symonds donned a gas mask and entered one of the rooms but before his search was completed word came that the children were safe, that they had not been in the house. The word did not come any too quick as Symonds came staggering out overcome by the smoke and had to be laid out on the lawn for several minutes before he finally came to.

In the meantime, even though the police ambulance was on hand, residents became excited and called for the hospital ambulance, anticipating the possible finding of children in the house. The hospital ambulance responded to the call.

As another evidence of the "mob cru" the work quickly went the rounds from those who did not see Symonds carried out the front door of the hose that he had fallen from the roof. The fire and combining circumstances furnished an evening of human drama not often seen.

Discovered by Children

None of the Chakalos family was home at the time of the fire which was discovered by children of Ira O. Willard on Congress Street who saw smoke pouring out of the house. Someone at the Willard residence called the fire station by telephone and a still alarm was sounded.

Bernard Willard, who later rang in the box alarm, said his sister informed the firemen that the blaze was at the corner of Baker and Congress Streets but they evidently misunderstood her and went to the corner of Adams and Baker Street and were trying to find the fire when the box alarm, 182, at the farther end of Congress Street was sounded.

When no apparatus showed up after several minutes a second telephone call was made to the station and at the same time Bernard Willard ran to the box and sounded the alarm.

As the bell alarm came in the driver of the first piece of apparatus went to the same place as did the chauffeur on the still alarm, the corner of Adams and Baker Streets. Another

truck went down Marlboro Street beyond Baker Street.

Chief Riley followed one truck through Dartmouth Street from Marlboro Street and upon reaching Baker Street the truck turned west toward Main Street, and Chief Riley turned east to Congress Street and found the blazing house and much to his amazement, no apparatus. One of the trucks finally arrived and a chemical line was quickly put onto the fire until other firemen finally got things straightened out.

With the interior of the house a mass of flames the firemen seemed to make up for "lost time" and keeping it form breaking through the roof or walls. Smoke and flames were pouring out of several windows on both floors at one time.

Fire Starts Near Stove

The fire evidently started from behind the stove in the chimney and spread with lighting-like

rapidity down stairs, into partitions upstairs, and into the ceiling and floors which burned through.

No Insurance on Furniture

Mr. And Mrs. Chakalos and four children left their home about 7 o'clock to visit with friends for the evening. According to Mr. Chakalos he left a wood fire in the stove. Chief Riley lays the fire to an overheated chimney, probably caused by wood fire. There is no insurance on the furniture, according to Mr. Chakalos, as it expired six months ago. The house is partially insured. The firemen had to tear down the walls separating the kitchen and other rooms to get at the heart of the blaze. The kitchen is a mass of charred ruins.

Patrolman Fred J. Bergeron, one of the first on the scene, tried desperately to attack the driver of the truck which turned west on Baker Street, and it was only his insistent blowing of a siren on the police auto that finally attracted the driver of the Marlboro

Street truck which had turned back towards the center of the city.

A man who lives on Baker Street almost across from the burning house, sent in a telephone call giving

The location of the fire as Baker and Congress Streets, and was informed that the apparatus was on its way.

Bad Traffic Jam

Traffic became so jammed on Baker Street that the ladder truck could not get through until several cars had been moved.

Two lines of hose were laid from the Congress Street hydrant almost directly in front of the house, a line was laid from the booster pump and another line from a hydrant on Marlboro Street, near Martin Street. Officer Harry Mentor did traffic duty at Marlboro and Baker Streets. Chief Harold E. Tibbetts helped to keep the crowed back at the scene of the fire and assisted Chief Riley in making an investigation of the fire.

The delay of the firemen was partially due to the bell and whistle going "haywire," a broken ratchet on a fan causing the bell to keep sounding. The first two rounds sounded all right and registered on the tape at the fire station in proper manner, but went wrong on the last two rounds, so "fire fans" as well as firemen had to hunt for the fire.

———————

As Reported by the *Keene Evening Sentinel* on May 8th, 1935:

'FIRE'
Misreading Box Number Sends Fire Department Apparatus to Wrong Box

Firemen Go To Box 57 on Pearl Street Instead of Box 571 on Avon Street, Sounded by Sprinkler "Trouble"; There Was No Fire

Firemen had to "pull out of bed" shortly after 2 o'clock this morning anticipating a fire that wasn't," although they had to make an intensive search of the Sprague and Carleton chair factory storage building on Avon Street before they satisfied themselves that the alarm was due to trouble with the sprinkler system which automatically rang Box 571 at the factory, and started a gong outside to sound and water to pour through a pipe outside the building.

This was the first call the department had from this box which known as an automatic master box, the only one if its kind in Keene, only a few of which have been installed in the state.

It is a special system that furnishes protection without the need of a night watchman.

The whole affair came near being a "false alarm" in more ways than one as the firemen first went to Box 57 on Pearl Street anticipating this number as 571 is a new box, and not waiting for the single stroke to be recorded on the "tape" at the fire station.

Upon arrival there was an inspection of Box 57 and the firemen practically decided that a false alarm had been sounded, when someone heard the factory alarm gong sounding. The firemen quickly retraced their travels to West Street into Avon Street where Box 571 is located.

There was no damage at the factory as no sprinkler "heads" went off.

The trouble, according to Mr. Wallace Redish, General Manager of the chair factory, was due to scale getting inside the pipe and catching underneath the valve when the pressure was pumped up Thursday, and this caused a slow leak and when low pressure was reached the alarm was automatically sounded and the gong started. A watchman was placed on duty for the remainder of the morning and will remain on tonight until repairs to the system are made. An expert from the Gamewell system is expected in Keene, Thursday to make necessary adjustments and valve change to prevent a repetition of the difficulty.

"Fire fans" as well as firemen became confused, many of them taking the call as Box 57, and others at 71. The Box 571 is not listed on some of the fire alarm cards, and they're being no Box 71 added to the mix-up.

Mr. Redish was notified of the trouble by Sentinel reporter and made a quick response to the call.

_____

Personnel Of Fire Department

Board of Engineers

Remain the same as 1934

Captains

Remain the same as 1934

Permanent Drivers

Remain the same as 1934

Steamer Hose Company

Remain the same as 1934

Deluge Hose Company

Remain the same as 1934 except with the addition of R. C. Swan

Hook & Ladder Company

Remain the same as 1934 except for the addition of T. C. Auger.

Apparatus And Equipment

Ahrens-Fox Triple Combination No. 1
Ahrens-Fox Triple Combination No. 2
Ahrens-Fox Triple Combination No. 3

A 600 Gallon pump, 1,200 feet of 2 ½ inch fire hose, 100 gallon booster tank, 150 feet chemical hose and one soda-acid and one Foamite extinguisher, one 20 foot extension and one 12 foot roof ladder, two shut-off nozzles, and all other necessary equipment.

Resolutions for the year ending 1935

An Ordinance relating to salary of Chief Engineer of the Fire Department.

Be it ordained by the City Councils of the City of Keene, as follows:

Amend Chapter XXXIV, Section 13 of the City Ordinances by striking out the words "two thousand" in line 2 and substituting therefore the words "twenty-four hundred".

Passed February 7th, 1935.

1936 [from *City of Keene Annual Report*]

Report of the Chief Engineer of the Fire Department.

To His Honor the Mayor, and Board of Aldermen:

I hereby submit my report for the year ending November 30th, 1936.

There were 24 bell alarms, 373 still alarms, making a total of 397 alarms, 14 of these calls were out of town.

The estimated value of buildings damaged by fire, $291,300.00

Damage to buildings, $9,870.04
Insurance on said buildings, $233,400.00
Insurance paid $9,870.04.
Value of contents of buildings, $180,220.09
Damage to contents, $11,621.60
Insurance on said contents, $161,800.00
Insurance paid $11,621.60.

The number of alarms the department has answered for the year is 51 less than that of last year. Chimney fires are still the large part of the alarms. The board of Engineers and the Committee on Fire Department are working out a regulation on chimney fires.

The fire loss is quite a little less than that of last year and I will say that our citizens are becoming more fire minded and are using more care to prevent fires, but quite a number show that losses would run from $1,000 to $3,000 dollars.

The Building inspections by this department have been carried out through the year in the business sections, with the result that the report shows that the Stores, Basements, Hotels and mills are kept in very good condition with very few exceptions.

The motor fire apparatus and its equipment are in very good condition, except Engine No. 1 which needs new leathers and valves in its pump. There has been installed on Engine No. 2 four new tires, also two new front tires on the Kissel. There has been installed on the Kissel Combination a 136 gallon booster tank and a booster pump of 75 gallons capacity, this truck can draft water from a brook or pond and it has two outlets for two 1 ½ inch streams. This makes this truck much more valuable for the outside area of the city and for forest fires.

There has been a new Chiefs car purchased to replace the 1927 coupe, which was requiring a number of repairs.

The department has on hand 10,700 feet of 2 ½ inch double jacket rubber lined hose, also 1,200 feet of linen unlined hose at South Keene in hose house, and 950 feet of 1 ½ inch single jacket rubber lined hose. There has been turned over to the water department 400 feet of unserviceable hose.

The Fire Alarm system and its equipment are in very good condition. The alarm boxes have been painted during the year, also two new fire alarm boxes have been purchased and installed; Box 24 Beaver corner Dover and Box 32, Elm Street corner High.

Deaths

One death occurred in the department during the year, Thomas R. Pickett, Hook and Ladder Company, died September 20th, 1936.

At a meeting of the Board of Engineers, May 13th, 1936, it was voted to reduce the call men of the department form fifty to forty-five call men. This reduction was to be automatic, by resignation or discharge. The Board of Engineers recommended the purchase of 1,000 feet of fire hose; to continue the purchase of two fire alarm boxes each year until all the old type boxes have been replaced and to renew the leather packing and valves on Engine No. 1 pump.

To His Honor the Mayor, Members of the City Government, Joint Standing Committee on Fire department, Officers and members of the Fire Department and to the Police Department, I extend my sincere thanks and appreciation for the aid and support rendered me during the year.

Respectfully submitted,
EUGENE B. RILEY,
Chief Fire Department

Personnel Of Fire Department For 1936

Board of Engineers remains the same except for the addition of Elwin H. Applin 2nd Assistant due to the death of Assistant Fred W. Towne.

Captains

Remain the same except for the addition of Lewis H. Dean when Elwin H. Applin became an Engineer.

Permanent Drivers

Remain the same as 1935

Steamer Hose Company

Remain the same as 1935

Deluge Hose Company

Remain the same except for the addition of W. R. Messer and C. P. Woods.

Hook and Ladder Company

Remain the same as 1935

Apparatus And Equipment

Ahrens Fox Triple Combination No. 1
    Ahrens Fox Triple Combination No. 2
    Ahrens Fox Triple Combination No. 3
    Mack Ladder truck and Chemical
    Reo Combination Chemical and Hose
    Kissel Combination Chemical and Hose
    Chiefs Car
    Oldsmobile Coupe
    Relief Ladder Truck 357 feet of ladders
Horse drawn
    Forest Fire Equipment

Fire Alarm Telegraph
NOTE: Box blown

122 for Brush, 12 for Military call, 4 for Legion call, 3 for Fire out and 2 for a still alarm.

School Signals

Three Blasts: at 8:05, no morning session; 11:05, one session; 1:05, no afternoon session, High School, 7:05, no session.

[*Compiler's Note:* For the year 1936 Keene had the unenviable record of more chimney fires per capita than any other New England city.]

The fire selected for 1936 was on October 10th, 1936. The Store house of Johnson Lumber Co. with a loss of $3,713.28. As Reported by the *Keene Evening Sentinel:*

'FIRE'

Fire in Shed of Johnson Lumber Co. Menaces Area on Cypress Street in Night

Thousands of Feet of Finished Lumber Is Destroyed, But Damage Not Estimated; Patrolman Walter M. Barnard Discovers Blaze and Sounds Alarm; Fire Chief Believes Fire Originated Around Truck

A menacing fire, in which flames shot high in the sky, caused several thousand dollars damage in the sheds of the Johnson Lumber Company in the east railroad yard off Cypress Street, shortly after midnight, Friday. A company truck was charred beyond use, thousands of feet of finished lumber for building purposes were destroyed and there was considerable smoke and water damage which company officials are unable to estimate until after Inventory.

A storage truck of the Keene Oil Company was quickly removed from the end of the building where the fire started, and railroad officials were early on the scene ready to move three tank cars of road surfacing material if the firemen considered it necessary, as the fire was an unusually hot one when the fire trucks arrived.

Policeman Discovers Blaze

Prompt discovery of the blaze by Patrolman Walter M. Barnard and lack of wind were considerable help in preventing a serious conflagration as there are other lumber sheds in that area. There were also freight cars filled with chairs and others with coal, and the Spencer Hardware Company has storage buildings in that section and the Keene Oil Company buildings and Sunshine Feed stores are nearby.

Officer Barnard was making his rounds on Railroad Street, near the Spencer Hardware Company buildings, when he saw sparks and made a quick dash to the corner of Main Street and sounded an alarm form Box 8. The fire broke through the roof into roaring flames which could be seen in practically all sections of the city. Reginald F. Howe of the Granite State Studio was among the early arrivals and leaning against the side of tank cars already hot, he made what he hopes are good color pictures of the flames at their height.

The heart of the fire was in the second section of the warehouse from the east end and the entire roof was burned off. The fire evidently spread in both directions, considerable damage being caused to pile of match spruce, in 12, 14 and 16 feet lengths, in the extreme east end of the building. The fire also spread westerly along the top of the sheds through practically the entire upper sections of the building. The lumber's company's truck was in the section where the worst of the fire occurred and Fire Chief Eugene B. Riley is inclined to believe that it started from that source. He does not discount however the belief of Clyde C. Clark manager of the lumber company that it might have been caused by "canned heat" users who have been of considerable bother by making the buildings and yard a hangout. The shed door where the automobile was located was securely padlocked, however, and other doors were locked and the firemen had to use hooks and other force to open them.

Stone Bridge, Court St., Keene NH.

East Side Main St., Keene NH.

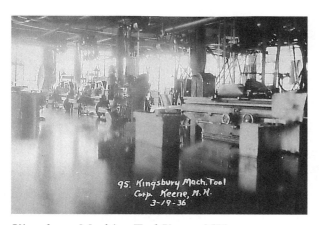

Kingsbury Machine Tool Keene, NH.

Landslide at So. Keene, NH.

Two lines of hose were laid from Main Street in front of Johnny's diner and two others from a hydrant in the yard alley, or yard by the Robertson Motor Company, making a total of nearly 2,000 feet. Chief Riley expressed himself as really fearful when he was on the way to the fire as he saw the flames rolling up.

Officer Barnard and fellow patrolmen Clifton A. Smith and Fred J. Bergeron did an excellent police job in handling the large midnight crowd and they also worked cooperatively with the firemen in guiding them about the area. The onlookers who joined with Chief Riley in expecting to see "a real fire" had considerable praise for the promptness with which the flames were confined to the inner sheds. Representatives of the companies in that section were on hand to look after their interests.

Insurance Covers Loss

The loss is covered by insurance, but the lumber will have to be replied and taken from the sheds before even a rough estimate of damage can be given, according to the officials of the lumber company. It doesn't take much fire in finished limber to cause considerable financial loss they say, and it is hard to gauge the amount of lumber on hand. Approximately one-third of the building was considerably charred.

———

[*Compiler's Note*: March 1936 was a rough month. Between March and April it rained every day for two weeks. There was 12 inches of snow cover and the rain melted all of the snow. The entire lower sections of Keene

Faulkner & Colony Mill, West St., Keene, NH. Photos from Fire Department Scrapbook. HSCC collection.

were flooded as the pictures in the Keene Fire Department Scrapbook shows.]

1937 [from *City of Keene Annual Report*]

Report of the Chief Engineer of the Fire Department

I hereby submit my report for the year ending November 30th, 1937.

There were 21 Bell alarms, 360 Still alarms, making a total of 381 alarms. 16 of these calls were out of town.

The estimated value of buildings damaged by fire, $498,750.00

Damage to buildings, $15,317.33
Insurance on said buildings, $376,500.00
Insurance paid $15,317.33.
Value of contents of buildings, $185,429.00
Damage to contents, $19,554.33
Insurance on said contents, $169,700.00
Insurance paid $19,554.33.

The number of alarms the department has answered for the year is 16 less than that of last year.

I think that a number of house owners have kept their chimneys cleaned in the past year, as we have not had as many chimney fires.

Grass, Automobile, Roof and partition, Dumps, and out of town fires makes up nearly fifty percent of the still alarms.

The fire loss will be quite a little more than that of last year, for the reason of the water damage at the Princess Shoe Co. on Church St. This happened on April 2nd, after the closing of the garage on the first floor the night before, a small fire started on the top floor, and this started the sprinkler which practically extinguished the fire, but the cause of the damage was that some time, probably that evening, a car or truck in the garage had hit, and broken off a small pipe, near the main valve that operates the alarm bell on the outside of the building, so as the sprinkler started there was no alarm outside to ware anybody that there was a fire. The fire department was not notified until about five o'clock in the morning. The water had leaked through the floors and damaged a good many pair of shoes to the extent of more than $12,000. The garage has protected this pipe so this should not occur again.

The building inspections by the department have been carried out through the year in monthly inspections of the fire precinct with very good results.

A Demon Called Fire

The motor fire apparatus and its equipment are in very good condition. All pumping engines have been tested out for their capacities. Engine No. 1 has had new leather packing and valves installed in its pump and is in A-1 shape. Engine No. 3 has been equipped with two new rear tires which was getting too smooth for safety, these tires were three and one half years old, but this machine makes about eight percent of the runs for the year. On all other pieces of apparatus we get about six years of service. In the coming year the tires on Engine No. 1 and the rear tires on Combination No. 2 should be renewed.

A Cambridge wind-shield has been installed on Combination No 2 as this piece had no wind-shield before.

An H-H Inhalator of the Mine Safety Appliance make, with two extra tanks has been purchased by the department. This is a valuable piece of equipment to the city and to the department. The Inhalator has saved a good many lives in a number of cities and towns. Namely: Drowning, Electric Shock, overcome by Gas and Smoke. The Inhalator is used in conjunction with artificial respiration.

The department has on hand 9,900 feet of 2 1/1 inch double jacket rubber lined hose, 700 feet of pores hose, 1,950 feet of 1 ½ inch single jacket rubber lined hose, and 1,200 feet of linen unlined hose at South Keene in hose house. There has been 450 feet of pores hose turned over to the Water Department.

The Fire Alarm system and its equipment are in very good condition. The two boxes purchased this year for replacement are Box 15, Water Street corner South Lincoln; and Box 23, Roxbury Street corner Beech. The department now has 29 of these 51 old type boxes replaced with modern ones.

Deaths

One death occurred in the department during the year. Fred A. Russell, Steamer Hose Company, died April 22, 1937.

There has been added to the permanent force another man, making six permanent men besides the chief. The call force has been reduced from 50 to 45 call men.

The board of Engineers recommended the purchase of 1,000 feet of fire hose; new tires on Engine No. 1; two rears on Combination No. 2 and the two fire alarm boxes.

To His Honor the Mayor, Members of the City Government, Joint Standing Committee on Fire Department, Officers and members of the fire department, and to the Police Department, I extend my sincere thanks and appreciation for the good support and co-operation rendered me during the year.

Respectfully submitted,
EUGENE B. RILEY,
Chief Fire Department

Personel Of Fire Department For 1937

Board of Engineers remains the same as 1936.

Captains

Remain the same as 1936.

Steamer Hose Company

Remain the same as 1936.

Deluge Hose Company

Remain the same as 1936.

Hook and Ladder Company

Remained the same as 1936 except for the addition of L. M. Pickett

Apparatus And Equipment

Ahrens-Fox Triple Combination No. 1
  Ahrens-Fox Triple Combination No. 2
  Ahrens-Fox Triple Combination No. 3
  Mack Ladder Truck and Chemical
  Reo Combination Chemical and Hose
  Kissel Combination Booster and Hose
  Chief's Car
  Oldsmobile coupe
  Relief Ladder Truck
  Horse drew 357 feet of ladders
  Forest Fire Equipment

Fire Alarm and Signals remain the same.

The fire selected for the year 1937 is a fire which occurred in the Buffum Block on June 11th, 1937. As reported by the *Keene Evening Sentinel*:

'FIRE'
Fire In Closet In Buffum Block Discovered In Night And Blaze Quickly Subdued

Officer Dennis and Truck Driver John Ryan See Smoke Pouring From Building in Center of Business Section and Summon Firemen; Blaze Believed to have Originated in Waste Basket; Damage not Estimated.

Timely discovery of a fire in a closet in the Buffum block, 59 Main Street, shortly after 1 o'clock, by Night Officer John Dennis and a truck driver, John Ryan, probably prevented a serious blaze in the business section of the city. The fire is believed to have originated in a wastepaper basket in the closet at the head of the stairs on the second floor, according to firemen. The loss has not been estimated.

The fire in this block recalled to firemen and others the conflagration which occurred there during the winter of 1917-18, when firemen combated a blaze in below zero weather. Many thousand dollars of damage resulted from the blaze in nearly 20 years ago.

See Smoke Coming From Building

Officer Dennis and Mr. Ryan were talking in front of the Latches theatre and noticed smoke coming from the direction of the Buffum block. They believed that it was smoke from a chimney in one of the nearby blocks, but immediate investigation disclosed that dense smoke was pouring from the Buffum block and Officer Dennis went to the corner of West and Main Streets and sounded a general alarm from Box 7 and then returned to the building to awaken tenants and locate the fire. Mr. Ryan accompanied the officer into the block. There was no one sleeping in the building.

Use Hand Extinguisher

Dennis and Ryan secured a hand fire extinguisher in the hallway and when they opened the closed floor flames shot out against them and Mr. Ryan suffered slight burns up on one hand and Office Dennis hands were singed. The contents of the extinguisher were poured upon the flames which were checked until firemen arrived and subdued them.

Firemen carried the booster hose line from one piece of apparatus into the building and within a few minutes the fire was under control. The basket containing burning waste paper was carried down the stairs into the street. Papers closely pressed together in the basket were still smoldering after the fire in the building had been extinguished.

When the firemen arrived the smoke was pouring out of all sides of the building on the upper floor and the fire at first appeared to be of greater proportions than it later proved to be. Water ran through the flooring into the Royal Fur shop owned by Abraham Fine on the first floor. The goods and cases were covered with rubber blankets which the firemen carry. Mr. Fine reported recent purchase of a valuable carpet.

Smoke also entered the store of Goodnow Foods, Inc. The second floor of the Buffum block is occupied by the law offices of Howard B. Lane and of John Elliot, the owner of the block. The rear of the second story is occupied by Mr. Fine for the repairing of furs. The greater part of the third story is occupied by Mr. Fine in conducting his fur business. A portion of the third story is occupied by the Full Gospel mission.

The interior of the closet was badly charred; also the door and some of the outside woodwork, but due to early discovery the blaze had broken through the top part of the closet in only one place. Before leaving the building the firemen chopped away boards to make sure that no fire remained between the partitions. A large wooden box used for storage of supplies was considerably burned. The fire appeared worse from the outside due to the smoke pouring through a ventilator fan on the third floor, in the alley beside the Cheshire National Bank.

Officer William J. Wheelock had different business tenants notified Mr. Fine, who lives across the street from his business establishment was early on the scene and helped the firemen get into the different parts of the building. He placed a man on duty there for the rest of the morning.

Police Chief Robert E. Tucker responded to the call and was ready to direct traffic in the square if an extensive blaze had required it. Only a small crowd gathered through this is one of the "danger points" in the square.

———

1938 [from *City of Keene Annual Report*]

Report of the Chief Engineer of the Fire Department

To His Honor the Mayor and Board of Aldermen:

I hereby submit my report for the year ending November 30th, 1938.

There were 17 bell alarms, 390 still alarms, making a total of 377 alarms. 14 of these calls were out of town.

The estimated value of buildings damaged by fire, $251,700.00

Damage to buildings, $8,420.95
Insurance on said buildings, $205,800.00
Insurance paid $8,420.95.
Value of contents of buildings, $100,000.00
Damage to contents, $3,049.56
Insurance on said contents, $71,600.00
Insurance paid $3,049.56.

The number of alarms the department has answered for the year is four less than that of last year.

The fire loss for the year will be only about one-third that of last year, as there has been no large fires during the year, or any damage of water from sprinkler systems.

The inspection of buildings has been carried out during the year in monthly inspections, with the exception of October, with very good results with a few exceptions.

The Motor Fire Apparatus is in very good condition.

Engine No. 1 has had the four tires renewed also Combination No. 2 has had the two rear tires replaced.

Engine No. 3 has been touched up and given a coat of varnish; this makes its finish in very good shape.

Combination No. 1 has been remodeled and made into an emergency or "Squad truck." It carries first aid supplies, gas masks, inhalator, Salvage covers, flood lighting outfit and invincible nozzle.

The department has purchased a portable flood lighting plant which consists of a 1250 Watt Engine and Generator and three portable lights, two of these are 500 Watts each, and one a 250 Watt Spot light, three 50-foot extension cables, and a distributing board, this makes a very valuable unit for lighting up at fires and all other emergencies.

The department has also purchased and installed at the junction of Vernon and Washington Streets a Beacon Signal light, this is a three way light, the Green faces Vernon Street for clearance of cars that might be on that end of Vernon Street, and the two red lights facing up and down Washington Street which holds traffic either way. This makes a big improvement in safety of traffic in answering an alarm.

The department has on hand 10,250 feet of 2 ½ inch double jacket rubber lined hose and 1,950 feet of 1 ½ inch single jacket hose, also 1,200 feet of linen unlined hose at Couth Keene in hose house.

There has been 300 feet of unserviceable hose turned over to the Water Department.

The Fire alarm, its circuits and its equipment is in very good condition. The hurricane of September 21st wrecked the alarm circuits, it requiring about eight miles of wire to replace that which was broken up so much that it could not be used over again. The total amount of wire in the alarm system is about twenty-seven miles.

The Highway department's portable air compressor was loaned to supply air to the fire whistle, and Larry Pickett loaned his sound truck outfit so we could charge the storage battery until the Public Service Company restored its electrical service.

The two boxes purchased this year for replacement are Box 26, Spring Street and corner Brook, and Box 37 Mechanic Street corner Pleasant.

The Board of Engineers recommend the purchase of 1,000 feet of fire hose, also the two fire alarm boxes for replacement, and also the apparatus rooms be repainted, as these rooms have not been painted for eleven years.

To His Honor the Mayor, Members of the City Government, Joint Standing Committee on Fire Department, officers and members of fire department, and to the Police Department, I extend my sincere thanks and appreciation for the good support and co-operation rendered me during the year.

Respectfully submitted,
EUGENE B. RILEY,
Chief Fire Department

Personel Of Fire Department For 1938

Board of Engineers remains the same as 1937.

Captains

Remain the same as 1937.

Permanent Drivers

Remain the same as 1937

Steamer Hose Company

Remain the same as 1937.

Deluge Hose Company

Remain the same as 1937 Except for the addition of George Shepard to the company.

Hook and Ladder Company

Remained the same as 1937

Apparatus And Equipment

Ahrens-Fox Triple Combination No. 1
　　Ahrens-Fox Triple Combination No. 2
　　Ahrens-Fox Triple Combination No. 3
　　Mack Ladder Truck and Chemical
　　Reo Combination Chemical and Hose
has been changed to the Reo Emergency truck. This truck now has First aid supplies, gas masks, inhalator, Salvage covers, flood lighting outfit, and invincible nozzle, 1,100 gallons, and two shut-off nozzles.
　　Kissel Combination Booster and Hose
　　Chief's Car
　　Oldsmobile coupe
　　Relief Ladder Truck
　　Horse drawn 357 feet of ladders.
　　Forest Fire Equipment
　　Fire Alarm and Signals remain the same.

[*Compiler's Note*: The fire selected for the year 1938 is a fire which occurred on February 10th, which was a brick building occupied by Russell & Foster for the storage of Autos.] As reported by the *Keene Evening Sentinel*:

'FIRE'
Gasoline Stove Explodes And Fire Damages Automobile Salesroom Conrer Elm And Mechanic Streets

Building Used by Russell & Foster Sustains Damage Estimated Not Over $5,000; Flames Originate in Office and Employee Calls Firemen From Nearby Station; Quarters Are Used for Storage of Used Cars

Five or six cars were damaged and about 50 others were threatened by flames shortly before noon today when fire broke out in the two-story brick building owned by the Keene

Development company on the corner of Elm and Mechanic Streets. The building is used by Russell & Foster, Inc., as salesroom for used cars. The loss is not expected to exceed $5,000. Fire originated from a gasoline stove which exploded in the office.

Firemen kept the flames confined within an area a short distance from the office which is in the center of the building on the Mechanic Street side of the structure. The office and fixtures were practically destroyed by flames. Firemen laid several lines of hose from nearby hydrants.

In the office at the time the gas online stove ignited and set fire to the wood work nearby were Richard Hudson, sales manager in charge of the department and Deputy Sheriff Edward Bonnette of Troy. Sibley Darling, an employee of the company was in the garage and attempted to quell the flames by using a hand fire extinguisher, while Mr. Hudson ran to the fire station, which is not far distance, and instructed firemen to "bring everything you've got".

Great Volume of Smoke

When firemen arrived, smoke was pouring out of the building on all sides and flames were eating their way into the main garage from the office enclosure.

The automobiles which were damaged by the fire were standing on either side of the office. Firemen had difficulty in working their way into the building owing to the volume of smoke which emitted from the doors and windows as soon as one was opened or broken.

The flames were under control in about 10 minutes and in another five minutes were entirely extinguished. Several firemen managed the second floor of the building by means of ladders and a few lines of hose where carried into the second story of the building where flames had worked their way. A considerable quantity of water stood on the garage floor after the flames hand been extinguished.

Many onlookers expected to witness or hear a gasoline tank on one or more of the cars explode. Hundreds of men, women and children thronged Mechanic Street to watch the progress of the flames and the firemen in their work extinguishing the fire.

The fire occurred in the building which was for many years owned and used by the Nims-Whitney company for the manufacture of window sash and blinds. The structure was later used for the manufacture of textile goods by the Wassookeag Manufacturing Company. The building was sold at auction several years ago to the Keene Development Company. The Lower part has been used the past few years by Russell & Foster, Inc., for the storage and sale of used automobiles.

Police officers were on hand to keep the onlookers at a safe distance so as not to hamper the work of firemen.

During the past 24 hours firemen were called out three times once Wednesday night for a chimney fire in the building owned by the New Hampshire Mica & Mining Company between Washington and Giffin Streets, but the call proved to be needless.

————

1938 was a rough year for the entire North East due to the Hurricane on September 22nd, 1938. On Friday September 23rd, 1938 the *Keene Evening Sentinel* published an Emergency Edition Printed on Commercial Press Operated by Gasoline Engine due to the Hurricane. Headlines Read:

"Keene Swept by Hurricane; Water Drives Hundreds from Homes; Damage Cannot Be Estimated."

Keene caught in the tentacles of the 90 mile per hour hurricane which swept north from the Atlantic at New York City late Wednesday afternoon; has sustained losses which cannot be estimated. Every

Official unit is working to bring resumption of activity. Electric current is stilled and no definite idea is offered when it will be resumed. Flood waters made it necessary to evacuate many families. About 225 persons are being sheltered and fed, by the Keene Chapter of Red Cross. There was no loss of life and few injuries. Flood waters are receding rapidly. Gasoline and oil supplies are being conserved.

Scene Of Demolition

Scores of automobiles were crushed in the streets by falling trees. Many houses are wrecked. Hundreds of the city's beautiful elms lie toppled in the streets. All industry is crippled, factory roofs torn off and water running through plants. The First Church spire was blown down. State and federal aid will probably be sought for rehabilitation.

There have been many stories and pictures published in reference to this Hurricane. This writer elects to give you a few pictures and to let you know that all the safety services were used during this trying time for the citizens of Keene.

———————

As Reported by the *Keene Evening Sentinel* on February 11th, 1938:

'FIRE'
ONE BELL AND SIX 'STILL' ALARMS IN CITY IN ONE DAY

Keene Firemen Kept Busy Thursday; Two Blazes in Garages

Thursday was a busy day for Keene firemen as they responded to six "stills" and one box alarm, the latter from the used car garage on Mechanic Street operated by Russell & Foster, Inc. Thus far the present fiscal year firemen have responded to 125 still alarms and two bell calls.

During the afternoon Thursday, firemen were recalled to extinguish a blaze that had rekindled in the building on Mechanic Street, where the fire had occurred several hours previously. The "smoke eaters" were also called to extinguish a fire at Tucker's garage on Pinehurst Avenue, but the fire was extinguished on arrival of firemen. Chimney fires were extinguished in houses owned by Mrs. Alice Sparks, 22 Carroll Street and Mrs. Herman chickening, Sylvan Way, North Swanzey.

Soon after the fire was discovered in the barn the flames spread rapidly and within a short time the house, which was about 25 feet distant, caught fire from the intense heat.

The Keene fire department was called and a motor pumper responded with several firemen. No water was available and the firemen were unable too safe the house, as they could have done had there been a supply of water in the vicinity of the buildings.

Besides the buildings, Mr. and Mrs. Crain lost between 40 and 50 tons of hay, two horses, about 40 hens, two dogs, farming implements and tools, wagons, harnesses, furniture, potatoes and nearly 500 cans of fruits, vegetables and berries which Mrs. Crain had canned during the summer. The barn was 40 by 60 feet in size and the house was a two and a half story structure.

———————

1939 [from *City of Keene Annual Report*]

Report of the Chief Engineer of the Fire Department

To His Honor the Mayor and Board of Aldermen:

I hereby submit my report for the year ending November 30th, 1939.

There were 24 bell alarms, 380 Still alarms, making a total of 404 alarms. 38 of these calls were out of town.

The estimated value of buildings damaged by fire, $389,900.00

Damage to buildings, $12,154.67

Insurance on said buildings, $305,650.00

Insurance paid $12,154.67.

Value of contents of buildings, $359,750.00

Damage to contents, $6,128.82

Insurance on said contents, $334,550.00

Insurance paid $6,128.82.

The number of alarms the department has answered for the year is 27 more than that of last year.

The fire loss for the year will be larger than last year, as there have been a number of fires that resulted in quite a loss, and some from sprinkler systems.

The inspections of buildings which is carried out monthly, continues to show very good results, as there is a better understanding between the business men, merchants, and the fire department.

The motor fire apparatus and its equipment are in very good condition. The pumping engines have been tested for their pumping capacities and all of them showed a good reserve over capacity.

Engine No. 2 will need to have the leather cups or packings and also the valves changed the coming year as ten years is very fair service for them.

The department has purchased a forest fire pump, with all the necessary equipment, two lengths of 1 ½" suction with strainer, one Wye with gate valves, one relief valve and two nozzles with three sizes of tips, also 1,000 feet of 1 ½" single jacket rubber lined hose. This makes 2,500 feet for forest fire use, and the forestry department has 2,500 feet here also with a portable pump. This gives very good protection from forest fires, also there is a C.C.C. Camp in West Swanzey of 200 young men, which we can call in case of a large forest fire. The department has also purchased a cellar pump with a capacity of 250 gallons a minute or 15,000 gallons per hour.

There will have to be purchased new tires for the City Service Ladder Truck and the Emergency truck, as these tires are six years old.

The department has on hand 10,750 feet of 2 ½" double jacket rubber lined hose and 2,900 feet of 1 ½" single jacket rubber lined hose, and 1,200 feet of linen unlined hose at South Keene in hose house.

There has been 200 feet of unserviceable hose turned over to the Public Works Department.

The fire alarm, its circuits and equipment are in very good condition. There has been installed a new seven pair cable from fire alarm room to the pole outside, this is a lead covered cable. The fire alarm boxes have been painted during the year.

The two new alarm boxes purchased this year for replacement are Box 46 Court Street Corner of School, and 115 Church Street corner Valley. There will be some changing over on No. 1 circuit on Marlboro Street from Eastern Avenue to South Keene, as the Telephone Co. have changed their lines over on new poles, and will take down the old ones, which the alarm circuits are now on. Fire Headquarters is now in very fine condition, as the Land Building Committee have painted the Station inside and out, and have repaired the roof which had been leaking, also remodeled the Shower Bath and tiled the same.

The Board of Engineers recommend the purchase of 1,000 feet of fire hose, two fire alarm boxes for replacement, also tires for the city Service Ladder Truck, and Emergency Truck, also repacking the pumps and renewing the valves on Engine No. 2.

To His Honor the Mayor, Members of the City Government, Joint Standing Committee on Fire Department, Land and Building Committee, Officers and members of Fire Department, and to the Police Department, I extend my sincere thanks and appreciation for the good support and co-operation rendered to me during the year.

Respectfully submitted,

EUGENE B. RILEY,
Chief Fire Department

Personel Of Fire Department For 1939

Board of Engineers remains the same as 1938.

Captains

Remain the same as 1938.

Permanent Drivers

Remain the same as 1938

Steamer Hose Company

Remain the same as 1938.

Deluge Hose Company

Remain the same as 1938 Except for the addition of G. H. Fish to the company.

Hook and Ladder Company

Remain the same as 1938 Except for the addition of F. E. Winn to the company.

Apparatus And Equipment

Ahrens-Fox Triple Combination No. 1
    750 GPM with 60 Gallon Booster Tank
    Ahrens-Fox Triple Combination No. 2
    750 GPM 80 Gallon Booster Tank
    Ahrens-Fox Triple Combination No. 3
    600 GPM 100 Gallon Booster Tank
    Mack Ladder Truck and Chemical in title has been changed to the City Service Ladder Truck with 239 feet of ladders still a 40 gallon Chemical tank and tools.

    Relief Ladder Truck with 357 feet of ladders, trailer drawn

    Reo Emergency truck, flood lighting outfit and first aid supplies, Salvage covers and 1,100 gallon Morse Gun and other equipment.

    Combination No. 2 For forest fires and still alarms, 2,500 feet of 1 ½" hose, a 75 gallon booster pump, 136 gallon booster tank, and 40 gallon portable pump.

    Chief's Car
    Oldsmobile Coupe
    Cellar Pump

Capacity 250 gallons per minute or 15,000 gallons per hour

    A Foam Generator with 1,400 lbs. of foam powder.

    Reserve Forest Fire Equipment

    One 35 gallon portable pump, with all necessary equipment, 2,500 feet of 1 ½" hose, 17-2 ½" gallon extinguishers, 14-5 gallon and 5-4 gallon pump tanks, 67 shovels, 14 hoes, 30 4 quart water pails, and two tubs for relaying from pumps

    Fire Alarm and Signals remain the same.

[*Compiler's Note:* The fire selected for the year 1939 is a fire which occurred on May 19th, which was a wood building on Court Street and Vernon Street occupied by A. E. Fish & Co.] As reported by the *Keene Evening Sentinel:*

'FIRE'
FIRE IN PLANT OF A. E. FISH CO. QUICKLY SUBDUD

Flames Originated Near Blower on Roof of Wood-working Concern

Fire which threatened the block bounded by Court & Vernon, Elm and Mechanic Streets, broke out about 9:40 Friday night in the blower system of A. E. Fish Company on Elm Street, but prompt and efficient work of the firemen checked the blaze. The loss has not been estimated.

It is believed that a spark ignited the dust which had accumulated in one of the blowers on top of the woodworking establishment and was burning for a time before it broke through and could be seen. Several persons saw the flames about the same time but two boys rushed into the fire station and informed Firemen Fred S. Morse of the fire and Mr. Morse sounded Box 22, which is at the fire station. This Box except for a test had not been sounded for a long period.

Two lines of hose were laid from a hydrant at the corner of Elm and Mechanic Street and taken to the fire from Mechanic

Street; two lines were laid from the hydrant in front of the Methodist Church on Court Street and taken to the rear of the fire and two lines were laid from the hydrant near the corner of Court and Vernon Street and carried from Vernon Street. Thus the fire was surrounded on three sides and firemen had water on the blaze in short order. Many words of praise for the firemen for the prompt work were heard from many onlookers.

Three trucks in the area near where the fire was burning were removed to safety. Two of the vehicles were owned by the A. E. Fish Company and the third by an individual who had left it there temporarily.

The fire not only damaged the blowers but also some dried lumber which had been stored in one of the buildings.

A large number of persons gathered at various advantages points and watched the progress of the fire and the work of the firemen.

The company trucks were moved out of the fire zone by "Al" Lavasseur and Laurence Thompson, the later an employee of the Fish Company before the arrival of the firemen; giving them a clear ent4rance to the fire.

———————

A second fire of interest was a fire at Sprague & Carleton on November 8th, 1939. As reported by the *Keene Evening Sentinel*:

'FIRE'
FIRE IN FACTORY IS SUBDUED BY SPRINKLERS

Water Does Damage in Sprague & Carleton Furniture Plant

An honest to goodness fire was raging on the second floor of the Sprague & Carlton Chair Company on Avon Street about 8 o'clock Wednesday night when the firemen arrived at the scene in response to box alarm 571 which is on the factory building. The sprinkler system had the fire practically extinguished when firemen arrived. A blanket smothered the remaining fire which was blazing in two pails of paint. The loss from fire was small but, The water damage may amount to several hundred dollars.

The fire started near paint pails and wiping cloths in the finishing room in the middle of the second floor of the building and heat put the automatic water sprinkler system in operation which kept the fire well in hand. Firemen who arrived at the scene early tossed a blanket over the two burning pails of paint and extinguished the blaze.

Water released through the sprinklers damaged unfinished chairs on the second floor and also on the first floor. Firemen removed many chairs to dry areas prior to the water in the sprinklers being shut off.

Many "fire fans," believing that the alarm was another false one did not go to the scene and as a result the usually large number of cars did not "chock" West Street.

———————

1940 [from *City of Keene Annual Report*]
Report of the Chief Engineer of the Fire Department

To His Honor the Mayor and Board of Aldermen:

I hereby submit my report for the year Ending December 31st, 1940:

There were 56 Bell alarms, 520 Still alarms, making a total of 576 alarms. 31 of these calls were out of town, and 16 were false alarms.

The estimated value of buildings damaged by fire, $480,800.00

Damage to buildings, $35,208.18
Insurance on said buildings, $404,100.00
Insurance paid $35,208.18.
Value of contents of buildings, $174,093.12
Damage to contents, $43,622.51
Insurance on said contents, $150,767.45
Insurance paid $39,840.38.

The department has answered for the year more alarms than any one year in its history. In the twelve months there has been answered 54 Bell alarms, and 477 Still alarms, a total of 531 alarms, and for the thirteen months with 45 more making a total of 576 alarms.

The fire loss will be large this last year, as there were several fires in the business districts, with quite large losses, like the Consumers Market, Carpenter's Tobacco Store, Dexter's Optical Co. and the Golding Keene Co.

The Fire Department inspection of buildings continues to show very good results, as the basement and cellar fire are at a minimum.

Last Spring the Department had a Vocational training course for Keene and all Cheshire County, consisting of eight lessons, or a series of eight weeks, with instructors from our own department. This was sponsored by the New Hampshire Fire Chiefs' Club and the State Board of Education. This training course consisted of the following: 1, ropes, knots and hitches; 2, extinguishing and forcible entry; 3, elementary ladder work; 4, elementary hose work; 5, combined hose and ladder work; 6, gas masks; 7, ventilation 8, examinations.

The Motor Fire apparatus and its equipment are in very good condition. All three pumping engines have been tested for their capacities and all show a fair reserve over capacity. Engine No. 2 has had its valves and packings renewed, also Engine No. 3 pump has been repacked.

The Department has on hand 10,900 feet of 2 ½" double jacket rubber-lined hose and 2,900 feet of 1 ½" single jacket rubber lined hose. There is 1,200 feet of 2 ½" linen unlined hose at South Keene in hose house.

There has been 500 feet of unserviceable hose turned over to the Public Works Department.

The Fire Alarm System is in very good condition.

There has been quite a lot of work done on the alarm circuits during the year. The circuit on Marlboro Street at Eastern Ave. has been changed over to follow the highway to South Keene Chair Shop. Also extensions have been made on the several circuits for the installing of the new alarm boxes. Box 38 Gilsum Street opposite house 208, Box 48 Russell Street cor. Wheelock; Box 172, Main Street cor. Manchester, and a private Box 523 at Golding Keene Company's plant on Ralston Street. The two boxes for replacement are Box 13, Railroad Street at Beaver Mills, and Box 17 Main Street corner Baker.

Also the fire alarm has had a new storage battery installed.

The Board of Engineers recommend the purchase of 1,000 feet of fire hose, two fire alarm boxes for replacement, also tires for the Emergency trucks, and two front tires for Engine No. 3, with two spare tires to be replaced. We also recommend that the four inch connected hydrants in the center of the City be replaced with six inch connected hydrants.

To His Honor the Mayor, Members of the City Government, Joint Standing Committee on Fire Department, officers and members of the Fire Department, and to the Police Department, I extend my thanks and appreciation for the support and co-operation rendered me during the year.

Respectfully submitted,
EUGENE B. RILEY,
Chief Fire Department

Board of Engineers remains the same as 1939.

Captains

Remain the same as 1939.

Permanent Drivers

Remain the same as 1939.

Steamer Hose Company

Remain the same as 1939 Except for the addition of A. S. Hobson to the company.

Deluge Hose Company

Remain the same as 1939.

Hook and Ladder Company

Remain the same as 1939 Except for the addition of R. A. Reason to the company.

Apparatus And Equipment

Ahrens-Fox Triple Combination No. 1
750 GPM with 60 Gallon Booster Tank
Ahrens-Fox Triple Combination No. 2
750 GPM 80 Gallon Booster Tank
Ahrens-Fox Triple Combination No. 3
600 GPM 100 Gallon Booster Tank and tools

Mack Ladder Truck and Chemical in title has been changed to the City Service Ladder Truck with 239 feet of ladders still a 40 gallon Chemical tank

Relief Ladder Truck with 357 feet of ladders, trailer drawn

Reo Emergency truck, Flood lighting outfit and first aid supplies, Salvage covers and 1,100 gallon Morse Gun and other equipment.

Combination No. 2 For forest fires and still alarms, 2,500 feet of 1 ½" hose, a 75 gallon booster pump, 136 gallon booster tank, and 40 gallon portable pump.

Relief Ladder Truck with 357 feet of ladders, trailer drawn

Reo Emergency truck, Flood lighting outfit and first aid supplies, Salvage covers and 1,100 gallon Morse Gun and other equipment.

Combination No. 2 For forest fires and still alarms, 2,500 feet of 1 ½" hose, a 75 gallon booster pump, 136 gallon booster tank, and 40 gallon portable pump.

Chief's Car
Oldsmobile Coupe.

Cellar Pump
Capacity 250 gallons per minute or 15,000 gallons per hour

A Foam Generator with 1,400 lbs. of foam powder.

Reserve Forest Fire Equipment

One 35 gallon portable pump, with all necessary equipment, 2,500 feet of 1 ½" hose, 17-2 ½" gallon extinguishers, 14-5 gallon and 5-4 gallon pump tanks, 67 shovels, 14 hoes, 30 4 quart water pails and two tubs for relaying from pumps

Fire Alarm and Signals remain the same.

[*Compiler's Note*: In the Chief Report for the year 1940 a list of fire losses by years from 1910 to 1940 was published on page 137 of the Annual Report.]

The fire selected for the year 1940 is a fire which occurred on April 28th and was a brick building on Roxbury Street occupied by Consumers Food Store and Puritan Clothing Company. As reported by the *Keene Evening Sentinel*:

'FIRE'
FLAMES DAMAGE TWO STORES ON ROXBURY STREET

Consumers Food Store and Puritan Clothing Company Sustain Loss Estimated Above $10,000 Sunday Night; Fire Believed to Have Started in Basement

Damage from fire and smoke estimated at more than $10,000 was caused in a store building and contents on Roxbury Street Sunday night and five families who occupy apartments on either side were driven out by smoke. The origin of the flames which started near the center of the east store occupied by the Consumers Food Store has not been determined. The block is owned by Mrs. Fanny Medvidofsky. The store at the west side of the building is occupied by the Puritan Clothing Company. Several firemen were overcome by smoke and ammonia fumes.

Still Alarm

The fire was discovered between 8:30 and 9 and a still alarm was sounded. A general alarm followed shortly after from Box 9. It so happened that Roxbury Street was free from automobiles at the time but spectators swamped into the street and the police had a difficult time in keeping the people at a safe distance from the firefighters. When ropes arrived the police officers strung these across the street and kept the spectators at a safe distance. Several special officers were called to duty to aid the regular officers.

Hard Fire to Fight

The fire was one of the most stubborn the firemen have had to combat in recent years. Dense volumes of smoke poured out of the front and rear of the building and drove the firemen back every time they attempted to enter the store. No blaze was seen by the people as the fire appeared to be burning in the floor stringers giving the opinion the fire originated in the basement and had probable been burning for a considerable time before it was discovered.

Six Lines of Hose

Five lines of hose were laid from hydrants on Roxbury Street and one in the rear of the Knowlton and Stone block. Volumes of water were poured into the store and into the basement front two windows in front and the bulkhead in the rear. It was a considerable time before firemen could enter the store and chop a hole in the floor in order to use the cellar pipe. This kept the fire down so that firemen could enter the building and fight the flames from a closer range. A Cellar pump was used in the rear.

Had Large Stock

The manager of the Consumers Food Store told newspapermen that there was about a $16,000 stock of goods in the store and basement.

The floor in the center of the food store gave away during the progress of the fire and this aided the men in pouring water into the basement.

Stock Protected

Smoke entered the establishment of the Puritan Clothing Company and most of the goods were moved to the west side of the store and covered with blankets. Dense smoke filled the store causing considerable damage. Fire worked its way up the partitions between the two stores and holes were cut in the walls to pour water into a hole was chopped in the roof of the building to permit smoke to escape rather than have it pour out the front and rear entrances and bother the firemen.

Legionaries aided firemen and police in keeping people at a safe distance from the fire.

Arron Good is manager of the food store and Edmond Fleming manager of the clothing store.

The building exterior is brick. The Wright building adjoins the store building but is separated by a brick wall. This building is occupied on the ground floor by the Wright Brothers who deal in carpets and window shades. Clarence F. Stickney plumber has the east store. Three families occupy apartments on the4 second and third floors.

A Brick house is just west and slightly to the rear of the building which is of brick.

Over 3 Hours Battle

The "all out" signal was sounded about 1 o'clock this morning; more than three hours after the fire was discovered. Firemen remained on duty all night to prevent any outbreak of flames.

Members of the ladies Auxiliary of the fire department performed valiant service for the firemen by serving hot coffee and doughnuts. Firemen went in relays to the fire station for their refreshments. The women remained on duty until all the firemen were given food.

Overcome by Gas

Late during the progress of the fire connections at a gas motor melted causing gas into the building and several firemen wee overcome. Clarence S. Dean collapsed and he was rushed to Elliot Community Hospital in the Police ambulance. He regained consciousness soon after 2 o'clock this morning.

Among those who temporarily were overcome were Maurice Waling, Samuel Thompson, George Shepard, George Fish, George Erwin, Albert Mason and Fordyce J. Thomas. Several of the firemen required attention of a physician and were treated at the fire station by Dr. J. B. Daniels.

Chief Eugene B. Riley has not been able to enter the building today to make an examination of the floor to determine the cause of the blaze owing to the quantity of water in the cellar. The cellar pump was to be used to eject the water so the examination could be conducted.

————

Noted: Another short story about the firemen on a daily run as reported by the *Keene Evening Sentinel* on February 15th, 1940.

'FIRE'
FIREMEN ARE KEPT BUSY ANSWERING STILL ALARMS

Strong Wind Causes Many Blazes in Chimneys

Firemen had a busy time today there being an unusual number of chimney fires due to the strong wind as householders were "pushing" their fires to capacity to keep homes warm. One general alarm was sounded from Box 28 for a chimney fire in the house at 30 Douglas Street owned by Harry A. Page of Marlboro. A "general" was not necessary as the blaze was being successful handled by firemen who had responded to a still alarm call.

A thimble in the chimney on the third story of the house was either taken out or blown out, and the top of the building filled with smoke giving the appearance that the house and not the chimney was ablaze. The house is occupied by three families.

Chimney fires were extinguished, houses owned by the following

Persons; Kingsbury Manufacturing Company, 107 Foster Street; Forrest Carey, 64 Spring Street; Peter Cota, 25 Giffin Street; M. E. Cantlin, 28 Harrison Street; Jessie M. Greenwood, 23 Sullivan Street.

————

As Reported by the *Keene Evening Sentinel* on April 30th, 1940:

'FIRE'
FIRE NEAR BLOWER OF LYNN WOOD HEEL PLANT

Firemen Quickly Subdue Blaze on Roof

The third fire around the blower on the roof of the Lynn Wood Heel Company factory within the past two weeks resulted in the sounding a general alarm shortly after 2 o'clock this afternoon.

Danger was slight and the fire was quickly extinguished with booster lines. The sounding of Box 6 brought a large number of spectators to the scene but police handled the crowd in an efficient manner.

Fire Chief Eugene B. Riley told newspapermen that he had given orders to the factory management to have a spark arrester put on the blower equipment to eliminate the existing danger.

Between the time of the sounding of the general alarm and the "all out" signal there was a still alarm calling firemen to extinguish a grass fire on land owned by Mrs. Grace Ellis at 50 Arch Street.

Mr. Crain is undecided as to whether he will rebuild.

————

As Reported by the *Keene Evening Sentinel* on April 30th, 1940:

'FIRE'
GRASS AND BRUSH FIRES KEEP KEENE FIREMEN BUSY

Flames on Summit Road Necessitate Calling Extra Firefighters.

Keene firemen were kept on the jump Monday afternoon and within the space of a few hours were called upon to subdue three grass and brush fires, two in Keene and one in Roxbury. No serious damage resulted but all three could have easily become serious woods fires if they had not been cornered promptly.

Conditions existing throughout the state Monday were favorable to fires and firemen in all sections were kept busy. Humidity and other conditions determining the class of fire danger are relatively the same today as Monday, according to the state district fire chief's office in this city.

Conditions Dangerous

Fire conditions are expected to grow more dangerous within the next week or two and in another few days fires will spread much more rapidly that at present, Fire Chief Eugene B. Riley stated today.

Fire on Summit

Between 50 and 60 men combated a woods fire which burned over 10 to 12 acres of land owned by Henry Barrett of Keene near the Keene Surry line just beyond the underpass on the summit. Although permit burning has been in progress on Barrett's land for several days Monday's blaze is reported to have started 400-500 feet away from where burning had taken place.

Fire Chief Riley, who received work of the fire, called the fire station and asked for a crew of about 35 men. Box 122 was sounded for the first time this year and two truckloads of men were sent to the scene along with the department's brush fire truck and pump crew.

A brook close at hand enabled the firemen to operate one of their portable forest fire pumps and some 800 feet of hose was used. The fire started some distance north of the highway but burned down to the road and in one place a small area burned south of the road. It is believed that the fire on the south side of the road was started by a cigarette or match tossed from a passing car as the wind was blowing from the south.

Eastern Avenue Blaze

Firemen were called by Box 15 to Eastern Avenue for a grass and woods fire said to have resulted from the burning of grass on land owned by Charles Wyman.

The flames jumped a wall at the edge of Mr. Wyman's cornfield and spread quickly in dry pine needles up Beech Hill. A line of hose was laid from a hydrant on Eastern Avenue. A large number of citizens assisted firemen in helping to extinguish this fire, brooms and other articles being used to "knock down" the flames.

Roxbury Blaze

A brush fire, which burned briskly for a while on land owned by Harry Menter in Roxbury, was put out by firemen from Marlboro and Keene, although only one crew was needed.

Robert Bolster, lookout at Hyland Hill, reported this fire and notified the district chief's office in Keene. Marlboro was asked to send men to the scene, as was Keene.

Lookouts Open

The lookout stations at Mt. Monadnock and Pitcher Mountain in Stoddard were officially opened today. The other two stations in this section, Hyland Hill in Westmoreland, and Sam's Hill in Charlestown, were opened last week.

Minor Blazes

In addition to fires in brush and grass which firemen extinguished on Monday afternoon they were called out to extinguish grass and chimney fires at the following places: Harry J. Menter, Branch Road, brush; Frank Pratt, Beaver Street grass; Elmer E. Stinson,

Keene's Engine, 3, comes to grief while answering a call for chimney fire in Surry Sunday night. The apparatus hit a utility pole and overturned. No one was injured and the costly equipment was but slightly damaged. Pictures from Keene Fire Depart Scrapbook. Photo by Granite State Studio.

562 Washington Street, grass; Leonard-Swift Land Company, Wagner and Wood Streets, grass; Bernard Streeter, 51 Beech Street, grass; Kingsbury Machine Tool Company, Myrtle Street, grass and debris; Keene Development Company, Belmont Avenue, grass. The chimney fires were in houses at 75 Beaver Street and 24 Probate Street.

Thus far this year there have been 315 still and 25 bell alarms.

As Reported by the *Keene Evening Sentinel* on November 3rd, 1940:

'FIRE TRUCK ACCIDENT'
Fire Truck Disabled

The Ahrens-Fox pumper was disabled Sunday night in responding to a call to a fire in the house in Surry owned by Fred Gardner. No one was hurt. The truck was returned to the fire station about 11:30. A second truck was sent to the Gardner home where a chimney fire was in progress.

The accident occurred near the Hollis Harvey farm above Surry Village near the point where the new and old roads come together. The driver of the fire truck, Frank Reid, did not notice that turn into a field which would lead to the main highway but continued along the old section of the road where there has been a fill to take care of the new road. The truck struck a service pole and then tipped over on its left side. The front bumper was bent. Lawrence Pickett was the only fireman on the truck besides the driver.

Volunteer fire fighters from Surry loaded milk cans filled with water into trucks and automobiles and were combating the blaze when Keene's second truck arrived. The chimney fire was in progress nearly an hour.

The Gardner home is a short distance south of where the home of Thomas Northway was destroyed by fire about two months ago.

1941 [from *City of Keene Annual Report*]

Report of the Chief Engineer of the Fire Department

To His Honor the Mayor and Board of Aldermen:

I hereby submit my report for the year Ending December 31st, 1941

There were 34 Bell alarms, 422 Still alarms, making a total of 456 alarms. 24 of these calls were out of town.

The estimated value of buildings damaged by fire, $569,800.00

Damage to buildings, $14,373.47

Insurance on said buildings, $482,350.00

Insurance paid $14,325.47.

Value of contents of buildings, $184,866.00

Damage to contents, $5,377.35

Insurance on said contents, $155,26670

Insurance paid $5,226.30.

The number of alarms the department has answered for the year will be quite a number less than that of last year.

The fire loss also will be quite a lot less, as there have been no large fires during the year.

The Fire Department inspection of business and industrial places in the fire precinct continues to show good results.

The Fire department is starting a series of lessons on vocational training for auxiliary firemen, which consists of seven or eight lessons on firemanship, ten hours of first aid, also instructions on the handling of incendiary bombs.

The Motor Fire apparatus and its equipment are in very good condition.

All three pumping engines have been tested and all showed reserve capacity.

There has been purchased for the department an Emergency Squad truck.

This truck replaces the old Kissell Combination which has been in service since September, 1917. This truck has a 200 gallon pump, 150 gallon booster tank, also two hose reels with 200 feet of booster hose each. Carries 2,500 feet of 1 ½" rubber lined hose, a 35 gallon portable pump, also Indian knapsack tanks, shovels, forest fire rakes, and pails. This truck is completely equipped for forest fire service, also still alarms and small fires.

The Department has on hand 10,550 feet of 2 ½" double jacket rubber lined hose and 3,700 feet of 1 ½" single jacket rubber lined hose. There is 1,200 feet of 2 ½" linen unlined hose at South Keene in hose house, all unserviceable hose has been turned over to the Public Works Department.

The Fire Alarm System is in very good condition.

There have been any extensions and very little repairs on the system for the year.

There have been no new boxes installed this year on account of the Federal priority rating.

To His Honor the Mayor, Joint Standing Committee on Fire Department, Officers and members of the Fire Department, and to the Police Department, I extend my thanks and appreciation for the support and co-operation rendered me during the year.

Respectfully submitted,

EUGENE B. RILEY,

Chief Fire Department

Board of Engineers remains the same as 1940.

Captains

Remain the same as 1940.

Permanent Drivers

Remain the same as 1940 except for the addition of Walter R. Messer. Messer was assigned as permanent driver of the new Emergency Squad No. 1.

Steamer Hose Company

Remain the same as 1940 Except for the addition of C. W. Johnson to the company.

Deluge Hose Company

Remain the same as 1940 except for the addition of M. G. Waling to the company.

Hook and Ladder Company

Remain the same as 1940.

Apparatus And Equipment

Ahrens-Fox Triple Combination No. 1
     750 GPM with 60 Gallon Booster Tank
     Ahrens-Fox Triple Combination No. 2
     750 GPM 80 Gallon Booster Tank
     Ahrens-Fox Triple Combination No. 3
     600 GPM 100 Gallon Booster Tank and tools
     Mack Ladder Truck and Chemical in title has been changed to the City Service Ladder Truck with 239 feet of ladders still a 40 gallon Chemical tank
     Relief Ladder Truck with 357 feet of ladders, trailer drawn has been removed from service.
     Emergency Squad No. 1.
     Flood lighting outfit and first aid supplies, Salvage covers and 1,100 gallon Morse Gun and other equipment.
     Emergency Squad No. 2
     For forest fires and still alarms, 2,500 feet of 1 ½" hose, a 75 gallon booster pump, 136 gallon booster tank, and 40 gallon portable pump.
     Chief's Car
     Oldsmobile Coupe.
     Cellar Pump
     Capacity 250 gallons per minute or 15,000 gallons per hour
     A Foam Generator with 1,400 lbs. of foam powder.
     Reserve Forest Fire Equipment
     One 35 gallon portable pump, with all necessary equipment, 2,500 feet of 1 ½" hose, 17-2 ½" gallon extinguishers, 14-5 gallon and 5-4 gallon pump tanks, 67 shovels, 14 hoes,
     30 4 quart water pails and two tubs for relaying from pumps

Emergency Squad 2 was used for brush fires, which carried additional equipment. It was also used for multi-fires due to the booster pump and ladder, which it carried. This truck was traded in the early 1960s for another pumper. Photo taken by Ronald Amadon.

Fire Alarm and Signals remain the same.
[*Compiler's Note*: In the Chief Report for the year 1941 a list of fire losses by years from 1910 to 1941 was published on page 143 of the Annual Report:]
     Fire Alarm Telegraph and Signals remain the same.

Joint Resolutions for the year ending 1941

A JOINT RESOLUTION relating to Fire Hydrants.
     Resolved by the City Councils of the City of Keene as follows:
     That the Joint Standing Committee on Public Works causes a fire hydrant to be installed on Gardner Street and a fire hydrant on Nelson Street, the locations of hydrants to be approved by chief engineer of Keene Fire department, cost of said project to be charged to Water Department
     Passed January 2, 1941

1941

As reported by the *Keene Evening Sentinel*:

Board of Engineers Is Authorized to Place Men on Retired Firemen's List

City Government Places Responsibility of Putting Inactive or Aged Firemen on Honorary Roll on Certain Officials upon Recommendation of Fire Department Committee; Routine Business Is Transacted

The responsibility of releasing from the fire department rolls and placing on the retirement, or honorary list, members who it is believed are not capable of carrying on their duties, was placed on the shoulders of the board of engineers by the passage of a joint resolution at the city government meeting Thursday night.

Ordinances Amended

Passage of the joint resolution calls for an amendment to Chapter 8, Section 3, of the city ordinances and provides that the following be added to the ordinance: "It shall be the duty of the board of engineers to retire or place on the honorary list any member of the department who in their opinion shall because of age, physical condition, inefficiency or inactivity, be unable or fail to perform the duties required of him as a fireman."

Committee Explains Recommendations

Alderman Reginald F. Howe, chairman of the joint standing committee on fire department explained to the upper body that the board believes there are several men in the department who are no longer capable of helping. The engineers, he said, don't feel that they want to release these men without the backing of the city government. The resolution makes it a duty of the engineers to do so, he declared.

A Joint Resolution was passed on September 4th, 1941 relating to pensions for fireman, and police officers or constables.

An Ordinance relating to pension for fireman, police officer or constable

Be it ordained by the City Councils of the City of Keene, as follows:

Section 1. A pension may be granted, by the city councils, to any fireman, police officer or constable, who by reason of permanent disability directly incurred in the performance of his official duty, is no longer able to perform services in such capacity, or who has served faithfully for not less than twenty-five years.

Section 2. No pension shall be granted for more than one year at a time.

Section 3. The maximum amount of such pension shall be in the case of a permanent man one half of the pay received by him at the time of his retirement or disability, and in the case of a part-time, call man or special man, five hundred dollars.

Section 4. All applications for pensions under the provisions of this ordinance shall be made by joint resolution to the city councils.

Section 5. NO fireman or police officer who is at the time of his retirement or disability eligible to receive benefits under Chapter 154 Laws of 1939, An Act Creating a Retirement System for Firemen, and/or Chapter 166 Laws of 1941, An Act Creating a Retirement System for Policemen, shall be eligible for a pension under this ordinance.

Passed September 18th, 1941

A Joint Resolution was passed on October 2nd, 1941 for the purchase of a Fire Truck for the sum of $2,500 which will be raised by taxation in the year 1942.

————

[*Compiler's Note*: 1941 was an important year for America. As the *Keene Evening Sentinel* published:]

US DECLARES WAR ON JAPAN

UNAMIOUS VOTE IN SENATE AGAINST JAPAN; HOUSE HAS ONE "NO"

Washington, Dec 8, (AP) Congress voted a formal declaration of war against Japan today after Pres. Roosevelt requested immediate action as an answer to Japan's "unprovoked and dastardly attack" on Hawaii.

A united congress acted swiftly after the president had revealed that the American forces lost two warships and 3,000 dead and wounded in the surprise dawn attack yesterday.

The house vote was 388 to 1. Miss Jeannette Rankin (R-Mont), who voted against a declaration of war with Germany in 1917, was the lone member casting a negative vote. Rep. Harold Knutson (R-Minn), who also voted against the 1917 declaration, voted for war against Japan.

———————

The fire selected for the year 1941 is a fire which occurred on December 16th, which was a wood & brick building on Main Street occupied by the Eagle Hotel. As reported by the *Keene Evening Sentinel*:

'FIRE'
EAGLE HOTEL FIRE SENDS OCCUPANTS FROM THEIR BEDS

Occupants Flee From 40 Rooms When Blaze Starts in Hotel Kitchen But Damaged Is Not Estimated to Be Heavy; No One Injured; Blanchard Barn Burns in North End of City.

Occupants of 40 rooms in the Eagle hotel on Main Street were forced to leave their beds at 5 o'clock this morning when fire broke out in the kitchen. The flames did not reach the floors where the occupants were sleeping. Two alarms were sounded for the blaze. The firemen had just returned to their beds after combating a fire which leveled the barn owned by Joseph Blanchard located on the "ledges" between Sullivan and Charles Street. The losses at both fires are not reported very large.

Fire in the Eagle hotel

The first one in the building under the management of Daniel E. O'Neil, started near the kitchen stove and a flash resulted which spread the flames about the kitchen. Fire worked its way into the wooden ventilator in the roof over the kitchen, which is a one story building. The flames also followed up the vent pipe over the stove and the heart from the pipe set fire to the roof.

Firemen responded first to a still alarm. When they arrived the blaze appeared to be serious and Officer William C. Hadley sounded Box 6. After Assistant Engineer John H., Simpson reached the scene and the flames were spreading about the kitchen he instructed Officer Carl W. Swanson to sound a second alarm as a precautionary measure.

The alert work of the firemen soon had the fire under control but they worked for nearly an hour before the flames were entirely extinguished.

As soon as the fire was discovered James O'Neil started making a round of the rooms awakening the occupants. The guests fled into the hallways and down stairs into the lobby. Fire did not enter any of the rooms on the second or third floors where the people were sleeping. Smoke entered a number of rooms.

Some of the metal ceiling in the kitchen had to be torn away by firemen to get at the flames.

After the smoke had cleared away, occupants to the hotel returned to their rooms. No one was injured in their haste to dress and leave their rooms.

———————

'FIRE'
Blanchard Barn Fire

At 3 o'clock this morning fire leveled the barn owned by Joseph Blanchard which is located between Sullivan and Charles Streets. This fire had made much headway that firemen were not about to check it. The building is about 20 to 25 feet in size. There was a ton of hay in the barn according to Mr. Blanchard. No animals were in the barn. Firemen were summoned to the fire by a transmitter call on Box 25.

Other buildings in the neighborhood were endangered but firemen kept a close watch that none caught fire. The roofs of several of the buildings were covered with snow which afforded protection from the flying embers.

Only a few "fire fans" went to the barn fire but many went to the Eagle Hotel fire on hearing the second alarm. The Blanchard fire was spectacular as the flames illuminated the sky and could be seen for a number of miles.

Another Fire noted for 1941 was the fire of October 2nd, in the Cheshire County Grain Company Building on St. James Street:

'FIRE'
BLAZE FROM OIL BURNER IN GRAIN COMPANY OFFICE

Fire Causes Damage at Cheshire County Grain Company Building

Fire which firemen claim originated about an oil burner in the office of the Cheshire County Grain company off St. James Street, caused considerable damage to the office building and contents shortly before 8 0'clock this morning. Firemen responded to a general alarm sounded on Box 512 St. James Street, opposite Holbrook Grocery Co., and in a short time had the fire under control.

Ray A. Wright, the manager of the grain company was in the main building working when he discovered the fire and he closed the door into the main building to prevent the fire and smoke from damaging the grain.

Fire charred the floor about the heater, the counter and some of the furniture. Some of the goods in the office building were damaged. Clouds of black smoke from the oil poured from the open door giving the appearance of a worse fire.

Wednesday night firemen were called by a still alarm and extinguished a fire which was burning in a chair in one of the apartment of the Main Street Sentinel building. This was noticed by an observant citizen from across Main Street, and thus prevented a serious blaze. No one was home in the apartment at the time.

As Reported by the *Keene Evening Sentinel* on December 16th, 1941:

'STORY'
Over 500 Men Attend Air Raid Wardens School

Responding to the "call to arms" with the serious purpose of effecting an efficient working organization designed to protect civilian life and property, between 500 and 600 men of this city and surrounding towns assembled in Spaulding gymnasium at Keene Teachers College Monday night for the opening session of the local Civilian Defense Committee's school for air raid wardens.

Members of the local auxiliary police and firemen joined with the air raid wardens in the initial meeting but will hold separate training sessions hereafter.

Mayor Holbrook

Dr. Lloyd P. Young, president of Keene Teachers College, who expressed gratification at the large turnout, opened the school with preliminary remarks.

Just as the attack on Pearl Harbor was unexpected, so might be an air raid in this city, the chief executive stated, adding: I feel that we would be very lax if we didn't do our utmost to develop a thorough and efficient defense organization in the city."

Any organization, declared the mayor to give effective protection must be a working unit from the top to the bottom and he emphasized the importance of those in the defense units to learn their assignments so well that if emergency does come they will act instinctively. He urged that every effort be made by the men to attend all of the instruction classes. In closing, he suggested that the local Civilian Defense groups adopt as their watchword and slogan: "Remember Pearl Harbor."

Films Shown

While the air raid wardens were waiting for arrival of the auxiliary police and firemen a motion picture of London fire raids were shown.

First of the instructors to address the meeting was Alpheus B. White, deputy air raid warden and one of the two Keene men to secure an instructor's rating at the school conducted in recent weeks by the State Council of Defense.

Addressing the men from the outside towns, Mr. White told them that they would have to pattern their organization on the material given out during the course. He stated that the auxiliary police and firemen had been invited to the meeting in order that they might get an over-all picture of the different Civilian Defense organizations and the parts that each would play in the set-up.

After asserting that the purpose of air raid precaution are to protect life and property and keep the morale of the civilian population at a high point, Mr. White explained in detail by the aid of blackboard diagrams and a map, just what the Air Raid Warning Service is, how it operates and how it differs from the Air Raid Wardens Service.

Other than to understand the set-up of the warning service, the air raid wardens were told that they could forget about it.

The very vital nerve center of the Air Raid Wardens organization, the report center, was discussed in detail and the men were given a clear picture as to how this function and what officials are connected with this center.

————

The ladies auxiliary has served the Keene Fire Department and the Fire Department has benefited from their dedication. Over the years the Ladies have purchased and paid for the above display case, built by Ronald Amadon. The ladies auxiliary has also purchased tables, chairs and other items used by the fire department. Photo by Steven Goldsmith.

[*from the compiler*, Steve Goldsmith, 2011:]

Keene Fire Department Ladies Auxiliary

After December 7, 1941, the attack on Pearl Harbor changed the course of history for our country and the Keene Fire Department was no different. Men were drafted into the war effort, and men enlisted into all branches to defend our country. This created a shortage of men.

A small band of ladies, wives of firefighters decided to form a Ladies' Auxiliary to assist the fire department during fires and other emergencies. The Ladies became known as the Keene Fire Department Ladies Auxiliary. They assisted at fires, the annual dinner, and other sponsored events.

These ladies, Elsa Messer, Mather Towne, Tina Messer, Judy Thompson, Betty Symonds, and the list goes on and on. These faces could be seen serving coffee, donuts, sandwiches at fires and other events. As time went on newer members joined, firefighters' wives, daughters, etc. And the list of ladies goes on. If not for the smiling faces of this organization the times when they were most needed would have created an additional burden to the department and others during the emergencies that the fire department responded to. For this organization, the Keene Fire Department Ladies Auxiliary, we thank you.

1942 [from *City of Keene Annual Report*]

Report of the Chief Engineer of the Fire Department

To His Honor the Mayor and Board of Aldermen:

I hereby submit my report for the year Ending December 31st, 1942.

There were 21 Bell alarms, 347 Still alarms, making a total of 368 alarms. 11 of these calls were out of town, and three of them were false alarms.

The estimated value of buildings damaged by fire, $345,830.00

    Damage to buildings, $11,879.62
    Insurance on said buildings, $283,050.00
    Insurance paid $11,879.62.
    Value of contents of buildings, $167,100.00
    Damage to contents, $3,446.08
    Insurance on said contents, $154,000.00
    Insurance paid $3,446.08.

The Department has answered 88 less alarms during the year, than was answered the year previous. The fire loss will be some less this year.

The Fire Department inspections continue to show very good results, as there

Emergency Squad 1 was used for all types of night firefighting due to the lighting that it had on it. The Morse gun on the rear of the truck was used when master streams were needed on a defensive attack. The Fire Department still owns this truck today. Photo by Ronald Amadon.

The Reo Combination was converted into a forestry unit carrying the states equipment for Keene and Cheshire County area. This truck now belongs to Keene Parks and Recreation Department and gives fire truck rides for children. Photo by Ronald Amadon.

are very few cases of any large amount of rubbish found in the inspections. Also you will note that the basement fires have been reduced to a minimum.

The Department is continuing the Vocational lessons to the Call Firemen so that all firemen will have the benefit of this training. This also includes first aid instructions.

The Motor Fire apparatus and its equipment are in very good condition. All Pumping engines were tested for their capacities last October, and all showed a reserve capacity.

There has been purchased for the Department another Emergency Squad truck. This truck replaces the Reo Combination which was placed in service August 15th, 1923. This truck has a small pump of 75 gallons, 150 gallon booster tank, 200 feet booster hose, 400 feet 1 ½" hose, first aid supplies, inhalator, gas masks, flood lighting outfit, Salvage covers, 2 stretchers, 1,100 gallon Morse gun. Also the department has a Rockwood water fog applicator, which is very effective on small gasoline and oil fires, especially automobile fires.

The Reo Combination now carries the State Forestry equipment for forest fires.

The Department has on hand 11,500 feet of 2 ½" double jacket rubber lined hose and 3,500 feet of 1 ½" single jacket rubber lined hose. There are 3,800 feet of 2 ½" and 3,200 feet of 1 ½ " hose that is loaded on the trucks at all times. There is also 1,200 feet of linen unlined hose at South Keene in hose house.

The Fire Alarm System and its equipment are in very good condition. There has been very little repairs or line work done on the system during the year, but repairs will have to be done the coming year as the telephone is setting quite a number of poles that will have to be changed over by fire alarm.

The Board of Engineers recommend that two more permanent men be added to the force, and suitable rooms be provided for them, as the manpower of the permanent force is not sufficient for keeping the station covered at all times.

To His Honor the Mayor, Joint Standing Committee on Fire Department, Officers and members of the Fire Department, also the Police Department, I extend my thanks for the co-operation rendered me during the year.

Respectfully submitted,
EUGENE B. RILEY,
Chief Fire Department

As Reported by the *Keene Evening Sentinel*, February 11, 1942.

Board of Engineers Changes with Simpson Registration

CHIEF RILEY AND FIRST ASSISTANT

(Photo by Granite State Studio)
CHIEF EUGENE B. RILEY

Changes in the personnel of the board Have been made recently. John H. Simpson, who has been a member of the department for a long period of years and a member of the board of engineers for more than 20 years, resigned and his place on the board is being taken by Thomas B. Wallbank, who was formerly Captain of the Washington Hook and Ladder Co.

Mr. Simpson was named as an associate member Of the board of engineers in recognition of his long and faithful service as a member of that board. He served as its clerk.

Mr. Wallbank's promotion and the recent Retirement of John A. Denison, captain of the Keene Steam Fire Engine & Hose Company. Leaves tow captain posts vacant.

A review of the personnel old and new engineers is as Follows:

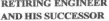

RETIRING ENGINEER AND HIS SUCCESSOR

(Photo by Granite State Studio)
JOHN H. SIMPSON

(Photo by Granite State Studio)
ELWIN H. APPLIN

Mr. Simpson is a native of Yonkers, N.Y., and Has been a resident of Keene about 48 years. He was employed in the hardware store of Knowlton & Stone Company for a time and Then entered the employ of the Pearson Bros., Plumbing department and was later the Nims Plumbing Company.

Mr. Simpson, as a member of the Keene Steamer Company rose through the ranks To become captain of the company and was Named member of the board of engineers About 23 years ago.

He is a member of the Masonic fraternity, Eastern Star Chapter, Odd Fellows. Lodge Rebedahs, Elks lodge, Spanish War Veterans and Keene Firemen's Ass.

"Tom" Wallbank

THOMAS B. WALLBANK

Thomas B. Wallbank, new member of the board of engineers is a member of the Washington Hook and Ladder Company. He has been a member of the company since 1914. He has risen in the ranks as Lieutenant and at the time of his promotion held the rank of Captain.

Mr. Wallbank was born in Kent, England, and came to this country when a small boy. He is a member of the Keene Firemen's Association. Mr. Wallbank is the groundskeeper at Alumni-field.

"Ike" Applin

Elwin H. Applin has been a member of the Keene Fire department for 42 years and has served as member of the board of engineers the past four years.

Mr. Applin was a member of the Deluge Hose Company and served as captain of the company for 23 years before being prom0pted to the board of engineers. He is a member of the Elks lodge and Keene Firemen's Association.

Mr. Applin is a native of Swanzey and has lived in Keene the greater part of his life. He employed by the Beaver Mills Company 16 years before he entered the automobile tire business in 1910.

———

Board of Engineers remains the same as 1941.

Captains

Remain the same as 1941.

Permanent Drivers

Remain the same as 1941.

Steamer Hose Company

Remain the same as 1941.

Deluge Hose Company

Remain the same as 1941.

Hook and Ladder Company

Remain the same as 1941.

Apparatus And Equipment

Ahrens-Fox Triple Combination No. 1
750 GPM with 60 Gallon Booster Tank
Ahrens-Fox Triple Combination No. 2
750 GPM 80 Gallon Booster Tank and tools
Ahrens-Fox Triple Combination No. 3
600 GPM 100 Gallon Booster Tank and tools
Mack Ladder Truck and Chemical in title has been changed to the City Service Ladder Truck with 239 feet of ladders still a 40 gallon Chemical tank
Emergency Squad No. 1.
Flood lighting outfit and first aid supplies, Salvage covers and 1,100 gallon Morse Gun and other equipment.
Emergency Squad No. 2

For forest fires and still alarms, 2,500 feet of 1 ½" hose, a 75 gallon booster pump, 136 gallon booster tank, and 40 gallon portable pump.
Chief's Car
Oldsmobile Coupe
Cellar Pump
Capacity 250 gallons per minute or 15,000 gallons per hour
A Foam Generator with 1,400 lbs. of foam powder.
Reserve Forest Fire Equipment
One 40 gallon portable pump, with all necessary equipment, 2,500 feet of 1 ½" hose,
23 5-gallon pump tanks; 5 4-gallon, and 6 3-gallon, 3 2 ½-gallon extinguishers 26 14 quart water pails; 65 shovels; 12 hoes; 12 Fire rakes; 12 Pulaski's, and two tubs for relay from pump to pump.
Fire Alarm and Signals remain the same.
NOTE: In the Chief Report for the year 1942 a list of fire losses by years from 1910 to 1942 was published on page 80 of the Annual Report:
Fire Alarm Telegraph and Signals remain the same.

Joint Resolutions for the year ending 1942

NOTE: On January 6th, 1942 a Joint Resolution was passed for $75,000 Dollars by issuing and selling bonds of the City of Keene for said sum. The purchase is for appropriation for the purchase of land in Swanzey, New Hampshire to be used as an air craft landing area, and the erection of incidental buildings thereon for the carrying on of an air craft landing area, The Keene Airport.

A Joint Resolution Relating to Water Pipes at Fire Station The sum of Three Hundred ($300) Dollars was appropriated for new water pipes for the Fire Station. Passed March 19th, 1942

A Joint Resolution was passed on April 2nd, 1942 for the sum of Five Hundred Dollars for maintenance of fire apparatus.

NOTE: On April 2nd, 1942 A Joint Resolution relating to the purchase of land be purchased any parcel or tract and/or parcels or tracts of land in Swanzey, New Hampshire, for the City of Keene, Which the Airport Committee deem necessary as new sites for buildings acquired in the purchases of land on the proposed Airport site in Swanzey.

An Ordinance relating to the preparation for and conduct during black-outs and air raids.

Be it ordained by the City Councils of Keene:

Finding and declaration of necessity—It is hereby found and declared that the interest of the City of Keene in the public safety of its citizens and in the National Defense compel the enactment of rules and regulations with reference to blackouts and air raids and t is further found and declared that a black-out is one of the most important phases of passive defense. That it is one of the most difficult to achieve successfully. That it requires planning and advance preparation as well as the fullest cooperation, from the people at large. That the purpose of a blackout is to deprive enemy airmen of all possible reference points which might aid them in locating targets such as air fields, utilities, industrial plants and centers of population. That the objective to be achieved by black-out procedure and regulations is to have all exterior lights so controlled that they can be immediately extinguished upon the sounding of the blackout alarm or the air raid alarm or upon the issuance of a command to extinguish them and to have all lights and buildings so controlled that upon the alarm these lights can be immediately extinguished or by the use of screens or other blackening devices no light can be observed from the outside. It is further found and declared that the public safety demands rules and regulations as to the conduct of individuals and motor traffic during black-outs and air raids.

For Definitions the Annual Report of 1942 on page 19 has both the ordinance and definitions of Black-outs and Air Raid Alarm

A Joint Resolution was passed on May 7th, 1942 relating to repairs to the Fire Station. These repairs would cost no more than $214.50 for the roof on the hose tower at the Fire station.

Also on May 7th, 1942 a Resolution was passed relating to the Purchase of a Boat for the sum of $300.00 dollars with an outboard motor and will be for the use of any City Department, to be housed at the fire station. This purchase will be by the Police committee.

As Reported by the *Keene Evening Sentinel* on January 5th, 1942:

'FIRE'
BOX 19 SOUNDED BUT NOT NEEDED FOR AUTO FIRE

Firemen Called Out for short Circuit Blaze on Marlboro Street

Someone did as they were told Saturday night and as a result the entire fire department and a large percentage of motorists in the city went to lower Marlboro Street after Box 19 sounded.

A motorist's car was a fire from a short circuit and he called to a passerby to "call the firemen." Instead of telephoning for a single truck the man sounded a general alarm from Box 19, which was nearby. The fire was out before the department arrived.

The going and coming of the autom9biles up and down Marlboro and Baker Streets caused more or less of a traffic jam but no accidents were reported.

Firemen answered two still alarms on Sunday who extinguished a fire in the house at 24 Pearl Street, which was caused by putting hot ashes in a wooden container, and a fire among rags in the house 9 Madison Street.

_____

As Reported by the *Keene Evening Sentinel* on January 7th, 1942:

'FIRE'
FIRE DAMAGES 3-FAMILY HOUSE ON MARLBORO STREET

Apartment Occupied by Earnest Richards Has Blaze in Basement

Three families in the house at 691 Marlboro Street were driven out about 11 o'clock Tuesday night by fire and smoke. The damage to the building, which is owned by Councilman J. Henry Southwell, is estimated at several hundred dollars. Firemen combated the blaze in below-zero weather. The general alarm was sounded from Box 65, which is in front of the Keene Chair Company Factory.

Fire started in the basement of the section of the three-apartment house occupied by Ernest Richards and was making headway when discovered by Mr. Richards who detected the odor of smoke and discovered a brisk blaze.

When firemen arrived flames were issuing from the door and windows leading to the basement. A booster line of hose from one of the trucks was laid and the water kept the flames quelled until a large hose line was laid from the hydrant near the factory of the Keene Chair Company plant. Flames did not reach any of the apartments as the firemen made a good stop. A large number of burlap bags, pine box wood and felting in the basement burned, causing an unusual amount of dense smoke which filled all the apartments.

Forest A. Crossman and Frank Wheeler occupy the other two apartments. There are three children in the Richards family and one each in the Crossman and Wheeler families.

A number of "fire fans" followed the trucks to the scene of the fire but they remained only a short time owing to the extremely cold weather.

Tuesday October 13th, 1942 Keene's Amoskeag Steamer took its ride to the Scrap heap for the war effort as reported by the *Keene Evening Sentinel*:

'STORY'
Keene's Amoskeag Steamer
KEENE STARTS BIG 3-DAY CAMPAIN TO COLLECT OLD METALS FOR WAR NEEDS

As Keene today swung into an all-out drive to slap the Jap with a huge amount of scrap, two trucks were busy collecting the waste materials which citizens have placed at the edges of sidewalks in the first section of the city to be covered.

An effort will be made, the Public Works office reported, to complete the first-day area collection on this day to avoid overlapping into the second day when the second sections will be covered.

In the meantime, two significant contributions to the local scrap drive were made over the long weekend. On Monday the old octagon reservoir on Beech Hill was taken down. This has been estimated to provide about 10 tons of scrap in it.

Containing much valuable brass and other metals, the old Amoskeag steam fire engine, owned by Ellis Robertson, has been turned over by Mr. Robertson to the scrap campaign. The steamer was made in Manchester, bought by the city in 1883 under the mayoralty of Horatio Kimball, sixth mayor, and was used for many years by the fire department. Mr. Robertson's farther, the late George Robertson, was engineer in charge of the steamer.

Follow up to the story as research has brought up in 1942 the Amoskeag Steamer was owned by the Keene Fire department? A question which has not truly been answered. The record shows that prior to 1942 Ellis

Robertson has purchased the Steamer due to new equipment purchased by the Department, possible the chiefs' car or a new truck. In 1942 on the Cities scrap drive the Amoskeag Steamer was taken to the scrap pile on its last ride by members along with Mr. Ellis. The Steamer was hooked up to a team of horses and paraded down Main Street to lower Main and back to the scrap pile.

Mr. Ellis Robertson rescued the Steamer from the scrap pile and was moved to a garage for storage possible on Roxbury Street. The reason the Steamer was removed was due to public pressure that this once historic part of Keene should be saved.

In 1943 Mr. Ellis Robertson made an offer to the Society for the Preservation of New England Antiquities out of Boston Mass. To Donate and partially sell the Old Amoskeag Steamer.

The Letter from the Society for the Preservation of New England Antiquities is as follows:

Dated December 27th, 1943:

Dear Mr. Robertson:

It is with the greatest pleasure that I learn from our member, Mr. F. H. Reed that you are selling to the Society for $35.00 dollars the old fire engine, which you had in your possession. Mr. Reed and I are delighted to acquire this contribution to the collection of fire apparatus being formed by this Society for the Preservation of New England Antiquities.

As you so very kindly shaded the price for our benefit, we are going to consider this piece to be partly your gift, and partly the gift of Mr. Reed and also of myself. So that when in the fullness of time this piece is exhibited where it belongs it will have a large label bearing the name of each one of us three as joint donors. It will be a great satisfaction to be permitted to be a donor of so valuable apiece.

Enclosed please find a check for $35.00 dollars in full payment.

Signed sincerely yours, Henry Appleton

In 1949 Mr. Ellis Robertson sent a letter to the Society for the Preservation of New England Antiquities on Cambridge Street Boston, Mass.

Here is the reply from the letter dated January 29th, 1949.

Dear Miss Addison,

Your letter received as from Mr. Robertson who wanted to know the whereabouts of the Steam Fire Engine that he sold to Mr. Appleton in 1944.

This old engine (Amoskeag #580) I moved from Keene, New Hampshire to Ipswich, New Hampshire and was the one there in the barn on Mr. Johnson's Estate.

The Amoskeag Mfg. Co. Manchester New Hampshire built it for Keene New Hampshire in 1883, was number 580. It was a second size engine with double piston pumps. It had been given over for scrap drive at Keene by Mr. Robertson, but due to the protests of the Society and others, including myself, was returned, but not until it had been almost stripped of many accessories and gadgets and equipment.

It was still deemed worthwhile saving as a relic, and Mr. Robertson sold what remained of it to Mr. Appleton in 1944. I myself moved it, hiring a trailer truck, from Keene to Ipswich, and recall the perilous ride we had with chains holding the huge piece on thru the hills of Peterborough.

After the death of Mr. Johnson, vandals again robbed the machine of other accessories and parts, and as the place was sold, it was a question of either moving the machine at further expense to another location or of turning it over to Mr. James Filleul, 619 South Main Street, Manchester, New Hampshire who was getting up a collection of Steam Fire Engines to go with the historical collection of Manchester. With my sanction and that of Mr. Little, it was turned over to Mr. Filleul on the condition it was not to be sold, but restored by Mr. Filleul and added to his collection of Steam Fire Engines.

He has already done some work on the Steamer, and hope in time it will be at least partially restored. I think Mr. Filleul would be glad to cooperate with the people in Keene if they wish to borrow the engine or photograph it; no doubt he may have other interesting data concerning it. The Steamer is to remain in Manchester where it was built and can be seen at any time, I should imagine.

It is just an interesting story of how an ancient fire engine escaped from being destroyed thru the kindly ministrations of interested parties, including Mr. Appleton and myself, so that it might be preserved for future generations.

The letter was sent form South Weymouth, Mass., 59 Torrey Street on January 29th, 1949 by James Filleul.

It wasn't until early 1983 that Mr. Charles J. Hanrahan of Keene and Robert Mason who was a member of the Keene Steamer Company tried to find the whereabouts of the Amoskeag Steamer.

On November 15th, 1983 a letter was sent to Mr. Charles J. Hanrahan of Keene from the Society for the Preservation of New England Antiquities of 141 Cambridge Street Boston, Massachusetts 02114, and reads as follows:

I am writing in response to your letter regarding the Amoskeag Steamer that Ellis Robertson sold to SPNEA in January 1944. I spoke with Mr. Robertson's son at least six or eight months ago, and he has already given you all the information we have.

Enclosed is a copy of the letter written in 1949 regarding the history of the engine, which was given to James Filleul in 1948. Our files indicate that Mr. Filleul died sometime before 1973 without restoring the Amoskeag Steamer. He possible may have used parts of it to restore other engines in his collection.

I suggest you try to contact his descendants to find any addition information. We do not have a photo of the engine.

Sincerely, Penny J. Sander Assistant Curator

Through the work of Charles J. Hanrahan and Robert Mason Mathew J. Spinello purchased the Keene's Amoskeag Steamer somehow from the late James Filleul Estate.

2126 Barton Blvd., Rockford, Ill. 61103. To our knowledge this is where the Keene's Amoskeag is today. It was noted that after Mr. Filleul had died his estate was auctioned off without knowing that at least the Keene's Amoskeag Steamer was not there's to be sold.

Into the scrap heap goes one of Keene's historic relics, the old Amoskeag Steamer, owned by Ellis Robertson, who several years ago took it in trade on a new piece of apparatus. Mr. Robertson (left) is shown here taking a final glance at the old steamer with Salvage Chairman Russell F. Batchelder. Photo by Keene Sentinel.

Keene's Amoskeag Steamer #580 took its last ride with a team of horses from Ellis Robertson Garage down Main Street to just beyond Rt. 101 and turned around and drove back to Emerald Street and Main where a large scrap pile was being built. The Old Amoskeag was fired up for its last time. As you read and saw, the Steamer stood proudly on Main Street with the sign "We're Steaming it up for the Japs!"

There is no documentation as to following up on its retrieval except that the now owner would return it if another one could be found and this would be an exchange.

————

[*Compiler's note*: The 70th Annual Report of 1943 has made changes as to the way the Annual Report is done by Chief Riley.]

1943 [from *City of Keene Annual Report*]

Fire Protection

EUGENE B. RILEY, Chief

Expenditures in 1943 $27,749.79

The night before Christmas, 1943 gave every indication that it was going to be a cold, cold holiday. After the Christmas tree trimmings had received their final touch,

the man of the house took a peak at the thermometer outside the kitchen window, quickly bedded down his furnace for the night, dug out a couple of extra blankets and proceeded to enjoy the comforting warmth of his bed.

At approximately two-thirty Christmas morning, the first of three fire alarms sounded and house lights went on all over town as citizens contemplated "going to the fire." Probably a third of Keene's adult population, deciding to brave the below zero weather, hurriedly donned their cloths, added an extra sweater for good measure and dashed off for the general vicinity of Alarm Box 6.

By the time people arrived at the scene, the Robertson Motor Company building was already well on its way to being completely

A Demon Called Fire

gutted and the worst and most expensive fire since 1934 was underway.

"Efficient Work"

In the department chief's annual report to the city government regarding this fire, he merely commented, "It was efficient work on the part of the firemen to hold the fire in the building in which it started." But to those persons who were on the scene, it was much more that simply "efficient work".

No fewer than 13 lines of hose were used in combating the blaze, many of the lines being used slowly to prevent a spread of the fire to adjoining business buildings and homes, some of which were within four feet of the blazing inferno. Despite the fact that there was no wind blowing, it was a superlative feat of fire-fighting that the blaze was confined to the one building. Oil soaked floors and exploding gasoline tanks of automobiles stored in the garage helped to create an intensely hot fire, and though the adjacent buildings were scorched by this radiated heat, they were saved only because of hoses constantly played on them.

The Christmas morning fire served as an excellent example of the fire-fighting capabilities of Keene's firemen,-regulars, call men and the auxiliary group. It gave the onlookers a dramatic illustration of the protection the tax payers are buying when they invest in proper equipment and obtain willing and "efficient" personnel.

388 Alarms in 1943

During 1943, there were 16 bell alarms and 372 stills, 13 of which were for out –of town fires. There were 20 alarms more than during 1942, and in the financial loss, the most severe since 1934. Other large individual losses were occasioned by fires at the Golding-Keene Company and at the Norman's Motor Transportation terminal.

Statistically, 1943's fire report is:

Estimated value of buildings damaged by fire, $384,800.00.

Damage to these buildings, $39,704.68
Insurance on these buildings, $299,550.00
Losses paid by insurance, $39,704.68.
Value of contents, $561,114,
Damage to contents, $92,442.48
Insurance on contents, $483,275.00
Insurance paid on contents, $92,324.62.

Pressure Tests

In October a test was made to prove that if a broken water main crippled the usual supply, water could be pumped into Central Square from Mill Pond or from Beaver Brook with good pressure maintained. Using 2,150 feet of hose, from the Faulkner & Colony mill to the square, engine No. 2 at the pond had 210 pounds pressure through 1,350 feet of hose to the point where engine No. 3, carrying 160 pounds pressure, brought the water through 800 feet of hose to the square.

With a one-inch nozzle at 70 pounds pressure, it was delivering 247 gallons of water per minute, and in a second test engine No. 2 alone, with 410 pounds engine pressure, with the 2,150 feet of hose, delivered the same amount of water at the same nozzle pressure.

All the motor fire apparatus and its equipment are in very good condition as well as the fire alarm system, and for the latter, two replacement boxes were purchased.

Business District Inspection

As a preventative measure, the department engineers continue to inspect the business district for fire hazards. While the value of this procedure cannot be determined in dollars and cents, it is recognized by fire-fighters that a maintenance of these inspections save countless fires which could be course, prove to be costly. Basements of buildings and adjacent alleys are inspected once a month as part of the local program.

Two men Added

During the past year, two more men were added to the permanent force, there now being eight men on duty. New rooms have been provided these men and a big improvement is noticeable in fire service.

Note: that the Number of Alarms and Fire Losses during the Past Decade; from 1934 to 1943 was placed on page 25 of the chiefs report for the year.

Joint Resolutions for the year ending 1943

A Joint Resolution Relating to the Transfer of Funds. That a balance of the amount, Three Hundred Fifty-four and 38/100 Dollars ($354.38) be transferred to the Fire Department Fund to pay for labor and material used to provide a suitable depository for Civilian Defense apparatus loaned by the Federal Government. Passed December 16th, 1943.

NOTE: A short note on the Municipal Airport.

MUNICIPAL AIRPORT

After weeks of effort in purchasing land in North Swanzey, Keene's new municipal airport' began to take form in Fall of 1942. On September, 17th, the city government formally voted that it "shall be known and bear the title "Dillant –Hopkins Municipal Airport" in honor of Thomas David Dillant, Keene New Hampshire, and Edwin Chester Hopkins of Swanzey, New Hampshire, who willing gave their lives in defense of their country in the early months of the year 1942 of the Second World War."

Soon after the airport received its name, ground-breaking exercises were held and construction got underway. By the time it was accepted by the city, approximately $1,100,000 were spent, $71,800 by the city and the remainder by the United States government.

Officially dedicated Sunday, October 31st, 1943, an estimated 5,000 persons witnessed an impressive program, taking a part in which were Governor Robert O. Blood, the entire New Hampshire congressional delegation and representatives of the army and navy.

Two long runways greet the aviator to Keene's new municipal airport, located in North Swanzey, New Hampshire.

The fire selected for 1943 is the Robertson Garage, as reported by the *Keene Evening Sentinel* on Monday, December 27th, 1943.

'FIRE'
KEENE HAS ITS WORST FIRE IN 10 YEARS

Robertson Garage Destroyed By Fire; Int. Narrow Fabric Damaged; Loss of $200,000

Keene's worst fire since the Goodnow store block blaze in August 1934, occurred Christmas morning when the Robertson Motor Company garage on Eagle Court was almost completely gutted and more than a score of automobiles were burned or damaged with an estimated loss of $100,000; and the top floor, occupied by the International Narrow Fabric company, suffered an equal amount of damage, the total loss being estimated at close to $200,000.

The garage started salvage operations today and the textile concern absorbed its 30 or more idle employees in other departments, as members of the board of engineers of the fire department met with Ellis Robertson, officials of the International Narrow fabric Company, the watchman and Insurance agency representatives to try to determine the cause and make a more accurate estimate of the damage.

While the loss was large and the fire was fought under the handicap of below-zero weather, citizens in general consider it fortunate there was not a general conflagration and there is widespread praise of the firemen in keeping the fire confined within the brick wall, and saving at least a half-dozen tenement and rooming house properties in the area bounded by Eagle Court, Main Street and Dunbar Street, many of which were within few feet of the inferno of blaze.

The firemen made an excellent stop in the rear, preventing the spread of the fire across a bridge connecting with the main plant of the International Narrow Fabric Company. Lack of wind also helped as the sparks, smoke and flames rolled skyward, although reports were received of cinders as far away as Beaver street.

Thousands of persons were attracted to the scene by three alarms and visited the fire ruins on Christmas Day and Sunday.

Customers Cars Burned

Among cars owned by customers of the garage which were lost were those of Daniel O'Neil, Miss. Vivian Rockwood, Miss Doris Wilder, Carl Manhall, Catherine Campagna, cars to two transients, one owned by a New York woman, American Express company, Ruth Avery.

The paint on a car owned by Leo McInnis, chief clerk of the rationing board, was burned and three customer's cars were damaged by water. It is reported that all of the privately-owned vehicles were covered by Insurance.

Repair Shop Established

Under the direction of Mr. Robertson, a repair shop unit was being set up today and the company's used car reconditioning room is made ready so that needs of customers can be met. The first floor of the new part of the building which escaped damage by fire will be usable at once. Telephone connections have been reestablished. The stock room of the garage is also intact.

New Autos Saved

Several new automobiles owned by the Robertson Motor Company, which were in the show room and a considerable distance from the burning building, were removed during the progress of the flames by volunteers. Fire did not enter the show room as metal covered doors were closed between the garage and the building used as a stock room, office and show room.

Probably one of the first persons who live in the immediate neighborhood of the fire, to discover the blaze was Joseph Gallagher, 136 Main Street who had a room in the rear of the Gallagher rooming house which is next adjoining the Robertson building. He called the central telephone office and asked the operator to call the fire station.

Houses Evacuated

The magnitude of the fire in the early stages caused 10 or more families on Dunbar Street to remove their valuables and most of their belongings from houses in the immediate vicinity of the blaze. Mayor Richard L. Holbrook was among the volunteers who helped remove the volunteers who helped remove articles from the threatened houses. There were more than 25 persons in the Gallagher house and all of these make a hurried exit with their valuables.

Houses on Main Street and Dunbar Street were within 30 feet of the blazing building and two of the houses on Dunbar Street are within four feet of the razed structure.

Firemen in relays kept the houses drenched with water but several of the houses were scorched. Other firemen poured water from all sides of the burning buildings. One line which was used to good advantage was the nozzle mounted on the rear of a truck in Eagle Court and manned by one man. Three lines of water were poured through this nozzle and this kept from burning the covered passage way between the main building of the International Narrow Fabric Company plant and the Robertson Motor Company's garages, the top floor of which was occupied by the International Narrow fabric Company and where there were a number of valuable looms, machinery and stock.

Three Alarms

The first alarm was sounded from Box 6, Main and Emerald Streets, sounded from the fire station following a telephone call and a still alarm. Almost simultaneously, Police Officer Daniel D. Henderson on Main Street noticed the flames leaping skyward and rang Box 7, Main Street corner of West Street. Upon arrival at the scene, fire Chief Eugene B. Riley ordered a general alarm and Box 6 was sounded again.

After firemen arrived they could see that more help, hose and apparatus was needed to combat the worst blaze which had been experienced in Keene in many years.

Firemen began laying hose and combating the blaze from all sides of the fire. No less than 13 lines of hose were laid from nearby hydrants.

Police Service

Chief of Police Joseph L. Regan personally directed police service during the fire. In addition to the regular officers the auxiliary police responded and showed the benefit of the training in emergency action. They not only remained on duty during the fire but were detailed to keep sightseers from getting too close to the ruins over the weekend.

Blaze Spectacular

The blaze was spectacular and the flames shot high into the air and sky was illuminated for miles. Billows of black smoke and flames followed gas tank explosions. The elevator shaft acted as a huge chimney for the flames and the floors being more or less saturated with oil through the long years the building has been used for garage purposes, furnished fuel for the flames which mushroomed through the entire building within a short space of time.

Gants W. Hall who is on duty at the garage until late at night left the building about midnight, when he shut off the compressor and did not see any signs of fire at that time. The firemen on duty for the International Narrow Fabric Company who remains on duty all night in the main factory did not see any blaze at 2 o'clock in the morning and Officer Fred J. Bergeron who passed along Eagle Court on his tour of duty between 2 and 2:15 a.m. did not notice any sign of a fire at that time.

According to Ellis Robertson treasure and manager of the Robertson Company, nine automobiles owned by customers and 10 owned by the company were destroyed. No new cars or tires owned by the company were destroyed. The company lost a large number of tools and much equipment and the company's loss he estimated will probably reach $100,000, and a similar loss by the International Narrow fabric Company is estimated. There was some insurance on the vehicles and building according to Mr. Robertson. The International Narrow Fabric Company's loss is largely covered by insurance.

Quick Flare Up

As is often the case no two stories agree as to how or where the fire actually started but one of one thing all are sure that the flames gained such headway that it was practically impossible to get onto the first floor and save any equipment. The blaze had reached through the roof before it was discovered but how long it had been burning one could hardly tell and the chief effects of the fire centered on the second floor, The explosions of the gas tanks of some of the autos helped to spread the fire quickly to all parts of the garage.

30 Motor Vehicles

More than 30 motor vehicles were in the building at the time and many of these were destroyed or crushed under the falling timbers.

Several vehicles in the rear part of the garage were damaged only by smoke and water. One vehicle, the "wrecker" owned by the Robertson Motor Company, was removed to safety. There were four trucks owned by the American Express Company in the building and these were damaged, one considerably. One tank truck, containing 1,000 gallons of fuel oil, in one section of the building, did not burn, but was damaged by smoke and water.

There were many looms and other pieces of machinery on the top floor of the building and several of these looms fell to the ground floor; some in the rear of the building remained in place but are covered with ice. Most of the machinery lost by the International Narrow fabric Company is irreplaceable. It is reported. This Company is engaged in the manufacture of braid used on service uniforms.

Families forced to flee from their home were given refuge in the Eagle Hotel, Hotel Ellis and in the homes of neighbors.

To Open Repair Shop

Mr. Robertson will establish a repair shop in a nearby building until necessary repairs are made to the burned structure.

About 30 persons employed in the International Narrow Fabric Company part of the building will be given work in the main factory and the manufacturing of goods will not be greatly affected, it is reported. Company officials hope that some of the machinery may be salvaged and repaired.

Members of the Red Cross Canteen and Keene Firemen's Auxiliary carried coffee to the firemen during the fire. Dion's Restaurant and the Eagle Hotel furnished coffee to firemen and police.

Many of the auxiliary policemen were called in for duty as were a member of regulars not on duty. Auxiliary firemen reported for duty and were of great assistance to the regulars.

While one of the fire trucks was engaged in laying hose on Main Street an automobile driven by Mrs. Elizabeth Webster of Keene collided with the vehicle. Mrs. Arthur Laurent of 20 Marlboro Street, an occupant of the Webster car, sustained head injuries and was treated in Elliot Community Hospital.

Robertson Aroused

Ellis Robertson treasure of the Company is evidently a sound sleeper for friends tried for a long time to get him by phone with no avail, and neighbors were almost equally hard to arouse but some of them finally answered and made and made special messenger service to notify him. Mrs. George B. Robertson whose late husband founded the company was early on scene.

The inset photo (top left) shows the close proximity of the buildings, which were endangered by the Robertson Motor Co. fire. The main picture (left) shows not only the fire damage, but indicates the zero weather. Taken from City of Keene Annual Report.

Salvage Radio

Almost a Leon Errol comedy was that enacted a the Robertson Motor Company fire Christmas morning when a well-known Keene man was trying to retrieve his belong from the Robertson block. He carefully carried a radio down stairs to the street and found a dry place to set it. When the apartments no

longer seemed in danger, the owner picked up the radio to take it back upstairs and fell over a fire hose landing face down in ice and water with the precious radio under his stomach, with the man who so carefully carried it out looking on.

Neither was in a mood to say much, but finally each broke out in laughter, for after all it was Christmas Day, and the incident could have been worse.

_____

(Lower photo:) Show right corner of the Robertson garage building and the bridge connecting with the main International Narrow Fabric Company building, where the firemen centered their efforts to prevent the spread of the blaze. Both photos by Reginald R. Stebbins.

⚜   *A Demon Called Fire*

1944 [from *City of Keene Annual Report*]

Fire Department

To His Honor the Mayor, and Board of Aldermen:

I hereby submit my report for the year ending December 31st, 1944.

There were 21 Bell Alarms, 400 Still Alarms, making a total of 421 alarms. Eighteen of these alarms were out of town.

The estimated value of buildings damaged by fire, $319,750.00

    Damage to buildings, $13,210.69

    Insurance on said buildings, $274,900.00

    Insurance paid $13,210.69.

    Value of contents, $131,500.00

    Damage to contents, $2,473.87

    Insurance on contents, $122,040.00

    Insurance paid $2,473.87.

The Department has answered 33 more alarms during the year, than last year, and the fire loss will not be half that of last year.

There were more large forest fires during the year than usual, as the Spring season was very dry. Most of these fires were caused by the Railroad.

The fire inspection of public buildings is still showing very good results as regards to store and basement fires, as these inspections are carried out monthly by the permanent men.

The Motor Fire Apparatus is in very good condition, with the exception of Engine No. 3, which needs its pump reconditioned as it is beginning to wear and does not pump capacity. This pump answers 80 percent of all alarms, and the Ladder Truck which is 24 years old, should be replaced by a modern piece of equipment, as it is in the obsolete class in a number of ways.

The Pumping engines have been tested for their capacities, and all passed the test except Engine No. 3.

All fire hose has been tested to 200 pounds pressure, 750 feet was discarded as not being fit for use. This hose will be turned over to the Public Works Dept. There has been purchased by the department 1,000 feet of 2 ½ inch hose and four new 36 x 8 tires for Engine No. 1. The tires of the Chief's car have been recapped, and three more salvage covers have been purchased, this makes ten covers in all.

The department has on hand 11,250 feet of 2 ½ inch hose, and 1,200 feet of linen unlined hose at South Keene in Hose house.

The Fire Alarm and its circuits are in very good condition. The battery plates will need replacing this year as they are five years old.

There is quite a little work to be done on the underground circuits this coming year.

The Board of Engineers recommend the purchase of an aerial ladder truck, 1,00 feet of fire hose, new tires for Engine No 3, two fire alarm boxes, and new plates for the fire alarm battery.

To His Honor the Mayor, Joint Standing Committee on Fire Department, Officers and Members of the fire department, Auxiliary Firemen, and the Police Department I extend my thanks for the food cooperation rendered me during the year.

EUGENE B. RILEY, Chief Fire Department.

Apparatus and Equipment:

Engine No. 1-750 gallon triple combination, 60 gallon booster tank

Engine No. 2-750 gallon triple combination, 80 gallon booster tank

Engine No. 3-600 gallon triple combination, 100 gallon booster tank

Emergency Squad No. 1-75 gallon pump, 150 gallon booster tank, flood lighting outfit, first aid supplies, salvage covers, inhalator, gas masks, stretchers, 1,100 gallon Morse invincible nozzle.

Emergency Squad No. 2-200 gallon pump, 150 gallon booster tank, 2,000 feet of 1 ½ inch hose, 35 gallon portable pump, pump tanks, shovels, axes, pulaskis, fire rakes, cross cut saw, and peavey

City Service Ladder 239 feet ladders, Eastman deluge gun, 1,100 gallons, and foam generator.

Stewart Panel Body Truck for transporting men, hose and equipment.

Reo Speed Wagon 2,500 feet 1 ½ inch hose, 40 gallon portable pump.

This equipment is furnished by State Forestry Department.

Chief's Car Oldsmobile Coupe.

Foam Generator For large gasoline and oil fires, 2,000 lbs. foam powder

Forest Fire Equipment 65 pump tank, 3 extinguishers, 6 pulaskis, 6 forest fires rakes, 47 shovels, 12 hoes, 18 14-quart water pails, and two tubs for relaying water from pump to pump.

Note: That the Number of Alarms and Fire Losses by Years from 1910 to 1944 was placed on page 38 of the chief's report for the year.

The Fire selected for 1944 is the G. Baker Dairy Farm on the Summit Road, as reported by the *Keene Evening Sentinel* on June 29th, 1944:

'FIRE'
FLAMES DESTROY 2 BARNS AND PART OF HOUSE ON G. BAKER DAIRY FARM, SUMMIT ROAD.

Twenty-five head of cattle were rescued from two burning barns during the fire this morning which destroyed the farm buildings owned by Gordon Baker on the Summit Road opposite the old airport. The loss is estimated at from $8,000 to $10,000 and is partially covered by insurance. Alfred Durant, hired man, told the firemen that the fire started near an electric light bulb close to hay. The light was not burning at the time, Durant said. A Holstein bull and one heifer were destroyed.

The fire broke out shortly before 5.45 o'clock and one piece of apparatus was sent when the still alarm signal was sounded. A few minutes after the still alarm a general alarm from Box 49 was sounded and the department trucks and firemen responded to the call.

Mr. Durant had gone to the barn to begin milking and Mr. Baker was in the house at the time. When the fire was discovered the two men began liberating the cattle and they drive them into a pasture in the rear of the barns. The men were not able to save the bull and one heifer in another part of the barn.

The two barns were about 50 by 100 feet in size and there was from 40 to 50 tons of hay in the two structures, some old and some of newly-harvested. The modern milk house, which contained the milk cooling system and bottling plant, was saved. This was quite close to the barns but firemen kept the building wet with a stream of water from a booster tank.

Included in the farm machinery burned were a homemade tractor and many tools. Some of the farm machines were in the hayfield or door yard.

When firemen arrived one pumper was set at the brook between the farm and airport. Water was forced to the buildings from a time and then one of the lines is reported to have broken and this had to be replaced before the pressure at the nozzle could be resumed. While the pressure was cut off fire made a good headway into the house. The ell and rear of the house was burned and smoke and water entered the front part of the structure.

When firemen arrived the barns were in flames, nothing could be done to save the barn structures and firemen devoted their efforts to saving the house. Firemen and volunteers removed what furniture they could from the house. Some of the furnishings on the second floor was passed out a window onto the piazza roof and then lowered to the ground.

Flames destroyed 2 barns and part of the house on G. Baker Dairy Farm on the Summit Road in Keene. Photo by Granite State Studio.

The first floor was occupied by Mr. And Mrs. Baker and their three children, Ronald, Gerald and Janice. The children were taken to the home of Arthur D. Mosher, a neighbor and former owner of the Baker farm.

The upstairs tenement was occupied by Mr. And Mrs. Alfred Durant and Mrs. Durant's father, Charles Pratt.

Firemen used more than 2,500 feet of hose in conveying water from the brook to the fire.

1945 [from *City of Keene Annual Report*]

Your Fire Protection

EUGENE B. RILEY, Chief Engineer
  1945 Expenditures $28,792.06

Every Citizen is concerned with the Fire Department. We all listen when the alarm sounds, we all stop to look when a red engine dashes by, and unfortunately too many of us get into our cars and speed to the scene of the fire, a very bad practice in the eyes of the department. But most people have no other concern with firefighting or fire prevention.

It is commonly supposed that the firemen lead a pleasant and idle life, with the right amount of excitement when a fire occurs, but the truth is that they are busy men, for there is a lot to do in keeping the equipment in first-class condition, besides maintaining

Each and every day the permanent firefighters maintained all of the equipment and as you may see always spotlessly cleaned. Engine 3 the Ahrens Fox, which is the front line response piece 1945.

the station in such spike and span condition as the housewife might envy. There is a great deal of equipment to be kept in order too.

The Keene Fire Department has three fire engines, a 75-foot aerial ladder truck, an emergency squad car equipped especially for first aid with stretchers, gas masks, inhalator, flood-lighting equipment, etc., a second emergency squad car, primarily for brush fires, a Stewart panel-body truck for transporting men and equipment, a cellar pump, a foam generator for large gasoline and oil fires, the Reo Speed Wagon with equipment furnished by the State Forestry Department for fighting forest fires, and other extensive equipment for the same purpose.

When the Alarm Rings

The first step to ringing in an alarm is a street box being pulled, which in turn rings the bell at the fire station and punches a tape, which gives you a number. That number corresponds with the box that is pulled.

KEENE FIRE SIGNALS

5—Main, Hospital
6—Main, corner Emerald
7—Main, corner West
8—Main, corner Railroad
9—Central Square, City Hall
13—Princess Shoe Company
14—Water, corner Grove
15—Water, corner So. Lincoln
16—Main, corner Marlboro
17—Main, corner Baker
18—Marlboro, corner Kelleher
19—Lower Marlboro
113—Railroad, corner 93d
114—Dalbolt, Inc.
115—Church, corner Valley
118—Marlboro, corner Martin
142—Willow
143—Kingsbury Machine Tool Co., Myrtle
161—Adams St., opp. Adams Court
172—Main, near Manchester
174—Main Street, at Edgewood
182—Congress
21—Mutual Aid
22—Vernon, at Fire Station
23—Roxbury, corner Beech
24—Beaver, corner Dover
25—Washington, near Giffin
26—Spring, corner Brook
27—Washington, cor. Wash. Avenue
28—No. Lincoln, corner Beaver
252—Washington at Schleicher & Schuell
31—Washington, opp. Pine
32—Elm, corner High
33—Washington, corner Cottage
35—Court, corner Prospect
36—Elm, corner North

37—Mechanic, corner Pleasant
38—Gilsum, at No. 208
491—Summit Road & Hastings Avenue
41—Middle, opp. Schoolhouse
42—West, corner School
43—West, opp. Faulkner & Colony Mfg.
44—National Grange Ins. Bldg., West St.
45—Castle, corner Barker
46—Court, corner School
47—Court, at Allen Court
441—Peerless Ins. Bldg., Maple Ave.
48—Russell, corner Wheelock
49—Park Ave. at Arlington
51—Winchester, corner Blake
52—Emerald, corner Ralston
53—Winchester, corner Winchester Ct.
54—Island, opp. New England Box Co.
57—Pearl, 3d Pole So. of Track
512—St. James St., opp. Holbrook Groc.
521—Central Screw Company
523—Ralston St., at Golding-Keene Co.
571—Avon St., at Sprague & Carlton
65—South Keene
72—West, corner Park Ave.
73—Park Ave., corner Arch
721—West, near Bradford
731—Arch & Bradford
733—Hurricane Road & Hastings Ave.
2—Still Alarm
3—Fire Out
4—American Legion
12—Military Call
122—Brush Fire Call

The boxes in Keene were displayed on calendars sent out or little pocket booklets that were given to Keene Firefighters, so that when the whistle was blown and the box number was transmitted, all they had to do was to look up the number of blows on the whistle to determine the location where they need to report to. For example: Box 5 – 5 blows on the whistle, four rounds of five, Cheshire Hospital, Box 28 – 2 blows on the whistle, eight blows on the whistle which sounds twenty eight, four rounds on the whistle as you count box 28 you would respond to North Lincoln Street, corner of Beaver Street. This is before they had radios that everyone carried.

When you pull a box alarm, everyone in the city counts the number, but aside from you, the most interested people are the men always on duty at the fire station, and they have to wait just as you do until one round had been completed. The whistle sounds automatically from the station, (but the red light and siren at the corner of Vernon and Washington Streets for fires north of Vernon Street and the siren in the square) if the fire is south of the square, are controlled manually. The alarm also serves to inform the volunteers of the location of the fire, and sometimes when the size of the fire warrants it, a telephoned alarm may be turned

Everyone glances as the whole department swings into action, responding down Washington Street towards Central Square. Sometimes multiple pieces respond, depending on the call.

into a box alarm from the station to inform these men that they are going to be needed.

In a matter of a few seconds the equipment is on its way, and since no one at the station knows the extent or type of the fire, the same pattern is always followed. Two pumping engines, a ladder truck, and one emergency squad car are speeding to the fire. Time is too precious a factor to fool with insufficient equipment. As soon as the alarm sounds, an extra man comes to the station to relieve the man still left there, which frees him to go to the scene of the fire with the Stewart panel truck…Therefore there is always someone at the station in case a second fire should occur, an ever-present worry to the department. By the law of averages it shouldn't happen in Keene, but it may.

When you telephone your fire instead of using the box alarm, the fireman at the desk endeavors to learn not only the exact location and house number but something about the size and type of the fire, and thus it is wise to control your excitement enough to give a clear account in order that the proper equipment may go out at once. Above all, be sure to give your street clearly, because there are several streets in the city with similar names.

As many picture it, "sliding down the pole" is the main thing when the department gets a call, but that is a very minor factor in the careful planning required to get the correct fire-fighting forces to your burning house speedily. And it is done speedily, for under normal conditions of traffic and proper road conditions, the department will reach the scene of the fire in any section of Keene within a two-mile radius of the station in not more than three minutes.

Putting Out the Fire

Not only does the Keene Fire Department get there quickly, but it knows what to do once it gets there. If the dimensions of the fire seem to warrant it, the first engine will have a line of hose laid by the time the rest of the equipment has reached the burning building. The professional fireman sizes up the situation almost instantly and proceeds to get at the real source of the fire. We expect a doctor to make a speedy diagnosis of an acute illness, but the firemen have to make their diagnosis in a split

A Demon Called Fire

second. Attacking at the right spot and in the right way saves your house. Not only does the department know how to fight the fire, he sees also what is to be done to save damage to the contents of the building, and lays salvage covers to protect goods, etc.

Once arrival on the scene of the fire hose lines are connected to the City Hydrants. The fire engine then lay's hose to the fire or to the pumper at the fire so that water can be disbursed.

The firemen know too when the fire is really out, and they have signs and test, such as the smell and quality of the smoke, the feel of heat in the walls, so that they are sure that the flames are not going to burst out again when they have left. You do not need to worry, for if there is any doubt, one or more firemen may remain on the scene until certainly is doubly sure. It is difficult for people to realize that amid the noise, the speed, and smoke and flame, the fire department is proceeding

according to an orderly plan, calculated to hold your loss to a minimum.

What This Means to Keene

People do not need to be convinced that a professional fire department is a good thing, but most do not fully realize how fortunate they are to live in a community with such protection. Last year in Keene the value of buildings damaged by fire was $381,275, but the actual damage was only $30,022.54, which is a mere 8% of the possible loss. Of course you might extinguish the fire with a bucket brigade of your neighbors or a cloudburst might do the work for you, but you know how slight such chances are. Saving 92% of the value of the buildings which catch fire is a very remarkable achievement, when one stops to think about it, and one which is repeated in about the same proportions in Keene year after year.

It Is Also the Fire Prevention Department

No citizen wants to replace even 8% of the value of his house, and it isn't much fun living with the neighbors while repairs are being made. Thus it is a matter of vital concern to all that some agencies should always be on the job to see that we have as few fires as possible. Thus we have building ordinances and zoning codes and electrical codes with this objective high among others. For example, a fire-resistant roof is not a fire-proof roof, but it reduces the chances of spreading a fire. If you clean your chimney annually or more often with certain types of fuel, you help to reduce the chances of the most common type of fire in Keene. And most realize that if it were not for the efficiency of the department, many chimney fires would not be "just another chimney fire".

The fire chief and the building inspector work closely together to make sure that new buildings and alterations observe the safest practices. Insurance companies constantly

Equipment displayed from L to R, Keene Fire Station: 1945 Cgrave 75' Ariel ladder, 1930 Ahrens Fox, 1924 Ahrens Fox, 1942 Diamond T, 1942 Diamond T, 1934 Ahrens Fox (engine #3), the Chief's coupe.

send out agents and inspectors with hints for the greater protection of their policy-holders, and frequently they urgently request them to take certain precautions; for example, a manufacturing plant might be urged to make it possible for the fire department to bring its equipment more speedily to its buildings by removing obstructions.

Within the business district the firemen make a monthly inspection to make sure that the city ordinances are being closely followed, and they make suggestions, and may even be forced to insist that such things ashes, rubbish piles, etc., should not exceed the minimum described in the ordinances. Incidentally the fireman in inspecting a building also gets to know "the lay of the land" just in case he has to come on serious business.

Therefore it may safely be said that a considerable part of the fireman's work is in fire prevention, and a large part of prevention is education property owners in the best ways of saving their own buildings from fire. Those

in authority say frankly that they would like to be able to do even more of this work. Fire prevention is a job, which requires 365 days a year; unfortunately for most of us fire prevention is only a week, including a parade of fire equipment.

There were 20 Bell Alarms and 361 Still Alarms with a total of 381 Alarms for the year.

The estimated value of buildings damaged by fire, $381,275.00

Damage to buildings, $30,022.54
Insurance on said buildings, $285,600.00
Insurance paid $30,022.54.
Value of contents of buildings, $71,613.38
Damage to contents, $14,933.69
Insurance on said contents, $51,350.00
Insurance paid $14,933.69.

There were 40 fewer fires than in the previous year, but the loss was approximately twice as much though in only three fires was the loss described as total.

A Demon Called Fire

Board of Engineers

Chief Engineer Eugene B. Riley, Asst. Engineers Thomas B. Wallbank, Elwin H. Applin and Associate Engineer John H. Simpson

CAPTAINS

Remain the same as 1944.

Permanent Drivers

Chauffeurs Lyman O. Cass, Frank M. Reid, Samuel J. Guyette, Charles M. Ballou, Elton P. Britton, Walter R. Messer, Harry F. Hammond, Paul E. Gallup.

Steamer Hose Company

Remain the same as 1944.

Deluge Hose Company

Remain the same as 1944.

Joint Resolutions for the year ending 1945

A Joint Resolution Passed on February 1st, 1945 relating to the fire department for the purchase of a new aerial ladder truck.

[*Compiler's Note:* Fire for the year ending 1945 is the fire of the Nazarene Church on Vernon Street across from the Central Fire Station.] As reported by the *Keene Evening Sentinel* on December 17th, 1945:

'FIRE'
NAZARENE CHURCH SUFFERS HEAVY DAMAGE BY FIRE

Rev. L. G. Strathern and Family Lose All Possessions in Flames

In near zero weather, firemen this morning combated a stubborn fire in the Nazarene church at 19 Vernon Street within 150 feet of the fire station. The loss which was estimated at several thousand dollars is partially covered by insurance.

The fire caused by an overheated chimney on the second floor of the building. Rev Leslie G. Strathern, the pastor and his family lost all their clothing except that which they were wearing.

Mr. Strathern, who discovered the fire, said that at first it did not seem to be serious. He was on his way to the fire house across the street when the general alarm from Box 22 started sounding at 10 o'clock. He returned to the building but was unable to save any of the family possessions.

Flames Spread Rapidly

The fire mushroomed rapidly to the third floor which made it difficult for the firemen to combat, the roof of the building being slate. The cupola, which is in front of the building provided a chimney for the flames and within a short time the entire third floor was an inferno. Six lines of hose were laid and firemen fought the blaze from all sides of the building.

Firemen with a line of hose were on the roof of the Perkins Machine company building in the rear of the church and several times the flames and dense smoke which poured out the rear window on the third floor drove firemen from their posts temporarily.

Roof Caves In

Water from the six lines of hose did not seem to have much effect on the flames at first. The fire broke out shortly before 10 o'clock and about an hour afterward the roof caved in. Fire at times broke out in all corners of the building and in the cupola. Slate from the building fell and at times barely missed firemen who were holding hose.

The first floor, which is used for the Sunday school rooms, seemed undamaged by fire. The coal furnace which is used for heating auditorium and the parsonage quarters is on the second floor. It was at the point where the flue enters the chimney that Mr. Strathern saw first evidence of the flames. There at two rooms on the second floor in front of the building.

Two rooms on the third floor are used by the pastor and his family. The rear section of the third floor is an open attic.

Child Removed From House

When Mr. Strathern discovered the flames he instructed his father and mother, Mr. And Mrs. William Strathern of Bayonne, N.J., who had come to Keene to spend Christmas, to take his seven-months-old son Bernard out of the building. William Strathern carried the child across the street to the fire station. Henry Gillespie, also of Bayonne, who came to Keene with his wife to spend Christmas with the Stratherns, was in the building at the time. Mr. Gillespie is the brother-in-law of Mr. Strathern. Mrs. Gillespie and Mrs. Leslie Strathern were shopping at the time the fire was discovered.

Mr. And Mrs. Strathern's daughter, Phyllis, age 5, was in kindergarten at the time.

Salvation Army workers brought pots of hot coffee, which they served, to firemen, and members of the auxiliary of the Keene Fire Department served hot coffee and luncheon to firemen who went to the station to get warm or change clothing.

Work In Relays

Firemen who handled the hose nozzle were covered with ice after a short time. Owing to the extreme cold firemen had to work in relays at the nozzle.

State and local police were on hand to direct traffic on nearby streets and keep onlookers at a safe distance from the burning structure.

During the general alarm fire in the church, firemen were called by still alarm to extinguish a chimney fire in the house owned by the Keene Development company at 346 Marlboro Street. Other Chimney fires were extinguished over the weekend in housed owned by C. S. Brigham, 173 North Street and George K. Brinton, 35 High Street.

Parishioners of the Church of the Nazarene will meet tonight at 7:30 o'clock to consider what action they will take in their present emergency; it is announced by Rev.

Leslie G. Strathern, Pastor. The meeting will be held in the vestry of Grace Methodist Church.

It is announced by Rev. James F. Quimby that the Methodist church trustees are extending an official invitation to the people of the Nazarene Church to use the facilities of the Methodist Church.

————————

[from *Keene Evening Sentinel:*]

CHURCH COUNCIL TO AID STRATHERNS

Rev. C. Barnard Chapman, chairman of the Keene Church council, has called a special meeting of the members for 7:30 o'clock tonight in the Baptist church parsonage to discuss ways and means by which the organization can assist Rev. Leslie G. Strathern, pastor of the Church of the Nazarene, who lost many of his personal belongings in this morning's fire which badly damaged the church building on Vernon Street.

Mr. Chapman makes the request that all members of the council attend the meeting.

[*Compiler's Note*: The building still stands on the Corner of Vernon and Elm Streets with the 3rd floor gone.]

————————

NOTE: On December 5th, 1945 the *Keene Evening Sentinel* published this Headline and reads as follows:

FIRE CHIEF RILEY WILL QUITE AFTER 24 YEARS IN POST

Walter Messer Is Held Probable Successor Among Local Men

Fire Chief Eugene B. Riley today announced his intention to retire on pension Jan 1st.

Firemen battle flames at Nazarene Church. Several thousand dollars damage was done by fire discovered shortly before 10 o'clock in the Nazarene Church on Vernon Street just opposite the fire station. An overheated chimney was said to have caused the fire.

Chief Riley has been head of the fire department for 24 years and a member of the department for 44 years.

Chief Riley has been head of the fire department for 24 years, and a member of the department for 44 years. He is a past president

of the New Hampshire Fire Chiefs association and a past president of the Cheshire County Forest Fire Wardens association.

Messer Mentioned

All speculation this morning on Chief's Riley's probable successor centered on Walter R. Messer, veteran engine driver. However, certain members of the incoming city government who preferred not to be quoted by name, suggested the possibility that a fire chief might be selected from professional ranks outside Keene. It appeared to be agreed that if a successor to Chief Riley were appointment would probably go to Mr. Messer.

Chief Riley's interest in the fire department has been of such long standing that few residents of Keene can remember when this was not one of his principal preoccupations. He was appointed a call fireman in 1901. When the Stark fire alarm telegraph system was installed in 1912 he became city electrician in charge of the system, and the first regular member of the fire department.

Then he first entered the department Chief Riley was a member of the Washington Hook and Ladder Company. He was promoted to the position of deputy chief at the time Chief Louis A. Nims retired in July 1919, and in January, 1922 he was promoted to chief, a post he has occupied since that time.

The 73rd Annual Report gave a full two page dedication to EUGENE B. RILEY as follows:

1901 joined the hook and ladder company as a callman.

1912 became electrician as a regular.

1919 Became Assistant Chief Engineer.

1922-1946 served Keene as Chief Engineer and thus has served the Fire Department 45 years has been at the fire station for 34 years and Chief Engineer 24 years.

He has seen many methods of firefighting, been a part in many improvements and responsible for most of them.

A splendid record of public service.

———

[from *Keene Evening Sentinel*:]

MAYOR AND ALDERMEN PICK MESSER TO SUCCEED RILEY AS FIRE DEPARTMENT CHIEF

Walter R. Messer of Keene, NH – New Chief of the Keene Fire department, succeeded Chief Eugene B. Riley, retired.

New Fire Chief has Been Regular Driver 5 Years

Walter R. Messer, nearly elected chief of the fire department, was born in Keene April 27th, 1906, a son of Martha Randall Messer Towne and the late Arthur T. Messer. He was graduated from Keene High School in 1926 and was a member of the Keene High School football team and manager of the basketball team.

He was employed as a mechanic for the F. J. Bennett company for five years and then went to Glen Cove, Long Island, N. Y., where has conducted a garage of his own for four years and on returning to Keene was employed as mechanic for the Robertson Motor Company. He was appointed a regular driver April 1st, 1941. He had been a call fireman, with the exception of the time he was in New York, since January, 1926.

He is a member of the Masons, the First Congregational church and the various organizations in the fire department.

In December, 1942, Mr. Messer was selected to attend the chemical warfare school for civilian defense officers at the Edgewood arsenal in Edgewood, Md.

Mr. Messer is married. His wife the former Elsa Nordin of Winchendon, Mass is chief clerk in the Selective Service office. Their son Bruce is a member of the Keene High school football team.

In support of the candidacy of Mr. Messer a resolution signed by a large number of members of the fire department was submitted by Don W. Cook, chairman of the joint standing committee on fire department.

Alderman Frederick D. Mitchell of Ward 3 sought to delay the election, stating that he felt opportunity should be given other candidates to come forward and present their qualifications. He was found voting for Mr. Messer however at the conclusion of the discussion.

Cook Nominates

Mr. Messer's name was placed in nomination by Alderman Cook and Alderman William H. Shea seconded the motion. Both spoke for Mr. Messer and urged his election.

1946 [from *City of Keene Annual Report*]

Fire Department

Walter R. Messer,
 Chief Engineer 1946

During 1946 the Keene Fire Department answered 380 alarms, as compared with 381 the previous year. The department answered 354 still alarms and 26 bell alarms. Of these 21 still and 3 bell alarms were calls from neighboring towns for which the city was reimbursed. The table at the end of this report shows the damage incurred by these fires, the real damage when the insurance is taken into account, but it may be pointed out that, as was true last year and in many preceding years, the prompt work of the department gives a very fine percentage of loss in comparing the actual loss with the total value of the property affected.

The monthly inspections of buildings in the Fire Precinct have been carried out, and the suggestions of the inspectors have been welcomed by most occupants, and in general the conditions have been found excellent in most properties.

New Apparatus

In March the new Seagraves Aerial Ladder arrived and was put in service. This unit enables one man to raise a ladder 75 feet in less than one minute. It also carries 200 feet of ground ladders, axes, hooks, shovels, a 500 gpm ladder pipe, booster tank and 100 gpm pump, fire foam equipment, protective clothing for the firemen, and other small equipment. In partial payment for this the 1919 Mack Ladder truck was sold to the Bellows Falls Department.

All the motor apparatus is in good condition. One pumping unit was revalved and new piston leathers and seals installed. The Department also purchased two Scott Airpack masks early in the year, and they have proved very satisfactory. The booster hose for Engine 3 has been replaced, 800 feet of 2 ½ inch rubber-lined double jacket hose, 2 reserve extension ladders 35 and 40 feet long, 2 carbon dioxide extinguishers to assist in handling oil, gas, and auto fires, the equipment from the War Assets Administration, 2 fog nozzles, and applicators were purchased during the year. The Department also has on hand 11,500 feet of 2 ½ " rubber lined hose, 3,500 feet of 1 ½ " rubber lined hose, and 1,200 feet of 2 ½ " linen hose at the South Keene hose house.

Fire Alarm Circuits Repaired

The Fire Alarm circuits are in good condition. Some repairs have been made during the year. Four boxes, which had been in service over twenty-nine years, have been

Friday March 22, 1946 New Aerial Ladder — This new fire department truck with 75-foot aerial ladder was scheduled to be publicly demonstrated for the first time this afternoon at 4 o'clock at the Newberry block. The schedule also called for a demonstration of the ladder pipe at the end of Railroad Street. Photo, made for the Sentinel before today's demonstration, shows ladder against roof of the old Sentinel building on Main Street.

replaced with new boxes. One set of batteries were reconditioned with new plates and acid. During 1947 there will be some relocation of wires because of changes by the utility companies whose poles we also use.

Recommendation

Upon the recommendations of the Board of Engineers and authority of the City Councils a new man will be added to the regular force at the station January 1st, 1947. The Board of Engineers have also called to the attention of the proper authorities the need for tying in dead ends and increasing the size

A Demon Called Fire

of some water mains for better fire protection, especially in the West Keene area, and attention should be given in any water supply studies to this important consideration.

Summary of Fire statistics for 1946

The estimated value of buildings damaged by fire, $448,900.00.

Damage to buildings, $33,433.81
Insurance on said buildings, $338,100.00
Insurance paid $25,933.81.
Value of contents of buildings, $210,415.93
Damage to contents, $73,861.57
Insurance on said contents, $148,350.00
Insurance paid on contents $35,240.39

As Reported by the *Keene Evening Sentinel* on February 20th, 1946:

'FIRE'
BLAZE IN BOILER ROOM OF COLONIAL THEATER BLOCK

Melting Telephone Cable Flashes Warning, Many Concerns Suffer

Melting of the telephone cable in the basement of the Colonial Theater building on main street which flashed signals on the switchboards of the telephone exchange about 2:15 o'clock this morning, resulted in telephone operators, Mrs. Verna L. Bissel ad Miss Helen R. Manch to call the Keene Police station and inform Sgt. Michael T. Griffin who was at the desk that a fire was burning in the Colonial Theater block. The fire was confined to the basement and the stairway leading to the balcony of the theater. Smoke and tenants in the building suffered water losses and residents in the block had to leave. The combined losses have not been ascertained.

Sgt. Griffin radioed Officer Orlando Boccia who was in the police cruiser to investigate which he did and about the same time Patrolman Daniel D. Henderson arrived on the scene and he sounded the alarm from Box 6, corner of main and Emerald Streets.

Flames on South Side

When firemen arrived at the scene flames were issuing from the basement on the south side of the building where the boiler is located. Smoke was pouring from the windows and doors on the south side of the building next to the Exchange block and from the Hy-Grade Automobile store, front door. This store is located on the south side of the building.

Several lines of hose were laid from the hydrant in front of the building and the hydrant across Main Street.

Occupants Awakened

Officers' Henderson and Boccia went through the block to awaken the occupants in the apartments on the second and third floors. Mr. and Mrs. William E. Cyr, owners of Olga's Beauty parlor, have rooms on the second floor and Peter Latchis one of the owners of the block, also has an apartment on the second floor, but were not in their rooms. Mrs. Helen E. Alden is the only person having rooms on the third floor. The Cyrs and Mrs. Alden left there rooming quarters and sought refuge in the lobby of the Hotel Ellis, where they remained for the rest of the night.

The fire will not affect the holding of shows in the Colonial Theater.

Other Losses

Ye Goodie Shop, the candy store on the north side of the building, suffered losses from smoke in the store and water in the basement. The store suffered a water loss several weeks ago.

The Colonial Barbershop and the Colonial Shoe Repair shop are in the basement and these places of business suffered losses from water and smoke. In some places in the basements there were from four to eight inches of water.

The Hy-Grade Automotive store sustained the greatest loss from fire, and smoke and water as this store is located on the south side of the building and the rear of the store is near the boiler room in the basement where the fire was burning.

Called Wire Chief

When the telephone operators discovered there was trouble in the Colonial Theater block they called Wire Chief Walter Kennedy and he instructed them to call the police which they did without delay.

————

As Reported by the *Keene Evening Sentinel* on April 4th, 1946.

'FIRE'
BAKER STREET FIRE DAMAGE
$1,000

Origin of Bardis' Home Blaze Undetermined

Fire of undetermined origin, discovered shortly after 3 o'clock Thursday afternoon, caused damage estimated at more than $1,000 to the house and furnishings at 177 Baker Street owned by James D. Bardis, proprietor of Bardis Fruit Company.

A set of overstuffed furniture in the Bardis living room was completely destroyed and a piano was seriously damaged. Every room in the house suffered smoke damage and on the ground floor hears seared the paint on the walls and fire burned a hole in the living room floor. Evelyn Bardis, 15 year-old high school freshman discovered the fire that had apparently been smoldering for some time without breaking into flames, when she arrived home from school. Heat and clouds of smoke repelled her when she opened the front door. Unable to enter the house to telephone the fire department she ran to the home of Charles Lyon, 194 Baker Street and put in the call.

A few moments before she called George Kellogg Jr. driver of a bus carrying four passengers saw smoke issuing from the house and saw the girl running across the street. He drove to Baker and Main Street and sounded Box 17. The box alarm was sounded just a few minutes after firemen had pulled a general alarm from the same box at the fire station. After sounding the alarm, Mr. Kellogg drove his bus and passengers back to the Bardis home to offer his services if needed.

Among the apparatus answering the alarm was the new aerial ladder truck, driven by Lyman Cass. Only the smaller ladders were used. Quick action prevented the fire from spreading beyond the living room at the front of the house although the penetration of smoke through all the rooms up to the roof gave the first intent that the entire house was involved.

According to firemen, the blaze apparently originated in or near a chair at the right of the front entrance. Mr. Bardis owner of the house, told fire officials that he had been at home during the noon hour and found no sign of fire. When he left, he said, there was no other person in the house, which he locked on leaving.

The loss was covered by insurance he said.

————

The fire selected for 1946 is the fire of Carey Factory on Victoria Street on September 4th, 1946, Box 15. As reported by the *Keene Evening Sentinel*:

'FIRE'

Keene firemen fought a hot blaze in one of the Carey Manufacturing company buildings early last evening, making good stop and preventing the fire from spreading to other parts of the factory. Damage is estimated at $15,000.

Fire in Carey Factory Causes Loss of $15,000

Fire believed to have started from an explosion in a dust collector and which rapidly spread through kilns where stock was being dried, caused damage estimated at $15,000 at the Carey Manufacturing company plant on Victoria Street shortly after 6 o'clock Wednesday night.

Although confined to a brick addition, approximately 130 by 60 feet, the fire gave firemen a stubborn battle and tons of water were poured into the building, the interior of which was badly gutted. The all out signal was not sounded until 10:26 o'clock.

Employees Salvage Material

Employees of the company pitched in to assist in moving machinery and salvaging stock and as a result considerable material will be saved. The loss on the stock will run about $10,000 while the damage to machinery is estimated at $5,000 by Mr. Koritz.

Fire did not get into the boiler room proper as it was separated from the burning building by a firewall.

Firemen were first called to the scene by still alarm which was follow by a general alarm from Box 15. The fire had made great headway before the truck arrived Chief Walter R. Messer sized up the situation quickly and dispatched a truck to the station for additional hose.

Miles of Hose Is Laid

Approximately a mile of hose was laid from hydrants on Water Street. Firemen fought their way through thick billowing clouds of smoke to reach advantageous points to combat the blaze. Some hose lines were carried to the roof of a nearby building.

The fire endangered the main part of the plant also nearby log and lumber piles. Most of the roof of the building, which housed a dry room and finishing department, was burned through.

Thousands of spectators witnessed the fire and police officers had a busy time keeping the crowd back at a safe distance and from hampering the firemen. The smoke was visible for miles around.

The Carey Company employs about 200 personal.

———

September 4th, 1946 as reported by the *Keene Evening Sentinel*:

'STORY'
STEAM MISTAKEN FOR SMOKE, FIREMEN CALLED

Firemen were called this morning to the home of Mrs. L. Martell, 465 Main Street but no fire was found. Steam was escaping from one of the radiators into the room and occupants of the house believed it to be smoke and summoned the firemen.

At 10.30 o'clock firemen extinguished a chimney fire in the building by John N. Carr, 37 Armory Street. A fire in an automobile owned by Lewis Buntlin of Surry was extinguished on Court Street late Tuesday afternoon.

———

As Reported by the *Keene Evening Sentinel* on October 11th, 1946:

'STORY'
Fire Department Praised At Inspection Day Dinner

Customary praises given members of the Keene Fire Department on the occasion of their annual banquet was supplemented at the inspection day event Thursday night at the fire station by mayor James C. Farmer said others who commended Chief Walter R. Messer upon the way he had conducted the department during his first year.

The "police stole the show" however with Chief Joseph L. Regan making the surprise announcement that his department will give an extra police two-way radio to the fire department provided the city government will take care of the $150 expense of installation of the equipment in Chief Messer's car. Mayor Farmer unofficially pledges the appropriation.

When Alderman Don W. Cook chairman of the fire department committee took credit for getting added remuneration for the firemen, who had said feel they are now well paid. Chief Regan in his short talk indicated the police did not share the same view and he served notice on the city government members present that additional pay will probably be asked.

Alderman Cook praised the cooperation of the police in making it possible for all fire department units to join in the parade for the first time with the police two-way radio cruiser filling in to take any calls of an emergency nature and ready to contact the fire officials in the parade if necessary.

"City Fathers" Speak

Four of the five aldermen present and many of the common council praised the fire department officials and men and in turn received praise for their part in providing appropriations.

While Chief Messer received commendation, the former Chief Eugene B. Riley who has attended the banquets over 40 years was not forgotten and came in for his share of praises as did the retired firemen and veterans of many years.

Chief Messer in the role of toasting master called on Mayor Farmer as the first speaker ad he complimented the entire force on their splendid spirit which he said "contributes to the building of Keene in ways you don't realize." He called on Former Chief Riley to stand and in a gesture toward Chief Messer stated that while the department had good chiefs the success was due to the support of the men who worked with them.

The mayor assumed his share of credit for promotion of Chief Messer stating that he answered those who suggested bringing a man from outside by insisting on the policy of developing someone within the department. Other speakers joined him in emphasizing that Chief Messer had lived up to expectations in adopting this policy.

Mayor Farmer stated that the men were doing a good job and that he was proud of the department demonstration. After citing the appalling figures of fire destruction throughout the country "Sunny Jim" stated that he brought the greetings and appreciation of the people of Keene for the security they have in their department in keeping fire losses at a minimum.

100 Seated For Dinner

The Banquet was served in the assembly hall of the Central Fire Station and was attended by more than 100 firemen, members of the city government and guests. Following the banquet, Laurence M. Pickett led in group singing with Eric Crowther at the piano and ending with a song for their Chief. "For He's a Jolly Good Fellow"

Don W. Cook alderman from Ward 1

Said the department is one of the best in the state and through the cooperation of the city government the men are well remunerated for their work. He said that it is the plan to send firemen to schools where firefighting is taught. He gave credit to the firemen for the fine appearance at the fire station, noting the painting and the regular firemen had done cleaning.

Councilman Walter Royal a member of the fire department committee asked that all the men give their full cooperation to Chief Messer and said he hopes the time will come when one or two more regulars will be on duty at the station to relieve men who now have to spend 120 hours or more each week there.

Councilman Arthur Kingsbury, senior member of the fire department committee spoke briefly and said that he was on the committee which purchased the new ladder truck. He said he thought it was turning out very good and will be even more appreciated in the future.

Praises Public Spirit

Alderman Bernard A. Streeter from Ward 2 expressed the opinion that the voluntary firemen are public spirited in their service and added that as chairman of the city government finance committee, he will help the department in every way possible. He cautioned against expecting everything in one year, however, but promised a long-range policy of some improvement each year.

Alderman Robert M. Saers of Ward 4 member of the city government the past seven years expressed his pleasure at being present.

Former Chief Eugene B. Riley who had served the department as firemen, electrician and chief for more than 40 years, said that he knows Chief Messer will carry on in a manner which will make all proud of him.

Chief Joseph L. Regan of the police department; George Whitney superintendent of the Public Works department; Elmer S. Britton superintendent of cemeteries; Elliot Wright of the tax collector office; Charles Farrar of the recreation program of the city and Sidney S. Frissell city comptroller were called to take a bow.

Many Guests Present

Other guests present included Postmaster Carl D. Roche, Harold T. Packard, former chairman of the fire department committee; Harry N. Aldrich, former assistant engineer of the department; Rev A. Norman Janes, member of the city government and former firemen, some of who are on the retired list. Mrs. Alice D. Matthews, a councilman from Ward 1 attended the meeting. All the aldermen were present except Frederick D. Mitchell of Ward 3.

Among those who spoke briefly were Rev. A. Norman Janes, Chief Regan and City Solicitor Harry C. Lichman.

Among the retired firemen present were: Frank J. Bennett, Thomas Roche; S. Elliot Witham, Frank Streeter, John Seawall, Cleon Symonds, Fred S. Morse, John A. Denison, also ex-chief Riley.

————

[from *Keene Evening Sentinel:*]

FIREMEN'S BALL IS BIG SUCCESS

Proceeds of Ball Go For Relief Purposes

Firemen from surrounding towns and city government officials were guests of the Keene Fire Department at the annual Firemen's Ball in the City hall Wednesday night when 500 persons danced to the music of Herm Reed and his orchestra with vocalist, Carl Decker. Proceeds from this semi-formal event went to the Firemen's Relief Association.

Bellows Falls Vt., Peterborough, Troy, Swanzey and other communities in New Hampshire and Vermont were represented at the gala affair which had not been held during the war.

Mayor James C. Farmer and members of the city government participated in the grand march held during the evening. Chief Walter R. Messer led the traditional march and Mrs. Farmer followed by the mayor and Mrs. Messer, members of the Fire Department and guests. Laurence M. Pickett was the prompter.

Members of the three fire companies all in uniform, and the bright gowns worn by the members of the firemen's auxiliary and dancers added much color in the evening entertainment.

The music was broadcast a half-hour over Station WKNE.

During the intermission many of the dancers left to participate in the entertainment furnished at the local fire station by Eric Crowther pianist. Refreshments were served.

Many persons watched the evening's dancing and listened to the concert.

The dance was under the general supervision of Chief Walter R. Messer. The chief was assisted by the following committee:

General Chairman, John O'Neil, tickets, Francis Donovan; music, Gerald McCarthy; publicity Alfred L. Castaw; invitations and program, Donald Trask, and reception Samuel Guyette.

1947 [from *City of Keene Annual Report*]

Fire Department

Walter R. Messer,
  Chief Engineer 1947

During the year 1947 the Keene Fire Department answered 269 alarms. There were 254 still alarms and 15 bell alarms.

Twenty stills and on bell alarm were for calls to the outside communities. Charges to these communities have been promptly taken care of.

The monthly inspections of the fire precinct have been carried out with conditions found to be nearly perfect. During the year approximately 175 oil permits were issued, after thoroughly examining the premises to see that rules and regulations had been complied with.

One of the pumps purchased from the Federal Government was mounted on the Reo chassis so we could have a good size pump for brush fire service. This unit is able to fill in for other pumping jobs as well. All of the pumps were tested during the year and were found to be in good condition with the exception of Engine 3. While this unit will still deliver capacity, the engine has to run at near the danger point and we intend to recondition this pump next year.

Working clothes of the call men have been put in individual bags that are carried on the Ladder truck. These are numbered so that each man can locate his own equipment.

The Department purchased 600' of 2 ½ inch underwriters hose during the year and also some 1 ½ inch iron pipe thread couplings to change over thread on the hose that was

purchased from the Federal Government. The department has on hand approximately 11,400 feet of 2 ½ inch rubber lined hose and 3,500 feet of 1 ½ inch rubber lined hose.

The kitchen at the Fire Station was remodeled by the permanent men. A larger stove and a new sink were purchased to round out the project.

Two replacement boxes were installed during the year. The lines were cleared of interference of tree and brush, and all the boxes and poles were painted. The circuits are in good condition. A survey by an engineer of the Gamewell Company was made and he recommended enlarging the circuits with an increase in the number of boxes for better coverage, and also suggested replacing some of the other equipment.

A new firemen was added to the permanent force the first of the year. Training sessions were held at different intervals during the year and in September when the State Fire College was held, 18 firemen attended the 3 day session.

There follows a table comparing 1947 fire loss with those of 1946. A further break-down of fire with damage above $1,000 is indicated for 1947 on page 31 of the Annual Report.

The estimated value of buildings damaged by
  Fire, 1946 $448,900.00 for 1947 $481,200.00
  Damage to buildings, 1946 $33,433.81 for 1947 $26,589.70
  Insurance on said buildings, 1946 $338,100.00 for 1947 $446,600.00
  Insurance paid on buildings, for 1946, $25,933.81 for 1947 $26,589.70.
  Value of contents of buildings, for 1946 $210,415.93 for 1947 $349.625.02
  Damage to contents, for 1946 $73,861.57 for 1947 $18,936.07
  Insurance on said contents, for 1946 $148,350.00 for 1947 $332,075.02
  Insurance paid on contents for 1946 $35,240.39 for 1947 $18,936.07.

[*Compiler's Note:*The fire selected for 1947 is the fire at Pastime Bowling Alleys on the corner of Pleasant Street and Mechanic Street on March 1st, 1947, Box 37.] As recorded by the *Keene Evening Sentinel* on March 1st, 1947:

'FIRE'
FIRE TRAPS 7 PERSONS IN BOWLING ALLEYS

Loss in Early Morning Blaze May Reach $30,000

Two of the seven persons trapped in the Pastime Bowling Alleys, leaped to safety and five were rescued by ladders early this morning when a flash fire which firemen battled for nearly five hours damaged the two story brick building on Mechanic Street owned by Verne C. Swan and occupied by the Pastime Alleys and R. C. Swan Company. The loss may reach $30,000.

Fire is reported by Manager Gordon Bemis of the bowling alleys to have started about the fuse box. Two of the groups trapped in the building suffered lacerated hands. All seven were treated in Elliot Community Hospital and later released.

Caught in the building besides Manager Bemis were six "pin boys." Mr. and Mrs. Robert Short and Leo Short of Swanzey, David and Ralph Pelligrine of 215 Church Street and Andrew O'Donnell of Martell Court.

Two of the pin boys leaped to safety into snow banks from a window on the north side of the building. Four were taken down the new aerial ladder on the Pleasant Street side and Mr. Bemis descended a ladder raised to a window at his office at the corner of Mechanic and Pleasant Streets.

Two Receive Cut Hands

Robert Short and Ralph Pelligrini sustained severe lacerations of their hands when they smashed windows in the building on the Pleasant Street side. The injured were given first aid treatment at the Sprague & Carleton Chair Company plant on the opposite side of the street by Police Officer Daniel D. Henderson and others before they were taken to the hospital in a police cruiser by Officer Harold E. Savage.

Other Police officers were in vicinity of the fire directing traffic, and keeping the fire fans at a safe distance.

Mr. Bemis and the "pin boys" remained in the building after the bowlers had left, cleaning up in preparation for the weekend business. Mr. Bemis said that one of the young men called to him that there was a fire in the west end of the building and Mr. Bemis saw what looked like a ball of fire about the fuse box.

Formed Bucket Line

He said that they formed a bucket line and began throwing water on the fire when suddenly the lights in the building went out. They groped their way to the east end of the building where they were rescued by firemen. Mr. Bemis said that he went to his office to telephone the fire station when the alarm sounded from Box 37, which is located on the building.

When the firemen arrived police officers directed them to windows where the people were trapped and aided in the rescue. Dense volumes of black smoke poured from practically every window on the second story of the building where 15 bowling alleys are located. About an hour after the fire started it broke through the roof of the building in several places and flames shot skyward.

Cover Valuable Machinery

Tons of water were poured on the raging flames and a considerable amount leaked into that part of the building occupied by the R. C. Swan Company and containing valuable woolen manufacturing machinery. Some of the machines were covered with waterproof tarpaulins.

The bowling alleys are owned by the John Monahan estate of Marlboro Mass. A fire occurred in the bowling alleys about two years ago after which the building was refinished.

The fire resulted in the first general alarm this year. The last general alarm was in December. The alarm from box 37 was sounded about 12:15 o'clock this morning and the all-out was blown at 4:55 o'clock.

Salvation Army on Hand

Representatives of the Salvation Army Corps furnished coffee and doughnuts for the firemen.

Gilbert D. Oliver, watchman for the Sprague and Carleton Company in the building located across the street from the fire, said when he made his rounds at midnight and went outside of the factory to go to the office building, there were no signs of any fire.

Lay 3,000 Feet of Hose

More than 3,000 feet of hose in six lines were laid at the fire by the 40 call firemen and the six regulars who answered the general alarm. The smoke-eaters were handicapped by sub-freezing temperatures and ice on the ladders and roof-top providing dangerous footing as firemen scaled the building on all sides.

The rescue of the pin boys trapped on the east end of the second floor was the first of its kind affected with the department's aerial ladder truck which was purchased more than a year ago.

A large crowd gathered in the early stages of the conflagration and numerous spotlights from the various pieces of apparatus lighted up the towering pillars of smoke and steam, contributed to the spectacle.

Chief Walter R. Messer of the Keene Fire department and Driver Elton P. Britton attended the meeting of the New Hampshire Fire Chiefs association in Concord Friday night and arrived in Keene at the height of the blaze. They were able to see the flames as they descended Concord Hill.

———

NOTE: Chief Walter R. Messer receives new Radio for his 1947 sedan. The messages transmitted are received through the Police Department but the Fire Department will soon be equipped with its own transmitter and receiver.

New Fire Department Equipment: Fire Chief Walter R. Messer is pictured above testing the radio-telephone equipment, which was recently installed in his car. Messages are relayed through the Police Department to the Fire Station. Chief Messer first joined the department as a volunteer in 1926.

The article which picture shows Chief Walter R. Messer talking on his new radio in his car reads as follows.

Fire Chief Began Career During His School Days

by Jack Teehan

"Others firemen may be ardent pi nochle fans but here in Keene they like to play cribbage."

I was talking to Fire Chief Walter R. Messer, a fireman from his boots up and a fan with a long tradition of firefighting in his family. A youthful man with ruddy complexion and a ready smile, Walter Messer has come a long way since his high school days when he had a written excuse from school ready for use whenever the fire whistle sounded.

A volunteer in the Steamer Hose Company at the age of 20, Walt was appointed to his present position by the Mayor and Board of Aldermen.

January 5th, 1946.

Newspapermen talk about great fires they have seen, murders and all sorts of accidents and disasters. Firemen talk only of fires and they can remember the smallest detail of a fire that occurred 20 years ago.

The second floor of the fire station on Vernon Street contains a large hall used for meetings and whist parties. The walls are covered with pictures of fires which raged in Keene many years ago. Proud firemen of the Eighties and Nineties, many boasting large handlebar moustaches, look down upon the modern apparatus of today.

Used Horses in 1926

All of us remember seeing Currier & Ives prints of pot-belled steamers being drawn to fires by a snorting team of hoses. I asked Walt how they worked. "It was simple," he replied. "they built a fire as soon as the steamer left the station on the way to a fire.

The steamer was always equipped with a heap of wood shavings and oil rags and by the time the firemen arrived at the blaze the water was hot enough to generate steam. They used coal after the fire was high enough but it was a tedious job cleaning the equipment after each fire.

No one recalls the exact date on which horses were last used but the horse stalls in the fire station were blocked off in 1926 after THE FIRE.

The Fire was, you guessed it, in the fire station. The men and equipment were out at another fire and many an incredible eyebrow was raised when the alarm for the fire station sounded. It was true enough as things turned

out and a section of the second story was destroyed.

Station Is Modernized

Men arrived soon after the alarm sounded and two horses were rescued from the burning building. The fire was soon under control and perhaps it was a blessing as the was a blessing as the fire station was modernized soon afterward. Horses were kept in the city barns at the rear of the station after that and were used for many years to pull snowplows and rubbish wagons.

Walter's farther, Arthur T. Messer, who died in 1910 was a volunteer fireman for many years as a member of the Steamer Hose Company. His stepfather, Fred W. Towne, was fire chief twice though in those days there was no permanent chief, they were all call chiefs.

Eugene B. Riley was the first permanent fire chief and he was appointed in 1922 to succeed Fred Towne. He held the post until his retirement Jan. 1st 1946.

The worst fire in Walt Messer's memory is the Goodnow store fire on Main Street the night of Aug 17th, 1934. It started in the basement where ammonia tanks for refrigeration were stored and firemen were unable to get near the blaze because of the terrific heat and ammonia fumes.

Three stories were gutted in the blaze and the loss was more than $100,000. The entire business district was endangered but the fire was kept from spreading to adjoining buildings.

Accident Record Good

No men have died in the line of duty with the department in Walt's memory, and only one has been seriously burned. The record points to adequate safety measures and modern equipment to protect the lives of those who guard a city.

Walt doesn't have any special hobbies unless you count the jitter bug racing he used to do before the war on icy ponds in the Monadnock Region. He worked in a local garage in the years when he was a volunteer and became a permanent member of the department in 1941 after six years as a call fireman with the Deluge Hose Company.

He lives in an apartment with his wife who served as clerk of the District 11 Selective Service board through the war. Apartment house dwellers don't have gardens to tend so Walt contends himself with his work and leaves the hobbies for others.

Two brass poles are still in use at the fire station and on one wall hangs a fire warden's staff topped with a brass knob which was carried by all firemen back in 1789. The staff identified fire officials who were always on hand to prevent looting. A simple badge and distinctive hat has replaced the staff but the duties are still the same.

Walt is assisted in supervising fires by the Board of Engineers which he heads. Three men, Elwin H. Applin, John H. Simpson and Thomas B. Wallbank comprise the board. The group makes all decisions on policies and work as a team at major fires.

Has Radio Now

Today the fire chief rides in a 1947 sedan equipped with a two way radio with which he can relay messages to the fire station through the Police Department. The department will eventually be equipped with its own transmitter and receiver.

There are nine regular firemen, three call engineers, 42 call men and six substitute call men ready to answer a general alarm at the first blast of the whistle. They use a modern aerial ladder truck three pumpers, two squad wagons, several auxiliary pump, oxygen masks and other modern apparatus.

During the war Walt went to a special training school at Aberdeen, Md. Where he learned to fight incendiary bomb fires and how to battle the havoc spread by enemy air raids. A fire chief's training never ceases and Walt will attend a special conference in

Washington early in May at the invitation of President Truman.

While the city sleeps the Fire Department is ever alert to hidden dangers. The next time you see Walt on the street say hello and remember he's your fire chief.

————

During the year 1947 the Keene Fire Department answered 269 alarms. There were 254 still alarms and 15 bell alarms. As Reported by the *Keene Evening Sentinel* on April 8th, 1947:

'STORY'
FIRE COMPANIES ELECT OFFICERS

Members Enjoy Banquet After Business Session

Officers of the three companies of the Keene Fire department were elected at the annual meetings held Saturday night in the Central Fire Station. The meetings were held prior to a banquet served by the auxiliary with Mrs. Eugene B. Riley as general chairman.

Chief Walter R. Messer was toastmaster. Loyd W. Hewitt showed several members spoke and motion picture secured by John O'Neil a member of the department.

The elections resulted as follows: Deluge Hose Company Arthur D. Irwin, Captain: Stephen W. Pollock, first Lieutenant; Paul E. Symonds Clerk and George E. Fish treasurer.

Washington Hook and Ladder Company Edward l. Reason, Captain Samuel V. Thompson, first lieutenant; Francis J. Driscoll second lieutenant; Clare H. Symonds, Clerk and Francis J. Driscoll, treasurer.

Keene Steam Fire Engine and Hose Company Ralph H, Turner, Captain, Earl W. Little, first lieutenant, Carl W. Johnson, second lieutenant, Albert I. Little clerk and Bertrand G. Harvey treasurer.

Twenty stills and on bell alarm were for calls to the outside communities. Charges to these communities have been promptly taken care of.

The monthly inspections of the fire precinct have been carried out with conditions found to be nearly perfect. During the year approximately 175 oil permits were issued, after thoroughly examining the premises to see that rules and regulations had been complied with.

One of the pumps purchased from the Federal Government was mounted on the Reo chassis so we could have a good size pump for brush fire service. This unit is able to fill in for other pumping jobs as well. All of the pumps were tested during the year and were found to be in good condition with the exception of Engine 3. While this unit will still deliver capacity, the engine has to run at near the danger point and we intend to recondition this pump next year.

Working clothes of the call men have been put in individual bags that are carried on the Ladder truck. These are numbered so that each man can locate his own equipment.

The Department purchased 600′ of 2 ½ inch underwriters hose during the year and also some 1 ½ inch iron pipe thread couplings to change over thread on the hose that was purchased from the Federal Government. The department has on hand approximately 11,400 feet of 2 ½ inch rubber lined hose and 3,500 feet of 1 ½ inch rubber lined hose.

The kitchen at the Fire Station was remodeled by the permanent men. A larger stove and a new sink were purchased to round out the project.

———

1948 [from *City of Keene Annual Report*]

Fire Department

Walter R. Messer,
    Chief Engineer 1948

Fire Department in 1948

Permanent personnel 10
Expenditures $46,141
Monthly cost per person 25c
Total Fire Loss $102,500
Fire Loss Per Capita $6.83
Total Alarms 291
Still Alarms 254
Box Alarms 25
False Alarms 7
Oil Permits 160
Pieces of Apparatus 8

Majority of Fires Reported by Telephone

In 1948 The Fire Department responded to 291 alarms, an increase of 22 over the previous year. The fact that eighty-eight percent of the alarms were reported by telephone stresses the importance of giving clear information to the Fire Department when confronted by a fire emergency. The Fire Department is able to reach almost any point in the city within three minutes provided that the correct street is known.

Fire Prevention plays an increasingly important role in the department's activity. By having each men in the department take part in inspections, the fire fighters become familiar with the various buildings in the city and hazardous conditions are brought to the attention of property owners. Over 1665 inspections were made in 1948 and recommendations for the elimination of fire hazards noted in 22 cases were followed.

The Severe Drought in 1948 created an unusually long forest fire danger period. Through the cooperation and carefulness of the public, however, no serious conflagration occurred. Your department assisted surrounding communities in controlling severe fires. Although such

Assistance is reimbursed by a cash payment, this service can not be measured in dollars and cents when an emergency arises.

STONES FOUND IN HYDRANTS

Several Times through the year firemen have discovered stones in nozzles when using the first line of hose from a hydrant. This is caused by malicious stuffing of stones into hydrants. Such vandalism can be the cause for loss of valuable time in fighting fires. Steps are being taken to remedy this situation.

In The Annual Inspection of the department in October, a public demonstration of ladder handling and hose connecting was had on Central Square. Late in the year the fire station ramp was replaced by the Public Works department and new doors were constructed at the fire house. Much of the work on the doors was performed by the firemen at the station house.

The Old Doors of the central fire station were replaced with new doors that were made out of Mahogany. In 1966, the door glass was changed to 3 full panes of glass and remained in place until the steel overhead doors were installed in the mid 1990s.

All The Fire Apparatus is in good condition. With the addition of a four wheel drive "power wagon" for use in fighting forest fires and as a utility vehicle the department now has greater flexibility in its operations. In all the fire department has the following equipment:

APPARATUS & EQUIPMENT

Engine No. 1-750 Gallons triple combination, 60 gallon booster tank.

Engine No. 2-750 gallon triple combination, 80 gallon booster tank.

Engine No. 3-600 gallon triple combination, 100 gallon booster tank.

Emergency Squad No. 1 1-75 gallon pump, 150 gallon booster tank, flood lighting outfit, first aid supplies, salvage covers, inhalator, gas masks, stretchers, 1.100 gallon Morse invincible nozzle.

Emergency Squad No. 2-200 gallon pump, 150 gallon booster tank, 2,000 feet of 1 ½ inch hose, 35 gallon portable pump, pump

Tanks, shovels, axes, pulaskis, fire rakes, cross cut saw, and peavey.

Seagraves Aerial ladder-75 feet aerial with 200 feet of ground ladders and a 600 gpm ladder pipe.

Dodge 1 ton 4 wheel drive power wagon-200 gallon tank with auxiliary pump and hose reel for grass and brush fire fighting, and for transportation of men, hose and equipment.

Reo Speed Wagon-2, 500 feet 1 ½ inch hose, 40 gallon portable pump. This equipment is furnished by State Forestry Department.

Chief's Car-Chevrolet coach with two-way radio.

Foam Generator-For large gasoline and oil fires, 2,000 lbs foam powder.

Forest fire equipment-43 pump tanks, 11 pulaskis, 11 forest fire rakes, 40 shovels, 14 hoes, 15-14 qt, pails and two tubs for relaying water from pump to pump.

The annual hose testing disclosed a large amount of hose unable to withstand the minimum pressure. As a result thirteen hundred feet of hose was taken out of service. This was replaced with 700 feet of 1 ½ inch hose bringing the department's complement of hose up to 11,000 feet of 2 ½ inch and 4,100 feet of 1 ½ inch hose.

NOTE: On page 17 of the 1948's Annual Report, the fire losses for 1940 to 1948 totals were listed as shown below.

FIRE LOSSES 1940-48

As Reported by the *Keene Evening Sentinel* on February 1st, 1948.

'FIRE'
16 HEAD OF CATTLE PERISH IN SUNDAY AFTERNOON FIRE

Sixteen head of cattle, most of them registered Gurnseys, were burned to death late Sunday afternoon when fire destroyed the barn of Mrs. Henry S. Hoisington on the West Surry Road. The MacKenzie family of upper Court Street owned the cattle. The loss, which is expected to exceed $10,000, is partially covered by insurance.

Origin of the fire has not been determined. Keene firemen saved the house which was connected with the barn and nearby storehouse, were 18 tons of hay, two tons of beet pulp, a quantity of grain, and farm imple-

ments. The Hoisington automobile and a harvester were removed to safety.

Had Big Start

When the fire was discovered it had a tremendous headway and the entire interior became a raging inferno within a short time. The fact that the barn was covered with metal roofing prevented an early discovery of the blaze.

One of the heifers destroyed was a prize animal owned by Warren and Lawrence MacKenzie and valued at more than $1,500. This prize heifer had been exhibited at the Eastern States Exposition in Springfield, Mass., last fall and at the 4-H club national exhibit in Waterloo, Iowa, last fall. The youths had refused an offer of $1,500 for this animal. They lost ten other prize animals. The farther, Elmer L. MacKenzie, who operates a large dairy farm about a half a mile away from the Hoisington property, owned the other five cows burned. The Hoisington barn was used to house the overflow of stock from the MacKenzie dairy.

Mrs. Hoisington occupies the downstairs apartment and Frank Jacobs, his wife and three children occupy the upper tenement. Mr. Jacobs is herdsman for the MacKenzies and was at the dairy farm when the fire broke out, Mrs. Jacobs and the three children were in the house at the time. She had been in the shed that connects the hose and barn after some wood about ten minutes before the discovery of the fire. She did not notice anything wrong at that time.

Robert M. Clark Jr., John Brosnahan and Edward Madison, who were passing the Hoisington house in an automobile, saw the fire and attempted to get into the house to notify the occupants. Finding the door locked, they broke a window and entered the house, one calling the fire station while the others searched the house for occupants. Being unable to locate anyone, they started removing furnishing from the building. It was later learned that Mrs. Jacobs had taken her three children to the Mitchell home across the road.

Firemen Save House

Firemen laid three lines of hose from two hydrants on the road and water was played on the flames from two sides of the building. While the water pressure was not too good as the hydrants are the last two on the line, there was sufficient water to enable firemen to check the flames from entering the house.

Mrs. Hoisington, who is the mother of Mrs. MacKenzie, was not at home when the fire broke out as she was staying at the MacKenzie farm while Mr. and Mrs. MacKenzie and their three children were in Boston attending the Sportsman Show.

Large Crowd Attracted

Motorists swarmed to the scene after the alarm but police officers were able to stop most of the cars at the junction of the Old Walpole Road and the West Surry Road.

The all out signal was not sounded until after 9 o'clock. The first call, a still alarm and this was followed ten minutes later by a general alarm from Box 47.

––––––––––

The fire selected for 1948 is the fire on July 4th, 1948. The Bloomer and Haselton Fire at 23 Winter Street. As recorded by the *Keene Evening Sentinel* on July 4th, 1948.

'FIRE'
BLOOMER & HASELTON FIRE CAUSES $60,000 DAMAGE; OWNER PLANNING TO REBUILD.

Sunday's Blaze is Spectacular; Cause Unknown.

Five Businesses Are Affected Also State Welfare Department

One of the most spectacular fire which Keene has experienced in years gutted the Bloomer and Haselton

Property at 23 Winter Street early Sunday afternoon and damaged the nearby residence of Mrs. Marie Pratte, 10 Center Street, causing a loss estimated in excess of $60,000.

Every available piece of firefighting apparatus in the city was used to combat the blaze which was not brought under control until firemen had fought desperately for more than two hours. Five business concerns suffered losses. The New Hampshire Department of Public Welfare offices were also damaged.

Plans To Rebuild

Carl R. Bloomer, president and treasure of the Bloomer & Haselton Company Inc., furniture dealers said today that he expects to rebuild a two story structure on the present site. His plans however, are indefinite.

The tower on the front of the building on Winter Street will be torn down. Winter Street is barricaded to prevent motorist from passing as it is feared that the cupola, which was weakened by the fire, might topple. Center Street is also made a one-way street.

Discovered by Miss Foster

The fire was discovered by Miss Marium E. Foster who lives in the Pratte house. Hearing what she believed was popping firecrackers investigation revealed flames leaping up from the platform on the east side of the building. She called the fire department. Other neighbors saw the flames about the same time, Box 41 was sounded.

The fire started near the metal containers on the platform in the rear of the brick addition occupied by the Colony shop which fronts on Winter Street. Within a short time the flames were shooting high into the air and dense volumes of black smoke were rolling skyward.

Fight From Four Sides

Firemen combated the blaze from Center and Winter Streets, the grounds of the Central Junior High School on the west and the Court House property on the east.

Barn Fire: Sixteen head of prize cattle perished in this barn fire early Sunday night at the residence of Mrs. Susan E. Hoisington on the Surry Road. Photo shows barn reduced to a skeleton. Firemen saved home after a three hour battle.

Pumpers were stationed on Middle Street at the end of Center Street; Winter Street and in Central Square. Engine 1, which was stationed in Central Square for a time was transferred to Court Street. The pumpers forced water though nine lines of hose to the fire. The aerial ladder was brought into use on Winter Street in order to throw water on the tower on the building.

Practically Total Loss

The building, owned by Mr. And Mrs. Carl R. Bloomer, is practically a total loss. The store of Bloomer and Haselton Associates and the Bloomer & Haselton Inc., furniture of which Carl R. Bloomer is the president, suffered the largest loss. Mr. Bloomer said that his losses will exceed $50,000. Loss of the Lindsey Plumbing & Heating Company, owned by William F. Lindsay, was estimated between $4,000 and $5,000 by the owner.

The Store occupied by the Keene Screen and Awning Company was damaged by smoke and water only. The fire did not reach his store which is in the northern part of the building.

Rooms occupied by the New Hampshire Department of Public Welfare on Center Street were damaged.

Remove Store Stock

The colony Shop on Winter Street owned by Mr. & Mrs. Thedore Kohler received some damage. Dresses and garments were removed during the height of the fire. Clerks and volunteers assisted in moving the stock.

The Reliable Laundry in the basement of the building and owned by Edwin Budd received a water damage. A pump was used the greater part of the night Sunday to clear the water from the basement.

Firemen remained on duty all night.

Before the all out signal had sounded a still alarm was sounded about 5:30 o'clock for a small blaze which had broken out in the attic of the house owned by Mrs. Marie Pratte. A hole had to be punctured in the roof near the eaves to get at the fire.

Garage Damaged

The Pratt house, less than 30 feet from the Bloomer building was scorched by the heat and the two car garage which stands between the Pratte house and the Bloomer building was badly damaged.

Chief of Police Regan had a number of regulars and specials on duty during the fire to keep the spectators at a safe distance. The local police were also assisted by members of the Sheriffs department.

The part of the building which fronts on Winter Street was dedicated as a church on Sept. 17th, 1839 and was used by the Baptist denomination for nearly 40 years. The building was used for various other purposes including a state armory, the large space in the rear being used as a drill hall, roller skating, basketball and dancing.

Salvaging of the merchandise by the business firms hosed in the building was started Monday.

Crowd Scatters When Aerial Ladder Swings

Plagued by acrid smoke fumes most of the afternoon, the crowd of spectators on Winter Street had time for a few laughs at the height of the blaze.

The humorous incident occurred when Chief Messer ordered the aerial ladder truck to move in closer to the building. The firemen directing the stream of water from the t op of the ladder was unable to shut it off as the ladder swung around to a descending position.

A few dozen persons found themselves in the path of the high pressure stream and were forced to flee in the direction of Central

Battle Fire From Roof: Firemen fought the flames from all sides. The above shows hosemen on top of the Colony Shop roof in rear of the Pratte house garage. Note: containers of bottled gas on loading platform at side of building. Police kept spectators at a safe distance. Photos by Jack Teehan.

Aerial Water Tower: Two firemen aim stream of water into burning tower of Bloomer and Haselton building from top of aerial ladder, which was brought into play by Chief Messer as the fire worked to the front of the building. The blaze was the most spectacular in the city in several years.

square. A hose clamp was used to shut off the water.

Note: Fighters Fly Over City in Formation

Spectators at the Bloomer & Haselton fire Sunday afternoon were momentarily distracted by a flight of 15 F-47 fighters which flew low over the city in formation of three V's.

It is believed that the Thunderbolt fighters are assigned to the New Hampshire National Guard with headquarters at Grenier Field, Manchester.

NOTE: Praises Efficiency of Keene Fire Department.

Theodore W. Gunn of Peterborough, inspector, New Hampshire Fire Underwriters, had nothing but praise for the Keene Fire Department and Fire Chief Walter R. Messer after he inspected the fire damage Monday morning.

Gunn told Messer his department had done a "wonderful job" and said the fire proved once again that an aerial ladder is all invaluable piece of equipment.

Card of Thanks

I wish to sincerely thank Fire Chief Walter R. Messer and the members of the Keene Fire Department, the Keene Police Department Miss Marium E. Foster and all others who assisted to save my residence at the time of the Bloomer & Haselton fire, July 4th,

Mrs. A. A. Pratte
Keene New Hampshire July 12th.

_____

1949 [from *City of Keene Annual Report*]

Fire Department

Walter R. Messer,
Chief Engineer 1949

Fire Department in 1949

Statistics

Permanent personnel 11
Expenditures $46,820
Monthly cost per person 28c
Total Fire Loss $66,117
Fire Loss Per Capita $4.25
Total Alarms 281
Still Alarms 256
Box Alarms 25
False Alarms 3
Pieces of apparatus 8

The Fire Department of the City of Keene is a protective organization, set up for the protection of live and property against fire, on a 24 hours a day basis. There are 11 permanent men and 45 call men. The permanent men operate and repair the equipment and maintain the Fire Station and property. They also make routine inspections of all the property in the Fire Precinct in search of fire hazards and observe changes in building construction that take place from time to time. They recommend changes to eliminate fire hazards and for safer housekeeping conditions where they feel they are necessary, and in general improve conditions around the properties in inspected.

The Fire Department issues permits for the storage of flammable fluids; the location of this material is inspected and safety installations are recommended.

The Fire alarm system maintained by the permanent men, is of the type where warning would be given audibly should any breaks occur in the system. There are 56 Fire Alarm Boxes dispersed throughout the City. The outskirts are covered to a fair extent as well as the more heavily populated central sections. In case of fire, if the call comes over

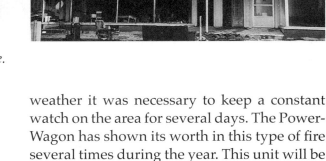

Photo shows the aftermath of the Bloomer block fire.

the telephone, two permanent men with equipment respond. If the fire is of proportions greater than they can handle, a call for more men and equipment is sent to the Fire Station, usually by radio, and a box alarm is sounded and the call men respond to give the support in man power as needed.

The call men are also available for special duty and assistance at brush fires. They are trained in the use of fire fighting equipment and salvage work, such as covering property with salvage covers and removing debris that will keep the fire loss as small as possible. The call men are all volunteers-in varied activities other that the Fire department for their livelihood. They like to fight Fire!

Slight Decrease In Number Of Alarms In 1949

The Fire Department responded to 281 alarms of varied nature during the year of 1949. There wee 25 bell alarms and 256 still alarms and 256 still alarms, of which 18 wee for out of town assistance. The fire loss for 1949 was $66,117, about 35% less than the 1948 figure of $102,500.

There were 65 calls for grass and brush fires, one being of good size before we were able to reach it. With the aid of the Power-Wagon we were able to carry water to the top of the hill where the fire was and to keep it limited to that area. Because of the dry

weather it was necessary to keep a constant watch on the area for several days. The Power-Wagon has shown its worth in this type of fire several times during the year. This unit will be equipped with a radio, enabling to be in direct contact with the station.

In January the State put on a training session in brush fire control and the meeting were very well attended. The department had training sessions during the year and handling of tools and equipment was stressed as well as question and answer periods. About 20 men attended the sessions of Firemen Training that were held in Concord under the sponsorship of the N.H. Fire Chiefs Club. The men attending these sessions were able to act as instructors for the local sessions. Several Keene firemen attended a school at the Framingham Police Barracks, sponsored by the Mass. State Fire Marshal and the Mass. Fire Chiefs Association, for oil burner fire control as well as bottled gas fire control.

New Radio Equipment

The Fire Alarm circuits are in good condition. The lines have been cleared of brush at different intervals during the year. Three new boxes were placed in the circuits as replacements. No serious interruption of service occurred during the year, and while some of the call men complain of being unable to hear the

Permanent Men of the Keene Fire Department 1949. L to R: Back Row: Charles M. Ballou, Prescot M. Little, Lawrence E. Thompson, Robert C. Callahan, Paul E. Gallup, Harry F. Hammond. L to R, Front Row: Lyman O. Cass, Captain Samuel J. Guyette, Chief Walter R. Messer, Captain Elton P. Britton, Frank M. Reid. Picture from Keene Fire Department Records.

whistle in different locations, this condition is more or less climatically.

The inspection of business places and properties within the fire precinct was carried out. The low percentage of fires starting in basements or from rubbish in or around properties shown that this service is very successful. Recommended changes have been complied with by the occupants. 170 oil permits were issued during the year. All of these locations were inspected as to the proper installation.

The apparatus is in good condition.

Some of the pieces of equipment are now getting to a ripe old age and replacement is being considered. The pumps have been tested and found to deliver their rated capacity. The hose was tested and 600 feet, found to be porous, was taken out of service and 1,000 feet of new hose purchased. A smoke ejector was purchased to enable us to remove smoke from very heavy atmosphere. This device will enable us to enter smoky areas more quickly to locate the seat of the trouble.

All of the plastered ceiling on the second floor of the station were painted and repaired as necessary. The permanent men painted all of the woodwork on the exterior of the building. The lavatories and shower room were completely refinished as well as several floors in the different rooms.

The annual inspection and ball was held during Fire Prevention Week. Schools were visited and checked as to the ability of the children to conduct a satisfactory fire drill. Several spot talks on fire protection and prevention were given on the radio, and trailers were run in the theatres. The Fire Department put on a parade, with an exhibition of equipment and man power operation in Central Square for the general public. The most spectacular fire of the year, the Crocker storehouse call out the whole fire department and left the station without good coverage. The Town of Troy was called for assistance and they brought in a pump that "stood by" in the station in case any more trouble developed. These situations arise occasionally and about 25 departments and Towns in the area from New Hampshire, Vermont and central Massachusetts have been working on a system of mutual aid to assist each other. This system will begin to operate in the very near future. The main dispatching station will be in Greenfield.

The Fire Department wishes to thank the Ladies Auxiliary of the Fire Department for their efforts in feeding the members at the several fires; also the Red Cross for their assistance at the brush fire on the Hurricane Road, and to all the City Department for their cooperation and assistance in combating fires this year.

Alarms

From Box 10
By Telephone 268
At Station 3
Total 281

Fires

In Buildings 160
Brush or grass 62
Motor vehicles 18
Other 13
Total 253

False Alarms 3

Rescue/Emergency 6

Fire Loss $66,117

Investigations 141

Inspections 1,357

The fire selected for 1949 is the fire on March 4th, 1949. The Fire on 268 Gilsum Street. As recorded by the *Keene Evening Sentinel*.

'FIRE'
One Man Dies, Two Others Seriously Burned When Oil Heater Explodes In Gilsum St. House This Morning.

Wilbur L. Mayou Declared Victim of Suffocation

William C. Gauthier and Clifford Mayou Are Hospital Patients

Explosion of an oil heater in the home of William C. Gauthier, 268 Gilsum Street, about 1 o'clock this morning, resulted in the death of one man and put two others in Elliot Community Hospital with serious burns.

The dead:

Wilbur L. Mayou, 37 of 433 Elm Street.

Injured:

Mr. Gauthier, 65, second and third degree burns of face and hands.

Clifford Mayou, 46, of 268 Gilsum Street, second degree burns of face and hands.

Hospital authorities reported this morning that the condition of both Mr. Gauthier and Mr. Mayou is "only fair."

Dr. Walter F. Taylor, acting medical referee, said that Mayou's death was caused by suffocation due to smoke inhalation. The burns, he said, were no worse that those received by the other two men. The victim was visiting his brother, Clifford, who lives in the Gauthier home.

The medical referee quoted Gauthier as saying that a flash occurred as he was placing a refilled oil tank on the stove in the living room.

Gauthier is reported to have aided Clifford Mayou from the house but it is believed that Wilbur was trapped in the kitchen as he attempted to make his way to a door leading to a shed.

Find Raging Inferno

Firemen responded to a still alarm call and while enroute to the scene radioed the fire station to sound a general alarm as flames could be seen shooting skyward. Box 38 was sounded. When the firemen arrived they found the house a blazing inferno. A dog owned by Mr. Gauthier was burned to death.

Myrl Blanchard, night dispatcher for Town Cab, told a Sentinel reporter that one of his drivers was called around midnight to make a delivery at the Gilsum Street address.

The driver, Blanchard said, reported that no lights were on in the home and he was unable to rouse anyone after repeated knocking at the door. This was less than an hour before the alarm sounded.

Cab Driver First or Scene

Charles A. Forest, another town Cab driver, said he was the first man on the scene. He was making a call at 61 Woodbury Street when he saw the flames leap skyward.

"Bill Gauthier (one of the two men who received severe burns in the fire) was outside the house." Forest said, "and he was coal black as black as the ace of spades."

Forest said Gauthier was incoherent and obviously dazed soon after he left the building. But he finally told Forest that he had called the Fire department.

The Cab driver radioed his dispatcher with instruction to relay a warning to the fire station. A telephone operator advised the dispatcher that fire trucks were already on the way.

The all out was sounded at 4:17 a.m. It was the first bell alarm of the year.

Another fire selected for 1949 is the fire on November 9th, 1949. The Fire off Water Street. As recorded by the *Keene Evening Sentinel*:

'FIRE'
SPECTACULAR FIRE DESTROYS WAREHOUSE OFF WATER STREET

One of the most spectacular fires here in recent years destroyed the three-story frame building owned by Harry Crocker, off Water Street, late Wednesday afternoon. The loss is estimated at $12,000 by the owner.

Firemen combated the blaze, which threatened houses in the vicinity for more than five hours.

Police said that the fire was apparently started by four teenagers, two boys and two girls, who are to appear later in juvenile court.

According to information secured by Chief Joseph L. Regan the youngsters were playing in the building and while using a cigarette lighter to illuminate a narrow passage between two piles of baled rags, accidentally started the fire. It was reported that one attempted to extinguish the blaze with a pail of water.

Florian J. Madore, who is employed at the Gay's Express terminal nearby, discovered the flames and telephoned the fire station. About the same time an unidentified person passing by rang Box 14 at the corner of Water and Grove Streets.

The building, approximately 100 feet square, was filled with new roofing material, baled paper, rags and junk. Mr. Crocker had owned the property the past two years, having purchased it from Arthur Whitcomb Inc.

Attack From All Sides

When the firemen arrived, the building was an inferno. The blaze was attacked from all sides to keep the flames from spreading to the nearby houses on Grove, Water and Myrtle Streets. A shed which had been used for the drying of lumber and the grass in

Deluge Hose Company 1949. L to R Seated: S.W. Pollock, A.D. Erwin, P.A. Barrett. 1st Row: P.E. Symonds, C.M. Ballou, P.M. Little, C.F. Caldwell, R. Henry, G.E. Fish, L.F. Curtis, J.J. Keating. 2nd Row: R.C. Calahan, G.H. Seaver, E.P. Britton, C.P. Woods, J.G. McCarthy, F.R. Dovovan, M.G. Waling, G.H. Sheppard.

the vicinity caught fire at various times but firemen quickly extinguished these.

The intense heat hampered fighting the blaze during the early stages. One fireman, Maurie G. Waling, was treated by a physician late Wednesday night.

Many lines of hose were laid from hydrants on Myrtle, Grove and Water Streets. All apparatus was brought into the except the Emergency Squad truck, which was left at the fire station. This was pressed into use when calls came for a grass fire and a fire at the Federal Lunch on Lamson Street.

Troy Truck Covers

A large fire truck summoned from Troy remained at the station to "cover" any fire, which might develop while the Keene Firemen were engaged at the Water Street conflagration.

The all out signal was not sounded until after 11 o'clock. Some firemen and one piece of apparatus remained at the scene all night.

Thousand of persons were attracted to the scene by the dense smoke which could be seen from many miles around.

The building was used at one time for storage of chairs and stock used by the C. L. Russell & Sons, chair manufactures. Later it was used by Arthur Whitcomb, Inc.

Members of the Women's auxiliary furnished coffee and food to firemen at the station.

————

I think it only fitting to add this short Brush fire, which was interesting to read. As reported by the *Keene Evening Sentinel* on August 8th, 1949:

'FIRE'
BRUSH FIRE GIVES CREW HARD FIGHT

Ten Acres Are Burned Over Off Hurricane Road.

About 75 firemen and volunteers combated a forest and brush fire which burned over an estimated ten acres of land owned by Leon Ellis and located between the Hurricane and summit road Saturday afternoon. The fire is believed to have originated by lightning, which struck an old pine tree a few days previous, causing a smoldering fire among pine needles, according to District Fire Chief Fred J. Baker.

The fire was discovered shortly before 4 o'clock Saturday afternoon.

The flames were under control before 7 o'clock but a crew of men remained at the scene Saturday night to combat any outbreak. About a dozen men were on duty Sunday.

Firemen Battle Hornets

The emergency squad truck carried firemen and water tanks to within a quarter of a mile of the fire. From this point the firemen had to "fight" their way through heavy underbrush and hornets nests. Several of the volunteers were stung by the insects.

Lt. Elton P. Britton took charge of the fire until Walter R. Messer and district Fire Chief Baker arrived. Cold drinks, coffee and food were taken to the men on duty. In order that the emergency truck might reach a point near the fire trees, brush and stones had to be removed from the old tote road leading to the scene.

In order to get enough help to fight the fire two still alarms and three bell alarms were sounded. The first still alarm came at 3:20 o'clock and the first bell alarm was sounded at 4:20 p.m. A second still alarm was sounded at 4:30 for a truck to convey equipment, water tanks and men. The second bell alarm was sounded at 4:35 and the third bell alarm at 4:50 o'clock.

Spotted By Pilot

Robert Hayes a pilot for the Bowman Flying Service, spotted the fire and reported it to the Fire Department. Later in the afternoon he flew Fire Chief Walter R. Messer over the area.

This was the second fire spotted and reported by Pilot Hayes this year.

Firemen were called Sunday morning for a brush fire on land of Forest L. Carey on Beech hill in the rear of the ski jump. It is believed the fire had been started from a boys camp fire.

————

As Reported by the *Keene Evening Sentinel* on November 28th, 1949:

'FIRE'
Firemen Are Called 4 Times This Morning

Firemen responded to four still alarm calls this morning. One was for a fire about an oil burner in the house owned by George Miller, 26 Elm Street, the second was to secure aid in lowering the body on Island Street following a fatal accident.

The third call was for a fire about the motor of a washing machine in the home of Roger Thayer of 59 Pine Avenue. The fire was controlled and the firemen were recalled by radio before they arrived.

The fourth call was for a fire in the flooring in John's IGA store in West Keene.

————

The Past

The Present

The Future

PAST, PRESENT, FUTURE

The glamour, pride and dedication of those who made history and forged ahead with innovations has given direction for the present, so future generations can reap the benefits. Our traditions maintain the pride and honor we feel for the privilege to serve the public and to save lives and property. This is what the men and woman of the fire service hold so dear.

1950–1986

Past – Present – Future

1950 [from *City of Keene Annual Report*]

FIRE DEPARTMENT

Walter R. Messer,
    Chief Engineer 1950

Fire Department in 1950

Statistics

Permanent personnel 11

Expenditures $47,729.48

Total Fire Loss $29,028.00

Total Alarms 314

Still Alarms 302

Box Alarms 11

False Alarms 2

During the year 1950 there was a slight increase in the number of alarms compared to 1949. A total of 314 alarms were answered in 1950, while 281 alarms were answered during the previous year. Three people died during the year in Keene from the effect of fire. Mr. Wilbur Mayo suffocated and burned at a cottage on upper Gilsum Street. Mrs. Oleson and Mrs. Bennett also died from the effects of burns resulting from a gas explosion in a tourist cabin in Keene.

The permanent men in the department started testing hydrants early in February with the aid of the power wagon, which was equipped with a radio. This service was carried on for about two months. During this period these men were called back to the station 5 times to cover for a still alarm.

It took up to four minutes for the men to get back to the station. This service was called off the last of March.

Reported by the *Keene Evening Sentinel* March 29th, 1950:

"FIRE"

Two Alarms Given For Hyde Street Fire

The names of two Keene Streets Hyde and High are often confusing when spoken over the telephone.

This fact was responsible for the sounding of two still alarms this morning fore an oil burner fire at 55 Hyde Street in the home of Mrs. Irene Sullivan.

The firemen who took the call thought the location was 55 High Street and a truck was dispatched. It was recalled by radio when the mistake was discovered.

_____

From the *Keene Evening Sentinel*:

"FIRE"

Grass Fires Keep Department Busy April 10th, 1950

All Started From Burning Refuse, Says Fire Chief

Firemen had a busy time Saturday extinguishing grass fires in various sections of the city. One call Sunday was for a chimney fire.

According to Chief Walter R. Messer of the Keene Fire Department all of the eight fires which occurred on Saturday caught from outdoor incinerators which were not properly supervised.

The grass fires Saturday, which burned over only small areas, were on land owned by John DiLorenzo, 51 Butler Court; Forrest L. Carey,

Eastern Avenue; Fred Fields, North Lincoln Street; Roy Champagne, North Swanzey; A. LeClair, 443 Elm Street; Robert Monroe, 164 Baker Street; Ray T. Tarbox, 88 Baker Street and Michael Mitchell, 439 Elm Street.

The Sunday chimney fire was in a house owned by Mrs. Minnie S. Howard, 217 Elm Street. The grass fire was on land owned by Robert Rice, 113 Cross Street.

This morning a grass fire was extinguished on land owned by the Boston & Main railroad near the Tidewater Oil Company's plant on Water Street.

Watch Incinerators

Would you take the family papers out of the strong box and dump them into the incinerator? Would you stuff that heirloom painting, bedspread, or tapestry into the wire basket in the back yard and set it a fire?

No? Of course you wouldn't - willingly. But every time you light your backyard incinerator and go off and leave it, you're taking a chance of doing just that.

There were eight grass fires in Keene over the weekend. Any one of them, if not caught in time, could have taken the house along with the grass.

And they all started from improperly watched incinerators. An incinerator, especially an open wire one, is a major hazard in windy weather. It doesn't take much to plant a spark in the middle of dry grass nearby.

Than the grass catches fire, and unless someone sees it quickly, the house can catch fire from the grass.

And when the house goes, so do the heirloom painting, tapestry and the papers in the family strong box. It's just like stuffing your home in the wire basket and letting go with the matches.

The only thing that is needed to prevent trouble is a little care. If you will wait until the wind dies down and watch the incinerator like a hawk while it is burning, there will be no danger.

It cost money to send out the fire department. It cost more money to replace a burned out home, or even a burned over garden. But all it takes to prevent these costly mistakes is a little care in when and how you burn rubbish.

————

Reported by the *Keene Evening Sentinel* April 23rd, 1950:

"FIRE"

Fire Damage Put at $5,000 Ellis Bros. Greenhouse Office Gutted Sunday

Fire early Sunday morning resulted in damage of more than $5,000 to buildings and property of Ellis Bros. Company, florists, at 203 Winchester Street.

Fire broke out in the office building and was discovered about 5:30 o'clock. Firemen were quickly on the scene and checked the flames from entering the ten large green houses. Smoke, however seeped into the greenhouses and the damage to the plants and flowers has not been determined.

During the fire an explosion took place, but no firemen were injured. It is believed that a container of insecticide exploded.

A buzzer in the apartment of Mr. and Mrs. Arthur Colton awakened Mrs. Colton who gave the alarm. It is believed that someone passing discovered the fire about the same time and started to sound the alarm from Box 53 as the door of the box was opened. The damage was covered by insurance.

––––––––

Reported by the *Keene Evening Sentinel* on May 31st, 1950:

"STORY"

Tidbits of information New Street Names Concern Fire Chief

Fire Chief Walter R. Messer is keeping an eye on the names suggested for new streets in Keene.

The fire chief fears his trucks may some day rush to the wrong street unless names are chosen with care.

The City Council will be asked to change the name of Summit road, which was recently accepted as the official name for a street in proposed housing development off Fox Avenue.

Messer pointed out that a section of Route 12 in Keene is already known as Summit Road. The road could also be confused with Summer Street on telephoned alarms, he said.

––––––––

Reported by the *Keene Evening Sentinel* on June 2nd, 1950:

"STORY"

On a Fox, a Tail Is Called a Brush

Councilman Joseph H. Johnson was willing to accept the name Fox Circle for the extension of Fox Avenue in his new subdivision development.

Fire Chief Walter R. Messer preferred it to the name approved last week, Summit Avenue, because he feared firefighters might

confuse it with Summit Road or Summer Street.

Mayor Ford Suggested Johnson Avenue.

Councilman Clair E. Wyman suggested Hound Avenue.

City Solicitor Kenneth J. Arwe said Fox Circle might be confused with Fox Avenue.

The newly-accepted street is an extension of Fox Avenue which ends in a large circle.

"It's a circle with a tail on it," Arwe said.

That ended the discussion. The new Street will be known as Fox Circle.

––––––––

Reported by the *Keene Evening Sentinel* on June 9th, 1950:

"STORY"

Fire Alarm Boxes Get Coat of Paint

Picture of John Phillips painting a fire alarm box. About every twenty years, the boxes get redone by the department. In the late 1970s, the department repainted all the fire alarm boxes lime green. They are being brought back to the original fire alarm red.

The city's fire alarm boxes are getting a new coat of paint.

A biennial chore, the 56 boxes will be painted bright red.

No paint is needed for the "phantom" alarm system however.

Whistle signals are assigned to areas where no boxes are located.

When an alarm is telephoned, volunteer firemen know the approximate location by the number blown on the whistle, hence the name phantom alarm.

———————

Reported by the *Keene Evening Sentinel* July 7th, 1950.

"FIRE"

Eight Flee House In Night Clothes, Firemen Are Called To Foundry Street

Eight persons were driven into the street in their night clothes shortly before 5 o'clock this morning by fire in the two-tenement house at 48 Foundry Street.

Cause of the fire, which originated in a shed, is undetermined. The loss is estimated at $1,200 by Chief Walter R. Messer.

Occupants of the house include Mr. and Mrs. Charles L. Rivers, owners of the property, and Mr. and Mrs. Norman R. Clark and four children who live in the north apartment.

Mrs. Clark detected the odor of smoke and awakened her husband who discovered the fire. He went to the home of Ellsworth Rouleau and called the fire station. Firemen responding to a still alarm radioed for more help and a general alarm was sounded on Box 53.

———————

Reported by the *Keene Evening Sentinel* November 28th, 1950:

"FIRE"

Firemen, Barred From Entering House, Turn to Police for Aid

Keene firemen are well trained but nobody ever told them what to do when the occupant of a burning house wouldn't let them in.

So they called the police. Firemen responded to a still alarm at 16 Sullivan Street Tuesday night. Flames were coming out of the chimney.

Fire Chief Walter R. Messer reported that the occupant, William F. Melvin, a tenant, refused to open a locked door.

Firemen Frank M. Reid, who was on the scene, said "We couldn't get in so we tried to talk with him through the window.

They finally gave up, went back to the fire station for council and were advised to call police.

Reid said "Mrs. Melvin finally opened the door when police arrived. The blaze was quickly extinguished.

Reid quoted Melvin as saying, "his landlord had refused to clean the chimney so he decided to burn it out."

Other calls Tuesday were for a blaze in a hot air duct in the house owned by Edward Sutton, 103 Pinehurst Avenue, and a fire about an oil burner in the house owned by Reginald Stebbins, 70 Prospect Street.

———————

Reported by the *Keene Evening Sentinel* June 12th, 1950:

"STORY"

Firemen Pay Tribute To Deceased Members

Memorial Service Held Sunday at Fire Station

Tribute to deceased firemen was paid at the annual memorial service Sunday morning in the assembly hall of the fire station. Rev A. Norman Janes, Pastor of the First Congregational Church, the department chaplain, gave the address, Chief Walter R. Messer presided.

The honor roll of 55 deceased members was read by Stephen W. Pollock. There were no deaths during the past year.

A trio from Keene High School, the Misses Barbara Jennison, Anne Kirk and Ruth McNeil, with Jeananne Farina, at the piano, gave three selections.

Following the service firemen decorated the graves of deceased firemen.

Mayor Leroy S. Ford attended the service.

The committee, in charge of the service included Arthur D. Irwin, Stephen W. Pollock and George E. Fish of the Deluge Hose Company; Edward L. Reason, Francis J. Driscoll and Lawrence M. Pickett of the Washington Hook and Ladder Company; Ralph H. Turner, Earl W. Little and Carl W. Johnson of the Keene Steam and Fire Engine Company.

From *City of Keene Annual Report*:

In charge of decorating the graves were Edward L. Reason, Francis J. Driscoll, Stewart Hobson, Carl Johnson, H. William Sanderson, Frank M. Reid and Chief Walter R. Messer. Phillip A. Farrett was in charge of the music.

The inspections of the business places in the fire district were carried out and very good conditions were found in practically all locations. The checking of locations and installations of containers for flammable fluids also installations of oil burners for safety conditions was carried out. There were 180 oil permits issued in 1950. Several classes from the different schools in the city visited the fire station and received instruction in fire prevention and protection by the chief and firemen. The equipment was taken to different schools for demonstration of fighting special types of fires with special equipment. The 2½" fire hose was tested and 500' was taken out of service. On two different occasions we pumped water out of cellars where we felt there was a distinct emergency. The parking meters were reconditioned with new parts supplied by the meter Company.

Several training meetings were held for the whole department for explanation and use of smoke ejector and portable foam equipment and fire inspection day activities. Ten men attended the training sessions at Concord, N. H. sponsored by the N. H. Fire Chiefs Club. All of the schools in the city were visited during Fire Prevention week and fire drills were held for the benefit of the chief and fire prevention committee.

From Keene Fire Department Records:

The Fire Mutual Aid System was put in operation March 15, 1950 throughout the Connecticut Valley and we were called for assistance once for a fire at the Winchester Tannery.

NOTE: On May 5th, Box 21 was struck at 12:20 for help to Winchester for a Fire at the Tannery. This was the 1st call to be used under the new Mutual Aid System.

New equipment put in service this year includes the radio in the power-wagon; a 1950 two door Chevrolet chiefs car; a device for hoisting hose in the hose tower; 1,000' of new underwriters grade of Fabric fire hose; and ten uniforms purchased for the call men. The civil defense trailer was painted and lettered. A new 80 gallon Electric hot water heater was installed. All of the metal ceilings were painted by a local contractor. The permanent men washed all of the walls in the station and painted the steam and water pipes and all the main cement floors.

The fire alarm system received a few changes and also minor trouble developed during the year. Box No. 142 and No. 25 were replaced during the year. The lines were relocated on Vernon Street, all the fire alarm boxes and pole markers were painted. Brush was cleared from the fire alarm wires over the whole system, also the different bells in the station were rewired to have them all on different circuits. An air raid signal box was built into the system. Falling trees and limbs broke the system on two occasions.

A survey by the N. H. Board of Underwriters was taken with the assistance of the several departments related to the work.

The civil defense organization was reactivated and the fire department was given its part to carry out. The Chief was appointed chairman of the fire section, Capt Britton vice-chairman, Capt. Guyette in charge of the auxiliary firemen.

STATUS OF FIRE PROTECTION

The following conclusions refer to a detailed 1950 report on fire protection in the City. The detailed report is on fire in the City Manager's Office and is available for inspection. If sufficient interest is shown, it can be duplicated for wider distribution.

"In 1918, a grading of Keene was established for the N. H. Board by the National Board of Underwriters, and comparison to the current survey in each respect proves to be interesting and revealing. The comparisons in brief are as follows:

Water Supply: Less adequate, but somewhat more reliable than formerly indicated. The net change in this phase is slightly negative.

Fire Department: Vast improvement, primarily due to the acquisition of ladder and pumping apparatus, also minor and special equipment of many varied types.

Fire Alarm: No net change, as improvements in box design and condition, Fire Alarm Headquarters, etc. have been offset by the even more limited extent of the system in general (due to growth of the city and its population). It is significant that where the city has expanded almost 50% during the interval, no additional circuits and only a handful of boxes have been installed.

Building Laws: Slight improvement in existing ordinances and their enforcement.

Fire Prevention Ordinances: No change.

Structural Conditions: No change. During the 32 year interval just completed, the net overall change in fire protection available to the citizens of Keene had been one of moderate improvement.

THE NEW HAMPSHIRE BOARD OF UNDERWRITERS

Report No. 12, November 1950 F. H. Krauss, Engineer

FIRE LOSS STATISTICS, 1950

Value where fire occurred in Buildings, $187,750.00 and Contents $60,550.00 for a total of $248,300.00.

Insurance on where fire occurred in the Buildings, $129,250.00 and Contents, $48,650.00 and the total is $177,990.00.

Loss where fire occurred in Buildings, $26,270.33 Contents $2,757.17 and the total is $29,027.50.

Insurance paid where fire occurred in buildings $23,770.33 and the total for Contents $2,741.34 and the total is $26,511.67.

———

Fire selected for 1950 is the fire on October 5th, 1950. The Fire at 508 Washington Street at the Keene Cabin Court. As recorded by the *Keene Evening Sentinel*:

"FIRE"

One Woman Dead, Another Is Critically Burned When Gas From Heater Explodes

Washington Street Cabin Scene of Tragic Accident

Mrs. Georgiana Oleson of Fond du Lac, Wis. Dies in the hospital.

One woman was fatally burned and another is in critical condition at Elliot Community Hospital today following a gas explosion shortly after 5:30 a. m. in an overnight cabin at Keene Cabin Court, 508 Washington Street.

Mrs. Georgiana Oleson, 47, of Found du Lac, Wis., died several hours later at Elliot Community hospital.

Mrs. Annie Bennett, 68 of Rockland, Me., foster mother of the dead woman, is being treated at the hospital for burns of the hands, face and head and severe smoke inhalation.

Attempted to Light Heater

Fire Chief Walter R, Messer said the room was apparently "well saturated" with bottled gas which is used to heat the cabins. The explosion occurred when Mrs. Oleson attempted to light the gas heater. It was reported that the heater was turned off when the tow women retired.

Chief Messer said bottled gas "supposed" to have an odor but added that the sense of smell can be detected by a slow leak.

Escaped Through Window

Detective Sergeant William T. Bridgham investigated and reported that Mrs. Oleson rescued her foster mother by pushing her out through a window.

He talked with Mrs. Oleson before she died and said she was unable to find the door lock or a light switch in the smoke filled room but managed to locate the window through which both women escaped.

Mrs. Bennett was in bed when the gas ignited. The window shades were drawn at the time.

Heat Starts Fire

Heat from the explosion set the mattress and bed clothes ablaze and scorched wood in the cabin which consisted of a room and bath.

The women were taken to the hospital by ambulance.

Mrs. Oleson had spent the summer in Rockland with her foster mother where the estate of the latter's husband, who recently died, was being settled.

Were on Way to Wisconsin

They were returning to Found du Lac in a taxi owned by John J. O'Sullivan of Rockland, an acquaintance. He was accompanied by his wife.

O'Sullivan and his wife occupied an adjoining cabin. He told the Sentinel he heard "an explosion" and that fire broke out immediately. The tow women had escaped by the time he reached the scene.

The tourist cabins are owned by Frank B. Colvin.

Sgt. Bridgham said the intensity of the heat was confined to the upper portion of the room. There were no marks of fire on the floor or three to four feet up the walls.

Matches Not Ignited

The untreated portions of wooden matches placed head down in a holder were scorched but the heads had not ignited. The bottom of a paper bag on a table was untouched but the upper half was scorched.

Chief Messer explained that the gas needs oxygen to burn and that the actual explosion occurred at a level where the mixture was adequate for combustion. The great heat which was generated forced the gas lying on the floor to the upper portions of the room. The gas is heavier than air.

———

NOTE: In 1950 the City of Keene published its last Annual Report book as was published in the past. This Annual Report became smaller and smaller as each year moved from the 30's and 40's to where the council deemed the price of publication was to high. After the 40's rolled into the 50's all reports were loose and Ordinances and Resolutions were with the Council meetings.

As Reported by the *Keene Evening Sentinel* on October 7th, 1950:

"STORY"

Annual Inspection of Keene Fire department Set For Thursday

National Fire Prevention week (October 8-14) will be observed here with the annual inspection of the Keene Fire department.

A parade of Fire Department personnel and equipment will precede a demonstration n Central Square at 2 p.m. Thursday afternoon.

The annual Firemen's banquet will be held at 5:30 p.m. at the fire station.

Topping off the day's program will be the annual Firemen's Ball in the city hall auditorium.

Fire Chief Walter R. Messer injected a serious note into the observance, however urging local residents to rid their cellars, attics, back halls, sheds and barns of all combustible materials.

"Take advantage of the Clean-Up week service offered by the Public Works department." Messer said, "and avoid the danger of fire during the winter months ahead."

The chief also called on Keeneites to check electrical wiring, oil furnaces, all types of stoves, chimneys, accumulations of leaves in roof gutters, etc.

"A few minutes checking your home may prevent a disaster," he concluded.

———

Friday, October 14th, 1949 fire alert as reported by the *Keene Evening Sentinel*:

"STORY"

A stream of water gushes high into the air in Central Square. Thursday afternoon as members of the Keene Fire Department go through their paces in a National Fire Prevention Week exhibition. Chamberlain block below is "on fire" and a hose team attacks blaze from roof. Hordes of school children watched the show.

Firemen Demonstrate Equipment And Skill at Annual Inspection

Demonstrations of rescue work and hose laying by the Keene Fire Department featured the Thursday afternoon program of the annual firemen's inspection. The day's events include a parade of firemen and apparatus lead by a 50-piece Keene High School band, demonstrations in Central Square, tug of war, banquet and ball, Chief Walter R. Messer was in general charge.

Thousands gathered in the square to watch the simulated rescues in which two persons were "rescued from the Chamberlain block. The firemen also demonstrated the efficiency of a water gun mounted on one of the trucks.

The parade moved at 1:15 o'clock. Following the band was Chief Messer and Assistant Engineers Thomas Wallbank and John H. Simpson and riding in the chief's car were Assistant Engineer Elwin H. Applin and Capt. Samuel J. Guyette. More than 40 firemen marching with the eight pieces of apparatus.

Companies Parade

The line of march was through Central Square and south on Main Street to Wyman Way and return, the department passing in review before Mayor Frederick D. Mitchell, City manager Goodnow and members of the City Council in front of city hall. Members of the city government and public inspected the fire station during the afternoon.

The Steamer and Deluge Hose Companies made practice runs. Hose was laid from a hydrant in front of the courthouse to Central Square. The Steamer Company, according to unofficial timers, made the best time.

Stage Tug of War

After the demonstrations selected teams of firemen participated in a tug-of-war in the rear of the high school building. Charles Farrar, city recreational director, was in charge.

Members of the team were: Fred S. Bing ham, H. William Sanderson, Merton Mills, Stuart Hobson, and Kenneth Conant, Steamer Company; Francis Donovan, George Shepard, Clarence Caldwell, Paul Symonds and Linwood Curtis, Deluge Hose Company; John O'Neil, Francis Winn, Robert Faubert, Earl Smith and Laurence Pickett of the Washington hook and Ladder Company. The Steamer Company team was declared the winner.

Children in the upper grades of the public schools were dismissed early so the children could witness the demonstrations.

Firemen Have Banquet

About 100 persons, including firemen, members of the city government and guests, attended the banquet in the assembly hall at the fire station. Members of the Ladies' Auxiliary of the Keene Fire Department prepared the meal. Chief Messer was master of ceremonies. Speakers included Mayor Frederick D. Mitchell, City manager Goodnow, Rev. A Norman Janes, department chaplain; former Chief Eugene B. Riley, Alderman Vena DiLuzio, Councilmen Alton Coller, Arthur Kingsbury, Harold Nims, Clair Wyman, Robert Calef, John McGrath, Clarence Ewins and Burleigh Darling, City Solicitor Kenneth J. Arwe, Park Commissioner Wright Carter, Laurence m. Pickett, Walter M. Hubbard of the Public Works Department, Postmaster Carl D. Roche, George Stevens, fish and game conservation officer and Capt. William J. Corbett ,of the Lowell (Mass.) Fire Department.

Mr. Corbett told the group that he hopes to see New Hampshire adopt a training program for prospective firemen. The speaker said cooperation and coordination is most important in combating fires and said that investment in fire fighting equipment is money well spent.

———————

FIRE ALERT, A stream of water gushes high into the air at the J. J. Newberry Co. building Thursday afternoon as members of the Keene Fire Department go through their paces in the National Fire Prevention Week exhibition. Chamberlain block as shown above is "on fire" and a hose team attacks the blaze from the roof. Hordes of school children watched the show. Picture taken by Keene Fire Department.

1951 [from *City of Keene Annual Report*]

As the Keene City Council moved into another decade and took on another approach as doing business, the department heads gave reports to the Council.

The Council received a report form Walter R. Messer, Chief Engineer of the Fire Department, of storage of gasoline underground. This report was the total amount of gasoline stored throughout the City of Keene and was reported 250,635 gallons through out the city stored in underground tanks.

In 1951 a motion was made by Councilman Wyman that the Chief Engineer of the Fire Department, and the City Engineer, City Manager and City Solicitor be instructed to examine Fire Department Ordinances for further fire protection.

On Thursday September 20th, 1951 a regular meeting of the City Council was held and called to order by His Honor Mayor Ford. A communication relating to the Fire Department was brought forward by Chief Engineer Walter R. Messer. The communication reads as follows: Communication received from Walter R. Messer, Chief Engineer Keene Fire Department, extending invitation to City Council members to attend annual inspection of Keene Fire Department on Thursday October 11 at 2:00 P.M, and banquet at 5:30 P.M. in Assembly Hall in Fire Station. One motion Councilman Cook voted that invitation be accepted and all attend.

As in the past and as in the future this Annual Inspection continues today.

It was noted by council and brought up that 102 requests received for permits to store inflammable liquids, location approved by Walter R. Messer, Chief of Fire Department. It was voted that City Clerk be authorized to issue permits.

Also a request was received from Descoteaus Brothers to store gasoline in two 1000-gallon tanks, location approved by Walter R. Messer, Chief of Fire Department. On motion of Councilman Barrett voted that permit be granted.

Let it be noted that two large books are kept within the Keene Fire Department archival collection which lists the gasoline and oil storage tanks of house and commercial properties. These books hold by date and address of the tanks for the past 40+ years.

———

As the Fire Department moved into 1951 it was not on moving forward with EMS First Aid training but still continued to keep a good Civil Defense organization. On January 4th, 1951 a notice was printed in the *Keene Evening Sentinel* and reads as follows:

Fire Department to Run Test Of Air Raid Signal Saturday

The Fire Department will test-repeat-test a Civil Defense air raid warning signal here Saturday at 12:05 p.m.

Object of the test is to determine whether a special whistle mechanism made in the department will prove satisfactory.

Fourteen blasts on the fire whistle will signal the test. Each whistle blast will be of the same duration as a regular fire alarm blast, but the tempo will be speeded up so that the public can immediately identify the special warning sound.

Keene Civil Defense Director John H. Griffin stressed that in no way is the signal to be construed as a real air raid warning test and the public advised to continue business as usual.

Regular test will not begin until definite instructions and advance warnings have been given and until such tests are approved by the proper officials.

———

[*Compiler's Note:* In 1951, the country was still fearing possible attack from Russia or other 3rd world countries. The Air Raid Signal system was still up and in operation. A new special whistle mechanism made by the members of the Fire Department was to be tested. The *Keene Evening Sentinel* ran this article on January 4th, 1951 and it reads as follows:]

The Fire Department will test-repeat-test a Civil Defense air raid warning signal here Saturday at 12:05 p.m.

Object of the test is to determine whether a special whistle mechanism made in the fire department will prove satisfactory.

Fourteen blasts on the fire whistle will signal the test. Each whistle blast will be of the same duration as a regular fire alarm blast, but the tempo will be speeded up so that the public can immediately identify the special warning sound.

Keene Civil Defense Director John H. Giffin stressed that in no way is the signal to be construed as a real air raid warning test and the public is advised to continue business as usual.

Regular tests will not begin until definite instructions and advance warnings have been given and until such tests are approved by the proper officials.

For those who lived in the decades of the 40's, 50's and 60's, Air Raid Drills were common and taught in all the schools. Children would upon the directions of teachers would leave their desk and go into the hall-ways and face the inside walls on their knees. Another drill was children would kneel under their desks. This was performed as was fire drills throughout the year.

Positioned throughout the City of Keene were Bomb Shelters, The Keene Fire Station, the Keene Middle School, the Keene City Hall just to mention a few.

———

Reported by the *Keene Evening Sentinel* on January 5th, 1951:

Civilian Defense

If Saturday afternoon's scheduled air raid warning test had been run without advance public notice, as was at one time discussed, public apathy to the importance of Civil Defense might have disappeared overnight.

Those who survived the resulting panic of having the raid warning cut into their daily lives would have realized that Civilian Defense means a lot more than an excuse for appropriations and committees.

Imagine yourself returning from a quiet lunch at a local restaurant. As you walk up Main Street the fire siren cuts loose with 14 frantic and rapid fire blasts. There's no mistaking the possible meaning. It has emergency written all over it.

What would you do? It's completely unexpected. You can't help thinking that nobody said anything about a test. You'd do the same thing all the other people in hearing would do. You'd head for cover.

There might be a panic. There might not. But you wouldn't quickly forget your helpless feeling and the need for Civilian Defense organization.

They aren't going to do it that way. Too much danger of panic. They're going to give warning. They have given warning.

But we can't help regretting that some of our follow citizens didn't get the jolt that would knock them out of there, compliance. Then they might realize the reason and the need for everyone, including them, to participate.

For it is acute. Saying that there isn't any danger doesn't make it so any more that saying there is danger will make planes appear overhead.

Saying anything isn't going to help. It's what you are willing to do that count.

There may never be need for Civilian Defense forces in Keene. Heaven grant there never is. But we can't count on it.

You carry fire insurance on your house not in the expectation that it's going to burn down, but in case it does. If it does burn and you aren't covered your previous complacency is very little help. It doesn't replace or save the house.

We need a complete Civil Defense organization with the active support of every single citizen. Complacent, "It can't happen-here" individuals are just so much dead weight.

It's too late after it's happened. And we won't have much warning in this air age.

Maybe we need something like a surprise siren blast, if the sirens of our consciences won't sound off in time. In war complacency kills people. And we are just as much at war as if we had formally declared it.

Some time ago we ran an editorial captioned "Wake Up Keene" in which we appealed to citizens to offer their services to the local CD organization. Volunteers are still needed and, as time goes on, more and more helpers will be needed.

————

From the *Keene Evening Sentinel*:

Air Raid Signal Is Satisfactory Locations for Sirens Are Being Examined

Civil Defense officials were satisfied with the Saturday performance of a mechanical device which blows 14 quick blasts on the fire whistle to signal the air raid warning.

A few complaints were received from persons who reported they did not hear the red alert signal but Civil Defense spokesman pointed out that plans are underway to blanket the city with siren alarms in the near future so that all residents will hear the alarms.

————

Chief Walter R. Messer placed in the budget for 1951 a new pumper for the department. The *Keene Evening Sentinel* reported on February 8th, 1951 the bids for the new Fire Engine:

"STORY"

Nine Concerns Submit Bids For Keene's New Fire Engine

Nine companies submitted bids on a new Fire Department pumper truck, City Manager Goodnow reported today.

Low bid, $12,797.67, was submitted by the Howe Fire Apparatus Company of Anderson, Ind. The bid included the trade-in of the present pumper, a 1925 model, but did not include a separate bid of $664.32 for special equipment for special equipment.

High bid ($18,220) came from the Stevens Fire Equipment Sales and Service Company of Terryville, Conn., which submitted three bids on three models. The figure quoted did not include a bid on special equipment.

Goodnow explained that some bids do not meet specifications. A study was being made today to determine which bidder came closest to filling the bill.

Trade-in offers on the 1925 truck included two for $100, one for $200, one for $350, three for $500, one for $800, and one for $2,500. The later was in connection with a high-priced truck.

Delivery offers averaged about 150 days.

Purchase of the equipment has not been officially approved and the city reserved the right to reject all bids.

————

A Demon Called Fire

Picture taken on the delivery of the 1951 Pirsh in front of the Central Fire Station, Vernon Street Keene. This engine was later converted to Keene's tanker, the hose bed was removed and a 1,000 gallon steel tank was inserted. Courtesy of Keene Fire Department.

Each fire engine before it's acceptance is tested to specific specifications as to its delivery of water at fires. This test falls under NFPA and ISO guidelines. Courtesy of Keene Fire Department.

Reported by the *Keene Evening Sentinel* on February 9th, 1951:

"FIRE"

Firemen Battle Stubborn Blaze Washington Street home badly damaged

Firemen combated a stubborn blaze in the house owned by Richard T. Smith, 369 Washington Street, and Shortly before 1 o'clock this afternoon.

The loss will be several hundred dollars. Origin of the fire had not been determined at press time.

The fire was in the upper part of the house, but the entire house was filled with smoke.

Firemen responded to an alarm from Box 252which followed a still alarm.

It was the first box alarm this year.

————

Reported by the *Keene Evening Sentinel* March 19th, 1951:

"FIRE"

M.S. Perkins Jr. Dies of Burns Received in Explosion Saturday

Melvin S. Perkins Jr., 27 of 324 Water Street, an executive of the M. S. Perkins Machine Company Inc. and the Perkins Pump and Engine Company Inc. died early Sunday morning at Elliot Community Hospital from extensive body burns he received in an explosion Saturday afternoon at the Perkins Pump and Engine Company plat on Emerald Street.

Heat Ignited Vapor

Firemen said the heat from Perkins acetylene torch apparently ignited vapor in a 55-gallon drum from which he planned to remove the head. The drum formerly contained naphtha.

The explosion blew the other end of the drum out and fired Perkins clothing and a small section of the wall where burlap had been stuffed into a hole to keep the wind out.

Employees ripped the young man's clothing off and he was taken to the hospital in an ambulance in an unconscious condition.

The Explosion and Fire was on March 17th, 1951.

————

Reported by the *Keene Evening Sentinel* on Friday March 28th, 1951:

"FIRE"

Fire at Monadnock Appliance Center Causes $5,000 Damage

Fire originating on the second floor of the Monadnock Appliance Center building at 19 Vernon Street, caused damage estimated in excess of $5,000 early Friday night. The building is owned by Henry and Johnson.

Mrs. Ethel H. Stanton, bookkeeper at the store, discovered the fire when she heard the roar of flames and explosion of electric light bulbs. As she started to run across the street to the fire station to give the alarm fireman Laurence E. Thompson spotted the flames from his position at the desk in the fire station and pulled Box 22.

Firemen combated the flames from two sides and carried one hose line into the building from the rear. The flames were confined to the second floor, which was used for storage purposes.

Water seeped into the first floor display rooms but the merchandise was protected by salvage covers. Heat cracked one of the large plate glass windows in the front of the store and sprung the steel support of another.

Origin of the fire has not been determined.

———

A couple of stories reported in the *Keene Evening Sentinel* on April 7th, 1951:

"STORY"

Fire Whistle Mistaken For Whistle on Train

Ernest R. Humphrey, 69, of Windsor, VT thought it was a train whistle.

But it wasn't. It was a fire whistle and Humphrey was right in front of the station on Vernon Street.

Police estimated damage to the fire truck and Humphrey's car at $50.

The truck was operated by fireman Lawrence E. Thompson, 30, and kept right on going to a grass fire.

———

From the *Keene Evening Sentinel*:

Box 113 Is Sounded For Chimney Blaze

Firemen were called out shortly before 3 o'clock this morning by a general alarm sounded on Box 113 for a blaze in the large chimney at the plant of the Lynn Wood Heel Company on Railroad Street.

A man on Church Street who saw the flames believed the flames were coming from the roof of the building and sounded the alarm.

One truck and several firemen were all that was necessary to take care of the flames and the other trucks immediately returned to the fire station.

———

The *Keene Evening Sentinel* reported on July 7th, 1951 this article:

Third Fire Truck Gets 2-Way Radio

A third Keene fire truck was equipped with a two-way radio today.

Fire Chief Walter R. Messer said the VHF (very high frequency) radio was installed in Engine 1 and will be transferred to the replacement for Engine 1 which is expected to be delivered in January of 1952.

A fourth radio used by the department is installed in the Chief's official car.

The equipment transmits on the Police Department frequency.

———

As reported by the *Keene Evening Sentinel* on July 25th, 1951 a warning from the fire department:

Messer Sounds Warning On Filling Oil Tanks

Keene Fire Chief Walter R. Messer and the State Fire Marshal's Office today warned against improper filling of oil bottles and tanks used in space heaters, stoves and other appliances.

Oil containers filled from a source of supply in an outside shed or cold location must never be poured full, Chief Messer explained, because as the cold oil warns it expands and will spill from the container.

The fire officials advised that at least two or three inches of air space be left when filling such containers.

———————

Reported in the *Keene Evening Sentinel* on October 9th, 1951 by Jack Teehan:

"STORY"

Chief Messer Says That Most Of Keene's Fires Preventable

Why didn't you try to prevent that oil burner fire you had last year? Didn't you care enough about your home and family to clean the soot out of your smoke pipes? Why was your burner improperly adjusted?

These questions run through the mind of Fire Chief Walter R. Messer after every fire.

The Fire Department heard 287 people cry "Fire", in their telephones last year, usually because an oil burner had flooded or a chimney had caught fire.

It's the same story year after year; carelessness, negligence, ignorance, laziness. Fire chief's don't like to use those words because the public resents them. Instead they say the fire was preventable. It means the same thing.

The common oil burner fires usually start in ranges, room heater, or oil-fired hot water heaters. The power-driven oil burner unit for furnaces rarely causes trouble.

Don't Invite Trouble

When your oil heater is not clean or is improperly adjusted you are inviting trouble.

Did you know that an inexpensive safety device is on the market which will automatically shut off the flow of oil in the event of fire? We don't know why they're not standard equipment-but there not.

The device works when the heat melts a piece of lead in a spring loaded valve, thus shutting off the oil flow. The replacement lead costs 15 cents, cheap protection? Yes but few people take advantage of it.

How long does it take to clean your furnace and stovepipes and to replace corroded sections? But how many people bother to do it?

———————

As reported by the *Keene Evening Sentinel* on October 12th, 1951:

"FIRE"

Fire Breaks Out in Vacant Building

General Alarm Sounded For Federal Street Blaze

Fire broke out shortly before 11 o'clock today in the vacant building at 17-19 Federal Street formerly the home offices of the Peerless Casualty Company, the National Grange Fire Insurance Company. The loss has not been determined.

The fire believed to have started in the chimney above the oil burner, worked its way to the first floor.

The fire quickly extinguished filled the entire building with smoke.

Firemen responded to a still alarm call and this was followed closely by a general alarm from Box 512.

———————

FOREST STREET FIRE

Keene firemen battle to check the spread of flames to a house occupied by Councilman Fred D. Laurent of 29 Forest Street, after a fire broke out Saturday afternoon in a shed connected to the main building. Fire Chief Walter R. Messer said damage was under $5,000. Laurent said he believed insulation between the shed and the house slowed the progress of the flames. June 6th, 1951. Photo by Jack Teehan.

"FIRE"

HOUSE AND GAS STATION FIRES KEEP KEENE DEPT. ON THE JUMP

Keene Firemen had a busy afternoon Saturday combating a stubborn fire in the house of Mrs. Arthur Laurent, 29 Forest Street in response to a general alarm sounded and a fife in the rear of the Speedway gasoline filling station at 507 Main Street.

The damage at the Laurent property will not exceed $5,000. The Speedway Petroleum Company's damage is under $500, according to estimates of Chief Walter R. Messer.

The Fire at the Laurent home originated in the shed where a quantity of cartons and boxes were stored. The fire was mostly confined to the shed and ell but the smoke penetrated the entire house and occupants were forced to leave.

Firemen called by a general alarm on Box 46 had to combat the blaze from both sides of the building.

Two trucks responding to still alarms were needed at the fire at the filing station fire. The fire is reported to have originated in debris in the rear of the building. The building was damaged.

The cause of the fires have not been determined. There was some insurance on the properties.

Firemen were called Sunday June 10th, 1951 for a fire in an automobile at the corner Winchester Street and Butler Court. The vehicle owned by Leo Bedaw, was destroyed, according to firemen.

___

Permanent Company 1951

Pictured form left to right front row L.O. Cass, S.J. Guyette, W.R. Messer Chief, E.P. Britton, F.M. Reid, Back row standing from left to right, C.M. Ballou, P.M. Little, L.E. Thompson, R.C. Calahan, P.E. Gallup, H.F. Hammond. Picture from Fire Department Records.

☙ *A Demon Called Fire*

Washington Hook and Ladder Company 1951

Seated 1st, Row from left to right M.I. Pishon, L.H. Cass, C.H. Symonds, L.M. Pickett, 2nd, Lt. E.L. Reason Captain, F.J. Driscoll, 1st, Lt. F.W. Sharkey, R.L. Piche, R.F. Driscoll, 2nd, Row Standing from left to right R.W. Faubert, B.J. Thompson, J.H. Dennis, J.H. O'Neil, E.A. Smith, R.A. Reason, F.J. Foley, F.E. Winn. Picture from Fire Department Records.

1952

From Keene Fire Department Records:

"STORY"

The Keene Fire Department Mascots

Like most departments Keene fire had a Mascot too, his name was "Billie", and another one was named "Smokey". Before you read the stories about our Mascots let me pass a little history as to why we had a Mascot.

Mascots all began in the days of stagecoaches. Horse thefts were common in those days and stagecoach drivers used to sleep behind the stalls where their horses were kept to guard against theft of their horses.

If a stagecoach driver owned a dog and in those days it was a Dalmatian, the driver of the stagecoach could sleep in the way house or the hotel. Dalmatians seemed to form an amazing bond with the horses.

When this tight bond between the horses and the Dalmatian became a team, no one would dare lay a hand on the horses without fear of being attacked.

Once the bond between horse and dog became a team and the knowledge of this trait more stagecoach drivers would go to great lengths to obtain a Dalmatians to watch over their team of horses. This practice of Dalmatians became so popular the dogs were known as "coach dogs".

It's been known for a long time that Dalmatians have always gotten along well with horses. As we know every fire house back in the days of horse drawn fire equipment had horses and their always seemed to be a Dalmatian.

The Dalmatians guarded the firehouse and the horses as well as keeping the horses company during their long, boring wait between fires. When the bell would ring the Dalmatian would be as eager as the horse to run and along side the steamer they would run.

There is no mention in the books of the city or the fire department that Keene's Fire Department ever had a Mascot until February 2nd, 1931. "Billy" was known as the first Fire Department Mascot and he was born on Ground Hogs day February 2nd, 1931 is when he joined the fire department as the first canine. His master was Fred Morse, a firefighter who called his dog a funny little dog. He was a lovable dog and was liked by every one young and old. All but the first few weeks of his life he would chase the fire apparatus to the fires. He would run along side the fire engine barking all the way. He was a great little worker at fires. He spent all his time barking and chasing children away from the fire trucks. It was not known whether he was jealous or that he felt it was his job, but he was performing a duty to great advantage. "Billy was known as a faithful fireman as he had not missed a fire for three years that he was Mascot to the Keene Fire Department. He was a shaggy white haired dog that everyone loved."

Billy was a mascot of the Keene Fire Department. Photo courtesy of the Keene Fire Department.

After fires he would often ride back to the fire station, until one day he fell from the engine. Although he was not injured, after that he would only occasionally ride back to the fire station on the engines.

Finally one day "Billy" was unable to answer his last fire call as he became sick and died during an operation for Acute Indigestion. Several phone calls were made to the station when he was not seen chasing the fire apparatus and when these people were told of the sad news, they were stricken with grief as the men of the fire department were, because they missed the little fellow chasing them to all the fires.

It wasn't until December 1951 that the fire department had received another mascot, a "Dalmatian" named "Smokey". He was presented to Chief Walter R. Messer, by Mrs. Elmer L. MacKenzie of MacKenzie Dairy Farm on upper Court Street.

Smokey was another mascot of the Keene Fire Department. Photo courtesy of the Keene Fire Department.

"Smokey" lived at the fire station and answered all fire calls make by the department. He would ride to the fires in the front seat of the fire apparatus. Like "Billie" this dog lived a short life also. After returning from a fire on the Belvedere Road, he had wandered to Union Street just north of the fire station and was struck by an automobile and killed on November 3rd, 1952.

Another Dalmatian was soon donated by Mrs. Doris Harris, to replace "Smokey." This dog was also called "Smokey" as this became a trade name for the fire dogs.

This dog like the others lived here at the fire station and performed his duties, as the other firedogs had done in the past, for six years before he died of liver trouble and old age.

Since then there has never been another Mascot. With the number of permanent firefighters now at the fire station a dog would have a hard time getting out of the way from the running feet of the firefighters hurrying to their apparatus upon the ringing of the fire bells.

———————

From *City of Keene Annual Report*:

1952 The year proved to be a year filled with activity, and a year which the fire department would say business as usual.

There were 102 requests received for permits to store flammable liquids, located and approved by Walter R. Messer, Chief of Fire Department. It was voted at the February 21st, 1952 Meeting by Council that the City Clerk be authorized to issue permits.

On March 13th, 1952 a motion by Councilman Proulx it was voted that personal services, Fire Department, be changed from $49,199,00 to $49,599,00 changing a total from $61,833.00 to $62,233.00, by eliminating item "Other" $100.00 and changing item "Other" amount $407.00 to $513.00.

———————

NOTE: In time each member that has put more than 20 years within the Keene Fire Department, either Carrier or Paid Call, is entitled to a Fire Department Funeral. It is without question that any member of the department that giveS his life in the line of duty, regardless of time, is entitled to that Honor. In 1952 these final honors were paid to veteran fireman Elwin H. Applin. As recorded in the *Keene Evening Sentinel*:

DEATH OF A FIREMAN

The casket bearing Elwin, 76, member of the Keene fire department for 52 years and an engineer for 17 years, is carried atop old Engine No. 3. Three blasts on the fire whistle sound the "all out" signal Wednesday afternoon. All trucks stood in the ready position beneath doors draped with crepe. Photo by Jack Teehan.

"STORY"

Final Honors Paid Veteran Fireman

Department Attends Service for Applin

The Keene fire department paid a final and impressive tribute to Engineer Elwin H. Applin, 76 a member of the department for 52 years, who died last Saturday. Funeral services held Wednesday afternoon in the First Congregational Church.

Rev. Edward W. Meury, pastor and Chaplain of the fire department, conducted the services and Mrs. John Pike was organist.

Members of the department including permanent firemen, board of engineers, Deluge Hose Company, Washington Hook and Ladder Company, Keene Steamer Company and retired firemen attended in a body. Retired firemen present were Frank J. Bennett, George C. Symonds, Charles E. Witham and Daniel E. Hathorn.

The City of Keene was represented by Mayor Laurence M. Pickett and Councilman Francis Callahan, Chairman of the fire department committee.

Following the services the casket was carried from the church to Engine 3 of the Deluge Hose Company of which Mr. Applin was Captain for 24 years. Escorted around the common, up Washington Street and thence to Vernon Street the procession halted in front of the fire station where three blows on the alarm system, "all out" signal were sounded by Captain Elton P. Britton.

The procession then proceeded to the F. J. Foley Funeral Home on Court Street Burial took place this afternoon in Fair View Cemetery in Hyde Park, Mass. Rev Meury, department chaplain, officiated.

Honorary bearers were Chief Walter R. Messer, Engineer Thomas B. Wallbank, Associate Engineer John H. Simpson, Captain Arthur D. Irwin of the Deluge Hose Company, Dr. James H. Grimes of Sullivan a former member of the department and Sherman Hadlock of the Mack Motor Company of Manchester, N.H.

Active bearers include Captain Samuel J. Guyette, Frank M. Reid, Lyman O. Cass, Charles M. Ballou, Paul E. Gallup, department drivers and 1st. Lt. Stephen W. Pollock of the Deluge Hose Company.

From the *Keene Evening Sentinel*:

FIRE TRUCK DELIVERY IS EXPECTED IN MARCH

Delay in Getting Parts Holding Up Production

Delivery of the city's new $15,000 fire truck is not expected until March.

Fire Chief Walter R. Messer said a shortage of vital parts at the Peter Pirch & Sons, Inc., factory in Kenosha, Wis., was responsible for the delay.

The pumper scheduled to replace a 1925 model, was originally to be delivered in December.

According to word from the factory, all vital parts except the motor have been delivered. The motor has been promised for delivery in February.

January started off with a fire at 562 Washington Street as the *Keene Evening Sentinel* reported on January 28th, 1952:

"FIRE"

FIRE GUTS HOME OF E. J. STINSON

Flames Drive Eleven Persons Into Street

Eleven persons were forced to flee from the home of Mr. and Mrs. Elmer J. Stinson at 562 Washington Street about 8 o'clock Sunday night when fire gutted the house.

The loss by fire, smoke and water will amount to several thousand dollars. The house was insured.

Mr. and Mrs. Stinson and their eight children, ranging in age from 15 months to 18 years and Mrs. Stinson's father, William Miller, were in one of the downstairs rooms when the electric lights failed. Believing that a fuse had burned out, Mrs. Stinson started to replace it when she detected the odor of smoke. On opening the door leading to the upstairs bedrooms she discovered the fire.

Mr. Stinson telephoned the fire department and a general alarm on Box 25 was sounded.

Fire burned its way to the second story where there is one finished and one unfinished room.

Firemen laid two lines of hose and used one booster line.

Members of the Stinson family were given temporary home by neighbors and relatives.

Washington Street was choked with several hundred cars which had raced to the scene when the general alarm sounded. Although police routed northbound traffic off Washington Street south of the scene of the fire, dozens of cars had crowded in behind the fire trucks before police arrived.

————

SUNDAY FIRE. Eleven persons, including Mr. and Mrs. Elmer J. Stinson and eight children, were forced to flee their home at 562 Washington Street Sunday night when a fire of undetermined origin broke out on the second floor. Flames are shown breaking through the roof (top center) as firemen battle the blaze. Loss was estimated at several thousand dollars. The home was insured.

On January 31st, 1952 Officials Stirred By False Alarms as reported by the *Keene Evening Sentinel*:

Police Investigation Has Been Inaugurated

Fire Chief Walter R. Messer and Chief of Police Thomas J. Qualters were sharply critical today of the unidentified youngster or adult who sounded a false alarm from Box 18 at Marlboro and Kelleher Streets Wednesday afternoon.

A serious accident was narrowly averted when a fire truck hit the corner of a snow bank at Main and Marlboro Streets to avoid a car, which had stopped at the junction.

The bump tilted the truck to the right but the driver managed to retrain control. The driver of the car had not been identified this morning.

Chief Qualters said a person can be fined up to $20 upon conviction of sounding a false alarm.

The false alarm was the second to be sounded from Box 18 in the past two weeks and police are investigating the incident.

The box is located near Wyman's garage and the Granite State Cleansers' plant.

————

As reported by the *Keene Evening Sentinel* February 1, 1952:

"FIRE"

TWO FAMILIES MADE HOMELESS BY FLASH FIRE IN WEST KEENE

Six persons in two families were made homeless Thursday night when flames destroyed the interior of the house owned by Ralph L. Follansbee at 28 Stanhope Avenue. Fire is believed to have originated from an oil burner in the apartment in the rear. The loss is estimated at $1,500, not including contents, by Fire Chief Walter R. Messer.

The front part of the house was occupied by Mr. and Mrs. Marcel Follansbee and child and the rear tenement was occupied by Mrs. Velma Clark and her two children. Mrs. Clark's husband, Ralph Clark is in the service. Mrs. Clark and children were visiting in the home of her parents at the time.

Mrs. Follansbee risked her life in an attempt to save some clothes and was forced to leap through a front porch screen into a snow bank to escape the licking flames.

Three neighbors were also endangered when flames leaped out the front door as they were removing a love seat from the front porch. They broke through a screen door to make a hasty exit.

Flash Fire

The fire, of the flash type, was discovered by neighbors. Fire raced through the building in a short space of time. Flames burned a hole in the roof of the house in the rear and were shooting skyward before firemen arrived. The alarm was telephoned in and the Box 49 alarm was rung from the fire station.

Mr. Follansbee and neighbors removed some furniture, but much of it was burned.

Before the fire was extinguished the Salvation Army was on the scene with hot coffee for firemen. The Salvation Army and Red Cross also offered aid to the two families. The American Legion gave aid to one of the families.

Police were called upon to handle the usual amount of traffic.

Salvation Army Lassie Wears Fireman's Boots

The Salvation Army's Lt. Ina Petz looked like a genuine smoke eater at the Stanhope Avenue fire Thursday night at least up to her knees.

Fire Chief Walter R. Messer spotted Lt. Petz as she distributed coffee and doughnuts to firemen. But he noted her feet weren't dressed for duty in the water soaked area.

The Chief gallantly offered a pair of fireman's boots.

The offer was graciously accepted.

WEST KEENE FIRE. An oil burner was believed responsible for the flash fire, which made two families homeless at 28 Stanhope Avenue Thursday night. Firemen are shown moving in through the thick smoke, which poured from the dwelling. Damaged to the house was estimated at $1,500 by Fire Chief Walter R. Messer. Photo by Jack Teehan.

On Monday February 25th 1952 a Sprinkler Extinguishes a Small Fire in Factory as Reported by the *Keene Evening Sentinel*:

"FIRE"

Minor Damage Reported At Roberts-Hart Plant

A small fire in a pile of rubbish on the second floor of the Roberts-Hart Shoe Company plant on Water Street was extinguished by a sprinkler head system Saturday afternoon.

Fire Chief Walter R. Messer said only minor water damage resulted.

Firemen were on their way to the blaze in response to a telephoned alarm when a resident near the plant spotted smoke and rang a general alarm from Box 14.

Office equipment and some stock was protected from water damage by firemen who covered it with large tarpaulins.

⚜   *A Demon Called Fire*

On January 23rd, 1952 the *Keene Evening Sentinel* reported:

"STORY"

For information on the Civil Defense as the Keene Auxiliary Firemen.

Auxiliary Firemen Elect E. G. White, Paul Bergeron Chosen To Captain Hand Tub Edward G. White was elected president of the Keene Auxiliary Firemen Monday night.

Other officers are: George Vorce, vice-president; Alton Weagle secretary; Howard Wakefield, treasure; Edward White, Paul Bergeron, Clearence Bouffard, John Graham and George Vorce, committee on special events; John Graham, Paul Bergeron and Russell Driscoll, auditing committee; Walter Royle, John Graham and David Ringland, committee on bylaws.

Paul Bergeron was elected Captain of the hand tub with William Strongren, First Lieutenant and Walter Royle, second lieutenant.

A buffet lunch was served by Edward White, Alton Weagle, John Graham, George Vorce, Howard Wakefield, William Strongren and David Ringland.

Practice tests will be made with the hand tub as soon as the weather permits.

The next meeting will be held Feb. 5th, at 7:30 p.m.

Sixty-five members of the Keene Auxiliary Firemen and Auxiliary Police joined for an evening of entertainment in the fire station last Saturday night. Dancing followed and a lunch was served.

———

On Fridays in January and February and March, the City Council had Lengthy Sessions, reported by the *Keene Evening Sentinel*. The portion related to the Fire Department as follows:

City Council
Messer Reappointed

Fire Chief Walter R. Messer and assistant Chiefs Elwin H. Applin, Thomas Walbank and John H. Simpson were reappointed, for 1952.

City Budget Hearing is Set for Tomorrow, March 4th, 1952.

The annual public hearing on the Keene city budget will be held at 7:30 p.m. Wednesday in the city hall auditorium.

Up for consideration is a $700.336 budget, down $68,486 from 1951 all time high.

Final adoption of the budget is slated for Thursday night, date of the first March City Council session.

Council to Act On Budget Bill.

———

From the *Keene Evening Sentinel*:

"STORY"

Public Hearing Draws Only a Few Taxpayers

It was the same old story at the annual public hearing on the city budget Wednesday night.

About 30 members of the general public- less than one-half of one percent of the registered voters appeared at the hearing. And of these, two men, Carl R. Bloomer, president of the Keene Taxpayers association and former Alderman Bernard A. Streeter asked 90 percent of the questions.

The $700,336 budget will come up for final adoption at a Council session tonight.

Bloomer called for a cut in the Police Department budget, noting the department spent $43,000 five years ago, not proposes to spend more than $60,000.

Police Commissioner John P. Wright said that more than $52,000 of the budget is for salaries, added the department must compete with private industry. He also cited an increase in the number of school children and a "tremendous growth" in the traffic volume as reasons for the advance.

Fire Chief Quizzed

Fire Chief Walter R. Messer was quizzed by Bloomer who wanted to know whether local fire insurance rates had been reduced as Fire Department expenses rose. Messer said he understood rates were cut 10 percent within the last two years.

Mayor Laurence M. Pickett closed the meeting by promising the city a conservative administration. He said no attempts had been made to impair services formerly enjoyed by taxpayers.

Thanking those present for their interest the mayor said he hoped they would exhibit the same interest attending the annual Union District meeting later this evening. The hearing closed at 9:30.

————

From the *Keene Evening Sentinel*:

"STORY"

KEENE'S NEW PUMPER DELIVERED

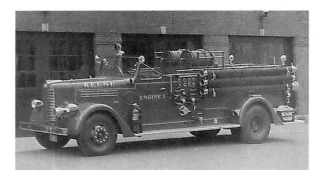

Keene's 1951 Pirsch. Engine 1, 750 GPM Pumper. Photo courtesy of Keene Fire Department.

Performance of City's New Fire Engine Praised by Underwriters

Like kids with a new toy, Keene firemen can't take their eyes away from a new addition in the fire station.

The $15,000 pumper with a capacity of 750 gallons-per-minute was ordered in March 1951, and was delivered Last Wednesday.

Manufactured by Peter Pirsch & Sons Co. of Kenosha, Wis., the truck carries 1,500 feet of 2 ½-inch hose, 500 feet of 1 ½-inch hose, two booster lines, a 300 gallon water booster tank for small fires, a 28-foot extension ladder and a 16-foot roof ladder.

Powered by a 200 horsepower engine, the truck weighs nine tons loaded, is 25 feet long and eight feet wide. Four hoses can be attached to the pumping unit for fire-fighting purposes.

Already checked by Fred N. Krauss of Concord, a Board of Underwriters engineer who praised its performance, the truck is expected to be approved this week by Fire Chief Walter R. Messer and the City Council's fire department committee.

The new engine replaces a 1924 model. The department is equipped with three standard pumpers, the other two having been purchased in 1929 and 1934. Other equipment and dates of purchase include: 1923 model truck with new portable pump; two light squad trucks, used mainly for brush fires, 1941 and 1942; aerial ladder, 1946; four wheel drive power wagon 1948.

Old Engine 1 has been sold to the town of Pembrook. The truck is now being repainted and will be delivered after the new truck is accepted.

————

From the *Keene Evening Sentinel*:

Firemen's Memorial Service Tomorrow

Rev. Edward Meury Will Give Address.

Firemen, former firemen, members of the city government will meet in the Assembly Hall of the fire station Sunday at 9:a.m. for annual Memorial service of the department.

Rev. Edward W. Meury, pastor of the First Congregation Church will give the message. There will be special music in charge of Mayor Laurence M. Pickett.

Following the service graves of deceased firemen in Keene and vicinity will be decorated.

Firemen of the three companies will wear their uniforms along with the permanent fire department members.

————

As reported by the *Keene Evening Sentinel* on June 30th, 1952:

"FIRE"

Fire Stanhope Ave. House Gutted

Sunday Night Fire Loss Put at $4,000

The seven-room house at 21 Stanhope Ave., owned by Mrs. Theresa Holt of Maple Ave. and occupied by Mr. and Mrs. Franklin O'Neal and family, was gutted by fire Sunday night.

The fire, according to Mrs. O'Neal, started from the electric wiring in one of the up stair's rooms. The three second-floor rooms were badly damaged and all furnishings were destroyed. Members of the house hold also lost all their clothing and personal belongings.

Damage to the down stairs rooms was confined to smoke and water. Firemen estimated that the damage might run as high as $4,000. There was some insurance on the building, but none on the furnishing.

Most of the furniture was removed and stored in a vacant garage nearby.

FIRE ALARM MIXUP

Box 49 was sounded and while it registered correctly in the fire station, the whistle signal failed to sound properly due to transmitter trouble.

Call firemen had to go to or telephone the fire station to find the location of the fire. Others followed the apparatus.

————

1953

As the department moved into 1953 to ready itself for the upcoming Annual State Firemen's Convention which was slated to be held in Keene the second week of September.

Plans Underway For Convention

State Firemen's Assn. Meets Here Sept. 11-12

Fire Chief Walter R. Messer is general chairman of committees making plans for the State Firemen's Association annual convention here September 11-12.

This will mark the second consecutive year for the convention in Keene Mayor Laurence M. Pickett invited the association to meet here as part of Bicentennial year activities.

Kenneth G. Conant is head of the convention's publicity committee. Other committee chairmen named to date include William Sanderson registration and housing, and Clarence Caldwell, entertainment.

The State Firemen's Convention is a big deal with firefighter throughout the Sate and gives support and direction for the fire service community.

————

Keene plays Convention up big as the *Keene Evening Sentinel* Reports on September 10th, 1953:

"STORY"

600 Firemen Are Expected In City

Annual State Convention Gets Under Way Friday

Between 500 and 600 members of the New Hampshire State Firemen's Association are expected to attend the annual state convention in Keene Friday and Saturday, according to the local committee on arrangements.

The Firefighters will register at the Central Fire Station Friday and Saturday and the formal program will get underway with a round table discussion Friday night at the station followed by a free public dance at city hall auditorium.

Music will be furnished by Herm Reed's Orchestra who's services are being donated by the local musician's union.

Mayor Laurence M. Pickett, incumbent president of the state association, will conduct the business meeting in City Hall auditorium Saturday morning at 10 o'clock during which election of officers and other business will be transacted.

A parade will get under way at noon. After forming on Washington Street above the high school the parade will move across Mechanic Street to Court Street, down Court to Main down Main to Water where it will swing back up Main Street and return to the station vial Washington Street.

Starting at 1:30 Saturday after noon a chicken barbecue will be served at the youth agricultural building in the south end of the Cheshire Fair Grounds in North Swanzey.

An old building in the northern section of the city will be deliberately burned at about 3:30 p.m. following a brief school of instruction in the proper methods of combating house fires. An alarm will be sounded and the Keene fire apparatus will converge on the burning building to climax the two day convention.

Members of the Fire Department met last night to discuss the annual inspection and Firemen's Ball to be held this year October 8th.

For the Convention Chief Walter R. Messer purchased a battery-operated amplifier which carries his voice to the top of a four-story block as seen in picture below.

————

TAKE 'ER DOWN! Fire Chief Walter R. Messer orders his men to remove a hose from the aerial ladder during annual National Fire Prevention Week exercises Thursday afternoon in Central Square. He is using a battery operated amplifier, which carries his voice to the top of a four story block. The picture was taken by Jack Teehan of the Keene Evening Sentinel.

Firemen To Set Several Blazes

Old House Will Be Burned in demonstration

Keene firemen will try their hand at arson during the annual convention of the

N.H. Firemen's Association hers September 11-12.

The smoke eaters plan to destroy a frame house by setting several blazes.

But it's all perfectly legal, Fire Chief Walter R. Messer explained today.

The old house (its location is a secret) was slated for razing anyway, and the owner offered it to the firemen for experimental purposes.

Chief Messer said the use will be used to demonstrate fire-fighting techniques. After the last demonstration it will be allowed to burn to the ground.

————

1953 was a busy year for the Keene Fire Department as a few fires follow. As reported by the *Keene Evening Sentinel* March 2nd, 1953.

"FIRE"

Firemen Report Busy Weekend

Two Calls Result From Partition Fires

Keene firemen had a busy weekend responding to still alarm calls.

Saturday afternoon firemen were called for a fire in the city dump on Main Street and later for a fire about an oil burner in Fred Hook's home at 24 North Lincoln Street.

Sunday calls were at the home of Evans Barrett of the Summit Road for a fire in the chimney and partition. A stovepipe blaze in the house at 26 Park Street owned by the Arthur Barker estate and a grass fire on land owned by the Union School District on Newman Street.

This morning calls were for a chimney and partition fire in the house owned by Mrs. Horace Bond at 17 So. Lincoln Street and for a dust fire about the boiler in the building owned by Heald Bros. at 29 Island Street.

————

As reported by the *Keene Evening Sentinel* on April 8th 1953.

"FIRE"

Firemen Battle Sawdust Blaze

General Alarm Sounded For Railroad Street Fire

Firemen combated a stubborn smudge this morning in a sawdust pit building on Railroad Street. The building is used jointly by the Princess Shoe Company and Keene Wood Heel Company.

Firemen remained on the scene more than an hour before the burning sawdust was extinguished.

A freight care on a siding between the main plant and the building were the sawdust pit is located was moved by volunteers.

The building is located near the spot where the boiler of Beaver Mills exploded in 1893.

The fire was discovered by Ralph Avery, an employee of the Keene Wood Heel Company. A general alarm from Box 13 was sounded.

Firemen responded to a still alarm call Friday afternoon and extinguished a chimney fire in the house owned by Walter L. Moor on Concord Hill, off Route 9.

————

As reported by the *Keene Evening Sentinel* on April 9th 1953.

Sawdust Fire Starts Again

Keene Firemen Have Long Sunday Battle

Firemen worked in shifts Sunday combating a second smudge in the sawdust container at the old Beaver Mills plant now being used by the Keene Wood Heel Company and the Princess Shoe, Company. Firemen were on duty from 5:15 a.m. until the "all out" was sounded about 4:30 p.m.

The fire, smoldering in partitions and flooring of the sawdust pit, was difficult to reach.

The Sunday fire was discovered by local police officers who saw the smoke rising above the buildings while cruising on Main Street. Firemen were notified by radio and a still alarm was sounded at 5:15 and a general alarm at 5:27 a.m.

Firemen were called by still alarm Saturday for a grass fire on land owned by Emile Herbert, 685 Main Street and a fire about an oil burner in the house owned by Bert Enwright, 606 Court Street.

Insulation on Wires Burn

About 2:20 p.m. Saturday firemen responded to a general alarm from Box 512 on St. James Street for a fire in insulation on electric wiring on the outside of the storage warehouse owned by the Holbrook Grocery Company on Railroad Square. The building was formerly owned by the Abbott Grocery Company.

A single truck could have taken care of the fire, but the person calling the fire station gave firemen the idea that the building was in flames.

Firemen notified the Public Service Company.

––––––––

As reported by the *Keene Evening Sentinel* July 26th, 1953:

"FIRE"

Fire Guts Small West Keene Bldg

Investigation Started As to Origin of Blaze

Investigation is being made into the origin of a fire early Sunday morning which gutted the unoccupied building at 43 Arlington Ave. owned by Clyde A. Goodrich.

As far as known the building, a one-story, two-room structure, had not been occupied in recent months.

The loss will be several hundred dollars, according to Chief Walter R. Messer. The building was formerly owned and occupied by Nathan Moultrop and recently acquired by Mr. Goodrich.

Chief Messer received an injury to one knee when he fell through an open trap door.

Firemen also responded to a fire Sunday afternoon which is reported to have originated from a short circuit in the wiring in the house at 290 Pearl Street owned by Christopher D. and Roene L. Guinnane.

The damage is estimated at several hundred dollars.

––––––––

The Holbrook Grocery Fire was a large fire for 1953 and the *Keene Evening Sentinel* Reported as follows on September 12th, 1953:

"FIRE"

Fire Guts Holbrook Grocery Warehouse On Railroad Square. Loss Is In Excess Of $50,000

Flames Threaten Other Buildings In City's Center

Hundreds of Visiting Firemen Watch Local Dept. Make Good Stop

Keene firemen battled a hot and stubborn blaze in the warehouse of the Holbrook Grocery Company on Railroad Square last night as hundreds of visiting firemen from all sections of New Hampshire here for the 56th annual convention of the New Hampshire State Firemen's Association, watched from the sidelines.

The fire, which was discovered at 10:57 p.m. gave the department a four-hour workout and caused damage which Richard L. Holbrook, president of Holbrook Company, Inc. estimated this morning will be in excess of $50,000. Origin of the fire has not been determined.

The alarm from Box 512, sounded during the height of the firemen's ball which was in progress in City Hall Auditorium, interrupted the social program of the convention and sent firemen hustling to the scene to battle the fire in their dress uniforms.

Several of the visiting firemen made the run with apparatus and assisted the local department. The fire was brought under control about 1:30 o'clock, but the all out was not sounded until 3:30 o'clock.

Although many residents in the city thought at first that the alarm was a "false", news of the fire and its location brought many to the scene. The area was roped off and Chief of Police William T. Bridgham ordered special officers to the scene to aid firemen.

The fire appeared to have originated near the center of the 150-foot three-story frame building. It spread toward what was the office section of the building when it was owned by the Abbott Grocery Company. The east end of the building is badly damaged and most of the contents destroyed.

The building had a frontage on Railroad Square of about 150 feet and 75 feet on St. James Street. Two spur tracks separate the storehouse from the main building where the business of the Holbrook Grocery Company is conducted.

The west end of the building was not reached by the flames, but the contents where damaged by smoke and water.

A large quantity of cereals, paper towels, tissue paper, twine and canned goods were stored in the building.

Many Hose lines Used

Approximately 10 lines of hose were laid from hydrants on Railroad Square, St. James, Federal and Main Streets. Good pressure was maintained by pumpers throughout.

Firemen combated the flames from two sides. The frame building owned by Peter Latchis on Railroad Square, about 15 feet away, although threatened, did not catch fire. The main office and warehouse of the Holbrook Company is less than 25 feet from the old Abbott building.

The aerial ladder was brought in to use in combating the flames from the roof on the Railroad Square side of the building.

Has Narrow Escape

One fireman, Paul E. Symonds, fell through the roof, but caught himself and held on until fellow firemen pulled him back to safety. He escaped injury. Another, Captain Stephen W. Pollock, was hit on the head by a falling slate.

West Swanzey Covers

Soon after the fire broke out a telephone message was sent to the center for Mutual Aid System in Greenfield, Mass. And within a short time West Swanzey firemen with one piece of apparatus moved to the Keene Station to "cover" and Winchester, the next town south of West Swanzey, sent firemen and apparatus to West Swanzey to protect that town.

Keene Dept. Praised

Many of the visiting firemen aided the Keene Department and were high in their praise for the way in which the situation was handled.

Several firemen remained on duty until after daylight. The area in the vicinity of the fire was roped off to prevent spectators from interfering with firemen.

Fire Sidelights

While the unannounced fire gave visitors a demonstration of what their host firemen could do, they will also have a chance to watch a deliberately planned fire in an old building in the north end of the city at 3:30 this afternoon. This is a part of the convention program.

While Officer Mervyn C. Frink was making his rounds in Railroad Square he discovered the fire and while on his way to the nearest available telephone the general alarm from box 512 started sounding. This box is on the west side of St. James Street opposite the Holbrook property.

Engine No. 2 was in the paint shop at the time, but was taken out under orders of Chief Walter Messer and stationed on Federal Street.

———

Midnight Fire. Keene firemen battle a hot blaze in the Holbrook Grocery Company warehouse on Railroad Square early this morning as visiting firemen in the city for a state convention watch local department make good stop of flames in highly congested business area. The loss is estimated by the owners in excess of $50,000.

As reported by the *Keene Evening Sentinel* on October 17th, 1953:

"FIRE"

Flash Fire Burns Garage Employee

Anthony Toscano, 32 of 87 Church Street received first degree burns on both arms, face and knees during a flash fire Saturday in the grease pit at the Woodward Motors Garage on Church Street.

Toscano's condition is reported as satisfactory by officials of the Elliott Community Hospital where he was taken for treatment.

Firemen were also called by still alarm Saturday afternoon to the house owned by C. R. Lyle at 130 School Street for a fire around a broiler.

———

Reported by the *Keene Evening Sentinel* November 16th, 1953:

"FIRE"

Firemen Are Called To Sullivan Street

Four Alarms Sounded Here Over the Weekend

Firemen responded to a general alarm from Box 25 about 10 o'clock Sunday night for a fire in the house in the rear of 23 Sullivan Street owned by Wilfred J. Begin and occupied by Mr. and Mrs. Homer J. Gosselin and family.

Most of the damage to the building was from smoke. A section of wall board was burned around the chimney.

On Saturday night firemen went to the plant of the Central Screw Company on Emerald Street where a sprinkler head let go and set off the fire alarm.

Sunday noon firemen responded to anther still alarm for a fire about the electric motor in Bruno's restaurant on the Troy Road in Swanzey.

Shortly after 11 o'clock Sunday night firemen were called for a chimney fire in the house of Mrs. Verna Bissell, 523 Court Street. This morning firemen returned to the Bissell house where the fire had broken out a second time.

———

From the *Keene Evening Sentinel*:

"STORY"

Keene Fire Mutual Aid System known as South Western New Hampshire Fire District Mutual Aid

Keene Fire Mutual Aid System known as South Western New Hampshire Fire District Mutual Aid System is a very important part of the emergency services. Established in 1953 by then Keene Fire Captain Robert Callahan and Walter R. Messer Keene Fire Chief. It was Robert Callahan's vision and the help of Walter R. Messer than Chief of the Keene Fire Department that made a vision a reality which changed the way the fire service does business. Chief Robert Callahan changed hats form a Keene Fire Captain to the Chief Coordinator of South Western New Hampshire Fire Mutual Aid in 1962 and SWNHFMA began as we know it today.

The dispatch center is housed within the Keene Fire Department Central Fire Station on Vernon Street and has been there since it's incipient.

It's only fit to add them to the History of the Keene Fire Department.

———————

1955

In 1955 the *Keene Evening Sentinel* published the following article by Herb Allen:

Keene a Local Center

Mutual Aid System Cuts Fire Hazards.

During a civil defense test, on paper, fire apparatus bearing such strange names as Peterborough, Jaffrey or Keene was seen theoretically by people as far away as Connecticut.

During an actual disaster it could happen, although people might wonder how the apparatus responded to calls so far away and how a small town like Jaffrey could spare its equipment.

System Spreading

Mystery? Not at all, when you know about the Mutual Aid System that has spread and is spreading among New England towns and has become the basis for civil defense commitments between states as far apart as New Hampshire and Connecticut.

It is not just a neighborly gesture when the Hancock tank truck shows up at a Peterborough fire as it did when the Four Winds farm burned recently. It is part of a chain reaction that may involve movements of fire apparatus in three states or half a dozen towns.

It is called "covering in" and is much more thoroughly organized than even a reporter who has gone to many fires realized. It actually has taken two years to solve the problem presented by a mutual aid system in Southwestern New Hampshire.

Center At Keene

Keene is the center for the system involving 35 cities and town from Antrim and Langdon on the north and west to Brattleboro, Vt., and Winchendon, Mass, on the west and south. Bob Callahan of the Keene Department is secretary of the system and head problem-solver.

One major problem-keeping track of the apparatus-Callahan has solved with a big peg board. Opposite the name of each community he has placed different colored pegs representing the types of apparatus available. Every time a truck "rolls" a peg is moved by the Keene Fireman on duty at the alarm desk. And sometimes the pegs jump around the board like a cribbage score.

Some of the most exciting scores Callahan can reel off from memory. For instance Keene is also in the mutual aid system centered in Greenfield, Mass., where there was an "awfully, good example" last spring.

Phones-Out

On May 29th, Callahan said, there was a fire in Winchester, where the local department reported its situation to the Greenfield department. Ordinarily Greenfield would have notified Brattleboro to send a truck to Hinsdale while Hinsdale sent a piece to Winchester. But a bad electrical storm had put so many phone circuits out of commission that Greenfield could not call either of these towns. At the same time, Greenfield apparatus was tied up at a fire in Northfield that also required apparatus from Bernardston. So Greenfield, relying on its mutual aid arrangement with Keene, called for apparatus from Keene and West Swanzey to "cover in" at Winchester.

In a theoretical case, so far, the two systems might work together in the same way to draw apparatus out of Greenfield or even farther south if Keene assisted at a fire in Antrim.

The real virtue of the system is that all these moves are calculated in advance.

Important Role

Among the rules of this serious cribbage game is that no town is asked to send more than one piece of apparatus, although it may receive as many as it needs for any emergency. And no town is left without at least a 500-gallon capacity pumper for any alarm at home.

"In the past," Callahan said, "departments would send all they had to a fire in a neighboring town, not knowing whether it would be needed or not, and leave their own town exposed. They don't have to do that now. Town after town covers in, all along the line until we get back to one that can spare the equipment."

He moved pegs around to demonstrate, a yellow peg for a 500-gallon pumper, a blue peg for a 600-gallon pumper, and so on.

"Two weeks ago Alstead had an alarm that called for Walpole to cover the Alstead station with a piece. That left Walpole without a 500-gallon pumper we consider minimum protection, so Westmorland sent a truck to Walpole. That left Westmorland in the same position, and Keene sent a 600-gallon pumper over there," Callahan explained.

Can Sleep Better

One of the results is that a small town fire chief can sleep better knowing that there is material backing him up to match any emergency. Callahan had just completed an inventory revealing such resources in the Southwestern system as 84 pumpers 12 lighting units with their own generators and an average of three big floodlights apiece, 23 resuscitators, more than three tons of the foam powder used to smother petroleum blazes, 167,000 feet of woven hose in good condition, 17 of the tank trucks so indispensable in some rural area and more than 1,000 trained firemen.

When Peterborough reported the fire at Four Winds farm, all the operator had to do was call for aid number one and two, key words indicating that a pumper, from Jaffrey was needed to cover the station and a 1,000-gallon tank truck from Hancock was needed at the fire.

New Problem

Organized in 1953 after Keene's satisfactory experience in the Greenfield group, the Southwestern mutual aid system is now working smoothly, and has applications for membership by Ashburnham, Mass., Townsend, Newfane and West Dummerston, Vt. The latter would create a problem because the Connecticut River separates them from most of the system, but this might be solved by providing the nucleus for a new system.

Chief Walter R. Messer of the Keene department has this to say about the success of mutual aid in the Cheshire county area:

"Until a fire department has actually experienced the benefits of mutual aid, it feels sort of uncertain and out in left field. But the morning after a real test of available equipment--and everyone is sold on it completely."

The next step, Chief Messer said, will be radio control of equipment. The Greenfield system is trying to organize radio communication now with the handicap always faced by small towns when there is a question of expense. On the other hand, Keene has five radio-equipped vehicles and Greenfield even more radio power.

Radio Jeep

One of the last pegs added to the control board for the system represent a radio jeep added to the model little Meadow Wood Fire Department in Fitzwilliam, bringing radio contact to nine neighboring towns when needed, and emphasizing the new forces brought to bear against the old bugaboo of country fires.

And at the other end of the scale, the state fire marshal only has to send a brief message to Keene to mobilize fire resources in this whole section of the state against disaster.

Officers of the Southwestern New Hampshire Mutual Aid system include Chief Messer, president; Chester Nason of Marlboro, vice president; George Porter of Langdon, second vice president; Walter Post of Spofford, treasurer; Homer Tillson of Gilsum, Robert Parent of Swanzey Center, Hermand S. Woods of Peterborough, Winston Cray of Chesterfield and Ralph S. Hoyt of Rindge, directors.

————

On December 21st, 1955 the *Keene Evening Sentinel* reported as follows:

Mutual Fire Aid Helped By Radio

KEENE-Mutual Fire Aid received further advancement with the completion of a radio survey in the area bounded by Athol, Mass., west to Munroe Bridge., Mass., north to Brattleboro, Vt., east to Keene and the surrounding area. Monitors in Keene, Brattleboro, Athol and Monroe Bridge, showed that the signals of the main transmitter in Greenfield also a ca with mobile radio could all be heard equally well and the car, from any section.

The purpose of the survey, which was conducted by the Tri-State Mutual Aid Fire association, (Massachusetts, Vermont and New Hampshire) was to determine how much radio could be used in summoning aid from other towns and also control fire vehicles en route with assistance, or even to save time in directing such vehicles to a fire through unblocked streets.

The survey followed a meeting of the Tri-State group in Greenfield, when a complete report of the radio committee was made. It was revealed at that time that mobile radios could be purchased by towns so desiring, at $300 and permanent base installations at $400. This is of course using matching funds from the Federal government which are available to towns desiring the added protection of radio communications on fire fighting equipment.

It was pointed out by Dep. Chief Edmond F. Tetreault of Greenfield, that the Tri-State organization and the South western

New Hampshire associations worked closely together and that many were members of both organizations. Tetreault was accompanied on the survey Monday by General Electric engineers.

New Hampshire directors of the Tri-State Mutual Aid Fire Association and Chief Dexter Royce of Hinsdale and Harry Worcester of Swanzey, Chief Walter R. Messer of Keene, is a past president of the organizations.

————

1956

In 1956 the *Keene Evening Sentinel* reported as follows:

Radio Service Fire Aid Plan Moves Ahead

Approval of 46.14 Megacycles Received; Engineering Tests Next Step

Greenfield August 11- Deputy Chief Edmond F. Tetreault, Secretary of the Tri-State Mutual Aid today received approval for use of 46.14 megacycles for the fire radio service to be used by the more than 40 departments in the Fire Mutual Aid system.

On August 30th, 1956 The Mutual Aid Radio Tower was installed.

A radio antenna installed stop the Keene Fire Station is another step in the local department's radio coordination with Tri-State Mutual Aid System.

As soon as radio equipment is received from the factory the coaxial type antenna and the radio equipment will tie Keene in with the Tri-State dispatcher at Greenfield, Mass.

The radio equipment has been held up for a critical part and will be installed sometime in the near future, Secretary Robert C. Callahan of the Southwestern New Hampshire Fire Mutual Aid said.

Installation of the radio equipment which will work on dual frequency will also put Keene in contact with some Southwestern departments. A more powerful antenna to be located in the Keene area sometime in the future will complete the Southwestern network, Callahan said.

On September 13th, 1956 Fire Station Radio Setup is completed.

A 60-watt dual frequency radio base station set installed at the Keene Fire Station now puts the department in direct radio contact with 12 base stations and 58 mobile units of the Tri-State Fire Mutual Aid System, plus three departments of the Southwestern New Hampshire Fire Mutual Aid System.

The equipment is financed with matching funds by the city and by the federal government under the Civil Defense setup.

The equipment will also put the Keene station in contact with Manchester, Nashua, Hudson and Bedford for Civil Defense purposes.

Member departments in the Southwestern system which may be reached are Fitzwilliam, Meadowood and West Swanzey.

————

MUTUAL TOWN FIRE AID, now working in 34 towns of southwestern New Hampshire, will overcome many obstacles with establishment of proposed radio network. Shown here are Fire Chief Walter R. Messer of Keene, director of Civil Defense for Keene and president of Southwestern

A Demon Called Fire

New Hampshire Mutual Aid System, and Robert Callahan, secretary of the system, at control pegboard in Keene fire station.

As reported by Don Gross of the *Keene Evening Sentinel*:

Radio Network to Speed Mutual Aid During Fires.

An appropriation of $2,500 recently approved by the delegation for Cheshire County for radio equipment in Keene to permit establishment of a countywide radio communication network for fire mutual aid, Civil Defense work and natural disasters is one of a number of steps in the mutual aid between 34 towns of Southwestern New Hampshire, four towns in Vermont and one in Massachusetts.

Although the 39 fire departments of the Southwestern New Hampshire Fire Mutual Aid System have been working together since the pact was organized in 1953, many of its obstacles will be overcome by the completion of a radio communications setup between the Keene dispatch station and various town fire departments.

Present System Has Faults

To illustrate one glaring deficiency in the system's present method of communication, Robert C. Callahan of Keene, Secretary of the fire mutual aid system, posed the situation that a fire truck on the way to a fire in an outlying part of its territory gets mired in mud or snow, or that the fire I of such a nature that additional equipment is needed. At present, it is necessary to send a man to make a telephone call.

The property on fire in an instance like this is often a total loss before equipment can get there. The ability to communicate directly by a radio transmitter receiver right in the truck however will obviate the problem of the mired truck and fire apparatus can be brought to the fire scene, perhaps from some other route, in time to save the property.

How It Will Work

In explaining the proposed radio communications setup, which can be brought into direct and immediate action for Civil Defense and mutual disaster alerts as well as for day to day fire calls, Callahan outlined the method in which the mutual fire aid system is presently working.

Assume that fire equipment of one of the 39 departments in the system is called to a fire in its area, and needs assistance from another town. A telephone call is made to the dispatch base in the Keene Fire Station. The dispatcher has an index of each of the 39 fire departments and the priority with which aid should be sent to the town calling for assistance. He checks the index orders the department selected to go to the needy town, and diagrams this movement on a peg board to show where the movement has taken place.

If the moved equipment leaves the assisting department without necessary equipment to care for minimum emergencies, additional equipment is then dispatched to this town from another town. An intricate number of movements have been simplified by the ready-reference and the peg board.

Put to Test Recently

The operation of the system was put to a test in the recent Sprague & Carlton fire when equipment of seven departments of the Southwestern New Hampshire system and that of three departments of the Tri-State system were moved into strategic locations while the fire was being fought.

Equipment of four of these companies was at the scene of the fire while equipment of six more were moved in to cover vacated stations and were readied to move into the fire area if needed. One of the covering pieces was at the Keene station which had been emptied of local equipment because of the fire.

This mutual aid, entirely without charge to towns of departments calling for assistance (there is a $5 per year membership fee) is presently working with telephone communications and limited radio facilities with installation of proposed radio equipment in Keene's fire station which will have two frequencies, however Fire Chief Walter R. Messer points out that Keene will be a base of radio dispatching in the Southwestern N. H. pact as well as being tied in with the Tri-State Mutual Aid System operated out of Greenfield, Mass.

Plan Tower on Hill

The $2,500 county appropriation with an equal amount from federal civil defense funds will provide for a 250-watt transmitter and auxiliary tower unit on some local hill to which signals will be relayed from headquarters, making the entire operation independent of wires in case of disasters.

Along with establishment of this departments in the system will acquire radio equipment according to their needs. Some towns have already appropriated equipment, including Marlboro and Keene. Fitzwilliam and Meadowood will be in as well as Troy, West Swanzey, Winchester and Hinsdale. In addition to truck-mounted units in all towns, there will be local base stations in certain towns.

First in State

With completion of the radio system, the Southwestern New Hampshire Fire Mutual Aid System will be the first countywide mutual aid system in the state to complete radio communications, and the second in New England.

The operation entails a lot of paper work Callahan says; necessitating approval of moves on county, state and city levels. The matching civil defense funds are cleared through the state CD office. When the system is completed, however he says the system "will be a tremendous benefit to the small towns."

————

On Tuesday October 16th, 1956 22 Towns Participate in radio testing. The report read as follows:

Radio Test Results Please Fire Chiefs of Mutual Aid

Radio testing between Hyland Hill and member towns of the Southwestern New Hampshire Fire Mutual Aid System was completed Secretary Robert C. Callahan said. The Fire Chiefs are enthusiastic with the success of the tests.

Callahan said that Hyland Hill will make an ideal location for the mutual aid system's transmitter. He indicated that negotiations will be made with the State Forestry Department for permission to use the position. The possibilities of getting electric power to the position are also being studied.

The tests where conducted with the aid of engineers of a radio manufacturing company who traveled from town to town in radio cruiser cars picking up fire chiefs who sent and received between critical locations in the towns and Hyland Hill tower where a temporary transmitter was used.

————

From the *Keene Evening Sentinel*:

Real Fire Proves Value of Keene Radio Tests

A Fire Department radio test in 22 towns was declared successful yesterday when one of the test cars discovered a real fire.

Fireman Robert Guyette of Keene and Ray Minichielllo communications engineer were cruising on Route 9 in West Chesterfield when they discovered a well-developed brush fire beside the road. They were in radio communications with the temporary test transmitter on Highland Hill in Westmorland.

———————

CAPT. ROBERT CALLAHAN OF THE FIRE DEPARTMENT. He has high hopes for the proposed control center.

Saturday, February 10th, 1962 the *Keene Evening Sentinel* published the Item in County Budget by Harvey Dodd, Staff Writer:

Proposed Control Center: 24 Hour Emergency Help

Six towns in Cheshire County have no telephones numbers listed for fire departments. In four others, the fire department telephone is on an eight-party line.

In most of the towns, an expensive setup of "red network" telephones cost about $450 for each fire department. These phones are dial less instruments, spotted in homes throughout town, which ring simultaneously with the fire house phone. The theory is that somebody, in at least one of the houses, will be around to answer it...

Many police vehicles have no radios, because around the clock communications

system would require the installation of a station on a mountain in the town and a dispatcher both day and night.

The control center for emergency calls as proposed in the Cheshire County Budget would service the county with 24 hour dispatch service.

It would eliminate the need for the "red networks" and would serve as a coordinating agency for police and fire activities.

Central Agency

It would make it possible for a person in trouble to get help dispatched by a central agency. Capt. Robert Callahan of the Keene Fire department, who is the local spokesman of the sponsoring Southwestern N. H. Mutual Aid association, says:

"We hope to set up a nerve center for the benefit of all the people in the county, a place you can call in any kind of trouble and be taken care of."

The Mutual Aid group has proposed an $11,500 item in the Cheshire County budget no being study by the County Convention and soon to be acted on. The figure represents the estimated expense of setting up the control center and staffing it for half a year. Capt. Callahan hesitated to guess at a figure for annual costs, but said that the annual figure would include three or four salaries for dispatchers, the telephone bill, and equipment maintenance and repair.

Equipment Ready

Much of the equipment needed is already owned by the county, Capt. Callahan said. He pointed out that no new radio station facility would be required since the equipment on Highland Hill in Westmorland used by the sheriff, the Keene Fire Department, and others could handle the added burden of the control center.

Capt. Callahan said that the central dispatching system would make it feasible for every town to have police, fire and other emergency vehicles equipped with radios without the necessity of base station on a mountain in each town.

Another factor, he said was the added security police officers in cars with radios would have in checking large stores and in stopping suspicious cars. In a car without a radio, in a town with no radio setup, the officer is, in a sense, isolated. With a radio, he can at least tell the dispatcher that he is about to stop what may be a stolen car, enabling the dispatcher to send aid if the officer does not call back in a few minutes. The description of the car can also be given to the dispatcher so that, if anything happens, there will be a description of the care on record.

The sheriff's radio now is staffed, of necessity, only during the day. For this reason, and also because the sheriff's staff would not be able to handle the load, very few local towns are equipped with radios tied into it.

The control center would make it possible for every car to have two-way radios by furnishing a base station through which communications could be routed.

In an emergency call, the person seeking aid would dial the one Elmwood number of the control center.

The dispatcher would answer the phone, simultaneously turning on a tape recorder. He would get the information from the caller.

If it was a fire, he would sound the siren in the appropriate fire house, triggering it by means of a radio tone. The firemen in that area, responding, would call the control center by FM radio or by telephone to get the location of the fire.

At the present time, it usually works this way; the caller dials the town's "red network" in case of a fire, and some other number for police emergencies. One of the persons with a red network phone answers, and then sounds the alarm through a switch and phone wire link with the station. The firemen, arriving at the station call the red network again, and

the person with the location information answers and tells them where the fire is. The information is posted in the fire house for late arrivals.

The central control station would do the same job, Capt. Callahan said, without the necessity of red networks in each town.

Police calls would be the same. The dispatcher would have a list of all area police officers and could reach one by radio or by telephone. Capt. Callahan said, incidentally, that the telephone company completely discounted the possibility of the trunk lines out of a town being so jammed up that a distress call could not be placed.

One trouble is expected with fire calls: 18 of the county towns have direct dialing to Keene. Four do not. In the four that do not, Callahan expects there will be too much confusion inherent in going through an operator, and says it may be best for these few towns to retain their present fire system until they get direct dialing to Keene. The control center, of course, would still remain available to these towns for emergency calls.

The tone system for sounding the alarm is remote control would cost about $250 at the control center, and costs would vary in the outlying towns depending on the amount of equipment already on hand.

In effect, Capt. Callahan said, the control system would place a 24-hour dispatcher and base station radio equipment at the disposal of every town in the county. The County Convention will vote on the budget Feb. 17th, 1962.

————

On February 5th, 1962 Harvey Dodd a *Sentinel* Staff Writer wrote about the Budget Hearing:

☙ *A Demon Called Fire*

Mutual Aid Plan Aired At Couty Budget Hearing

The proposed improvements to the mutual aid fire system, including the addition of a central dispatching station for the surrounding towns, provided the only major interruption at the Cheshire County budget hearing held Saturday afternoon at the Court House.

The hearing was attended by 46 persons, including members of the Cheshire County Convention.

Louis S. Ballam of Walpole, chairman of the county convention, read the budget figures while Sheldon L. Barker, county commissioner, answered questions.

The reading proceeded with only short discussion until additional mutual aid appropriation of $11,500 was reached.

Explains Item

Capt. Robert C. Callahan of the Keene Fire Department and secretary of the Mutual Aid Assn. explained the item. He said that the mutual aid system as proposed would set up a central dispatching station in Keene that would service 18 towns in or near the county that have extended local dialing in their telephone systems.

The central dispatching system would eliminate the red network in the small towns, and people at the hearing were told it should be a financial savings as well as more efficient.

An example was cited; a person in Troy wishing to report a fire would pick up the phone and dial an Elmwood number instead of a Circle number. The dispatcher in Keene, on 24-hour duty, would answer the phone and get the information, which would be simultaneously tape recorded. He would then sound the whistle at the Troy fire station by remote control, and the firemen on duty there, or the first to arrive, would get in touch with Keene by two-way radio to get the information.

Capt. Callahan said that the sheriff's radio would also be tied into the system, to provide dispatching service for that department and also for ambulances.

Towns Billed

Out-of-county towns participating in the central dispatching system would be billed at the same rate as in-county towns, although, in the county, the money would be raised by county taxation. The funds sought would provide equipment to set up the center and pay manpower to operate it for one half of a year.

Sheriff Frank Walker spoke, endorsing the idea, and Mayor Robert L. Mallat and City Manager Donald Chick also said they favored it.

Harrisville fire chief Francis Parker said he was enthusiastic about it.

Capt. Callahan said after the hearing that an engineer from the telephone company had told representatives of the mutual aid system that a busy signal caused by busy circuits from one town to the other was rare and lasted only for a matter of seconds. He said that many people with four or eight party lines thought the trunk circuits were busy because they didn't get a dial tone when they picked up their phone but in reality it was caused by someone talking on the other half of the party line.

He Opposes It

Kenneth Colby, a former councilman, voiced opposition to inclusion of the $11,500 item. He based his opposition, he said, on the fact that a large portion of the budget at the present time consists of expenses over which the county commissioners have no control. He was also critical of the fact that some of the towns in the association are outside the limits of Cheshire County.

The county convention will vote on the budget at its annual meeting Feb. 17th. The budget this year is $438,971.00. Last year it was $391.085.00. The largest increase was the boost from $155,500 to $170,000 in the County Farm item.

NOTE: The February 17th, 1962 County Budget was passed and South Western Mutual Aid moved forward as follows:

————

News Release Monday March 25th, 1962 by the Directors Fire Mutual Aid:

New Chief For Fire Mutual Aid

Robert Callahan of Spofford, N.H. has been appointed Chief Coordinator for the Southwestern New Hampshire District Fire Mutual Aid System.

Sheldon Barker, Chairman Executive Committee, Board of Directors Fire Mutual Aid and County Commissioner made the announcement here today. Callahan, now a Captain in the Keene Fire Department, will serve at present on a part-time basis helping organize the new Dispatch Center. It is anticipated by July the Dispatch Center will have been completed and Chief Callahan will then devote his whole time to this operation, as well as new duties prescribed under the recently voted Fire Mutual Aid Program.

————

Mutual Aid Space Added to Keene Fire Department.

Fire Addition May Go To City Council
Lack of agreement among members of three City Councils committees over how big a proposed addition to the fire station should be is expected to send the question to the full council to be resolved.

The question is whether to authorize a one-story addition to provide room for central-dispatcher equipment, or a two-story addition to provide for that, plus room for beds for the department's expansion.

Discussing it last night were the Fire, Finance and Land and Buildings committee, the mayor, the city manager and the fire chief.

The one-story cost estimate is about $6,000. The two-story estimate, $12,000 to $14,000.

The central-dispatcher system to handle fire calls on a county-wide basis has been approved by the County Convention and the city has approved making space available as a headquarters.

The City Council, too, in approving the 1962 city operating budget, made provision for four new firemen in what was described as the first step in bringing the department up to the strength recommended by the Fire Underwriters.

To make room for the new men, it is planned to use a room that has been the fire chief's office. This would give space for four beds.

The Council committeemen who favor the two-story addition argued last night that to build the one story addition now would be a false economy.

The one-story addition would provide for immediate needs, they said, but within a relatively few years the second story would have to be put on, and the cost of doing part of the job twice is not a necessary cost. It could be done all at once, more economically.

Those who favored the one-story addition said that since two-story space is not needed now, spending money for it is not justified. A flat roof that could later become a first floor ceiling and a second story floor could be put on, and the top story built when needed.

Generally speaking. Fire Committee members favored the two story addition and Finance Committee members favored the one. The makeup of the committees makes a definite lineup difficult, since some men are members of one or the other besides being on the Land and Buildings Committee.

☗   *A Demon Called Fire*

Louis Simon and James A. Mugford are on the Finance Committee. H. Franklin Guild, who has resigned, was the third man. The Fire Committee is Jeremiah J. Keating, Francis P. Callahan and George E. Fish. The Land and Buildings Committee is Mugford, Callahan and Evans H. Barrett.

Regardless of which plan is approved, it is proposed to add about 200 square feet of floor space to the current fire-alarm room, which itself is housed in a one-story addition to the east side of the fire station, facing Vernon Street.

The two-story plan would add 400 more square feet of space; the 200 above the proposed addition and 200 above the existing fire-alarm room.

Robert Callahan, Chief Coordinator of the new system, which he envisioned for years.

Following reported by *Keene Evening Seninel* June 20th, 1962:

Bids Opened For Addition To Firehouse.

Less than $200 separates the two lowest bids for the contract to build a two-story addition to the Central Fire Station to house the proposed mutual-aid central dispatcher fire-alarm communications system control center.

The lowest of three bids open yesterday came from the r. E. Bean Construction Co. at $13,373. Next, $184 higher was from the MacMillin Co., at $13,557. The third was from Ivah Ballou at $15,990.

Authorization to award the contract is expected to be considered by the City Council tomorrow night.

Chief Dispatcher Robert C. Callahan said today that operation of the control center will be ready to start as soon as the construction is finished. This is expected to be toward the end of August, 1962.

In 1963 *Yankee Magazine* out of Dublin, New Hampshire published an article as told by Robert Callahan to Daniel H. Larker.

Over 30 towns in New Hampshire's Monadnock Region have banded together in devising a system the only one of its kind in New England to meet efficiently all emergencies:

Small Towns With Big City Service

WHEN A FIRE IN MANY small New England towns becomes too large for the local volunteer department to handle, a call for help must be made to one of the neighboring towns. Sounds like a simple and neighborly procedure but, in many cases, it isn't. First of all, the town which sends its equipment and manpower must also, subsequently, send a bill. Due to this often considerable expenditure, some town fire chiefs are compelled by local laws to confer with the Town Selectmen in order to obtain the authority to call for aid! Others are reluctant to summon assistance due to both to this extra cost and to a basic pride and independence typical of any small New England community. There are other assorted complications, too. For instance, when the Dublin, New Hampshire, fire department was fighting a blaze several years ago, one of those present at the scene figured help was needed. Without notifying the Dublin fire chief, he phoned the Harrisville fire department which responded quickly and later sent Dublin a bill for something over a hundred dollars. Dublin, in turn, responded by saying that they hadn't asked Harrisville for aid, that they hadn't needed aid, and those they wouldn't pay the bill. Well, there was a lot of water over the dam before that one was resolved.

In the Monadnock Region of New Hampshire, none of these problems has existed since 1958. At that time, the Southwestern New Hampshire District Fire Mutual Aid System, which now includes thirty-three towns as members and ten as associate member, became effective. Like many similar agreements set up around New England, this plan meant that all member towns would aid each other in fighting fires, if called upon, without charge. But whereas the usual procedure was to call the specific department needed by telephone, this new organization set up one central control station in the Keene Fire Station, the only manned station in the group, from which the entire operation could be coordinated. A base radio station, purchased with County Funds, was build on nearby Hyland Hill by volunteer members of the various fire departments (plus a "Repeater" Station on Pack Monadnock Mountain) and by the following year most of the member towns had, by appropriations obtained at their Town Meetings, purchased mobile radio units for their fire trucks.

While the "red network" telephone number system is still in sue (by which three or four homes in a town are equipped with a special number used for fires, plus equipment to activate the local fire alarm in which case the base station in Keene is notified by the local truck radio), many of the member towns (21 departments at this writing) can report a fire directly to the base station in Keene. After Town Meetings are held this month, it is expected more will be able to do away with the more costly and less efficient "red network" system.

When the man on duty at the base station receives a call from someone who had discovered a fire in any of the member towns, this base station operator activates by radio tone the local fire alarm of the town in which the fire is reported and he may activate the alarm of the fire station in another town if it happens to be nearer to the actual fire. Currently, a zoning system is being worked out whereby the caller will report his zone or street number to the base station operator who will then, in turn, automatically activate the alarm nearest to the fire regardless of town lines.

An automatic covering procedure is the next step. That is, after any fire apparatus has been dispatched from a given town, the base center operator would notice on his board which lists all available equipment in each town whether less than a 500 gallon–per-minute apparatus remains. If this is the case, he will direct a truck from a point geographically away from the fire with at least five men into the town. There they will remain until the home company returns.

Since last year, however, this wonderful and efficient system has gone much further. Under the able leadership of Robert Callahan, a Keene fireman with seventeen years experience and a rating of Captain in the department, a Control Center for every emergency has been organized. Since the costly base station with all its equipment had already been set up for the fire mutual

A Demon Called Fire

aid system, it naturally followed that the police, ambulances and doctors of all the surrounding towns could take advantage of it. Certainly few towns could afford a base station, in operation 24 hours a day, of their won. Hardly any of the local towns, for instance, had radios in their police cars a dangerous situation, needless to say. But, without someone to talk to, what good where radios? Some towns, such as Keene, had a Base Station for County-Town Police, but even these did not have 24-hour coverage. At present, eight towns have bought radios for their police cars and other towns will be joining the system after Town Meeting Day this month.

All telephones in member towns have been, or will be, equipped with a red sticker with instruction to call 352-1100 for any kind of emergency whether it be fire, an accident, an illness, or a crime. A good illustration of the value of such a set-up was demonstrated recently in town of Stoddard, New Hampshire. A lady driving home at night passed a serious highway accident. At the first lighted house beyond she telephoned the above number and gave the operator on duty at the Control; Center in Keene the information Immediately both an ambulance and police car were dispatched to the scene. When the injured arrived at the hospital, doctors, having also been alerted by the Control Center, were on hand to administer specific treatment for the injuries described over the ambulance car radio. What would have happened in this situation a few years ago, without the Mutual Aid System, is difficult or perhaps easy to imagine.

Additional services will be offered to industry and private business in the form of monitoring burglar alarms and sprinkler alarms. In other words a bell and light activated at the Control Center in Keene will alert the dispatcher that a sprinkler system has been triggered, a door or safe has been entered, a boiler is malfunctioning, or what ever and it will tell him exactly where. He will then activate the appropriate department. All income received from these services will be used to defray the costs of operating the Center, thereby decreasing the amount of taxpayer funds required from the county budget.

Chief Callahan's Control Center is, surprisingly, the only one of its kind in New England, yet it has already proved to be the answer to efficient fire, police and ambulance service in small towns which cannot afford these services on their own. Perhaps this example can show the way at a few Town Meetings this month..?

As we approach the 21st century the Southwestern Mutual Aid Dispatch Center dispatches for more than 75 town covering three states in New England. Its dispatchers are highly trained professionals, with a computerized up to day form of dispatch to insure that you receive the best and quickest response to your emergency.

Since 1953 when SWNHFMA started, and in 1962 when it moved into 24 hour coverage there has only been three (3) Chief Coordinators the 1st being Chief Robert Callahan and 2nd being Chief John Marechal and now filling the Chief Coordinators position is Chief Paul Szoc.

Southwestern Fire Mutual Aid Dispatch Center is the 1st line of communications to expedite the call from beginning to end. Without them we the emergency services would be in the dark ages.

––––––––

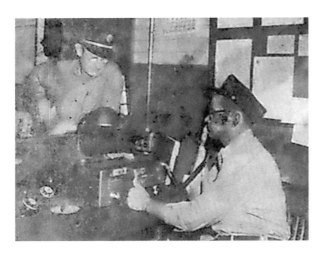

Radio Communications Center – Mid 1950's. Radio Communications linking the Southwestern Mutual Aid (fire) and the Tri-State Mutual Aid were installed at the Keene Fire Station Wednesday. The Keene station is the dispatching center for the Southwestern association. The equipment enables the dispatching center to monitor (listen) or talk to either of the two mutual aid systems. Over the new radio system Keene has talked to Manchester and Swanzey, and to Athol, Greenfield and Ashfield MA. Shown seated at the transmitter-receiver is Richard Pollock, while Elton Britton (captain) listens as Fitzwilliam reports on a fire in that town. Photo taken by Howard F. Morse.

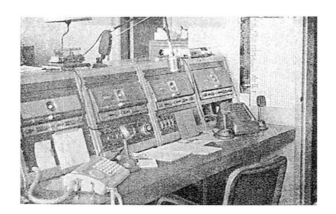

Communications Center – Mid 1960's. This is the Control Center in Keene, base station for 33 member towns. The radio sets include frequencies

for fire, police, ambulance, Civil Defense plus their many subdivisions.

This picture of the dispatch center shows several members of the Keene Fire Department discussing the call of a fire that had just been dispatched. Seated: dispatchers Phil Toureill and Bonnie Johnson. Standing: Mr. and Mrs. Charlie Harris(in background), and Captain Steven Goldsmith.

1954

1954 Started off with activity as reported by the *Keene Evening Sentinel*:

"FIRE"

Firemen Combat Stubborn Blaze

Chester L. Kingsbury's Home Badly Damaged

Keene firemen combated a stubborn and disastrous fire on New Year's eve in the house owned by Mr. and Mrs. Chester L. Kingsbury, 189 Court Street. Loss to the building is estimated at $15,000 and the loss placed on the contents has been tentatively put at $10,000.

Fire had gained a good headway when firemen arrived and dense smoke throughout the house made it difficult to locate the blaze. Firemen were driven back when they first attempted to enter the building.

Some clothing was removed from upstairs rooms and carried to the home of neighbors.

Mr. and Mrs. Kingsbury were visiting in the home of friends when the fire was discovered. They had been away from home about an hour.

According to Chief Walter R. Messer, the fire is believed to have originated in a closet under the stairway.

Guy F. Rurrill, Keene High Instructor, called the firemen from his home at 95 Cross Street after seeing smoke pouring from the house.

The still alarm was sounded at 9:21 o'clock and a general alarm on Box 46, located at the corner of Court and School Streets was sounded at 9:25 o'clock. The all out signal was sounded shortly after 12:30 Friday morning.

———

On Friday January 8th, 1954 the *Keene Evening Sentinel* reported that an Early Morning Fire Caused Heavy Loss to the Bon Ton Kitchen:

"FIRE"

Flames Damage Bon Ton Kitchen

An early morning flash fire in the kitchen of the Bon Ton Restaurant 45-47 Main Street caused damage in excess of $5,000 to the restaurant and building.

Occupants of the apartments in the block over the restaurant were alerted and left their rooms.

The fire is reported to have originated about deep fat frying equipment.

The kitchen and most of the equipment is badly damaged. Smoke also permeated the dining room, lunch counter section and rooms in the apartments.

Officers Carl R. Decker and Maurice Olmstead, who were on duty alerted the occupants of the apartments in the block.

Firemen responding to a still alarm call at 6:01 o'clock, radioed for more equipment and men. Box 18 at the corner of Marlboro and Kelleher Streets, was sounded by mistake. Box 8 was then sounded.

Peter Booras, one of the owners of the restaurant, says that new equipment will be rushed to Keene to replace that which is damaged. He plans to resume business early next week.

———

Reported by the *Keene Evening Sentinel* on January 18th, 1954:

"FIRE"

Firemen Combat Blaze In Studio

Frinks lose Building Photographic Equipment

Keene firemen combated a stubborn blaze in near zero weather Sunday morning in the photographic studio of Mr. and Mrs. Edward A. Frink at 702 Main Street.

The studio building was badly damaged and the Frinks lost valuable photographic equipment. Damage to the building was estimated at $2,000 by Fire Chief Walter R. Messer.

According to firemen the blaze originated around a space heater. The studio was located about 30 feet in the rear of the Frink home. The house did not catch fire although during the early stages of the fire the wind was blowing toward the house.

The Frinks, who attending church services at the time, arrived home during the progress of the fire.

Arthur Laurent, who lives at 650 Main Street served the firemen with coffee at the scene.

———

On January 25th, 1954 the *Keene Evening Sentinel* reported:

"FIRE"

Smoking In Bed Caused $1,500 Loss

"Smoking in bed" was recorded on the firemen's bulletin as the cause of the $1,500 fire Sunday in the house at 541 Washington Street. Property is owned by the Beauregard estate.

One upstairs room was badly damaged by the flames and some permeated the entire building.

Firemen responding at 2:35 o'clock Sunday morning to a still alarm call, radioed for more equipment and men. Box 252 was sounded three minutes later.

As reported by the *Keene Evening Sentinel* on April 6th, 1954:

"FIRE"

Elderly Women Led To Safety

Fire Caused $1,000 Damage to Home

Two elderly women were led to safety here late Monday afternoon as a fire caused damage estimated at $1,000 in a first floor living room at the residence of Julia L. Withington, 119 High Street.

Robert J. Norton, of 54 Armory Street, a sentinel newsboy, first noticed the fire while delivering papers and warned the occupants.

Fire Chief Walter R. Messer said the two women, who lived upstairs, were led down a back stairway by firemen.

Messer said he believes the fire was started when a male tenant inadvertently dropped hot pipe ashes in a bureau drawer.

One fire truck was sent to the scene in response to a still alarm.

Firemen used gas mask and fog nozzles to enter the burning room and place the fire under control.

Also reported on April 10th, 1954 Keene Firemen extinguished a chimney fire at the home of John Tasoulas, 8 Franklin Street at 8:47 Friday night and a grass fire on the land of Wallace at 298 Main Street at 1:37 p.m. Friday. As reported by the *Keene Evening Sentinel* on April 30th, 1954:

"STORY"

Motorists Hinder Fire Department

False Alarm Points Up Serious Problem

A restless four-year old youngster, waiting for his parents who were visiting a patient , sounded a general alarm Thursday night which brought several pieces of apparatus to Elliot Community Hospital.

But it wasn't the unintentional false alarm that bothered fire and hospital officials, it was that perennial fire hazard, the motorist who tries to get to the fire before the department.

Fire Chief Walter R. Messer reported today that he and several of his drivers were forced to use the left hand side of the street because motorists absolutely refused to pull to the side when the fire warning sounded as required by law.

He said the traffic jam at the hospital would have been a serious detriment to the firefighters if there had been a real fire.

The congestion of cars caused by curious motorists also prevented call firemen from reaching the scene as quickly as they might have, Messer reported.

Miss. Dorothea W. Rice, hospital administrator, said the experience showed her that a different method must be used at the hospital to assure that those ECH personnel who are trained for such emergencies are not prevented from reaching the building.

Miss Rice said that least two trained hospital people wee prevented from doing the emergency duties assigned to them because of the crowd.

———

From Keene Fire Department Records:

"STORY"

Fire Department Holds Memorial Service

Rev. Clinton L. Morrill Of Concord Gives Talk

Reported June 14th, 1954: The Rev. Clinton L. Morrill of Concord delivered the address at the annual memorial service for Keene firemen in the assembly hall of the fire station Sunday morning. Rev. Charles Austin, Pastor of the Court Street Church and chaplain of the department, presided.

Mr. Morrill's wife is a daughter of the late Lt. Earl W. Little, one of the firemen who died during the past year. Only other death during the past year was that of Dennis Driscoll, an auxiliary fireman.

The honor roll was read by Lt Francis Driscoll.

Following the services firemen decorated graves of deceased firemen in cemeteries in Keene and nearby towns. Members of the decorating committee included, William H. Sanderson, Lt. Jesse Little, Lt. Francis Driscoll, Capt. Edward L. Reason, George Shepard and Clarence Caldwell.

A group from the Barbershop Chorus, in charge of Gardner H. Barrett, sang two selections.

Members of the city government were guests.

———

From the *Keene Evening Sentinel*:

Lightining Blamed For Sounding Box

On September 7th, 1954 the *Keene Evening Sentinel* reported that Firemen did not find any fire at the Elm City Grain Company building, 93 Railroad Street shortly before noon today when the automatic box alarm 113 sounded during an electrical storm.

Lightning was given as the cause of the sounding of the alarm.

———

Reported by the *Keene Evening Sentinel* on November 4th, 1954:

"STORY"

Police Will Probe False Fire Alarm

A police investigation was ordered late Wednesday by Chief of Police William T. Bridgham as the second false alarm in four days was sounded shortly before 10 p.m. from Box 53 on Winchester Street near the railroad crossing.

The first false alarm, sounded late Saturday night, October 30th, was believed to be the work of Halloween pranksters.

———

On November 11th, the *Keene Evening Sentinel* reported:

Firemen Answer 3Rd False Alarm

The sounding of a false alarm shortly before 7 o'clock Monday night, the third in nine days, is under investigation by members of the Keene Police Department.

The Monday alarm was Box 51, located at the corner of Winchester Street and Blake Streets.

The other alarms were on Box 53 on Winchester Street near the bridge over the Ashuelot River. One was sounded on the night of October 30th, and the second on the night of November 3rd.

———

On December 2nd, 1954 the *Keene Evening Sentinel* reported:

"STORY"

Firemen Answer 5Th False Alarm

Another false alarm, the 5th, since October 30th, was sounded at 5:48 o'clock Wednesday on Box 57, south of the railroad crossing on Pearl Street.

Fire fans turned out in force along with the department.

The following is the list of false alarms: Oct. 30th, box 53; Nov. 3rd, box 53; Nov 8th, box 51; Nov. 9th, box 53; Dec. 1st, box 57.

_____

NOTE: During World War 2 and the Koran Conflict the Civil Defense was a major part of every one's lives. This continued into the Cold war decades as well. In 1954 the state and counties moved forward with the Civil Defense program as reported by the *Keene Evening Sentinel*:

City And County Civil Defense Directors Ask Cooperation

The week beginning Sunday, Sept. 9th, and through Sept. 15th, is National Civil Defense Week, designated by the President of the United States.

Gov. Lane Dwitnell had requested all the people of New Hampshire to join in its observance and County Civil Defense Directors Casper C. Bemis Jr., is seconding this request by urging all town directors in Cheshire County to a renewed effort to make their organization as complete in efficiency as possible.

In Keene, City Director Walter R. Messer pointed out that the week is a good time for everyone to give thought to the need of supporting the Civil Defense program.

County Director Bemis said that anyone who is interested in volunteering for any one of the Civil Defense teams in his community should contact the town or city director and talk over the situation with the director.

Both Bemis and City Director Messer pointed out that Civil Defense has a constant purpose over and above sneak enemy attack. Civil Defense is the best possible protection against large-scale fires and floods and hurricanes.

Bemis said that an increasing need to be protected against nuclear "fallout" should be considered by residents and business people in this area.

"This area probably would not be singled out for direct attack" he said, "but it would very likely be affected by the danger or radiation if our larger New England cities were bombed."

Such an attack would present two immediate needs which must be prepared for; (1) to shelter area residents against "fallout" and (2) to care for refugees evacuated from critical area of bombing.

State Civil Defense Director C. A. Brinkmann said that "survival requires the willing cooperation of all people."

"Our Civil Defense Act is most comprehensive, and provides the necessary legal basis for relief measures. But survival in disasters is not something that can be provided by law," he said. "Our citizens must learn train organize Civil Defense begins with the individual, the family circle and progresses upward through the neighborhood, the community, the state, the nation."

_____

From the *Keene Evening Sentinel*:

"STORY"

First State Wide Civil Defense Test Reasonable Successful, Director Brinkmann Reports

Respond To Cd Alert In Keene Satisfactory

Public response to the 15 minute, statewide Civil Defense test here this morning was termed "remarkable cooperative" after it was over by Fire Chief Walter R. Messer, Civil Defense director.

Messer said that except for a "few little holes," the test was reasonably successful." One of the bugs was in communications where the red alert was sounded on the fire whistle before a radio warning was sent out to police cars. A simultaneous warning is more desirable.

Twenty-eight members of the Civil Defense auxiliary police force directed by Gordon L. Phillips helped regulars curb traffic at key intersections and more than half the fire department's auxiliary and call force reported for duty.

Messer said West Keene was "reasonable covered" by the signals from the fire station and Sprague & Carleton, Inc., thanks to an east wind. But the east side of the city was not covered well for the same reason, he added.

All Clear at 9:46

Keene police received the test yellow warning signal at 8:32 a.m. and the red alert flash came at 9:31, 59 minutes later. The all clear came at 9:46 a.m.

Mayor Laurence M. Pickett spent nearly an hour in Wheelock Park, waiting for the red alert signal.

He was in a public works truck equipped with a public address system.

Preliminary reports indicated the voice amplification did not carry any great distance, however.

From the *Keene Evening Sentinel*:

Keeneites To Get Civil Defense Tags

Civil Defense identification tags will be available for Cheshire County men, women and children in the near future, county Civil Defense Director Casper C. Bemis announced to day.

The tags, which will list the wearer's name, emergency addressee, religious preference and blood type, will be available at cost in grocery stores.

The Federal Civil Defense Administration said the tags will be of invaluable aid both in wartime and peacetime disasters. Bemis Said

[*Compiler's Note*: This writer can say that as a child growing up in the 50's and 60's, I can remember the air raid alert drills, which were indicated by the Fire Department's whistle. I can also remember practicing at Roosevelt School to go under the desks, then move to an inside hall wall and face the wall on your knees. It was like practicing fire drills, but was not as common.]

From the *Keene Evening Sentinel*:

"FIRE"

Partition Fire Causes Damage

On December 6th, 1954 the *Keene Evening Sentinel* reported Two fire trucks from Keene and one from Surry responded for a partition fire Saturday afternoon in the house owned by Merton Tenney on the Old Walpole Road. Defective wiring was given as the cause.

Most of the damage estimated at several hundred dollars, was caused by smoke and water. The fire was hard to reach. Firemen remained on the scene for more than an hour to prevent any outbreak. Some of the furniture was removed from the building.

From the *Keene Evening Sentinel*:

"STORY"

Two Persons Escape When Plane Crashes

CLOSE CALL, Pilot James C. Gillespie, a 52 year-old Northfield Mass. farmer and his passenger, 18 year old Milton Deane of Bernardston, Mass. walked away from this crash off the Base Hill Rd. Gillespie lost a front tooth and received only slight cuts on the face. Deane was uninjured. Gillespie said that the engine of the plane, rented from Bowman Flying Service, conked out. Unable to make airport in glide, Plane clipped treetop and spun into field.

Rented Piper Cub's Engine Conks Out Off Base Hill Road.

Two persons narrowly averted serious injury this morning when a rented light plane in which they were flying crashed just off the West Hill Base Road southwest of the airport.

James C. Gillespie a 52-year-old Northfield Mass farmer who was flying the two-place Piper J-3 plane rented from Bowman Flying Service, received only minor injuries.

His passenger 18-year old Milton Deane of Bernardston, Mass escaped injury.

Gillespie a veteran of 2,000 flying hours and an instructor in World War II, said that the engine conked out. He tried to glide the ship into a field but struck a tree top.

The plane spun around and crashed about 15 feet short of a bank. Both wings were damaged and the nose of the plan buckled by the impact.

A fire engine was dispatched to the scene of the crash.

———

From the *Keene Evening Sentinel*:

"STORY"

Important Note: Fire Substation

During the years since World War II, though it began before that, there has been a shift in the population location of Keene.

Anybody seeking to locate the center of population, as statisticians sometime do with an arbitrary point, would find that the pinhead had moved west across Keene's map.

The heavy building in the West Keene area has been largely residential, although there has been in the motor lodge and in the retail field, certain other valuable construction.

It does not seem as if the trend were gong to reverse itself. There is still considerable build able land unoccupied in that area, but serviced by the city water and sewer lines.

It appears as if the expansion of Keene, residentially at lease, will continue to follow the trend to the West. The school district voters recognized this trend when they called for the erection of the new junior high school plan in the West Keene area.

The increase in residential building has jumped the total valuation of the West Keene area considerably of the community.

Yet much of this new area is more than two miles from the central fire station over a road system, which does not allow much in the way of alternate routes.

Within a couple of years, whole the bridge on Routes 9 and 12 over the Ashuelot was being reconstructed, the department decided to station an auxiliary engine on the West Keene Side of the bridge. In doing that, the department took cognizance of the fact that the e routes to West Keene are not a matter of much choice. It's West Street or nothing, practical, that is.

With the propensity of Keene people to clutter the highways the moment the fire whistle blows, the use of a single access road for the fire department to any such valuable area as West Keene is sheer hazard. A traffic jam caused by an accident between eager fire buffs could prevent the engines form arriving in time.

The time has come, because of all these factors, when the city should consider the establishment of a branch fire station with one or two pieces of equipment, in the West Keene area.

A branch station's complement of men and equipment could extinguish all but most stubborn of fires. It would be in constant radio contact with the main station and would be on call as auxiliary equipment in case of need elsewhere.

Recently an insurance regulation was placed in effect, reducing the rate materially for those homes and buildings within two road miles of the fire station. Much of the West Keene area does not qualify. With a branch station established in the area, money could be saved house-holders to compensate for the extra tax burden such a station would entail.

With so much of our tax valuation in threat area, it is good investment for the city to protect it better than it now can be protected. Our junior high school would thus be closer to help in case of fire that is not the case.

The use of a local alarm system would do away with the long runs from the central fire house and cut down the possibility of accident on our highways.

From any aspect, convenience, safety, economy and others, the establishment of a branch fire station in West Keene is called for as a matter of priority business for Keene.

NOTE: This was published early May in the *Keene Evening Sentinel* in 1954. A sub station within West Keene has not been new, just a long time coming.

————

1955

The 50's brought to the entire country a new outlook on Civil Defense. In 1955 Keene moved forward as a new year rolled around.

On January 13th, 1955 the *Keene Evening Sentinel* wrote:

"STORY"

1955 City Fire Losses Decrease In 1954

Estimated fire losses, in 1954 dropped nearly $70,000 from 1953, Fire Chief Walter R. Messer said today.

Messer said estimated damage totaled $93,134.45 compared with $148,134.45 a year ago.

And more than $60,000 of the total was attributed to the disastrous Davis Oil Co. fire which destroyed a lower Main Street Garage and several tractor units and trucks.

The estimated value of buildings and contents in which fires occurred was $1,300,800.

Insurance paid added up to $93,924.24.

The department reported 273 alarms during the year, 42 less than the preceding year. An unusually wet summer held the total down. Only 22 grass and brush fires occurred, 25 less than the 1953 total.

Firemen answered nine false alarms during the year and 16 calls outside the city.

————————

On May 6th, 1955 the *Keene Evening Sentinel* carried the story of the MacKenzie Dairy Barn fire on Court Street:

"FIRE"

MacKenzie Dairy Burns Causing $30,000 Loss

A fire, which caused damaged at some $25,000 to $30,000 swept through a section of the MacKenzie Dairy on upper Court Street early this morning.

The main damage area included the boiler room, milk processing room, a three car garage uses as a bottle receiving room and the dairy bar.

Fire Chief Walter R. Messer said the fire is believed to have originated in the boiler room area, but the cause has not been determined

The fire was discovered at 3 a.m. by Mrs. Henry Hoisington, mother of Mrs. Elmer L. MacKenzie, who lives near by and happened to be up at the time.

She called Mrs. MacKenzie who in turned summoned firemen. A clock in the milk processing room was stopped at 2:50 a.m. indicating the fire was underway at least 15 minutes before firemen arrived.

Firemen Praised

Elmer MacKenzie, who operates the dairy with the aid of his wife and family said "firemen deserved great credit" for saving a big barn which adjoins the heavy damaged area.

Although flames had already made their way into the structure, which contained a small amount of hay, a small hose line quickly checked the blaze in that area.

Fireman Injured

Firemen Clare Symonds 62 of 12 West Street received chest injuries when a roof caved in on a ladder on which he was standing. He is in satisfactory condition at Elliot Community Hospital.

MacKenzie's son Warren who also lives near the dairy and Frank Jacobs an employee led 80 head of cattle from a smoke filled barn to safety in a field outside.

Milk stored in a cooler for early morning delivery was not damaged by the fire and was delivered today.

MacKenzie and local dairies cooperated to speed milk deliveries and temporary cold storage facilities were offered by Clark Distributors and the General Ice Cream Corp.

None of the dairy truck were damaged in the fire as they are not garaged on the premises MacKenzie said, regular deliveries will resume tomorrow.

Mrs. MacKenzie said Ralph W. Payne will begin immediate reconstruction of the damaged buildings and the contractor was on the job early this morning.

Since dairy bar damage was mainly confined to the roof it is expected to be reopened very soon. The property and equipment was reported covered by insurance.

Box alarm 471 was sounded at 3:05 a.m. and four trucks were sent to the scene. The all clear sounded at 6:49 a.m.

————————

From the *Keene Evening Sentinel*:

A Demon Called Fire

MACKENZIE DAIRY FIRE. A fire of undetermined origin caused damage estimated at between $25,000 and $30,000 at the MacKenzie Dairy on Upper Court St. early this morning. This view, taken from a crane owned by contractor Ralph Payne, shows heart of the fire area at upper right, fire was centered in the boiler and milk processing rooms. Eighty cattle were led to safety and milk was delivered this morning.

In January of 1955 The Civil Defense Director Walter R. Messer proposed City's CD Budget which Figured at $4,705.

Civil Defense Director Walter R. Messer will submit a $4,705 budget for City Council approval, nearly double the 1954 total.

Messer recalls only too well that his predecessor, John H. Giffin, resigned last year after the Council applied the ax to his budget. But he believes he is acting in the best interest of the city and will leave the final decision to the Council.

Two major items share responsibility for the hike - a new warning horn system and a new ground observer post atop the old Sentinel building at the corner of Main Street and Railroad Square.

Cost of the warning horn installation on the public works garage lower main street is estimated at $1,400. Directional horns would cover present "dead space" area in South Keene and West Keene, Messer believes. It would supplement the present whistle at the Central Fire Station.

If some $1,000 is earmarked for the new ground observer post, a number of objections to the present unmanned post on Meadow Road off Pearl Street are expected to be eliminated.

Chief objection came from women volunteers who disliked the isolation. The new post would be in a central, easily accessible location with an adequate stairway leading to the roof and heating facilities.

————

From the *Keene Evening Sentinel*:

"STORY"

Chief Messer Explains Civil Defense Work

Fire Chief Walter R. Messer, director of civil defense, explained the civil defense program in this area at a meeting of the Soroptimists Tuesday night February 8th, 1956 at the home of Mrs. Raphael J. Shortlidge.

He stressed the need for more committee workers and ground observers. The civil defense program is divided into service committees including fire fighting, health and sanitation, industrial, medical, police, rescue and evacuation and transportation.

He stated that the civil defense unit is organized to take over in war times and also in major disasters such as fire and floods. The speaker was introduced by Mrs. Mary Lane, program chairman.

A supper preceded the meeting. Those on the committee were Miss Elizabeth Foley, Mrs. Jan Larson and Miss Margaret Sadoques.

————

1956

In 1956 the City of Keene had constructed a new Civil Defense Aircraft spotting post atop of the old Sentinel building as published in the *Keene Evening Sentinel* January 16th, 1956.

Civil Defense Construction is Underway

Construction of a new Civil Defense aircraft spotting post atop the old Sentinel building and installation of supplementary warning horns on the roof of the new public works department garage is now underway.

NEW SPOTTING POST. Three Keene Civil Defense officials are silhouetted against the sky in this rooftop view of the city's new Ground Observer Corps airplane spotting post located on the old Sentinel building at the Corner of Main St. and Railroad Square. Room beneath observation deck is heated. Shown (l to r) are Keene Civil Defense Director Walter R. Messer, Chief Observer Edward F. Myers, and Ground Observer Corps Director Albert B Stroshine who asked volunteers to meet tonight at the Fire Station. Photo taken by Jack Teehan.

Keene Civil Defense Director Walter R. Messer said the warning horns, to be tied in with the city fire whistle, are expected to cover the lower Marlboro Street, and South Keene area, Edgewood, and possibly sections of West Keene.

The horns are not expected to be tested this week, Messer said.

The new observation post at Main Street and Railroad Square will replace a site on Meadow Road off Pearl Street.

Funds for both projects were appropriated early last year.

———————

Sprague & Carlton Fire February 21st, 1956. Article by Herb Allen, *Manchester (N.H.) Union Leader* February 22nd, 1956:

"FIRE"

MILLION DOLLAR FIRE SWEEPS KEENE PLANT

Million Dollar Keene Fire started in the mid-section of the main production building of Sprague & Carleton, Inc. Furniture manufacturing plant on Avon Street. Photo by Allen.

Furniture Firm Hit As Five Towns Battle General Alarm Blaze

KEENE - Fire damaged approaching a million dollars at the Sprague & Carleton, Inc., furniture manufacturing plant here early yesterday afternoon crippled one of the city's major industries and threw 300 Greater Keene residents temporarily out of work.

Representatives of management last night indicated that rebuilding would begun as soon as salvage operations are completed. Franklin Peart, Vice president of the company, estimated the loss at between $750,000 and $1,000,000.

Blame Short Circuit

The fire one of the largest in the city's history, started in the main building of the seven-unit plant late in the noon hour, just a few minutes before the employees were due to return to their jobs.

Believed to have started from a short circuit near an electric motor above a sealer-spray booth in the finishing room midway of the 300-foot long main building, the flames raced in both directions along a conveyor belt loaded with furniture in process of manufacture and enveloped the entire building.

As employees in the yard out side ran to procure fire extinguishers and to pull fire alarm boxes, the sprinkler system in the huge plant set off an automatic alarm from Box 571, a general alarm call in Keene.

NOTE: Sprague & Carlton Furniture Co. was the first to be equipped within the city of Keene, with a fire alarm system, to trip the Master Fire Alarm Box. This would intern notify the fire department, without pulling the fire alarm box or by calling the fire department via phone.

General Alarm

The general alarm sounded at 12:52 and all available local apparatus and firemen responded. Fire Chief Walter R. Messer soon after ordered a second call, bringing apparatus from Marlboro, Troy, Winchester and West Swanzey. Mutual Aid System of Southwest New Hampshire and Tri-State Mutual Aid System, embracing Brattleboro, Vt., and Greenfield, Mass., also moved up apparatus

into the area to cover in for apparatus in nearby communities that had been sent to Keene.

Flames broke through the roof of the main building in a matter of minutes after the blaze was discovered and heavy thick smoke engulfed the factory yard, attracting hundreds to the scene and posing a traffic problem.

Very Hot Blaze

So hot was the fire that the flames burst through firewalls into the upholstery department occupying two floors in the center of the main building. Here tons of cotton and other upholstery material and unfinished furniture fed the flames, leaving this part of the plant a mass of twisted steel.

Water mains near the burning plant were found inadequate to supply the many hose lines and water was relayed by two stages of pumpers from the Ashuelot river, nearly a quarter-mile away. Hose lines blocked trains on the Boston & Main railroad for several hours and traffic on Highway Routes 9 and 12 had to detour through Swanzey.

Sprague & Carleton, Inc, view of warehouse, Avon Street. Photo by Allen

Save Warehouse

Firemen, using a wall of water, succeeded in keeping the blaze from the new warehouse wing adjoining the upholstery department, although the fire doors had melted under the intense heat of the flames.

They were also successful in keeping the fire from the large dry kilns and the hundreds of thousands of feet of lumber stored there.

Only a handful of employees were actually in the building when the fire started. Recapping the sequence of events, Philip McGinnis, in charge of the sealer-spray booth, near where the fire started, said that Marcus Bean, a fellow employee had just thrown the switch on the motor as the workmen were preparing to come back to work at the end of the lunch period. He said that there was a flash of flame as the short circuit arced, and that the sides of the spray booth, covered with dry sealer, immediately burst into flame. About 35 gallons of sealer in the booth helped feed the fire, he said.

Flee From Fire

As Bean and McGinnis fled from the path of the flames, they joined other employees Wesley Peats, Kenneth Fisher, Raymond Colburn and Joseph Hart in manning fire extinguishers, and they managed to save some pieces of completed furniture near the exit.

Several thousand dollars worth of finished furniture, and upholstery supplies were moved from the first floor of the upholstery department during the height of the fire. The salvaged stock was stored in a nearby shed which was protected by a water curtain.

The removal of stock and equipment was directed by Chester Pollicks, foreman of the upholstery room.

Minor Injuries

Several firemen suffered minor injuries and others were temporally overcome by smoke. Ladder man Rudolph Piche was blinded briefly by cinders spread by one of several hot air explosions during the fire. Auxiliary Fireman Robert Lincoln suffered a lacerated nose from falling glass.

During the fire, Cheshire county chapter, American Red Cross provided ambulance and canteen service for the firemen. The Salvation Army also had a canteen corps at the scene, serving the firefighters hot coffee, doughnuts and sandwiches.

State Police and many volunteers aided local police and their auxiliaries in handling traffic near West Street and Central Square during the fire.

Firefighters were still at the scene late last night, soaking down the ruins.

––––––––––

The next day the *Keene Evening Sentinel* continued with the fire as follows:

Sprague & Carleton Moving Fast to Resume Operations

Some Employees Will Shift to Milford Plant.

Sprague & Carlton Inc., dealt a staggering blow by the fire which swept through its furniture manufacturing plant on Avon Street Tuesday afternoon, is back in business today.

Even as the ruins of the factory still smoldered Wednesday company officials were making plans to resume many of their operations immediately.

Franklin S. Peart, company vice president in charge of production told the *Sentinel* that many of the company's 300 employees, will be transferred to the company's Milford plant and that others will be shifted to the S. & C. building on Marlboro Street where an upholstery operation has been carried on.

Plan Multiple Shifts

Peart said that space is available in the Marlboro Street building where manufacturing process can be started. Operations in the Milford factory, now employing about 200 persons, will be stepped up and put on a two and possibly three shift basis.

Although the fire precipitated many gave and serious problems into the laps of company officials they already have given some thought to rebuilding. No definite decisions will be reached, however, until Howard E. Page president and general manager of the company returns the later part of the week from Palm Beach, Fla. Where he was vacationing at the time of the fire.

Worried About Water

One of the problems giving grave concern and uppermost in minds of company executives, is whether or not any adequate city water supply can be secured, this factor having an important bearing on whether or not insurance companies will underwrite fire risks. The supply now available is insufficient to take care of existing sprinkler line requirements and provide water for fire fighting equipment. There are two supply lines to the plant, both six inch mains.

Company official are outspoken in their belief that the fire could have been stopped in its early phases had there been enough water.

Loss Not Determined Yet

Officials are loath to give out any figure as to the estimated loss resulting from the fire Mr. Peart said that all previously published figures were at their best rough estimates that there has not been time to yet make a through check. Company executives say however that the amount will be several hundred thousand.

The company is "well covered" by insurance, Mr. Peart said and it also carries insurance covering loss of business caused by the fire.

If everything proceeds according to plan the company expects to have its boiler room, which was undamaged, back in operation today. This will provide heat for the rough mill room which also escaped the flames. The company's large battery of modern dry kilns and material in process of curing was not damaged and no lumber in the yard was lost.

Machines Motors Checked

Damage to heavy equipment was confined to a comparatively small section of the plant. A check is not in progress on other machines and motors and it is believed that many of them will be found in running condition.

300 Foot Building

The two story main building, where the fire started is some 300 feet long, running north and south on the east side of Avon Street.

The bottom floor was devoted to furniture part cutting and shaping operations and was crammed with tons of hard wood, chair and table legs, chair seats and backs, and tabletops.

Finishing operations were conducted on the second floor. In this section parts were sprayed with wood sealers and various finishes. It is the most hazardous section of the plant due to the high flammability of the materials used.

Ceiling Holds

Despite the intense heat generated on the second floor where the roof finally collapsed, the first floor ceiling held in most places except for the extreme south end of the building where it was completely burned out along with a three story structure housing the upholstery and shipping departments.

The fire also destroyed the wooden stairwell and elevator shaft at the north end of the building and burned through the ceiling along the extreme west side of the building.

Much of the hard wood and the first floor was drenched with water and not stands sheathed in ice. More than six inches of water was drained out of the first floor area yesterday.

Still Burning

Small fires are still burning in the debris and two firemen on duty at the plant this morning had to wet down one area, which broke out this morning.

No "all out" signal has been sounded on the fire. Four firemen were on duty at the plant in shifts until 7 a.m. today when the standby staff was cut to two men.

Insurance inspectors were inspecting the plant this morning.

The main factory building was entirely gutted and the three story addition at the rear was completely demolished, even to the walls. All stock in process of manufacture is considered lost. Water poured into the new addition and pumps were operating to cleat this area of the factory yesterday.

Furniture Moved

Cartooned furniture valued at thousands of dollars was removed from the first floor section of a three story building at the south end of the plant before the building was devoured by flames.

The furniture was moved into an adjacent warehouse with the help of employees and bystanders. Trucks were loaded with upholstery stock from the warehouse but it was never necessary to clear out the warehouse during the course of the fire.

Employment Situation

Many employees were set to work Wednesday morning on salvage operations and putting machinery not destroyed by fire back into shape.

In speaking of the employment situation Mr. Peart said "the best help we can give our employees is to get them back to work as soon as possible." He said that employees will be notified as quickly as possible concerning the availability of work at Milford and the Marlboro Street plant.

Many Offers of Help

Mr. Peart said that the company is most appreciative of the many offers of assistance it has received from business firms and friends.

Edward Ellingwood, executive vice president of the Keene Regional Industrial Foundation, was in touch with Mr. Peart Tuesday afternoon and stands ready to assist in what ever way is possible.

Sprague & Carlton has a big backlog of orders and secured a large volume of new business at the recent furniture show in Chicago. The company's annual payroll is well over a million dollars.

Sidelights on the Big Fire

Except for a few scratches, no firemen were seriously injured fighting the fire.

Fire Chief Messer said a number of men became sick as a result of excessive smoke inhalation, but quickly recovered.

Sentinel Photographer Jack Teehan took 155 pictures at the scene of the fire Tuesday and Wednesday. Forty 35 mm. negatives were selected for printing and the best eight were used for publication.

West Keene was isolated by the big fire. Traffic detours set up by police routed through traffic through Swanzey and around the Five Mile Drive via Maple Ave.

Shortly after 5 p.m. in West Street traffic was backed up to Central Square. One way traffic was permitted on West Street in a westerly direction, police said.

Keene firemen almost "lost" a ladder at the fire. The ladder used early in the fire to check conditions in the finishing department were the fire started was left untended outside the building as the smoke eaters moved to another location. It was "rescued" just in time as tongues of flame licked out a window near the ladder.

Former Mayor Laurence M. Pickett and Councilman George E. Fish were among the firemen battling the flames.

———

NOTE: Due to the water problem during the fire at Sprague & Carlton a Special Session was called to talk the situation over. From the *Keene Evening Sentinel*:

Water Supply Probe Starts

A special meeting was called here this morning by Mayor J. Alfred Dennis. in an effort to determine whether the city water system was adequate to meet the needs of the disastrous Sprague & Carlton fire Tuesday and if not what steps can be taken to remedy the situation.

Even before the hour of the meeting was set Superintendent of Public Works George E. Hawkins said the present city water system is adequate only to meet normal needs and to fight house fires.

Hawkins said the present system can supply enough to feed four hose lines the exact number tied into the system Tuesday but that 30 hole lines are required to fight a "conflagration" similar to the Sprague & Carlton fire.

When firemen arrived at the scene of the Avon Street Fire Tuesday they found the plant sprinklers system had been actuated in areas where the temperature had gone high enough to start water flowing.

Find Pressure Low

Chief Messer said as soon as firemen connect4d a hose to an Avon Street hydrant they found the pressure was insufficient, due to the sprinkler system demand. Firemen even tried a smaller hose in an effort to build up the stream.

It was immediately apparent that four hoses had to be obtained from hydrants away from Avon Street where the water main was only six inches in diameter.

Firemen ran hose out to West Street hydrants which, according to Superintendent of Public Works Hawkins, are fed by an eight-inch main.

Pump From River

Four hoses were laid in this manner and an additional four lines were laid to the Ashuelot River, using pumpers to make a total of eight hose lines on the fire.

In Chief Messer's words "There was plenty of water but not enough pressure". In other words, water will come through an eight inch pipe only so fast, providing a limited amount of pressure. A 20 inch main would have provided more pressure for example.

Walls No Protection

Messer also disclosed that none of the firewalls in the furniture plant "functioned as firewalls". This was due to the fact that the walls had been breached with holes make, in at least one instance, for a conveyor belt.

The chief said legislation in the state is inadequate to properly control such procedures.

Chief Messer said that if he had had a 12-inch main, and enough hydrants, he might have been able to check the fire on the fire side of some fire walls.

The firefighter were able to keep the fire away form the warehouse at the southwest end of the plant as the fire door at the east end of the building, aided by water from hoses, withstood the onslaught of heat.

Sprague & Carlton had a sprinkler system throughout the plant and an automatic alarm system. Five automatic devices were located on sprinkler risers, any one of which would trip the alarm for Box 571 at the fire station.

Four of the fire automatic alarms had been tripped, an investigation showed after the fire, and three of six manually operated alarms were tripped presumably by employees.

Chief Messer said the sprinkler system was not actuated on the first floor of the main building, although the heart of the fire, at the outset, was on the floor above. The heat on the first floor never reached the point required to set off the system.

Messer also pointed out that a sprinkler system becomes useless as soon as a falling girder breaks a sprinkler line.

Some 100 firemen battled the blaze, including companies form Marlboro, Winchester, Troy and West Swanzey.

"Now is the time to really do something." Superintendent of Public Works George E. Hawkins exclaimed this morning.

Recommendations Were Made

Hawkins said that he made recommendations in 1946, and the Boston engineering firm of Camp Dresser & McKee, made similar recommendations a few years later, which would have provided adequate pressure at the fire Tuesday.

He said a main trunk line should traverse the city and the city should build a 5,000,000 gallon storage reservoir on West Hill which could be supplied by the gravel packed well in West Keene.

Hawkins said he believed a five million gallon reserve would cover any firefighting requirement in the foreseeable future.

Results of Meeting

A study of the city's water system was initiated following the meeting.

Dennis met with Fire Chief Walter R. Messer, Superintendent of Public Works George E. Hawkins, Councilman Karl R. Beedle, chairman of the Council's fire department committee, and Joseph R. Bruce, foreman of the water department.

Avon Street, Main entrance in the center of the main building, shown fully ablaze. Photo by Allen.

Twisted Tangle of metal and ice marks the spot where flames roared from main building into the upholstery section of Sprague & Carleton, Keene furniture factory, Tuesday when firemen could not get enough water. Photo by Allen.

A Demon Called Fire

Pictured is Box 571 of Sprague and Carleton chair factory. This was the first business within the City of Keene to put a Master Box on its building. There was confusion as you read the above article Misreading Box Number Sends Fire Department Apparatus To Wrong Box. Since 1935 other companies added Master Boxes to their buildings, which have been activated by the sprinkler system going off when a sprinkler head fusible link melted from heat tripping the box. Picture by Steven Goldsmith.

Reported by the *Keene Evening Sentinel* on April 4th, 1956:

"FIRE"

Early Morning Fire Causes Estimated Loss of $50,000 In Wayside Furniture Store

Flames Make Big Headway before Alarm

Fire, which was probably caused by a defective gas heater, damaged furniture; appliances and the building of the Plotkin's Wayside Furniture Store located at the junction of Routes 9 and 12 early this morning. The estimated loss is more than $50,000.

Keene firemen responded to a telephoned summons at 6:20 a.m. and seven trucks from the Keene station and one from West Swanzey went to the scene.

The fire had consumed much of the interior of the insulated building before the alarm was sounded. Fire Chief Walter R. Messer said. Foggy weather conditions probably concealed the fire from being discovered sooner.

Thick billowing smoke rolled out of the building delaying attempts at entry by firemen.

The firefighter smashed windows and chopped holes in the roof to help clear the air and got into the front section of the building about two hours after the fire started.

Called Total Loss

The property, owned jointly by Charles Sherman and Sylvia Plotkin of Athol, Mass was described as a total loss.

No one was in the building at the time of the fire.

Manager of the store Richard L. Lane of North Swanzey.

One of the owners Charles Plotkin, was notified and arrived in Keene from Athol about 10 o'clock. Sherman and Sylvia Plotkin, on their way to a furniture show, were reached in Worcester, Mass., and arrived in Keene about 11 o'clock. Owners and manager were in conference with insurance adjusters following the fire.

Water Pressure Reasonable

Water pressure for fighting the fire was described by Chief Walter Messer as reasonable, considering the long hose lines used. The all out was officially out at 10:30 o'clock.

The furniture and appliances store has been operated by the Plotkins since January 1, following purchase from Jack P. Magner formerly of Keene. The business was known as Parker Pines Wayside Furniture, Inc. under it former ownership.

No Plans Yet

The Plotkins could immediately express no plans as to reestablishment of the business, either in its present location or elsewhere in Keene. The local store employed five persons, including the manager.

Marlboro Covers

A truck from the Marlboro Fire Department covered the Keene station during the furniture store fire and the Keene department responded to a chimney fire at the home of Guy Thompson 333 West street at 8:03 a.m.

Keene firemen last night responded to alarm for fire caused by a flooded oil burner at the home of Laurence Marcus, 76 Island Street, at 8:45 p.m.

————

Plotkin Fire, Keene firemen pour water through holes in the roof of the Plotkin Wayside Furniture store at the junction of Park Ave. & Arch St, early this morning as flames caused damage estimated at $50,000. A defective gas heater was believed responsible. Photo by Jack Teehan.

Reported by the *Keene Evening Sentinel* on April 9th, 1956:

"FIRE"

Firemen Called For Truck Fire

Keene firemen responded to a fire in the body of a pickup truck owned by M. E. Prouis of Keene which was parked near the Cheshire National Bank Saturday morning at 11:48. The fire was caused by hot ashes on other rubbish, fireman said.

On Sunday firemen responded to a call for a stove pipe fire at the home of Eli Chabot on 109 Island Ave, at 7:34 a. m. Another fire at the home of Eli Bouffard, 39 Colorado Street was responded to at 4:37 p. m. caused by a flooded oil burner.

A fire in a wastebasket, started when cigarette ashes were dumped into the basket, was extinguished at the home of Joseph Cristiano, 171 Court Street at 9:25 this morning.

————

Reported by the *Keene Evening Sentinel* on April 13th, 1956:

"STORY"

Chief Messer Elected Head Of Chief Club

Fire Chief Walter R. Messer of Keene was elected president of the NH Fire Chiefs Club last night when about 60 persons attended the annual meeting at the Congregational Church in New Ipswich.

Attending from Keene in addition to Chief Messer were City Manager Donald E. Chick, Fire Captain Elton Britton, Robert Callahan and Walter Royal.

————

Reported by the *Keene Evening Sentinel* on April 25th, 1956:

"FIRE"

Fire Damages Grocery Store On Church Street

A fire of undetermined origin did considerable damage to the interior of Fairbanks Handy Shop, a grocery store at 217 Church Street, early this morning.

The fire started in the back part of the store, which was owned and operated by Arnold E. Patnaude of 168 Washington Street.

Keene fire department firemen arrived on the scene shortly after an alarm was telephoned in at 5:37 a.m. by Leo Rose Sr. and Louis Trombley of 215 Church Street who saw the smoke about the same time.

The building, which is owned by Phileas Fontain of 90 Valley Street, was burned in the back storage room and in the attic. An unofficial preliminary estimate of the building damage was set at $4,000.

The Keene fire department responded to an alarm for a space heater fire at 16 Pine Street belonging to Clifford Reynolds at 8:06 p.m. Tuesday.

The Keene Department following an alarm at 11:40 a.m. today extinguished a grass fire, which started from an incinerator at the home of George Goodrich, 8 Crescent Street.

————

Reported by the *Keene Evening Sentinel* on May 3rd, 1956.:

"STORY"

County's Civil Defense Communications Setup Does Good Job in Test

A statewide Civil Defense communications test alert Wednesday was responded to by all but one town in Cheshire County. Director Casper C. Bemis Jr. county director, said. The county towns were checked within a period of seven minutes after the red alert sounded at 1:33 o'clock Wednesday afternoon.

Keene CD Director Walter R. Messer reported that the alert went off better here than previously and added that there is still room for improvement.

Although stopping off traffic or taking shelter generally were not enforced, an awareness of the red alert which was signaled from both the fire station and the city high way garage was noted downtown where pedestrians took cover in the stores and doorways and waited till the all clear was given.

Drills held in Schools

All schools of the city which were alerted through the School Department by Chief Messer, cooperated in the alert by carrying out prescribed drills which required pupils to take cover at predetermined locations.

Among units contacted were Richard Palmer, refugee committee; Radio Station WKNE; Weldon Stanford, communications officer; Elliot Community Hospital, medical teams; Red Cross disaster teams, the Public Works Department rescue and evacuation work; Health Officer, Evan C. White, biological control; the municipal Airport, and the City Police department.

The alert was received at the police station from Manchester at 1:30 and it was 1:40 when county towns had received the alert.

No Answer in Marlow

Marlow was the lone town where the telephone was not answered.

The "all clear" whistle was sounded at 2:04 p.m. by three long evenly spaced blasts.

Messer said there were complaints in certain areas that the signals were not heard, but he said that the new whistle at the city garage aided in a definite improvement over previous alerts.

————

Reported by the *Keene Evening Sentinel* on May 9th, 1956:

"FIRE"

Fire From Car Spreads to Grass

Fire burned out the inside of a junked car and about a half acre of grass at the Forsyth Auto Company establishment at 451 Winchester Street Tuesday afternoon.

The Keene fire department responded to the alarm for the fire at 4:41 p.m. The fire was caused when someone was cutting a fender from a junk auto with a welding torch. Owner of the property is Morris Forsyth.

Fireman responded to an alarm for a grass fire on land of Forrest I. Carey on Damon Court at 12:47 p.m.

———

Reported by the *Keene Evening Sentinel* on May 19th, 1956:

"FIRE"

Fire Destroys 2-Car Garage In West Keene

A two-car garage belonging to Charles Grace of 310 Park Ave. was destroyed by fire Friday afternoon. The loss was estimated at about $1,300.

Firemen responded to an alarm shortly following detection of the fire by Mrs. Cora Grace, 79 mother of the property owner, around 3:30 p.m., Grace's wife telephoned in an alarm and the fire box in the vicinity was pulled by two men of the Public Service Company.

Four fire pieces made quick work of the fire and kept it from spreading to the house which two families live. Mr. and Mrs. Clayton Gray and three children, who live in the upstairs apartment, were away when the alarm was sounded.

Some garden tools were stored in the garage, but there was no car at the time of the fire. Origin of the fire is not known.

———

Reported by the *Keene Evening Sentinel* on June 5th, 1956:

"FIRE"

Fire Damages Ice Creamery, Garage Office

Fire of undetermined origin burned out the interior of Richard's Ice Creamery and did considerable damage to the service station office of Chiovitti's Garage at 394 Washington Street early this morning.

The damage estimated unofficially at $6,000 included an ice cream storage plant and other restaurant fixtures. Fire, smoke and water also damaged office fixtures in the garage.

Fire Chief Walter R. Messer said that the fire originated in the top part of the southwest corner of the restaurant and spread down through the partitions and floors.

Firemen and equipment of the Keene fire department responded to the alarm, which was pulled in at Box 27 on Washington street and Washington Ave. about 3:57 a.m. The all out was sounded at 5 a.m.

The fire was discovered and the alarm was pulled by a Main couple Mr. and Mrs. Douglas Anner, of Monmouth, Main who had stopped nearby in their car to rest and noticed the smoke coming from the building.

The ice creamery and garage is owned by Chiovitti Enterprises, Inc., whose president is Angelo Chiovitti, Richard Chiovitti, a son and Mrs. Glady's Chovitti, wife of Angelo and mother of Richard, operated the restaurant.

———

Reported by the *Keene Evening Sentinel* on June 12th, 1956:

"STORY"

Underwriters Making Fire Flow Tests Here

The first complete fire flow test made here by the NH Board of Underwriters since 1950 will be completed within the next 10 days.

Requested by the City Council as an aid in making a decision on recommended improvements to the city water system, the tests will be made by Walter M. Fife, a NH Board of Underwriters engineer.

One expected result will be to show the effect of improvements to the water system since 1950.

Another feature will be to show what effect the turning on of the Goose Pond water supply would have had on water pressure in the vicinity of the Sprague & Carleton Inc., plant partially destroyed in a fire Feb. 21. The auxilary supply was not used during the fire.

Fife tested four hydrants Monday but no further tests are scheduled this week due to a conflict of commitments involving both Fife and Fire Chief Walter R. Messer.

The Board of Underwriters engineer will return next Monday June 18th, and is expected to complete the tests within two or three days.

Working with Fife and Chief Messer on the tests is Joseph R. Bruce, head of the city water department.

Fire Insurance Rates in Keene Second Lowest

Keene's fire insurance rating, second to that of Manchester which is the lowest in the state, is the same as that of Nashua which has a bigger fire department and crew that Keene. Charles W. Clark, insurance salesman revealed at a meeting of Keene Rotary Club Monday at Wildey Hall.

He attributed the low rate to the efficiency of the Keene Fire department. The statement came at the conclusion of an explanation of the Southwestern NH Fire Mutual Aid System by the Keene Fire Chief Walter R. Messer and Fireman Robert C. Callahan, secretary-treasure of the system.

The fire mutual aid system was described as one whereby 33 communities in this area are able to exchange firemen and equipment in emergencies without leaving any station or community inadequately protected.

The Keene Fire Department is the dispatch base fore the system, and Keene and four other departments of the system are also members of the Tri-State Fire Mutual Aid System whose dispatch base is Greenfield, Mass.

The preliminary organization of the system required inventories of equipment and resources of individual departments cooperating in the system, and company has a lost of five possible towns to call, enumerated in terms of priority.

Control Equipment

Control of equipment from station to station is by the dispatch station with a system of a pegboard and colored pegs, which have a quantitative meaning. The pegs are switched from one spot to another as fire trucks and equipment are sent to corresponding communities in the system.

The fire mutual aid system eliminates prohibitively expensive charges of independent assistance. The departments make no charges to the community affected.

The fire mutual aid system will be brought to further efficiency with the advent of a radio system.

Community County and Civil Defense funds will pay for the system Callahan indicated. The radio system will be used in CD and other community emergencies as well as fires, and trucks will be equipped with apparatus with which to readily contact the dispatch station by telephone

Features Cited

A number of features of the fire departments in the mutual aid system were brought out in a question and-answer session conducted by Chief Messer, among them:

Existing agreements between fire departments would continue under the fire mutual aid system.

A "pilot" at a strategic spot directs firemen of the visiting department to the town into which it comes to assist.

Community fire departments fight forest fires only as an emergency, and withdraw to protect real estate property. The State Forest Fire service has this responsibility.

Keene's volunteer or call firemen receive $150 a year from the city and many of them are not paid for time away from their regular jobs.

There are 5,500 deficiency points on which the Board of Fire Underwriters determines insurance rates, and 1,500 of them are dependent on the efficiency of the community's fire department.

———

Reported by the *Keene Evening Sentinel* on June 29th, 1956:

"STORY"

Jet Damage Estimated May Be $9,000

The unofficial damage estimated to the T33 Air National Guard Jet-trainer which came to rest off the runway of Keene Airport Wednesday night was "way off", according to Capt. William Kordas maintenance officer of the 133d Fighter Squadron who is supervising removal of the plan to Grenier AFB, Manchester.

An unofficial estimate given the *Sentinel* Thursday was put at $250,000.

"The plane itself only costs $160,000'" Capt. Kerdas said. He added that repairs would run between $8,000 and $9,000.

The plane whose nose will be removed, will be transported on a flatbed trailer under State and Air Police escort about 4 a.m. Saturday.

———

Landed at wrong field: Mechanics today were dismantling the T33 jet Trainer, the landing gear of which was extensively damaged when its pilot, Col Clayton E. Hughes of Air Force Headquarters, Pentagon, put his plane down at the Keene Airport Wednesday night by mistake. The Shop went off the runway. Photo by Granite State Studio.

Reported by the *Keene Evening Sentinel* on July 13th, 1956:

"FIRE"

Restaurant Fire Causes $10,000 Loss in Block

Fire which started from an overheated fryolator in the kitchen at the rear end of Libbares Spa. At 26 Washington Street about 6 p.m. last night jumped through a ventilator fan in a window and spread to an open shed and adjoining storage shed, doing smoke and water damage estimated at around $10,000 by George Libbares.

Four apartments in the block occupied by 15 persons and two other business, were damaged with smoke.

Firemen saw the blaze from the fire station, a short distance away, and Box 22 was sounded. Engines 1 and 2 and Ladder 2 and Squad 1 responded. Firemen used gas masks to enter the front of the restaurant.

Application of fog effectively contained the fire to the kitchen of the four-story block's restaurant and damage to a storage room adjoining the garage of Richards Motors was of smoke and water.

No one was in the kitchen when the fire started, but George Libbares, who with his brother Fred L. (Fortes J.) Libbares, owns the restaurant discovered the flame and turned off the heat of the fryolator.

A number of patrons were driven from the restaurant by the fire and residents of apartments overhead got out of the building safely.

Residential apartments in the building are those of families of Robert Burbank and Daniel R. MacLean. Office buildings were those of J. J. Viette Construction Co. and Scott Lumber & Supply Co.

Reported by the *Keene Evening Sentinel* on August 3rd, 1956:

"FIRE"

Firemen Called For Roof Blaze

Sparks from welding torch-ignited sawdust on the roof of the shipping room of Sprague & Carleton Inc. off Avon Street Thursday afternoon.

The Keene Fire Department responded to the alarm at 3:45 o'clock and the fire was quickly extinguished.

Firemen also extinguished a brush fire on land near the Pako Park development between Court and Armory Streets at 8:43 o'clock last night.

Reported by the *Keene Evening Sentinel* on October 6th, 1956:

"STORY"

Fire Prevention Week Program Is Announced

A schedule of events for Fire Prevention Week Oct 7-13, has been announced by Fire Chief Walter R. Messer and other city officials, as follows:

Rubbish pickup days in the city. Tuesday, Wednesday and Thursday. Fire Drills at all schools of the Union School District Wednesday morning and afternoon.

Thursday, Inspection Day, with a firemen's parade, maneuvers, and annual banquet in the afternoon and the Firemen's benefit ball in the evening.

The semi-annual citywide rubbish pickup is being conducted by the Public Works Department to give residents an opportunity to rid their homes of unwanted rubbish which might also prevent a fire hazard.

Supt. George E. Hawkins has announced the following schedule:

Tuesday Marlboro Street and north of Marlboro street to and including Gilsum Street.

Wednesday-All territory between Gilsum and West Street, also Arlington Ave.

Thursday-All territory between West and Marlboro Streets.

School fire drills on Wednesday morning and afternoon will give students an opportunity to view pieces of fire equipment. Chief Messer will direct demonstrations and educational phases for the benefit of the children.

On Thursday, Inspection Day-a time-honored annual occasion of the fire department-the Keene department personnel and trucks will parade beginning at 1:30 p.m. from Central Square down Main Street to Wyman Way and return.

At City Hall the parade will be reviewed by members of the City Council, mayor J. Alfred Dennis and City manager Donald E. Chick.

The fire station will be open for inspection by council members and city officials following the parade.

A demonstration of fire-fighting equipment will be conducted on the east side of Central Square from 2:30 to 4 p.m. Thursday at which time the public will be able to see fire men lay lines of hose and shoot water at a target.

Several trucks will take part in the demonstration. Traffic flow around the Square will be handled in as nearly normal a manner as possible, Police Chief William T. Bridgham said. Plans are to route northbound traffic if necessary from main to Roxbury to Spring to Washington Street.

Banquet Planned

A banquet prepared by the Ladies Auxiliary of the Fire Department will be served to the firemen and quests at 5:30 p.m. at the fire hall.

The Firemen's Ball the annual benefit for the Firemen's Relief Association will take place at the State Armory from 8 p.m. to 12 midnight, with a concert and dance by the recording orchestra of Ted Herbert.

A Grand march will be part of the ball. Tickets may be procured from any of the firemen.

Reported by the *Keene Evening Sentinel* on October 10th, 1956 by Don Gross:

"STORY"

Keene Chief Wants Special Group Named

Fire Chief Walter R. Messer in a Fire Prevention Week interview with Sentinel reviewed progress, which the Keene fire department has made during his 10 years as chief and revealed some of the improvements he would like to see, made in the future.

Messer said that he would like to see:

1. An active fire prevention committee which would work along the same lines as the planning board.
2. A house to house inspection by the department.
3. The Chief, who was appointed in 1946 to succeed Chief Eugene B. Riley, touched on the following improvements, which have been made:
4. Adoption of the oil burner ordinance by the city.
5. Coordination of radio with police department.
6. Institution of county area and interstate fire mutual aid.
7. Use of fog, which takes less water and cools fire more rapidly.
8. Addition to the number of permanent fire roster from eight men to 13 men.
9. Addition of the power wagon to the department equipment.

Wants Committee

Messer indicated that he will suggest the fire prevention committee to the mayor, with the hope that it will become a reality sometime next year.

"This committee could give us a lot of good ideas," he said. The members would be Keene residents, not necessarily connected with the fire department.

Messer said that limited personnel makes it impossible for the department to make an annual house to house inspection with the idea of eliminating fire hazards. He said that added personnel could make the precautionary measure a reality.

At present, with the 13 permanent fire crew and chief, the number of men on duty at one time is limited to six, which he said is needed in case of fire.

Served as Call Fireman

Chief Messer's fire experience began in 1926 when he became a call fireman.

In 1930, he became a garage owner and operator in Long Island, NY. And rejoined the Keene Fire Department in 1935 as a call fireman. He became a permanent man in 1941, and was appointed chief in 1946.

He attended the Civil Defense Fire School at Edgewood Arsenal, MD. in Dec 1941.

He is president of the NH. Fire Chiefs Club, a director and past president of the New England Division of International Association of Fire Chiefs, a past president of both Tri-State and Southwestern New Hampshire Fire mutual aid System, and is presently director of civil Defense for Keene.

Reported by the *Keene Evening Sentinel* on October 13th, 1956:

"STORY"

Firemen Stage Demonstration For the Public

Firemen's Inspection Day Thursday meant many things to many persons. Events included a parade of men and equipment to the music of the Keene High School band an inspection of the fire station by city councilmen and officials and a demonstration of fire equipment on the East Side of Central Square.

If the firemen's chests seemed more expanded than usual in their flashy blue uniforms, their pride was well justified.

A clear, cool autumn day helped to attract persons from all walks of life, schoolboys on bikes, farther with two-year-olds astride their shoulders, and old timers who could make some drastic comparisons between present day equipment and that of only a few years ago.

Fire Chief Messer led the parade of firemen and trucks.

In demonstrations, ladders were erected at the four story Bridgman Block and firemen descended from windows with safety slings.

Firemen from the three companies knocked thrown a target with water, an event that was not officially timed, evidently to allow for friendly argument.

Deluge Guns demonstrated the power and effectiveness of regular water and fog spray nozzles.

At their dinner at the firehouse later, firemen were hosts to city councilmen and other city officials. The dinner was prepared and served by the Ladies Auxiliary of the Firemen's Relief Association.

Festivities culminated with the Firemen's Ball at the State Armory, with music by Ted Herbert's recording orchestra.

Reported by the *Keene Evening Sentinel* on October 17th, 1956:

"FIRE"

Fireman Hurt Early Today in Garage Fire

A Keene fireman suffered a foot injury early this morning in a fire that leveled a garage and the ell of a house owned by Abraham Cohen of 185 Appleton Street. Cohen estimated loss at $1,000.

Lawrence Thompson, 35 was treated at Elliot Community Hospital at 6 a.m. for a puncture wound in the right foot, which he suffered at the fire. He was released from the hospital following treatment.

The fire and the front windshield was cracked charred the paint on the front end of a car belonging to Clifford Blanchard, a boarder at the address.

Machinery Lost

The fire destroyed a piece of farm machinery situated in the ell adjacent to the garage and a quantity of lime. In the garage two children's bicycles and two auto mobile tires were destroyed.

The blaze was discovered about 4 a.m. by Blanchard, who with his three children boards with Mrs. Daisy Bailey at the home.

He awoke around 3:30 a.m. and smelled burning rubber but could not determine from where it was coming.

————

Reported by the *Keene Evening Sentinel* on November 19th, 1956:

"FIRE"

$5,000 Fire Destroys Garage on Surry Road

A father of 10 watched his part time garage business go up in flame this morning on the Surry Road because it was too far from the last water main to get enough water to the fire.

George Guillet who works as a machinist at Burr & Nichols Co. said that the loss of the garage tools and equipment and two vehicles would run in excess of $5,000.

Firemen of the Keene fire department were at the scene shortly after an alarm was telephoned in about 8:30 and poured 1,100 gallons of water in vain effort to save the wood frame building, which is adjacent to Guillet's residence.

Surry Stands By

A truck and firemen of the Surry fire department stood by with water to safeguard the home, while Keene's 800 gallon Squad 2 truck shuttled back and forth from the last hydrant near Harry F. Knight's home on the Surry Road.

A pickup truck which Guillet had planned to work on and a heavy farm vehicle were removed from the area of the fire, but a 1948 beach wagon, his property, and a 1941 Ford sedan went with the flames.

The beach wagon was inside the building and the sedan was parked in the rear of the building.

Cause of the fire was not immediately determined. Guillet said one of his six sons Ivan 15 had built a wood fire in a drum stove in the rear of the garage about 7:40 a.m. and had gone back into the house.

Spotted From Car

The next thing he knew, Ivan said smoke was pouring from the building.

Elliot Cummings of Surry, who saw the fire as his car passed the house, called the Keene fire department and alarmed the Surry department of which he is a member.

Guillet said he first knew of the fire when he returned from Keene where he had gone for parts, about 8:30.

The Surry volunteers ran a line of hose from the Ashuelot river and gave aid with a portable pump.

Included in the fire loss, Guillet said were $1,500 worth of hand tools. Two welding tanks exploded in the flames but no one was injured. A quantity of lumber stacked alongside the garage was also lost.

Guillet bitterly recounted that three petitions had been circulated by residents in the area since 1950 in an effort to get the water main extended to the neighborhood.

Thwarted Each Time

Each time he said, they had been thwarted because the amount each resident would have to put up to bring the water main in was more that he could afford

"The city wanted $2,000 apiece from each resident" he said. "We just couldn't put up the money."

The Keene department dispatched a fire truck to Surry under the fire mutual aid system and West Swanzey covered in with a truck at the Keene station.

The firemen were still standing by at 10 o'clock this morning.

The building is covered by some insurance. Guillet said but he indicated that the vehicles and tools and equipment would be a total loss.

Guillet came to Keene from a little Vermont town where he had operated a garage and found supporting his family a difficult proposition.

––––––––

Fire Takes Garage: Volunteers help George Guillet of Surry Rd. remove a pickup truck from the fire, which destroyed his garage business Saturday morning. A beach Wagon and a sedan were destroyed in the fire, which burned property valued at $5,000. Photo by Gross.

Reported by the *Keene Evening Sentinel* on November 21st, 1956:

"FIRE"

Plant Firemen Hold Down Putnam Fire

Quick work by volunteer plant firemen and safety devices kept a flash fire at the F. A. Putnam Mfg. Co. division of Markem Machine Co. at 150 Congress Street from getting out of hand Tuesday at 4:51 p.m.

The fire started after a kettle in which varnish had been cooking boiled over. The area is hooded for safety, and the room is sectioned off to safeguard against fire and explosion.

The room was immediately closed off by a fire gate and volunteer firemen under the direction of Bob Goodale used fire extinguishers in addition to a number of sprinkler heads which went off.

The Keene Fire Department responded with four trucks. The fire was extinguished on their arrival.

Damage was estimated in excess of $200, and was mostly caused by water.

Cause of the fire was not immediately ascertained.

––––––––

Reported by the *Keene Evening Sentinel* on December 3rd, 1956:

"FIRE"

Girl Is Quick To Spot Fire

Quick action by Kathleen N. Schneider, 10 a fifth grade student at the Franklin School, brought the local Fire Department on the run this morning about 8:30 to extinguish a chimney blaze at a three story apartment building on the corner of Brook and beach Streets.

According to Fire Chief Walter Messer the little girl daughter of Mr. and Mrs. Louis N. Schneider was on her way to school when she noticed flames erupting from the chimney and immediately pulled the handle on a nearby fire alarm box.

Chief Messer said a truck was quickly dispatched to the scene and the fire brought under control. The building was owned by John Smith.

––––––––

1957

Reported by the *Keene Evening Sentinel* on January 5th, 1957 by Don Gross:

"FIRE"

$9,000 Fires Hit Two Keene Homes

Fire struck two Keene homes Thursday afternoon causing an estimated total damage of $9,000.

The first fire occurred around 12:30 at the home of Alton O. Weagle, 13 May Ave. when his father, Jason 75 discovered the kitchen walls ablaze.

The second alarm occurred shortly before 4 o'clock at the home of James F. Fleming 27 Colby Street when Mrs. Fleming, who was in the living room with her three small children when she heard the crackling of flames in the living room closet.

Time Lost

At the Wagle fire some minutes were lost when according to Fire Chief Walter R. Messer, two inexperienced volunteer helpers tried to turn the water on at a hydrant from Washington Street and abandoned the effort when the believed the hydrant was frozen.

Water Supt. Joseph Bruce who arrived at the scene while the fire fighting was in progress told a Sentinel reporter the hydrant definitely was not frozen, and said he had been able to get water from the hydrant without difficulty.

He indicated that the fault was in leaving the job to inexperienced men.

A hose was run from another hydrant at Giffin Street and water was pumped from nearby Beaver Brook following expenditure of the 300 gallon tank on the department's Engine 1.

Furnishings Gone

The six-room one-story wooden frame house was destroyed along with all the house furnishings on which no immediate evaluation could be made.

The 75-year old father was sitting in the living room of the Weagle home shortly before he found the adjacent kitchen wall in flames.

He was burned about the forehead, hair and eyebrows. He was alone in the house at the time.

Residents of the home were Alton O. Weagle, his wife and two teenage children, who were in school at the time of the fire. Booth Alton and his wife were working.

Mrs. Nina Smith, Alton's mother of Groveton, who was visiting the family was shopping.

Chief Messer said the fire apparently started near a smokepipe in the kitchen Weagle said his kitchen stove had been recently cleaned and was in good working order.

Checked Dailey

He expressed consternation at the inability of the fire department to get water from the Washington Street hydrant prior to learning that the cause was not attributed to a freeze as had been thought before Bruce made an inspection.

City Manager Donald E. Chick said "daily checks are made to detect frozen hydrants except on Saturdays and Sundays. It's a very important procedure."

Four men are assigned to the work; two work in outlying sections out of a pickup truck and two cover the business district and nearby residential areas on foot.

Any hydrant found to be frozen are thawed out with steam. Freezing is usually caused by ground water seepage, Chick said.

Fire In Closet

The Fleming fire originated in a two door clothes closet in the living room of the home in which they have been residents about a year.

The home is a new Cape Cod type built by Pako Homes. Firemen were successful in covering furnishings in a number of the rooms. Damage to bedrooms, ceilings and closet interiors was extensive.

Total damage estimate given by Chief Messer was $4,000. He said the cause of the fire had not been determined.

The fire department was notified by telephone when Mrs. Fleming took her three children Katherine age three months, Bryan, 2 and Mark, 5 to a neighbors house.

Two other children had not arrived home from school at the time of the alarm. Her husband a telephone company worker was notified of the fire while on duty.

────────

Home Burns: The six-room home of Alton O. Weagle at 13 May Ave., was destroyed by fire Thursday afternoon with a damage estimated at $5,000. Photo taken by Gross.

Reported by the *Keene Evening Sentinel* on January 9th, 1957:

"STORY"

Family Highly Praises Keene Fire Department

James F. Fleming, whole home at 27 Colby Street suffered $4,000 damages by fire last Friday, had high praises yesterday for Fire Chief Walter R. Messer and his department.

Fleming, who is presently living in a model Pako Home with his wife and two of his five children, had warm praise for a lot of other persons, too.

Fleming contacted the Sentinel Monday night following publication of criticisms by Alton O. Weagle for what Weagle described as the "Slipshod" method in which a $5,000 fire at his home at 13 May Ave. was handled.

Weagle claims that the fire at his house which occurred earlier Friday, was hampered when 30 minutes ensured before hydrant water was put to the burning home.

Fire Confined

Fleming told the Sentinel that the fire department took care of the fire at his home in good shape. The fire was confined to the bedroom and closet where it apparently began, he pointed out.

He praised the way the fire department cleaned up after the fire and added that he was impressed with the firemen's overall courtesy and consideration.

In fact, Fleming told the Sentinel, he was overwhelmed with the way "people have helped us" with furniture, furnishings, loans and outright gifts.

He spoke highly of Chief Messer, who Weagle also described as "one of the best fire chiefs in the state."

Praises Paquette

Another person Fleming couldn't praise too highly was Armand Paquette, who immediately set the family up in the model Pako Home.

Chief Messer indicated that an additional man is being asked in this year's budget to supplement his 13-man permanent firefighting force.

The chief has previously stated that added permanent personnel might have averted the type of delay experienced in the Weagle fire.

————

Reported by the *Keene Evening Sentinel* on January 12th, 1957:

"STORY"

Samaritans, and the Fire Budget

The fire last week at the home of Alton O. Weagle, 13 May Ave., was unfortunate in more ways than the fact that it destroyed the home of a family of five.

A considerable amount of time was lost when volunteer helpers tried to turn on the water at a hydrant on Washington Street, and abandoned it when they believed the hydrant to be frozen. Water was eventually pumped from a hydrant on Giffin Street and from Beaver Brook.

A Check by the water department superintendent, however, revealed that the hydrant had not been frozen after all.

There are precious few o his fellow citizens who do not sympathize with Mr. Weagle in the loss of his home, and when he voiced criticism of the method in which the operation was handled, he was simply making use of his inalienable right to publicly express his opinion.

We're happy, however, that he saw fit to temper his comments with a good word for Fire Chief Walter Messer, whom, we believe is a good chief.

The most important point that Mr. Weagle made, however, was when he asked, "If the regular (fire) department is shorthanded, why don't they get more men?"

The fact is, the chief is asking for the salary of an additional man in this year's budget. The department is presently a 13 man permanent force. Obviously, all of these men can't be on duty all the time. Like all fire departments, they must work in shifts. And like all small fire departments the Keene force must depend to some extent upon auxiliary firemen, and volunteers.

We hope that Chief Messer will be allowed a budget that will enable him to add another man to his department. The city is constantly growing, there are a lot of industrial buildings here, and the down town business section is pretty closely packed. We believe a larger permanent fire department is warranted.

As far as the Weagle fire itself is concerned, while Mr. Weagle would be abnormal if he were not extremely upset over the situation, what actually happened could happen anytime anyplace and it's understandable.

The persons who have been described as "inexperienced volunteers" were merely trying to help. Their intentions were the best. Also it's the most natural thing in the world that when others, more experienced at the fire saw them working on the hydrant, the assumed the volunteers knew what they were doing.

It's simply one of those situations where it's difficult to blame anyone.

When a man's car is stuck in the snow and a Good Samaritan comes along and offers to give him a push, it's pretty hard for him to get angry when the Samaritan's bumper rides too high and crashes through his trunk.

As we see it, the "inexperienced volunteers" are in pretty much the same situation as the well-meaning but ill fated Samaritan.

————

Reported by the *Keene Evening Sentinel* on January 8th, 1957:

❧   *A Demon Called Fire*

"FIRE"

Firemen Put Out 2 Motor-Fires

Monday - generally a busy day for washing machines was also a busy one for the Keene Fire Department which responded to two separate alarms for overheated motors in washing machines.

The first alarm was at the home of Mrs. Melvin Perkins, 324 Water Street at 11:44 o'clock in the morning. The second was at the home of Howard B. lane, 441 Main Street at 2:12 o'clock in the afternoon.

Motors in both residences were reported burned out.

————

Reported by the *Keene Evening Sentinel* on January 15th, 1957:

"FIRE"

Two Fires Caused by Cold Weather

Attempts by Keene residents to combat frigid weather last night resulted in two fires, one for a car which was being warmed by an electric light bulb and the another for paper insulation which ignited when a resident was thawing out a water pipe.

The Keene Fire Department was called to the home of Elwyn Beard at 14 Sweeney Road, at 10:25 o'clock last night about an hour after he had placed an electric light bulb under the hood of his car to keep the motor warm.

Beard, who said that the car was not in a garage, was awakened by the smell of smoke. He called the Fire Department, and threw snow into the motor of the car. A fog line extinguished the fire, which burned through the dashboard.

The damage, which included a burned out wiring system, heater and radio, was not estimated this morning.

Capt. Elton Britton theorized the fire began when the electric cord shorted-circuited. A blanket had been placed over the motor and was burned.

The fire which ignited when someone at the home of Richard J. Paristo was thawing out a water pipe was extinguished before firemen arrived following an alarm at 8:32 o'clock Monday night.

————

Note: Reported by the *Keene Evening Sentinel* on February 25th, 1957:

"STORY"

Mutual Aid System to Use High-Band Frequency

Fire department members of the Southwestern New Hampshire Fire Mutual Aid System who have yet to procure their radio equipment will be using a high band radio frequency, Secretary Robert C. Callahan of Keene Reports.

The switch from the low band 33.78 megacycles originally assigned the system is being made because the Federal Civil Defense administration will no longer authorize matching funds for fire service low band equipment.

A high degree of interference in the low meter band is the reason Civil Defense is not authorizing matching funds.

To Retain Equipment

Four communities which have already procured dual frequency equipment for both the Southwestern New Hampshire and Tri-State systems will retain the equipment and their frequency will be coordinated with the frequency assigned by the Federal Communications Commission to Southwestern in the near future.

The coordination point will be a radio tower at Hyland hill, Westmoreland. The four departments, which will retain the assigned fire frequency of 33.78 megacycles, are Keene, West Swanzey, Winchester and Hinsdale.

Fitzwilliam and Meadowood are presently working this frequency, but they may change to the higher band, it is believed.

Local mutual aid system men have been working with two radio manufactures to test out high band equipment before drawing up specifications, Callahan said.

The high band, ranging between 152 and 174 megacycles, has the advantage of not-interference, minimizing "skip" a phenomenon now being experienced whereby foreign and far –reaching U.S. stations some times interfere with local short wave communications in the low band.

No efficiency in communications has been lost, Callahan said and he pointed out that the directive on the high band came at a fortunate time so that most of the departments can avail themselves of the better medium.

A factor in the low quality of "bend" on the high frequency, he pointed out, may necessitate another base station on the Western boundary of the Southwestern New Hampshire-system.

The "bend" quality of high frequency radio, he said, may be compared in characteristic to television "straight line" reception.

The "bend" in the lower radio frequency ban, which is greater, also is the chief reason for so many stations being heard on the same frequency and thus defeating the emergency purpose to the network.

––––––––

Reported by the *Keene Evening Sentinel* on March 16th, 1957:

"FIRE"

Truck Burns In Blaze at Dairy Garage

Quick action by employees of the MacKenzie Dairy on Upper Court Street in removing a flaming truck from a garage and prompt response from the Keene Fire department were this morning credited for saving buildings at the dairy from igniting early last night.

Elmer L. MacKenzie said the van-type rout truck, which ignited as a mechanic was draining the gas tank, was pulled partially out of the garage with a jeep Keene firemen answering a call from Box 471 at 7:33 p.m. quickly extinguished the flames, MacKenzie said.

Damages to the truck were estimated at $1,000. Damage to the building was limited to smoke and window breakage.

The fire call to the MacKenzie Dairy brought many spectators to the scene. The dairy was the scene of a disastrous fire last year.

Paul Frechette, a part time mechanic at the dairy, was drawing gas from the tank to make repairs when fumes from the gas were ignited probably by a cigarette, MacKenzie said.

A front tire on the truck blew during the fire. MacKenzie said he and employees were able to get the vehicle about two-thirds of the way out of the garage before firemen came.

––––––––

Reported by the *Keene Evening Sentinel* on March 28th, 1957:

"STORY"

Fireman Felled

Chester E. Dubriske, a member of the Keene Fire Department was admitted to Elliot Community Hospital shortly after noon today when he was overcome by fumes while painting the inside of an air tank at the Fire Station

He managed to crawl out of the tank before he became unconscious. Fire Chief Walter R. Messer said and the fire department's resuscitator was used in applying oxygen to revive him.

———

Reported by the *Keene Evening Sentinel* on April 5th, 1957 by Don Gross:

Fire Hits Barn, Home
Firemen Find Two Buildings Ablaze at Once

Fire late last night destroyed a barn and gutted a house on property owned by Arthur Houghton on the Old Walpole Road Fire Chief Walter R. Messer estimated total damage around $5,000.

Firemen were called at 11:37 p.m. after Houghton's neighbor, Robert A. Smith, reported the barn fire to the Keene Fire department.

Messer said firemen, who found the barn burned to a point beyond saving, started pouring water on the house located about 75 feet away, as a preventive move. He said firemen then found the house was already burning inside when it started steaming.

Messer said this morning he is looking into the cause of the fires.

Houghton a limberman and widower, was visiting a brother, Rufus Houghton in Greenfield Mass, at the time of the fire Messer said. Houghton had been notified and he understood he was back in Keene this morning.

Morton Wheeler, Houghton's hired man who lives in a nearby cabin, was alerted by Smith and saved four draft horses and a cow housed in the barn.

Messer said the 26-by-34-foot barn was destroyed. The four-room bungalow, he said was pretty well burned internally.

———

Destructive Fire: Keene firemen battle a blaze, which last night destroyed a barn owned by Arthur Houghton. Another fire at Houghton's house about 75 feet away gutted the interior of the building. Photo by Don Gross.

House, Barn Blazes Under 3-Way Probe

Fire Chief Walter R. Messer said today that an investigation into a house and barn fire at the home of Artemus N. Houghton on the Old Walpole Road Thursday night is being continued.

In an effort to determine why there should be two fires, one in the house and one in the barn, with no immediately apparent connection. Chief Messer is being assisted by the state fire marshal's office and Keene Police Department.

The fire, which did damage estimated at $5,000, according to Chief Messer occurred while Houghton was visiting his brother in Greenfield Mass.

Neighbor Wakes

Robert A. Smith a neighbor, said he woke Thursday night and thought the fire was in his house. He alarmed the Keene Fire Department and Houghton's hired man Morton Wheeler, who lives in a nearby cabin, and together they took four horses and a cow from the burning barn.

The house fire, which was centered in a bedroom closet on the side of the hose farthest away from the burning barn, was discovered when firemen put the water hose onto the roof and it began to steam.

Inspector Ernest Jenkins of the state fire marshal's office arrived in Keene Friday afternoon to investigate the circumstances of the fire.

Houghton Questioned

Houghton, who returned from Greenfield early Friday morning was questioned by both fire and police officials. Messer said thee is no suspicion against any one person in the investigation.

Houghton, whose wife Margaret died last October after a lingering illness, expressed discouragement to a neighbor about the fire. He had lived at the home for 28 years, he said.

————

Reported by the *Keene Evening Sentinel* on April 25th, 1957:

"FIRE"

$8,000 House Blaze Splits Up Family of 9

Fire Cause Not Known, Chief Reports by Don Gross

Fire ate its way hurriedly through a two-story frame house at 78 Wood Street, late Wednesday afternoon, leaving destruction estimated at $8,000 and splitting up temporarily the nine-member family of George S. Tetreault.

Keene Firemen were hampered in fire-fighting operations by dense smoke and intense heat. The house was sided with asphalt shingles, which contributed to billows of black smoke.

A passing neighbor who told Mrs. Tetreault smoke was pouring from front windows of the house discovered the fire. A general alarm was sounded.

Starts in Stairway

Fire Chief Walter R. Messer said the blaze started in the stairway area in the center of the house and progressed through the second floor rooms and into the roof.

The chief said that the cause of the fire was not determined.

The house was enveloped in smoke and flames had progressed rapidly by the time fire trucks arrived. Firemen however, managed to save a breezeway and a storage garage.

The house was well-furnished Chief Messer said, and practically all the furnishings with the exception of pieces of a living room set were destroyed.

Fight Fire Tow Hours

The fire was discovered about 5 p.m. and firemen fought stubborn flames which licked through the partitions of the attic and roof. The all-out was sounded at 7 p.m.

"It was an awful shock," Stephen said.

Mrs. Terreault said the three smallest children, Kenny, 10 Cheryl, 7 and Kathy, 4 were playing near Cleveland School close by when the fire broke out.

Two other children, Raymond, 14 and Jerry , 13 were working in the back of the house. The Tetreaults have another daughter , Dorothy, 17.

"What do you do in a case like this?" She asked, looking on at the burning house.

She indicated that the family could stay with her mother, Mrs. Emillenne J. Blaine, a widow, on the Meadow Road overnight.

Tetreault said this morning he is looking around for a tenement until he can rebuild. He said that his other-in-law Mrs. Blaine, had made plans for sale of her house, which means that they would need another place to stay.

————

Smoky Fire: Damage amounting to $8,000 was estimated by Fire Chief Walter R. Messer to the home of George S. Tetreault of 78 Wood St, Wednesday afternoon. The fire made a family of nine temporarily homeless. Photo by Don Gross.

Reported by the *Keene Evening Sentinel* on April 30th, 1957. Story and Photo by Don Gross:

"STORY"

Keene, Let's Get Acquainted With Your Fire Department "After the fire, God and the firemen are forgotten."

There's more than a little truth in the saying, but so we'll be more aware of who makes up the Keene Fire Department, let's get acquainted.

Chief Walter R. Messer of the Keene Fire Department has held this position since Jan 1944, when he took over from the Chief Eugene Riley.

A call fireman since May, 1926, Messer joined the permanent force in 1941 and performed every mechanic's job in the department during this time.

Keene Fire Department. 1st Row L to R - Robert C. Callahan, Laurence E. Thompson, Richard E. Pollock, Robert N. Guyette, Frederick H. Beauchesne, Chief Walther R. Messer, Capt. Frank M Reid, Capt. Elton P. Britton; 2nd Row L to R – Edwin F. Ball, Harry F. Hammond, Prescott M. Little, Paul E. Gallup, Lyman O. Cass and Chester E Dubriske. Smokey the dog, is the departments mascot. Photo by Don Gross.

An auto mechanic before joining the permanent crew, he operated a repair shop in Glen Cove Long Island, from 1931 to 1934.

Keene Native

The fire chief is a Keene native. He is married to the former Elsa Nordlin and they have one son Bruce, a veteran of the Korean War, who is employed with the National Grange insurance Company.

The fire chief is a member of a number of organizations, which include:

New Hampshire Fire Chiefs Club (of which he is president). Massachusetts Fire Chiefs Club, Cheshire County Forest Fire Wardens Assn., New England Assn. Of Fire Chiefs, International Assn. Of Fire Chiefs, International Municipal Signalmen's Assn., State Board of Fire Control, State Firemen's Assn.

He is a past president of both the Tri-State and Southwestern New Hampshire Fire Mutual Aid System.

He is director of Civil Defense for Keene and is a member of the Lions Club, Elks and Masonic lodges.

Capt. Frank M. Reid, 64 of 22 Harrrison Street was born in Nova Scotia and moved to Keene when he was two years old. He joined the fire department in 1926, and was made captain in 1954.

His wife, also a Nova Scotian attended Keene Normal School before they were married. They have a son, Robert, who is an assistant superintendent at Homestead Woolen Mills, a daughter, Margaret, wife of Capt. Reid Puckett, in Germany.

Capt. Reid served in the Yankee Division in France in World War I.

Captain in 1949

Capt. Elton P. Britton who lives at 157 Gilsum Street, became a permanent fire fighter in March 1937, and was made captain in 1949.

Born in Westmorland, he lived most of his life in Keene.

He served in the Navy during World War I, prior to which he served in Company G. New Hampshire National Guard, in the Mexican Border Incident.

He is a member of the American Legion, new Hampshire Fire Chief's Club and County Forest Fire Warden's Assn.

He was married to Roamond Frizzell in 1921. Their four children now grown, are Mrs. Margaret Kingsbury, Holbrook Mass., Mrs. Pauline Courchesne, Concord, Mrs. Bertha Bressett, Keene, and Carl, a student at Keene teachers College.

38th Year

This May will mark the 38th, year for Lyman O. Cass with the Keene Fire department. The joined the department in 1919.

He served in the U.S. Army Signal Corps during World War I and is a member of the American Legion.

He was born in Richmond, and still owns a homestead there.

Harry F. Hammond of 46 Lynwood Ave., Received his permanent appointment to the Fire Department in May, 1943. Prior to this he was a route salesman for Cheshire Oil Company.

Harry served three years in the Army Quartermaster Corps from 1926-29. In 1930, he married Margaret O'Neil. They have one daughter Martha Jane, who is employed with the Telephone Co.

He took over the duty of working with the Auxiliary Fire department in 1954 on the death of Capt. Samuel Guyette and still holds this duty.

He was born in Manchester, but lived most of his life in Keene. His father, Albert Hammond, is retired and lives in Gardner, Mass.

He is a past master of Lodge of the Temple No. 88.

"Kelley" Man

If you hear anyone mention "Kelley" at the Keene Fire Station, they're probably referring to the "swing man" who alternates to balance the two shifts of fire fighters.

Paul E. Gallup of 75 Pinehurst Ave. is the "Kelly" man. He joined the permanent crew in May 1943. Born in Grafton, VT. he came to Keene in 1935.

Before coming with the department, he was employed as a service station man at the Emerald Street Socony station.

Lawrence E. Thompson, 36, joined the permanent department in January 1946. He was a call man in 1942. Born in Keene he attended Keene Schools, and served in the marines on the Aircraft Carrier Essex in the Pacific Theater during World War II.

Besides other duties, he maintains Fire Alarm circuits systems.

⚜ *A Demon Called Fire*

Joined in 1947

Robert C. Callahan, 7 Vernon Street joined the permanent crew in 1947. He was graduated from Keene High School in 1938 and from St. Johns Preparatory, Danvers, Mass in 1939.

One of the persons who pioneered the mutual aid firefighting system in the county, he is presently the secretary of the Southwestern New Hampshire Fire Mutual Aid System.

He recalls that one of the first fires in which mutual aid was used was that of a farm house in Troy Feb. 13, 1955 in which Matti Kunttu, lost his life.

He is married to the former Evelyn Peer of Rutland, VT.

He is a fourth degree member of the Knights of Columbus and a member of the Cheshire County Forest Fire Warden's Assn.

Born in Keene

Prescott M. (Pep) Little, of 44 Madison Street, joined the Fire Department in 1949. He was born in Keene and was graduated from Keene High School in 1942.

Following service in the Navy in the European Theater, where he was given two Purple Hearts and three Bronze Stars for action in the Sicilian and Southern France Invasions, he married Lucy Colantonio of Keene in 1946.

They have two children, Larry 8, and Linda, 5.

He is a member of the American Legion, 40 and 8, Veterans of Foreign Wars, Fourth Degree of Foreign Wars, Fourth Degree Knights of Columbus, and the New Hampshire Trapper's Assn.

Robert N. Guyette, 29 of 198 Church Street became a call fireman in 1949 and joined the permanent crew in 1952. He was born in Keene, attended Keene Schools, and married a Keene girl, the former Lois Kerbaugh. They have three children, Mary Lou, 7, Jody, 5, and Robin 3. He saw service in the Navy in

European waters during World War II, and worked as a mechanic before joining the fire department.

Father Is Volunteer

Richard E. Pollock joined the department in 1952. His father, Stephen W. Pollock Sr. is Captain of the Volunteer Deluge hose Co., one of the three volunteer fire companies in Keene.

He was graduated from Keene High School in 1950 and was employed with Johnson Drug Co., where he still continues to work on a part-time basis, before coming with the fire department.

During two years in the Army from 1954-56, he attended an arson investigation school. He was with a military police criminal investigation outfit in the Army.

Edward F. Ball, 28 of 435 Washington Street joined the Fire Department in Sept. 1954. Before this he operated a bus for Whitney Service between Concord and Keene. He is married to the former Gwendolyn Frazier of Keene and they have three children, David 8, Jean, 9, and Carol, 1.

Has Two Boys

Frederick H. Beauchesne, 33 of 95 Colorado Street joined the fire department in Dec. 1954. He is a native of Keene, and was graduated from Keene High School in 1941.

During World War II, he served in the Army in the Persian Gulf Command. Before coming with the fire department, he was employed with Robertson Motors. He is married to the former Sallie Taylor of Hinsdale, and the have two boys Gary, 10 and Kevin ,6.

Chester E. Dubriske, 31, of 26 Edwards Street, joined the Fire Department in April last year. He was born in Ashuelot and attended Thayer High School, Winchester. During World War II, he was a paratrooper attached to the 82d Airborne. He is married to the former Betty Smith of Winchester and they have three children, Gail , 8, Paul, 4 and James, 1.

Some Bad Fires

A number of memories of bad fires, changes in firefighting methods, and personnel stand out in the minds of the members of the Keene Fire department.

The chief describes his group as an organization in which there is "no absenteeism because all the men are interested in their jobs."

If fire-fighting gets "in the blood" it's no wonder that firefighting should be passed down from father to son. The chief's father, Arthur Messer, who died when the son was four, was a member of the department.

Fred W. Towne, who served as chief from 1900 to 1906, then returned to serve again in 1919, following Chief Louis A. Nims' term of service, was Chief Messer's step father.

Towne was succeeded by Chief Riley in 1922.

Fire Horse Passed On

The phrase, "fire horse" has been passed on to describe a human characteristic, but prior to 1919, a fire horse was a literal object.

The Keene Fire Department made its first change from a horse drawn to mortised fire engine in 1917. The second came in 1919.

A chemical hose wagon was added in 1923, and the first automobile pump engine which was gas driven came in 1926. Before this, pumps were activated by steam generated from a quick-burning charcoal fire.

A second gas driven pumper came in 1930, and a third in 1934. Taking another look back to 1926, Chief Messer recalls how one of the horse-drawn steamers was converted to a tractor-drawn vehicle.

Emergency squad engines came in 1941 and 1942, and it was during this period that the present ladder truck was negotiated for. When it came in 1946, following the war, it replaced a 26-year–old ladder truck.

The present power wagon which is used for brush fires and service work, was acquired in 1948, on the trade-in of a "Black Maria" which formerly belonged to the Police Department.

The department's present Engine 1, a Pirsch pumper with 750 gallon capacity, was acquired in 1952 as a replacement for the first automotive pumping engine bought in 1926.

Among call firemen inducted into the service in World War II are listed Paul E. Symonds, Lawrence E. Thompson, Herbert W. Sanderson, Francis R. Donovan, Maurice G. Waling, Charles J. Woods, Harold L. Curtis, Rupert A. Reason and John G. McCarthy.

During World War II the auxiliary fire department was organized for civil defense purposes.

Although the fireman's workday is still a lone one, the addition from six to 13 permanent men has changed the hours from 96 per week in 1943 to the present 78 hours per week.

Looking into the immediate future, Chief Messer would like to see the department have a fire prevention committee similar to the city planning board. A house to house inspection by the department to prevent fires.

————

Reported by the *Keene Evening Sentinel* on May 14th, 1957 by Don Gross:

"FIRE"

Child Warns of Fire Blaze Leaves Family of Six Without Home

A five-year-old girl who told her mother her throat hurt alerted a family of four children and their parents to a fire which made them homeless around 2 o'clock this morning

The father Richard C. Drew of 32 Park street took the children out of the smoke-filled house while his wife, who is expecting another child, ran to a neighbors to notify the Keene Fire department.

The fire started in a built-in cloths hamper in a downstairs bathroom Fire Chief Walter R. Messer said. It progressed upstairs under partitions into a second-floor roof and into the roof.

Damage to the house and furnishings was temporary estimated by Chief Messer at $6,000.

The house is the property of Robert H. Stone. The Drews, who rent from Stone lost practically all their clothing.

The father said their three-year-old daughter Patty came into the parents bed in the front of the second floor followed by Peggy, 5 who complained that her throat hurt.

The throat irritation was caused by smoke from the downstairs fire.

Drew said he tried to put out the smoking cloths hamper with a kettle of water. A pop sounded, he said and all the lights in the house went out.

The two girls and two boys Richard 2 and Raymond 8 months were taken to his brother Lester Drew's house at 37 Madison Street.

A neighbor Louis R. Lembardi of 38 Park Street, ran a garden hose into the house in an attempt to keep down the fire.

Drew is an assembly floor machinist employed at Kingsbury Machine.

Drew praised the work of the fire department, which saved furnishings in the front part of the house.

He said there was insurance on the furnishings. He indicated that the most pressing need for the family was for clothes for the children.

The fire destroyed all the children's clothes, except what they had on.

———

Night Fire: Keene firemen confined a fire last night at the home of Richard C. Drew of 32 Park St., to the rear of the house fire made family of six temporarily homeless. Photo by Don Gross.

In the *Keene Evening Sentinel* on Tuesday June 18th, 1957 the Safford Inn Fire was reported By Don Gross:

"FIRE"

Safford Inn Fire Leaves 7 Homeless, Loss Set at $12,000

Fire swept through the first floor living room of a Keene landmark, the Safford Inn at 154 Main Street last night, traveled through the partitions of three floors and did damage estimated by Fire Chief Walter R. Messer at $12,000.

Seven roomers and the manager of the inn, Mrs. Marion I. Thompson, were made homeless, and personal belongings and furnishings were destroyed in the fire, smoke and water damage.

The fire was believed to have started from defective wiring in a television set in Mrs. Thompson's apartment.

Other residents of the inn were David F. Sentabar, George Perham, and Mr. and Mrs. Henry Howland, Harry Cheney, Armand Lamy and Paul Dakomas.

33 Room House

Cheney and Dakomas were the only two persons inside the house at the time the blaze was discovered.

Mrs. Thompson said the wood frame house contains 33 rooms, which include her seven-room apartment.

Mrs. Thompson was out on an errand at the time the alarm was set off about 10:30p.m. and returned while firemen were fighting the blaze.

The fire was first discovered by Cheney, employed as a fireman at Wallisford Mills, who was in a second floor room. Cheney ran downstairs and yelled to Sentabar and Perham, who were sitting on the front porch, that the place was on fire.

Sentabar said that when he and Perham opened the door to Mrs. Thompson's apartment a blaze was coming from around the television set.

Hundreds of Spectators

A still alarm was sounded, and was almost immediately followed by a box alarm. The alarm attracted hundreds of spectators.

Dakomas, who lives in a front room apartment, was the only person in the building when the firemen arrived.

Dakomas, who has a heart condition and was the victim of a knife stabbing last summer in his former pool room establishment on Church Street said that he had gone to bed about 9 p.m.

He was awakened by the noise of firefighters and got out of the house.

Roof Problems

The fire traveled from the middle room up through the partitions of the upper floors, spreading and mushrooming through the carved outer slate roof of the house.

Firemen experienced some difficult in arresting the blaze because of the slate roof. The fire was under control at 12:30 a.m.

Firemen from Meadowood Fire Department responded to the alarm, and equipment from the West Swanzey Fire Department covered in for the Keene department at the local fire station.

The fire was centered in the rear of the building which estimated to be about 145 years old, but firemen kept the blaze from traveling to the adjacent building which contained stored bottled gas.

Soft Drinks

Perley F. Safford of Swanzey Center, owner of the inn, said that the property is taxed for $47,500. He said that the furniture worth $7,600 was purchased for the inn a few years ago, and additional purchases have since been made.

Safford said that he has owned the rooming house for about 25 years. The house was at one time the property of Governor Hale, and was given to a son, William Hale, Safford said.

Firemen, who battled the blaze under prevailing warm, humid weather and under extreme smoke conditions, expressed high appreciation for soft drinks which were passed out by the Salvation Army.

———

Reported by the *Keene Evening Sentinel* on June 24th, 1957:

"FIRE"

Fire sweeps 3rd Floor of Marlboro Street House

Black charred ashes were all that remained today of a third floor apartment at 50 Marlboro Street following a fire early Sunday morning. The remaining two floors were a mass of smoke-and-water damage representing a total loss unofficially estimated at $12,000.

Fourteen occupants of the apartment house, most of whom were roused from sleep when the fire was discovered on the third floor, reached safety.

According to other occupants of the house, Maurice Boomhower, who discovered the fire suffered burns.

Mrs. Hazel Blake was the tenant of the third floor apartment according to the owner Lester M. Fairbanks.

Lorraline Deegan, 24 who occupied a first floor rear apartment with her mother, said that she and a friend Thomas G. Carroll of 16 Willow Street were sitting in a car outside the house when Boomhower ran down stairs and notified them of the fire.

Carroll roused other occupants of the house while Miss Deegan awakened her mother, Mrs. Ruth Deegan, and another occupant of the apartment, Eric Crowther, about 55, and called the fire department.

Members of an American Legion drum corps who were staying at Keene Teachers College helped occupants remove some furnishings.

Other occupants of the house include Mr. and Mrs. Richard Putnam and three children, Lila, 3 months, Lucille 5 and Karen 8, and Mr. and Mrs. Joseph Guyer and their great granddaughter, May, 11, all on the second floor, and Mrs. Edna Robbins on the first floor.

A barbershop operated by Peter Mills of Marlboro is situated in the front of the first floor.

Fire Chief Walter R. Messer said that the cause of the fire has not been determined.

Firemen confined the blaze to the third floor apartment, but water and smoke pervaded the remaining two floors.

———

Reported by the *Keene Evening Sentinel* on August 2nd, 1957:

"FIRE"

Dog Wakes Keene Family As Fire Starts

The growl of their mixed cocker spaniel, Poochy, roused the family of Mr. and Mrs. Emile P. Spiess Jr. at 243 Court Street early this morning to a fire which started under the floors of the kitchen and traveled up the partitions.

Spiess, father of David 4, and Diane 2-1/2, called the Keene Fire department at 4:54 a.m. Damages were held to an estimated $400, Fire Chief Walter R. Messer said.

The kitchen of Mr. and Mrs. Sidney Collins which is situated directly below the Spiess kitchen was slightly damaged by water.

The apartment of another tenant, Mrs. Rose DeRosier, who was away on vacation was apparently unharmed.

The four members of the Spiess's family were asleep in front rooms of the two-story house when the dog's growl woke Mrs. Spiess. The two children were taken to the home of his mother.

Spiess said that the house is covered by insurance.

Chief Messer said the fire may have started from a rat nest. The fire traveled from the underneath of the second floor boards and up the partitions on the outer side and up into the roof.

Spiess had high praise for the work of the fore department.

———

Reported by the *Keene Evening Sentinel* on August 19th, 1957:

"FIRE"

Lighter Causes $300 Loss in House Blaze

Fire from a cigarette lighter ignited a mattress in a second story bedroom at 10 Green Ct. shortly after 3 o'clock this morning, destroying two beds and a number of articles of clothing and furnishings.

Mrs. Elsie C. Minch, who occupies the small wood frame house which is the property of the Arthur Wheeler Estate. Said none of the bedding and clothing was insured.

The fire started when a companion staying with Michael Minch 16, used a cigarette lighter to find an article which dropped under the bed. Materials in the under part of the mattress quickly ignited.

Michael hopped on a bicycle and pulled a box alarm at the Keene Fire Station, about three blocks away.

Deputy Fire Chief Elton Britton estimated damage to the room, at about $300.

The Minch family had returned from Bellows Falls, Vt., shortly before the fire, Mrs. Minch said.

The fire was extinguished by crew on Engine 1.

Fire in the popcorn machine at the Scenic Theatre to which the Fire Department was alarmed at 6:55 p.m. Sunday was put out by a hand extinguisher.

Francis E. Winn, a call fireman who happened to be passing by, moved the machine to the street.

———

Keene Fire Department Utility & Deputy Vehicle 1957.

Reported by the *Keene Evening Sentinel* on October 24th, 1957 by Don Gross:

"STORY"

West Keene Receiving Four New Fire Alarms

Four new fire alarms boxes are presently being installed in the West Keene area, and a fifth will be installed sometime in the near future, Fire Chief Walter R. Messer said yesterday.

The creation of the new alarm boxes paves the way for a continuous alarm circuit with which the west Keene area has not previously been equipped.

The continuous alarm circuit, based on a system of dual wires will assure that the alarm will go off at the fire station when an alarm box is pulled despite the fact that a storm-blown tree or other object.

Chief Messer said that the setting up of the continuous circuit would also make possible the installation of a fire alarm whistle in the West Keene area.

New Alarm Boxes

The four new alarm boxes and their numbers are:

No. 491-Hastings Ave and Summit Road.

No.-733-Hastings Ave and Hurricane Road.

No.-731-Bradford Road and Arch street.

No.-721-West Street near Bradford Road.

The fifth alarm box, which is awaiting parts, will be no 441 at Maple Ave near the new Peerless Insurance Co. Building.

Messer said that the West Keene area would be the second of four sections of Keene to have a continuous circuit. The other continuous circuit is in the Court, Baker, Allen Ct. Elm, Upper Washington and George Street areas.

The continuous circuit would act in an emergency as follows. When the wire to the alarm box is snapped, the whistle at the fire station blows once. The circuit which is affected is then detected at the fire station and a ground connection is automatically set in motion at the station rejoining the circuit.

This emergency connection is continued only till the line can be repaired.

Messer said future plans call for having continuous circuit service in all four sections of the city.

———

Fire Circuit Control: Fire Chief Walter R. Messer of Keene is shown examining Keene's four fire circuit indicators. When a wire to a fire alarm box is broken in a storm, the break is indicated on one of the four circuits by a flag. Two circuits will

shortly be made continuous, giving continuous protection in those sections of the city in case of a broken wire. When the break is detected a ground is established at the fire station, thus resuming the connection between the fire box and the fire station.

Reported by the *Keene Evening Sentinel* on November 12th, 1957:

"STORY"

Firemen Plan Annual March For Dystrophy

A brief meeting on the Keene Firemen's March on Muscular Dystrophy will be-held Tuesday November 5th, at 7:30 p.m. at the fire station. Harry Hammond, chairman of the drive announced today.

The firemen, with assistance of members of the Gordon-Bissell Post, American Legion, and Cheshire County Volture, 40 & 8, will conduct the house-to-house campaign on Thursday, Nov. 7 between 7 and 9 p.m.

Muscular dystrophy is a disease, which affects more than 200,000 Americans, two-thirds of whom are children.

Proceeds from the drive are used in research to find a cure for the disease, and for clinical work and patient services.

———

Reported by the *Keene Evening Sentinel* on November 12th, 1957:

"FIRE"

Firemen Battle Blaze at Dump For 5 Hours

A fire which got a good headway at Keene's sanitary-fill rubbish dump required five hours of firefighting and tons of sanitary-fill earth to bring under control last night.

The Keene Fire department was called to the fire at 5:46 p.m. A dozen firemen were employed in combating the fire, which had spread over the whole east side of the dump.

Two portable pumps and line from water in the area were used in attempts to stem the insidious blaze.

City Engineer Robert G. Shaw said that 100 tons of sanitary fill were used by the Public Works Department crew men.

A smog condition existed in the dump area this morning will continue to clean out "hot spots" in the smoldering dump.

One of the arguments which has been used against the present dump is that the fire chief would have to close the dump up if it ever caught fire.

This argument has been voiced by City Councilman William H. Shea, who has been advocating a burning dump in another location.

Fire Chief Walter R. Messer said this morning that if would be necessary to close the dump under present conditions if they occurred during a woods fire ban.

He said that the present situation does not merit closing the dump, which "is reasonably safe."

Chief Messer said that the dump is supervised by the crew of the Public Works Department and that they will continue to soak down spots where the fire breaks out.

The Fire Department was called to a chimney fire at 50 Terrace street property of Leon Benkosky, at 5:15 o'clock this morning.

————

Reported by the *Keene Evening Sentinel* on December 21st, 1957 by Don Gross:

"FIRE"

Fire Guts City Home, Injures Man and Wife
Keene Hospital List Condition As Satisfactory

Parents Save Children In Early Morning Blaze

A Keene father and mother, badly burned when fire gutted the interior of their home on the West Surry Road early this morning, are in "satisfactory" condition at Elliot Community Hospital where they are being held following treatment.

They are Vernard J. Wirein, 44 who is suffering second degree burns of the body, and his wife, Julia L. 43 suffering second degree burns of both lower arms, hands and left foot.

A 12-year-old-son, Donald (nicknamed Mike), and a 17 year-old daughter, Joanne, were roused from their beds and brought to safety by the parents.

Fire Chief Walter R. Messer estimated the fire damage to both the one-story wood-frame house and its furnishings in excess of $8,000.

Fire Started in Chair

Chief Messer said the blaze started from an overstuffed chair situated in the living room right outside the parents bedroom.

The blaze of the smoldering fire burst into the parent's bedroom when the father opened the door sometime around 3 o'clock.

Wirein broke open a back window leading from his bedroom and managed to get Mike and Joanne, who were in other parts of the house, out to safety.

Neighbors Help

A neighbor, Elijah A. Robbins, and his wife Bessie, who heard calls for help assisted the badly burned couple into their house.

Both telephone and electric lights were dead along the street, and Mrs. Robbins got into her car and drove to the Keene Fire Station.

An ambulance of the Foley Ambulance Service took the parents to the hospital.

Two fire trucks, a 300-gallon capacity pumper, and an 800-gallon tank truck were used in fighting the fire.

The blaze was confined mostly to the interior. The house is insulated, and a steady downpour of rain had kept the fire from spreading to the outside.

Chief Messer said that the house is located about 2 1/2 miles beyond the nearest city water hydrant.

Central Screw Employee

The family had lived at the house about two years. The father is employed as a machine operator at Central Screw Co.

Mike, who said his father woke him up from a sound sleep, is a student at Fuller School. Joanne is a student at Keene High School and works partime at Woolworth's.

The parents bedroom was gutted from the blaze. Two house pets, a dog and cat were lost in the fire.

Friend starts Fund for Wireins

A friend of the family of Vernard J. Wirein made homeless early this morning by a fire which hospitalized both father and mother was quick to respond to their dilemma.

The woman, who wished to remain anonymous, called *The Sentinel* asking if there were someone who would hold a $10 donation for the family.

At presstime, arrangements were being attempted to secure a volunteer organization for anyone else who wishes to donate to their cause.

Most of the furniture and clothing of the family was lost in the fire. Members of the family were in night clothes when the fire was discovered.

_____

1958

Reported by the *Keene Evening Sentinel* on January 5th, 1958 by Don Gross:

Keene Fire Department Receives New Frequency

Smokey Testing. The Keene Fire Department yesterday changed its radio units over from the frequency tied in with the Keene Police Department. To a frequency assigned for the Southwestern New Hampshire Fire Mutual Aid System. Smokey, the fire department's Dalmatian mascot 'tests' one of the walkie-talkie units with the help of Fireman Robert Guyette.

_____

Reported by the *Keene Evening Sentinel* on January 7th, 1958:

"FIRE"

Firemen Battle Flames In City, Sullivan Homes

A fire which apparently started inside a bathroom hamper damaged the house of Mr. and Mrs. Ralph O. Warner of 45 Rule Street, to the extent of $5,000 before Keene firemen brought it quickly under control around 8 o'clock this morning.

The fire traveled from the hamper to partitions between the bathroom and kitchen eating its way through the kitchen and into the upper partitions.

Both Warner and his wife had left for work shortly before 6:30 o'clock when smoke was seen by neighbors Mrs. Ernest J. Fish called the fire department and Paul A. Jarvis called Warner at the City Public Works department.

Box Alarm Sounded

Engine 1 radioed for a box alarm on arrival at the scene, bringing four additional trucks to the fire. The fire was brought under control in less than an hour.

Fire Chief Walter R. Messer said that the estimated of $5,000 damage would cover the house and furnishings. The structure of the house is intact, but panels and furnishings were blistered by heat and smoke.

Warner said that there is insurance on both the house and furnishings. His wife, Marie S. Warner, had just returned to employment at Wallissford Mills following recovery from a medical operation

----

Reported by the *Keene Evening Sentinel* on January 11th, 1958:

"FIRE"

Budget Stalls Fire Station In West Keene

A sub fire station in West Keene mentioned by Mayor Richard P. Gilbo in his inaugural speech appears out of the picture for this year.

Councilman Ralph W. Wright, chairman of the fire committee, said that the sub station is not one of the requests being made in the Fire Departments budget requests.

This negative decision is no rebuff at the new mayor, Fire Chief Walter R. Messer said, and he added that eventually there will be a sub station in West Keene.

Mayor Gilbo, in his inaugural address said "It may be something in the distant future. In order to protect the many thousands of dollars worth of buildings that has been going on there."

West Keene residents may get a fire alarm whistle, however. A request for the whistle ($1,500) is being made in the Civil Defense capital fund budget.

Chief Messer said that the recent extension of the fire alarm system has made possible the tie-in of the fire alarm whistle. Many West Keene residents cannot hear either the alarm at the fire station or the public works building with accuracy.

Messer said his eye is set on a location for a future station in West Keene "when people feel they want and are willing to pay" for its establishment.

His choice is the intersection of Rts. 9 and 12. If the land can be procured, he is requesting that it be made available for this purpose.

The location for the fire alarm whistle has not been definitely decided, he said, but both Lash's and Winding Brook Lodge service station are being considered.

[*Compiler's Note*: This is where Parks on Park Ave. and the Summit Road intersect today.]

On Thursday January 30th, 1958 a *Keene Evening Sentinel* Staff Writer wrote the story of the burning Assembly of God Church on Park Ave.:

Narrow Escape: Wilfred O. Levasseur of 18 Charles St., left points to the narrow basement window through which he and Gerdon Stone of 18 Arch St., right made their escape from the cellar of the burning Assembly of God Church on Park Ave. Photo by Thibault.

Unhappy Congregation Begins Cleanup Task

The Rev. Roy B. Suhl and his congregation at the Assembly of God Church on Park Ave. will begin today the heartbreaking task of cleaning up ruble left by a $16,000 fire that struck the still unfinished church structure yesterday afternoon.

The Suhls, who came to the parish three years ago, said this morning they had hoped the church might be completed for dedication on Easter Sunday but extensive repairs of damage created by the fire will now set the project back considerably. They said the loss may run as high as $16,000 to $18,000 and is partially covered by insurance.

In the meantime the congregation will have the use of facilities of the Keene Unitarian Church until repairs can be made. The Rev. Richard Gross, pastor of the Unitarian Church, said today he has offered the use of his church to the Assembly of God Parish on authorization by church trustees.

Two plumbers, Gordon Stone of 18 Arch Street, and Wilfred O. Levasseur trapped in the basement of the church where the fire broke out as a gasoline can burst into flames, fled through a 10-inch deep cellar window after the exit was blocked by flames. Both escaped serious injury, but Stone suffered a small cut on one hand as he broke the escape window.

Levasseur, who was doing plumbing

The main entrance and shut the door in the cellar in an attempt to prevent flames from spreading to other sections of the church.

Two other men working in the auditorium of the church at the time also escaped without injury. They were the Rev. Philip Anderson, pastor of the Assembly of God Church in Brattleboro, Vt., one of 15 volunteers who have been assisting in construction of the church, and Ted Holbrook of Matthews Road, an electrician. Holbrook sounded the alarm from Box 73.

The Keene Fire Department which responded with four pieces of equipment including the ladder truck, plus cleanup equipment, kept the flames from spreading into the blind attic of the church auditorium.

City Firemen Plan Dance To Aid Church

An "Old Folks Dance," a revival of round and square dances of years gone by is planned for Feb. 7th, by the Washington Hook and Ladder Co. of the Keene Fire Department to assist the Assembly of God Church on Park Ave., heavily damaged by fire yesterday.

Laurence M. Pickett, general chairman for the event, said today the fire company will ask a $1 subscription from those attending and the entire proceeds will be turned over to the church to assist in repair work.

Pickett said the Keene Lodge of Moose has donated the use of its home on Park Ave. for the affair and the hook and ladder company is appealing to musicians and callers to donate their services and perform their abilities at the dance.

The volunteer musicians will form an orchestra to play for such old time dances as the Prize Waltz, luck spots, and others reminiscent of years gone by.

Pickett noted that while the dance will particularly bring back fond memories for the older folks, it will be equally enjoyable to young people.

The dance he said will get under way at 8 p.m. and continue "until exhausted."

Reported by the *Keene Evening Sentinel* on February 5th, 1958:

"STORY"

Fire Chief Seeks Members For Auxiliary

If you're one of those who still cherishes dreams of riding on a fire engine Keene Fire Chief Walter R. Messer is looking for you.

The fire department is currently calling attention to its Civil Defense Auxiliary fire department through a special display of fire fighting equipment in the Public Service Co. Window on Central square.

Chief Messer explained that the auxiliary is shooting for 60 additional members, who would supplement the regular fire force in case of emergency.

Members of the auxiliary receive regular fireman's training at meetings held every second Tuesday. The next meeting is slated for Feb. 11.

Those interested in joining the auxiliary are asked to call Chief Messer or Fireman Harry Hamond at EL2-1100.

Call For Help: Elton Britton, deputy fire chief, dons an old time hat and uses an old-fashioned speaking tube to call for volunteers to the fire department's civil defense auxiliary. Equipment is part of old and modern fire paraphernalia in the Public Service Co., window. Photo by Auran.

Reported by the *Keene Evening Sentinel* on February 7th, 1958:

"FIRE"

Flames Rout Family of 8 From Home

Fire routed a family of eight out of their home at 109 Island Street at 5:24 this morning.

Left without a home as a result of the blaze was the family of Richard Drew. In addition to his wife, his mother and five children lived in the three-story frame house.

It was the second time within a year the Drews have been struck by fire.

Damage was estimated at "no more than $4,000" by Chief Walter R. Messer after the blaze was brought under control shortly after 6:30 a.m.

The house, part of the Papile estate was partially covered by insurance, according to Arthur Olson, his son. Arthur Olson Jr., is the administrator of the estate.

Three fire engines responded to the alarm. When the first engine arrived at the scene it found a shed in the back of the house completely ablaze. It was then that two other engines were called to help quell the flames.

Chief Messer said this morning that the fire apparently started in tome rubbish in the shed, burned through a partition into the second floor and then into the attic.

One of the Drew children discovered the fire when it awoke and smelled smoke. The child woke up his grandmother and all members of the family in the house at the time were able to evacuate through the front door without injuries.

The father was at work at the time the fire broke out. The Drew family-the children range from 5 years to 3 months-is temporarily housed at the Salvation Army until arrangement can be made for new quarters.

It is the second time within a year that the Drews have been struck by fire.

The Salvation Army also provided for firemen last night. Shortly after the alarm went off, Capt. Alfred Milley rushed coffee to the scene of the blaze.

Freezing temperatures made the firemen's job more difficult. Water running over the street soon froze and created slippery conditions. The department of public works sanded the street after the firemen left.

————

Reported by the *Keene Evening Sentinel* on March 1st, 1958:

"STORY"

Area Firemen Will Revamp Mutual Aid System

Representatives of 35 towns are expected in Keene March 10th, for a reorganization meeting of the Southwest New Hampshire Fire Mutual Aid System. Fire Chief Walter R. Messer said today.

The reorganization is necessary to conform with a law enacted at the last state legislature making the fire mutual aid system a state recognized function.

The meeting was called by state Fire Marshal Aubrey G. Robinson, who said only slight changes will be necessary to make the organization conform to state law.

The Southwestern Fire Mutual Aid system is the largest in the state covering all of Cheshire County and parts of Sullivan and Hillsboro Counties. Keene is the dispatch center for this system.

Hooked together by radio it uses a system of "running cards" anticipating the disposition of every piece of fire equipment under almost every type and degree of emergency.

————

Reported by the *Keene Evening Sentinel* on March 17th, 1958:

"FIRE"

City Firemen Probe $2,000 Keene Blaze

Keene firemen today are investigating the cause of a $2,000 blaze which burned an upstairs tenement at 656 main Street yesterday morning.

Deputy Fire Chief, Britton said the fire started in a sofa in the second floor apartment of Mr. and Mrs. Everett Lounder. He said the fire probably was started by a cigarette. No one was in the house when the fire began.

Ronald Safford, a member of the Keene Fire Department, discovered smoke coming from the house while he was off duty and sounded a general alarm at 11:38 a.m. Engines No. 1 and 2, the ladder truck and Squad No.1 responded to the alarm.

The flames spread to a partition above a first-floor porch on the south side of the house, but firemen quickly brought the blaze under control. The all-out signal was sounded at 12:45 p.m.

Mrs. Vera C. Wright, 86 Spring Street said the house is owned by her daughter and son-in-law, Mr. and Mrs. Bayard B. Mousley of Melbourne, Fla. She said the house is insured for about $12,000.

————

Reported by the *Keene Evening Sentinel* on May 7th, 1958:

"STORY"

Civil Defense Force Wins Praise in Keene

Bridgham Cites Cooperation in 12-Minute Test

Keene's Civil Defense personnel awaited the end of a two-day simulated attack today amid applause by Director Walter R. Messer and Police Chief William T. Bridgham.

Messer lauded the efforts of city and county CD units during the exercise, which began here yesterday at 10:43 a.m. when a yellow alert was sounded.

Public cooperation during the 12 minute red alert, which came at the height of a noon-hour rush yesterday, was termed "satisfactory" by Police Chief Bridgham.

Bridgham cited only two instances where citizens were slow in taking cover. "We also got a little trouble from a motorist on Washington Street who insisted he had to get home immediately," he added.

Traffic was stopped during the red alert but citizens were allowed to remain in their cars. Pedestrians were required to take cover. The alert snarled traffic throughout the city's business district.

The noon-hour red alert also caused some difficulty in the city's schools.

One secretary at Keene High School was home for lunch when the alert came leaving only three to notify the junior high school and the elementary schools. Under the alert plan high school officials were ready to call all other schools in Keene after being notified by the fire department.

John Day, assistant superintendent of schools, said the line was busy at Keene Junior High School when a secretary twice called the school after the alert had sounded. About five minutes had elapsed before the school was finally notified.

Another delay resulted at Tilden School when no one was on hand to take the call. School had been dismissed five minutes before the alert came. A teacher who was on duty in the lunchroom however ushered the children into shelters after hearing the fire whistle.

Some Confusion

Some confusion was reported in area towns during the initial phase of the mock war. Richmond, Harrisville and Sullivan were slow in getting the word when CD officials in those towns were not on hand to receive a telephone message from Keene Police officers at the start of the alert.

Sixteen other towns in the county had been notified of the alert less than 10 minutes after Keene was alerted.

Joseph Burke and Robert Shaw, co-chairmen of rescue and engineering reported to the city fire department soon after the test started yesterday morning. Also reporting early at the fire department was Gordon Sargent, chairman of transportation.

Reporting at other station in Keene were Michael Carbone, head of the auxiliary police; Harry Hammond, auxiliary firemen; John Frain, county coordinator and Evan C. White health officer.

Fourteen Keene High School students reported at the city health office early in the alert. They heard a lecture by White on local health problems, which would result from an influx of evacuees from Massachusetts.

Radio operators, manning radios at a "secret" communications center in Keene, have been working in shifts throughout the alert. Weldon R. Stanford of Keene Area 1 radio officer directs them.

––––––

[*Compiler's Note*: I remember this drill, as others during this area will. I was in 2nd

A Demon Called Fire

grade at Roosevelt School on Washington Street when the alert was sounded. We as students were directed to enter the hall and kneel and face the interior wall until the all clear was given.]

Reported by the *Keene Evening Sentinel* on July 23rd, 1958:

"FIRE"

Keene Firemen Battle Blaze in B & M Train

Seeks Fire Source: Fire Chief Walter R. Messer (with white cap) climbs into Boston & Maine locomotive to find the source of the fire, which continued to endanger the engine even after flames had been extinguished by Keene Firemen. Photo by Auran.

Fire in the electrical system of a Boston and Main diesel locomotive hauling a 21-car milk train brought out Keene firemen shortly after 1 o'clock this morning.

A general alarm and a call from the police department sent firemen to the Eastern Avenue crossing where the train had stalled.

The fire was brought under control in about 45 minutes.

H. Welch, engineer, told Fire Chief Walter R. Messer that he had been experiencing electrical troubles for several miles in the first unit of the two-unit locomotive.

The train had started to cross Eastern Avenue when a generator "flashover" filled the cab with smoke and brought the train to a halt.

The engineer then changed to the second unit and backed the train, which was heading toward Boston, to the west side of the crossing before going for help.

He flagged down a car driven by a woman, who agreed to report the fire, but refused to give him a ride. She went to the police station to relay the message.

Sounds Alarm

Shortly before she reached the station Welch reached the fire box at Martin and Marlboro Streets and sounded the alarm.

When firemen reached the scene they found a series of ports below the main body of the locomotive aflame. These were quickly extinguished.

However, the heat which originally caused the fire persisted. Sparks continued to come from beneath the locomotive.

It was this that kept firemen on the job for almost 45 minutes.

Chief Messer with the aid of Welch finally located the source of the current which continued the short-circuit. This was eliminated by disconnecting a series of storage batteries.

The train, which originated at White River Junction, continued on its way to Boston after another locomotive was brought to Keene from either Boston or Fitchburg.

Chief Messer said he had no estimate of the damage caused by the fire. He said wiring, insulation, relays and switches were damaged. He said there was also a possibility of damage to the main generator.

About 50 to 60 firemen turned out to help in fighting the blaze.

————

Reported by the *Keene Evening Sentinel* on August 21st, 1958:

"STORY"

Siren Accidentally Set Off at Station

Wires, accidentally crossed during maintenance work on the fire alarm system, set off the fire siren for several minutes yesterday afternoon.

Fire Chief Walter R. Messer said today that the steady blast was "unintentional", and that the alarm system was operational again with in 10 minutes after the trouble occurred.

————

Reported by the *Keene Evening Sentinel* on October 10th, 1958:

"STORY"

Firemen End 'Week' on Musical Note

Wet But Fun: Squirting water at the rate of a thousand gallons a minute proved to be a damp experience for firemen on Inspection Day yesterday. Operating the big nozzle on Central Square were Emile DeRosier, George Shepard, Linwood Curtis, Russell Driscoll and Paul J. Rushlow. The firemen wound up their day with a banquet and ball last night. Photo by Auran.

The Keene Fire Department's efforts during Fire Prevention Week ended on a musical note at the Firemen's Ball last night at the armory.

Firemen old and young danced until midnight after participating in the traditional Inspection day banquet at the fire station.

The banquet for more years than any fireman can remember, has consisted of backed ham, escalloped oysters, cabbage, salad, rolls, coffee and apple pie.

The banquet, which was attended by city officials and regular, volunteer and retired firemen was prepared by the department's Ladies Auxiliary.

Yesterday afternoon saw the department parade down Main Street. Led by the Keene High School band, the parade consisted of eight pieces of equipment and more than 60 firemen-marchers.

The toot of sirens marked the beginning of each demonstration on the east side of Central Square.

In the hose-laying and accuracy contest the volunteer group of Roger Conway, Paul Benoit, Eldon Loisell, Ronald Amadon and Irwin Clark distinguished itself by its speed in knocking down a sign.

The demonstration ended with a demonstration of the department's heavy artillery, including a stationary nozzle fed by three hoses.

The "heavy artillery" demonstrated how the department could pour more than 2500 gallons of water a minute on a fire.

————

Reported by the *Keene Evening Sentinel* on October 21st, 1958:

A Demon Called Fire

"STORY"

Keene's Civil Defense Group Gets Tough Duck for Half Cent a Pound

Army Truck to Aid In Rescue Work

Strange Duck: H. Franklin Guild, chairman of the City Council's finance committee, and Fire Chief Walter R. Messer, Civil Defense director in Keene, are dwarfed by the city's new "DUCK" and amphibious truck weighing seven tons and assigned to the Civil Defense Rescue Services here. The Army vehicle was purchased for $50 and driven here from Toledo, Ohio. Photo by Peck.

Reported by the *Keene Evening Sentinel* on December 3rd, 1958:

"FIRE"

$2,500 Damage In Garage Fire

Damage estimated at $2,500 was caused in a fire at the U.S. Army Corps of Engineers garage at Otter Brook Dam yesterday afternoon.

Two engines of the Keene Fire Department answered the alarm.

The fire started when the exhaust pipe of an auxiliary power unit over-heated and set a partition aflame. The fire spread into a blind attic before it could be put out.

The damage estimate came from Fire Chief Walter Messer. The damage was to the building only.

The department also answered an alarm on Water Street when a coal car had caught fire shortly after noon yesterday. The fire was put out in less than four minutes.

Reported by the *Keene Evening Sentinel* on December 4th, 1958 by Phyllis Peck:

"STORY"

School Board Will Get Fire Inspection Report

Fire Safety Check: Fire Chief Walter R. Messer, left and Theron L. Yost, agent of buildings for the Union High School District express satisfaction with the boiler system at Keene High School. Messer is making a fire safety inspection tour of all Keene schools in the wake of the Chicago school fire. Here they consider the oil burners at the high school building. Photo by Peck.

The Keene School Board will get a report next Monday night on fire safety conditions in the city's 10 public schools.

Theron L. Yost, agent of buildings for the Union /School District, said today he will present to board members results of a special inspection tour of schools currently being conducted by Fire Chief Walter R. Messer along with other information pertaining to fire precautions in the district.

Yost said the inspection prompted by the Chicago school fire, which took 90 lives, was called by Mario G. Farina, school board chairman. The matter had been brought to the attention of the board during a special meeting Tuesday night.

Messer said he also plans an inspection of St. Joseph's Parochial School.

Inspection Warranted

While Keene's schools are under surveillance for any fire hazards both Yost and Messer said an extra inspection is certainly warranted particularly at a time when parents are understandably alarmed as a result of the Chicago tragedy.

Messer said he makes checks at all Keene schools each year, although not usually in one inspection trip. He revisits schools when questions arise.

Yost said any recommendations entered by the fire chief concerning the safety of schools are promptly acted upon.

Inspections involve primarily a matter of "housekeeping," since basic data such as adequacy of exits and fire escapes are known factors. Messer said. Checks are made to see that rubbish or combustible materials aren't left around the schools.

Any time changes are made at schools inspections are made by the chief to establish safety, Yost said.

Adequate Exits

Messer considers exits in the city's schools adequate and feels that necessary precautions are being taken against fire.

In addition to inspection by the chief boilers in the city's school safe inspected once a year.

Asst. Supt. John W. Day said fire drills are held at the city's schools many of them surprise drills. Franklin School, one of the larger elementary schools empties in 59 seconds and Keene High School in a little over a minute, Day said.

Messer said Yost yesterday inspected Keene High School, Tilden and Lincoln Schools and Keene Junior High School. They will complete the inspection rounds before next Monday night's board meeting.

————

From the *Keene Evening Sentinel*:

Tilden School Parents Protests Fire Hazard
Board Hears Basement Area Listed as Trap

A complaint by a Tilden School parent that a basement all-purpose room at the school would be a trap for children and teachers in the event of fire will be investigated by the Keene School Board's land and buildings committee.

Joseph T. Cristiano told the board last night he thinks the room poses a "serious condition." Two normal exits require children to pass up stairways through the building and the only other means of escape are two ladders leading to grade-level windows so small children would have to "crawl through," he said.

"If we had a fire very few if any would get out alive if they were down there," he added.

Cristiano noted that "the building is old and probably should be condemned and abandoned. But if were going to use it as a school building let's make it safe. Its within the board's control now. Do something about it."

Two Recommendations

The board also received two recommendations from Theron L. Yost, agent of buildings, stemming from a recent inspections of schools with Fire Chief Walter R. Messer.

1. Training of teachers and adults in each building to close all doors at each fire drill to create "small areas."

2. Use of obstructions during fire drills to break up the normal pattern in order to make both pupils and teachers realize that abnormal conditions can develop. Neither teachers nor pupils should know where these obstructions would be before a fire drill.

Expense 'Secondary'

Cristiano said expense in such a case is purely secondary. "The prime consideration." He said is the safety of children. If you don't look into it and do something about it you will be derelict in your duties and obligations not only toward children but to the people."

Cristina said his complaint was not prompted by the recent school catastrophe in Chicago. "I've been complaining about it ever since I was PTA president in 1956 and 57."

Yost had this to say about the basement room.

Chief Messer has inspected the room in the past and exits were considered adequate.

Exits from the room are separated by a brick fire wall. The ladders to grade level windows were installed as an additional safety measure. If it were deemed advisable the front of the basement could be knocked out and an exit built extending out in front.

Fire Escape Complaint

Cristiano also complained of the fire escape at Tilden School noting that it is uncovered and might be hazardous in snow and ice conditions. He said it would also take care of only the two rooms at the rear of the building, being of no value to the two front upstairs rooms.

Yost assured the board that all fire escapes and other exits are salted in freezing weather and kept clear of ice and snow as far as possible. He said the fire escapes are not used during fire drills "no fire escape is easy to go down in the best weather."

Yost indicated in his report that Keene Schools are considered safe. He said several suggestions by the fire chief to further insure against "possible or remotely possible hazards" have been attended to.

These included buildings on several basement openings changed to make easier exit, changes in some ductwork, changes on fusible links for boiler room doors, patching on one basement ceiling and covering over vents in one storage room.

Supt. L. O. Thompson told the board fire drills are held regularly in all schools. "We try to have them monthly." He said.

Questioned by Dr. Howard M. Oliver Thompson said in most cases the drills are held unannounced ahead of time. He said reports on results of drills in the various schools are filed at his office.

Mario G. Farina, board chairman suggested that fire drills be made regularly at all schools and monthly reports on results be made to the school board.

Permanent Company 1958

Front row from left to right L.E,. Thompson L.O. Cass, Capt. F.M. Reid Deputy Chief, W.R. Messer Chief, E.P. Britton Deputy Chief, P.E. Gallup Capt., H.F. Hammond, Back row standing from left to right E.F. Ball, R.N. Guyette, F.H. Beauchesne, R.C. Callahan, P.E. Crowell, P.M. Little J.N. Phillips, C.E. Dubriske.

1959

Reported by the *Keene Evening Sentinel* on January 2nd, 1959:

"FIRE"

Keene Firemen Answer 3 Calls

The Keene Fire Department answered three calls for help since noon Wednesday.

At 7:18 p.m. Wednesday's chimney fire was extinguished at 698 Marlboro Street. The house owned by Michael Lis.

At 2:12 a.m. yesterday the department answered a call to Gilsum Street where the car in which Francis M. Sullivan died had caught fire. The Keene Police Department put out the flames before the firemen arrived on the scene.

At 6:03 p.m. yesterday the department answered another call to an automobile fire, this one on Jordan Road. The owner of the car was not identified.

Reported by the *Keene Evening Sentinel* on January 31st, 1959:

"FIRE"

Fire Damages Emerald Street Storehouse

Firemen battled flames and dense smoke this morning in a one-story brick storehouse on Emerald Street.

The building, owned by the Crocker Metal Co. was still burning at press time.

Fire Chief Walter R. Messer estimated damage at several thousand dollars.

Lloyd Hewitt purchasing agent of the Central Screw Co discovered the blaze. Hewitt telephoned the fire station and a general alarm was sounded at 9:54 a.m.

Hewitt said he saw the smoke in the building when he "happened to be out in the yard."

Two engines, a squad trucks and ladder truck responded to the call. About a hundred spectators watched firemen fight the stubborn flames.

Michael Crocker of 45 Willow Street administrator of the metal company could not be contracted this morning.

Reported by the *Keene Evening Sentinel* on February 2nd, 1959:

"FIRE"

Flash Fire Injures Woman, 91, Child

Washington Street Fire: Keene firemen battle smoke and flames in front part of Amos Castor home at 523 Washington St., The fire, believed to have been caused by an exploding oil burner, injured 91 year old Mrs. Sara Cutts and Bonnie Lee Castor, who is observing her second birthday today. Photo by Keene Fire Department.

A flash fire swept a Washington Street home this morning and injured a 91 year-old woman and her two-year-old granddaughter.

Injured were Mrs. Sara Cutts and Bonnie Lee Castor, who is observing her second birthday today.

Bonnie's brother Bobby, 4 were also in the 1-½, story house but he escaped uninjured. They were the three occupants of the house when the fire started.

The house is owned by Amos Castor of 523 Washington Street.

Mrs. Cutts and Bonnie were given first aid treatment for burns and smoke inhalation by Keene Police and Firemen. They were later removed by ambulance to the Elliot Community Hospital.

A hospital official said this noon that both victims suffered "quite severe burns." They were removed from the emergency room shortly after noon.

Castor said he thought the fire was started from an exploding oil burner.

Fire Chief Walter R. Messer said fire, water and smoke damage to the asbestos-covered building would probably run into several thousand dollars. At press time the fire was still burning.

The front part of the building appeared to be completely destroyed. Huge columns of white smoke billowed from the roof.

A general alarm was sounded at 10:38 a.m. Several persons telephoned the fire station to report the fire.

Engines 1 and 2, Squad 1 and Ladder 2 responded to the call.

More than a hundred spectators lined the street to watch the firemen battle the flames.

Police routed traffic down Giffin Street to Sullivan Street and the Concord Road. Police also rushed a resuscitator to the scene.

————

From the *Keene Evening Sentinel*:

Fire Victim Dies of Burns In Hospital

A 91-year-old Keene Woman died at the Elliot Community Hospital this morning the victim of severe burns she received in a fire at her Washington Street home two day ago.

The death of Mrs. Sarah Cutts was the first in the city caused by fire since Christmas Day, 1957, when Fred Wirein died after fire destroyed his home on the West Surry Road four days earlier.

Mrs. Cutts great granddaughter, Bonnie Lee Castor, remained in critical condition at the hospital. The girl was observing her second birthday when the fire swept the Castor's seven-room house Monday morning.

State and local fire officials said the blaze started in the kitchen, probably from a flooded oil range.

Fire Chief Walter R. Messer estimated damage at $9,000.

Bonnie's brother, Bobby, 4 and half-sister, Helen Phelps, 17, escaped injury. Six other members of the family were not at home.

————

From the *Keene Evening Sentinel*:

Fire Victim, 2 Off Critical List

Bonnie Lee Castor, 2 daughter of Mr. and Mrs. Amos Castor of 523 Washington Street, who was seriously burned Feb. 2 in a flash fire, which swept her home, has been taken off the critical list at Elliot Community Hospital.

Her great grandmother, Mrs. Sara Cutts, 91, who was also injured in the fire, died later at Elliot Community Hospital. Bonnie's brother, Bobby, 4 who was in the house when the fire broke out, escaped uninjured. They were the only occupants of the hose at the time of the fire.

————

Reported by the *Keene Evening Sentinel* on February 6th, 1959:

"FIRE"

Firemen Answer 3 Still Alarms

Keene firemen responded to two still alarms this morning and one yesterday afternoon.

At 10:56 a.m. firemen were called to a truck fire at the city dump.

A fire in a power burner at 4:51 a.m. sent firemen to the Bur and Nichols Machine Co. 76 Railroad Street.

At 2:17 p.m. yesterday firemen were called to put out a couch fire at the home of Mrs. Josephine Davis on Swanzey Factory Road.

———

Reported by the *Keene Evening Sentinel* on March 11th, 1959:

"FIRE"

Fire Drives Patrons From Town Diner

A fire caused by defective wiring at the Town Diner, 371 West Street yesterday morning drove patrons from the restaurant and caused heavy some damage.

Neither firemen nor owner Gerald Sweet were able to give a reliable estimate of the dollar damage, they said. Firemen said fire damage was almost completely confined to the basement, where the fire started but that it appeared that the inside of the restaurant on the ground floor was so heavily damaged by smoke that renovations may be necessary.

Firemen said basement timbers, which support the floor of the restaurant, were charred. Flames reached the ground floor level through a hot air duct but were kept from spreading.

The fire was burning rapidly in the basement when firemen arrived and had set off about 20 cases of matches. Hundreds of Sunday morning watchers viewed the fight against the fire, which broke out at about 8:40 a.m.

———

Reported by the *Keene Evening Sentinel* on March 23rd, 1959:

"FIRE"

Fire Partially Destroys Home on George Street

George Street Fire: Keene firemen battle flames in rear wall of house owned by William C. Fisk of 135 George St. Most of the fire was contained to upstairs bedroom. The $1,500 blaze was caused by an overheated chimney. Photo by Thibault.

Fire caused by an overheated chimney partially destroyed the home of William C. Fisk at 135 George Street this morning. Fire Chief Walter R, Messer estimated damage at $1,500. The house was partially insured.

Messer said the fire started around a chimney in the kitchen, located downstairs in the rear of the seven-room frame building.

The flames spread quickly into an upstairs bedroom located over the kitchen. Most of the fire damage was confined to the bedroom. Smoke and water did other damage.

Nobody was home when the fire broke out. Fisk and employee of Putnam Manufacturing Co. and his wife, Anna was working. Mrs. Fisk is employed by Miniature Precision Bearings, Inc.

Their two children Lawrence E. 16, and Rose Anna, 14, were in School.

Two neighbors discovered the blaze and called the fire department. A third call was received shortly after the box alarm was sounded at 9:49.

Ladder 2, Squad 1, and Engine 1 and 2 were dispatched to the fire scene. A hose was connected to a hydrant located a short distance from the house.

The all out was sounded at 10:30

————

Reported by the *Keene Evening Sentinel* on March 30th, 1959:

"FIRE"

Fire Injures Keene man on Sullivan Street

Flames injured a Keene man early this morning in a fire first-floor porch fire on Sullivan Street.

Roland R. Davison, 36 of 23 Sullivan Street was discharged from the Elliot community Hospital after treatment for burns received in the fire.

A hospital, official said Davison suffered burns on his back when he went through a flaming doorway.

Deputy Fire Chief Elton P. Britton said a smoldering overstuffed chair caused the fire. He said Davison had placed the chair on the porch after apparently putting out a fire in the chair earlier in the evening.

Engine 1 was summoned to the scene by a still alarm at 1:18 a.m. Davison was removed to the hospital by Police Officer Richard H. Patton.

Theodore Clough of 82 Billings Ave owns the house.

————

Reported by the *Keene Evening Sentinel* on April 22nd, 1959:

"FIRE"

Fire Destroys End of Henhouse

A fire at the farm of Dr. Thomas Lacey on West Hill Road destroyed one end of an empty, 50 foot henhouse at about 9:30 a.m. today.

Firemen said the fire started in leaves and brush and worked its way to the henhouse. They said there was no damage to any other buildings.

Answering the alarm were a pumper, a hook and ladder and crews No 1 and 2 on tank trucks.

————

On Tuesday April 14th, 1959 *Keene Evening Sentinel* reported with a picture by *Sentinel* Photo-Thibault of the fire at 287-293 West Street:

"FIRE"

Four City Firemen Hurt In West Street Blaze

West Street Blaze: Smoke billows from four-apartment West Street building in fire yesterday afternoon, which caused an estimated $8,000 damage. Four families were forced to flee the building. The fire was caused by an overheated chimney. Most of the fire damage was confined to the roof and attic. Firemen on ladder are Top of ladder-Ronald Amadon, Paul Crowell and George Shepard. Photo by Thibault.

Four firemen received minor injuries yesterday in an $8,000 apartment house blaze at 287-293 West Street caused by a chimney fire that smoldered from before 7 a.m. until the noon hour when it burst into flame and was discovered.

Injuries reported were to William Sanderson, nail in foot; George Shepard, bruised scalp; Paul and Wayne Crowell, cut hands.

Four families were driven from their homes. A dog in the basement, with help from firemen, came out unscathed.

Hundreds gathered to watch as billows of smoke and steam arouse when firemen poured tons of water into the attic. Traffic on West Street was slowed but was not halted at any time.

The fire broke out under the roof at the east end of the building and made its way under the ridge the length of the structure. Firemen confined the glaze to one apartment and the attic, but smoke and water damage was heavy.

Two grass fires and a brushfire also were put out yesterday, one while firemen with fighting the apartment house blaze.

A grass fire was reported at 10:53 a.m. at the home of Everett Patria, 202 Gilsum Street; a brush fire at 12:42 p.m. at the home of George Coburn on Stanhope Avenue and a grass fire at 3:25 p.m. at 84 Carpenter Street.

———

Reported by the *Keene Evening Sentinel* on April 14th, 1959:

"FIRE"

Fire Drives 4 Families Into Street

Four families of a two and a half story four apartment frame house at 293-287 West Street were driven out by fire at 12:30 p.m. today.

The fire started in the attic or second story but its origin was not determined immediately. Flames and huge billows of smoke were issuing from the building at 12:45 p.m.

Owner of the building is the Cheshire Oil Company.

Occupants were Mrs. Margaret Lougee and her 3 1/2-year-old son Kevin; and the families of Alfred Druin, Robert St. John and Mrs. Sophie M. Lambert.

Mrs. Carl Curtis, co owner of Curtis's Texaco Station 281 West Street, notified the fire department.

The blaze was confined to the top floors and was under control at 1 p.m., Fire Chief Walter R. Messer said.

———

Keene's new engine, a 1959 Ward LaFrance 750 GPM Pumper.

Reported by the *Keene Evening Sentinel* on May 2nd, 1959:

"FIRE"

Fire Does $4,000 Damage To Pine Street Apartment House

Fire of undetermined origin caused $4,000 damage to a barn and adjoining unoccupied two-apartment house at 55 Pine Street yesterday afternoon. Fire Chief Walter R. Messer said today.

The fire was one of five yesterday afternoon. The others were grass fires.

Chief Messer said the fire started in the garage where teenage boys had been working for the owner. Carl Johnston, to get the house ready for occupancy.

The blaze was almost entirely confined to the barn, but tongues of flames licked through a partition and caused damage to the corner of the ceiling in the kitchen of the down stairs apartment.

The inside of the barn and storm windows store there were destroyed. There was minor smoke and water damage to the inside of the apartments.

Firemen put out the blaze in 43 minutes.

The grass fires were 3:21 p.m. at the home of David Prevost, 140 Armory Street.

4:22 p.m. on property owned by Sheldon Barker off River Street and at 5:16 p.m. at the Holbrook Realty Co. on Bartholomew Court. Another at 5:16 on Boston & Maine Railroad Co. property on Davis Street.

───────

Reported by the *Keene Evening Sentinel* on June 16th, 1959:

"STORY"

Hold Services For Deceased

The Keene Fire Department held its annual memorial service Sunday in the assembly hall at the Fire Station and then members went to 57 Graves of deceased firefighters in Keene and four other county towns to place flags on final resting places.

The Rev. Leo Descolos of St Bernard's parish delivered a memorial prayer and Capt. Jesse O. Little read the roll of honor at the services in the fire station. Twelve members of the Keene Chapter SPEBSQSA led by Dino Hopus provided music for the ceremony.

Graves were decorated at all of Keene's cemeteries and in Harrisville, West Swanzey, Marlow and Hinsdale.

Flags for decorating graves of former Keene Firefighters buried out side the state also were sent out, Fire Chief Walter R. Messer said.

───────

Reported by the *Keene Evening Sentinel* on June 16th, 1959 by Bill Gagnon:

"FIRE"

Torch Sparks Sets Factory Fire, Loss Set at $15,000

Island Street Fire: Heavy smoke rolled hundreds of feet skyward drawing spectators from all over town this morning as fire hit the old New England Box Co. building on Island Street, Firemen poured tons of water into the building, despite the heavy smoke, which hampered their efforts. Photo by Gagnon.

Blower System Spreads Fire As Dust Ignites

Smoke and fire caused by an acetylene torch spark in a blower system dealt $15,0000 damage to the old New England Box Co. building on Island Street this morning. Also damaged, but to an undetermined extent were partially finished, and finished and packaged juvenile furniture stored there by the Marlboro Manufacturing Co., present owners.

Hundreds gathered to watch as smoke billowed skyward in huge rolls, black at first and then gray and white after firemen poured tons of water into the building.

The Marlboro manufacturing Co. had been using the structure as a warehouse according to John L. Ohman, president.

Working inside on remodeling this morning were two company employees, Dudley Bailey and Clifford Wilson Jr. Also at work inside were Wilfred Vorce and Frank Burgmaster of the Crocker Metal Co.

Dust Ignites

Bailey said that Vorce and Burgmaster were cutting away parts of the old blower system with an acetylene torch when sparks got into the system igniting dust that had accumulated for years and spreading smoke and fire throughout the building.

The structure consists of a central two-story brick building and three long low wooden warehouse type buildings, all connected. The fire spread through the whole cluster in a matter of minutes.

Two witnesses who work nearby said that they had passed the building three minutes before the alarm was sounded at 8:56 a.m. and that there was no sign of smoke or fire.

Then they said they looked again on hearing the alarm and saw smoke pouring from windows and from under the eaves of all parts of the building.

60 Fight Fire

About 60 firemen-using Engine's 1,2 and 4 and Ladder Truck 2, with other equipment all from the Central Fire Station fought fire and smoke.

At 10:06 they were able to radio the fire station that the fire was "pretty well under control" but that there was a lot of cleaning up work yet to be done.

Firefighting was hampered by the fact that one plant hydrant had been covered with lumber and gave forth no water when turned on. All city hydrants were operating.

The initial spread of the fire was unchecked because the sprinkler system had been out of operation for some time.

A Reuben Ohman. Marlboro Manufacturing Co. vice president was on the scene shortly after the fire broke out.

He said that the company stocks of partly finished and finished stock were stored in almost all parts of the building.

The property, which has an assessed valuation of $40,900, was purchased by the Marlboro Manufacturing Co. of Fitchburg, Mass., which had bought it about a year ago from the New England Box Co.

Reported by the *Keene Evening Sentinel* on June 30th, 1959 by Thibault:

"STORY"

71 years of service
Keene Firemen Honor Deputy Chief, Captain

Memory Lane was a busy street last night when two veteran firemen were honored at a party at the Keene Fire station.

The two Keene Firemen who retired Jan 1st are Frank M. Read Deputy Chief and Lyman O. Cass Captain. About 80 members of the department attended the party. Reid and Cass together have served more than 71 years in the department.

Veteran Firemen: Lyman O. Cass, left and Frank M. Reid, right swap stories of old fires with Fire Chief Walter Messer in front of Reid's old truck a 1930 Ahrens-Fox pumper. Cass and Reid retired January 1st after serving a total of more than 71 years in the Keene Fire Department. Photo by Thibault.

Read was elected a permanent fireman Sept. 27 1926 and was made captain Oct. 7 1954. He became deputy chief June 7, 1957.

Cass joined the department as a permanent firemen May 13, 1919 and was promoted to captain July 7, 1957.

Cass recalled that when he joined in 1919 the department had only one chemical wagon. He served 36 years, however, before he fought what he termed the biggest fire in his career the Sprague & Carleton fire in February 1956.

I was never so cold in my life he said but a moment later he remembered an earlier ordeal. It was 22 below zero when the old Carey Chair factory burned in January 1919 he said.

Reid also said the Sprague & Carlton fire was the biggest one in his career. Flames caused an estimated million dollars of damage to the furniture plant.

Reid and Cass were presented traditional purses and retired badges at the party by Chief Walter R. Messer.

Reid who lives at 22 Harrison Street said he has "no plans" for the future Cass intends to work around his home in Richmond.

John O'Neil was the master of ceremonies at the dinner. Rev Leo A. Desclos assistant pastier of St. Bernard's Catholic Church and fire department chaplain gave the invocation.

Representing the permanent firemen on the arrangements committee were Deputy Chief Stephen Pollock, Deputy Chief Alton Britton and Capt. Paul Gallup. Representing the volunteers we Capt. George Fish of the Deluge Co. Capt. Frank Driscoll of the Hook and Ladder Co., Capt. Jesse O. Little of the Steamer Co. and Irving Clark, President of the Auxiliary firemen.

————

Reported by the *Keene Evening Sentinel* on July 2nd, 1959:

"FIRE"

Cigarette Fires Gas Fumes at Service Station

A service station attendant's cigarette ignited gasoline fumes resulting in a fire, which caused several hundred dollars damage early this morning at the Gulf Station at Island and West Streets.

The Keene Fire Department, answering a call at 7:30 a.m. quickly extinguished the flames at the station owned by Raymond Stinson of Woodside Avenue, Keene.

Firemen said that the attendant, Peter Bergeron, was smoking as he was filling the tank of a car driven by Eugene Trubiano of 5 Wood Street, Keene. The cigarette apparently ignited fumes around the tank, burning the gas pump hose and the rear section of Trubiano's car.

The attendant, Bergeron received burns after the fumes ignited.

————

Reported by the *Keene Evening Sentinel* on September 10th, 1959:

"STORY"

City Fire Department Hits Deluge of Phone Calls

A false alarm from a box at the Peerless Insurance Co., coupled with a telephone mix-up which sent two departments to a car fire in Munsonville, plus scores of curious callers, brought a situation last night that has result4d in a plea from Keene Fire deportment officials for the public not to call the Fire Department except when necessary.

Officials said that Keene is the communications center for a 43 department mutual aid system.

Last night while the Sullivan and Nelson fire departments were trying to straighten out their mix-up through the radio center in Keene, a general alarm was sounded from Box 441 at Peerless.

While fire crews were manning the four pieces of mobile equipment that go to general alarm calls, the telephone started ringing as curious residents tried to find out where the Keene fire was and what is entailed.

It turned out to be a false alarm. Fire officials, disturbed at the risk to property involved when a real fire report might be unable to get through because of the calls from curious residents, appealed today for an end to the practice.

"The day is coming when someone is going to have a fire and won't be able to get through on the telephone especially under the present dial system where an operator cannot break in when there's an emergency," a department official said.

————

Reported by the *Keene Evening Sentinel* on October 6th, 1959:

"STORY"

Keene Firemen Schedule Events to Mark 'Week'

Highlighting activities in Keene will be the annual firemen's banquet Thursday and a big parade and ball Saturday. But these features are only a part of the week's program, which in turn is only a part of the departments continuing fire prevention program that operates the year around.

The week is proclaimed each year so that it will include Oct. 9, the anniversary of the fire that 88 years ago swept through Chicago.

That fire, started in Mrs. O'Leary's cow barn, caused $168,000,000 worth of damage and killed 250 persons. On the same day in Peshtigo, Wis, a brush fire swept over 1,280,000 acres and killed six times as many persons-1,500.

The Peshtigo fire in a rural area received little public attention because word of it did not get out for days since communications were knocked out and because of the great stir caused by the Chicago fire.

Focus for Efforts

The double tragedy has been used in more recent years as a focus for fire prevention efforts.

In Keene this year, the week's program starts today, in a sense, with the Public Works Dept.'s three-day fall cleanup drive, timed to help make fire prevention easier at a time when emphasis is being put on fire prevention measures.

Special emphasis this week is put on the year-around fire prevention educational program conducted in the schools. Posters are being made by students in some grammar schools. Fire drills are being held and fire trucks will visit all grammar schools tomorrow.

Fire drills also will be held in the high school and the junior high school. In grades up to 6, children have taken home to parent's inception blanks giving points to be checked for fire hazards in the home.

Throughout the week emphasis is being put on quick notice to fire departments in case, despite precautions, a fire does get started. Fire Chief Walter r. Messer said a strong head start by a fire is the most difficult obstacle to effective firefighting.

————

From the *Keene Evening Sentinel*:

"STORY"

Banquet Thursday

The annual fireman's banquet for permanent and volunteer firemen and city father's is scheduled for Thursday at 6:30 p.m. in the Central Fire Station.

In a departure from the pattern of previous years, the program of public activities will be held Saturday. It previously was Thursday. On Saturday afternoon there will be a big parade starting at 2 p.m. It will form at the Court House, march down Main Street to a point past Elliot Community Hospital, and return to Central Fire Station.

Invitations have been sent to the 42 member departments of the Southwestern New Hampshire Fire Mutual Aid District, and about 12 to 15 are expected to send tankers, pumpers, ladder trucks or squad cars.

The Keene High School Band will lead the parade. Next will come firemen marching on foot, followed by the trucks.

Between 2 and 3 p.m. city officials will inspect firemen's quarters and at 3 p.m. trucks will go to Robin Hood Park pool for a pumping demonstration. The climax will be water spraying simultaneously from trucks pumping from all sides of the pool.

The wind up of public activities will come from 8 p.m. to midnight Saturday with the fireman's ball in the new National Guard

Armory on Hastings Avenue. Music will be by Ted Herbert's orchestra.

Normal, year-around fire prevention work, the chief said, includes inspection of each building in the city's fire precinct in (the downtown area) at least once every two months; supervision of burning permits; drills and educational talks in the school; maintenance of the fire alarm system and firefighting equipment training sessions, talks by specialists and other measures.

————

From the *Keene Evening Sentinel*:

Ladder Show for Students

Children of the Symonds School gave rapt attention to Keene Fire fighter Larry V. Wood perched on the ladder truck two of Keene's Fire Department. The demonstrations are being presented at all public and parochial schools as part of fire drills in connection with fire prevention activities. Taking part in the program are Chief Walter Messer, Wood and Clare Symonds, Firemen and custodian at Keene High School, representing the school district.

————

Messer Says Parade Will Be Extended

Keene Fire Chief Walter R. Messer has announced an extension in the route of the firemen's parade Saturday, part of the celebration honoring "Fire Prevention Week."

Starting at 2 p.m. at Cheshire County Court House, Court and Winchester Streets, the parade will proceed down Main Street to Gates Street, Gates Street to Adams Street, Adams Street to Marlboro Street, Marlboro Street to Main Street and the up Main Street to Keene City Hall for review by city government officials.

Following will be the order in the parade of the participating organizations: Keene Police escort, Keene High School Band, color bearers, Chiefs, officers and firemen marching, Chief Messer's car, visiting fire trucks from Brattleboro, Vt., Chesham, Francistown, Jaffrey, Marlboro, three from the Meadowood department, Newfane, Vt., Peterborough, Stoddard. Surry, West Swanzey Center, Troy, Westmorlan, Williamsville, Vt., Winchester and Keene Fire Department, apparatus.

The public will have an opportunity to inspect fire department head quarters and fire equipment. There will also be a pumping demonstration at Robin Hood Park after the parade.

More than 100 regular and volunteer firefighters and city officials gathered in the Central Fire Station last night for the Keene Fire department annual dinner.

Fire Chief Messer was master of ceremonies for an informal program of short talks and introduction of city officials.

Among those who spoke briefly were Mayor Richard P. Gilbo, City Engineer Robert G. Shaw, Public Works Supt. Joseph F. Burke, Tax Collector Elliot A. Wright, members of the City Council and the heads of the city's volunteer fire companies.

Dinner was served by the Fire Department's Ladies Auxiliary.

There were no fire calls yesterday but this morning at 5:15 firefighters went to the YMCA building on West Street to extinguish a small fire in some cushions, Damage was light.

———————

Reported by the *Keene Evening Sentinel* on December 4th, 1959:

"STORY"

Civil Defense Test Tomorrow

Fourteen short rapid blasts of the fire alarm signal will be sounded tomorrow at 12:05 instead of the usual few Saturday check blasts, Fire Chief Walter R. Messer said today.

The blasts will simulate one round of the four-round Civil Defense alert alarm, he said. This signal system test will be made as a substitute for a statewide Civil Defense alert scheduled for Monday in which Keene will not participate on a wide scale.

CD Communications Director Weldon Stanford said that Monday from 6:30 to 7:30 p.m. the county CD communications headquarters will operate to be in contact with state headquarters in Concord to receive any messages.

———————

1960

Reported by the *Keene Evening Sentinel* on January 14th, 1960:

"FIRE"

$2,500 Damage In House Fire

Fire from a flooded oil burner caused about $2,500 damage to the home of Mr. and Mrs. John Hope, 137 Eastern Ave, yesterday afternoon.

Thick black oil smoke happened firemen in fighting the blaze that crept up the partitions from the first floor kitchen to the attic.

According to firemen, Mrs. Hope had been cooking at the kitchen stove when the oil apparently flooded the burner. Flames and heavy smoke went up the chimney catching fire to the partitions.

A still alarm was sounded at 3:23 p.m. and a general alarm followed at 3:40. All out was sounded at 4:45.

———————

Reported by the *Keene Evening Sentinel* on January 26th, 1960:

Firemen Extinguish Car Blaze

Keene firemen today were credited with preventing what could have been a serious automobile fire.

Herbert J. Nokes of 109 School Street said, "that fire department is okay. They were Johnny's on the Spot," this morning. It seemed like no time when they arrived and had the blaze out."

At 7:30 this morning Nokes got into his two-week old care and started it. He keeps it in his garage over night. "I got in, started the car and backed out of the garage to let it warm up a little before I left on a trip."

He said he heard a slight explosion and noticed the hood began smoking. Rushing out of the vehicle he lifted the hood. "When I put up that hood flames shot up about 13 feet into the air. It was a good thing I took the car out of the garage first."

Engine 4, under the direction of Capt. Paul Gallup, went to the scene and quickly extinguished the fire.

————

Reported by the *Keene Evening Sentinel* on February 19th, 1960:

"FIRE"

Three Alarms Are Answered During Storm

A false alarm and two still alarms sent Keene firemen out early this morning in the worst storm of the season in three widely separated sections of the city.

The false alarm sounded at 2:34 a.m. at the Peerless Insurance Co., Maple Ave. The building's electrician, Phil Moran, is presently checking the wiring system of the building in an attempt to determine the cause. This was the second time a false alarm has been set off due to mechanical error in the building since it was built.

The second alarm sounded at 5:12 from 391 Winchester Street the home of Harry F. Kingsbury. According to the fire department report, faulty wiring caused a minor blaze in the cellar.

Wiring in the cellar was also called the cause for the third alarm which came from the home of Hugh F. Waling, 99 Douglas Street. The alarm sounded at 7:38 for this small fire.

Damage in both homes was slight.

————

Reported by the *Keene Evening Sentinel* on February 20th, 1960:

"FIRE"

Five Persons Flee Fire on Church Street

Five persons fled into the storm last night as a fire swept through one room of a boarding house at 61 Church Street.

Ernest Tasoulas owner, said today he estimates the fire damage at approximately $400 or $500 dollars.

Firemen reported that a hot plate located too near a wall started the wall on fire and a part of the floor in a room occupied by Sylvester Kivisto.

At 8:52 after the still alarm was sounded, Box 8 rang and four pieces of apparatus answered the call, including the squad emergency truck. Firemen confined the fire to the one room on the first floor.

Tasoulas said the room was completely destroyed.

The other residents who sought safety in the storm were able to return to their rooms for the night.

————

Reported by the *Keene Evening Sentinel* on March 11th, 1960:

"FIRE"

Firemen Answer 2 minor Fires

Keene Firemen were called out twice yesterday afternoon for minor fires.

At 12:22 p.m. Engine four, under the direction of Deputy Chief Harry Hammond, went to the home of Petrone Kraucunas, 33 Wilford Street to fight a small chimney fire.

One hour later Engine 1 under Deputy Hammond's direction extinguished an automobile fire at the corner of Spruce and Howard Streets. The car belonged to Roger Croteau of Keene. A short circuit in the wiring of the vehicle was blamed for the fire.

————

Reported by the *Keene Evening Sentinel* on March 30th, 1960:

Fiske Hall Fire Damages at $75

A neglected cigarette is blamed for a fire in a second floor room of Fiske Hall at Keene Teachers College early this morning that caused about $75.00 damage.

Dr. Lloyd P. Young president of the college, said that one of the girls forgot to put out a cigarette when she left her room for breakfast in a first floor dinning room.

The girls pulled the burning mattress out of the building and called the fire department. Firemen quickly extinguished the smoldering bedding.

————

Reported by the *Keene Evening Sentinel* on April 9th, 1960:

"FIRE"

Small Fire Extinguished At Abbott Co.

An undetermined amount of water damage was caused when a small fire set off the sprinkler system in the Abbott Co., Railroad Street just before midnight last night.

Capt. Robert Callahan of the Keene Fire department said today the fire was caused by spontaneous combustion of refuse and paint residue on the third floor of the Furniture Company.

The automatic sprinkler system was set off quickly dousing the blaze as firemen arrived but also sending water cascading down through the next two floors of the building. The company makes wooden furniture and much of the wood stock became water soaked.

Another sprinkler system sent firemen scurrying to the Markem Machine Co. at 5:42 a.m. today. For some unknown reason the sprinkler system went off sounding the automatic fire alarm.

————

Reported by the *Keene Evening Sentinel* on April 15th, 1960:

'FIRE

2 False Alarms Sounded at Glass Firm

Two false alarms at Pittsburgh Plate Glass within an hour this morning caused a traffic snarl and brought about an investigation.

The first alarm sounded at 6:37 a.m. When firemen arrived on the scene they discovered that a malfunction in a heating control system in the paint room of the company set off the automatic sprinkler which in turn set off the alarm.

Within 20 minutes the firemen had returned to their headquarters at 7:34, the alarm sounded again. This time Fire Chief Walter Messer went to the company alone to investigate.

Maurice Wright, general foreman, said that an air compressor in the paint room was not working for some reason. The compressor controlled the heat in the paint room and the temperature went up, setting off the alarm.

The resulting confusion of call firemen trying to get at the scene, early risers going to work and the curious, tied up traffic the entire length of Marlboro Street for about half an hour in both directions.

Company officials and Chief Messer are investigating investigation into the cause of the double false alarm.

Also on May 12th, shortly after 8:30 last night a general fire alarm sounded sending about 40 firemen and hundreds of residents to the Pittsburgh Plate Glass Co., plant on Marlboro Street.

The rapid influx of firemen and the curious tied up traffic on the thoroughfare for more than 45 minutes. The firemen dashed in to the building fearing that a blaze had broken out in the company's paint storage room.

They figured they had arrived in time, as no smoke was visible. Once inside it was noted that the smell of a fire was missing so a quick search was made and the cause for the false alarm found.

The culprit...loose mercury switch on the automatic alarm system. The all out was sounded.

———

[*Compiler's Note*: Growing up in the 50's and 60's was an ongoing "ALERT" because of the atomic age after World War II. Each and every state follows the Civil Defense agency as the mediation to the local civilians.]

As reported by the *Keene Evenning Sentinel* on May 2nd, 1960 by *Sentinel* Staff:

"STORY"

CD Test Alert Slated; Cooperation Is Asked

Civil Defense authorities have asked that Keene residents participate in the nationwide test alert tomorrow as well as cooperate with it.

Fire Chief Walter R. Messer, local CD director, said that a local civil defense program will get under way at 8:30 p.p. after the nationwide alert. "The first alert will sound at 2p.m., making the Yellow warning and the switch of radio stations to the Conelrand channels," he said. "The Red Alert will sound at 3, which means citizens should seek the nearest shelter until the all-clear, which will sound at 3:15."

The Conelrand system will stay in effect for half an hour, during which time all regular radio broadcasting and television stations will be off the air. Only those stations on the Conelrand frequencies of 640 and 1240 will be allowed on the air.

Urge Citizens

Chief Messer and Police Chief William T. Bridgham ask that all citizens attempt to pick up the Conelrad broadcast. They suggest the use of car radios, portable radios (including transistors) and ask people to notify them of the reception.

"We would like to see if the residents will get information if all electrical power is knocked out," they said. "Use a postcard, brief note or some other method, but please let us know if you receive the Conelrad broadcast."

An emergency telephone has been set up in the fire station (CD headquarters for the alert) in case of any case of an emergencies. "Call Elmwood 2-2800 in case of any emergency during the test," Chief Messer said.

Police Chief

Bridgham said that during the afternoon, alert, his men have been instructed to halt traffic and drivers to take cover along with the pedestrians. He added; "I am going to utilize all my manpower during the tests. There will be 25 auxiliary police men and 18 regular officers, on duty. I urge the public to take part and cooperate."

Prior to Alert

Prior to the "Red Alert", a practice evacuation will be held at Lincoln, Tilden and Roosevelt Schools. "The pupils will be sent home at 2 when the Yellow Alert sounds, and will return to school immediately." John W. Day, assistant superintendent said.

At 8:30 p.m. local disaster problems will be sent up. A mass drowning will take place at Wilson Pond, and the West Street Bridge between Pearl and Island Streets will be washed out in a flood.

"These simulated problems might be rather grim but they will help in case we ever get a real alert." Chief Bridgham said.

At the "drowning" site, the CD personnel will practice rescue through the use of skin divers and the Civil Defense "duck," amphibious vehicle.

Reported by the *Keene Evening Sentinel* on June 11th, 1960 by Bill Gagnon:

"FIRE"

Early Morning Fire Loss Set at $10,000. One Occupant Jumps From Second Floor

Flames believed to have sprung from a rubbish bin under a stairway shot up through a narrow space between the stairway and an outside wall then mushroomed to spread through the top floor of the building at 87-87 1/2 Main Street early today causing damage unofficially estimated to be at least $10,000.

One occupant of living quarters on the top floor jumped to safety and firemen carried another down. Both were in "satisfactory" condition at Elliot Community Hospital this morning.

RESCUE OPERATION: Firemen and volunteers (right photo) struggle down ladder to truck with Mrs. Ruth Price, 49 of 87½ Main St, after rescuing her. Suffering from smoke inhalation from the top floor of the burning building, they whirled her quickly (left photo) into a waiting ambulance that took her to Elliot Community Hospital. Her condition there this morning was 'satisfactory'. Photo by Gagnon.

Harold Fowle, 36 of 87 1/2 Main Street cut his feet forehead and hands and was treated for smoke inhalation. He jumped from the second story.

Carried to Safety

Mrs. Ruth Price carried to safety by firemen, also was treated for smoke inhalation. Firemen reported no serious injury to any of the 50 regular and volunteer firefighters who fought the blaze from 12:27 a.m. until 3:45 a.m. but minor cuts were reported by two or three.

Hundreds of watchers's lined Main Street and blocked traffic at Railroad Square as firefighters poured thousands of gallons of water into the flaming smoldering building.

Firemen confined fire damage to the rear portion of the top floor of the building, which contained six or seven rooms of living quarters on the top floor. Driven out besides Fowles and Mrs. Price and her daughter was an unidentified woman who lived in a rear room.

Water Damage

There was water damage but no fire damage to the three front top floor rooms and to the business establishments on the ground floor.

Most downstairs damage was borne by the former Monadnock Grill, which was being remodeled to make space for Berkeley Stores Inc. women's apparel shop that was to move into the quarters from 32 Washington Street.

Also receiving some water damage were the What Not Shoppie at the front and a bakery at the back where cooking was done for the grill and for the Crystal Restaurant next door.

Besides gutting the living quarters at the rear of the second story, flames also ate their way through the roof at the rear portion of which collapsed.

Owners of the building Paul and Theodore Evangelo former operators of the Monadnock Grille were not available this morning to give a definite estimate of the loss or replacement cost or to say how heavily the building might have been insured.

While Keene firefighters with five trucks fought the blaze a truck from the Marlboro Fire Department stood by at the Keene Fire Station to cover for the Keene crews, and a truck and crew from the Meadowood Fire Department helped out at the scene.

————

From the *Keene Evening Sentinel*:

Fire Victim Dies After Long Illness

Mrs. Van R. Rice 49 rescued from her smoke-filled apartment during the early morning fire Saturday at 87 ½ Main Street died last night in Elliot Community Hospital.

She has been ill for some time and her death was attributed to the long illness. Dr. Robert M. Hamill said that smoke inhalation was only a coincidental factor.

Mrs. Price the former Ruth Tupper, was born in Burlington Vt. Dec. 7, 1910.

Her husband two sons, Alonzo and Daniel of Keene; a daughter, Mrs. Walter Boudreau of Burlington, a brother, Bert Tupper of Burlington and two sisters, Mrs. Elizabeth Reed and Mrs. Edith Hattin of Burlington survive her.

————

Reported by the *Keene Evening Sentinel* on June l 8th, 1960:

"FIRE"

Quick Action Saves Barn on East Surry Road

Aubrey and Ellis Barrett of the East Surry Road were credited last night with saving their barn, hay and cattle from possible destruction by taking a fire out of their barn.

The brothers had pulled a wagon loaded with hay into their barn at about 7:30 last night when the hay ignited from friction from a flat tire on the wagon. They fought the blaze with had extinguishers. When the fire began to get away from them they pulled the wagon into the center of the East Surry Road and called the Keene Fire Department.

Engine 1, squad and Engine 4, raced to the scene. Five minutes later they called for a tanker and Squad 2 responded. About 100 cars and boys on bicycles hampered call firemen getting to the fire.

Cars were parked back a full mile from the scene.

The wagon loaded with about five tons of hay was dumped onto the highway and the firemen extinguished the blaze. They remained at the fire until 9:15p.m. to insure the safety of the barn.

The barn contained 130 head of cattle and 7,000 bales of hay. The Barrett brothers said they had no time to let the cows go free.

———

Reported by the *Keene Evening Sentinel* on July 5th, 1960:

"FIRE"

Fire Damage $1,500 at Abbott Company

The plants sprinkler system, functioning quickly dampened the fire before it could get well started. Damage of $1,500. to partly processed children's furniture stock and the building itself. Photo by Gagnon.

Damage estimated at $1,500 was caused by fire in the Abbott Co. Railroad Street yesterday. It was the fourth fire to break out during the day.

Firemen responded to the alarm the 21st, bell alarm this year, just before 8 p.m. A fire had broken out in the third floor paint spray booth of the building. It started on a sheet of burlap material.

Fire Chief Walter R. Messer said that the fire was confined to the booth but water caused damage on all three floors of the building. The automatic sprinkler system was set off and water ran throughout the building. The chief said the fire could have been caused by spontaneous combustion.

Two Minor Fires

Wiring caused two other minor fires yesterday in Keene. Chief Messer said that one fire was caused by overloading the circuits.

The fires were the 100th and101st still alarm sounded this year.

The home of Harold Black Jr. Route Gilsum Road was slightly damaged when a fire broke out Chief Messer said overloaded circuits caused the fire. He said that the demand from appliances nowadays is getting greater than the wiring can carry and the fuses used are not always the right size. If the fuse gives out before the wiring, fires can be avoided he said.

A short circuit caused a fire at 272 West Street in a tenement owned by the Heald Brothers. The fire swept through the partitions of one room causing extensive damage inside the walls. The blaze was quickly extinguished.

The 102nd still alarm this year was sounded when a mattress caught fire in the Lane Block on Main Street. Firemen reported that Frank Henery, a tenant was smoking in bed when the mattress caught fire. Damage was slight.

———

Reported by the *Keene Evening Sentinel* on August 18th, 1960:

"FIRE"

$300 Damage In Fire at Carey Chair

A fire of unknown origin caused about $300 damage to the roof of the Carey Chair Mfg. Co. this morning. Franklin Carey said he did not know what might have caused the blaze.

The roof over the boiler room of the plant caught fire shortly before 10 a.m. Firemen put the blaze out before it could spread out of one corner.

Late last night firemen were called to the Markem Machine Co. when heavy smoke was spotted in the Inking room of the plant. The smoke was caused by a chemical reaction in a can of acid. There was no damage reported.

—————

August 21st, 1960 the *Keene Sentinel* ran a story of a fire at the Marlboro Mfg. Co., at Island Street property in Keene. A picture taken by Bill Mahan-Berkshire Eagle was in the Sentinel with a caption under the picture. Reported by the *Keene Evening Sentinel* on August 21st, 1960:

"FIRE"

Fire Damage Is Set at $4,000

BLAZE DESTROYS SHED: Late last night a fire of undetermined origin destroyed a shed off Island Street causing an estimated $4,000 in

damages inside the shed were 20 tons of stoker coal and two coal loaders. Heat from the building melted shingles on buildings some 20 feet away from the fire. The shed was the property of the Marlboro Manufacturing Co., of Marlboro.

Fire Damages Estimate Is Set at $4,000

An estimated $4,000 damage was caused last night by a fire of undetermined origin that swept through a large shed on Island Street owned by the Marlboro Mfg. Co., of Marlboro.

The building, located along side the Boston and Main Railroad tracks, was completely destroyed by the blaze. Fallen wires hampered firemen fighting the blaze.

Eli Chabbot, owner of the Hope Coal Co., who had stored two coal loaders and 20 tons of coal in the shed, said-today that the intense heat from the fire melted one of the loaders.

He said the coal was ruined and the other loader badly damaged.

John Ohman of the Marlboro Manufacturing Co., said that one of his company's buildings located across the railroad tracks from the burning building, was damaged by the intense heat.

"The heat melted the shingles on the front of the building. We will have to re-do the entire front of the building." He said.

At one point during the fire a freight train was stopped at the Island Street crossing to prevent it from running over the fire hoses in the street. The train was delayed about 15 minutes. Firemen put flares along side the tracks warning the train to stop. When the train stopped firemen clamped off the hoses and removed the section across the tracks to let the train continue.

A little after 9 this morning the firemen were once more called to the scene as some of the smoldering timber broke into fire again. This was quickly extinguished, preventing it from spreading into nearby sheds.

Earlier yesterday firemen were called out to extinguish a blaze in a storage room in the cellar at 279 Marlboro Street. The home is owned by Christine Boucher. Damage was slight.

The second fire was at 34 Franklin Street when a television set belonging to Antoinette Casillo broke into flames. This was also quickly extinguished with minor damage.

Reported by the *Keene Evening Sentinel* on September 13th, 1960:

"FIRE"

Minor Fire Blamed on Donna Threat

While Hurricane Donna threatened Keene, three local residents faced a closer threat of minor fires, one of which could be indirectly blamed on the impending hurricane.

At 7:15 p.m. last night Box 721 sounded and firemen under the direction of Deputy Chief Harry Hamond responded. A candle sitting on a deck at the home of A. R. Chase, 621 West Street ignited several items on the desk. The area was blacked out in a power failure caused when a tree fell across wires. The fire was extinguished after inflicting minor damage.

In other minor fires during and after the heavy winds and rain hit the city, firemen were called to the Central Shoe Repair store at Central Square. A fire had broken out under a machine. Damage was minor. A power burner caught fire at the home of Charles Diluzio, 87 Davis street, but was quickly extinguished by a fire crew led by Deputy Hammond.

Reported by the *Keene Evening Sentinel* on October 6th, 1960 by Charles Knee Jr.:

"STORY"

Fire Inspections Drop Tax Rate Prevention Week Listed On October 9-15

In the last 10 years the number of fires in Keene has dropped because of a stepped-up inspection program by the Keene Fire Department, Chief Walter R. Messer said today.

Next week the local department will observe National Fire Prevention Week. During that week the department will inspect all schools in the city for fire hazards.

During the rest of the year, besides a periodical check on the schools in the city for fire hazards.

Buildings throughout the business district check all oil burner installations in the city and flammable in the city and flammable bulk fluid storage's and run a special series of inspections at the convalescent homes, state welfare agency homes and nursing homes in Keene.

Refresher Training

Each fireman is required to take periodic refresher training on the different types of fire fighting equipment.

Chief Messer said that while national Fire Prevention Week is in progress, it would be a good time for people to check their homes for fire hazards.

He said the most frequent causes of fires, nationally as well as locally were smoking and matches, defective, overheated heating and cooking equipment; electrical wiring, rubbish (ignition unknown); flammable liquids; open lights, flames and or sparks chimneys and flues; lightning; children with matches and incendiary materials.

136 Still Alarms

This year up to yesterday noon, a total of 136 still alarms were listed in Keene as well as 28 Box alarms. "The majority of these were from matches, defective and overheated equipment," Chief Messer said.

The total still alarms last year was 183 as compared with 233 in 1956 and 229 in 1955. "The reason for this apparent decrease in total number of fires is because of our inspection system. The majority of fires in Keene 10 years ago were chimney fires, caused by wood burning instead of oil.

"The majority of oil burner fires are no caused by defective equipment. It is usually a cause were the person using the equipment is not too careful of what he or she is doing." Messer said.

Chief Messer has a complement of 15 permanent firemen, 48 call firemen two deputies and 25 Civil Defense firemen. His regular firemen work a 24-hour shift every other day from 7 a.m. to 7 a.m. During their tenure of duty the firemen check all the fire alarms systems, clean the fire house and equipment if used the night before, check all firefighting equipment including radios, overhaul and repair stand-by generators and check operate and maintain the fire trucks. Each man must be adept with each piece of equipment he may be use during his tour of duty.

Jack of All Trades

"The firemen are jacks-of-all-trades. They are carpenters, electricians, mechanics, diesel and automotive and radio operators. They also know first aid techniques." Chief Messer said.

During Fire Prevention Week the local firemen will participate in the observance planned in Central Square on Tuesday.

Special Program

Special radio programs will be held Tuesday locally in conjunction with nation-wide programs. The school visits and inspections will be held Wednesday and a parade in Keene Saturday will highlight the week-long activities. More that 50 fire-fighting units are expected to take part in the parade and muster. The parade begins at 1 p.m. in front of the Cheshire County Courthouse, Court Street and the Muster will be held at Alumni Field, West Keene.

The route for the parade will be down main Street, North on Adams Street to Marlboro street, West on Marlboro Street, to main Street and back up Main Street where it will pass in review at the flagpole.

The Week will end with the annual Firemen's ball and dance Saturday from 8 p.m. to midnight in the National Guard Armory Hastings Avenue.

———

Reported by the *Keene Evening Sentinel* on November 4th, 1960 by Charles Knee Jr:

"STORY"

Lt. Verry Says Korean Orphans Badly in Need of Winter Clothes

Key developments in Operation Orphans today shifted from Keene to Korea.

First Lt. Horace D. Verry, Keene athlete who is supervisor of a 74-children orphanage near Seoul, came through this morning with a list of specific needs.

The *Keene Evening Sentinel* requested the list earlier by telephone, radio, Red Cross cable, and airmail.

Here is the list of things needed by the Pub Won Orphanage: List is cut short due to space. All types of Winter Clothes Jackets etc. sizes 4 to 16. Blankets, Musical Instruments, Books Grades 1-6 and Dehydrated Foods and Rice, potatoes, vegetables etc.

———

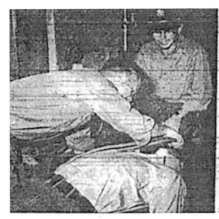

Firemen to Dieselmen: Fire Chief Walther R. Messer (left) along with Capt. Paul Gallup and firemen Robert Guyette roll up their shirt sleeves to repair the huge diesel generator. Picture on right K C E – 579 over Lawrence V. Wood, Keene firemen mans the main desk at the Keene Fire Department central headquarters for the southwestern NH Mutual Aid. Photo by Keene.

Practice Session: (left) Keene Deputy Fire Chief Harry Hammond (right) looks on as 2 of the regular firemen practice using the resuscitator. The victim is Firemen Lawrence V. Wood. Firemen maintain constant readiness for any emergency. Alarm System Check (right) Lawrence Thompson one of Keene's 15 regular firemen makes his daily check of the fire alarm control board at Central Fire Station Headquarters. The board is the controlling center of Keene's 67 alarm boxes which, use 39 miles of wiring.

LEND A HAND: Keene firemen Laurence Thompson (left) and Edwin Ball help to unload a People's Linen Truck full of clothes donated to "OPERATION ORPHANS" yesterday. The firemen are helping to store the clothing, canned goods and toys being send in from all over the country for the 1st Lt. Horace Verry's Korean Orphans. The donations are being stored in the upstairs hall of the Fire Department until they can be packed and flown to Korea.

Reported by the *Keene Evening Sentinel* on November 5th, 1960.:

"FIRE"

Wire Break Starts Fire, Cuts Power

An unexpected break in a 12000-volt wire at Bradford Road this morning left Chesterfield Westmoreland and sections of West Keene, without electrical power.

The wire arced when it hit the ground along the Boston and Main Railroad Tracks, just east of the Keene Country Club grounds at Bradford Road, and burned a patch of railroad and Public Service Company land about 300 yards long and 5 yards wide.

Keene firemen were called out shortly after 6:20 this morning to fight the fire. Public Service crews quickly repaired the wire.

Power was restored to Chesterfield and Westmoreland within 25 minutes of the break, but some sections of Keene were without power for an hour.

Roger Hunt western division manager for the PSC, and Wilburn Francis, PSC engineer inspected the area this morning in an attempt to determine the cause of the break.

————

Reported by the *Keene Evening Sentinel* on November 29th, 1960:

"FIRE"

Damage Set At $1,000 After Fire

Burning rubbish caused an estimated $1,000 damage to the home of Mrs. Harry Shamoon, 49 Fox Circle last night.

Fire Chief Walter R. Messer said today that the rubbish was in the cellar of the home and that the cause of the fire has not been determined.

Heavy smoke billowed from the house sending tears down the faces of the firemen who were trying to locate the cause of the blaze.

The fire damaged rafters of the cellar and caused extensive smoke damage to the rest of the home before being extinguished. Mrs. Shamoon and her youngest son were at home at the time. She has three sons. No one was injured.

Shortly after the Shamoon fire, a false alarm sounded at Box 72 corner of West Street and Park Avenue. The Police Department is investigating.

————

Reported by the *Keene Evening Sentinel* on December 12th, 1960:

"FIRE"

Fire Department Gets 7 Calls In Three Days

Keene firemen in the past three days have been called out to extinguish seven minor fires through the city.

The last in the rash of small fires was a chimney fire yesterday afternoon at 343 Washington Street in a home owned by Max Benkosky. Damage was slight.

Earlier yesterday the firemen were called to 70 Davis Street, a home owned by George Stavrow, to fight a cellar fire. The home received minor smoke and water damage.

A flooded space heater sent firemen to an apartment owned by Ernest Tasoulas at 82 Church Street yesterday morning.

Sunday night firemen put out an oil burner fire at the home of Mr. and Mrs. Roland J. Robitaille at 45 Oak Street.

Late Saturday night a clogged stove pipe caused firemen to be called to the home of Sanford Williams, 161 High Street.

A flooded oil burner caused a minor fire at the home of Mr. and Mrs. Thomas Roche, 27 Gates Street.

Shortly after noon Saturday firemen extinguished a grass fire at 71 Valley Street on property owned by Mrs. Jeanette Wilder.

————

1961

Reported by the *Keene Evening Sentinel* on January 9th, 1961:

Firemen Answer Emergency Call

Firemen responded to an emergency call yesterday at 1:33 p.m. from the home of Mrs. Agnes Venette, 16 Martin Street where gas leakage from a refrigerator in the cellar was reported.

Firemen found sulfur dioxide fumes in the air. They carried the refrigerator outside and used pan-of household ammonia to neutralize the remaining gas fumes in side

———

Reported by the *Keene Evening Sentinel* on February 17th, 1961:

Keene Girl, 7 Heroine in $8,000 Fire

Elana Houpis 7, daughter of Mr. and Mrs. Constantine N. Houpis of 17 Baker Street was the heroine last night in a fire that caused about $8,000 damage to her home.

Her father said today that Elana was upstairs with her brothers, Nicholas 5, and Christy 2, when their mother discovered a fire in their living room divan. The children were getting ready for bed.

The mother's cry apparently frightened Nicholas who crawled under a bed. Elana prodded him out and took his hand. She also picked up Christy under her arm and all three went downstairs and outside.

The mother and her three children escaped without injury but a pet parakeet died, apparently overcome by smoke. The father who owns the Crystal Restaurant was working at the time.

Fire Chief Walter R. Messer said he was uncertain of the cause of the fire but that it could have been a cigarette.

Shortly after firemen responded to the still alarm they sounded a general alarm and

Engines 1 and 4 responded along with Ladder 2 and Squad 1. The fire was extinguished within a half an hour.

———

Reported by the *Keene Evening Sentinel* on February 21st, 1961:

Fire Department Budget Cut Discussed

Firemen and city officials discussed a firemen's protest over proposed cuts in the Fire Department budget for 1961 in a meeting at the Fire Station last night, but nothing was resolved.

Fire Chief Walter R. Messer had recommended an increase of $4, a week for permanent firemen and an increase of four firemen. The firemen supported both measures and the New Hampshire Fire Underwriters had recommended the additional men.

During budget discussion, City Manager Donald E. Chick and the City Council's Finance Committee recommended increasing salaries for permanent firemen by two percent for a average of a little than $2 a week and recommended against adding more men this year.

The mayor, the Finance Committee, the council's Fire Committee Messer and Chick heard protests from all permanent firemen who wanted to speak. Chief spokesman for the firemen was Lawrence Thompson president of the permanent firemen's organization.

———

Reported by the *Keene Evening Sentinel* on February 23rd, 1961:

False Alarm Brings Out 50 Firemen

Keene's second false fire alarm of the year was rung in late last night sending more than 50 regular and call firemen to the Gilsum Street area.

Fire Chief Walter R. Messer said that whoever was ringing in the false alarms seems to like the late hours. He said the first false alarm of the year was a little after 1:15 a.m. Jan 15. Last night's alarm was recorded at 11:15 p.m.

Chief Messer said "that Box 38 near 208 Gilsum Street had definitely been pulled. The box had evidence of being actuated. It was not a malfunction in the alarm system. The police were there and they are now investigating the incident."

Police Sgt. Albion Metcalf is in charge of the investigation.

———

Reported by the *Keene Evening Sentinel* on April 27th, 1961:

Civil Defense Alert Set for Tomorrow

Civil Defense Operations Alert 1961 will be held in this city starting at 3 p.m. tomorrow and will continue through noon Saturday. This is a statewide practice alert.

Fire Chief Walter R. Messer Keene's Civil Defense director said today, local residents will be asked to take cover tomorrow when the signal is sounded at 4 p.m. All streets will be cleared and motorists will be asked to pull to the side of the street and to fake cover.

"At 4:15 the all-clear will sound but the actual alert practice will continue until noon Saturday. During that time our communications systems (RACES) the contact between state, county and local Civil Defense units will be in operation. Radiological personnel and Civil Defense police will also be taking part." Messer said.

Messer said that the Conelrad radio channel will be operating from 4-4:30 p.m. tomorrow. He urged all residents to listen in for instructions. Conelrad supposedly would be the only communication system working during and after an actual attack.

All other radio stations and television channels will go off the air during that half-hour. Conelrad frequencies are 640 and 1240.

———

Story by Steve Goldsmith:

Keene Musters

On October 8th, 1961 the Keene Muster was held at the Cheshire Fair Grounds which was an annual event, as was, and still is the Annual Fire Prevention Parade. The musters aren't held anymore as the muster team no longer exists, but during Keene Fire's 60's and

KEENE FIREMEN at the annual Firemen's Muster at Cheshire Fair Grounds. From Left to Right standing, Wayne Crowell, Ervin Vorce, Larry Cutter, Earl Wilber, Wesley Peets, George Vorce, Larry Thompson, driver, Bob Murry, Bob Raymond and Ronald Amadon; kneeling, Robert Mason and Winston Wright. More than 4,000 attended musters. Seventeen teams from four states competed. Photo by Roger Packard, Union Leader.

through the 70's, Musters were a big event for the tri-state fire departments.

————

Reported by the *Keene Evening Sentinel* on November 25th, 1961:

Summer Street Garage Fire Investigated

Fire in the garage of Dr. James M. Ballou, 53 Summer Street is under arson investigation.

After extinguishing flames shortly before 8 last night firemen found that there had been two fires 10 feet apart along an inside wall.

One had started in a coca mat and the other had started in a bundle of papers and suitcases. Both were near the floor. An odor of kerosene was detected in the burned substance. Fire Chief Walter R. Messer said; and Police Chief William T. Bridgham confirmed Messer's statement.

Chief Messer notified the police department and Sgt. Albion F. Metcalf and Officer Francis J. Donahue Jr. are investigating.

The flames damaged inside garage wall surfaces, but did not get through the wall sheathing into the partitions, firemen said. The blaze blistered ceiling paint and damaged the casing around a door leading from the garage to the house.

There was no indication whether there was this morning, a particular arson suspect.

About 11 a.m. today firemen responded to a call from 51 Arlington Ave. to put out a grass fire.

————

Reported by the *Keene Evening Sentinel* on December 4th, 1961:

Fire Destroys Matthews Road Machine Shop

A fire that broke out before dawn this morning destroyed a small machine shop on Matthews Road making precision parts for the defense effort.

Damages were unofficially estimated in the neighborhood of $24,000. The precision turret latches and other machines were owned by Clarence Bergeron who ran the business in a building owned by John Scobi.

Bergeron's two full-time employees and other part-time help made close tolerance parts for missiles, submarines and airplanes. The value of the machines was roughly estimated at $20.000.

Although the cause of the fire was not ascertained, it was thought that it may have broken out in a faulty refrigerator. The Keene Fire department was called at 4:40 a.m., and returned to the station at 6:39 a.m. Four trucks were sent.

Bergeron said that the shop had just been moved to the location three or four months ago. He had been making parts in his basement, but had had to expand and buy new machinery.

————

Reported by the *Keene Evening Sentinel* on December 8th, 1961:

Dense, Choking Smoke. Firemen from the Keene Department were hampered Friday by heavy

smoke in their efforts to put out this fire. The fire alarm was sounded at 10:22 for the blaze, which was at 82 Church St. in the building owned by Ernest J. Tasoulas. Tasoulas had his law office in the front, the rear was occupied by tenants. The fire was confined to the rear of the building. Photo by Dodd.

Fire broke out at about 10:30 this morning in the rear of the house on Church Street in which Ernest J. Tasoulas had his law office.

The blaze was brought under control by the Keene Fire Department in about half an hour, although damage to the rear portion of the house was heavy.

Because of the dense and acrid smoke, the department's air breathing masks were used by some of the firemen who had to stay in the smoke.

Books and office equipment were carried out of the smoke-filled law office on the street front, and tarpaulins were spread over the furniture.

The fire appeared to be centered in the rear attic, and firemen pried off slates to get to the stubborn blaze which kept breaking out afresh in the corners and edges of the roof. The cause of the fire and the amount of damage could not be learned this morning.

The building is at the rear of the A and P supermarket parking lot and hundreds of spectators watched.

———

Reported by the *Keene Evening Sentinel* on December 13th, 1961:

Fire Alarm System Bid To Moran

Low bidder on the public school fire alarm system for which the School Board approved the contract this week is Philip D. Moran, Keene electrical contractor.

The base bid was $5,199 and his alternate bid for an alarm-box installation at Thompson Hall was $419, bringing the total for boxes at all public schools and the two at the high school to $5,618.

The only other bidder was Fred H. Hamblet whose total bid was $6,044.

The Board voted to charge about $500 for the Thompson Hall alarm to the High School Building Account; a like amount to the Fuller Addition Account for the alarm there: $4.500 to the budget account set aside for the project; and the balance of about $100 to the Land and Building Committee's General Account.

———

1962

Reported by the *Keene Evening Sentinel* on January 2nd, 1962.

"FIRE"

KTC Paint Shop Loss Estimated at $4,000

A fire at the Keene Teachers College paint shop did about $4,000 to $5,000 damage early Sunday morning. The alarm was sounded at 3:44 a.m.

Investigators from the state fire Marshall's office were looking over the charred interior of the shop this morning, but it was speculated unofficially that the blaze may have been caused by defective wiring in a heating fan. The damage estimate was also unofficial.

The fire was in a barn behind the Theta House, a boy's dormitory, on the East Side. The barn housed the plumbing and paint shops of the college and only the interior of the paint shop was charred although the plumbing shop was damaged somewhat by water as the firemen strove to quench the blaze in the near zero cold. Four trucks had been dispatched by the fire department, and they returned to the fire station at 5:48 a.m.

A college spokesman said that some paint had been destroyed by the blaze, but quite a lot would still be usable, although the painters would have to pry the lids off to see what was in the cans. The labels were burned off.

———————

Reported by the *Keene Evening Sentinel* on February 15th, 1962:

Refrigerator Starts $10,000 Hi-Hat Fire

A fire apparently started by the explosion of a defective refrigerator caused damage unofficially estimated at $10,000 at the Hi-Hat restaurant, 711 Marlboro Street this morning.

One tenant of an upstairs apartment jumped out of a window.

The Keene Fire Department was called at 7:01 a.m. and fought the blaze for two hours. Four trucks and the ladder truck were sent. The rescue truck from the Meadowood Fire Department also came.

Going Up: *Keene firemen climb the aerial ladder to get close to a Hotspot on the roof of the Hi Hat restaurant. The fire broke out at about 7 am and is thought to have been caused by the explosion of defective refrigerator. (Photo by Dodd)*

Clouds of Smoke: *The stubborn blaze at the Hi Hat restaurant this morning was eventually, quenched by floods of water from the hoses of the Keene Fire Department. Smoke and fumes billowed upward as the blaze tenaciously clung to life in the floors, roof, and partitions. (Photo by Dodd)*

From the kitchen, where the refrigerator was located the fire spread into the upper story of the one-and-a-half story frame building. Firefighters used ladders and the aerial ladder truck to direct streams of water into the upper windows and onto the roof, where there were occasional puffs of flames.

The owner of the restaurant is John Patenode of the same address, who was present at the fire although he was away at the time it started. One of several tenants in the apartments above the restaurant discovered and reported the fire.

Fireman Laurence Wood suffered burns and blisters when hot roofing tar splattered on his hand as flames melted the shingles.

Trucks at the fire were Engine 4, Engine 1, Ladder 2 and Squad 1 as well as the Meadowood rescue unit, Firemen and a number of volunteers fought the blaze for several hours. The all –clear was sounded at 9:04.

Local radio stations broadcast a plea by Police Chief William Bridgham to motorists to avoid if possible, the road between Marlboro and Keene. The fire slowed traffic, but police control was thorough and no lasting tie-ups developed.

———

Reported by the *Keene Evening Sentinel* on March 5th, 1962.:

"FIRE"

Police Investigating $5,000 West Street Fire In Unoccupied House

Holes in the Ceiling. Chief Walter Messer of the Keene Fire Department surveys damage in the ceiling of the second floor hallway in an unoccupied house at 550 West St., the fire, which broke out Saturday night, did an estimated $5,000 in damage. The Keene Police Department is investigating the cause. Photo by Dodd.

Keene police today were investigating a fire which did an estimated $5,000 damage to a stately, unoccupied house at 550 West street near Park Ave.

The house is the one used by the players at the Keene Summer Theater as a dormitory.

The fire, which spread in the space between the attic floor and the ceiling of the second story, was reported at 9:41 p.m. Saturday.

It apparently had been burning for some time since the heavy frame members of the attic floor were deeply charred.

Rubbish Heap

After the attic fire had been extinguished, firemen surveying the house discovered a smoldering heap of rubbish in the cellar that could have had no connection with the attic fire. It had been quenched by water leaking into the cellar as firemen fought to bring the attic fire under control. The owner of the house was said to be George Hanna of the law firm of Faulkner, Plaut, Hanna and Zimmerman.

The Keene Fire Department had four trucks at the scene. The first alarm was sounded at 9:41 and the second was sounded at 9:44. The trucks returned to the station at four minutes before midnight.

While the firemen were at this blaze a chimney fire erupted at a house owned by Donald Wyman and occupied by tenants at 39 Armory Street. The alarm was sounded at 10:57 p.m. and a truck was dispatched from the fire station and put the fire out.

At 9:23 Sunday morning a chimney fire broke out in the same house again and at 3:51 p.m. Sunday at the same house a chimney fire and a third chimney fire broke out at 2:37 p.m. and the firemen put it out again.

The fire out and firemen found it extinguished when they there were two other fires reported on Sunday at 2:37 p.m. a truck was dispatched to Dino Houpis at 81 Main Street for a car fire. The truck returned to the station at 2:41 and Sunday morning there was a sprinkler alarm sounded at the national Grange Mutual Insurance Co. building on West Street. A pile of boards stacked near the furnace caused it. They had caught fire and set off the sprinkler above them. The sprinkler put arrived.

———

Steamer Company: *Seated from L to Rt: W. Sanderson, J. Little, C. Johnson. 1st, Row L to R: A. Little, K. Conant, W. Peets, R. Safford, G. Vorce, N. Trask. 2nd, Row: J. Little, W. Stromgren, A. Jacques, C. Rowell, M. Mills, P. Trask.*

Deluge Company: *Front row seated from L to R: Russell Driscoll, Bruce O'Neil, Everett Symonds, George Shepard, Paul Symonds Sr., Clarence Caldwell, Paul Bergeron, Linwood Curtis. Second row standing from L to R: Wilfred Begin, Paul Rushlow, Charlie Woods, Harold Nash, Robert Murray, Stephen Pollock Jr., William Omstead, Robert Raymond, Earl Wilbur. 1962 Washington Hook and Ladder picture is on page 656.*

On April 1st, 1962 Chief Messer added 4 new firefighters to the department. Reported by the *Keene Evening Sentinel* on April 1st, 1962:

"STORY"

4 Men Join Fire Department Full Time

Four men have joined the Fire Department as full-time firemen Chief Walter R. Messer said Monday.

They are Homer L. Atkins of 50 Castle Street, Allan O. Collier of 29 Oak Street, Ronald P. Amadon of 19 Hillside Ave. and Robert A. Symonds of 116 Roxbury Street.

Atkins was formerly an officer with the Keene Police Department. The other three have been "call" or part-time firemen.

Chief Messer said that the addition of men to the full time rolls of the department was a step toward the improvement of the city's insurance rating. The council and the city manager had backed the addition, he said.

————

Reported by the *Keene Evening Sentinel* on April 5th, 1962:

Keene Fire Companies Will Meet

The annual meetings of the Keene Fire Companies will be held Saturday afternoon, and will be followed by a dinner at 6:30 at the fire station.

The companies that will meet are the Deluge Hose Co., the Washington Hook and Ladder Co., the Keene Steam Fire Engine and Hose Co., the Permanent Co., and the Civil Defense Auxiliary Co.

Explaining the role of the companies. Chief Walter r. Messer said that all of the permanent full time firemen are members of the Permanent Co. The call firemen who are summoned for general alarm fires are members of the Deluge Hose Co., The Washington Hook and Ladder Co., the Keene steam Fire Engine and Hose Co. and the Civil Defense Auxiliary Co.

The Deluge Hose Co. and the Keene steam Fire Engine and Hose Co. are the crews in charge of four of the fire departments pumpers, and the Washington Hook and Ladder Co., is the crew of the ladder truck.

Each group elects officers yearly, Chief Messer explained including a captain.

————

Reported by the *Keene Evening Sentinel* on April 17th, 1962:

False Fire Alarm Investigated

Keene police this morning were investigating a false alarm turned in at the alarm box at the intersection of Arch and Bradford Streets at 9:29 Monday night. The Keene Fire Department sent four trucks to the box.

At 6:35 p.m. Monday, the department was called for a fire in a garage belonging to Carl Atkins at 23 Perham Street. The garage used partially to house sheep was badly damaged. The trucks returned to the station at 7:30 p.m.

At 4:57 p.m. Monday there was a fire at the home of Marion Poisson at 22 Gardner Street. It was in a shed at the rear of the house, and was badly damaged. The firemen kept the fire from spreading to the house. The trucks returned to the station at 5:20.

————

Reported by the *Keene Evening Sentinel* on May 9th, 1962:

Fire Addition May Go to City Council

Lack of agreement among members of three City Council committees over how big a proposed addition to the fire station should be is expected to send the question to the full Council to be resolved.

The question is whether to authorize a one-story addition to provide room for central dispatcher equipment, or a two-story addition to provide for that, plus room for beds for the department's expansion.

Discussing it last night were the Fire Finance and Land and Buildings committees, the mayor, the city manager and the fire chief.

The one-story cost estimate is about $6,000; two-story estimate, $12,000 to $14,000.

The central-dispatcher system to handle fire calls on a county wide basis has been approved by the County Convention and the city has approved making space available as a headquarters.

The City Council, too in approving the 1962 city operating budget, made provisions for four new firefighters in what was described as the first step in bringing the department up to the strength recommended by the Fire Underwriters.

To make room for the new men it is planned to use a room that has been the fire chief's office. This would give space for four beds.

The Council committeemen who favor the two-story addition argued last night that to build the one story addition now would be a false economy.

The one-story addition would provide for immediate needs, they said but within a relatively few years the second story would have to be put on and the cost of doing part of the job twice is hot necessary cost. It could be done all at once more economically.

Those who favored the one-story addition said that since tow-story space is not needed now, spending money for it is not justified. A flat roof that could later become a first floor ceiling and a second story floor could be put on and the tip story built when needed.

Generally speaking, Fire Committee members favored the two story addition and Finance committee members favored the one. The makeup of the committees makes a definite lineup difficult since some men are members of one or the other besides being on the Land and Buildings Committee.

Louis Simon and James A. Mugford are on the Finance Committee, H. Franklin Guild, who has resigned, was the third man. The Fire Committee is Jeremiah J. Keating, Francis P. Callahan and George E. Fish. The Land and Buildings Committee is Mugford, Callahan and Evans H. Barrett.

Regardless of which plan is approved it is proposed to add about 200 square feet of floor space to the current fire alarm room, which itself is housed in a one-story addition to the east side of the fire station, facing Vernon Street.

The tow-story plan would add 400 more square feet of space; the 200 above the proposed addition and 200 above the existing fire alarm room.

————

From the *Keene Evening Sentinel*:

"STORY"

Fire Station Contract to Be Considered

The City Council tonight is expected to consider awarding the contract for the proposed fire station addition and if it does, it may have uncluttered a cluttered situation.

The actual low bidder withdrew his bid, but it appeared today the withdrawal came after, not before Tuesday's bid opening. This raised at least the theoretical question of whether the Council might be able, legally, to hold the low bidder to his bid.

The Bergeron Construction Co. Inc. put in a bid offering to build the two-story addition to house a countywide fire alarm communications control center for $9,795. He contacted City manager Donald E. Chick to say that his figuring had left out an item that would increase the cost, and he wanted to withdraw.

This was not reported prior to the bid opening, however, but the other three bidders agreed that something must have been omitted and they would not oppose the withdrawal.

Other bidders were R. E. Bean Construction Co. Inc., $13,373, reported yesterday as; low since Bergeron apparently had withdrawn, the MacMillin Co., $13,557; and Ivah Ballou, $15,990.

———

From the *Keene Evening Sentinel*:

"STORY"

Fire Station Addition Job Goes to Bean Co.

The City council last night approved unanimously and without comment authorization for the city to contract with the R. E. Bean Construction Co. for construction of a fire station addition at Bean's bid price of $13,373.

The action followed City Manager Donald E. Chick's explanation that the low bidder had withdrawn. Chick did not elaborate.

The Bergeron Construction Co. bid of $9,795 was the lowest of four submitted but it was withdrawn because some elements had been omitted.

The Council also authorized borrowing up to $16,000 for the addition to be repaid next year. Chick said that besides basic contract cost the expense would include $790 for electrical installation $750 for plumbing and heating lines, $500 for architect's and supervisory fees and $125 for underground telephone lines.

The two-story addition is to house the countywide communications control center and provide room for anticipated fire department expansion.

———

Reported by the *Keene Evening Sentinel* on September 1st, 1962:

Fire System Being Installed Mutual Aid Center in Operation

As the culmination of seven years of planning the Mutual Aid system went into operation this week from its control center on Vernon Street. It is the only center of its type in New England. Mutual Aid is the short title of the southwestern New Hampshire District Fire Mutual Aid System, which acts as a nerve or control center for 48 fire departments in New Hampshire and Vermont border towns.

The control center is prepared to handle all emergency services in New Hampshire and Vermont border towns.

The control center is prepared to handle emergency services in the area and early this morning had its first test in other than a fire situation.

When the Foley Ambulance responded to a call at the site of this morning's accident on Route 12, the ambulance driver radioed the dispatch center and reported that a rescue team was needed at the scene where a car had gone over a 50 foot rocky embankment.

On a separate network the dispatch center alerted the nearest rescue unit which in this case happened to be the Meadowood County Fire department. That organizations rescue team was sent to the accident scene to lend assistance.

The Mutual Aid center is the coordinator for county police service, ambulance service, and county sheriff departments. Vehicles of these services are linked to the center by radio and are dispatched by the center as needed in coordination with other department.

Robert Callahan chief coordinator is in charge of the Mutual Aid center. The telephone number is Elmwood 2-1100.

———

Reported by the *Keene Evening Sentinel* on November 24th, 1962:

"FIRE"

Boiler Room Fire Halted At Abbott Co.

Fire broke out last night in the boiler room of the Abbott Co. on Railroad Street.

The fire started in a pile of sawdust close to the front of the boiler for reasons not yet known, Keene Fire Chief Walter Messer said this morning. It spread slightly to the room's partitions.

The fire apparently heated the room to the point where the sprinkler alarm system on the furniture company was set off. The sprinklers took care of most of the fire before Keene firemen arrived on the scene around 7:20 p.m.

Mrs. William F. MacPhail first reported the fire. She said she heard the Abbott Co. alarm ringing for 20 minutes from her home on 68 Water Street and fiscally went to investigate. She saw smoke so called the Keene Police.

The police called Fire Mutual Aid and also sent a cruiser patrol down which found nothing suspicious.

Keene Engine 4 responded to the call and spent about an hour and a half on the scene. The firemen had to cut through some of the partitions. They also had to get rakes and rake through the pile of sawdust.

At 9:05 p.m. Engine 4 returned to station and Keene Engine 6 set out for Abbott Company with a special portable cellar pump. The boiler room was flooded by water from the sprinklers and also from the firemen's hoses. Engine 6 pumped out the room and was back in service at 10:30 p.m.

Damages were slight Arthur I. English vice-president and general manager of Abbott Co. said this morning.

Both Chief Messer and Mr. English said they had no idea what caused the fire. Messer is investigating. Also the Abbott Co. alarm system is not connected with the fire station Messer said.

———

Reported by the *Keene Evening Sentinel* on December 12th, 1962 by Jon McLaughlin Sentinel Staff Writer:

"FIRE"

9 Engines Fight Blaze 3 Hours

Firefighters Battle Blaze in Near Zero Weather: *Keene firemen fought this blaze at the Carey Chair Mfg Co. last night while the temperature slowly dropped below zero. The fire started before midnight, and quickly roared out of control in the two-story wood and concrete structure. Photo by McLaughlin.*

A general alarm fire completely destroyed the east wing of Carey Chair Manufacturing Co. on Victory Street last night and injured one Keene fireman.

Franklin Carey president of the company this morning estimated damages at $50,000 and said 35 employees are temporarily out of work as a result of the fire.

Icicles on Fire Site: *Coated now with icicles (firemen poured 350,000 gallons of water on the building) the remains of the fire-gutted Carey Chair Mfg Co. on Victoria St. are shown here as they looked yesterday afternoon. Flames, which rose 20 feet high on the night before last caused $50,000 in damage to the east wing of the building and caused the unemployment of 35 of the 55 company workers. A case of dynamite inside the building, near the doorway, had to be removed by firemen. Photo by McLaughlin.*

The only injury was received by Keene fireman Wesley Peets who cut his knee by knee by falling on a nail and had to be taken to Elliot Community Hospital for a tetanus shot.

All six fire engines of the Keene Fire Dept. two Meadowood fire trucks and a Marlboro fire engine teamed up to quench the blaze that was first reported at 11:45 p.m. Keene Fire Chief Walter Messer said firemen had the situation under control at around three o'clock this morning.

Carey said the wing was completely covered by insurance and would be rebuilt in the indefinite future. The main building and another wing of the Furniture Company escaped damage.

Messer said the fire started in the sanding room on the first floor of the two-story east wing. Sparks from the sanding machine ignited wood dust o the floor. Messer attributed the rapid spread of the fire to the lack of a sprinkler system and large amounts of wood dust throughout the building.

The only people on the premises when the fire broke out were two watchmen and the man operating the sanding machine who quickly left the building without incident.

Cary said all the company shipping assembly and sanding was performed in the east wing which in now a "total loss." Large quantities of furniture stored on the second floor were burned. The machinery received water damage but not fire damage he said.

The wood working is handled in the main building where business will resume next week.

Four Keene fire engines responded to the general alarm at 11:46 p.m. More and more trucks were called in as the fire spread until nine engines and their crews were fighting the fire by one o'clock in the morning as a large crowd of bystanders looked on.

The units at the fire were Keene Engines 1,2,3,4, Ladder Truck 2 and Emergency Squad 1. Marlboro Engine 1 and Meadowood Ladder Truck 1 and the Meadowood Rescue and Squad Car. Chief Messer was in charge of the entire operation.

Brattleboro Engine 4 covered the Spofford station; Spofford and West Swanzey Engine 2 covered the Keene station.

The all-out signal came at 8:10 a.m. Messer said the last five hours of the firefighting were devoted mainly to overhaul and dousing stray flames.

———

Reported by the *Keene Evening Sentinel* on December 20th, 1962:

"STORY"

Fire Chief Cautions On Yule Decorations

The Keene Fire Dept. is not only responsible to put out fires but to help prevent them.

And as the Christmas season nears its Tuesday climax, Fire Chief Walter R. Messer had requested that due caution be observed in handling and decorating Christmas trees.

Messer asked the public to use a flame retardant "of sorts" on their trees and to keep inside trees immersed or set in water.

Several years ago he noted the sentinel ran an article that recommended the use of a solution combining borax and boric acid with water that can be sprayed with a "fit gun" on trees or if a tub is available in which trees can be immersed.

The recommended mixture, the article said, included nine ounces of borax and four ounces of boric acid mixed with one gallon of water. It can then be sprayed on a tree by any means that will thoroughly saturate all the limbs. The mixture is orderlies, does not discolor the tree and will not stain.

Messer also gave particular emphasis to the so-called "Coconut Grove Law" which requires those Christmas trees in places of public assembly is flameproof.

Noting an increase in the use of metal trees, Messer said that these present a hazard if the electric lights are placed on them. He recommended that lights not be draped over such metal trees but that lights are so arranged as to reflect on the tree. As for lights on regular Christmas trees the Chief urged that the wiring be checked and double-checked and that lights be kept from leaning on needles of the tree limbs in order to prevent rapid drying.

Christmas trees set in water, Messer noted, will remain in a damp condition to some extent and thus will present a lesser fire hazard.

———

Reported by the *Keene Evening Sentinel* on December 21st, 1962 by Jon McLaughlin Sentinel Staff Writer:

"FIRE"

Fire Destroys Two-Family House; Three Firemen Hurt

Two families lost their home yesterday when fire gutted the house at 40 Winchester Court, injuring three Keene firemen and causing an estimated $15,000 damages.

Eight Keene and Meadowood fire trucks and their crews had the blaze in the empty house under control after more than one and a half hours of fire-fighting in bitter 15 degree cold.

The wooden dwelling was described as a "total loss." It had been occupied by the families of Richard E. Dunn, the owner and Edwin Bourassa of the Keene Police force.

George Shepard jr., Emile DeRosier and Prescott M. Little, all of the Keene Fire Dept., had to be taken away for emergency medical treatment during the fire.

Keene Firemen Battle Blaze at 40 Winchester Court: *A Keene fireman brings up another ladder in order to go to assistance of companion on the porch roof of the house at 40 Winchester Court. Another fireman bends over choking with smoke, right foreground. Fire caused an estimated $15,000 in damage. (Photo by McLaughlin)*

ﷲ *A Demon Called Fire*

Keene Fire Department Acrobatics: *A Keene fireman here balances at the end of a ladder of Keene Ladder Truck 2 and chops a hole in the house wall at 40 Winchester Court in order to get a hose onto the flames n the attic. Another fireman has a precarious foothold on the icy porch roof as he helps hold a high-pressure hose being operated in the second story. (Photo by McLaughlin)*

Treated at Hospital

Shepard was treated at Elliot Community Hospital for smoke inhalation received by staying too long inside the house. He was held overnight for observation and released this morning.

Little received spark burns to his face and left eye when struck by an unidentified falling object while coming out the front door, and Emile DeRosier was overcome by smoke. Neither required hospitalization.

Keene Fire Chief Walter Messer said the fire did so much damage because it had been burning for an undetermined time before a neighbor telephoned a report to fire Mutual Aid at 12:05 p.m. Two other neighbors called in within the minute.

When the first Keene Firemen arrived on scene, they found flames roaring out of control in the partitions and cellar, and the whole rear of the house was a smoking inferno.

Messer said the fire started through a "malfunction in an oil burner installed this fall."

Officer On Duty

Patrolmen Bourassa was on duty at the time and his wife and three pre-school age children were at Bourassa's father's, Leon Bourassa, 430 Marlboro Street where they have now moved. Bourassa is looking for a new apartment.

Dunn and his wife were at work and their son was at school. The Dunn's are staying with Edgar J. Durling, 35 Winchester Court.

A television set and a few armfuls of clothing were all that could be salvaged. All other furniture, clothing, and Christmas gifts were destroyed by either fire, smoke, or water. Walls and partitions were gutted and half of the roof is gone.

In the duplex arrangement, the Bourassa's occupied the rear or east portion of the house and the Dunn's lived in the front. Messer said fire-fighting was hampered because there was no interconnection between the two apartments.

Assistance Given

The Salvation Army is furnishing the Bourassa's with a crib this morning and a spokesman said it is organizing further assistance. The Army yesterday gave coffee to the firemen whose faces, helmets and protective clothing were

———

1963 [from *City of Keene Annual Report*]

1963 Report of the Chief Engineer of The Keene Fire Department

The Permanent force of the Fire Department consists of 19 men, including the Chief, 2 Deputy Chiefs and 3 Captains. The Call forces consist of 50 men including 2 call Deputy

Chiefs, 3 Captains, 3 First Lieutenants, and 3 Second Lieutenants. Out of this group the Chief, 2 Permanent Deputy Chiefs and 2 Call Deputy Chiefs make up the Board of Engineers.

During the year 1963 there were 291 still alarms and 48 box alarms for a total of 339 alarms received and answered by this department. There were 279 fire calls of which 20 were Mutual Aid calls. There were 60 non-fire calls, which includes rescue or emergency (32), false alarms (18), smoke scares or wrong location or accidental (9) and one special call (American Legion Test). Total number of inspection, made by permanent men, through the fire precinct and oil burner inspections were 1,628.

The automotive equipment housed in the one Central Station consists of, one 1961 Ford Chiefs car, one 1959 Ward LaFrance (750 gallon per minute centrifugal pump), one 1952 Pirsch (750 GPM centrifugal pump), one 1934 Ahrens Fox (600 GPM rotary pump), one 1930 Ahrens Fox (750 GPM piston pump), one 1946 Segrave (75' hydraulic operated aerial ladder), two 1941 Diamond T trucks (one equipped as a tanker and the other as a rescue unit), one 1948 Dodge Power Wagon for grass and brush fires. All of these units are two way radio equipped except the 1930 Ahrens Fox and the 1946 Segrave which have receiver radios only. Also one 1923 Reo (equipped with State of N.H. portable pump, hose, fittings, etc., for forest fires and this Reo truck also carries a mounted Willys 4 cyl. 500 GPM skid pump), one Twin Coach Trailer Pump. In addition to the above auto motive equipment there are portable pumps, lighting plants, smoke ejectors, Scott Air-Pac equipment, Deluge sets, Emerson resuscitator, foam inductors, hose, nozzles and fittings, powersaw, ladders, etc. All of the pumps were tested and all of the permanent men are instructed in their operations and maintenance. The rest of the equipment was also tested, operated and maintained by the permanent men. All of the pumps and equipment were found to be in good condition. There is 11,300 feet of 2 1//2 " hose and 6,100 ft. of 1 1/2 hose and all of this fire hose went through a 250 pound pressure test during May.

All of the cement floors on the ground floor were painted during the year and all of the fire alarm boxes were painted. The fire alarm circuits were kept in condition during the year; these involved running wires above and underground, brush trimming, testing circuits, etc. There were five fire alarm boxes replaced with modern automatic grounding type boxes and 4 new boxes were added to the circuits. These new boxes were located at Beaver & Page Streets #215, Woodbury Street & Fox Circle #235, Marlboro Street & Eastern Ave. #151 and Maple & Pako Avenues #442.

Training was held here in the station for the permanent men 1 to 2 hours daily regularly scheduled. The permanent men participated in the N. H. Chief's Club school held at Meadowood as instructors. The permanent men also helped train the nurses and employees of the hospital and nursing homes in evacuation and first aid fire fighting procedures. Also information and training was given to three of the large manufacturing plants in Keene to help them with there in plant fire brigades.

During the year there was a study and report made by the N. H. Fire Underwriters, which brought a reduction in the rating from class 5 to 4 for the City of Keene. Basically this was to give the manufacturing and industry insurance a reduction in base rates. The fire precinct in the central part of the city was increases making a much greater area to be inspected by the permanent firemen.

The number of permanent men should be increased to coincide with the recommendation of the Underwriters report as fast a s possible. A sub station with training facilities should be considered in the West

A Demon Called Fire

Keene area but only with no loss of manpower in the central station. The doors on the Fire Station should be replaced in the near future.

A Fire Prevention Division with inspector and clerical help should be provided as soon as possible.

	Value	Insurance Carried	Insurance Pd
Buildings	$435,700.00	$400,000.00	$59,521.56
Contents	$43,188.00	$30,044.00	$21,776.94
Totals	$478,888.00	$430,044.00	$81,298.50

Respectfully submitted
Walter R. Messer, Chief

————

Reported by the *Keene Evening Sentinel* on January 21st, 1963:

Family Lost 'Everything' During Fire

Fire destroyed the interior of a two-and-one-half story wooden house at 261 Water Street Saturday night causing damage estimated "in the thousands of dollars."

Owner Haerbert V. Braley said today as he surveyed the wreckage. "I've lost nearly everything I had."

Fire, smoke or water from the hoses destroyed nearly all furniture and clothing inside the house.

The Braley family moved into the home of Mr. and Mrs. Ernest Thoin in Marlboro.

Harley E. Folsom of 275 Water Street first reported the fire by telephoning Fire Mutual Aid at 6:31 p.m. Firemen and engines from Keene and Meadowood fought the blaze for ore than an hour and managed to salvage the exterior of the house.

A Keene fire official said fire started in a television set in the downstairs living room. Braley and his wife and three children were visiting the Thoins at the time.

————

Reported by the *Keene Evening Sentinel* on January 30th, 1963:

Quick Action By Plumber Saves House

Quick thinking by a plumber from the Gordon E. Davis Plumbing firm, 55 Washington Ave. saved the house at 225 Pearl Street after a tank of acetylene fuel caught fire in the cellar around 8:30 a.m. today.

Owner Karl P. Brown and two tenant families occupy the house. It is being remodeled and plumbers were at work in the cellar this morning when the hose of an acetylene torch ruptured. The torch flame ignited the fuel coming out of the length of hose attached to the tank, according to Keene Fire Chief Walter Messer. The tank itself caught fire after the hose burned up.

Messer said consequences might have been serious if Clarence E. Webber of 170 Gilsum Street had not tipped the blazing tank over onto its side on the dirt-covered cellar floor where the fuel burned with out causing any damage to the house.

Four Keene fire engines came to the scene. Firemen cooled the tank off and took it outside Messer said. No one was hurt.

————

Reported by the *Keene Evening Sentinel* on February 5th, 1963:

"FIRE"

Student Nurses Annex Destroyed On Wyman Way

Fire, which started in the cellar where several Elliot Community Hospital maintenance men were thawing water pipes with a blowtorch today substantially damaged Wyman Way Annex, student nurse quarters at the hospital. The two and one half story wooden house was valued at close to $40,000.

Nurses' Quarters Ruined. Firemen here fight the fire, which destroyed Wyman Way Annex, Elliot Community hospital student nurses' lodging. Estimate of damage has not been reported. The building was worth $35,000 - $40,000 according to hospital. Photo by McLaughlin.

A hospital spokesman said the Wyman Way Annex was vacant this year, though being readied for possible use by the new class this fall. It houses 12.

President of the hospital board of trustees Robert F. Babcock said, "The building was pretty well ruined, at least half gone. He valued the structure at $35,000 to $40,000.

Official cause of the fire has not been given. Babcock said "two or three" plumbers were at work in the upper story when they smelled smoke in the cellar. They ran downstairs and found a partition ablaze.

The plumbers, whom Babcock described as "well experienced" had been thawing frozen pipes with a blowtorch in the cellar shortly before.

Nine Keene and Meadowood fire engines came to the scene and firemen battled the blaze until the all-out signal came at 11:16 a.m. Keene Fire Chief Walter Messer was assisted by Meadowood Fire Chief Donald Holbrook in directing fire-fighting operations.

When Deputy Keene Fire Chief Harry F. Hammond arrived with the first three Keene trucks on the 9:15 a.m. still alarm; he found the flames had shot up through the partitions and set the entire attic ablaze. Hammond called Fire mutual Aid and ordered Box 17 sounded.

Other Keene and Meadowood fire engines came to find dense smoke billowing hundreds of feet into the air from the roof. Firemen had to use oxygen masks inside the house. No injuries have been reported. Firemen had to hack through walls and smash windows to get their hoses onto the flames. Many emerged choking from the house.

Marlboro Engine 1 covered the vacated Keene fire station.

Hospital authorities said it was discovered several weeks ago that the heating system in the annex was off. Recently frozen pipes were found in the cellar. The maintenance men were working on these defects. Hundreds of persons came to watch the firemen at work.

———

Reported by the *Keene Evening Sentinel* on February 6th, 1963:

"STORY"

City's Fire Insurance Rates Cut

Major improvements triggered by a disastrous factor fire which threw some 300 out of work nearly seven years ago, have made possible a six to eight percent reduction in fire insurance rates for commercial and industrial buildings in Keene.

Notice of a new classification for Keene from Class 5 to 4 was made public today by the N.H. Board of Underwriters here, through the Insurance Information Officer of N.H.

Keene City Manager Donald Chick told the IIONH that city had added some $30,000 a year to its fire department budget in taking on the equivalent of six new men; had installed new water mains and hand constructed a new $3,000,000 gallon reservoir.

Fire Alarm Additions

These improvements, plus additions to the city fire alarm system made the classification possible, according to W. Harrison Ferris superintendent of rating for the N.H. Board.

"It proves any community can earn better fire insurance rates", he explained, "by working with our engineers to make necessary improvements."

Crediting Fire Chief Walter R. Messer with a lion's share of the labors to bring about the new rating, Chick said that four men have been added to the department's staff, plus two more assigned to the county mutual aid system, which is headquartered in a new addition to the central fire station.

"We will be able to improve our training and inspections" he added, "because of the additional men. We are already sending three trucks on every first alarm, which is an improvement over the old system. This with added water power makes our department much more efficient.

"And we aren't going to stop here," he went on. "We are now aiming for a Class 3 rating". Only Manchester and Nashua now enjoy this classification.

Retroactive to Jan. 1st

Ferris said that because the insurance coverage figures are not available he could not estimate the total savings in premiums. He said the new rate was to be retroactive to January 1, and that it applies only to unsprinklered mercantile buildings, plus churches, schools and other public buildings. It does not apply to homes.

Much of the engineering work on the project was conducted by Carl B. Smith Jr., assistant manager of the board, working closely with Chick and Messer.

Keene suffered a major fire loss in 1956 when the Sprague and Carlton furniture factory was destroyed.

Reported by the *Keene Evening Sentinel* on February 11th, 1963:

"FIRE"

Lumber Company Destroyed by Fire

Fire of unknown cause Saturday night destroyed the Perkins Lumber Co. building at 31 Ralston Street. The flames, which sometimes danced more than 100 feet into the air from the wooden frame building, burned the structure almost down to the ground within 45 minutes.

Keene firemen Ernest Selby and Prescott M. Little were injured.

Selby was poisoned by smoke, treated at Elliot Community Hospital and released in time for him to return to the fire. Little received two cracked ribs when the fire truck on which he was riding went over a severe bump in the road on the way to the fire. He was treated and released from the hospital Sunday morning.

Lumber Company Fire: *Flames that shot over 100 feet in the air, sparks and smoke could be seen throughout most of Keene as firemen fought a fire at Perkins Lumber Co. on Ralston St., The scorched partition in the upper left finally fell to the ground. Cause of the $15,000 fire had not been determined. Photo by State News Service.*

Battling the Blaze: *Two Keene firemen play water on a portion of the Perkins Lumber Co. at 31 Ralston St., as fire spread through the wooden frame building and almost reduced it to ashes within 45 minutes. Photo by McLaughlin.*

Keene Fire Chief Walter R. Messer estimates damage at more than $15,000. The loss was fully covered by insurance according to the company assistant treasurer Cleon A. Nims.

Fire started inexplicably in a small office on the main floor, according to Messer. A still alarm report was given at 6:15 p.m. and the general alarm sounded two minutes later.

Keene fire engines and three Meadowood units came to the scene. Their crews kept the flames from spreading to the company's main office building at 29 Ralston Street and to other company sheds in the yard.

Used for storage and mill working Machinery tiles, plywood, Masonite and other materials stored Nims said company business would go on as usual. The 31 Ralston Street building was there was destroyed.

Edward H. Paquette, who leased a carpentry shop on the premises, is out of business. He made cabinets and doors and leased machinery from the company.

Nims said the building was termed a "total loss" by insurance appraisers. He said there are no plans for rebuilding. The company will salvage what it can from the rubble and then have the structure torn down.

No company employee is jobless because of the blaze, he added.

A crowed, estimated at over several hundred, gathered at the scene of the fire. State and local police set up a roadblock at the junction of Winchester, Pearl and Island Streets to prevent traffic from coming east into the city on Winchester Street. This was to claimant traffic congestion and allows the free access of fire department trucks responding to the fire.

———

Reported by the *Keene Evening Sentinel* on March 15th, 1963:

"FIRE"

Hay Barn Is Leveled; Nearby House Saved

Barn Fire. Keene firemen play hoses on the burning barn owned by Kenneth D. Cornwell, 436 Winchester St., fire leveled the barn. No persons or Livestock were hurt. Photo by McLaughlin.

Playing With Matches

Children playing with matches yesterday caused fire that leveled a hay barn owned by Kenneth D. Cornwell of 436 Winchester Street.

Cornwell said the fire destroyed 30 tons of hay, a hay bailer, two wagons, and two low wheel trucks all inside the barn. He does not have an estimate of total damage yet. No persons or livestock were hurt.

The Keene Fire Department lists "children playing with matches" as cause of the fire. Cornwell said if that were the cause they were neighborhood children because neither he nor his wife and child were home when fire broke out.

'Very Lucky'

The 42 x 60 foot barn was within 15 feet of the Cornwell house and Deputy Keene Fire Chief Robert N. Guyette who commanded the fire fighting, said the Cornwells were "very, very lucky" the towering flames didn't spread to the house.

The flames didn't spread Guyette said, because the wind was blowing away from the house and the first Keene firemen on the scene played their hoses on the side of the barn next to the house. When these firemen came, they found the whole barn wrapped in flames.

The barn, a familiar landmark was leveled within half an hour. Cornwell said the structure was fully insured against fire.

Inspector James G. Small of the Keene Police Department said five or six Keene Police and State Police officers worked at relieving traffic jams caused by the fire apparatus most of which stayed parked on Winchester Street during the first half hour.

Fire started shortly after 4 p.m. and the box alarm was sounded at 4:19 p.m. Five Keene engines came to this fire. A Meadowood engine came was not needed and returned to the station.

The last Keene engine returned to station at 4:13 a.m. today according to the Fire Mutual Aid log. Firemen stood on guard at 436 Winchester Street all night because the barn rubble was still smoldering.

Reported by the *Keene Evening Sentinel* on April 8th, 1963:

"FIRE"

In $10,000 Fire 2 Policemen, Fireman Rescue Five Children

Two Keene Policemen and a fireman braved dense smoke early yesterday morning to rescue from a $10,000 fire the five children of Mrs. Marion Yoerger of 463 Washington Street.

At home with chicken-pox when fire broke out in the early morning were Billy 9, Shirley, 4, Brenda, 3, and twins Dennis and Donald, aged 18 months. Mrs. Yoerger was away at the time.

The youngsters and their rescuers all suffered smoke inhalation but did not require treatment. The baby sitter also escaped uninjured.

Patrolmen Robert Donovan and Edwin F. Bourassa were in cruiser patrol about 3:50 a.m. when they spotted smoke coming from the on e-and a-half story wooden structure that contained the Yoerger apartment and also the Mark Toppan Co., a tiling firm.

Dashed Inside

Donovan and Bourassa dashed inside and each brought out two children. They could not return to rescue Shirley because they were overcome by smoke, they said.

The children were rescued from upstairs bedrooms that were gutted before firemen could quench the blaze. Fireman Keith Randall was taken to Elliot Community Hospital with smoke inhalation.

To Police Station

Keene police took the children to the police station where they waited until their mother was notified. Mrs. Yoerger and her children today are staying with Mrs. Yoerger's mother. Mrs. Eunice M. Cushing of 87 Pinehurst Ave.

Keene Fire Chief Walter R. Messer today estimated total property damage at about $10,000. Fire burned through the roof, ruined the upstairs, part of the apartment, and caused some damage downstairs. The Mark Toppan office received water damage and part of its ceiling was burned, Messer said.

The Keene Fire department alerted by the police, sent four engines and Meadowood sent squad and rescue truck.

Messer said today he though faulty electrical wiring in the ceiling of the Toppan office started the blaze that whipped upstairs through a partition.

The Salvation Army said today that the Yoergers lost everything they owned in the fire except a washing machine and refrigerator. The family badly needs clothing, according to the Salvation Army.

––––––––––

Reported by the *Keene Evening Sentinel* on July 2nd, 1963:

"FIRE"

Tenants Flee $4,000 Fire Here Sunday

Careless use of smoking materials caused a $4,000 fire at 21 Damon Court yesterday, forcing tenants to flee a tenement house fire.

According to Fire Chief Walter Messer embers from a cigarette or pipe apparently ignited a bed on the second floor porch of the two-story house, owned by Herbert and William Smith of Swanzey. The fire broke out at 1:39 a.m.

Flames spread from the porch into the attic at the rear of the building making Mutual Aid assistance from Meadowood necessary. Three Keene trucks and one from Meadowood responded along with rescue-squads from each department.

While firefighters were at the scene of the Damon Court fire a box alarm was rung in

from West Street and Bradford Road. Engines 2 and 3 were sent and reported back a false alarm. A Marlboro truck on the way to Keene was sent back.

––––––––––

Reported by the *Keene Evening Sentinel* on August 15th, 1963:

"FIRE"

Firemen Extinguish Partition Fire

Keene firemen were called to 28 Green Street yesterday afternoon after a still alarm was telephoned in saying that a house was on fire.

Firefighters put out a fire in a wall partition on property belonging to Lester Fairbanks. The alarm was sounded at 1:56.

The department had been called on July 23rd, to extinguish a bed fire at the same address according to records.

Chief Walter Messer said that the fire apparently started in the basement and went up through the partition and into a wall on the first floor. Gas masks were needed to get into the frame building, which is tenanted by three families.

The fire is still under investigation according to Chief Messer.

––––––––––

Reported by the *Keene Evening Sentinel* on October 4th, 1963:

"STORY"

Fire Department to Face Busy National Week

Besides the New England Championship muster, the Keene Fire Department has a number of activities planned for next week which is by proclamation national Fire Prevention Week.

A Demon Called Fire

Scouts Get Tour. As part of National Fire Prevention Week, Keene firemen showed cub scouts (Dens 1 and 6, pack 348 Symonds School) about the Fire station. Here they are on the hook-and-ladder truck. Photo by McLaughlin.

The New England Championship firemen's muster on Sunday, at the Cheshire Fair Grounds is to be preceded by a giant parade of fire tucks down Main Street.

Fifty fire trucks from Keene, outlying towns, other counties in the State of Connecticut, Massachusetts and Vermont are due to parade.

So are the Gordon-Bissell post American legion Band, the Keene High School Band, and the St. Michael's High School Band of Brattleboro, Vt.

At the muster, scheduled to start at 3:15 p.m., events will include centrifugal and rotary pumping contests, and the midnight alarm, in which firemen put on fire fighting equipment, from a pile of boots, coats and helmets and leap onto trucks, and race to a finish line.

About 30 entries from New Hampshire, Connecticut, Massachusetts, and Vermont are due to compete, said Fire Chief Walter R. Messer. The Keene muster Team will be among them.

Next week, the Keene Fire Dept. will have firemen visit every Keene School to exhibit fire-fighting gear, to supervise fire drills, and to answer questions on fire prevention.

At Elliot Community Hospital on Tuesday, the Fire Department. And the hospital will sponsor a day-long Fire Safety Workshop with Herbert Whitney, Deputy Fire Marshal, attending.

Some patients are to be evacuated, fire extinguishers are to be used to put out real fires, and firemen in fire prevention techniques, according to hospital administrator Robert K. Wood will drill hospital employees.

Some 60 employees from local nursing homes and from the Keene, Peterborough, Winchendon, Mass., and Brattleboro and Bellows Falls, Vt. Hospitals will attend. A Keene engine will be on hand.

The annual banquet of the Keene Fire Department is scheduled for Thursday night. The night before, Messer said, some Keene firemen and trucks may participate in the Fire Prevention Parade in Greenfield, Mass.

Saturday night is the night of the 115th annual ball for the Keene Firemen's Relief Assn.

————

Keene Fire December 24th, 1963 by *Keene Sentinel* Staff:

"FIRE"

Pair of Fires Battled by Firefighters

Fire from an overheated fire place and chimney swept up through partitions into a blind attic at the home of Raymond F. Merritt of 17 Burr Ave., yesterday afternoon.

As firemen fought the blaze from inside the house and squelched it before it broke out under the eaves and through the roof, police directed car traffic carrying curious spectators around the scene so that firemen could work unhampered.

Winter Work. Firefighters took precautionary measures from the outside of the Raymond Merritt residence at 17 Burr Ave while their fellow workers battled the blaze from the inside. Flames from an over headed fireplace worked up through partitions into a blind attic. Each year winter's cold puts more demand on heating facilities and the fire rate climbs. Photo by Gagnon.

At the same time Gilsum firefighters were busy putting out a fire in the home of Henry Gauthier, in Gilsum.

The first alarm for the Merritt residence fire came at 3:12 p.m. at 3:15 the Gilsum alarm sounded.

Merritt and a younger daughter, noticing smoke from around the fireplace in a new addition to the home, called for firefighters. A first truck and crew was joined by more crews four minutes later as the general alarm was sounded.

Firefighters stayed at the scene until 4:32.

In Gilsum, where the fire broke out of a stove, firemen worked only 12 minutes before returning to their station and reporting slight damage.

The Merritt family, consisting of the father, mother, stayed in the house last night.

Fire Chief Walter R. Messer set the first tentative estimate of the loss at about $2,000.

From the *Keene Evening Sentinel*:

"FIRE"

Fire Damages Home In Keene

Blazes that damaged the home of a Keene firefighter and destroyed a pump house attached to the home of the police chief in Spofford were the most serious of weekend fired in the county.

Fire of undetermined origin that broke out at 8:30 a.m. yesterday drove Keene firefighter Prescott M. Little and his family from their home at 44 Madison Street. Also burned out were a mother and child who lived in an upstairs apartment.

Little and his son, James, 5, were in the living room when fire broke out in the kitchen and Little carried the boy outside to safety, Fire Chief Walter R. Messer reported. Little said the fire seemed to "puff up" from the kitchen.

Mrs. Little and two other children, Larry, 15 and Linda. 11 were in church.

Walls Burned

A general alarm brought fire crews, who were able to keep the entire house from going up, but inside walls were burned or badly scorched.

The cause of the blaze still was being studied this morning, Chief Messer said.

The family moved to the home of Mrs. Little sister on Water Street right after the fire and later in the day moved again into the home of Prescott's mother at 21 Elliot Street.

The family lost all its clothing and personal belongings, included Christmas gifts already purchased. There was insurance coverage, but to what degree had not been determined early today. The loss estimate was several thousand dollars.

Mrs. Jay Marsh and her daughter, Debbie 4 also lost all their clothing and personal belongings including Christmas presents.

1964

As reported by the *Keene Evening Sentinel* January 20th, 1964:

"FIRE"

Firemen Called Thrice Sunday

Keene firemen were called out on three occasions Sunday.

At 1:59 pm, a still alarm brought firemen to MacKenzie Dairy Bar in the Keene shopping plaza. The call was caused by a smoke scare with Engine 4 returning to the station at 2:09 pm.

At 3:57pm, the department responded to a chimney fire at the Loren E. Livingood residence on Carroll Street.

No damage was reported and firemen returned to the station at 4:25 pm.

Finally, at 4:42 pm., a box alarm brought firemen to Central Square, where a car operated by Gordon Rudolf had caught fire. The damage was light and firemen were back at the station by 4:47p.m.

As reported by the *Keene Evening Sentinel* January 30th, 1964:

Operating Expenses

Police, Fire Requests Up By About $17,000

Budget requests for 1964 submitted by the police and fire departments total about $18,000 more for operating expenses than was budgeted last year. but these figures do not reflect an anticipated increase in police pay requests.

A "working budget" containing department heads requests is currently being used by the city council's Finance Committee and the city manager as a basis for their 1964 recommendations. Shows total city wide requests increases of $244,000 of which $135,000 is for higher operating costs and $109,000 is for increases in capital improvement requests

The Breakdown

Fire: Requests under salaries are increases of about $15,000. Of which $1,450 is asked for the chief and about $13,550 would be spread between two deputy chiefs, three captains, 13 fire fighters, and the call men. Besides providing two new firemen.

Among other items showing increased requests are; Uniforms $500, and supplies $300. (For requested new men), and $200 for new alarm system.

Capital improvement request are down $650 fro police department and up $1,100 for the fire department. Here's the detail:

Fire: New requests for this year are for Scott air masks, $970 and air cylinders $150.

As reported by the *Keene Evening Sentinel* March 2nd, 1964:

"FIRE"

Blaze Destroys Barn at Dairy Farm Cause is still Undetermined

Search for clues to the probable cause of a fire which destroyed a barn of the Winding Brook Dairy Saturday night continued late this morning

The barn, connected to a two story house, was engulfed in flame when Keene firemen reached the scene at about 11:20 p.m. Saturday

The initial call came from Mrs. Clinton Wilder who awoke from the sound of coughs from her grandson. Smelling smoke Mrs. Clinton notified the fire station after first awaking her daughter and another grandchild and three elderly tenants who moved to the street.

En route to the fire at 44 Maple Ave., Deputy Chief Robert Guyette called for reinforcements. Reporting that he could see the glow from along Park Ave. However at nearly the same time, a neighbor had pulled an alarm in front of the Peerless Insurance Co.

By 11:38 pm. Chief Walter Messer reported that the barn was destroyed and all firemen concentrating efforts on saving the house.

Successful attempts contained damage to a porch of the house, and a bathroom.

Three injuries were reported by firemen. Admitted to Elliot Community Hospital were David Adams, 32, mutual aid fire dispatcher, who suffered a bruised left hand, and puncture wound. Lee Tommila, 21, who reportedly slipped on ice and suffered an abrasion of his left hand, And, Phillip Davis, 23, who had two teeth broken when the force of water through a hose pushed him against a well. All three were treated and discharged

Milk bottling equipment at the dairy was not destroyed, but, it was impossible to bottle the dairy milk there for delivery this morning. The dairy had its milk bottled for delivery today in Brattleboro.

The 100 year old structure was reportedly insured, but, the amount was not known immediately.

Meadowood rescue units responded to the call at 11:25 pm. returning to the station at 12:21 am. All Keene units were back in service by 2:14 am.

Fire noted above of a Barn Destroyed: *A barn of the Winding Brook Dairy was destroyed by fire late Saturday night. Cause of the blaze*

was unknown following investigation yesterday and this morning. The fire sent eight people fleeing from the home of Clinton Wilder. Photo taken by Warren MacKenzie.

Fire noted below of 7 people left homeless: *Seven members of the Rodney Horton family were left homeless following this fire, gutted the inside of their four room house and attached garage yesterday. Cause of the blaze is undetermined. Photo taken by Reed.*

———

As reported by the *Keene Evening Sentinel* March 20th, 1964:

"FIRE"

7 Homeless after Fire Ruins House

A family of seven is homeless today following a wind swept fire that destroyed their four room house on the Daniels Hill Rd off route 9.

Mr. and Mrs. Rodney Horton and their five children aged from 1 – 7 were away from the house when fire broke out shortly before noon.

Dr. Thomas Lacey, who first noticed the fire, contacted Keene firemen who rushed to the scene. West Swanzey units were also called in. But attempts to save the house and an attached storage garage were fruitless. The insides of both structures were badly burned.

Horton who had left his house about an hour before the blaze to get some gasoline for a machine . He said he thought the house was insured, but was not sure for how much.

Cause of the fire believed to have started in the garage, was unknown.

———

As reported by the *Keene Evening Sentinel* April 13th, 1964:

"STORY"

Fire warning Is Issued by Chief Messer

Keene fire department and fire departments linked to the fire mutual aid network located in Keene were busy battling blazes in buildings, cars, grass, fields, and brush areas.

Caution

As a result, Keene fire chief, Walter R. Messer has offered a few words of caution to residents.

He said this morning that this is the time of year, just before the grass, brush, and leaves turn green that fires break out and burn readily. A combination of balmy weather, gentle and sometimes brisk winds and dry grass and leaves are just the combination to make one spark a firemen's nightmare.

Permits Required

Chief Messer said that permits are required for burning in the open. This aids in fire control, he pointed out, and keeps firemen alerted to the whereabouts of controlled burning.

But, he added, there is the problem of incinerators. No permits are required, Messer said, and asked that those who use them to carefully watch the burning to prevent accidental fires from their use.

———

As reported by the *Keene Evening Sentinel* April 13th, 1964:

"FIRE"

Weekend Blazes Keep Firemen on the Run

An 8 am. Box alarm on Sunday was a call to the most serious of number of fires that kept Keene firemen on the go through out the weekend.

The Sunday box 13 alarm from outside the Princess Shoe and Abbott Companies brought firemen and equipment to the Monadnock Cutlery Co. Inc. off Railroad Street, where fire broke out, Chief Walter R. Messer Said. Apparently from sparks imbedded in woodwork from previous operations of the company

Sprinklers helped to hold the blaze in check; Messer estimated damages at $3,000 to $4,000.

Engines one and four, ladder truck two and squad one answered the call. The all out sounded at 8:33 and all units were back in service at 9 am.

Still alarm at 1:34 at Robert Wilcox property occupied by tenants on Marlboro Street and Keene-Marlboro town line.

Two engines, the ladder truck and emergency squad were called out to the second box alarm (Box 252) at 2:36 for a car fire in a garage at 524 Washington Street.

At 2:49, engine one responded to a car fire at 203 North St.

———

As reported by the *Keene Evening Sentinel* May 20th, 1964:

City Firemen Called Out Three Times

Keene firemen were called out three times within the past 24 hours and all three resulted in no fires.

Lighting struck a house owned by Lawrence Paquette at 109 Royal Ave. at about 4:30 pm. The still alarm was caused because of the lingering smell of smoke.

Tracing the path of the bolt, the firemen said it apparently struck a garage first, cracking timber, and then traveled to the house where it blew fuses and grounded in the kitchen plumbing.

Shortly before 3am today, box 43 was sounded, near the corner of Ashuelot and West Street. Upon investigation it was found that a faulty alarm in the colony mill had been tripped by the fire detection system.

At 5:11 am. A still alarm sent firemen for a smoke scare at 21 Brook St. Investigation of the smoke found that a radio had burned out and some fuses had blown.

Finally, at 10:54 this morning, firemen were called to the Cheshire lunch for a minor blaze in the motor of a refrigerator unit. Minor damage resulted and the firemen returned to quarters at 11:15 am.

———————

Reported by the *Keene Evening Sentinel* May 22nd, 1964:

Hose testing moved from being pressurized by pumper, to a new "hydro-pneumatic hose tester.

Firemen use new device in hose tests.

Keene-Pressure-proofing 10,000 feet of hose at Keene fire station without using a fire engine pumper will be possible this year because of an ingenious device recently installed by firemen, directed by fire chief Walter R. Messer.

Annual Fire Hose Testing at Keene Fire House will be done without the roar of a fire engine pumping water due to a new device recently installed. Above, firemen John Phillips and Ernest Selby restrain nozzle as 250 pounds of water and air pressure are released. In background, Deputy Chief Robert Guyette, left, holds water valve with right hand and air valve with his left had, as fireman Larry Wood, and Larry Wood Jr., observe. Compressed air from tank between Guyette and Wood boosts normal water main pressure, making hose rock hard. Photo by Perrotta.

Equipment maintenance is a constant job at firehouses, with the facility at Keene no exception, as firemen above demonstrate. After pressure-proofing, the two and one half inch hose was carefully packed back into Engine 4, department workhorse, by, left to right, Larry Wood, Allan

Collier, Capt. Lawrence Thompson (bending over a truck) Chester Dubriskie, and Edwin Ball (On truck). Photo by Perrotta.

A combination of copper tubing, valves, and wood framing, the device can be best described as a "hydro-pneumatic" hose tester, Chief Messer said. It uses normal line pressure in the city water system, about 85 pounds, and added compressed air, bringing the total pressure in the hose up to required test load of 250 pounds per square inch.

Messer thinks the idea, originated during a Massachusetts fire chiefs meeting he attended, and developed by himself and Chief James Casavant, of Gardner Mass., may be unique in the country. "I don't know if we got the only one." Messer said, "But I've never seen one anywhere else."

Installation of the tester became possible when a large air compressor recently installed in the fire house for filling "Scott Air Packs", self-contained breathing devices. The compressor also fills large portable tanks with air to 2,000 pounds pressure.

On a convenient corner of the fire house, the fire men built a detachable wooden platform to hold valves for the air and water. Water is piped to the appropriate valve from inside the building. The pressurized air tank is brought along side the hose reloaded onto Engine 4 after being tested.

Each piece of hose is tested and inventoried. Each hose has been marked and numbered and date when purchased. Hose testing is completed each year. The hydro-pneumatic hose tester that was made in the early 60's was replaced in 2000 fro the tune of $5,000 dollars. Hose testing was always done prior to this by hooking directly to a fire truck and building pressure via the pumper. This new way makes it safer and easy to perform the daily task of hose testing.

As reported by the *Keene Evening Sentinel* June 8th, 1964:

"FIRE"

Lighting Source Of Still Alarm

Lighting was given as the cause of a still alarm last night at 10:39 at Cheshire Oil Co. Keene firemen found a small fire had ignited in a vent of a storage tank.

Minor damage resulted and the unit returned to quarters at 10:55pm.

———

As reported by the *Keene Evening Sentinel* July 1st, 1964:

"FIRE"

Blast Rocks Building; Man On Critical List Co-Worker Is Also Burned

A North Swanzey man remained in critical condition this morning in Elliot Community Hospital from burns received yesterday noon in an explosion which caused upwards of $50,000 damage to Dalbolt Inc. A textile manufacturing company, which leases space in the former Faulkner and Colony Mill.

Parker patch Jr., 36, superintendent of production for the West St. and Water Street plants of Dalbolt Inc. was working near a large gas oven at the time of the explosion at about 12:30 pm. He suffered burns over most of his entire body, according to the hospital.

A co-worker, 62 year old Joseph Soucy of 65 Appian Way, who was standing nearby, suffered burns to some 25 percent of his entire body. He was listed as in fair condition this morning.

Every window on the third floor of the section occupied by Dalbolt, Inc., was blasted during the explosion yesterday. Debris on West Street caused a detour by there for more than an hour. Photo by Reed.

At the site of the explosion. Keene Fireman Laurence V. Wood (right) discusses damage to drying oven at the scene of explosion that rocked the Faulkner & Colony Mill building. Photo by Hipple.

Rocks Building

The explosion on the third floor of the mill, owned by Barker Reality co., rocked the entire building, sending glass and debris more than 100 feet away.

There were nine men on the floor at the time of the blast. Plus Frederick O. Daley president of Dabolt Inc., who was in the southwest corner of the third floor?

Only Patch and Soucy were seriously injured, even though all of the workers were knocked to the floor. Patch and Soucy were standing near the end of the 120 foot drying unit where the explosion took place.

Estimates of damage to the mill building and contents this morning ranged from $50,000 to $250,000, no one being able to give more than a guess.

Sheldon Barker, senior partner of Barker Reality Co. Inc., owners of the mill building which has a full value of $180,000 for tax purposes, said that it would be three or four days before an estimate of damage could be made.

"As of right now, I couldn't even make a guess." He said.

Damage Extent

Engineers, insurance men, personnel from the fire department and the state fire marshals office have been in and out of the building in effort to determine the extent of damage, the amount of dollars damage, and the actual cause if the explosion.

Daley, the Dalbolt official, said that in looking at the firms' new automatic screen printing machine, an individual did not know whether it could be dried out and put back to work or whether he was looking at $100,000 piece of junk.

Rebuilding started almost immediately.

Last nigh, while watchmen were on guard around the building, temporary shoring was put up, and blocking off of windows began.

All electrical controls were blown out, according to Daley, who added that the back wall appeared to be held to the building by the electrical conduits.

The explosion apparently originated inside of the oven curing unit, part of the drying machine that runs the length of the front o the building on the third floor. It would cost $35,000 to replace the machine, Daley said. It appeared to be totally destroyed.

Damage to goods ready for shipment could not be estimated, Daley added. There are just no dollars and cents value of damages available today, he said.

Robert Caldwel, office manager of Douglas Toy Co., located in the same building, said he was heading up the stairs to prepare for inventory when he heard the blast. He said he thought it was a "sonic boom" at first.

Alarm Garbled

The force of the explosion damaged the alarm system, thus garbling information at the fire station.

However, Cal Frink, operator of the service station across the street from the building, phoned the department immediately. A call from the Mutual Aid Fire Center also went out to the Meadowood department in Fitzwilliam.

The force of the blast shattered every window in that section of the building, including 15 on the West Street side. Cars parked in a lot across the street were hit by debris, as was several automobiles passing by. None were damaged seriously. A section of West Street was closed for more than an hour while debris were cleaned up.

The force of the blast lifted the roof of the plant, caving in one section.

Damage Extensive

Damage to the second floor was extensive, mainly caused by water from the sprinkler system set off by the fire and explosion. The floor is used for printing and storage, also by Dabolt.

Other businesses in the building, including Douglas Co., Traxion Co., Bergeron Machine co., Keene Electric and plumbing supply Inc., and Keene Mill End store, were virtually undamaged.

Keene firemen, directed by Deputy Chief Robert N Guyette, arrived on the scene at 12:32 pm. They centered efforts on the oven and on about a dozen open drums which contained paints used in the printing process.

An investigation continued this morning.

————

As reported by the *Keene Evening Sentinel* July 24th, 1964:

"FIRE"

Fire Damages West Surry Road Home

A late afternoon fire severely damaged the West Surry Road Home of General Court Rep. Ellen Faulkner yesterday

Fire officials said that the blaze started in a car which had been parked in the garage of the colonial structure.

A passerby, Richard Toomey of Springfield, Mass., noticed the fire and alerted Miss Faulkner's aunt, who was inside he house, unaware of the fire. She was assisted from the house by Toomey and city assessor Edward F Greene who was also driving by.

Fire spread from the car to the garage and a section which separates the garage from the house.

Units from Keene were called first by still alarm, for the car fire, but upon arrival at 4:15pm. Surry, Swanzey Center, and Marlboro in that order, were called to the house.

Fire damage to the house was minor, but extensive smoke damage was caused. Several items classified as "valuable antiques "were carried to safety.

The "all out "was sounded at 5:27pm.

————

As reported by the *Keene Evening Sentinel* July 24th, 1964:

Firefighters Respond to 4 small Fires

There were several small fires in the area yesterday.

At 7:53a.m. A still alarm was sent to Marlboro via Mutual Aid Center for a flooded oil burner at Dodges on Main Street. The unit returned to quarters at 8:04 a.m.

At 10:23 a.m., Keene firemen were called to Mrs. B's Restaurant on lower Main Street for electrical trouble and returned to the station at 10:47 am,

A smoke scare in the library was cause for a still alarm at 7:20 p.m. A ballast in the lighting was found to be the cause and both units were back in service by 7:32 p.m.

A car fire in front of the Ellis Hotel this morning brought out Keene firefighters again. The blaze, however, was under control and firemen returned to the station at 12:42. The car, owned by, Mark Parker, was slightly damaged.

As reported by the *Keene Evening Sentinel* September 19th, 1964:

Two Persons Injured In Light Plane Crash One Hospitalized

Two Keene residents were injured when their light plane, a Piper Colt, crashed in a field, which was formerly the Keene airport.

Mrs. Robert K. (Mary) Fairbanks, of 317 Park Ave. is listed in satisfactory condition this morning in Elliot Community Hospital. She received a fractured upper jaw in the accident. Joseph O. Trombley of 56 Birch St. was treated for minor bruises and discharged.

Two are injured. A woman student pilot received a fractured jaw, when the plane she was operating crashed in a field, which was once the Keene Airport. Mrs. Mary Fairbanks is listed in satisfactory condition at Elliot Community Hospital. Her instructor Joseph O. Trombley, was treated for bruised and cuts and discharged. In the foreground is shown the burrow caused by the nose wheel. (Photo by Reed)

Student Pilot

A student pilot, Mrs. Fairbanks was reportedly practicing "sideslips", a form of landing developed for a small airstrip. In "sideslipping" the pilot comes into the area at a greater angle, leveling of at the last moment. Mrs. Fairbanks craft apparently came in to low, with the nose wheel making contact with the ground. The nose wheel gouged the field for about 40 feet and then apparently broke, causing the plane to flip over.

The front end of the plane was badly damaged, but Trombley, an instructor for Bowman Flying Service, was able to get himself and Ms. Fairbanks from the craft. There was no fire.

Taken To the Hospital

Trombley then went to nearby Wyman road to the home of Dr. Charles L. Putnam. There, he contacted Bowman's headquarters and went back to the field with Mrs. Putnam in a car. Mrs. Fairbanks was taken to the hospital.

Firemen were called to the scene as a precautionary measure.

The plane had taken off from Dillant-Hopkins Airport in North Swanzey. Mrs. Fairbanks, who had 35 to 40 hours of student flight time, needed only a few hours of flying experience before she would have qualified for an operators' license, according to her husband.

The plane, which cost $7,600, was termed a total loss. It was owned by Bowman Flying Service.

————

On September 16th, 1964 *The Sentinel* staff photographer Frank Perrotta took the picture of Emile DeRoaier, left and Russell Cloutier coding 675 telephone poles to identify fire hydrants in the city of Keene.

Coding 675 Telephone Poles

Coding 675 Telephone poles in Keene to give firemen long-view assistance in locating hydrants are Fire Department members H. Emile DeRosier, left and Russell Cloutier. Poles near hydrants are banded and a large white dot is sprayed on the side of the pole toward the hydrant. Reflective glass beads sprayed on the paint before it dried will aid nighttime identification. Photo by Perrotta.

Coding 675 telephone poles in Keene to give firemen long-view assistance in locating hydrants are firemen members Emile DeRoaier, left and Russell Cloutier. Poles near hydrants are banded and a large white dot is sprayed on the side of the pole towards the hydrant. Reflective glass beads sprayed on the paint before it dries will id nighttime identification. In the mid 70's the department went from spraying to an aluminum yellow florescent with a florescent diamond on the side of the telephone pole facing the hydrant. You can still see these through the city as you drive around.

————

As reported by the *Keene Evening Sentinel* October 9th, 1964:

Firemen's Muster, Parade Are Planned

The New England Firemen's Muster Team Championships, which will begin Sunday at 3 o'clock at the Cheshire Fairgrounds, will open with a parade through Central Square at 1:30 pm.

Participating in the parade and muster championships will be fire department competitors from Vermont, Massachusetts, and New Hampshire.

The parades route of march will be from Vernon Street to Court, through Central Square to Main Street, past the reviewing stand, across from Dunbar Street, and down Main Street to the Public Works area on lower Main.

Bands participating in the parade will be Keene High School, Gordon Bissell American Legion Post 4, New Hampshire State AMERIAN Legion Championship Band, the Scarlet Marauders of West Swanzey, the Hinsdale High School Band, and Saint Michael's High School Band from Brattleboro, Vt.

Apparatus and equipment appearing in the parade will come from East Swanzey, East Swanzey, Bellows Falls, Chester, Mass., Cummington, Mass., Alstead, East Alstead, Williamsburg, Mass., Westmoreland, Troy, Walpole, Hinsdale, Mass., Harrisville, Surry, Lee, Mass., Hatfield, Mass., Marlow, Fitzwilliam, Whately, Mass., Hudson, Brattleboro, Vt., West Dummerston, Vt., Chesterfield, Erving, Mass., Greenville, Stoddard, WINCHESTER, Sunapee, South Deerfield, Mass., Warwick, Mass., Tully, Mass., Meadowood County.

The parade will be judged by members of the Gordon-Bissell Post 4, American Legion, and prizes will be awarded to the best fire department with music and without.

On the reviewing stand will be city officials, fire department Chief Walter Messer, retired deputies and Revs James Moran and Fay Gemmell.

Participating in the Muster Championships will be teams from Warwick, Mass, Dublin, Marlborough, West Swanzey, Chester, Mass., Cummington, Mass Williamsburg, Mass Winchester, Meadowood, Erving, Mass., Greeneville, Tully, Mass., Forge Village, Mass., Whately, Mass., and Hudson.

———

1965

As Reported by the *Keene Evening Sentinel* January 11th, 1965 by Doug Reed, *Sentinel* Staff Writer:

"FIRE"

Young Brothers Die

Tragedy in the form of fire snuffed out the lives of two young boys here this morning. Ronald George Morse, three, and his brother, Keith Scott, 15 months old, were trapped on the second floor of a four tenement apartment building on Baker Street as flames raged out of control.

Keene Tragedy: Keene firefighters are show battling the flames, which raged through one end

of a four-tenement apartment building on Baker Street. The fire caused the death of two young boys where were trapped upstairs in the building. Cause has not yet been determined. Photo by Reed.

Two Children Killed: Tragedy in the form of a mid-morning fire took the lives of two young children this morning. Ronald, three and Keith, one; Sons of Mr. & Mrs. George Morse were killed in this blaze at 102 Baker Street. Every available piece of equipment and nearly every man in the Keene Fire Dept. were called out.

Their parents, George and Beverly, are in Elliot Community Hospital, being treated for injuries received when they leaped from the second story.

The children were reportedly trapped in an adjoining bedroom.

The origin of the fire is thought to have been a defective stove on the first floor of the Morse apartment. The initial call was received at 8:20 a.m. by the fire department. A box alarm was sounded less than three minutes later.

Mass of Flames

Upon arrival, firemen said they found the Morse apartment in a mass of flames. Approximately 10 residents of the other three apartments were evacuated.

The bodies of the two brothers were not found until some 25-30 minutes after the first arrival of firefighters.

Other tenants include Gilbert W. Rouleau, Robert B. Worcester and Mark W. Messer, and Ellsworth E. Rouleau.

Other Damage

The Worcester-Messer apartment was also extensively damaged; the other two received smoke damage.

According to reports, X-rays were taken of both Mr. and Mrs. Morse. Listed as in satisfactory condition with possible pelvic injuries is the 21-year –old Beverly. Her husband, George Henry, 23, is listed in fair condition. He suffered face lacerations.

Authorities could not immediately determine whether the youngsters died of burns or of asphyxiation. At least half a dozen fire departments members were continually going in and out of the smoke-filled fire ravaged apartment with oxygen masks before the bodies were discovered.

Shroud of Smoke

A shroud of smoke hovered over the city as the blaze was being contained, but the flames had reaped their tragic toll.

It was the first fire resulting in the loss of life since June 30, 1964 when a gas explosion in the West Street Dalbot Inc. building took the life of Supt. Of Production Parker Patch Jr., 36 A co-worker, Joseph Soucy of Appian Way, was hospitalized as a result of the same tragedy which was estimated to have caused well over $50,000 in damages.

No immediate property damage estimate could be given this morning, though it's expected to run well into the thousands of dollars. Nothing was salvaged from the Morse apartment.

The entire building was appraised at a value of $14,000, and is owned by Ward 5 Councilman Philip D. Moran.

Fire chief Walter R. Messer directed fire fighting operations. He said it was not definite as yet as to how the blaze did begin, but it apparently ignited in the kitchen. A probe of the ruins was continuing late this morning.

As Reported by the *Keene Evening Sentinel* January 20th, 1965:

"FIRE"

Firefighters Respond to 3 Still Alarms

Keene firefighters answered four still alarms yesterday, with none resulting in serious damage. At 9:02 a.m., a car fire on the Old Homestead Road in North Swanzey brought response from Engine four. Upon arrival, the blaze in the car owned by Saul Mariaschin was found extinguished. The unit was back in service at 9:13 a.m. A welder's torch apparently ignited canvas and plastic covering at the building site in the rear of Keene High School shortly before 10:45 a.m., with engines one and four responding. Minor damage resulted and the firemen were back at the station by 11:05 a.m.

A tenement house at 311 Winchester St, owned by Lloyd E. Richards, was filled with smoke at 12:30 p.m. bringing a quick response from engines one and four again. Both units were back in service by 12:56

Wiring in a washing machine at 127 Washington St., the residence of Dr. Albert C .Johnston, was given as cause for alarm at 3:19 p.m. with engine four responding. The unit was back at the station at 3:28 p.m.

As Reported by the *Keene Evening Sentinel* February 25th, 1965:

"STORY"

Firemen Add Pumper to Department

Keene's new fire truck, a 750 gallon pumper, shown with Chief Walter Messer and Deputy Chief Robert Guyette. Photo by Reed.

Keene has a new addition to its fire department, today a 1965 Ward LaFrance, 750 gallon pumper fire engine. Fire Chief Walter R. Messer, along with Deputy Robert N. Guyette and Chester E. Dubriske returned from Elmira N.Y., with the vehicle. It will replace the department's 1934 Engine No.3. Described as "very easy to handle" by Guyette, the truck has a carrying capacity of 1,800 feet of 2 ½" hose. It is quite similar in appearance to the most recent addition to the department purchased in 1959. That, one, the present Engine 4, is surpassed in weight by the new engine, which also has a safety windshield for firemen riding on the rear, and several less noticeable advantages. Cost to the City is about $24,000, which had already been appropriated. The engine will undergo scrutiny and testing by a representative of the Insurance Underwriters in Concord.

As Reported by the *Keene Evening Sentinel* March 1st, 1965:

"FIRE"

Cattle Destroyed by Blaze

A blaze which is under investigation as to its cause leveled a barn and destroyed 16 head of cattle on the farm of Robert A. Smith on the Old Walpole Road early this morning.

The structure w2as reported ablaze to fire department officials at 1:27 a.m. and upon their arrival, they found the building a mass of flames it was reported.

Efforts were concentrated on adjacent buildings. All available equipment and manpower from the Elm City department were sent there.

The barn was burned to the ground in less than half an hour, although firefighters remained at the scene until 3:45.

No estimate of damage has been given.

As Reported by the *Keene Evening Sentinel* March 1st, 1965:

"FIRE"

Blaze Causes Damage to Keene Home

Keene firemen were called by still alarms to different locations simultaneously yesterday afternoon at 2:37.

Engine three responded to 9 Ashuelot Court while Engine four rushed to the Abbott Co.

Engine one was also called to the Ashuelot Court residence listed as owned by Lester Fairbanks. Several hundred dollars in damage was caused by smoke in the upper section of the building. The cause is still under investigation.

Squad one also responded to Ashuelot Court with the under control noted at 3:08 p.m.

Meanwhile, the Abbott Co. blaze was found to be in a blower system with minor damage resulting.

Earlier, at 1:29 p.m., a hot water heater was cause of a still alarm at 15 Park Ave. Engine three responded to the residence of Mrs. Julia S. Keating. They returned at 1:36 p.m.

As Reported by the *Keene Evening Sentinel* March 19th, 1965:

"STORY"

"Fire Training" 18 Men Complete Course

Eighteen members of the Keene Fire Department recently completed the Cheshire County Civil Defense medical and self-help course. CD director, Hector Holm of Richmond announced yesterday.

"Similar courses are now under way at Franklin Pierce College and the Elliot Community Hospital School of Nursing," he said.

The graduating firemen were Harry F. Hammond and Robert N. Guyette, deputies; Laurence E. Thompson and Frederick H. Beauchesne, captains; Edwin F. Ball, Chester E. Dubriske, Laurence V. Wood, Allan O. Collier, Owen T. Holden, George H. Shepard Jr., Bernard N. Blancato, H. Emile Derosier, Homer L. Atkins, Ronald P. Amadon, Ernest M. Selby, Russell P. Cloutier, and Paul E. Crowell.

Another course, Holm said, will begin at Marlborough High School March 22. Omer Dumont will be in charge.

As Reported by the Keene Evening Sentinel April 8th, 1965:

"STORY"

City Picked 1st Winner From State

Keene has been named an All-America City by the National Municipal League and Look magazine, co-sponsors of the annual competition for the nation's cities. It becomes New Hampshire's first All-America City. South Portland, Maine, was the second New England city named today in the official announcement. The All-America City designation is given each year to 11 cities whose citizens have made outstanding progress in solving community problems. The winning cities were picked from more than 100 by a jury headed by Dr. George H. Gallup, director of the American Institute of Public Opinion and chairman of the council of The National Municipal League.

————

As Reported by the Keene Evening Sentinel March 28th, 1965:

"FIRE"

Firemen Called Out Early Today

Keene firemen from Engines 3 and 4 made an early morning run today at 7:00 o'clock to the Keene Paving Co. at 315 Winchester St., where an electric spark from a gas pump ignited gas and oil spills. Firemen were at the scene for 35 minutes. Theodore R. Bergeron and Emile W. Bergeron, owners of the business, said about $75 was done in damage to the gas pump, a wall and roof of a building.

————

As Reported by the Keene Evening Sentinel April 24th, 1965:

"FIRE"

House fires fought in Keene

The fire Mutual Aid Center reported the following area calls Thursday: Engines three and four responded to a still alarm from 67 Winter St. and extinguished a partition fire at 11:34 p.m. The building is a rooming house owned by Mrs. Nellie Peabody. Minor damage resulted.

————

As Reported by the Keene Evening Sentinel June 5th, 1965:

"STORY"

"Modern Fire Department"

Keene's Modern Fire Department is one of New Hampshire's Best

Those All-America City firemen are in a hurry when dispatched on an emergency call. Time, measured in scant minutes, is vital when human lives or valuable property may be in peril.

Keene has one of the most modern fire departments in New Hampshire, and one with which the city government has always been generous for needed and up-to-date equipment.

Departments new Ward LaFrance, in front of Central Fire Station. Engine 3, Engine 4 and Engine 2. All Ward LaFrance Engines.

Money set aside annually for this purpose has eased the transition from old to new for taxpayers, a policy that was started about 20 years ago.

The city began motorizing its equipment in the early 1920's, when it bought its first Ahrens-Fox pumping engine. In the Central Fire Station now are four pumping engines, an aerial ladder truck, two emergency squad trucks, brush fire truck and trailer, inspection station wagon and chief's sedan.

New Addition

Newest addition to the line of apparatus is a 1965 Ward LaFrance 750-gallon-per-mintute pumping engine purchased at a cost of $25,800, and the chief's car which is also a 1965 model.

But it is more than serviceable apparatus and equipment that make the Keene Fire Department operate with outstanding efficiency. It is men with an interest in doing a good job for the community, sometimes at the risk of life and limb.

Keene's firemen, under the leadership of Chief Walter R. Messer, have developed a unique attitude about working together as a unit. Often they volunteer for unpaid service when it means helping a fellow fireman or improving standards.

"Many hours of work by off-duty regulars and call men, at no recompense, have frequently been logged just because of a feeling of civic pride in the community and the department," Chief Messer said.

Not So Prominent

Decades ago this work-together attitude was not quite as prominent as it is today. The fire station used to be partitioned off in three sections, each one occupied by a different company-Washington Hook and Ladder, Deluge Hose, and Keene Steamer. At times there was said to be considerable rivalry between the companies in the line of duty.

Keene is the only city in the state, according to Chief Messer, to recently receive better insurance rates through improvements in the fire department and the city water supply system.

Each city is assigned a grade from one to 10 by the State Board of Underwriters. The grading schedule is a yardstick, which can be used to measure the efficiency of municipal fire protection services. Keene has lowered its rating from Grade 5 to Grade 4.

The Keene Fire Department's permanent force of men is 19, including the chief and all except the latest recruit have at least three years of experience. There are 50 call men in the department's three companies and 30 men available in the auxiliary.

There is also the two men credited to the department due to the fact that all emergency calls come through the Southwestern N.H. District Fire Mutual Aid System's dispatch center located next to headquarters. The dispatch center is manned around the clock. This coordination also gives Keene a Class A fire alarm system rating.

$25,800 Truck Aids Firemen, the newest addition to the Keene Fire Department is a $28,500 piece of equipment. It is a 1965 Ward LaFrance 750-gallon-per-minute pumping engine. Chief Walter R. Messer, also has a 1965 car.

The other equipment in the Central Fire Station includes three pumping engines, an aerial ladder truck, two emergency squad trucks, brush fire truck and trailer, and an inspection wagon.

Chief Engineer

According to City statutes, the head of the fire department is titled Chief Engineer and his Deputies are known as Deputy Engineers.

The Chief is appointed by the City Manger for all indefinite periods of time and is required to give his entire time to the department. The Deputy's, two Full-Time men and two call men, are also appointed for an indefinite period of time by the City Manger and must be technically qualified by training or experience.

The present line of command in the department under Chief Messer is Senior Deputy Harry Hammond, Deputy Robert N. Guyette, Capt. Paul E. Gallup,

Captain Frederick H Beauchene, and Fire Alarm Captain Lawrence E. Thompson.

The permanent force, according to seniority, includes Edwin F. Ball, Chester E. Dubriske, Paul E. Crowell, John N. Phillips, Lawrence U. Wood, H Emile DeRosier, Homer L. Atkins, Allan O. Collier, Ronald P. Amadon, Ernest M. Selby, Owen T. Holden, George H. Sheppard Jr., and Russell P Cloutier who is the newest member of the force.

Keene Native

Chief Messer is a Keene native and has had a long association with the department. Actually, he was exposed to the functioning of a fire department at a very early age. His step-father, the late Fred W. Towne, served in the Keene Fire Department from 1900 to 1906 and was the last call chief, serving 1918 until 1923.

Messer joined the department as a call man in 1926 and became a member of the regular force in 1941. In January of 1946 he became chief succeeding Chief Eugene Riley.

Chief Messer has held several organizational positions all concerned with fire-fighting service. He is a past president of the N.H. Fire Chief's Assn., past president of both the Tri-State and Southwestern N.H. Mutual Aid System, present chairman of the State Board of Fire Control, present secretary-treasurer of the New England Division of International Association of Fire Chiefs, current president of the Keene Firemen's Relief Assn., and chairman of this committee in charge of the annual fire school training program.

Chief Messer also heads the Keene Civil Defense program and is the City Forest Fire Warden.

General Duties

In general the duties of the chief are that he shall have the care and supervision of all equipment and apparatus of every description used in connection with extinguishing fires whether belonging to or loaned by the city.

His responsibility also includes insuring that all regulations regarding the prevention of fires are enforced. This means regular inspections every two months of all business, professional and apartment buildings in the fire precinct.

Also there is the inspection of nursing homes, places of public assembly, all public buildings, installation of oil burners and flammable liquid storage containers. Members of the department give instruction on fire prevention at the public schools from time to time.

The firemen do their own mechanical repair work, plus maintenance of the station including carpentering, steam fitting, plumbing and electrical work.

A Demon Called Fire

Alarm System

Fire Alarm Captain Thompson supervises the maintenance of the Class A fire alarm system. There are 95 fire alarm boxes in the city and more than 40 miles of wiring.

The permanent force works in two shifts of nine men each, 24 hours on duty at the station and 24 hours off duty 7 a.m. and one day until 7 a.m. It amounts to about 72 hour week.

There are about 50 radio monitors located in the homes of firemen so they can listen for calls for assistance whenever needed.

The permanent firemen spend a small percentage of time in the actual fire fighting. Part of their on-duty day is spent on in-service training, maintenance of equipment and apparatus, maintenance of fire station itself, and the chores of housekeeping.

Training Program

The in-service training program for permanent men is directed by Senior Deputy Hammond, who has recently completed a training course for instructors at the University of New Hampshire. Deputy Guyette is the department's instructor on maintenance of equipment and apparatus, Keene firemen also attend the annual fire school at Meadowood in Fitzwilliam for training.

In 1964 the Keene Fire Department answered 347 calls for its services. A total of 288 calls came in over the telephone, 39 by radio communication and 20 were box alarms.

The estimated fire losses last year amounted to $220,617 and about $190,000 of that figure was attributed to one industrial fire and explosion that occurred at the Dalbolt Manufacturing Company plant located in the former Faulkner-Colony Mill building. Losses in 1963 totaled about $104,000 and in 1962 they were $82,000.

Forest Fires

The fighting of forest fires in the area comes under the direction of Chief Messer, who is the District Chief as well as City Forest Fire Warden.

Keene has a 75-foot all-steel aerial ladder truck; a 1946 Seagrave. Other pieces of apparatus include a 1959 Ward LaFrance engine, a 1952 Peter Pirsch engine, both 750-gallon-per-minute pumpers (so called triple combination units containing booster tank, hose and pump)

In addition to the 1965 chief's vehicle and Ward LaFrance pumper, the department has a 1956 Chevrolet station wagon used as a second car for inspections, a 1948 power wagon and two 1941 Diamond T emergency squad trucks. A 1923 Rio engine (about the third piece of motorized equipment that the city purchased) is used for brush fire fighting and has a 500 gallon pump and a 500 gallon portable pump trailer.

One of the older pieces of apparatus is a 1930 Ahrens-Fox 750-gallon-per-minute positive displacement pumper, affectionately known as "Old Rosie". It is in first-class operating condition, although relegated to second line duty.

The department has its own emergency power plant, a semidiesel army surplus generator, and air compressors to activate the fire whistles; also portable field kitchens, all of which are stored in the basement of the station.

What actually happens when a call comes into the department? The Mutual Aid dispatcher determines the nature of the service required if possible, the men are assembled and they take what ever is needed to handle a medium or large fire.

Unless the call can be identified as one-unit fire, two or three unites leave the station to handle the situation. If the call requires more than one unit out side the fire precinct, then two pumpers are dispatched. In the same instance, inside the fire precinct, two pumpers and the ladder truck are dispatched.

The radio communication more equipment and off shift men can be called in quickly either to cover the fire itself or the station. Mutual aid assistance may also be sent in motion if necessary.

Muster Team

One of the extra activities of the Keene firemen for which they display enthusiasm is the muster team. Muster competition among fire departments in the region and the tri-state area is keen.

The team practices on its own time perfecting the pumping technique, midnight alarm drill and other muster events. Deputy Guyette is in charge of the 10-man unit (roster varies), and their apparatus is a 1924 Ahrens-Fox-600 gallon per minute pumper.

Future of the Department

In the future for the Keene Fire Department, as the city continues to grow, will be construction of sub-stations in some of the outlying neighborhoods. Plans now are being considered for such a sub-station in the northwestern part of the city and the hope is to construct a training area next to the station.

Chief Messer also said one of the objectives of the future is a permanent force of 27 men at the present station to meet the minimum standards of the Underwriters Grading Schedule. This would further lower Keene's grade to get better insurance rates.

————

As reported by the *Keene Evening Sentinel* August 1st, 1965:

"FIRE"

Cause of Fire on Valley Street – Undetermined

Barn Blaze: Keene Firemen battled a fire in a barn, adjoining 84 Valley St., yesterday afternoon and managed to save the house. Although the barn itself was Heavily damaged. Two youngsters were already allegedly playing darts in the barn when the blaze broke out. There were no injuries from the fire. Photo by Selkowe.

Fire Chief Walter R. Messer said this morning that positive cause of a fire, which caused considerable damage yesterday at 84 Valley St., "can not be determined as yet" Messer added that investigation is continuing.

According to witnesses, the two oldest sons of Mrs. Janice Arsenault (Steven, 8 and Brian, 7) were playing darts in a barn attached to a two and a half story frame house when the fire broke out early in the afternoon.

The boys ran from the barn to notify an aunt, Mrs. Linda Robinson, who was in the house with the youngest of the Arsenault children, four-year old Christopher.

A reported explosion resulted after the occupants had left the house.

A number of passers-by ran into the structure, bringing out personal belongings and stacking them on the front lawn.

The property is owned by Mrs. Charles H. Wheeler. Authorities described the barn as a total loss, with some fire and smoke damage to the adjoining house.

As Reported by the *Keene Evening Sentinel* August 25th, 1965:

"FIRE"

Fire Destroys Keene Residence

An early Sunday morning fire almost completely destroyed the inside of a residence at 83 Rule Street. Keene Fire Chief Walter R. Messer estimated the loss at around $5,000.

A box alarm sent engines one, three and four and squad two to the residence of Mr. and Mrs. Earl. C Wilson Jr. at 3:12 a.m. Upon arriving on the scene they found the structure already burning extensively.

The Wilson family was not at home at the time. Messer said the fire started under a stairway in the living room. All of the family's possessions were lost.

As Reported by the *Keene Evening Sentinel* September 27th, 1965:

"FIRE"

Fire Damages House Sunday

A Keene family reportedly lost all possessions in an early Sunday morning fire that caused considerable damage to a Jordan Road house.

Box 153 was sounded at 12:23 a.m. to the residence of Mr. and Mrs. Haven Hall. They were reportedly coon hunting at the time of the blaze, while their seven children were at a neighbor's house.

No cause was given and officials said that the blaze was contained mostly to the lower sections of the structure.

The fire was brought under control at about 1:30.

As reported by the *Keene Evening Sentinel* October 4th, 1965.

"STORY"

Fire Safety Week Starts with Parade

Young forest fire warden salutes Smokey the Bear on top of ladder truck during start of fire prevention week in Keene. Photo by Barndollar.

More than 50 pieces of fire control apparatus, marching units and bands participated in a parade marking the start of Fire Prevention Week in Keene yesterday.

The parade down Main Street viewed by an estimated 5,000 persons, included apparatus from every town within the Tri-State and Cheshire County Mutual Aid Systems.

Judges for the parade and firemen's muster at the Cheshire County fairgrounds in North Swanzey sponsored by the Keene Firemen's Muster Association were =Chief Walter Messer and members of the Gordon Bissell American Legion Post headed by Karl "Gubby" Underwood, and Albert LaFountain. Frank Barrett, Evan White, Guy Bailey and Warren Barrett.

A first-place prize was awarded to the Hinsdale Fire Department marchers and their band. A top prize was also awarded the Warwick, Mass., Fire Department for its marching unit. Parade marshal was Paul E. Symonds.

Muster winners included: Rotary pumping; Whately, Mass., 32.8 seconds; Erving, Mass., 34 seconds; Dublin 38 seconds.

Centrifugal pumping: Cummington, Massl., 38.6 seconds; Meadowood County Area, Fitzwilliam, 39, and Tully, Mass 46.

Med, midnight alarm: Worthington, Mass., 34.4 seconds; Meadowood, 36, Whately, 37.3.

Women, midnight alarm; Ashburnham, Mass., 29.5 seconds; Warwick, 32; Worthington, 34.

As reported by the *Keene Evening Sentinel* December 6th, 1965:

"FIRE"

Keene Firemen Collapses, Dies Wile Fighting Fire

A fire last night swept through three rooms of a house on North Lincoln Street and took the life of a Keene firefighter.

Fire Victim: Keene firemen rush a stretcher with the body of Captain Francis J. Driscoll to a waiting ambulance after he collapsed Street last night. He was pronounced dead on arrive at Elliot Community hospital. Photo by Selkowe.

Taking care of their own: In a funeral procession down Main Street to St. Bernard's Church this morning, members of the Keene Fire Department escorted and casket of Captain Francis J. Driscoll on top of Engine 4. Photo by Miller.

Dead on arrival at Elliot Community Hospital was Captain Francis J. Driscoll Sr., 62, of 63 Spring St., who collapsed inside the house while fighting the fire.

The cause of death was determined this morning by Dr., Charles E. Schofield, medical examiner. Driscoll died of a coronary thrombosis, a form of heart attack, he said.

The scene of the death was a three-story, two-family, frame building near the corner of Roxbury Street and North Lincoln Street, home of Ainslee E. Phillips. The ground floor apartment is empty.

Fire Damage

The fire extensively damaged the two upper floors, though flames were confined to a bathroom, the kitchen and the attic.

Fire Chief Walter R. Messer said this morning that the blaze was first discovered by Phillips shortly after 7:20 p.m. when he returned from walking his dog. The fire started, Messer said, in a bathroom and spread to the kitchen and upstairs to the attic.

How it started is not known. "I cannot find a positive condition as to how it started, "Messer said. Damage was estimated to be at several thousand dollars. The building is owned by a Kenneth Ames of Lynn, Mass.

No Flames Visible

About 200 persons were attracted to what appeared to be just a house fire. At no time were flames visible from the street although inside the heat was so intense that it melted or scorched objects in every room.

All available pieces of equipment in the Keene department answered the call at 7:23 and at 11:44 engines 3 and 4 returned for one hour when the fire rekindled itself. The first indication that some one was injured came as a fireman virtually slid down a ladder to the second story to summon an ambulance.

Ambulances Arrive

Shortly after that two ambulances arrived and two stretchers were readied and placed at the front door, as firemen rushed in with resceitators and other gear. Driscoll was evacuated in a fire department wire mesh stretcher because it was more maneuverable.

About a dozen firemen thronged around the stretcher when it was brought from the house and rushed it the 30-feet to the waiting ambulance, which sped off even before the back door could be closed. Driscoll was born in Keene on December 13th 1902, the son of Cornelius and Hannah (Lombard) Driscoll.

He became a member of the Washington Hook and Ladder Company April 14, 1932 and was made Captain of that company on November 15, 1956. He has also served as treasurer of the company. He as also a member of Keene Council 819 Knights of Columbus and had been employed for several years by the Fletcher Paint Store in Keene.

He s survived by his widow, the former, Lucille Larmay, two daughters,; Mrs. Mary A. Smith and Linda Driscoll, both of Medford Mass.; three sons, Francis J. Driscoll Jr. of Munsonville, Joseph W. Driscoll of Fort Ord, California, and Lawrence L Driscoll of Keene; three sisters, Mrs. Margaret Goggin of Keene, Mrs. Helen Ware of West Swanzey and Annie Driscoll of Keene; 10 grandchildren, several nieces and nephews.

The funeral will be held Thursday morning from the Frank J. Foley Funeral Home, 49 Court St., followed by a solemn high mass of requiem in St., Bernard's Church at 9 o'clock. Burial will be in St. Joseph Cemetery. Friends may call at the funeral home Tuesday and Wednesday from 2 to 4 and 7 to 9 p.m.

————

Keene Fire December 23rd, 1965 by *Sentinel* Staff Writer Mike Miller:

"FIRE"

Fire Department Battles Winter Street Blaze

Winter Street Fire: Firemen battled fire and smoke last night at 85 Winter Street, but the blaze extensively damaged a 16 room building owned by George W. Stone Construction Company, who was making the structure over into a professional building. An electrical breakdown in the cellar entry was believed to be the cause. Photo by Miller.

Two firemen received minor injuries while fighting a hard to get at fire which extensively damaged a 16-room, wood frame house at 85 Winter Street last night.

Robert W. Raymond, 24 of 37 Wright Street and Wesley Peets, 38 of 82 Dover Street were both treated at Elliot Community

Hospital for a cut hand and nail puncture, respectively.

The alarm was first sounded from a box at the corner of School and West Street at 7:57 p.m. and a second time shortly after that when Dr. Leroy S. Ford phoned from his home on School Street across from the fire.

Equipment Responds

Four pieces of city equipment, engines 3 and 4, ladder 2 and emergency squad 1 responded but the fire was not declared under control until 45 minutes later.

According to firemen, the blaze started from "an electric breakdown in the cellar entry" and spread to most parts of the Winter Street side of the house, damaging the first and second floors and the attic. The north side of the house was untouched by flames, but suffered severe smoke damage.

The building was owned by the George W. Stone Construction Company and was largely unoccupied. It was in the process of being remodeled into a professional building with three offices and tow apartments, the latter upstairs.

Ready to Move

Donald Stone, president f the company, said this morning that the remodeling was about 45 percent finished with one doctor scheduled to move his offices there the day after Christmas.

The only tenant of the house was Jesse Lewis of Gardner, Maine, who was living there temporarily until he could move his family to Keene. He was out at the time of the fire. He is a production manager at the Monadnock Press, a Stone-owned business.

Stone this morning described damage to the building as "very extensive." He said he did not know whether the fire would change his ultimate plans for the building.

Brosnahan Home

Before being acquired by Stone, the house was the home and offices of the late Dr. John

J. Brosnahan. It was sold in 1951, two years after his death, by his sons to G. Allen Mott who in turn sold it to the Stone Construction Company. Stone leased it to the Keene State College Kappa Delta Phi fraternity until they moved to the campus property last June. Until that time the building had been largely unoccupied.

———————

1966

As Reported by the *Keene Evening Sentinel* January 19th, 1966.

"FIRE"

Electric Heater Causes Fire on Cross Street

An electric heater being used to thaw pipes caused extensive fire, water and smoke damage to a three-story house at 127 Cross Street yesterday afternoon.

Cross Street Fire: Keene firemen extinguished a fire, yesterday afternoon in the rear of this three story house at 127 Cross St., Cause of the fire was believed to be an extension cord attached to an electric heater to thaw frozen pipes. Photo by Frank Perrotta.

The elderly owner and upstairs tenant fled the blaze. Quick action like shown above confined the fire mainly to half the third story of the wood frame structure. Damage expected to exceed $5,000. Photo by Frank Perrotta.

The fire itself was confined mostly to the rear of the wood frame house, having started on the ground floor where an electric heater was placed to thaw water pipes in a second floor crawl space.

The fire had a good start before it was discovered by the Rev. and Mrs. Burton G. Robbins, second floor tenants of Roger A. Witham, who owns and lives in the house. According to deputy fire Chief Robert Guyette, the Rev. Robbins opened a door to the rear of the house and was confronted with scorching heat.

Before the fire was under control it had swept up the three stories at the tear of the house and broken through portions of the roof.

Deputy Chief Guyette said this morning that in addition to fire damage three ground floor and three second floor rooms were damaged by water. The whole house received smoke damage.

The first alarm was called in by the Rev. Robbins at 3:22 p.m. and a second call came from a nearby alarm box three minutes later. Engines 3 and 4 answered the call at once and

Ladder 2 and Squad 1, moments later. The last piece of equipment did not return to Central station until 5:50 p.m.

Due to incidental damage to the front of the house the Rev. and Mrs. Robbins, upstairs and Witham, downstairs, were not able to spend the night at 127 Cross Street.

Witham left yesterday to stay with his daughter in Dover and the Robbins are living with their daughter, Mrs. Alice R. MacKenzie at 16 Hardy Court.

———

As Reported by the *Keene Evening Sentinel* March 16th, 1966:

"FIRE"

House fires fought in Keene

Fire of undetermined origin did an estimated $20,000 damage to the Laplant Used Furniture and Appliance Center at 133 Water St last night.

Keene firemen and three pieces of equipment answered a call at 5:30 p.m. yesterday when a truck filled with furniture parked at a loading platform caught fire.

According to Merrill J. Laplant, president of the Laplant Moving and Storage Co., Inc., the fire did $750 in damage to the pickup truck and $9,000 damage to the furniture in the truck. An additional $10,000 in smoke damage was done to the building and its contents, Laplant said.

———

And reported on March 28th, 1966:

"FIRE"

Firemen Called Out Early Today

Keene Firemen from Engines 3 and 4 made an early morning run today at 7 a.m. today to the Keene Paving Compan at 515 Winchester Street, where an electrical spark from a gas pump ignited gas and oil spills. Firemen were at the scene for 35 minutes. Theodore

R. Bergeron and Emile W. Bergeron, owners of the business said about $75 damage was done to the gas pump, a wall and roof of a building.

————

As Reported by the *Keene Evening Sentinel* May 6th, 1966:

"FIRE"

Four Calls In One Night

Keene firemen were called out four times yesterday, shortly after 8:00 p.m. Engines 3 and 4 and Ladder 2 sped to the Wallisford Mill on Emerald Street for a fire caused by an electric motor in a carbonizer. The fire was confined to the machine and an exhaust duct.

At 5:30 p.m. Engine 3 was called to the home of Ernest F. Beauregard at 14 Greenwood St. to extinguish a grease fire in the kitchen. There were also two grass fires in Keene yesterday.

————

As Reported by the *Keene Evening Sentinel* June 11th, 1966:

"STORY"

"Memorial Service"

Memorial services for deceased firefighters will be held tomorrow morning at 9 o'clock in the Assembly Hall at Central Fire Station.

Fire Chief Walter R. Messer said yesterday that the fire department's two chaplains, the Rev. Fay L. Gemmell and the Rev. William L. Quirk will officiate at the services. Music will be provided by a chorus from the Barber shoppers, conducted by Dino Houpis.

Mayor Richard F. Bean and all of the City Councilmen have been invited to attend the memorial service.

Messer also said that the graves of all deceased firefighters have been decorated including four who have died during the past year.

————

As Reported by the *Keene Evening Sentinel* July 5th, 1966:

"FIRE"

Fire damage extensive to Keene Home

Extensively Damaged: Keene firemen pump water into the home of Mr. & Mrs. Herbert Lambert during an afternoon fire that extensively damaged the residence.

Fight Blaze: Four pieces of equipment from Keene Fire Department battled the blaze at the Royal Ave home. The fire was brought under control after 30 minutes, but still resulted in extensive damage

Fire of undetermined origin extensively damaged the home of Herbert C. Lambert at 61 Royal Ave. here yesterday.

Keene Fire Chief Walter R. Messer estimated damage to the structure between $18,000 and $20,000.

The five Lamberts had left the house to visit friends about a half hour before the alarm was called in by a neighbor across the street at 4:11 p.m. A box alarm was also sounded.

According to Messer the blaze apparently started inside the garage attached to the two-story wood frame house, although it has not been determined what originally kindled the fire. By the time firemen arrived with four pieces of equipment, flames had worked up to the roof and were visible through second story windows. Messer said.

It was 30 minutes before the blaze was brought under control, and the last piece of equipment left the scene one and one half hours later. Nothing was carried out of the house due to intense heat, Messer said.

One man, Captain William H. Sanderson, a "call" fireman, was overcome briefly by heat exhaustion, and smoke inhalation, and was treated with oxygen at the scene.

Firemen used mostly fog nozzles to bring the blaze under control.

The air inside the house was so hot, Messer said, that firemen could stifle the blaze with steam from evaporating fog.

Four pieces of equipment, Engine 3 and 4, Ladder 2 and Squad 1, answered the alarm, and laid down hundreds of feet of 2 ½ and 1 ½ inch line and booster line.

While the four pieces of equipment were out on the call and while the fire was still burning out of control, Engine 1 was summoned to 41 Pleasant Street for another fire in a garage. That fire was put out quickly.

Later in the evening Engine 3 was called back to Royal Avenue when the fire was reported active again. It turned out, however, an observer had mistaken copper colored weather stripping on the roof of the burnt house for flickering flames.

The Royal Avenue fire marked the climax of a busy three day weekend for Keene firemen. In addition to contending with separate fires minutes apart yesterday, firemen extinguished car fires Sunday morning and Monday night.

Engine 3 went to a fire in the rear seat of an auto at 26 Butler Court owned by Joseph Levasseur Sunday at 9:53 a.m.

———

The Old Doors of the central fire station were replaced with new doors that were made out of Mohogany. In 1966, the door glass was changed to 3 full panes of glass and remain in place until the steel overhead doors were installed in the mid 1990's. Photo by Robert DiLuzio, Sr.

———

As Reported by the *Keene Evening Sentinel* October 5th, 1966:

"FIRE"

False Alarms pulled by juveniles

Keene Firemen were called out by three false alarms last night apparently turned in by juveniles pulling outdoor alarm boxes.

Locations and times were The Peerless Insurance Company at 10:02 p.m., Bradford Road and West Street at 10:12 p.m. and Castle Street and Barker Street at 11:51 p.m.

In each case firemen from Engines 3 and 4 answered the calls.

A legitimate call to 14 Forest Street to attend to an overheated stove at 7 o'clock was answered by the same personnel.

Fire Chief Walter Messer, said this morning that the alarms were probably turned in by "kids with an automobile" and has turned the matter over to the Keene Police department for investigation.

———

As Reported by the *Keene Evening Sentinel* October 8th, 1966:

"STORY"

"Muster, Parade" Muster, parade set for Keene Sunday

A parade and muster Sunday will mark the opening of the Keene Fire Department's Fire Prevention Week program.

More than 50 pieces of visiting front-line and muster apparatus, along with marching units and bands, will participate in the day's events, which start at 1:35 p.m.

The parade will begin at the Vernon Street parking lot go through Central Square and don Main Street to the Public Works garage. Judges, members of the Gordon-Bissell Post American Legion, headed by Karl Underwood Jr., will review the marchers and prizes will be awarded at the Cheshire

Fair Grounds in North Swanzey, during the muster.

The muster will begin at 3 p.m. with a dry and wet hose competition included in the program for the first time in this area.

In addition there will be a midnight alarm contest for ladies teams only and rotary and centrifugal pumping competition. Cash prizes will be awards.

Admission to the fairgrounds is free and food concessions will be available.

Chief Walter F. Messer is in charge of the day's events, with Deputy Chief Robert Guyette directing the muster and Mutual Aid coordinator Robert Callahan handling the microphone during the parade.

33 Fire units participate in event here

Fire truck fanciers of Keene turned out in force yesterday and lined Main Street 3,000 strong before adjourning to the Cheshire Fair Grounds to observe the doings of the men who operate teams.

The weather was good for the traditional event which this year marked the beginning of Fire Prevention Week.

The 45-minute parade down Main Street attracted units from 33 fire departments in New Hampshire, Vermont and Massachusetts, and six area bands.

At the fairgrounds 12 departments competed for a total of $5600 worth of prizes in five different events. A crowd estimated at 2,500 by Keene fire Chief Walter R. Messer filled the fair grounds bleachers to watch.

Hamburgers and hot dogs were sold by the Ladies Auxiliary of the Keene department in the infield for hungry spectators and to raise money for cash prizes.

'Winning wet and dry hose teams were the Hudson and West Groton, Mass., departments, placing over 14 teams participating in the event. Prizes were $25.

In the centrifugal pumping contest the Tully Fire Department of Orange Mass., placed first and the Meadowood Fire Department in

Fitzwilliam placed second, winning $50 and $25 in cash prizes.

Women of the Keene Fire Department won the $15 prize in the Ladies Midnight Alarm.

_____

As reported by the *Keene Evening Sentinel* October 21st, 1966:

"STORY"

Fire Chief Walter R. Messer, left, receives a portrait of himself from H. Emile DeRosier on behalf of the Permanent Men's Company. Messer has been chief for 20 years.

_____

As Reported by the *Keene Evening Sentinel* November 2nd, 1966:

"FIRE"

House fires fought in Keene

Fire caused by "improper discarding of smoking materials," according to fire officials, caused several thousand dollars damage to an eight-apartment house located at 75-77 Beaver St., this morning.

Beaver Street Fire: Keene firemen lead hose into the third floor window at 75-77 Beaver Street. Photo by- Clark.

According to Chief Walter R. Messer the fire started in an unoccupied room on the top floor in the apartment house. It burned a hole in the floor and spread to the ceiling and into the attic. Messer said that salvage covers were used in the house.

The fire was first spotted by the man operating the public works street sweeper and was called into the public works office. The fire department was notified at 8:27 a.m. and the fire was termed out at 8:56 a.m.

Two pumper trucks, a ladder truck, and a squad car were summoned.

The building is owned by Frye of Keene. Tenants in the house were Mrs. Rita Scarborough, Audry Vanhorn, and Mrs. A. Cagill, Messer said. The remaining apartments were unoccupied.

_____

As Reported by the *Keene Evening Sentinel* November 17th, 1966.

"FIRE"

Making Candles starts Blaze at Beech Street

Children making candles touched off a fire, which left a family of six at 31 Beech Street homeless last night.

Fire officials at the scene estimated that damage to the house, owned by Mr. and Mrs. Frederick C. Mohr, would amount to $10,000.

For Keene firemen it was one of three calls last night, all of which occurred within the space of an hour.

At 8:50 p.m. Engines 3 and 4 were summoned to the Chabott Coal and Oil Co. to extinguish a fire caused earlier in the day by sparks from an acetylene torch.

Two Calls

Seven minutes later the Beech Street alarm was turned in. While firemen were fighting that blaze, Mutual Aid received a call to North Swanzey to administer the department's resuscitator to a choking baby.

The five-week old child of Mr. and Mrs. Allan Cantlia of James Road in North Swanzey was reported to be doing well after receiving first aid treatment and did not require hospitalization.

Fire Chief Walter R. Messer said that although the two-story, wood-frame house on Beech Street was not gutted, almost every room received considerable damage.

Spreads Quickly

Messer said the fire spread quickly in the kitchen and raised the temperature inside the house to such an extent that one window on the first floor was blown out. Painted surfaces in nearly every room were scorched, Chief Messer said.

Other materials in the house with low kindling temperatures were ignited by the heat, the chief said.

About 50 firemen were summoned to the fire after a "Code 3" was sounded by Mutual Aid at Central Station.

All available firefighters, both volunteers and permanent personnel off duty, were called to the scene one minute after the first engines arrived. Flame was reported to be coming from both ends of the house.

Chief Messer said the fire was brought under control buy using fog nozzles to create steam and lower the temperature inside the house. Direct streams of water were played on visible flames.

———

As reported by the *Keene Evening Sentinel* November 18th, 1966:

"FIRE"

Fire Destroys house on Beaver Street

Fire completely destroyed an unoccupied two and half story building on 77 Beaver Street early this morning.

The blaze, which had spread to virtually all sections of the 20-room house by the time fire trucks first arrived, was visible the city over.

Intense Heat

So, intense, was the heat from the blaze that the first task confronting the first two units of firemen was to play water upon neighboring houses at 87 and 75 Beaver Street. They received no damage. Later units attacked the fire proper.

The first alarm was sounded at 3:54 a.m. and a Code 3 was turned in almost immediately to summon the city's entire fire-fighting force, except a small standby crew.

Almost all neighborhood residents watching the blaze spoke of being awakened by an explosion and of seeing the glow of the blaze through their bedroom windows.

Deputy Chief Robert N. Guyette said this morning that the explosion was probably caused by a bottled gas tank with a faulty safety valve. The ruptured form of a bottled gas tank could be seen lying near the basement of the building.

Another bottled gas tank with an operative safety valve discharged several times with an ear piercing roar during the course of the fire.

The only occupants of the large wood-framed building had moved out shortly after a previous fire. The morning of November 2nd two engines were called to extinguish an upholstery fire, which had subsequently burnt through the floor and a wall and had made its way into an attic crawl space.

"We were lucky that time" Guyette said this morning. At the scene of the fire earlier this morning, Chief Walter R. Messer said it was also fortunate that the fire contained itself within the Beaver Street building.

The roof did not collapse owing to the sturdy construction of the building, Messer said, and an evening's rain prevented nuisance fires developing from the airborne embers.

Messer was hesitant in saying what may have caused the fire, but it was known that a kerosene-burning "salamander" was being used to heat the building.

Workmen were remodeling apartments in the house and repairing damage caused by the first fire. The "all out" was sounded at 5:57 a.m., two hours after the first alarm, but two trucks stayed at the scene well into the morning for "mop up" operations.

The building was owned by Nathan Goldberg and Charles Frye, both of Keene.

———

As Reported by the *Keene Evening Sentinel* December 15th, 1966:

"FIRE"

Bardis Fruit Company Fire. Firemen fight the general alarm fire, which destroyed the building of Abraham Cohen and rented by the Bardis Fruit Company yesterday. The total loss was estimated at $60,000. Over 75 firemen and six trucks were called to the blaze. Photos by Alexander Baker.

A fire, which grew progressively worse despite the presence of 75 firemen, completely destroyed the building that housed the Bardis Fruit Co. on Emerald Street yesterday.

Firemen from Keene, Marlborough and Meadowood fought the blaze for three hours before finally bringing it under control. The last piece of firefighting equipment did not leave the scene until 10:10 – seven hours after the first alarm was sounded.

Mr. and Mrs. Elias J. Bardis, treasurer and president of the company, said at the scene late last night that they would not know3 the extent of their loss until they could run an inventory today.

Although the building, owned by Abraham Cohen, was completely gutted, some of the Bardis produce is believed salvageable.

Unofficial estimates place the total loss at $60,000

Mrs. Bardis said the fire was discovered in the basement of the Bardis half of the 150 by 70-foot building by an employee. The other half was formerly occupied by the Cheshire Beef Co. which moved to their present location on Railroad Street several years ago.

Deputy Chief Harry F. Hammond, who supervised firefighting operations in the absence of Chief Walter Messer, said that the fire is believed to have started near an air compressor of a refrigeration unit at the base of an elevator shaft.

Both Upstairs

Both Mr. and Mrs. Bardis and two employees were upstairs at the time. Mrs. Bardis stayed in the building until the first trucks arrived. She was helped through a front window by firemen when the path to the front door was blocked by thick smoke.

Deputy Hammond said this morning that the heat apparently built up in the basement until a hot air explosion spread flames and gasses up the elevator shaft and throughout the building. The explosion knocked several basement windows out.

Rapid Succession

These developments occurred in rapid succession and "what appeared to be just a routine deal turned out to be a major fire," Hammond said.

Three Keene trucks answered the first alarm, but additional equipment was called within minutes, along with the alarm for all available personnel.

A Marlborough fire engine was sent by Mutual Aid to Central Station in Keene to cover for the absent Keene trucks, until it too was summoned to the fire. A West Swanzey truck was called to take its place.

Rescue Truck

A Meadowood rescue truck was also requested by Mutual Aid and arrived at the scene shortly after 4:30 p.m.

All told, more than 75 firemen and six trucks were at the scene by 5 o'clock, but the building burned out of control for another hour.

Even so, firefighters were fortunate in keeping ammonia tanks in the basement from exploding and confining the fire within the building, Hammond said. Also firemen were able to remove two cases of business records while the building was still on fire.

Less fortunate was a local newscaster who was unable to phone dispatchers to his radio station. The lines ere tied up with youngsters phoning Santa Claus.

Only one injury requiring medical attention was reported as a result of the fire. A Keene fireman, Robert Mason, was burned on the hands by hot melted tar and treated at Elliot Community Hospital. Several other firemen sustained cuts, scratches and minor burns.

No cases of smoke inhalation were reported, although most firemen at the scene spent the better part of the last night breathing the black, greasy smoke.

Several hundred spectators attended the fire, drawn by innumerable sirens and a blanket of smoke that was spread over the center of town by West wind.

Bardis Fruit Firm Still in Business

Mrs. Elias J. Bardis, President of the Bardis Fruit Company, which was destroyed by fire, said that she and her husband are still in business.

"We are definitely in business; In fact we sent a truck to Boston for fruit the night of the fire" Mrs. Bardis said.

The fruit company has located behind the Perkins Lumber Company on 29 Ralston Street in a garage formerly occupied by Law Motor Freight, Inc.

Two men and equipment from the Keene Fire station were standing by at the former location of the company. One engine was called early morning to douse the still moldering embers.

A crew of Keene firemen was at the scene all day to conduct mop-up operations.

Mrs. Bardis said that the only things saved were office equipment and trucks, which were moved to make way for the fire fighting equipment. "All perishables have been condemned by the City and State health officials", she said. Mrs. Bardis declined to estimate the loss.

"We wish to thank all of the people who were so helpful and thoughtful, including the fire and police departments, the Meadowood and Marlboro fire departments, the Crystal Restaurant for the coffee they sent and our many friends, " Mrs. Bardis said.

———

1967

As Reported by the *Keene Shopper News* February 9th, 1967:

"STORY"

A Word of Praise

Rev. Gerard J. Vallee congratulated by Fire Chief Walter R. Messer on appointment as Fire Department Chaplain Photo by Keene Shopper News.

The members of the local Fire department deserve an editorial work of praise and commendation from this newspaper. The Keene Fire department and it Mutual Aid System coupled with a fine Rescue Squad is on the ball. Read accounts of fires in Keene. Split second action occurs. In record time, Keene firemen are dousing fires, putting them under control and preventing major catastrophes in our city. We citizens should be proud of our men on Vernon Street.

We smile when we hear the whistle blow and see the "Red Lights Brigade" cutting sharp corners, speeding to the scene of tragedy. We need be thankful for their high sense of concern for our properties and lives.

A new addition was made to the KFD five months ago. The Newman Chaplain, father Ferard J. Vallee at Keene State College accepted Chief Messer's invitation to join the Department and act as Catholic Chaplain. In the early hours of the morning or late at night, a priest now joins the firefighters to help. When interviewed by this newspaper about where he finds the time to do so many things, the new Chaplain responded casually: "There is plenty of time. It's a question of knowing how to use it and use it well."

This newspaper was informed that the Fire Chaplain caught a bad cold when he joined the firemen at the Bardis Fruit Company in early December. Reportedly, the Chaplain was clad in his clerical black suit, heartless, wearing no rubber boots or gloves. Men of the department took notice of this, and were determined to outfit their Chaplain. Anonymous firemen purchased a Chaplain's fire wardrobe.

We want to be on record for not wanting fires in our city of Keene, but, if and when the fire whistle blows a general alarm, look for the new Chaplain. He will be clad in white coat, helmet and boots.

Men of Vernon Street, you are doing a fine job. We congratulate you.

As Reported by the *Keene Evening Sentinel* February 18th, 1967:

"STORY"

Chasing fires gets in chaplains blood

Holy Smokes: Father Gerald Vallee turns his back to the camera and models the latest accoutrements of his office fire

It gets into your blood, this business of chasing fires!

If you have any doubts, just ask the Rev. Gerard J. Vallee, Keene priest who is the director of the Newman Center at Keene State College.

Fr. Vallee is in a position to know whereof he speaks for he is the Catholic chaplain of the Keene Fire Department and takes his job seriously.

When first named by Fire Chief Walter R. Messer to the post, Fr. Vallee didn't think too much about it, but he said that when the first general alarm rang after his appointment "I almost jumped out of my trousers."

Since that time Fr. Vallee has made it a point to answer every general alarm.

Fr. Vallee's car is equipped with the customary red blinker light and siren. And what is more he dons his fireman's helmet and raincoat, the back of which is stenciled the words "Chaplain, Fr. Vallee" before the first round of the alarm is sounded.

Should his services as a clergyman be needed in any emergency at the scene of a fire, Fr. Vallee stands ready to fill that need. Happily however, most of his duties as a chaplain are in a different area.

He attends the annual memorial service of the department, the yearly banq1uet of the firemen, company meetings held to honor retiring firemen and visits department members when they are ill. He is also active during the observance of Fire Prevention Week.

By coincidence Fr. Vallee's Protestant counterpart in the department chaplaincy, the Rev. Fay L. Gemmell, is also connected with Keene State College, being the Protestant campus minister.

The Keene Fire Department has had both Protestant and Catholic chaplains for many years, the first dating back to the appointment of the Rev. Norman H. Janes, pastor of the First Congregational Church on June 10, 1948.

The first Catholic chaplain was the Rev. Roland Montplaisir, a curate at St Bernard's Church whose father was a lieutenant on the Manchester Fire Department.

Others who have served as chaplains include the Rev. Edward Meury, the Rev. Charles Austin, Capt. Albert Milley of the Salvation Army, the Rev., James Moran, the Rev. William Quirk, the Rev. Francis Curran and the Rev. Leo Desclos.

As Reported by the *Keene Evening Sentinel* April 5th, 1967:

"STORY"

"New Truck" City's newest fire truck in operation

New Fire Engine: Keene's newest fire fighting unit arrived on April 5th after being purchased from the Wethersfield, CT Fire Department. It is a 1957 Ward LaFrance 1,000 gallon unit. Photo by Steven Goldsmith.

Keene's newest fire truck, Engine 2, was placed in service last week.

The new vehicle, a 1957, 1,000 gallons-per-minute pumper, was purchased from the Whethersfield (Conn.) Fire Department at a cost of $6,025.

The previous Engine 2 is a 1930 Ahrens Fox 750 gallons-per-minute front end piston pump. Fire Chief Walter R. Messer was in the process of purchasing a new commercial truck to replace the 1941 Diamond T 800 gallon tanker and had anticipated an approximate $18,000 cost for the new vehicle, before receiving a notice on the 1957 pumper available in Connecticut.

Chief Messer said, "This engine will be far superior to the commercial vehicle we had first planned to buy." Keene firemen have been very busy in the past few weeks, cleaning, painting and transferring equipment. All tests have been made by Messer, and met all standard requirements for operation.

The 1951 Pirsch 750 gallons-per-minute pumper and hose truck will be converted to a 1,000 gallon tanker," Messer said.

The City Council approved the bid for the Ward LaFrance pumping engine on March 16. The money was supplied through the capital reserve fire equipment fund.

———

As Reported by the *Keene Evening Sentinel* April 9th, 1967:

"FIRE"

Damage by vandals amounting to $700 was reported by Keene Police today to have occurred at a house being constructed by Contractor Ovid A. Carrier at the corner of Elm and Court Streets.

In confirming the report, Carrier said his house was actually damaged twice – Monday night and Wednesday night.

Carrier said someone spent a portion of Monday night destroying outside shutters and doors and throwing rocks through windows.

Wednesday night someone threw a rock through the picture window of the house, Carrier said.

Entrance to the house, which has been under construction all winter was not gained, Carrier said. Some $480 of his loss is covered by insurance, he added.

———

As Reported by the *Keene Evening Sentinel* April 17th, 1967:

"FIRE"

Emerald Street Fire. Wallisford Mills and Cheshire Oil Building. Photo by Clark.

A warehouse fire on Emerald Street Saturday afternoon resulted in "several thousand dollars" damage to the first and second floors of the wooden structure.

Engines 3 and 4 and ladder truck 2 of the Keene Fire Dept. were summoned at 3:53 to the wooden warehouse owned by Realties Inc. The building housed the Cheshire Oil Co. retreading plant and Wallisford Mills merchandise.

The fire was caused by a faulty compressor on the first floor, according to fire officials, and swept up through the outside partitions to the second floor. Sprinkler systems on the second floor prevented the blaze from spreading further.

At 4 p.m. a truck from the Marlborough Fire Dept. was called to the fire scene and West Swanzey was used to cover the station.

Damage was to the compressor and sprinkler control room, the second floor and wall, rubber stock and ties belonging to Cheshire Oil, yarn, spindles and bales of wool belonging to Wallisford Mills.

———

As reported by the *Keene Evening Sentinel* June 17th, 1967:

"STORY"
Trucks

Fire Department Lineup Three latest Ward LaFrance engines in front of Keene's Central Fire Station. The first two from left to right are 1965 and 1959 750 Gallons-per minute pumpers. At right is the newest truck, a 1957 1,000 gallon-per minute pumper.

City Newest Fire Truck In Operation Keene's newest fire truck, Engine 2, was placed in service last week.

The new vehicle, a 1957, 1,000 gallons-per minute pumper, was purchased from the Whethersfield (Conn.) Fire Department at a cost of $6,025.

The previous Engine 2 is a 1930 Ahrens Fox 750 gallons-per minute front end piston pump. Fire Chief Walter R. Messer was in the process of purchasing a new commercial truck to replace the 1941 Diamond T 800 gallon tanker and had anticipated an approximate $18,000 cost for the new vehicle before receiving a notice on the 1957 pumper available in Connecticut.

Chief Messer said, "This engine will be far superior to the commercial vehicle we had first planned to buy." Keene firemen have been very busy in the past few weeks, cleaning, painting and transferring equipment. All tests gave been made by Messer, and met all standard requirements for operation.

"The 1951 Pirsh 750 gallons-per-minute pumper and hose truck will be converted to a 1,000 gallon tanker," Messer said.

The City Council approved the bid for the Ward LaFrance pumping engine on March 16th. The money was supplied through the capital reserve fire equipment fund.

———————

As Reported by the *Keene Evening Sentinel* June 22nd, 1967:

"FIRE"

Barrett Barn was completely destroyed by fire at 5:18am this morning on East Surry Road. All Cattle were removed and later nearly 100

volunteers constructed a temporary structure to house the milking equipment to house the dairy herd. Photo by Finning.

Spontaneous combustion has been blamed for a fire early this morning, which leveled a huge barn and silo and caused other damage on the Brentwood Farms property of Aubrey W. and Ellis E. Barrett on the East Surry Road.

The fire, which started in a wooden hay storage silo, was discovered by Ellis Barrett around 5 o'clock and quickly spread to the nearby barn.

Seventy-three dairy cows and some young stock, housed in the barn, were led to safety. The blaze completely destroyed the barn and silo, caused some damage to a sugarhouse, burned some hay and wing of a plane, which was in storage.

The barn, according to the Barretts, was large enough to accommodate 100 cows, with some young stock.

Heat from the burning structures was so intense that it ignited the lawn in front of the Barrett home across the road.

The initial fire call was issued to Mutual Aid center at 5:18 with Engines 3 and 4 responding. Later Squad 2 and Ladder 2 sped to the scene, closely followed by two Surry Fire Department vehicles.

In addition to housing cows, the structure contained milking equipment and was used for hay storage. The Barretts plan to set up temporary milking equipment on the grounds and are contemplating building a shelter for the equipment.

Milking equipment was being sent to the scene this morning from R. N. Johnson in Walpole for use in an emergency milking setup.

A Keene fireman, H Emile DeRosier, 40 of 65 Stanhope Ave., was overcome by smoke at the scene and taken to the Elliot Community Hospital. He was treated for smoke inhalation and returned to his home.

The Barrett herd of registered Jerseys was one of the larger dairy herds in the county. The cows were being tested under the Dairy Herd Improvement Association.

Old fashioned working bee

As Robert Frost once said, "Good fences make good neighbors." New barns apparently do too.

The New England Yankee spirit of work bees and barn raising, evident 100 years ago, was rekindled yesterday at Brentwood Farm on the East Surry Road.

Nearly 100 neighbors, friends and even total strangers pitched in to help Aubrey W. and Ellis E. Barrett after a fire had destroyed their barn and milking equipment in an early morning fire yesterday. As soon as the flames had died down the crew set to work.

Big Job

There was a big job at hand because the 73 head of dairy cattle remained to be milked.

The newer extension of the barn had not suffered as much damage as the main structure and it was decided to set up the temporary milking apparatus in this area. With a flourish saws, hammers and nails, a building team under the direction of James A. Mugford erected a makeshift barn to house the milking equipment transported from R. N. Johnson of Walpole.

A rough structure was built after ashes and charred wood has been swept up and carted away by the helpers. At 4:30 p.m. the milking had started.

Mrs. Ellis Barrett said ham sandwiches, lemonade and coffee arrived from nowhere.

"The cows did not want to go into the milking machines because the cement was still hot and they were not familiar with the surroundings." Mrs. Barrett said. "But finally we got them milking by using three shifts."

Pretty Amazing

"This is all pretty amazing to me," she said. "I am deeply appreciative of the concern shown by the people. I had no idea people would turn out like this."

Mrs. Barrett explained that the temporary facilities will suffice until a more permanent plant is working out. However, she said she did not know when everything would be back to normal at the farm.

Spontaneous combustion was blamed for the fire which was discovered by Ellis Barrett around 5 a.m. in a wooden hay storage silo next to the barn. The first call to Mutual Aid came in at 5:18.

Fully Involved

The barn was fully involved by the time trucks from the Keene and Surry Fire Departments arrived and firemen concentrated on saving nearby structures.

The Keene department sent Engines 3 and 4, Squad 2 and Ladder 2, and Surry dispatched two trucks to the scene. Water was obtained from a nearby pond.

Seventy-three head of registered Jersey cows and some young stock were led to safety. In addition to destroying the main barn and wooden silo, the fire damaged a sugar house. Some hay and a stored airplane wing were also lost.

There is still no estimate of damage but the Barretts had insurance coverage.

————

As Reported by the *Keene Evening Sentinel* July 17th, 1967:

"FIRE"

The Keene Fire Department responded to three calls on Saturday and two more Sunday. A still alarm ran at 2:08 a.m. for a short in the battery cable of a truck at Cheshire Oil Co., Inc.

A smoke detector, which picked up the mist from a deodorizer sounded an alarm at the National Grange Mutual Insurance Co. Saturday morning at 9:11 sending engines three and four and the ladder truck to the scene.

A fire in a car on Route 10 called out engine 3 at 4:26 p.m.

On Sunday engine 3 responded to a sprinkler alarm at Frazier and Son, 678 Marlboro St., at 5:16 p.m.

A chlorine leak at the city pumping station on Lower Main Street sent engine 3 out last night at 9:32.

———

As Reported by the *Keene Evening Sentinel* August 29th, 1967:

"FIRE"

Heavy smoke battled. Firemen battle heavy smoke during a fire in the basement of the Keen Tiki on 45 Main Street in early morning

Several thousand dollars damage was done to the Keen Tiki restaurant in an early-morning fire that completely gutted the cellar below the restaurant at 45 Main St.

Tenants above the restaurant smelled the smoke, reported the fire, and Engines 3, 4 and the ladder truck were called out for a still alarm at 1:49 a.m. A box alarm followed at 2:02 sending the squad.

Starts in Cellar

The fire is believed to have started in the area of the cellar near the walk-in refrigerator and freeze3r, and may have been caused by electrical wiring. The cellar extends the entire length of the restaurant and is used for storage and preparation of food.

According to Harry Moy, owner of the Keen Tiki, the restaurant will be closed until smoke damage has been repaired. He said the entire restaurant area was covered with a film of smoke and all the food had spoiled.

The fire was confined to the cellar, and the partitions. No flames were visible from the street, but heavy smoke poured from the restaurant's rear entrance.

Smoke Damage

The restaurant, apartments upstairs, and Miller Brothers Newton all received smoke damage. Slight water damage was reported to G. H. Tilden and Co.

Firemen stayed at the scene to clear out smoke until 7 o'clock this morning.

The Keene Fire Department is still investigating the fire.

A fire yesterday afternoon did several thousand dollars damage to the home of Richard Walsh on Silent Way. The blaze believed to have been started by a short circuit in an electrical lamp, broke out just after 1 p.m.

According to Keene firemen, all the contents of a second-floor bedroom were destroyed and other rooms were damaged by smoke and heat.

Material stored in a garage was believed to have been the cause of a fire at the home of Clarence Castor on 22 Cottage St., yesterday at 5:19 p.m. Engines 3 and 4 responded and were back in service at 5:30.

———

As Reported by the *Keene Evening Sentinel* September 11th, 1967:

"FIRE"

The charred remains of the Bloomer Block, which housed Cut Rate Shoe Mart, Bloomers Furniture, The Colony Shop along with Chute & Page Refrigeration and 20 private apartments took almost five hours late Saturday night to bring the Elm Cities downtown block under control. Photos by Bill Gagnon and The Keene Evening Sentinel.

Fire of undetermined origin, which appeared to have started on a loading ramp and rear stairway swept through a downtown business block Saturday night and caused a reported $100,000 in damage.

The multi-alarm fire was reported at 10:58 p.m. in a two-story building owned by Carl R. Bloomer and housing the Cut Rate Shoe Mart, Bloomer & Haselton, Inc., Colony Shop, Inc., Chute & Page Refrigeration Service and 20 private apartments, rented by Bloomer.

1,000 Onlookers

More than 1,000 onlookers watched as Engines 2, 3 and 4, Ladder 2 and Squad 1 of the Keene Fire Department, Engine 1 of the Marlborough Fire Department and the hose and ladder truck of the Meadowood Fire Department of Fitzwilliam battled for nearly eight hours trying to quell the fast-spreading blaze.

"It was like many fires in one," Robert N. Guyette, deputy of KFD said. "Actually there were three general alarm fires in the one building."

He said first indications were that the fire had been stopped but it had so many blind spots that it started right up again."

Several times firemen, concerned about their fellow workers in the thick smoke, hollered, "they're taking a licking up on that roof. More water over here."

When the firemen arrived at the scene they found fires in the hall of the apartment building, in a garage connected to a building housing the law firm of Bell and Kennedy and in the attic on the Center Street side of the building.

Atty. Ernest L Bell, 3rd and several others carried important records from the law firm's office.

We had planned what to do in case of fire for a long time," Bell said. "We knew exactly what to take out."

"People were hanging out their apartment windows when we arrived," Guyette said. "Three people had to be taken out by ladders because of the blaze in the corridors. We were damn lucky we did not lose anybody."

The blaze then gained access into the blind attic and soon spread throughout the building. Both Winter and Center Streets were virtual seas of water as the firefighters pumped thousands upon thousands of gallons on the blaze.

"We were concerned about the fire spreading to the law offices and the court house." Guyette said. "With all that heat the court house could have gone up so we had a truck and four hand hoses in the alley between the two buildings."

The deputy explained that the department had a definite plan and pattern of fighting the fire as they installed two ladder hoses to shoot water down on the fire and hand hoses to shoot up.

"When we decided that we could not stop the blaze our main concern was not to let it spread," Guyette said. "If we didn't have the ladder hoses it could have."

He said the firemen were "beat" because they had been fighting a brush fire earlier in the day and the final truck did not leave the scene of the Winter Street fire until 6:45 a.m. Sunday.

Trucks from Troy and West Sw2anzey covered Keene during the fire.

The last fire of such intensity was in the same building 20 years ago according to Guyette. "That was the same to a tee as this one was,:" he said.

Several firemen received injuries while fighting the blaze. Suffering from cut hands were Herman Trombley and Keith Randall. Paul Symonds Jr. stepped on a nail, Phillip Davis lost a toenail when a ladder fell on it and John Dennis, Jr. suffered a cut on the left wrist.

Jerry Merrill from the Meadowood Department suffered a cut left index finger.

One of the tenants, Frances Waldron, collapsed from smoke inhalation and heat after she escaped from the blaze.

Guyette reported that more than 5,500 feet of hose were used.

"We were damn lucky we didn't loose anybody in the fire," Robert N. Guyette, deputy fire chief, said today.

Guyette was talking about the fire which swept a downtown block Saturday night and Sunday morning causing thousands of dollars in damage.

"I usually take a swing around a building when I arrive at the scene and there were people hanging out of their apartment windows because of the flames." He said. "We had to take three people down ladders."

The building, owned by Carl R. Bloomer, housed 20 apartments along with the Cut Rate Shoe Mart, Bloomer & Haselton Inc., the Colony Shop and Chute & Page Refrigeration Service.

The police department got most of the people out of the building. "I'd say the people were taking it quite well, but they were nervous," Guyette said.

The fire came within 45 minutes of having tragic consequences.

"If that fire had broken out 45 minutes earlier," Guyette said, "there might have been lives lost."

The deputy explained that trucks and men from the Keene Fire Department had been summoned to an alarm on South Lincoln Street. When they arrived at the box they learned it was false. "That was box 15," Guyette said.

"I don't know if it will do any good," he said, "but tell the readers about this. If the fire had started with the men and equipment on the east side of town it would have been very serious."

The possibility of expanding the County Court House onto the land occupied by the Bloomer block occurred this morning to

County Commissioner Harold O. Pierce of Walpole.

"We don't know if Mr. Bloomer wants to sell," he said, "but it's something to be considered."

———

As Reported by the *Keene Evening Sentinel* October 3rd, 1967:

Fire Line Coming Down: Capt. Laurence E. Thompson of the Keene Fire Department works at the end of a ladder taking down fire line as part of West Street construction. Line will be placed underground. Photo by Rafford.

———

As Reported by the *Keene Evening Sentinel* October 13th, 1967:

"STORY"

Fireman recognized at banquet

Albert Little, clerk of the Keene Steam Fire Engine and Hose Company for 36 years, was presented a token badge for service last night at the Keene Fire Department banquet.

Chief Walter R. Messer made the presentation to Little who resigned October 1. He plans to move to Connecticut.

Retired Deputy Chiefs Elton Britton, Ralph Turner and Stephen W. Pollock were special guests of the department.

Laurence M. Pickett, House minority leader, spoke briefly of his past experience while a member and lieutenant on the Washington Hook and Ladder Company.

Mayor Richard E. Bean, along with other city officials, attended the banquet.

The ladies auxiliary prepared the banquet dinner and it was held in the assembly hall.

The observance of "Fire Prevention Week" will continue this afternoon with the testing of a 1,000 gallon pumper at Robin Hood Park. The annual firemen's ball is scheduled tomorrow night.

———

As Reported by the *Keene Evening Sentinel* December 6th, 1967:

"FIRE"

Car Fire Extinguished: Rosamond Alberti talks to police as firemen inspect her car, which caught on fire on Main Street in front of Keene State College shortly before 9 a.m. Photo by Selkowe.

"I stopped to ask the officer how to get to the airport and he grabbed me and said 'get out'."

Rosamond Alberti of Hancock did just that, and watched smoke and flames pour from under her cars hood. The fire was quickly extinguished by the Keene Fire Department, which was called by Officer Leon M. Daby. He was directing Main Street traffic in front of Keene State College where the fire occurred shortly before 9 this morning.

———

As Reported by the *Keene Evening Sentinel* December 21st, 1967:

"STORY"

Pumping Again on the Flame Front. Driver Laurence Wood carefully removes smudgy fingerprints from shiny new paint of Engine 4, now back in action for the Keene Fire Department after a six-week overhauling.

Gleaming in a shiny new red coat trimmed with 24-karat gold, Engine 4 got its overhauled pump back in action last night after a six-week respite when a Christmas tree caught fire at 192 Winchester Street.

The blaze started at 7:59 p.m. in the home of Keene Police Inspector Robert F. Donoval. Engine 4, its rust holes, dents, chips and scratches gone for the first time since 1959, rushed to the scene, accompanied by Engines 1 & 3.

Within minutes the fire was brought under control and all engines were back at the station by 8:35 p.m. The fire did a minor damage to the living room of the house.

———————

As Reported by the *Keene Evening Sentinel* December 26th, 1967:

"FIRE"

Fire Damages Home, Level Camp Here

Christmas Eve Blaze. William Olmstead goes up ladder to assist firemen on roof of home damaged by flames Christmas Eve at 67 Summer Street. Photo by Rafford.

Fire alarm and firemen helped Mrs. Daniels and her mother, Mrs. G. A. Weaver, from the burning building. The two women escaped injury.

Fires leveled a camp on the Gunn Road and caused thousands of dollars damage to a house at 67 Summer St. over the holidays.

An alarm shortly after 7 o'clock last night sent Engines 1 and 3 of the Keene Fire Department to the unoccupied camp owned by Mr. and Mrs. William Sawyer of North Swanzey. Observers in the downtown area reported a glow was still visible in the sky above the camp site 45 minutes later.

Firemen returned to the station around 8 p.m. but rushed back at 8:33 to battle the rekindled blaze for another hour.

The camp contained building materials.

On Christmas Eve a fire swept through two downstairs kitchens and rear upstairs rooms of the home of Mrs. Philip B. Daniels.

The blaze apparently broke out when Mrs. Daniels tried to light the oven of a gas stove in one of the kitchens. It got into the partitions and spread to the second floor.

Engines 3 and 4 responded to the alarm and firemen helped Mrs. Daniels and her mother, Mrs. G. A. Weaver, from the burning building. The two women escaped injury.

Engine 3 returned to the scene around 9:10 p.m. after the blaze apparently rekindled.

Mrs. Daniels is the mother of the late Jonathan M. Daniels, Episcopal seminary student who was killed about three years ago while working for civil rights in Hayneville, Ala.

1968

As Reported by the *Keene Evening Sentinel* January 8th, 1968:

"FIRE"

Gas Station Damaged by Flames

Washington Street Blaze. Fire caused thousands of dollars in damage to a gas station this morning, Fire officials blamed an overheated furnace for the blaze. Photo by Selkowe.

Fire flashed through Streeter's Citgo gas station and store early this morning after its steam furnace overheated, ran out of water and ignited the underpinnings of the building at 384 Washington St., Keene Fire Chief Walter R. Messer said. The fire spread to the partitions and got into the walls, he said, but firemen wearing smoke masks were able to contain it within the structure. Firefighters had the blaze under control in about a half

hour, Messer said, but it was nearly two hours before the fire was completely out. The chief said damage depended on how much of the store's stock was salvageable.

As Reported by the *Keene Evening Sentinel* January 27th, 1968:

"FIRE"

House Damaged On Main Street

Several hundred dollars fire damage was caused a residence at 707 Main Street last night at 5:40.

The fire, officials said caught n a partition between the bedroom and bathroom on the second floor of the house owned by Fay E. Small.

It was believed to have started from a wiring problem and firemen were forced to pull down the ceilings. No estimate of damage was given but Small said he had insurance coverage. Engine 3 and 4 answered the call.

As Reported by the *Keene Evening Sentinel* March 1st, 1968:

"FIRE"

Firemen Answer Minor Calls

A malfunctioning oil burner sent Keene / firemen to Burr an Nichols Machine Company 76 Railroad Street at 3:16 a.m. today.

Engines 3 and 4 responded to the alarm.

Smoke from an incinerator at the rear of the Cheshire National Bank prompted someone to sound an alarm there at 6:45 p.m. yesterday. "Fire authorities chalked it up as an honest mistake."

On Wednesday Engines 3 and 4 went to 74 Carroll Street for a kitchen range oil burner fire at 3:36 p.m.

As Reported by the *Keene Evening Sentinel* March 5th, 1968:

"FIRE"

Fire Damages Home On Monday

Bedroom Charred. Fire caused extensive smoke and heat damage to the home of the Ernest Sargent family at 33 Park Ave. Yesterday. Photo by Zachary.

A fire shortly after noon yesterday charred a bedroom and caused heat damage to the entire first floor of an old Park Avenue home.

Kim Sargent, 8-year-old daughter of Mr. And Mrs. Ernest Sargent of 33 Park Ave. discovered smoke in the home when she came home fro lunch. She called the Fire Department from a neighbor's.

Authorities said the blaze was probably electrical in origin. It was confined primarily to the floor, walls and furniture of the bedroom on the Russell Street side of the house. However, heat damage was widespread throughout the first floor and the fire caused smoke damage through the entire building.

Engine 3 and 4 responded to the alarm at 12:21 p.m. and were there for about an hour.

Fireman Laurence Wood was injured slightly when a piece of glass from the bedroom window gashed the back of his right hand. The building is owned by E. J. Bergeron

————

As Reported by the *Keene Evening Sentinel* March 15th, 1968:

"FIRE"

Fire Destroys Dwelling on Spruce Street

Keene Home Destroyed. Keene firemen scramble up ladder in the hopes of halting flames, which destroyed home of the Kenneth Buffums at 17 Spruce Street early this morning, Contents in the house were also lost. Photos by Selkowe.

A family of seven escaped unharmed as fire swept their home at 17 Spruce Street early this morning. The house and its contents were a total loss.

Mrs. Kenneth Buffum awoke and smelled smoke around 1 a.m. and roused her husband. He went downstairs in the two-story wood frame structure to investigate and found heavy smoke through the first floor.

Buffum woke his five children and got them and his wife safely outside. Then he pounded at doors of three neighbors before he was able to arouse someone to call the fire department.

By the time firemen reached the scene the house including the porch was engulfed in flames, authorities said. They fought in vain for nearly three hours to save the building, which was left with only the outer walls and roof standing.

The family was unable to get any of its possessions out. "They were lucky to get out themselves," Deputy Chief Harry Hammond said. He had no estimate of the value of the loss.

Hammond said the fire is believed to have originated in a bathroom storage cabinet, the top of which was used for medicine and the bottom for storage.

The building was owned by Roy Buffum, farther of the occupants.

————

As Reported by the *Keene Evening Sentinel* April 11th, 1968:

"FIRE"

Fire Damages Old Colony Lumber Company

A fire early this morning destroyed several thousand dollars worth of renovations to the Old Colony Lumber Company building at 599 Main Street.

Keene Fire chief Walter R. Messer said the fire apparently was caused by a counter which had been left over the floor furnace. The automatic furnace overheated, he said, igniting the floor and the counter and burning up into the ceiling before flames were spotted by police who turned in the alarm at 3:40 a.m.

Engines 3 and 4 responded and remained at the scene nearly two hours.

Daniel Humphrey, proprietor of Mr. Take Out, has been remodeling the building into a restaurant. The structure, formerly occupied by the Old Colony Lumber Company is owned by William DiMeco.

Estimating damage, Messer said the floor and heating system would have to be replaced and the interior of the building refinished.

————

As Reported by the *Keene Evening Sentinel* by Carolyn Zachary April 20th, 1968:

"FIRE"

Fire Sweeps Nearly 25 Acres in Keene

After all-night vigil firemen began early this morning to check and wet down 25 acres in Keene forest fire.

The fire broke out in a remote area, necessitating the use of planes to pinpoint the location.

The blaze erupted just before 4:30 p.m. between Old Gilsum Road and Drummer Road, an extension which crosses a field between Old Gilsum Road and the East Surry Road. Deputy Chief Robert Guyette was flown over the area and helped guide firemen to the scene.

Chief Walter R. Messer said the fire, on land which may be state-owned, was inaccessible to fire trucks; firemen took only one truck and a power wagon to the area. He said they fought the blaze, which burned 20 to 25 acres, mostly with hand tools, using some water carried on the power wagon.

We actually used very little water on it," he said. "We were able to knock it down with hand tools, outlining it first for perimeter control.

Fire Battled

About 50 men battled the fire in shifts for several hors, with members of the Ladies' Auxiliary supplying sandwiches and coffee.

Firemen were reported" moping up" by about 8:30 p.m., and several stayed into the night as a check against possible rekindling.

Keene state college students joined firemen and volunteers fighting the fire.

————

As Reported by the *Keene Evening Sentinel* by Carolyn Zachary April 20th, 1968:

"FIRE"

Spectacular Blaze Levels Barn As Fires Continue to Take Toll

Barn Burns Like a Tinderbox. Flames erupt from the roof of a barn on Winchester Street moments after the first hint of fire became visible Saturday afternoon. Within five minutes, and before firemen arrived, the structure collapsed. Photo by Selkowe.

A spectacular blaze razed a barn in the heart of Keene. The fire erupted around 3:45 p.m. Saturday, apparently caused authorities said. By children playing in the barn at 322 Winchester Street adjacent to Riverside Shopping Plaza. The barn, loaded with hay, went up like a tinderbox, observers said. It collapsed in minutes before firemen arrived.

The surrounding area was quickly mobbed with lines of parked cars and spectators, many of them taking pictures of the raging general alarm fire, as others flooded the Fire Mutual Aid Centers with calls reporting the blaze

Winds from the east fanned flames towards the house, owned by Mrs. M. Doris Shechan, just to the west of the barn. Using fog lines, firemen were able to confine damage to two sections of the attic and some scorching on outer walls of the house. No one was home when the fire occurred.

Fireman Robert Croteau slipped and fell down a flight of stairs while fighting the blaze. He was checked at Elliot Hospital and found to have only a bruised arm.

He returned to the scene before the fire was out.

The fire spread to the dry grass around the barn, keeping firefighters hopping to stamp out freshly burning patches.

Firemen were on the scene well into the night, bulldozing about 30 tons of hay and overhauling the area. The last unit returned to the station just before midnight.

There was no actual estimate of damage.

————

As Reported by the *Keene Evening Sentinel* by Carolyn Zachary April 23rd, 1968:

"FIRE"

Heat Damage Results From Chair Fire

A smoldering overstuffed chair caused heat damage to an apartment at 249 Marlboro Street last night.

The fire, in a second floor apartment occupied by Joseph Dubois, caused heat damage to the living room furniture walls and ceilings before firemen snuffed it out. Little water was used keeping water damage to a minimum.

Engines 3 and 4, Ladder 2 and Squad 2 responded to the alarm at 8:02 p.m. and stayed on the scene about an hour. The building is owned by Albert W. Drogue.

At 3:45 a.m. Keene firemen also were called to the OK Fairbanks Market on West Street after a malfunctioning sprinkler system triggered a sprinkler alarm.

————

As Reported by the *Keene Evening Sentinel* Writer June 7th, 1968:

"FIRE"

Fire Damages Hose Basement

Sentimental Ruins. Firemen carry remains of keepsakes destroyed by fire in the cellar of Donald C. Sterns family house at 74 Franklin Street. Photo by Zachary.

A fire, apparently caused by spontaneous combustion, destroyed the contents of the basement of the Donald C. Stearns residence at 74 Franklin Street.

Stearns said only objects of sentimental value were lost in the blaze, which was extinguished soon after the alarm came in at 5 p.m. Firemen were able to confine burning to the cellar of the building owned by the Rev Hubert Mann.

Chief Walter R. Messer said the fire apparently was caused by the spontaneous combustion of painting materials in the basement.

————

As Reported by the *Keene Evening Sentinel* Writer July 4th, 1968:

"FIRE"

Five-Year Old Gives Alarm; Fire Doused

A five-year old boy, who spotted smoke coming from his neighbors window early last night prevented a living room fire from growing into a more serious blaze. Eric Goodenough went home and told his parents, Mr. & Mrs. William G. Goodenough of 35 American Ave., that the house next door might be on fire because he had seen smoke. They turned in the alarm at 6:43 p.m.

Authorities said the fire, which apparently started in an overstuffed chair in the unoccupied home of the Edward Caouette family at 31 American Ave., had burned the chair, rug, hardwood floor and the end table by the time firemen arrived and quickly extinguished the blaze. Paint in the living room was also blistered by the heat.

Caouette arrived home while firefighters were there and said his wife, who had been out earlier in the day had stopped home about and hour before the fire was reported. She had picked up clothes for the children and had taken them out of town for the weekend he told authorities.

————

As Reported by the *Keene Evening Sentinel* Writer July 4th, 1968:

"FIRE"

Keene Fire Department Responds to house Explosion

Two eight-year-old boys apparently were responsible for the explosion which burst through an unoccupied house at 16 Garrison Ave. early last night,

The house, currently up for sale, is owned by Major Leroy Z. Page, who is stationed at Fort Belvoir, Va.

Results of Gas Explosion. This home at 16 Garrison Ave was blown apart last night after escaping gas from propane tank ignited. Blast blew out windows and walls and caved in the roof. Photo by Hicks

Keene Home is Ripped Apart by Explosion, 2 Boys Blamed

Police Chief Albion E. Metcalf said two tanks of propane gas were turned on " by some unknown means" and gas was allowed to fill the house. He explained that the appliances to which the tanks had been connected had been removed.

Authorities questioned two boys, one of whom admits to having built a small fire at a rear corner of the house, according to the chief. Then the youngsters got on their bikes and left the area, he said, telling "several people that the house would blow up-and it did."

Mrs. James H. Fish, whose home at 269 Pako Ave. is on the corner of Garrison Avenue, said she and her husband were just sitting down to dessert when the explosion occurred at about 7:10 p.m.

"We heard the explosion-very loud explosion-and then saw the roof lift up and the house come apart," she said. "Then a flash of fire went up through the center of it."

Mrs. Fish said they telephoned the Fire Department, but another family in the neighborhood had reported the blast just before they called.

The explosion blew the windows and walls out of the structure, caving in its roof and scattering glass and debris over several hundred feet of ground. The front and one side were completely torn off the building.

The house reportedly was on the market for $25,000 although its original cost allegedly was about $18,900.

As Reported by the *Keene Evening Sentinel* Writer September 27th, 1968:

"FIRE"

Blazing Truck Gets Drive-In Fire Service

I was in the Neighborhood. A fire erupted this morning in the load of a rubbish truck operated by Ken's Trucking. The driver spotted the smoke and made for the nearby fire station. Photo by Zachary.

No need to chase fire trucks nowadays to be where the action is-not when the fire comes right to the door of the department.

At 8:15 this morning a white rubbish truck came barreling down Vernon Street, horn wailing, with smoke billowing from its garbage compartment. The driver wheeled right up the Fire Department ramp.

Firemen quickly escorted him across the street between the Elm Street Parking lot and the Olson and McMahon Law Offices. Engine 3 pulled up in front of the truck and fire fighters quickly extinguished the blaze.

Donald Murdock was driving the truck owned by Ken's Trucking Co.

About 40 minutes earlier firemen had been summoned to a house at 32-34 Victoria Street where an electric motor on the hot water system's circulating pump had malfunctioned and had begun to smoke. The building, occupied by tenants, is owned by Allen Sweeney

---

As Reported by the *Keene Evening Sentinel* Writer October 10th, 1968:

"STORY"

Surprise Fire Drills 'Orderly'

It took only 38 seconds to empty Roosevelt School yesterday in one of nine surprise fire drills held around the city in conjunction with Fire Prevention Week.

The annual tests were run by Russell Johnson, superintendent of buildings and maintenance, who sneaked into the school and pulled the alarms, and Capt. Frederick Beauchesne of the Keene Fire Department, who accompanied a ladder truck to the scene of each drill demonstrating the equipment and speaking briefly.

Beauchesne was pleased with the results and said all the times were "good" and the drills "orderly." He said he considers 45 to 50 seconds a "good time" for emptying a school explaining that longer times yesterday usually involved extenuating circumstances, such as a child on crutches who was on the second floor when the alarm rang.

Only St. Joseph's School wasn't timed- purely by accident. Johnson said he had trouble turning the alarm off at the parochial school and therefore was unable to make a time check.

Roosevelt tipped the list of the school which were clocked. Franklin School was second with 40 seconds, followed by Jonathan Daniels and Lincoln both 45. Wheelock and the Junior High School both 60 seconds and Symonds, 75 and Fuller 90.

All the grammar schools were drilled in the morning. The Junior High drill in the afternoon was not followed by a demonstration and talk; nor will be the Keene High School drill, scheduled for sometime today or tomorrow.

As Reported by the *Keene Evening Sentinel* October 21st, 1968:

"FIRE"

Kitchen Fire

A pan caught fire on a stove and burned the cabinets, walls and ceiling in Mrs. James Muchmore's kitchen Saturday morning.

Engines 3 and 4 responded to the 10:59 a.m. alarm at 28 Allen Court. The fire was under control minutes later and all units were back at the station by 12:40 p.m.

Keene firemen used a smoke ejector yesterday morning to clear the Michael D. Zaluki home after an oil burner fire. Engine 3 went to 8 Roosevelt Street after the alarm came in at 10:19 a.m. Fire fighters were on the scene about half an hour.

Burning ballast in a light fixture sent firemen to Ye Country Store, 520 Washington Street at 5:33 p.m. yesterday.

As Reported by the *Keene Evening Sentinel* Writer October 24th, 1968:

"FIRE"

Floor Damaged

A fire yesterday morning damaged flooring at Princess Shoe Co., 115 Railroad Street.

Authorities said the blaze probably was caused by a cigarette tossed from a second or third floor window. It landed on the wooden threshold of the rear and burned under the first floor.

A Demon Called Fire

Engines 3 and 4 responded to the alarm at 9 a.m. and used a small amount water to bring the fire under control within minutes. A four-foot section of flooring was removed.

———

As Reported by the *Keene Evening Sentinel* Writer October 24th, 1968:

"FIRE"

Garage Fire "Old Chesterfield Road, Keene"

Keep the Faith, Firemen. Father Gerard J. Vallee, KFD Chaplain, and two other firemen in the thick of a garage fire on Chesterfield Hill yesterday. Structure belonged to Howard E. LaClair. Connected tool shed was also damaged, as well as a car. Photo by Hicks. As Reported by the Keene Evening Sentinel Writer Carolyn Zachary November 11th, 1968 All fire photographs by Sentinel staff reporter Jim Hicks, Carolyn Zachary and Tom Kearney.

———

As Reported by the *Keene Evening Sentinel* Writer December 16th, 1968:

"FIRE"

Estimated at $500,000 As Fire Destroys Eagle Block Businesses

Blaze Originates In Paint Store

Battle Scene After Three Hours. Firemen pour tons of water on Sport Shop and Fletcher's Paint Store from Main Street. Fire apparently began in paint store and spread upward into Eagle Hotel room and laterally to Sport Shop. Main Street was blocked off to all traffic.

Through Front Window: *Water is poured into Fletcher's Paint Store through broken front window. Firemen, kneeling to escape smoke, were in constant danger from exploding paint cans.*

Rooftop Battle: *Firemen train hoses on front of Eagle Hotel building from roof of Sport Shop. Firefighters used power saw to cut through roof so blaze could be hosed from above.*

A general alarm fire raged through the Eagle block in downtown Keene this morning causing damage conservatively estimated at $500,000. It was one of the worst fires in the city's history.

Destroyed in the blaze were the Sports Shop, Fletcher's Paint Store, where the fire originated, Benny and Frenchy's Barber Shop and the old Eagle Hotel above them.

GMA Finance Corp., The Bell Shops, the N.H. Welfare office on the second floor and Goodyear received slight smoke and water damage.

The alarm was turned in at 7:11 a.m. by David Marshall, who lived in an apartment above Fletcher's Paint Store. His wife, who woke up just before 7 a.m. smelled smoke and spotted it coming from under the carpet.

Marshall ran outside and pulled the box alarm by Robertson Motors. An upstairs alarm which was supposed to ring through the building was broken, he said, so he , his wife and Andrew Chylk, who lived with them banged on doors to arouse 15 other tenants

The Marshall's lost everything including their cat. Keene firemen first on the scene, said the fire originated in the ceiling of Fletcher's Paint Store probably in the heating system or light fixture, according to Chief Walter R. Messer. It apparently spread through the ceiling partitions to the upper floors and into the other shops.

Items Saved

Volunteers and firemen helped store owners carry merchandise from the shops, but nothing was saved from Fletcher's and only a few items including the cash register were rescued from the Sports Shop.

First to be carried from the Sports Shop was ammunition. Other items were moved first to the barber shop next door, than further up the street when Benny and Frenchy's began to fill with smoke.

Clesson J. Blaisdell, part owner of the Sports Shop with Isadore Borosky, worked to remove as much stock as possible and then watched as firemen moved in with hoses.

"That's my whole life 25 years of hard work," he said. He estimated his stock alone was worth about $150,000, including a large shipmen of Christmas merchandise which had just arrived.

At least half a dozen firemen were given quick breaths of oxygen by Foley's Ambulance Service and Keene Police, but none were injured or overcome.

Hundreds Watch

Several hundred spectators watched from the sidewalk on the opposite side of main street which police roped off about mid-morning to keep the crowd back. Others lined windows of the Ellis Hotel and the Exchange Building as firemen brought the blaze under control around 10 a.m.

Firefighters cut through the rear roof with a power saw to wet down the interior of Fletcher's and the Sport Shop. Armed with Scott Air Packs, firemen spewed water on the blaze from two extension ladders at the rear of the building and one in the front. Others manned hoses from the ground along Main Street.

Bricks began to crumble and walls sagged in the Eagle Hotel's upper stories around 10:30 a.m. The fire was pretty well out by noon, but firemen were expected to remain on the scene most of the day.

Woman from the Keene Fire Department Auxiliary set up an urn around 9 a.m. in front of the Bell Shops and distributed coffee and donuts to cold, wet firemen. After an hour the store filled with smoke and refreshments were moved up the street to the front of the Keene Co-operative Bank.

The Eagle Hotel had occupied the site since 1806. The Sports Shop, previously located on Railroad Street, moved to the Eagle Block six years ago. Fletcher's Paint Store, a branch of Fletcher's Paint Works of Milford; opened in the block 1959.

The Eagle Hotel has operated continuously at the same location on Main Street since May 1806. Built by Luther Smith a clockmaker, Keene's first brick tavern house was opened to the public when Thomas Jefferson was President. At that time the population of Keene was about 1,600.

It was named Eagle Hotel by its patriotic owner , Col. Stephen Harrington of Nelson, in 1823.

A popular stopover for stage travelers in the early 19th, century, famous lodgers included Daniel Webster; Commodore William Bainbridge, Commander of the frigate "Constitution;" the duke-of-Sax-Weimar; Henry Rowe Schoolcraft; Franklin Pierce, afterwards president of the United States; Horace Greeley; Baynard Taylor; Oliver Wendell Holmes and "the great" John L. Sullivan.

The Eagle has, up to now, escaped any serious fire damage. Wooden additions were destroyed by its greatest blaze in 1836 and Colonel Harrington then built his second addition connecting the original hotel with an adjoining three story leather store.

Keene's last major fire occurred a little more than a year ago, on Sept 11th, when the Bloomer Block on Winter Street was destroyed in a $100,000 blaze. The building housed the Cut Rate Shoe Mart, Colony Shop Inc, Chute and Page Refrigeration Service and 20 private apartments rented by Bloomer.

Firemen from four departments battled the Bloomer blaze for eight hours before bringing it under control.

12 Left Homeless By Blaze

Fresh snow this morning helped cover the stench of fiery destruction which clung to the air following a blaze that wiped out three business and left 12 persons homeless.

The General alarm fire, discovered around 7 a.m., gutted the old Eagle Hotel Block.

Destroying the Sports Shop, Fletcher's Paint Store' Benny and Frenchy's Barber Shop, a ware house for the Goodyear store and the Eagle Hotel rooms and apartments on upper floors.

Goodyear, GAC Finance Corp., the Bell Shops and Robertson Motors received smoke and water damage, and hot cinders fell on Robertson cars parked in a lot behind the hotel block.

A rough estimate fixed damage at $500,000. The hotel building itself, excluding property, was appraised at $80,000.

Investigators from the State Fire Marshal's Office were to inspect the charred ruins today. Authorities said yesterday the fire apparently originated in the ceiling of the paint store, either in the heating system or light fixtures.

Keene Fire Chief Walter R. Messer said the building had been remodeled several times and had false ceilings, which enabled the fire to get a head start before it was discovered.

Firemen from Keene Meadowood, Marlborough and Walpole pumped between 600,000 and 800,000 gallons of water on the blaze, which was brought under control around 10 a.m. and was pretty well out by noon. A truck from the Surry Fire Department covered the Keene Station for the duration.

Firemen Return

Keene fire fighters returned to the scene at 6:04 a.m. today to douse some debris which had rekindled in the rear of what was the Sports Shop. They were on the scene only a few minutes.

The water used to battle the blaze flowed as much as a foot deep for more than a block on Main Street. Public Works director Robert G. Shaw said the large quantity used had little effect on the city's water supply.

"We lost less pressure that we did in a pipe break a few days ago on Appian Way," he said. "Yesterday we turned on the well pumps right away and practically kept even with the firemen. All the storage tanks are full again this morning."

Clesson J. Blaisdell, part owner of the Sports Shop, spent the afternoon and this morning with volunteers loading soggy, ash laden woolen sportswear and heat damaged equipment into pickups trucks. The goods are being stored temporarily in the vacant Newberry building.

Hit Hardest

Blaisdell, Isadore Borofsky, his partner in the Sport Shop and owner of the entire building; N.H. Executive Councilor Fred Fletcher, owner of the paint store, and Joseph A. Campagna and Vena Diluzio, proprietors of the barber shop were hit hardest by the fire.

Blaisdell reportedly told friends yesterday that the Sport Shop's recent large shipment of winter stock intended for purchase by Christmas shoppers, was not insured. But Borofsky said he believed their policy covered all merchandise "as soon as it came through the door." He added, however, that he couldn't be sure until they meet with their insurance company representatives.

Blaisdell said the Sport Shop employees five full and two part-time workers, none of whom would be out of jobs. "We'll all be working, starting this morning," he said. "We're going to start again-today, in fact."

Blaisdell and Fletcher share another common misfortune both lost political races this year, Blaisdell as a Democratic candidate for State Senate and Fletcher as a candidate for the Republican gubernatorial nomination.

Fletcher, a Milford resident visited the remains of his Keene shop yesterday afternoon just before 3 p.m. He said he had sent a truck carrying $3,000 worth of Christmas stock to the branch store on Friday, but had no estimate of his total loss.

"I own seven stores and a paint factory and I'm getting old," he said with a touch of humor. "I don't mean to be evasive, I just don't remember these things. All I know is we had a very nice store here." Shortly after Fletcher's arrival all the gutted store fronts were boarded over with plywood.

The paint and wall paper store employed three full and one part time worker. Manager Lenard R. Haubrich was to meet with Fletcher this afternoon to discuss the situation. He was unsure of the owner's plans, but said, "If we can find another location, we'll probably get going again but it's hard to say. Haubrich said he was still employed, but he didn't know about the other workers.

The destruction of Benny and Frenchy's Barber Shop, located there for nine years, put one part and four full time employees out of work. "W were covered by insurance," DiLuzio said this morning. "I think we'll be all right."

That the partners will relocate and open again together is doubtful he said, since he had been thinking about retiring in a year or two. How ever, he said Campagna might reopen at another site.

Losses Confined

Phillip G. Taaffe, proprietor of the Goodyear store, was happy his major losses were confined to a warehouse behind the barber shop. It contained a refrigerator and 700 to 800 snow, truck and farm tires, as well as customer's tires to be recapped.

His store, built in 1954 on what once was a parking lot fore the Eagle Hotel, erected in 1806, withstood the fiery onslaught because of its modern construction.

Taaffe's appliances and the store itself suffered smoke and slight water damage.

He said he got his records out right away, but no stock was removed.

The fire was not without its humorous moments. "While it was going a woman was giving me heck because I wouldn't put her snow tires on," Taaffe said.

Goodyear reopened today. "We're here without electrical power, but we're open," a salesman said this morning.

GAC employees also were back on the job today. They had electrical power but were a bit chilly doors were open and fans were going in order to clear the last of the smoke from the office. Their part of the newer building adjacent to the Eagle Hotel received only minor smoke and water damage to the rear hall.

Next door the Bell Shops, and branch of a Boston corporation, did not reopen. Mrs. Douglas Page, assistant manager, said

yesterday there was "so much water on the roof that they're afraid it will give."

The store stock was moved out by employees, neighboring merchants and Keene State College fraternity men yesterday

———

As Reported by the *Keene Evening Sentinel* Writer December 16th, 1968:

"FIRE"

KSC Family Loses Belongings in Fire

House Fire. Low temperatures and high winds hampered firemen trying to douse this fire at 47 Park St., the blaze began in the heater in the garage and spread to the house. Photo by Kearney.

A fund has been started to aid a Keene State College sophomore and his wife who were left homeless last night after a fire gutted their rented house at 47 Park Street.

Caused by a space heater in the adjoining garage-workshop, the blaze destroyed most of the belongings of Mr. and Mrs. Richard Albright. Damage to the building owned by Mrs. Elizabeth M. Foley, was estimated at $4,000.

Authorities said the fire swept through the garage and to the house via the breezeway. In the house it spread through the partitions, helped by very flammable insulation and ceiling tile.

Keene Fire Chief Walter R. Messer said Albright was able to rescue his school books and a few other items from the first floor of the 1 ½ story structure. But most of the couple's other possessions were either burned or soaked in the fight to save the house.

Engine 3 and 4 and Ladder 2 answered the alarm at 8:05 p.m. Smoke was heavy and the roof was scorched, but flames never came into view from outside the house. Brisk winds and low temperatures created less-than ideal fire fighting conditions. Water from fire hoses froze when it hit the ground.

Firemen were on the scene for almost two hours.

While the blaze was in progress, the annual Keene State College Christmas concert began at Keene Junior High School. During intermission the Rev. Gerard J. Vallee, fire department men and KSC Newman Center chaplain announced that a fund would be started to aid the Albrights. A collection of $77.28 was taken up.

During the night calls to the Newman Center offered three apartments to the couple. They will move into one tomorrow. The Popular Club of Keene donated a $50 certificate for clothing for Mrs. Harriet Albright and a bellows Falls, VT individual called with an offer of clothing for her husband.

Minutes before the Park Street blaze broke out last night Keene Engines 3 and 4 returned from the corner of Maple and Pako Avenues where a car fire was reported.

On Saturday, Keene firemen were called out twice for a kitchen fire at 54 School Street at 6:28 p.m. and, while that was still in progress to the Keene Manor on Main Street where the smell of smoke had been reported.

1969

As Reported by the *Keene Evening Sentinel* January 6th, 1969:

"FIRE"

Minor fires are reported in Keene area

A series of minor fires were reported in the Keene area over the weekend.

Late yesterday afternoon Engine 3 and Ladder 2 were called to the Eric J Kromphold, Jr. residence at 208 Main St. for a chimney and fireplace fire. The alarm was sounded at 5:27 p.m. and firemen were on the scene about 30 minutes.

Just before 1 p.m. yesterday Engine 3 responded to an alarm at 40 Wilford St. for a malfunctioni8ng power burner. The building, owned by Leo Howland, is occupied by tenants.

At 10:20 a.m. a water surge in the Keene Shopping Plaza sprinkler system triggered an alarm. Engines 2 and 3 responded, firemen spent about 45 minutes checking the system.

At 10:20 p.m. Saturday John F. Mooney of Harrisville drove up the Keene Fire Department ramp to report a car fire in his car. Firemen quickly extinguished the smoldering front seat. The fire apparently was caused by a cigarette.

Engine 3 was called to 39 Brook St. at 11:20 a.m. Saturday where a space heater had started a fire in a building owned by Morton Whippie and occupied by tenants.

At 10:31 p.m. Friday oil salamander and boards ignited at the Keene State College Student Union building. Engine 3 responded to the alarm.

As Reported by the *Keene Evening Sentinel* March 8th, 1969:

A Demon Called Fire

"STORY"

County Having Problems With Ambulance Service

On The Rescue Scene. Foley Ambulance Service attendants Robert J DiLuzio, left and Miles Carothers prepare to lift a highway accident victim into the ambulance after administering first aid. Photo by Zachary

Private ambulance services nationally have reached a crisis and Cheshire County, though in better shape than most places, is not without its problems either.

The Frank J. Foley Funeral Home in Keene handles most of Cheshire County's ambulance calls. One of only four private services still operating in New Hampshire, it has managed to survive despite financially tough standards imposed by the federal Medicare law. But without an eventual subsidy from some source—most likely the federal government—Foley, too, might fold his ambulance business.

Foley took over the Elliot Community Hospital ambulance service June 1, 1953, after the hospital was forced to drop it ECH officials explained at the time that their equipment was obsolete and their ambulance old; sending the vehicle out often left the hospital with insufficient manpower to operate properly.

Bystanders, Too

Bystanders can cause major trouble. When rescuers were at work at the scene of the fiery crash on Route 10 that killed Gary B. Filiault of Keene, firemen nearly has the blaze out when a bystander flicked a cigarette in a pool of gasoline. The resulting explosion showered the crowd with bits of hot metal; additional trucks had to be called in, and firefighters had to go to work all over again to douse the blaze.

In 1962 A Keene State College girl was badly mutilated in an accident that killed her companion on Route 101 in Marlborough. Police thought the girl was dead too, and threw a blanket over her. Foley discovered a pulse, however, and he began to administer first aid.

But as soon as the crowd learned she was alive, bystanders began yelling for the attendants to stop fooling around and get her to the hospital.

"Most people think we're just supposed to pick up victims, throw them in the ambulance and go," DiLuzio said.

They don't realize we're trained to administer first aid—and how important emergency care is.

In this case, Foley ignored the critical crowd and took the time to insert a breathing tube in the girl's throat. Doctors later credited him with saving her life—without the tube, they said, she would have strangled on her own blood.

———

As Reported by the *Keene Evening Sentinel* May 13th, 1969:

"FIRE"

Area Firemen Respond to Five Calls

Area firemen answered five calls yesterday, including an alarm at a Keene wholesale grocery.

Engines 3 and 4 and Ladder 2 of the Keene Fire Dept. responded to an alarm at Holbrook Grocery yesterday at 2:09 a.m.

Firemen said the alarm had been triggered by a broken sprinkler head.

Engine 3 extinguished a telephone pole fire at 8:23 p.m. yesterday on Route 32.

Keene's Engine 3 also cleaned up gas spillage made by a delivery truck early today at the West Street Esso Station at 12:03 a.m. Firemen hosed the area as a precautionary measure.

Quick work by Keene firemen was credited with short-circuiting a blaze in the attic of a duplex at 22 Wilford St. this morning.

The house was occupied by the Frank D. Wilson family, received smoke, fire and some water damage in the attic but conservative use of water in containing the smoke blaze prevented damage on the first two floors of the wooden frame building.

Three trucks from the Keene Fire Department responded to the alarm shortly before 11:30 a.m.

————

As Reported by the *Keene Evening Sentinel* June 3rd, 1969:

"STORY"

Insurance Rates, Firemen's Pay Topics at Public Safety Meeting

Fire insurance rates and firemen's salaries were the primary topics yesterday at a meeting of the City Council Public Safety Committee.

William Propler of the New Hampshire Board of Fire Underwriters reviewed the city's insurance status and the slim possibility of a rate reduction if a new substation is erected in West Keene.

On Firemen's salaries, Chief Walter R. Messer pointed out the salary range parity his men achieved with Police Department employees in 1966 has vanished, and urged the committee to consider reestablishing the practice.

Proper told the committee the latest survey his group did on Keene was in 1962 when the city was moved up one class from five to four, reducing fire insurance rates for industries but having no effect on residences.

"A West Keene fire station is entirely up to the community," Proper said, emphasizing his agency is supported by insurance companies and has no authority to impose fire protection improvements on a community. "I would hope, though, that the communities will keep improving themselves. You have had substantial growth in the western side of the city."

Rate Drop Doubted

Proper said he doubted whether the city could top another class in insurance rated with just a new substation, since about 400 deficiency points would have to be eliminated before a new classification could be issued. In fact, he said, it is "conceivably possible" the city could slip back one class because of fire protection problems around shopping centers. The grading system encompasses the fire department, water supply, alarm system, prevention techniques and building conditions.

"The huge floor areas in many shopping centers are too large for many fire departments to cover, and construction is frequently inadequate with incomplete fire partitions and a partial sprinkler system," Proper said.

"Probably by the time we get a substation it will just about be enough to keep us in class four," James A. Masiello, committee chairman, said.

"Instead of thinking only of insurance rates,: Proper said, "you might think of fire protection improvements to protect your tax base. The rebate on insurance rates is really gravy, but the real roast beef is the tax base."

No Action Taken

The two members of the committee who were present, Masiello and Richard W.

Louis, took no action on Proper's report since the session was strictly for informational purposes.

The third member of the committee, Chris J. Tasoulas of Ward 1, has not attended any of the bimonthly committee meetings during the last three months.

On the salary issue, Chief Messer pointed out a pay ordinance passed earlier this year granting city employees an 8.1 per cent pay boost included elevation of several classes of policemen to new salary ranges, eliminating parity between comparable police and fire positions, set up from a 1966 study of salaries in the state.

James C. Hobart, city manager, said the new ordinance does not set salaries for the police, since salaries are entirely under the jurisdiction of the Police Commission, but only reflects the current payroll.

Masiello said although the city gave an 8.1 per cent increase this year, the big shift came in 1968 when the commission increased salaries an average of 16 per cent.

Increase Did Nothing

"It was big enough to make the Finance Committee swallow it hard," Hobart said of the payroll schedule introduced in the 1968 budget hearings which were closed to the public. "So in terms of parity, our 8.1 per cent increase really did nothing."

And we get socked in the nose with this because we have no control over salaries." Masiello said.

"I've been shooting for equality in grades of work between police and firemen since I became chief in 1946," Messer said. "I hesitate to sit back now because it can get too far out of line. For the morale of our service, we should get it straightened out."

Louis said a member of the Police Commission told him informally the Police Department's goal is to have a force composed entirely of college graduates with a $10,000 minimum salary.

Keene, Not Harlem

"But this is Keene, N.H., not Harlem," Hobart argued.

"We're shooting for parity," Messer said, "whether you do it now or the first of next year, but I bring this up just so you know what's going on. We're not going to stop work just because it isn't so."

We not only have to fight for this but against the other (additional police salary increases granted by the Police Commission,") Masiello said.

The committee chairman also indicated there have been some problems in issuing courtesy tickets since the council have the police authority to use discretion in issuing them. The ordinance was changed at the request of Police Chief Albion E. Metcalf to provide ammunition for prosecution for "flagrant violators" of the law, which at that time made issuance of courtesy tickets mandatory for out-of-state vehicles.

"We left it to their discretion but I think we should set some criteria for them, since obviously there is no discretion," Masiello said. "We could make up the criteria and if they (the police) don't like it, we could change the ordinance back."

———

As Reported by the *Keene Evening Sentinel* June 26th, 1969:

"FIRE"

Fire damages Wilder House

Fire caused extensive damage to the interior of the Raymond Wilder residence, 198 Carroll St., Yesterday at 3:15 p.m.

Fought From Above. Keene firemen broke through slate roof tiles yesterday to attack a blaze in the Raymond Wilder residence on Carroll Street. Bad wiring was believed to have been the cause.

Keene's Engines 3 and 4 responded to the alarm, and a call for additional crew and equipment brought out Ladder 2 and Squad 1.

The fire in the one-and-a-half story building may have been caused by faulty wiring, Deputy Chief Robert N. Guyette said.

Guyette reported smoke damage throughout the house with heavy water damage in the rear section of the house.

————

As Reported by the *Keene Evening Sentinel* July 26th, 1969:

"FIRE"

Old Summit Road Dump Burns Underground Like a Volcano

"It stinks." "It smells horrid."

These were some of the remarks made by people in the Pako Avenue area about the recent outbreak of smoldering flames at the Summit Road dump.

On Tuesday, July 22, at 6:12 a.m. Keene firemen went to thee old dump site on the Summit Road upon a call from neighbors of the area. The fire was reportedly smoldering beneath the debris.

On Friday morning, July 25, three days later, city bulldozers were still attempting to seal off the dump area by covering it over with three to four feet of dirt.

"We surveyed the area hoping to arrive at a solution," said Fire Chief Walter R. Messer. "We put over a thousand gallons of water on it to slow it down, but it didn't amount to a thing. It's like using a tea cup to fill a swimming hole."

"It was burning like a volcano, 60 to 70 feet in the ground," said Public Works director Robert G. Shaw after inspecting the smoky dump.

"The only way to smother a fire like that is to seal it up with dirt."

According to Messer a Public Works payloader worked on the burning debris eight hours the first day spreading mud and slush over the smoldering flames.

The next day a bulldozer and payloader from R.W. Payne, Inc. began covering the 20-acre dump area with dirt from the hillside, and by 4 p.m. Friday, the job had been completed.

"We can't be positive as to what gave ignition to this material", Messer said. "It's a combination of heat that has accumulated plus the right temperatures and wind."

Messer explained that when the city stopped using the area as a dump 11 years ago, they leveled it off for a landfill. In doing so they spread over a pole of old tree stumps and wood that had accumulated but hadn't been burned. This dry wood slowly began decomposing, heated by the smoldering dump debris below it. This debris had not been covered daily by layers of dirt like the modern sanitation landfill on Winchester Street.

————

As Reported by the *Keene Evening Sentinel* September 11th, 1969:

"STORY"

Mutual Aid emergency Medical Plan Part of National Study

Always Alert and Awake. One of the dispatchers who man' the Emergency Control Center of the Mutual Aid System on Vernon St., listens to a radio call. The center is manned 24 hours a day, 365 days per year. Photo by Zanes.

The National Association of Counties has announced that the Southwestern New Hampshire District Fire Mutual Aid System will be studied as an example to be included in a forthcoming safety program action guide.

The study will be conducted by the National Association of Counties Research Foundation of NACO under a research contract from the National Highway Safety Bureau.

The particular aspect of the Mutual Aid System which the association will study is the emergency medical services program.

The guides will incorporate concepts outlined in federal highway safety standards. The general purpose of the guides is to provide information and assistance to locally elected and appointed policymaking officials in the development of effective highway safety systems.

The local district will be one of about 60 programs studied in the preparation of the projected guide.

"The situation here is unique," said Warren Howe, researcher assistant for the national association, who spent several days in Keene. "It is a regional approach to the problem."

The Mutual Aid control center on Vernon Street, is in communication with a number of area ambulances. Since it is also in communication with the Cheshire County Sheriff's Department and with police departments in 22 towns, for a total of over 80 two-way radio equipped vehicles, it is in at least indirect contact with emergency rescue vehicles in the entire area.

Mutual Aid serves a population of approximately 67,000.

The system consists of 45 towns. Seven neighboring towns in Vermont and Winchendon, Mass, are included in the system.

The emergency communications center of Mutual Aid is operated 24 hours a day, 365 days a year.

"Our emergency control center is not restricted to fire calls only," Chief Robert C. Callahan said. "We operate an all-emergency center to serve the people of this area."

———————

As Reported by the *Keene Evening Sentinel* October 3rd, 1969:

"STORY"

Parade, Muster Set Sunday in Keene

A parade and firemen's muster Sunday will kick off Fire Prevention Week in Keene.

The parade, featuring between 40 and 50 pieces of fire equipment and marching bands, will begin at 1 p.m. and stretch from the fire house on Vernon Street to the Keene Public Works Building below the bypass on main Street.

A regional firemen's muster the last of the season, will be offered at the Cheshire Fair Grounds free to the public, after the parade. The muster, scheduled for 3 p.m.

Keene Fire Chief Walter R. Messer. *Stands with trophy's that will be given out during Keene's parade and muster on Sunday.*

City Firemen Will Visit Grade Schools

The Keene Fire Department continues its observance of Fire Prevention Week today with visits to all public grade schools in the city.

According to Chief Walter Messer, an exercise will be performed with the ladder truck at each of the schools.

The inspection day banquet will be Thursday at 6:30 p.m. to midnight in the National Guard Armory on Hastings Ave. Dance music will be provided by Leo Daniels Orchestra.

As Reported by the *Keene Evening Sentinel* October 6th, 1969:

"FIRE"

Keene Firemen Answer 2 Calls

Engines 3 and 4 of the Keene Fire Department went to a box alarm at the intersection of Spring and Brook Streets shortly after noon yesterday

The fire, believed started by a pipe or matches, was in the Louette Johnson residence at 64 Spring Street. It was under control when firemen arrived.

Engines 3 and 4 responded to an alarm Saturday in Carle Hall at Keene State College. The fire confined to the rubbish room of the new men's dormitory, had been extinguished by an automatic sprinkler when firemen arrived.

As Reported by the *Keene Evening Sentinel* October 21st, 1969:

"FIRE"

Knoll Avenue Fire Kills Man, 83

A Keene man died early this morning after discovering a fire in the living room of his home at 5 Knoll Ave.

Charles Charnella was found by firemen in the bathroom of his home. Death was by smoke inhalation, according to Dr. James M. Ballou, Cheshire County medical examiner.

Officials theorize that Charnella was awakened by the fire which they believe was started by a cigarette in an overstuffed chair in the living room, and tried to get water from the bathroom to douse the flames. A coffee pot was found near the body, indicating the man was overcome by smoke before he could return from the bathroom.

The blaze was reported to the Keene Fire Department at 3:14 a.m. and four engines responded to the scene. Firemen remained on the scene until 4:55 a.m. The fire has been burning for some time before it was reported, officials said.

The flames were confined to the living room area, burning two holes in the floor and causing damage to the furnishings and walls of the room. However, intense heat was generated by the smoky fire, causing heavy damage to other parts.

There was no exact estimate of damage available, but fire officials said damage to the house was extensive.

Mr. Charnella, who was born June 3, 1886 in Ansonia, Italy, a son of Bernardo and Rose Charnella, was president of the Paper House of New England for 45 years prior to his retirement in 1953.

He was a resident of Springfield, Mass. For many years before moving to Keene in 1962.

Survivors are his wife, the former Adelene Fortenbaugh whom he married in the Little Church Around the Corner in New York City in 1916 and a niece, Mrs. Harold Stevens of North Swanzey.

A prayer service will be held in the Fletcher Funeral Home Thursday morning at 11 with burial in Hillcrest in Springfield, Mass.

————————

As Reported by the *Keene Evening Sentinel* December 15th, 1969:

"FIRE"
Elderly Man Killed in Spring Street Fire

Flames out, but smoke remains. Keene firemen breathe fresh air at the door of a Spring Street home before re-entering smoke filled building. One resident died, another was injured.

Oscar W. Blake, 78, of 64 Spring Street died when fire swept his second floor apartment early Sunday morning.

Blake was pronounced dead at the scene by Cheshire County medical referee Dr. James Ballou, who said death was caused by smoke inhalation.

Hubert Sprague, who lived in the apartment below Blake's suffered first-degree burns in an unsuccessful attempt to rescue the elderly man. Sprague was released from Elliot Community Hospital after treatment for burns of the face, neck, chest and left hand.

Two engines of the Keene Fire department responded to the initial call at 12:22 a.m., and two more answered a box alarm sounded two minutes later. The blaze was under control at 12:51 a.m., less than half an hour after it was discovered.

A Fire Department spokesman said the entire upstairs area of the two-story wooden frame house was damaged by fire, heat and smoke, while some smoke and water damage was reported to Sprague's first-floor apartment. Most of the contents in the second floor apartment were destroyed.

Fire officials reported they found tools and a bicycle pump near a kerosene heater in Blake's living room. Apparently, Blake was trying to blow out the oil line on the heater with the pump when the fire started.

His body was bound in the kitchen adjoining the living room. He had a slight burn on his chin.

Blake was born November 2, 1891, in Alstead, the son of Welsey O. and Edith M. (Wilder) Blake.

He lived in Alstead until moving to Keene in 1923, where he was employed by the Wheeler and Taylor Dairy until his retirement.

He is survived by one brother, Robert W. Blake of Keene; three nieces, Mrs. Albert Schultz of Keene, Mrs. Edwin Croteau of Surry and Mrs. George Trnaritis of Limassol, Cyprus; several grand nieces and grand nephews.

Funeral services will be held in the Fletcher Funeral Home Wednesday afternoon at 2 p.m. Burial will take place in Centennial Hill Cemetery in Gilsum.

————————

PERMENANT MEN 1969. *Seated Row from Left to Right, FF Paul Crowell, FF Chester Dubriske, Capt. Laurence Thompson, Deputy Chief Harry Hamond, Chief Walter Messer,Deputy Chief Robert Guyette, Capt. Fred Beauchene, FF Edward Ball, FF John Phillips. Standing Row from Left to Right, FF Owen Holden, FF Herm Troumbly, FF Bernard Blancarto, FF Russell Cloutier, FF George Shepard Jr., FF Robert Symonds Sr., FF Allan Collier Sr., FF Emile DeRosier, FF Francis Driscoll Jr., FF Laurence Wood, FF Ronald Amadon, FF Robert Croteau, FF Philip Davis Sr., FF Homer Atkins.*

1962 Washington Hook and Ladder Company. *Seated from L to R: FF Robert Diluzio, FF Grover Howe, FF Evert Symonds, Lt. Rupert Reason, Capt. Francis Driscoll, Lt. "Huck" Francis Winn, Clerk Clare Symonds, FF Fred Sharkey. Standing from L to R: FF Jack Dennis, FF Jim Brown, FF Steve Gibson, FF Earl Smith, FF John O'Neil, FF Irving Vorce, FF Harry Russell, FF Bob Driscoll, FF Robert Symonds, Sr.*

♛ *A Demon Called Fire*

1970

As Reported by the *Keene Evening Sentinel* April 1st, 1970:

"FIRE"

Fire Damages Basement of Store

An early morning fire damaged the basement of the Olson Cosmetics store and the smoke damaged Lantz Jewelers next door.

The fire was discovered in the Main Street store at 2 a.m. by Keene police officer Hugh McLellan, who smelled smoke as he patrolled his beat. McLellan and a second officer checked out the entire Roxbury main Street block and then called the Fire Department.

Deputy Fire Chief Robert N. Guyette said the fire department doused the blaze in the basement of the Olson store, but not before fire damaged storage shelves, items stored in the basement and backboard for electric boxes.

The deputy said the cause appeared to be malfunction and flooding of an oil burner. No estimate of the damage has been completed. The building was owned by the Ellis Estate.

———

As Reported by the *Keene Evening Sentinel* June 8th, 1970:

"FIRE"

House fires fought in Keene

A metal clad structure at 203 Winchester St. was totally destroyed by fire shortly after 9 a.m. today.

Keene firefighters arrived at 9:10 a.m. and battled the blaze for about one hour. One fire engine remained at the scene for mop-up operations.

Winchester Street Blaze. Keene Fire Department members douse mid-morning fire today at 203 Winchester St. The structure owned by Ellis Bros Florists was totally destroyed. Photo by Haley.

Keene Fire Chief Walter R. Messer said workmen were in the process of dismantling the building when the fire was probably set by accident. The structure was part of the former Ellis Bros. Florists facilities. A house on the same property received some smoke damage.

No one was reported injured in the fire, and no damage estimate has been released.

———

As Reported by the *Keene Evening Sentinel* October 7th, 1970:

"FIRE"

Cigarette Sparks Fire in Apartment

A cigarette sparked a fire last night at 8:53 p.m. in an apartment occupied by Eric Krieson at 145 Church St. according to the Keene Fire Department.

According to police Erickson said he fell asleep on a couch while watching television and smoking a cigarette.

Police officers Eugene Rosin and Charles A. Norcross said they guided several children and a woman out of the building.

A fire department spokesman said today the furniture, floor and one wall were damaged by the fire. Two other apartments in the building received smoke and water damage. The building is owned by Leon Bergeron.

The fire department units returned to the station at 9:36 p.m.

————

As Reported by the *Keene Evening Sentinel* October 10th, 1970:

"STORY"

Fire Prevention Week Capped by 122nd Annual Fireman's Ball

Firemen on Parade. *Fire Department marching unit leads Main Street parade, which yesterday opened Fire Prevention Week. Crowds lined street to watch marching bands and fire equipment pass by. Photo by Haley.*

Fire Prevention Week 1970 winds up tonight with the 122nd annual Firemen's Ball at the National Guard Armory on Hastings Avenue.

For Keene firemen, tonight is one of the first moments to relax after a busy week of helping the community learn how to prevent fires and save lives and property.

This week's events were kicked off with a Main Street parade with 45 fire departments from a four-state area participating with men, equipment and music.

At one time in Keene's history, the day was called "Fire Inspection Day" and Chief Walter Messer recalled the chief crow gathering event was a hose spraying contest pitting local firemen versus the steeple of the United Church of Christ.

How did that work? Well, Messer said, a steamer truck was drawn up to Central Square and connected to a hydrant there. Then the firefighting team attempted and often did, squirt the hose higher than the steeple.

Batten the Hatches

One year, the chief recalled someone forgot to close the church doors and he said "that ended that event."

Today, the hose pumping events are only one part of muster exhibit at the Cheshire Fairgrounds. South Deerfield, Mass., walked away last Sunday with the 1970 Muster Association trophy.

Keene, with Phil Davis at the head of the muster team; piled up enough points to win first place in the rotary pump and dry hose events, but as host team passed the trophies on to Williamsburg, Mass., and South Deerfield.

Monday, the fire department began 30-minute tours of the station for local elementary, junior high and special schools.

Yesterday, 50 youngsters—the last of the weeks' parade of schoolchildren—left the firehouse. They had learned how men cooperated to fight fires, how equipment was put to work and that a firemen's tour of duty is 24 hours with the next 24 hours off.

Inside View

The wide-eyed youngsters also peeked at the firemen's living quarters and meeting and training areas. They also were encouraged to work out escape routes in case of fire in their own houses.

"I encourage them to take anything like a chair and break a window to escape from a burning house," Firefighter Homer L. Atkins, Jr. said. "We also tell them to sit down with their parents and work out possible exit paths from their houses.

Twenty five members of the Ladies Auxiliary worked over the firehouse stove Thursday and cooked up a dinner for city officials and department heads. City Manager James C. Hobart and City Councilmen Thomas P. Wright, George M. Rossiter, Richard W. Louis, Ronald G. Russell and James A. Masiello were among the 95 guests who enjoyed the featured oyster stew.

Ladder Upped

Also during the week, fire department members visited all but three local schools to demonstrate aerial ladder escape equipment.

At Keene High and Junior High, the men conducted a fire drill for the two larger schools.

The fire department set up a Fire Prevention Week exhibit in the Public Service Co. Central Square window—one week early. But Messer said, next year with proper scheduling, "It'll be right on time."

Tonight Fire Prevention Week ends with the ball at the National Guard Armory. Admission is $1 per person and dancing to the strains of Perry Borelli will last from 9 p.m. to 12.

The ball benefits the Fireman's Relief Fund.

———————

As Reported by the *Keene Evening Sentinel* October 16th, 1970:

"FIRE"

Fire Damages House on Elm Street

Heavy Smoker. Keene fireman endures smoke from hole axed in roof of house at 33 Elm St., Early morning fire caused several thousand dollars damage, and its cause is under investigation. Photo by Kearney.

A fire of undetermined origin caused several thousand dollars damage early this morning to a two-and-one half story house at 33 Elm Street.

According to records in the city assessor's office, the two apartment buildings are owned by Gierald M. Miller of Keene.

Six trucks from the Keene fire department were called to the scene about 4:30 a.m. to fight the fire which reportedly began in the middle section of the house at the top of the ceiling stairs.

Fire Chief Walter Messer said the blaze was contained in the stairway area and did not spread to either side of the house to any great extent. The fires spread upward, but Messer said it did not burn through the roof of the house.

Lack of an escape route for heat and smoke due to containment of the fire, made the interior of the house extremely hot and smoky. However, though use of artificial breathing apparatus and face protections, no firemen were reported suffering from smoke inhalation. Firemen were hampered briefly by a broken hydrant in front of the house.

Both apartments in the wood frame house had been vacant for some time.

Messer said the fire is being investigated "with a fine tooth comb" by the Keene Fire Department.

Units from Surry, Marlborough and Meadowood were called to cover the Keene station during the fire.

———

As Reported by the *Keene Evening Sentinel* October 21st, 1970:

"FIRE"

House Fire at 550 West Street

West Street Fire. Keene firefighters battle smoke on third floor of unoccupied hose at 550 West Street last night. Fire was second in two weeks in vacant Keene Hose. Photo by Haley.

Keene police are investigating the cause of a fire last night in an unoccupied house at 550 West Street near Park Avenue.

Deputy Fire Chief Harry F. Hammond said today the fire began on the first floor then spread to the second floor and then to the attic. He said no damage estimate was available. The house had been vacant "for many years."

Fireman Paul Rushlow of 61 Adams Street was injured when he fell and stuck his head while fighting the fire. An Elliot Community Hospital spokesman said today he was treated and released last night.

Firemen reached the scene at 10:45 p.m. and remained there for two hours.

The property is owned by the 912 Realty Corp. The fire last night was the second in an unoccupied house in Keene within two weeks.

———

As Reported by the *Keene Evening Sentinel* November 20th, 1970:

"FIRE"

Fire Damages Residence on Eastern Ave

Fire yesterday damaged the John Corliss residence at 127 Eastern Ave.

The fire broke out at 8:34 p.m. and according to Fire Chief Walter R. Messer, consumed "household items stored in a second-floor ell at the north end of the house.

The chief estimated damage to the house at several thousand dollars.

The fire spread into the rafters and water from fire hoses damaged part of the first floor.

The fire, Messer said, may have been caused by children bringing in a portable light to the area and placing it on the divan while they were playing.

———

As Reported by the *Keene Evening Sentinel* November 20th, 1970:

"FIRE"

No Extensive Damage in Fire

A broken hydraulic line in a vulcanizing machine caused a fire at 1:24 p.m. yesterday at the Markem Edgewood Operation plant.

Deputy Fire Chief Robert N. Guyette said today the damage was not extensive and was limited to the ceiling, a wall and the electric boxes.

He said the Markem fire brigade had the blaze well under control when the fire department arrived. The units returned to the station at 1:48 p.m.

———————

As Reported by the *Keene Evening Sentinel* December 7th, 1970:

"FIRE"

Beaver Street Market

Beaver Street Market destroyed by Fire

Only charred shell remained today after fire swept through the Beaver Street market building early this morning.

The fire which broke out at 12:11 a.m. today, just after the store had closed, destroyed the market, two apartments and a storage ell. No one was injured in the fire which, according to Deputy Harry F. Hammond of the Keene Fire Department "apparently started in a rubbish area in the rear of the building."

Beaver Street Market Fire. *Firemen from three area companies battle early morning fire, which destroyed Beaver Street Market building.*

High winds and gusty smoke make firefighting difficult. Photo by Haley.

Hosing Down. *Fireman soaks down one area of Beaver Street Market building. Fire started in rubbish in rear of store. Photo by Haley.*

Firefighters from Keene, Meadowood and Marlborough battled the blaze for almost six hours and were hampered by a strong wind which coated the area with ice. Blinding smoke blanketing the area also blocked firefighting efforts.

The building was owned by Alfred P. Masiello of 92 Beaver St. who also operated the market for 25 years. Mrs. Masiello was in the store when the fire broke out, Hammond said.

James A. Masiello, son of the owner, said today the family had made no decisions yet about rebuilding the store. He is handling post-fire details for his father, whom he said, has been ill for a week.

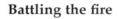

Battling the fire   **The aftermath**

One of the two apartments was occupied by James E. Champney, Barbara A. Logan was listed as the occupant of the second apartment.

Firefighting equipment from West Swanzey, Surry, Spofford and Walpole was brought into town to cover the Keene Station.

All equipment was back in service by 6:45 a.m. with Keene making a return trip to the scene at 6:35 a.m. and returning to the station at 7:20 a.m.

───────

As Reported by the *Keene Evening Sentinel* December 14th, 1970:

"FIRE"

Fire Damages Keene Market

Market Damaged by Fire. An early Sunday morning blaze caused several thousand dollars damage at Streeter's Superette on Washington Street, An electric heater was named as the possible cause. Photo by Wallace Baker.

An early Sunday morning fire caused several thousand dollars damage to Streeter's Superette at 265 Washington St.

The market is owned by Bernard A. and Thompson C. Streeter.

According to a Keene Fire Department spokesman, Keene units responded to a box

alarm at 5:45 a.m. The fire began in a back storage room and spread to the second floor before being contained.

The spokesman said no one was in the building at the time of the fire and no one was injured.

All units were back in service at 8:42 a.m.

An electric heater may have caused the fire, according to fire department officials.

───────

1971

As Reported by the *Keene Evening Sentinel* January 15th, 1971:

"STORY"

Quarter Century of Service

Mayor Robert M. Clark, left presents 25-year service certificates to Keene Fire Department Captain Laurence Thompson and Chief Walter Messer in ceremonies at City Hall. Photo by Baker.

───────

As Reported by the *Keene Evening Sentinel* February 11th, 1971:

"FIRE"

Fire Damages House on Woodburn Street

Fire Controlled Quickly. Keene firemen takes hose to douse flames in two-story house at 43 Woodburn St., owned by Edward L. Curtiss. Damage was reported as Heavy in second story. Photo by Kearney.

A fire discovered at 8:12 a.m. caused heavy damage to a two-story house at 43 Woodburn St. City records list the owner of the house as Edward T. Curtiss.

Keene Fire Chief Walter R. Messer said flames and heat "pretty well cooked" the second story of the house, which contained two apartments. The fire started in the kitchen of the second floor apartment and spread through the other rooms, but the cause of the flames has not been pinpointed. The only damage to the first floor was from water, which seeped through from the second story.

Messer said insulation along the ceiling kept flames from breaking through to the attic and roof and helped control the fire.

A woman and her dog were in the first floor rooms when the fire was discovered, but they escaped safely.

Four engines responded to the scene, and firemen wearing artificial breathing apparatus entered the smoky house to eject smoldering material after hoses directed through windows quelled most of the flames.

Messer said damage would exceed several thousand dollars because of the extent of upstairs damage.

———

As Reported by the *Keene Evening Sentinel* February 12th, 1971:

"STORY"

Keene firemen go to college to learn tactics and strategy

Educated Firefighters. Returning from training courses at Greenfield, Mass., Community College, Keene firemen Roland Amadon, left and Emile DeRosier, right, discuss their studies with Chief Messer. Photo by Rousmaniere.

Gone are the days of firefighting when all a fireman needed to know was what he learned on the job.

It still takes water to put out fires—that part has not changed—but today the science of controlling and dowsing flames has developed to the point where some colleges are offering degrees in fire engineering.

One such institution is Greenfield Community College in Greenfield, Mass., and for the past four years the Keene fire department has been sending some of its men there to study.

The courses on hydraulics, fire tactics and fire protection systems last 15 weeks, with a three hour evening session once each week. The tuition for each course, which is worth three college credits, is $63 per student. The city of Keene pays the tuition of the volunteer students, just as it does in almost every department in the city.

The courses are taught by a member of the Greenfield Fire Department who is working toward a fire engineering degree.

7 Keene Firemen

Seven Keene firefighters took the most recent course the college offered, which is a slight decrease from the average 10 men who usually volunteer for the program.

The course was called "Fire Tactics and Strategy." Most of the course involved classroom lectures, but an important part of it was a work project each student had to do.

The projects were "preplanning," fires in selected buildings in Keene. Each of the seven firemen-students had to choose a large building in Keene and write a paper on how a fire could be put out if one started within it.

Fireman Ronald Amadon's case is an example. He chose the Barker Realty building at 210 West Street. "Pre-planning" a fire there involved more than just knowing how to get to the site and hooking onto a hydrant.

Amadon had to chard the building's sprinkler system, study its structure, check out its alarm system and record what contents there are in all parts of the building.

He spoke to the owners of the building to find out more about it, went to the Public Works Department to get figures on what kind of water pressure he could expect from surrounding hydrants, and drew up a map locating all hydrants and all means of access to the grounds around the building.

He also located a number of "hazard areas" where fires can conceivably start. Hopefully, Amadon's paper will never have to be used by the fire department, but if a fire ever starts in the Barker Realty building, the officers in charge will have advance knowledge on the conditions inside, thanks to the "pre-planning" work project.

None of the reports have been put to use yet since all but one of the bui9ldings studied have not been touched by flame yet.

That one cause was Streeter's Market on Washington Street, and it was hit by fire two weeks before the reports were submitted to the course instructor in December.

Fireman Robert Symonds' had chosen the market for his work project, and the accuracy of his work was illustrated in the fact that the fire started in a part of the building he had earlier identified as a "hazard area." The flames claimed $30,000 of inventory and building before the fire department could put it out.

If the fire had waited a couple of week, before striking the market, Symonds' report would have been in the hands of the department and might have helped cut down the losses.

———

As Reported by the *Keene Evening Sentinel* April 7th, 1971:

"STORY"

Keene Fire Companies Elect Officers

The Keene Fire Department and its three call companies met for an annual dinner meeting Saturday.

Officers chosen for the permanent company are Homer Atkins, president; Alan Collier, first vice president; George Shepherd second vice president; and Francis Driscoll, Secretary.

The Keene Steam Fire Engine and Hod call company reelected William Sanderson captain, Merton Mills first lieutenant and Wesley Peats secretary.

The Washington Hook and Ladder Company elected Robert Driscoll captain, Jon Driscoll lieutenant and Owen Holden secretary.

The Deluge Hose Company elected Russell Driscoll captain, Paul Bergeron lieutenant and William Olmstead secretary.

Chief Walter R. Messer said the Rev. Denis F. Horan was installed as Catholic chaplain and Chaplain Fay I. Gemmell spoke to the firemen at the next meeting.

———

As Reported by the *Keene Evening Sentinel* April 13th, 1971:

"FIRE"

Fire Damages New Apartment

Four Keene fire engines answered a call at the Perham Street low income housing project at about 10 a.m. today to douse a fire in one of the new apartment complexes.

At 11:30 a.m. two of the trucks were still at the scene.

The only damage visible from outside the building which is still under construction was a hole chopped in the roof by the firefighters. Smoke filled the interior of the two-story structure and billowed out of the windows.

Fire department officials were not available for comment on the cause and nature of the fire.

———

As Reported by the *Keene Evening Sentinel* May 1st, 1971:

"STORY"

Walter Messer Never Forgot First Fire

The Chief on his last day. *Chief Walter Messer checks "Old Rosie" the department's 1930 model pumper before leaving. The chief retires May 1 after 47 years of service to the fire department. Rosie is the Department's pride and joy.*

A Brighter Retirement. *Retiring Keene Fire Chief Walter Messer displays to his wife, Elsa, an alarm box lamp presented to him by his department. In front of Elsa are roses presented to her by auxiliary.*

Messer is paid a tribute at Keene Testimonial

The temperature soared to 106 degrees that day, July 6, 1911. Keene residents were talking about the summer heat wave, which had gripped the Ashuelot Valley for days.

Then fire erupted at the Impervious Package Company's sawmill. It spread over the "Patch" neighborhood on lower Emerald Street.

The blaze raged in the summer heat for days. Steamers rolled into town from West Swanzey and Marlborough to help. Doctors ordered exhausted firemen to rest.

A Keene mother took her toddler in a stroller to watch the firefighters at the scene. Five year-old Walter R. Messer never forgot the fire which left an entire neighborhood in ash. It was his "first fire."

By the time Keene Fire Department Chief Walter Messer retires May 1st, he will have logged 47 years of service which saw the fire engines zoom to trouble spots over 15,000 times.

As a youngster, Messer grew up with the sound of fire alarms. His dad, Arthur T. Messer was a volunteer fireman with the Keene Steam Engine and Hose Company.

After his dad died, his mother Martha Randall Messer married Fred W. Towne who was the department's chief for almost ten years.

The history of Keene's 20th century firefighting is also Walt Messer's own story. He recalls the time the fire station was damaged for the first time by fire in 1914. The blaze began in the horse stables, ignited the hay stored there and before it was put out it caused $4,500 damage.

The horse shed was never locked and arson was suspected.

As a Keene High School student, Messer scrambled out of the classroom and onto the fire engine every time the alarm rang. Headmaster Willis O. Smith excused his student from classes because Messer had already achieved substitute fireman rank in the Keene Steam Fire and Hose Company.

After which school graduation he was elected as a volunteer to the company. Before joining the Navy, he worked as a mechanic for the F.J. Bennett Co.

Messer then opened his own garage in Glen Cove, N.Y., but he decided to return to Keene in 1934. This time he was elected to another fire company, the Deluge Hose Company.

Chief Messer joined the fire department as a permanent man in 1941 and in 1946 was appointed to the chief's rank-the second permanent chief of Keene's Department since its organization in 1808.

In the early days of Keene firefighting, Messer said chimney fires were the most frequent call. On cold winter days, the men would go out about 15 times a day to put out those fires.

His first major fire as chief was July 4, 1948 at the Bloomer Haselton building on Winter Street. The blaze caused $60,000 worth of damage to the building and five businesses located there.

When the New Hampshire fire chiefs convened in Keene back in 1953, the Holbrook warehouse went in flames. Two firemen, Paul E. Symonds and Captain Stephen Pollock were injured in the fire. Damage was about $50,000 and a department historian noted, "there were as many visiting firemen as spectators at the scene."

No cause has yet been determined for a spectacular 1954 fire at the Davis Oil Company which caused over $100,000 in damage. A second $100,000 fire damaged the Sprague and Carleton furniture plant in 1956.

The Southwestern New Hampshire Fire Mutual Aid System which Messer helped to organize in 1953, supplied men and equipment from three states, Firemen worked all night to contain the factory fire. They remained at the scene for a week.

A 1964 explosion at the Dalbolt Company on the site of the former Faulkner and Colony mill took the life of a production engineer and caused $125,000 damage. The blast and fire started in a gas drying oven and the cause remains undetermined.

The chief has been active in firefighting professional organizations. He has served as president of the Keene Firemen's Relief Association, the Keene Firemen's Memorial Association, the Cheshire County Fire Wardens Association, Mutual Aid, Tri-State Mutual Aid and the New Hampshire Fire Chiefs Association.

He has also been director of the New Hampshire Firemen's Association and was appointed to the State Board of Fire Control on which he later served as chairman.

[*Compiler's Note*]: This complier would like to pass on what Chief Messer had to say at the end of his testimonial.

At the end Chief Messer closed out his long and distinguished career with his characteristic humility by expressing his gratitude to "all the men and women in the fire service who have served him well." He thanked all those responsible for and present at the testimonial dinner.

At the completion of his brief speech, he presented the gold chief's badge to his ex-deputy, Robert M. Guyette, with the hopes "he enjoys wearing it as much as I did."

The badge that was passed down from Chief Messer to Chief Guyette has been worn by Chief's Towne, Nims and Riley as well. The badge carries a history with it and a privilege to wear. The last Chief to wear the badge was Chief Guyette who retired in 1992.

———

As Reported by the *Keene Evening Sentinel* May 1st, 1971:

"STORY"

Guyette Appointed Fire Chief

As of May 2nd, Robert N. Guyette will be chief of the Keene Fire Department.

Guyette has been appointed by City Manager James C. Hobart as successor to Chief Walter R. Messer, who will retire as of May 1st after 25 years as Keene Fire Chief. Guyette, 43, was a spare driver for the department in 1950, and became a member of the permanent firefighting force in 1952. He worked his way up through the ranks, and now is deputy chief of the department.

He is a native of Keene, was graduated from Keene High School and served in the U.S. Navy. He lives with his wife, Lois, and their four children three girls and a boy at 198 Church Street.

The pay range for the fire chief's post is $11,027 to $14,086.

Messer will be honored May 1st, at a testimonial and banquet at the state armory on Hastings Avenue. Messer was a call fireman for 10 years, a permanent firefighter for five years and chief for 25, a total of 40 years in the Keene department.

Tickets for the ham dinner are $5.50. Reservations may be made through Deputy Chief Harry F. Hammond at the Keene Fire department. Executive Councilor Bernard Streeter, Jr. will be the speaker.

————

As Reported by the *Keene Evening Sentinel* May 13th, 1971:

"FIRE"

Arson Suspected In Apartment Fire

A locked door may have saved two lives and kept a house from burning this week in a case involving arson.

The new investigations unit of the Keene Police said a juvenile was responsible for setting two fires in an apartment building g on 20 Wilford St on May 12.

The fires were discovered by Donald W. Murdock and Harry Murdock, Jr., of Don's Trucking. They came to the building at 9 a.m. to collect refuse when they found a Public Service Co. agent trying to disconnect the power for one of the apartments which had just been vacated.

The front door was locked so the Murdocks led the agent to the outside basement door. When they opened it they found smoke billowing inside.

A fire was burning in a coal bin, and once they had put it out and carried a coal barrel outside, they began an investigation of the house to see if there were any other fires burning.

They found one in a second floor apartment. After the Murdocks had put out that one, they discovered two Keene State College students sleeping in an adjacent apartment.

Upon investigating the fires, the Keene Fire Department said they had been going approximately 40 minutes before the Murdocks arrived. The department said arson was involved.

The juvenile responsible for the fires will appear in juvenile court at a date not yet set by the court.

Clyde J. Dicey, of 135 High St., has made no damage claim, police said.

————

As Reported by the *Keene Evening Sentinel* May 17th, 1971:

"FIRE"

Matches, Rubbish Bin causes fire

A child playing with matches and a rubbish bin were the causes of two fires in Keene Saturday night.

At 8:43 p.m. the Fire Department answered a call at 15 Hanover St. to put out a fire originating in a mattress. Officials said a four-year-old boy started the fire while playing with matches. The house is owned by Ronald Holden.

Fire Chief Robert Guyette said the fire caused "considerable" smoke damage throughout the house. He said it is difficult to make a financial estimate of the damage. The fire was put out in less than 30 minutes.

At 9:57 p.m. two fire engines were called to the William H. Kennedy home at 67 Cross St. to put out a barn fire.

Guyette said the blaze started in a rubbish barrel in the barn, which adjoins the house. He said Mrs. Kennedy discovered the fire as she was checking over a charcoal burner near the driveway.

The fire spread up the stairs onto the second floor before firemen were able to put it out. Smoke from the blaze got into the house, but there was no damage there.

The firemen returned to their station at 11:01 p.m. Guyette estimated damage to the barn at $3,500.

A Keene firefighter heads into a blaze, which damaged a barn at 67 Cross St. Saturday night. Officials said the fire started in a rubbish bin.

A Barn A'Blaze. *A Keene firefighter heads into a blaze, which damaged a barn at 67 Cross St., Saturday night. Officials said the fire started in a rubbish bin. Photo by DiLuzio.*

As Reported by the *Keene Evening Sentinel* October 2nd, 1971:

"STORY"

Beauchesne Deputy Chief of Fire Unit

Fred H. Beauchesne

Fred H. Beauchesne of 95 Colorado St. has been appointed deputy chief of the Keene Fire Department.

Beauchesne, 48, fills the vacancy left by Robert Guyette, who was made chief of the department last month following the retirement of Walter R. Messer.

The new deputy joined the department in 1952 when he was elected to the auxiliary department. One year later he was appointed to the permanent department. He was elevated to captain in 1962.

Beauchesne lives with his wife, Thelma, and a son, Gary at 95 Colorado St. His other son, who is married, is at vocational school in Claremont.

As Reported by the *Keene Evening Sentinel* October 2nd, 1971:

"STORY"

An Oldie But Goodie

With the 123-year old hand-pump apparatus they will exhibit in Sunday's parade and muster are Keene firemen (Paul Crowell pushing; Emile DeRosier and Phil Davis pulling). Photo by Rousmaniere.

Vintage Fire Pumper Will Emit No Chugs

While a score of fire engines drive down Main Street Sunday at the Fire Prevention Week parade, there'll be one piece of fire equipment making nary a chug.

Perhaps the wooden wheels will squeak a little. And perhaps the firemen pulling it will wheeze.

But that's the only sound coming from the clean machine, a hand-drawn, hand-pumped tub vintage 1848, the oldest piece of fire equipment in the Keene Fire Department.

The Deluge apparatus will be making its first public appearance in more than 13 years when it joins the caravan down Main Street and then is put to work at the New England muster championships at the fairgrounds.

Back to Work

For the last decade of its 123 year history, the hand tub has been in storage, but this summer a few energetic Keene firemen led by muster team captain Phil Davis rescued the machine from neglect and restored it to working order.

The hand tub is a tradition in the Keene Fire Department and in fact it is older than the department itself. In the days when it first went to work, it was owned and run by the organizations predecessor, the Keene Fire Society.

The Deluge hand pump has been a showpiece ever since it came to Keene. Sometimes that was a liability.

One late night in 1856, when the Deluge and Neptune Engine Company was holding its second annual levee in the town hall, the party, apparently, was so joyous that the firemen dragged the hand pump upstairs to join the dancers in the hall.

Downstairs

Sometime during the wee hours of celebration, however, a report came in of a large fire in the north part of the village.

The hand pump and the firemen got downstairs somehow and over to the fire. They were fast enough to keep the blaze from spreading, but nowhere in subsequent history of the fire department is there record of the tub ever doing duty in the dance hall upstairs at the annual levee.

The apparatus continued in regular use through the purchase of steamers in 1883 and 1890.

As Reported by the *Keene Evening Sentinel* October 4th, 1971:

"STORY"

3,000 People Watch Firemen Parade; Muster Draws Crowd

Crowds turned out to honor area firemen Sunday at the start of this year's Fire Prevention Week

Threats of rain failed to dampen the enthusiasm of spectators, who lined up six deep along Main Street for a fire prevention parade and later filled the stands at muster competitions at the fairgrounds.

More than 50 fire trucks, ranging in age from 123 years old to less than one year, traveled the parade route down Main Street amid the marching band sounds of six area schools.

The annual event, sponsored by the Keene Fire Department, drew firemen from as far away as Nowank, Conn., and Stephentown, NY. Firefighters from Massachusetts and Vermont also participated in the parade and muster.

Monadnock band Tops

Most of the 3,000 parade watchers were children, whose eyes were glued to the flashing lights of passing fire trucks and who raced for the lollipops thrown by some firemen.

Parade results announced at the fairgrounds put Monadnock Regional High School as the best marching band in the event. The bands sponsor, Swanzey Center Fire Department, also picked up first prize as the best fire unit with a band.

The fire contingent from Guilford, Vt., was selected as the best unit without a band. The Stephentown, NY firemen won honorable mention in the competition.

That was not Stephentown's only award, however. In muster competition, the New York team picked up first place trophies in both the portable pump and oil pit tests.

Team Trophy

Other first place winners were Whately, Mass., in rotary pumping and South Deerfield, Mass., in centrifugal pumping.

South Deerfield's placing in that event and in other competitions earned it the Cheshire County Muster Team Association season trophy.

The award has been won twice by the Keene muster team. The local unit placed in a number of the events Sunday, but because it was sponsoring the competitions, it was ineligible for trophy awards.

The parade and muster events began the 50th year of fire preventing observances in North America

President Nixon has called special attention to this year's celebration noting that fires each year in the United States kill more than 12,000 persons and cause property losses exceeding $2 billion.

The President's proclamation has been seconded by state Fire Marshal Herbert L. Whitney. In a news release Whitney said 16 persons have been killed in fires so far this year in New Hampshire. Last year, he said, 37 fatalities were caused by fire in the state.

The fire marshal urged state residents to visit their local fire stations during the week. The Keene Fire Department has planned visits to the city's elementary schools to demonstrate fire equipment during the week and the fire station is open for tours.

The final results of the muster competition are:

Rotary Pumping: Whately, Mass., first; Lanesboro, Mass., second; West Swanzey, third.

Centrifugal Pumping: South Deerfield, Mass., first; Williamsburg, Mass., second; Stephentown, NY, third.

Portable Pumping: Stephentown, first; South Deerfield, second; Williamsburg, third.

Oil Pit: Stephentown, first; Whately, second; Williamsburg, third.

Sportsmanship: Nowank, Conn.

————

As Reported by the *Keene Evening Sentinel* October 5th, 1971.

"STORY"

Reasons Evident for Fire Prevention Week

Firefighters in Cheshire County, and some home towners and businessmen too, can point to more than one good reason why Fire Prevention Week is held each year.

There have been some big fires in the county since the last Fire Prevention Week, which itself is pegged to the anniversary of one of the greatest conflagrations of American history, the Chicago Fire of 1871.

As fire departments across North America use the annual observances to show off their equipment, they are reminding their spectators that firemen's services are still in need.

A record of the big fires during the last 12 months shows the need is apparently still as great as it ever was.

On December 7, 1970, an early morning fire razed the Beaver Street Market in Keene. Two apartments were also destroyed in the blaze.

Christmas morning brought 19 separate fire units to Peterborough Consolidated School for a blaze which caused more than $2 million damage.

On Jan. 19 of this year, downtown Winchester caught fire, and firemen called out by the Southwestern New Hampshire Fire Mutual Aid system worked along with Winchester firefighters in sub-zero temperatures to control the blaze. Four stores and six apartments were destroyed in the fire.

On February 24 three children died in a pre-dawn house fire in Marlborough, and 19 hours later an Alstead man was critically injured when his house burned down. He died a few days later at Elliot Community Hospital.

200 Keene Calls

The following month, on March 17, the Flock Fibers, Inc. building in North Walpole went up in flames. Damage exceeded $100,000.

Those were not the only fires of the last 12 months. The Keene Fire Department alone was called out for more than 200 fires during the period, and while few of them qualify as "big" in an historical sense, each had large dimensions in the eyes of property owners and relatives of the injured. Some of the "big" blazes of the year rival in size the great conflagrations in the city's history.

The most recent of them was the Eagle Hotel Block fire of 1968. Three businesses on Main Street were destroyed and 12 persons were left homeless in the blaze, which registered a damage of more than $300,000. A testimony to that fire remains in downtown Keene today. The block has lost its charred remains, but most of it is as lifeless now as it was when the fire finished in that cold November day.

Firemen from Keene, Meadowood, Marlborough and Walpole pumped up to 800,000 gallons of water on the blaze and in some parts of Main Street the water flowed a foot deep.

The only other conflagration of any comparable size in Keene was the E.F. Lane Block fire of 1934. Damage estimates exceeded $500,000.

Firemen were called to the scene late at night and remained until the following day. They succeeded in containing the fire to the block building, but not until after flames spread into the upper story of the Spencer Hardware Co. storeroom, where ammunition was being kept. Several hundred rounds exploded, but nobody was hit.

There were no major injuries in either of those fires, but in another major blaze, in 1964, a man lost his life.

An explosion rocked the Barker Realty building in West Street at noon on July 30, production superintended for a cloth factory in the structure, was fatally injured in the blast.

The blast occurred inside a gas drying oven and scattered debris more than 100 feet from the building. The rood of the structure was lifted in the explosion, and damage was estimated at $125,000.

A spectacular 1966 fire gutted the Bloomer Block on Winter Street, causing more than $100,000 damage while a large crowd of spectators watched firefighting efforts from the Winter Street parking lot.

Other major blazes caused more than $100,000 damage each at Sprague and Carleton, Inc. on Avon Street in 1956 and at Davis Oil Co in 1954. In 1925, Burdette Chair Shop received $100,000 damage and Lane Chair Shop sustained $30,000 damage in 1933

As Reported by the *Keene Evening Sentinel* October 23rd, 1971.

"STORY"

Dogs Once Led the Fire Trucks, But Time Has Passed Them By

As more than 50 Dalmatian-less fire trucks passed by on parade last Sunday, a little boy tugged at his father's sleeve and asked "How come there are no fire dogs riding along?"

'Because they're out chasing your sister's cats, probably," was the fatigued reply.

As a comment on domestic affairs, his answer may have been accurate. But as far as the absence of "fire dogs" is concerned, the explanation was less than complete.

Firemen's Friend of Yore. Smokey, the Keene fire station's first Dalmatian, sits proud in his favored seat of fire engine now used only for musters.

The reason there were no Dalmatians riding beside fire engine drivers at the Fire Prevention Week parade Sunday was that the age of "fire dogs." Like many other things, is gone.

In cities across the nation a few dogs still ride to the flames, and in some fire departments pet cats do the Dalmatians' duty. Even monkeys have been known to be firemen's mascots.

Casualty

But the days of mascots are dying. In Keene, those days died in 1939 when Smokey, the department's Dalmatian for six years, succumbed to a liver ailment.

Smokey was preceded by a Dalmatian of the same name. The first Smokey's tenure with the fire department was cut short after less than two years when, after returning from heroic duty at a fire, he was run over by a car.

The only other official mascot in the Keene fire station was a little shaggy dog named Billie. He rode to his first fire in 1931 and didn't miss a blaze for three years straight. Acute indigestion laid him low in the year 1934.

The history of the Keene Fire Department casts a fond light on the three mascots, and other accounts of firefighting in America are filled with eulogies to faithful Dalmatians.

Too Confusing

Why, therefore, are they no more?

The reason, according to Keene Fire Chief Robert N. Guyette, is that most fire stations today are too confusing for most mascots. In olden days a "fire dog" could stay close to his master and get to know all the men of the department.

But these days, when different shifts alternate on a 24-hour duty, mascots have a difficult time, he said. The station is just too busy with unfamiliar faces.

"Fire dogs" started out as real members of fire companies when they led horse drawn pumpers and ladder coaches through crowded streets.

But then the internal combustion engine came along, out speeding both horses and Dalmatians.

Despite that, the dogs retained one important job at fires—keeping spectators away from the action—but gradually their role lapsed into mascot hood.

And now even that fate is deprived the proud Dalmatian.

———

As Reported by the *Keene Evening Sentinel* November 1st, 1971:

"STORY"

Northeast DC-9 in Inaugural Flight into Keene's Airport

Keene's First Jet Service. People view Northeast DC-9 at Keene airport. The 92-passenger plane will fly one round-trip daily between Keene and New York. Plan began regular service Sunday.

People used to laugh at the kind of town where the biggest event each day was the arrival of the train. In Keene, only the technology has changed.

About 100 people showed up Sunday at Dillant-Hopkins Airport to watch the arrival of the first DC-9 jet flown in by Northeast Airlines to serve the Keene-New York City route.

About four people got on the plane to fly to New York.

The jet came a little late carrying only crew and Arthur Fairbanks, vice president in charge of public affairs for Northeast Airlines. The plane was ferried to Keene especially to make its inaugural run to New York.

It came screaming and whining over the fields of North Swanzey, and once on the ground the jet taxied up to the terminal to the waiting crowd and the four passengers.

Fairbanks got off the plane and chatted for a while with Keene Mayor Robert M. Clark Jr., and City Councilmen Thomas P. Wright and George M. Rossitter.

Community leaders in Keene have been pressing hard for a long time for improved air service to the city, and the coming of the DC-9 was the latest result of their efforts.

————{End extract *Keene Evening Sentinel*]

As Reported by the *Keene Evening Sentinel* November 1st, 1971:

"FIRE"

Fire at Keene Landfill Lasts For 17 Hours

Firemen worked through the night Sunday to quell a blaze, which began in Keene's sanitary landfill off Winchester Street.

Engine 1 and a large tanker were called to the scene about 1:15 a.m. to begin a work detail, which didn't end until 6 that night.

Though the blaze was quickly under control, the 16-hour vigil was necessitated but the nature of the rubbish fire, which continues to burn below ground, according to Fire Chief Robert N. Guyette.

A bulldozer was called in late in the morning: by alternately pushing the smoldering refuse forward and dousing it with water from the 2,000 pound tanker the men slowly worked at the flames.

"This was the only way we could have handles it," said the chief, "otherwise, it would have kept starting up again."

About 2,500 feet of hose were laid and the men worked in shifts of three and four men. As of 9 a.m. today it was still not certain whether the blaze was completely extinguished, said Guyette.

The cause of the blaze was undetermined.

————

As Reported by the *Keene Evening Sentinel* November 19th, 1971.

"CRASH"

Vermont Man Alone in Plane

Final Flight, Wreckage Checked. *Debris in foreground shows where plane, piloted by Robert C. Howe Jr. of Northfield VT skidded in the field off of Winchester Street. Howe was killed in the crash. Picture by Kearney.*

Robert C. Howe, Jr., 36, of Northfield, Vt., died Tuesday when his twin-engine private plane crashed in a field southeast of the intersection of Route 9 and Winchester Street.

Howe, who was alone in the Super-V modified Beechcraft was pronounced dead on arrival at the Elliot Community Hospital by Cheshire County medical referee, Dr. James A. Ballou.

Dr. Ballou said Howe received multiple fractures of the skull, ribs, and both legs.

Officials from the National Transportation Safety Board, the New Hampshire Aeronautics Commission and the Federal Aviation Administration were at the site this morning investigating the cause of the accident.

The crash occurred at about 1:45 p.m. Tuesday. Two men at Surry Mountain Dam said they heard and saw a plane fly over the area at about 2,500 feet and they said the plane sounded like it was having engine trouble.

A bystander at the Riverside Plaza in Keene said he saw the plane circling and then plummet to earth about one-half mile from an airport runway. Marks in the field indicated the plane hit, bounced, turned 180 degrees and then skidded a short distance. The plane's fuselage and cockpit were intact, but the engines were smashed, wings heavily dented and nose broken open.

Origin Unknown

Howe's point of origin and destination were unknown, although officials at the airport assumed he was planning on landing in Keene. Caryl Lane, Keene Air Service manager, said there was no radio contact with Howe prior to the accident.

Pennsylvania Registration

Members of the Keene Civil Air Patrol chapter stood watch over the plane in the field Tuesday night.

Howe carried no identification, and his identity was derived from a flight log found in the aircraft, Dr Ballou said.

The twin-engine plane is registered as belonging to Don F. Yenko of Canonsburg, Pa., in the Federal Aviation Administration's registry of airplanes.

Little Fuel

At press time, a number of circumstances surrounding the crash were undetermined. For instance, it has not been revealed where the plane was coming from. It only assumed that the plane's destination was Keene, since there was little fuel left in the plane's tanks. However, there was no radio contact between the plane and the Keene airport prior to the crash.

The last fatal plane crash in this area was on September 2, 1967 when F. Nelson Blount of Dublin was killed when the plane he was piloting crashed in Marlborough.

———

As Reported by the *Keene Evening Sentinel* November 19th, 1971:

"STORY"

3 Promotions Made in Fire Department

Fire Department Promotions. The Keene Fire Department has three new officers of higher rank, Promoted to the new positions are from left to right: Lieutenant Chester Dubriske, Captain John Phillips and Lieutenant Paul Crowell. Photo by Rousmaniere.

Keene Fire Chief Robert N. Guyette has announced promotion of three permanent members of the fire department.

John N. Phillips of 105 South Lincoln St., has been appointed captain, and Chester E. Dubriske of 65 Valley St. and Paul E. Crowell of 73 Douglas St. have been raised to the new position of Lieutenant.

Phillips, 47, joined the fire department in 1958 as a member of the ladder company. The same year, he became a fulltime member of the department. His appointment fills a vacancy created last summer when Frederick

Beauchesne was elevated to the rank of deputy.

Phillips is married to the former Harriet Randall of Keene and has two children.

Dubriske, 45, joined the steamer hose company in 1952, and four years later he was appointed to a permanent position in the fire department. He is married to the former Betty Smith of Winchester and has three children.

Crowell, 43, has been with the Keene Fire Department since 1957. He is married to the former Florence Britton of Keene and has four children.

As Reported by the *Keene Evening Sentinel* November 30th, 1971:

"STORY"

Swanzey Man Rescued After Falling Through Ice

Keene Firefighters rescue Walter Rosin and Enoch Sherwood safely to shore. Firefighters on ice are Ronald Amadon and Homer Atkins. Photo by Wallace Baker.

A North Swanzey man was saved from possible drowning Monday afternoon in Bent's Pond, between Hurricane Road and Alumni Field.

Enoch Sherwood, 71, was fishing from the thin ice on the pond when the ice gave way, plunging him into the cold water.

Two brothers, Walter and Eugene Rosin, tried to rescue Sherwood first, but the ice sank slightly. The Keene Fire Department pulled all three men out, and all three were treated for the effects of immersion at Elliot Community Hospital and released.

The Rosins, both former Keene police officers, were driving on Arch Street when they were hailed to aid Sherwood. Walter Rosins edged out on the ice with two shovels, a fallen tree and a rope using the shovels on the ice to distribute his weight and tossing the rope around Sherwood.

His brother also pushed onto the ice, using a ladder supplied by an off-duty fireman on the scene. But, after Walter Rosin tied the rope to himself to pull Sherwood out onto the ladder, the ice gave way.

The Keene Fire Department arrived as the men slipped into the water. Using ladders and ropes, the firemen first pulled Eugene Rosin to shore; then worked their way out to Walter Rosin and Sherwood.

Sherwood told police he knew the ice was thin when he cut holes for fishing. It soon gave way, and he was plunged into water that was over his head. However, he was able to keep his arms, head and shoulders above water until the Rosins arrived, an interval he estimated at 45 minutes.

Sherwood said he had waved for help to a number of passing cars, but no one had stopped until the Rosins did.

Keene police officer Robert Hardy reported "the two Rosins saved the man's life."

Engine 2 responded to the alarm at 2:16 followed seven minutes later by Ladder 2. Four firemen and three Keene policemen helped in the operation, Fire Chief Robert N.

Guyette said. Guyette praised the men's work as well as three off-duty firemen who heard the alarm and rushed to the scene.

Though no serious accidents resulted, Eugene Rosin said he may have injured his back when he rolled over on the ice to avoid falling in the water.

––––––––

As Reported by the *Keene Evening Sentinel* December 11th, 1971:

"FIRE"

Two Rooms Gutted in Keene House

Two Rooms Gutted. Smoking chair in foreground is where fire at 43 Main Street is believed to have started. Flames damaged two rooms of Harold I. Chandler's house. Photo by Wallace Baker.

Flames gutted two rooms of a home at 431 Main St. this morning, with heavy smoke damage reported throughout the residence, which is owned by Mr. Harold I. Chandler.

Keene Fire Chief Robert N. Guyette estimated damage at "several thousand dollars" to the two-story building.

The blaze was reported at 9:37 a.m. and answered by Keene engines 3 and 4, the emergency squad unit and ladder 2. It was quickly under control.

Guyette said the fire may have been started by a burning cigarette left in a stuffed chair.

All the furniture, the woodwork, walls and ceiling were heavily damaged in the living room where the fire was believed to have started. The dining room was also damaged extensively.

––––––––

1972

As Reported by the *Keene Evening Sentinel* January 1st, 1972:

"FIRE"

Garage Hit in New Year's Fires

New Year's Day Blaze. Keene firemen observe the smoldering ruins of a garage owned by Dr. James Ballow on the Old Concord Road. Fire swept through the structure Saturday. Photo by Quinn.

New Year's Day fires destroyed a garage, three cars, two dogs and a medical bag in Keene.

A fire reported at 6:26 a.m. destroyed a garage and its contents owned by Dr. James M. Ballou on Old Concord Rd.

A passing neighbor spotted the blaze and reported it to firemen. The Ballous were asleep at the time in their home, a short distance from the garage.

Keene engines 1,3 and 4 and ladder 2 responded. The entire department force of 22 men and about 35 volunteers helped in the minus seven degree cold. They used 1,600 feet of hose to pump water from the foot of Concord Hill

Dr. Ballou said the garage and automobiles were insured. He estimated total damage at $60,000.

In addition to the other damage, Dr. Ballou lost tools, hunting and fishing equipment and chain saws.

Several boxes of ammunition and cans of oil, along with three partially filled automobile gas tanks, lasted through the blaze without causing an explosion.

All units were back in service at 8:52 a.m.

———

As Reported by the *Keene Evening Sentinel* January 19th, 1972:

"STORY"

Keene Fire Department Seeks New Truck

Addition to Station

Keene Fire Chief Robert N. Guyette presented the City Council Finance Committee Tuesday night with his 1972 budget request of $319,126.

The fire department's 1971 budget appropriation was $297,398.

The major increase requested by Guyette is in the area of salaries, where he proposes to promote two firefighters to fire lieutenants, a position created by the 1971 city council.

Also included in the 1972 budget request is a provision for $20,000 for capital equipment reserve.

As part of the department's five-year plan for replacing fire equipment, Guyette plans to purchase a new ladder truck in 1972. He also plans to construct an addition to the fire department's building to house the new truck.

Guyette told the committee Wednesday night that he had received a letter from the New Hampshire Board of Underwriters saying that the city does not need a fire sub-station in West Keene at this time.

The board said that the department had "liberalized" its "response distances" and was able to serve adequately the West Keene area from its present facility on Vernon Street.

Guyette told the committee Tuesday night that it would be at least five years before a sub-station would be needed in the West Keene area.

City Manager James C. Hobart has recommended minor cuts in the fire department budget request in the areas of Civil Defense communications equipment and pensions.

Hobart's recommended fire department budget for 1972 total $317,357.

———

As Reported by the *Keene Evening Sentinel* January 19th, 1972:

"FIRE"

Gas Fire. An explosion and fire at 2:37 p.m. Friday caused considerable damage to the Getty gas station at 205 West St., but Keene firefighters brought the blaze quickly under control and only minor burns reported by an employee of the Getty gas station. The fire was believed to be caused by

drilling on the gas tank of an auto, which was being repaired.

———

As Reported by the *Keene Evening Sentinel* January 29th, 1972:

"FIRE"

Keene House Damaged by Friday Fire

A fire Friday afternoon in the living room of a house belonging to Dr. Norris Robertson off the Jordan Road caused extensive damage to the house.

Three engines from the Keene Fire Department responded to the fire at 4:19 p.m. and remained at the scene until 5:47.

The house was occupied by Frank B. Eastern 3rd.

According to fire department reports the fire caused major damage to the living room and one side of the house. No cause of the fire has been determined.

———

As Reported by the *Keene Evening Sentinel* February 22nd, 1972:

"FIRE"

Fire Produces Heavy Damage in Cheshire Oil Co. Structure

Fire swept through the upper stories of the Cheshire Oil Co. building on Emerald Street Monday night, sending white smoke billowing in to the night sky.

Ten fire trucks from three fire departments responded to the blaze, which took 90 minutes to bring under control.

Damage figures were unavailable today, but Keene Fire Chief Robert N. Guyette estimated the loss "will be over several thousand dollars."

The four-story wooden structure houses the company's tire retreading operations. The fire was contained to a section of the building where old tires are kept.

Third Fire

Guyette said the fire probably started from a malfunction in a metal chimney running up through the building from a high-pressure boiler in the lower floor.

While firemen from Keene, Marlborough and Meadowood were fighting the blaze, Surry firefighters, covering the Keene station were called to a fire in a circulator motor at an apartment building at 29 Elm St. They had the situation under control within minutes.

The Emerald Street building has been hit by fire three times in the past seven years, but Guyette said the blaze last night was the largest of them all.

The flames were contained to the third and fourth floors at the east side of the building. "It was a hard one to get," Guyette said. "The fellows had to battle their way on the third floor through a lot of smoke."

Heat from the fire set off most of the sprinklers in the structure, producing a shower in the lower floors and a river flowing through mushy snow into the street.

Plant manager Phillip G. Taaffe credited the firefighters with cutting water damage to the company's new stock on the lower floors by covering all equipment and materials with tarpaulins.

Taaffe, who was at the fire from the time the alarm went off at 6:44 p.m. to the time the firemen left almost four hours later, said, "One irony of this is that earlier in the day the Meadowood truck was up here and we put on four new tires.

Taaffe said the company is operating today, but he said it will take a couple of days to clean up the damage.

Wilfred Begin, a Keene fireman, was the only casualty of the day: he stepped on a nail in the firefighting effort.

Fire on the Roof. *A Keene fireman makes his way up a ladder to fight the flames, which swept through the upper stories of the Cheshire Oil Co., building on Emerald Street. Ten fire trucks were called. Photo by Ferriter.*

In addition to the five Keene fire trucks on the scene, Guyette called in five units from the Meadowood department and the Marlborough truck.

"We didn't need them all, but we just wanted to have them there in case the fire got away from us," Guyette said.

———

As Reported by the *Keene Evening Sentinel* May 23, 1972:

"FIRE"

Barn, Antique Shop Destroyed by Flames

A spectacular fire destroyed a barn and antique shop at 460 Winchester St. Monday.

While no exact damage estimate has been released, a Keene Fire Department official called the barn, owned by Perry A. Kiritsy of 110 Court St. a total loss.

The structure housed an antique shop called "Trash Treasures." The contents of the antique shop were destroyed.

The alarm for the barn fire was turned in at 3:20 p.m. and four Keene Fire Department engines responded, but the blaze was too far along for the building to be saved.

Red Hot. Flames roar from loft of barn at 460 Winchester St., in Monday afternoon fire that demolished the structure. Smoke from spectacular blaze could be seen several miles away. Photo by Fossel.

Smoke billowed high into the sky above the Winchester Street site and could be seen for several miles. Traffic clogged Winchester Street as people tried to get a close look at the blaze, which was clearly visible from the street.

Other people congregated on the side of the Route 9-12 bypass to watch the fast-burning fire and others stood on their cars to view the flames from the Riverside Shopping Plaza parking lot.

Firemen said the barn was only 15 feet from a house, but prevailing winds carried the flames east, away from the house into a field.

Grass and brush in the field around the barn was ignited by sparks and ash particles from the building fire, but the Keene department's power wagon was able to outflank the grass fire and douse it.

The cause of the fire has not been determined yet.

————

As Reported by the *Keene Evening Sentinel* July 3rd, 1972:

"STORY"

Police, Fire Chiefs Preparing for High-Level Rescues in City

If you're wedged on one of Keene's "skyscraping" windowsills in the not-too-distant future there may be a specialized unit to rescue you.

A rescue squad is in the offing for the city of Keene.

"It would be a new thing for Keene, but the city deserves the service," Fire Chief Robert N. Guyette said.

Presently, when rescues from high altitude locations are made a fire engine is employed.

"There are several tenements in Keene, and if there's an upper story disaster there ought to be seven or eight specialized men to carry out the rescue" Keene Police Chief Donald G. Ficke said.

Ficke explained that three people were needed downstairs and three upstairs plus a leader to coordinate their efforts.

The men should be trained in climbing techniques, the use of ropes and repelling Ficke said, "and this is just one type of rescue where specialization would help."

Ten thousand dollars has been earmarked in the 1973 Keene Fire Department budget for the rescue squad. The plan is part of a five-year capital reserve schedule.

Although the fire department already has much of the necessary equipment, according to Guyette, the money will pay for a rescue vehicle and supplemental equipment.

Ficke and Guyette concur that the new unit will be a combination Fire Department – Police Department operation.

"It could be the first combined rescue department in New Hampshire," Guyette said.

————

As Reported by the *Keene Evening Sentinel* July 18th, 1972:

"STORY"
Out of Order Use Telephone

Storm Casualty. Out of Order fire alarm on St. James Street is casualty of Sunday's electrical storm. It's being repaired. Photo by Kearney.

————

As Reported by the *Keene Evening Sentinel* July 20th, 1972:

"STORY"

Angels' Jet Skids off Runway

The visit of the Blue Angels to Keene got off to a rocky start Wednesday afternoon when the advance plane for the U.S. Navy precision flying team slid off the end of the main runway at Dillant-Hopkins airport and tipped over on its back.

Neither of the two men aboard the F4 Phantom aircraft was injured in the accident.

According to witnesses, the airplane's braking chute failed to open as the plane taxied south on the airport's main runway after landing. The accident happened about 4:40 p.m. Wednesday.

Also, contributing to the mishap was a runway made slick by a shower earlier in the afternoon.

Out to Dinner

Lt. Gary Smith, Pilot of the plane, said this morning that neither her nor CPO Keith Chambers was injured seriously in the accident. They were treated at Elliot Community Hospital for minor cuts and went out to dinner immediately afterward.

"I plan to be back flying tomorrow," Smith said.

Smith said he could not comment on the cause of the accident until an official team of Navy investigators arrives in Keene this afternoon.

The jet had not been moved from the scene of the accident about 30 feet south of the end of the 6,500 foot north-south runway and was guarded this morning by a team of eight Marines from the Quonset Point, RI Naval Air Station.

Not too bad

The Blue Angels are scheduled to perform in the Keene Air Show this weekend at the airport. Smith and air show spokesmen said the accident would have no effect on plans for the show.

Smith said he would attempt to arrange for another plane to come to Keene from the Pensacola, Fl headquarters of the Blue Angels to take the place of the damaged plane.

He added that the plan involved in the mishap Wednesday was certainly salvageable.

"It isn't damaged as badly as it looks," Smith said.

————

Marine Guards Blue Angels' Jet, which skidded off end of runway at Keene airport due to chute failure. Photo by Wallace Baker.

As Reported by the *Keene Evening Sentinel* August 2nd, 1972:

"STORY"

Bids $16,000 High for Planned Addition to Keene's Fire Station

Keene Fire Chief Robert N. Guyette was philosophical this morning after a second round of bids on building an addition to the city fire station came in Tuesday about $16,000 above the budget for the project.

"These things will happen," Guyette said.

"I really can't say what we're going to do," Guyette said. "It doesn't look as if we'll reject the bids; it's a matter of figuring out where we can get the money."

The first advertisement for bids for the fire station project elicited only one response, from M.W. Goodell Construction, Inc.

The bid, for the complete constructions project, was for $52,776, or almost $23,000 more than the budgeted amount of $30,000. It was rejected and the project was re-advertised.

$5,700 savings

The bids opened Tuesday were for three separate portions of the addition, and resulted in a saving of about $5,700 if only the low bids are considered.

The addition to the fire station would provide an additional bay for a new ladder truck expected to arrive shortly, additional dormitory space, a conference room and a new had quarters for Southwestern NH Fire Mutual Aid.

Two bids were opened for electrical work connected with the proposed addition, from Olympic Electric Co for $4,967 and from Harold Johnson Electric Services, Inc. for $1,998.

Only bid for the plumbing and heating work connected with the project was submitted from Rivers and Henry Plumbers for $4,200.

$4,049 Total

For general contracting, Goodell submitted a bid for $40,861 and Hoard Aho submitted a bid for $45,100.

The low bid total for the three portions of the contract is $47,049.

City Comptroller Raymond P. Tracy said this morning that the fire department has only about $31,000 in its budget, which could be allocated toward construction of the addition.

The only way the project could be financed this year, he added, would be for the city to borrow the $16,000 and pay it back from the 1973 budget.

Guyette said he would take the problem of financing the fire station addition to the Keene City Council Finance Committee next week.

Guyette said the new ladder truck is expected to be delivered by the end of the month and temporary quarters will have to be found for the ladder truck the department now uses.

————

As Reported by the *Keene Evening Sentinel* September 21st, 1972:

"STORY"

The Keene Fire Department has received its new ladder truck, purchased at a cost of $63,000. A new bay is being built at the fire station to accommodate it. Photo by Wallace Baker.

———

As Reported by the *Keene Evening Sentinel* October 5th, 1972:

"STORY"

Busy Fire Prevention Week Planned by City's Department

Next week is Fire Prevention Week, and the Keene Fire Department is planning "a much greater effort than ever before," according to Fire Chief Robert N. Guyette.

The activities for the week begin Sunday with a parade and firemen's muster.

The parade will begin at 1 p.m. in the Elm Street parking lot opposite the city fire station. At least six marching units will take part in the parade, which will also include about 50 pieces of fire apparatus from neighboring towns.

The parade will follow a route down Court Street, through Central Square and down Main Street to the Public Works Department garage, where it will disband.

Muster Follows

Immediately following the parade, the firemen's muster will begin at the Cheshire Fairgrounds on Route 12 in Swanzey.

There will be no admission charge at the muster.

Beginning Tuesday, members of the fire department will begin visiting local schools and demonstrations of fire equipment will be held daily at Robin Hood Park.

Students will be bused to the demonstrations and parents are being urged to attend. The demonstrations will begin at 9:30 a.m.

The annual inspection dinner will be held Thursday with members of the fire department and city government invited to partake of the traditional scalloped oysters served by the ladies auxiliary of the fire department.

The annual firemen's ball will close out the activities of Fire Prevention Week Saturday at 9 p.m. at the National Guard Armory on Hastings Avenue.

———

As Reported by the *Keene Evening Sentinel* October 10th, 1972:

"STORY"

Goal of Fire Inspector is Keeping People Alive

Safety Check. Keene Fire Inspector Homer L. Atkins Jr., left checks fire extinguisher location with Richard W. Frazier of Frazier and Son, Inc. Photo by Ferriter.

Exposed light bulbs in the wrong places, a three-foot clearance between stored materials and overhead sprinklers, fire extinguishers marked at eye level—"A lot of these things you'd never even think about," said Richard W. Frazier.

Frazier has shielded light bulbs, cleared safety paths, installed fire doors, marked fire extinguishers and done a number of other things to meet requirements of state and local fire codes at the Frazier and Son finishing plant in the former Princess Shoe Co. building on Railroad Street.

It is the job of Homer L. Atkins, Jr., inspector for the Keene Fire Department, to find things other people would overlook—and make sure that potentially hazardous situations are corrected.

Making It Better

"When you come into an old building like this one," Atkins said during an inspection tour of the Frazier operation on the third floor of the Princess building, "you don't try to get everything done at once."

"But every time you do through, you try to make things a little better."

Atkins and Frazier have developed a working relationship during the last six months that has led, in Atkins opinion, to major improvements in fire safety conditions on the third floor of the Princess building.

"They made up their recommendations and we went ahead and complied," Frazier said. "That's about all there is to it."

Frazier concedes that improvements his company has made to comply with fire codes have cost a good deal of money, but points to some advantages he has noted by complying.

Nothing Wrong

"We've seen some savings on our insurance rates," he said, and when the federal inspectors from OSHA (Occupational Safety and Health Act) were here, they couldn't find anything wrong. All the things we've done for the city have helped.

Keene's fire-inspections program has been under way on its present basis for about a year, according to Fire Chief Robert N. Guyette.

The department has two inspectors, each of whom spends about half his time on fire inspection work. In addition, each firefighter spends one day a month doing fire inspections in the city's business district.

The intent of the inspections program, Guyette said, is to prevent fires and confine them if they occur.

Key Interpretation

"Training for fire inspectors is mostly on-the-job," Guyette said, adding that he and his two inspectors have attended courses and professional meetings to improve their efficiency.

"The toughest part of fire inspections," Guyette said, "is interpreting the intent of the codes." The codes consist of state and local fire regulations and the city adopted BOCA

(Building Officials Conference of America) code.

Especially in older structures, Guyette said, the letter of the codes is often unenforceable, and the job of the inspector is to make sure that safety conditions are upgraded as much as fire department officials consider feasible.

The inspections program covers all buildings of public assembly, including schools and meeting halls, industrial buildings and buildings within the fire precinct, which includes most of the commercial and industrial uses near the center of the city.

Also watched closely are buildings under construction, to determine that safety factors are built into them and to avoid costly renovations after buildings are completed.

The "essential elements" an inspector looks for when he enters a building, Guyette said, are occupancy, type of use, fire detection systems, fire separations, exits, potentially hazardous materials and safety equipment such as sprinkler systems and fire extinguishers.

Inspectors Alternate

The Keene department follows a general policy of alternating inspectors for each building visited.

"Every inspector has particular things he looks for," Atkins said. "I'll catch things somebody else might miss and vice versa."

It is hard, or even impossible, Guyette admits to evaluate a fire-inspections program like the one operating in Keene.

"You can't point out a building and say it would have burned if we didn't have it inspected," he said. "But sometimes when you have a fire and you're able to get to it and contain it, you can be thankful you made them put in a fire door."

———

As Reported by the *Keene Evening Sentinel* October 12th, 1972:

"STORY"

City Firemen Take Program to School

Fire Hats for Fire Prevention. Elizabeth and Albert Christian, 6-year-old twins of Mrs. Carolyn Christian of 406 Court St., try on the firemen's hats they got during a fire prevention week demonstration. Photo by Wallace Baker.

Keene firefighters are going back to elementary school this week as part of the fire department's Fire Prevention Week program.

But Fire Chief Robert N. Guyette said Wednesday that the department's fire prevention effort in local schools will carry well beyond the end of this week.

"The schools are the prime target in our whole fire prevention effort," Guyette said. "We try to get to the kids and they'll get to the mothers and fathers."

Guyette said that this year, for the first time, the educational program will be conducted during several months in elementary schools with special programs for junior high and high school students planned for later in the school year.

This week, the fire department is giving daily demonstrations of firefighting apparatus at Robin Hood Park for elementary school pupils and is "taking the program into schools" with presentations of fire-prevention programs.

The elementary school program has been organized this year by Firefighter Robert Symonds and Franklin School Principal Michael White.

Guyette said a second program would be started in the junior high school later this year, and added that he was trying to work out a program for high school students. "This is a program we'll be working on throughout the year," he said.

The elementary school program begun this week is expected to continue through December, and consists of films and material supplied by insurance companies on fire dangers and prevention.

The fire department will hold a dinner tonight as part of Fire Prevention Week and will cap the week's activities with the annual fireman's ball Saturday.

———

As Reported by the *Keene Evening Sentinel* November 8th, 1972:

"FIRE"

Five Persons Homeless After Blaze

At least five persons were left homeless today in the wake of an early morning fire that destroyed the upper floors of a two family house at 41 Wilson St.

Occupants of the wood frame structure included Clayton R. Duhaime and his wife Judith, Leroy Hollis, his wife Eleanor and her mother. None of the residents reportedly had fire insurance.

Four fire trucks responded to the 1:52 a.m. alarm which caused "many thousands of dollars" damage, according to Deputy Fire Chief Frederick H. Beauchesne. The fire, which apparently began in the attic, gutted the top two floors and resulted in considerable smoke and water damage to the first floor.

Five Homeless. Firemen await water as blaze guts a two-family house on Wilson Street. Photo by Kearney.

Capt. Wesley J. Peets of the Keene Fire Department received a slight injury to his foot when he stepped on a nail.

It took firemen about 30 minutes to bring the blaze under control, but mop-up operations lasted nearly another four hours, according to Chief Robert N. Guyette.

Guyette was unsure of the cause of the fire.

———

As Reported by the *Keene Evening Sentinel* December 6th, 1972:

"CRASH"

Keene Man Killed; Car Seen in River

Investigation. Rescue workers probe the wreckage of a car in which a Keene man died this morning after it was pulled from the waters of the Ashuelot River. Photo by Baker.

A Keene man was killed sometime this morning when his car left the Route 12 bypass, north of West Street, leaped two deep ditches and plunged into the Ashuelot River.

The dead man was identified as Raymond Ramsey of 116 Roxbury St.

The accident was reported to Keene police shortly after 9 a.m. today, but rescue workers at the scene of the accident said Ramsey's watch had stopped at 1:15 and speculated that the man may have been in the water for hours.

The accident was reported by the driver of a Public Service Co. of NH truck, who noticed gouges left in the snow beside the highway by Ramsey's car after it left the road.

Ramsey was headed north at the time of the accident and the car was discovered upside down in the icy water about 200 yards from the point where it left the road.

Rescue workers from the Brattleboro, Vt., fire department were searching the water near the car late this morning in an effort to determine whether there may have been other occupants of Ramsey's car.

Only a small portion of the vehicle was visible when police arrived at the scene.

————

As Reported by the *Keene Evening Sentinel* December 18th, 1972:

"STORY"

$385,652 Asked by Firemen

The Keene Fire Department's budget could be hiked $55,845 in 1973—from $326,807 in 1972 to $385,652—if the city council approves the proposed budget of Keene City Manager Peter L. Cheney.

Included in the sum` is $3,806 for a new airport crash truck required by the Federal Aviation Administration (FAA), and $32,435 in additional salary costs. The department this year asked $239,734 for salaries, and Cheney's 1973 budget is seeking $272,169.

Firefighters' salaries now range from $6,900 per year to $8,387, but the city manager is calling for a three per cent across-the-board salary raise for city employees.

Keene Fire Chief Robert N. Guyette is asking for two additional training officers, two new fire inspectors, a new fire alarm superintendent and one less firefighter.

Costs of fire equipment including hoses, hydrants, communications, pensions, and office supplies among other things, amounted to $64,668 this year in estimated costs. Cheney is seeking $76,683 for 1973.

————

As Reported by the *Keene Evening Sentinel* December 27th, 1972:

"FIRE"

Marlboro Street Fire Kills Man; Woman Hurt

Fatal Blaze. Firemen struggle against smoke and flames to rescue women from the second floor of 75 Marlboro street apartment house. One man dies in the two-alarm fire as Keene firemen rescue one of several cats caught in the night blaze. Photo by Fossel.

A two-alarm fire in an apartment house at 75 Marlboro St. claimed one life Tuesday night and left another Keene resident in critical condition in Elliot Community Hospital today with 90 percent burns over her body.

Andrew Pelletier, 57, died in the blaze which began in a first floor bedroom and quickly engulfed a hall and staircase, blocking the only means of escape from the second floor.

The injured woman, Nellie Willard, 76, was discovered in a second-floor room by firemen with air tanks who fought their way up the staircase and through second-floor windows.

Smoking in Bed

According to Keene Fire Chief Robert N. Guyette, evidence indicated the fire was caused by someone smoking in bed.

The first alarm was rung at 7:37 p.m. and the second alarm two minutes later brought a total of four fire trucks and about 45 firemen to the Lewis Block blaze.

Damage to the building, owned by Richard B. Lewis, was listed by Guyette at "several thousand dollars" and at least five apartments were destroyed or damaged in the fire, forcing eight persons out of the building.

When firemen arrived, the first-floor hallway and staircase were engulfed in flames, but the fire was contained in the west end of the building and was under control within 30 minutes.

Guyette said he was told of the possibility that there were still persons on the second floor minutes after he arrived and said his men made "all attempts that were humanly possible" to get through the flames to the second floor.

Mrs. Willard was rescued about 10 minutes after fire trucks arrived and oxygen was administered immediately in an effort to save her life.

Guyette said he had no doubt that the woman could have escaped if a second means of exit from the building was provided, as required under city fire codes.

Details were not available today on the cause of Pelletier's death.

Another resident of the apartment house, Eva MacKenzie, 52, was treated for hysteria at Elliot Community Hospital and released.

Firemen remained at the scene nearly three hours trying to extinguish spot fires hidden in the walls and ceilings of the building.

"It was a hell of a good effort," Guyette said. "The whole building could have gone up."

Guyette said his "big regret" is that his department does not have the manpower for strict enforcement of city fire codes which require apartment houses to have at least two means of escape from all floors.

The fire chief said he would consult with city officials in an attempt to find a solution—possibly more inspectors—for his department.

Keene's last fatal fire was on December 14, 1969 when an elderly man was killed in a house fire on Spring Street.

————

From the *Keene Evening Sentinel*:

Marlboro Street Fire Claims Second Victim

The Keene apartment house fire which killed Andrew Pelletier, 57, Tuesday night, claimed its second victim Wednesday when Nellie Willard, 76, died of burns received in the blaze.

Mrs. Willard was apparently trapped in the second floor of the wood frame building at 75 Marlboro St. when flames swept up a staircase blocking her only exit. She had been hospitalized with burns over 90 per cent of her body, and died at 6:25 p.m. Wednesday.

The apartment house was owned by Richard J. Lewis, who could not be reached for comment today, and it apparently failed to meet city fire and building codes requiring two exits from the upper floors of apartment buildings. Keene Fire Chief Robert N. Guyette said Wednesday the woman might have escaped if another exit had been provided.

The Lewis Block building, where the fire occurred, was last inspected by city officials in 1967—three years before Keene adopted strict new life-safety codes concerning apartment houses and places of public assembly.

Guyette said evidence indicates the fire may have resulted from smoking in bed and spread from a first-floor room down a hallway and up the only staircase.

Owen T. Holden, Keene's superintendent of inspections, said the building had not been inspected since 1967, when tenants complained of overloaded fuses and rubbish in the cellar.

Holden's department, which has one fulltime and three part-time inspecto0rs, has been busy this year with new building construction in Keene, he said and has had time to act only on complaints.

The fire department has two inspectors, each part-time, who have been tied up this year with oil burner and storage inspections, along with new building checks, according to Guyette.

Guyette said today there were "most definitely" other apartment houses in Keene which violate the requirement for two exits, "but we just don't have time to get them all," he said.

Guyette is seeking money for two additional fire inspectors in the city's 1973 budget, but said he couldn't ask for more since "the taxpayers won't buy it." The salary scale for full-time inspectors is $6,900 to $8,387 this year—the same as for firefighters.

Holden is also seeking an additional inspector for his department next year at a salary of $6,258.

Holden said, "The city has so much new construction this year that our inspectors have only had time to act on the two or three complaints we get each week."

He said he had received no complaint recently of a lack of fire exits in apartment houses, and suggested that many apartment-house owners may be unaware of the requirement.

He said he would take action to see that another exit is constructed in the building; which had five apartments destroyed or damaged by smoke and fire Tuesday night.

"That kind of sounds like closing the door after the horse has escaped," he said. "But what else can we do?"

Mr. Pelletier was a native of Jaffrey and had lived there until moving to Keene about five years ago. He had been employed at the Robert Hart, Inc. shoe factory in Keene.

He was born April 4, 1915, son of Andrew and Eliza (Yergeau) Pelletier.

————

As Reported by the *Keene Evening Sentinel* December 29th, 1972:

"STORY"

Rossiter Asks for Fire Facts

The chairman of the Keene City Council Finance Committee has asked City Manager Peter L. Cheney for "a complete explanation of why the apartment building at 75 Marlboro St. where a fire killed two persons this week, has not been inspected since 1967.

At-large Councilman George M. Rossiter asked for an explanation and verification of statements made by Fire Chief Robert N. Guyette and Superintendent of Inspections Owen T. Holden that the Marlboro Street building had remained uninspected for five years because of a shortage of inspections man-power.

Rossiter said such statements "are completely new to me during the past three as a member of the city council."

Only One Exit

He added that he was not "trying to stir up a tempest in a teapot. I think Bob Guyette's doing a hell of a job, but I'd like to know the reasons why he's complaining about a lack of manpower."

Killed in the fire which struck the Marlborough Street apartment house, Tuesday night were Andrew Pelletier, 57, and Nellie Willard, 76.

The building had one means of egress from the second floor, contrary to a city fire code regulation which requires at least two exits.

Guyette currently employs two part-time fire inspectors and Holden employs one full-time inspector and two part-time inspectors.

Holden is seeking one more inspector in his 1973 budget request and Guyette is requesting two more. Guyette said Thursday that he was reluctant to ask for more inspectors "because the taxpayers won't but it."

No Excuses

Rossiter said, "It is my opinion the city council, with the support of the taxpayers, wants an excellent inspection system and will gladly pay for it with dollars, but at the same time we will not accept excuses for poor management or gross negligence, if that is the case."

Holden said his inspectors had been unable to make significant progress during 1972 with a five-year program aimed at inspecting every housing unit in the city because of the press of new construction.

He said his personnel were so busy overseeing new building that the projected comprehensive housing inspection program had been held back.

Rossiter, in his letter to Cheney, said, "The city council has been told for the past three years by the former city manager (James C. Hobart) and his staff that an excellent inspection job was being done and could be continued with existing staff."

If the staff wants more manpower to perform its tasks adequately, Rossiter said, requests should have been made in previous budget hearings.

Holden submitted a request for an additional part-time inspector in 1972, but the request failed to win Hobart's approval and was not reinstated by the city council.

Guyette said this morning he did not wish to comment on Rossiter's request for an explanation, adding he would explain the matter to Cheney if requested to do so.

Holden was not available for comment.

Cheney said he would not comment on Rossiter's statements until the next meeting of the city council January 4. He said he would study the matter in the meantime.

————

1973

As Reported by the *Keene Evening Sentinel* January 23rd, 1973:

"STORY"

Inspection Program Scrutinized

The specter of a fatal fire loomed Monday night as the Keene City Council Finance Committee scrutinized the Keene Fire Department's inspection program.

The review came at the committee's third meeting on sections of the proposed 1973 city budget.

The department proposes several changes "aimed at increasing prevention activities," wrote City Manager Peter L. Cheney in his budget message released December 18.

But after the city budget was presented, a fire at the Lewis Block at 75 Marlboro St. caused the death of two persons, and Cheney

confirmed that the building failed to meet city fire and building codes requiring two exits from upper floors of apartment buildings, and that the building had not been inspected since 1967.

Since the fire, criticism of the entire city inspections program has ranged from claims that it is inadequate to charges of nitpicking. The finance committee wanted to know how the program functioned and how budget proposals would improve that situation.

The proposed fire department budget of $382,652 includes $10,000 for a new rescue vehicle plus funds for additional salaries. The 1972 fire budget was $326,807.

Fire Chief Robert N. Guyette said he had no one in mind to add to the department's inspection staff.

Presently, two firefighters are doubling as fire inspectors and two are training officers. The four men are paid firefighter's wages plus $5 per week assignment pay. Guyette proposes raising the four men four pay classifications on the city wage scale, creating two inspector and two training officer positions.

Guyette has also requested adding a fire alarm superintendent to be paid in the same range as a deputy chief. In proposing the new position, Guyette said it had become "quite a job" to install fire alarms in new areas and still upgrade the existing system.

Presently, a fire captain is doubling as a fire alarm man and Guyette would promote him to superintendent. That means someone would be moved up to a captain's position. The new fire alarm superintendent would retain firefighting responsibilities.

Guyette said he wanted to establish a stable "top structure" in his department.

"We're trying to overcome 10 to 15 years of deficiency," Guyette said, referring to the inspections program, "and we can't do it in one or even two years. If we do it in five years, I'll be happy."

Finance committee chairman George M. Rossiter questioned Guyette about two firefighters moonlighting as part-time inspectors for the city inspections department.

What happens if one of the men fights a fire all night; then goes "off duty" and reports to the city inspections department, Rossiter asked.

But Alfred H. Merrifield, director of the department of health and inspections, said neither of the two men had missed a day of work because of fighting a fire.

The regular inspector, Guyette said, focused on foster homes and day care centers, places of assembly, storage tanks, gasoline and propane installations, investigations for other city departments, oil burners and new construction,

Cheney said it was necessary that the council approve a request for four additional firefighters to compensate for promotions and to meet new Federal Aviation Administration (FAA) regulations at Dillant-Hopkins Airport.

Starting May 21, the city must provide a fire crash truck manned by two firefighters for every arrival and departure of a commercial airplane.

Furthermore, Guyette disclosed new insurance requirements for the city. With a new ladder truck and increased city population, the insurance underwriters have required the department to increase its manpower from the present 24 to between 32 and 34.

Guyette wants to add four men this year, four next year and two in 1975.

————

As Reported by the *Keene Evening Sentinel* January 29th, 1973:

"FIRE"

Fire Forces Family into Snow

An early morning fire at 289 Court St. forced a Keene family with six children into a blowing snowstorm today as firefighters with air tanks battled a blaze in the basement for nearly 90 minutes.

The fire at the William D. Horne residence resulted from a water boiler malfunction and caused at least $4,000 damage to the three-story home, according to Fire Chief Robert N. Guyette.

It took firemen 30 minutes to bring the blaze under control after the alarm was rung at 6:04 a.m. and the family was able to return to the house when firemen left at about 7:30 a.m.

Capt. John N. Phillips said, after returning from the blaze, that damage was restricted to the basement but smoke filled the entire house.

"It was really burning when we got there," he said, "and we had to send men in with air packs to get to the basement."

Four trucks responded to the fire and smoke ejectors were used to clear the house.

There were no injuries reported to firemen or the family, which had so stand in 10 inches of snow while firefighters extinguished the blaze.

————

As Reported by the *Keene Evening Sentinel* February 12th, 1973:

"FIRE"

Flames Hit Spring St. Apartment

Fire in a second-floor apartment at 77 Spring St. kept Keene firefighters busy for more than two hours this morning.

There were no injuries reported in the blaze, and the burned-out apartment occupied by Robert Miller and his wife was empty when the fire was reported about 10:50 a.m.

The blaze in the four-family house began near a bedroom heater, according to Miller.

Apartment Burns. Smoke belches from second story apartment, occupied by Robert Miller family at 77 Spring Street this morning, no one was hurt. Photo by Wallace Baker.

Three Keene fire trucks and one ladder truck responded to the blaze and appeared to have the flames under control within 20 minutes.

Miller said he had no insurance on his possessions.

The apartment house was equipped with a second-floor emergency exit staircase near where the fire broke out.

———

As Reported by the *Keene Evening Sentinel* February 12th, 1973:

"STORY"

Battle Between City Employees and Council Finance Committee

It is important to note that it was the fighting of those firefighters and others who have made the department today a very good paying job.

75 City Employees Vote to seek $750 pay raise.

Instead of a 3 percent cost of living pay raise, more than on-third of Keene's city employees gathered at St. Joseph's School Sunday afternoon to protest a Keene City Council Finance Committee recommendation to eliminate the 3 percent pay raise.

The $750 request, along with four other proposals, was discussed at a closed meeting this morning between employee representatives and City Manager Peter L. Cheney.

Representatives of each city department were selected Sunday to attend today's meeting and to voice specific departmental grievances on the finance committee budget reductions.

The meeting Sunday followed three weeks of finance committee review of Cheney's proposed city budget. The committee looped about $200,000 from Cheney's proposed total of $4.2 million.

The committee decision to eliminate Cheney's request for $41,000 to give city employees 3 percent cost-of-living raises caused the employees to organize the Sunday meeting.

Besides their proposal for a $750 raise, the 75 employees voted to seek time and a half overtime pay for employees working more than a normal work day or work week. Not all city departments work eight hours each day, or 40 hours per week.

The group also voted to request 5 per cent merit increases (retroactive to Jan 1 for 28 city employees who would otherwise receive no pay raise at all this year.

The 28 employees (17 percent of the city's work force) have reached the top step on the city's five step wage scale for their jobs. The finance committee has recommended budgeting $15,000 for a professional evaluation of city salaries, including funds to bolster where recommended, and this will be conducted within two months, Cheney has said.

The employees voted to "give 100 percent support" to City Comptroller Raymond P. Tracy, who has been criticized by Major James A. Masiello for "statements which, incidentally, were made without permission, and the contents certainly exceeded his realm of responsibility as a comptroller."

Masiello disagreed with Tracy's figures on annual salary increases in local private industry.

Similar backing was accorded Cheney by employees several of whom voiced support for Cheney's efforts to improve employee salaries.

"I agree with everything that's been said," said Keene Police Sgt. Hugh McLellan, "but if we come with 99 demands we'll lose out."

"We've got the people behind us, and let's put a little faith in Cheney," McLellan said.

Several employees said they thought percentage wage raises were unjust.

The proposal for an across-the-board $750 pay hike first came from George H. Shepard, Jr., spokesman for Keene Fire Department employees.

"It is unfair to give 3 percent pay raises because the employees at the top of the pay ladder will benefit most," Shepard said, "it should be the same amount for all employees."

Shepard also criticized the finance committee recommendation to increase city councilmen salaries from $200 to $400.

"A conscientious councilman deserves more than $200, but the increase this year is inconsistent with other budget reductions," Shepard said.

Frank H. Hughes, a master mechanic for the Public Works Department, said he had checked three local garages and mechanics received an average of 52 cents more per hour than city mechanics.

Hughes said the local mechanics received the same benefits city employees received.

Keene Police Officer Robert F. Silk, who chaired the Sunday meeting, said the budget reductions "lowered everyone to second-class citizens."

"We can't go to the council alone, but we stand a lot better chance together," Silk said.

Silk said he was satisfied with the employees showing at the meeting. Of 178 employees, he said, about 15 could not attend because they were working on city jobs and another 20 department and assistant department heads were not invited.

"This means well over half attended," he said.

The finance committee will conduct a public hearing on the budget Tuesday night, but Chairman George M. Rossiter said Sunday night he would ask the committee to meet if Cheney formally requests a special meeting to consider city employees proposals.

Cheney said this morning before the employee meeting he was not sure he would request such a meeting with the finance committee.

————

As Reported by the *Keene Evening Sentinel* March 1st, 1973:

"FIRE"

Damage Extensive in Keene Fire

A fire of undetermined origin did extensive damage to four rooms of a two-story apartment house at 368 Court St., Wednesday afternoon.

Three Keene fire trucks responded to a 2:46 p.m. alarm at the house owned by Walter I. Bourassa of East Swanzey, and had the blaze under control within 30 minutes, according to Deputy Fire Chief Fred H. Beauchesne.

The fire, which reportedly started in a first-floor bedroom, caused no injuries.

Beauchesne said the structure, containing two apartments, was purchased Wednesday by Bourassa and was covered by insurance.

Firemen were at the fire about an hour and contained heat and fire damage to the first floor.

————

As Reported by the *Keene Evening Sentinel* March 19th, 1973:

"STORY"

Fire Alarm Supervisor

Fire Department Promotion. Laurence E. Thompson, has been promoted to newly created position of fire alarm superintendent. Photo by Kearney.

Prior to March 1973 Laurence E. Thompson along with others shared the load of assisting Larry Thompson in keeping the system up and running, but Larry was the key to its operation.

The Keene Fire Department now has a full-time fire alarm supervisor.

Laurence E. Thompson, a captain in the department since 1966, has been promoted to the new position, according to Fire Chief Robert N. Guyette.

Guyette had requested the new position in making his 1973 budget proposal, and the Keene City Council approved it.

Thompson will be responsible for maintenance of overhead and underground fire alarm wires, all fire alarm boxes in Keene, planning new installations and fire alarm revamping.

The new job is not new to Thompson. He's been working on the fire alarms for 26 years, in addition to handling his other responsibilities as captain, and earlier as a firefighter.

But now it's a full-time job.

Elated with his new job, Thompson said Friday, "You just can't run a shift and concentrate on the fire alarms."

Since May, Thompson has had full charge of one of the department's shifts. As fire alarm supervisor Thompson will still be on call to fight fires.

Thompson explained that all of Keene's 120 alarms must be checked every 60 days according to state regulations, but he also will start replacing about two miles of wiring.

Over a period of two or three years Thompson hopes to bring the entire alarm system up to date with new wiring.

Tomorrow Guyette will announce a promotion to deputy fire chief.

————

As Reported by the *Keene Evening Sentinel* March 20th, 1973:

"STORY"

Phillips Promoted to Deputy

New Deputy Chief. Keene Fire Chief Robert N. Guyette congratulates newly promoted Deputy Chief John N. Phillips. Photo by Baker.

Captain John N. Phillips has been promoted to the position of Deputy Fire Chief by City Manager Peter L. Cheney. The promotion is effective on March 20, and follows the recommendations of the Board of Engineers, a specially convened Oral Examination Board and Fire Chief Robert N. Guyette.

The new deputy chief has been a captain in the department since November 1971, and a permanent member of the department for nearly 15 years, having become a permanent firefighter in September of 1958. For three years prior to that time he was associated with the department as a call man. Phillips lives at 105 South Lincoln, is married to Harriet Phillips, and has two sons.

In his new position Phillips will have responsibility for half of the personnel in the fire department and with Deputy Frederick N. Beauchesne will act as fire chief in Chief Guyette's absence.

With Phillips' promotion and the filling of the position of Fire Alarm Superintendent by former Captain Laurence Thompson, two captain positions in the fire department are now vacant.

———

As Reported by the *Keene Evening Sentinel* April 5th, 1973:

"STORY"

Keene Firemen Learn What They'll Do at Fire

Richard Allard's house on Beech Hill is about as far from conventional fire protection as any place in Keene.

The nearest fire hydrant is almost a mile away by road, and the house itself is a long way from the city fire station on Vernon Street.

Until recently, Keene firemen didn't know how long it would take them to reach Allard's house, how much pressure they would find in the nearest hydrant on Beech Hill or exactly what kind of equipment they would need to fight a fire in Allard's house if one ever did break out.

Now they know.

The fire department recently staged a mock alarm at Allard's house after notifying Allard and his neighbors to find out exactly what would be needed to respond to trouble in the area.

Pre-Planning Program

The mock alarm, worked out in conjunction with the Swanzey Center fire company, is part of a new training program for local firemen known as pre-planning.

Under the new program the fire department prepares maps and floor plans for key fire-prone areas of the city and works out a firefighting strategy for each area.

Each pre-plan is prepared by fire department officers, presented to firemen in daily training sessions, put down on paper and filed with dispatchers for Southwestern New Hampshire Fire Mutual Aid.

When a fire alarm is sounded for any site which has been pre-planned, the dispatcher will know which engines to send out and which will stand in reserve. The firefighters will know where each unit will go and what each man is supposed to do when the unit arrives at the scene.

Battle Strategy

So far, according to Fire Chief Robert N. Guyette, only a few "key areas" in the city have pre-plans, but he hopes eventually to cover the entire city with the program.

"It's kind of like fighting a war, "Guyette told the city's Safety Board of Review this week. "You have to know how many men you need and where to send them. You have to have a battle plan."

The Swanzey Center company was essential to Guyette's battle plan for the Allard mock fire because it is the only nearby fire department with a truck that can carry 3,000 feet of four inch hose.

One thing Keene fire officers wanted to learn from the practice session on Beech Hill was how close that hose could bring them to Allards house, how long it would take the Swanzey men to arrive at the scene and what Keene firemen would have to do while the Swanzey unit was on its way.

Near Perfect

At least one of Keene's pre-plans has already been tested in action at a real alarm.

Firefighters answered an alarm last Saturday at Cheshire Hospital and following the pre-plan strategy worked out in advance, had the building covered almost immediately.

The alarm turned out to be a minor malfunction with the heating system at the hospital, but the pre-plan program is being directed by George H. Shepard and Ronald P. Amadon, who were recently named training officers for the fire department.

Members of the safety board pronounced themselves "very impressed" with the new program.

"People don't realize what a tremendous amount of time and effort have gone into this," Guyette said. "It has to be a very well-thought out operation.

As reported by the *Keene Sentinel* Monday April 16th, 1973:

Bomb Scares, Fires Mar Weekend at Keene State College

Keene firemen are investigating the possibility of arson in connection with four minor fires at Dwight Carle Hall, a dormitory on the Keene State College campus this weekend.

Meanwhile, Keene Police and campus official are continuing the investigations into the epidemic of bomb scares on the campus, which showed another upsurge during the weekend.

Beginning early Friday afternoon there were seven weekend bob scares on the KSC campus in addition to the four fires in the rubbish bin at Carle Hall.

Fire Chief Robert N. Guyette said this morning there was "no positive way to tell" whether the four fires were set deliberately, but added that "it would be asking an awful lot of coincidence" to conclude that they broke out spontaneously.

"All appearances are that they were set," Guyette said.

The first of the rubbish fires this weekend was reported at about 10 p.m. Friday, and occupied firemen for about 30 minutes. This was followed by another fire late Saturday night and two more early Sunday morning.

Guyette said he was "looking for full cooperation" from college officials in his investigation of the fires but added, "All I can say right now is the investigations after on going."

The bomb scares included five at Carle Hall and one each at Huntress and Monadnock Hall, all dormitories.

A Keene police spokesman said today the college officials are handing the investigations of the bomb-scare wave on the campus, but city police respond to each bomb threat individually.

More than a month of investigation by campus security personnel has so far apparently proved fruitless.

Dr. Thomas D. Aceto, dean of students at KSC could not be reached for comment this morning.

————

As Reported by the *Keene Evening Sentinel* June 4th, 1973:

"FIRE"

Fires Hit Two Keene Buildings

Going Up. Three Keene firemen scramble up ladder Sunday morning to douse mattress fire in third floor bedroom of house owned by Sheldon Barker Sr. Photo by Baker.

Two fires Sunday morning both of undetermined origin kept Keene firemen busy for four hours.

At 3:57 a.m. units were called to 136 Winchester St. where flames had started in a rear upstairs shed and spread to a blind attic above the second floor in an apartment building owned by John T. White.

The blaze seared part of the roof and did extensive damage to the second floor of the building according to Fire Chief Robert N. Guyette.

Both the Jason Crook family, which occupies the second floor, and Edward Bossieau and Steven Zimmerman, who rent the ground floor, were home when the fire started.

No estimate of damage was available this morning. The fire is being investigated by Keene firemen who stayed at the fire scene for three hours.

Firemen had a short break before they were called to a bedroom fire at the Sheldon Barker, Sr. residence at 210 West St.

Guyette said the fire reported at 7:30 a.m. apparently started in a bed on the third floor and did minor damage to the bedroom.

Barker said he had no idea how the fire started. The third floor is seldom used, he said, and he and his wife had been away the previous day.

Barker said they lost a bed, a mattress and a rug, with a total value of less than $1,000.

————

As Reported by the *Keene Evening Sentinel* July 3rd, 1973:

"STORY"

Thomson Vetoes Fire Truck Bill

Gov. Meldrim Thomson, Jr. has vetoed a bill which would have given Keene $31,00, half the cost of a new fire truck which the city purchased a year ago.

The veto was reported by Sen. Clesson J. Blaisdell, D-Keene, this morning. Blaisdell and City Manager Peter L. Cheney called the veto unfair.

Blaisdell said the legislature had paid half the cost of a fire truck for the town of Plymouth four years ago because the town's fire department was responsible for protecting students at Plymouth State College.

Since Keene protects a state-operated college, Keene should be given the same benefits, said Blaisdell.

Blaisdell said the bill vetoed this morning also included an appropriation for half the cost of a fire truck for the city of Concord, because of the large number of state government buildings there.

The Concord portion of the bill was passed by the NH House of Representatives, but the Senate amended it to include the appropriation for Keene. The amended version of the bill was sent to the House-Senate Conference Committee where it was okayed.

"This is something due the city of Keene," Blaisdell said.

"I'll be calling the governor's office in about two minutes," he said.

Cheney said the appropriation had not been included as anticipated revenue in Keene's 1973 budget, but added it seems only "equitable" that if one city can get state help, Keene should too.

"It's a way for the legislature to repay Keene for protection of buildings which provide no taxes for the city," he said.

————

Keene Firemen Phil Davis, dressed in fireproof suit aims nozzles from new airport crash truck. City firemen are undergoing daily training sessions on the vehicle, which stands ready at

Dillant-Hopkins Airport for all major commercial flights. Photo by Baker.

As Reported by the *Keene Evening Sentinel* August 11th, 1973:

"FIRE"

Firemen Answer Two Calls

A cellar fire and a broken power line fire Friday kept Keene firemen busy part of the day. Around 12:50 p.m. Keene units responded to a call at the Richard Austin residence at 189 Pako Ave where a dryer was reported on fire.

Brian Austin, 12, was reportedly cleaning his bicycle and had spilled some gasoline in the cellar.

Keene firemen believe the gas fumes ignited the nearby gas dryer. While extensive damage was reported to the dryer and parts of the cellar, the fire was confined to the laundry and furnace room in one corner, reports indicate.

Damage was estimated at $1,000.

Keene units were bank in service at 2:21 p.m.

At 7:52 p.m. they were called out again, this time to the Keene Country Club where a power line near the swimming pool had broken. The line was believed to have fed tennis court and pool lights.

The units were back in service at 8:40 p.m.

————

As Reported by the *Keene Evening Sentinel* September 25th, 1973:

"FIRE"

Two Persons Hurt Slightly as Fire Hits Housing Project

Two persons, including a fireman, were injured slightly Monday afternoon when flames swept a two-story apartment at 112 Gilsum St. occupied by Mrs. Charlotte Miller and her three children.

Keene Fire Chief Robert N. Guyette, who estimated damage at "several thousand dollars," said the two-alarm fire was caused by a child playing with matches.

Mrs. Miller was treated for shock at Cheshire Hospital and released. Fireman Ralph Newell received hand and thumb cuts when a light fixture fell on him, according to Guyette.

Roger Miller, 4, was rescued from an upstairs bedroom where the fire started by a neighbor at the low-income family housing project, Mrs. Elizabeth Supernor. Two other Miller children were not at home when the blaze broke out.

Guyette said flames had reached outside and into a blind attic when firemen arrived.

The chief said he was "positive" the entire building would have been destroyed if it weren't for fire separation walls in the attic.

He said the separations were installed on the recommendation of the fire inspector when the building was constructed.

The apartment's second floor was gutted by fire and the first floor suffered water damage, Guyette said.

He said the fire was under control within 10 minutes. Engines 3 and 4, ladder truck 1 and a squad car responded to the two alarms.

Firemen used air packs to reach the second floor and Guyette said he was struck, but not injured, by a falling ceiling.

The first alarm was at 3:17 p.m. and all units were back in service at 4:38 p.m.

Guyette said Monday's fire was the second in the same apartment within the last year.

The family has been given temporary quarters in an adjacent apartment, according to Stanwood R. Searles, executive director of the Keene Housing Authority, which owns the project. However, neighboring tenants report the family still requires a permanent apartment.

As Reported by the *Keene Evening Sentinel* October 2nd, 1973:

"STORY"

Overtime Firefighting Pay Being Sought

For the first time in Keene's history, fulltime firemen will get overtime pay for responding to fire calls while off-duty if the Keene City Council approves a finance committee recommendation.

The committee, in a unanimous vote Monday, recommended the new overtime pay policy for city firemen and a new overtime policy for city public works and parks and recreation departments.

For employees on a regular 40-hour work week, the committee proposed time-and-a-half compensation for working extra hours. Present policy pays overtime only for working more than eight hours a day.

Fire Department personnel are on a 63-hour work week and in the past have voluntarily responded to alarms when not on duty and have received no pay for this.

The suggested overtime policy would compensate full-time firemen if they voluntarily responded to 75 per cent of the fire alarm calls while off duty.

It would be mandatory for off-duty firemen to respond to second alarm fires, but they would still receive overtime pay for time spent on the job.

The finance committee is withholding formal recommendation to the city council on the overtime pay policy until ordinances have been written for the employee handbook. The council may consider the recommendations when it meets October 18.

The new overtime policy was recommended in the $7,500 study of city wages by Arthur D. Little, Inc.

In other business Monday, the committee recommended that the city purchase Albert

C. Whitaker's general store at 589 Court St. across from Cheshire Hospital.

The Keene Planning Board proposes to redesign the intersection where the store is and the plan entails demolition of the building.

The proposal is to extend New Acres Road from Court Street through Whitaker's store and to make Allen Court one-way northbound. Acquisition of the store was also recommended by the council's Planning Health and Welfare Committee.

In other action, the finance committee recommended spending $5,500 to appraise 11 parcels of land east of Main Street for the Wells Street parking lot.

The proposed 200-car lot would be located on both sides of Wells Street between Church and Railroad Streets.

The appraisal money, which must be approved by the City Council, would come from the city's parking meter fund.

According to City Manager, Peter L. Cheney, if the funds are approved at Thursday's council meeting, appraisal work could be completed in about two months and then land negotiations could begin.

Two Winchester Street property owners came to the finance committee to urge the building of a road from north of Clarke Distributors, Inc, 472 Winchester St east to the railroad tracks.

The proposed 60-foot right of way would open up about 100 acres of land for industrial use, according to Perry A. Kiritsy of 110 Court St. and Theodore R. Bergeron of 515 Winchester St.

Bergeron owns 47.5 acres of land divided into 21 parcels South of Clarke Distributors. Kiritsy owns 21.3 acres of land adjacent to Bergeron's and wants to divide them into 8 tracts. George M. Gline, city publics works director, estimated that the 2,150-foot road would cost about $130,000 to build.

Committee members questioned whether increased tax revenue from new industry or higher assessments on the road would be worth road construction costs.

"The main thing is to get together and keep the land cost down so industry can move in," Bergeron said.

He indicated that if he and Kiritsy had to build the road themselves, price of the land would have to increase to compensate for the road cost.

George M. Rossiter, committee chairman, said he didn't think the city would want to invest $130,000 in the road without having control over the development. Rossiter said auto body shops which are allowed in industrial zones would probably not add to Keene's tax base.

Both the Greater Keene Chamber of Commerce and the Keene Regional Industrial Foundation support the road to augment Keene's industrial development.

Rossiter suggested meeting with City Manager Peter L. Cheney and City Planner Jerry F. McCollough before making a decision on the road and the committee agreed.

————

As Reported by the *Keene Evening Sentinel* November 13th, 1973:

"STORY"

With Wood Burning on Rise, Fire Officials Urge Caution

One of the hottest heat sources is wood, and many area residents are preparing for the day when they might have to rely on it.

Chances are the day won't come, but the thought of it scares local fire department officials.

"There's not so much to worry about with the old timers," said fire Inspector Laurence V. Wood of the Keene Fire Department.

What Wood is concerned about are people who don't make careful plans before supplementing their heat with a wood stove or fireplace.

First, Wood says, a wood burner should not be vented through the same chi8mney as an oil heater.

So figure on building a new chimney if you don't already have one for wood burning.

If you do have one, your problems are not over.

Many chimneys in the Keene area are 50 to 100 years old, Wood says. They were build with a single layer of bricks connected with mortar, and don't have liners. They're just not made for central heating systems, the inspector says.

Plus, there may be holes in the chimney where stovepipes were once connected. The holes are often plugged with sheet metal when they should be plugged with masonry, Wood says.

Some chimneys are just too small to handle an additional stovepipe. Some are eight inches wide with liners less than seven inches wide, and it stands to reason, Wood says, that an eight-inch stovepipe is too large for them.

Lately, the inspector says, he has heard about people cutting holes in the wall for stovepipes.

That's scary, he says. Houses aren't built the way they used to be, Wood says: they have lighter materials which born quicker.

Non-combustible materials should surround a franklin fireplace or stove, he said, and chimney liners for both wood and oil heat ought to be checked. A flashlight or mirror can be used for the check or people can call the fire department for help, he says.

Officials of the Meadowood County Area Fire Department suggest using seasoned wood in fireplaces, cleaning chimneys and making sure there is no blockage of flues.

After the fire is going, flues can be closed to conserve heat.

Pipes of all heaters should be checked for blockage; you never know when they've become home for a pack of mice.

Wood says there's only one thing that won't burn—the human soul. So, he suggests checking everything else.

————

As Reported by the *Keene Evening Sentinel* November 14th, 1973:

"STORY"

Overtime for Firemen Recommended in Keene

Call it a Christmas bonus or a gift from heaven—Keene firemen may have a chance to earn an extra $800 a year if the Keene City Council approves a new overtime pay policy for full-time firemen.

The council's Bills, Lands and Licenses Committee, after much deliberation Tuesday, recommended unanimously that the city adopt the new overtime pay policy for firemen.

Off-duty firemen would have to respond to 75 percent of first-alarm and still alarm fires to earn overtime pay. Overtime for up to 130 hours per man per year will be paid, or about $800 per fireman, depending on individual salaries.

The policy would cost Keene taxpayers about $20,000, according to Keene City Manager Peter L. Cheney.

The council is expected to vote on the policy Thursday. Full-time firemen in Keene have never been paid overtime.

Fire department personnel are on a 63-hours work week—most spend 24 hours on duty, then 24 hours off duty—and in the past have responded voluntarily to first and still alarm fires when off duty.

According to Keene Fire Chief Robert N. Guyette, a still alarm fire is a "definitely known minor fire when one piece of fire equipment is sent out." A first-alarm fire is in a dwelling and two fire trucks are sent to the scene.

It is mandatory for firemen to respond to more serious second-alarm fires when off duty, but firemen have never been paid for this. Under the new policy, firemen would receive overtime pay for time spent on the job.

But only when they respond to three of every four first and still alarms would they get time-and-a-half pay for up to 130 hours of their regular salary.

Cheney said about half the off-duty firemen—or roughly five of ten men—usually respond voluntarily. He said he thinks it's time these men were paid for this, and looks upon the new policy as an incentive to get more men to respond to calls during off-duty hours.

At-large Councilman George M. Rossiter, a committee member asked why firemen's pay should go from nothing to time-and-a-half, since they had never been paid for responding to first alarm and still alarm fires before.

Cheney explained that other city departments have been paid time-and-a-half for overtime work, and he thinks it's time the firemen were too.

———

As Reported by the *Keene Evening Sentinel* December 3rd, 1973:

"FIRE"

Grease Fire Damages Residence

A grease fire at 103 Pinehurst Avenue early Sunday morning caused extensive damage to the Henry P. Miller residence.

Miller fell asleep after putting French fries on the stove to cook, firemen said. When he awoke, he found hot grease had set the wall behind the stove on fire, so he threw water on it, according to Deputy Fire Chief John N. Phillips.

Phillips said the water made the flames jump higher and the ceiling caught fire.

About five rooms upstairs, plus the kitchen, suffered smoke, heat and water damage estimated to be several thousand dollars.

Miller and his wife were not injured, according to fire department reports.

Four fire units were called to the scene at 3:52 a.m. and returned to the station at about 5:30 a.m.

———

As Reported by the *Keene Evening Sentinel* December 12th, 1973:

"FIRE"

Fire Causes Damage to Trailer

A Monday afternoon fire caused extensive damage to a mobile home at 40 Maple Ave.

The fire damaged the entire roof of the home owned by Frank A. Gline, Sr.

Keene Fire Chief Robert N. Guyette said it appeared the fire started in a broom closet located between a refrigerator and stove.

The exact cause of the fire is unknown.

Besides damage from the flames, there was extensive smoke and heat damage, Guyette said.

He said the afternoon blaze was easily extinguished by two fire department engines, which responded on the first alarm.

———

As Reported by the *Keene Evening Sentinel* December 24th, 1973:

"STORY"

$1.5 Million Damage Estimated From Flood

Water Gone; Boat's Job Over on Church Street. Photo by Fossel.

Firemen Pump Water From Water Street House. Photo by Terry.

Cleanup Continues

Keene cleanup operations continue today in the aftermath of a flood that did about $1.5 million worth of damage to an estimated 120 homes, 20 businesses and numerous streets on the east side of Keene.

About three inches of heavy rain Friday combined with melted snow pushed Beaver Brook over its banks and into basements.

A sharp temperature drop contributed to both flooding and cleanup problems.

City Manager Peter L. Cheney says the city has asked Gov. Meldrim Thomson, Jr. to declare Keene a disaster area, so homeowners and industries could quality for low-interest loans. The city would be eligible for road improvement reimbursement.

Cheney said this morning he had not received approval yet from the governor's office, but he hoped it would come soon.

Mayor James A. Masiello said many people told him they hadn't seen such extensive flooding since the 1938 hurricane.

"The result is similar to that of a 100-year flood in damages and water depth," Masiello said.

Keene firemen, policemen, police Explorers, public works crews and volunteers spend Friday and Saturday pumping out basements, helping several families evacuate homes and patrolling streets to clear plugged drains and aid motorists stranded in puddles.

Firemen from about 15-area towns and NH National Guard troops were called in Saturday to help man pumps and relieve local crews which had worked all night Friday.

Ted W. Kehr, battery commander of the NH National Guard Battery C, First Batallion of the 172 Artillery, said 57 local guards men were activated Saturday morning and worked through Sunday afternoon.

About 250 acres, including 20 to 25 streets, were hit by flood damage, according to Public Works Director George M. Gline.

"We're in pretty good shape; it's strictly cleanup from here on," Gline said today. "Crews were removing ice from streets and debris from the Beaver Brook channel today.

Gline said he thinks the flood was caused by the sharp drop in temperatures Friday evening. Debris that had been carried downstream got caught in culverts when the water turned to ice.

It was about 53 degrees at 5 p.m. Friday, but had dropped to 28 degrees by 10 p.m.

The clogged culverts backed up the brook from Myrtle Street on Keene's east side all the way to Beaver Brook Falls near Route 9 in the northern part of the city.

Several outlying roads, including Belvedere Road off Route 10, West Street near the Keene Country Club, Daniels Hill Road, Stearns Road and Hurricane Road were all washed out, Gline said.

In Keene's east side, Water and Church Streets and side streets between them near Beaver Brook were hit hardest.

Henry Bent, maintenance supervisor for the state highway department, reported about $10,000 worth of road damage just in the Alstead-Acworth area.

All roads were reported open as of this morning, according to Bent and Gline.

Trying to get flood insurance for Keene has been a major problem, according to Masiello. Neither homes nor businesses are eligible for federal flood insurance now.

The federal government has told Keene that there are too many buildings in what are considered flood-prone areas, the mayor said.

Three to four feet of water covered the manufacturing area of the Pneumo Precision Products Inc. building at 40 Carpenter St.; the company offices in a higher section of the building, had about eight inches of water on the floor.

"It's hard to assess damage," said Donald A. Brehm, company president. All the firm's machine tools were at least partially underwater, but William H. Hall, an employee working on the company cleanup today, said he thinks all machines will be in working order.

Brehm said he hopes the city application for disaster relief funds is approved.

Efforts by an emergency organization of employees "saved the day" at Kingsbury Machine Tool Corp, at 80 Laurel St., according to Peter Warren, a company official.

One of the firm's buildings straddles Beaver Brook," and the brook crested to inches to a foot above our floor level," Warren said. "You could imagine the mess that would have been."

However, the employs emergency team got sandbags from the Keene Fire Department, got help from a pay loader and dump truck from Ball and Wixon, sandbagged and blockaded all doors and dealt with leaks inside the building with pumps and more sandbags.

"The disaster squad group saved the day," Warren said," and other volunteers are giving up their long weekend to get things straightened out."

Warren said he had no doubt that the company would be back in operation Wednesday. The firm was to have been closed today anyway.

At Kingtool, a division of Kingsbury's which is primarily an assembly area at 131 Water Street flooded and the Kingtool building had about a foot of water covering the floor. But because it's an assembly area, rather than a manufacturing operation, cleanup should be easier and things should be nearly normal when work resumes Wednesday, Warren said.

At Roberts Hart Inc., at 92 Water St, 12 to 18 inches of water covered factory and office floors.

Damage was heaviest to raw materials and work in process, according to Alan E. Richardson, vice president and general manager of the shoe manufacturer.

"We're trying to salvage all we can and I think we'll make a pretty good job of it," Richardson said. "We'll be back making shoes Wednesday.

Portable heaters were drying materials out today, he said, and some work in process was moved to the parent company in Fitchburg, Mass., to be dried out.

The Roberts-Hart factory store had about 12 inches of water on the floor, and many finished goods there were soaked, Richardson said.

On Sunday, the sound of gurgling sump pumps filled the air on Keene's east side.

Oil and gas dealers' trucks lined the streets, as workmen restored heat in homes whose basements had filled with water.

Children were skating on iced-over lawns and streets, and a ribbon of ice about three feet off the ground hung on cars, trees and houses.

One man from the Church Street area, who owns a bulldozer, was cleaning ice from driveways voluntarily.

That kind of incident was typical of what happened all weekend, Cheney said. Things got cleaned up and taken care of very quickly, considering the amount of flooding, he said.

Masiello said he wanted to thank all volunteers who helped in the weekend flood work.

————

1974

As Reported by the *Keene Evening Sentinel* February 4th, 1974:

"STORY"

$177,000 Lopped from City Budget

The Keene city budget proposed for 1974 took some sharp blows Saturday.

The Keene City Council Finance Committee chopped $177,000 from City Manager Peter L. Cheney's budget proposal of $4.7 million and the committee's still holding the ax.

Although it met from 8 a.m. until 6 p.m. Saturday, the committee didn't get through the entire budget. It will meet again tonight to complete the chore.

The cuts already except last year's $150,000 total and are believed to be among the largest slashes in the history of Keene budgets. The cuts came from police, fire, public works and general government budgets.

Total reductions will almost certainly top $200,000, the goal set last week by committee Chairman George M. Rossiter, and could approach $300,000. The most significant action the committee took Saturday may have been refusing to add new employees to the city payroll.

The committee reviewed requests for 11 new employees but approved only one—a new animal control officer, or dogcatcher. Committee action on the employee was considered a formality because the post was approved last year by the full council.

Mayor James A. Masiello has been a strong opponent of hiring new city workers this year, and Rossiter said the committee "should authorize few, if any, additional personnel."

The fire department budget was cut $21,125 from the $456,125 proposed. Wiped out were four new firefighters requested by Fire Chief Robert N. Guyette, since federal legislation is expected to reduce firemen's work weeks.

Keene Firemen now work a 63-hour work week, and the proposed federal legislation would reduce it to 40 hours by 1979.

Two committee members, Lane and John M. Croteau, said they don't think the department needs new men now, and another, Robert A. Candello, said he wouldn't favor adding firefighters until Congress actually passes the law.

If Congress passes the law the request will get top priority next year, Rossiter said.

————

As Reported by the *Keene Evening Sentinel* February 14th, 1974:

"STORY"

Taxpayers Urge Budget Cuts; City Employee Defends Pay Raise

It was supposed to be city employees' night, but the Keene Taxpayers' Group stole the show at a public hearing on the Keene city government's proposed 1974 budget Wednesday.

Employees were expected to protest a cut in their 3 per cent cost-of-living raise recommended by the Keene City Council Finance Committee.

However, George H. Shepard Jr., head of the city's Personnel Advisory Board and a Keene firefighter, was the only city employee to speak against the proposed reduction. He urged the council to reconsider.

Members of the taxpayers' group clearly dominated the hearing. Taking turns speaking on each section of the budget, they proposed widespread cuts totaling about $132,000, according to group spokesman Roland G. Gray.

The finance committee has already lopped $255,000 off City Manager Peter L. Cheney's $4.7 million proposal.

The tax group supported the cost-of-living increase for employees and improvements along Beaver Brook to reduce flood hazards on Keene's east side. It also drew praise from city officials for interest and concern.

But some cuts the group suggested irked city officials, and one suggestion—no city departments heads and immediate assistants get merit raises—got little support. Police and fire department heads were excluded because of their "hazardous duty."

————

As Reported by the *Keene Evening Sentinel* March 5th, 1974:

"STORY"

Special Emergency Vehicle is expected to Cost $18,000

A man pinned under a 15 tog rock, a woman trapped on the fourth floor of a burning building, hikers stranded in the woods—they'll all be getting special treatment in Keene soon.

Invitations for companies to submit bids for a new rescue vehicle will be sought in advertisements Wednesday.

The vehicle will be equipped for numerous potential emergencies, and will cost $18,000 with all the equipment.

Included will be tools which can cut people from smashed vehicles, four-ton and 10-ton "spreaders" and jacks capable of listing weights from five to 20 tons.

The rescue wagon will carry litters, resuscitators, blankets, ropes and first-aid equipment.

It will not be used as an ambulance, except to remove someone from an area inaccessible to other vehicles.

Although the rescue truck will be available to the Keene Fire and Police Departments, exactly who will make up the rescue team has not been decided.

"I'm hoping there will be a team in each department which could be combined in a major emergency," said Fire Chief Robert N. Guyette.

"We've had numerous accidents where it could have been used," he said.

But Police Capt. Thomas N. Lacroix said last week he thinks the fire department should be in charge of the rescue program, so it would be in one department only.

The logistics are currently being worked out.

————

As Reported by the *Keene Evening Sentinel* March 23rd, 1974:

"STORY"

Firefighting a Way of Life for Keene's Chief Guyette

Fire Chief Robert N. Guyette.

Keene Fire Chief Robert N. Guyette pored over the fire department scrapbooks and talked about the life of a fireman.

The books chronicle many of the men and events of this century. They're old and yellowing, but the stories in them have been handed by generations of firefighters.

"Firefighting is a game really:" Guyette says. "It's not thought of as a job by me or any of the other men in the department. I think that it's just something that you're born with and grow to love."

Firefighters are a special breed of men, he says, who are completely devoted to their work.

It's a way of life for me, and if you ask my wife, I'm sure that she will agree with me. It's just not the kind of a job that you can walk away from at the end of the day.

As a boy growing up in Keene, Guyette held the affection for firemen and their apparatus that most young boys have.

His uncle, Sam Guyette, served on the department and that made it a little more special for him.

As a teenager, he would "chase the fires," and he would lend a hand in fighting grass fires. He loved the excitement and never forgot it.

During World War II, he served in a Navy amphibious crew in Europe. When the war ended, he returned to Keene and went to work for the old Sargent Motor Co. as a jack-of-all-trades.

His job required that he travel frequently to Boston, and he would often stop in and visit his Uncle Asa, who was chief of police in Waltham, Mass.

"Asa was quite a colorful character and a hell of a good policeman. He was tough, but fair, and people respected him."

If old Asa McKenna had been just a little more persuasive, Keene's fire chief might have been pounding a beat in the Boston suburbs.

"My uncle had me in the talking stages of joining the force, and I suppose if I hadn't become a firemen then I would have joined the police force," said Guyette.

At any rate, in 1949 he joined a call fire company in Keene. In 1950 and 1951, he was a spare driver and filled in for firemen on vacation.

Finally, he was appointed to a permanent position April 1, 1952.

When Chief Walter R. Messer retired in 1971, Guyette was named to succeed him.

Looking back on his 25 years on the force, Guyette shrugs off the close calls he has had.

"It's just a part of the job in the back of your mind you realize that each fire could be your last, but you can't think about it.

Still, some brushes with disaster stay with him.

"About the closest I ever came was the day that the old Marlborough Town Hall burned down," Guyette says.

"I had just been appointed a deputy and it was my day off. The alarm came in and I went out there.

"We had six men in the rear of the building and in sizing up the fire, I was afraid that the third floor would collapse, so I ordered the men out.

"To double check, I followed the line to the third floor and as I was preparing to leave the floor collapsed beneath me.

"Fortunately I landed near the staircase and made it to the fire escape safely.

"The other men had just made it out when the building went."

As Guyette continued through the scrapbooks he and some of the other men talked about the fires and the stories that surrounded them.

Finally, the discussion came down to what it is that makes a man take a job where his life in on the line every time the alarm goes off.

"A large part of it is a real desire to help people when they're in trouble," Guyette said.

"When you first start out, they're also the tension and the excitement of the job. You never know when there will be a call or how bad the fire will be.

"As you get older, though, you mellow a bit and you're thankful at the end of the day when the alarm hasn't gone off.

There have been many bad fires in the area since Guyette joined the department, but he says the worst was the Sprague and Carleton fire in 1956.

"The size of the fire was overwhelming as we got there it was obvious that the building was lost.

"To make things worse, there was very little water pressure.

"As a result of the fire, the town installed a major water main," Guyette said.

Today, fires, fire trucks and the men who fight the flames still fascinate people. Children still listen to sirens sail and daydream about sliding down the pole, pulling on the coat, helmet and boots and racing to the fire.

Maybe one of them will be Guyette's successor. If they're as satisfied as Guyette seems to be, they'll be happy.

––––––––––

As Reported by the *Keene Evening Sentinel* March 25th, 1974:

"FIRE"

Fire Levels Barn; Truck Destroyed

Blackened Ruins Under Control. A Keene firefighter wets down smoking ruins of a barn destroyed by flames Saturday on the Hurricane Road. Photo by Fossel.

Keene police are investigating the cause of a fire, which destroyed a barn and truck on Hurricane Road Saturday, according to Fire Chief Robert N. Guyette.

No injuries were reported in the 3:30 p.m. blaze, which leveled the barn in a matter of minutes and destroyed a truck parked alongside.

"I have no reason to believe the fire was set: Guyette said, but added he has found no natural explanation for the fire and the barn had no electrical connections, he said.

The one-and-a-half story barn was owned by Frederick Zeitler of New York City and apparently contained little of value. The truck was owned by George T. Giannette; a neighbor.

Mrs. Giannette reported the blaze at about 3:30 p.m. when the farm was fully engulfed in flames, Guyette said.

The barn was nearly four miles from the fire station in downtown Keene.

Water was trucked to the scene by tankers from Surry and Westmoreland. Keene engines 1, 3 and 4 responded to the alarm and the last firemen left at the scene were not back in service until 7:30 p.m.

Guyette said the pickup truck was probably the most valuable item lost. He did not know if the barn was insured.

————

As Reported by the *Keene Evening Sentinel* April 17th, 1974:

"FIRE"

Recovery Operations Started After Knight Farm Barn Fire
Smoke and Flame Billow over unalarmed cow at Knight Farm

The family of Robert H. Knight was back to the business of farming today, a business interrupted by a spectacular fire Tuesday afternoon, which severely damaged a year-old barn.

"We'll go right through 'til we get back to where we were," Knight said this morning, referring to rebuilding of the barn.

With professional and volunteer help, it should take about two weeks, Knight estimates.

About 75 firefighters battled the blaze, which started early Tuesday afternoon in a sawdust bin at the eastern end of the barn. Keene Fire Chief Robert N. Guyette, who directed the firefighting operation, figures a spark, from a sawdust-blowing machine caused the fire.

A piece of metal probably went through the machine, Guyette says, causing the spark. When farm workers returned from lunch, the eastern of the barn was burning and fire was running in the eaves through the rest of the barn.

After firefighters arrived just after 1 p.m. it was "nip and tuck," Guyette said.

"We were right on the edge of losing it," the fire chief said.

Firemen attempted to "catch the fire" from the east end soon after their arrival, but 3,000 bales of "the best hay we had" were on fire, the heat was trapped inside the barn and temperatures were building.

It was just a matter of time until there was a heat explosion, Guyette said.

"The heat builds up, picks up oxygen, then bang."

One Keene firefighter, Allan Scott Collier, received the brunt of that "bang." He was blown backwards from the top of a ladder, where he had been trying to extinguish flames at the end of the barn.

Collier landed on a corn grinding machine and dislocated his shoulder and received cuts. He'll be out of action for several weeks.

Two other firemen, Philip Davis of Keene and Paul Kirouak, an auxiliary fighter were treated for minor burns and released from Cheshire Hospital.

At 1:40 p.m. the roof buckled, then collapsed, and flames shot up through the gaping vent.

Before the roof caved in, billows of black smoke rushed through a door on the second floor of the east end of the barn and about 100 excited cows milled around on the floor.

They were all evacuated unharmed. The Knight farm milks 90 cows—50 of which were in the new part of the barn destroyed by fire.

Knight said a large bull had to be released and, in its excitement, badly injured

Knights Recover. Crane removes ruined hay and debris, as farm of Robert H. Knight on West Surry Road is put back into shape after fire Tuesday Afternoon. Photo left by Hannah and Photo right by Pitfield.

a cow. The cow will have to be used for beef, Knight said.

Neither Knight, his wife Betty A. Knight nor son James were in Keene until more than three hours after the fire broke out.

"It's just as well," Knight said, "I probably couldn't have helped and I would have been mighty nervous.

Wind favored the firefighting operation. It blew briskly to the east, away from an older barn and the Knights' home.

The strategy, according to Guyette, was to cut off the fire at the junction of the old and new portions of the barn. It Worked.

Departments from Keene, Surry, Marlborough, Swanzey Center and Meadowood were at the fire while Spofford and West Swanzey men covered the Keene station.

Water was drawn from the Ashuelot River, the Knights' swimming pool, a hydrant near Maple Avenue and a hydrant on Route 12A.

Knight and several neighbors spend today evaluating damage and continuing the routine farming operation. The Knights have the only full-scale dairy farm in Keene.

There will be no way to determine the exact damage for several weeks.

Besides loss of the new portion of the barn, 3,000 bales of hay, and the cow which

will have to be slaughtered, others cows may be lost because of the fire.

A couple of cows may have "picked up hardware," nails or other metal which could puncture their stomach walls, said James H. Knight, son of Robert. A few older cows may not live through the stress caused by the fire, he said.

The full extent of damage to feeding, gutter cleaning equipment and wiring has not been determined, Knight said.

The Knights' milk processing plant next to the barn received minimal damage.

As Reported by the *Keene Evening Sentinel* June 5th, 1974:

"FIRE"

Beauty Shop Damaged by Fire

A fire Tuesday night damaged Unique Hair Styles at 382 West Sat.

According to Keene Fire Chief Robert N. Guyette, the fire started in the back of the beauty parlor when a dryer caught fire and ignited a real well.

It then spread to a rear partition in the building. Firefighters were at the scene for more than 90 minutes because the partition fire was inaccessible and difficult to extinguish, Guyette said.

Mrs. Gail M. Leville of the beauty parlor said insurance adjustors were estimating damage costs today. She said some damage from soot and smoke occurred outside the burned area, but the shop opened for business as usual this morning.

As Reported by the *Keene Evening Sentinel* June 10th, 1974:

"FIRE"

Fire Doused at Factory in Keene

Watering Down. Keene firemen attack roof of Central Screw Co on Emerald Street to reach fire beneath surface. Flames were controlled within 20 minutes. Photo by Baker.

Keene firemen controlled a fire in the ceiling of one section of Central Screw Co. at 149 Emerald St. within 20 minutes this morning.

The fire started at about 10:45 a.m. in the ceiling over the casehardening furnace—the furnace used to harden screws.

Emp0loyees theorized that a spark flew from the furnace into the ceiling. A protective zone is located between the ceiling and roof to contain flames.

Two alarms were turned in at 10:50 a.m. Using chain saws, firemen cut through the roof of a one-story section of the building, located at the west end of the factory, where the fire started. By 11:15, much of the smoke had escaped and the flames had been doused.

As Reported by the *Keene Evening Sentinel* July 10th, 1974:

"FIRE"

Fire Guts Trailer in Tanglewood

Fire destroyed a double-wide mobile home at 186 Tanglewood Estates early this morning.

The home was completely engulfed in flames by the time firefighting units arrived at about 3:30 a.m., according to Keene Fire Chief Robert N. Guyette.

The sole occupant of the home, Mrs. Shirley Bickford, was taken to Cheshire Hospital for observation and was reported in satisfactory condition late this morning.

Cause of the blaze is still under investigation by the Keene Police and Fire Departments. Guyette estimated the loss at $18,000 to $20,000.

Since Tanglewood has no fire hydrants, tanker trucks from Surry, Marlborough, Spofford and the Meadowood Fire Departments joined Keene firefighters in battling the blaze.

No one was in the mobile home when firefighters arrived at the scene.

As Reported by the *Keene Evening Sentinel* November 1st, 1974:

"STORY"

Clang! Keene's first firefighting Woman

Felicity Crowell. Photo by Haley.

Felicity Crowell is a member of both Keene Fire Department Auxiliaries—the men's and the women's.

She has been a member of the women's auxiliary since she was six years old.

There wasn't anything formal about her joining. Her mom, Florence B. Crowell, also a member of the women's auxiliary, simply took her daughter to a fire.

That was 12 years ago and Felicity recalls "I served coffee and sandwiches and made sure I stayed out of the way."

It took a little more doing to join the men's auxiliary. Firefighting seems to run in the Paul E. Crowell family. Crowell is a permanent (full time) city fire captain and his two sons are members of one of the three call companies.

Keene Fire Chief, Robert N. Guyette explained the 45 members of the call companies are paid $200 each for their years work. "It doesn't matter how many fires they go to or how many hours they work. They do it for love, really."

The men's auxiliary was formed during World War II as a civil defense unit. It was revived during the Korean War.

More recently, Frank Driscoll, a full-time Keene firefighter, was appointed auxiliary adviser and the group was expanded to 32 members.

"The auxiliary is a good place for interested people to find out what the fire department is all about without getting over their heads. It also gives us a chance to see how capable and interested someone is."

Enter Felicity Crowell. Born under the pioneering sign of Aquarius, Felicity looked up Frank Driscoll the day she turned 18 last January.

"I kept checking back. I was bound and determined to follow it up. I think the fire department and civil defense by-laws were being checked out to see if it was legal to admit me—to see if insurance would cover me. And the other members have to vote you in."

Six months passed. So in August, Felicity, took a deep breath and walked in on an auxiliary training session at the fire station.

"And they gave me a membership card." What did her co-members say to her:

Well, most of the auxiliary guys are pretty good about it. A couple of guys tried to talk me out of it. They said "You're not strong enough to carry a person out of a building and you are taking a job away from a man."

The auxiliary meets once a month for training sessions and so far Felicity says "I've been learning basic things like how to handle a hose and other basic equipment.

She expects to leave her data processing work at Cheshire Hospital when the alarm for a major fire sounds. And how do her hospital superiors feel about this volunteer? They think it's a good idea," Felicity said.

The young firefighter hasn't actually fought a fire yet because she's anxiously awaiting arrival of her hear--$150 worth of helmet, bunker coat, night hitch, short and hip-length boots and mittens.

Felicity paid for her own gear because the fire department budget doesn't extend as far as auxiliary equipment. Guyette said the fire department, companies and auxiliary operates like a big family and surplus equipment may be occasionally passed onto junior members.

Meanwhile, she has been assigned station duty putting trucks back in to service after calls.

What does her firefighting father think of all this? "Dad never discouraged me. He always said, "Do what you really want to do. And when I made up my mind to go ahead, he was happy about it."

Asked if she did it to help the cause of equal opportunity for women, Felicity said no. "Being a fireman is too dangerous to do to prove a point. I did it because I always wanted to.

And what does she want to be called? Fireperson? Firefighter? Firewoman?

Felicity laughed. "No, I am a fireman—just like one of them."

————

As Reported by the *Keene Evening Sentinel* December 28th, 1974:

"FIRE"

Porch, Apartment Damaged by Fire

Firefighters at Work. Firemen converge on apartment and porch at 36 Marlboro St., Friday night. Firemen brought the blaze under control swiftly, but two people suffered minor injuries. Photo by Hebert.

A two-alarm fire damaged a porch and second floor apartment at 36 Marlboro St. Friday night and left two people with minor injuries.

Fireman William Durin was taken to Cheshire Hospital for smoke inhalation, and later released. Edward Weeks, in whose apartment the blaze started, received second degree burns of his hands, according to Deputy Chief Fred H. Beauchesne of the Keene Fire Department.

It is not known if Weeks required medical treatment.

Box 16 alarm on Marlboro Street came in at 5:51 p.m. and firemen had the blaze under control in less than 25 minutes. Beauchesne said. The firemen were at the scene cleaning up until 7:49 p.m.

Beauchesne said he could not estimate the cost of the damage, but that it would amount to probably more several thousand dollars.

Fire damage in the house beside the post office was limited to Weeks' apartment and an adjoining porch on the west side of the building. Smoke, heat and water damage spread through other parts of the house.

There are eight apartments in the main part of the apartment house where the fire began. A wing, undamaged, contains five apartments.

The building is owned by Frances Ash of West Surry Road.

The fire started "from an electrical problem" in the apartment when Weeks was downstairs changing a fuse, according to Beauchesne.

Weeks apparently burned his hands when he threw a smoldering mattress out the door of the apartment. The mattress apparently set fire to the porch.

Occupants of the apartment house were able to make their way out of the building without difficulty, except for an elderly woman.

Firemen helped Mrs. Ruth Deegan evacuate the building by some back stairs from the second floor.

Mrs. Ash could not be reached for comment.

————

Fire Chief's car and Deputy Chief's Car added to the Fire Department Fleet.

Keene's New Fire Alarm Truck to fit the new full time fire alarm Superintendent.

1975

As Reported by the *Keene Evening Sentinel* January 2nd, 1975:

"FIRE"

Two Fires are Probed by Police

Two fires that did slight damage to a shed behind 309 Water St Wednesday have been labeled as suspicious and are under investigation by the Keene Police Department.

Firemen were called out at 9:15 a.m. and 12:46 p.m. to put out fires at the shed spending several minutes on the scene each time to 0065tinguish the blazes.

Damage to the structure was slight, according to Keene Fire Chief Robert N. Guyette.

Keene Police Chief Harold A. Becotte said today police are seeking the cause of the fire.; the shed is located at the rear of the three-unit apartment building.

———

As Reported by the *Keene Evening Sentinel* January 22nd, 1975:

"STORY"

Supreme Court Ruling Affects Need for More City Firemen

A U.S. Supreme Court decision, temporarily blocking Congressional legislation requiring stricter overtime pay provisions for local fire and police departments, may postpone the need for four more Keene firefighters and one inspector.

Members of the Keene City Council Finance Committee, reviewing part of the proposed 1975 city budget Tuesday night, reacted to the news with wary pleasure.

Although the postponement could save city taxpayers at least $30,000, committee members don't know what the final Supreme Court ruling will be, and they don't want to get caught violating federal law in mid-year with no money to remedy the situation.

The court ordered a "stay" of federal legislation which would require local governments to pay time-and-a-half overtime pay to firemen working more than 60 hours during a seven-day shift. Currently, firefighters at the Keene Fire Department work 63-hours over seven days.

City Manager Peter L. Cheney and Fire Chief Robert N. Guyette said that for about the same amount of money it costs to pay firefighters overtime, the city could hire four more firemen and improve coverage.

Cheney proposed spending slightly less than $500,000, up more than $55,000 from last year's budget, to run the fire department in 1975. Depending on the council's reaction to the court stay, the total may be reduced.

The federal legislation, entitled the Fair Labor Standard Act, was to take effect January 1 this year.

Cheney told committee members that he will try to find out when a final ruling may be issued by the high court.

At-large Councilman George M. Rossiter, chairman of the committee, asked Cheney to supply the committee with information about the city council's authority to raise money for additional firemen, and not use it.

The question still to be determined by the court is whether the federal government can constitutionally set the number of hours worked by state and local government employees.

The committee raised several questions about Guyette's requests for large budget increases for Nomex firefighting costs and other uniforms, replacement of minor equipment, tires totaling a cost of more than $3,000 and construction of a training ground on city-owned land at Dillant-Hopkins Airport.

But committee members did not indicate where they would recommend budget cuts.

The federal law on overtime pay also affects the city's inspection's department, which employs part-time Fire Inspector Laurence V. Wood. Under the law, Wood's work for the inspections office would be considered overtime, at a time-and-a-half rate.

Consequently, Cheney recommended hiring a full-time inspector to replace Wood, but the court's action this month postpones the need for a full-time inspector.

————

As Reported by the *Keene Evening Sentinel* February 28th, 1975:

"FIRE"

Fire Sends Homeowner to Hospital

Keene Fire. City firefighters douse blaze that struck Meadow Road home when cement ignited during home improvement project. Photo by Baker.

A fire that apparently resulted from a home-improvement project did considerable damage to a Meadow Road home Thursday afternoon and sent its owner, James L. McPhail, to Cheshire Hospital for treatment of burns.

The fire apparently began when McPhail was cementing a piece of formica onto a kitchen surface and the pilot light on a gas stove ignited the cement, according to Fire Chief Robert N. Guyette.

Guyette said McPhail was out of his home at 126 Meadow Road by the time firefighters arrived at the scene. He was taken to the hospital for treatment of arm and hand burns and later released.

Guyette said several thousand dollars worth of damage was done to both stories of the home. The burned areas were confined to the downstairs living room, dining room and kitchen, but the upstairs suffered considerable smoke and water damage. It took firemen about 10 minutes to bring the blaze under control.

Guyette urged anyone using highly flammable glue for home improvements to turn off the stove pilot light and open all windows to insure that explosive fumes are dissipated.

———

As Reported by the *Keene Evening Sentinel* May 13th, 1975:

"STORY"

Jaws of Life

As Reported by the *Keene Evening Sentinel* June 2nd, 1975:

"FIRE"

Two fires in Keene during the weekend caused extensive damage to portions of two houses

A fire early Saturday morning severely damaged one of nine apartments in a two-story structure at 88 High St on the corner of Carroll Street.

The apartment house is owned by Howard B. Lane Jr., according to Keene Fire Chief Robert N. Guyette. Fire officials still have not determined how the blaze started.

The Keene department arrived at the fire slightly after 2:30 a.m. Saturday and had it under control in less than half an hour. But Guyette said one apartment and the attic were badly burned, while the other apartments received some smoke and water damage.

Flames were pouring out of the roof of the building when firemen arrived.

The fire apparently started in a partition on the west side of the house, Guyette said today, but fire officials are investigating the cause.

New Machine. Keene Firemen-Ronald P. Amadon, tests new extricator on junk car as instructor David Mills looks on. The tool can tear metal and helps rescue workers get accident victims out of wrecked cars. The machine has been donated to the Keene Fire Department by Bruce and James Pollock and Hubbard Farms of Walpole in memory of Mr. & Mrs. Stephen Pollock, who died in a car accident in Keene last year. Photo by Baker.

Another fire also forced firemen out of bed about 2 a.m. this time on Sunday.

The fire damaged the cellar and a partition to the garage at the home of Steward M. Holmes at 10 Ward Circle.

Guyette said fire officials have determined that the blaze started in a pile of rags. The cause was labeled spontaneous combustion.

The rags were located near a work bench in Holmes' cellar.

Firemen had the fire under control soon after 2 a.m. Sunday.

————

As Reported by the *Keene Evening Sentinel* September 9th, 1975:

"STORY"

City Busy in Preparing for Ford's Appearance

Limousine Sparkles in sun as Ford wades into crowd. Photo by Baker.

The Keene city government; working under the wing of federal officials, has shifted into hi8gh gear in preparing for President Ford's visit here Thursday.

The President's eight-seat JetStar aircraft is scheduled to land at Dillant-Hopkins Airport at 9:30 a.m. Fort and U.S. Senate candidate Louis C. Wyman will then begin a cross-state motorcade, following Route 101 east, which will begin with a drive along Main Street in Keene and a brief address by the President at Central Square.

Mayor James A. Masiello said city officials have been very busy with preparations. Final plans for rerouting traffic and closing off streets will be available Wednesday, the mayor said.

In other matters related to the presidential visit:

—The mayor briefed downtown businessmen this morning about the trip, saying it will be up to storeowners to decide whether to close when the President's in town.

—All Keene schools will be closed Thursday. Some other area schools will close and some will remain open,

—Most Keene industries are giving employees time off from work to see the President.

—A spokesman for Cheshire Hospital said the hospital has been contacted by White House staff members and appropriate plans are being readied for any medical emergency that might arise, both for the President and the mass of people expected in Keene Thursday morning.

—"The gray cloud" hanging over the event, in the mayor's words, is the traffic problem which a large influx of people might cause.

Masiello told businessmen at a meeting this morning that Main Street will be closed to car traffic while the eight or nine-car motorcade travels through Keene between 9:45 and 10 a.m.

Rope and barrel barriers will be set up in the street so the crowd viewing the President can fill part of the street.

Central Square will be open for on-lookers, but Masiello expects that area to be filled early. The President will be easily seen anywhere on Main Street, and he is expedited to stop briefly from time to time to shake hands, said Masiello.

Folding chairs will be set up i9n front of the United Church of Christ for elderly people wishing to see Fort. The Keene City Council, the Keene Board of Education, the Cheshire County Legislative Delegation and Commissioners, Swanzey selectmen, and their families, along with local Scouts, will gather in front of the Sears store. The President and Wyman will speak from the President's limousine at about where Central Square meets Court Street.

That spot was chosen, Masiello said, because national television officials like it.

A proposal by local officials would have had the President speaking at Joyce Field on the Keene State College campus, but Ford prefers to mingle with the crowd on the street, said Masiello.

In a vote by about 45 downtown businessmen, one-third said they'd stay open during the motorcade visit, one-third said they'd close, and one-third apparently hadn't made up their minds, because they didn't raise their hands on the vote.

The President will be accompanied by a small staff, dozens of Secret Service men, many of whom have been in the Keene area since last Friday, and scores of newsmen.

Two limousines will be flown here in a cargo plane, and the newsmen will arrive via a chartered Boeing 737 aircraft. Federal officials will set up a temporary tower at the Keene airport to control air traffic. Planes will be banned from the airport one hour before the President is scheduled to land.

Masiello said nearly all Keene police will be working Thursday and there will be heavily-concentrated crowd control measures for obvious reasons.

Most Keene industries and the city's two large insurance offices are making provisions to let their employees see the President if they want to.

The motorcade will consist of two limousines, with Ford and Wyman riding in one and presidential staff members in another, plus Secret Service cars, a van of state and local Republican dignitaries and two busloads of newsmen.

————

As Reported by the *Keene Evening Sentinel* October 10th, 1975:

Fire Prevention Week

Fire Demonstration. Keene Fireman Steve Goldsmith explains rescue equipment during Fire Prevention Week to students at Wheelock School. Others on fire department demonstration team are Larry Thompson, Paul Symonds and Jack Dennis. Photo by Baker.

————

As reported by the *Keene Sentinel* Monday October 13th, 1975 by Ernest Hebert, Staff Writer:

Alarm Clangs, Firefighters Jump, trucks Leave in 30 Seconds

When the alarm rings, Keene firefighters are out of the firehouse faster than kids are out of the classroom on the last day of school.

That point was made clear to this reporter Sunday night at the Keene fire station, when the alarm rang for a third story apartment blaze in the Colonial theater building on Main Street.

The fire, caused by a short-circuit electric stove, was put out very fast, and damage was slight.

As John Phillips, who was crew chief last night, put it, the blaze was "more smoke than fire."

Phillips, a big calm middle-aged man with spectacles, was smoking his pipe and had just finished chatting with the reporter when the call came in to dispatcher Edwin Mattson of Southwester N.H. Fire Mutual Aid.

Mattson made a few notes than pressed a button. The fire bell went off in the quiet station. Within seconds the building was alive with running men.

By the time this reporter could reflect on the matter three fire trucks and six men were already out of the building. About 30 seconds had elapsed since the alarm bell went off.

Just routine for Keene firefighters Deputy Fire Chief Fredrick N. Beauchesne said crews are expected to be out of the building and on the way to the blaze between 30 and 45 seconds from the time the alarm bell rings.

Preparation makes it possible. Each man knows his assignment in advance. Boots helmets and bunker coats are kept in a certain place. All tools are kept in compartments on the trucks.

At night when firefighters are sleeping at the firehouse, a "night hitch" hangs beside each bunk. A night hitch is a pair of boots rigged to a pair of pants so a fireman can jump into his boots and pants at the same time.

There are two fire poles at the Keene fire station to slide down.

At the alarm, Phillips ran to the dispatcher's desk Mattson gave him the location of the probable fire and a few details. By that time the doors were open for engines 3 and 4 and the hook and ladder truck. Seconds later the trucks were gone.

Firefighters have routines for every area in the city. When Mattson said "third floor Colonial Theater," Phillips knew that under procedures worked out earlier the hook and ladder truck might be needed and he sent it to the blaze.

A fire in a different location might require different equipment and procedures.

Phillips and his crews reached the fire moments after the call came in. One of the first things they did was open the window and place a gasoline powered smoke ejector (a big fan) on the sill. That started to remove dense smoke in the apartment.

The fire itself was slight, and firefighters were able to extinguish it with a pan of water drawn from a faucet in the apartment. Had the fire been more serious a one-inch hose line could have been run from a water-carrying pumper truck upstairs to the fire. Meanwhile another crew could have begun rigging a line to a nearby hydrant.

Had Phillips seen orange in the windows showing a blaze in progress chances are he would have immediately called in a second alarm.

When that occurs off duty regular firemen head for the station for instructions. Part time firemen monitoring the fire frequency on their radio scanners would already be on their way to the fire.

A Demon Called Fire

Some don't even wait for a second alarm said Beauchesne.

The result is that a sizeable crew can be at the scene in minutes, although just six firefighters answered the original call.

Phillips crew was one man short last night. During the day theoretically 10 men are on duty. But it doesn't work out like that in practice. One man is usually on vacation at any one time and two often are covering the airport. One might be conducting a building inspection.

Fire officials would like to have one driver and two tail men for each engine, but that is not practical because of the man shortage.

Driver and other assignments are rotated so that each man can do many jobs if necessary.

There are hundreds of kinds of fires and buildings and a firefighter has to depend on his training, his nose and his intuition in deciding what is the right thing to do in any given situation.

Equipment on trucks includes an electrician's kit, forcible entry tools that would make a burglar envious, hoses, fittings, a water vacuum cleaner and all sorts of lights, first aid kits and may other items.

There are all sort of subtle things a firefighter must learn for example, how much water pressure to use and the water pressure in particular hydrants.

The firefighters returned from Sunday night's fire in a good mood. Phillips was kidded about being "an old man running up three flights of stairs." There were a few other jokes then calm again. A few minutes work in the life of Keene firefighters had gone by.

————

As Reported by the *Keene Evening Sentinel* October 30th, 1975:

"FIRE"

Two Fires in Area Extinguished

Area firefighters extinguished minor blazes at 39 Trowbridge Road in Keene and at the Hampshire Country School in Rindge Wednesday.

Keene firefighters pulled down a burning wall partition behind a fireplace at the home of Edward T. Dowling before extinguishing the blaze.

Fire officials said the fire was limited to the wall partition but the house was filled with smoke. The fire started at about 4:45 p.m. and firemen were at the scene about 50 minutes.

The blaze apparently started from heat from a metal fireplace.

The fire at the Hampshire Country School was in a dormitory-classroom building called the Coach House, according to Rindge fire officials.

A rug over a furnace grate caught fire and filled the building with smoke. The fire began about 7 p.m. Wednesday.

Rindge firefighters contained the fire to the rug and a small area near the grate.

No injuries were reported.

————

As Reported by the *Keene Evening Sentinel* November 17th, 1975:

"FIRE"

Fire Hits Office; Damage $15,000

A two-alarm fire Friday night destroyed between $15,000 and $20,000 worth of office equipment at Chamberlain Office Equipment Inc., located at Lamson and Federal Streets.

Keene firefighters were able to contain fire damage to the single large room in the Beedle Block building where the office-equipment is located, but smoke damage was reported throughout the building, which extends to Main Street.

Keene Fire Chief Robert N. Guyette said the fire appeared to have started in a workbench area where volatile cleaning materials were stored, but he did not know what caused the fire.

"It's still under investigation," he said. "We may never know.

The fire was reported at midnight Friday from the Tiffany Tavern, which, like the Chamberlain office, is on the first floor of the Beedle Block.

Guyette said the fire was under control in 15 minutes, but firefighters didn't leave the scene for two more hours.

George B. Chamberlain Jr., owner of the Chamberlain business, said he would review the damage today with an insurance representative. He said typewriters and other office equipment destroyed in the blaze had a wholesale value of roughly $15,000.

Talbot R. Hood, vice president and general manager of radio station WKBK, whose offices are on the second floor of the Beedle Block, said the station equipment appeared to be undamaged, but there was some smoke and water damage to the offices and damage to a stairwell.

The fire did not affect WKBK's normal broadcasting schedule.

Richard W. Conway, owner of the Beedle Block, said he didn't know this morning how much it will cost to repair the building.

————

As Reported by the *Keene Evening Sentinel* November 23rd, 1975:

"FIRE"

Arson Suspected in Fire Which Guts Warehouse

Warehouse Gutted. Flames leap from the abandoned, three-story building formerly owned by Elm City Grain Co., Inc. on Railroad Street. Keene police are investigating the blaze, which they think was set by an arsonist Sunday night. Photo by Fossel and Hebert.

Arson is the suspected cause of a towering fire which destroyed the vacant warehouse of Elm City Grain Co. on Railroad Street Sunday night.

While about 100 firemen battled the spectacular blaze, the Keene Fire Department was called to a second fire in the same area, this time on Church Street. Walpole, West

Swanzey and Keene trucks went to the second fire, which was put out immediately.

"We are confident both were set fire," Keene Police chief Harold A. Becotte said this morning.

Becotte said the police department has suspects, but no one had been arrested late this morning.

Hundreds of spectators surrounded the huge gray warehouse soon after the first Keene fire engine arrived on the scent just before 8:00 p.m.

Fire Chief Robert N. Guyette had one strategy in fighting the fire, which could be seen several miles away: contain it in the warehouse.

Firemen concentrated on the east end of the building, only about 15 feet from the former Princess Shoe Warehouse, now MGF Appliance Warehouse.

It worked.

"A fire is like an orchestration—a few bad musicians and the sound is awful, but last night was a pretty good song," said Guyette in praising the firefighters' work.

Besides Keene, Walpole and West Swanzey, Meadowood, Surry, Swanzey Center and Marlborough Fire Departments were either at the scene of the fire or helped cover the Keene station.

There was no damage estimate, but the building was considered a total loss. In 1974, the structure was valued by the city assessors at $20,400.

Firemen had to contend with three heat explosions, the first of which occurred when they opened the large front door to the warehouse.

Guyette said the fire was roaring through three floors by the time fire trucks arrived. It started on the ground floor at the west end of the building, he said, and rose through openings in the upper levels.

There were no serious injuries, but Guyette said two Keene Firefighters became trapped in the building when the second floor collapsed on them.

Paul E. Symonds Jr. and Steven Goldsmith were "mopping up," meaning they were dousing hot spots, when the second floor came toppling down on them.

They were buried in wood, said Guyette, but several men pulled them out, and they received only a few scratches.

Water was drawn from eight hydrants located on Railroad, 93rd and Church Streets and behind the Keene Co-Operative Band and on Central Square.

Keene firemen were at the scene throughout the night and this morning, watching for spot fires. Their efforts were aided this morning by a steady rain.

The City of Keene claims ownership because of the failure of a Connecticut firm to pay taxes on the building.

————

On Wednesday, February 26th, *The Keene Sentinel* published the article below:

The Last Alarm

It would be futile to lecture those troubled souls who go about setting fires in buildings, vacant or otherwise. Arson is an irrational act and no rational plea in this space to the area's firebugs is likely to dampen their inflammatory ardor.

But it may be worth reminding ourselves just how irrational these blazes can be.

Sunday night's warehouse fire in Keene, which authorities strongly suspect was set, came very close to restoring our perspective when a floor collapsed on two city firefighters.

Paul E. Symonds and Steven Goldsmith were pulled from the debris suffering only bruises and scratches. Had their luck been shorter, however, two men might have answered their last alarm.

That's how irrational life and death can be—something to remember the next time we hear the fire horn.

————

As Reported by the *Keene Evening Sentinel* December 16th, 1975:

"STORY"

Subsidy for Ambulances Proposed to City Council

Either the ambulance service of Foley Funeral Home Inc. is subsidized by public funds or it will cease operations Sunday.

This was the message taken to the Keene City Council's Finance Committee Monday night by City Manager Peter L. Cheney.

Members of the committee weren't pleased by the time pressure, but all five decided they had no choice and recommended that the council pay $3,500 to keep the private company's two ambulances going for another 10 weeks.

In addition, Cheney will recommend that the city government subsidize the ambulance service on a regular basis.

In 1976, Cheney figures, the firm will need about $25,000 in public money.

The ambulance service, according to its director, Robert J. DiLuzio, lost $21,942 during the first nine months this year. The service's expenses totaled $45,378, but income amounted to only $23,436.

If the firm had been paid its customary fee of $45 for every call, it would have exceeded its expenses by $161. That doesn't mean a profit of $161. Cheney pointed out, because the two ambulances need to be replaced, and the firm did not consider depreciation in its expense account.

Running in the red is nothing new to the ambulance portion of Foley's business, DiLuzio said today.

Until his death last year, Frank J. Foley Jr. operated the business for 23 years and, in recent years it has been a losing proposition. The ambulance service has been financed by the funeral business.

DiLuzio said the firm had considered seeking city help last year but did not because of the extra work load caused by Foley's death.

A decision on whether to subsidize the private service will be a major policy question for the new council when it takes office January 1. The question will be debated by the finance committee during its deliberations on the 1976 city budget. The budget is expected to be unveiled Wednesday.

DiLuzio says most other cities in New Hampshire use public funds in the operation of their ambulances.

Laconia pays $72,000 in subsidies to a private operator and Claremont pays $37,000, according to Cheney.

Foley's financial problems stem largely from the failure of customers to pay their bills. And, if federal Medicare is billed, the payment is only $28, not the full fee of $45 which is the amount needed to cover expenses.

The finance committee's recommended temporary subsidy will cover ambulance attendants' salaries (which average about $300 per week) and fuel costs for 10 weeks. If the council approves the stop-gap measure Thursday night, Foley's will obtain its gasoline from city pumps.

The firm came to the city when it was refused a temporary bank loan, Cheney said .

"On December 1 we had zero in our checking account," DiLuzio said.

"We're in a unique situation of not having a choice," remarked Ward 5 Councilman Richard P. Peloquin, a member of the committee.

The service needs upgrading, according to DiLuzio, who says that besides needing new ambulances, the firm should hire around-the-clock-staff to be on duty at Foley's headquarters at 49 Court St. Response time is a problem now, he said. Ambulance attendants currently stay at home, and when there is an emergency call they travel from home to 49 Court Street, where the ambulances are kept.

"We don't have the money to keep them there all night," DiLuzio said today.

———

As Reported by the *Keene Evening Sentinel* December 19th, 1975:

"STORY"

Ambulance Service Subsidy Approved by City Council

The Foley Ambulance Service will receive a temporary $3,500 subsidy from Keene city funds while officials try to figure out some way of continuing ambulance services in the area.

Unless the service is subsidized by the city and surrounding towns it will go out of business, according to Robert J. DiLuzio Sr., president of the company.

The temporary subsidy, approved by the Keene City Council Thursday, is expected to be enough to keep the ambulance service going until the council acts on budget expenditures for 1976 in February.

City Manager Peter L. Cheney has included $25,000 in his proposed budget for an ambulance subsidy, but how that money is to be spent, if it is approved has not yet been determined.

Cheney, who is not ready to recommend how the problem is to be solved, listed a number of alternatives—subsidize the Foley Ambulance Service: have the fire department or police departments perform the service: let Cheshire Hospital have the problem put the service out to competitive bidding with a promise of a subsidy: or do nothing.

DiLuzio, in a November 7 letter to Cheney, indicated the reason the service is losing money is because many people don't pay their bills; either because they can't afford to or because federal Medicaid and Medicare payments cover only part of the bill.

———

As Reported by the *Keene Evening Sentinel* December 27th, 1975:

"STORY"

Keene City Manager Peter L. Cheney is not the only city official who sees the cost of government rising dramatically in 1976. With one exception, budget requests by city department heads are higher than last year, and in some cases they are substantially higher.

Cheney made some city councilmen and local taxpayers gulp when he asked for $5.8 million to run Keene government next year— an increase of $1.6 million over the current budget. If Cheney's budget is approved by the Keene City Council in February, he says the city's share of the local property tax rate will rise from $6.80 per $1,000 of assessed evaluation to $8.61.

Some city councilmen say the requests will have to be reduced, but they aren't sure how cuts can be made. They'll have their chance when the council's Finance Committee begins its budget review next month.

Cheney made a lot of changes in requests by department heads, but many of those were minor, and on the whole the city manager's budget reflects the department heads' budgets.

Keene Fire Chief Robert N. Guyette is requesting $53,107 for 1976, up from $449,309 appropriated this year. Cheney cut Guyette's requests to $513,898.

Guyette asked for $24,570 for new personnel, but Cheney approved just $12,000 for that item. The chief wants $16,000 for overtime pay, up $10,000 over this year. Cheney is recommending $13,500 for overtime pay.

Cheney and Guyette say the city needs more firefighters, and that the ones it does have work too many hours.

Cheney, in one of his top priorities in his budget message, asks for four additional firemen to cut firemen from their current 63-hour week to a 56-hour week.

Cheney is also asking for another accountant in the finance department and a part-time city prosecutor. Both positions are recommended by department heads.

According to Cheney's estimates, if the council approves his budget some $2.2 million will have to be raised by local property taxes. That's an increase of about $667,000 over this year.

————

As Reported by the *Keene Evening Sentinel* December 29th, 1975:

"STORY"

New Ambulance Firm Plans to Open

A new ambulance service is scheduled to open in Keene January 2, possibly eliminating the need for a $25,000 public subsidy the Foley Funeral Home ambulance service in 1976.

Donald Bingham, a former ambulance driver in Woodsville, is preparing to open a new service with a fully equipped vehicle leased from a Concord ambulance firm, and will require no subsidy from the city, he said today.

Bingham has applied for state licensing, and said he will hire two full-time and seven part-time staff members.

The 24-hour service is scheduled to cost $35 per call within the city limits plus $1.50 per mile when a patient is being transported, Bingham said.

He predicts he will have one fully-equipped emergency ambulance, together with another vehicle for transporting non-emergency cases.

Under state law, the service must obtain a state license, have vehicles inspected by state officials and employ state-licensed attendants.

The operations license has been applied for, and will probably be granted in the immediate future, according to an official of the Emergency Medical Services Division of the N.H. Department of Health and Welfare.

Currently, Keene has only one ambulance service—operated by Foley's Funeral Home. The Keene City Council has been asked to subsidize that serviced next year, and City Manager Peter L. Cheney has asked for $25,000 for that purpose.

The council last week approved an emergency appropriation of $3,500 to keep the Foley ambulance running temporarily.

It is uncertain what effect a new ambulance service will have on the subsidy for Foley's, or whether both services will continue at the same time.

However, Bingham made it clear today that he will compete with the Foley Funeral Home on a business basis.

————

As Reported by *Boston (UPI)* December 30th, 1975.

"STORY"

Fire Deaths Rise in 1975

Nearly 12,000 Americans died in fires during 1975, according to the National Fire Protection Association.

Fire-related deaths rose by 200 over 1974, the Boston-based research group said Monday. Fire-related property damage during the year amounted to about $3.8 billion.

————

1976

As Reported by the *Keene Evening Sentinel* January 15th, 1976:

"STORY"

Ambulance Policy to be Discussed

Cressey Goodwin, director of the state Emergency Medical Services agency, will talk about ambulance service and emergency medical treatment in Keene, Jan. 22.

Goodwin will address interested officials and citizens at a meeting sponsored by the Cheshire County Emergency Medical Services District in cooperation with Cheshire Hospital and the Keene city government. The meeting will begin at 7:30 p.m. Jan. 22 in the hospital auditorium.

Thomas R. Morton, chairman of the county emergency medical services district said the meeting is an attempt to answer questions that have arisen about ambulance service in Keene and towns in the area.

Morton hopes the meeting will help his group meet its obligation of planning and coordinating emergency medical services in the region.

Keene City Manager Peter L. Cheney said the meeting will give local government officials and area hospital and medical personnel a chance to learn more abo0ut ambulance service and its relationship to other medical services.

Cheney said the meeting is tied to changes in the financing of ambulance service in the area. Keene's only ambulance service, the Robert J. DiLuzio Ambulance Service, has asked the city government for a substantial subsidy this year, saying financial problems will force the service to shut down without city help.

Morton said the emergency medical services district will also hold its annual meeting Jan. 22, and will elect new officers.

More information is available through the city manager's office or through Morton, who can be reached at 352-0310, extension 246, from 7 a.m. to 3:30 p.m. or 352-3356 after 3:30.

_____

As Reported by the *Keene Evening Sentinel* January 21st, 1976:

"STORY"

Cheney, Chief Defend Request for Four New Firefighters

Should Keene have four more firemen? The fire chief thinks so, and so does the city manager. But it will be up to the Keene City Council to decide on Feb. 25.

Meanwhile, the council's Finance Committee is continuing its review of a $5.8 million budget proposed for this year by City Manager Peter L. Cheney, an increase of $1.6 million from 1975. On Tuesday night, the committee covered requests for fire prevention inspections, mental health, and retired persons in the fourth of ten planned review sessions.

Cheney's budget is up in nearly every area, but the increase for the fire department is substantial and Chief Robert N. Guyette and Cheney spent about two hours explaining their requests to the committee.

Budget requests in the fire department are up from $449,309 in 1975 to $513,896 proposed this year, an increase of $64,598.

The addition would also boost the budget in other areas, such as uniforms and training.

Guyette says the four new firefighters would increase this coverage of the Keene fire station during the day and reduce the workweek for firefighters from 63 hours to 56 hours.

If you're going to have a fire in Keene, have it after 9 p.m., please—that's Guyette's ironic message. Under the present system, an eight man shift covers the city during the day, but two of those men are at the airport, one is inspecting buildings, one is repairing fire alarm systems spread throughout the city, and another might have the day off. And if someone is sick, that means only three men can answer a first alarm from the Keene fire station.

Since a first alarm in some areas—downtown, for example—calls for two engines and a ladder truck, Keene firemen may have to head for a fire with too few men and too little equipment.

Coverage gets better at night, Guyette says, because men come back from fixing alarms, inspecting buildings and covering the airport.

Under the present system, there are two shifts of firefighters. Each works 24 hours and then has 24 hours off. Every third working day, a firefighter takes a day off. It all amounts to an average 63-hour week for Keene firefighters.

If the council approves the request for four new firemen, a new system will be inaugurated. There will be three shifts. Each will work two ten-hour days, two 14-hour nights and take two days off. That will average out to a 50-hour week and give Guyette additional coverage in the Keene station.

Cheney said cutting the length of the work week will bring Keene into line with other cities in the state, and a proposed federal law may require that the 63-hour work week be abandoned anyway.

In another large request, Guyette said it's time to buy a new fire engine. There is already $34,000 in reserve fund for that expenditure, and Cheney wants to add $30,000 to the fund this year.

In other business, the finance committee reviewed requests by the city inspections department for $67,724, an increase of $2,288;

$10,329 for Monadnock Family and Mental Health Service, the same sum as last year; and $1,850 for the Retired Senior Volunteer Program, and increase of $925.

The finance committee will make its recommendations on all budget requests at the last review session Feb 7.

———————

As Reported by the *Keene Evening Sentinel* January 22nd, 1976:

"STORY"

Keene Ambulance Service Requests Subsidies From Towns in the Area

The Robert J. DiLuzio Ambulance Service in Keene is seeking operating subsidies from area towns this year, in addition to $25,000 of aid being considered now by the Keene City Council.

In letters being send out today, DiLuzio has requested a total subsidy of about $15,000 from towns in Cheshire County.

Without the funds, he said, the ambulance service will be in serious shape and may be forced out of business.

DiLuzio's is the only ambulance service in Keene, and it serves 18 towns in Cheshire County which do not have their own ambulance.

A county-wide meeting will be held tonight at Cheshire Hospital to discuss emergency medical service coverage in Cheshire County, and town officials have been urged to attend the session.

Cressey Goodwin, director of the N.H. Emergency Medical Services Agency will address the meeting on ambulance service and emergency medical treatment.

———————

As Reported by the *Keene Evening Sentinel* February 9th, 1976:

"STORY"

Committee Won't Endorse New City Staff Positions

Keene city government may grow a little this year, but probably not as much as City Manager Peter L. Cheney thinks it should.

The Finance Committee of the Keene City Council, at its all-day budget review session last Saturday, recommended that four firefighters be added to the fire department, but other proposals by Cheney to add employees to the city's labor force were either not recommended or were reduced.

The council is expected to act on the recommendations when it adopts a budget Feb. 25, following a public hearing Feb. 18. Cheney's budget package is set at $5.8 million, $1.6 million more than the 1975 appropriation. Much of the sum will be paid by other revenues, so city taxpayers will be asked to raise $2.2 million, an increase of $680,000 over last year.

The finance committee recommended reductions of more than $320,000 Saturday and still has not finished its work, but is expected to do so by Wednesday.

———

As Reported by the *Keene Evening Sentinel* March 19th, 1976:

"FIRE"

Fire Guts Barn at Keene Home

Fire gutted a combination barn and garage at 127 Washington St. late Thursday night, and one fireman was injured slightly when a slate shingle fell on him during the blaze.

The fireman, Edmund E. Hutchins of 47 Meadow Road, was treated for an arm injury at Cheshire Hospital and released.

Cause of the blaze, and the full extent of damage, was not immediately determined.

The barn is attached to a house and office owned by Dr. Homer L. Ash at Washington and Beaver Streets. The building was gutted and fire turned through the roof, but the structure remained standing.

Mrs. Ash reported the fire at 11:21 p.m. Thursday, and firemen were at the scene until 1 a.m. putting out the two-alarm blaze.

The interior of the two-story building was charred, windows were broken out and sections of the slate roof were burned through.

———

As Reported by the *Keene Evening Sentinel* March 29th, 1976:

"STORY"

First Safety Awards are Presented in Keene

Award Winners – Patrolman Bruce Boucher, left and firefighters Steve Goldsmith and Ronald Amadon were the recipients of exceptional service awards in the Keene Safety Service Awards breakfast Saturday. Photo by Hackler.

Twenty-Year Awards were given by Rev. Kenneth Bachelder (center) to four firemen during the Keene Fire and Police Awards breakfast Saturday morning, receiving awards were, from left: Homer

L. Atkins, Frederick, H Beauchesne, Wesley J. Peets Jr. and Clark Rowell. Photo by Latamore.

Keene started a new tradition Saturday as it held the city's first safety service awards program.

The event, thought to be the only one of its kind in the state, got off the ground at 7 a.m. Saturday in the Keene Fire Station with a breakfast. The presentation of awards followed, with men receiving certificates, medals and citations bars in five of the six safety award categories.

Michael J. White was the sole recipient of the citizen's award, which goes to persons who initiate and carry out community safety programs, mostly directed toward school children.

Two men received the community service award. Paul E. Crowell was named for 14 years of service to the Boy Scouts and Keene Police Sgt. Hugh M. McLellan for five years work with the Keene Boys' Basketball Association.

The educational achievement award went to three men. Sgt. Blaine M. McLellan was honored with this award for being the first member of the Keene Police Department to obtain an associate degree in law enforcement. Two other men, Fire Inspector Homer L. Atkins and Fire Capt Chester E. Dubriske, were named for their work toward degrees related to safety services.

Three men were recipients of the exceptional service award, which is given to persons who help improve the safety program. Ronald P. Amadon, a Keene firefighter, was named for off-duty time spent preparing the training field and tower for the fire department, firefighter Steven W. Goldsmith, Jr., was honored for off-duty time working with children and teachers in fire safety, and Bruce J. Boucher, a Keene police patrolman, was named for the capture of two burglary suspects in two separate cases, within an 11 day period. Both men were convicted.

In all, 58 persons received honorable service certificates. Nine of those persons, who have served more than 20 years on the police or fire departments, also received medals and citation bars.

William H. Sanderson tops the list with 35 years of service as an on-call fireman. Laurence E. Thompson was named for 30 years as a permanent fireman and Frederick S. Bingham for 30 years as an on-call fireman.

Fire Chief Robert N. Guyette was honored for 35 years of service.

Named for 30 years of service were Homer L. Atkins, (permanent fireman), Clark R. Rowell (call fireman), Robert F. Donovan (policeman), Wesley J. Peets Jr. (call fireman) and Frederick H. Beauchesne (fireman).

Eleven persons were named for 15 years of service, 14 for 10 years of service and 24 persons for five years of service.

This year, no one received an award in the sixth category, which is a medal of honor for persons who risked or gave their lives in a heroic act beyond the call of duty.

For 15 years' service:

Allan O. Collier, Robert F. Driscoll, Ronald P. Amadon, Paul E. Crowell, Laurence V. Wood, John W. Little, John N. Phillips, Chester E. Dubriske, H. Emile Derosier, John J. Byrnes and Thomas N. Lacroix.

For 10 years' service:

Bernard N. Blancato, Russell P. Cloutier, George H. Sheppard Jr., John H. Dennis Jr., Robert J. DiLuzio, Harold D. Nash, Robert W. Raymond, Edward P. LaBounty, Everett W. Simonds, Armand R. Jacques, Douglas K. Fish, Blain M. McLellan, David C. Robinson and Frank W. Smith.

For five years' service:

Allan S. Collier, Phillip L. Davis, Francis J. Driscoll, John S. Marechal, Paul E. Symonds, Jr., Barry G. Pearston, Wayne A. Spofford,

James A. Beauregard, Bruce N. Cloutier, James E. Harris, Harry H. Johnson, Frederick R. Laffond, Thomas R. Morton, Wilfred E. Begin, Alexander W. Matxon, Sr., Robert A. Mason, William J. Olmstead, David G. Hackler, Hugh M. McLellan, William K. Sargent Jr., Robert S. Snow and Robert H. Hardy.

As Reported by the *Keene Evening Sentinel* April 14th, 1976:

"STORY

The Accident: What Happens After You Call Out for Help?

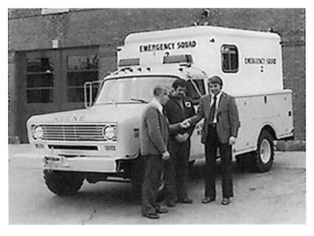

Rescuers - Delivery of Keene's new Emergency Rescue Squad, acceptance (from L to R) Chief Robert N. Guyette, Dealer Bob Bergavin of the International Garage, and Jack Saum from International Harvester Dealer.

You've just wrapped your car around a tree. You're pinned behind the steering wheel, not in pain exactly, but reality seems strange—sirens, voices, lights. It occurs to you that you may die, and then everything darkens.

What happens next involves many people much equipment and an intricate communications system. It's society's best try in this area to save your life.

A single accident in Keene may involve the police department, fire department,

Southwestern N.H. Fire Mutual Aid, a private ambulance service, and Cheshire Hospital.

It's likely that emergency service will be set into action by a telephone call to the police, 352-2222, or to mutual aid, 352-1100. Police and fire numbers are on the inside flap of your telephone book.

Mutual aid, centered in the Keene fire station, is the control center for Cheshire County, plus other parts of the state and some of eastern Vermont.

It's a complex system, uniquely suited for this area, according to Robert C. Callahan, chief coordinator of mutual aid, which began on a much smaller scale back in 1955.

Mutual aid and the Keene police can monitor each other's phone calls, so if a call goes to the police, mutual aid will receive the information within seconds. Mutual aid, informed of a personal injury accident, will dispatch the Keene Fire Department's new emergency rescue truck—it went into service last December—and Robert J. DiLuzio Ambulance Service, which has a crew on call 24 hours a day and three ambulances available.

Meanwhile, the police dispatcher has already directed a police cruiser to the scene.

In the case of a fire, mutual aid can broadcast on the home monitors of firemen to inform them of the problems, and also ring the fire bell at the proper fire station.

With the help of charts, a clever filing system and a lot of radio equipment, the two mutual aid dispatchers on duty know who to call for which incidents, and they can keep track of several emergencies simultaneously. They also have a backup system in case a fire or ambulance group is already busy. They also keep track of some 300 burglar alarms from various businesses and homes which are wired into the control center.

The control center is full of equipment, buttons, switches, lights, tapes and panels. This equipment is hooked up to lines, leased from the New England Telephone Co. which run to mutual aid's radio towers in Hyland Hill in Westmoreland. From there, messages are transmitted and received for miles around.

Each city and town is assessed a certain sum depending on it size and wealth, by the county government to pay for mutual aid.

Now back to the accident. The policeman arrives at the scene, but he can't get into the car because the door is bent shut against the unconscious driver. The police officer relays the information to his dispatcher, and the information is monitored by mutual aid.

A fire truck and rescue truck are already on the way and the firefighters are notified by radio of what to expect.

The fire truck arrives and firefighters wash away the gasoline. Meanwhile, a fire officer and two firefighters in the rescue truck see they'll have to force the door open to get the victim out.

He's alive, and they take his pulse and perform necessary first aid before taking the door off.

The officer in charge decides they'll have to use a Hurst tool to open the door. This device—Deputy Fire Chief John Phillips calls it the "jaws of life"—is the biggest, strongest, most expensive can opener in this area.

Handled by two men and running on portable power with a variety of attachments, the "jaws of life" can cut open a car door, rip off a dashboard or pry into a wreck. The Hurst tool cost more than $5,000 and was donated by Hubbard Farms of Walpole and Bruce and James Pollock of Keene.

The Hurst tool is the most glamorous of the tools on the lime green emergency truck, but not the only one. In fact, the truck is crammed with hundreds of pieces of first aid and rescue equipment, including a respirator, portable power tools and hand tools.

"There's about $25,000 sunk into that truck," said Keene Fire Chief Robert N. Guyette. Of that sum, $10,000 was put up by

the state and $10,000 locally. The donation for the Hurst tool accounts for the rest.

Although the truck has been in operation only since late last year, the Hurst tool has been used several times, and "it works just fine," said Phillips.

Guyette says the truck has already proven its value and should continue to do so. The department is currently training all its men to use equipment of the emergency truck.

Guyette noted that training for firefighters is becoming more extensive every year.

At our hypothetical accident, the police are directing traffic and trying to determine what happened. The firefighters, with the help of the "jaws of life," have opened the front door so that the driver can be removed. But for the moment he stays where he is.

"People at the scene expect you to load the victim on a stretcher and haul him to the hospital right away, but that's not often the best thing to do," said Robert J. DiLuzio, president of Keene's only ambulance service.

The two-person ambulance crew examines the victim to get some idea of injuries. They take his pulse and perhaps his blood pressure. They look for symptoms of broken bones or internal injuries. They try to stop bleeding.

But before they move the victim, they call the emergency room at Cheshire Hospital by radio and talk to the doctor on duty. The doctor listens to the radio report and advises the ambulance personnel on how the victim is to be moved.

If spinal or neck injuries are suspected, the victim may have to be completely immobilized on the spot, with the help of up to a dozen special splints, before being moved.

Sometimes fire or ambulance officials have to apply mouth-to-mouth resuscitation, or perhaps a resuscitator is used.

Hospital authorities, in touch with officials on the scene by radio, have a pretty good idea of what to expect by the time the ambulance reaches the hospital.

The percentage of what DiLuzio calls DOA's (dead on arrival) is down to near zero these days, thanks to improved equipment and training among police, fire and ambulance personnel.

DiLuzio credits a state law, passed in 1971, for improved emergency service in the area. The law forced ambulance services to get new equipment and provide medical training for their personnel.

Ten years ago, the numbe3r of victims dead on arrival was much higher that it is today, DiLuzio said.

Towns outside of Keene are served by other rescue squads and ambulance services, and mutual aid can call upon the right unit for any particular emergency at any time.

————

As Reported by the *Keene Evening Sentinel* April 19th, 1976:

"STORY"

4 at KSC Charged on False Alarms

Three Keene State College students and a KSC residence director were arraigned in Keene District Court this morning on charges connected with false fire alarms at the college.

All the cases were continued by Judge James S. Davis.

The students were charged in connection with two separate incidents of apparent false alarms at KSC last month, and the residence director was accused of blocking the apprehension of two of the students.

Arraigned on a single count of false public alarm were Dean N. Kontinos, 20 of Nashua, William J. Welch, 20 of Manchester and John D. Thaute, 19, of Swampscott, Mass.

All are full-time students at the college, according to the registrar's office.

The residence director, Raymond Holz, 25, of Dean's Hall on Butler Court, was formally charged with hindering the prosecution of Welch and Kontinos.

The court warrants charge Welch and Ko0ntinos with setting fire to a piece of paper in the Owl's Nest, a KSC dorm, causing sufficient heat and smoke to set off a smoke detector which summons Keene Fire Department equipment.

The incident allegedly occurred at about 5:50 p.m. March 29.

The charge against Holz states that he allegedly was aware of the false alarm, but told a Keene police officer and Keene Fire Chief Robert N. Guyette that he knew nothing about it.

Thaute is charged with a separate incident of turning in a false alarm. Court records show he is charged with setting off a false alarm March 6 at 12:30 a.m. in Carle Hall, another KSC dormitory. His case was continued.

The charges against the four men were made following a Keene Police Department investigation headed by Inspector John J. Byrnes.

Meanwhile, City Manager Peter L. Cheney is preparing a report analyzing the sharp increase in false alarms for a Keene City Council committee.

Cheney said this morning he plans to complete the report sometime this week and forward it to the council's Public Safety Committee.

False alarms are up sharply this year from comparable periods a year ago; according to fire department statistics, and Cheney said more false alarms have been coming in from KSC, although he declined today to estimate the percentage of false alarms from the college.

In the first three months of 1976, the fire department registered 14 false alarms, while the same three month period in 1975 saw just 6, the fire department report stated.

––––––––

As Reported by the *Keene Evening Sentinel* April 29th, 1976:

"FIRE"

MPB Fire Does Little Damage

A small fire at MPB Corp. early this morning caused little damage but a lot of smoke, as about 20 employees on the third shift had to clear the building for about one hour.

No injuries were reported, and damage to the building was listed as minor by company officials, although a $1,000 unit which clears oil mist from automatic screw machines was ruined.

Company employees had extinguished the fire when Keene firefighters arrived about 2:30 a.m. according to James A. Levins, company general manager. But the firefighters remained to clear smoke for about an hour.

The fire began after an electrical short circuit in a "Percipitron Unit," which clears oil mist, Levins said.

The automatic screw machine itself was not damaged.

––––––––

As Reported by the *Keene Evening Sentinel* May 18th, 1976:

"STORY"

DiLuzio to Halt Ambulances Without Subsidy from City

The Robert J. DiLuzio Ambulance Service will stop running if the Keene city government doesn't renew its subsidy for the service.

DiLuzio, on the advice of his attorney, plans to present argument to the Keene City Council Finance Committee, which meets tonight to consider the ambulance question.

Meanwhile, an ambulance question appointed recently by Keene Mayor George M. Rossiter met for the first time Monday night: its job is to recommend the future of city ambulance service.

DiLuzio said today that his lawyer and accountant will attend the finance committee meeting tonight, and that his attorney has advised him to prepare a notice to terminate ambulance service unless the city subsidizes the service.

Early this year, the city council voted 8-7 to put $25,000 in the city budget to subsidize an ambulance service, and later voted to pay a month-to-month subsidy to DiLuzio, who runs the only ambulance service in Keene.

The council approved two months' worth of subsidy, but DiLuzio hasn't been subsidized since April 30th.

At the last council meeting May 6, at large Councilor L. Edward Reyor introduced a resolution asking that no further subsidies be paid to DiLuzio until completion of a certified audit of the company's books at the time DiLuzio took over the former Foley Ambulance Service.

DiLuzio said this morning he has done everything the city has asked, and that an accounting firm has prepared a certified financial statement for the books of the former Foley service and of the present DiLuzio service. The statement should satisfy the council, he said and that an audit would be both costly and time consuming.

City Manager Peter L. Cheney declined comment on the ambulance subsidy question this morning.

On Monday night, the six-member ambulance study committee—chaired by Ward 3 Councilor Phillip G. Taaffe—discussed options the city government can pursue for ambulance service.

♕   *A Demon Called Fire*

Alan C. Merrill, a committee member and chairman of the Winchester Ambulance Department, said there are only a few options to pursue. Have a municipal service operated by either the police or fire departments, subsidize a private operation like DiLuzio's or have a volunteer force to man a city owned ambulance.

However, Cheney said another possibility would be to form a new municipal agency for ambulance service or to seek county government ambulance service.

The committee was formed after the council approved the $25,000 subsidy Councilors said they didn't want to subsidize a private operation if better and more efficient service were possible if the city invested its money elsewhere. Mayor Rossiter appointed the study committee to advise the council on possibilities for ambulance service.

Late last fall, DiLuzio announced that his ambulance service was losing money and would be forced to close if Keene and several nearby communities didn't supply a subsidy.

All but two communities asked for a subsidy supplied one, although Troy agreed to subsidize DiLuzio only until its own municipal ambulance arrived. The ambulance was delivered in late April.

Some towns in Cheshire County have their own ambulance services, but many rely on DiLuzio. Merrill urged committee members considering ambulance service in Keene to remember that their recommendations could have an impact on service in nearby communities.

Without getting into specifics, committee members discussed ambulance services they were familiar with and kicked around some suggestions for Keene.

Merrill recommended that the city think in terms of something more than a volunteer force because of the number of calls (700 – 800 a year) in Keene.

He and Cheney also said some charge should be levied for any service because without one, Merrill said, "people would call for a toothache."

Cheney said the city could provide strictly emergency service, with one vehicle and let a commercial business, like DiLuzio's, serve as a back-up to handle other calls.

Rossiter pointed out one problem with that system.

"How do you separate an emergency medical problem from someone wanting a free ride across town? How do you say no?" he said.

Subsidizing a service can be costly. In Laconia, Cheney said, which is smaller than Keene, the cost is $72,000 a year; in Nashua, a larger city, the cost is $120,000.

DiLuzio said today his operation meets all the standards set for ambulance service.

"The only thing I can't meet is my payroll," he said.

DiLuzio disputed allegations that he needs the subsidy because of mismanagement. His books are open to the public, he said, and anyone can look at them.

In addition, he said, he has turned over $14,000 in unpaid accounts to a collection agency and said the city can't tell him he's not trying to collect from individual persons he serves.

DiLuzio said he will accept the subsidy payment "anyway the city wants to disperse it," including through a bank.

And, while the ambulance committee debates alternatives like police or fire department service, DiLuzio said several large cities have shifted away from that system—finding it too costly—in favor of subsidized or contracted service.

————

As Reported by the *Keene Evening Sentinel* May 20th, 1976:

City Panel Favors 4-Month Subsidy for Ambulance Service by DiLuzio

Tuesday was a difficult but successful night for Robert J. DiLuzio.

The Keene City Council Finance Committee conducted a lengthy grilling of DiLuzio but in the end, voted 3-2 to recommend that the council approve a $2,200 a-month, subsidy for the DiLuzio Ambulance Service through August.

DiLuzio's subsidy request goes to the full council Thursday, and another close vote is expected.

On Tuesday morning, DiLuzio said he would stop serving Keene if the city didn't renew its subsidy, which ran out April 30.

The warning angered Ward 5 Councilor Richard P. Peloquin, who said Tuesday night that DiLuzio had promised early this year to continue serving g the city, whether the council agreed to subsidize his service or not.

However, DiLuzio said he can't continue to operate in Keene without a city subsidy, and if the council doesn't approve the money, he will serve only those communities which subsidize his service.

If that happens, it's doubtful that Keene would be left without ambulance service, although the closing of DiLuzio's service would cause chaos and could cost the city more than the amount of the subsidy, said Alan C. Merrill, secretary of the Cheshire County Emergency Medical Services District.

Merrill said the district board would act quickly to ensure some sort of ambulance coverage for Keene, but that he couldn't guarantee coverage.

———

As Reported by the *Keene Evening Sentinel* May 21st, 1976:

DiLuzio Gives City Ultimatum: Extend Funds for the Rest of Year

Members of the Keene City Council felt like Robert J. DiLuzio was pointing a gun at their heads Thursday night.

And unless the council acts quickly, DiLuzio says he'll pull the trigger in ten days.

DiLuzio, in a letter read to the council Thursday night, cited "antagonism… far more than we can tolerate," and gave council members an ultimatum: Subsidize his ambulance service through December, or face loss of his service as of May 31.

Councilors expressed shock that DiLuzio hadn't given them any warning about the cutoff of ambulance service.

The council voted 13-2 Thursday night to extend a $2,022-a-month subsidy for the DiLuzio Ambulance Service through August—but City Manager Peter L. Cheney informed councilors that DiLuzio had informed him 90 minutes before the council meeting started that the four month subsidy wouldn't be enough.

Service would be stopped May 31 if the council didn't approve a subsidy through December, DiLuzio said in a letter which Cheney read to councilors.

DiLuzio said this morning he suggested to Cheney last week that the subsidy he extended through December, and then decided Monday that without the full-year subsidy he would stop serving Keene at the end of this month.

Neither DiLuzio nor Cheney made that point at a meeting of the council's Finance Committee Tuesday night. DiLuzio said he didn't mention the matter to the committee because he thought Cheney would.

Cheney refused all comment on the ambulance situation this morning.

"On the advice of our attorney, Richard J. Talbot, we regret to inform you that we will terminate emergency ambulance to the residents of Keene at midnight on May 31, 1976, unless we can be assured of subsidy payments through December.

"We will, however, be most happy to furnish any information to the city ambulance committee and to work with them in any way to resolve this problem."

DiLuzio said the decision to terminate servide3 without the full subsidy was made on the advice of his attorney on Monday.

He said he assumed Cheney would bring his request for a full subsidy before the finance committee Tuesday night, but since the city manager didn't, he decided against mentioning it himself.

"I'm not putting them against the wall. I'm not trying to hide anything. But I don't need the hassle. I've given them everything they wanted. It's a personality conflict now." DiLuzio said this morning. He added that he has been receiving threatening telephone calls.

————

As Reported by the *Keene Evening Sentinel* May 26th, 1976:

"STORY"

The Ambulance Subsidy Controversy: Six-Month Question Nears Resolution

The same questions, the same answers and the same arguments have marked Robert J. DiLuzio's six-month quest for an ambulance service subsidy.

Only a handful of the 15 members of the Keene City Council have changed their stance on the issue since it surfaced last December. Most, for one reason or another, admit the dispute has left a bitter aftertaste.

Each time the subsidy question has arisen, the funds have been approved, mostly on close votes. And, in every instance, at least one councilor has cited a "lack of alternatives" as the reason for his endorsement.

An unaudited financial statement pegs DiLuzio's net loss for 1975 at $26,694. It is this money he hopes to recoup from the city in the form of a subsidy.

DiLuzio's financial battles with his ambulance service publicly surfaced last month when he asked for and received a temporary ten-week subsidy to tide him over until the 1976 city budget was finalized. Without it, he said, he would have to close up shop.

He gave the council six days to act on his request.

In the meantime, DiLuzio's March-April subsidy had run out and the city had taken no action to renew it. At-large Councilor L. Edward Reyor, however, had introduced a motion asking that DiLuzio be given no further payments until a certified audit had been done of both the ambulance and funeral home financial books from the time he bought the business from Frank J. Foley, Sr.

On May 18, the finance committee met to act on motion and on a four-month extension of DiLuzio's subsidy. That morning, DiLuzio said he would cease city service unless the subsidy was renewed.

The four-month extension was granted by a wide margin, and Reyor's resolution was defeated by the same 13-2 vote, but the council failed to muster a two-thirds majority to suspend its rules and act on the full subsidy.

————

As Reported by the *Keene Evening Sentinel* May 28th, 1976:

"STORY"

DiLuzio Wins Battle, Gets City Ambulance Subsidy for Rest of Year

Robert J. DiLuzio won a long-fought battle for a city ambulance service subsidy Thursday night as the Keene City Council, on a 9-4 vote, promised to pay him $2,022 a month through December.

In return, DiLuzio has promised to serve the city through next February—to give the council's ambulance study committee time to recommend a permanent solution for city ambulance service and to ensure service through finalization of the 1977 city budget.

The council, after hearing comments from DiLuzio's attorney and from Frank Foley, Jr. approved the subsidy extension with no debate; Richard P. Peloquin, Ward 5, Bruce R. Anderson, Ward 3, L Edward Reytor, At-large and Priscilla F. Bachelder, Ward 4 cast the opposing votes.

———————

As Reported by the *Keene Evening Sentinel* June 11th, 1976:

"FIRE"

Barn Fire Destroys Building

Firemen douse remains of Walsh Barn on Silent Way, Thursday afternoon. Photo by Kearney.

A two-alarm fire Thursday afternoon destroyed a story-and-a-half barn belonging to Richard F. Walsh on Silent Way in south Keene.

The barn, about 50 by 20 feet in size was used to house horses and store garden equipment. However, no horses were in the barn at the time of the fire and no injuries to persons or animals were reported, according to Keene fire officials.

The cause of the blaze is unknown, Keene Fire Chief Robert N. Guyette said, and the matter is under investigation.

The fire was first reported at 2:37 p.m. by a NH State Trooper who spotted smoke rising in south Keene. Moments later officials received a call from Walsh. Smoke was visible more than five miles away.

The fire had gotten a strong start by the time, firefighters reached the scene, Guyette said. Firefighters from Keene, Swanzey Center, and Marlborough fought the blaze until 4:25, although it was under control within 20 minutes after firefighters arrived.

Units from Surry covered the Keene fire station while Keene firefighters were at the blaze.

———————

As Reported by the *Keene Evening Sentinel* June 18th, 1976:

"STORY"

Brand New Fire Truck Due Soon

Keene's new Fire Truck has arrived. Photo by Steve Goldsmith.

The City of Keene is going to get itself a better fire truck for the same amount of money planned in the 1976 city budget, but in less time.

That was the good news delivered to the Keene City Council Thursday night in a written memo from City Manager Peter L. Cheney.

The council budgeted $64,000 this year for a new fire truck, expecting to wait nine months to a year from the signing of a contract until the actual delivery of the truck. In addition, it expected to pay a sale price based on materials and manpower costs at the time of delivery.

No so, according to Cheney's report.

Cheney, in his communication, said that under a new program started by two fire equipment manufacturers "stock models" can be bought as they come off the assembly line.

It is one of these pumpers that the city is buying.

Cheney figures that the city will save between $8,000 and $10,000 because it will be bought at today's costs and that Keene will be getting a better fire truck in the bargain.

The new pumper will cost $68,500 and will be paid for with the $64,000 already in the budget and the returns from the trade-in of the fire department's 1957 Ward LaFrance truck. He figures that the city will get at least $5,000 for the trade-in.

"We're getting a better truck for the budgeted amount," he said this morning.

What's "better" about the truck is list in his communication; a larger pump, a diesel engine, automatic transmission, improved pump gauges, mou7nted deck gun and an enclosed five-man cab, which Cheney said is safer because it lets firemen ride inside the truck instead of on the tailboard.

The new pumper will be delivered in the next two to three weeks.

————

As Reported by the *Keene Evening Sentinel* July 1st, 1976:

"STORY"

State Official Outlines City Ambulance Options

Already chock-full of potential alternatives, Keene's ambulance study committee plans just one more information-gathering session before it sits down to hammer out a plan for future city ambulance service.

Wednesday night Cressey Goodwin, director of the N.H. Emergency Medical Services agency, filled the committee members heads with suggestions and warned them that their task is not an easy one.

Goodwin said there are three basic categories of ambulance service. The city can provide the service for itself, the city can contract for the service or a volunteer force can be trained.

The committee however, has just about ruled out volunteer service for a city the size of Keene and is concentrating instead on several options of contracted or municipal services.

Although volunteer forces provide almost 80 per cent of the ambulance service statewide, they are for the most part in rural areas. Goodwin said, however, there are six other options he said.

Of all commercial services the combined funeral-ambulance business is the most prevalent. Goodwin said, but there are also some commercial services p0-rovided strictly for a profit.

Municipal service provided through a city police department is rapidly on the wain, Goodwin said, while services run by fire departments are rapidly growing.

The committee's two other alternatives are to either create a separate municip0al ambulance department with its own chief or develop a hospital-based service. Trustees at Cheshire Hospital, however, have already said they're not interested in providing the service.

Goodwin suggested that the committee decide exactly what ambulance service it wants and then draw up a list of specifications required from the provider. He warned against having an existing ambulance service operator draw up the list to avoid the possibility that he may later bid on his own specifications.

The committee will decide what training personnel should have the type of vehicle and equipment needed, where the service will be based and several other questions before it sits down to "cost things out," Goodwin said.

City Manager Peter L. Cheney said if bids are sought, the city would be the victim of the low bidder. He asked Goodwin how it could make judgment about the capabilities of an unknown commercial operator.

If the service is put out to bid, Goodwin said, the city could require the provider to post a performance bond guaranteeing the required level of service.

Goodwin said collection rates for municipal services are usually higher than those that are commercially operated. While a commercial operator may collect only 30 per cent of his bills, the rate for municipal services is often around 80 or 90 per cent, he said.

Robert J. DiLuzio, the city's current ambulance service provider, received a $25,000 city subsidy for his service this year after he told city officials he could no longer afford to operate his business without one.

DiLuzio earlier estimated that he collected about 40 per cent of his bills. However, his May activity schedule—which goes to the Keene City Council tonight—shows he took in $213 of the $4,000 in bills he sent out during May, or only five per cent.

A questionnaire is being sent out to ambulance service operators in cities about the same size as Keene in New Hampshire,

Vermont and western Massachusetts to help the committee's study.

Included are questions concerning the number of vehicles, hours of coverage, manpower, financing and the number of bills collected in those towns.

————

As Reported by the *Keene Evening Sentinel* July 11th, 1976:

"STORY"

Keene Parade July 11; Biggest in City's History

Yes, Virginia, there will be a parade in Keene celebrating the national bicentennial.

In fact, local officials believe the parade July 11 will be the biggest in the state during the bicentennial year and the biggest in the history of the city.

"Some people seem to be wondering whether we're going to have a parade at all," said Robert A. Candello of the American Revolution Bicentennial Commissions Parade Committee. "I don't understand it. We've been working on this for two and a half years. This is going to be the biggest parade in the state. I guess it's time to get out the publicity.

If the weather is good, officials expect 30,000 or more people to line Washington, Main and Marlboro Streets to watch the parade.

The parade is scheduled to start at the Keene Parks and Recreation Center on Washington Street at noon, proceed south on Washington Street, march around the square, then south on the west side of Main Street to Marlboro Street and break up on the vast grassy areas in the industrial park on Optical Avenue.

It may take as many as four hours before the parade is over.

The parade will include 34 bands, 50 floats, 20 marching units not including scouts and youth baseball teams, horse and ox-drawn wagons, 16 divisions and 162 units in all at a cost of $11,000.

The money already has been raised by various programs by the local commission.

Wednesday night the commission met to consider some of the hundreds of details involved in the bicentennial celebration.

————

As Reported by the *Keene Evening Sentinel* August 3rd, 1976:

"FIRE"

Mattress Fire Put Out in Keene

Keene firefighters responded to a double alarm at 81 Marlboro St just after midnight this morning, but found the fire there wasn't as serious at first expected.

The blaze turned out to be a smoldering bed mattress that firemen were able to take out of the apartment and extinguish, according to Keene Fire Department Deputy Chief Frederick H. Beauchesne.

The upstairs apartment at the Lewis Block was unoccupied at the time of the fire, and firemen are still trying to determine what caused the blaze, Beauchesne said.

The apartment suffered no damage from the fire, he added.

Beauchesne explained that the second alarm was called in because flames were seen through the window and fire officials wanted all available men and equipment in the event of a serious fire at the densely populated block.

————

As Reported by the *Keene Evening Sentinel* August 5th, 1976:

"FIRE"

Sawdust Shed hit by fire

An early-morning fire of suspicious origin struck a sawdust storage shed at Abbott Industries Inc. on Railroad Street.

Keene firefighters brought the two-alarm blaze under control within a half-hour of the alarm, but remained at the scene until about 5 a.m. to extinguish the stubborn blaze in the sawdust pile.

Keene Fire Chief Robert N. Guyette said that the fire was "of suspicious origin" and has called the state fire marshal's office to investigate the cause.

The story-and-a-half shed measured 30-by-20 feet and was burned severely on the inside.

It had been condemned and was scheduled to be pulled down this morning, according to Guyette.

Keene police are investigating a possible link between the blaze and an apparent burglary attempt at the former Princess Shoe building. A door there was discovered kicked open by a patrolman this morning.

The shed had probably been on fire for some time before it was discovered by a Keene policeman at about 3:30 a.m., according to Guyette, but an automatic sprinkler system that had been activated helped to keep the fire down.

————

As Reported by the *Keene Evening Sentinel* October 4th, 1976:

"STORY"

Parade, Muster, Open House Draw Big Crowds in Keene

About 5,000 people lined Keene streets Sunday for a massive parade that kicked off Fire Prevention Week in Keene.

Later, about 4,000 people went to the Cheshire Fairgrounds in North Swanzey and watched 16 teams of firefighters compete in a muster.

On Saturday, more than 1,000 people—at least half of them children—took a good look at Keene's Central Fire Station on Vernon Street.

A total of 73 fire vehicles were included in the parade, including 13 Keene trucks. Some 16 marching units, including nine bands, also participated.

In the end, two local units came away with awards, after judges examined the two-hour line of March.

The Alstead Fire Department's Ladies Auxiliary, whose members wore colonial costumes, won the "best appearance" award for auxiliaries. The award for best appearance for marching firemen went to Swanzey Center's contingent.

The Brattleboro, VT Union High School band won first prize for best musical organization, and the judges picked the Bissellville, MA unit as the best appearing muster team.

Units from Unionville, CT and Avon, CT traveled the farthest of any parade participants, and many units from Vermont and Massachusetts, as well as New Hampshire, joined the line of March.

After the parade ended, 16 muster teams competed for honors in six events, all involving speed, timing and accuracy in laying out hose, connecting it to a water source, and being ready to douse a potential fire.

When Keene firemen began planning an open house held Saturday, the believed it was to be the first in the department's history. However, it turns out the open house was at least the second for Keene's fire fighters.

Whatever number it was, it was a success, according to Keene firefighter A. Scott Collier, who organized the event. It turned out so well that similar programs probably will be arranged in the future, he said.

Collier estimated that more than 1,000 persons, at least half of them children, walked and ran through the central fire station during the six-hour open house Saturday, consuming at least 57 dozen doughnuts and lots of coffee and soda.

"The turnout was good, the weather was good, and the success of the open house showed us it would be a worthwhile thing to repeat in the future." Collier said.

There were generally few problems as children and adults inspected fire equipment, rang a bell or two, inspected the second story fire pole and talked to firemen.

Refreshments were served by members of the Keene Fire Department's Ladies Auxiliary and most of the edibles were donated by Keene merchants.

On display was firefighting equipment spanning 70 years.

————

As Reported by the *Keene Evening Sentinel* October 20th, 1976:

"FIRE"

Fire Guts Garage; Keene Man Injured

A Keene man received first aid for his second-degree burns late Tuesday afternoon when a gasoline fire raced through a garage at 187 Park Ave.

Bradford Crocker was tre3ated for burns on his legs at Cheshire Hospital and later released, a hospital spokesman said today.

Four pieces of equipment and about 30 men from the Keene Fire Department responded to the two-alarm blaze at the Richard D. Duhaime residence shortly after 5 p.m. and were able to bring the fire under control in less than half an hour.

The garage was gutted in the fire, and the attached house suffered extensive heat and smoke damage. Keene Fire Chief Robert N. Guyette said today. Also lost in the blaze were a pickup truck and several appliances, producing damage estimated in the thousands of dollars.

Guyette said the fire started when an electric lamp fell to the floor of the garage, breaking and igniting a pool of gasoline on the floor.

Crocker and David Wesson, another Keene man, were using the light while fixing the truck and apparently had the fuel line disconnected at the time the fire started, according to Guyette.

Both men are employees of Ed's Appliance Center Inc. of 238 Church St., of which Duhaime is a proprietor.

Guyette said Crocker was standing between the front end of the truck and the engine when the gas caught fire and had to jump out of the truck's front end to escape the flames.

"I consider him very lucky to have no more injuries than he had," the fire chief said.

Although the attached house had heat and smoke damage, firefighters were able to stop the fire at the breezeway between the house and the garage.

———

As Reported by the *Keene Evening Sentinel* October 28th, 1976:

"STORY"

Emergency Ambulance Service Will End in February: DiLuzio

Rescue Operation – A Walpole man is placed in the back of an ambulance for transport to Cheshire Hospital Sunday afternoon after he apparently skidded on a wet patch of road and ran through a guard rain on Route 10 in Swanzey. Photo by Perry.

Faced with too many problems and too many headaches Robert J. DiLuzio has decided to quit the emergency ambulance business.

The result is that the Keene city government which currently pays DiLuzio $25,000 a year in a subsidy to provide emergency ambulance service, probably will have to pay more for the same service in the future according to Mayor George M. Rossiter.

City Manager Peter L. Cheney has estimated that a city-run emergency ambulance service would cost about $64,500 a year Cheney, without making an outright recommendation, suggests in a report to a study committee that negotiating with a private ambulance business or accepting bids from firms may be a better way of dealing with the ambulance problem than getting the city into the ambulance business.

DiLuzio whose three ambulances currently serve Keene and some surrounding towns, will terminate emergency service Feb 28, 1977 DiLuzio indicated he will continue to provide non-emergency transfer service.

DiLuzio informed the city government of his decision in a letter from his attorney,

Richard J. Talbot to City Councilor Philip G. Taaffe, chairman of the city ambulance committee.

"This decision is final and unequivocal, regardless of whatever recommendation the study committee may take or whatever subsequent action may take or whatever subsequent action may be taken by the Keene City Council Emergency Services will not be provided to either the city of Keene or any of the surrounding towns. He does anticipate at this time providing non-emergency transfer service," Talbot wrote in the letter.

In the letter, DiLuzio offers to help the city study committee find an alternative to his ambulance service. DiLuzio recommends that the city provide emergency ambulance service.

"His personal feeling is that the best alternative would be to have the city of Keene provide emergency ambulance coverage, and he would like to have the opportunity to discuss this in detail with the committee." Talbot wrote.

DiLuzio this morning referred reporters to his lawyer on the ambulance matter.

Talbot said a combination of factors led to DiLuzio's decision. The factors included financial problems, and DiLuzio resented inquiries into his private business affairs after he accepted the subsidy funds.

At one point recently, a private citizen "walked in off the street and asked to see the books of DiLuzio's funeral business, Foley Funeral Home, Talbot said.

"There were just too many problems and too many headaches," Talbot said.

Rossiter sees DiLuzio's decision as causing problems and headaches for the city and town governments which DiLuzio now serves.

It's a big surprise and a big disappointment," Rossiter said. DiLuzio has provided "top quality professional service, and this tells me that if we want the same service, it's going to cost us more money."

"It's not just a city problem but an area problem," Rossiter said, and as a result, he has decided to invite selectmen of towns currently served by DiLuzio to meet with him Nov 8 to try to resolve the problem.

The DiLuzio decision will probably affect most towns in Cheshire County. DiLuzio either serves the towns directly, or—as in the case of Winchester, Marlborough, Harrisville, Troy, Fitzwilliam, Marlow, Peterborough and Jaffrey—he serves as a backup service to the towns regular service. Backup service is important because in many town services, ambulance drivers have other jobs and often are not available for emergencies.

DiLuzio currently provides regular emergency service in Swanzey, Surry, Sullivan, Nelson and parts of Chesterfield.

Another problem is that the city doesn't have much time to come up with an ambulance plan. The city council has been working on the problem for about ten months, but has failed to adopt a permanent policy.

Rossiter said he wants the ambulance committee to come up with a recommendation soon.

"We've been talking about this for ten or eleven months, and it's time we wrapped it up" Rossiter said.

If the city government decides to start its own ambulance business, the expenses will certainly be more than the $25,000 a year it currently pays DiLuzio, Rossiter believes.

If the city provides emergency ambulance service through the fire department, it could cost $64,500 a year, according to a report from Cheney to the ambulance study committee.

The projected costs include $37,500 for personnel and $11,500 for operating costs.

Cheney suggested in his report that "consideration is given to the private subsidized service. The process of selecting a provider of ambulance service would probably be either by negotiation or sealed comparative bids.

The Cheney report was compiled before DiLuzio released his decision to quit the emergency ambulance service business.

———

As Reported by the *Keene Evening Sentinel* November 9th, 1976:

"STORY"

2 Ambulance Options for Keene: Hire a Firm, or Start City Service

Out of Business – Robert J. DiLuzio's decision to stop emergency ambulance operations Feb 28th has left at least seven towns and the city of Keene scurrying to provide an alternate service before that date. Photo by Baker.

A committee studying Keene's ambulance needs has whittled down its suggestion list to two recommendations.

Philip G. Taaffe, Ward 3 member of the Keene City Council and chairman of the ambulance study committee, said this morning he plans to present both recommendations to the council for consideration.

The special study committee meets Wednesday night and Taaffe hopes to present its recommendations to the council Nov. 18.

Two broad choices will face the council Ambulance service provided by a municipal agency or ambulance service provided by a private contractor.

City Manager Peter L. Cheney, in a report the committee has not yet been discussed, estimates that it will cost $64,000 to have the Keene Fire Department run an ambulance service, using the Robert J. DiLuzio Ambulance Service as a backup.

Cheney said Monday night that DiLuzio who plans to end emergency service in March will stay in the nonemergency transfer business, will keep at least two of his ambulances, and that the city can probably contract with him to provide backup service.

DiLuzio said this morning he is willing to provide backup for a city run ambulance service. He said he plans to reduce his staff from twelve to four persons, sell one of his three ambulances, and keep his transfer service.

DiLuzio said he would want Keene and nearby towns to guarantee payment for any emergency calls he makes on a standby basis. However, he said he does not want to accept any more public funds—he currently receives a $25,000 a year subsidy from Keene, and subsidies from all the towns he serves—and would prefer to send his bills to the city or town served, and have them collect it.

DiLuzio, in requesting a subsidy last year, said he was losing money because people were not paying their bills.

The study committee will also meet Wednesday night with a person interested in providing ambulance service to Keene and towns that need it.

Gordon R. Davis of Troy, a former employee of DiLuzio and a trained emergency medical technician had told Taaffe he would provide coverage to Keene for $43,000

Taaffe said the person the committee was meeting with Wednesday he did not name Davis was offering 24-hour service, seven days a week, using two ambulances.

The $45,000 would cover the contract with Keene and other towns could work out arrangements for service, Taaffe said. In addition persons using the service would be charged $35 per call.

At a special meeting Monday night seven towns said they were dependi9ng on Keene to provide some form of emergency ambulance service. A dozen other towns said they were already adequately covered by their own squads, most of them manned by volunteers.

Mayor George M. Rossiter said this morning that the council must decide which option it wants to pursue. It will be easier and more manageable for the city to run its own service, he said, but it will also be more expensive.

If the council opts for a private contractor, Rossiter said it will probably want to negotiate with someone who has a proven track record. He suggested that if the council picks a private contractor, several nearby companies should be contacted to determine if any are interested in serving Keene.

"I'm leery of any organization not currently in business. It's too vital a service to go with someone's dreams. We can't afford to have low bidder when it comes to ambulance service." Rossiter said.

The city usually seeks bids on projects and awards the contract to the low bidder. However, Rossiter said that system will not work for ambulance service where quality is vital.

Although the mayor said he has not yet decided which option he prefers, he suggested it will be even harder for the city to conduct bills than it is for a private firm.

———

As Reported by the *Keene Evening Sentinel* November 16th, 1976:

Ambulance Committee Report Favors City-Operated Service

Five of the six members of Keene's Ambulance Study Committee favor a city run emergency ambulance system which would cost about $64,500 a year.

The committee neared the end of its career Monday night as it endorsed a report the Keene City Council will get Thursday night.

The report carries no recommendations on future ambulance service, but like the committee members, it means toward the municipal ambulance plan. The other option the committee will present to the council hiring a private ambulance firm is not discussed as favorably.

Committee members viewed the report compiled by City Manager Peter L. Cheney, for the first time Monday night and congratulated Cheney for his work.

The report concludes that "there are two alternatives available for providing ambulance service Municipal service or private service. If a private service is chosen, the report states the provider can be selected by either negotiation or open bidding, although it carries no recommendation.

The report doesn't answer all the questions the city council hoped it would.

The council authorized Mayor George M. Rossiter to appoint the study committee April 1. During committee deliberations on the matter Cheney suggested that the study committee consider three questions. Whether the city should have a municipal or private service, if a private service, whether the contractor should be selected by negotiation or open bidding, and what level of service should be provided.

The committee is recommending 24 hours coverage with two private or city owned ambulances, with backup service available immediately, that the present level of high quality service be maintained, and that service for surrounding towns be considered.

The report outlines what the committee has been doing for the past six months, and presents the two options, their impact, and the advantages and disadvantages of each.

However, there are no real disadvantages listed under the city run ambulance plan, and the few "advantages" mentioned about the private firm plan carry warnings about the method.

That section of the report contrasts with an Oct 18 report from Cheney to the committee, which appeared to lean toward a private ambulance firm. It asked that "consideration is given to the private subsidized service."

Since then, however, the Robert J. DiLuzio Ambulance Service has announced plants to end emergency ambulance service to Keene and the surrounding towns in early March.

DiLuzio suggested that the city consider running its own service, and offered to provide backup for the city coverage. He said he did not want to accept any more public money but would like the city to collect any emergency service bills for him.

DiLuzio said he would keep at least one and probably two ambulances and a crew of four persons to handle non-emergency transfers and so would need no "standby" fee from the city.

If the council decides to hire a private firm to provide the service, DiLuzio plans to close up shop entirely, the committee report states.

DiLuzio received a $25,000 subsidy from the city this year, but council votes on the subsidy agreement were usually closed and always followed heated argument.

The word "subsidy" has been systematically eliminated from Cheney's report and replaced by the phrase "purchase of service," a term the report states the committee prefers.

The report praises emergency service under the DiLuzio operation, and says the $25,000 "purchase service agreement has been extremely favorable for the community…an extremely good buy…a good buy that will never be available to the community again."

At least two persons have expressed interest in providing private ambulance service for Keene.

Gordon R. Davis, a Troy police officer, emergency medical technician and former employee of DiLuzio, offered to serve the city for about $50,000.

In addition, a Claremont contractor has expressed interest in Keene. Neither party is mentioned in the first draft of the report, and members suggested—and Cheney agreed—that they should be included.

One thing that both the earlier Cheney report and the present report agree on is that maintaining the current level of quality service is essential. However, the reports differ on how to do that, with the first appearing to lean toward DiLuzio—without mentioning the name—and the second toward a municipal service.

Although the present report lists few advantages of a private firm operation, the October report points out benefits of negotiating with a private contractor.

Cheney wrote, "Negotiations would assure…(it) is possible to select the provider of service who is a known quantity to Keene." Costs could be monitored and analyzed, and the level of service could be prescribed for the dollars being spent on the service, the October report states. It also mentions that although negotiations may cost more than an open bidding process, competitive bidding could provide a contractor who's not well-known.

In discussing private service, the committee's current report states that although it is often felt that a private firm could offer service at a lower cost to the public, "this judgment cannot be validated without knowing the specific price that a private service would charge…"

There is no advantages listed in the current report for a contracted ambulance service, but disadvantages are numerous: Private firms are ineligible for federal or state aid or grants: there would be no direct selection of personnel by the city government; there would be no assurance on service to surrounding towns since a private firm wants to make a profit, it may "skimp on services" if the operation starts losing money.

A municipal service, the reports state, should carry a "lower total cost because there is no need to make a profit."

Advantages listed are numerous: The city does not pay business taxes; the city can qualify for aids and grants; continuity of service and cooperation with the towns is guaranteed.

The only disadvantage listed for a city-run service is the "some may consider that the addition of any new public employment jobs would be a disadvantage, even though there may not be any increase in total public costs."

However, the report also states that "direct public control by a public body would be more appropriate…than indirect public policy involvement that would result in the implementation of service with a third party contract.

———

As Reported by the *Keene Evening Sentinel* December 1st, 1976:

"STORY"

A majority of the Keene City Council favors a city run emergency ambulance system

Eight councilors—members of the council's Public Safety and Finance Committees—voted Tuesday night to recommend to the full council that the municipal service plan be approved "in principle."

Committee members stopped short of seeking establishment of the new service because they first want to study up-to-date cost estimates and draft a service policy.

City Manager Peter L. Cheney Tuesday night gave councilors a glimpse of how a municipal service would be operated.

Cheney said the city will probably have one vehicle, probably a van, that will be housed at the fire station. Full-time and part-time workers will be employed to provide 24-hour service to Keene and nearby towns that want to participate.

He said the city government would raise enough money to cover the cost of having 24 hour standby service, and charge persons using the system $45 per call, which is the amount now charged by the Robert J. DiLuzio Ambulance3 Service. DiLuzio plans to halt emergency service next March that's why the city is making plans for a new service.

After a year of operation, the city could either raise or lower the per-call cost, based on the average cost of making a call. Residents of towns outside Keene using the service will be charged the same fee as city residents, plus mileage.

Cheney would also like towns participating in Keene's service to appropriate their share of the cost of having 24-hour emergency service available.

Keene's ambulance will participate in a mutual aid agreement with other town ambulances, he said. That means that it will respond to a call in another town if the town's vehicle is unavailable or a second ambulance is needed.

DiLuzio, Cheney said, will provide back up service to the city. DiLuzio plans to continue an ambulance transfer service, which makes money, emergency service loses money, he says.

Earlier this year, Cheney estimated a municipal ambulance would cost $64,500. However, that figure was drawn up before DiLuzio announced plans to halt emergency ambulance operations in March, and so does not include any income from towns which may now want to contract with Keene for service.

Representatives from eight towns told city officials last month they were looking to Keene for service after DiLuzio closes up shop.

Rossiter suggested Tuesday night that the municipal operation not be approved until new cost estimates and a policy are prepared. The policy, he said, should cover how the city will deal with nearby towns.

Rossiter said he will call a special meeting of the council—probably at the end of December—so that the ambulance question can be laid to rest.

Cheney told councilors it is important to include in the policy some statement about which towns Keene is willing to serve. He doesn't want town ambulance services to decide now that their operations are too much bother, and dump the matter in Keene's lap.

————

As Reported by the *Keene Evening Sentinel* December 6th, 1976:

"FIRE"

Fire Guts Bedroom in Keene

Fire gutted a bedroom and caused extensive smoke and water damage Sunday afternoon to a two-story home on Terrace Street in Keene, but there were no injuries.

The blaze, reported at 3:15 p.m. at the home of Robert S. Pierce at 45 Terrace St., is believed to have started in a faulty baseboard heater in a second-story bedroom, but officials say the fire is still under investigation.

The house was occupied by Pierce, his family, and the family of his son-in-law, but all escaped injury.

Fire officials said four trucks answered the call, and controlled the fire before it spread beyond the second-story bedroom.

The bedroom was gutted. No exact damage estimate has been compiled.

————

As Reported by the *Keene Evening Sentinel*, December 15th, 1976:

"STORY"

Youth is Rescued From Culvert Trap

No Exit – Jason Wood, 7 got stuck in this West Hill Road culvert for more than half an hour. John Phillips (above) deputy chief of the Keene Fire Department and other fire rescue squad members freed the youth. Photo by Baker.

A Keene youth was treated for exposure and released from Cheshire Hospital this morning after being wedged in a culvert on West Hill Road for more than half an hour.

Jason Wood, age 7, son of Mr. and Mrs. Laurence Wood of West Hill Road, crawled into a 30-foot long culvert this morning and just before reaching the other end, was trapped by an ice build up, according to H. Emile DeRosier of the Keene Fire Department Rescue Squad.

According to DeRosier, the youth crawled apparently on his stomach about 25 feet along the culvert before he got stuck. After hitting the ice build up, the youth was unable to either proceed or turn around in the 12-inch wide culvert.

Wood's sister apparently ran home to notify her parents when she became aware that her brother was stuck in the culvert.

The rescue squad was on the scene shortly before 8 a.m. and had to chip away all the ice blocking the first six feet of the culvert before they could free young Wood. According to DeRosier, the boy was in good spirits when he was pulled out.

He was rushed to Cheshire Hospital shortly after 8:30 a.m. and treated for exposure. A hospital spokesperson said the youth was lucky that his sister was able to get assistance so quickly.

————

As Reported by the *Keene Evening Sentinel* December 28th, 1976:

"STORY"

City-Run Ambulance Plan Backed by Finance Panel

A policy governing a proposed municipal ambulance service got a stamp of approval from the Keene City Council's Finance Committee Monday night,

Finance committee members and one member of the Public Safety Committee agreed unanimously to recommend to the council tonight that the policy be adopted.

If it is, Keene will have 24-hour emergency ambulance service provided by a new division of the city fire department. Six new employees will be added to the city payroll to staff the vehicle, which will be housed at the fire station.

City Manager Peter L. Cheney has estimated it will cost $93,488 to provide the service for 12 months to Keene and nine surrounding towns. His proposal calls for the city and towns to share the cost of having 24-hour standby service available. Persons actually using the service will pay $45 per call, plus mileage for calls outside Keene. Towns will be responsible for paying what their residents do not.

Towns wishing to use the city service will have to appropriate funds at annual town meetings March 3. Cheney hopes to have the service in operation March 1.

Keene's share of the total cost is $60,330 under Cheney's proposal $38,280 for having the standby service and $22,050 as the city's share of paying anticipated unpaid bills. Cheney estimates that only 30 per cent of the total billing will be collected. On an estimated 700 emergency calls per year the actual amount received from individuals and sources like Medicaid would be only $9,450, meaning that the city will have to pick up the tab for the other 70 per cent. Cheney's figures include both persons that don't pay bills and the difference between the $45 cost of the call and the amount that Medicaid and Medicare will pay toward it, which is less.

A similar formula has been set up for the nine towns. Each town pays a standby cost on the basis of its population. For example, Roxbury would pay $331 for having the service available while Swanzey would pay $8,672 under the Cheney plan.

In addition, towns must pick up their share of unpaid bills. Cheney's estimates show $4,725 coming from the towns based on 150 emergency calls made in one year.

These are projected figures; if all bills are paid in full, there will be no need for towns to pay the difference. However, according to Cheney, experience has shown emergency service collection rates to be low.

The council has already approved, in principle, the idea of a municipal ambulance service.

Keene and many surrounding towns were left in a pinch when the Robert J. DiLuzio Ambulance Service announced plans to fold in late February. In Keene, however, a special committee was looking into the question of ambulance service in the aftermath of a dispute over paying DiLuzio a $25,000 subsidy. The council approved the subsidy but asked that a committee be appointed to develop long range plans.

When DiLuzio decided to close, the committee leaned heavily on the municipal service plan.

The nine towns included in Cheney's proposal and their share of the standby costs are: Surry $939, Chesterfield, $1,878; Sullivan, $828; Nelson, $718; Westmoreland, $1,933; Roxbury, $331; Gilsum $1,050; and Stoddard, $608.

1977

As Reported by the *Keene Evening Sentinel* January 21st, 1977:

"STORY"

Man Dies in Car Accident

Jarvis Car Wedged under truck off Winchester Street. Photo by Kearney.

A 73 year-old Keene man was dead at the scene of an accident Thursday in which his car left Winchester Street and struck a parked truck.

It was not clear this morning, however, whether the man died of injuries received in the accident or if he was dead before his car went out of control.

Paul A. Jarvis, of 8 Gemini Drive, was pronounced dead at the scene by deputy medical referee James M. Ballou, Jr.

According to police, Jarvis' late-model Pontiac went off the left side of Winchester Street while traveling south near Old Colony Lumber Company.

The car went through the Old Colony parking lot apparently with the accelerator pedal still down and struck a large parked truck.

The car drove under the truck and had its windshield smashed, leaving it still accelerated, with its rear wheels spinning.

Police, fire and ambulance units were called to the scene, in addition to Ballou. There was no fire.

No one else was injured in the accident, which is still under investigation by officials.

He was born in Keene December 22, 1903, son of Alfred and Josephine Rule Jarvis and had been a lifelong resident of the city. He was employed as a builder for Pako Homes of Keene for many years.

————

As Reported by the *Keene Evening Sentinel* January 31st, 1977:

"STORY"

Girl, Operator Honored at Keene Awards Event

Citizen Awarded – Allison Woods, Age 6 receives her award from Keene's Fire Chief John N. Phillips. Photo by Ingleheart.

A 6-year-old-girl was the star of the Keene Fire and Police Department's awards breakfast Saturday, as she was honored for quick action, which helped to save the life of her 7-year-old brother last December 15.

Allison Wood ran to get help when her older brother, Jason, became stuck in an icy culvert near their home on West Hill Road.

Allison, daughter of Mr. and Mrs. Kenneth W. Wood, received a citizen's award from the master of ceremonies police Sgt. Hugh McLellan. She also won the applause of 75 firemen, policemen, city officials and their families, who attended the awards breakfast early Saturday morning. If the boy hadn't been rescued promptly, his life would have been threatened by exposure in severely cold weather.

Harriet M. Moore, a telephone operator, received the other citizen's award give at the annual ceremony. She helped to calm a hysterical woman last April, who called because a man was breaking into her house.

Mrs. Moore was able to obtain needed information from the woman, notifying police quickly, and thus preventing what police said was an attempted burglary and rape.

Keene Police officer Robert H. Hardy received an exceptional service award for climbing into an attic to apprehend a felon who was thought to be armed, and Officer Randall LaCoste and police chaplain Rev. Kenneth A. Batchelder got exceptional service awards for their actions in disarming a man with a shotgun who threatened to kill himself. The shotgun went off during the man's scuffle with LaCoste, destroying part of a wall, but no one was injured.

Sgt. Blaine M. McLellan received the fourth exceptional service award for coordinating an elementary school education program.

Honorable service awards were presented to firemen Thomas L. Loll, Ralph W. Newell, Jr. Bradley B Payne, Michael J. Driscoll, Peter J. Masiello, Phillip L. Davis, Francis J. Driscoll, Wilfred E. Begin, William J. Olmstead, Robert A. Nason, Edward P. LaBounty, Robert W. Raymond, Everett W. Simonds, Chester E. Dubriske and Clark H. Rowell.

Policemen receiving honorable service awards included Romain Martin, Lawrence D. Smith, David Rajaniemi, Robert H. Hardy, Frank Smith, Karl Brown, and Paul E. Brown.

Officer Lawrence D. Smith also received the police department's educational award while Firemen Laurence E. Thompson and Wayne Guyette and Policeman Stephen T. Nash received community service awards.

Police Chief Harold A Becotte gave citations of appreciation to Officers Douglas K. Fish, David G. Hackler, Hall G. Brown and Bruce Saari.

Sgt. Hugh McLellan cited two Keene man, Dennis D DiTullio and John DiBernardo, members of the Italian Club's William Marconi Society, for continuing financial support of police and fire department programs. DiTullio and DiBernardo donated at least half of the necessary funds for the annual breakfast and awards.

———————

As Reported by the *Keene Evening Sentinel* February 8th, 1977:

"FIRE"

Cause Investigated in Church St. Fire

Bedroom Blaze- Firemen get ready to fight a fire which broke out Monday afternoon on the third floor of an apartment building at 176 Church St. No one was hurt, but damage was extensive. Photo by Weeks.

Keene fire officials were investigating this morning the cause of a fire, which destroyed a bedroom and caused several thousand dollars damage to a three-story apartment building on Church Street.

Three fire engines, a rescue vehicle and about 35 firemen responded at 3:20 p.m. Monday to the smoky fire on the third floor of 176 Church St.

The fire started in a third-floor bedroom, according to Keene Deputy Fire Chief Frederick H. Beauchesne, burned through the ceiling, and scorched some of the rafters in the attic of the building.

Firemen contained the blaze before it burned through the roof.

The building, which Beauchesne said is owned by Acre Realty of Keene, suffered "extensive damage."

Beauchesne would not speculate on the cause, but estimated repairs will cost several thousand dollars.

There were four families living in the apartment building, and the deputy chief said he thought all were still able to live in the damaged building.

He said smoke damage affected other rooms on the third floor, and two floors suffered some water damage.

It took firemen about one hour to extinguish the blaze; there were no injuries.

———————

As Reported by the *Keene Evening Sentinel* February 11th, 1977:

"STORY"

Ambulance Bids Opened; Lowest is $16,263 for City

Park Superior Sales Inc. of Connecticut was the apparent low bidder, at $16,263 to supply the city of Keene with a van-type ambulance.

Five bids received from the four different ambulance companies invited to bid on the project were opened in City Hall Wednesday. Robert J. Wyman, city purchasing agent, and Robert N. Guyette, city fire chief, are now reviewing the bids. Their recommendation will go to City Manager Peter L. Cheney Monday.

The Keene City Council has already voted to go into the ambulance business. Ambulances will start running in Keene March 1, when Robert J. DiLuzio ceases service to city residents. DiLuzio will continue to serve outlying towns until annual town meetings are held.

Several towns in the area must appropriate funding at town meeting this year to either start up their own service or pay Keene to use the city's service. A funding formula has been devised for them.

DiLuzio will continue to provide transfer ambulance service while the city vehicle answers emergency calls only DiLuzio will also allow city ambulance personnel to use his vehicle, for a certain fee, if back up is needed. Keene will enter into mutual aid agreements with existing ambulance services like the Marl-Harris squad at no charge.

Four of the five bids opened Wednesday were for a maxi-van ambulance, including the bid from Park Superior. Delivery dates ranged from 10 to 90 days. Park Superior promises 10-day delivery.

Other bidders include:

Southern of New England, of West Hartford, Conn., bid $16,345 to supply a Dodge Tradesman van with delivery in 30 days. The company also bid $16,865 to supply a Dodge maxi-van by April 1.

Miller Motor Sales of Brookline, Mass., bid $17,249 to supply a maxi-van within 90 days.

S&S of New England, Inc. of Lowell, Mass., bid $17,450 for 90-day delivery on a maxi-van.

The vans come equipped with basic ambulance equipment although other equipment will have to be put out to bid and purchased, according to Cheney.

The city is trying to get $7,500 in federal funding to help offset the cost of purchasing the vehicle. Some $77,500 is included in the 1977 city budget proposal to cover the cost of buying the vehicle (12,500) and providing the 24-hour emergency service ($65,000)

The service will be operated under the wing of the city fire department.

_____

As Reported by the *Keene Evening Sentinel* February 16th, 1977:

"FIRE"

City Plans to Buy 2 Ambulances

The Keene city government may buy two ambulances instead of one this year.

The Keene City Council Finance Committee agreed Monday night to recommend that a used ambulance be purchased from the Robert J. DiLuzio Ambulance Service for $4,000.

The city government had originally planned to rent the vehicle from DiLuzio for "backup calls." Using city workers to man it, but insurance problems make that idea nearly impossible, according to City Manager Peter L. Cheney.

The municipal service is slated to start March 1. Six new employees have already been hired and will start work next week. Bids have been received for a new ambulance and they are now being reviewed.

The used vehicle should last two years if used strictly for backup activities, according to Keene Fire Chief Robert N. Guyette.

_____

As Reported by the *Keene Evening Sentinel* February 26th, 1977:

"STORY"

Keene Inaugurates Ambulance Service Early Tuesday Morning

Ready to Roll — Keene's new six-man crew, a rented vehicle and a backup ambulance are ready to start service. From left to right: Robert A. Campbell, Thomas H. Chase, Clayton R. Stalker, Scott B. Taylor, Gary R LaFreniere and George W. Shepard. Photo by Baker.

Starting Tuesday at 7 a.m., Keene residents who need emergency ambulance service can get it by calling Southwestern N.H. Fire Mutual Aid at 352-1100.

Then, the mutual aid dispatcher will send the Keene city government's own ambulance to provide the necessary help.

Keene will enter the ambulance service Tuesday morning with two vehicles, a six-man crew and a $77,500 first-year appropriation from the Keene City Council.

The council decided to start a municipal ambulance service after the Robert J. DiLuzio Ambulance Service of Keene—it and its predecessor, the Foley Ambulance Service, have provided emergency service in the Keene area for many years—announced plans to end emergency service, staying only in the profitable ambulance transfer service.

That left a major void in area ambulance service, and the council decided the city government was most able to fill it.

Residents in towns near Keene will continue to be served by DiLuzio only through town meeting day March 8.

"The respective town meetings will have an opportunity to raise and appropriate funds for alternate service," said Richard J. Talbot, DiLuzio's lawyer, in a letter to selectmen of Swanzey, Surry, Nelson, Chesterfield, Sullivan and Roxbury. The alternatives will not include any extension of service from DiLuzio.

"All emergency services will terminate after the town meetings, regardless of what action they do or do not take," Talbot said.

If voters in towns now served by DiLuzio decide to join Keene's ambulance operation they will have to raise a specific amount of money based on each community's population to support the cost of having 24-hour coverage available.

In addition, residents will be charged $45 per call plus $1.5 per "loaded" mile, which means the person pays the mileage from his house to the hospital. Towns will be held responsible for paying any ambulance bills its residents do not pay, according to a funding formula adopted by the council.

In Keene, residents will be charged a flat $45 per ride.

The municipal service will become a wing of the Keene Fire Department and the two vehicles will be housed in the fire station.

The city government's primary vehicle has not yet been purchased because officials are waiting to see if federal funds are available to buy the van-type ambulance. At most, the city government can get $7,500 toward the $16,263 vehicle; Park Superior Sales Inc. of Connecticut, the low bidder, will be selling the vehicle to Keene, according to City Manager Peter L. Cheney. The firm has promised ten-day delivery.

In the meantime, Keene is renting a vehicle for $150 a month on a month-to-month basis while awaiting word on the federal funding.

The city government recently purchased a backup vehicle from DiLuzio for $4,000, and that ambulance is now being painted.

Although both vehicles are designed to carry one passenger, each can carry two and possibly three passengers if necessary. The Keene service—as yet officially unnamed—will participate in mutual aid agreements with ambulance services in surrounding towns on a basis similar to fire mutual aid.

The city government has already purchased $2,500 worth of equipment and has obtained licenses for the two vehicles from the N.H. Emergency Medical Service Coordinating Board.

Six new city employees have been getting acquainted with the new service all week, according to Robert N. Guyette, fire chief.

Guyette said the six men are all emergency medical technicians (EMT's) and each has had experience in the emergency ambulance field.

The six were chosen from among 26 applicants.

The ambulance crewmen will be classified as grade 11 employees on the city's pay scale, the same classification used for firefighters and patrolmen. Starting pay for that grade is $8.391.

Emergency service will be available 24 hours a day. The ambulance squad will work two 11 and 13-hour shifts, as the fire department now does, putting in a 56-hour work week.

————

As Reported by the *Keene Evening Sentinel* March 4th, 1977:

"STORY"

Fire Prevention Project Set

A program on fire prevention will be held in the Keene High School cafeteria March 9,

sponsored by the Keene Fire Department's fire prevention group.

The program starts at 7:30 p.m.; there is no admission charge.

A film, "Another Man's Family," will be shown, and speakers from the fire department will answer questions and give tips on fire safety, wood stoves, and other subjects.

"How Not to Burn" is the title of the fire prevention program. Statistics show, for instance, that one child is seriously burned every four minutes in the United States, and children who are burned spend 18 million days each year in a hospital.

The fire prevention program is aimed at lowering such statistics.

————

As Reported by the *Keene Evening Sentinel* March 16th, 1977:

"STORY"

7 Towns in Area Join City Ambulance Service

Seven towns have joined Keene's new ambulance service, contributing a total of $25,299 toward the cost of having 24-hour emergency service available.

The $25,299 is the towns' share of the $55,237 cost of having standby service available. The Keene city government expected to pay $38,250, but thought Gilsum and Stoddard would be paying $1,650 toward the total bill.

Towns will also be charged for any of their resident's unpaid bills. Some towns appropriated funds this year to cover bad bills; others will wait until the city government bills them and take action at town meeting next year.

Keene launched its municipal ambulance service March 1, filling the void left when the private Robert J. DiLuzio Ambulance Service curtailed the emergency end of its operation.

DiLuzio continues to provide transfer service to Keene and the surrounding towns.

City officials have estimated it will cost about $343,486 a year to run the new ambulance service. More than $65,000 of that total covers salaries and fringe benefits for the six employees, pays for part-time billing clerk and back-up service.

Another $10,000 pays for operating costs. The city has picked out its primary ambulance vehicle, but has not yet bought it because officials are waiting to see if federal funds will be awarded to pay a portion of the purchase price. A rented ambulance now serves as the primary vehicle and the city government has bought a back-up ambulance from the DiLuzio operation for 4,000.

In its first two weeks the ambulance service made 34 calls, 31 in the city and the other three to surrounding towns. Everyone is charged $45 per ride and non-city residents also pay a mileage fee.

The back-up vehicle has been used twice. As soon as an ambulance leaves on a call—manned by two trained ambulance workers—two more workers are called into the station. If a second call for assistance is received, they take out the back-up vehicle. If additional assistance is needed, it is supplied through mutual aid agreements with other ambulance services in the area.

Stand-by costs raised by the towns this year are based on population. Swanzey raised the lion's chare. Voters there raised $12,600; $8,672 as their share of the stand-by costs and $4,000 to guarantee payments of resident's bills.

Swanzey voters defeated a VFW plan to start their own volunteer service. The VFW bought an ambulance, personnel were trained and the service would have been offered free from 6 a.m. to 6 p.m. Voters were asked to raise $4,400 to pay Keene for coverage from 6 p.m. to 6 a.m. and $20,000 to expand the fire station so the vehicle could be housed.

All towns raised the amount of money the city government requested for standby service, Chesterfield raised $2,978, $1,178 for standby costs and $1,100 to cover bad debts; Westmoreland raised $2,500, with $1,933 covering standby costs; Sullivan raised $828 for standby; Nelson raised $1,100, with $718 covering its standby share; Roxbury raised $331 for standby; and Surry raised $939 for standby.

City officials originally thought Gilsum and Stoddard would sign up, contributing $1,050 and $608 toward the standby operation. They are already covered by other ambulance services.

————

As Reported by the *Keene Evening Sentinel* April 21st, 1977:

"STORY"

Ambulance Services Stabilizing in Region

Emergency ambulance service, in a state of change for more than a year in some area communities, appears to be stabilizing. Indeed, service may be better than ever.

Keene, Swanzey, Troy and Westmoreland—four communities with problems providing ambulance service a year ago—now appear to have solved, or are on the verge of solving, their problems.

The reasons are twofold; The Keene city government established a city-run emergency ambulance service and town volunteer groups mobilized to form their own ambulance and rescue units.

The Keene ambulance service, which aids local towns for a fee, is located at the Keene Fire Department under the jurisdiction of Fire Chief Robert N. Guyette. The arrangement has worked well.

The ambulance crew of six full-time trained emergency medical technicians—two are on call at the station at all times—have "dovetailed beautifully" with the fire department, said Guyette. "They live together, eat together, joke together. They're part of the team.

Since the Keene emergency service began March 1, with two ambulances and a $77,500 first-year operating budget, the crews have answered an average of 2.7 calls per day.

Under the Keene emergency ambulance system, two medical technicians are always at the first station, two are free but on call to cover the station when those on duty respond to an emergency, and two are off duty.

Since the headquarters for Southwestern N.H. Fire Mutual Aid—where all emergency calls in the area eventually wind up—are located in the same building as the Keene ambulances, technicians can respond to a cry for help as soon as possible.

It's "a good system," and so far it has worked very well, said Guyette.

The Keene ambulance budget is offset somewhat by revenues from area towns, which appropriate some funds in return for service, and from a $45 per person fee, charged residents in Keene, and $45 per person plus $1.50 per mile from out-of-town calls to the hospital.

The ambulance crisis arose when the Robert J. DiLuzio Ambulance Service announced plans to end emergency service—primarily because of rising costs and the difficulty of raising the necessary subsidy funds from Keene and area towns.

Since then Keene and the towns have been scurrying to establish their own systems to answer emergencies. The towns are moving well toward such systems—thanks to an outpouring of donations and the enthusiasm of volunteers.

Ambulance officials in Swanzey, Troy and Westmoreland are optimistic. Their only cautionary note is they hope the enthusiasm of volunteers—none of whom are paid—remains strong after the novelty wears off. So far, raising money necessary to buy ambulances and train technicians has not been a tough problem for the town ambulance systems, all of which are independent from the town government, but which in some cases get small subsidies from town voters at town meeting.

————

As Reported by the *Keene Evening Sentinel* April 25th, 1977:

"FIRE"

Damage Heavy in Keene Fire

Winchester Street House Damaged Heavily By Fire. More than 60 firemen from Keene and Swanzey Center battled a fire at a house at 515 Winchester St. late Sunday night for more than three hours. Photo by Lorinczi.

A smoky fire of undetermined origin caused extensive damage Sunday night to a two-story house at 515 Winchester St., despite efforts by almost 60 firemen to control the blaze.

The fire was reported at 10:09 p.m. Sunday, and firefighters from Keene and Swanzey Center responded. It took more than three hours to get the blaze under control, and most of the house was damaged by the fire.

The first and second floor and the attic were reported extensively damaged, by flames, and those parts of the house, which weren't burned suffered heavy smoke, heat, and water damage.

Fire officials investigating the incident this morning said the fire started on the first floor in a small middle bedroom, but no other details were available.

There was no one living in the house at the time of the fire.

An attached barn was saved, but fire officials are not sure the rest of the house is repairable.

One fireman, Lt. Emile Derosiers, was treated at Cheshire Hospital for a minor smoke injury to the eye, and two other firemen were given oxygen by emergency personnel at the scene, according to fire officials.

———————

As Reported by the *Keene Evening Sentinel* June 27th, 1977:

"FIRE"

Mattress Fire Put Out in Keene

Keene fire officials this morning were investigating a pre-dawn mattress fire which caused smoke and water damage to a Roxbury Street apartment building.

The fire was reported at about 2:10 a.m. in a second-floor apartment.

Fire officials would not identify the tenants of the burned apartment, saying it might hamper their investigation.

The fire burned a mattress and several clothing items before firemen brought the smoky fire under control at about 2:40 a.m.

The apartment is located at 106 Roxbury Street.

Second and third-floor tenants were evacuated from the building while firefighters put the blaze out. Fire officials reported some smoke and water damage to the second floor.

———————

As Reported by the *Keene Evening Sentinel* July 2nd, 1977:

"RESCUE"

Keene Man is Pulled from Bottom of Wilson Pond in "Textbook" Rescue

Keene Firemen Who Performed Rescue. Four members of the fire department rescue team that saved a drowning man Tuesday stand near the city ambulance. They are (L to R) Gary "Spanky" LaFreniere, Clayton Stalker, Phillip L. Davis and Alex W. Matson Jr. Photo by Lord.

A Keene man was listed in critical condition at Cheshire Hospital this morning after being rescued from the bottom of Wilson Pond by two Keene firemen Tuesday afternoon.

Donald Hillock, 30, was saved from drowning by the combined efforts of area police, Keene Fire Department , and James A Sibley of Keene, whose citizen's band radio call initiated the rescue.

Sibley said Tuesday that he was traveling north on Route 32 in Swanzey just after 1 p.m. when he was flagged down near the public swimming area at the south end of Wilson Pond in North Swanzey and was told that a man was in trouble about 50 feet offshore.

"I immediately called the Keene police on emergency channel nine when I saw the man floundering in the water," Sibley said.

Keene police relayed the call to the Southwestern N.H. Fire Mutual Aid dispatcher at the Keene Fire Department, who in turn alerted firemen Alex W. Matson Jr. and Phillip L. Davis, who were on duty at Keene's Dillant-Hopkins Airport near Wilson Pond.

Sibley placed a second call when he saw the man "go under."

"I told them I was going in after the man, and they said that assistance was on the way," Sibley said.

"Just then the fire truck came around the corner. I couldn't believe it. It had been less than three minutes since the first call." Sibley said.

Matson, a strong swimmer, dove in immediately after the man began searching beneath the water in an area where several bystanders had seen him so under, Matson said Tuesday.

"At first I couldn't see anything, then I spotted something on the bottom." Matson said.

"He was lying face down in the mud about 12 feet under water, and it was all I could do to pull him up."

Davis met Matson halfway from shore and helped pull Hillock in. By the time they reached the shore, the Keene city ambulance and fire rescue vehicles were arriving.

"The timing was unbelievable," Matson said.

The ambulance crew began cardio-pulmonary respiratory treatment and took Hillock to Cheshire Hospital, where a team of physicians continued to treat him, a hospital spokesman said this morning.

"It was a textbook rescue," Matson said.

"Credit should be given to the Keene police, the Swanzey police, the Cheshire County Sheriff's office, Mike Willard, a Swanzey rescue man who helped and others whose names we didn't get," a Keene Fire Department official said Tuesday.

"Everyone worked together to save the man, and we appreciate all the assistance."

Sibley said witnesses said Hillock was at Wilson Pond with his three children and had gone out to retrieve a beach ball for one of them when the near-drowning occurred.

Matson said Hillock was wearing pants but no shirt when he dragged the man from the bottom of the pond.

———————

As Reported by the *Keene Evening Sentinel* July 14th, 1977:

"FIRE"

Garage of Store Hit by Fire

The Carroll's Variety Store building at 661 Marlboro St., at the corner of Route 101 and Swanzey Factory Road, was heavily damaged by fire early this morning.

Damage to the store itself was not extensive, according to Keene Fire Department officials, but the garage portion of the building was gutted. No one was injured in the blaze.

The fire was reported at 12:52 a.m. by a Keene police officer who had been called to the scene by a complaint from the store's owner, Alex Carroll of 659 Marlboro St.

Carroll reported two suspicious persons in the area at 12:45, but the suspicious persons complaint was not related to the fire, Keene police said this morning.

The cause of the blaze is under investigation, fire officials said.

Four Keene units fought the fire until 2:17 a.m., when all units were reported back in service; however, two firemen remained on the scene all night to monitor the smoldering building, fire officials said.

———————

As Reported by the *Keene Evening Sentinel* July 18th, 1977:

"FIRE"

Fire, Vandalism Reported in Keene

A bedroom fire on Sullivan Street, vandalism on Franklin Street and a theft at Keene State College were among the few incidents, which marred an otherwise quiet weekend for police and fire officials in Keene.

The fire at 8 Sullivan St. broke out Saturday at about 2:30 a.m. at the residence of Alfreda Flagg. The smoky blaze was confined mainly to the first floor bedroom where it started, and firemen were at the scene for about 70 minutes.

According to Keene Fire Department Captain Paul E. Crowell, the fire may have been started by "improper disposal of smoking materials."

No one was injured, but smoke and water damage was heavy on the first floor of the building, and smoke damaged parts of the second floor, according to Crowell.

Two movie projectors valued at about $1,000 were reported stolen Saturday evening from the student union building at Keene State College.

Keene police reported no evidence of forced entry at the building. The projector theft was reported by Keene State College security officers.

Vandalism and attempted burglary reported at 49 Franklin St. early Sunday morning are under investigation by Keene police. Mrs. Lillian Drouin reported the incident at about 1 a.m. Sunday.

Police reported entry into the building was gained through a window, and rooms inside were damaged with sprayed water, but nothing was reported stolen.

————

As Reported by the *Keene Evening Sentinel* August 2nd, 1977:

"FIRE"

Keene Wood Heel Building Damaged by Fire; Two Firefighters Are Injured

Keene Firefighters Battle Fire at Keene Wood Heel Co., Inc.

Fire early Monday evening extensively damaged Keene Wood Heel Co., Inc. at 158 Water St. and sent two Keene firefighters to Cheshire Hospital with apparently minor injuries.

Firefighters Robert Meagher and Armand Jacques were rushed to Cheshire Hospital by ambulance, but both soon were released. Meagher had an ear injury, Jacques a puncture wound in his foot.

Damage to the sprawling industrial building was limited—by an in-house sprinkler system and the swift work of Keene firefighters to a 50-by-50 foot area.

The two-alarm fire was reported at about 6:45 p.m. and it was two hours before it was brought under control. Thick smoke billowed up into a graying sky. A violent thunderstorm hit Keene at about 7:30, and sent more than 100 spectators scurrying for cover. The onlookers stood along nearby railroad tracks, while some of the more adventuresome climbed atop rail boxcars for a better view.

The last fire truck left at about 10 p.m., although a crew remained during the night to keep an eye on the embers.

This morning, fire officials were back at the scene, trying to determine what had happened.

The fire apparently started in a trash barrel after workmen had gone home, said

Deputy Chief John N. Phillips. Most of the damage was to the roof.

Firefighters cut through the roof with a ten-inch circular saw to get at the flames. They poured water into the area sealing the fire off from the main shop. The fire was limited to a storage area, where lumber is ripped (cut in strips). Firefighters were aided by a sprinkler system which cooled part of the building.

Some 60 Keene firefighters, six fire trucks and two ambulances were at the scene. Firefighters from Swanzey Center and Surry covered the Keene station during the fire.

The Wood Heel Company makes pine, maple and birch heels for women's shoes. About 23 persons are employed in the building.

Owner David Court said he hoped to resume production soon, but he wasn't sure this morning when that would be.

Court said he couldn't estimate the losses.

"Most of the damage is to the roof," Court said, "and we have a lot of cleanup to do.

————

As Reported by the *Keene Evening Sentinel* August 26th, 1977:

"FIRE"

Fire Damages Shed, House

Elm Street Fire. A fire that broke out this morning did extensive damage to the back portion of a house at 83 Elm St. Keene firefighters were able to bring the fire under control soon after their arrival, but were still mopping up late this morning. Photo by Wallace Baker.

Fire damaged a shed and a portion of a house at 83 Elm St. Friday morning.

Keene firefighters were called to the multi-family dwelling owned by Mr. and Mrs. Randall S. Nearing shortly after 10 a.m. and had the fire under control about 20 minutes later.

The shed and most of its contents suffered extensive damage; the rear of the house was also burned, and the rest of the building had smoke and water damage.

No cause for the fire was listed on fire department reports.

————

As Reported by the *Keene Evening Sentinel* September 23rd, 1977:

"STORY"

Keene Fire Ladder Damaged; New One to Cost $32,000

100 Foot Long Ladder on Keene Fire Truck Twists to Right, Gouges Show where Ladder was hit. Photo by Kearney.

The Keene City Council approved an emergency appropriation of $32,000 Thursday for repairs to the Keene Fire Department's aerial ladder truck.

The truck was damaged as it left the fire station at 4:32 a.m. in the process of answering an alarm from Cheshire Hospital, City Manager Peter L. Cheney reported to the council.

As the truck left its bay, the driver "apparently turned toward the left onto Vernon Street too soon and hit the end of the ladder on the steel door casing of the fire station," Cheney stated. In doing so, the side rails of the three section of the 100-foot ladder were damaged to such an extent that the ladder is no longer useful above about 50 feet, according to Keene Fire Chief Robert N. Guyette.

When the ladder is extended, it bends to the right and twists clockwise. Guyette said a fireman atop the ladder would be in danger of falling off because of the ladder's position, and it's also structurally unsafe, the chief said.

The truck was purchases in 1972 from the Maxim Fire Truck Co. of Middleboro, Mass., at a cost of $68,500, Cheney said. Representatives from the firm have been in Keene to examine the ladder and concluded that the ladder cannot be repaired and must be replaced, he said.

Since fire trucks are manufactured on a custom-made basis, a ladder for Keene's truck would not normally be available. However, the firm has a new ladder under construction to go on another truck, and would be willing to use it to replace Keene's ladder if the truck is delivered to them within a few days, Cheney said.

The cost of replacing the ladder will be between $28,000 and $32,000, while a new truck similar to Keene's would now cost between $140,000 and $160,000, according to Cheney.

Replacement of the ladder will take from two to three weeks, Cheney said.

The 1977 city operating budget includes a capital reserve fund for fire equipment of $40,000. About $6,000 has been spend, and $13,500 had been earmarked for a new power wagon and a new deputy's car this year.

If those purchases are delayed, the reserve fund could cover the ladder replacement, Cheney said, and the planned replacement program for fire equipment could be reevaluated during preparation of the 1978 budget.

Some councilors were reluctant to spend so much money on such short notice Thursday, but Guyette explained that since the Maxim firm is the only company that manufactures a ladder that would fit the Keene truck, he sees no alternative.

Councilor Timothy N. Robertson said that he would like to consult with a structural steel expert to see if the $32,000 cost is justified.

This morning, Robertson, Councilor Philip G. Taaffe, and two steel experts viewed the bend and twisted ladder.

"I just had to some see it. You can't really tell from a piece of paper" what the damage actually is, Taaffe said.

"After looking the whole thing over, I don't think we have any choice but to buy a new ladder," Taaffe said. "I certainly wouldn't want to climb it with that crick in it.

"And if you got it fixed, you'd always wonder whether it was really safe."

Taaffe said Peter G. Warren of Kingsbury Machine Tool Corp, and Eugene D. Mellish of MacMillin Co., Inc. examined the ladder this morning, and agreed that the best thing for the city to do is buy a new one.

"If that was a crane, it would tip over," Warren said this morning while looking at the ladder.

———————

As Reported by the *Keene Evening Sentinel* September 29th, 1977:

"FIRE"

Hospital Employees Quell 'Fires'

Dousing The Flames – Holly Simpson of the Cheshire Hospital Staff trains fire extinguisher on fire. Ronald Amadon, right of Keene Fire Department offers advice. Photo by Baker.

Nurses, clerks and administrators manned the fire extinguishers at Cheshire Hospital this week, as the hospital conducted its annual two-day training session in firefighting.

Hospital employees took turns extinguishing fire under the guidance of the Keene Fire Department.

The training session is part of a year-round safety program at the hospital, and is also required by the Joint Commission on Accreditation, according to Frank Webinski, director of plant and safety.

"This demonstration gives employees hands on experience on the use of a fire extinguisher," Webinski said. "It's amazing how many people do not know the weight of an extinguisher, how to activate it, and how to approach a fire."

In addition to the annual training the hospital conducts monthly fire drills, requires employees to learn procedures for reporting and extinguishing fires, and holds monthly safety checks.

————————

As Reported by the *Keene Evening Sentinel* November 7th, 1977:

"STORY"

New Rules for Fires Outdoors

Keene residents will no longer be able to burn brush, leaves and other non-household waste on wet or rainy days.

Keene Fire Department rules limit the burning of brush to the hours before 9 a.m. and after 5 p.m., but firemen previously allowed such burning during days when damp weather minimized the danger of fire spreading out of control.

City fire officials have tightened up the rules to cooperate with aims of the N.H. Air Pollution Control Commission.

A city ordinance forbids the open burning of household wastes like garbage and limits the burning of brush to small branches no greater than five inches in diameter.

Keene residents can contact the Fire Department for further permit information.

————————

As Reported by the *Keene Evening Sentinel* December 12th, 1977:

"FIRE"

Pipe-Heating Attempt Starts Fire

Morning Fire. A home on Stearns Road suffered extensive damage in a mid-morning fire today when insulation underneath the home caught fire. Photo by Baker.

A home on the Stearns Road was heavily damaged in a midmorning fire today.

The blaze started when Edward Neatwawk, who was renting the house from owner Donald Stone, was attempting to thaw out water pipes that had frozen in a crawl space underneath the house, according to Keene Fire Chief Robert N. Guyette.

Guyette said that the propane torch Neatwawk was using for the job apparently ignited some insulation and bits of paper in the crawl space.

The flames spread throughout the space and into the partitions, moving through the partitions into the roof.

Guyette characterized damage to the house as extensive. The fire was out by 11:30 a.m.

As Reported by the *Keene Evening Sentinel* December 14th, 1977:

"FIRE"

Garage Destroyed by Flames

Garage Destroyed – (L to R) Call firefighter James St. Laurent, permanent firefighter Ralph Newell and Stevens Goldsmith battle the blaze. Photo by Baker.

Keene firemen prevented a fire from spreading to the living quarters of a Manchester Street home Tuesday, but were unable to save any portion of the garage and patio area where the blaze started.

The fire was reported at 1:09 p.m. at 52 Manchester St. in the garage of a house owned by Raymond Jay, Jr. A second alarm was rung a few minutes later.

According to Capt. Chester Dubriske of the Keene Fire Department, the garage was "in total flames by the time firemen arrived and was destroyed along with tools and assorted household furnishings stored in the area."

Jay told firemen he had been working in the garage, repairing a car, when flames broke out. Jay managed to get out of the structure seconds before an explosion engulfed the building in flames.

Dubriske theorized that either gasoline vapors or a very small leak in the car's gas tank caused the fire.

Three trucks fought the blaze, which was extinguished just before 1:30 p.m., Dubriske said.

As Reported by the *Keene Evening Sentinel* December 27th, 1977:

"FIRE"

Fire Damages Keene House After Smoke Detector Test

An otherwise peaceful three-day Christmas weekend in the Monadnock Region was marred by fires in Keene and Jaffrey.

Five Keene Fire Department units responded to a house fire just before 4:30 p.m. Monday at the home of Frederick B. Parsells.

Although the fire took only 20 minutes to control, it took firemen more than another hour to clean up, and damage to the two-story house "was extensive" according to John N. Phillips, deputy chief.

Ironically, the fire broke out as the owner was installing and testing a smoke alarm system.

Phillips said Parsells told him he was following the manufacturer's instructions and was igniting a small bunch of cotton balls to set off the alarm. However, Parsells told firemen the several ignited cotton balls fell from the container and one landed on the couch, which immediately was consumed in flames.

"When we got there, flames were pouring out the front window," Phillips said.

Phillips said the fire destroyed the living room and its furnishings, and quickly spread into the partitions on the south side.

"The heat was so intense on that side, it peeled the paint on the upstairs south wall," he said.

Smoke and water damage were extensive throughout most of the house, although a rear apartment wasn't hurt at all, Phillips said.

The tenant was spending the holiday in Florida.

One of two pet dogs, was killed in the blaze.

In Jaffrey, details are sketchy about an early morning fire that destroyed a storage garage and truck belonging to Donald Baird of 30 East Brook St.

The fire broke out at 2:30 a.m. in the structure, which housed equipment for Baird's small paving company, according to Jaffrey police.

No one was injured in the fire, which was still under investigation late this morning.

———

1978

As Reported by the *Keene Evening Sentinel* January 3rd, 1978:

"FIRE"

Fire Destroys Shed on Elm Street

A New Year's Day fire destroyed a storage shed owned by Wayne R. Bissell of 364 Elm St., according to Deputy Keene Fire Chief Frederick H. Beauchesne.

No injuries were reported.

Bissell said he had once housed livestock in the shed, which was partitioned into three stalls—14 feet square, but recently had stored building supplies there. Some of the materials lost in the blaze included hardwood flooring, windows, shingles and roofing and construction supplies, Bissell said Monday.

When neighbors reported the fire to Keene firemen at 4:18 p.m., Bissell and his family were out of town for the afternoon.

Beauchesne said the fire was out within 45 minutes, but much of the damage had been done before firemen arrived.

Officials are investigating the cause of the fire.

———

As Reported by the *Keene Evening Sentinel* January 17th, 1978:

"FIRE"

Garage, Car Destroyed by Flames

A fire destroyed a Graves Road garage and a car, motorcycle, riding lawnmower and a number of other items inside it Monday night.

No serious injuries were reported as a result of the fire in the two-bay garage near the home of Douglas Parker, officials said. However, a fireman, Jack Dennis, was treated at the scene by Keene ambulance attendants for a bruised hand.

Fire officials this morning did not know the cause of the blaze, which was reported at 11:30 p.m. nor was a damage estimate available. An investigation is under way.

Keene firemen fought the fire for about two hours, but were unable to save the contents of the garage.

The Surry Fire Department stood by at Keene while four of Keene's fire trucks went to the Graves Road scene.

————

As Reported by the *Keene Evening Sentinel* January 25th, 1978:

"FIRE"

Trailer Destroyed by Fire; Dog Dies

Trailer Burns – Firemen inspect the scene of a fire this morning. A dog died in the blaze at 413 Tanglewood Estates. Mrs. Sylvia Youngman was not at home when the fire broke out. Photo by Baker.

Fire destroyed a mobile home and killed a dog this morning before firemen arrived to put out the flames which had completely engulfed the inside of the trailer at Tanglewood Estates.

Keene fire officials reported no other injuries.

When Keene and Surry firemen arrived at the home of Sylvia Youngman at 413 Tanglewood Estates minutes after 7:55 a.m.,

the fire had spread throughout the trailer, according to Keene Fire Chief Robert N. Guyette.

Although firemen had the blaze under control by 8:10 a.m., the crew remained at the scene of the fire until nearly midmorning wetting down the charred ruins.

Guyette said the fire probably began in a central part of the mobile home before spreading to other parts. An investigation was being conducted today to determine the cause, he said.

Mrs. Youngman was not at home at the time, but a car parked in the driveway led neighbors to believe someone possibly was inside, according to an ob server, Dennis Dubois, who was clearing snow from the roof of a nearby trailer.

Dubois said that he and several others saw flames and smoke pouring out from a window on the north side of the trailer and "screamed" through broken windows and the door to see if anyone was inside.

"The smoke was so thick, you couldn't get in," he said, "it was wicked."

Dubois said the smoke was everywhere inside the one-story trailer, except for an area about a foot off the floor.

"We broke some of the windows to let the smoke out. We saw the parked car and were worried that someone was inside," he said.

With the windows broke and the door opened, the smoke was replaced with fire, he said, which eliminated any chance of entering the burning building.

The small black poodle, apparently killed by smoke inhalation, was removed by firemen and police.

Chief Guyette said Surry's fire department was called in to stand by with additional water, but Surry firemen helped Keene crews put out what was left of the fire.

————

As Reported by the *Keene Evening Sentinel* February 4th, 1978:

"FIRE"

Store, Ten Apartments Damaged in Keene Fire

Firefighters combat flames in upper windows of Sentinel Block. The fire seen Saturday afternoon was from a helicopter. Photo by Manlove.

A three-alarm fire at 55 Main Street Saturday afternoon left the tenants of 10 apartments homeless and forced the temporary closing of G. H. Tilden Inc., a stationery and office equipment store.

No one was injured in the fire, which apparently started when a plumber attempted to thaw a frozen water pipe on the ground level at the rear of the four story brick building, according to Keene fire officials.

Tilden's store was not badly damaged, according to Mildred Jaynes, a spokeswoman for the store. Gordon Edmunds, who owns the store which has occupied the building for 12 years, plans to reopen for business on Tuesday.

The 10 apartments on the second, third and fourth floors above the store were quickly evacuated Saturday, although some tenants objected to leaving because the fire began in the rear of the building.

Firefighters from Keene, Swanzey Center, Westmoreland, Meadowood and Brattleboro, VT, fought the flames and smoke, while Walpole and Surry crews covered Keene's fire station in case another alarm came while city equipment was at the Main Street fire.

Keene Fire Chief Robert N. Guyette said the fire began at the rear of the building, and shot up quickly through a wooden shaft housing water pipes and electrical wires. The shaft acted like a chimney, creating a draft, which carried heat and flames into the floors and walls of the 85-year old building which once was the headquarters for The Keene Sentinel.

Tilden's store was closed this morning, and employees were cleaning up damage caused mainly by water and some smoke.

The building and the apartments are owned by George T. Kingsbury of 700 West Street his wife, Marjorie Kingsbury, said that the building is adequately insured and that only problem now is to see that the apartment dwellers get back into their homes quickly.

Guyette said about four apartments on the second and third floors were damaged extensively by fire, smoke, and water.

Firemen remained in the burned building throughout the night Saturday to make sure the fire did not rekindle.

No tenants were allowed to return to their apartments during the weekend, but fire officials thought some would return to undamaged rooms today or Tuesday.

———

As Reported by the *Keene Evening Sentinel* February 23rd, 1978:

"FIRE"

Fires Doused on Wyman Road and Washington Street in Keene

Firemen leave scene of Washington St. fire. Photo by Baker.

Keene firemen, assisted by a crew from the Surry Fire Department, extinguished a garage fire on Wyman Road and Old Walpole Road Wednesday afternoon before any damage was done to the small home attacked.

No in juries were reported, but the garage was gutted, according to Keene fire officials.

The two-=story wooden house is owned by Marion Wilson of Westwood Apartments, but was occupied by Robert and Sandra Cunningham, according to officials.

The cause of the fire, which took firemen some 15 minutes to put out, was undetermined as of this morning, but fire officials were at the scene conducting an investigation today.

Everett D. Simmons, a neighbor, reported the fire to Keene police and then firemen at 4:51 p.m.

When firemen arrived, the garage was burning inside with flames and smoke billowing out through windows, the door of the garage and through parts of the walls, firemen said.

Damage to the garage was described at "total" and it will probably have to be torn down and rebuilt, a fire official said.

The shed between the garage and the house was also damaged by fire and a 275-gallon oil storage tank in the shed was heated to the point where the plastic fuel gauge on the top melted off, the spokesman said.

The Cunningham family was not in the house at the time of the fire, and are still living in the undamaged house.

No estimate of the cost top repair the shed and garage was available this morning.

Keene firemen also responded to an attic fire at the Carl Chamberlain residence at 355 Washington St at 8 a.m. this morning.

The fire was out before any serious damage was done, however, Capt. Chester E. Dubriske of the Keene Fire Department said no one was injured.

Dubriske said minor smoke and water damage was done to part of the attic area and the ceiling just below it.

A passing motorist, who noticed smoke coming through the roof, alerted the Chamberlains who were at home to the fire. The Chamberlains reported the fire to authorities.

The cause is unknown and is under investigation.

As Reported by the *Keene Evening Sentinel* February 27th, 1978:

"STORY"

Firemen Honored for Action

The two Keene firemen who pulled a drowning victim from 12 feet of water at Wilson Pond in North Swanzey last summer were presented Exceptional Service Awards Saturday morning at the third annual Safety Services Awards Ceremonies held at the Keene Fire Station.

(L to R) Firemen Phil Davis and Alex Matson.

Some 26 other firemen and policemen also were recognized and presented with citations for safety service in Keene.

Phillip Davis, 37, of 34 Dale Dr, who has been with the Keene Fire Department since 1963, and Alex Matson, Jr., 21 of 22 Colby St., who has been a fireman since 1974, were cited for rescuing Donald Hillock from Wilson Pond on June 28. Hillock, however, died several days after the drowning from which he was revived temporarily by efforts of the rescue and fire crews.

Matson and Davis were on duty at nearby Dillant-Hopkins Airport when they received a call informing them of the drowning. Within three minutes of receiving the call, the firemen arrived at the shore of the pond and Matson swam out and pulled Hillock from the bottom. Davis helped bring the drowned man to the shore where they managed to restore the man's vital signs.

They were assisted by other rescue crews which showed up at the scene within minutes of the first call from a witness who had a citizens band radio in his car.

Fire Chief Robert N. Guyette told nearly 100 firemen, policemen, rescue crewmen, some city officials and members of the Explorers Scouting group that the decision to single out one or two from such a large group was next to impossible.

"How do you pick out a hero among heroes?" he asked.

"They don't work singly, they work collectively," he said. "If somebody fails then somebody else has to pick up the loose ends."

Guyette, praising the Keene Police Department, said the recent fire at G.H. Tilden stationery supply store on Main Street exemplified the cooperation firemen and policemen incorporate into their work.

"The men on the third floor depended on the men on the second floor to do their part in controlling the fire. The men on the second floor depended on the men on the first floor," he said.

Guyette praised police for traffic and crowd control and for filling in within the building to help firemen "who were shorthanded".

"You did one heck of a job and I want you to "appreciated it," he told them.

City Manager Peter Cheney, speaking briefly also praised both departments, the rescue squads and the young Explorer Scouts who intend to go on to police work when they are old enough.

Police Chief Harold A Becotte presented citations of appreciation to policemen William Sargent, Thomas Cunningham, Michael Keller and Frederick Parsells for "doing just a little bit more than is expected of them."

He, too, said choosing a few among so many who all deserved awards was a hard decision.

Patrolman, Michael Mack, was presented the community service award for his contributions to Keene's Pee Wee football program.

Firemen Laurence Thompson was given a certificate of appreciation for his 33 years on the department.

Officer Robert Donovan of the police department was recognized by serving 25 years on the force.

Certificates recognizing 30 years service to the fire department were given to Paul

Crowell Sr., H. Emile DeRosier, Laurence Wood and Robert Driscoll.

Certificates for 15 years of service went to George Shepard, Jr., Armand Jacques, John Dennis, Jr., all firemen and to Blaine McLellan, a policeman.

Ten-year awards were presented to Officers Hugh McLellan and David Hackler of the police department.

Those receiving recognition for five years of service included Gary Bergeron, Robert Crowell, Bruce Pollock and Robert Spicher, who are firemen.

As Reported by the *Keene Evening Sentinel* April 24th, 1978:

"FIRE"

Wind Whips 3 Brush Fires; George St. House Fire Halted

Fire Halted – Keene firefighters move to control fire in second story of Fred W. Harriman Jr., residence at 101 George St., as smoke seeps from eaves. Fire was halted quickly. Photo by Oliver.

A light but brisk spring breeze fanned three brush fires fought Sunday by Keene firefighters.

Firefighters responded to the first brush fire at 11:53 a.m. in a wooded area behind a housing project at North and Gilsum Streets.

Frederick H. Beauchesne, deputy fire chief, said the blaze—which was put out in

less than five minutes—started in a mattress, which had been thrown into the woods.

A second grass fire occurred just before 2:30 p.m. at 411 Champman Road. That fire was put out in 30 minutes, Beauchesne said.

The causes of the fires were unknown this morning.

Keene police are assisting firefighters in investigating a third grass fire reported shortly after 4:30 p.m. on North Lincoln Street, opposite the north gate to Woodland Cemetery.

Two fire trucks had to be called in to douse that blaze, which firefighters say is of suspicious origin.

At about the same time firefighters were responding to the North Lincoln Street brush fire, two alarms were called in for a fire at the residence of Fred W. Harriman, Jr., of 101 George St.

Beauchesne said the blaze began in a second-story room, which the family used as a storage area.

Because firefighters were able to respond quickly and spray inside the house with portable machinery, only minimal smoke and water damage occurred, Beauchesne said.

The outside of the roof was spared serious damage but "the inside ceilings are pretty messed up with heavy soot," Beauchesne said.

The cause of that fire was undetermined this morning.

As Reported by the *Keene Evening Sentinel* May 17th, 1978:

"RESCUE"

City Worker Hospitalized after Cave-In on Cross Street

A Keene Public Works Department worker was listed in fair condition at Cheshire Hospital late this morning after being caught in an earth cave in on Cross Street Tuesday afternoon.

Glenn Priest, 25, of 72 High St was working in a newly dug ditch when the sides caved in. Although Priest's face was not buried by the earth, said John W. Ranagan, acting director of the Keene Public Works Department, the weight of the caving walls of the ditch caused injuries. Priest was brought to Cheshire Hospital shortly after the incident about 4:30 p.m.

Priest is in the intensive care unit being treated for multiple injuries, according to a hospital spokesman.

The trouble began when the city public works department got a call that a sewer was plugged up at 57 Cross St.

Ranagan said Priest, a sewage treatment plant operator, and an assistant engineer were dispatched to the scene along with employees from Park Construction Corp. of Rindge.

The company, in the last several weeks, laid a water main in the area and was called in because city officials suspected that work may have damaged sewer pipes.

Under the city's contract with the company, it is responsible for repairing damage accidentally caused to sewer lines, said Ranagan.

The backhoe operator for the Park Company dug a ditch about six feet deep and four feet wide, Ranagan said, and Priest was in the hole trying to find where the house's sewer line linked up with the city sewer main.

Apparently some of the earth on the sides of the ditch was loose from the digging in the last few weeks and that's why it suddenly gave way, Ranagan said.

_____

As Reported by the *Keene Evening Sentinel* July 3rd, 1978:

"FIRE"

Fires Doused in Keene

Fires in Keene Saturday damaged an attic room at 40 Forest St.

The fire at 40 Mechanic St was contained to a rear attic by Keene firefighters, who responded to the call at 8:19 p.m.

The building, a two-and-a-half story, four apartment house, is owned by George Trahan.

The fire apparently started from defective electrical wiring, according to Keene Deputy Fire Chief John N. Phillips.

There were no injuries reported. Firefighters remained on the scene until 9:00 p.m., but returned early Sunday morning to extinguish a minor rekindling of the blaze.

_____

As Reported by the *Keene Evening Sentinel* July 19th, 1978:

"STORY"

Fire Prevention Workshop Topic

Six hour-long workshops focusing on fire prevention, exit drills and safety measures in the event of a fire will be held at the Keene Fire Department at 32 Vernon St. on Friday, Saturday and Sunday.

The workshops, one at 7 p.m. and repeated again at 8:30 p.m., each of the three nights, will feature talks on fire prevention, movies and leaflet handouts with safety tips for households, according to Keene firefighter Bruce Polluck, who's coordinating the program.

The public is urged to attend, Pollock says, and admission is free.

The mini-course will include information on smoke detectors and planning escape routes from a burning house. Pollock says the course will remind people to take a few seconds to examine the layout of public buildings, too so an escape route might be envisioned in the event of an emergency.

He said several recent fatalities resulting from fires in the area may have been prevented had the victims been protected by smoke detectors and if they'd had escape routes from their homes.

Such planning "only takes a few minutes of your time," Pollock says, "and they are life-saving techniques."

Children, more importantly, should be aware of how to get out of a house in case of fire, he says.

As Reported by the *Keene Evening Sentinel* August 21st, 1978:

"STORY"

Fire Prevention Meetings Begin

The first of six fire-prevention workshops will be held at 7 o'clock tonight, with another one following at 8:30, at the Keene Fire Department at 35 Vernon St.

The hour-long sessions are designed for the public and will be held twice a night through Wednesday.

Information on smoke detectors, planning of escape routes and other safety measures will be discussed.

The workshops are free, and attendance will be limited to about 100 people per session.

As Reported by the *Keene Evening Sentinel* September 20th, 1978:

"FIRE"

Motel Fire Guts Room; No Injuries

A fire in the Valley Green Motel at 379 West St early this morning destroyed the furnishings in one second-floor room, according to Deputy John Phillips of the Keene Fire Department.

The fire was reported at 3:43 a.m., according to Southwestern NH Fire Mutual Aid, and three units from the Keene department responded.

The occupant of the room, George Speers, of East Haven CT, woke up when the room was filled with smoke and exited through the window, Phillips said.

Although Speers broke through the glass to get to the balcony outside the window, he didn't receive any cuts or other injuries.

After alerting the desk manager to call the fire department, Speers woke up the people in adjacent rooms.

The construction of the building fireproof cement block floors and ceilings prevented the fire from spreading, Phillips said.

The fire was under control in a few minutes, but firefighters remained at the motel until about 8:30 a.m.

Phillips said the cause of the fire is not known at this time and is under investigation.

As Reported by the *Keene Evening Sentinel* October 7th, 1978:

"STORY"

Fire Prevention Tips

Fire Prevention Week will be observed from Sunday to October 14 around the county, according to the National Fire Prevention Association.

The association says that nearly 10,000 Americans died in fires in 1977 and an estimated 7,800 of those were in their homes.

Going Down. Keene firefighter Ronald Amadon makes his way down rope suspended from 100-foot ladder at Lincoln School. This is Fire-Prevention Week and fire officials are visiting schools to tell youngsters how fires are fought and how they can be prevented. Photo by Wallace Baker.

The Insurance Information Institute is offering some suggestions for saving lives and property:

Have a family escape plan and a prearranged meeting place outside the house for use in the event of a fire.

Be careful to clean grease from the stove area and not to leave dish clothes, towels or other items near a hot stove or oven.

Leave a window open near any portable gas or oil heater.

Have any experienced serviceperson check out your central heating system and any chimneys or flues in your home.

Don't clean stained clothes with lighter fluid or gas, the dry cleaner is a lot safer.

Don't use kerosene or other flammable liquids to start fires.

Don't let old newspapers, trash or old furniture pile up and create a fire hazard in attics or basements.

Keene Steam and Hose Company 1978. *Seated from L to Rt. FF Armand Jacques, Clerk nFF Douglas wright, 2nd Lt. William Peets, Capt, William Sanderson, 1st Lt. Merton Mills, Lt. Fredrick Birgham, FF Clark Rowell, Standing from L to Rt. FF Wayne Guyette, FF Robert Mason, FF Wayne Crowell, FF Wayne Spofford, FRF Gordon Davis, FF Jack Little, FF Berry Pierson, FF Donald Blanchard.*

As Reported by the *Keene Evening Sentinel* November 16th, 1978:

"FIRE"

Lots of Smoke, Not Much Fire

Firefighters from Keene and Peterborough dealt more with smoke than fire Wednesday and early this morning.

In Keene, firefighters spent more than two-and-a-half hours hosing down a smoldering tree near Keene High School Wednesday afternoon.

The fire apparently started when someone stuffed a burning item into the old hollow tree. The fire did not spread beyond the tree.

In Peterborough, firefighters from three departments responded when heavy black smoke was spotted at Gates, Inc. on Main Street in West Peterborough at 1:32 this morning.

There never was any real fire present, though, just lots of smoke from the oil preheater in the boiler room, according to an official at Southwestern N.H. Fire Mutual Aid in Keene.

_____

1979

As Reported by the *Keene Evening Sentinel* February 3rd, 1979:

"STORY"

Study of City Pay Scale Urges Increase to Lift Wages to Local Industry Level

A detailed study of pay scales for Keene city government employees calls for salary increases to bring city wage levels up to those of local industry and comparable cities elsewhere.

The report, prepared by Yarger and Associates Inc. of Falls Church, VA, is now being considered by City Manager J. Patrick MacQueen and the Keene City Council for possible implementation this year. However, city officials have said that any pay increases will have to be considered in light of their impact on local property taxes.

The consultants have offered city officials two options for increasing salaries. One would hike the city payroll by 5.5 percent the other would result in an 11.6 percent rise in the annual payroll.

Firefighters currently get $8,769 to$12,291. The proposed budget would bring it to $10,457 to $13,422.

The city's employment policies and benefits are comparable to those of local industry for the number of hours worked, overtime pay practices, holidays, vacations, hospitalization and life insurance.

The city has a slightly more favorable policy for sick leave than the selected local industries, but contributes less toward a retirement fund than the industries do.

_____

As Reported by the *Keene Evening Sentinel* February 22nd, 1979:

"STORY"

Keene Adopts $6,423,831 Budget; Taxes for City Government Drop

The Keene City Council giveth, and the Keene City Council taketh away.

On a unanimous vote Wednesday night, the council voted to give the city a $6,423,831 operating budget for 1979 and, although the budget is 11.7 percent higher than last year's, the council has taken away 1.5 percent of the property taxes needed to be raised to support city government.

Last year, property taxpayers contributed $2,463,944 to run the city government. This year, that figure is actually down by $36,870, despite a $673,284 increase in spending. The savings come from increased revenues and a healthy surplus from last year's operating budget.

Based on the adopted budget, the tax rate for 1979 will be $7.83 for each $1,000 of assessed value, down from $8.50 last year. However, special appropriations later this year or changes in the city's tax base could alter the tax rate, which won't be set until late this year.

City Wages Up 8.7 Percent

The Yarger firm proposed two methods to bring Keene's salaries up to competitive levels. The first would have added 5.5 percent in wages to the payroll. The second would have cost 11.6 percent more for salaries than was paid last year.

Under the first method, an employee whose present salary is below the proposed minimum pay will be given an increase to the recommended level. An employee whose present pay is the same as that on the proposed pay scale, will receive no increase in pay, but employees whose salaries are between steps will get raises to the next step in the proposed scale. If an employee's present pay is above the proposed maximum for his job, there will be no change in his pay.

If the second method is used, an employee whose present salary is below the proposed minimum will be given an increase to one step above that minimum. An employee whose present salary falls on a step in the proposed pay scale will get an increase to the next step, while an employee whose present pay falls between steps in the proposed pay scale will be given an increase to the second step above his present salary.

Peloquin said that the old city pay plan "has been stale for a long time." He said that the raise will make Keene competitive with other towns again, but that Keene should update its wages and salaries every year to avoid the problems that necessitated the major overhaul this year.

The 8.7 percent increase is substantially more than any granted in recent years, Peloquin said.

———

As Reported by the *Keene Evening Sentinel* March 14th, 1979:

"FIRE"

Fire Burns Tanglewood Trailer

Firemen double-checking after trailer fire. Photo by Del Trost.

Fire of an unknown origin caused extensive damage to a house trailer Tuesday night at Tanglewood Estates, according to Keene fire officials.

The home of Henry Wellington of 165 Tanglewood Estates burned for about 30 minutes before firefighters brought the blaze under control at about 9:45 p.m., said Deputy Fire Chief Frederick H. Beauchesne.

The fire started beneath the floor, Beauchesne said, and firefighters used water underneath the trailer and fire-smothering fog inside the home to put out the flames.

The extra wide trailer was unoccupied at the time of the fire, and no injuries were reported as a result of the incident.

Beauchesne said most of the damage was caused by flames, smoke and heat. He said damage to the home appears repairable.

Keene fire officials are continuing an investigation into the cause of the blaze.

———

As Reported by the *Keene Evening Sentinel* March 29th, 1979:

"STORY"

Nuclear Plant Accident Contaminates 3 workers

3-Mile Island will forever change the way nuclear power plants do business for all communities within a ten-mile radius.

Photo by Steve Miller.

————

As Reported by the *Keene Evening Sentinel* March 31st, 1979:

"STORY"

Keene Needs to Set Up Disaster Plan to Cope With Emergency, Official Says

Nuclear reactor. Radiation. Evacuation.

Those four words have suddenly become firmly linked in the public consciousness in the aftermath of problems at the Three Mile Island nuclear power plant outside Harrisburg, PA.

The Keene City Council reopened its file on emergency preparedness about a month ago, anticipating what could happen in the city if a significant amount of radiation escaped from the Vermont Yankee Power Plant in Vernon, VT., about 12 miles away on a direct line from Keene.

City Councilor Barbara B. Battenfeld of Ward 1 raised the issue at a council meeting February 15. She recalled that a letter from Jay Adams of Stoddard has been received by the council, referred to committee, and than apparently lost. Mrs. Battenfeld called the letter out of the Public Safety Committee where it had been since February 2, 1978, and it was then referred to the committee on which she serves; Planning, Health, and Welfare.

At its last two meetings, the planning committee has discussed issues raised by Adams and others, and City Manager J. Patrick MacQueen has also become involved.

MacQueen said Friday afternoon that Keene now has no detailed plans for coping with a disaster or coordinating an evacuation Fire Chief Robert N. Guyette, who heads the city's civil defense network, has a direct radio link with the Vernon plant through Southwestern N.H. Fire Mutual Aid. Nevertheless, the city needs to begin work on a disaster plan, MacQueen said.

He has talked with Guyette, Health Officer Alfred H. Merrifield and heads of other city departments in recent weeks, MacQueen said, but so far it has been "just talk."

MacQueen said he hopes to devise a working plan with the help of city staff members and then present it to the council. He added that the plan is just one of many projects facing the city. The Pennsylvania incident may not push the planning to the top of the priority list, but it "won't slow it down any," he said.

Any Keene plan would include agencies such as schools, hospital, police, fire, and public works departments, MacQueen said.

The city is also looking into monitoring the atmosphere for radiation. MacQueen sees the problem as one the region might confront as a whole.

According to Councilor Gordon S. McCollester of Ward 1, the nearest monitoring device is in Concord; Merrifield has written to state health officials about the value and cost of such devices, McCollester said Friday.

Mayor Richard P. Peloquin said more conventional disasters pose a more immediate threat to Keene's safety than the Vernon power plant does.

"My concern was, and still is, in the hazardous materials that pass through this town every day," Peloquin said, citing the volatile goods carried by trucks on Route 101 and the gas shipped by rail through the center of Keene.

Jay Adams' letter was never reported out of committee last year, as it should have been. Two weeks after the Public Safety Committee received the letter in February, 1978, the committee asked for more time to study the safety issues. The letter apparently was then forgotten about, and the committee members changed.

Adams attended a council meeting December 11, 1978, and asked to be allowed to speak during the "citizens forum" section of the meeting. Because he is not a Keene resident, he was denied the opportunity, but then chairman of the Planning, Health, and Welfare Committee, Timothy N. Robertson, invited Adams to address his committee.

Adams did so, and the letter is now officially in the hands of the planning committee.

Mrs. Battenfeld said Friday that she hopes the council will come up with an emergency plan, adding that she thought the Three Mile Island accident "will get us all to thinking" about nuclear power.

————

As Reported by the *Keene Evening Sentinel* April 4th, 1979:

"STORY"

If Keene Faced a Disaster, There Would be Problems

What would happen if:

A serious accident occurred at the Vermont Yankee nuclear power plant in Vernon, VT and high levels of radiation req2uired a full-scale evacuation of Keene."

Or another kind of disaster occurred in the Keene area—fire, flood or traffic accident in which nuclear material was spilled—that required immediate relocation of dozens of families:

Right now, city and state officials have some rough ideas, but nothing definite.

State disaster officials say it's unlikely that the Vernon plant would have an accident requiring serious safety measures in Keene, since the city is outside the area in which harmful levels of radiation would occur.

But what if the more than 22,000 residents of Keene, plus thousands more from nearby communities, had to be evacuated possibly within just a few hours"

There would be problems according to David W. Hayden, protection planner for the N.H. Department of Civil Defense.

Hayden said there's no plan for a full scale evacuation of the Keene area because there is little need for one.

If fact, according to Keene Fire Chief Robert N. Guyette--who's also the city's Civil Defense director—present evacuation plans for emergency at the Vernon plant call for people to head for Keene. There is nothing in the system about people being shipped out of the area.

The federal Nuclear Regulatory Agency requires evacuation plans only for towns within a three-mile radius of the Vernon plant. Keene is about 12 miles away. The NRC is considering extending that evacuation area to 10 miles, but that still leaves most of Keene out.

Hayden admitted that, despite the federal guidelines, it's possible that an accident at the Vernon plant could be serious enough to affect Keene.

A major problem in that case would be transportation and traffic, Hayden said. There aren't very many roads leading out of Keene, and most could not handle safely the rush that an evacuation would cause, he said. And some of those roads couldn't be used because they head toward the nuclear plant.

And what about evacuating Cheshire Hospital patients, or caring for people injured in the hustle of an exodus?

Hayden said the state government would assist city officials in the case of a nuclear disaster, although if an evacuation was ordered, it would have to be carried out by Keene officials.

Hayden noted that, in any disaster plan, an evacuation is always a last resort because it is dangerous and confusing and inevitably some people would be hurt.

"You've got to weigh the disaster against the difficulties of evacuation," he said. "The dangers of evacuation have got to be less than the dangers of staying."

But if there were an evacuation, the city would depend heavily on the Red Cross, Hayden said. The American Red Cross can produce the manpower, equipment and the organization to cope with a major emergency in Keene; it could get trained people to help find housing and to help care for the sick and injured.

It may be a good idea for the Keene City Council to come up with a plan for dealing with a large-scale crisis—but not just a nuclear disaster, Hayden said.

He said the city should have plans for coping with any kind of disaster; relocating families threatened by flood, finding shelter for people who lost their homes in a major fire.

In a non-nuclear disaster, Guyette would be in charge of emergency action, and he, the major and other city officials would become an emergency, temporary government.

Planning for a disaster can eliminate a lot of trouble, Hayden said, and settle a lot of thorny questions.

For instance, if people have to be moved out of Keene, do city officials have the authority to commander buses? That's a legal question, Hayden said, and when the emergency is at hand, there is no time to consult a lawyer and negotiate.

"You would just have to take the buses and get yelled at later," Hayden said. But if Keene had a good plan when a disaster occurred, those kinds of questions would have already been answered.

Edward H. Wyman, president of Cheshire Transportation Co., said his firm has 60 buses, and each could carry about 50 people in an emergency. He said the buses would be available in a crisis, but no city officials have talked to him about making that official.

A disaster plan would also assign specific responsibilities to departments and individuals, making it clear who's in charge, Hayden said. He speculated that Keene officials might not know today who would be in charge in a disaster.

Keene should also establish where people would go in an evacuation, Hayden said. Keene is an isolated community, he noted, and there are not many places nearby where people could go for shelter. In the case of a disaster in Vernon, he said, people would probably be moved to the Peterborough-Jaffrey area, or perhaps to the Claremont-Newport area.

Without a full-scale disaster plan, the question of what happens if Keene residents must evacuate remains unanswered. City officials said last week that they are studying the possibility of a plan, and Hayden said his office is available to prepare it.

———

As Reported by the *Keene Evening Sentinel* April 10th, 1979:

"STORY"

City Role in Nuclear Accident at Vernon will be Explained

Representatives of the N.H. Civil Defense Department will be in Keene in a few weeks to answer questions about how Keene citizens should react to a serious accident at the Vermont Yankee nuclear power plant in Vernon.

The open meeting is being organized by the Keene area Citizens'

Forum with the assistance of Keene Mayor Ricard P. Peloquin.

Forum representative Kenneth P. Altshuler said today that the meeting is tentatively scheduled for late this month or early May. He said discussion will center on a possible evacuation of Keene as a result of an accident in Vernon.

State officials will explain what kind of accident would force such an evacuation, how the evacuation would be handles and where people would go, Altshuler said.

In addition, the forum hopes to get representatives of the Vermont Yankee plant to attend the meeting.

Altshuler emphasized that there will be no discussion about the pros and cons of nuclear power. The aim of the nonpartisan forum is to get information to the public, he said.

Peloquin is helping the forum get in touch with state disaster officials, He talked with Eileen Foley, head of the state's civil defense office, and she has been very helpful in setting up the meeting, he said.

Mrs. Foley will send representatives from her office to explain disaster plans and to demonstrate radiation monitoring devices, Peloquin said.

The Citizen's Forum was organized in January as a nonpartisan group with the goal of bringing information about important local issues to the public.

Altshuler said the steering committee for the forum, which was named last week, includes himself, Elizabeth L. Brown, Peloquin, David Sutherland, Jackie Thiele, Allan N. Kendall, Mark D. Russell and Cecile Goff.

———

As Reported by the *Keene Evening Sentinel* August 9th, 1979:

"MOTOR VEHICLE CRASH"

Woman Dies of Injuries in Keene

Fatal Crash. Norman Scofield of Walpole is placed on a stretcher for trip to Cheshire Hospital after Route 12 accident Wednesday. He is in good condition today, but his wife, Ruth died from her injuries. Photo by Wallace Baker.

A Walpole woman was killed and her husband injured in a one-car accident on Route 12 in Keene Wednesday.

Ruth Schofield, 68, of Walpole died at 3 p.m. Wednesday in Cheshire Hospital as a result of injuries suffered in an accident nearly two hours earlier. The exact nature of Mrs. Schofield's injuries were not available this morning.

Mrs. Schofield's husband, Norman, 71, was admitted to Cheshire Hospital for treatment of multiple cuts and bruises he received in the accident; he was reported in good condition this morning.

Keene police said Norman Schofield was driving the car south on Route 12, between Maple Avenue and West Street, when the vehicle went out of control at 1:05 p.m., flipping over several times.

The car was extensively damaged.

Funeral arrangements were incomplete this morning, and will be announced Friday by the Fenton and Hennessey Funeral Home of Bellows Falls, VT.

———

As Reported by the *Keene Evening Sentinel* August 21st, 1979:

"FIRE"

Fire, Water Damage Crystal

A small fire in the Crystal Restaurant Inc. at 81 Main St. forced police to divert southbound Main Street traffic onto Gilbo Avenue for about 45 minutes Monday.

The fire, which started in a storage area on the second floor of the restaurant, was reported at 3:48 p.m. and was nearly extinguished by the restaurant water sprinkler system when firefighters arrived, according to officials of the Keene Fire Department.

Extensive water damage was reported in the restaurant, but little fire damage. When firefighters arrived at the restaurant they plugged the sprinkler head to shut off the flow of water, but a considerable amount of water had already seeped through the ceiling of the restaurant's main dining room, according to fire officials.

As a result, firefighters had to ear down a portion of the ceiling to allow the water to drain.

The fire may have started when combustible material was left near a light bulb, fire officials reported. Keene firemen were back at their station by 4:37 p.m.

———

As Reported by the *Keene Evening Sentinel* September 4th, 1979:

"FIRE"

Man Burned Critically in Keene Fire

A Munsonville man was listed in critical condition this morning, suffering from burns he received in a fire early Saturday morning in Keene.

Mitchell Hughes, 29, was injured when flames destroyed a mobile home at 136 Tanglewood Estates. Three other occupants of the mobile home escaped with minor injuries.

Hughes was listed in critical condition today in the intensive care unit at Mary Hitchcock Memorial Hospital in Hanover, with second-degree and third-degree burns on his face, hands, arms and back, according to a hospital spokesperson.

The other occupants of the trailer—John Mooney, the owner of the mobile home, and Warren Mooney and Susan Komos—reportedly suffered minor burns and other injuries, but apparently refused hospital treatment in Keene.

Keene firefighters said the trailer was completely engulfed in flames when they arrived at the scene at 4:30 a.m. Deputy Fire Chief John N. Phillips said the occupants managed to escape the inferno in their underwear, but lost all their possessions to the flames.

The cause of the blaze is under investigation.

The trailer next door, at 137 Tanglewood Estates, was damaged by heat from the fire, but firemen sprayed water on it to prevent it from catching fire.

The Keene Fire Department was aided at the scene by Surry firefighters, Phillips said. The fire was put out in about 30 minutes.

————

As Reported by the *Keene Evening Sentinel* September 7th, 1979:

"STORY"

Keene Fire Illustrates Need for Smoke Alarms: Officials

A fire in Keene Saturday in which a Munsonville man was burned seriously, and which destroyed a mobile home is further evidence of why every home should be equipped with at least one smoke detector, according to Keene fire officials.

Keene Fire Chief Robert N. Guyette and firefighter Bruce W. Pollock said that, in many fires, injuries could be avoided and property damage reduced if smoke detectors had been installed.

Saturday's fire is a case in point, Pollock said.

The mobile home at 136 Tanglewood Estates was engulfed in flames when firemen arrived at 4:30 Saturday morning. The four occupants of the mobile home—John Mooney, the owner, and Warren Mooney, Susan Komos and Mitchell Hughes—managed to escape the inferno in their underwear, but lost all their possessions to the flames.

Hughes, 29, of Munsonville was transferred to the intensive care unit at Mary Hitchcock Memorial Hospital in Hanover with second-degree and third-degree burns on his face, hands, arms and back. He was listed initially in critical condition; on Thursday afternoon, hospital officials said Hughes was in fair condition.

The other occupants of the mobile home suffered minor burns and other injuries, but refused hospital treatment in Keene.

If the mobile home had been equipped with a smoke detector, Pollock said, the four occupants probably would have been alerted early enough so that Hughes could have escaped with less serious injury.

"A smoke detector is the most inexpensive form of life insurance," Pollock said, noting that prices can range from $15 to $60, depending on the model.

The National Fire Protection Agency lists four classes of fire protection setups in houses, ranging from a single smoke detector to a master system that runs throughout the house Pollock said. He believes that every house should be equipped with at least one smoke detector, and electrically operated smoke detectors should be equipped with a battery backup system in case of a power failure.

If a house has only one detector, it should be located in a hallway outside the main bedroom, Pollock said, and the bedroom door should be closed at night so that the people inside can escape through a window once the detector sounds an alarm.

Families should have plans of action in case a fire breaks out, Pollock said.

Pollock said some insurance companies give discounts for residences properly equipped with smoke detectors.

————

As Reported by the *Keene Evening Sentinel* October 8th, 1979:

"STORY"

Residents Line Street for Firemen's Parade

The only thing missing Sunday from a parade to kick off the Keene Fire Department Fire Prevention Week was a fire, as some 40 fire trucks and several bands and muster teams paraded down Main and Marlboro Streets.

More than 1,000 people lined the streets on a cool, gray fall afternoon to watch the show, which featured trucks and muster teams from many local—and some not so local—towns, along with several marching bands and groups.

After the parade, a firefighters' muster competition at the Cheshire Fairgrounds in North Swanzey gave part-time, volunteer firefighters a chance to show their skills.

The parade started in the Vernon Street parking lot, moved south on Main Street, turned east on Marlboro Street and ended on Optical Avenue. Judges sat on a stage near Davis Street and gave the following awards;

Best appearing ladies auxiliary; the Rockingham VT\ Old Town Firefighters Ladies Auxiliary.

Best musical organization: the Brattleboro, VT Union High School band.

Best marching unit: the Hinsdale Fire Department.

Longest distance traveled to the parade: the Lenox Dale Mass Fire Department.

Other activities scheduled for this year's fire prevention week are a firefighter's dinner at Central Fire Station on Vernon Street Thursday evening and the annual Firefighter's Ball at the N.H. Armory on Hastings Avenue on Saturday.

————

As Reported by the *Keene Evening Sentinel* October 27th, 1979:

"FIRE"

Fire Doused at Factory

The Keene Fire Department was called to a minor fire just before midnight Thursday at Sprague and Carlton Co. Inc. on Avon Street.

Two units responded to the first alarm at 11:48 p.m. Officers found evidence of a small fire near a vent in the boiler room, but it appeared that the building's sprinkler system had put it out. A department spokesman said Friday that the engines left the scene at 12:56, but at 1:01 the officer in charge at the scene called an engine back: He had spotted some more fore on the roof.

That was quickly put out, and all units were back in service at 1:42. The spokesman said that steam from the boiler may have obscured the fire from view. Damage to the building was minimal, he said.

————

As Reported by the *Keene Evening Sentinel* November 8th, 1979:

"STORY"

Keene Needs Updated Plan for Disasters, Panel Says

Keene's city manager should call a meeting to discuss disaster plans, particularly what would happen if the city had to be evacuated.

That recommendation was made unanimously Wednesday by the Keene City Council's Health, Welfare and Safety Committee, which is studying two issues raised at a council meeting last week; how well Keene is prepared for a radiation accident at the Vermont Yankee nuclear power plant in Vernon VT, and the safety of the plant's operation.

P. Susan Blair, a Keene State College student, asked the council November 1 to set up a task force to coordinate disaster plans for the city and the college. The existing plan, which state officials wrote in 1972, calls for evacuating about 3,000 people to KSC, and 200 more to Monadnock Regional High School in Swanzey Center.

However, committee chairman Gordon S. McCollester said Wednesday that neither college nor Monadnock officials seem prepared for such an evacuation. He noted that the state government is revising its disaster plan, and will probably change the evacuation procedures. KSC was made a haven for evacuees because, in 1972, Elliot Community Hospital was right next door. However, that building is no longer a hospital; it now houses KSC offices and classrooms, and a new hospital opened five years ago on Court Street.

City Manager J. Patrick MacQueen said the city staff has been working on a plan to cover any type of disaster affecting Keene, using existing emergency organizations and city departments. Those groups would respond to any crisis, whether there is a plan or not, he said.

After the plan is completed, a committee should meet quarterly to update it, MacQueen said, preventing the document from becoming outmoded and also keeping emergency officials aware of their responsibilities and the need for teamwork.

"This project has not been a top priority of the city staff," MacQueen said, but the city council could order him to concentrate on it. MacQueen suggested a meeting of all people working on the city and state disaster plans, plus other officials, such as representatives of the college, the Red Cross, and Vermont Yankee.

That way, he said, the groups could learn about the various disaster plans.

Jay Adams of Stoddard, an-anti-nuclear-activist, suggested that city officials get more information about disaster planning from the federal Nuclear Regulatory Commission, Department of Energy, and Environmental Protection Agency. He also urged formation of a disaster task force.

Councilor Barbara B. Battenfeld said nuclear safety is a legitimate concern for the city, especially in light of the Kemeny Commission Report which concludes that the nuclear plants can be dangerous.

"We should keep the pressure on them (Vermont Yankee officials) to follow the recommendations that are coming out of the Kemeny report," she said. She promised to submit a resolution on the subject at the next committee meeting.

————

As Reported by the *Keene Evening Sentinel* November 19th, 1979:

"FIRE"

Smoke Detector Saved Keene Man

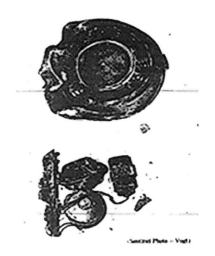

Charred Remains of Smoke Alarm. Photo by Vogt.

A smoke detector saved the life of a Keene man Saturday morning, according to both the man and Keene fire officials.

Russell Cloutier of 42 Cottage St. was asleep on the upstairs front bedroom of a two-story house owned by Robert Dionne of Keene when a smoke detector on the wall outside the bedroom sounded an alarm shortly after 6 a.m. Saturday, fire officials said.

Cloutier called the fire department, and when tracks arrived minutes later, the upstairs part of the building was burning rapidly.

Fire officials blamed the blaze on improper installation of a wood stove on the first floor. A fire began in a partition behind the stove, and swept up to the second story of the house.

Bruce R. Pollock of the fire department said Cloutier might have died if the smoke detector hadn't awakened him, and Cloutier told firemen that he agreed.

The fire caused extensive damage to a second-floor partition and the attic, and smoke and water damage was reported throughout the house.

However, no one was injured. Firemen returned to the station by 8:39 a.m.

As Reported by the *Keene Evening Sentinel* November 30th, 1979:

"FIRE"

Perkins Building is Ravaged by Fire

Keene Firefighters Work Amidst Smoke and Heat. Photo: L- dousing the fire, R- assessing

the damage. A metal building full of lumber and building materials burns Thursday night in a fire at Perkins Home Center on 29 Ralston St. The metal building shown here was destroyed along with a truck and some lumber stored nearby. No injuries were reported. Photo by Minard.

A metal frame building filled with lumber and a large delivery truck at Perkins Lumber Yard on Ralston Street were destroyed by fire Thursday evening.

No injuries were reported, but dense smoke temporarily sickened some firefighters.

Fire officials aren't sure at this point how the fire started or the cost of the loss.

John N. Phillips, deputy chief of the Keene Fire Department, said today that the storage building was "fully involved" with flames when Keene firefighters arrived at the scene at 7:01 p.m. Some members of the crew stayed at the lumber yard until after midnight, he said.

The storage building was filled with finished pine lumber according to Stephen Clark, assistant manager of Perkins.

A large new truck used to haul lumber, parked in front of the storage building during the blaze, was ruined by the heat, Phillips said.

A glass door on the lumber yard office, some 30 feet from the blaze, shattered from the heat, Phillips said.

Phillips wasn't sure this morning how the fire started, but he said it is under investigation. Neither Clark nor Phillips had damage estimates, but Phillips said loss was considerable.

The fire also spread to a few stacks of wood outside the building, Phillips said, but other buildings in the Perkins complex were spared. Flames from the blaze could be seen throughout downtown Keene.

The Surry Fire Department sent a truck to the Keene station to cover for the Keene trucks at the fire scene, Phillips said.

That was a good thing, too, he said, because seven other fire and medical emergency alarms were sounded while Keene units were at the fire.

Keene firefighters were called to extinguish two other minor fires last night at 5:50 and 8:50.

A fire in a trash dumpster at Franklin Elementary School at 217 Washington St. was extinguished about an hour before the Perkins fire was reported.

Less than two hours after the Perkins fire, a second dumpster fire was reported behind Roussell's Inc of Keene, at 9 Elm Street.

Little or no damage occurred as a result of the dumpster fires.

Police said arson is suspected in both dumpster fires.

———

As Reported by the *Keene Evening Sentinel* December 1979:

New City Ambulance December 17, 1979. *Keene City government receives new ambulance this week. Cecil B. Taylor, right sales representative for ambulance firm, hands over keys to Capt. Chester Dubriske; others, from L to R are Lt. John Marechal, Thomas Chase and George Shepard. Ambulance service is operated through Keene Fire Department. Photo by Baker.*

Landfill Burns December 29, 1979 *.For a while Friday, the Keene landfill, in which trash was burned. Several large piles of rubbish caught fire Friday, sending heavy smoke pouring skyward from the landfill off Route 12 near the Surry town line. Photo by Baker.*

———

Keene's new 1979 Dodge Power Wagon Brush Fire truck. Picture by Dave Symonds.

Keene's 1947 Dodge Power Wagon Brush truck to assist with the new Power Wagon. Photo by Ronald Amadon.

1980

As Reported by the *Keene Evening Sentinel* January 21st, 1980:

"FIRE"

Fire Destroys School Shack

A small wooden shack on Daniels School property was destroyed by fire shortly after midnight Friday.

According to a spokesman for the Keene Fire Department, the shack was built behind the school by children.

The building was about 15 by 15 feet in size and contained a crude wood-burning stove, which apparently was the source of the fire. No injuries were reported.

―――――

As Reported by the *Keene Evening Sentinel* January 27th, 1980:

"FIRE"

KSC Dorm Destroyed by Fire

Former Dormitory Destroyed: An early morning fire Sunday destroyed this vacant Keene State College dormitory. The building had been scheduled for demolition to make room for construction of new dormitories. Photo by Baker.

Fire did a job slated for a demolition crew when it destroyed a former Keene State College dormitory at 45 Butler Court early Sunday morning.

The building was vacant when the fire broke out and no one was injured in the blaze.

Keene firemen responded to an alarm at 5:21 a.m. Sunday to find the building engulfed in flames, according to fire department officials.

The building, owned by Keene State College, had been used as a dormitory until Christmas vacation.

After the vacation, students who live there were transferred to other quarters, because the college planned to demolish the building as part of a project to build new dormitories in the area.

College maintenance men were in the process of salvaging timber and other items of value in the building before the fire broke out.

The cause of the fire is under investigation, according to fire department officials.

Firemen were back at the station by 7:20 a.m. although they had to return briefly to

Butler Court to douse a rekindling of the fire shortly after 2 p.m.

————

As Reported by the *Keene Evening Sentinel* February 1st, 1980:

"FIRE"

Fire Doused at Keene Residence

Fire caused minor damage to the Charles Town residence on Peg Shop Road this morning.

Firefighters from Keene, Marlborough, Sullivan and Surry were called to the scene at 2:43 a.m., but the fire turned out to be less serious than initially believed, according to Keene fire officials, and the additional firemen weren't needed.

The fire may have been caused by faulty installation of a wood stove, fire officials said. It started near the stove and spread along a wall and through the ceiling near the chimney.

Firemen had to pull down part of the ceiling to douse the flames, and some smoke and water damage was reported. The last truck on the scene returned to its station by 5 a.m.

Robert Noyes, a caretaker living at the house, turned in the alarm. The West Swanzey fire department covered the Keene station during the fire.

————

As Reported by the *Keene Evening Sentinel* February 29th, 1980:

"STORY"

Areas Near Vernon Nuclear Plant Work to Update Evacuation Plans

You're in Hinsdale when a siren goes off. Do you hear it? Do you know what it means? Do you know what to do?

That siren could be signaling an emergency at the Vermont Yankee nuclear power plant in Vernon, VT, right across the Connecticut River from Hinsdale and only a few hundred yards from the town's two schools.

Hinsdale officials test the siren on the last Friday of every month, but if it sounds at any other time, it could be calling for evacuation of all persons within 10 miles of the plant.

Right now, a calm, rapid, efficient evacuation of the area would be impossible.

However, federal, state and local government officials, as well as Vermont Yankee representatives, are working to remedy that situation. The U.S. Nuclear Regulatory Commission has proposed new, tougher regulations for evacuation needs and procedures. The NRC has just finished gathering public comments on it proposals, and, after reviewing those comments, will issue its new rules in June.

Meanwhile, towns near the Vernon nuclear plant are developing their own evacuation plans, and state plans are being worked out for Vermont, New Hampshire and Massachusetts.

Vermont Yankee officials may be more concerned that anybody about emergency plans. Unless federal standards are met before NRC set deadlines. It's conceivable that the Vernon nuclear plant could be shut down.

The federal government is moving toward stricter controls on nuclear plants, in part because of an accident at the Three Mile Island nuclear plant in Pennsylvania last year. The federal push has put some pressure on state and local governments.

By June 30, the NRC expects to receive emergency plans from Vermont Yankee, from state officials in Vermont, New Hampshire and Massachusetts, and from towns near the Vernon plant. The NRC aims to approve emergency plans by next January 1, and emergency procedures must be firm by May 1, 1981.

The 10-mile zone was proposed to protect people who live near the plant. The 50-mile zone was proposed to protect food sources that could be affected by a nuclear accident, and emergency plans in that zone involve such things as cattle, milk and crops.

In an emergency, the proposed rule says, nuclear plant operators have 15 minutes to notify state, local and other officials; those officials then have 15 minutes to notify everyone within 10 miles of the plant. Thus within 30 minutes after an emergency is detected, everyone within 10 miles of the plant must know about it.

In a rural area such as Cheshire County, that's easier said than done. Vermont Yankee officials question whether the requirement can be met, and whether it's necessary.

Vermont Yankee has asked the NRC to prove that the 10-mile zone and the 30-minute notification requirement aren't just arbitrary figures, said company spokesperson Stacey Weaver.

The Vernon plant can already meet the 15-minute deadline for notifying state and local officials; some credit for that goes to Keene-base Southwestern N.H. Fire Mutual Aid system. Robert C. Callahan, chief coordinator for mutual aid, said he decided to set up emergency communications with the plant because no one else seemed to be doing anything.

If there's a problem at the Vernon plant, Vermont Yankee personnel will radio the mutual aid office in Keene; Mutual aid dispatchers will independently confirm the nature of the emergency, and then notify emergency officials in the Vermont and New Hampshire communities which are part of the mutual aid system.

That can be done in about three minutes, Callahan says. Meanwhile, Vermont Yankee can use a microwave radio system to contact N.H. State Police in Concord.

But Vermont Yankee officials are concerned about notifying everyone within 10 miles of the plant half an hour after an emergency is detected. Mc. Weaver said Vermont Yankee engineers are working on different figures and timetables that apply specifically to the Vernon plant.

David W. Hayden of the N.H. Department of Civil Defense agrees that the NRC time limit might be needlessly tough.

New Hampshire officials have told the NRC that the 30-minute notification limit cannot be met, Hayden said; they feel 40-45 minutes is more realistic.

State officials are consulting town officials to determine how quickly people could be notified, and the best way of doing it.

Overall, though, Hayden says the proposed regulations are "certainly a far cry better than the original disaster planning." Most of the proposals are based on common sense, he said, and present no problems.

It's vital to have good emergency plans both statewide and in towns near the nuclear plant, Hayden said. Those plans must cover all factors, Hayden said; wind direction, population centers, traffic patterns, road capacities, evacuation facilities, and other items. The plans must also be coordinated among three states, and evacuation time estimates are needed.

We're going to do the best we can to reflect present capabilities in the towns and at state level," Hayden said. New Hampshire officials want to finish their plan by May.

————

As Reported by the *Keene Evening Sentinel* March 22nd, 1980:

"FIRE"

Fire Doused at House on Court Street

Keene firemen extinguished a house fire at 234 Court St Friday evening before extensive damage occurred.

Fire officials said a second-story porch and several bedrooms were damaged by fire, smoke and heat, but the rest of the home, rented by Carole Reid and her children was not severely damaged.

No injuries resulted; the cause of the blaze is under investigation.

Deputy Fire Chief Frederick H. Beauchesne said the house was empty when the fire started: it was reported at 6:02 p.m.

"It was one of those where there was a lot of fire showing, but the guys got in and did a pretty good job of getting the fog to it" Beauchesne said.

He said the upstairs porch was damaged extensively by flames, and several upstairs bedrooms and the family's furniture was damaged by heat and smoke. The only damage on the first level of the wooden house occurred only in one room, where water ran through the floor, Beauchesne said.

While firemen battled the fire, traffic was diverted off Court Street.

————

As Reported by the *Keene Evening Sentinel* March 22nd, 1980:

"STORY"

Emergency plan Okayed by Keene City Council

The Keene City Council last Thursday night put its stamp of approval on an emergency operations plan for the city.

Councilors also approved a new vacation policy for city employees, upped the rates for city-owned parking spaces that are rented to the public and authorized several minor traffic changes on a few city streets.

The city's disaster plan has been the focus of a special committee working since last fall to compile a list of names and addresses of key persons and organizations that should be contacted in case of an emergency.

City, police, fire, safety and other officials who wrote the city's disaster plan intend to add to it evacuation plans for Keene, in addition to emergency procedures that would be followed should an accident occur at Vermont Yankee nuclear power plant in Vernon, VT.

Officials deleted from the city plan evacuation procedures for getting large numbers of Keene residents out of the city, because they are waiting for regional and statewide evacuation plans, currently being compiled by state Civil defense officials in Concord.

The council's Health, Welfare and Safety Committee, which has already endorsed the plan, noted in it's recommendation to the full council that one of the most important aspects of Keene's new emergency procedure plan is to keep it updated.

Officials have said that communications and well-organized emergency procedures are the key to the city's response to any disaster, and that's the aim of the new disaster plan does.

The document also lists churches, schools and other buildings suitable for temporary housing for residents who might be forced from their homes by a major disaster such as a major flood, fire, storm or nuclear contamination resulting from an accident at Vermont Yankee.

————

[Compiler's Note: May 21st, 1980 was a special day indeed for the author of this book, as it was the day that he became Keene's first fire protection college graduate.]

Keene's First Fire Protection College Graduate Stevens Goldsmith. Fire Fighter Stevens Goldsmith is the first firefighter to graduate from the New Hampshire Vo-Tec College with an Associate's Degree in Fire Protection. Attending classes two nights a week, four classes per semester, three semesters a school year, for a total of 5 years to graduate. Since his graduation other firefighters have joined the program and will be graduating in the near future.

As Reported by the *Keene Evening Sentinel* August 7th, 1980:

"STORY"

Firemen to Solicit Funds

Members of the Keene Fire Department will be soliciting donations on behalf of the New Hampshire Chapter of the Muscular Dystrophy Association Saturday, August 16 from 10 a.m. to 6 p.m. at Kings and Central Square Common.

Firefighters will be giving away replica firefighter helmets and will be showing one of their trucks at three of the four locations.

The association provides medical services, orthopedic appliances, physical therapy, recreation and support for the victims of 40 different diseases while aiding research into the causes and cures of the diseases. The New Hampshire MDA Clinic is at Mary Hitchcock Memorial Hospital in Hanover.

As Reported by the *Keene Evening Sentinel* August 8th, 1980:

"FIRE"

Smoky Fire Causes Extensive Damage to 5 Businesses in Court Complex

Firefighters battle smoky fire in Court Street complex. Photo by Kearney.

Fire caused extensive damage this morning to five businesses in the Old Town Shops building—formerly MacKenzie's Ice Cream shop—on upper Court Street.

Two Keene firefighters were injured in efforts to control the blaze.

The fire was reported at 6:56 a.m. and flames were pouring out of the structure when trucks from Keene, Marlborough and Swanzey Center arrived.

The fire apparently started in a first-floor storage room shared by businesses in the building, said Keene Fire Chief Robert N. Guyette.

"From there it worked its way up to the second floor, through the partitions," he said.

"It was a mean cuss to get at," Guyette said, because much of the fire was inside the wall partitions. Firefighters had to tear apart a lot of the building's interior to extinguish all of the fire.

Most shops in the building were damaged by smoke and water, and some were virtually gutted by flames.

Expressions in Flowers, a florist shop, suffered some fire damage and extensive heat, smoke and water damage, Guyette said.

Cecil's Produce-a-Party, a produce shop that had just opened its doors, was pretty much burned out, the chief said, and Monadnock Flooring had quite a bit of smoke damage.

Cricket's Crafts was damaged by smoke and water; fire got into the roof over Harnport, a beauty salon, and the rest of the shop was damaged by smoke. Also damaged was a vacant store that, until recently, housed The Apothecary North.

No estimate of damage was available this morning.

Two Keene firefighters were injured on the scene; Bruce R. Pollock cut his arm while breaking through a window, and a number of stitches were required to close the cuts. Another fireman, Wayne Ericson, was treated for smoke inhalation. Both were treated at Cheshire Hospital, and then released.

Smoke billowed out of the building as firefighters labored to bring the flames under control, some firemen used air masks and tanks that allow them to enter the smoky building, while others ventured briefly inside the structure without air packs and emerged coughing.

More than 100 people gathered to watch the fire, emerging from mobile homes in Tanglewood Estates or The Court condominiums just across Court Street from the complex of stores; tenants of the nearby Maple Court apartments watched from their outdoor balconies.

Police had to close part of Court Street while fire hoses were strung along the street to fire hydrants, and heavy morning traffic was detoured around the area.

Guyette said the cause of the fire was not determined immediately, an inspector from the state fire marshal's office was to inspect the building today.

While most of Keene's firemen and fire trucks were at the Court Street fire, trucks and crews from the West Swanzey, Spofford and Meadowood departments covered the Keene fire station.

When a minor electrical fire was reported at Allan Kendall's Office Specialists Inc. shortly after 7:30 a.m., the West Swanzey and Spofford trucks responded.

————

As Reported by the *Keene Evening Sentinel* September 11th, 1980:

☙   *A Demon Called Fire*

"STORY"

ICI, Life Saving Decal, is Here!

New ICI Home Window Decal.

The Keene Fire Department has launched a new fire safety project—"ici is here"—on behalf of invalids and children.

The department, with the help of local donations, has "ici" decals for area residents. The letters stand for "invalid or child inside." An "ici" sticker on the front of a house will alert firefighters to the presence of people inside who might need special assistance. Additional stickers on bedroom windows will pinpoint their locations.

Most fatal fires occur between midnight and 6 a.m. when people in a household are asleep. More than half the victims of such fires are children and elderly persons who become confused or can't move quickly enough to escape.

Some 10,000 of the stickers were donated to the fire department by State Farm Insurance agents George Liebl and Edward Kingsbury.

The stickers and a folder telling how to use them are free from the Keene Fire Department. For more information, interested persons can telephone the department at 352-1291.

————————

As Reported by the *Keene Evening Sentinel* October 1st, 1980:

"STORY"

Keene Firefighters to Hold Parade, Muster on Sunday

The Keene Fire Department will hold its annual Fire Prevention Activities Sunday.

A firemen's parade will begin at 1 p.m., and muster competition will start at 3:15 p.m. at the Cheshire Fairgrounds in North Swanzey.

Six or more school bands will lead various divisions of marching firefighters and their equipment. The host band will be the American Legion Gordon-Bissell Post 4 Band.

The line of March will start on Vernon Street, proceed south on Main Street, east on Marlboro Street and end at Optical Avenue.

Admission to the muster competition is free. Members of the ladies auxiliary will operate a food booth.

————————

As Reported by the *Keene Evening Sentinel* October 9th, 1980:

"STORY"

Keene Fire Department Draws 500 to Open House

Checking it Out. *Clayton R. Stalker of the Keene Fire Department checks the blood pressure of David Parody of Keene. The blood pressure check is just one of the many services provided by the fire department and rescue squad. Photo by Baker.*

Now here's what to do in case of a fire.
Keene Fireman Scott Collier explains to Lynne Rust and son Nicholas of West Swanzey what to do in the event of a fire and how to use some firefighting equipment. Photo by Baker.

They come from far-away cities, such as Kenosha, Wisc., Columbus, Ohio, and Elmira, New York, and they have strange names, such as Diamond T. Maxim, Ahrens Fox and Pirsch, but they all have one thing in common.

They reside in Keene and are here to protect the city's residents.

They're the fire trucks of the Keene Fire Department, and on Wednesday afternoon, they were all polished, shined and proudly displayed as part of the department's open house.

This is national fire prevention week and the members of the Keene Fire Department thought residents should have a look at the men and equipment that fight the city's fires.

Residents apparently agreed. A fire department spokesman said some 450 to 500 people attended the open house between 2 and 8 p.m. Wednesday. It was only the department's second open house in 50 years; the last was in 1976.

Several trucks were moved out of the six-bay building that houses the department to make room for people to walk about, and dozens of wide-eyed youngsters looked on in amazement as firemen demonstrated the department's "sky genie."

The genie is part of ladder truck No. 1 and allows a man in a special harness to be suspended from a rope as high as 100 feet off the ground. The genie is used to get firemen to particularly difficult points to fight a fire or as part of rescue operations.

Inside, parked precisely on spotless floors, were the rest of the department's trucks.

There are ladder trucks, pumpers, a tanker, rescue trucks and vans, forest fire trucks, an emergency squad truck with massive spotlights and, like any good fire department, a muster truck for competitions against other fire departments.

The pride of the department is a 1930 Ahrens Fox front-end pumper that Fireman Clayton R. Stalker said "will probably still out pump anything else we've got."

The trucks range in age from brand new to 50 years old, and the changes in firefighting methods are obvious. The older trucks have wooden parts, limited instrumentation and conventional fire extinguishers strapped to the running boards.

The newer trucks have more equipment, are often designed for a specific job, and feature a vast array of dials and gauges to control and monitor such things, as water pressure and flow rates.

The fire station itself is typical. There are coats and boots everywhere, but in a very neat fashion, and one of the first rooms one notices when walking in is the kitchen where, when waiting for calls, the firemen sit, have a cup of coffee and solve all the problems of the world, as one fireman put it.

Also in the kitchen are three vending machines, two of which the department owns. All profits from the machines go toward buying the firemen niceties such as comfortable chairs and other accessories the firemen wouldn't feel justified in asking the city to pay for Stalker said.

The second floor of the department has a large open meeting room where firemen set up a display of firefighting equipment. There were different types of hoses and fire extinguishers, a full set of firemen's clothing,

A Demon Called Fire

a fire alarm box, a pair of melted smoke detectors that had saved some lives, and information about what to do if a fire breaks out or if a person is on fire.

One wall of the room is taken up by a case containing hundreds of trophies and plaques the department won or has been awarded over the years. A special table was set up with the 16 trophies won by the department's muster team so far this year.

Also set up in the meeting room was a table for youths who'd like to join the department's Boy Scout Explorer unit captain Paul Crowell said the program has 15 youths involved and he'd like to see another 15 join.

Off the meeting room are the firemen's bedrooms. Small mostly two men rooms that look very much like college dormitory rooms. In fact the firemen refer to the one large eight man bedroom as the dorm.

Also upstairs are the offices of the chief and his deputies, the fire prevention officer, and other department officials.

There is also a newly completed recreation room, complete with carpeting, soft lighting and overstuffed recliners Stalker said the chairs were paid for by the firemen. The room is very comfortable, so much so that firemen aren't allowed to use it during the day, and do so only at night after all the station chores are done.

The room was used Wednesday for a slide show on the daily life of a fireman to Keene. The show was put together by Bruce Pollock and featured scenes of firemen both in the station and out fighting fires. All photographs in the show were taken by department members.

The second floor also has showers, and of course, the traditional brass poles for firemen to slide down and get to the trucks in a hurry.

The firemen themselves are much like the equipment they use. They're from various places and backgrounds, but they have a common purpose, to protect the residents of Keene.

Some of them are ex-policemen, one's an ex-marine, another was trained as a teacher but turned to firefighting when he couldn't find a teaching job, and others have been fire truck chasers, the kind of people who wanted to be firemen since their youth.

The range in age from early 20's to mid 60's, but a walk through the station with an ear open to their conversations will convince anyone of one thing. These men know and care deeply about what they do, and most of them wouldn't be happy in any other job.

———————

As Reported by the *Keene Evening Sentinel* October 13th, 1980:

"FIRE"

Weekend Fire Damage Restaurant

A Keene restaurant and a Jaffrey farmhouse were damaged heavily this weekend in separate fires.

About 350 people had to leave the Hungry Lion restaurant at 667 Main St when fire broke out at about 7:40 p.m. Friday. The fire began in an open grill in the main dining area, and spread upward through the building's ventilating ducts.

Deputy Fire Chief John N. Phillips said firefighters controlled the flames quickly, but crews spent several hours pumping out the cellar and cleaning up some of the mess.

The dining grill area suffered extensive water damage, Phillips said; the ceiling, roof rafters and ductwork were burned and also suffered water and smoke damage.

Even so, the restaurant was open for business the following night. As soon as the flames were extinguished, Hungry Lion owner, Lawrence A. Colford, called in a private cleaning firm, local electricians and his own employees; they worked through the night and the next day, cleaning and making repairs.

More repairs are still needed, Colford said today. He won't have a complete estimate of damage for several days.

The Greater Keene Pops Choir was to have begun its fall season Friday night by serenading people at a Kingsbury Machine Tool Co. banquet at the Hungry Lio0n. However, choir members arriving for the concert found the parking lot full of fire trucks, and chair and tables sitting on a side lawn.

––––––––

As Reported by the *Keene Evening Sentinel* November 24th, 1980:

"FIRE"

Fire Burns Barn, but House is Saved

Early Morning Blaze Fought. Keene firemen haul hoses about trying to get a better vantage point to fight a fire that destroyed a two-story barn at 248 Washington St., early in the morning. The barn and one room of an attached house were gutted, but quick action by firemen saved the rest of the house. Photo by Kyte.

As early morning fire today gutted a two-story barn and destroyed one room of an attache3d house at 248 Washington St Monday, but quick action by Keene firefighters saved the rest of the nine-room house.

Keene fire units responded to the fire at the David J. Avery residence about 2:19 this morning, and when they arrived the barn was fully in flames, according to Keene Fire Department Deputy Chief Frederick Beauchesne.

Firefighters were able to contain the fire to the barn and one room of the house, Beauchesne said. The rest of the house received heavy heat and smoke damage, he said, but did not catch on fire.

No one was in the house at the time of the blaze, Beauchesne said. The state fire marshal's office is investigating the cause of the fire.

Firefighters and equipment from Swanzey aided the Keene department in fighting the blaze.

––––––––

As Reported by the *Keene Evening Sentinel* December 1st, 1980:

"FIRE"

Smoke detector saves house and lives of a Keene family

Three members of a Keene family consider themselves lucky to be alive today and have a smoke detector to thank.

A fire started early Saturday morning in a shed attached to the rear of a house at 22 Cross St. owned by Randall and Heather Locke, and caused extensive fire and smoke damage in the house.

But the family was awakened by a smoke detector, and escaped to safety along with six dogs and two cats.

The Lockes and their 12-year-old son, Jeff, were sound asleep at about 5 a.m. Saturday when the smoke alarm went off.

"We initially thought it was Monday morning," Mrs. Locke said today. We were half asleep and thought it was the alarm clock.

But when the alarm didn't shut off, Locke went downstairs to investigate and discovered that the house was filling with smoke from the fire in the shed. They didn't know until later that the flames were creeping up back stairs that lead to the bedrooms, and into a wall next to the kitchen.

Mrs. Locke tried to call the fire department, but a telephone upstairs didn't work and there was too much smoke and heat in the kitchen to use an extension there. She took her son, their dog and its five puppies outdoors, the two cats took care of themselves.

Meanwhile her husband had pulled an alarm box on the street and firefighters arrived quickly to quell the blaze.

Deputy Fire Chief Frederick H. Beauchesne said damage was heavy in the shed and in parts of the house, but thanks to the smoke alarm—no one was injured.

————

As Reported by the *Keene Evening Sentinel* December 24th, 1980:

"FIRE"

Fires Destroy Van in Keene

Too Much Heat. The heating unit in this van was a little over-active at about 8pm Tuesday night and started a small fire that quickly spread to the vehicle's magnesium engine and gave Keene firefighters a tough battle for almost an hour and a half. Photo by Kyte.

Stubborn fire occupied Keene firefighters for a few hours Tuesday night.

A Volkswagen van owned by John Franklin of Westmoreland was destroyed when it caught fire at the Route 9-10-12 intersection in West Keene at about 8 p.m. The blaze wasn't fully extinguished for more than an hour.

Deputy Chief John Phillips said the fire began in a gas heater inside the van, then spread into the engine block. Firemen had to stand idle while the fire inside the engine burned itself out, and eventually were able to extinguish the fire at about 9:15 p.m., Phillips said.

————

1981

As Reported by the *Keene Evening Sentinel* January 8th, 1981:

"FIRE"

Firefighters Save Two Pets, Douse Flames at Keene Home

Smokeout. Keene firefighters open eaves of Davis Street house so smoke can escape. Fire crews halted flames and saved two pets. Photo by Baker.

Keene firefighters were able to control a smoldering, smoky fire at a Davis Street residence Wednesday. They also saved the life of a cat overcome by smoke, and rescued a dog.

Firefighters were called to the Delia M. Theriault residence at 75 Davis St. at noon after a neighbor spotted smoke seeping from a cellar window. They found that the house and cellar were full of smoke, since a fire had apparently been burning in the basement for some time, said Fire Capt. Francis J. Driscoll.

Driscoll said the fire spread up one wall of the basement and into the first floor of the house, but firemen were able to prevent it from spreading any further.

No one was home when the fire was discovered, Driscoll said.

However, a cat had been inside the house, and was overcome by smoke. Firemen revived the animal by administering oxygen and pumping its legs to pull air into its lungs.

Firemen also carried a dog out of the house, resting comfortable in his favorite chair, which he was reluctant to leave.

No injuries were reported. Officials aren't sure yet how the fire began.

―――――――

As Reported by the *Keene Evening Sentinel* January 27th, 1981:

"MOTOR VEHICLE ACCIDENT"

Four Injured in Keene Accident

Four people were injured Monday afternoon in a two-car accident at Route 101 and Optical Avenue in Keene.

The collision involved cars driven by Linda M. Stone, 26, of Highland Street, Marlborough and Fannie V. Shea, 78, of 26 Colorado St., Keene. Police said the Stone car was westbound on Route 101, while the Shea car had been eastbound on the highway and was turning left onto Optical Avenue.

Both drivers and two passengers in the Stone car were taken by ambulance to Cheshire Hospital.

A passenger in the Stone car, Muriel Bach, 53, of Keene, was admitted to the hospital with a fractured leg; she was listed in good condition this morning.

Released after treatment were Mrs. She, whose left arm was fractured; Mrs. Stone, who had a cut on her face; and her son, Matthew D. Stone, age 1, who had a bruised forehead, a hospital spokeswoman said.

Police said both cars were damaged extensively. The investigation of the collision is continuing, but no charges have been filed.

———

As Reported by the *Keene Evening Sentinel* February 23rd, 1981:

"FIRE"

Sprinkler Controls Blaze in Sears Block Apartment

Firemen attack downtown apartment fire. One fourth-floor apartment was gutted by fire and several others damaged by water Saturday morning. Two Keene firemen suffered minor injuries, when their feet were pinches by extending aerial ladder. Photo by Manlove.

A high-pressure sprinkler system, pumping 200 gallons of water a minute, kept a serious fire from becoming worse Saturday morning in the four-story Sears block at 41 Central Square, Keene.

A fourth-floor apartment was gutted by flames and at least four other apartments suffered water damage in the blaze reported at 10:50 a.m. Saturday in the brick building.

Keene fire officials estimate that the Sears store, directly below the apartment that burned, suffered $30,000 in water damage.

No serious injuries occurred, but three firemen received minor injuries. Keene firefighters Raymond Hadley and Ronald Dunn were hurt when their feet were pinched in an aerial ladder while they were more than 50 feet above the sidewalk, and firefighter William A. Manwaring was treated at the scene for a cut hand, said Deputy Fire Chief John N. Phillips.

Keene Police Sgt. John J. Byrnes said the fire was caused accidentally by a 5-year-old boy.

Fire officials and Robin Severance—the manager of the building, who lives in a third-floor apartment—said the sprinkler system kept the blaze under control until firemen doused it completely.

Without the seven sprinklers—each spraying 23 gallons a minute—in the apartment rented by Lisa Norton and her son, Eric, the fire probably would have spread quickly through the entire building, Phillips said.

"It would have been one great, empty hole inside the building," Phillips said.

Severance and several other residents of the building alerted other tenants to the fire. They said the sprinklers tempered the heat and reduced smoke, but even so, smoke formed a thick, black cloud on the top floor, hovering 4 feet above the hallway carpet, Severance said.

While fire crews contained the blaze within a few minutes, they spent several hours trying to protect Sears merchandise from water that cascaded down through walls and ceilings. Some firefighters scraped water out of the building with rubber floor squeegees, while others collected water in large plastic trash cans.

A dozen tenants from apartments on the building's upper floors, some still in nightclothes and bare feet, huddled on the sidewalk along with more than 200 onlookers who gathered in Central Square.

The Sears building is owned by Frederick Fletcher of Milfore, who had insurance on the building. Insurance on the contents is the tenants' responsibility, Phillips said.

One fourth-floor tenant, Ted Lombard, is blind, but he escaped from the building safely.

Police said the fire started in an apartment rented by Ms. Norton, who wasn't at home when the fire broke out. Gayla Kilyanczik, who lives in the apartment next door to Ms. Norton's said she learned of the fire when she hear Ms. Morton's 5-year-old son run up and down the hallway, calling for his mother. The Norton apartment was engulfed in flames by that time, she said.

The Kilyanczik apartment received minor water damage. Severance lives with his wife and 3-year-old daughter in an apartment directly below the Nortons'; his apartment received extensive water damage. He has moved temporarily into a vacant apartment down the hall.

Apartments rented by Gary Bond and Phillip Powley also received some water damage, according to Severance.

Keene Police Patrolman Gene E. Cuomo aided in the investigation of the Sears block fire.

Suddenly, Flames Poured out of the Bedroom Door

Robin Severance was watching television with his young daughter Saturday morning when he saw a wisp of smoke drift past his front window.

Gayla Kilyanczik had stayed up late Friday night, and was lazing in bed at 10:55 Saturday morning when she heard 5-year-old Eric Norton in the hallway, screaming for his mother, who'd gone to the laundromat.

Most of the other occupants of 10 apartments in the Sears block at 40-44 Central Square, Keene, were still asleep Saturday morning when the fire started in apartment 8.

Somehow, everybody got out of the four-story building safely, thanks largely to people who spotted the fire and to a sprinkler system that held the flames in check until firefighters arrived.

The blaze started in the Norton apartment on the top floor, next-door to Miss Kilyanczik's apartment.

"I heard Eric screaming up and down the hall…just yelling for his mother," Miss Kilyanczik recalled later in an interview, She got up to see what the boy was screaming about and "just as I was going out the door, I heard something crash."

Suddenly, she could see flames just pouring from the bedroom of the Norton apartment.

The boy rushed downstairs, still searching for his mother.

Although the fire gutted the Norton apartment, the building's powerful sprinkler system kept the flames under control, and even extinguished most of the blaze by the time the Keene Fire Department arrived moments later.

But Saturday morning was terrifying for apartment dwellers; they didn't know how bad the fire would be.

"That was the closest I've ever been to a fire," Miss Kilyanczik said. "It scared the hell out of me."

Miss Kilyanczik said she and others moved swiftly in the next few chaotic moments, but "I was thinking in circles, going around in circles." She'd thought about what she might do in case of fire, but the plan "just went out of my mind," she said.

Later, she would pray that her two cats would be all right. They were.

While a friend, Robert Lombard, began banging on doors to wake other tenants, Miss Kilyanczik rushed downstairs to tell Severance about the inferno in Lisa Norton's apartment. She pounded on his door at about the same time he saw the wisp of smoke.

Severance and tenant Lynn MacKay both called the fire department within seconds of each other. Miss Kilyanczik said. Severance then ran upstairs, looking for young Eric, who he didn't know had gone downstairs already.

Severance said he wrenched a fire extinguisher off the wall on his way to the burning apartment, but the intense flames and heat prevented him from getting even close to the door. If the boy had still been inside the apartment, there would have been nothing he could have done about it, Severance said.

The fire set off seven sprinklers inside the apartment and one in the hallway. As the water did its job, thick black smoke began to pour out of the apartment.

Satisfied that people in other apartments were on their way out—including a blind man, Ted Lombard, who lives on the fourth floor—Severance, Roger Lombard and Miss Kilyanczik crawled to safety beneath the thick, black smoke that hovered 4 feet above the floor.

The tenants who fled the burning building huddled in a group on the sidewalk below, some in bare feet and nightclothes, as firemen dragged 1-¼ inch hoses up four flights of stairs to put out what was left of the fire.

The worst part of the ordeal was the feeling that came over Miss Kilyanczik when she saw the fire raging in the apartment and realized "it was something you couldn't put out. There was no way to stop it."

But the fire was stopped, and later in the day, most of the tenants returned to their wet apartments. But Saturday night, looters stole some of the things that had been moved into hallways, Miss Kilyanczik said.

Several apartments ended up with wet floors and carpets, and the smell of stale smoke and soot lingered in the air throughout the building.

The Severance apartment directly below Ms. Norton's was soaked so badly that the family—Severance, his wife, Miriam, and their daughter Rhapsody Lynn, who's almost

three, had to move into a vacant apartment down the hall.

Severance talked about the fire Saturday as he contemplated his daughter's ruined bedding and his soaked stereo-color television console, which he doubts will work again. Chairs, a couch and many other things in the Severance apartment were ruined by sooty water that gushed through the ceiling and walls from the burned-out apartment above.

Frederick Fletcher of Milford owns the four-story brick building; he carried enough insurance to cover his losses, according to Keene fire officials.

But for Severance and others whose property was damaged, there is nothing. None of the tenants had renters' insurance.

Four hours after the fire, Severance, his wife and a friend were clearing out the soggy apartment, saving what could be saved, discarding the rest.

Water still trickled and dripped as they worked. The air stank.

Severance, 25, is a slim man who works at A.C. Lawrence Leather Co. in Winchester. On Saturday, he was subdued and spoke slowly and quietly.

"I've been down here trying to clean it up all day," he said. "A lot of our clothes got soaked with sooty water. Everything got soaked," he said, as he picked up a wet pillow from an equally wet twin bed. Brown stains and black char streaks led from the ceiling and walls to the light blue sheets and pillow on the bed.

"Everything got wet, my daughter's clothing…" he said.

"You just have to pick up the pieces," he said. "It's going to set up back a little bit financially, but we'll make it, of course."

————

As Reported by the *Keene Evening Sentinel* March 1st, 1981:

"FIRE"

Fire Doused at KSC Shanty

A small fire broke out Saturday night in a protest shanty at Keene State College.

Police are investigating what caused the blaze, which was controlled quickly. They declined to say if there was any evidence indicating how the fire started.

Campus security officers reported the fire Saturday at 11:20 p.m. in the shanty in front of Elliott Hall on Main Street. Police said the fire was confined to a small area. Police officers were able to control the fire with a fire extinguisher until firefighters arrived moments later to extinguish it.

Students built the shanty to protest the University System of New Hampshire's investments in companies that do business in racially divided South Africa. After meeting with college officials laws week, the students in the group People for a Free South Africa agreed to post a person at the shanty during the day to avoid possible safety problems. College officials said the shanty could be a safety hazard for children walking to and from school.

College officials and representatives of the group were not available this morning for comment on the fire.

––––––––

As Reported by the *Keene Evening Sentinel* March 2nd, 1981:

"FIRE"

Fire Destroys Keene Cabin

Keene police are investigating a fire of suspicious origin that destroyed a small cabin in the woods behind the Donald Patnaude residence at 415 Woodburn St., Keene.

The fire was reported at 10:55 p.m. Saturday, and the cabin was beyond salvage when Keen firefighters arrived.

––––––––

As Reported by the Keene Fire Department March 10th, 1981:

"STORY"

On March 10th, Valerie D. Coleman Keene Police Dept. Animal officer nominated Fire fighter Steven Goldsmith for the hero of the year award for an incident at Brickyard Pond of Appleton Street in Keene. The letter follows after the incident.

Mrs. Carroll Bringham
Monadnock Region Humane Society
P.O. Box 243 , West Swanzey, N.H/ 03469

Dear Mrs. Bringham; know I am aware of your societies annual Hero of The Year award which is present at your annual dinner. I realize that so far these awards have always been presented to animals who have rescued or warned their endangered owners or have in some way heroically served people.

I would like to ask you to consider awarding the Hero of The Year award this year to a Keene fireman at risk of his own life saved a dog from drowning.

Yesterday the Keene Fire Dept. was called to Appleton St. where a Golden Retriever belonging to Charles M. Davis Sr. of 30 Appleton St. had fallen through the ice into Brickyard Pond. "Sammy" had been in the water for quite a while when we arrived and was in a real bad way. He was about 20 yards from shore with ice separating him from the shoreline. I really believe he would have drowned shortly had Fireman Steven Goldsmith not gone into the pond and literally pulled the dog out. As the ladder was extended out some 20 feet above "Sammy" Fireman Steven Goldsmith went down a rope into the water and pulled him out. All the Firemen at the scene were extremely efficient and competent but Steven was the one who actually went swimming.

I am happy to report that both "Sammy" and Steve have recovered admirably from their ordeal. Since yesterday several people have told me boy how wonderful they thought it was for Steve to go into the water after a dog! They usually follow up with "if he'll do that for a dog, what would he do for a human?"

All the firemen involved deserve a round of applause. Their calm cool concentration in spite of the emotional trauma all around them is a credit to their ability to do the job they were hired for. However this incident was certainly above and beyond the call.

I would sing their praises for hours but by now you should get the picture. Of course "Sammy" is one of my favorite clients as I may tend to be emotional, but if I know if Steven hadn't risked himself that dog would have been in the grave today.

Thank you for your consideration.
Sincerely,
Valerie D. Coleman

Firefighter Steven Goldsmith was invited to the Hero awards dinner and was honored. But the awards are for animals and if the same incident occurred again he would still do it all over again for any living animal.

_____

As Reported by the *Keene Evening Sentinel* March 25th, 1981:

"RESCUE"

Swanzey Boy Rescued from Pond After 20 Minutes Under Water

Rescuers bring Wilson Pond victim to shore. Ice gives way under 15 year old boy who was riding on the ice. Keene firefighters Phillip Davis & Henry Memmerschiemer hold the line to the small boat, upper right were Fred Beauchesne & Peter Rokes of Keene Fire Department began CPR on Ronald Carter. Divers Hal Brown (in water) and Gary LaFreniere (on ice) assist. Photo by Manlove.

A 15-year-old North Swanzey boy, pulled from beneath the waters of Wilson Pond Tuesday afternoon, was clinging to life late this morning in Cheshire Hospital's intensive care unit.

Ronald W. Carter of Wilson Pond Road, North Swanzey, was listed in critical condition late this morning.

Authorities said he fell through soft ice on the pond's surface just after 2:30 p.m. Tuesday, and remained submerged for 20 minutes before being pulled from the water.

The Carter boy is the son of Alfred and Norma Carter; he lives on the east side of Wilson Pond, half a mile from the point where he fell through the ice.

A second boy, Ivan Walker Jr., 14, of Lake Shore Road, North Swanzey, plunged into the bitingly cold water in an unsuccessful effort to reach Carter with a broomstick. However, Walker managed to scramble back onto the surface of the thin ice, about 100 feet from shore, and to reach safety.

As soon as the Carter boy was pulled from beneath the water, and into a shaky aluminum boat, Keene Fire Department rescue workers began cardiopulmonary resuscitation. The boat floated in water that filled the hole where the youth fell through the ice.

The Walker boy said Carter had ridden his bicycle onto the ice, and had stopped for a moment. The ice gave way, and the boy, still on his bicycle plunged into the water, Walker said.

As Carter floundered in the 30 degree water, Walker ran to shore, found a broomstick, and rode his bicycle out near the hole in the ice. But Carter had vanished.

Walker said the soft, honeycombed, 2-inch-thick ice sagged as he walked and rode his bicycle on it.

Robert J. Stiles of Lake Shore Road, North Swanzey, was the first to see the Walker boy riding his bicycle onto the ice in a rescue attempt. Stiles had returned home unexpectedly for a few minutes Tuesday afternoon, and saw the Walker boy riding toward the hole in the ice about 150 yards from his home.

"The next thing I knew, I didn't see Ivan and I didn't see the pole," Stiles remembered. Then, "I saw Ivan trying to scramble out of the hole. He was trying to get back up onto the ice."

Stiles called to his wife, Eva, who called Keene police at 2:48 p.m. Four minutes later, Keene fire and rescue officials arrived.

Other officials called N.H. Fish and Game Department officers and Keene Police Sgt. Hal G. Brown, a trained rescue-recovery scuba diver. In the meantime, Deputy Keene Fire Chief Frederick H. Beauchesne and Peter M. Rokes, an emergency medical technician with the Keene Fire Department, found a small aluminum boat on the shore, shoved it onto the ice and slid it with them as they walked across the soft, sagging ice toward the hole and Walker's bicycle, which had been left on the ice when the boy finally ran for help.

As a growing crowd of friends and neighbors watched in horror from shore, the two firemen began searching the bottom with a pole and hook.

At one point, Rokes thought he caught the boy's jacked with the hook, but it slipped off. Rokes then moved the pole back and forth in the water—8 to 9 feet deep at that point— until he got a solid hold and pulled the youth into the boat.

It took about five minutes to locate the boy, officials estimated. By then, Ronnie Carter had been submerged in the frigid water for 20 minutes, and Rokes said he could detect neither a heartbeat nor a pulse.

While Beauchesne tried to stabilize the wobbly boat, Rokes started CPR, and kept it up until the boy reached the hospital emergency room.

The boat "definitely wasn't build for three people our size," Rokes said, and several times water sloshed over the side and into the boat.

But rescuers couldn't get the boat out of the water and back onto the ice surface, and the ice surface was too soft for anyone to walk out from shore to help.

Then the divers showed up. Brown and Gary LaFreniere, a Keene firefighter, both wearing wetsuits, waded into the water, hammered the ice with their elbows, and began towing the boat on an agonizingly slow journey back to shore.

Reporter Manlove, also a diver, helped Brown and LaFreniere break a channel to shore.

Once the pram reached shore, the boy was placed in an ambulance as Rokes continued CPR. The ambulance rushed through intersections police had cordoned off between North Swanzey and Cheshire Hospital; the trip took seven minutes, according to Keene Fire Chief Richard N. Guyette.

At the hospital, a team of doctors and technicians was waiting anxiously to go into action. Four doctors, six nurses, a respiratory therapist, several laboratory technicians and others went to work.

In the next six hours, the team worked nonstop to revive Carter. A hospital official said the team took turns administering heart massage for about two hours, and then trying to bring his body temperature from 85 degrees to a normal 98.6.

At the same time, the boy's breathing was aided and monitored by a respirator, to make sure he got the right amount of oxygen and maintained regular, although assisted, breathing, said one doctor.

While some members of the medical team kept the boy breathing, others forced warm fluids into his stomach and warm oxygen into his lungs, and injected warm fluids into other abdominal areas.

Reviving cold-water drowning victims is relatively new territory for the medical world, doctors say. New discoveries about the human body's reaction to frigid water makes it possible, in some cases, for victims to be underwater for up to 45 minutes and still be revived with few adverse effects, according to some medical reports.

Rescuers and medical authorities hope this will be one of those miraculous cases.

Finally, at 9 p.m., Carter was transferred from the emergency room to the intensive care unit. Hospital officials said late this morning that Carter's condition was considered critical.

————

From the *Keene Evening Sentinel*:

Boy, 15, Dies 26 hours After Falling in Pond

A 15-year-old boy pulled Tuesday from the frigid waters of Wilson Pond in North Swanzey died Wednesday afternoon.

Ronald Wayne Carter of Wilson Pond Road, North Swanzey, was pronounced dead at 4:10 p.m. Wednesday at Cheshire Hospital. An autopsy was scheduled today to determine the exact cause of death.

The boy was riding his bicycle on the pond's thin ice Tuesday when he fell into the 39-degree water. Keene police and firefighters reached the boy after he'd been underwater for about 20 minutes, and rushed him to Cheshire Hospital.

————

As Reported by the *Keene Evening Sentinel* March 26th, 1981:

"STORY"

Police Seek Diving Team for Rescues

A few extra scuba divers might have speeded up the rescue Tuesday of a North Swanzey boy who fell through ice on Wilson Pond, and a Keene policeman would like to start a police department underwater rescue team to assist in such rescues in the future.

Keene Fire Department rescue workers pulled the boy from the water, after he'd been on the bottom of the pond for about 20 minutes, but scuba divers were needed to break the ice so firemen and the victim could return to shore in a small boat.

Ronald Carter, 15, of Wilson Pond Road in North Swanzey fell into the pond about 100 feet from shore after his bicycle broke through soft, thin ice. Carter died Wednesday, after being partially revived by rescuers and Cheshire Hospital officials.

At the scene of the accident, though only three divers turned up to help bring the youth and his rescuers to shore. More than 50 people, including neighbors and law enforcement and rescue officials, stood waiting on shore to rush the youth to the hospital.

But the swift rescue operation was slowed by ice in the pond that was too soft to support people who might have walked from shore to help, yet thick enough to stop the boat.

Additional divers could have speeded the process of breaking a channel in the ice for the boat, saving 10 minutes or more during the rescue, several workers agreed afterwards.

As divers worked to break the ice, firemen began cardiopulmonary resuscitation as soon as they pulled the boy into the boat on the pond. That provided a spark of hope that the youth could be revived.

One of the divers Tuesday, Keene police Sgt. Hal G. Brown, is proposing a police department underwater rescue-recovery team to help out in rescue operations in Keene and throughout the county.

The team would have about 20 members who would respond quickly to water accidents, with their own diving equipment, and help at emergency scenes, Brown has suggested.

Brown began laying plans for the team last fall, but the key to organizing the team is money, Brown said Tuesday.

Ironically, Brown submitted a proposed budget of $1,433 for the team in the fiscal year 1981; 1982 on Tuesday morning, just hours before Ronald Carter fell into Wilson Pond.

Brown said the $1,433 he's requesting from the Keene City Council in May will pay for insurance for divers, some equipment and other miscellaneous expenses. The council is expected to consider that request, along with the entire Keene Police Department budget proposal sometime in May, during city government budget deliberations.

City Councilor Robert F. Wilber supports Brown's proposal wholeheartedly and said he'll try his best to usher it through the council budget process.

If the $1,433 for the diving team isn't included in the police budget, Wilber said this morning, "I'll bring it up" as an addition to the budget, he said.

Brown said the proposed team's quick response to drowning accidents or people trapped underwater, for example, in a car that's gone off the road and landed in water, could save lives.

"It is my hope that this team would set a new trend in underwater rescue operations," Brown said, "as we dive for a survivor, not just a body."

There is no organized rescue recovery team in the county, Brown said.

N.H. Fish and Game Department divers are usually called to recover people after drownings. Because of a shortage of manpower and the distance that's often involved in drowning accidents, Fish and Game divers generally can't respond to drownings immediately.

Brown says a rescue-recovery diving team could get to potential drowning victims quickly and, in some cases, prevent death.

Recent medical discoveries now show that cold-water drowning victims can be revived after as long as 45 minutes under water, without serious brain damage, Brown said.

Brown has a list of about 20 divers waiting to join the team. They're certified scuba divers and would be trained in CPR and first aid, Brown said.

"I figure if they're willing to use their own equipment and donate their time the cost of insurance is pretty inexpensive to be saving some lives," Wilber said.

On Wednesday, Keene Fire Chief Robert N. Guyette said he, too, supports the concept of Brown's proposed rescue team and said such a time "would make a difference and could be very beneficial" during water rescues.

Wilber thinks other towns in the region should share the cost of the diving team, but said Keene should foot the whole bill for the first year, since towns have already adopted budgets this year.

Brown said the cost of the team would be lower in the second year, since initial costs include some money for rescue equipment.

———————

As Reported by the *Keene Evening Sentinel* on March 30th, 1981:

"FIRE"

Fire Hits Home in Keene

Fire Seriously damaged a house in Keene Sunday night.

One person was injured and several thousand dollars of damage resulted from the Keene fire, reported just before 11 p.m. Sunday in a two-apartment house at 86 George Street. The house is owned by Mary Boomhower, who lives on the second floor.

The first floor occupant Thomas Boomhower, 25, Mrs. Boomhower's, grandson suffered minor burns when he apparently used kerosene in trying to start a fire in a wood stove, according to Keene Deputy Fire Chief John N. Phillips.

The first floor kitchen was damaged heavily, and other rooms on the first and second floors were damaged by smoke and water. Keene firefighters finished dousing the fire by about midnight, but had to return shortly after that when a hot spot flared up in a kitchen wall. The Boomhowers have moved out temporarily, during cleanup work, according to Phillips.

Keene police said Boomhower is scheduled for arraignment April 2 in Keene District Court on disorderly conduct charges in connection with the fire. He was released on personal recognizance bail.

———————

As Reported by the *Keene Evening Sentinel* on June 5th, 1981 by George Manlove, Sentinel Staff Writer:

"STORY"

City Disaster Plan Set up

Keene fire, safety and government officials have finished a disaster plan for Keene.

A handbook listing emergency procedures in the event of a major disaster or emergency in the Keene area has been complied, and the Emergency Operations Advisory Committee of 15 to 17 members currently is being formed. The group will establish a chain of command and outline what each person will do in the event of an emergency.

City Manager J. Patrick MacQueen said Tuesday the panel will include representatives from the Keene Police and Fire Departments, Keene School District, Keene State College, the Red Cross, Civil Defense, utility companies, and city and county government heads.

Communications is the most important aspect of any disaster plan, MacQueen said, and that's the main feature of the local plan. MacQueen said the plan will grow in detail as it is updated, and the advisory committee will meet at least twice a year to see that the plan and procedures are current.

The disaster plan offers no great departures from current procedures. Under the plan, the steps that would be taken in case of a disaster are about the same as they are now, without the plan.

However, written down for the first time in recent years are provisions for evacuation of neighborhoods I Keene to schools and churches, where families could go for food and shelter.

A city-wide and regional evacuation is absent from the plan, officials said because state civil defense authorities are in the process of working out a comprehensive evacuation plan.

Also, the plan has no particular provisions from dealing with a nuclear disaster at the Vermont Yankee nuclear power plant in Vernon, Vt.

In the event of a major emergency the advisory committee would meet at the Keene Fire Department, the designated command post.

Keene Fire Chief Robert N. Guyette, who is also the Keene Civil Defense coordinator, said that the plan tells officials what should be done in case of emergency, but it doesn't spell out exactly how to respond to the disaster itself.

Such details won't be known until an emergency occurs, he said.

"If you could say how or what to do, you could be set up before it happened," Guyette said. Under the plan, "You have your people, you know where you go for your resources, and then you get down to the knitty-gritty."

Guyette said fire, police and Red Cross officials know from experience and training how to handle a disaster or accident. The procedures would be essentially the same.

Guyette said the communications system includes new media and public address system that would be driven around the city to alert residents of emergency procedures.

Eventually, he said, the public should be familiar with the basic plan, although cost will prevent printing copies of the plan so everyone can have one.

The Keene City Council will be asked tonight to endorse the plan. Guyette said that tests and drill are planned in the near future, to see how well the network of communications works.

"It's a start," he said. The handbook for the plan will measure at least an inch thick once more details are added to it.

Currently, Keene has no formal disaster plan. The city had one in the 1950's Guyette said, but it's out of date.

Keene's most recent disaster was a flood in 1976, MacQueen said, when many residents on Keene's east side had to evacuate their homes temporarily.

Robert C. Callalhan, chief coordinator of Southwestern N.H. Fire Mutual Aid and a member of the disaster plan committee said that officials have been talking about starting the emergency plan for several years.

"Now we're actually getting something on paper," he said.

The committee began work on the plan last fall, Callahan said.

———

As Reported by the *Keene Evening Sentinel* on September 16th, 1981 by Elane Cushman, *Sentinel* Staff Writer:

"STORY"

Horrifying Plane Crash Successful

A disastrous airplane crash Tuesday at Keene's Dillant Hopkins Airport in North Swanzey was a success because it was just a drill for area rescue squads and it went smoothly.

The drill gave a frightening taste of disaster for area emergency squads.

But making abrasions, burns, and other chilling injuries and then tipping them off

☙   *A Demon Called Fire*

with a generous dose of blood are run of the mill assignments for Roger Packard of Harrisville and his cohorts.

Tuesday, Packard and other transformers of healthy human bodies into grisly disaster victims made up an extra large batch of blood, using red food coloring, corn starch, water, and dental adhesive (added as needed to achieve the desired consistency) for their deed.

Packard and company, all members of the Monadnock Moulage Simulated Disaster Specialists, made up some 22 volunteers who posed as victims in the mass casualty drill. The drill was called a success by fire, police, victims, ambulances and hospital workers involved at a critique held after it was finished at about 8 p.m.

"We provide our services to hospitals, ambulance services and other on a small or large scale," Packard said. "We've been known to put on some fabulous Halloween costumes as well disaster by design."

As Packard, head of the Harrisville Rescue Squad, put the finishing touches on simulated burns on the legs of one victim, Cindy Lord of new York, he explained why members of the disaster service volunteer their time to make simulated injuries at least a dozen times a year.

"Our role is to try to make the scene as realistic as possible. We want to give the ambulance and hospital crews a closer look at reality, so they can react more as if it were an actual emergency.

"In drills, sometimes it's hard to get the adrenaline going that you would have if you were dealing with people who were actually injured," said Packard. "This is the type of thing the military has been doing for years."

All six members of the disaster service, who put in about four hours work on their victims at the Keene Fire Department airport station Tuesday, are emergency medical technicians and have seen most of the injuries they

simulate. "It mostly comes out of practice. We do a lot of reading and looking around. Some of us did take a basic simulation course, " said Packard.

Lord, an education major at Keene State College, looked down at the "second and third degree burns" on her legs and said; "They look so gross. I think it's going to be hard to get all this stuff off. I was going to go out after this."

"It's all theatrical equipment. Most of it comes off with soap and water." Said Packard reassuringly, as he patter yellow and red globs under the blisters" on Lord's legs. This drill is one of the biggest and our best efforts."

While the disaster service was making up the victims, Ronald P. Amadon, training officer for the Keene Fire Department, was preparing the scene of the crash, southwest of the main runway on the site of the new sewer plant.

With the help of a private contractor who volunteered his services, Amodon dug two ditches, 60 and 80 feet long, in the shape of a cross roughly the size of a Fairchild 227 aircraft.

The 6-foot wide ditches were then leveled off with water and topped with 800 gallons of donated fuel oil and gasoline. The ditches were set on fire, and as flames and smoke billowed upward, the alarm went in.

A fogger set a cloud of white fog into the area, simulating chlorine gas. The drill had begun.

Artists add to horrid drama at Keene Airport 'disaster'

Amadon said he was pleased with the performance of the two-man fire department crew at the airport who responded to the alarm in the department's engine 10 a crash fire rescue truck

"Overall, I thought it was excellent. We made some mistakes, but those involved know what they did wrong and will learn from it. Their response time was about two minutes to put that fire out." He said. "They used the correct foam to fight the fire and made the approach upwind they had been taught to use."

Once the fire was extinguished, victims took their places scattered around the crashed plane and were given final sprays of blood from disaster service volunteers.

One volunteer victim, Brenda Bernard of Keene, is a nurse at Cheshire Hospital. "I've always been on the other end of these drills," said Bernard, a simulated amputee.

"I think the drills are basically good. They keep people on their toes something like this could really happen and they should be ready."

Ambulance crews from Keene, Swanzey and five other towns arrived and began assessing the screaming, moaning or silent victims according to the seriousness of their injuries.

Amadon said, "This was also a good test of our use of a triage or sorting system, its kind of hard to see someone who's injured and not want to transport them to the hospital right away.

"You can't do that in a mass casualty. You have to take the most seriously injured first with the triage system you decide who has to go first.

First or last all the victims were transported to Cheshire Hospital in Keene as police and volunteers for KARES Keene Area Radio Emergency Services directed traffic.

Frank Webinski, director of plant and safety for the hospital, said that from the hospitals standpoint the drill went very well.

"There were some minor problems. There was good communication in all respect and good cooperation. The emergency room was handled very well we've learned a lot from our past drills."

The hospital is required to have two drills every year to maintain its accreditation with the Joint Commission of Hospitals.

"There were a lot of positive comments about the drill" at the critique held later he said."

Nothing major showed up; there were no major errors. Everyone felt that if it had been a real disaster, it would have been handled very well.

————

As Reported by the *Keene Evening Sentinel* on October 16th, 1981 by Martha Burdick, *Sentinel* Staff Writer:

"STORY"

Keene City Council approves hike in ambulance service rates

New rates for the Keene Fire Department's ambulance service will take effect soon and they'll be up to 47 percent higher than previous rates.

The new ambulance rates were approved unanimously Thursday by the Keene City Council.

The new rates will affect Keene and seven outlying towns that use the ambulance service.

The service now charges a base fee of $45.00, plus $1.50 a mile for trips outside Keene. The new rates set at $62.50 base fee and hike the per-mile charge to $2.50. The new system also establishes a separate $12.50 charge for oxygen that isn't used by all ambulance rides.

City Manager J. Patrick MacQueen said the new rates will go into effect as soon as he can send out the necessary notifications.

The new rates will hike fees by about 38 percent for service provided in Keene and by 47 percent for the two most distant towns.

Here's a list of the seven towns that use the service, the current cost and the cost under the new rates (not including the extra oxygen fee):

Chesterfield; $63, ($92.50); Westmorland, $63, ($92,50); Nelson, $57, ($82.50); Sullivan,

$57, ($82.50); Swanzey, $55.50, ($80.00); Roxbury, $52.50, ($75); and Surry, $52.50, ($75). The rate increase is the first since the city took over the ambulance service that had been provided by the Robert J. DiLuzio ambulance Service of Keene until March of 1977, according to city fiscal officer Raymond P. Tracy.

Rate payments are supposed to cover 50 percent of the cost of service, but that percentage has slipped in recent years to about 39 percent with taxpayers picking up the difference, according to Tracey.

We're in the hole now MacQueen told councilors Thursday. But he said the increased rates will cut Keene's "standby" cost for the ambulance service from about $30,000 to $21,000 and the towns standby costs from about $15,000 to $11,000.

City officials said the new rates don't exceed the maximum payment allowed under Medicaid and Medicare, which pay ambulance fees for about half of the service clients.

A survey of 10 other New Hampshire ambulance services initially indicated that only Bristol's service charged less than Keene, according to city purchasing agent Robert J. Wyman.

But he said he later learned that Bristol's service receives a subsidy from some towns, and that distorts the comparison of the Bristol fee to Keene's.

Wyman said the highest fee among the services surveyed is charged by a Nashua firm. American Ambulance and medical Rescue Service, which charges an $80 base fee, plus $4 a mile, up to $30 for oxygen and additional fees, if applicable for use of special equipment.

Only councilor Ruth R. MacPhail complained about the rate hike, but she voted with the other 12 councilors to approve it.

Councilors John W. O'Neil and Robert F. Wilber were absent and didn't vote.

As Reported by the *Keene Evening Sentinel* on October 19th, 1981:

House Fire Hits Keene

Keene firefighters responded at 9:35 p.m. Sunday to the Joseph Begin residence at 100 Arlington Ave. in Keene, where a wood stove had ignited a partition.

Keene Fire Captain George Shepard said it was a tough fire to douse, and required that the wall and ceiling be torn out to get at burning embers. The house was damaged extensively firefighters were on the scene until 11:14 although the fire was under control within half an hour after crews reached the Begin house.

————

As Reported by the *Keene Evening Sentinel* on November 13th, 1981:

House Fire

House Fire – Fire caused heavy damage late Thursday morning to a house at 35 Shady Lane owned by Robert H. Tullar. Keene fire officials said smoking materials in a mattress apparently caused the blaze. No injuries were reported. Photo by Janice Johnson.

————

As Reported by the *Keene Evening Sentinel* on December 14th, 1981 by Elaine Cushman, *Sentinel* Staff Writer:

Two Killed in Keene

Rescue workers administer first aid to Keene accident victim Elisabeth Blaudschun at the intersection of School Street and Gilbo Ave Saturday morning. Mrs. Blaudschun died hours later of massive injuries. Photo by Wallace Baker.

Two Keene residents were killed in separate accidents in Keene and Winchester.

Elisabeth Blaudschun of 124 Elm Street died several house after her car collided with a pickup truck at the intersection of Gilbo Avenue and School Street intersection in Keene at about 8:48 a.m. according to Keene Police.

Police said the accident occurred as Mrs. Blaudschun, 69, the mother of Nelson Police Officer Michael W. Blaudschun, was heading south on School Street and apparently failed to stop at the red blinking light at the intersection.

The pickup, heading east on Gilbo Avenue, rammed the driver's side of the car, and then spun around pushing the compact car into a snow bank, police said.

Police said Keene Fire Department and ambulance crews used the "jaws of life" to free Mrs. Blaudschun from the wreckage and administered first aid there.

Departments throughout the nation transferred from riding the tailboards of the fire engines to riding inside, the main reason being that firefighters were getting hurt by falling off the back of the truck while responding and returning from emergencies. Therefore, NFPA (National Fire Protection Association) passed rules to govern firefighter safety. Riding the tail of Engine 3 is firefighter Paul Symonds on ground and firefighter Thomas Loll.

She was taken to Cheshire Hospital in Keene, where she was treated for massive internal injuries, a hospital spokeswoman said. Mrs. Blaudschun was transferred to Mary Hitchock Memorial Hospital in Hanover, where she died at about 2:45 p.m. officials said.

Police said the driver of the pickup truck Daniel A. Skousen of 10 School Street Marlbourough, was not injured in the crash.

————

1982

As Reported by the *Keene Evening Sentinel* January 25th, 1982:

"FIRE"

Blaisdell Fire Called Suspicious

The origin of a two-alarm fire that caused "thousands" of dollars in damage early Sunday to Junie Blaisdell Sport-A-Rama in Keene is considered suspicious.

The blaze, which was discovered at about 4 a.m. Sunday by an off-duty Keene firefighter, extensively damaged the basement of the two-story concrete building on Roxbury Street.

"I never thought it could happen again." *Clesson J "Junie" Blaisdell above assesses fire damage of his sporting goods store just before*

dawn Sunday. A store that Blaisdell ran was destroyed by fire 14 years ago. Photo by Cushman.

Thousands of Dollars in Damage. *Basement floor of sports A Rama suffered heavy damage and sports equipment was charred – including tennis racquets at right. Officials said fire doors later opened for ventilation prevented the blaze from reaching the main floor. Photo by Cushman.*

Keene Fire Chief Robert N. Guyette said the blaze apparently started in the basement of the building near a cash register and display.

"We have found no definite cause," Guyette said, "it is being considered suspicious.

Firefighters from West Swanzey, Surry and Meadowood assisted Keene at the scene, which, because of its location, "was a hard fire to get at," Guyette said.

No estimate of the damage was available this morning, but he did say the dollar figure would be in the "thousands."

He said firefighters had to wear oxygen tanks to get through the thick smoke that witnesses said was pouring out the back doors of the building.

"You go in with a hose line and you stay with it," Guyette said as he stood in the burned-out basement shortly after the fire had been extinguished.

Pointing with a flashlight to two fire doors that had been opened to provide ventilation, he said, "Those fire doors at the foot of the stairs (between floors) and the concrete floors are responsible for keeping the fire in the basement."

As steam, tinged with a sharp biting smell of smoke, poured out through the front entrance, Clesson Junie Blaisdell, who has run the Roxbury Street sporting goods store sine 1969, shrugged his shoulders and said: "I never thought it could happen again. It's nowhere near as bad as last time."

In November 1968, a sporting goods store that Blaisdell helped run—The Sports Shop—was destroyed in a fire that came to be known as the Eagle Hotel fire, a blaze that destroyed the Main Street hotel.

The sporting goods store was reopened a year later at the current site.

"It's not the end of the world, although it seems like it right now," said Blaisdell, who also runs a sports shop in Peterborough. "It's just great the way the Keene Fire Department handled this."

Blaisdell, a state senator, was at the store this morning where he and other family members were tallying the loss.

Lawrence H. Sanderson, the Keene firefighter who discovered the blaze as he was returning home from a party and then stayed at the scene to help fight the fire, said "he couldn't see anything inside the building because of the dense smoke."

"In a fire, you go in on your hands and knees and try to find your way around. You're following a hose line and have a good amount of air in the Scott Airpaks," he said.

"It was awfully hot," Sanderson said, "I couldn't even really see the fire because the smoke was really dense. Inside, you could hear popping sounds. I don't know if it was ammunition or tennis balls exploding."

The state fire marshal and the Keene Police Department are helping the fire investigation.

———

From the *Keene Evening Sentinel*:

Blaisdell Fire Probe Continues

Arson is possible in an early Sunday fire that destroyed the basement floor of Junie Blaisdell's Sport-A-Rama in Keene.

Keene fire Chief Robert N. Guyette said, "It appears there was a break in at the store prior to the fire, but it isn't confirmed."

He said, "a glass door in the basement was found smashed when firefighters arrived at the scene moments after the blaze was discovered at about 4 a.m., indicating a possible break-in.

Guyette said the fire is believed to have started in a display area, near a staircase leading to the upper floor of the concrete structure.

He said the fire is not being considered a case of arson at this point, but is still being listed as "suspicious" in origin.

Beverly Blaisdell said she and her husband, Clesson—also known as "Junie," a state senator have not been able to come up with a dollar figure on the damage.

The store at 25 Roxbury St. will reopen in "another week or two," Mrs. Blaisdell said.

The state fire marshal, who is also investigating the fire, could not be reached for comment this morning.

———

As Reported by the *Keene Evening Sentinel* February 8th, 1982:

"FIRE"

Patrolman Saves Elderly Man From Smoky Court Street Fire

A Keene policeman spend almost two days in the hospital this weekend after suffering smoke inhalation early Saturday morning while rescuing an elderly man from the smoke-filled basement of a Court Street apartment building.

A Demon Called Fire

Patrolman Randall M. LaCoste, 31, was taken to Cheshire Hospital Saturday for treatment of smoke inhalation. He was released from Cheshire Hospital Sunday.

The man rescued from the smoky basement at 11 Court St., Raphael "Trapper" Dow, 73, wasn't injured, according to police.

The building houses the Foodstuffs store and about 10 apartments on the second and third floors.

LaCoste, along with Patrolman William Sargent and Capt. Paul Crowell of the Keene Fire Department, prevented the fire—which was reported by a passerby at about 1:30 a.m. Saturday—from spreading from a burning easy chair to the basement walls.

When he arrived at the fire, LaCoste said, he went to look for Dow after remembering from a previous visit that the man lived in a basement room.

LaCoste said the smoke was just thing enough to see through, and he found Dow slumped, semiconscious, in a chair outside his room.

LaCoste dragged the elderly man to the bulkhead, up the steps and to an unidentified person who helped carry the man to safety.

Then Crowell, Sargent and LaCoste went back into the basement, found and removed the source of the fire—a burning cushion on an overstuffed chair, a few feet from the chair Dow was in.

After LaCoste returned to the police station, he went to Cheshire Hospital for a checkup for aftereffects of smoke inhalation, which hinders the lungs ability to absorb oxygen.

LaCoste has been a patrolman in Keene for about eight years.

Fire officials said this morning that it's fortunate that the fire was discovered early, because any fire "in a block like that is serious," said the Capt. George Shepard.

———

As Reported by the *Keene Evening Sentinel* March 22nd, 1982:

"FIRE"

Keene House Damaged

Keene House Damaged Heavily – Residence of Eric J. Kromphold Jr. suffered heavy damage in two-alarm fire Sunday morning. Fire started between chimney and wall of house was extinguished. Then rekindled later. Photo by Trachido.

A chimney fire that refused to be extinguished resulted in a two-alarm fire Sunday morning that caused extensive damage to the Eric J. Kromphold Jr. home at 331 Pako Ave.

No one was home at the time of the fire and there were no injuries reported, although Keene firefighter Harry Nelson suffered a twisted knee after he fell through deep snow around the house.

Capt. Chester E. Dubriske of the Keene Fire Department said more than half of the Kromphold home was damaged by fire, smoke and water.

Dubriske said firefighters were first called to the house just after 1 a.m. Sunday for a chimney fire. Part of the wall around the chimney was torn away by firefighters to make sure the fire hadn't spread, but apparently some sparks traveled up the wall and started a second fire that was reported by neighbors at 5:47 a.m.

When firefighters arrived, they immediately called for a second alarm.

Dubriske said the first fire started because there wasn't enough space between the chimney and the wall of the house, He said the fire smoldered for about a day, because the chimney hadn't been used for at least that long, according to a girl who reported the first fire.

————

As Reported by the *Keene Evening Sentinel* January 25th, 1982:

"STORY"

Two Men Killed in Route 9 Crash

Two area men were killed Thursday in a head-on collision on Routes 9 and 10 in Keene, about 1 mile east of the Washington Street exit.

Also, a Surry woman was listed in good condition at Cheshire Hospital in Keene this morning after a accident in Keene early today.

Nell C. Phillips Jr., 19, or 20 Fowler St., Keene, and John T. Hardman, 69, of West Street, Antrim, were both killed in the two-car crash at about 12:30 p.m. Thursday, Keene police said.

Both men were pronounced dead at the scene by Dr. Charles E. Schofield, a Cheshire County medical referee, police said.

Police said Phillips was heading east in his sub-compact car and Hardman was traveling west in a full sized sedan at the time of the crash.

The crash occurred in the eastbound lane, police said.

Police said there were no passengers in either vehicle and no witnesses to the accident.

Traffic was rerouted through the area for several hours while police and rescue workers cleared the scene.

Keene police are investigating the accident.

Police said it took Keene fire department rescue workers nearly 30 minutes to free Belinda Reney of Surry from her car after an accident on Route 9 near Winchester Street in Keene at about 2 a.m. today, her 21st birthday.

She suffered a dislocated hip and scrapes on her forehead and legs in the accident, a hospital spokesman said.

Witnesses told police Reney was traveling west in the eastbound lane when her vehicle hit the rear wheels of a tractor-trailer truck that was trying to get out of her way.

The driver of the truck, Robert Wade of Mt. Holy, Vermont, was not injured, police said.

Reney faces charges in connection with the accident, police said.

————

As Reported by the *Keene Evening Sentinel* March 26th, 1982:

Fire Department's New Rescue Boat

Chilly Trial – Keene Fire Department Capt. Ronald P. Amadon pulls Firefighter Scott Taylor out of Ashuelot River in test of department's new ice and water rescue boat. The boat has skids on the bottom for use on ice. Photo by Baker.

————

As Reported by the *Keene Evening Sentinel* May 24th, 1982:

"FIRE"

Fire Damages Apartment

Keene firefighters quickly doused a Sunday morning fire in the bedroom of a Gilsum Street apartment, but they couldn't prevent the blaze from causing serious damage.

No one was injured in the blaze, which was reported at 10:56 a.m. in the first-floor apartment of Arleen Johnson at 114 Gilsum St., according to Capt. George Shepard of the Keene Fire Department. But the bedroom, where the fire started, was gutted by flames, and the rest of the apartment was damaged by smoke, water and heat, he said.

The cause of the fire, which started in a clothes closet, is under investigation, he said.

Ms. Johnson and her children were at home when the fire started, but escaped unhurt. Tenants in a second-floor apartment were temporarily evacuated, officials said.

The apartment, owned by the Keene Housing Authority, is one of several in a public housing complex between North and Gilsum Streets.

———————

As Reported by the *Keene Evening Sentinel* August 22nd, 1982:

Mud Football Team

Front Row, Seated: Marty Wilson, Gary Lamoureux, Steve Goldsmith. Second Row, Kneeling: Gary LaFreniere, Clayton Stalker, Carl Collier, Paul Scoz, Harry Welson, Bruce Pollock. Third Row, Standing: Bob Symonds, Brad Payne, Phil Davis, Alex Matson, Dave Symonds.

The Keene Fire Department sponsors each year a fundraiser for the Muscular Dystrophy Association. Mud football was the game of choice between the Keene Fire Department and the Keene Police Department which raised over $1,000; Keene Police won 8—0. A good time was had by all.

———————

As Reported by the *Keene Evening Sentinel* September 13th, 1982:

"FIRE"

Fire Damages Apartments in Keene; Man Escapes When Wakened by Smoke

Aftermath – Keene call fireman James A. Beauregard relaxes after helping to douse a fire that damaged two apartments and left one family homeless Saturday. Photo by Elaine Cushman.

Keene officials are trying to determine the cause of a two-alarm blaze that forced a Keene man to flee his smoke-filled apartment and caused considerable damage to two apartments in a Marlboro Street building.

The fire started in the closet of a ground-floor apartment shortly before 1 p.m. Saturday and spread up a pipe chase into a second-floor apartment, according to Keene Fire Chief Robert N. Guyette.

Keene firefighters fought the blaze in the 80-degree temperatures for more than an hour before bringing it under control, while firefighters from West Swanzey and Marlborough covered the Keene station.

Guyette said fire, smoke and water damage to the apartments was considerable.

Maureen A. Gibson, who lives in the damaged first floor apartment, said she and her 4-year-old daughter, Jeneca, will have to stay with friends or family.

"I don't know what I will do right now," Ms. Gibson said as she sat in the badly damaged apartment Saturday.

Guyette said this morning that the cause of the blaze in the two-story wooden structure, which has six apartments, has not been determined.

One breath of the thick, acrid smoke was all it took to bring Jon Lounder to his feet.

"Lounder, the only person who was in the building at 259 Marlboro St. when the fire started, was asleep in his second-floor apartment Saturday when he "rolled over and took one breath."

"When you first wake up, you don't really want to wake up. I'm a pretty sound sleeper. I didn't know what woke me up, I just took a breath and that was it. I started I started choking," said Lounder, who works at American Optical in Keene.

Lounder said he didn't panic, but he did move quickly.

"You read about people dying of smoke inhalation so I just held my breath. There was a lot of smoke, I couldn't even see my hand in front of my face. I just felt my way to the door: I've lived here for several years and I knew my way around pretty well," he said Saturday, as he stood watching firefighters spraying water on a pile of charred furniture and toys outside the building,

He said he "didn't even have time to put on my clothes. It was kind of embarrassing sitting in the car with a blanket around me until I get some clothes. I'm okay; I'm safe.

───────

As Reported by the *Keene Evening Sentinel* October 1st, 1982:

"STORY"

Parade and Muster Sunday Begin Fire Prevention Week

The Keene Fire Department will recognize Fire Prevention Week, October 2-9 with a parade Sunday at 1 p.m. with bands and 50 to 75 pieces of fire equipment, old, new and antique. The parade route will include Central Square, Main Street, and Marlboro Street, ending on Optical Avenue.

A muster will be held at 3 p.m. at the Cheshire Fairgrounds in North Swanzey, with eight to 10 teams from New England and New York competing. There will be no admission charge, and refreshments will be available.

A supper for fire department members only, put on by the ladies auxiliary, will be held Thursday night.

The week will end Saturday, October 9, with the annual Firefighter's Ball from 9 p.m. to 1 a.m. at the National Guard Armory on Hastings Avenue in Keene. The cost is $2.50 per person, and people can bring their own alcoholic beverages. Tickets will be available at the door.

As Reported by the *Keene Evening Sentinel* November 18th, 1982:

"STORY"

Workers Mopping up Beaver Brook Oil Spill; Keene Truck Driver Remains in Fair Condition

Officials trying to clean up as much as 2,000 gallons of No. 2 home heating oil that gushed into Beaver Brook in Keene Wednesday after a delivery truck careened over a bridge estimated this morning that cleanup costs might reach $100,000.

Meanwhile, the driver of the truck, Philip Lagerberg, 26, of 108 Tanglewood Estates in Keene, was reported in fair condition with a broken leg, broken ribs and multiple lacerations this morning in the intensive care unit at Mary Hitchcock Memorial Hospital in Hanover.

Where the spill started. *Keene police Master Sgt. David Hackler takes measurements while Patrolman Bruce Boucher looks on at scene of accident off upper Knight Street in Keene Wednesday, where oil deliver truck crashed in Beaver brook and spilled 2,000 gallons of heating oil in brook. Photo by George Manlove.*

Ronald Dunn of Keene Department of Public Works uses vacuum to draw oil from Beaver Brook after truck that crashed Wednesday spilled 2,000 gallons of oil in the brook. Oil absorbing booms, snow fences and hay were also used to control the spill. Photo by George Manlove.

He was initially taken to Cheshire Hospital after the accident at 11 a.m. but was transferred to Hanover later in the day.

Keene Fire Chief Robert N. Guyette, who joined Keene's fire department in 1950, called Wednesday's spill the worst he's seen since I've been around.

State, federal and local officials plus a professional on spill cleaning outfit from Massachusetts—converged on Keene Wednesday afternoon to deal with the slick mess that drifted slowly down Beaver Brook. When the oil reached the first of eight floating, oil-catching dams set up at the Railroad Street Bridge over the brook, the tumbling trip down the brook and over a small waterfall at Railroad Street had turned the oil into a brown, scummy mess.

Guyette said both local officials and cleanup crews from Jet Line Services Inc. of Stoughton, Mass. might spend the rest of the week cleaning up residual oil left on the surface and the banks of Beaver Brook.

Floating booms set up on the brook and sucked off with water vacuums.

He also estimated that the cleanup cost may reach $100,000.

"That's the figure I hear being thrown around yesterday" by N.H. State Police and officials from the N.H. Water Supply and Pollutants Central Bureau who came to Keene Wednesday, Guyette said. The Federal Environmental Protection Agency sent representative to the cleanup site at Railroad Street.

Workers including employees of the Keene Department of Public Works and Keene Fire Department worked Wednesday afternoon sucking off the water, and crews from Jet Lane Services stayed on the job until at least 10 p.m., officials said.

The end got into the water less than a mile upstream from the main cleanup site, at a bridge at the intersection of Old Concord Road and Upper Knight Street. The truck, operated by Lagerberg was headed down Old Concord Road according to Keene police, when it shot through the intersection, broke through steel guardrails and landed upside down in the brook coming to rest about 10 feet downstream of where it left the road.

Police Lt Hugh MacLellan said this morning that officials still don't know what caused the accident.

"There's so many things it could have been," MacLellan said.

The 1,800 to 2,000 gallons of oil officials estimated was still in the truck poured directly into the brook. The truck was later pulled out of the brook by two cranes, officials said.

Workers floated special absorbent pads called "booms" on the brook to sop up much of the oil, which floats on water. The water and some oil passed beneath the booms, which also included bales of hay floated in the brook and kept in place by snow fences erected across the stream by public works crews and firemen wading in the water.

"The contaminated booms helped tremendously in containing the spill," said Paul Keough of the Environmental Protection Agency.

He credited state trooper Stuart Bates for calling in local police and fire units immediately and getting the booms from the Keene Public Works Department. The officials checked downstream from the spill and put the booms in place before the oil could seep far from the truck, Keough said.

A few hundred yards downstream Kingsbury's Machine Tool officials also set up a floating dam system with two "sump sucker," water vacuums, to collect what oil got by the six dams, further upstream.

Gary N. Langley, a plant engineer of Kingsbury, said the company provided several employees to help with the cleanup, and they also offered use of company coolant pits to store the oil pulled off the brook until it can be disposed of.

Guyette said that long term effects of the oil spill on any aquatic life in Beaver Brook will be negotiable once the cleanup is complete. He doubted that there was much life in the brook in the area of the spill. Keough also said the spill apparently caused no permanent damage in the brook.

The fire chief praised the work of area volunteers and officials who participated in coordinating the cleanup effort.

"You couldn't ask for better cooperation," Guyette said.

———

As Reported by the *Keene Evening Sentinel* November 24th, 1982:

"FIRE"

Fire Damages House in Keene

Keene firefighter s battle blaze on Old Walpole Road. Photo by Martha Burdick.

An early morning fire today that fire officials attributed to an overheated chimney caused heavy damage to an Old Walpole Road home and left owners Phyllis and William Matson at least temporarily homeless.

The fire was discovered by Phyllis Matson, who awoke before smoke detectors went off at 95 Old Walpole Road. The blaze was reported at 3:42 a.m. today.

"We feel pretty strongly that it was an overheated chimney that caused it, Keene Fire Chief Robert N. Guyette said. The chimney served a fireplace, the home didn't have a wood burning stove.

Neighbors reported flames shooting out of windows four feet to the roof before firefighters arrived. The fire left huge gaping holes in the roof and considerable smoke, fire and water damage, particularly in the roof area, which was heavily damaged and where Guyette suspected the fire began.

No injuries were reported as a result of the fire.

1983

As Reported by the *Keene Evening Sentinel* January 10th, 1983:

"FIRE"

Keene Building Catches Fire

Several Keene Fire Department units were called to a fire at Whitney Bros. Co. toy manufacturers at 93 Railroad St. late this morning after Keene police reported a fire in the building.

The smoky fire appeared to be in the third floor of the brick building. A Whitney Bros. employee said the fire apparently started when sparks from a welding-operation were carried up to the third floor. The worker said it appeared everyone in the building was able to escape without injury.

Two alarms were sounded; traffic was diverted from Railroad Street and a Marlborough unit was called to cover the Keene station while Keene units responded to the fire.

As Reported by the *Keene Evening Sentinel* January 11th, 1983:

"FIRE"

Fire Damages Toy-Making Factory in Keene; 5 0f 150 Firefighters injured, 1 in "close call"

Nearly 150 firefighters worked for more than three hours Monday to extinguish a stubborn 3-alarms blaze at Whitney Bros. Co., Inc. toy manufacturers on Railroad Street to Keene.

But for company officials, the work has just begun.

Many of about 40 company employees, who hurried from the large brick building at about 11:35 a.m. Monday, were back at the factory this morning, beginning to clean up and assess damage left by the fire.

Smoke Everywhere: Fire began Monday in this end of building at rear of 93 Railroad Street., Keene, when a spark was apparently carried up a dust exhaust pipe from lower floors of the building to upper stories. Photo by Elaine Cushman.

Making the best of it: Workers at Whitney Brothers Toy Company on Railroad Street clean top floor of factory that was damaged by fire Monday. Photo by Mark Van Wehrden.

Keene Deputy Fire Chief, John N. Phillips, said the fire apparently started when a spark was carried up an exhaust fan and blew back into the building.

The fire which drew hundreds of spectators after it was reported by a Keene policeman on patrol was brought under control at about 2:00 p.m.

Five Keene firefighters suffered minor injuries—one of them in a "very close call"—fighting the fire that started in the east end of the building at the rear of 93 Railroad St.

Keene firefighters Gary E. Bergeron and Harry Nelson were treated at Cheshire Hospital in Keene and released, a hospital spokeswoman said. Two others were treated at the scene for smoke inhalation and a fifth was treated for an ankle injury, Phillips said.

He said a 500 to 600 pound weight on the metal fire escape at the east end of the building fell from the third floor and just glazed Nelson's fire helmet and shoulder.

"If it had been a few inches different… I don't know," Phillips said.

Cherolyn W. Robinson, company clerk, said she was in the office area working when workers "came down from the second floor and said "Fire, there's a fire.

"My boss ran upstairs to see and I called mutual aid," she said. We covered everything in the office and then went out. Apparently they already know about it by then.

Mrs. Robinson said the company is run by Griffin M. Stabler of Swanzey Center and Bernard M. Barrenholtz of Marlborough and employs 35 to 40 people. "Many of those employees were at the factory this morning," she said.

The company moved into the Railroad Street building, which is more than 100 years old, from Marlborough between two and three years ago, she said.

She said Whitney Bros. makes easels, storage cabinets, blocks and other wooden "early learning" materials. Which it sells to school distributors.

The fire "could have been worse. Fire is something that a woodworking factory always has to fear. We work with wood and wood burns," Mrs. Robinson said.

She said it's too soon to tell if the company will be able to reopen.

Phillips said fire caused heavy damage to the top or attic floor and considerable damage to the third floor. Fire also burned through the roof in several places. The bottom two floors, where the actual manufacturing takes place suffered water damage, he said.

The fire took hold in the attic area that has only two entrances, which made it difficult for firefighters to get at the blaze, Phillips explained. "We had to cut some holes in the roof to get at it," he said.

He said that with the help of a fire wall, which divides the building nearly in half, firefighters were able to contain the damage to the east end of the building. A sprinkler system in the building also went off, but was not able to put out the fire. The sprinkler system has no feeding ducts outside so the water pressure probably dropped too much when it went off to make it effective, Phillips said.

He said he was told that a fire door between the two halves of the building had been left open, but had apparently closed through an automatic mechanism that reacts to heat.

If something has been placed in front of the door to hold it open, the fire probably would have spread the entire length of the building, he said.

Phillips said Keene Fire Chief Robert N. Guyette directed firefighters from Keene, Marlborough, Meadowood and Swanzey Center at the scene of the fire. Fire companies from Spofford, West Swanzey, Harrisville and Brattleboro, Vt. were called in to cover for companies at the scene.

"We had a crew down there all night just to keep checking the fire. We didn't want to have to put it out the second time, Phillips said.

He said the building is part of the old Beaver Mills factory and is more than 100 years old.

_____

From the *Keene Evening Sentinel*:

After The Fire

After a Lot of Help, Keene Factory Damaged by Fire Plans to Reopen

Thanks to a fire door, firefighters and the help of a lot of people in the community, Whitney Bros. toy manufacturers in Keene is expecting to reopen Monday—just a week after it was damaged by fire.

Griffin M. Stabler, president of the company that makes wooden materials used in day care centers and elementary schools across the nation said that some of 35 to 40 employees will be back at their regular jobs Monday.

Many of those employees have been at the factory since Monday's blaze, but instead of making the parts, or assembling them, they've been cleaning up the machines and clearing out debris.

Community members have also been a great help to the company, he said.

"We have a lot of people to thank. The help has been just great. We've been very appreciative of the effort," Stabler said. "It really is sort of amazing that we'll be back in work only a week after that terrible fire.

He said the first floor, where the parts are made, will be reopened Monday and the assembling division on the second floor will reopen later.

The three-alarm fire brought nearly 150 firefighters to the scene at about 11:35 a.m. Monday, Stabler said the efforts of those firefighters is greatly appreciated.

The fire started when a welding spark on the first floor was carried up a dust exhaust system which blows the hot air back into the top floors of the building. The system apparently carried the spark along with the hot air back into the building, officials said.

Fire officials said that they were able to keep the fire from spreading to the west end of the large, four-story brick building because the two ends of the building were divided by a fire door.

The fire door had been left open, but closed through an automatic mechanism that reacts to heat, Stabler said.

"We still have half a factory that was untouched by the fire. That is one of the reasons we will reopen so soon, "he said.

Part of the roof of the building was burned off and Stabler said he was lucky there was no rain or snow this week because it left the building open for exposure to the weather.

A temporary roof is being installed over the third floor and comp0any officials don't anticipate that the snowstorm expected this weekend will be a problem

Stabler said a dollar figure of the loss has not been estimated, but that we feel that we were adequately insured.

The company has been located at the rear of 93 Railroad St since it moved from Marlborough two years ago.

————

As Reported by the *Keene Evening Sentinel* February 16th, 1983:

"FIRE"

Shoe store fire 'tough way to go'

After 37 years of business and with less than a week to go before the last pair of shoes was to be sold, the Boccia & Grout Shoe Store on Roxbury Street was hit by a fire Tuesday morning that damaged the shoe repair shop and much of the store's remaining stock.

The two-alarm fire also struck at a time when the store's owners, Eurelis Boccia and Frederick Grout, had been packing up much of their remaining repair machinery and inventory for sale. A buyer of the material had already been lined up, Boccia said.

Under Control. *Firemen fight a fire that broke out in the repair shop of Boccia & Grout shoe store on Roxbury Street, Keene. The fire was controlled, but damaged equipment materials and inventory. Photo by Martin Frank.*

"Most of what was to be sold was destroyed," he said.

"When you work week after week and then have this happen to you…we were trying to get everything done in an orderly fashion and then this thing came up," said Boccia.

No damage estimates were available and no cause has been determined for the fire, although Keene Deputy Fire Chief John Phillips said smoking material—a cigarette, for instance—is suspected.

Fire damage was confirmed to two rooms in the rear of the building attached to the retail front.

The building at 30 Roxbury St. had been sold to Roxbury Street Elderly Housing Associates, the partnership that will construct the planned elderly housing project on Roxbury Street and Central Square, said George Moylan, executive director of the Keene Housing Authority.

The structure was scheduled for demolition early this year, he added.

Among the items destroyed in the burned-out repair room and storeroom were stitching machines, a finishing machine, shoe materials, and tools.

Also damaged from the smoky fire were many of the remaining shoes in the retail part of the store, Boccia said, adding that the store was insured for its contents.

The first alarm for the fire went out at 11:26 a.m., Phillips said, and the fire was brought under control in about a half-hour.

The fire started in the repair shop under a workbench against the building's east wall, Fire Chief Robert N. Guyette said. No one was in the repair shop when the fire broke out, Boccia said.

"The shoe glue fueled it," said Phillips. "It only took a minute to build up the heat, and then it really got going.

"I looked up and noticed smoke coming from the repair shop," said Gail Trubiano, Grout's daughter, who was working in the store at the time. "My father went for the extinguisher and I called the fire department. As I went out the flames really started shooting out from the repair shop into the hall. It happened very quickly.

"It filled the place up with smoke so quickly, I didn't even have time to go in the office and get my coat," Boccia said.

He said he and Grout had planned on finishing their close-out business on February 19 and vacating the building at the end of the month.

Boccia said that the store will be closed temporarily to allow the fire marshal to make an inspection and might reopen for a short time at the end of the week.

"This is a tough way to go out," Mrs. Trubiano said.

————

As Reported by the *Keene Evening Sentinel* February 22nd, 1983:

"FIRE"

Man dies, 10 are injured in city rooming house fire

Firemen hose down rooming house fire.
Keene firefighters on ladder aim stream of water just above second-floor apartment at 82 Spring St. where one man died Monday. Photo by George Manlove.

City and State fire officials suspect an unattended hot plate caused the fire Monday on Spring Street that claimed one life, critically injured a second person and resulted in minor injuries to more than 10 people.

The house had been cited by city officials for fire safety code violations.

About 14 people were left homeless and eight firefighters were injured as a result of the two-alarm blaze at Four Seasons rooming house at 82 Spring St, which broke out in a second floor apartment just before 1:53 p.m.

The name of a 69-year old white male found dead in his second-floor room on the south side of the house was being withheld late this morning, pending notification of the man's relatives and an autopsy to determine the exact cause of death.

A second victim, Alice Jevne, 59, was rescued, unconscious, by firemen from her third floor apartment, directly above the room where the fire started, officials said. She was listed in critical condition this morning at Cheshire Hospital, where she was being treated for smoke inhalation.

Another elderly woman whose name was unavailable today was rescued from her second-floor apartment by firemen on an aerial ladder, after she pushed out her window screen to escape.

Keene Fire Chief Robert N. Guyette said the fire didn't appear to be to have been set. State Fire Marshal Raymond Dewhurst said an initial search of the charred apartment here the fire started indicated that an unattended hot plate started the blaze.

Where it all started. *Charred room at 82 Sprint St. is where fire began Monday afternoon and where man was killed. In addition, a woman was critically injured and eight firefighters suffered minor injuries. Photo by George Manlove.*

Watching. *Soiled and soggy George Shepard of Keene Fire Department, watches progress of battle against blaze at 82 Spring St., where Four Seasons rooming house was damaged extensively by fire that killed an elderly man Monday afternoon. At right is fireman Gary LaFreniere. Photo by George Manlove.*

"The cause of the fire was accidental," Dewhurst said, "It appears to be a hot plate that was left unattended with some cooking material on it.

The building didn't appear to have smoke or heat sensors, fire officials said. It had no fire sprinkler system and had been cited by city fire safety code inspectors for safety violations.

The building's owner, Francis A. Dostillio, who also lived at 82 Spring St had been warned about the violations by city officials, said Owen T. Holden, director of code enforcement.

Holden said code violations lodged against the building, "by today's standards, would be a major violation."

"We have been trying to get something done since 1975," Holden said. "We exhausted all our avenues and referred (the matter) to the city attorney for appropriate action."

That action included a letter from City Attorney Charles H. Morang to Dostillio Realty Co. Inc. of 82 Spring Street in 1979, Holden said.

Holden said the fire "is what people in our profession dread. We don't sleep nights worrying about this happening. We know it can happen and it does happen," he said. "It makes you feel so damn helpless."

Dostillio couldn't be reached this morning to comment on the alleged safety violations or on the damage the fire caused.

A smoke alarm probably wouldn't have helped the man who died in his room, said Keene Police Det. Lt. Douglas K. Fish, who is assisting in the investigation.

Circumstances at the scene "indicated he was aware there was a fire in his room," Fish said. The man was not entirely ambulatory and may have been unable to get out or deal with the flames, Fish said.

A charred cane was found in the man's room.

One firefighter at the scene described both rescue and firefighting efforts a difficult and hampered by smoke because of the maze-like interior of the three-story rambling wooden house.

"It was a nasty fire," Guyette said. "It was hard to get at. She was well into the attic when we pulled in. It was over the third floor ceiling... and meant going onto the third floor" and working at the blaze from below, he said.

From the second level, "We (took) the walls out of a majority of the apartments to get at the fire in that blind attic," Guyette said.

Meanwhile, firefighters wearing breathing devices hauled hoses into the burning house, looking for flames and victims.

Keene's Deputy Police Chief Thomas N. Lacroix and Sgt. Hal G. Brown were among the first to arrive at the house. They and firefighters went into the building to help clear it.

Smoke "burned your eyes, it burned your lungs," Brown said. "You couldn't stay in there very long." After the initial search, any one without a breathing unit had to leave the building. "If there was anyone else in there, we couldn't have found them because the smoke was so severe," Brown said.

Many of the tenants were elderly, officials said. While about six people escaped from the building on their own, Keene Police and firemen also carried one elderly man to safety.

Mrs. Jevine was discovered in her room by Keene firefighters Scott Taylor and Edward Lamoreaux, who passed her out through the third-floor window to Alex "buddy" Matson, who was manning the aerial ladder, Fish said. Matson carried the woman below, where other firemen began cardiopulmonary resuscitation in an effort to revive her.

As a thick plume of smoke swirled upward over the neighborhood, between 300 and 500 spectators gathered at the scene to watch, while members of KARES, a volunteer CB radio club, helped police control crowds and traffic, and about 65 firefighters attacked the fire.

The fire was finally brought under control and extinguished at about 3:30 p.m., Guyette said.

The attic and two rooms in the house were damaged by flames and the rest of the house was damaged by water and smoke, officials said.

Police, fire, Cheshire County Red Cross and Keene Salvation Army officials worked into Monday night cleaning up at the scene and trying to find lodging for the fire victims left homeless.

Witnesses at the scene said that, at first, the fire didn't appear to be too bad. A neighbor, Darrin Koski of 64 Spring St. said he watched the woman on the second floor push out her window and try to escape as smoke poured out the window from behind her.

"It looked like it was pretty much under control" from the street, he said, "and all of a sudden, the flames just shot right up" through the roof.

"It was terrible," said one girl who lives nearby. Rumors spread as fast as the fire, and it wasn't long before word of two deaths circulated, incorrectly, through the crowd below.

"All we could see was the top (of the building) smoke in the front part of the roof," said another neighbor who watched from the street before fire trucks arrived.

Keene firefighters were caught off guard when the report of the fire came in. A truck and crew had moments before been dispatched to 114 Greenwood Ave. for a reported chimney fire.

Only three firemen were on hand to rush to Spring Street for the first alarm, Guyette said. Others arrived moments later.

Fire equipment and personnel from Meadowood County Area Fire Department in Fitzwilliam also went to the scene, while Swanzey Center, Meadowood, Walpole and Marlborough fire department sent equipment and personnel to cover the Keene fire station.

Most injuries suffered at the scene were the result of smoke inhalation. Several firefighters suffered cuts and burns.

Treated at Cheshire Hospital and released a short time later were call firefighters, Alex Matson Sr., James Seavey, Michael Blanchard, Michael Bergeron, Joseph Gallup, Robert Spicher and Time Mason, Lt Philip Davis, a full-time fireman, was also treated at the hospital.

Names of tenants injured in the fire were unavailable late this morning.

"The law of averages catches up with you after awhile," said Guyette. "We've had a pretty good record" thus far.

Holden said city officials have mounted an aggressive campaign to make rooming houses in the city safer. "I hope (this) makes a lot of people wake up to what we've been trying to do" in the way of fire prevention measures, he said.

In addition to the state fire marshal's office inquiry, Keene fire Capt. Laurence V. Wood is investigating the cause of the fire.

From the *Keene Evening Sentinel*:

Keene house fire victim named; investigation of cause continues

Searching for the cause. *Keene Fire Department Capt. Laurence V. Wood checks burned appliance wires in the 82 Spring St., apartment of John Howland who died in the fire Monday. Officials suspect unattended hot plate caused the blaze in which one other person was critically injured and 10 others suffered minor injuries. Photo by George Manlove.*

Keene police have identified the victim of the fatal fire Monday at Four Seasons rooming house in Keene as John Howland, 69, a semi-handicapped man with no apparent local relatives.

A second fire victim, Alice Jevne, 59, who lived on the third floor directly above Howland's apartment, was listed in critical condition at Cheshire Hospital today. She is being treated in the intensive care unit for smoke inhalation.

Meanwhile, Keene Fire Prevention Officer Capt Laurence V wood said investigators believe an unattended hot plat probably started the fire that caused extensive damage to two rooms, the attic and roof of the rambling building at 82 Spring St. The fire started in Howland's second-floor apartment, officials said.

"There's no way in God's world we're going to say, that's it," Wood said this morning of the hot plate. "There are too many other factors that may have contributed to the blaze.

But officials believe the hot plate is the likely cause.

Howland's death resulted from smoke inhalation, an autopsy showed Tuesday. He was found dead in his room by firefighters.

Howland was described by social workers who knew him as a bright man who suffered a stroke several years ago. He had difficulty getting around, even with a cane.

Jean Wollert, an outreach worker for Home Health Care and Community Services Inc. said Howland, a tall, slim man, insisted on maintaining independence, despite his condition.

"He loved music and played the guitar and accordion," she said. "I believe years ago he played the banjo.

"We were sending him meals and everything, but nobody k new anything about his family," said Alice Crays, a social worker at the health care agency in Keene.

They said Howland was a quiet but friendly man, quite bright and a voracious reader. "I would say his door was always open to people, who wanted to come in" and talk, Wollert said.

Howland also enjoyed painting and walking, when he could, to the Unitarian Church on Washington Street, from which Friendly Meals operates, the women said.

Funeral arrangements for Howland were still incomplete today and hampered by so little information about him. Attempts were being made this morning to locate Howland's relatives.

The building in which Howland died Monday afternoon did not have visible smoke or fire detectors, investigators said, but officials indicated Tuesday that such devices probably wouldn't have helped Howland. Police Det. Lt. Douglas K. Fish indicated Howland may have tried to put out the fire himself when it broke out.

City officials had cited the building, owned by Francis A. Dostillio of 82 Spring St, for fire safety code violations, but officials declined to discuss specific violations.

One investigator said that the 82 Spring St. fire could have happened in almost any home in the city. The lack of fire detectio9n equipment did not necessarily cause Howland's death, he said.

Dostillio couldn't be reached to comment on the condition of the building or the fire.

Eight firemen and several other people suffered minor injuries as a result of the fire Monday.

————

As Reported by the *Keene Evening Sentinel* April 12th, 1983:

"STORY"

Keene firefighter snuffs out habit

'After the first meeting, I just wanted to get out and light up. But I decided I had come this far, so I'd throw away my pack and give it a chance. I've never had a cigarette since' Capt. George H. Shepard Jr. Photo by Steve Goldsmith.

What's the best reason to quit smoking? There are many, as any firefighter can tell you. More than half of all fires are caused by careless use of smoking materials.

But Captain George H. Shepard Jr., of the Keene Fire Department and most of the men on his shift agree; a smoke-free environment is better for their health and for the health of their families and co-workers.

"I started smoking when I was in high school," recalls Capt Shepard. "It was the "in" thing then—peer pressure. And then I kept smoking for 21 years.

Capt. Shepard and his wife found the motivation to quit when they learned their son was asthmatic and needed a smoke-free atmosphere. "My wife quit by herself, but it didn't work for me. I kept needing a smoke until I finally went to the 5-day Quit Smoking Clinic.

Dependency on nicotine develops in subtle and complex ways. There are more ordinary situations and common foods associated with the desire to smoke than s smoker realizes.

"During the five days of the clinic, we gave up coffee, spicy foods, anything that reinforces the desire to smoke. We substituted fruit juice—it counteracts nicotine. After the first meeting," recalls Shepard," "I just wanted to get out and light up! But I decided I had come this far, so I'd throw away my pack and give it a chance. And I've never had a cigarette since." That was four years ago.

The 5-Day Plan to Quit Smoking, co-sponsored twice each year in Keene by the Seventh-Day Adventist Church and the Cheshire Unit of the American Cancer Society, reports a high success rate among its graduates. One reason for the success is that the plan educates people about the complex motivations for smoking and situations to avoid.

"It's easier to stay away from cigarettes on the job now," says Capt. Shepard, "since so many people have quit. Only one man on my shift of eight still smokes. The majority prefer a smoke-free work place.

A firefighter's job includes a lot of routine work between the intensely demanding situations of firefighting. "There's a lot of tension in the smoke-filled building. The

body uses up its supply of nicotine. When we relax afterward, the body wants to replenish its supply. This is the hardest time to resist the urge to smoke. But the five days the clinic lasts is about the length of time the body needs to cleanse itself of nicotine." Meeting every evening provides moral support during the most difficult period for the motivated quitter.

Capt. Shepard is so impressed with the effectiveness of the 5-Day Plan that he continues to attend the clinics twice a year to help others to quit. The next clinic will be held May 2 to 6 at Keene Junior High School.

Interested persons may call 239-4571, 352-4587 or 256-6521, or write Box 51, West Chesterfield, NH 03456, to register. There is a registration fee of $5.

"There are many more expensive programs you can try," agrees Capt. Shepard, "but I don't know of any that are more successful."

————

As Reported by the *Keene Evening Sentinel* April 14th, 1983:

"STORY"

Keene committee wants smoke detectors required in every apartment building

Every lodging, rooming or apartment house in Keene should have smoke detectors, A Keene City Council committee agreed Wednesday.

It will recommend next Thursday that the city council change building codes to require smoke detectors in all apartment houses, including duplexes, said Aaron A. Lipsky, chairman of the Health, Welfare and Safety Committee.

Fore safety codes now require smoke detectors only in those apartments build after 1978, Lipsky said. The committee wants to apply the same rule to buildings constructed before that, to improve safety.

Terry A. Bishop was the only councilor on the five-member committee to oppose the proposal.

In addition to re1quiring smoke detectors, councilors are trying to help streamline the way in which codes are enforced, so landlords and building owners who don't comply with safety requirements will be prosecuted more quickly than they are now.

Owners of apartment buildings will have until Jan. 1, 1984, to install smoke detectors if the council adopts the ordinance.

Lipsky said committee members debated whether to allow battery operated smoke detectors, then decided to require equipment that's connected to each building's electrical system. That will be safer, they said since batteries can run out of power or be removed.

"While no protection can be perfect, much greater protection would be afforded by detectors wired to the house," Lipsky said. "It not only protects the lives of the tenants, which everybody should be concerned with, but it protects the landlord's property."

Lipsky said the ordinance allows a landlord to appeal if he thinks a particular smoke detector is adequate, but city inspectors don't.

———

As Reported by the *Keene Evening Sentinel* May 17th, 1983:

"STORY"

Keene panel gets budget requests of commissions, fire, ambulance

The feasibility of spending $10,000 on the Southwest Region Planning Commission and another $10,000 on the Keene Conservation Commission were added to the Keene City Council Finance Committee's list of considerations Monday night.

Along with the two $10,000 budget requests, the committee also reviewed the fire and ambulance department budgets, which account for more than $1 million of the city manager's $9,377,885 proposed budget for 1983-1984.

In past years, the commission has received $23,000 a year from the city.

Keene Fire Chief Robert N. Guyette faced the committee to explain the fire department budget of $893,700, up 14% from the current year; and the $178,086 ambulance service budget.

Guyette's salary doesn't contribute to the requested increase; he's been with the city for 32 years, has reached the top of the pay scale for the position and will receive the same salary he has for the past three years.

Along with pay increases for most of the 37-member department, Guyette said the department needs money to repair a dilapidated ladder truck.

The department also needs $900 for air bags, which are portable rescue devices, and $10,000 for the replacement of Scott Airpaks, some of which are more than 20 years old, Guyette said.

The Keene area municipal ambulance service budget is up about 11.8% from last year's and includes a first-time administrative cost of $5,500/

———

As Reported by the *Keene Evening Sentinel* June 27th, 1983:

"FIRE"

Policeman douses fire in Keene; fireworks damage, thefts reported

A potentially serious fire behind Monadnock Cutlery Co. Inc. at 155 Railroad St, Keene, was prevented by Keene police Friday night.

Police also received more than a half dozen reports of fireworks being set off during the weekend in various places, including in a mail drop at the US Post Office on Main Street.

Police Lt. Lawrence D. Smith emptied a fire extinguisher on the blaze, then called in the Keene Fire Department to finish dousing the fire when the extinguisher's contents couldn't quite handle the job.

Damage was minimal, but Smith said the flames might have spread to the building had the fire gone unchecked.

He said he found an empty marijuana bag at the scene and believes someone dropped a marijuana or tobacco cigarette onto the pallets. Smith saw no one around when he spotted the fire.

Many people complained to police that they were awakened at various times during the weekend by fire works.

The most damage was reported in the mailbox incident, in which the door to the mailbox was blown open early this morning by what police described as an "explosive device." Postal officials are investigating.

———

As Reported by the *Keene Evening Sentinel* June 27th, 1983:

"FIRE"

One hurt late this morning as fire breaks out in Keene

A Keene firefighter was reported injured late this morning in a two-alarm fire reported in a garage at 29 North Lincoln St. Keene.

Officials rushed to the fire scene at about 11:30 a.m. The building was described as being fully ablaze when firefighters arrived. Further details were unavailable at press time.

———

As Reported by the *Keene Evening Sentinel* August 22nd, 1983:

"FIRE"

Fire doused in Keene

Testing hose 1983. *During the fall of each year, all hose was tested. If a hose passed the pressure test, it was restacked on the truck or rolled and placed in racks. This extra hose was used to reload fire engines with dry hose after a fire. Hose was rolled to remove air for easy loading; all shifts tested hose. Pictured are A shift FF Campbell and FF Loll in the hose bed of Engine 3. Standing on the tail board are Capt. Shepard and Lt. Goldsmith. Rolling hose is FF Spofford, and feeding hose are FF Rokes and FF Memesheimer, to the left.*

A two-alarm fire caused minor damage to a house on Kelleher Street Saturday night before it was extinguished by the Keene Fire Department.

A second-story smoke detector sounded just after 7 p.m. in the home of Bruce E. and Susan R. Thielen at 45 Kelleher St., said Deputy Fire Chief John N. Phillips. Apparently, an electric fan was blown out of the window of a second-story storage room and fell onto a file of clothes, Phillips said. The blade of the fan became caught in the clothes and the fan overheated, igniting the clothes.

Mrs. Thielen heard the smoke detector, found the smoke upstairs, and called the fire department, Phillips said. The fire was confined to the attic-like room where it started; some structural damage was reported to the walls and roof, Phillips said, and there was also some water damage in the house.

Five units responded to the3 scene, with crews from West and East Swanzey covering the Keene station, Firefighters spend about two hours at the fire scene, Phillips said.

————

As Reported by the *Keene Evening Sentinel* September 3rd, 1983:

"FIRE"

Shed burns up in Keene

A shed behind a house at 12 Sullivan St, Keene, caught fire Thursday evening and created billows of smoke that could be seen for blocks.

The shed, about 12 feet square, was engulfed in flames when Keene firefighters arrived on the scene a few minutes before 7 p.m. Firefighters had the blaze in the wood frame, shingled shed under control within minutes.

No cause for the fire had been determined this morning. Firefighters said damage was limited to thee shed and its contents.

————

As Reported by the *Keene Evening Sentinel* September 8th, 1983:

"FIRE"

Fire ruins Keene barn; cause unknown

A barn containing hay behind Timothy N. Robertson's house on Faniels Hill Road in Keene was destroyed by a fire early this morning, but the cause of the blaze is still under investigation.

Keene firefighter hoses down smoldering remains of barn. Photo by Mark Van Wehrden.

Two Keene fire trucks responded to the fire at 5:36 a.m., but the barn was already engulfed in flames, when they arrived. About 10 minutes later another truck was sent to assist with the fire. It was under control within a half-hour, firefighters said.

"All we could do is contain it and make sure it didn't spread to nearby structures," said Keene Fire Department Lt. Bernard N. Blancato.

He said a small garden tractor and utility trailer were in the 40-by-60 foot barn and were destroyed in the blaze, as were tools and other contents of the barn. The front end of a nearby car was damaged by heat.

Firefighters were still on the scene at 10 a.m. today dousing the barn spreading out hay and looking for embers.

————

As Reported by the *Keene Evening Sentinel* December 21st, 1983:

"FIRE"

Fire doused fast at housing complex

A small fire at a 75-apartment complex for the elderly was contained quickly Tuesday by Keene firefighters, but one fireman suffered frostbite in the numbing cold.

Keene firemen use truck – mounted ladder to reach roof of six-story apartment building. Photo by Martin Frank & Michael Knell.

Deputy Phillips of the Keene Fire Department checks air handling machine where fire started. Photo by Martin Frank & Michael Knell.

Equipment that keeps hallway air fresh malfunctioned and burst into flames on the roof of the six-story Cleveland Housing for the Elderly on Roxbury Plaza, said Edward A. Kingsbury Jr., controller for Emile J. Legere Management Co., which operates the federally subsidized housing project.

A little after 3 p.m., Millard L. Blanchard, who supervises the building's maintenance, noticed that something was wrong with the air circulation, checked the machine and saw flames, Kingsbury said.

Blanchard called Southwestern NH Fire Mutual Aid at 3:28 p.m. which dispatched Keene firefighters; they scrambled up a truck-mounted ladder to reach the roof.

Keene Fire Chief Robert N. Guyette said he used thee building's intercom system to ask the 14 residents of the top floor to come to the lobby. Some weren't at home, but those who were, went downstairs quickly. Some of them were escorted down stairs by firefighters. Blanchard then checked all the apartments to make sure no one had been left behind, Kingsbury said.

On the roof, firefighters found that flames from the machine had spread to the timbers that supported it and to the roof itself. Guyette said. A hose was hauled up the long ladder, and water was poured on the flames for about 15 minutes. Once the fire itself was under control firefighters peeled back a section of the roof to make sure the flames had not spread.

The fire damaged the machine and the roof around it, and a sixth-floor apartment suffered minor water damage, Guyette said.

However, the building's heating system was never threatened, Kingsbury emphasized—a major concern, since temperatures at the time were only in the teens, and hit zero overnight.

The air in the building might be a little less fresh with the air recirculator out of commission, but repairs will be completed by this weekend, Kingsbury said.

Firefighter Wayne A. Spofford, 37, of 51 Stanhope Ave., Keene, was treated at Cheshire Hospital for minor frostbite on both hands and released. Spofford had been manning the truck-mounted ladder.

———

Keene Steam and Fire Engine and Hose Co. #1 1983

1st Row L to R: Larry Sanderson, Carl Collier, Mike Rochleau, Clerk Jack Little, 2nd Lt. Robert Spicher. 1st Lt. Armond Jacques, Captain Robert Mason, Ronald Leslie, Raymond Hadley, Allen Welsh. 2nd Row, L to R: Treas. Paul Szoc, Fred Hale, Tim Mason. 3rd Row: Deputy Chief W. Peets, Jr.

June 12, 1983. Washington Hook and Ladder Company No. 1

Front Row, Seated L to R: R. Davis, Lt. Johnson, Capt. J. Dennis, 2nd Lt. R. Driscoll, D. Symonds. Standing, L to R: L. Burt, N. Skantze, R. DiLuzio, R. Symonds, W. Kingsbury, E. Labounty, T. Morton, J. Gallup.

Keene Deluge Hose Company 1983

Front Row, L to R: Edward Lamoureux, Lt. Alex Matson, Sr., Captain Robert Raymond, Lt. Wilfred Begin, Wayne Crowell. Back Row, L to R: Neil Collier, James Seavey, Sheldon Fifield, James Laurent, Mark Carrier, Gary Bergeron, Harry Nelson, Gary Lamoureux.

As Reported by the *Keene Evening Sentinel* December 30th, 1983:

"FIRE"

Chimney Fire

Up on the Housetop. *Keene Firefighter, Scott Collier lowers a "snuffler" to extinguish a chimney fire Thursday afternoon at the home of Richard and Gayle Arsenault on Billings Avenue in Keene. Like leaf-bore trees and ice encrusted roads, the sight of firefighters on housetops is one of the signs of the chilly season as area wood stoves heat up. Photo by Mark Van Wehrden.*

1984

As Reported by the *Keene Evening Sentinel* January 14th, 1984:

"FIRE

Fire heavily damages home on Sullivan Street in Keene

A fire badly damaged a Keene family's home on Sullivan Street Friday afternoon.

Keene Deputy Fire Chief John N. Phillips said an investigation was underway to determine the cause of the blaze.

Phillips said Richard and Allison Fairbanks and their two children were not at home when a neighbor spotted smoke coming from the windows of their house at 31 Sullivan St.

The neighbor, Elmer W. Caldwell, reported the blaze at 1:51 and six minutes later the firefighters had arrived and called for reinforcements, Phillips said.

Entering the house, firefighters wearing breathing apparatus found the first floor of the two and a half story residence engulfed in flames.

"The flames came right up to us at the door," Phillips said. You know how these things are—when they get a good start they keep on going.

About 35 firefighters fought the fire to a standstill pouring water on it from two hoses on the ground floor and another carried by firefighters entering through an upper story window.

By 2:29 the fire was under control due to what Phillips called "a good team effort," but the Fairbanks home had suffered extensive damage.

"What the fire didn't get the head did," Phillips said. "The telephones melted. The wiring melted. Anything plastic went."

According to Phillips, the house, although not a total loss, will not be livable until it undergoes substantial renovation.

The family has been forced to temporarily move into the Keene home of Richard Fairbanks' father, Phillips said.

Phillips said the fire began somewhere in the center of the house, but not apparently in the stove.

————

As Reported by the *Keene Evening Sentinel* February 16th, 1984:

"FIRE"

No one hurt when gas explodes

AFTER THE BLAST. *Keene firefighters enter the cellar of an apartment house at 309 Water St., Keene, where gas explosion Wednesday moved the building off its foundation. Photo by William Fosher.*

An explosion blew a Keene house off its foundation Wednesday afternoon, scattering building materials and shattered glass in all directions.

The blast occurred just after 4:00 p.m. at 309 Water St., a three-apartment wood-frame house owned by the Keene Housing Authority. The explosion apparently caused a small fire in the basement.

One tenant said the explosion blew off the cellar's bulkhead door, and he saw a flame leap across the driveway—a distance of about 25 feet.

No one was injured.

Laurence V. Wood, Keene's fire prevention officer, said the incident was still under investigation this morning, but apparently occurred after a "heavy concentration of gas"

had collected inside the building. The gas may have been by an electric water heater in the basement.

Wood said Keene Gas Corp. crews had tentatively determined that a leak in the gas main under Hancock Street was to blame for the accumulation of gas. The main has been shut off, Wood said.

Apparently, the leak was caused by the movement of the ground around the gas main.

"It happens a lot this time of year," said Robert F. Egan, distribution manager for Keene Gas. "The gas apparently migrated through the soil and entered the basement. The house doesn't have an all-concrete basement,: and the gas must have come into the basement through the ground.

Several residents of the house said they had reported a gas smell to the gas company earlier in the afternoon, but a Keene Gas Corp spokesman said no reports had been received.

"We're pretty touchy about reports of gas leaks," Egan said. "We send people immediately."

Brian Boucher, who lives at 334 Water St., said "We've been reporting these things for two years, and we had the police up there trying to pin it down, and we couldn't." Boucher said his house had been converted from gas years ago, but still has gas lines leading into it.

George J. Moylan, executive director of the Keene Housing Authority, said the gas lines into the house at 309 Water St. had been capped, and he thought the has had entered the cellar through cracks in the foundation.

One resident said she had been telling the Keene Housing Authority "for weeks" that something was wrong with the furnace and believed the explosion was related to those complaints.

Moylan said he didn't know of any complaints, but it was possible that a staff member, who has been in the hospital, might have received them.

_____

As Reported by the *Keene Evening Sentinel* February 17th, 1984:

"FIRE"

Keene house damaged in fire; tree service garage protected

A two-alarm fire did extensive damage to an unoccupied Keene house Thursday night

A passerby noticed smoke coming from the two-story house at 686 Court St., owned by Raymond L. Harris, and called Southwestern NH Fire Mutual Aid at about 8:15 p.m.

Keene firefighters arrived less than four minutes later, found flames engulfing the home's living room, and called for reinforcements at 8:19.

A number of firefighters entered the smoky structure, wearing breathing gear: others hooked hoses to nearby hydrants. Chester E. Dubriske, deputy fire chief, said about 45 Keene firefighters fought the blaze for more than an hour before bringing it under control.

Harris is president and treasurer of Chase Tree Service, Inc., and the house is connected to a garage used by the tree service, but firefighters managed to confine fire damage to the house.

"The good weather made it easy," Dubriske said, "But there was considerable damage. There was a lot of heat and smoke through the whole house.

Dubriske said the house was fully furnished, but Harris had not lived there since about Christmas.

The fire is still under investigation, Dubriske said; no cause was immediately apparent.

_____

As Reported by the *Keene Evening Sentinel* February 29th, 1984:

"STORY"

Keene promotes 3 firefighters

Three Keene firefighters have received promotions.

David Osgood of Old Richmond Road in East Swanzey is now a captain.

Bradley Payne of Route 10 in Winchester is now a lieutenant.

Bruce Pollock of 32 Partridgeberry Road in Swanzey Center is the department's new training officer.

The decision to promote the three was made by the Board of Engineers, the department's governing body, comprised of Fire Chief Robert N. Guyette and his four deputies.

_____

As Reported by the *Keene Evening Sentinel* May 17th, 1984:

"FIRE"

Barn, house damaged in Keene fire

Three families were forced out of their apartments at 77 Elm St., Keene, on Wednesday afternoon when a fire swept through a barn attached to the house.

Paul E. Crowell, deputy fire chief, said the cause of the fire has not been determined, and he declined to speculate on the cause until an investigation is completed. He would not say whether it had a suspicious origin.

The property is owned by Leonard W. Tichy of Peterborough.

Crowell said the barn was "fairly burned out" and smoke and water caused damage throughout the house, though flames were largely confined to the barn. The barn is still standing, but is gutted.

Quelling the flames. *Carl Collier of Keene is one of about 30 firefighters who fought a blaze that gutted a barn and damaged an attached apartment house Wednesday afternoon on Keene's Elm Street. Three families were forced out of their apartments temporarily, but should be able to move back in after repairs. Photo by Mark Van Wehrden.*

No one was injured in the fire, extinguished by about 30 full-time and call firefighters in less than two hours.

The barn had been used primarily for storage, Crowell said.

An estimate of damage was not available this morning. According to city records the apartment house was assessed last year at $40,400.

Residing in the building's three apartments—one on the first floor and two on the second—were the families of Barbara Serpico, Cynthia Bush and Anthony and Jackie Olivo. Approval from city safety officials will be needed before they can move back into the apartments.

Crowell did not know if anyone was home when the fire broke out. He called the blaze "a good working house fire," one of the worst in Keene in several months.

As Reported by the *Keene Evening Sentinel* May 29th, 1984:

"FIRE"

Fire damages mobile home

Firefighters doused a fire at a mobile home in Keene Saturday morning.

The mobile home is owned by John D. Smith Sr., and is at 420 Tanglewood Estates. A malfunctioning oil burner started the blaze, said Capt. George Shepard of the Keene Fire Department.

The fire was reported at 8:23 a.m. and was under control by 9:30.

Shepard said the mobile home can probably be repaired, and was covered by insurance. Smith, who was home when the fire broke out, is staying with relatives, Shepard said.

As Reported by the *Keene Evening Sentinel* May 31st, 1984.

"STORY"

Four-day rain may end tonight

Finally, the rain may stop tonight in the Monadnock Region, ending a siege that has flooded homes and businesses, forced people to flee, closed roads and caused heavy damage.

The flooding in southwestern New Hampshire is the worst since the 1930's, a state official said.

The floods have closed a number of major roads, and blocked sections of many streets and roads.

This morning, state highway officials began closing Route 10 between Keene and Massachusetts because of high water, said Robert N. Dodge, head of Swanzey based Division 7 of the NH Public Works and Highways Department.

Extra Day – More than 100 workers of Kingsbury Machine Tool Corp volunteered to work on their holiday, Wednesday to put up sandbags walls in an effort to stem the flow of Beaver Brook through the company's Marlborough Street Keene Plant. Trucks moving through the city to move out people and furniture made it difficult. Photo by George Manlove.

In Keene, firefighters distributed sandbags by the thousands, said Deputy Fire Chief Chester E. Dubriske. More than 75 people were added to the regular eight-man shift to handle flooding problems. Dubriske said the department is still tallying the figures on how many people were affected by the storm.

As the clouds begin to thin, state officials are preparing to appeal for federal help in the cleanup.

Gov. John H. Sununu will ask the federal government to declare a state of emergency to Cheshire and Merrimack counties, and maybe Grafton County, too, if the Connecticut River hits hard in West Lebanon. The declaration would allow low-interest loans to help rebuild water damaged communities.

However, the money won't arrive right away, Frank J. Haley, a Civil Defense spokesman, said the request for money can't be submitted until damage estimates are compiled—and that can't really happen until the flood water recede.

The rain that started Monday morning has dropped from 5 to 7 inches of rain on southwestern New Hampshire. National Weather Service radar indicated this morning that the clouds were beginning to thin over the Monadnock Region and the end of the storm was in sight. New rain will dwindle to showers this afternoon and tonight; spotty showers are possible Friday, and the drying out should begin this weekend.

From the *Keene Evening Sentinel*:

Keene begins to resurface from water

The waters began receding on Keene's east side late Wednesday night, but electricity is still off in a hundred homes, dozens of people had to spend the night with friends on higher ground and still hadn't been able to return home this morning, and a number of industries and businesses are salvaging what they can after the flood.

Up to 4 feet of water flowed atop streets on Keene's east side on Wednesday, lapping at the front doors of several hundred homes and businesses.

"Beaver Brook, I think, has backed off, but I think the Ashuelot River is getting overloaded," said Keene police Detective Sgt. Robert H. Hardy. "What you've got now is a tremendous amount of surface water, and it's got nowhere to go," referring to the Winchester Street-Key Road area.

Keene's east side is bisected by Beaver Brook, which gnawed hungrily at its banks and rushed over the top of concrete flood-control channels Tuesday and Wednesday. The brook has returned to the confines of cement today, but the mess it left behind, was evident in litter-strewn back yards, water soaked cars and trucks, and hoses poling out of cellar windows.

At 44 George St, a 200-year-old barn owned by Margaret and Phillip Croteauy tilted into Beaver Brook, as the water had eroded the earth beneath it. Thick cables, connected by city public works crews, kept the broken building from tipping completely into the brook.

Elsewhere in Keene, damage was concentrated in cellars and some foundations. Furnaces, washing machines, dryers and stored clothes and toys were soaked as water poured into basements.

Many homes nowhere near a street had water trouble, too, as the saturated earth—soaked by up to 7 inches of rain since Monday—couldn't absorb any more water.

Keene officials urged people to ease up on sewer use today, since the flood-choked city sewer system simply can't keep up with demand.

Dozens of east-side residents fled Wednesday as water climbed up the foundations of their homes. Keene firefighters and volunteers used boats to move out those who wanted to leave. Others paddled canoes and aluminum boats up and down Church, Brook, Spring and Water Streets.

As Reported by the *Keene Evening Sentinel* June 7th, 1984:

"FIRE"

Small fire at furniture firm

Keene firefighters snuffed out a small fire in a sawdust trailer at Sprague & Carleton Co., Inc. on Avon Street early today.

The fire was reported at 3:43 a.m., and was under control within a few minutes, according to Southwestern NH Fire Mutual Aid. A night watchman discovered the fire.

There was no damage to the trailer and the furniture company is open today, according to a Sprague & Carleton spokesman.

As Reported by the *Keene Evening Sentinel* August 22nd, 1984:

"FIRE"

Smoke fills nursing home in Keene; no one injured

Clothes in a dryer ignited a fire in a laundry room early this morning at the Westwood Healthcare Center—a nursing home—at 298 Main St., Keene.

Keene Fire Capt. David B. Osgood said the fire was discovered at about 2:56 a.m. Firefighters had doused the blaze within minutes after arriving; all it took was a few buckets of water." Osgood said.

However, while the fire was limited to the clothes dryer, it produced lots of dense smoke and a choking smell of burned rubber, and it took several hours to restore the air inside the nursing home to normal.

No one was hurt and no patients at the nursing home was evacuated Osgood said, although about 15 people who had been sleeping downstairs were moved upstairs while firefighters worked near the laundry room.

Osgood said nine firefighters, four fire trucks and two Keene police officers responded to the alarm.

The cause of the fire is being investigated, Osgood said, but it's highly doubtful that the blaze was set.

A Demon Called Fire

As Reported by the *Keene Evening Sentinel* September 8th, 1984:

"STORY"

Emergency Medicine Week set in Keene

Keene Mayor L. Edward Reyor has declared Sept. 16-22 as Emergency Medicine Week.

Emergency medicine, the newest medical specialty, is the evaluating, stabilizing and treating of life-and-limb-threatening illnesses or injuries. Emergency physicians and nurses provide that type of care—as well as treating less serious illnesses and injuries—24 hours a day, 365 days a year at Cheshire Hospital in Keene.

The week long observance will be sponsored by the hospital's emergency care center, in cooperation with the Keene Fire Department and is designed to encourage people to learn more about the emergency medical resources in their community.

To help accomplish that, hospital personnel and emergency medical technicians associated with public and private ambulance services in Keene plan an exhibit at the Colony Mill Marketplace, West Street, Keene, on Thursday and Friday, Sept 20 and 21, from 6 to 8 p.m. and on Saturday, Sept 22 from noon to 6 p.m.

———————

As Reported by the *Keene Evening Sentinel* December 5th, 1984:

"FIRE"

Apparent wood stove fire leaves family homeless

A Keene family was burned out of their home Tuesday night when a wood stove apparently overheated, starting a fire in one room of the house.

Charles and Kim Care and their children returned to their house at 32 Royal Ave. about 9 p.m. to find it full of smoke, said Chester Dubriske, deputy chief of the Keene Fire Department.

Firefighters put the blaze out within an hour, he said, but damage to the inside of the house was extensive.

"The inside was pretty well burned," Dubriske said. "The fire was basically contained in one room, but two or three rooms had fire damage." "There was smoke and water damage in other parts of the house.

No one was injured in the fire.

Dubriske said he believed the Careys were staying with relatives for now but the family could not be reached for comment this morning.

Firefighters were going to return to the house today to complete their investigation into the cause of the blaze.

In addition to firefighters, there were lots of other participants in Sunday's Fire Department Parade and Muster in Keene, launching Fire Prevention Week. A young man rides in a passenger seat of one of the many fire trucks that drove down Main Street during the parade, left, while Smokey the Bear took a higher seat to greet the hundreds of people lining the route. Photo by Virginia Ryan.

———————

1985

As Reported by the *Keene Evening Sentinel* January 19th, 1985:

"FIRE"

Fire Doused

A quickly extinguished fire on the back porch of a third story apartment did minor damage to materials on the porch and the p0orch itself in a fire reported at 9:41 Friday night a Keene Fire Department official said. The building at 84 Davis St., Keene is owned by Henry Lehrmann, the apartment is occupied by Michelle Arlan. No cause had been determined late Friday night. Photo by: Jim Coppo.

————

As Reported by the *Keene Evening Sentinel* February 7th, 1985:

"FIRE"

Making sure it is out

Keene firefighters check in the rafters for any remnants of a fire that caused minor damage to a Washington Avenue parsonage Wednesday morning. Officials said it apparently was ignited by smoldering ashes. After being dispatched to the Sturtevant Chapel property at 11:29 a.m., firefighters were able to extinguish the fire completely by 12:24 p.m., said Keene Deputy Fire Chief, Chester Dubriske. Damage was limited to the door casing, a wall and ceiling, and some smoke and heat damage, Dubriske said; estimating necessary repairs at a few thousand dollars. The resident, Rev. Peter L. Michaels, "told us that there's a wastebasket near the door where he disposed of some ashes," Dubriske said. "We don't know for sure (that was the cause of the fire). Everything was consumed to the point where it was hard to tell," Dubriske said it was lucky that smoke and a burning door were noticed by a passerby and reported to the fire department. Photo by: Martin Frank.

————

As Reported by the *Keene Evening Sentinel* February 14th, 1985:

"FIRE"

Where there's fire, there's smokes, Keene police allege

A fire in their cellar was double trouble for two Keene residents. Not only did the fire cause minor damage, but police arrested the pair on charges of growing marijuana in their basement.

Brian K. Dodge, 24, and Margaret L. Dodge, 21, of 33 Page St. were charged by Keene police with manufacturing a controlled drug. They were arrested Wednesday and were to be arraigned today in Keene District Court.

The cellar fire was reported Tuesday night at 9:55; police returned with a search warrant at 1:15 Wednesday morning and said they seized three pots of marijuana growing under lights. The Dodges were arrested later that morning.

―――――――

As Reported by the *Keene Evening Sentinel* February 20th, 1985:

"FIRE"

Smoky fire damages Keene firm

Into The Inferno – Deputy Chief Paul Crowell, Lt Bruce Pollock and firefighter Gary LaFreniere, from left to right all of the Keene Fire Department prepare to enter the smoky interior of Frederick A. Farrar Inc while fighting the blaze Tuesday night. Photo by: John Baptista.

A smoky fire caused extensive damage Tuesday night to parts of Keene business that works on electric motors.

It took three hours for Keene firefighters to extinguish the stubborn fire at Frederick A. Farrar Inc., at 15 Avon St.

A passerby reported the fire at 10:34 p.m., after seeing flames coming through the roof of the masonry building, said Capt. George Shepard of the Keene Fire Department.

"The fire started in the boiler room area," he said. "The boiler room walls are fire-resistant, so the fire was contained in that room until it came through the roof."

Firemen had to take the entire roof off the boiler room to get at material that continued to smolder, Shepard said. "It took a long time."

The fire was out at 1:41 a.m.

Shepard said Keene fire investigators are inspecting the building today, trying to determine precisely what caused the blaze.

Extensive fire damage was reported to the boiler room and the roof, and smoke damage was reported throughout the building, Shepard said.

The company was open for business today, despite the damage, said one of the company's employees.

―――――――

As Reported by the *Keene Evening Sentinel* February 28th, 1985:

"FIRE"

Fire damages railroad car

A railroad box car used for storing wooden products at Kingsbury Machine Tool Corp. in Keene burned Tuesday on an old spur track behind the company's building between Marlboro and Water streets.

Firefighters worked about 30 minutes to control the fire, which was reported at about 4:30 p.m.

Cause of the blaze had not yet been determined this morning, said Deputy Fire Chief Paul Crowell.

Kingsbury has five box cars for storing polystyrene patterns used in casting metal fixtures. There was no damage estimated this morning, either.

Juveniles are suspected of causing the fire, said Roger W. Hetherman, vice president for employee and community relations at Kingsbury. Three youngsters were seen bicycling away from the area about 10 minutes before the blaze was discovered, he said.

————————

As Reported by the *Keene Evening Sentinel* March 23rd, 1985:

"FIRE"

Explosion, fire destroy Keene home; owner says she's lucky she escaped

A fire caused the windows of a house in Keene to blow out destroy the home of Lucinda M. Bouffard Friday afternoon. At left Keene firefighters ventilate the house. Photo by Virginia Ryan.

Lucinda M. Bouffard was sitting one of the few chairs on her porch that wasn't in front of a door or window; lucky for her.

Without warning her Friday afternoon repose erupted with a loud crash as the windows of her house blew out.

"I was sitting on the porch and all of a sudden, the first thing I knew, all this glass was out here and black smoke. I said "what is that?" I couldn't believe it." Bouffard said as she sat on the lawn, watching firefighters extinguish the two-alarm blaze that destroyed the home she had lived in most of her life.

"I've got to simmer down and realize that this has happened," she said. "It's a nightmare."

The fire began in or near a bathroom in the rear, first floor of Bouffard's two-family home at 81 N. Lincoln St., Keene, according to Deputy Fire Chief Chester E. Dubriske.

Although it was not discovered until about 1:41 p.m., Dubriske said the fire in the house must have been burning for quite some time to have built up enough heat to cause the windows to explode.

"It's just like if you put something in the oven (and leave it)—it keeps going and going and going and then it just goes like wildfire," he said.

Although both arson and electrical wiring have been ruled o0ut as causes for the fire, Dubriske said there was so much damage inside that the real cause may never be known.

The white house, which had been in the Bouffard family for more than 80 years, was "more or less" gutted, Dubriske said. He said the house apparently was insured.

A couple who rents a second-floor apartment from Bouffard, Mr. & Mrs. Bruce Pride, were not home when the fire broke out.

Only one of the more than 40 firefighters who were called to the scene was injured, and that was for a cut finger that was treated in time for him to return from the hospital to the scene of the fire.

Firefighters began leaving the scene around 3:20 p.m.

Bouffard sat on the lawn, watching firefighters carry some of the things in her home that were not completely destroyed. She said perhaps she was lucky—she could have been sitting in front of one of the windows, or worse, had been inside. And after all, she mused, this was the first fire the home had ever suffered.

Despite her losses, she maintained a sense of humor. When asked it she needed anything, she replied, "yes, how about $1 million?" Bust as for where she was going to go now, she said, "I don't know, I was going to ask the same thing."

However, her daughter, Shirley Boucher, said she would stay with one of her children or grandchildren who live in the area.

Finally, when the firefighter brought over her charred pocket book, its handles burned and material charred, she said "I was going out to dinner tonight and was going to take this," she said.

———

As Reported by the *Keene Evening Sentinel* April 26th, 1985.

Smoky Fire Probed. *Keene firefighters were called out at 12:31 this morning to fight a blaze in a 1 1/2 story frame home at 87 Beaver Street. A second alarm was sounded at 12:33 am to call*

additional help to the scene. The house, which wasn't occupied was heavily damaged by the fire. Investigators were returning to the home today to try to determine how the blaze started, said Keene Fire Department Deputy Chief Paul Crowell. Photo by John Baptista.

———

As Reported by the *Keene Evening Sentinel* May 23rd, 1985:

Accident Wreck. *Firefighters clean up after a car slammed into both sides of the Maple Avenue overpass of Route 12 in Keene Wednesday night and burst into flames. Photo by John Baptista.*

———

As Reported by the *Keene Evening Sentinel* July 15th, 1985:

"FIRE"

Fire damages building

A smoky fire at 17 Dunbar St. late Saturday night was put out by Keene firefighters in about an hour.

A tenant in a neighboring building first spotted the blaze at 11:42 and called firemen to the scene. A second alarm was sounded a few minutes later, sending a total of four trucks to the building.

The fire apparently started in wooden ductwork on the o0utside of the structure, said a spokesman for the Keene Fire Department. The building was occupied by Commercial Business System, but the ductwork had been built by a previous occupant and wasn't currently being used.

The ductwork was destroyed by fire and the building received some smoke and water damage.

————

As Reported by the *Keene Evening Sentinel* August 5th, 1985:

"STORY"
$5,000 more needed for heart-attack gear in ambulance

Top photo: Lt Bruce Pollock tests defibrillator equipment, which sends heart information to Cheshire Hospital E.R. Bottom photo: Receiving that data is Secretary Sheryl Beckta at the hospital. Photos by: John Bapista.

A difference between life and death is only about $5,000 away.

That difference is a piece of ambulance equipment called a defibrillator, and it produces an electric shock that can be crucial in smoothing out the heartbeats of heart-attack victims.

Dr. Kimball B. Temple, a Keene cardiologist, said the device could conceivably save 50 percent of heart-attack victims in Keene last year, 72 of 81 such heart attack victims died.

Keene ambulances can reach any point in the city within four to six minutes says Lt. Bruce Pollock, training officer for the Keene Fire Department, and that can be quick enough for a defibrillator to make a difference to a heart attack victim.

The Keene ambulance also serves Chesterfield, Nelson, Roxbury, Sullivan, Surry and Westmoreland, and the time it takes to reach those points may make defibrillators less effective.

Until now, defibrillators have been used mainly in the hospitals. Moving the equipment into ambulances is a logical response to emergency seizures, but getting enough trained personnel and lining up insurance coverage isn't easy, Keene officials say.

The fire department operates the city's ambulance service, and fire officials are relying on the Keene Lions Club to raise enough money-$10,000—to buy a defibrillator.

Cardiac Resuscitator Corp., which manufactures defibrillators, is loaning one to the fire department until the Lions Club can finish raising the money. However, Keene Fire Chief Robert N. Guyette said he does not want to use the equipment until the money to make the purchase is in hand.

So far, the Lions Club has raised about $5,000, said the club's Wallace A. Reney. He said efforts have been aimed so far at other service clubs, though there have been several small donations from private citizens.

Keene's ambulances are staffed by firefighters who are certified as emergency medical technicians. Pollock said the Keene department has 23 EMT's and retrained to use the defibrillator. The 15 are spread over four shifts, so four are on duty two to an ambulance most of the time.

The EMT's who will use the defibrillator have taken a 24-hour training program required by the N.H. Board of Registration in Medicine. The board says that with the course, trained EMT's can use defibrillators safely.

Sets of instructions guide EMT's in using the equipment, depending on the patient's condition.

"You've got to follow them by the letter A, B, C, D, E, F," Pollock said.

————————

As Reported by the *Keene Evening Sentinel* September 28th, 1985:

"STORY"

Damage is minimal in region from Hurricane Gloria

Hurricane: Arthur Borousseau stands near falling tree that blocked West Street in Keene. Sand gags were placed around Terry O'Connor's Furniture store to keep flood waters from entering the building. Photo by: Medora Hebert.

Hurricane Gloria slammed into southern New England and Long Island with predicted ferocity, but did little more to the Monadnock Region than ruffle its fall foliage.

The hurricane's winds and drenching rains forced the evacuation of hundreds of thousands of shoreline residents from North Carolina to Maine. At least six deaths were blamed on the storm, including three in Connecticut, and nearly 2 million homes lost power.

But Gloria spend most of her energy before she hit the Monadnock Region, and caused less damage to property than to the reputations of meteorologists and headline writers. No injuries were reported locally.

Whatever remained of Gloria's eye came through the southern towns of Cheshire County between 4 and 4:15 p.m., said Raymond Mosher of the New Hampshire bureau of the National Weather Service. The eye had grown so large that it covered several counties, and the hurricane was breaking apart, he said.

The general path of the widening eye was in a line from Keene to Concord. The storm continued to dissipate as it passed over the White Mountains.

————————

As Reported by the *Keene Evening Sentinel* November 1st, 1985:

"STORY"

Oil spill at Keene plant contained, cleaned up fast

About 75 gallons of No. 6 heating oil spilled into Beaver Brook on Keene's east side Thursday at about 2 p.m.

The oil came from a stream discharge pipe at Kingsbury Machine Tool Corp, at 80 Laurel St., and was caused by a leak in a machine that heats the thick oil to a temperature where it will burn, said Roger Hetherman, a Kingsbury official.

The oil worked its way into the stream discharge pipe, which funneled the oil into Beaver Brook.

"Ordinarily, the pipe only discharges water condensation," Hetherman said.

As soon as the leak was discovered, Kingsbury contacted the Keene Fire Department, which installed three booms—flotation devices intended to contain oil spills. One was installed at the Kingsbury plant, one in Beaver Brook, and a third in the Ashuelot River, into which the brook feeds.

Some oil did reach the Ashuelot.

Firefighters worked into the evening until 9 p.m. when Jetline—a Portland, Maine, company that specializes in oil spill cleanups—took over the job.

"They saw the oil had been contained, and decided to start cleanup work in the morning" said Fire Chief Robert N. Guyette.

"This morning," Hetherman said, "they installed three vacuum trucks, two on Beaver Brook and one on the Ashuelot River, to vacuum the oil off the surface of the water. The latest word I've gotten is that it's practically all cleaned up.

As Reported by the *Keene Evening Sentinel* November 22nd, 1985:

"STORY"

Car-truck collision on bypass kills one

A 33-year-old Keene man died at about 8:40 Thursday night when his sedan collided with a tractor-trailer truck on the Route 9-10-12 bypass near West St., Keene.

The crash ripped off the whole left side of the car. Photo by Nathaniel Stout.

William R. Wallis of both 22 Blake St., Keene and Old Keene Road, Walpole, was pronounced dead at the scene of multiple injuries. Blood samples from the victim were taken Thursday night and an autopsy on Wallis was to be performed today.

The truck driver, Richard E. Bergeron, 48, also of Keene, was uninjured in the accident, police said.

Wallis' 1962 Mercury Comet was traveling north on the bypass when it struck the southbound tractor trailer, police said. The collision occurred between the northbound exit for West Street and the West Street overpass.

A team of Keene police officers were still investigating the accident this morning. But officials said their initial investigation indicates that Wallis was not braking his car before impact, indicating that he may not have seen the truck coming. His car had veered partly into the oncoming southbound lane for reasons police have not yet ascertained.

The car's left front side was torn off, and Wallis was thrown outside the car. The car was demolished. Debris from it was strewn about 100 feet beyond the point of impact.

The truck cab's lower-left front section was badly damaged, though no estimate had been made yet this morning of the damage.

Both vehicles had to be towed from the scene. The truck is owned by Sanborn's Motor Express Inc. of Portland, Maine.

Traffic was blocked on the bypass for roughly three hours as police, fire and ambulance personnel worked at the scene. Helping direct traffic around the scene were volunteers from the Keene Area Radio Emergency Service

---

As Reported by the *Keene Evening Sentinel* November 8th, 1985:

"FIRE"

Fire truck damaged

A four-wheel drive fire truck belonging to the Keene Fire Department, which had gone to woods near Drummer and Green Acres roads to put out a bonfire was damaged when a vandal threw a large rock into its door this morning.

The area where the fire was spotted at about 12:45 a.m. is used by teenagers for partying.

As firefighters were cleaning up from the bonfire, the rock was thrown from a wooded area. When police looked in the area, though, whoever had thrown the missile had gone.

Damage was estimated at about $100.

As Reported by the *Keene Evening Sentinel* December 2nd, 1985:

"FIRE"

Lightning hits 2 homes

Two houses in Keene were apparently hit by lightening bolts early this morning, but no damage resulted.

The lightning was part of a thunderstorm, that moved over the Monadnock Region at about 3 a.m.

The lightening strikes were reported at 105 Castle St., and 55 Wilder St. Keene firefighters rushed to the two residences, but found neither fire nor damage.

As Reported by the *Keene Evening Sentinel* December 6th, 1985:

"FIRE"

Fire doused at KSC president's home

Quick Stop. *In this morning's snow, Keene firefighters move quickly to douse a fire in the President's house at Keene State College. Photo by Jim Coppo.*

An electrical heating unit malfunctioned early this morning, causing a fire in the historic home of Keene State College's president.

However, the fire was doused before it could do serious damage.

The heating unit was in the ceiling of a second-floor bedroom at the house, located at Main Street and Appian Way. The house has been the college president's residence since the school was founded in 1909, and is listed in the National Register of Historic Places.

Firefighters took pains to protect the contents of the building, which include valuable antiques. No one was injured.

No estimate of damage had been compiled by late this morning. However, the fire was restricted to the space between the bedroom ceiling and the attic floor, said fire Capt. David B. Osgood. One floor joist was burned out.

Fire-retardant insulation in the ceiling probably kept the fire from spreading, he said.

KSC president Barbara J. Seelye and her mother, Mami Seelye, the only people in the house, were awakened by smoke detectors, which also sent an automatic alarm to Southwestern N.H. Fire Mutual Aid at 5:16 a.m.

When firefighters arrived, there was no sign of fire in the basement or first and second floors, but the attic was filled with smoke, Osgood said.

In the second-floor bedroom, firefighters found that a small area of the wall was charred, and removed parts of the wall and ceiling to get at the fire. To minimize damage, they also removed much of the furniture in the room and covered the floors with canvas, and used little water.

"The fire department was extremely competent in the way it handled the whole thing," said Robert L. Mallat Jr., KSC's vice president for resource administration.

"We believe it was the wiring" that caused the fire, said fire Capt. Lawrence V. Wood. "We don't know what happened to the heating system.

The fire was under control about a half-hour after firefighters arrived. In case the fire was more serious, two engines, a ladder truck and 15 firefighters were sent to the house. The last crew left the house at 7:06 a.m.

———

1986

As Reported by the *Keene Evening Sentinel* January 31st, 1986:

"FIRE"

Two fires reported in Keene

A smoke detector's scream alerted members of a Keene family to a wood stove fire early today, allowing them to keep the fire from spreading until firefighters arrived to finish the job.

Debris from the dryer was removed along with other burnt items from 33 Gates St. Photo by Michael Moore.

On Thursday, a Keene woman suffered second-degree burns on her left hand trying to pull burning clothes from an electric dryer.

This morning's fire was reported at 1:53 a.m. to Southwestern N.H. Fire Mutual Aid, which sent four firefighters and a fire truck to the Cray home at 63 Rule St, according to Paul E. Symonds of the Keene Fire Department. Owner David G. Cray had already used a fire extinguisher to help control the flames.

The blaze started when materials beside the wood stove ignited, and spread into the nearby wall.

On Thursday, Helen O'Brien of 33 Gates St. told firefighters she smelled smoke, found the clothes in the dryer were burning and hurt her hand while trying to pull them out, Symonds said. Damaged were the dryer, some plumbing, electric wiring and a number of items stored in the cellar, Symonds said.

———

As Reported by the *Keene Evening Sentinel* February 8th, 1986:

"FIRE"

Fire doused in Keene

Workmen using a torch on plumbing in the basement of a three-apartment building at 20 Park St., Keene, started a fire Monday night.

Three trucks from the Keene Fire Department responded to the call Monday at 10:08 p.m. Firefighters had the blaze under control within an hour, and stayed until 11:45 to mop up.

The fire spread up the walls of the wooden structure to the second floor, and also caused smoke damage to contents of the apartments. The building is owned by James A. Mugford of Keene.

No damage estimate was available this morning.

————

As Reported by the *Keene Evening Sentinel* March 3rd, 1986:

"FIRE"

Fire doused at KSC shanty

A small fire broke out Saturday night in a protest shanty at Keene State College.

Police are investigating what caused the blaze, which was controlled quickly. They declined to say if there was any evidence indicating how the fire started.

Campus security officers reported the fire Saturday at 11:20 p.m. in the shanty in front of Elliot Hall on Main Street. Police said the fire was confined to a small area. Police officers were able to control the fire with a fire extinguisher until firefighters arrived moments later to extinguish it.

Students build the shanty to protest the University System of New Hampshire's investments in companies that do business in racially divided South Africa. After meeting with college officials last week, the students in the group People for a Free South Africa

agreed to post a person at the shanty during the day to avoid possible safety problems. College officials said the shanty could be a safety hazard for children walking to and from school.

College officials and representatives of the group were not available this morning for comment on the fire.

————

As Reported by the *Keene Evening Sentinel* March 16th, 1986:

"FIRE"

Suspicious fire at Boston & Maine Railroad freight depot

Photo by: Nathan Stout.

A suspicious fire was reported as Keene firefighters rush to fight the flames in a vacant building where vagrants have sometimes taken shelter and from which youths have frequently been chased. Sunday afternoon's fire at 24 Cypress Street in Keene, might have been set, investigators say. The fire was under control in about 20 minutes. The former Boston & Maine Railroad freight depot has been empty for more than five years.

————

As Reported by the *Keene Evening Sentinel* March 20th, 1986:

"FIRE"
Collision on West Street sends two men to hospital

A collision on West Street injured two people Wednesday. Photo by: Jim Coppo.

A two-car crash on West Street, Keene, sent two men to the hospital Wednesday.

Sheldon L. Barker, 85 of 19 Robbins Road, Keene was in fair condition with broken ribs this morning at Cheshire Hospital, according to a hospital spokeswoman. Wayne L. Fisher, 44 of Reavely Road, Hancock, was treated for a muscle strain in his back and released.

Police said Barker was headed west on West Street as Fisher was leaving the parking lot of D'Angelo's Sandwich Shop at 189 West Street. A westbound car with engine trouble was parked in the right hand lane, apparently blocking Fisher's view as he tried to pull around it into the eastbound lane, the report said.

Barker's car and Fisher's pickup truck collided, and both were badly damaged, police said.

As Reported by the *Keene Evening Sentinel* May 24th, 1986:

"STORY"
Old dump is toxic waste site

City Manager J. Patrick MacQueen points out problems at City Dump. Photo by Medora Hebert.

Oil-Spill control equipment installed at the site of river contamination. Photo by Michael Moore.

An old chemical dumping ground in Keene contains high concentrations of industrial solvents, oil-derived chemicals, and at least some polychlorinated biphenyls—PCB's—,which are widely believed to cause cancer.

One of nine chemicals found in the soil at the site, 1,1 dichloroethylene, has been found in the Branch River, in an area where an oil film covers the water's surface. More chemicals, most of them suspected of being carcinogenic, were found in nearby ground in much higher concentrations.

The site is on the north side of the river, behind Keene Public Works Department buildings, east of Lower Main Street and south of Route 101. Tests were taken there in April by the N.H. Water Supply and Pollution Control Commission. City and state officials met this week to discuss the findings.

The conclusion: Levels of contaminants already found are "enormous," said Kenneth W. Teague, assistant director of the state pollution control commission's test laboratory in Concord.

"There's something very wrong there," Teague said.

Teague said he doesn't believe a person walking through the site would face an immediate health threat, but "I wouldn't want to pitch a tent there and sleep overnight."

George M. Gline, who was a public works engineer from 1956 to 1966 and headed the department during much of the 1970's, said the Lower Main Street site was used as a public dump during the early part of the tenure with the city.

He recalled an incinerator on the site that was used to dispose of dead animals. Ashes were dumped to the rear of the incinerator.

In the late 1950's, a new city dump was opened off Route 12 in West Keene, near the current city landfill site. After that, Keene residents dumped their trash at the end of Bradco Street, which runs off lower Winchester Street. And when the dump on Bradco Street was closed, city dumping was moved back to the site in West Keene, where residents currently dispose of their trash in a state-approved landfill.

Though most of the city's trash was dumped in the various landfills and dumps, local industries were permitted to dump liquid waste in a pit on the public works land, which is where the hazardous chemicals have been found, said City Manager J. Patrick MacQueen.

Pollution-control booms and pads set up by the Keene Fire Department are containing most of the oily materials leaking into the Branch River, though a little oil seeps around the downstream end of the barrier.

———

As Reported by the *Keene Evening Sentinel* July 19th, 1986. Throughout the decades the *Keene Sentinel* reported all types of newsworthy motor vehicle accidents. Some of these could be classified as bizarre, while others have been quite serious and have reported fatalities:

"STORY"

Bizarre crime is investigated

Big Hole – Vandals drove a van through this fence at the Keene Gas Corp. parking lot on Emerald Street and then stole five vehicles. Photo by Will Fay.

In a bizarre act of vandalism, a truck and a van stolen from Keene Gas Corp. were set afire early Saturday morning and a company car was found upside down in Ashuelot River. Two other trucks stolen from the company were recovered by police. One was slightly damaged, police said Sunday.

No arrests have been made and police investigating the case said today they have yet to determine a motive.

According to police, in the early morning hours Saturday, someone opened a hole in a 6-foot-high fence around the Keene Gas Corp. parking lot on Emerald Street by driving a van through it.

Stolen from the company's fleet were two small S-10 Chevrolet pickup trucks; a large, 1-ton pick-up, and a Chevrolet Citation car. A van that police said belonged to a company employee also was stolen.

Police were alerted at 3:30 a.m. Saturday to reports of a fire along the Ashuelot River in woods behind the Harper Acres housing complex on Castle Street in Keene.

Keene firefighters found the van and one of the small trucks engulfed in flames on a gravel road cutting through the woods.

Police found the Chevrolet Citation floating upside down in the river near the flaming truck and van.

Because a light was on inside the submerged car, the Connecticut River Valley Underwater Rescue Team was called to the scene. Divers found no one inside the car.

Police said the interiors of the truck and the van were gutted by fire, and the tires on both vehicles were burned off.

Police saw someone driving the 1-ton pickup down Colorado Street, but when they caught up to it the truck had been abandoned. The other small pickup also was found abandoned, on Castle Street.

Kenneth Wood, a Keene Gas Corp. spokesman, estimated the total cost of damage at $10,000. Wood said that his "gut feeling is that it's strictly vandalism" and that the thefts and arson are not the acts of anyone specifically trying to hurt the company.

Vandals have certainly destroyed cars before, said Keene Fire Capt. George H. Shepard, "but it usually doesn't get as malicious as this."

––––––––––

As Reported by the *Keene Evening Sentinel* June 12th, 1986:

"FIRE"

His 103rd birthday sets off fire alarm.

When Conray Wharff puffed up his cheeks and blew out the 103 candles on his birthday cake Wednesday night, alarms went off, lights flashed and a Keene fire truck pulled up at the front door of his home at the Country Way Retirement Care Center.

What caused the ruckus was not that Wharff was celebrating his centennial-plus three birthday. Rather, it was that all those candles, blown out over one sheet cake, sent up a mighty plume of smoke that set off the building's fire alarm.

Keene firefighters said their alarm went off at 5:54 p.m. and a fire truck immediately headed for the Court Street nursing home. Before it arrived, the nursing home reported the false alarm.

Even so, firefighters kept going. "When the alarm goes off, we have to go," a captain said.

Besides, the fire crew was invited to help eat Wharff's birthday cake.

––––––––––

As Reported by the *Keene Evening Sentinel* September 15th, 1986:

"STORY"

Motorcyclists lose leg, foot in accident

Police assist motorcyclists after a collision with a car seriously injures two. Photo by: James Coppo.

One woman lost a leg and another lost a foot when the motorcycles they were riding were struck by a car Saturday afternoon on Route 9 in Keene.

Robin A. Romaine, 29, of Salem and Susan B. Southwick, 27, of Allston, Mass., were rushed to Cheshire Hospital in Keene. Both were listed in serious condition this morning, a hospital spokesman said.

Romaine's left leg was severed above the knee and Southwick's left foot was cut at the ankle, the spokesman said.

Both women underwent surgery Saturday to cleanse their wounds. There was "no possible way to reattach" their severed limbs, a hospital official said.

Another motorcyclist, Alice C. Kitselman, 25, of Jamaica Plain, Mass., checked into Cheshire Hospital several hours after the accident for treatment of a bruised shin, the spokesman said. She was subsequently released.

Police say William M. Kazakis, 39, of Nashua lost control of his 1984 Lincoln when he tried to avoid a pickup truck that was waiting on Route 9 to make a left turn onto South Sullivan Road. The two vehicles were eastbound.

Police said Kazakis's car swerved into the westbound lane, where about 80 female motorcyclists participating in Fox Run, New Hampshire's first all-women's motorcycle tour, were riding into Keene. The group had planned a party Saturday night at the Coach and Four Motor Inn on Route 12 in Marlborough.

The impact of the crash smashed the women into a guardrail, police said.

It is not clear whether Kitselman was hit by the car or another motorcycle, police said.

Kazakis and his wife, a passenger in the car, were not injured in the accident, which occurred shortly before 4:23 p.m., police said.

————

As Reported by the *Union Leader Correspondent* October 2nd, 1986 by John Scibelli:

"STORY"

Keene firefighters will host big parade, activities day

Finishing Touches: Capt. David Osgood applies some paint in preparation for tomorrow's parade. Photo by John Scibelli.

Harry Nelson adds the elbow grease to make the front and shine. Photo by John Scibelli.

More than 20 communities from New Hampshire and Vermont will be represented at tomorrow's firemen's parade, hosted by the Keene Fire Department.

Deputy Chief Paul Crowell said six bands will march and more than 25 pieces of fire apparatus, some vintage and some now, will be in the four division parade.

The parade begins at the Central Square Fire Station at 1 p.m. It will proceed through the square, go down Main Street, turn left onto Marlboro Street, and end on Optical Avenue in the industrial park.

During the parade, the Keene Fire Department will display its 1930 Ahrens-Fox hose and pumper truck, "Rosie," one of the few of its kind in the country. The truck has been repaired after being out of service for two years and can still serve as a pumper. Its last fire response was November 11, 1968.

For the first time in the history of the parade, fire prevention day activities will be held behind the American Legion Hall on Upper Court Street, from 3 to 5 p.m.

Capt. Bruce Pollock said firefighters will take part in an auditorium raise, in which they erect a 45-foot extension ladder so it is pointed straight up, secure it with safety lines then climb it. The exercise may be cancelled if there are heavy winds or bad weather, Pollock said.

There will also be demonstrations of firefighting tools, master stream appliances and foam equipment, and firefighters will be available to answer questions on woodstove safety, kerosene heater regulations, and other topics.

In addition, there will be a juvenile fire setter program, a concession stand, "Learn Not to Burn" pamphlets will be distributed, and a raffle for two five pound multi-purpose fire extinguishers and two smoke detectors.

———

As Reported by the *Keene Evening Sentinel* October 27th, 1986:

"FIRE"

Church Street & Sullivan Street fires

Keene firefighters doused a fire in a Church Street apartment Saturday morning just in time to join firefighters at a second fire at 9 Sullivan St.

No injuries were reported in either blaze.

A call at 5:36 a.m. sent three firefighters to 153 Church St., where Linda Marotto and Diane Nuzzo had already put out a blaze in a bedroom, said Capt. David B. Osgood. The fire started when a candle burning on a bureau melted down then ignited the wall and ceiling.

Firefighters cut into the ceiling and wall to extinguish the blaze completely.

From Church Street, they joined firefighters who had been called at 5:55 a.m. to 9 Sullivan St. A second alarm at 6:01 sent additional firefighters and equipment to help at the scene.

Osgood said the fire started behind the furnace chimney, where the stack pipe had rusted through. The blaze burned through the exterior wall and spread up the chimney to the roof. The house is owned by Robert J. Wyman, whose son and a friend were there when the fire broke out. Wyman's son discovered the blaze and reported the fire, officials said.

The fire, under control by 5:30 a.m., resulted in damage to the exterior wall and an upstairs bedroom.

————

As Reported by the *Keene Evening Sentinel* November 1st, 1986:

"FIRE"

Halloween fire at former Keene drive-in

Photo by Medora Hebert.

On October 31st flames ripped through a wooden platform supporting the giant screen at the former Keene Drive-in Theater Friday night for 20 minutes before firefighters brought the blaze under control according to a city emergency squad worker.

The fire burned a 3-foot wide by 10-foot high hole in the wooden structure that supports the screen said Raymond Claisson of the Keene Area Radio Emergency Squad.

The big screen reportedly wasn't damaged.

Keene firefighters and police were called to the scene at 9:22 p.m. when an emergency squad worker spotted the blaze at the former theater on Optical Avenue. Because of possible Halloween pranks, the emergency squad had stepped up its patrols around the city. The quick alert to the fire enabled firefighters to prevent a lot of damage, a squad worker said.

"They put it out just in time. The whole thing could have burned down," Claisson said.

He also said that the boys were seen running from the vacant lot surrounding the former theater and were pursued by Keene Police officers, who were unable to apprehend them.

————

As Reported by the *Keene Evening Sentinel* November 8th, 1986:

"STORY"

Emergency landing ends safely at city's airport

City fireman eyes Sandra McDonough's plane at Dillant-Hopkins airport. Photo by Medora Hebert.

On November 8th Sandra McDonough had no plans to fly her airplane into the Dillant-Hopkins Airport Friday afternoon, but she was glad she could when she did.

McDonough, a lawyer from Fairfield, Conn., was completing the second leg of a roundtrip solo flight from Montpelier, VT to

Bridgeport, CT, when her single-engine plant lost a cylinder.

She was about 12 miles north of the Keene airport and 8,000 feet in the air when it happened; the aircraft immediately started losing power, she told the Sentinel shortly after the ordeal.

McDonough quickly called Boston center air traffic controllers in Nashua to report the emergency and they directed her to Dillant-Hopkins. About 2 miles away from the airport the plane lost power completely, she said, and quietly glided toward the runway. Once above it, the pilot broke through the clouds and began a lot corkscrew descent, landing safely on the runway. Then incident took less then 10 minutes.

A Keene fire truck and rescue service vehicle arrived just before McDonough landed, at about noon. Fire Chief Robert N. Guyette said the propeller wasn't moving when the plane touched down.

When McDonough emerged from the four-seater cockpit, Guyette said, "She looked toward the sky, put her hands up and said, "Thank you, I owe you one."

McDonough 47, smiling and calm, refused a ride from fire department officials, preferring to walk the distance from the south runway to the office to see if she could line up a ride back to Connecticut. "I need the walk," she said.

Behind her, smoke rose from the engine of her Piper Turbo Arrow IV plane. There was no fire, only smoke from burning oil and an overheated engine.

McDonough, a pilot for 10 years and a flight instructor, said this is the second time an aircraft has lost engine power in flight while she's been in the cockpit. But, she said, this was the first time she was flying a single-engine plane and had a back up.

James W. Ball of Keene, a pilot at the scene, was impressed by McDonough's flying. "It was a good bit of piloting," he said.

Guyette agreed. "I think she's a very, very good pilot," he said. "A real cool cookie as far as I'm concerned."

————

Keene replaced its old crash truck with this new 011A. It was one of the last 011A crash trucks in service. It was used for commercial flights (required by the FAA) and other petroleum-based emergencies. It was kept at Station 3, Keene Airport.

Segrave Ladder. In 1946 WWII Chief Messer ordered a ladder to replace the 1919 Mac Ladder. This Segrave Ladder came through with no frills (meaning chrome, etc.) and served the department for 3 decades.

Fire Training Tower. The training tower was a dream of Capt. Ronald Amadon, training officer. It was a long process to formulate and build the tower, which was constructed at the Municipal Airport. Construction was co-ordinated by Capt. Amadon, with help from some members of the department, and was used for nearly 2 decades.

Status Board. The Status board was made by Capt. Ronald Amadon to track on/off duty personnel and those who were out of the station. It was designed to follow all personnel and has grown along with the department.

1987–2003

Turn of the Millennium

Note: Beginning in 1987, the City of Keene stopped issuing Annual Reports.
*This section has only articles from the **Keene Evening Sentinel.***

1987

As Reported by the *Keene Evening Sentinel* January 26th, 1987:

"FIRE"

Major fire averted in Keene

A pickup truck that caught fire in a garage on Nims Road in Keene Sunday night was pulled out seconds before it became engulfed in flames, averting what authorities said would have been a major blaze.

"He got it out in just the nick of time," said Keene Fire Capt. David B. Osgood.

Michael L. Blair, owner of the truck, said he used a tractor to pull the 1983 Ford Ranger out of the garage. "I tried to pull it out by hand, but one of the tires had already blown." Fortunately, he said, the tractor "started right up" and got the truck out before it could damage the garage or home, owned by Harry Bolles of Clearwater, FL.

Osgood said Sunday that a heater used to keep the truck's engine warm is suspected as the cause of the fire. The investigation continued today.

The truck was destroyed, according to Osgood, but no damage estimate was available. A Keene police officer at the scene put the truck fire out with a fire extinguisher, and was later aided by firefighters who arrived on the scene shortly after 9 p.m.

As Reported by the *Keene Evening Sentinel* February 20th, 1987:

"FIRE"

Dryer linked to Keene fire

Keene firefighters spend about 16 minutes dousing a fire in an apartment at 21 Harmony Lane Thursday night.

The blaze broke out at 7:51 p.m., when an electric dryer in an apartment occupied by Ernest and Ethel Wood apparently burst into flames, according to a fire department spokesman.

No one was injured.

As Reported by the *Keene Evening Sentinel* March 19th, 1988:

"FIRE"

Damage estimated at $50,000 in fire at Keene businesses

Two alarm fire caused about $50,000 damage Wednesday night to a two-story office building at 85 Emerald St. in Keene Wednesday night. No one was injured.

About 75 firefighters worked for more than an hour to quell flames inside the building, which houses Economy Plumbing and Heating, Inc., Emerald Leasing Corp., an equipment rental company, and Carthotech, an energy management firm.

The owner of the building, Emerson H. O'Brien of Spofford, said during the fire that he hoped to be open for business today, but the cleanup hadn't been completed by this morning and investigators were still trying to pinpoint the cause of the blaze.

Fire engines arrived at the scene shortly before 10 p.m. and a second alarm went out 20 minutes later. But soon after that, Keene Fire Chief Robert N. Guyette said firefighters had succeeded in trapping the fire between the first and second floors near the rear of the building." It's just a matter of mopping it up," he said.

The fire was reported under control at 11:04, but smoke continued to drift slowly out of the building until shortly after 12:30 this morning.

At the height of the fire, smoke poured through cracks in the roof of the building from second-story windows and from the main entrance. Flames also curled out of an upper floor window on the east side of the structure.

Firefighters with oxygen tanks moved rapidly in and out of the building to battle the smoke and flames.

"There's smoke everywhere—you can't see a thing," said Tim T. Mason, a Keene firefighter, his face covered with soot and sweat as he came out of the building. Heavy smoke made it impossible to see more than a few feet inside the building from the front entrance.

"It's hotter than hell," puffed another firefighter, yanking off his oxygen mask.

The upper floor of the building was used for company offices. The floors of the building were carpeted, which may have accounted for the heavy smoke. Most of the damage occurred in the middle of the first and second floors. Parts of the first and second floor ceilings were destroyed, leaving nothing but charred metal bars.

At the present time, I would say it probably started in the supply closet of the ground floor," Guyette said today. The closet was used to store volatile chemical cleaners and maintenance equipment.

"There was a lot of damage on both floors, smoke and water," the chief said, putting the cost of repairing the building in the neighborhood of $50,000. City tax records value the building at $414,100.

Most of the first floor was also used for offices, though part of it was used for plumbing tool storage, including oxygen tanks, for acetylene torches. Firefighters quickly hosed down the tanks to keep them from exploding.

About 80 people watched the fire from across the street. Some had heard the fire call on their police scanners and wanted to see what was going on. Others, such as Salvation Army Capt. David E. Metcalf, showed up to serve coffee to firefighters, helping them to combat chilly temperatures Wednesday night.

Police cordoned off a two-block area around the building while firefighters fought the blaze.

Fire trucks from Marlborough, Surry and West Swanzey stood by at the Keene fire station in case others calls came in. A truck from Swanzey Center waited on Main Street to assist Keene firefighters if necessary, but was never called to the fire.

The last piece of fire equipment left the scene at 1:56 a.m., Guyette said. Some firefighters stayed through the night to check for hot spots that might rekindle the blaze.

"We've had them do that before," Guyette said. "I'd rather keep people there than have to go back."

———

Arson caused Keene fire

Someone set a fire that caused major damage last week at Economy Plumbing and Heating Supply at 85 Emerald St., Keene.

Thomas M. Norton, an investigator with the N.H. Fire Marshal's Office, said today that arson caused the two-alarm fire, but would not reveal what led to that conclusion or which direction investigators are taking now.

The building's owner, Emerson H. O'Brien of Spofford, was unavailable for comment this morning.

Initial reports indicated the fire at the two-story office building caused about $50,000 worth of damage, but Keene Fire Chief Robert N. Guyette said the total may reach $300,000.

Guyette said today that fire officials have "a pretty good idea" that the fire began in a first-floor supply closed, and that an insurance agency has also ruled that the fire was arson related.

———————

As Reported by the *Keene Evening Sentinel* April 6th, 1987:

"STORY"

Region flooding; evacuations ordered
More rain predicted for area

April rains raise havoc with Keene and surrounding areas. The Ashuelot River expands into Tanglewood Estates and creates an evacuation order. Photo above shows 1,260 cubic feet of water exits from Surry Mountain Dam Spillway. Photo by Michael Moore.

People along the Ashuelot River from Keene south to Hinsdale were being advised to evacuate their homes today because of expected flooding in the lowlands by this afternoon.

Based on the information we have we're telling people to get out now," said Keene Fire Chief Robert N. Guyette.

The warning went out to homes and businesses along Lower Main Street, Martel Court, Upper Court Street, West Street, Winchester Street and other low lying areas along the Ashuelot River in Keene as well as to Roxbury and the village of West Swanzey.

The Surry Mountain Dam, which holds back the Ashuelot River, was expected to reach capacity from the weekend's drenching rains, and spill over between 4 and 6 p.m. today, officials said. And Otter Brook Dam in Keene may flood by Tuesday afternoon, officials said.

West Swanzey, Winchester and Hinsdale will probably have some flooding by Tuesday afternoon officials said.

At a late-morning news conference emergency officials announced that Keene Junior High School was designated an evacuation center for people forced from their homes. Local Red Cross administrators also prepared to set yup shelters at area schools and churches. Rescue workers urged people to seek shelter at the homes of friends and neighbors.

Keene Fire Chief Robert N. Guyette said officials expect lower Winchester Street, south of the bypass, to be the hardest hit, sometime Tuesday, due to the combined effects of spillovers at the Surry Mountain and Otter Brook dams. Businesses along West Street have also been alerted, concluding offices at the Island Mill complex and stores at Colony Mill Marketplace.

"This is not going to be a one or two day deal," Guyette said. "This could be a week evacuation."

Two non-emergency numbers were set up for people to call for information about the flood emergency and evacuation plans; 357-1980 and 357-1981, both at the Keene Fire Department.

Guyette also advised people to stay tuned to a local radio station.

The local emergency preparations come after Gov. John H. Sununu declared a state of emergency in New Hampshire this morning because of drenching rain and flooding throughout the state.

More that 2 inches of rain have fallen since Friday, after more than 1 ½ inches last week that also melted a huge snow cover. Weather officials say the ground is saturated and unable to absorb any more rain, although light showers are predicted to continue through Wednesday.

————

Water expected to go over dam tops

Sunday at the Surry Mountain and Otter Brook dams. John F. Boyea knew by 7 p.m. that it was going to come over the top.

They are going to spill over unless we get an act of God," said Boyea, project manager for the U.S. Army Corps of Engineers two dams in the Keene area.

Instead the region has received continued rain—2 inches since Sunday. That's not necessarily a lot, except that the ground in this area has already been saturated from rain and melting snow last week. There's no place for the new rainwater to go but into local rivers and lakes.

This morning water collecting behind the Surry dam passed the record 62 foot level set during flooding in June 1984. It was expected to reach the 65 foot limit and begin pouring through the emergency spillway by noon today. The dam's flood gates had been opened slightly in an effort to delay the uncontrolled flood of water into the Ashuelot River above Keene.

Otter Brook Dam is expected to reach its spill over point sometime Tuesday, said Boyea from his offices below the dam. The water level was at 88 feet this morning, with its spillover point at 98 feet. The record there was also set in 1984 at 88,66 feet.

"We will be setting some records today," Boyea said. "It's going to be different. We've never spilled over before."

Although the current water levels are being compared to those recorded during severe flooding that hit the region in June 1984, the pattern of flooding is at least starting off differently.

That's because the flooding three years ago resulted from four days of intense rain that suddenly overcame the dams and other flood control structures in the region.

This time, the rain has been relatively light but insistent and it has come on the heels of rain and melting snow last week that has already saturated the ground. That leaves new rainwater no place to go but into the reservoirs.

Those reservoirs were rising as of this morning at a rate of about 4 feet per hour, Boyea said from 1.8 to 2.9 inches of rain were measured since Friday night at points throughout the region. The total for last week's storm was about 1.5 inches, plus the snow.

The National Weather Service in Concord, having issued a flood warning, said this morning that occasional periods of light rain will continue over the next two days.

Don't expect heavy rain, said the service's meteorologist, Joseph McCall, "but what rain we do have will aggravate the situation."

Water spilling into the Ashuelot River is expected to move at 2,000 cubic feet per second said Keene City Engineer Thomas F. Dutton.

That is likely to spend a surge down the river, with officials warning people in low lying areas from Keene down to Hinsdale that they should be prepared to leave their homes.

Some in Keene ready to evacuate

Their suitcases packed since Sunday night, some residents near the swollen Ashuelot River along Upper Court's Street in Keene were advised this morning to evacuate their houses, condominiums and mobile home parks.

Many were ready before the word came.

"They gold us to stay up, stay awake and stay alert," said Phyllis M. Baldwin who lives with her husband, William, at the trailer park at 515 Tanglewood Estates. "I didn't go to bed till 4 in the morning. They said they would notify us and give us time to get out. I went through this before as a kid in Surry."

The Baldwins and hundreds of other area residents were told Sunday night of possible flooding from Surry Mountain Dam which holds back the Ashuelot River. NH Civil Defense Agency predicted this morning the Surry dam was close to spilling over.

Emergency officials in Keene said residences and businesses on Upper Court and Winchester streets would likely be most affected by spillover, but they were making plans to aid anyone living along the 6 miles of Ashuelot that flows through Keene.

By late morning officials had no estimate of how many people would be encouraged to evacuate.

As Reported by the *Keene Evening Sentinel* April 20th, 1987:

"FIRE"

Dorm fire at KSC prompts evacuation

Students were evacuated from the Carle Hall dormitory at Keene State College when a fire broke out Sunday morning in a first-floor room.

Firefighters had to break into room 111 of the college dormitory at about 10 a.m. to squelch the fire, the cause of which is still being investigated a Keene fire Department spokesman said this morning.

The room is occupied by Warren Johnson of New London, who's studying for an associate degree; he was not there when the fire broke out. Since it was Easter Sunday, few students were in the dormitory, said Robert L. Mallat Jr., KSC vice president for resource administration.

The fire's heat cracked the room's windows, and heat and smoke damaged the walls and ceiling Mallat said. Damage to the room was estimated at $3,000.

The student's possessions also suffered an undetermined amount of damage, Mallat said.

————

As Reported by the *Keene Evening Sentinel* May 28th, 1987:

"FIRE"

Keene fire

Photo by Michael Moore.

At top, a Keene firefighter adjusts his outfit amid the rubble of the site of a Wednesday fire at 164 Roxbury St., while at left, three men look at the damage. The fire at the five-apartment building was reported at 1:19 p.m., and was doused within 20 minutes by Keene firefighters. Damage estimated at $200, was limited to the building's siding and a first-floor porch, according to Deputy fire Chief Chester E. Dubriske. No one was injured in the fire, which Dubriske believes may have been started by a cigarette. The building is owned by William Beauregard of 214 Franklin St.

————

As Reported by the *Keene Evening Sentinel* June 10th, 1987:

"FIRE"

Markem worker burned

A Keene man was in fair but stable condition this morning, under treatment for second-degree burns on his shoulders and face suffered in an industrial accident Tuesday.

Robert J. Campbell, 61, of 61 Congress St. suffered the burns Tuesday at 11:30 a.m. in an explosion at the chemical division of Markem Corp at 150 Congress St. He was being treated today in the intensive care unit of Cheshire Medical Center.

Campbell has worked at Markem for three years as an ink mill operator.

The accident occurred as Campbell was cleaning aluminum powder out of a 15-gallon drum, plant officials said. He was inside the chemical division's ventilation room, using a vacuum unit with a rubber-and-fabric hose.

Thomas P. Putnam, company president, said Campbell does not usually work in the chemical division, but was filling in there on Tuesday. Putnam said no one is sure yet what caused the explosion, but said it could have been a spark from static electricity.

So far, he said, there is no indication that Campbell was using incorrect procedures.

The ventilation room, where the explosion occurred, is a vault like room, 20 feet square with 15-foot ceilings. It has no windows and 6-inch-thick walls, with a roof skylight designed to pop out if an explosion occurs.

No one but Campbell was in the room when the explosion occurred.

The 2-inch-thick steel fire door—the only entrance to the room—was open, but no materials went out the door with the blast of air caused by the explosion.

Other production workers heard the blast and rushed to help Campbell, who had been wearing protective goggles, and a cloth apron. They laid him down on the floor, patted his clothing to put out the fire, then removed his clothing and rushed him to a nearby safety shower to cool his skin.

Campbell was rushed by ambulance to Cheshire Medical Center.

Putnam said a worker who was helping to put out the fire on Campbell's clothing suffered minor burns.

Five Keene fire trucks and 50 firefighters raced to Markem after the explosion, but the half dozen firefighters on the first two trucks to arrive doused the flames with water in six minutes.

Putnam sent the 40 production workers in the chemical division home after the explosion. The employees returned to work today.

The last accident this severe that Putnam could recall at Markem occurred 10 years ago.

Keene Fire Chief Robert N. Guyette said firefighters thought at first that magnesium had exploded. However, after chemicals did not extinguish the fire, the firefighters used water, and it worked.

Putnam said the bottom of the 15-gallon barrel was bubbled out from the explosion, the entrance door to the vault can no longer be closed because of some damage to the cinder block wall around it, and the skylight will have to be fixed.

The ventilation room also contained other drums—15 55-gallon drums and five 1-gallon pails—that held flammable chemicals, plus equipment to mix chemicals and to ventilate the room, but those were undamaged.

————

As Reported by the *Keene Evening Sentinel* June 23rd, 1987:

"FIRE"

Five stores still closed because of Colony Mill fire

Five stores remained closed today in the aftermath of a weekend fire at the Colony Mill Marketplace, Keene, but a sixth reopened for business.

The Pavilion reopened, but the five others will stay closed until insurance adjusters finish figuring out the damage estimates. Those five are Joe Jones Ski and Sports Shop, The Band Box, She of Keene, Faulkners Fine Menswear and The Gazebo. The Gazebo hopes to be back in business on Friday; the other stores were unsure when they will reopen.

A Pavillion spokeswoman said not much damage was done to the store, which glass separates from other parts of the west wing of the shopping complex, where the fire was located.

Most of the flame damage in Sunday's fire was confined to a counter area in the Joe Jones store, smoke and oil soot caused damage in nearby stores.

————

As Reported by the *Keene Evening Sentinel* June 25th, 1987:

"FIRE"

Keene fire evidence being tested

Police hope they moved quickly enough in sending evidence from last weekend's fire at Joe Jones Ski and Sport Shop in Keene to state laboratories in Concord for testing.

Police want to know if an accelerant—such as gasoline or kerosene—was used to spread the fire inside the store at Colony Mill Marketplace at 222 West St.

"Any accelerant will evaporate or dissipate quickly," Keene Police Sgt. Robert H. Hardy said. "If we got to Concord quick enough, they can probably find out if an accelerant was used."

Hardy said the remains of what appeared to be part of a rug were retrieved at the store Sunday morning and taken to the state laboratory, along with samples from what was probably a wicker basked full of corduroy hats.

Test results should be available in two weeks.

Meanwhile, fire sales are set to start Friday morning at three stores in the mill, a spokesman for the shopping complex said this morning.

While shoppers attack the racks Friday, police and fire officials will probably still be trying to determine what caused the suspicious fire.

"We don't know what caused it Hardy said this morning. "It just doesn't have the appearance of a natural fire."

The smoky fire—which initially closed six businesses because of smoke and soot damage—is being investigated by Keene police and fire officials. Police are interviewing people to try to glean information that could help them, Hardy said.

―――――――

As Reported by the *Keene Evening Sentinel* October 26th, 1987:

"FIRE"

Keene fire called suspicious

A Keene police arson unit is investigating a fire Monday that destroyed a storage trailer containing burning materials for the Drummer Hill housing project in Keene.

"I haven't concluded anything, but I will say I am extremely suspicious of it," police Sgt Robert H. Hardy said today of the fire at the trailer on Timber Lane Drive off Elm Street.

"Unless there's some element in the trailer that would give something to ignite it with I would say it needed something to help it along," Hardy said.

The trailer was owned by Page Street Trailer Rental Corp. It contained materials—tar, roofing paper, and cellar window encasements owned by Winter Panel Development Corp of Brattleboro, developer of the 54-home Drummer Hill project. According to Keene Fire Department Capt. David Osgood. The project, recently approved by city government is under construction.

The fire broke out around 3:30 p.m. Sunday. Six Keene firefighters, using an engine and a tanker, knocked the flames down within minutes but the damage had b been done, Osgood said.

Hardy estimated the damage at $600.

―――――――

As Reported by the *Keene Evening Sentinel* December 3rd, 1987:

"STORY"

New Engines

Keene Fire Department received an early Christmas present in the form of two new engines. Engine number 3 that has a six person cab and a 500 gallon tank and can pump 1500 gallons of water per minute. Engine number 4 has a 1000 gallon tank and can pump 1000 gallons per minute. Engine number 3 and 4 were manufactured by the Maxym Company for the Keene Fire Department. Fire Department Photo.

As Reported by the *Keene Evening Sentinel* December 12th, 1987:

"FIRE"

Keene fire leaves Sears with damaged hardware

A $10,000 worth of hardware was damaged to water Friday night at Sears Roebuck and Co in Keene, as firefighters extinguished an apartment fire above the store on Central Square.

About 15 Sears employees put in extra hours Saturday and Sunday, mopping up the hardware department and replacing soaked merchandise with in stock items, store manager James J. McGilvery said this morning.

The fire broke out in a bedroom of Joseph and Debra Moody's apartment at 40 Central Square and was apparently caused by a 4-year-old child playing with a cigarette lighter, fire officials said today.

About 50 Keene firefighters fought the blaze which caused smoke and heat damage to two other apartments and extensive water damage to Sears hardware department on the first floor of the building.

McGilvery said some items will be sold at a discount, but others are too damaged to sell and will have to be reordered. Sears' service department will test electrical devices to insure that they're safe to sell, he said.

As Reported by the *Keene Evening Sentinel* December 21st, 1987:

"FIRE"

No one hurt in Keene fire

Fire caused extensive damage to the kitchen of a single-family Keene home early this morning, but caused no injuries.

Keene firefighters responded at 12 a.m. to put out the blaze at 55 Graves Road that was caused by an overheated wood stove, said Deputy Fire Chief Chester Dubriske. Firefighters were back at the station by 1:14 a.m.

The cost of the damage had not yet been estimated this morning, but Dubriske said the ceiling and walls of the kitchen were heavily damaged and several windows were broken as a result of the fire.

Dubriske said the fire started near a stovepipe in the kitchen while the family of Kay Georgiana slept. The family discovered the blaze at about midnight and got out of the wood frame house safely.

1988

As Reported by the *Keene Evening Sentinel* January 6th, 1988:

"FIRE"

A fire at a Keene machine shop was extinguished by a sprinkler system early today before it got out of control, officials said.

The fire started at about 5:30 a.m. in the paint room of Al Melanson Co. Inc. at 80 Pearl St. That plant is a division of the company headquartered on West Street in Keene.

The machine shop filled with smoke and Keene firefighters had to use a smoke ejector to clear the air, according to authorities. No injuries were reported and damage was minimal.

The cause of the fire was unknown.

———

As Reported by the *Keene Evening Sentinel* February 9th, 1988:

"FIRE"

Keene High Evacuated

A pair of burning sneakers in a locker of Keene High School caused the evacuation of the entire 1,000 student school Monday at about 12:35 p.m.

The fire started in a locker in the school's east wing after someone dropped burning material through the locker's top vent said principal Charles A. Napoli.

"I don't suspect arson" Napoli said. "I do suspect it was a stupid move.

Smoke filled the corridor of the wing, causing the evacuation, although janitors had the fire under control before firefighters arrived.

———

As Reported by the *Keene Evening Sentinel* February 17th, 1988:

"FIRE"

Keene apartment damaged by fire

A two-alarm fire caused considerable heat, smoke and water damage to the bathroom of a first floor apartment at 67 Winter St. in Keene early this morning.

Keene fire officials said the occupant, who was not identified, was alerted by a fire detector shortly before 1 a.m. and escaped unharmed.

Three Keene State College students were evacuated from the apartment above the blaze. None were injured but their apartment suffered some damage when firefighters tore away parts of its floor to make sure the fire was out. The blaze was extinguished in about an hour.

The fire is under investigation.

———

As Reported by Steve Goldsmith in the *Keene Evening Sentinel* February 20th, 1988:

"FIRE"

Next time flashing light could be for you

It can happen to anyone, anywhere and anytime.

Every day we see the flashing blue or red lights of an emergency vehicle, but too often we don't pay sufficient heed to what those lights mean.

N.H. law requires all vehicles approaching an emergency vehicle—fire truck, ambulance or police cruiser—to pull over to the right and stop.

Photo by Steve Goldsmith.

All too often, however, many motorists try to beat the emergency vehicle to an intersection or side road. Many times, drivers will pull over to the right but maintain speed, which is in violation of the law.

The men and women in the emergency services are trained to save lives and protect property. They are trained to drive their vehicles to the emergency scene with all possible speed, but in a safe manner.

Many factors can delay that response, however, including unclear directions from a caller as to the type of help needed and where it should be sent.

An emergency can happen to any of us at any time. So, please remember that the person in the emergency vehicle can just as easily be responding to your house next time, to help you or one you love. The next time you see the flashing lights, red or blue, please obey the law. Pull over. Give them a fighting chance to do their jobs—and maybe save the life of someone near or dear to you. Thank you.

———

As Reported by the *Keene Evening Sentinel* February 26th, 1988:

"FIRE"

Tenants, firefighters, police acted heroically

At 12:34 a.m. on Wednesday, February 17, I was notified by the Keene Police Department that an office/apartment building I own on 67 Winter St. was on fire. Ten minutes later I arrived on the scene to find three policemen and 20-30 firemen hard at work. Apparently a fire had started in the first-floor apartment and had set off all the hard-wired smoke detectors. The second floor tenants, Dianne Bartlett, Sondra Bendel and Leigh Mann heard the smoke alarms going off and left at once. They stopped long enough at the first-floor apartment to kick in the door, get the other tenant and help her out of the building. If they hadn't had the courage and presence of mind to do so, I'm not sure what the result would have been. They should be commended for their actions and most certainly they have my sincere gratitude.

The Keene Fire Department also deserves my appreciation for their quick response, the care they took not to cause more damage than absolutely necessary, and the courtesy they exhibited while they were at the scene. They had the foresight to protect some expensive equipment in my office from water damage and the concern to rescue a hamster from the second-floor apartment.

The Keene Police were very helpful and also have my sincere thanks.

I wish to thank my heroic tenants, the men and women of the Keene Fire Department and the Keene Police Department.

For those of you who do not have smoke detectors or some that are not working I suggest you correct that situation at once. My tenants and I believe without them four lives would most likely have been needlessly lost on February 17.

————

As Reported by the *Keene Evening Sentinel* March 2nd, 1988.

"FIRE"

Keene fire likely arson

A small fire this morning on the second floor of an apartment house at 101 Main St. in Keene was probably set intentionally, fire officials said.

Firefighters were called to the fire at 1:58 a.m. and arrived to find a pile of burning newspapers at the top of a flight of stairs.

"The conclusion is that somebody probably set it," Keene fire Capt. Larry V Wood said.

"The fire was doused before any damage was done," Wood said. Keene police and fire officials are investigating.

————

As Reported by the *Keene Evening Sentinel* March 4th, 1988:

"FIRE"

3 fires in Keene blamed on arson

A series of small fires in downtown Keene has police and fire officials looking for an arsonist.

A small paper fire was set in an air shaft on the second floor of 12 West St. shortly before 1 this morning. The flames were doused before the fire could spread, but officials said it had the potential to cause significant damage because of where it was set.

The fire was the third this week that authorities think was set intentionally.

"If it hadn't been spotted quickly, it could have raced through the building," Fire Chief Robert N. Guyette said.

Although the fire was under control in minutes, three ground-floor businesses— Sotto Voce, Miranda's Verandah and Allan Kendall's Office Specialists—did suffer some water damage when the building's sprinkler system went off, police said.

A minor fire Wednesday at 101 Main St. was also set, said Fire Capt. Larry V. Wood, Firefighters arrived at about 2 a.m. to find a pile of newspapers burning on the second floor, at the top of a flight of stairs. No significant damage was reported in that fire, either.

On Thursday, newspapers were set on fire under some mailboxes at 23 West St. The fire went out on its own, and no damage was done. That building contains businesses and apartments.

Police have stepped up foot patrols of the area in an effort to prevent future fires. Police Lt. Larry Smith said residents in the Main Street area have been asked to be on the lookout for anything suspicious.

Smith said the recent fires have led residents to tell authorities of previously unreported fires. He declined to say how many fires are being investigated.

Other measures have been taken to stop the arsonist, Smith said, though he declined to say what those measures are.

"Whether it's kids' play or something else, it's not good," Guyette said.

————

As Reported by the *Keene Evening Sentinel* March 17th, 1988:

"FIRE"

Porch fire in Keene is under investigation

Keene fire officials are investigating the cause of a porch fire Wednesday night at a Sullivan St. home. Firefighters were able to quickly extinguish the small blaze on the back porch of Bruce DiCastro's house. No one was at home during the fire, officials said.

They declined to speculate on whether the fire may be another in a series of small blazes that have been set by an arsonist in the past few weeks in the downtown area. Three small fires that caused minor damage were set in buildings on West and Main Streets.

_____

As Reported by the *Keene Evening Sentinel* March 21st, 1988:

"FIRE"

Fire in Keene freight yard likely arson, fire chief says

A late-night fire that gutted an abandoned grain store in Keene was most likely the work of an arsonist, Keene Fire Chief Robert N. Guyette said today.

"All we can say at this point is that we are reasonably sure that someone set this. We have no suspects," Guyette said.

He declined to speculate whether Friday night's fire at a former Boston & Maine railroad freight yard off Main Street was set by the same person responsible for a recent series of small fires downtown.

Three suspicious late-night fires have occurred this month near Central Square.

Fire officials are working with detective Robert Hardy on the latest incident.

The aftermath of the Keene freight yard. Photo by Michael Moore.

"People should just keep their eyes open," Guyette said.

The blaze that destroyed the wooden building off Cypress St. was reported at 11:50 p.m. by a worker at the nearby Keene YMCA on Roxbury St.

A crowd gathered as 55 to 60 firefighters sprayed arcs of water on flames that shot up 20 feet. Smoke, illuminated by spotlights, curled over downtown as firefighters fought the blaze for 40 feet. Smoke, illuminated by spotlights, curled over downtown as firefighters fought the blaze for 45 minutes.

Freight yard fire was arson

Police say they are certain a fire that gutted an abandoned grain-storage building off Cypress St. in Keene March 18 was set intentionally.

Although authorities have not been able to determine what was used to start the fire at the building in the former Boston & Maine Railroad freight yard, the rapid spread of the flames has led them to believe the fire was set.

Keene police Sgt. Robert Hardy said he is still trying to determine whether the fire is connected to a recent series of small fires set in the Central Square area.

He declined to say if police have any suspects in the case.

———————

As Reported by the *Keene Evening Sentinel* March 25th, 1988:

"STORY"

Petroleum spill in Keene River contained; investigation underway

A petroleum spill floating on the South Branch River in Keene has been contained, a dispatcher for Zecco Inc. of Northboro, Mass. said this morning.

Cleanup crews from Zecco Inc. and the Keene Fire Department worked Wednesday and Thursday to contain the spill in an effort to keep it from spreading to the Ashuelot River, Keene Fire Chief Robert N. Guyette said.

The petroleum is apparently leaking from the Speedway Petroleum Co at 501-507 Main St in Keene and seeping from the south bank of the river, according to state officials.

Richard Berry, an engineer for the N.H. Department of Environmental Services said it is difficult to figure just how much petroleum has leaked into the river or what kind of fuel it is.

A spokeswoman for the Speedway service station, who declined to be identified, said this morning that the station's home heating fuel tanks have been emptied voluntarily.

Berry said an investigation has started, but it is unclear whether the fuel is coming from one of Speedway's six underground tanks or from a leak in the lines running from the tanks to the gasoline pumps.

Berry said monitoring wells will be installed in the area to determine the source of the leak and the extent of the contamination.

Guyette said a resident who lives near Beaver Brook reported a slick on the water Wednesday. The fire department responded initially and began efforts to stem the flow of the fuel using its own absorbent pads. Outside cleanup crews arrived Thursday.

Only a small amount of slick is on top of the water," Guyette said this morning. That slick will be soaked up with more absorbent pads.

Water samples were taken Thursday from the river between the gas station and Route 12 Berry said. Results are expected to show what kind of fuel is leaking.

———————

Probe continues into source of oil slick in Keene brook

Five monitoring wells will be dug in the next couple of days in an effort to determine if petroleum found last week in Beaver Brook in Keene is coming from any of the Speedway Petroleum Co.'s nearby underground tank, Speedway Manager Richard D. Stinson said this morning.

Stinson said he doubts that Speedway fuel tanks installed six years ago are the source of the leak.

Stinson who returned from vacation Monday, said he suspects that the film comes from pollutants contained by snow, now that the snow is melting, the pollutants are flowing into the water.

Inventories show no great loss of fuel from the Speedway tanks, Stinson said, but "we'll know more by the end of the week."

Crews from the Keene Fire Department and the N.H. Department of Environmental Services used absorbent pads last Wednesday and Thursday to contain a thin film of fuel floating in the brook.

State official Richard Berry said the slick spotted by a neighbor, may have come from one of the eight tanks at Speedway's Main Street service center.

Tests started last week; results won't be known for two more weeks, Berry said.

The absorbent pads were still in the brook Monday, said Paul Crowell, deputy chief of the Keene Fire Department—They are usually left in place until the source of a slick is determined and the pollutant is removed from the water.

As Reported by the *Keene Evening Sentinel* April 18th, 1988:

"FIRE"

Keene State College fire labeled suspicious

A fire that ravaged a dormitory room at Keene State College early Sunday and sent one woman to the hospital was labeled as suspicious today by Keene police.

The fire started at about 4 a.m. in the closet of a third-floor room at Carle Hall where freshman Charles Minnich told authorities he had been sleeping. Minnich's roommate was away for the evening.

"The fire is suspicious because of the fast, intense heat," said Sgt. Robert Hardy of the Keene Police Department. "The room is virtually totally destroyed."

Dorm room destroyed, this was the scene in a third floor dormitory room at Keene State College's Carle Hall. A fire early Sunday morning destroyed the room, caused damage to the rest of the dormitory and sent one woman to the hospital to be treated for smoke inhalation. The fire has been called suspicious. Photo by Medora Hebert.

All the objects in Minnich's room, including a bunk bed and television set, were melted or burned. Minnich said he was alone when the blaze started. College officials are not sure whether his door was locked.

Hardy said his investigation should be wrapped up in a few days. The N.H. Fire Marshal's office is also looking into the blaze.

Police are also investigating the vandalism Saturday of Minnich's car, and said the two incidents could be related.

Minnich's car was parked in a nearby commuter lot, and vulgar phrases and a sorority's emblem were scrawled in black paint across the vehicle.

College spokesman Ronald Paradis said school officials are working with fire and police to determine the causes.

The fire led to the evacuation of 150 students from Carle Hall. Minnich told police he awoke and alerted others on his floor.

Firefighters entered a third-story lounge and found one woman who had lost consciousness after inhaling the heavy black smoke.

Stephanie Evans, 18, of Plymouth had been visiting a friend at Carle Hall. She passed out from smoke inhalation and was rushed to Cheshire Medical Center in Keene, according to hospital and college officials.

"I can't remember what happened," Evans said from her hospital bed today.

She was listed in good condition, but could barely speak because of a sore throat.

Firefighters also rescued four students standing on an 8-inch ledge outside a third-story student lounge.

Students who lived on Munich's floor have been transferred to other rooms until the debris is cleared.

Munnich is staying with his parents in the Concord area, and could not be reached for comment.

The fire did not spread to other rooms in the hall, though nearby rooms were damaged by water and smoke. KSC officials estimate the damage at close to $20,000.

Paradis said college officials are trying to reassure students that there is no need for concern around campus.

"Our first priority is for the students, and our concern is for the students," he said.

Keene State fire called arson; message from president tries to calm fears

A fire that gutted a Keene State College dormitory room and left one woman hospitalized Sunday was the work of an arsonist, Keene police and fire officials said this morning.

In an effort to calm fear and contain rumors, college President Judith A. Sturnick issued a written message today to students, staff and faculty, urging students to cooperate with the police investigation and promising to keep everyone informed.

Sturnick said she has no reason to believe other incidents will occur, and said information gathered suggests that a group or organization was not responsible for the fire.

Police and fire officials said they are unsure what started the fire, which broke out in a double room at Carle Hall where freshman Charles Minnich escaped unharmed.

The blaze started in the closet of Minnich's room, and it is not clear whether the door was locked.

An investigator for the N.H. Fire Marshal's Office is expected to look at the room Wednesday.

The fire ravaged Minnich's room, caused smoke damage to other rooms and sent Stephanie Evans of Plymouth to Cheshire Medical Center in Keene for treatment for smoke inhalation. She was listed in good condition today.

Firefighters pulled Evans from a nearby student lounge, where she passed out after breathing the heavy black smoke.

They also rescued four students from an 8-inch-wide ledge three stories up, and evacuated 150 students from the building.

Minnich is staying with his parents in the Concord area, and has been unavailable for comment.

Man indicted in KSC fire

A Keene State College student was indicted by a Cheshire County grand jury Thursday for allegedly setting a fire in his dormitory room in April that injured one woman.

Charles H. Minnich, 4th, 18, of Dunbarton was indicted on one count of arson. He is to be arraigned October 21 in Cheshire County Superior Court.

A Demon Called Fire

Minnich is accused of setting fire to his third-floor room in Carle Hall on April 18, causing 150 students to be evacuated and injuring a Plymouth woman, then 18.

Stephanie Hall, who was in a third-floor student lounge, suffered smoke inhalation and was hospitalized.

The blaze stranded four students on a ledge outside the lounge, and gutted the dormitory room. Other rooms in the building received smoke and water damage. Damage was estimated at $20,000.

Minnich, who was a freshman when the fire occurred, allegedly told police he was alone in the room asleep when the fire broke out in a closet. He returned to his parents' home in Dunbarton after the fire, and did not return to classes this fall.

An indictment is not an indication of guilt or innocence, but rather that there is enough evidence to warrant a trial.

The arson charge in this case is a class A felony, police said, because the fire was allegedly set in an occupied structure, and is punishable by up to seven to 15 years in prison.

As Reported by the *Keene Evening Sentinel* April 25th, 1988:

"STORY"

Keene firefighter, 47, dies in fall from tree

Philip Davis Sr.

A 22-year veteran of the Keene Fire Department was killed Saturday when he fell from a tree in Keene.

Lt. Philip Davis, Sr., 47, of 34 Dale Drive worked part-time as a tree-cutter. He was trying to cut down a tree on Felt Road in Keene when the accident happened, police said.

Philip L. Davis, Sr.

Mr. Davis, 47, of 34 Dale Drive, Keene, died Saturday morning.

He was born in Keene August 23rd, 1940, son of George and Doris (Payne) Davis, and was a lifelong resident of Keene.

Mr. Davis worked for the Keene Fire Department for 22 years, and held the rank of lieutenant. He was also employed by Paragon Cable Co. for 20 years and also worked for Chase Tree Service.

He was a deputy warden with the N.H. Forest Fire Association and was a former member of the Keene Fire Department muster team.

Mr. Davis played softball in the city league with Mason Insurance Co. and in the senior league with the Old Timers.

Survivors include two sons, Philip L. Davis, Jr. and Michael F. Davis, both of Keene, two daughters, Brenda M. Rokes and Pamela J. Galford, both of Keene: his parents of Roxbury, four brothers, Charles Davis and Robert Davis, both of Winchester and Paul Davis and Richard Davis, both of Keene: two sisters, Jacqueline Reed of Keene and Carol Buffum of Roxbury, three grandchildren, his finance JoAnn M. Fairbanks of Keene and several nieces and nephews.

A mass of Christian burial will be celebrated Tuesday at 11 a.m. at St. Bernard's Church, 185 Main St. Keene. Burial will follow in St. Joseph Cemetery.

Friends may call today from 2 to 4 and 7 to 9 p.m. at Foley Funeral Home, 49 Court St., Keene.

In lieu of flowers, contributions may b e made in Mr. Davis' memory to Keene Firemen's Relief Association in care of Chief Robert Guyette, 32 Vernon St., Keene 03431.

———————

As Reported by the *Keene Evening Sentinel* May 23rd, 1988:

"STORY"

Keene budget cut; police, fire hit hardest

Keene's police and fire protection services took it on the chin Saturday.

The Keene City Council's Finance Committee recommended deleting money for new police cruisers, weapons and safety unit forms from the budget for the fiscal year that begins July 1.

The cuts would pare $136,082 from the fiscal 1988 budget that City Manager J. Patrick MacQueen proposed for the Keene city government.

Overall, the committee lowered the amount of property taxes needed to fund the budget by $206,983. down $162,070 from MacQueen's figure of $12.5 million.

The council will hold a public hearing on the budget June 14 at 7 p.m., then make final decisions June 21.

Ne boost on the budget's revenue side is $44,913 from increased fees at the Keene Recreation Center and from funds set aside to automate the city tax office. The system hasn't been set up, and the finance committee voted to use the money to lower property taxes.

Amid protests from a few councilors, the finance committee agreed with MacQueen's request to eliminate the resident tax as a revenue source. That means the $120,000 produced annually by the resident tax must be raised from property taxes.

The resident tax $10 a year on residents ages 18 to 65 requires a lot of paper work and city workers consider it an inefficient way to collect taxes. By shifting the assessment to the property tax base, businesses which don't pay the resident tax—would cover about 45 percent of the $120,000 total, resulting in lower taxes for individuals, city officials say.

The five committee members didn't debate much as they cut away at the budgets for the police and fire departments.

Taking the hardest hits were police services, with the committee denying requests for $15,000 for two cruisers, (maintenance and other expenses included), and $22,610 for a crossing guard at Keene High School.

The committee said it supports Police Chief Thomas F. Powers efforts to modernize the department, but some improvements could be delayed for a year or more.

Powers said the committee's actions pose problems, because several guns are outdated and the department doesn't have enough vehicles for its staff.

The committee voted to buy $6,000 worth of video equipment to modernize the way mug shots are taken and reluctant witnesses are interviewed.

Councilor Dean J. Eaton said video filming movements and recording voices is more effective in identifying suspects than mug shots are.

Left intact was a $66,892 request to set up a dispatch system operated by civilians—uniformed officers now field telephone calls and complaints—and $2,500 to buy a police dog, most likely a German shepherd.

Lost in the cutbacks was a request by Southwestern N.H. Fire Mutual Aid for $11,500 worth of repairs and renovations for an office it occupies at the Keene Fire Department. The structural work would spiff up the small office and enable the region-wide dispatch service to install a $100,000 communications console.

City Councilor Kendall W. Lane led the charge against the improvements saying the city should not foot the bill for Mutual Aid because the agency serves other communities in the Monadnock Region as well as parts of Vermont and Massachusetts.

MacQueen pointed out the improvements would amount to renovations that any landlord would do to a building, and said Mutual Aid provides services for free to the city, including handling calls for the fire department.

Keene Fire Chief Robert N. Guyette has estimated that, if Mutual Aid moved out of the fire department the city would have to spend at least $56,000 a year to replace its services. Debate is expected to continue when the city council reviews the budget.

The committee also reduced by roughly $40,000 funds to buy specialized uniforms to handle hazardous materials and for fire-safety training.

In other action, the committee:

Cut $4,000 from funds needed to pay for water. The money was to handle heating and fuel costs of a new water corrosion control building, which has not been built yet.

Increased MacQueen's salary to $56,500 from $52,000 and City Clerk Patricia A. Little's to $32,000 from $26,500.

————

As Reported by the *Keene Evening Sentinel* June 1st, 1988:

"FIRE"

Keene pedestrian suffers minor injuries

An 87-year-old Keene woman escaped serious injury Tuesday when she was brushed by a moving car on Main Street in Keene.

Edith F. Kelland of 127 Castle St. was treated at Cheshire Medical Center in Keene for bruises on her arms and legs, then released.

Keene police said Kelland was trying to cross Main Street, near Church Street, at 3:35 p.m. when she bumped into the side of a 1987 Buick driven by Ladonna Van Brocklin of Marcy Hill Road in Swanzey.

Van Brocklin, 44, was in the passing lane, heading north, when the accident occurred.

A brown pickup truck had stopped in the travel lane to let Kelland use a crosswalk; the truck blocked Van Brocklin's vision, police said.

Van Brocklin was cited for failing to stop for a pedestrian, police said.

————

As Reported by the *Keene Evening Sentinel* June 4th, 1988:

"STORY"

Bear magic is helping police and children

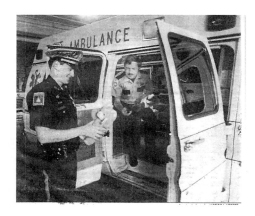

Furry Magic. Keene police officer Darryl Madden, left and Robert Crowell of the Keene Fire Department size up two Bear Buddies donated for distribution to children in distress. Photo by: Medora Hebert.

It's a little known fact that the amount of magic a teddy bear possesses is directly related to the amount of comforting a small child needs.

If the magic is needed just to help a youngster sleep at night, then only certain bears with limited magical skills are assigned to the task.

But when abused or traumatized children are in need of solace, special bears must be put on the job.

Fortunately, a number of very special bears have made their way to Keene and, for sexually or physically abused children, the magic of these new arrivals is omnipotent.

Suzanne Seaver of North Swanzey managed to coax the bears to the area, and she got them to go to the Keene Police Department.

Seaver, a self-proclaimed teddy bear lover who owned 200 of the cuddly stuffed animals before giving most of them away to needy children, suggested that Keene police use teddy bears to calm youngsters who have been victimized by adults or frightened or injured in an accident.

Keene Police Sgt. Hal G. Brown, who investigates reports of physical or sexual child abuse, said Seaver's proposal was just what he was looking for.

Although the program has just begun, Brown is already seeing happy faces on children who may not have smiled for a long time.

When a hurting child is given the new friend, the reaction in immediate, Brown said.

"It's a remarkable aid in getting a traumatized child to calm down," Brown said. "We've seen some sad little faces turn to smiling faces."

Brown has given out four bears in the first few weeks of the program, which officially kicks off next week. Keene police cruisers, along with ambulances from the Keene Fire Department, will each be equipped with two of the furry creatures, to help children who may be victims of accidents or crimes, or simply lost.

It's part of what a well-rounded police department should be, Brown said.

"We carry shotguns in our police cruisers," he said. "I think we also need some teddy bears in the trunk for the hurting kids we serve.

Brown said a bear comforts a child and lets him or her know that police and emergency personnel are friends who only want to help.

The child is asked to help name the bear, and once the bond is made, "I've found the child never puts the bear down," Brown said.

Seaver, who heard about a similar program in Colorado, coordinates the program and, with her penchant for stuffed bears, has convinced a number of local businesses to donate the fuzzy critters.

On Friday, Douglas Co. Inc. of Keene gave about 50 bears to the Keene Bear Buddies Program, which may be the only one of its kind in New Hampshire.

Aside from calming a child, the b ear can act as an investigative tool, Brown said.

"A creative approach to encouraging a child to communicate involves giving him or her a bear," he said, "restoring to the child even a small measure of security and trust is an end to itself.

"Moreover, as the child communicates more freely with us, we are also able to pursue a higher goal—learning the details necessary to protect the child and prosecute the abuser," he said.

While most of the bears will go to children under 15, a few will be reserved for mentally handicapped adults and teenage sexual assault victims, Brown said.

Bear magic knows no age limit.

———

As Reported by the *Keene Evening Sentinel* July 18th, 1988:

"STORY"

Keene's 1st firefighter, Lyman O. Cass, 94 dies

Lyman O. Cass.

Lyman O. Cass, 94, of Richmond died Sunday at McKerley Health Care Center in Keene.

He was born in Richmond December 17, 1893, son of Luther E. and Hattie M (Kempton) Cass, and was a lifelong resident of Richmond.

Mr. Cass served with the U.S. Army Signal Corps during World War I and was a member of the American Legion.

He became Keene's first fulltime firefighter when he was hired by the city May 13, 1919. He served the Keene Fire Department for 40 years, retiring as captain on January 1, 1959. After his retirement, he served as a lookout at Pitcher Mountain Fire Tower in Stoddard for 15 years, retiring at the age of 80.

Survivors include two sons, Lyman H. Cass of San Antonio, Texas, and Lawrence E. Cass of Phoenix, Arizona, two daughters Beverly J. Spearman of Fort Lauderdale, Florida, and Madalyn B. Carpenter of Hinsdale; 15 grandchildren, several great-grand children, several great-great grandchildren, and longtime friend Grace Whitney of McKerley Health Care Center.

The funeral arrangements are incomplete and will be announced Tuesday by Foley Funeral Home of Keene.

———

As Reported by the *Keene Evening Sentinel* July 27th, 1988:

"FIRE"

Keene kitchen fire doused

A minor kitchen fire in a Keene apartment was extinguished by firefighters soon after it began, at 8:30 Tuesday night.

Two trucks from the Keene Fire Department were on the scene at 37 Woodburn St. as firefighters doused a blaze that started when grease spilled on the stove, a fire official said.

The kitchen received minor fire damage and the apartment suffered some smoke damage, but no injuries were reported.

———

As Reported by the *Keene Evening Sentinel* August 12th, 1988:

"FIRE"

Man charged in KSC fire turns himself in to police

A former Keene State College student surrendered to police today after a warrant was issued for his arrest in connection with an April 17 dormitory fire that injured one student and caused more than $20,000 damage.

Charles Minnich, 4th, 18, of Dunbarton was to be released on personal recognizance bail later today, awaiting a hearing September 15 in Keene District Court, Detective Sgt. Robert Hardy said. However, a Cheshire County Superior Court grand jury will consider an indictment on an arson charge September 8, Hardy said.

More than 150 students were evacuated from the four-story dormitory after thick smoke filled a section of the third floor, and firefighters had to rescue four students stranded on a concrete ledge. Minnich's room was in flames.

One woman was treated at Cheshire Medical Center in Keene for smoke inhalation.

As Reported by the *Keene Evening Sentinel* August 22nd, 1988:

"FIRE"

Two fires doused Sunday in Keene

Keene firefighters extinguished two minor fires Sunday.

A brush fire burned an area 30 feet in diameter near baseball fields at Wheelock Park. Lt. Steven Goldsmith of the Keene Fire Department said the fire was probably started by a discarded cigarette. The fire was reported Sunday at 12:20 p.m. It was extinguished in about 30 minutes.

A second fire occurred at 8:36 p.m. at 32 Court St. when a plastic bowl was left atop a hot electric stove in the apartment of Denise Kershner. Some smoke damage resulted, but no one was hurt, said Acting Deputy George H. Shepard. The building is owned by Robert J. Lupien of 32 Monadnock St.

As Reported by the *Keene Evening Sentinel* September 15th, 1988:

"FIRE"

Storage barn burns at former farm; Keene fire chief won't rule out arson

Firefighters battle blaze Thursday evening at the former Knight Farm. Photo by Michael Moore.

A suspicious fire that destroyed a storage barn Thursday evening at the former Knight Farm on West Surry Road is being investigated by the Keene Fire Department.

Authorities don't know yet where the fire began or what caused it, Keene Fire Chief Robert N. Guyette said today. However, the fire appears to be suspicious, he said, and he is not ruling out arson. The barn was vacant and had no electrical wiring in it, he said.

Bretwood Golf Course of East Surry Road owned the barn.

About 50 firefighters from the Keene and Surry departments fought the fire, which was reported at 6:52 p.m. and was declared under control about a half-hour later. No firefighters were injured.

The 30-by-30-foot wooden barn was engulfed in flames when firefighters arrived, Guyette said. The building was in an out-of-the-way place where the fire could not be seen until the structure was completely ablaze, he said.

————

As Reported by the *Keene Evening Sentinel* October 4th, 1988:

"FIRE"

Keene house fire probed

A fire that damaged a vacant home on Winchester Street in Keene Monday night is being investigated by Keene fire officials.

Deputy Fire Chief George Shephard said the cause of the fire is unknown, and he is not sure whether it's suspicious.

No one was inside the two-story wood house at 291 Winchester St. when the fire was reported at 7:05 p.m., and no injuries were reported. According to city records, the property is owned by Lawrence R. Saunders of 188 Gilsum St., Keene.

Heavy smoke was pouring from the structure when firefighters arrived, and they were able to bring the blaze under control in 30 minutes, Shephard said.

The blaze damaged a major portion of the kitchen ceiling and flooring above it. There was also smoke and water damage in adjoining buildings, Shephard said.

————

No arson in Keene fire

Arson has been ruled out as the cause of a fire Monday at a Keene home.

An investigation by the Keene Police and Fire departments concluded that the blaze at 291 Winchester St. was caused by a transformer that overheated, Deputy Fire Chief George Shepard said Tuesday.

Shepard said the transformer was connected to a fluorescent light that had been left on for several days.

The fire damaged the kitchen ceiling and the floor above it. There was also smoke and water damage in adjoining rooms. No one was inside the two-story wooden house when the fire was reported.

————

As Reported by the *Keene Evening Sentinel* November 11th, 1988:

"STORY"

False alarms could cost Keene State $20,000

Keene State College should pay up for about 200 false fire alarms that firefighters have answered there since 1984, a Keene City Council committee decided Thursday.

If the 15-member council concurs next week, the college could get a bill for $20,000.

Under city policy, Keene State is supposed to be billed $100 every time fire crews respond unnecessarily to the campus—roughly 50 times a year. But city officials realized two weeks ago that Keene State inexplicably hadn't received a bill since 1984.

The bills for false alarms apparently stopped going out after a deputy chief left the fire department, City Manager J. Patrick MacQueen told the council's finance committee Thursday.

Normally, if the false alarm is in a residence hall, Keene State passes on the fees to the dormitory's residents, MacQueen said. But it will be impossible for the college to collect from dorm residents in previous years, MacQueen said; and he wondered if the college will be willing to pay back bills.

Fire Chief Robert N. Guyette had the same question.

"The college doesn't pay the bills—the building and students who are in the buildings are assessed for it," he said after the meeting, and students from those previous years have moved out.

College officials were not available for comment today, because of the Veteran's Day holiday.

Some committee members expressed frustration at the lapse in billing, and noted that the college pays no property tax.

Councilor Mary F. Penny called for raising the per-false-alarm charge to $250 for both fire calls and adding unnecessary police calls to the policy. Councilor Dean J. Eaton said he would support a false-alarm fee of between $500 and $1,000.

"It's a life-threatening situation every time they go out," Eaton said of firefighters racing to an emergency.

MacQueen said he wants to meet with college officials on financial and other matters, but no date has been set yet.

The committee recommended unanimously that the city try to recoup all the false-alarm money the college owes, and to ask Guyette and Police Chief Thomas F. Powers how high the per-false-alarm charge should be.

In other business Thursday, the committee:

Recommended unanimously that a full-time worker be hired to maintain Keene's downtown, dressed up with a $2.5 million renovation project completed during the summer, MacQueen said.

Recommended unanimously that the Keene Public Library be allowed to spend $4,000 to have Roche and Co., a Manchester fundraising consultant, study the feasibility of raising $50,000 to match the library's current $50,000-a-year book-buying fund.

———

KSC to be billed $20,000 by city for false fire alarms

Keene State College will be charged $20,000 by the city for false fire alarms over the past four years.

The Keene City Council voted unanimously Thursday night to collect on bills for phony fire calls at the college that were never sent out by the Keene Fire Department.

The college should have been billed $100 each time city firefighters responded unnecessarily to the campus—an event that occurs about 50 times a year, according to Fire Chief Robert N. Guyette.

Billings for false alarms stopped after a deputy chief left the department in 1984. Guyette said last week, he has declined to name the person responsible for accounts receivable since that time.

Councilors learned from City Manager J. Patrick MacQueen that police and fire officials have calculated the cost of false alarms today at between $175 and $200. MacQueen said he will recommend soon that the per-visit charge be raised.

KSC not promising to pay bill for false alarms

For now, Keene State College is making no promises on how much it will pay the Keene Fire Department on an estimated $20,000 bill for four years' worth of false fire alarms.

The Keene City Council ordered City Manager J. Patrick MacQueen last week to bill KSC for false alarms on which the city had forgotten to collect since 1984.

Typically, the fire department responds to 50 or more unwarranted emergency calls per year at Keene State; the city charges $100 when it has to respond to a false alarm.

When college officials receive the fire department's invoice, they will compare it with their own records said KSC spokesman Ronald S. Paradis.

"I'm not prepared to say we're not paying it, because we don't know that." Paradis said Tuesday. "We will work on it with the city though."

In the past, before the city's billing system faltered with the departure of a deputy fire chief, college administrators would try to determine who had activated the alarm and present him or her with the bill. If the search succeeded only in identifying which building the alarm came from. All students residing there shared the cost, Paradis said.

However, alarms dating back to 1984 could be the fault of students who have since graduated, and over whom the college has no leverage.

"If we know who did it, then that's who pays the false alarm fee, Paradis said. "If we don't know who does it, then we look at the number of people in the residence hall. We certainly are going to look at it and apply what we did in the past.

———

As Reported by the *Keene Evening Sentinel* November 29th, 1988:

"FIRE"

Keene wants gutted depot razed in 30 days

Official says city will sue if owner is late. Photo by Michael Moore.

More than two months after it was promised that a burned-out warehouse off Cypress Street in Keene would be torn down, it still partially stands.

And officials say the city government's 6-month-old promise to sue if the site isn't cleaned up soon also stands.

A fire in March destroyed a section of the abandoned railroad freight depot behind the public parking lot off Cypress Street. It was the latest in a series of blazes in different parts of the building which was last used about five years ago and has since become a hangout for city youths.

Authorities called the structure dangerous and an eyesore.

By June, the city was getting irked at the lack of response from Guilford Transportation Industries of Billerica, Mass., the buildings owner to letters requesting action. Assistant City Manager Alfred H. Merrifield, who also works as Keene's code enforcement officer, said the city would sue the company to get something done.

But in September, Keene officials thought they finally had an agreement.

On a visit to the city, Leonard Lucas, a Guilford real estate executive, promised to level the offending half of the building, fence in the remaining half and position no trespassing signs in the area.

Lucas, who had come to town to hammer out details on the city's purchase of several pieces of former railroad land, explained that the company had recently moved and thus did not receive Keene's correspondence earlier in the year.

He said he'd get right on it, Merrifield said. "So far, since that meeting, not much has happened."

Nothing, in fact, has happened and Keene had received no word from Guilford on the continued delay.

So by the beginning of next week, Merrifield said he will send Guilford a letter setting a 30-day deadline for action, after which court action will be started.

"We hope to get it taken care of on a voluntary basis," Merrifield said.

Reached by The Sentinel in Merrimack late this morning, Lucas said Guilford has held off doing anything about the warehouse because the firm hopes to close soon on the sale of the railroad property to the city, thereby making the burned-out building the city's responsibility.

————

As Reported by the *Keene Evening Sentinel* December 13th, 1988:

"FIRE"

Fire at Keene home causes smoke and water damage

Fire caused extensive damage in the kitchen of a home at 71 Woodland Ave. Tuesday night.

No injuries were reported.

Firefighters were called to the home at 9:52 p.m. and brought the fire under control within an hour, Deputy Chief Paul E. Crowell said.

Despite freezing temperatures Crowell said, the Keene department had no problem extinguishing the flames at the home of Gilbert Wyman, Crowell Said.

He said that the Wyman's were advised to leave the house after the fire because of the smoke and water damage.

Cabinets and kitchen appliances were damaged by the flames, but no dollar estimate of the damage were determined today, Crowell said.

The blaze is under investigation.

————

As Reported by the *Keene Evening Sentinel* December 27th, 1988:

"FIRE"

2 homeless in Keene after tree sparks fire

Two Keene residents were left homeless when their Christmas tree caught fire early this morning, destroying moist of their two-story apartment.

The blaze at the home of Nancy Buffum and Matthew Snow was one of two apartment fires reported in the Monadnock Region during the holiday weekend.

No one was injured in the fires, police said.

Snow and Buffum lived in apartment 107 of Cheshire Homes, off Pearl Street in Keene.

Snow called for help at 12:07 a.m. telling authorities the Christmas tree was on fire, said Deputy Chief George H. Shepard of the Keene Fire Department.

The cause of the tree fire is under investigation, fire officials said.

By the time the first two fire trucks had arrived, the second floor living room was ablaze, so more help was requested. In all, five trucks and 25 firefighters helped to quell the flames, Shepard said.

Although the blaze was quickly brought under control, it took firefighters two more hours to make sure the fire was out, he said.

The second floor of the apartment was gutted, and there was smoke and water damage in the first-floor bedrooms.

The couple spent the rest of the night at the Keene Ramada Inn.

Buffum, who works at Winding Brook Lodge in Keene, said the couple might be able to stay at that motel until they find another place to live.

A next-door apartment, rented by Stanley Lacoille, also received some smoke and water damage, but is still habitable, Shepard said.

In Keene, a fire that started Saturday morning, after ashes from a wood stove had been placed in a wooden box and left in a shed was put out before it had a chance to spread, firefighters reported.

Two engines were sent to 59 Sullivan St. and the fire, reported at 6:42 a.m., was out by 6:52 a.m., Capt. David B. Osgood said Monday. There was no damage to the shed. Authorities this morning did not have the name of the residents.

Osgood said the moral is: "Never put your ashes in wooden boxes, cardboard boxes or paper bags. Put them in the ash can."

Fire victims housed

A Keene family left homeless when a fire destroyed their apartment the night after Christmas are pulling themselves back together.

Nancy Buffum, her boyfriend, and her two children were forced out of their apartment at Cheshire Homes on Pearl Street when a short-circuit in some Christmas tree lights caused the ornamental light bulbs to explode and the tree to burst into flames early Tuesday morning.

But the family was not out in the cold for long.

Buffum, her boyfriend, Roy Ayotte, her 15-year-old daughter, Gretchen Snow and her 13-year-old son, Mathew Snow, spend the rest of Tuesday night at the Ramada Inn. They were told Tuesday that another apartment will be available in a week at Cheshire Homes, a subsidized housing project.

Shaine Kinson, a friend of Gretchen Snow, was also visiting when the fire broke out.

Until the new apartment is ready, the children are staying with their father in Dublin, and Buffum and Ayotte staying at Winding Brook Lodge, where Buffum works.

Buffum said she was able to recover most of the family's clothes, since the fire damage wasn't at bad downstairs, where the bedrooms are located. She also has home insurance, which will make it a lot easier to replace the personal items, furniture and utensils lost during the fire.

Gretchen Snow said the family presents were spared, since they'd already been removed from underneath the tree and placed in a downstairs bedroom.

Officials said today the fire was caused by faulty wiring in the family's Christmas tree lights.

"We looked it over yesterday and questioned everybody," said Deputy Chief George H. Shepard of the Keene Fire Department. "The Christmas tree caught fire from a short in the Christmas lights."

"It's really devastating," said Buffum. "You've just got to deal with it. I've got a lot of people being really concerned."

————

1989

As Reported by the *Keene Evening Sentinel* January 14th, 1989:

"FIRE"

Cause of deadly fire undetermined Officials don't know if cigarette was cause

The burned-out shell of 88 High Street gives grim reminder of what fire can do. Firefighter Ed LaBounty Jr. (left) and his father Ed LaBounty Sr. (right) assist at the scene of Saturday's fatal fire.

[*Compiler's Note*: January 14th, 1989 was a turning point for the Keene Fire Department and the City of Keene due to a tragedy that occurred on that day. The following is the account of the tragedy as written by the *Keene Evening Sentinel*. As the Captain on duty the morning of the fire, I have asked myself many times, "If only we had received the call earlier," or, "If I had found the family sooner," or, "If the building wasn't so cut up," or, "If we had the manpower to search and fight the fire at the same time..." The tragedy, as you can guess, was the needless deaths of a family of four. Also, let us not forget the firefighters, who in desperate vein tried to search with limited manpower and equipment. I would like to believe that we all did our best to try and save this family. Unfortunately for the family, but fortunate for the future of the fire department, we all learned from this tragedy. This was a turning point to the way we did business as a fire department operationally, and for those who had to live with the outcome of that tragic day. — Stevens Goldsmith. Captain of the Keene Fire Department]

Investigators were still trying this morning to determine the cause of a house fire that killed four people and left 15 homeless early Saturday morning in Keene.

Reports that it was caused by a cigarette are strictly speculative, N.H. State Fire Marshal William Toland said this morning.

"I was speculating at what might have happened," Toland said of a conversation he had with a reporter. "I was really surprised to hear it on the radio."

Toland said investigator Thomas M. Norton was to interview former tenants of 88 High St. this morning, in preparation for an announcement later in the day by Keene's police and fire departments.

Meanwhile, several people who lived in the nine-apartment dwelling are convinced that a breakdown in communications among tenants, police officers and firefighters may have cost four lives.

It's also possible that officials were notified too late to save any lives, officials said.'

Those who died in the Saturday morning blaze were Carl R, Hina, 49, his wife, Lori M. Hina, 26, his daughter by a previous marriage, Sara J. Hina, 12, and Lillian M. Hina, born Sept 19, 1988.

Tenants believe the fire; which started in the apartment of Sandra Walker, 41, was caused by a lighted cigarette that ignited a sofa or mattress.

Walker's apartment, at the rear of the building, was at the opposite end from the Hinas', which was in front. Both apartments were on the second floor.

Bruce Kennedy, 326, who lived in the apartment next to the Hinas' said he was playing cribbage when he heard a scream.

"It was Sandy Walker," Kennedy said, "I heard her yell, Fire! I'm not kidding! Help me!"

"I called the operator and said where the fire was. She said she would connect me with Southwestern N.H. Fire Mutual Aid, but I said there wasn't enough time because there was smoke everywhere, I had to hang up. I got out by the fire escape."

Southwestern N.H. Fire Mutual Aid, the regional dispatch center located just a few blocks away on Vernon Street, was notified of the fire at 2:25 a.m. by a telephone operator.

"I really thing the fire department was slow responding," Kennedy said. "It seemed like it took a long time from when I made the call."

According to Mutual Aid records, the first firefighters were on the scene four minutes later, at 2:29 a.m.

Between the time when Walker yelled for help and the time when firefighters arrived, Sean P. McCormick, 23, and his wife, Victoria 19, who lived in one of the first-floor apartments, were awakened by another tenant.

"We were sleeping when Betty LaCourse from up-stairs kicked the door in and told my daughter and my wife to get out, the building was on fire," McCormick said Saturday.

Donnie Abrams, a friend of tenant Edward L. Bussieres, 42, was on the roof of the porch and someone was screaming. He was trying to reach through the window to help, but he really couldn't get a reach."

The porch roof is about 6 feet from the front window of the Hina apartment. A broken window and a scorched curtain stood today as silent reminders of the fire and possible escape attempt.

McCormick said several tenants and a police officer tried several times to enter the burning building, but heat and smoke prevented them from reaching the Hinas' apartment.

McCormick said police were told, but did not seem to understand, that people were still in the building.

The police asked, "How do you know?" We said they smashed the window out. They were yelling and screaming.

"It was no one's fault," McCormick said. "There was so much confusion with nine apartments and 20 people yelling and screaming."

The person who got closest to the Hinas apparently was LaCourse, who was leading Sara down the stairs when she pulled away, perhaps to get the rest of her family.

"Betty didn't realize the girl wasn't behind her." McCormick said.

The first crew of firefighters on the scene made a search immediately and found no bodies, according to Deputy Chief George H. Shepard Jr.

Because the building was divided into so many rooms, it was easy in the heat and smoke to miss the room where the bodies were, Shepard said.

"There was zero visibility," he said. "It was like being in a pitch black closet. It's pretty easy with a cut-up building like that to miss a room."

Further attempts to enter the building were abandoned until conditions improved and a second crew of firefighters arrived on the scene, Shepard said.

No one was believed to be inside, Shepard said.

"The reports were everyone was out of the building," Shepard said.

"The police believed everyone was out of the building.

Shepard said no one in the crowd that gathered outside the burning building told him there still were people inside.

The bodies were found about 30 minutes later, after the fire was brought under control. Firefighters used a ladder truck to get into a rear window, Shepard said.

Three bodies were found in the rear bedroom, and a fourth was found in the kitchen, Shepard said.

The bodies were fully clothed indicating the Hinas may have thought they had time to get dressed, Shepard said.

Shepard speculated that, when the Hinas opened the door to the hallway, the heat and smoke rushed in, forcing them to retreat.

Cuts on Carl Hina's hands indicate he may have injured himself breaking the front window in an attempt to escape, Shepard said.

Shepard said he was not sure it would have made any difference if he'd known the Hinas were inside.

"Even with very heavy smoke conditions and high heat we'll attempt to search. We would have done our best," he said.

Four firefighters and two police officers suffered minor injuries.

Firefighter Henry Memmesheimer was taken to Cheshire Medical Center in Keene, where he was treated for smoke inhalation and released Sunday.

Lt. Paul Scoz of the Keene Fire Department was treated at the Keene hospital for a sprained neck, then released, firefighter Wayne A. Spofford was treated for smoke inhalation and released.

No police officers were taken to the hospital.

The building is owned by Thomas Yocono Jr. of Stoddard.

———

As Reported by the *Keene Evening Sentinel*:

Tenants homeless after Keene fire

Motorists slowed down to stare at the burned-out building at the corner of High and Carroll streets in Keene Sunday as Edward L. Bussieres of Apartment 1 prepared to remove his television and other valuables.

His videocassette recorder has been stolen Saturday night, and he wasn't about to take any more chances.

Bussieres, 42, who lived at 88 High St. for 17 years, was forced to leave after a Saturday morning fire killed four tenants and left the rest, including himself, homeless.

Bussieres said he knew the Hinas—the four people who died in their second-floor apartment—only in passing. But he fought back tears as he recalled how 12-year-old Sara J. Hina, a student at Keene Junior High School nearly escaped the fire.

She went back into the apartment to find the rest of her family, then perished.

Also killed were Sara's father, Carl R. Hina, 49, his wife, Lori M. Hina, 26; and their daughter, Lillian M. Hina, born September 19, 1988.

Bussieres said he was known as the "social director" of 88 High St.

It was obvious, even in the semidarkness of a building without electricity, that Bussieres had done some handiwork over the years—such as laying tile and installing wood paneling—to make his modest two-bedroom apartment into a cozy hideaway.

Bussieres, who works for Brickstone Masons of Keene, wasn't optimistic about finding another two-bedroom apartment for $100 a week.

Meanwhile, he's staying with friends, as are most of the former tenants.

Two former tenants, Bruce Kennedy and Wanda Fort, are staying at the Valley Green Motel on West Street, thanks to the Fraternal Order of Eagles.

The Greater Monadnock Chapter of the American Red Cross is also ready to provide food, clothing and essential furniture to the fire victims, Director Elizabeth A. Schesser said Sunday.

The neighbors also have been helpful.

Thanks to Aurea Parker of 104 High St, Victoria McCormick, 19, has diapers, pajamas, a bottle and a blanket for her year-old baby, Erinlee.

McCormick and her husband, Sean P. McCormick, were loading their car Saturday afternoon for a temporary move to Munsonville, where they'll stay with Mr. McCormick's parents.

Aurea Parker's mother, Claudia Parker of 32 Colorado St. in Keene, said Carl and Lori Hina got married on Christmas Eve.

─────────

As Reported by the *Keene Evening Sentinel*:

Funeral for family who died in Keene blaze

Carl R. Hina, 49, Lori M. Hina, 26, Sarah J. Hina, 12, and Lillian M. Hina, 4 months old, all of 88 High St., Keene, died early Saturday morning in an apartment fire.

Carl Hina was born in Lowville, N.Y., July 13, 1939, son of Earl and Lillian (Dickinson) Hina, and lived in Keene most of his life.

During the past 15 years, he worked for Ideal Taxi in Keene, at B&B Auto Parts, and McLaughlin Moving and Storage Swanzey.

Lori Hina was born in Hartford, Conn., March 2, 1962, daughter of Robert R. and Marcellene A. (Alger) Fuller. She graduated from Keene High School in 1981, and lived in Harrisville before moving to Keene in 1985.

Sarah was born in Keene January 26, 1976, daughter of Carl R. and Nancy (Hebert) Hina, and lived in Keene all her life. She was a 7th grader at Keene Junior High School, an office worker at the school, and associated with Big Brothers/Big Sisters of the Monadnock Region.

Lillian was born in Keene, September 19, 1988.

─────────

As Reported by the *Keene Evening Sentinel*:

Fire officials blame deaths on delay, no evacuation plan

A 15-minute delay in contacting the fire department may have cost four lives in a fire that destroyed part of a tenement building at 88 High St. early Saturday morning, according to a joint announcement Monday by the Keene fire and police departments and state fire marshal.

Other factors were lack of an evacuation plan, and doors left open in two of the nine apartments, allowing smoke to spread rapidly through the building.

The cause of the blaze was a lighted cigarette that had ignited a couch in a unit at the rear of the building.

The tenant, Sandra Walker, 41, escaped unharmed. She and 14 others were left homeless by the blaze.

Dead in the fire were Carl R. Hina, 49, Lori M. Hina, 26, Sara J. Hina, 12 and Lillian Marie Hina, just under four months. The cause of death of each family member was asphyxiation from smoke inhalation, according to Charles E. Schofield, Cheshire County medical examiner.

The Hinas lived in a front apartment on the second floor, at the opposite end of the building from Walker.

Since they were found fully clothed, authorities said they may have stopped to dress before trying to escape, which could have cost them their lives.

The fire was reported at 2:25 a.m.

The city's inspection department is trying to determine today if any building codes had been violated in the dilapidated, wood-frame building, owned by Thomas Yocono Jr. of Stoddard.

Inspectors are checking to see if devices that inhibit the spread of fire, such as springs that cause doors to close automatically, were installed in accordance with building codes, Fire Chief Robert N. Guyette said today.

Officials say they believe there were no sprinklers in the building. No other information was available today to indicate whether there were extinguishers or sprinklers in the building.

An employee at City Manager J. Patrick MacQueen's office said all questions concerning the fire should be referred to Guyette.

Guyette said he believes the fire had been burning for 15 minutes when the fire department made its first search of the two-story apartment house at the corner of High and Carroll streets.

Dispatchers at Southwestern N.H. Fire Mutual Aid on Vernon Street said the first call came at 2:25 a.m. from a telephone operator and that fire trucks arrived on the scene—just four blocks away at 2:29 A.M.

By that time the building was filled with smoke, and it was not surprising that the three firefighters who searched the nine apartment dwelling did not find the Hinas, who were trapped in a small bedroom on the Carroll Street side of the house, Guyette said.

According to Guyette, firefighters searched through what they though was the only bedroom in the Hinas' apartment, He said they checked the beds, floor and crib.

I can understand why in the preliminary search they missed them completely," Guyette said. :"They weren't in the room that was searched, and we didn't know there was another room until after we could see."

Visibility was zero, Guyette said. "You don't see a thing," he said. In nine0-tenths of preliminaries, it's as if you were locked in a closet. The only thing you use is your hands."

Bruce Kennedy, the tenant who first tried to notify authorities, said the delay may have been caused by his inability during the panic to call the fire department.

He did reach the operator, who offered to connect him with Mutual Aid. He gave her the address, then said he had to get out.

Tenant Edward L. Bussieres also called the operator.

No one knows for sure just how long it took the operator to contact Mutual Aid.

Another reason for the delay was that the fire started while Walker was sleeping, and by the time she woke up, flames were shooting out of her apartment windows.

Kennedy said he and other tenants, who were awake playing cribbage and darts, first realized the building was on fire when Walker ran out of her apartment screaming "Fire!" The buildings smoke alarms went off at the same time, Kennedy said.

Several tenants and neighbors who witnessed the fire have told reporters that police and firefighters ignored their pleas that people were trapped inside the burning building.

Tenants and police, who arrived earlier than the firefighters, tried several times to search the building but were repelled by heat and smoke.

Elizabeth LaCourse, a tenant, has said she attempted to lead Sara Hina out of the building, but that the girl pulled away from

A Demon Called Fire

her somewhere in the hallway, perhaps hoping to bring the rest of her family out.

Deputy Fire Chief George H. Shepard Jr., who was with the first of two crews to arrive on the scene, has said no one told firefighters or police anyone was left in the building.

According to Guyette, the same witnesses who claimed they had tried to tell rescue workers that tenants were trapped inside made no such allegations in statements to police.

Guyette said a preliminary investigation by the building inspection department has turned up no code violations.

All tenants had access to a fire escape, and there were smoke alarms. Some of the alarms were melted by the fire, and there's no way to find out whether they were functioning at the time.

Guyette said that tenants routinely ignored the fire alarms.

Tenants, such as Sean P. McCormick, 23, have said there had been many false alarms, and the smoke detectors were often ignored.

However, tenants did respond when the alarms went off on the night of the fire, McCormick said.

Kennedy said he and other tenants probably hadn't given much thought to what should be done if there were a fire.

The fire department recommends that people have a "home escape plan" in place, which should include at least two planned escape routes, Guyette said.

People should also be aware that closing doors can slow the spread of fire and smoke, he said.

The fire in the tenement house spread rapidly because Walker's door was open, Guyette said. And, the door left open at the Hinas' apartment probably led to their asphyxiation, he said.

————

As Reported by the *Keene Evening Sentinel*:

Keene fire probe centers on smoke detectors

Smoke detectors may not have given apartment residents any warning of a fire that killed four people in Keene Saturday morning.

Despite claims by several tenants—including one who is the building's manager—that the installed detectors did sound an alarm at 88 High St., documents filed in Keene District Court indicate the first police officers and firefighters on the scene did not hear any warning devices going off.

The documents were filed in connection with a search warrant issued Monday when a Keene housing code enforcement officer visited the burned-out building and removed two detectors for testing.

They were found to be inoperative.

City Fire Chief Robert N. Guyette said this morning that officials will go back into the building again, before the end of this week, to gather more evidence in what appears to be a growing investigation.

Smoke from the 2 a.m. fire Saturday killed newly married Carl and Lori Hina, the man's 12 year old daughter Sara, and the couple's 4 month old daughter Lillian. Mr. Hina was 49; Mrs. Hina was 26.

The loss of life makes it one of the worst fires in the Monadnock Region's history and the worst recent fire in the state, where two other fatal blazes have occurred within the past several months.

Officials have determined the blaze started when tenant Sandra Walker fell asleep on a couch while smoking a cigarette. Walker's apartment was at the other end of the nine-apartment building from the Hinas'. Fifteen people, including Walker, survived the disaster.

Walker has been unavailable for comment.

A growing investigation by Keene's police and fire departments and City Prosecutor Frank A. DePippo appears to be focusing on whether required safety equipment was installed and working in the apartment building, which is owned by Thomas Yocono Jr. of Stoddard.

Yocono, contacted Tuesday, declined to comment on the fire.

Accounts of whether smoke detectors worked at the time of the fire differ.

An affidavit filed along with the search warrant Monday states Keene Patrolman Joseph Collins was in the building before firefighters arrived and heard no smoke alarms. He also reported that no emergency lights were on in the smoke-filled hallways.

Guyette himself was at the scene a short time later and confirmed he also did not hear any alarms going off.

Guyette said at least two smoke detectors were not functioning when the fire broke out at about 2 a.m. Those alarms were taken from the building Saturday morning.

"We know some smoke detectors were not working," Guyette said. "We feel the tenants arte the ones who rendered them inoperative."

Guyette said Yocono is not responsible for making sure tenants do not tamper with smoke detecting devices. It's possible that the detectors regularly sounded off and after a time they were disconnected by tenants as a nuisance, one Keene official said.

Officials said a 15-minute delay between when the fire started and the fire department was called, the lack of an evacuation plan and open doors that allowed the flames to be fanned contributed to the deaths. Since the Hinas were found fully clothed in their apartment, officials also speculate that the family delayed fleeing the building to get dressed.

City officials are satisfied that the building had proper permits for a multi—family dwelling, said Alfred H. Merrifield, assistant city manager.

There are two apartments and 7 single rooms with bath in the building where 19 people lived.

Yocono bought the building for $60,000 in 1986, about two years after 13 smoke detectors were installed.

————

As Reported by the *Keene Evening Sentinel*:

Four victims of Keene apartment fire buried

More than 200 people attended funerals Wednesday for members of the Keene family killed in an apartment fire last weekend.

A line of Ideal Taxi cabs followed the hearse carrying Carl R. Hina's casket as it wound its way Wednesday afternoon from Trinity Lutheran Church on Arch Street to Monadnock View Cemetery in West Keene. Hina, who died along with his wife, daughter and stepdaughter in the smoky blaze Saturday morning at 88 High St., had worked for the cab company.

Earlier in the day, a separate funeral was held at First Baptist Church of Keene for Lori M. Hina, 26, who had married Carl Hina only three weeks before the deadly fire; the couple's 4 month-old daughter, Lillian; and Mr. Hina's 12-year-old daughter, Sara. The three were also buried in the family lot at Monadnock View Cemetery.

Meanwhile:

Investigators are continuing to poly through the rubble of the burned-out, nine-apartment building, searching for more information on one of the city's deadliest fires ever Officials suspect smoke detectors and emergency lights were inoperative when the fire broke out at about 2 a.m. They have already determined that the Hinas delayed leaving the building so they could get dressed, and that the fire started when another tenant fell asleep while smoking a cigarette.

Officials have all but ruled out tenants' charges that firefighters and police were slow to respond to the emergency call. Though two tenants say they called the fire in to a telephone operator and the Keene Police Department shortly after 2 a.m., records show the first calls to both came at 2:25 and 2:28 a.m., respectively. Firefighters were on the scene at 2:29 a.m.

Fifteen survived the blaze.

Keene Fire Chief Robert N. Guyette said this morning it may take some time to determine whether the smoke alarms were working at the time of the fire. An electrician will have to examine them, he said.

But court records indicate that when authorities arrived at the fire scene, no alarms were sounding.

Questions are also being raised about whether beefed-up safety codes should be applied to such old homes turned apartments as the one that burned on High St.

Assistant City Manager Alfred H. Merrifield said such buildings are difficult to protect from fire because of their age.

"The whole thrust of the city is for the health, safety and protection of the people who live here," Merrifield said. "You can do the best job possible but that doesn't mean there'll never be fire fatality."

He said Keene's building inspection codes follow national and state standards.

Guyette said those national standards could be stricter, but pressure from developers and landlords blocks tougher ordinances.

Rev Keith E. Enko, pastor of Trinity Lutheran Church, officiated at the services Wednesday for Lori, Lillian and Sara Hina. Music was directed by Elaine Pawski. Ushers were William Donaway and Thomas Britton.

Burial followed in the family lot in Monadnock View Cemetery in West Keene, where committal prayers were offered by Rev. Enko and Rev. Raymond Ball.

————

As Reported by the *Keene Evening Sentinel*:

Apartment fire may be arson

Arson—not accident—may have caused an apartment house fire that killed four members of a Keene family last weekend.

Authorities have been investigating reports that a man in his mid 30's told several tenants of 88 High St., the building where Carl and Lori Hina and their two children died, that he planned to set the building on fire.

The man subsequently told some of the 15 survivors of the blaze that he did start it, according to sources with knowledge of the investigation.

The man is reportedly a former tenant.

Officials ruled earlier this week that the fire began in a couch when tenant Sandra Walker fell asleep while smoking a cigarette.

But now they believe that Walker, 41, was in bed when the couch caught fire and that she was not responsible for starting the blaze.

Police officials would not discuss the investigation Friday night.

They also would neither confirm nor deny a report that a representative of the N.H. Attorney General's office would be in Keene this morning to review the evidence they have gathered.

The Attorney General's office routinely takes over from local officials in all cases where homicide is suspected.

Under N.H. law, death resulting from arson is murder.

Kathleen A. McGuire, assistant N.H. Attorney general, said late Friday night that authorities are still investigating the fire and have yet to rule it arson.

"Police aren't completely satisfied with their preliminary findings," McGuire said. "There are some issues that need to be addressed."

She declined to say whether evidence of arson would be reviewed today by the attorney general's office.

There was no information available Friday night about a possible motive for the alleged arson.

For the past three days, police and the N.H. fire marshal have been searching through the charred rubble at the two-story wood-frame structure looking for evidence to corroborate what the tenants have told them, sources said.

Dead in the fire were Mr. Hina, 49, his wife of two weeks, Lori, 26, Sara J. Hina, 12, and Lillian Marie Hina, the couple's four-month-old daughter.

The rest of the tenants managed to get out of the apartment house without injury.

Some of the former tenants have been staying in a Keene motel until they can find a new place to live.

Since the fire, tenants and authorities have been in disagreement about how the situation was handled.

While officials have said that some smoke detectors failed to warn tenants when the fire first broke out, some tenants have said the smoke alarms sounded loudly.

In addition, some tenants maintained that help was summoned long before it arrived. Official records indicate that less than five minutes passed between the time the Keene Fire Department was called and the time it arrived.

The building at 88 High St. is owned by Thomas Yocono Jr. of Stoddard.

————

As Reported by the *Keene Evening Sentinel*:

Some cities have stricter fire codes

Could a deadly fire such as the one at 88 High St. in Keene last Saturday happen in any city or town in New Hampshire? While some N.H. cities and towns have stricter fire safety codes for buildings than those in Keene, many are similar.

All start with a minimum standard required by the state.

After that, community officials are free to decide how stringent regulations should be to ensure the safety of residents.

In Keene, fire regulations for apartment houses, mandate smoke detectors, a second exit, special doors to protect the exits and emergency lights.

As it turned out at 88 High Street, at least two of the smoke detectors were not operational, officials said later. Emergency lighting, required since the regulation passed in 1986, wasn't there at all.

Carl and Lori Hina and their two children died in the blaze.

Alfred H. Merrifield, Keene assistant city manager and code enforcement officer, said he wasn't sure the building's owner, Thomas Yocono Jr., knew that emergency lighting was required.

The city doesn't notify landlords of such rules except when making an on-site inspection, Merrifield said.

The building at 88 High St. was last inspected in 1984, at the former owner's request, when new smoke detectors were put in.

Inspections aren't done annually, as in some municipalities, but only at the owner's request, a tenant's complaint or for new construction.

Merrifield said annual inspections have been suggested in Keene, but one of the problems is the amount of manpower it would take.

Also, he asked, "Are you really accomplishing anything? Would what happened have happened anyway" despite inspections and emergency lights?

Here's what other municipalities around the state would have required of a building like 88 High St.:

- Manchester requires rooming houses with more than 15 tenants to tie their fire alarm systems into the city fire department. Portsmouth strongly encourages that as well, though it's not a law there, said fire prevention and safety officer Brian P. Van de Meulebroecke.

  Keene officials said there was a 15-minute delay in reporting the High Street fire, which tenants had to telephone in.

  In Keene, tie-ins to the city's fire department are only required of buildings with 12 or more units.

  The problem of trying to fit this regulation to potentially hazardous situations is unsolvable, Merrifield said.

  "Where do you draw the line?" he asked. "Two units? Three units?"

  Unlike Keene, and many other cities and towns, Manchester requires some rooming houses—depending on size—to have outside the building an electronic box with lights indicating which floor the fire is on, said fire inspector George R. Lareau.

  Also, again depending on size the building could be required to have a full internal alarm system, meaning horns and lights, automatic and manual alarms and heat detectors, he said.

- In Portsmouth, 88 High St. would have been required to have "hard-wire" smoke detectors, which couldn't be shut off by tenants, in all rooms and common areas,

such as on each level of a stairway and in the basement.

  Keene's regulations are similar.

- In Salem, 88 High St. would have been required to have a "full" system—smoke detectors in the hallways and in each room, "pull" stations where people can manually set off an alarm, and possibly other items, depending on the house, said Fire Chief James J. Bliss.

- In Derry, 88 High St. may have ended up just as it did in Keene. Like Keene, Derry requires detectors and a second exit for rooming houses that size, said Fire Chief James J. Cote.

Sprinklers are the first-line fire weapon of choice for most fire chiefs.

————

As Reported by the *Keene Evening Sentinel*:

Keene pursues arson probe

Keene police have appealed for the public's help in determining whether a fire January 14 that killed four people was set intentionally.

Though police have acknowledged that an arson investigation is being conducted, they declined to comment further.

The Sentinel reported Saturday that a man in his mid 30's had allegedly told several tenants that he planned to set fire to their building at 88 High St. The man subsequently told some of the 15 survivors of the blaze that he did start it, according to sources with knowledge of the investigation.

All queries this morning were referred to the N.H. Attorney General's Office, but no one was available there this morning to discuss developments in the case.'

The attorney general's office handles local cases in which deaths occur.

Smoke from the fire killed Carl and Lori Hina, who'd been married for only two weeks; his daughter, Sara, 12, and the couple's four-month-old daughter, Lilli8an.

After the arson investigation was reported Saturday, Keene police issued a release Saturday night, asking anyone with information about the fire to come forward.

The release said investigators want to rule out the possibility of arson.

Preliminary findings were that the blaze was caused by a hot cigarette ash that had been dropped accidentally on a sofa. Two days after, the fire, authorities said Sandra Walker, a resident of the apartment house, fell asleep while smoking and awoke to find her rear apartment on fire.

However, officials now believe Walker was in bed when her couch caught fire, and was not responsible for starting the fire.

Walker and residents of seven other apartments managed to get out of the building without injury, but the Hinas were overcome by smoke before they could escape.

This morning, Alfred H. Merrifield, assistant city manager, said it will be several days before authorities decide whether to cite building owner Thomas Yocono Jr. of Stoddard for failing to have emergency lights in the two-story, wood-frame building. Keene requires that apartment houses have emergency lights in hallways.

Yocono said this morning his lawyer had advised him not to talk about the fire.

Arson report may be ready Monday
By Monday, authorities hope to have final results on an arson investigation in connection with a fire January 14 at 88 High St., Keene, that killed four members of a Keene family.

If the N.H. Fire Marshal's Office determines that arson caused the fire, a decision will be made about whether an arrest warrant should be issued, said Peter G. Beeson , assistant N.H. attorney general.

Smoke from the fire killed Carl and Lori Hina, who'd been married just two weeks:

Mr. Hina's 12-year-old daughter, Sara; and the Hinas' four-month-old daughter, Lillian.

Beeson said the findings of the investigation should be released to the public Monday, assuming they're ready by then.

Authorities began investigating the arson possibility after hearing that a man in his mid-30's had told several tenants of 88 High St. that he planned to set the building on fire, and later said he had done so.

At first, authorities said the fire started accidentally when a lighted cigarette ignited a couch.

———

As Reported by the *Keene Evening Sentinel* January 27th, 1989:

"FIRE"

Fire alerts Keene to dangers
Sometimes it takes a tragedy to drive home just how dangerous fire can be and just how vital it is to protect yourself and your home.

The apartment house fire January 14 that killed four Keene residents has heightened community awareness about fire safety, city officials say; local stores say sales of smoke detectors have risen; schools have stepped up their emphasis on fire safety.

If a fire breaks out at your house, fire officials say, the warning systems you've set up and the actions you take can often mean the difference between life and death.

Though many occupants of the apartment building at 88 High St. escaped unharmed, officials determined that at least two smoke detectors were not working and emergency lights, required since 1986, had not been installed.

Keene fire regulations for apartment houses require smoke detectors, two exits, special doors to protect the exits, and emergency lights. However, the rules vary somewhat, depending on how many apartments are in a building and when the structure was built.

What can apartment dwellers do if they suspect their building is unsafe?

First, talk to the landlord, says Alfred H. Merrifield, Keene's director of health and code enforcement. Make sure he or she knows the fire-safety regulations and is following them.

Another way to check is by calling the fire department or the city inspections office. Several people have done so in the past week, Merrifield said, and some suspect their buildings don't comply with safety laws.

In cases like that, a city inspector generally checks to see if there is a problem. If there is, the landlord is ordered to fix it within a specific period of time. If he doesn't, the case can be referred to the city prosecutor for court action.

Sometimes, Merrifield said, landlords call the city themselves to ask what they should be doing to ensure tenants' safety.

But no matter how many fire alarms or fire doors a building has, the ultimate responsibility for protection falls on the individual, Merrifield said. Each family should have a plan for evacuating their home in an emergency, and other fire-safety techniques need to be a top priority, too.

The earlier children begin learning about fire safety, the more likely the idea will remain with them, said Cynthia J. Day, a kindergarten teacher at Franklin School in Keene.

On the Monday after the High Street blaze, teachers at the school for kindergarten through grade 5 began stressing fire safety, which was already part of the curriculum.

The tragedy touched very close to home, Day said: Many of our students live near the High Street area."

Day gave the 39 children in her two classes a take-home assignment; check their smoke detectors to make sure they were operating properly, write down and memorize

the Keene Fire Department number (352-1100), and go over a home evacuation plan with their parents.

Day said she was amazed and pleased by parents' cooperation; most of them signed forms verifying that the assignment had been carried out.

Meanwhile, since the fire, some local retailers report a slight to moderate increase in the sale of smoke detectors and fire extinguishers.

At Hilson Home Center on Wet Street, clerk Edward P. Kane said sales of both smoke detectors and fire extinguishers have climbed in recent weeks, and some customers have mentioned that the High Street fire prompted their purchases.

Smoke detectors "have always been good sellers, but I noticed a big increase in the last couple of weeks," said Brenda Powell, a clerk at Bradlees department store on Winchester Street.

Basic fire safety can be divided into three areas, said Capt. Bruce Pollock of the Keene Fire Department; knowing how to protect yourself if a fire occurs, setting up an early warning system for fire and taking steps to prevent the fire in the first place.

"Exit drills are probably one of the most important but most overlooked" precautions, Pollock said.

Often, people aren't aware of just how fact, quick and deadly fires really are. Smoke and carbon monoxide gas can cause disorientation, and the better you know your surroundings, the better your chances of escaping unharmed, he said.

Families should devise a home evacuation plan, he said, and each member of the family should know his or her way out in the dark.

"Fire is black, and you literally can't see your hand in front of your face," Pollock said.

Most people simply don't know what a fire is really like, he said. For instance, television programs that show firefighters rushing into burning buildings are deceptive.

Hot air rises, and so does the choking smoke, so the safest place to be is near the floor. Crawling gives a person more light and air, he said.

Bedroom doors should be kept closed at night to prevent air currents that spread fire and smoke. For the same reason, you should close the doors behind you when you flee from a building.

Because fire spreads in a matter of minutes, early warning is essential. Buildings should have fire alarms on each floor level and in each bedroom, Pollock said, batteries should be checked or changed regularly.

Finally, people should make sure that certain appliances—portable heaters, irons and the like—are unplugged before they go to sleep or leave home, that matches and cigarette lighters are out of the reach of small children, and that nobody smokes in bed. Such measures can stop a fire before it starts, Pollock said.

Also, applying a little common sense can make your home safer; things as simple as not storing paint cans or other volatile items near your furnace. Often, taking a new look at your home from a fire safety viewpoint can really improve safety.

The fire department welcomes the chance to give fire-safety advice to community groups or organizations that ask.

Often, such requests are made during Fire Prevention Week in October, Pollock said, but fire safety should be a concern year-round.

————

As Reported by the *Keene Evening Sentinel* January 31st, 1989:

"FIRE"

Suspect in fatal fire is named in documents

Authorities don't know whether arson and manslaughter charges will be brought against a 32-year-old Keene man who allegedly bragged on January 14 he had "just torched 88 High St."

The early morning fire at the Keene tenement house left four people dead.

In court, documents released Monday, David McLeod, 32, a former tenant of the building emerged as the lone suspect allegedly responsible for starting the fire.

While police suspect arson killed Carl and Lori Hina, his daughter, Sara, 12, and the couple's infant daughter, Lillian, the N.H. Attorney General's office has declined to rule the fire was set intentionally.

Peter G. Beeson, assistant N.H. Attorney General, said this morning that the investigation will continue to see if charges should be filed in the case.

He said he had no idea when charges might be brought.

Officials came to suspect McLeod, now in Arizona, after three witnesses told police that he threatened to burn down the building earlier in the evening, and then later admitted to setting the fire.

Affidavits were taken by police on January 18, and made public Monday afternoon by Judge / Richard Talbot turned down a request by the N.H. Attorney General's office to keep the documents sealed.

Statements in the affidavit were made by Bonnie Faulkner, David Castor and Kurt Frazier, acquaintances of the suspect.

They told police that McLeod allegedly set the fire out of vengeance against his former lover, Wanda Ford, a tenant at 88 High St.

McLeod and Ford had shared an apartment in the building until he moved out last year. Witnesses alleged that McLeod held a grudge against male tenants in the building who knew his former girl friend.

According to the affidavits, Castor told Keene patrolman William Sargent that he and McLeod had walked to 88 High St. on January 14, where McLeod attended a party at about 10:30 p.m. until the fire was discovered, although he disappeared and reappeared," according to the affidavits. "He left the scene around 3 a.m. after a confrontation with Keene police. He then reappeared at Kurt Frazier's apartment on Elm Street bragging about the fire."

McLeod's own statements indicate he was in the apartment three weeks prior to the fire," court documents said.

The fire investigator said in the court documents; that revenge fires are frequently set without the use of accelerants using available materials.

Initially, officials ruled carelessness started the fire after tenant Sandra Walker fell asleep with a lighted cigarette.

Fire Marshal Thomas Norton said evidence gathered at the scene showed the fire started slowly, the affidavits said.

The fire marshal's office first ruled the fire accidental because the burn pattern was typical of a fire begun by a smoldering cigarette. On January 16 officials said the fire began on a couch in Walker's apartment in the back of the two-story wood-frame building. Smoke from the blaze enveloped much of the building, killing the Hinas.

But the next day, Keene police learned from people who knew McLeod that he allegedly threatened to burn down the building just before the fire broke out.

Keene and state investigators went back to the apartment house to check the burn pattern again. That investigation showed that the fire began more quickly than first thought, Beeson said.

The information would tend to rule out that a smoldering cigarette started the fire, he said.

Beeson said current findings show the fire started from an open flame as a result of an incendiary act from human involvement."

But he said that "it is not a conclusion of arson."

Beeson denied that officials are holding off on pressing charges because of a 180-degree change in the ruling of how the fire began.

No arrest is pending, Beeson said.

"We have to be satisfied that charges can be proved," he said.

————

As Reported by the *Keene Evening Sentinel* February 9th, 1989:

"STORY"

Suit possible over fatal fire Landlords' property attached

The first steps toward a lawsuit have been taken in connection with a Keene fire January 14 in which four people died.

Cheshire County Superior Court has ordered attachments—worth $3.8 million against Thomas F. and Agnes M. Yocono of Stoddard, who owned the two-story apartment house at 88 High St. that was destroyed by fire.

The attachments were sought by relatives of three of those who died, to keep the Yoconos from transferring any real estate holdings until a decision is made on whether a civil suit will be filed. Any such lawsuit would revolve around allegations of negligence.

The court action was taken by relatives of Lori Hina, her stepdaughter Sara Hina, age 12, and her infant daughter, Lillian. They and

Lori's husband of two weeks, Carl Hina, all died of smoke inhalation.

The attachments were requested January 31 and February 6. Attorney Ernest L. Bell 3rd of Keene, representing the estates of Lori and Lillian Hina, requested liens of $2 million on property owned by Thomas Yocono and $1 million on property owned by Agnes Yocono. Marcellene A. Halpin, Lori's mother and Lillian's grandmother, is administrator of their estates.

Attorney Susan Becker of Nashua filed for $80-0,000 in attachments against the two Yoconos on behalf of the estate of Sara Hina.

Thomas Yocono declined to comment on the issue this morning.

The requests for attachments allege the Yoconos were negligent and careless because the bu8ilding did not comply with city safety codes.

Keene city government officials are expected to confer next week with the city prosecutor, Frank A. DePippo, on whether to cite Yocono for failure to install emergency lights in the apartment building or for any other possible fire code violations, said Assistant City Manager Alfred H. Merrifield.

Many occupants of the wood-frame building escaped unharmed from the fire.

Fire officials determined that at least two smoke detectors in the building were not working when the fire broke out and that emergency lights, required since 1986, had never been installed.

Although officials first ruled the fire accidental, the result of a smoldering cigarette, witnesses told police a few days later that a 35-year-old Keene man had bragged he had set the fire to get revenge on a woman with whom he used to live in the building.

According to affidavits filed in Keene District Court, David McLeod, who lived in the building until last year, told acquaintances before the blaze that he planned to start the fire.

A special Cheshire County Superior Court grand jury is expected to hear testimony in the case on Friday.

———

As Reported by the *Keene Evening Sentinel* February 17th, 1989:

"STORY"

Official: No arrests are planned for fatal fire

Whether an accident or arson caused a Keene fire that killed four people January 14 is still no known, but no arrests are anticipated, a senior state prosecutor said today.

"The investigation remains open," said Kathleen A., McGuire, assistant attorney general. "We have pursued the leads; however, on the basis of the investigation thus far, we don't anticipate an arrest.

However, city officials are continuing an investigation on whether Thomas F. Yocono of Stoddard, who owns the burned-out apartment house at 88 High St., should be cited for failing to install emergency lighting or for any other fire code violations. City Manager J. Patrick MacQueen said today.

McGuire said a Cheshire County Superior Court grand jury questioned people in connection with the fire last Friday, but was not asked-to-return an indictment—a judgment that the prosecution had enough evidence to warrant a trial.

Asked if the fact that authorities changed their mind about the origin of the fire—first saying it was an accident, and then saying it may have been arson—contributed to the decision not to prosecute the case, McGuire said that was only one factor among many.,

"We have the burden of proving the case beyond a reasonable doubt," McGuire said. "We have to decide what impact each piece of evidence will have on the jury. We don't feel the evidence at this time warrants us presenting the case to the grand jury" for an indictment.

Authorities first said the fire resulted when a tenant fell asleep while smoking a cigarette. Two weeks later, they said the fire resulted from an open flame, "an incendiary act from human involvement." However, they said, that didn't mean it was arson.

Several people were subpoenaed to testify before the grand jury about their conversations with David McLeod, 32, a former tenant at 88 High St. Documents police submitted to Keene District Court alleged that, in those conversations, McLeod had said he'd started the fire.

However, authorities have apparently been unable to come up with evidence to back up the conversations.

All four members of one family died of smoke inhalation from the fire, which started at about 2:30 a.m. in a rear apartment of the two-story, wood-frame apartment house. Killed were Carl and Lori Hina, who'd been married only two weeks, Carl Hina's 12-year-old daughter, Sara, and the couple's infant daughter, Lillian.

Members of the Hina family, preparing for a lawsuit, have obtained a ruling from Cheshire County Superior Court, ordering attachments worth $3.8 million against Yocono and his wife.

———————

[*Compiler's Note*: In 2010, David McLeod, age 53, was charged with four counts of murder. He was extradited by the California State cold case unit and is awaiting trial.]

As Reported by the *Keene Evening Sentinel* January 27th, 1989:

"STORY"

City may bill college $250 per fire alarm

Keene State College may end up paying $250 for each fire alarm firefighters respond to if the city council adopts a recommendation made by the finance committee Thursday night.

"Seeing as the college does not contribute anything for fire protection, I think (the fee) should be for each alarm answered," said city Councilor Mary F. Penny, a committee member.

In voting to support the fee, the finance committee amended a previous proposal to charge the college $500 for each fire alarm.

City Councilor Kendall W. Lane, another committee member, said the original $500 figure was suggested as a penalty for false alarms. The city's actual cost of responding is $160, he said.

"As far as a fire down at the college, I would feel better if we came closer to charging the actual cost. I see no reason for charging a penalty when there is an actual fire in the city," Lane said.

Penny suggested that $250 be charged for all calls.

"There are too many false fire alarms occurring down there," she said.

Penny said the college should pay its fair share for using a city service.

Other N.H., colleges, such as Plymouth State and the University of New Hampshire, pay subsidies in lieu of taxes to their home communities o cover such services, she said.

The committee voted 3 to 1 to amend the proposal to include a $250 charge for each alarm, and voted 3 to 1 to recommend its adoption by the council February 2.

City Councilor Roger T. Zerba voted against both measures.

"Charging for all fire alarms to me just doesn't seem fair. I recognize the problem down there. I just don't think that's the soluti9on," he said, pointing out that the college contributes indirectly to the city through the impact of its payroll and students, and its cultural activities.

In other business, the committee:

Unanimously recommended allowing the Public Works Department to dip into other funds if the salt budget runs out. Public Works Director Robert J. Richards told the committee that the city has used 1,800 tons of salt on icy roads. That leaves only about 300 tons for the rest of the winter.

Since there has been little snowfall this year, Richards said the department has saved about $60,000 on equipment use, and overtime for plow crews. Money to buy more salt could be taken from those savings, he said.

Recommended that the city request $5,000 from the Emergency Shelter Grants Program to help the St. Vincent de Paul Society pay rent and other expenses to maintain the city's emergency shelter on Water Street. In the past two years, the city has received about $7,000 in grant money from the program.

Recommended appropriating $300,000 for a water corrosion control project.

Finance Director Raymond P. Tracy said the city is considering two other major projects as well to improve the water supply and service, but so far just the cost of the corrosion project has been determined.

He said the project could be covered from current funds until a bond is issued to cover all three projects. The water corrosion control project is expected to begin this spring, he said.

Briefly considered a $61 million, five year capital improvements program, the bulk of which outlines costs for solid waste management and upgrading city streets.

The plan also calls for a parking garage to overcome a shortage of parking spaces downtown. The finance committee plans to meet with planning officials February 13 to discuss the list of projects.

––––––––

As Reported by the *Keene Evening Sentinel* February 27th, 1989:

"FIRE"

Minor fire damages basement

Firefighters Hank Memmesheimer, Timmy Mason, and Mike Blanchard looking inside the apartment building checking the remains of the fire. Photo by Paul Montgomery.

Lint buildup behind a clothes dryer resulted in a minor fire Sunday afternoon on Beaver Street in Keene, officials said.

The fire broke out at about 12:50 p.m. in the basement of the three-story apartment building at 103 Beaver St.

Fire and smoke damaged the basement, and smoke damaged the inside of the wood-frame building, said Steven Goldsmith a Keene Fire Department captain.

Little water was needed to extinguish the flames, which were curling from under the basement door when firefighters arrived, Goldsmith said.

No injuries were reported.

The fire was put out in minutes and residents were able to return to their apartments.

––––––––

As Reported by the *Keene Evening Sentinel* March 4th, 1989;

"STORY"

Apartment landlord sued over fire-safety precautions

Keene has filed a criminal complaint against a Massachusetts realty company for alleged violations of the Keene building code.

The city filed the complaint Friday against LHM Realty of Sherbourne, Mass. which rents 14 apartments above the Sears Roebuck & Co. store at 41 Central Square.

City officials allege that the company failed to install adequate smoke-detectors in the apartments or fire alarm systems in the building.

Linda Melcher, an LHM trustee, was named in the criminal complaint. Arraignment is scheduled for March 6 in Keene District Court.

The city has been working with the landlord for several months to improve the building's safety, said Alfred H. Merrifield, Director of Health and Code Enforcement. Deadlines were set for certain standards to be met, but although some issues have been addressed, several serious ones remain unresolved, he said.

––––––––

As Reported by the *Keene Evening Sentinel* March 27th, 1989:

"FIRE"

Fire doused in KSC room

An electrical extension cord apparently caused a fire that damaged a Keene State College dormitory room this weekend.

Two students occupy the first-floor room at Randall Hall, but neither was in the room when the fire broke out Saturday at about midnight. No injuries were reported.

A smoke detector in the building set off an alarm at 12:08 a.m., and an automatic sprinkler system put out the fire before the Keene Fire Department arrived, Deputy Chief George H. Shepard said.

The fire damaged a combination desk and shelf unit in the room, and the students' clothing and personal items were damaged by smoke and water, Shepard said.

––––––––

As Reported by the *Keene Evening Sentinel* March 28th, 1989:

"STORY"

Hazardous scenario used to test emergency personnel

Say a delivery truck carrying kerosene, calcium hypochlorite and an insecticide called Dimetox spilled its load somehow, and all of the chemicals mixed together.

A highly poisonous vapor cloud would be created.

Say the truck's unlicensed driver ran away from the accident, leaving safety workers to figure out for themselves what the chemicals were and how they should be handled.

A highly dangerous situation would be created.

On Monday afternoon, 23 representatives from the Keene fire and police departments and from the Brattleboro, Peterborough, Swanzey and Meadowood fire departments were put up against just such a situation—simulated, in this case—after a 48-hour course led by the Keene Fire Department on handling hazardous wastes.

The students were told only that a vehicle fire had been reported in the Federal Express parking lot on Marlboro Street in Keene. They "discovered" the cloud when they arrived, and began putting their newly gained knowledge to work.

First, teams entered the spill scene—in $8,000 protective suits on loan from the state government—to learn by reading labels what chemicals had spilled. They relayed that information to other teams to learn how they should be handles, and then began "evacuating" the neighborhood.

The solution to the problem—removing the five 50-pound bags of insecticide, which caused the poison in the vapor—was reached in about 2 ½ hours, an "excellent" time, said Bruce Pollock, a Keene Fire Department captain who helped lead the course.

It might have taken longer if evacuation actually had to occur, he said. Removal of the bags probably would have taken an hour.

"Normally, these things take days," he said, noting it took eight days to clean up after a California incident in which pesticides spilled.

No major hazardous waste incident has happened yet in this area, Pollock said, though an accident on Route 9 late last year, in which a propane gas delivery truck was involved, could have been serious.

This was the first in-depth course the Keene Fire Department has held on handling hazardous waste, but more are planned, he said.

"This only scratches the surface" of the knowledge needed to deal with emergencies, he said.

Now that it has begun a team to handle hazardous waste spills, the fire department will ask for money to buy six of the $8,000 suits. Six suits are the minimum needed, Pollock said; two two-person teams would be needed, each working while the other was in decontamination, plus a backup two-person team.

"It's useless otherwise," Pollock said. "I know it sounds like a lot of money…but it really isn't if you look at what potential danger you're eliminating from the community.

The course, not counting labor, cost about $3,300 for the city to put on.

————

As Reported by the *Keene Evening Sentinel* April 1st, 1989:

"STORY"

Some people are born to serve, others are born to lead

Steven W. Goldsmith of Keene does both.

As a captain with the Keene Fire Department, Goldsmith helps oversee a crew of more than 30 firefighters.

He is also an emergency medical technician, a part-time police officer in Swanzey and an auxiliary trooper with N.H. State Police.

He teaches cardiopulmonary resuscitation, as well as fire prevention, to adults and schoolchildren.

And he still finds time to serve in the U.S. Marine Reserve in South Weymouth, Mass., where he was nominated recently by his commanding officer for U.S. Marine Reserve of the year. Out of 245,000 Reserves nationwide, 12 were nominated.

In the Reserve, Goldsmith is a quality control chief for jet fighters, making sure that all are in top notch condition before they leave the ground. He is also one of the few Reserves who flies in fighter jets.

Not surprisingly, Goldsmith is hard to get a hold of.

"I'm spread too thin," he said. "Sometimes I just try to do too much."

But he said he wouldn't trade public service for anything.

Personal tragedy led him to a career in emergency service, he said.

Goldsmith was raised by his grandparents in Keene, after his parents died in a car accident when he was 5.

When he was 17, a young cousin died in a Keene car accident. That was in 1968, when there was little-on-the-scene first aid.

Since the accident happened not far from his grandparents' home, Goldsmith went to the scene.

His cousin was taken to the hospital in the back of a station wagon, instead of an ambulance. Since there were no rescue squads to respond, there was just the driver to attend to her.

"Probably nothing could have saved her," he said. "It just struck me that she was all alone in the back of the station wagon.

"It seemed no one wanted to get into the emergency field."

Deputy Chief George H. Shepard, who has been with the Keene Fire Department for more than 25 years, said that, in the early 1960's, emergency services were lacking in the Monadnock Region.

"It was load-and-go," Shepard said. "You just threw them in the back."

Shepard said some people who died from injuries suffered in accidents might have lived if they had been treated on the scene.

Goldsmith said his experiences as a youth led him to want to help others. He started by joining the U.S. Marines in 1969.

After doing basic training at what many Marine recruits consider the most horrendous place on earth, Parris Island, S.C., Goldsmith was shipped out on the USS America for a year's duty in Southeast Asia.

He was discharged from the Marines in 1973 but went back in as a Reserve in 1980.

In the meantime, Goldsmith found his niche as a firefighter.

Following his discharge, Goldsmith was hired by H.P. Hood in Charlestown, Mass., working in its ice cream plant.

The pay was $175, with benefits, for a 40-hour week.

After just three weeks he left the plant—to work 56 hours a week for $106 as a Nashua firefighter.

"My (H.P. Hood) boss thought I was a real loony tune," Goldsmith said. "I said Nope, I just want to be a firefighter."

After two years of learning the trade, Goldsmith got his chance to return to Keene and work with the city's fire department.

The first fire Goldsmith fought in Keene almost turned out to be his last.

When the Elm City Grange burned on Railroad Street in 1975, Goldsmith charged into the building with another firefighter to battle the blaze.

Deep inside the burning building, the two got trapped under falling debris.

For nearly 10 long minutes, other firefighters concentrated their efforts on getting the two men out.

They managed to bring them to safety, but the building was destroyed.

Over the years, Goldsmith has seen tragedies, and bizarre incidents.

One of his strangest experiences came on a call to help a Keene woman supposedly injured in a domestic dispute.

When Goldsmith and another emergency medical technician arrived at the George Street home, they found the injured woman.

She was not the victim of an assault. She had a lawn dart stuck in her forehead.

"Nobody could believe their eyes," he said. "All she wanted to do was pull it out."

The dart had stuck nearly 2 inches into the woman's head, yet she was conscious and desperate to have it removed.

The emergency workers restrained the woman, who was insistent about getting the dart out of her head, then raced to Cheshire Medical Center in Keene.

The emergency room doctor was incredulous.

He asked if he could take a picture of the woman, so others would believe it had really happened.

She replied, "I don't care what you do, just take it out," Goldsmith said.

The woman recovered, but has a slight nasal problem now, Goldsmith said.

The once-popular lawn game has since been banned for sale because of fatal injuries caused by the darts.

In 1984 Goldsmith was named the Monadnock Region Humane Society's Hero of the Year. Usually, an animal wins the award.

Goldsmith won the honor for saving a golden retriever from the icy waters of Brickyard Pond at Keene State College.

The dog had fallen through the ice and was near drowning.

A crowd gathered as the rescue squad arrived, and it was Goldsmith who plunged into the water to bring the dog to safety.

It was a simple act, but it spoke loudly about the character of people like Goldsmith, who serve the public when quick action is needed.

Goldsmith said he isn't different from any of the firefighters in the department. All of them share a sense of service to the community.

On the two nights a week Goldsmith spends at the station house, calls for ambulances and fire trucks leave him and the other firefighters little time to rest, Shepard said.

"He's a real good firefighter," Shepard said. "He certainly doesn't lack for courage."

The only thing he lacks is enough time in the day, something he said he's working on.

Captain Goldsmith takes a break on the bumper of Keene Fire Departments Engine 1. Photo by Michael Moore.

As Reported by the *Keene Evening Sentinel* April 4th, 1989:

"STORY"

88 High St. owners are called poor neighbors

Noise, rowdy parties and obnoxious behavior were the norm at 88 High St. before the crowded Keene apartment house burned earlier this year, killing a family of four.

That's what neighbors told city zoning officials Monday, insisting that Thomas F. and Agnes Yocono of Stoddard be required to deal with those problems before being allowed to rebuild.

After a lengthy public hearing, the zoning board of adjustment voted 5-0 against granting the Yoconos' request to convert the two apartments and five boarding rooms in their damaged building into five apartments.

Under city zoning regulations, adopted after the building was turned into apartments at least a decade ago, only a single-family house can be build on a lot the size of the one at 88 High St. 'But also under the regulations, the Yoconos could rebuild the apartment house exactly as it was before the January 14 fire, without needing special permission from the city. The couple was before the zoning board only because they plan changes to the building that still do not conform to current zoning.

J.R. Davis, the Yoconos' lawyer, argues that since five apartments at the site would be less of a violation of current zoning than rebuilding the house to hold nine sets of tenants, the city should okay the plans.

But he also told zoning board members Monday that rebuilding the apartment house as it was would cost more than half the $136,700 assessed value of the building before the fire. That, he said, would have a sizable financial impact on the owners and still would not address the concerns of neighbors.

Zoning board members called the apartment building as it was at the time of the fire an "overuse of the land," and refused approval for the reconstruction plans.

Board Chairman Donald Askey said the Yoconos' have "not been a good neighbor" and advised Mr. Yocono, who was at the meeting, to work with residents of the High Street area to come up with a more acceptable plan.

Davis said afterward he was disappointed at the board's decision and would discuss with the Yoconos what action they want to take now. They can appeal the decision, first to the board and then to Superior Court.

The cause of the fire at 88 High St. has yet to be definitively determined, though authorities have indicated that arson is a possibility. Most of the building's occupants escape3d unharmed, but smoke killed Carl and Lori Hina, his 12-year-old daughter, Sara, and the couple's 4-month-old daughter, Lillian.

City officials have determined that several smoke alarms in the building were not operable at the time of the fire and that required emergency lighting was not installed.

Complaining that the landlords did not make enough of an effort to oversee conditions or conduct at 88 High St. before the fire, Artis D. Osborne of 31 Carroll St. told the zoning board Monday that she was awakened more than once at 2 a.m. by loud tenants in the two-story wood-frame building near her home. She said that she had to move her young son out of his bedroom because of profanity that wafted through the windows, and that she saw alcohol use and suspected drug use in the yard.

"Someone has to do something to convince me there will be a change," she said.

Three other neighbors who attended the meeting agreed, saying the lack of landscaping and the behavior of the mostly transient tenants who lived in the apartment building had been a blot on the neighborhood.

Since the fire, the house has been boarded up.

Neighboring property owner William Beauregard spoke in favor of the Yoconos' five-apartment plan, saying that doing away with the boarding rooms that were in the building would be a plus for the neighborhood.

But Mary Jo Fisher of Cross Street said five apartments is still excessive for the building and neighborhood, suggesting three be put in instead.

Davis responded that building three apartments into the house would not be profitable for the landlord and that the proposed plan would enhance the neighborhood. It would reduce the number of bedrooms from 11 to 7, which would reduce the demand for city water and sewer services, he said.

The new plan would also provide for more on-site parking by tearing down a barn at the rear of the building. In all, Davis said, the improvement night attract a more stable type of renter.

———————

As Reported by the *Keene Evening Sentinel* April 4th, 1989.

"STORY"

Keene officials silent on impending charges in fatal fire

More than two months after a fatal fire, Keene officials are offering no explanation on why they have not cited the owner of an apartment building at 88 High St.

A week ago, Assistant City Manager Alfred H. Merrifield said the city government intended to file a complaint against Thomas F. Yocono Jr., alleging safety violations.

To date, no complaint has been filed and Merrifield declined to comment on the matter Monday. He referred all questions to City

Prosecutor Frank A. Depippo, who could not be reached for comment Monday or today.

Contacted this morning, City Manager J. Patrick MacQueen said he could not offer any reasons why Yocono has not been cited. He said Merrifield and Depippo are handling the situation.

'Four people died in the fire January 14 that swept through the two-story, wood-frame building at 88 High St. Fire officials later determined that two of the building's smoke detectors were not working and that emergency lights, required since 1986, had not been installed.

Though many of the occupants of the building escaped unharmed, smoke from the fire killed Carl and Lori Hina; his daughter, Sara, 12; and the couple's 4-month-old daughter, Lillian.

———————

As Reported by the *Keene Evening Sentinel* April 19th, 1989:

"FIRE"

Markem fire creates toxic fumes; no injuries

Containers of Aluminum powder were carried by Capt Goldsmith and placed on the pallet, Call Firefighter Timmy Mason and Capt Goldsmith along with Wayne Spofford removed the chemicals to a safe location. Photo by Steve Hooper.

A flammable material used to make ink started smoldering and giving off toxic fumes Tuesday at Markem Corp. in Keene before being snuffed by firefighters.

No one was injured in the incident at 150 Congress St. at 6:35 p.m., but some people at the scene suffered eye irritation from the burning aluminum flake powder.

A night watchman at the plant called in an alarm after seeing smoke coming from an outdoor storage area, where empty barrels are stored. Firefighters later discovered a partially open 5-gallon container of the aluminum powder, which can ignite and explode when exposed to moisture. A sealed 30-gallon container and two sealed 20-gallon containers of the chemical were also stored ion the area, according to Deputy Fire Chief George Shepard.

Firefighters wearing protective gear used a dry chemical to extinguish the powder and removed it from the area using a dolly, Shepard said. The effort took more than an hour.

Markem President Thomas B. Putnam said the company plans to dispose today of all barrels of the material, which hasn't been used since last fall in making silver ink. The barrels were stored in the outdoor area because it was believed to be the safest place.

"It was in storage, outside, away from anything else." Putnam said. "Our intention was to send it back to the vendor for credit."

During the minor emergency Tuesday, work ceased temporarily for the 20 or so employees on the night shift at Markem, which makes industrial printing machines and print supplies.

The area was not evacuated, though police and members of the Keene Area Radio Emergency Service blocked off Optical Avenue and redirected traffic as a safety precaution.

Putnam said company officials will review their safety and storage procedures to make sure such an incident doesn't happen again.

———

As Reported by the *Keene Evening Sentinel* May 3rd, 1989:

"FIRE"

Apartment fire

A fire at 92 Beaver St. was reported at 3:53 this morning. Captain Steven W. Goldsmith of the Keene Fire Department said Prescott Dowland, a tenant at the wood-frame apartment house had put out a mattress fire Monday night that was caused by a cigarette. He then placed the mattress outside, against the building, and a few hours later the mattress began burning again and set fire to the building.

A neighbor saw smoke and called Keene police, who called the fire department. The mattress burned part of the building's exterior, and flames moved into a partition before the fire was put out.

———

As Reported by the *Keene Evening Sentinel* May 5th, 1989:

"FIRE"

Storage building badly damaged in suspicious fire

A suspicious fire in a storage building in Keene early this morning was doused before flames could raze it.

Keene firefighters were called to the building at 21 Railroad St. about 3:30 a.m. after flames were spotted. The building, owned by Roy O. Johnson, was used by store material for the nearby Johnson Motor Parts Ins., at 19 Railroad St.

The two-story wood-frame building was heavily damaged, officials said.

Arson Suspected – Flames, at top, rip through storage building for Johnson Motor Parts, Inc. as Keene firefighters, in both photos, train hoses on the burning structure. Photo by Steve Hooper.

It took firefighters about 90 minutes to extinguish the fire, which burned up much of the second floor and the attic.

Upon arrival, Captain Goldsmith requested a second alarm and ordered fire attack and salvage operations to begin.

However, firefighters were able to save a 1940 Cadillac that was being restored on the ground floor. It was not damaged, officials said.

As firefighters worked and a small crowd gathered, heavy smoke settled over much of downtown Keene.

This morning, fire officials would say only that the fire is of "a suspicious nature," and a police report also called the fire suspicious.

Both police and fire officials were investigating the cause of the blaze this morning.

A passerby called authorities after spotting the fire in the building.

A Keene police officer on patrol was the first official to reach the fire, and found the back of the building burning: "it appeared as though the flames were originating from inside the building," the police report said.

When firefighters arrived, the structure was engulfed in flames and smoke.

"It was going pretty good," said Lt. Robert S. Crowell of the Keene Fire Department.

However, no one was injured in fighting the blaze.

Johnson said this morning he did not yet know whether he could salvage the building. He said the structure was part of a five-building carriage house complex built at the turn of the century.

He used the building for dry storage and said nothing inside it should have started the fire, and nothing of value was kept there—except the Cadillac.

"That, thank God, was on the other end" of where the fire did most of its damage,

Johnson said. The car is just about completely restored, he said, and only got a little wet.

"(The firefighters) did a great job," he said. "I can't say enough about the fire department.

As Reported by the *Keene Evening Sentinel* May 16th, 1989:

"STORY"

3 youths accused of arson

Three Keene youths will be charged with arson in connection with a fire in a vacant building on Summit Road.

Police patrolling in West Keene Monday at about 5:30 p.m. noticed smoke coming from the unused building that was once the top floor of Jean's Pastry Shop when the business was on West Street. The pastry shop moved to Central Square several years ago, and the building's top floor was salvaged for future use. It's been sitting on a trailer off Summit Road ever since.

Police said they found a smoldering mattress inside the structure, and caught three teenagers as they tried to run away. The boys—one 14-year-old, two 13—were released in the custody of their parents, awaiting court action, police said. The boys names were not disclosed because of their ages.

Firefighters doused the mattress fire.

As Reported by the *Keene Evening Sentinel* May 19th, 1989:

"STORY"

Building owner is fined

The owner of the Sears building in downtown Keene has been fined $560 for violating city fire codes.

LHM Realty Trust of Sherborn pleaded no contest Tuesday to failing to install smoke detectors and fire alarms in the 11 apartments at 39-42 Central Square, above the Sears Roebuck & Co. department store.

The alarms and smoke detectors have since been installed, city officials said.

As Reported by the *Keene Evening Sentinel* May 25th, 1989:

"FIRE"

Fire ruled accidental; youths face no court action

A mattress fire in an abandoned building on Summit Road last week that resulted in the arrest of three teenagers has been ruled accidental, Keene Police said.

As a result, no court action will be taken against the boys—one 14 year old, two 13— who were found at the building May 15 at about 5:30 p.m.

Police said the boys had been playing with fireworks and accidentally ignited a mattress inside the vacant structure.

Police on patrol noticed smoke, found the three boys and arrested them. All were released to the custody of their parents.

Because they tried to douse the fire and pull the mattress out of the building, the boys were not charged in connection with the blaze, police said.

The building used to be the top floor of Jean's Pastry Shop on West Street. When the business moved to Central Square a few years ago, the top was salvaged and taken to Summit Road, where it now sits on a trailer.

As Reported by the *Keene Evening Sentinel* June 3rd, 1989:

"STORY"
MacQueen defends restructuring plan.

J. Patrick MacQueen

One rule from common wisdom, "if it ain't broke, don't fix it."

Keene City Manager J. Patrick MacQueen says that notion has become a primary obstacle to his plan to organize the city government, consolidating 13 departments into eight.

In MacQueen's eyes, the city government is not broken, but it could work a lot better.

"It's not as good, not as directed, as it could be, I believe," he said this week from his office at city hall.

MacQueen's plan is to form a public safety department overseeing fire, police and inspections services; an administrative services department for financing and data processing; and a community services department to head the juvenile conference program, and human and health services.

So far, his plan has met resistance from some city officials who complained he worked out the plan in secret, and from city workers—especially firefighters—who worry that an administrative head won't have enough expertise in their particular area.

The Keene City Council will vote June 20 on MacQueen's plan, as part of the $18.5 million city budget proposal for fiscal year 1990.

Heads of the new departments would be chosen from among existing department heads, MacQueen said. They would keep their existing jobs, but have expanded responsibilities.

Although MacQueen has declined to specify who he's considering for the jobs, many city hall workers and officials say he has already decided on Police Chief Thomas F. Powers for the public safety department, City Assessor Laurence Shaffer for administrative services, and Assistant City Manager Alfred H. Merrifield for community services.

Right now, all 13 department heads report directly to MacQueen, a setup he finds increasingly unwieldy.

The plan would cost an extra $4,100, to give raises to the three promoted department heads.

MacQueen said the easiest way to start his plan would also be the costliest: hire new administrators, instead of increasing the responsibilities of those already working for the city.

"We have good people. We should be challenging them to the maximum," he said. "There are few things we cannot do it we work together to accomplish them."

If the council rejects his plan, MacQueen said, he sees two options: keep things the way they are now, or hire more department heads.

"It's up to Keene," MacQueen said.

He wants to try his plan for a year, then ask the council to consider it again during next year's budget hearings. He believes in the idea: It's got to be proven to me that it can't work. And to do that, you have to try it.

For the critics, MacQueen has arguments on why his plan should be approved:

• By combining departments with similar functions under a single head, department workers will realize what MacQueen said should be a maxim: "You work for the city first, and your department second."

- The administrative structure now is unwieldy—while the new plan "would improve the ability to be sure that goals and objectives are agreed upon, and are in fact carried out down the structure," he said. Department heads "would end up being accountable for the whole thing, just as I am accountable for the whole thing now."

MacQueen's plan has been in the works for about a year.

First, he said, he listed functions the city should be doing, but isn't. He said he was surprised at how long the list was.

Then, he appointed department heads to task forces to see how these things could be accomplished. More than 10 task forces covered things that affected many city departments, such as community relations, data processing, building maintenance, emergency preparedness, and lobbying the Legislature.

About lobbying state lawmakers, MacQueen said, "When Concord's in session, we just put our arms over our heads and pray "Everything they do affects us."

Of emergency preparedness, MacQueen said it involves every department of the city, not just the fire department, to which the task is traditionally assigned.

As for the overall idea, MacQueen said he had shied away from working on restructuring in the past because he new it would be controversial.

The part of the plan meeting the most resistance would make the fire, police and inspections departments into divisions of the new public safety department.

Last week, a number of firefighters turned out for a city council committee meeting to oppose the restructuring plan. They said they were worried the move would jeopardize emergency services in Keene.

MacQueen assured them there's no plan to "cross-train" police and firefighters, so that their jobs would be interchangeable.

He also said that naming the fire chief or the police chief as head of the public safety department would not demean the one not names, nor would the promoted officials favor the departments from which they came.

MacQueen has also been criticized developing the plan in secret and announcing it after the city budget proposal had been firmed up.

He acknowledges he was secretive: "I admit that...knowing this would be controversial. I didn't want to put the city councilors in the position where they had to be pressed by the press about an ordinance they hadn't seen.

"I would also admit that, if this had been on the agenda (the Monday before the meeting where he unveiled the proposal), the councilors would have been besieged."

He said he talked with members of the council's finance committee individually, to tell them he would be adding money to the budget.

Critics are wrong, he said, when they charge that he waited until two weeks ago to announce the plan so he could slip it into the fiscal 1990 budget at the last minute.

He introduced the proposal at what seemed the logical time, MacQueen said, and the timing was not a means to limit debate.

When all is said and done, MacQueen said, he's doing what he gets paid for: "It's not my job to say (the city government) is adequate; let's live with it. My job is to continually attempt to provide improvement. When I stop doing that, they should fire me."

———

As Reported by the *Keene Evening Sentinel* June 13th, 1989:

"STORY"

Keene firefighters battle proposal

Confusion and controversy surrounding City Manager J. Patrick MacQueen's plan to reorganize the city government is mounting as the city council vote on his proposal draws near.

Most of the complaints are over MacQueen's plan to combine the fire, police and inspections services in one department; in all, 13 city departments would be reduced to eight.

Although MacQueen will only say that he's considering an existing department head for the job, many city workers and officials say that Keene Police Chief Thomas F. Powers has already been tapped for the job.

But city firefighters—who have been the most vocal critics of the plan—say they oppose the concept of the plan, not the candidate who's being considered for the job.

A public hearing on the plan is scheduled for Thursday at 7:25 p.m. in the city hall. The council will vote on the administrators' pay June 20, as part of the city's new budget.

Meanwhile, firefighters are circulating about 300 posters encouraging residents to turn out for the hearing to oppose the plan. They also are passing out petitions.

The posters show a man who is one-half police officer and one-half firefighter.

Above the figure is the statement "Public Safety Director; Don't Support a Failed Concept."

But MacQueen has said the poster is misleading. He said fire and police officers would not share duties.

The only change would be that individual department heads would report to the new administrator, instead of to MacQueen. The

administrator would also retain his existing post as department chief.

MacQueen said that it's possible some officers might be cross trained to take on other duties, though it's not something that he's seriously considering now.

"I never rule out anything," he said.

In their opposition, firefighters are warning that while an additional level of bureaucracy may work in other departments, it could jeopardize safety services.

They claim several national fire safety organizations, including the International Association of Fire Chiefs, the International Association of Firefighters, the Insurance Services Office, and the National Fire Protection Association, are against the concept of combining police and fire departments.

But MacQueen responded that the "delivery of services" would not change. His proposal is merely an administrative one.

Combining services is what that these national organizations are most likely opposed to, although the organizations are categorically opposed to anything that has a hind or possibility of consolidation, he said.

The firefighters said similar plans have failed in other New England communities, such as Augusta, Maine; Barrington, R.I.; Gardner and Portland, Maine; Springfield, Vt. and Exeter.

But officials from those cities and towns had mixed reactions about the plans, and in one case the system is still operating.

In Augusta, the Public Safety Department is alive and well, and has been for 10 years, said Paul Reitchel, who runs the police bureau there. Augusta has about 22,000 residents.

He said the Way Augusta's Public Safety Department runs is similar to what is proposed for in Keene, except Augusta has a full time Public Safety Director.

Fire and police functions are distinct, Reitchel said. But bringing them under one umbrella has advantages, he said.

"The officers are much more familiar with the inter-relation between the departments," he said. "I don't think you'll ever see a police officer fighting a fire, or a fire officer making an arrest," he said.

But at a fire, a police officer might help out with traffic, or "pull hose or help change a Scott Air Bag," Reitchel said.

Similarly, firefighters may help the police handle a bad accident by keeping people back, or helping control traffic.

"There's a vast amount of human resources that can be used," Reitchel said.

The officers wear similar uniforms, emblazoned with a patch that says "Augusta Public Safety," Reitchel said. But police officers wear a utility belt and a gun, as well as a police badge.

Firefighters' uniforms are flame-retardant, and firefighters wear a fire badge, Reitchel said.

In Barrington, the proposal was made five or six years ago, but it didn't get past the town council because of political opposition, said Town Manager Robert Schiedler.

In Gardner, the town used to have a fire and police deputy who reported to a public safety director. But because the town has only 7,000 people, town Manager Ken Kokernak said, it wads decided the town could save money by eliminating the public safety director and paying the deputies a little more to serve as chiefs.

He said the plan works better in a city the size of Augusta.

Springfield town Manager William Steele said the plan was tried in his town around 20 years ago, but failed because there was no support for it.

There was some cross-training of police and fire personnel, Steele said.

Steele, who said he's been town manager for around 10 years, said that the town is looking into bringing the departments under one roof again.

Portland had a public safety department, but it was different from what is being proposed in Keene, Josephine Burton, administrative assistant for the Portland Fire Department said.

The department combined ambulance services, airport security, and dispatching, she said. It failed because it became expensive, she said.

But the plan was successful on the islands of Casco Bay, Maine, where the fire, police and ambulance departments were combined.

There safety officers were cross-trained to work for the fire, police and ambulance departments.

Burton said the system in Casco Bay was dropped when Portland operations were revamped.

Powers used to be the public safety director in Exeter after working as police chief there.

Powers and a selectman from the town said the plan failed because it didn't have political support. They said the plan was a good idea that was not given enough time to prove its worth.

And given what Scott Collier said, Powers is a shoo-in for the Keene post.

"If this (reorganization) flies, my boss (Keene Fire Chief Robert N. Guyette) will more than likely retire," he said.

Lt. Thomas Loll of the Keene Fire Department said the wording of the plan would allow the public safety head to say "I'm going to make myself the fire chief," or "I'm going to make myself the police chief" even if he doesn't have the qualifications.

MacQueen said he did not build the plan around Powers; he has been thinking of it since he came to Keene more than 10 years ago.

"The structure (of city government) is awkward," he said.

The firefighters said they aren't necessarily opposed to the rest of MacQueen's plan.

"We're not against per se any kind of reorganization of the city government—we're not qualified to do that. But we are against putting the fire, police, inspections and city prosecutor departments all in one bowl," Loll said.

"My life is on the line every time that bell rings," firefighter Robert Meagher Sr. said.

"The man out on the street in the white hat (the fire chief) is the man who says "Get out!" or "Move them.' He's trained by the experience of seeing many different fires," Loll said.

They also said they don't like the power it would give the head of the public safety department—and to MacQueen.

"The power it would give MacQueen and the public safety director is just astronomical," Lt Allen S. Collier said.

Collier said other city employees, including most of the police officers, are opposed to the plan, although they aren't speaking out.

"It's incredible how MacQueen has spread a blanket of fear over city employees," he said.

MacQueen said he has not spoken individually to any city employees except for the fire and police chiefs.

Another concern of the firefighters is that whoever becomes the head of the public safety department might favor the bureau he runs.

"Your heart remains in the department you come from," Meagher said.

One of the departments could miss out on safety equipment when the time comes to crunch the budget, they said.

The firefighters also said the plan will lead to higher costs. The job of public safety director is too great for one person, and there will be related costs, because the director will end up hiring clerks and secretaries, they said.

A danger that is clear, they said, is that the plan, if passed, will clobber the morale of the fire department.

Meagher said that the fire department has received offers from residents to donate money. So far, Meagher said, the firefighters have dipped into a fund they raised, and have spent around $1,000 fighting the plan. Meagher said the firefighters are going to use some of that money to hire a lawyer, to help them fight the plan. "We'll be prepared in the next day or two. We'll get the questions clarified in our minds," he said.

The firefighters also said they opposed the secrecy in which MacQueen shrouded the proposal when he was working on it. They said it was an effort to ram it down the taxpayers' throats:

They said that there should be a lengthy study of the feasibility of creating a public safety department.

They said they want as many people as possible to go to the hearing—even people who want to see the public safety department formed.

"If someone can prove (the public safety department) is the thing to do, then bring them along. But with all the information, apparently (the proof) is not there," Collier said.

———

As Reported by the *Keene Evening Sentinel:*

Keene firefighters claim many oppose plan

Keene firefighters' media campaign against a planned reorganization of the city government is in full swing—complete with posters, petitions, press conferences and guest slots on radio shows.

The four firefighters in charge of the campaign—Lt. A Scott Collier, Lt. Thomas L. Loll and firefighters Alex Matson Jr. and Robert Meagher Sr. said on a radio show today they have encountered overwhelming opposition to the plan.

City Manager J. Patrick MacQueen proposed the plan, which would streamline the city government, and combine the police, fire and inspections services.

Firefighters said they oppose the plan to have those three departments report to a new public safety director.

The director would be chosen from among the heads of those departments, and city workers and officials said Police Chief Thomas F. Powers has already been tapped for the job.

The firefighters said they have gathered more than 500 signatures on petitions, and more than 200 of those signatures were gathered during the first 48 hours after the reorganization plan was announced.

Firefighters said they oppose the plan because, if adopted, it would lead to higher taxes, decreased morale and a greater risk to safety.

Meagher has said that the proposed ordinance calls for deleting the positions of deputy chiefs. But MacQueen said it would not.

The deputy chiefs would be needed in case there were no fire chief.

Firefighters have said that the public safety director, even if he is not qualified to do so, would direct firefighting operations at a fire.

While the proposal would allow for that, it probably wouldn't happen, MacQueen said.

The firefighters also have said the new public safety director—who would retain his former job as department chief—might also become the department head in the other two departments if the posts were vacated.

But MacQueen said that he would probably not approve such a move.

"My guess is one of the (deputies) would be appointed to act in the position if the vacancy were there," he said.

MacQueen has said that the plan is worth trying, to see if it can improve the delivery of city services to residents.

————————

As Reported by the *Keene Evening Sentinel* June 20th, 1989:

"STORY"

Keene budget vote is tonight

Whether and how to spend about $18.5 million will be the topic of discussion—and perhaps debate—when the Keene City Council meets tonight at 7.

Last month the city council's finance committee recommended a budget of $18,507,555, a 3.2 percent increase over current spending.

If that budget is adopted, tax bills are expected to increase 3.4 percent on average.

That means that, for every $1,000 of assessed property value, residents will pay $6.94 for the city government. School and county taxes come on top of that.

Councilors have noted that the budget increase is substantially lower than the annual inflation rate, estimated at 7.4 percent for the Boston area.

Although the meeting is open, the council will not allow comments from the public.

Their chance came last week when the council held a public hearing.

Only one resident, an official for a camp for handicapped children, attended.

One topic that may spark debate will be $4,100 slated for pay raises for two administrators who will be promoted too the positions of department heads if City

Manager J. Patrick MacQueen's proposed restructuring of city government is adopted by the council.

The plan will streamline the city's 13 departments into eight. The part of the plan that has been loudly criticized is a proposal to create a public safety department.

The director of that department would oversee the fire, inspections, and police departments. Speculation continues to mount that Thomas F. Powers, Keene police chief, will be named to the post if the restructuring passes the council.

A hearing on the proposal last Thursday night drew around 150 residents. Only one spoke in favor of the plan.

————

As Reported by the *Keene Evening Sentinel* June 27th, 1989:

"FIRE"

Fire burns Keene hayfield

A fire that started in a hay-bailing machine charred half to two-thirds of an acre of hayfield Monday before Keene firefighters brought it under control.

The fire was reported Monday at about 2:30 p.m. off Daniels Hill Road in Keene, and three Keene firefighters spent an hour putting out the blaze, said Fire Capt. Steven W. Goldsmith.

Firefighters believe the blaze started when loose pieces of hay got caught in the drive train of the machine that gathers cut hay from the field and presses it into rectangular bales.

Several bales appear to have been burning when they were ejected from the machine, Goldsmith said. About eight bales were burned in the fire.

————

As Reported by the *Keene Evening Sentinel* June 29th, 1989:

"STORY"

City hall proposal may get revised

The Keene government will likely be reorganized, but not in the manner City Manager J. Patrick MacQueen has proposed.

The city finance committee voted unanimously Wednesday night to delay making a decision on MacQueen's plan to combine several departments and name administrators to head them.

His plan has drawn a lot of criticism in recent weeks, particularly from firefighters. MacQueen's plan in part would combine the fire, police and inspections department into the public safety department.

The current police chief or fire chief would be named the new administrator, while continuing his duties as chief.

Wednesday night, the committee encouraged MacQueen to rework his plan.

"Some kind of reorganization will be forthcoming," but it probably won't include a public safety department, committee Chairman Robert E. Williams, a city councilor, said after the meeting.

The committee's vote came after Mayor Aaron A. Lipsky, Councilor Michael E.J. Blastos and several firefighters supported the plan's rejection.

"The reasons you are doing this (reorganization proposal) are absolutely appropriate. But reading this ordinance, I can't relate that to what you want to achieve," committee member Kendall W. Lane told MacQueen.

MacQueen has said the proposal would make the city government run more efficiently.

The city council does have the authority to take the issue out of committee and vote on it, even though the committee has yet to make its recommendation.

If the council rejects the plan, MacQueen would be free to draw up a new proposal.

Committee members said that some reorganization is necessary, but that MacQueen's plan is confusing.

For example, Lane said, the plan would allow for the public safety director to assume either the duties of police chief or fire chief, in addition to his duties as public safety director.

That issue has concerned firefighters enough that they have publicly campaigned against the proposal.

Although MacQueen said his plan doesn't call for cross-training officers to serve in all three departments, firefighters argued that the proposal rule allows for cross-training to occur.

Firefighters have said that such a change would crush their morale.

Finance committee members said the plan might not work because firefighters wouldn't allow it to work.

"But change usually doesn't come without pain," said committee member Dean J. Eaton, a city councilor.

Eaton said that although he supported MacQueen's plan, he has no problem with asking him to revise it, so as not to hurt the morale of city workers.

Department heads, not firefighters would see the greatest change under the plan, Eaton said.

Some heads would no longer report directly to MacQueen, but to an overseer who used to be their peer.

"Their positions and responsibilities wouldn't be changed, but the fact that they are one step away certainly would make them feel demoted," Eaton said.

Eaton expressed concern that rejection of the plan would hurt MacQueen's morale, but the city manager assured him that would not happen.

Committee member and councilor Roger T. Zerba said the structure of the city government is awkward, and that is should be reorganized.

"If we were going to set yup the city government from scratch, it certainly wouldn't be like it is now," he said.

"I think the idea of 'if it ain't broke, don't fix it,' makes no sense," he said.

With MacQueen's plan, "we have something to start with. We may have to modify it a little, but at least it's a start," he said.

Williams said he doesn't think the plan to create the post of public safety director would work.

"That part of the plan completely alienates one department, their spouses, and their supporters. It really doesn't make any sense to do anything like than," he said.

But MacQueen should get a chance to rework the plan before it is voted on, he said.

Committee member and councilor Mary F. Penny said she is opposed to the idea of a public safety director, but that reorganization might work for other departments.

Lipsky asked the committee to reject the plan.

"I think coming back with something new that doesn't include a public safety department is a good idea," he said.

After the meeting Lipsky raised a point that hasn't been explored, the potential legal problems that might arise from combining the police and inspections departments.

If the public safety director is the police chief, it would be possible for him to abuse his post, Lipsky said.

"It's important to keep civil inspections separate from criminal investigations. Inspections are not done with the intent of arresting anybody. And that's the way it should be," Lipsky said.

The public safety director would have access to information that can be gained by the inspections department, and may be tempted to use that information to make an arrest.

An abuse of power could result if the public safety director used an inspection as a pretext for an illegal search, he said.

Inspectors may enter homes to inspect, but police need search warrants, he said.

The public safety director might be confused as to whether to send building inspectors or police officers to check out a possible code violation, he said.

But Lipsky emphasized that this abuse is only a potential danger.

"I'm not saying the intent of this proposal is to use police as building inspectors any more than the intent is to use police as firefighters," he said.

Today Williams said that councilors haven't seen that as a concern; most of the attention has been focused on bringing together the police and fire departments.

"But (Lipsky) being a lawyer, he's probably delved into it a little more," he said.

Williams said the council will discuss concerns other than the firefighters' as MacQueen's revamped proposal unfolds.

Lipsky also criticized MacQueen for taking a corporate approach to city government in the case of reorganization.

"You want to run your city using good business principles, but you can't run it like a business—that's not the nature of democracy," he said.

The analogy that the city manager is to the city as a chief executive officer is to a corporation works to a point, "but it isn't complete. There's an important difference: we live in a democracy," he said.

Ultimately, the city government is answerable to "the will of the people," Lipsky said.

Committee members—and the mayor and other councilors present Wednesday night—also debated whether a committee

should be appointed to help MacQueen rework the plan.

Some residents, as well as the mayor, have suggested that a committee be formed.

"We have to oversee him, his progress, and his programs," Blastos said.

———

As Reported by the *Keene Evening Sentinel* July 1st, 1989:

"FIRE"

Fire damages Keene mobile home

Keene firefighters put out a furnace fire at 27 Schult St. Thursday night, after it had damaged the furnace, floor and electrical wiring in a mobile home owned by Bruce and Rhonda Phelps, fire officials said.

No one was injured in the incident.

Firefighters were called at 10:33 p.m., and spent more than an hour bringing the fire under control.

The fire was caused by a flooded oil burner in the furnace, fire officials said.

———

As Reported by the *Keene Evening Sentinel* July 9th, 1989:

"FIRE"

Family escaped injuries in fire

Early Morning Alarm. Fire damaged 2 motorcycles, garage and breezeway early this morning. At the home of Clesson and Cindy Jones on Liberty Lane, Keene the fire was stopped

before it spread into the Kitchen and the main house, it received some heat and smoke damage. The Joneses and their 2 children were not hurt. Photo by Michael Moore.

An early morning fire severely damaged a ranch home at 34 Liberty Lane in Keene today, but no one was hurt.

The two-alarm fire at Clesson C. and Cindy L. Jones' house was reported at 2:23 a.m. by a neighbor, Keene deputy Fire Chief George H. Shepard Jr., who later directed firefighters.

For Shepard, his work hit a little bit too close to home this time. "I don't ever want one of those again," he said.

Shepard offered this account of the fire.

He and his wife Claudette were awakened by a loud boom—either an explosion or the fire igniting. Shepard looked out the bedroom window and noticed an orange glow in the Joneses' garage across the street.

He then asked his wife to call the Jones house, unaware that another neighbor also had heard the noise, saw the fire, and warned the couple and their two daughters, who had been sleeping.

Shepard walked across the street to the house, and was relieved when he saw the family walking out the door. He then picked up a garden hose to douse the flames, but it was too late. They waited for the fire department to arrive.

"It was a futile effort to do anything because of the heavy volume of fire,' he said.

The fire caused heavy damage to the garage, where it started, and the breezeway, which connects the garage to the kitchen.

There was minor damage from the flames inside the house, but heavy heat and smoke damage.

Two motorcycles in the garage were destroyed. There were no cars parked inside.

The fire's cause is under investigation.

It was under control within about a half-hour after firefighters arrived, Shepard said.

———

As Reported by the *Keene Evening Sentinel* August 3rd, 1989:

"STORY"

Keene landlord fined $1,120 in fatal fire

The owners of a Keene apartment building where four people died in a fire January 14 have been found guilty of failing to maintain smoke detectors and fire doors.

Thomas F. and Agnes M. Yocono of Munsonville, owners of the 88 High St pleaded no-contest to charges of failure to maintain smoke detectors and failure to install self-closing devices on outside doors, where they are required to contain fire and smoke.

Judge Richard J. Talbot fined the Yoconos $1,120—$560 on each of the counts.

They also face civil suits in Cheshire County Superior Court stemming from the deaths of Carl and Lori Hina, who died of smoke inhalation during the fire.

Mr. Hina's daughter Sara, 12, and the couples' 4-month old infant daughter, Lillian, also perished, making it one of the worst fires in Keene's history.

"In February, a judge ordered attachments totaling $3.8 million against the Yoconos, pending the outcome of the civil action brought by relatives of the Hinas.

The rest of the building's tenants escaped unharmed.

Although the blaze at 88 High St. was investigated as arson, officials were never able to prove the fire had been set intentionally.

A Keene man allegedly admitted to friends that he started the fire to get revenge on a tenant there, but he was never charged.

In deciding to cite the Yoconos, fire officials determined that at least two of the building's fire detectors weren't working properly and that emergency lights, required since 1986, had never been installed. Also, lacking were automatic door-closing devices, which seal rooms from each other in case of a fire and prevent the spread of smoke and flames. The Hinas were overcome by smoke and unable to escape the building.

Although the case remains open, there is not enough evidence for the N.H. Attorney General's office to bring an arson charge.

This morning, Peter G. Beeson, an assistant N.H. attorney general, said the investigation is dormant.

"We're not anticipating criminal charges in the recent future," Beeson said, adding that the case remains open.

The attorney general's office has said the fire was started by "an open flame as a result of an incendiary act from human involvement."

Beeson said that statement does not necessarily infer that the fire was set intentionally.

A Cheshire County Superior Court grand jury heard testimony on the fire in February, but took no action.

————

As Reported by the *Keene Evening Sentinel* September 28th, 1989:

"STORY"

88 High St demolished

The Keene apartment building that burned in January, killing a family of four, has been demolished.

Thomas F. Yocono Jr. of Stoddard sold the building in late August to John H. Welch Jr. and Glenn W. Johnston for $25,000.

Four people died January 14 when fire swept through the two-story, wood-frame building at 88 High St. Many people escaped unharmed, but the fire killed Carl and Lori

Hina; Mr. Hina's 12-year-old daughter, Sara; and the couple's four-month-old daughter, Lillian.

The building was damaged, but not destroyed.

City Assessor Laurence Shaffer said the buyers bought the property for the lot, but had no intention of renovating the building.

————

As Reported by the *Keene Evening Sentinel* October 2nd, 1989:

"FIRE"

Incense blamed for fire at fraternity

Burned Out. A Keene State Fraternity brother surveys the rubble outside the Alpha Pi Tau house damaged by fire Sunday Morning. Photo by Michael Moore.

Twelve Keene State College students were forced out of the Alpha Pi Tau fraternity house early Sunday morning when burning incense ignited other materials and the building caught fire.

No one was injured. Residents of the fraternity house spend the rest of the night and Sunday night with friends, though they were to meet with KSC officials today to discuss other possible living arrangements.

The two-alarm fire at the three-story building at 6 Madison St. was reported at 1:45 a.m., and about 50 firefighters brought it under control within an hour.

Damage was substantial, though no dollar estimates were available as of this morning. The building is owned by the fraternity, not the college.

The incense had been left unattended, authorities said.

The fire started in a first-floor room and spread to part of the second floor. Much of the building received smoke and water damage, but it's considered salvageable, said Ronald S. Paradis, director of college relations.

————

As Reported by the *Keene Evening Sentinel* October 7th, 1989:

"STORY"

Keene firefighters, city negotiate union rules

Keene firefighters want to become the second group of city employees to unionize.

Firefighters voted overwhelmingly early last month to form a union, a move partly prompted by a plan to combine the police, fire and inspections departments into a single city department.

A union contract would guarantee that firefighters' health insurance and other benefits would be safe, said fire Lt. Thomas L. Loll, Jr.

"The benefits are just handed to us by the city," and could be taken away as easily if there's no guarantee, he said. "We want to protect what we have got now."

What shape the union takes is being worked out in meetings between organizers and City Manager J. Patrick MacQueen.

Once the union—organized as a local of the International Association of Firefighters—is formally approved by MacQueen and

state officials, organizers say their aim is to have a contract between the union and city government signed before the city's next budget goes into effect, July 1. "It is in its infancy stage," Loll said of the union, noting that the N.H. Public Employees Labor Relations Board must approve the union's form, once organizers and MacQueen hash out the details.

Organizers said they're unionizing to preserve their job benefits and improve communication between the fire department and city hall. They also said MacQueen's proposal to combine fire, police and inspections departments into a single city agency was a motivating factor.

Under MacQueen's plan, which has been postponed to allow the book of city laws to be revised, the three departments would have been combined into one and headed by a public safety director. Police Chief Thomas F. Powers was believed to be the leading candidate for that job.

Loll and firefighter Robert Meagher said they were impressed with how quickly firefighters organized to oppose MacQueen's plan in August. "When the chips were down with the public safety director, the firefighters stuck together like glue," Loll said.

Firefighters spend about $2,000 of their own money buying newspaper advertising, printing posters and getting legal advice on protesting the move.

MacQueen has said his main concern is that contract negotiations for fire fighters be separate from those of supervisors.

Keene's police patrolmen and supervisors are unionized, though the two groups bargain separately with city officials over contract issues.

————

As Reported by the *Keene Evening Sentinel* October 18th, 1989:

"FIRE"

School fire investigated

Police suspect two girls of starting a small fire inside the girls' bathroom Tuesday at Keene High School.

Police say they are looking into whether the girls, who are attendants, jammed wads of toilet paper in a toilet and started the morning fire.

The fire was put out by school janitors before the fire department arrived around 11:30 a.m.

The school was evacuated for 15 minutes while officials made sure the fire was out and checked the damage.

According to Keene fire Chief Robert N. Guyette, the fire was discovered by a female teacher whose classroom was beside the girls' bathroom.

The fire automatically set off the school's alarm, Guyette said.

"It looks like criminal mischief. There was nothing to burn except for toilet paper," he said.

There were no injuries and no suspects were arrested.

As Reported by the *Keene Evening Sentinel* October 31st, 1989 Halloween night. The Keene Sentinel Staff Writer Rowena Daly reported the fire in Wednesday, November 1st, 1989:

"FIRE"

Carved Pumpkin leads to fiery Halloween

On Halloween night the porches and windows around Keene glowed from the candlelight of hollowed pumpkins.

But a carved pumpkin turned out to be a haunting experience for the Nichols family, whose Adams Street home became engulfed in flames when it tipped over and set the living room and kitchen on fire.

Ernest and Diane Nichols of 61 Adams Street were celebrating Halloween with their three daughters and friend of the girls when they discovered that the front of their home was in flames.

The fire department was called at 7:43 p.m. Until firefighters arrived, neighbors from all around Adams Street jumped into action to control the flames.

According to Wayne Canwell, who lives next door to the Nichols, residents formed bucket brigades with buckets and trash cans to carry water to the fire. Another neighbor trained a garden hose on the flames.

"We had buckets, hoses; all the neighbors came running out. It was a community effort," Canwell said. "We had it out by the time the fire department arrived. They had to rip off shingles" to stop the smoldering fire.

"It took five to 10 minutes to put out and we had the hose squirting (on the flames) the whole time," Canwell said. "The sofa and chairs were destroyed. I have never seen a fire like this before."

Fire officials reported heavy damage in the living room and the kitchen, but there were no injuries.

"The pumpkin may have tipped over or heated up. It was just one of those freak accidents," said Keene Fire Captain Stevens Goldsmith.

The family stayed at a friend's house Tuesday night. None of the family members was available for comment today.

♛   *A Demon Called Fire*

As Reported by the *Keene Evening Sentinel* December 12th, 1989:

"FIRE"

Fire blamed on wiring

Faulty electrical wiring either in a wall switch or a fan switch caused a fire that left a Keene family homeless Saturday, fire officials said.

The fire started at about 8 a.m. in the family room of Gerald D. Moynihan's home on Trowbridge Road, Moynihan, his wife and son are staying with relatives until they can find housing.

The fire ripped through the house within minutes, killing the Moynihan's dog and cat, said Keene Fire Captain Steven Goldsmith.

The family had insurance, but all their belongings were destroyed in the fire, Goldsmith said.

———

Board of Engineers, Keene Fire Department 1990

L to R: Deputy Chief George Shepard, Deputy Chief Paul Crowell, Chief Robert Guyette, Call Deputy Chief Wesley Peets, Call Deputy Chief William Olmstead.

A-Shift: *Seated L to R: Lt. Thomas Loll, Capt. Stevens Goldsmith. Standing L to R: FF Mark Boynton, FF David Symonds, FF Wayne Spofford, FF Robert Campbell, FF Hank Memmesheimer, FF Chris Cram.*

B-Shift: *Seated L to R: Capt. David Osgood, Lt. Alex Matson. Standing L to R: FF Gary LaFreniere, FF Edward Hogdon, FF Art Johnson, FF Mike Driscoll, FF Harry Nelson, FF George Shepard.*

C-Shift: *Seated L to R: Lt. Scott Collier, Capt. Paul Symonds. Standing L to R: FF Jeff Morel, FF Ron Dunn, FF Robert Meghar, FF Clayton Stalker, FF Dean Ericson, FF Gary Lamoueus.*

D-Shift: *Seated L to R: Lt. Robert Crowell, Capt. Bradley Payne. Standing L to R: FF Brian Shepard, FF John Beckta, FF Scott Taylor, FF James Dubriske, FF Ron Leslie, FF Tom Chase.*

Washington Hook and Ladder Company: *From L to R Seated: FF Robert Diluzio Sr., Lt. Harry Johnson, Capt. Jack Dennis, 1st Lt. Robert Bounty. From L to R standing: 2nd Lt Harry Symonds, Clerk, FF Robert Davis, FF Robert Diluzio Jr., FF James Beauregard.*

Deluge Hose Company 1990: *Standing from L to R: FF George Potter, FF Ray Anderson, FF David Hackler, FF David Gaillardetz, FF Don Hackler, FF David Olmstead, FF Daniel Hackler, FF Barbra Johnson. Seated from L to R: FF James Seavey, Treas. FF Sanford Johnson, 1st Lt. Wayne Crowell, Capt. Edward Lamoureux, 2nd Lt. James Laurent, Clerk FF John Mullett.*

Steam and Hose Company: *From L to R: FF Philip Davis Jr., FF Michael Rochealeau, FF Charles Harris, Capt. Robert Spicher, FF Tim Mason, FF Alan Welch, FF Michael Blanchard, 2nd. Lt. Ray Hadley, FF Steve Dunchee.*

As Reported by the *Keene Evening Sentinel* December 28th, 1989:

"FIRE"

Toddler spots chimney fire at Keene home

A chimney fire at a house in Keene was spotted Wednesday by a toddler who can't talk.

But the little girl got the attention of her aunt, who alerted the homeowner and Keene firefighters.

Leslie Schnyer, who is two months short of her second birthday, noticed the flames coming from the chimney of Shirley Riley's house at 43 George St.

Leslie had been spending the day with her aunt, Lee W. Borden, who lives at 44 George St., when she became transfixed by the flames out the window.

Borden was giving Leslie her afternoon snack at about 4:45 p.m. when she saw the toddler pointing out the window.

Borden saw the flames and phoned Riley, telling her to get out of her house immediately.

"She was pointing. She can't even talk yet," Borden said of her niece.

Borden was babysitting the girl while her parents, Lona and George Schnyer, were away from their home at 38 Pako Ave.

The fire was extinguished in 45 minutes by the Keene Fire Department. Firefighters hung a narrow-bore hose, the size of a garden hose, down the chimney and sprayed water onto the fire, said firefighter Brian Shepard.

Soot and debris that had lodged in the chimney were ignited by the flames, Shepard said.

Lona and George Schnyer said they're not surprised that their daughter saw the flames. They said she's fascinated by the glow of Christmas lights and the flames from her family's fireplace.

Riley said the house suffered little damage.

1990

As Reported by the *Keene Evening Sentinel* January 3rd, 1990:

"FIRE"

Chimney fire leads to offer for back adjustments

Firefighters who doused a small chimney fire this morning at the Ridge Chiropractic Life Center on Court Street, Keene, may have missed out on an interesting offer.

David A. Ridge, a chiropractor in Keene for 25 years, said that, to repay the firefighters for putting out the blaze, he was considering offering each of them a free back adjustment. But they left before he could make the suggestion, Ridge said.

Ridge and his wife, Bonnie J. Ridge, run the office from their home.

The fire was reported to the Keene Fire Department at 8:20 a.m. by a police officer passing by in a cruiser.

Ridge said the fire was contained within the chimney, and the house remained smoke-free. He, his wife and their daughter, Dallas J. Ridge, stayed in the house during the half-hour it took to put out the blaze.

The fire was apparently caused by soot buildup in the chimney. The Ridges operate two wood stoves, and Ridge said he had meant to clean out the soot, but hadn't gotten around to it this year.

As Reported by the *Keene Evening Sentinel* January 18th, 1990:

"STORY"

Firefighters in Keene vote to unionize

Keene's firefighters have unionized, saying it enables them to bargain for wages and gives them power to fight any attempts by the city to combine their department with the police and inspections services.

Thirty one of the 34 firefighters voted in September to join the International Association of Firefighters, but waited until today to make an announcement because they had not received their charter from the union.

They are still awaiting state permission to become a bargaining unit.

Lt. Thomas L. Loll Jr. said the department unionized following an August 8 vote. The firefighters officially joined the union September 18.

There are two units—one for firefighters and one for supervisors up to captain.

The chief and his two deputies are not union member, Loll said.

"We have now got our charter. We have our cards and we've got stickers on the windows of our vehicles," Loll said.

He also said the firefighters have been reluctant to talk about the union because of bad feeling residents may have about protracted contract negotiations between the Keene teachers' union and school board. As a union, the teachers have had classroom work slow downs in the past year.

The city's police department also belongs to a union.

City Manager J. Patrick MacQueen was unavailable for comment this morning about the union, but Loll said MacQueen "doesn't seem to have any problem with it."

In a news conference this morning at the fire station, Loll said another reason to

unionize was to improve communication with city hall.

Now, if a firefighter has a complaint, he must tell the chief, who will relay the message to city officials. Union representatives will be able to take their complaints directly to city hall, he said.

Another reason to unionize is that the union will provide backing for lawyers in case a firefighter is injured.

But the major reason for joining the union was in response to MacQueen's plan to combine the fire, police and inspections department into a public safety department.

The reorganization plan, introduced in June, calls for combining 13 city departments into eight: Financing and data processing would become an administrative services department; a community services department would handle the juvenile conference program and heal and human services; and the fire, police and inspections departments would be run by a public safety administrator.

The fire department spoke out strongly against the most controversial aspect of the plan, the creation of a public safety administrator.

Now, the department heads report directly top MacQueen.

————

As Reported by the *Keene Evening Sentinel* January 22nd, 1990:

"FIRE"

Fire damages Keene home

A fire in Keene Sunday forced a family from its home on Colonial Drive.

Richard Le Beaux, of 53 Colonial Drive, and his family watched as about 30 firefighters battled a blaze that began at 3:15 p.m.

Firefighters got the fire under control quickly, but remained on the scene for four hours, to investigate the fire and make sure it was completely out, said Paul E. Crowell, Keene's deputy chief.

Crowell said that there was "extensive damage" to the Le Beaux basement and that there was smoke and water damage throughout the rest of the house. The cause of the fire is still under investigation.

————

As Reported by the *Keene Evening Sentinel* February 18th, 1990:

"FIRE"

Weekend fire burns out Keene restaurant

Clearing the Air. Two Keene firefighters use a fan to ventilate the stage restaurant on Central Square after a Sunday morning fire, no one was hurt but the restaurant suffered extensive smoke and water damage. Photo by Michael Moore.

Keene firefighters were kept busy early Sunday morning battling a blaze at a downtown restaurant, and a flood at the Colonial Theatre complex a short distance away.

Authorities won't know what caused the fire, which gutted the main dining room of The Stage Restaurant, 30 Central Square, until tests are completed at the state laboratory in Concord, Keene Police Capt. Hugh M. McClellan said late Monday afternoon.

The fire, which was reported at 1:20 a.m., did heavy smoke and water damage to the restaurant's kitchen and a smaller dining area. Owners say they will reopen the 60-year-old restaurant in about six weeks.

Nearby businesses also suffered smoke damage. Several businesses are located in the two-story building, including First Copy, Keene Gas, and the Bernina sewing machine store.

The fire was brought under control at 1:56 a.m. But firefighters were called back to the restaurant at 3:58 a.m. when a second fire ignited in the roof of the building, according to Lt. Scott Collier of the Keene fire department.

Meanwhile, a few blocks away, water seeping from a broken sprinkler pipe on the third floor of the Colonial Theatre, 95 Main St., set off an automatic alarm at 3 a.m.

Additional firefighters were sent to help contain the water, which had leaked from the third floor to the basement of the building, fire officials said.

No injuries were reported in either incident.

The restaurant fire is being investigated by a special investigations team comprised of members of both the Keene fire and police departments.

The restaurant's owners appeared in good spirits Sunday afternoon, though the fire occurred on a holiday weekend when business was expected to be brisk.

George Benik, a co-owner of the restaurant, said he didn't have an estimate of the damages.

"A lot of the antique stuff (was lost)—irreplaceable stuff, which is kind of sad," he said. "We're not closing down or anything. It's a matter of getting back on our feet.

Benik said the restaurant's tin ceiling may have kept the fire from spreading, though not in time to prevent antique lamps and woodwork in the dining room from being destroyed.

Customers who arrived at the restaurant Sunday morning for breakfast helped the Beniks carry out food and board up the front of the building, he said.

Another co-owner, Joan Benik, Benik's mother, was concerned that the restaurant's 12 employees would be out of work for several weeks, and joked that the non-smoking dining area of the restaurant was not gutted.

The new dining section was built last year when the restaurant expanded. A dinner menu was added and business had been good, George Benik said.

The Beniks said they had planned to have several specials on Monday's breakfast menu in celebration of Memorial Day, including "Red, White, and Blue Pancakes."

At the Colonial, water from the broken pipe seeped slowly through the theatre's lobby and through adjoining stores, apartments, and offices, before reaching the basement, co-owner Steven Levin said.

The business has remained open. Owners believe the pipe may have broken accidentally by someone playing.

Levin didn't know how much water had flooded the building, though he said it was "substantial."

Apartments received minimal damage.

Water dripped from chandeliers in the theater's lobby, and the gold leaf paint on the ceiling in the foyer is bubbling. Levin said the theater's owners wouldn't know the extent of the damage until the water dries.

Firefighters sopped up as much of the water as they could, and a professional cleaning service began mopping the rest Sunday afternoon.

The flood caused electrical problems with wiring in the building, Levin said, knocking out power to a cash register at Green Mountain Creamery, 97 Main St., and one of the chandeliers in the theater.

The chandelier suddenly began working later.

Water also damaged the ceiling and carpeting in the Mannequin dress shop, and books in the former Book Source store. The store recently closed.

The worst hit was Sykes Associates, Levin said. The office, which is located above the theater's outer lobby, was flooded.

————

As Reported by the *Keene Evening Sentinel:*

Stage fire cause not clear

Investigators have been unable to find out what caused a fire that ripped through The Stage Restaurant at 30 Central Square in Keene early on Sunday, May 27.

The cause might have been electrical, said Keene police Capt. Hugh M. McLellan, but because the evidence is sketchy, "we are classifying it as of undetermined cause."

The fire gutted the restaurant's main dining room and damaged part of the roof. There was smoke and water damage to the kitchen and a smaller dining area.

The 60-year-old restaurant has not yet reopened for business, but the owners, George and Eileen Benik of Keene, had said earlier they hoped to be back in business by mid-July. They could not be reached for comment today.

————

As Reported by the *Keene Evening Sentinel* February 23rd, 1990:

"FIRE"

Keene home damaged

It took Keene firefighters less than an hour Thursday to extinguish a fire that damaged the home of one of their own.

The blaze at the home of Wayne A. Spofford, 51 Stanhope Ave., was "possibly" started by a child playing with flammable materials, said Crowell, a fire captain.

The blaze started in the basement between the washer and the dryer and created thick black smoke according to Spofford.

Spofford, a firefighter and emergency medical technician for Keene, was in an ambulance returning from a call in Swanzey when he heard there was a fire at his house.

He was told that his family was unharmed.

But the ambulance headed to his house anyway.

By the time Spofford arrived, the blaze was extinguished, he said. He tried to go in, but his colleagues prevented him, because he wasn't wearing the right gear, he said.

The family didn't stay in the house Thursday night.

————

As Reported by the *Keene Evening Sentinel* February 26th, 1990:

"FIRE"

Fire damages Keene business

In Keene at about 1 a.m. Saturday, a computer printer and stack of paper were damaged in a computer room at Concord Laboratories on Kit Road.

Keene fire department Deputy Paul Crowell said the fire was extinguished quickly in the room by an automatic sprinkler system that sprayed a chemical called Haleon onto the equipment.

The fire was probably caused by an overload in the printer, he said.

————

As Reported by the *Keene Evening Sentinel* May 2nd, 1990:

"STORY"

Fatal fire prompts city inspections

Four Keene residents might not have died in a fire at a High Street apartment building last year had the structure been inspected for proper safety devices.

Though many of the tenants of the building escaped unharmed, smoke from the January 14, 1989 fire killed Carl and Lori Hina; Mr. Hina's 12-year-old daughter, Sara; and the couple's 4-month-old daughter, Lillian.

City officials late fined the building's owners, Thomas F. and Agnes M. Yocono of Munsonville, $1,200 for failing to maintain smoke detectors and failure to install self-closing devices on outside doors, where they are required to contain fire and smoke.

Keene officials hope to avoid a similar tragedy in the future through a new inspection program.

Beginning in mid-May, the city will start inspecting all multifamily buildings containing three or more apartments, said Michael B. Forest, Keene's code enforcement superintendent.

The program is aimed at ensuring that proper exit lights, smoke detectors, handrails and other safety devices are installed in public areas, he said.

Forrest estimates that roughly 370 apartment buildings in the city will be inspected during the next 18 months.

He said the last citywide inspection was done eight years ago, and that code enforcement officers will also be counting the number of apartments in each building to verify city records.

Since taking over the code enforcement job seven months ago, Forrest said he has made safety issues a top priority.

Though the inspection program is not directly related to the High Street fire, Forrest said he wished "it (an inspection) had been done two to three years ago so that wouldn't have happened." It's a "life safety measure to ensure safety of tenants."

Inspections should be done regularly, though the state does not require them, he said. "I feel very strongly it should be done regardless of what happened.

Landlords will soon receive notices in the mail telling them when their building will be inspected. It it's not convenient, they can call and reschedule the appointment.

Owners will be cited for safety violations, and will be prosecuted if problems aren't corrected, Forrest said.

In deciding to cite the Yoconos last August, city officials determined that at least two of the smoke detectors in the building weren't working properly and emergency lights, required since 1986, had never been installed. Also lacking were automatic door-closing devices, which seal rooms from each other in case of a fire and prevent the spread of smoke and flames.

The Hinas were overcome by smoke and unable to escape the building, fire officials said.

The blaze at 88 High Street was investigated as arson, but authorities were never able to prove their suspicions.

The building was razed, and the Yoconos later sold the High Street property.

Shortly after the fire a Cheshire County Superior Court judge ordered attachments worth $3.8 million against the owners of the building in court action brought by relatives of three victims.

Liens of $2 million were put on property owned by Thomas Yocono and $1 million on property owned by Agnes Yocono, in separate court cases filed by Marcelene A. Halpin, Lori's mother and Lillian's grandmother, who is administrator of the estates.

Nancy Holmes, Sara Hina's mother, had an additional $800,000 worth of attachments placed against the Yoconos on behalf of Hina's estate.

The cases were settled out of court: Halpin's in January, and Holmes' last month.

Court records about the suits are sealed, and terms of the settlements have not been divulged.

———

Saving Grace. *Apparently being freed from behind a window of the Latchis building in Keene was a religious experience for this pigeon (right), which lighted atop St. James Episcopal Church after being rescued. At left Keene Firefighter Thomas Chase performs the good deed. Photo by Steve Hooper.*

———

As Reported by the *Keene Evening Sentinel* May 12th, 1990:

"STORY"

Catalog jumps gun, combines Keene fire, police

From the looks of a badge catalog that Keene firefighters, police and city councilors are showing each other, the city has already combined the fire and police departments.

There it is, in the black and white pages of the Southern Emblem Co's catalog: "FIRE-POLICE" on the top line; KEENE," on the bottom; and the New Hampshire state seal in the middle.

And the fact that there was such a badge is either an extraordinary coincidence or a cynical conspiracy depending on who you talk to.

The reaction by city firefighters and police officers who saw the pictured badge was puzzlement and outrage. Puzzlement because they wonder who would order the badges when the two departments won't be merged unless the Keene City Council decides to do so, outrage because many in both departments are opposed to the city manager J. Patrick MacQueen's plan to join the two forces into one.

But according to the explanation of a Massachusetts company that made the original badge, most people may have to settle for the coincidence theory.

The badge—the one and only—was made three or four years before MacQueen ever proposed a city wide reorganization plan, according to Ronald O'Reilly, general manager of the B.H. Blackinton Co. of Attleboro Falls, Mass.

In a move that the city council has yet to approve—and maybe it never will—MacQueen has proposed combining 13 departments into eight, saying the changes would enable Keene's government to be more efficient in tight economic times.

Part of MacQueen's proposal calls for combining the city's fire, police and inspections department into a public safety department, to be run by a public safety administrator. Police and fire departments would continue to be run by separate chiefs, but overseen by the administrator.

Firefighters have opposed the plan, saying that one public safety administrator would not likely have the qualifications needed to run all three departments.

The fire department, which has unionized since the proposal first came up last May, mounted a massive protest last year against the restructuring plan, and have collected more than 1,700 signatures of residents also opposed to the move.

Some members of the police department have also opposed the plan.

After discussing MacQueen's reorganization plan Thursday, the city council's finance committee took no action, and probably won't until after the 1991 budget is adopted next month.

Also, after the meeting, Councilor Michael E.J. Blastos—an opponent of the reorganization plan—showed MacQueen the catalog and asked him whether he had ordered the badges.

MacQueen said he didn't order them; Police chief Thomas F. Powers also denied ordering the badges, as did city purchasing agent Robert Wyman, Blastos said.

Blastos said he called Southern Emblem Co. to see if he could find out who ordered the badges. Someone there told him that, because Southern Emblem is a distributor of badges from other companies, it didn't make the badge and wouldn't say who did.

But Blastos ordered two of the badges from Southern Emblem at his own expense.

The Sentinel learned that Southern Emblem put the badge in its August, 1989 catalog from the B.H. Blackinton Co. of Attleboro Falls, Mass., which actually made the badge, according to Southern Emblem general manager James Buck. Blackinton's general manager, Ronald O'Reilly, said that his firm gave Southern Emblem the artwork for the badge from its own September, 1987 catalog.

To prepare the catalog for publication pictures of the badges Blackinton makes were taken between 1985 and early 1986, O'Reilly said. The badge itself was probably made in 1985, he said, about four years before MacQueen proposed the reorganization plan to the city council in May, 1989.

To produce its catalog, Blackinton makes several sample badges, O'Reilly said. In doing so, it takes a sample badge style and puts lettering and artwork on it.

In this case, a secretary somehow picked out Keene, put the state's seal in the middle, and had "FIRE-POLICE" typeset on top, he said.

Both departments were picked either to see how they would look on the badge, or because many other cities have merged departments, he said.

Nobody from Keene's city government ordered the badge, no private individual ordered the badge, and there is no order by anyone for such a badge, he said.

In fact, according to Blackinton sales person Margaret Swiftak, the badge doesn't exist anymore. It was destroyed long ago, like all sample badges are after being photographed for the catalog, she said.

Swiftak said a secretary, for instance, will type "Supervisor – Fulton Fire Department" on a badge now knowing if there is a Fulton Fire Department or if there is a supervisor for it.

Another sample badge on the Southern Emblem's catalog shows one for the captain of the Cumberland, Calif., Fire Department. "Cumberland" on the badge, however, is misspelled—Cumberland,:

"It's an incredible coincidence," said O'Reilly after hearing of Keene's controversy.

After hearing the emblem company's explanation Friday, MacQueen said he wasn't surprised.

"Nothing surprises me any more," he said.

MacQueen said he wouldn't be surprised if some city workers didn't believe the explanation, opting instead to believe that someone in the city government ordered the badges.

Robert Meagher Sr., vice president of the firefighters' union, said before hearing the explanation that he and other firefighters were unhappy about the badge and wanted to know who in Keene ordered it.

"We're concerned with who's trying to put the cart before the horse," Meagher said. "It's really a shame that this happened."

After hearing Blackinton's explanation, Meagher said he still didn't believe it.

"It's too much of a coincidence, he said. "There's no way they could have just picked out Keene."

Blastos said the explanation was reasonable.

But if his order with Southern Emblem comes through, Blastos will have a memento of a plan he hopes is never realized.

————

As Reported by the *Keene Evening Sentinel* May 15th, 1990:

House fire on Hurricane Road

Fire Break – *A Keene firefighter above, adjusts his helmet as flames break through the wall of a vacant house on Hurricane Road, Keene, Monday afternoon. Left, two firefighters spray water on the blaze, which apparently started in the garage, spread to a breezeway, then to one room of the house and to a shed in the back; the rest of the house received smoke damage. No injuries were reported in the fire, which was under control in about 20 minutes. The two-story wood-frame house was owned by the late Edna Phelan, whose children had been removing her belongings gradually. Keene Fire chief Robert N. Guyette said the fire downed an electrical line and utility workers were called to turn off power. Family members told authorities that a lamp in the house was turned on by a timer, but Guyette said he didn't think that triggered the blaze. Photo by Steve Hooper.*

――――――

As Reported by the *Keene Evening Sentinel* June 4th, 1990:

Keene's public safety post is expected to raise hackles

The largest issue debated at a public hearing Tuesday may center on one of the smallest dollar items in Keene's $19.6 million budget: $4,400 for part of a plan to restructure city government.

Keene firefighters have hotly fought one aspect of the reorganization-a new public safety administrator who would oversee the city's fire, police and inspection departments—since City Manager J. Patrick MacQueen introduced it last May,

The plan's opponents believe that, if they can pressure the Keene City Council's finance committee to cut the $4,400 requested for the plan, they can undermine MacQueen's efforts.

The finance committee left the $4,400 intact two weeks ago when it slashed $37,858 from the $20 million budget MacQueen proposed in April.

Meanwhile, firefighters have revived a poster campaign against the reorganization and expect a large turnout by residents at Tuesday's hearing.

Although the hearing will also address the finance committee's controversial proposal to eliminate 17 jobs as part of a cost-cutting plan, firefighters are leaving that battle for others to fight.

"We don't like that one bit, but that's their problem," Robert Meagher, vice president of the firefighter's union said about the proposed layoffs. "We don't want to fight anybody's battles."

Firefighters unionized last year as a result of the reorganization plan.

Department members have flooded key locations throughout the city with posters, hoping residents will attend the budget hearing, Meagher said. Firefighters used a similar tactic last year to gather opposition against the restructuring.

"It's just a shame the city has to go through this a second time because one individual (MacQueen) wants his own way," Meagher said. "This is what it's boiled down to. We told them (the city council) last year they had to do the will of the taxpayers, not the will of one man,"

Firefighters say the public safety position, which they predict would be filled by Keene Police Chief Thomas F. Powers 3rd, would create another layer of bureaucracy and jeopardize safety services.

They also say the reorganization won't be cost-effective.

The committee's $19,624,871 budget would boost Keene's property-tax rate by $7.59 per $1,000 of assessed property, which means the owner of a house valued at $100,000 will pay $82 more in taxes for city services.

A total of $7,741,230 would have to be raised from property taxes—13.4 percent more than last year.

The council is not expected to vote on the reorganization until after the 1990-91 budget is adopted June 20.

MacQueen has proposed eliminating or combining 20 jobs in an attempt to restructure departments and balance the budget. The current budget deficit is $468,000 because of slumping revenues.

As Reported by the *Keene Evening Sentinel* June 7th, 1990:

"FIRE"

Keene fire 24 families burned out of apartments

Photo by Michel Moore.

At the Century Apartments complex in Keene this morning the smell of charred wood hung in the humid air.

Ernest F. Newcombe Sr., a resident burned out of his apartment by the blaze, was arranging paper bags full of clothing in the trunk of his cream-colored Cadillac.

Like other residents displaced by Wednesday afternoon's fire, he'd spent the night at the Days Inn on Key Road in Keene.

It's unclear exactly how many residents were displaced.

Newcombe said he counted himself lucky that he escaped injury and his belongings weren't damaged. His second-floor apartment was not one of the ones hardest hit.

"These six apartments are the ones that got it," he said, pointing to the building's western side.

Newcombe, who is retired, said he plans to stay with a daughter who lives in Keene, until the apartments are repaired.

"The people I feel sorry for are the ones with no homes who have nowhere to go," he said.

Other tenants rummaged through their damaged Park Avenue apartments this morning, gathering whatever belongings they could salvage.

The fire injured two Keene firefighters and left 12 families homeless, officials said.

Firefighters Wayne Crowell, 35, of 18 Speaker St., Keene, suffered a back injury; Paul Szoc, 38, of 7 River St., Keene, was burned on his back. Both men were treated at Cheshire Medical Center and released.

No other injuries were reported.

At least 24 families living in the 451 Park Ave. building spent the night at the motel.

Authorities this morning were still investigating the cause of the fire, though Keene fire officials have a "general idea of what happened, said deputy firechief Paul E. Crowell.

Crowell said the fire's cause is "not of suspicious origin."

Half the tenants were expected to move back this afternoon after the apartments were cleaned, said Peter P. Briggam, a custodian. The other 12 apartments are uninhabitable, officials said.

About 50 firefighters from the Keene, East Swanzey and Meadowood departments battled the flames for about two hours before bringing it under control.

As the fire raged Wednesday afternoon, tenants of the four-building, 96-unit complex, their families, and spectators milled outside on the lawn. Many sat stunned on picnic benches and in lawn chairs as firefighters worked on the building.

Helen Wheeler, an elderly tenant who lived on the other side of the building, was concerned about her daughter arriving late. Her voice was faint and hoarse from inhaling smoke as she worked her way out of the building.

She drank iced tea to try and clear her throat. "I thought I was going to collapse," she said.

Fire drills are conducted regularly at the complex and the tenants, most of whom are elderly, said they didn't think it was serious when the alarm system went off at 2:30 p.m.

"We have fire drills all the time. We're used to coming outside," said Lillian A. Bemis, 83, who lived in a 2nd floor apartment near where the fire was hottest.

Pale and quivering, Bemis sat on a picnic bench as family and neighbors tried to console her.

Bemis's granddaughter, Pam Russell of Keene, was at a store when she heard a report about the fire over a police scanner. She rushed to the complex.

"I knew it was her number so I came flying her," Russell said.

Bemis, who lived in the apartment complex seven years, was most concerned about oil paintings her son, Ken, had done. Ken died when he was 25, and the paintings had tremendous sentimental value, she said.

"I'm worried about those things—worried about the furniture that should go to my children," Bemis sad in a low voice.

No cost estimates of the damage this morning. Firefighters sifted through debris Wednesday night and were taking another look today.

"We haven't had a chance to really assess what we've got—without smoke," Crowell said.

Emile J. Legere, who owns the complex, was busy this morning meeting insurance agents and directing people in and out of the building.

He praised firefighters for containing the blaze3.

Tenants on Wednesday said the fire may have started in the basement.

The fire spread from the basement through the walls up to the attic on the 4th floor, said Keene Fire Chief Robert N. Guyette after the fire was under control.

Firefighters had to pull walls and ceilings apart to get at the flames, hampering efforts. For about 45 minutes, heavy smoke poured out of the side of the first floor windows, then suddenly 20 feet of flames shot through the 4th floor attic window.,

Robert and Glenna LeClair, who lived across the hall from Bemis, tried to keep their spirits up. Mrs. LeClair joked that the couple's apartment has just been redecorated with new carpeting.

"We didn't know it was bad—it got worse," she said.

One woman carried a tray with water to firefighters.

Keene fire caused by welding torch spark
Sparks from welding equipment probably caused the fire at the Century Apartment complex in Keene Wednesday that left a dozen families homeless, and did smoke damage to 12 other apartments authorities say.

A welder had worked on a furnace in the basement of the 451 Park Ave. apartment building sometime before the fire was reported, Deputy Fire Chief George H. Shepard Jr. said.

The sparks from a welder or heated chips from a machine used to grind pipes probably got into the basement wall and spread through the partitions to an attic on the 4th floor, Shepard said.

He said the investigation has been closed.

A different repairman was working in the basement when the fire was reported at about 2:30 p.m. Tenants interviewed at the scene said a welder had been working on the furnace.

The fire gutted six apartments and left six others badly damaged. Displaced tenants won't be able to move back until repairs are completed in about two months.

Twelve other families returned to their smoky apartments Thursday afternoon.

None of the tenants were allowed to stay in their apartments Wednesday night.

The fire was hard to get at because it was in the partitions. Keene firefighters remained at the complex overnight in case the fire rekindled.

Owner Emile Legere provided dinner, overnight lodging and breakfast for 20 of the tenants Wednesday night, said Robert L. Greene, general manager of the Days Inn on Key Road.

————

As Reported by the *Keene Evening Sentinel* June 27th, 1990;

"FIRE"

Stage fire cause not clear

Investigators have been unable to find out what caused a fire that ripped through The Stage Restaurant at 30 Central Square in Keene early on Sunday, May 27.

The cause might have been electrical, said Keene police Capt. Hugh M. McLellan, but because the evidence is sketchy, "we are classifying it as of undetermined cause."

The fire gutted the restaurant's main dining room and damaged part of the roof. There was smoke and water damage to the kitchen and a smaller dining area.

The 60-year-old restaurant has not yet reopened for business, but the owners, George and Eileen Benik of Keene, had said earlier they hoped to be back in business by mid-July. They could not be reached for comment today.

————

As Reported by the *Keene Evening Sentinel* July 19th, 1990:

"STORY"

Keene's reorganization excludes fire, police

Keene City Manager J. Patrick MacQueen's proposal to create a public safety director to oversee Keene's police, fire, and inspection departments is dead, and controversy over restructuring city government is, for the most, dead as well.

The Keene City Council's Finance Committee ended a yearlong debate Wednesday when it unanimously rejected the public safety job. That means the city's police and fire departments won't be grouped together. A majority of the committee said they still support changing city government in some way.

More than likely, the fire and inspections departments will be grouped together if a reorganization plan is approved, and police would be separate, committee members said.

While firefighters don't like what MacQueen want to do, the move to keep the police and fire departments separate, appears to have pacified them somewhat.

Firefighters could support being grouped with inspections if it came down to that, said Lt. Scott Collier of the Keene Fire Department.

Still, Collier said, changing the way the city runs is not needed.

"This structure has been in existence 12 to 13 years. If it was all that bad—why not 12 years ago when MacQueen was hired," Collier said.

Lt. Thomas L. Loll, president of Firefighters Local 3265, said the reorganization plan won't be forgotten.

"We're going to still watchdog the plan," Loll said. "We don't want it with another name on it."

Defeating MacQueen's efforts to lump the police and fire departments together "was the main target" of the firefighters' loud opposition, Loll said.

"We feel good about what happened last night," he said.

If adopted, the restructuring probably wouldn't take effect until next year because there's no money in the city's 1990-91 budget–which started July 1—for salaries.

Last May, MacQueen proposed consolidating 14 city departments into eight, and reducing the number of department heads who would report directly to him.

The committee Wednesday delayed making a recommendation to the city council because city codes are still being updated.

In their opposition, firefighters warned that while another level of bureaucracy may work in other departments, it could jeopardize safety services.

MacQueen offered the alternative restructuring plan to consolidate 14 departments into four, five or six, depending on whether police and fire are separate, and how other departments are grouped.

During a recess, MacQueen acknowledged that the alternative plan was a political maneuver to muster support for some kind of reorganization.

Nonetheless, giving up on the police and fire consolidation is "a step backwards for the fire and police departments," MacQueen said.

During an interview last month, MacQueen said opponents were confused. He said the new public safety post would have merely been administrative. The fire and police chiefs would have continued to run their departments.

He said that's different from a public safety officer—a person who is cross-trained to handle both fire and police duties.

Councilor Kendall W. Lane said after the 2 ½-hour meeting that a majority of the committee favored MacQueen's original plan with the public safety director, but the proposal would have been defeated by the 15-member city council.

At least two city councilors, Mayor Aaron A. Lipsky, and Keene firefighters, who vehemently fought the public safety post, said no reorganization plan would work. It would be expensive and cause internal problems for department heads.

"I'm afraid it's going to cost more money in the long-run and we will need to hire more people," said Councilor Mary F. Penny, a committee member.

Lipsky said the new administrator would be asked to make judgment calls and decide which departments in his group receive priority. Therefore, more people would have to be hired.

"In time of tight budgets, we can't afford a series of assistant managers," Lipsky said. "There are a lot of problems when you ask existing personnel to wear two hats."

The city council eliminated 17 positions in the 1990-91 budget, prompted by a $468,000 shortfall Keene's government experienced in the last fiscal year, which ended June 30.

Councilor Michael E.J. Blastos likened the city's current setup to a large corporation with one chief officer—MacQueen—and 14 vice presidents.

"It's not an unwieldy situation. It's a good separation of powers," Blastos said.

However, both Lane and Councilor Jeanie M. Sy said departments aren't coordinated well now and conflicts arise.

Though the new administrators' job will be more time consuming and it may be difficult to run more than one department, Lane said MacQueen is already doing that with 14.

As far as Lan and MacQueen are concerned, they both said that spending money to hire personnel is up to the city council—not MacQueen—to decide.

The committee will discuss the restructuring at its July 26 meeting.

————

As Reported by the *Keene Evening Sentinel* July 19th, 1990:

"STORY"

Propane tank fire exercise

It's not often that firefighters stand around and watch someone start a fire that they'll have to end up battling.

But Tuesday night, July 24, in a training session held at Keene State College's Science Center, more than 100 firefighters are expected to stand by while a fire is ignited in a 500-gallon propane gas tank.

Then, in shifts, they'll practice what they learned in a briefing session—the proper ways of controlling such fires.

The public is invited to come and watch the firefighters at work.

The school is being sponsored by the Keene Fire Department and the Propane Gas Association of New England. It's being conducted by the Ranger Insurance Co. of Houston, Texas.

A team of Ranger's safety technicians will provide instruction, working from a specially equipped van brought in from Oklahoma.

The fuel being burned will be provided by six local propane companies.

The session starts at about 7 p.m. Tuesday with a safety film and brief lecture on the proper methods of dealing with propane fires.

Then the group will move to an open area where the tank will be ignited. In teams of five, and under the close supervision of the Ranger safety personnel, the firefighters will then go into the fire behind water protection to control the fire by shutting off the safety valve.

————

As Reported by the *Keene Evening Sentinel* August 18th, 1990:

"STORY"

Final call for fire truck
Part of history is for sale

For sale: Sporty open-air vehicle, seats two. Low mileage, like new. 5 speeds, 12 cylinders. Fire-engine red, comes with 8 ladders. Must be seen.

Age before beauty, yes; but with Keene's 1946 Seagrave ladder truck, you can get both at the same time.

That's because the vintage truck, which made its last run three years ago, is for sale. Time has finally caught up with the truck's 75-foot hydraulic ladder, which was state-of-the-art when built 44 years ago. Today, the ladder is too old to be certified, and the truck's sleek lines won't help it fight fires.

So what was once the fastest truck on the force has responded to its last alarm. It now reposes at the far end of Keene's public works garage on Lower Main Street, mothballed among snowplows and other road equipment. It sits alone, covered with a thin layer of dust, its career with the city fast nearing an end.

"It's worth something to someone, but not in the fire department," said Keene Fire Chief Robert N. Guyette, who paid the Seagrave one last visit this week.

Bids to buy the truck will be accepted until next Thursday, when they'll be opened at 2 p.m. The lowest acceptable bid is $3,000. Whoever gets it has 10 days to take if off city property.

Not to say the truck's forgotten. As of Friday, the city's purchasing office had sent out 35 bid packages, mostly to other area fire departments.

The dark red truck has seen a lot of Keene history. It first shows up in the fire station's yellowing scrap books in photos taken just after World War II, when it was delivered brand new. Black-and-white snapshots tell the story; Crowds watch in Central Square as the Seagrave shows off its amazing aerial ladder. Pointed straight up, it rises higher than the buildings, Firefighters thrill spectators by climbing up and down.

Retired Keene Fire Chief Walter R. Messer remembers the truck's 1946 price tag: $17,500, what was then a princely sum.

"But they paid cash, so they got it for $17,200," he recalls.

Messer was chief from 1946 to 1971.

The truck then went to work. Some highlights of its four decades of faithful service: fighting the 1956 blaze which destroyed part of Keene's Sprague & Carlton furniture factory; playing the lead role in fighting in fighting the Elm City Grain fire on Railroad Street in the late 1960's; helping put out the fire which hit the fourth floor of Whitney Bros. in the early 16980's.

Messer, now 84, says the truck's finest moment came early on in the 1950's when it responded to a smoky blaze at a bowling alley on Mechanic Street. Six people were trapped in the building, but were rescued by firemen over the truck's ladder.

Messer said the Seagrave paid for itself that night long ago when several of those rescued were employed as pinboys.

Pages turn in the scrapbook. Years pass, crowds gather around other new trucks. In clippings, the Seagrave fades into the background, parked in the station behind posed shots, or in blurred photos taken at fires, doing what it was born to do.

Over the years, the truck earned the respect of firefighters; it's been on the force longer than any member of today's crew. In fact, it's older than many of them.

"If it could talk, it could tell you some stories," said Keene firefighter David E. Symonds, leafing through scrapbook pages.

Not to sentimentalize the Seagrave; for fighting fires, the truck was never perfect.

Guyette groans as he gets in the driver's seat one last time. As usual, he's caught his hip on the square door frame. It smarts.

"It was always a killer to get in," he says, shifting his position. The steering wheel is also too high.

It's easy to see why Guyette doesn't mind seeing the truck go. He said he'd be surprised to see "any bids higher than $3,001."

"I've never had any feeling for this truck," he says.

It's seen human error, too. Though it's never been in any accidents, its side bear the marks of several close encounters with the fire station's doorways.

Guyette explains: "Sometimes they cut the corner short and took a couple bricks out." But give the truck credit—it's stronger than the fire house.

That's one thing Guyette says he'll miss about the Seagrave: the metal. It's build like a battleship. Today's fire engines "are tin cans compared to what that is," he says, running his fingers along it.

And despite the dust, it's clean; there's not a speck of rust on it.

How fast can it go? Fire trucks aren't supposed to exceed 55 mph, but Guyette remembers the Seagrave once doing over 60 mph when he followed it to Bellows Falls on a call years ago.

Guyette says it still runs, but the 12-cylinder engine was always one of the toughest things to work on that the fire department owned. The transmission was rebuilt at some point—no one's really sure when—but the truck's small water tank needs replacing.

Keene's new Ladder 2, an American LeFrance 1972. This new truck replaced the '49 Seagrave ladder.

The truck comes with some extras; a small unrated fire pump which can supply water to a booster pump if needed. Bid documents list the condition of the pump as "unknown." A grab bag of tools and assorted bric-a-brac comes with the truck, and so do the eight wooden standing ladders. They range from 8 to 35 feet in length.

For good measure, a parts list is thrown in, too.

One thing the truck doesn't have is a nickname. Messer says that's not unusual in Keene; the only piece of equipment he recalls that had a name was a tanker in use during the 1930's which firefighters somehow dubbed "Rosie"

Of you buy the Seagrave, don't plan on using it to commute to work. Not only is the cab open to the weather, the truck gets only about 4 miles per gallon—of leaded gas. And if you find leaded gas, get out the wallet; the tank holds 50 gallons.

And then there's finding a place to park.

As Reported by the *Keene Evening Sentinel* October 16th, 1990:

"FIRE"

Keene fire out in 30 minutes

A fire damaged the upstairs apartment of a two-story apartment house at 209 Roxbury St. in Keene Monday evening, but no one was hurt.

The fire, reported at 6:25 p.m., apparently started in the living room of Peter Smith's apartment, said Keene Fire Lt. Robert Crowell. It destroyed the contents of the living room and caused beat and smoke damage to the rest of the apartment.

Officials are still investigating the fire's cause, Crowell said.

Air Time. David Gaillardetz, an on call Keene Firefighter, removes his self-contained breathing gear after the fire at 209 Roxbury St., was brought under control. Photo by Steve Hooper.

No one was in Smith's apartment when the fire broke out, though a woman who lives in a ground-floor apartment was home. A neighbor apparently reported the fire, Crowell said.

The house is only about half a mile from Keene's fire station on Vernon Street, and firefighters arrived within moments after the alarm sounded. The fire was "pretty well out" within about 30 minutes, and the last truck was back in the station by 9:19 p.m., Crowell said.

Part of Roxbury Street was closed for about two hours while firefighters clustered around the house.

———

As Reported by the *Keene Evening Sentinel* November 1st, 1990:

"FIRE"

Keene house fire doused

Fire damaged a single-family home at 28 Greenwood Ave. this morning before Keene firefighters halted the flames.

The fire at the home of Robert and Joyce Schoefmann was reported at about 10:15 a.m. The Schoefmanns were not home at the time.

A neighbor, David Lewcon, said he was doing paperwork at home when someone banged on his front door and said there was a fire next door. He called the fire department.

Then, Lewcon said, he and the other man went outside, saw smoke and flames coming out of a broken picture window in the Schoefmanns home, and tried to put out the fire with garden hoses.

Lewcon said that, when smoke began coming from the roof, it was obvious that the fire was worse than he had originally thought.

The Schoefmanns had recently added a second story to the house and the interior work was not yet finished, Lewcon said.

The cause of the fire and extent of damages were undetermined late this morning.

————

As Reported by the *Keene Evening Sentinel* December 10th, 1990:

"STORY"

Arrest in January 2011 made by Cold case NH Atty Generals office

1989 Keene fire deaths considered murder

Report: Family of four killed in High Street fire

The deaths of four family members in a Keene fire in January 1989 are considered homicides by N.H. State Police, though no charges have been brought and the blazes cause was never openly called arson.

The 88 High St. fire on January 14, 1989, killed Carl R. Hina, 49, his wife, Lori M. Hina,. 26,; his daughter by a previous marriage, Sara J. Hina, 12; and Lillian M. Hina, age 4 months.

This is the first time that investigators have said the fire was set intentionally, and that they consider the deaths to be murders.

The ruling on the Hina's deaths came in an annual statewide crime report for 1989 issued by N.H. State Police.

A Keene police captain who helped investigate the deaths said this morning he was surprised that the state considered them to be homicides.

Capt. Hugh M. McLellan said the High Street case is still open.

In terms of criminal wrongdoing in connection with the fire, "we never could prove anything," McLellan said. "I don't know why (the state) is calling it (homicide). That's not what we called it."

A Cheshire County Superior Court grand jury heard evidence on the fire in February 1989, but was not asked to return an indictment—a judgment that the prosecution had amassed enough evidence to warrant a trial.

A N.H, Fire Marshal's report said the fire resulted from an open flame, "an incendiary act from human involvement," and tenants who survived the fire reported that a former tenant admitted starting the fire for revenge.

However, "the fact that the guy had made statements—we could not substantiate them," McLellan said.

Despite the sworn affidavits from tenants and the fire marshal's ruling, no charges are pending.

Overall, the report said major crimes in New Hampshire increased 7.7 percent last year, with murders and reported rapes showing the biggest jump.

Cheshire County logged an increase of less than 1 percent.

————

1991

As Reported by the *Keene Evening Sentinel* February 4th, 1991:

"FIRE"

KSC dormitory evacuated

Students were evacuated from the Fiske Hall dormitory on the Keene State College campus early Monday morning after a small fire started in the basement, said Keene fire officials.

An automatic sprinkler system doused the fire, according to Deputy Chief George H. Shepard, Jr. of the Keene Fire Department. But following procedure the dormitory was evacuated as a result of the 2 a.m. fire, Shepard said.

He attributed the fire to "smoking materials" that were placed in a cardboard box in the basement. Students returned to their rooms within a half hour, and "everything was back to normal" in an hour, Shepard said.

————

As Reported by the *Keene Evening Sentinel* February 8th, 1991:

"FIRE"

Arrest near in KSC fire

A person suspected of setting a fire Monday in the basement of Keene State College's Fiske Hall dormitory is expected to be arrested in a couple of days, according to Keene police.

If not for a new sprinkler system in the dormitory, "the fire could have been disastrous," Keene Police Capt. Hugh McLellan said. More than 200 students live in the dormitory. The sprinkler system put out the fire in a matter of minutes, he said, spraying water only in the room where the fire started.

————

As Reported by the *Keene Evening Sentinel* February 23rd, 1991:

"FIRE"

Former KSC student faces arson charges

A former Keene State College student remains free after his initial court hearing this week into charges that he lit a February 2 fire at Fiske Hall.

Vernon L. Townsend Jr., a 20-year-old resident of Amherst, was ordered to reappear in Keene District Court on March 1. He is charged with arson in the February 2 incident, which forced college officials to evacuate the dormitory after a fire was started in cardboard in the basement.

No one was injured, and damage was minimal, said Ronald S Paradis, director of college relations for Keene State College.

Paradis said on Friday that Townsend, who was a junior, is no longer enrolled at Keene State. But college regulations prevent him from saying whether the student was expelled or dropped out, Paradis said.

The incident involving the fire in Fiske Hall will be or has been dealt with on campus through the judicial process," Paradis said. The maximum penalty for arson is expulsion from the college, he said.

———————

As Reported by the *Keene Evening Sentinel* April 12th, 1991:

"FIRE"

Fire truck bottoms out in Roxbury
Keene truck collapses bridge on way to fire

Photos by Steve Goldsmith.

"It just went crack, bang and down in went," said Keene Fire Capt. David B. Osgood, rubbing his sore jaw early Thursday evening.

Down it went, right through cracking pine timbers into Otter Brook—a $123,000

Keene fire engine heading for a burning truck at the former Pinnacle Mountain Ski Area in Roxbury. The truck dropped about a dozen feet, landing on the rubble of the beams.

Osgood said he and four other Keene firefighters got out and checked under the bridge to make sure it was sturdy enough before driving over it around 6 p.m. Thursday.

Then Osgood got back in the truck and headed across the bridge, making it halfway before things gave way.

From there, it was all down stream.

Except for the bruised jaw, Osgood apparently escaped serious injury.

Although the fire truck's predicament looked bad, a pickup truck owned by tenants at the hillside house probably received more damage, said Keene Fire Chief Robert N. Guyette.

The pickup truck was completely burned.

The bridge is not posted with a weight limit. "It's a 15-ton-truck on a 14-ton bridge, I guess" he said.

"I took a chance and lost," Osgood said. "I feel like a fool, believe me.

This morning, while about two dozen onlookers gazed and took pictures of the sight, Guyette and other fire officials waited at the former ski area parking lot for a crane from Yankee Crane Service Inc. of Merrimack.

By 11 o'clock this morning, the crane was still lumbering its way toward Roxbury to yank Engine No. 3 out of the brook.

Guyette said he was confident that the fire engine could be repaired and put back into service. The truck was insured. Just who will pay to repair the bridge has not been decided.

"Hopefully it's not hurt too bad," Guyette said. Hopefully we can get it out without doing more damage with the crane… All I want to do is get it out of there.

Before being hoisted out of the brook this morning, only a small corner of the rear bumper was actually in the water. The truck appeared to be resting precariously on fallen beams in the water and partially supported by its front end on the intact half of the bridge.

The right, rear corner of the engine's bumper was bent upwards, but other than that, there were few visible signs of damage.

The truck didn't appear to be leaking oil or fuel, and Guyette said he doubted there were any leaks.

Fire officials were also faced with another problem this morning: How do they get a fire deputy's car back with it stuck on the other side of the brook.

Deputy Paul Crowell had driven the car across the bridge just ahead of Engine No. 3 Thursday.

This morning, a group of firefighters drove a truck across the nearest bridge, almost a mile downstream at the Otter Brook recreation area, and were trying to drive up a wooded road parallel to the brook. Firefighters hoped they could bring the deputy's car back the same way.

After the fire engine fell through the bridge Thursday, Osgood got out and climbed to the "safe" side of the bridge.

The lower part of his firefighting outfit sopping wet, Osgood shook his head, rubbed his bruised jaw and reflected on the accident and his decision to drive across.

"Once you make a decision to cross, you go," he said "I can't wait 'til I can look back at this, I feel so stupid.

Guyette said that a crew of two firefighters stayed in the parking lot all night to watch the fire truck and be ready to cross the stream in case of a fire or medical emergency at the house.

Roxbury, which has no fire department, is covered by Keene.

It was unclear this morning who rents the house on the former ski slopes at Pinnacle Mountain. The name of the owner was also unclear.

The bridge to the former Pinnacle Mountain Ski Area also received notoriety a couple years ago when a replica of an old-fashioned style covered bridge was built on top of it. After the conversion, high winds knocked the covered portion of the bridge portion into the brook.

The rubble from the covered structure was taken out of the brook and the bridge was left without the cover.

————————

There's no place like home Keene truck is back on dry land after night in Otter Brook

After spending a night in the drink, a 15-ton fire truck was hoisted out of Otter Brook in Roxbury Friday afternoon and driven back to its quarters in the Keene fire station.

Now, the brook separates the residents of a house and their car; they're wondering how they'll get to work and school.

At about 6 p.m. Thursday, Keene's engine No. 3 was on its way to extinguish a burning pickup truck at the former Pinnacle Mountain Ski Area, when the fire engine crashed through the bridge's pine timbers and into Otter Brook.

After looking at the bridge's timber beams, the driver of the fire truck, Keene Fire Capt. David B. Osgood, thought the private bridge was strong enough to hold the weight. It wasn't.

Osgood, who was alone in the truck when it crossed, was bruised, but not seriously injured.

Meanwhile, David Joslyn's truck burned to a crisp outside the hillside home he rents with Debra Fournier.

The $123,000 fire truck that Keene bought two years ago remained with one end on a concrete bridge abutment and the other suspended on wooden rubble in the brook until 2:05 Friday afternoon.

That's when a giant crane hoisted the fire truck out of the brook and back onto the parking lot. The crane, owned by Yankee Crane Service, a division of the Hallamore Corp. of Holbrook, Mass., came from a job site in Merrimack.

Keene Fire Deputy Paul Crowell's car, which made it across the bridge before it collapsed, was also carried over the brook.

Joslyn's red Chevrolet station wagon was next.

While the crane operators prepared to lift the fire engine, dozens of spectators watched from the parking lot off Route 9. Many took pictures and filmed the event with video cameras.

During the operation, the tenants and their friends on the other side of the brook played loud music and watched from a porch.

Debra Fournier said she was frustrated that she, Joslyn and her young son were now stranded on the opposite side of the brook.

She said she asked a Keene fire official to let the crane stay longer and take some of the timbers out of the brook and set them across the abutments to make a walking bridge. The official told her the crane was all done, she said.

"They left us stranded," she said.

Employees of the property owner, Landis Atkinson of Stoddard, used some of the fallen timbers to create a makeshift bridge just over the water, Fournier said.

"But I would never go across it," she said. "Maybe a grown man would, but I wouldn't dare cross it."

Fournier also said that before the fire truck started crossing the bridge, Deputy Crowell asked her as she was half way up the driveway whether it was safe for the engine to cross.

She said she didn't know.

Fournier said a firefighter told her after the accident that firefighters disputed whether to cross.

Keene Fire Deputy George Shepard said there was discussion about crossing the bridge, but there was no dispute.

Damage to the fire truck, Shepard said, appeared to be mostly to the body. He said there was probably no damage to the frame.

The truck is at the Keene fire station but out of service until repairs can be made, he said.

————

As Reported by the *Keene Evening Sentinel* April 19th, 1991:

"STORY"

Keene State racks up big false-alarm bill
Students pay for pranks, but college refuses to pay $27,569 bill for city fire services

Every time a mischievous college student pulls a fire alarm as a prank, the Keene Fire Department responds to it. And, the college gets a $250 bill.

The college has been collecting the fines, from students, but it has refused to pay its now hefty $27,569 bill to the city.

college officials say they have no intention of paying the city, and have no legal obligation to do so—but will also continue to charge students.

The city government acknowledges the college may be right. It's not legally bound to pay, and Keene may have to write off the costs. Ronald S. Paradis, director of college relations, says the school's lawyer has argued that a city agency can't fine a state agency such as the college.

Keene City Manager J. Patrick MacQueen says that's true.

But the bills keep coming in for the average 10 false alarms per year at the college.

Jay Kahn, KSC's vice president for financing and planning, said the college fines students as a deterrent to false alarms, not to pay the city for responding to a false alarm.

Kahn said the fines are used to improve the college's fire safety program, and to install fire boxes that hinder vandalism.

Kahn said the city fines and college payments—if made—have been very sporadic over the past few years, mainly because the college didn't have a clear policy on how to deal with false alarms. Now, he said, it does.

The clarification was prompted two years ago when the city realized it hadn't billed the college for four years and on top of that, had raised the fine from $100 per call to $250. The college sought legal advice at that point, Kahn said.

The college isn't billed—nor are students fined—when the alarms are triggered accidentally by such things as heat, dust or cigarette smoke.

Kahn said he was unsure how much students were being billed per year.

And even though the city government is well aware that the college won't pay them, the bills keep coming.

"We hope the city council will reconsider the issue in the future," Kahn said, "and elect to stop billing us.

————

As Reported by the *Keene Evening Sentinel* May 9th, 1991:

"STORY"

Keene contract talks could take some time
New unions may prolong negotiations

With five separate union contracts to negotiate during the next seven weeks, it appears unlikely that pay raises for Keene city employees will be settled by June 30, when a new budget is supposed to be set.

Two unions have yet to put proposals on the table, and the city's top negotiator—City Manager J. Patrick MacQueen—said contract talks will take more time this year because the city has three new unions.

The city councilor in charge of budget hearings said "it doesn't really seem fair" not to give a pay hike to city workers when Keene teachers received a 5 percent raise earlier this week.

Things will be different and perhaps more difficult to address this year when it comes to settling the issue of pay raises because of new unions.

Last year, public works employees, firefighters and their supervisors voted to form a union. Along with police who were already unionized, that means approximately 44 percent of the city's 225-member work force is represented by unions.

Their wages and benefits will be decided at a bargaining table, rather than a city council meeting.

So far progress has been slow, according to union officials.

The public works union—whose workers average $10 an hour—has sat down several times with city officials, but the union representing firefighters and supervisors has yet to offer a proposal.

The police department's union president said despite some progress in negotiations, it's unlikely police will have a contract by June 30, unless the unexpected occurs.

"A bolt of lightening could come out of the sky and change everything," said Keene police Patrolman Timothy K. Peloquin, president of Chapter 66 of the State Employees Association of New Hampshire, which represents police.

This was the final year of a three-year contract that provided average annual raises of 8.3 percent to police officers and their supervisors.

Patrol officers now average $25,000 a year; police sergeants average $32,000.

Negotiators from both sides declined to talk publicly about specific wage requests.

For the other unions, which have to negotiate a contract from the ground up, it's likely to be slow going. Basic language covering work rules and procedures must be agreed upon, said MacQueen and union officials.

Making things more difficult is the poor economy, said Thomas L Loll Jr., president of the Professional Firefighters of Keene, Local No. 3265.

Firefighters average $25,000 while supervisors average $29,500 annually.

MacQueen, who union presidents say is a fair negotiator, will not characterize the talks. Nor would he stake out his strategy on raises, or say whether he is even seeking raises in his proposed budget.

But Robert E. Williams, the chairman of the council's finance committee, earlier this week signaled his willingness to consider pay increases.

Williams noted that Keene residents approved average pay hikes of 5 percent for teachers.

Considering that, "it doesn't really seem fair to tell city employees "this is a tough budget year, we're not going to give you a raise," Williams said.

Where money will come from for such a raise is another matter.

MacQueen has declined to say if his proposed $20.9 million overall budget contains money for across-the-board raises. Raises for union employees are negotiated behind closed doors, MacQueen said.

And he will not talk about raises for non-union workers.

————

As Reported by the *Keene Evening Sentinel* June 25th, 1991:

"STORY"

Keene firefighters at impasse in contract talks

More headaches have popped up in the Keene city government's relationships with employee unions.

The city has been found guilty of an unfair labor practice, and two more union chapters have declared an impasse in contract talks with the city.

The latest unions to ask for a mediator represent Keene firefighters and fire supervisors, and their lead negotiator said Monday that bargaining is going nowhere.

"A first contract, it's tough to get an agreement," said Glenn R. Milner, a Concord lawyer representing both the firefighters and fire supervisors. The supervisors' talks stalled last week, he said.

"We've met four times. After four times, you get a feeling whether you'll come to an agreement or not," Minor said after Monday's bargaining session on behalf of line firefighters.

The firefighter's chapters and a union for public works employees are negotiating a contract for the first time.

Already, unions representing police officers and police supervisors have declared an impasse and sought mediation.

That leaves only the public works union at the bargaining table without outside help.

"At this point, we are still having productive negotiations," said Harriett P. Spencer, a negotiator with the state chapter of the American Federation of State, County and Municipal Employees, which represents 59 public works employees in Keene.

So far, the city has held 14 negotiating sessions with public works employees, Spencer said. He said the union approached the talks with a "realistic outlook" on the economic and political problems facing Keene, he said.

The firefighters' call for a mediator came as a state board ruled the city government acted improperly in March, when it forced changes in a health insurance plan for fighters.

The N.H. Public Employee Labor Relations Board has ordered the city to abandon that plan, and discuss health coverage at the bargaining table.

"We aren't objecting to the plan itself. Our objection was the city forced it on us," Milner said.

City Manager J. Patrick MacQueen would not comment on the contract talks or the unfair labor ruling. Negotiators agreed at the beginning of talks not to divulge what goes on in closed-door negotiations, MacQueen said.

Mayor Aaron A. Lipsky is on a three-week vacation and could not be reached for comment.

According to the state labor ruling, the insurance changes for firefighters involved a new clause in an existing Blue-Cross-Blue Shield package that remains in effect for other city employees.

The change: a move to a managed-care plan, intended to hold down medical costs by requiring second opinions and approvals before most medical procedures begin.

City officials encouraged firefighters to accept the plan in early January. The firefighters refused, but the city adopted it anyway in March.

"It's kind of like: "What do you think of this guys? And we don't care anyways," Milner said of the city negotiators' attitude.

Under state law, issues such as pay and insurance are subject to negotiation with union members.

However, little headway seems to be occurring at the negotiating table.

Twenty-seven points still have to be settled between firefighters and the city, Milner said. Only four have been resolved.

The outstanding issues deal with management rights, grievance procedures, disciplinary hearings, incentives, education, pay and benefits, he said.

In proposing their contract, firefighters are drawing from language in Keene police and teachers contracts and from the city employee handbook, Milner said.

Because police have been unionized for years, it's not likely firefighters' pay and benefits will match police "dollar for dollar" in this contract he said.

––––––––

As Reported by the *Keene Evening Sentinel* June 27th, 1991:

"STORY"

Keene, Roxbury, owner trying to sort out bridge collapse

A wooden bridge over Otter Brook in Roxbury, which buckled and collapsed under the weight of a 15-ton Keene fire truck in April, has meant nothing but troubled waters between that town and Keene.

They're arguing about who will repair the structure, and why Keene responds to Roxbury fires in the first place.

The bridge collapse has also been a problem for the people who live on the other side of the bridge off Route 9 at the former Pinnacle Mountain ski area. They're forced to leave their cars on the road side of the brook, and carry food and other necessities across a narrow footbridge.

The homemade bridge fell into the water April 11, as Keene firefighters were on their way to extinguish a burning passenger truck on the other side of the brook.

A red-faced firefighter admitted his decision to drive the massive truck over the

☙   *A Demon Called Fire*

bridge was a bad one. He said he felt mighty stupid.

Anyway, the fire engine is being repaired—to the tune of about $15,000. The bruised ego of the firefighter has just about healed, and the jokes about his misfortune have died down.

Now, Keene City Manager J. Patrick MacQueen says it's up to the person who owns the land to replace the bridge.

That's the landlord's responsibility, as far as I'm concerned," MacQueen said. "It's certainly not the city's bridge.

No way, said the landlord. "We're not replacing the bridge right now because of the cost," said Landis W. Atkinson, secretary-treasurer of Bald Mountain Park Inc., which owns the property.

Struggling in these troubled waters is Debra Fournier and her 11-year-old son. They live in a cabin at Pinnacle Mountain, and the bridge leading to that cabin was the one that collapsed April 11.

So, ever since, she's been lugging groceries across a footbridge and up a steep hill to her door. It's cold showers for her and her son since she can't fill propane tanks located across the brook.

And now when it's summer, when she should be cutting and stacking firewood for the coming winter, she can only wait and hope the bridge is soon replaced—so the wood can be hauled across the brook.

"They should have known a 15-ton truck full of water would not come across that bridge," Fournier said. "These people are professionals. They should have known better.

So who's going to pay for the bridge?

That's a question for the insurance companies, say city officials and the property owner.

MacQueen said three companies—those who insure the city, the town of Roxbury and

the landlord—will have to "argue it out." That will take months, he predicts.

"They're still trying to determine who is at fault, just like any other accident," Atkinson said.

But Keene has already paid thousands of dollars in bills because of the accident. It cost $6,020 to hire a crane to lift the truck out of the brook; that bill has been turned over to the insurance companies. Estimates to fix the pumper truck—which is now at a body shop in Winchester, Mass.—amount to $15,000, said Fire Chief Robert N. Guyette.

As for the bridge, that will likely cost $8,000 to fix, Guyette said.

The accident has also prompted MacQueen to ask why the Keene Fire Department gives free fire protection to Roxbury. Since Roxbury has no fire department, there's not a mutual aid agreement between the two municipalities, he said.

And the city doesn't get any money from Roxbury for the fire protection, he said, so why are Keene taxpayers footing the bill for Roxbury fire protection?

He assigned the fire chief to investigate the issue and report to him.

For its part, Roxbury—the region's smallest community, with 248 residents—is worked up about how Keene owes Roxbury in taxes for city-owned land within the town.

Selectmen Chairman Robert L. Whipple said it's news to him that Keene is asking questions about city fire coverage in his town. "It's been that way since I've been in town, which is over 20 years," he said.

In the past, Roxbury has paid bills when other towns answered fire calls, he said. He doesn't know if it has so recently, because he doesn't see all the bills.

Speaking of taxes, Roxbury wants to collect from Keene. Roxbury had all its property reassessed last year, and Keene's property tax bill for 440 acres of land it owns in Roxbury jumped from $16,000 to $43,800, according to Laurence D. Shaffer, Keene tax assessor.

Keene balked at the increase and has appealed to the N.H. Board of Tax and Land Appeals. The city owns the property to protect two drinking water supplies—Woodward Pond and Babbidge Reservoir.

Roxbury says the property is worth an average of $1,293 an acre, a figure Keene says is way out of line.

"This isn't Vacationland U.S.A.," Shaffer said.

Whipple said state experts conducted the Roxbury revaluation and set the values for the Keene owned land.

Shaffer and MacQueen deny any link between Keene's reassessment of Roxbury fire protection and the squabble over taxes.

"I don't know," Whipple said when asked if he sees a link. "I don't have any idea."

—————

As Reported by the *Keene Evening Sentinel* July 2nd, 1991:

"STORY"

Keene adopts ordinances

Traffic will be slowing down and local businesses will be exempted from fees charged when their fire alarms are disconnected under ordinances adopted by the Keene City Council.

And when it comes to fire alarms, the city council exempted businesses from a $25 fire department fee charged when businesses hold fire drills for employees and disconnect their fire alarms.

—————

As Reported by the *Keene Evening Sentinel* July 14th, 1991:

"STORY"

Deadly drug found in makeshift lab

As operation in a Keene garage that was apparently intended to cook up an illegal drug similar to heroin went badly awry Thursday night, when two people feel seriously ill and catatonic after allegedly ingesting a toxic batch.

Friday afternoon, Keene police and federal drug-enforcement officials from Concord warned that the same or worse—death—could happen to anyone else who has synthetic drugs from that batch and takes them.

The officials said anyone who takes the grayish powder and starts to exhibit symptoms of Parkinson's disease—rigidity, immobility, a slowing down of body movements and functions—should go immediately to a hospital.

If they don't, "they could die," said John Ryan of the N.H. office of the federal Drug Enforcement Administration.

The two people who became ill from the drug Thursday night—Michael Cheney and Ann Collins, both of 43 Graves Road where the drug was allegedly being made—were in fair and serious condition, respectively, at Dartmouth Hitchcock Medical Center in Hanover Friday night.

Ryan said anyone who obtained drugs from the garage-lab would probably have been told that it was heroin.

In fact, it's believed to be a toxic substance known at MPTP, he said.

A DEA chemist was flown into Keene from New York Friday afternoon to analyze the drug remaining at the lab.

Ryan said it's believed that whoever was running the lab was trying to make MPPP, which is similar to Demerol, a synthetic morphine, MPPP has heroin-like effects and probably was being made to be marketed as heroin, he said. It can be injected, snorted or smoked.

Made right, the chemical is many times more powerful than morphine, said Jack Fasanello, senior forensic chemist with the DEA.

Made wrong, the drug sends the user into a frozen trance.

This batch was made wrong, Fasanello said, as he examined the chemicals outside the house.

The clandestine lab was discovered Thursday night, after relatives of either Cheney or Collins called Keene police and said there was trouble at the house.

Police entered the small white home and found the two in separate rooms. Both were practically catatonic and unable to talk, police said. Cheney, however, was able to point to a piece of paper that apparently indicated the drug he'd taken, police said.

The two were taken to Cheshire Medical Center in Keene, and then transferred to the Hanover hospital.

In the bathroom of the house, police found a syringe lying out in the open.

In the small detached garage next to the house, they saw what looked to be a lab, so a search warrant was obtained.

Ryan said the garage it contained numerous beakers, chemicals, glassware and other items used in making illegal drugs. "This was a major functioning lab," he said. It was also the first N.H. bust of a lab manufacturing MPPP clandestinely, he said.

The lab had been apparently operating since at least May, he said, though he declined to say how he knew that.

Police also said that at least two batches of the drug, including the bad one, had been made there.

Ryan and the police said they couldn't say yet who was operating the lab.

Ryan said the lab was almost certainly intended to produce drugs for sale. "People don't set up clandestine labs for just themselves," he said.

But he said police haven't tracked down anyone who may have bought or been given drugs from the lab. Keene police Capt. Hugh M. McClellan said there have been no reports of people falling ill from the drug, nor have there been any heroin arrests in this area.

He said police had no idea a lab even existed in Keene until they stumbled on it.

Thursday night and Friday, police and federal agents swarmed over the property, and lined the steeply-climbing narrow road with their vehicles. A hazardous waste crew arrived from Londonderry to carefully pick up and cart away everything used in madding the drugs.

Meanwhile, neighbors, who didn't learn the reason for all of the uproar until late Friday afternoon, said the incident was a tragedy.

The neighbor said it was hard to believe Collins, who is in her mid 30's, could have been involved in drugs, and described her as a warm and hard-working young woman who was a good mother to her two young boys.

The neighbor said Cheney, who is in his late 30's lived in the Graves Road home only periodically. The neighbor noticed a few months ago that Cheney was living there again.

"I'm just awfully surprised," said the neighbor.

No charges have been filed in the case.

———

As Reported by the *Keene Evening Sentinel* September 7th, 1991:

"FIRE"

Apartment fire leads to suit by owner, tenants

The owner of a Keene apartment building and occupants of two of his apartments are suing two companies that allegedly caused a fire there last June.

Emile J. Legere, owner of Century Apartments on Park Avenue, alleges in a suit filed last month in Cheshire County Superior Court that workers for two companies were responsible for starting a fire that temporarily displaced half of the 24 families living in one of the Century apartment buildings.

Adrian Pinney and his company, Pinney Plumbing & Heating of North Swanzey, and Irving Bruce, owner of North Country Welding of Chesterfield, are named as defendants.

"It was a very unfortunate fire, but we don't believe our client is at fault in any way," said Pinney's lawyer, Kevin C. Devine of Manchester.

Bruce's lawyer, Stephen B. Bragdon of Keene, could not be reached for comment.

According to the lawsuit, Legere hired Pinney Plumbing and Heating to perform annual maintenance work on a boiler in the basement. As part of that work, Pinney hired North Country Welding as a subcontractor to do some welding, the suit says.

Sparks from North Country's welding operation apparently entered a gap in a nearby wall and ignited a stud, according to the suit. The fire spread from there.

People who occupied two of the apartments—Leroy S. and Isabel A. Ford, and Lillian A. Bemis—are also suing the two companies separately, seeking an unspecified amount of money for property lost in the fire and for the risk of injury they faced.

As Reported by the *Keene Evening Sentinel* September 9th, 1991.

"STORY"

Contract for Keene firefighters may be coming later this week

Keene firefighters may decide on a union contract Thursday, but specific terms aren't being disclosed just yet.

A union official this morning declined to say what kind of pay and benefits are being considered for the 24 firefighters. Union members are also being kept in the dark about the proposed agreement until Thursday night, he said.

"It looks pretty promising, but you never know," said Robert Meagher, vice president for Keene Firefighters Local 3265 of the International Association of Firefighters.

The firefighters' union is the second of five Keene unions to come up with contracts, but whether this deal will be accepted is unknown.

Some things in the proposed contract are unfavorable, Meagher said, though he wouldn't say what they are.

The proposed agreement, which becomes binding only if accepted by firefighters, is the second to come out of months of talks between Keene officials and the fire unions that represent close to one-half Keene's public employees.

Firefighters, their supervisors and public works employees voted to organize last year. They joined police patrol officers and police supervisors.

Last month, the patrol officers' union agreed to a one-year contract that provided 2-percent pay raises and better language covering job protection in light of the botched firing of a police officer in November, a police official said.

At the time, union officials said they were hoping the economy would improve and with it, their chances at the bargaining table next year.

Whether firefighters will go for a short-term contract is unknown.

Police earn slightly more than firefighters. Last year, starting pay for a firefighter was $21,672 starting pay for a police officer was $21,930.

The firefighters' union was formed last year after a proposed reorganization in city government raised fears about how much bargaining power firefighters would have.

Still to reach agreement are public works employees, firefighters' supervisors and a union representing police supervisors.

————

As Reported by the *Keene Evening Sentinel* September 13th, 1991:

"FIRE"

'Prank' fire doused in time

A fire that may have been started as a prank could have turned into a disaster, had it been set at night instead of midafternoon, a Keene fire official said.

A grass fire, apparently started with a rolled-up sheet of paper, burned a 10-by-17 foot strip of grass Thursday as it moved toward the northeast corner of the former Sprague & Carlton furniture factory on Avon Street in Keene.

The flames actually licked up against the vacant 100,000-square-foot building and the heat cracked two windows before firefighters doused the flames, Keene Fire Department Capt. Steven Goldsmith said.

The damage could have been much worse, he said, as barrels containing flammable liquid were near the building. However, they were not set on fire and did not ignite.

The blaze burned for about 20 minutes. Because the fire was set in the middle of the day, and in a place that many passers-by can see, it was discovered quickly and put out. Had it been set late at night, the building might have been engulfed in flames, Goldsmith said.

He believes teenagers set the fire, and didn't intend to burn down the building.

————

As Reported by the *Keene Evening Sentinel* September 20th, 1991:

"STORY"

Keene fire supervisor talks hit impasse

The first-ever contract negotiations between Keene and 10 supervisors of the city's firefighters have hit an impasse and a fact-finder is being called in.

Fire Lt. Thomas L. Loll Jr., local union president, said a mediator from the N.H. Public Employees Labor Relations Board had worked to bring the city and the supervisors' bargaining unit together, but decided last Thursday the two sides were still at an impasse.

Now, a labor expert called a fact-finder, will come in, listen to the arguments from both sides and recommend a contract settlement. But, because there's no state law that makes such a ruling binding, either side could still reject the recommendation.

"In the end, we might still be in the end," Loll said. "In other words, it's kind of a vicious circle."

The 10 supervisors include the department's captains, lieutenants, fire prevention officer and fire training officer. The superintendent of fire alarms would also be in the bargaining unit, but that job is now vacant because of budget cuts, Loll said.

This is the first time the bargaining unit has negotiated a contract since it formed last year to fight a proposal for a public safety director to oversee Keene's fire, police and inspections departments.

Loll wouldn't comment on specific issues that blocked the negotiations but said the supervisors "tried very diligently to cut a deal with the city."

"We became frustrated when the city wouldn't agree to give us what we already have, let alone what they've given the police officers' union, he said. "We felt we've done all the giving with nothing in return."

Contacted this morning, City Manager J. Patrick MacQueen said he does not know what Loll is referring to, but added he would not comment on on-going contract talks.

Loll said MacQueen needs to look good to taxpayers and to sell the contract to city councilors, who might be even more interested in looking good to taxpayers with elections coming up.

Loll said the firefighter supervisors want to be fair to taxpayers, but to themselves, too. Many people might not realize the skills required of firefighters today, or the jobs they're asked to do, he said. It's not just "spraying wet stuff on red stuff," he said.

The city's 24 firefighters, a separate bargaining unit from their supervisors but members of the same union are also haggling over a contract.

———

As Reported by the *Keene Evening Sentinel* October 24th, 1991:

"STORY"

Keene unions still on hold

As the fourth month of Keene's fiscal year slips away, members of three city employee unions are still waiting for contract settlements.

"We're in never-never land," said Lt. Thomas L. Loll Jr., president of the union representing the 10 supervisors of Keene's firefighters. "We're waiting for the fact finder...I don't even know if one has been appointed yet."

Meanwhile, about 10 Keene police sergeants and corporals and the city's firefighters are still waiting for their union contracts to be settled.

Earlier this month, the police supervisors' union rejected a proposed contract in a "somewhat close" vote, said Cpl. Edwin F. Bourassa Jr., one of the union negotiators. Now that group too, is waiting for a fact finder to be brought in.

Firefighters rejected a proposed contract in mid September, sending those talks back to the bargaining table as well.

Representatives of all the unions say they know it's a tough year to negotiate because of the poor economy, and they insist their unions aren't making unreasonable requests.

"We're really used to striking it out for the long haul," said Loll of his group, which is negotiating its first-ever contract with the city.

———

As Reported by the *Keene Evening Sentinel* October 24th, 1991:

"STORY"

Roxbury bridge will be replaced

Temporary span planned for winter; new steel structure needs work

Landis W. Atkinson of Stoddard went shopping for steel beams to build a new stronger bridge to replace the wooden span demolished by a Keene fire truck in April.

Instead, he found a whole bridge for sale.

Now, the rusty, floorless steel structure, found in the Sunapee area, sits off Route 9 in Roxbury next to Otter Brook, which Atkinson hopes it will one day span.

But there are still many obstacles in the way. For one, the bridge, which Atkinson says was once used on a state highway, needs some repairs, general refurbishing and a cement deck. Atkinson says it's too late in the year to get all that done before bad weather sets in. Plus, he's out of money to spend on the project.

So, he's going to have another wooden bridge built—maybe by this weekend—so vehicles can get back and forth from the property this winter, he said Wednesday night. The steel bridge would be put in next spring, he said.

So far, Atkinson says, he has paid all the costs of buying the new bridge and hauling it down from Sunapee—more than $10,000.

But he hasn't given up on getting reimbursement from Keene, or from the city government's insurers. After all, a Keene fire truck, on its way to douse a pickup-truck fire on the other side of the brook, ruined the wooden bridge, he said.

But there are questions about who's responsible: Atkinson says city officials have pointed out to him that the wooden bridge wasn't posted for weight limits, thus relieving the firefighters of responsibility for breaking it.

But Atkinson said the city had told him before the incident that its fire trucks would never cross the bridge anyway because it hadn't been rated by the state. State officials told him it was impossible to rate the wooden bridge.

That didn't bother Atkinson, who thought smaller fire departments with smaller trucks could handle any problems at the one occupied house across the brook.

The wooden bridge worried some Keene firefighters when they arrived April 11. They took a look at it before crossing, trying to judge if it was strong enough, and several got off the fire truck to lessen the weight.

It wasn't enough. The 15-ton truck, its water tanks filled, crashed through and the pickup truck on the other side "burned anyway," Atkinson said.

Despite everything, Atkinson said he has no hard feelings toward the city.

"I admire firemen, I think they do a great job," he said. "It's an unfortunate accident. I think a misjudgment was made."

Now, he said, he's going to dump the matter in the lap of his insurance company and let it deal with city government's insurers.

Meanwhile there's the new bridge. Although a sign on the bridge announces as yard sale, that's now how Atkinson picked it up. He got it from a Wendell man whose former construction company happened to have several bridges for sale.

This one, nearly 75 feet long and 22 feet wide, used to be on a state highway up north, but was replaced when the state's standards called for bridges to be widened another six feet, said George Smith of Wendell.

Smith said it's a "helluva good bridge" and he had always intended to use it himself. But, after years in the construction business, he retired before he got around to it.

Atkinson said buying an entire bridge is "the oddest thing in the world."

Before Atkinson uses the bridge, he says he'll have it rated by an engineer. And he'll make sure it's strong enough to hold a fire truck.

————

As Reported by the *Keene Evening Sentinel* December 20th, 1991:

Fire chief retires from Keene force
Chief Robert N. Guyette

Robert N. Guyette, who worked his way up the ranks from firefighter to chief of the Keene Fire Department, is retiring Jan 1.

Guyette, 64, one of just a few city department heads who predates the arrival of City Manager J. Patrick MacQueen, said it's simply time to retire.

"I want to," he said, when asked why he's stepping down. "I don't plan on doing anything. I'm not going to retire to go to work."

Guyette was appointed chief in 1971, and oversaw modernization of the 36-member department.

This morning, firefighters said that, under Guyette's leadership, the department introduced an ambulance service, a rescue truck, firefighter training and fire alarm maintenance.

"What I saw in Bob Guyette was a fireman who could direct men and equipment and put out fires quickly and skillfully," said Keene Mayor Aaron A. Lipsky.

Firefighters say Guyette is a master at orchestrating firefighting.

But several people said this morning that he was less effective dealing with bureaucracy.

Guyette's relations with MacQueen soured a couple of years ago, when he fought MacQueen's proposal to put the fire and police departments under a single administrator.

Both firefighters and their supervisors subsequently organized unions.

Some critics say Guyette ran the fire department on a shoestring budget, delaying purchases of equipment.

"It's a funny thing about city employment," Guyette said this morning. "If you're in there to make a name for yourself, forget it, because you're only remembered as long as you're there."

At city hall, officials said Guyette told MacQueen last week he was retiring. Mac-Queen, vacationing in the Virgin Islands, could not be reached for comment.

Alfred H. Merrifield, acting city manager, said a search for a new chief will begin once MacQueen returns. The search will be nationwide, but local candidates will also be considered, he said.

The task of selecting Guyette's replacement will take several months. Advertisements will be placed in national magazines and trade journals, and a committee—possibly including fire professionals from other N.H. cities—will cull the applicants. Then the interviews will begin.

At the fire station this morning, feelings were mixed about Guyette's announcement.

"He had his drawbacks, but overall he was a good chief," said firefighter Henry Memmesheimer.

Capt. Steven Goldsmith echoed Lipsky's words—that the chief is an expert in the art of firefighting—adding that he lacked some administrative skills.

"Guyette would never create waves, never, ever create waves," Goldsmith said. Likewise, Guyette loathed city hall politics and would stay out of it, he said.

Guyette didn't like the unions, although his management style played only a small part in the decision to unionize, Goldsmith said. Most of the union momentum stemmed from MacQueen's attempt to reorganize the fire department, which was killed by the Keene City Council, Goldsmith said.

Today, Lipsky said the reorganization has "inherent problems" and saw no chance of it being revived after Guyette's departure.

————

As Reported by the *Keene Evening Sentinel* December 12th, 1991:

"FIRE"

Fire forces evacuation at Keene State dormitory

More than 300 students were evacuated from a Keene State College dormitory Wednesday night while Keene firefighters extinguished a fire that may have been started by an extension cord.

No one was hurt and damage was limited to a corner of a room in Carle Hall, said Christine M. Nerlinger, a college spokesman.'

Dormitory residents were evacuated for about an hour as Keene firefighters quenched the fire and cleared smoke out of the second-floor room in the building's west wing, Nerlinger said. Smoke and flames were seen by Keene State College security officers, who called the city's fire department.

While the cause of the fire remains under investigation, Nerlinger said it may have been started by an extension cord that was run under a mattress.

Possibly the insulation became hot and sparked a fire on some bedding, she said.

Keene fire Lt. A. Scott Collier termed the fire as "pretty run-of-the-mill." He did not want to ge3t into details until an investigator goes to the scene today.

————

1992

As Reported by the *Keene Evening Sentinel* February 25th, 1992:

"STORY"

New Keene chief still 3 months off

It could be three more months before Keene hires a boss for its 37 firefighters.

A 4-inch-thick folder of resumes from potential fire chiefs sits on City Manager J. Patrick MacQueen's desk, following Friday's deadline for applications.

MacQueen has yet to open the letters and begin the process to replace Robert N. Guyette, who retired January 1 after 20 years as Keene's firechief.

In the interim, the fire department is being run by Deputy Chiefs George Shepard and Paul Crowell.

While credited for his ability to make split-second decisions at a fire scene and move men and equipment effectively, Guyette loathed politics and avoided confrontations, critics said.

MacQueen said he'll sift through the applications and pick out those whop will get a follow-up questionnaire that poses several "what if" situations. From there, MacQueen said he'll narrow the field to five or 10 candidates.

By then, a committee will be ready to interview the would-be chiefs. MacQueen said the committee will likely include fire chiefs from other cities and local residents; he hasn't decided whether to name representatives from the city's two firefighter unions.

Though the committee will make a re commendation, the final decision is up to MacQueen.

"I certainly want to involve other people in the process, but ultimately it's my decision," MacQueen said.

If it comes down to two candidates of equal qualifications, MacQueen said he'd prefer hiring someone from within the fire department.

In advertisements published last month, the applicant is required to:

Have minimum experience of 10 years.

Be certified or able to be certified as a fire chief in New Hampshire.

Hold the minimum of an associate's degree in fire safety, emergency management systems or management; a bachelor's degree is preferred.

The salary will range between $44,700 and $54,800.

————

As Reported by the *Keene Evening Sentinel* March 2nd, 1992:

"FIRE"

Fire strikes condominium

An early morning fire at a Keene condominium was squelched by firefighters before it got out of control.

The Chestnut Green Condominiums, 210 Lower Main St., was evacuated while Keene firefighters doused flames in one of the apartments. Minor damage was reported.

Firefighters were unsure of the tenant's name this morning.

The tenant was asleep and was awakened by the smell of smoke from a burning log that had rolled out of the fireplace, said George Shepard, Keene's deputy fire chief.

The tenant called the fire department at 5:11 a.m.; by 5:25 a.m. the flames were out, Shepard said. No one was hurt, he said.

"Flames were starting to go down through the floor into the basement and to some beams down there" he said.

————

As Reported by the *Keene Evening Sentinel* April 4th, 1992:

"STORY"

Fire department contract near

Top city officials and bosses at the Keene Fire Department have reached a tentative agreement for a union contract, according to City Manager J. Patrick MacQueen.

After a Thursday morning session with negotiators, a tentative agreement was reached, which now must go to union members and elected city officials to be finalized.

Since the middle of last year, supervisors at the fire department have been working without a union contract. So have firefighters and police supervisors, though police patrol officers have a contract.

Other employees, including unionized police and public works department workers, received a 2 percent pay raise shortly after the Keene city budget was adopted in late June.

The agreement will first go to members of the fire supervisors' union—10 captains and lieutenants—and if they ratify it MacQueen said he will ask to the city council to approve it.

In the other two negotiations, a fact-finding session, in which a disinterested party recommends a settlement, is scheduled for May 22 with the firefighters and city officials.

————

As Reported by the *Keene Evening Sentinel* April 8th, 1992:

"FIRE"

Dinner goes up in flames

A burned leg of lamb sent Keene firefighters to an Ellis Court house Tuesday afternoon, making for a damaged oven, smoky house and one burnt entrée.

Firefighters spend nearly 30 minutes at 7 Allen Court, the home of Daniel Henderson. A babysitter called firefighters when the kitchen filled with smoke, said Keene fire Capt. Steven W. Goldsmith.

The Henderson's put a leg of lamb in the oven with a preset timer, and apparently it didn't work right, Goldsmith said. Four children were outside the house when firefighters arrived.

"The babysitter did a very good job of removing them from the house," Goldsmith said.

———

As Reported by the *Keene Evening Sentinel* April 13th, 1992:

"FIRE"

Candle-caused fire doused

A candle caused a fire in a Keene apartment building early Saturday, just a few hundred feet away from the fire station.

No one was hurt in the fire at 47 Mechanic St. The most severe damage was to a first-floor bedroom, authorities said; but other parts of the 2 ½-story building, which contains several apartments, also received smoke and water damage.

Firefighters said the fire was caused by an unattended candle in a first-floor apartment rented by Laura Martino and Laura Ward. Martino woke up and saw the fire before the smoke detector sounded, and woke Ward. Both got out of the building safely.

Other tenants also had to be evacuated from the building, owned by Ronald Subka of Peterborough.

Firefighters said the fire was reported just before 5 a.m.; they arrived at the building within 60 seconds, and doused the fire quickly.

———

As Reported by the *Keene Evening Sentinel* April 17th, 1992:

"STORY"

City narrows choices for fire chief

Keene may hire a new fire chief by the end of the month.

Nearly 90 people applied for the job, and that list was narrowed to 11 serious candidates, including members of the Keene Fire Department.

Now, the finalists' references and backgrounds are being checked, City Manager J. Patrick MacQueen said Thursday night. Sources say there are three finalists for the job, but MacQueen wouldn't confirm that number.

He said he hopes to hire a chief within a couple of weeks.

Fire Chief Robert N. Guyette announced in December he was retiring after 20 years in the job. He had worked his way up from firefighter to boss of the 37-member department.

MacQueen has said previously that, all things being equal, he would prefer to select a chief from inside the department. But sources said none of the three finalists is from Keene.

3 are finalists for Keene fire chief; 2 from N.H., 1 from Bradley airport

Two finalists for the Keene fire chief's job say they would consult the department's 37 members before making any changes. A third said it's too early to talk about specifics.

Interviewed by telephone today, the three men confirmed they are among the finalists for the job left open January 1 when Robert N. Guyette retired after 20 years as chief.

City Manager J. Patrick MacQueen hasn't said how many finalists there are.

This morning he said he has already made an offer, though he declined to name his choice. He said he expects a response by Friday.

The three known to be in the running are:

Robert P. Wood, chief of the 21-member Durham Fire Department, which provides fire protection to the town of 12,500 residents and the University of New Hampshire, with up to 20,000 additional students and staffers.

Peter R. Bumone, chief of the 40-member Bradley International Airport Emergency Services for the past nine years. The department handles fires, hazardous materials and paramedic services to the airport just outside Hartford, Conn.

William H. Pepler Jr., chief of the 18-member Exeter Fire Department, which covers the town of 18,000 in southeastern New Hampshire; Keene Police Chief Thomas F. Powers 3rd used to be Exeter's town manager.

Apparently, no local people are being considered at this point, although the applicants included at least one Keene firefighter.

Two of the three finalists interviewed today suggested they would poll firefighters and supervisors to see what can be done to make the department better.

The one thing I'm not going to do is go in and made changes alone, said Pepler, 39, Exeter's chief since 1986.

In Exeter, he has formed committees on research and development, health and safety, and advanced life support. The committees made up of firefighters and their bosses, come up with ideas and carry them out.

Pepler said the Keene job would mean a pay raise and career advancement as it's a larger community.

Bumone at Bradley, said he would also sit down with the firefighters and their bosses to see what changes are needed.

"The team concept, I think, is important," said Bumone, 45, "rank is not as important as accomplishing the goals of the agency."

Bumone wants out of Bradley because of fringe-benefit changes; in effect, he will be taking a pay cut if he stays there, he said.

The Bradley department is comparable in size to Keene's Bumone said. He would not say whether the Keene job would mean a pay raise.

Both Pepler and Bumone have fought their share of major fires—a downtown building and condominium converted mill building in Exeter; the explosion and subsequent fire of an Emery Air Freight 727 at Bradley.

Wood, while confirming he is a finalist for the Keene job, would not discuss his thoughts, saying the selection process is confidential. It would be a little premature to talk about a job he's applied for while he's still working in Durham, he said.

MacQueen reviewed the initial applicants, narrowed the field, and named a committee of fire experts, a local firefighter, and a city councilor to interview finalists. They'll make a recommendation, but the decision is up to him.

———

As Reported by the *Keene Evening Sentinel*:

New Keene fire chief coming from Exeter

Exeter's fire chief was named today to head the 37-member Keene Fire Department.

Keene City Manager J. Patrick MacQueen announced this morning that William H. Pepler, 39, will likely take over in Keene on June 22. Pepler has held the job of chief in Exeter since 1986.

He's the second Keene city department head to come from Exeter, a town of 18,000 in southeastern New Hampshire.

In December 1987, Thomas F. Powers 3rd took over as Keene police chief; he had been the police chief in Exeter.

MacQueen said today that Powers gave Pepler a good recommendation, but did not lobby for his employment.

"The candidates were, fortunately, very well qualified," MacQueen said. "It ends up being just a judgment call."

MacQueen doesn't have any marching orders for Pepler, he'll let the new chief make judgments about how the department should be run, MacQueen said.

Pepler heads an 18-member fire department in Exeter.

When contacted last week by The Sentinel, Pepler said he'd talk to firefighters and supervisors to learn what needs doing at the department.

"The one thing I'm not going to do is go in and make changes" alone, Pepler said then. He's big on committees.

Pepler was not available for comment this morning.

Pepler holds a bachelor's degree in business administration and a master's degree in public administration.

His pay will start at $50,300; he faces a six-month probationary period, like all city workers, MacQueen said. Last week, Pepler said the chief's job would mean a pay raise and promotion.

Since the beginning of this year, there's been no chief at the Keene fire station, since the retirement of Robert N. Guyette.

"I'm looking forward to working with the guy," said Deputy Chief George Shepard. "In fact, I welcome it at this point. Everything I heard about him he's excellent."

New fire chief says he's enthused about job in Keene

Becoming Keene's fire chief means an $11,000-a-year raise for William H. Pepler Jr., who will take over the 37-member department in June.

Pepler, interviewed Tuesday by The Sentinel, said the Keene job is a promotion, with more responsibility as well as higher pay.

He now earns $39,045 as Exeter's fire chief, a community of 18,000 in southeastern New Hampshire. In Keene, he'll be paid $50,200, the same as the former chief, Robert N. Guyette, who retired at the beginning of this year, said City Manager J. Patrick MacQueen.

When he moves into his Keene job, Pepler will be working again with Thomas F. Powers 3rd. Powers, now Keene's police chief, used to be / Exeter's town manager, and he hired Pepler as fire chief in 1986.

"Tom and I get along very well," said Pepler, 39. "I look forward to working with him because I think he's a true professional. He knows emergency services."

He sees Powers as a resource who will introduce him to Keene.

Powers returned the praise; "Bill did a very good and capable job."

Pepler doesn't seem to be one to withhold his views. He has already expressed his thoughts on a proposal to have a public safety director in Keene, which would add another level of government. Keene doesn't need a public safety director, Pepler said.

Again this year, MacQueen has hinted at the idea of reorganizing city government to reduce the number of department heads reporting to him. He'd like to cut the number from more than a dozen to about five or six.

Part of the change could be a public safety director to oversee fire, police, ambulance, inspection and related services.

In the past, the Keene City Council has shot down the idea, and firefighters have argued loudly against it.

Pepler concurs with those sentiments.

The way emergency services work best is when you have a separate police chief and separate fire chief," Pepler said Tuesday. Both should be able to report directly to the city manager, while a public safety director would be "another step in the bureaucracy that's not required.

Pepler said MacQueen did not mention a public safety director during discussions about the job.

Pepler was named fire chief on the day that three of his future subordinates explained their department's fiscal 1993 budget to a Keene city council committee.

He'll take over in late June, and the budget year begins July 1, so Pepler won't have any say in the budge—which means he'll run what's given him for 13 months.

But Pepler said that doesn't concern him. He'll have a year to look things over at the fire department and develop some long and short-term plans.

"You can't do the changes overnight," Pepler said. "You make the changes you need to make, but only after you make sure it's the right thing to do."

———

As Reported by the *Keene Evening Sentinel* June 5th, 1992:

"STORY"

Keene fire supervisors get contract, raises and back pay

After nearly a year of back-and-forth bargaining, the 210-member supervisors union at the Keene Fire Department has its first contract, providing a 5 percent pay raise in two steps.

The Keene City Council approved the contract Thursday. The supervisors will get a 2 percent raise immediately, retroactive to January 1992; the back pay will be issued in a lump sum.

And in July, they'll get a 3 percent raise.

Now, only two of five city unions –police supervisors and rank-and file firefighters— are working without contracts.

Fire department supervisors say their pay package isn't ideal. The retroactive 2 percent raise covers only six months, not the entire budget year, which began last July 1. All non-union city workers got that 2 percent raise.

However, the supervisors say they're happy about signing their first-ever contract, saying it gives them power and communication they didn't have before.

"We're certainly a lot more at ease dealing with the city," said fire department Lt. Thomas L. Loll.

"We're together. We're one unit now."

He said the contract will help preserve jobs, something members wanted "in these scary times." It also gives supervisors a say in promotion practices, though not about who should actually be promoted. And, as with any union agreement, it requires the city government to negotiate any pay or benefit changes.

Firefighters and their supervisors unionized about two years ago after City Manager J. Patrick MacQueen proposed reorganizing city government, and putting a public service director in charge of the fire, police and code enforcement departments. Firefighters opposed the setup, and it was never enacted.

Earlier this week, fire department supervisors approved the contract on a 7-2 vote. After discussing the package in secret Thursday night, the city council ratified the pact on a 14-1 vote. The dissenting vote came from Robert E. Williams, who chairs the council finance committee.

Williams said he opposed the retroactive pay.

"It's a tool I really don't want to play with," Williams said today. "You reach a settlement, you reach a date. It's not three, six, nine months before" the date of the contract.

MacQueen expressed pleasure that the contract was settled.

"It's been a long process," MacQueen said. "It being a first contract, it's probably the most difficult to reach.

He cautioned that people should not assume that the 3 percent raise for fiscal 1993 is a precedent for other contract negotiations, or whether non-union workers can expect a raise that size.

The fire supervisors' raises will cost Keene between $5,000 and $6,000 for the fiscal year that ends this month, and $16,000 to $17,000 for the budget year that begins July 1, MacQueen said.

Negotiations have been at an impasse between the city and the two unions that still have no contract—rank-and-file firefighters,

and police supervisors. Fact-finders have joined both negotiations, trying to settle the disputes.

The fact-finder's non-binding recommendations for firefighters have not yet been received. The police report has been received, and negotiations have started again, MacQueen said.

One police supervisor said today that retroactive pay is a key stumbling block in those talks. The police supervisors rejected a contract similar to the package just accepted by fire supervisors; it called for a limited retroactive pay increase and a larger pay raise fiscal 1993.

Keene's fire chief is on the job

Keene's new fire chief started work this morning.

William H., Pepler, 39, began his first workday by meeting with City Manager J. Patrick MacQueen and City Attorney Gerald Carney.

————

As Reported by the *Keene Evening Sentinel* June 25th, 1992:

"STORY"

Deputy Crowell to retire

After 35 ½ years of fighting fires in Keene and the Monadnock Region, Deputy Keene Fire Chief Paul Crowell is retiring.

Crowell, 64, said his decision has nothing to do with a changing of the guard at the fire department. A new chief, William H. Pepler Jr., has just replaced Robert N. Guyette, who headed the department for two decades before he retired.

"It's something I've considered for a while," said Crowell, who worked his way up the ladder from firefighter to deputy chief. "I'm not getting any younger."

About three weeks ago, he decided on his final day of work—July 1.

————————

As Reported by the *Keene Evening Sentinel* June 27th, 1992:

"STORY"

Pepler is ready for anything Keene's new fire chief steps in with a style that is hands-on

Once upon a time, the fire chief was the chief firefighter.

He was usually the guy who'd been with the department the longest. Who directed everyone else when it came to battling a blaze. Who was one of the oldest guys there.

Today's fire chief often gets stuck with different tasks—sorting through a blizzard of regulations, dealing with sometimes sticky community politics, negotiating spending plans in tough economic times and making sure the department and its personnel are working safely and efficiently.

A fire chief often ends up pushing more paper than pulling fire hoses.

And so the fire chief's qualifications are different these days, too. The trend is to younger, more educated chiefs who are viewed in the ways of administration, says William H. Pepler jr., Keene's new fire chief.

Take Pepler, for example. He's 39, his resume includes a long list of academic and professional educational achievements and, by more than one account, he was a whiz at running the fire department in Exeter where

he was chief for six years before taking the same job in Keene.

Seemingly more telling in his first few days on the job in Keene this week, Pepler, a friendly, mustached man, wore neat suits and ties and looked more the part of the accountant he one planned to be rather than the chief.

But some things never change. The suits were only because Pepler's new uniform wasn't in yet. And—though he hasn't directed a fire since March in Exeter—he still goes to fire scenes and had his fire-fighting gear on hand in case a blaze broke out in Keene.

Pepler replaces Robert N. Guyette, who retired January 1 at the age of 64 and after two decades as Keene's fire chief.

Guyette, though he oversaw modernization of Keene's department, would probably be considered from the old school of fire chiefs. Tops at running fire scenes, his critics said less proficient with the administrative end of things.

But that's a topic Pepler said to be a canny politician, won't touch with a 20-foot firehouse pole.

"He's certainly welcome here any time he likes," Pepler said of Guyette.

Holding steady

The new chief say he has no big plans yet for changes in Keene's department, though "It's safe to say, yes, there will be changes.

But, he said, those will come only after he has consulted the department's firefighters and asked them what they think needs to be changed and for their ideas about what to do.

"Everyone always says a new broom sweeps clean," he said. "But I don't want to change things overnight."

It will probably take a few months just to get the planning done, he said. And he's glad that he's starting the job at this point in the budget year—right when it starts—so he has plenty of time to learn and settle in before he has to submit his own spending plan for the department.

Pepler may have no plans for Keene yet, but a look at his six years heading up Exeter's smaller department might point the way.

There, he helped develop[standard operating procedures, a hazardous materials response team and an operational structure used any time there was an emergency and which let the first person on a scene take command and keep it, even when higher-ranking officers arrived.

"There's a lot of responsibility with that" operational structure, called an incident command system, said John Carbonneau, who worked in the Exeter department under Pepler and was appointed chief when he left.

The system—which grew out of a California forestry program—lays out how the command in a large incident can be broken down into areas of responsibility for different firefighters to handle. That way, the officer in command of the scene can oversee the big picture but doesn't have to deal with every detail.

It's a much more efficient way of handling situations, Carbonneau said.

It also gives lower-ranking firefighters the chance for more authority than they would otherwise have in an emergency.

The benefit is not only valuable cross-training, but boosted morale, he said.

Pepler also insisted that Exeter's firefighters upgrade their level of emergency medical training.

Pepler vigorously pursued changes to improve safety and efficiency, his top goals. But as he has promised to do in Keene, he first consulted firefighters at length to see what they had to say, Carbonneau said.

"He believes in participatory management," he said. "So there's involvement.

It paid off. Pepler was well liked and his ideas were well supported by Exeter's firefighters. And Carbinneau himself said,

"I really didn't want to see him leave—even though I'm thrilled to be chief.

Hot start

Pepler grew up with a fascination for fire departments. There was one at the foot of a hill he played on as a boy in Rhode Island, and he loved to watch the goings on.

By about age 15, the chief at that station would let him and his friends help fight brush fires. And by 16, Pepler was able to join as a volunteer junior officer.

By 18, he was an official member of the department.

He figured then that he would be a fire-fighter. Or a cop. Or, probably, an accountant. In college, on his way to a bachelor's degree in business administration, he realized an accountant's quiet life wasn't for him.

Instead, in 1980, he came to New Hampshire to teach firefighting and fire prevention courses at N.H. Vocational-Technical College in Laconia.

He stayed four years, then took a new job as supervisor of safety and security at the prestigious Phillips Exeter Academy in Exeter. There, he introduced new ways of doing the job, including standard operating procedures and an incident reporting system.

He also served in Exeter's call firefighter force.

Two years late, he was named chief of Exeter's department, which has 18 full-timers and 20 who are on call.

At the same time, he started working again for the voch-tech-college, teaching evenings in programs held off-campus.

Along the way, he also fulfilled another childhood goal—he became certified in New Hampshire as a police officer.

Through the years, Pepler has worked hard to increase his knowledge about firefighting and running a department. A few years ago, he became one of 28 fire service managers chosen from 2,000 applicants to attend an executive fire-officer program at the National Fire Academy in Maryland.

"It's probably the best training someone in a chief's position can get in the country," Pepler said at the time to an Exeter reporter.

He also managed to get his master's degree in public administration in 1989.

"He's highly educated and knowledgeable," Carbonneau said. "And he likes his people to be as knowledgeable as possible for safety's sake."

Of his attraction to firefighting, Pepler said, "When you're younger, it's the excitement of the whole thing—going down the street with the siren blaring.

For the mature man, though, it's about service. "I get great pleasure in helping people. I probably could make more money doing something else. But this is what I want to do."

Ironically, Pepler said, "fire departments have done such good jobs in teaching people how to prevent fires, they're putting themselves out of the fire-quenching business.

But he sees an ever-increasing demand on the department in two areas—medical emergencies and spills of hazardous materials.

————

As Reported by the *Keene Evening Sentinel* June 29th, 1992:

"FIRE"

Cause of gas leak still unknown

A poisonous, explosive liquid that got into Keene's downtown sewer system Friday night has not yet been identified, and fire officials are wary that it might return.

So far, "there's been no report of a reoccurrence. We think it's gone for now," George H. Shepard jr., Keene's deputy fire chief, said this morning. However, since no one knows where the material came from, "we can't rule out the possibility that it will be back. We're keeping our eye on it."

The unidentified liquid had the potential to blow up two downtown blocks it ignited, fire officials said.

It also caused fumes that forced evacuation of three businesses—including the announcers on radio station WKBK—and brought rush-hour traffic to a stand still. The bathroom area had been ventilated so that only a faint odor was present by the time our man arrived," said Gary M. Patnode, general manager of Keene Gas Corp.

The company's serviceman checked out the restaurant basement and other areas as a precaution and found no harmful levels of gas, he said.

Fumes forced the evacuation of Timoleon's, First NH Bank, and WKBK. Main Street's southbound lane was closed and traffic was diverted around Central Square for 2 ½ hours.

A high water table could have washed the liquid into the sewer system from a damaged or open container, Shepard said.

"Or somebody might just be dumping it into the sewer,' he said.

Kimberly A. Smith, a waitress at Timoleon's Restaurant, was the first to smell the strong odor of gasoline. After she caught a whiff of the odor in the women's bathroom of the restaurant at 3:35 p.m. Friday, she called Keene Gas Corp.

"The gas company came and said it wasn't gas; it was probably paint thinner. They said the smell was going away, so don't worry about it," Smith said.

But the smell got worse, so, at about 4:15 Smith called the Keene Police Department, which brought in the Keene Fire Department, she said.

"They had their gas-detection machines that beeped, too. But they were beeping like crazy," Smith said. "Two minutes later, they evacuated us."

————

As Reported by the *Keene Evening Sentinel* July 25th, 1992:

"FIRE"

Firefighters save River St. house

A three-year-old dog was among the prized possessions a Keene couple lost Friday when the house they rented burned.

When the fire started—shortly after 2 p.m.—no one but the dog was home at 98 River St. in Keene, which is rented by Benjamin JH. Brown, his girlfriend Kaaron A. Rohloff and her sister, Debra A. Rohloff.

A Keene firefighter carried the dog—a boxer named Abby—outside where a woman tried unsuccessfully to revive it with mouth-to-mouth resuscitation.

For Brown and the Rohloffs the greatest loss was the dog.

"I was coming home from work when I saw the (fire) trucks," Brown said as he stood on a neighbor's lawn. "Surprise, surprise."

Brown, who works at Markem Corp, in Keene, said he and Rohloff planned to stay with his parents in Keene.

Though the house had extensive heat and water damage, quick action by Keene firefighters saved the house from burning to the ground. Neighbors said firefighters arrived quickly and wasted no time dousing the fire.

The house is owned by John DeCoff of Manchester.

Firefighters were called to the fire by a neighbor at 2:12 p.m. They arrived in two minutes and called for more help—a second alarm—right away. They declared the fire under control at 2:45.

Keene Fire Capt., Clayton Stalker said the house can be renovated. Most of the damage was in the kitchen, though other rooms received smoke and heat damage.

"It was a good save," he said.

Though the fire probably started in the kitchen, Stalker said he's not certain what caused it. The Keene fire Department will investigate the fire over the weekend.

It is not believed to be of suspicious origin, he said.

Brown said he was confident that some of his possessions from the house were salvageable.

Fire traced to kitchen plug

A fire that damaged a home on River Street in Keene early Friday afternoon has been traced to an electrical outlet, the Keene Fire Department reported today.

The fire caused extensive damage to the building at 98 River St., owned by John DeCoff of Manchester. The home was rented by Benjamin A. Brown and Kaaron A. Rohloff. The couple's dog died of smoke inhalation.

Keene Fire Department investigators traced the blaze to a kitchen outlet where numerous appliances were plugged in. However, they haven't figured out exactly how the electrical outlet caused the fire.

———

As Reported by the *Keene Evening Sentinel* July 27th, 1992:

[*Compiler's Note:* Keene State College planned to knock down two buildings it owned on Madison Street, part of a project to increase parking space. Those plans fit well with the Keene Fire Department; the college let firefighters train by burning the two houses to the ground Saturday. The training helped, unless you were in a hurry: traffic jams resulted from people rubbernecking.]

"FIRE"

Practice effort licks flames

The thick smoke rising from a Winchester Street neighborhood in Keene Sunday morning likely caused some people to panic or at least wonder what the heck was going on.

Out on the roads that bypass the city, the curious strained and craned in their cars as wave after wave of white smoke rolled into the skies and drifted off to the north, giving Central Square a hazy, washed-out look.

Driving up to Madison Street near Keene State College, the smoke became even thicker, and flames leaped into view, ripping away at a rundown, former sorority house.

About 100 people turned out to watch the Keene Fire Department practice firefighting techniques by torching 44 Madison St., once home to the Kappa Gamma sisters.

Sean G. Laine of Westmoreland had participated in a similar exercise in his town last year to receive his firefighting certification.

"That's why I'm here, to learn something," Laine said. "I think it's very educational. I think everyone should know how a house burns. What a better way than this."

Keene fire Capt. Clayton Stalker said the drill went better than expected.

By purposely burning down a structure, firefighters can try out all kinds of techniques to improve their skills. In a real emergency, there's no time to learn new methods.

The fire department got to work early Sunday, getting the home fire burning at about 8 a.m. During the day, firefighters practiced searching smoke-filled rooms, making holes on the roof for ventilation. Fires were ignited with a torch, scrap wood, hay and old furniture, Stalker said. Gasoline was used for an arson investigation by Keene police, he said.

The only cost: paying overtime to about 20 full-time firefighters Stalker said that's "well worth the money spend," because the department rarely has a chance to burn down a house.

The 44 Madison St. house is one of nine houses the college has had demolished in the past two weeks. Another Madison Street house is expected to be leveled this week by a wrecking crew.

Some Hyde Street houses were knocked down to make way for a new art gallery. The Madison Street and Blake Street houses weren't scheduled to fall until March, making way for the new student union, said Carole

Sentinel *caption reads: What's wrong with this picture? Nothing, actually. Keene firefighters pose outside a flaming house at 44 Madison St. that they burned for practice. Firefighters asked that the photograph be taken after they spent Sunday morning on firefighting drills. Photo by Steve Hooper.*

♆   *A Demon Called Fire*

S. Henry, Keene State College director of residential life. But while Keene State officials were going through the houses with Stalker, "we found some safety situations we didn't feel comfortable with," she said.

Rather than spend money fixing the buildings to comply with city codes, college officials decided to raze them a bit early, Henry said.

Until construction begins on the new student union, the newly cleared area on Madison Street will be a parking lot for college commuters, faculty and staff. The lot won't be paved, she said.

The student union is expected to open in 1994.

————

As Reported by the *Keene Evening Sentinel* August 10th, 1992:

"STORY"

Keene police, fire chiefs get new wheels

Keene recently bought four new cars, and the officials using them include the fire chief and chief of police.

The cars, 1992 Ford 55A Crown Victorias, are loaded—power windows, locks and driver seats, AM-FM stereo and—in the case of one police car—cruise control.

The cars were bought 10 months after a blow up between city councilors and city officials over the use of city-owned cars. Many workers were taking their city-owned cars home at night; the council curtailed the practice after it was detailed in a Sentinel story.

In reviewing city policy, councilors said the fire and police chiefs had a legitimate need for a city-owned car because they're on call 24 hours a day.

When Keene officials bought four sedans this year, the two chief each got one.

The cars cost between $14,300 and $14,800, depending on various options.

William H. Pepler Jr., the recently appointed fire chief, got a car okayed in the current budget, which went into effect July 21.

It replaces the car used by former Chief Robert N. Guyette, who retired after January 1. Guyette's vehicle had 86,907 miles.

————

As Reported by the *Keene Evening Sentinel* August 11th, 1992:

"STORY"

Rough landing for pilot at Keene airport

Photo by George Shepard.

A physician in charge of the emergency room at Cheshire Medical Center in Keene ended up there Monday afternoon after the airplane he was flying flipped over and crashed at the Dillant-Hopkins Airport.

The accident occurred as the student pilot, Paul Barton, 44, of Amherst, was practicing takeoffs and landings on the main runway of the airport in North Swanzey, said Airport Director John M. Geisser.

Apparently no one saw the plane flip over and come to rest on its back about 200 feet off the north side of the main runway. It landed in a thick pile of swamp vegetation.

Barton crawled out a window of the plane and walked about a quarter-mile to an aircraft hangar, said Joseph A. Vogt, who operates a repair shop at the airport.

Barton approached Vogt and the office manager of Emerson Aviation, which sells fuel and teaches flying at the airport.

"He was shook up. He had a bump on his head," said Pat Blair, office manager for Emerson Aviation.

But "he wasn't hurt really bad," Blair said. Also, Barton was in good spirits, saying he hoped the crash wouldn't go on his record, Blair said.

Barton was taken to the Keene hospital's emergency room, which he runs. There was no word on the nature of his injury. He was released after about 90 minutes.

The physician, who was learning to fly, was doing touch-and-go landings in which the plan lands on the runway and then takes off immediately without stopping, Vogt said.

Most runways have a 250 foot-wide shoulder of smooth, flat, grassy ground on the side for safety purposes, Geisser said. But because of wetlands, the runway shoulder at the Keene-owned airport is 100 feet shorter, Geisser said.

Geisser speculated that Barton got into trouble, ran out of shoulder and into the rough ground and swampy vegetation, causing the plane to flip. The Cessna 172, which Vogt estimated to be worth $35,000, was slightly damaged.

———

As Reported by the *Keene Evening Sentinel* October 5th, 1992:

"STORY"

Firefighters strut stuff

Downtown Keene was the safest part of New Hampshire Sunday afternoon, at least in terms of fire protection.

Representatives of more than 40 N.H. and Vermont fire departments paraded down Main Street Sunday at 1 p.m., kicking off Fire Prevention Week.

Participants included firefighters and fire trucks from Keene, Bellows Falls, Marlborough, Stoddard and Swanzey, and the Meadowood County Area Fire Department in Fitzwilliam.

Also participating were marching bands from Gordon Bissell American Legion, Post 4 in Keene, Keene High School, Monadnock Regional High School in Swanzey Center, and Kurn Hatin School in Westminster, Vt.

Lt. Robert Crowell of the Keene Fire Department said about 1,000 people lined the street to watch the parade.

Afterward, firefighters headed for the American Legion softball fields off Court Street and competed to see which departments were quickest at putting on their gear, hooking up a hose to a hydrant, and hitting a target with water from a hose.

The Stoddard Fire Department won the competition.

Also, the Swanzey Center fire company won the Phillip Davis Memorial Trophy for the best-appearing fire truck in the parade.

———

As Reported by the *Keene Evening Sentinel* October 8th, 1992:

"STORY"

Acid spill under control

A chemical spill forced United Parcel Service to evacuate the northwest corner of its Krif Road building in Keene this morning.

At about 10 a.m. UPS workers unloading a truck spotted a leak in a container of hydrochloric acid, said Steven Goldsmith, a captain in the Keene Fire Department.

UPS called the fire department immediately.

The container, which had begun to smoke as acid corroded its exterior, was moved to adjacent parking lot to prevent the acid from seeping into the ground.

At 11, firefighters were preparing to pour the acid into a lime filled container, Goldsmith said lime neutralizes the acid, making it safe to haul away.

No one was hurt, Goldsmith said.

Fumes from the hydrochloric acid dissipated in the air

Goldsmith said he did not know why the container had leaked or where the acid—which can be used as a cleaning agent—was being delivered.

––––––––

As Reported by the *Keene Evening Sentinel* October 10th, 1992:

"FIRE"

Fire damages apartment

Children playing with matches sparked a fire Friday morning in an apartment on Woodburn Street, Keene.

Firefighters quickly extinguished the blaze, and no injuries resulted, according to a release from the Keene Fire Department.

The fire was limited to the laundry room off the kitchen at 86 Woodburn St.,
where Cindy Ford lives with her two young children. Fire investigators attributed the fire to children playing with matches.

Burned were a window, appliances, clothes, a wall and other items. Smoke also wafted into the second apartment in the two-family home, but smoke-related damage was minor.

The home is owned by Alan and Sharon Dean of Connecticut.

4 firefighters commended

Four Keene firefighters received commendations this week for their role in saving a man's life.

––––––––

As Reported by the *Keene Evening Sentinel* October 22nd, 1992:

"FIRE"

Chaos follows explosion
Downtown Keene rumbles from
electrical short-circuit

Computers shut down abruptly, many police radios stopped crackling, and buildings went dark when an underground explosion knocked out electrical power in downtown Keene Wednesday afternoon.

However, no one was hurt, and the juice was back on at most places in 45 minutes.

An old electrical cable buried in front of Keene City Hall simply failed at about 2:30 Wednesday afternoon, causing an explosion and fire, said Joseph E. Stevens, electrical superintendent for Public Service Co. of New Hampshire.

The utility plans to spend $750,000 in the next two years, replacing all older cables buried under the streets in downtown Keene.

The explosion sounded—and felt—like thunder, said City Manager Patrick J. MacQueen, who was working inside City Hall.

"It shook the building and everyone in it," MacQueen said. "At first, we were worried someone might have been hurt or killed."

He knew electrical workers had been down a manhole in front of City Hall. They had been removing asbestos insulation from underground cables, and the power was shut off while they worked.

Fortunately, when it was time to switch the power back on, it was done from above ground. No one was in the manhole when the cable blew, said Capt. Clayton Stalker of the Keene Fire Department.

Fire shot straight up out of the manhole when the cable exploded, witnesses said.

City Assessor Laurence D. Shaffer was on the telephone to his first-floor office when suddenly "there was a wall of flames outside the window. There was a pretty good concussion, too," enough to rattle his window.

I heard the bang and saw the light and I thought, "I'm in the tunnel, this is it." Shaffer said.

City Clerk Patricia A. Little, working in her first-floor office, heard "a big bang, I saw flames shoot up past the window."

Outside, three PSNH workers were standing around the manhole. They didn't seem too bothered by it; it was as though they see it every day," Little said.

Little said there was smoke in City Hall's basement.

When Peter C. Ryner, the city's planning director, heard the bang he let out a few choice words.

He'd been working on his computer for a day and a half on a complicated transportation model.

"It disappeared" when the power went off, and Ryner will have to rebuild it from scratch.

"This shows me the importance of having a backup battery," Ryner said; "I think I'll get on."

Stalker said firefighters attacked the underground blaze with fire extinguishers, "but they weren't up to the job. So they brought in two 100-pound cylinders of carbon dioxide and completely flooded the manhole," he said.

Stalker said his main concern was containing the fire inside the manhole, so it would not spread to other underground cables.

About 1,500 homes and businesses in downtown and eastern Keene lost power, Stevens said.

The explosion occurred at about 2:30, and Stevens said most places had power again by 3:15. However, City Hall and the Keene Police Department had to wait until 8:30.

City Hall's backup generator did not work during the power failure, so the police department had to reroute all its emergency calls around the corner, to dispatchers at Southwestern N.H. Fire Mutual Aid, said Thomas F. Powers 3rd, Keene police chief.

The incident also snarled downtown traffic, as police closed down the area at Washington Street and Central Square until about 5:30.

————

As Reported by the *Keene Evening Sentinel* October 27th, 1992:

"FIRE"

Toddler sparks fire

A 22-month-old toddler stuck something in a toaster oven this morning and ended up getting a visit from Keene firefighters.

The son of Holly Robarge of 122 Marlboro St., put an unidentified object in a toaster oven and then turned the oven on, authorities said. A towel atop the oven caught fire, and smoke filled the apartment at about 7:15.

Robarge got the boy and an infant out of the apartment immediately, and no one was hurt.

Keene fire Capt. Clayton R. Stalker said neighbors living above the Robarge apartment—Dawn Amer and Tim Merrill—heard smoke alarms going off in the building, raced to the apartment and were able to contain the flames with a fire extinguisher until firefighters arrived, according to Stalker.

A countertop and a cupboard were damaged slightly by flames, but the family was able to move back in, Stalker said.

Stalker said he doesn't know what the boy put in the oven, and "he can't talk, so he's not going to tell me."

————

As Reported by the *Keene Evening Sentinel* November 7th, 1992:

"FIRE"

Fire burns Keene garage

Fire hit a garage on Chapman Road in Keene Friday night, but firefighters were able to contain the flames before they ate through the rest of the house.

No one seemed to be home as flames licked along the garage eaves and fire trucks lumbered up the steep hill from Eastern Avenue. An older-model Datsun pickup truck, consumed by fire, was visible through the garage's open door.

Although the 2-car garage was in flames, firefighters first went into the one-story house to keep the fire from spreading.

At their height, the flames in the garage produced a blast of heat that could be felt on the street about 75 feet away.

After about 20 minutes, firefighters had beat down the flames in the garage.

Fighting a fire on Chapman Road—a residential street circling the southern and eastern sides of Beech Hill—is difficult because there are no hydrants. The street is so far above the city water system that fire hydrants wouldn't work.

Many fire tankers from nearby towns were called to bring water.

Late Friday night, fire officials were still at the fire and could not detail the suspected cause, the homeowner's name or other details.

The garage appeared to be demolished and the house apparently sustained smoke and water damage.

————

As Reported by the *Keene Evening Sentinel*:

Keene fire may be arson
Garage, truck are destroyed in Friday blaze

The Friday night fire that gutted the garage of a Chapman Road home may have been arson, according to the Keene Fire Department.

A dog trained to sniff out substances that can be used to start a fire was called in Saturday morning from the N.H. State Fire Marshal's office. Though the cause is still undetermined, Keene Fire Capt. Clayton Stalker said the fire is regarded as suspicious.

Stalker said he could not release the search results because that could undermine the fire department's investigation.

Firefighters from Keene, Marlborough, Swanzey and Meadowood County Area Fire Department were called to the home of Paul and Winifred Sullivan on Friday at 7:30 p.m.

According to fire officials, flames consumed the garage and a 14-year-old Datsun pickup truck parked inside. Though there was some smoke and water damage to the home itself, firefighters were able to prevent the fire from spreading beyond the garage.

The Sullivans were out of town at the time of the fire.

Anyone with information about the fire can contact Sgt. Frederick Parsells of the Keene Police Department at 3257-9815 or Stalker at 352-1291.

————

As Reported by the *Keene Evening Sentinel* November 13th, 1992:

"STORY"

Fire department presents wish list

When a fire was reported on Chapman Road last Friday night, most of Keene's fire department zoomed off.

Not the department's rescue truck, a 1973 International that carries a lot of rescue equipment and is supposed to respond to such emergencies.

It wouldn't start. Two firefighters had to push it out of the station and down Vernon Street to pop its clutch and get the motor to catch. That worked, and the truck got to the scene quickly.

But it's a situation that has happened more than once with a truck that Keene Fire Chief William H. Pepler Jr. says is in poor—now non-running—condition and that apparently has never run well since it was purchased.

So he has proposed replacing it—with a new truck costing $150,000.

That's not all, Pepler says other vehicles in his department's fleet need to be either refurbished or replaced this year—actions that he figures would cost the fire equipment capital reserve fund $340,000, including the new rescue truck.

Thursday night, Pepler presented the proposed spending to the city council's finance committee and won a 3-2 recommendation of his plan.

Councilors Roger T. Zerba and William A. Beauregard voted against the plan; they said it would leave the capital reserve fund with a too-skimpy $40,000.

But Councilor Kendall W. Lane said the city has to face up to the costs of maintaining its vehicles, or it will be saddled with much higher replacement costs.

"We are going to be looking at increased capital and maintenance costs as we fail to maintain equipment and infrastructure on a year-to-year basis," he said. "Every year we decide not to spend money we are simply kidding ourselves because the long-term costs are going to be substantially greater."

Another controversial aspect of Pepler's plan calls for adding a third ambulance to his department's fleet. The department also would replace two old pumpers with just one new one.

Pepler said that's in keeping with the department's changing mission—it now gets more rescue than fire calls.

The department could have used a third ambulance almost 100 times last year, he said. Instead, it had to rely on Robert J. DiLuzio's private ambulance service in Keene or on mutual aid from neighboring towns.

That doesn't cost Keene money, but sometimes DiLuzio's ambulances aren't available. And when ambulances have to come to Keene from other towns, it costs time in situations that may be life-threatening.

Some councilors attending the meeting said they agree that the department's oldest ambulance needs to be replaced, but they're not convinced it should be kept as a backup instead of being traded in.

But Councilor Randy L. Filault, who spends an eight-hour shift at the fire department every couple of months, said that in each of the three times he was there, both ambulances were sent out to calls at the same time, leaving the station empty. Once, one ambulance went to Swanzey and the other north to Stoddard.

"The thought always goes through the mind, what if my kid" gets hurt but there's no ambulance available in the city, he said.

"I know I've always been the one on this council to be the miser in the budget, but… this has to have my support," he said. "I just can't see a four to five minute wait."

Here are the specifics of Pepler's plan:

Spend $35,000 to refurbish Engine 1, which the chief says would add another 10 years of life to 10-year-old pumper.

Buy a new ambulance, costing $77,000.

Replace the rescue truck, costing $150,000, minus about $1,000 for the old truck.

Replace Engine 5—a 1959 truck, which has a small tank and pump fits only two people and doesn't meet any current safety standards—and Engine 2—a 1976 truck whose body is so rotten that the doors are now held shut with bungee cords. A new pumper would cost $220,000; the cost would be spread over three years.

That portion of the plan would seem to commit the city to returning to its one-time habit of placing $75,000 each year in the reserve fund, because the pumper would be paid for out of that fund. If Pepler's full plan is approved, it would leave just $40,000 in the fund next year.

———————

As Reported by the *Keene Evening Sentinel* December 16th, 1992:

"STORY"

2 accused of pulling alarm

Two N.H. men were arrested in Keene this morning, charged with setting off a phony fire alarm at Bradlees Department Store at Riverside Plaza.

Jason M. Rogers, 20, of Goffstown and Andrew W. Mackey, 19, of Greenville were scheduled to be arraigned today in Keene District Court.

They were arrested just after 4 a.m., moments after the alarm sounded, said Sgt. Edward F. Gross of the Keene Police Department. Rogers was freed on $1,500 personal recognizance bail; Mackey's bail was expected to be set this morning in court.

If convicted, the two could have to reimburse the city government for the cost of sending out a fire truck and rescue personnel, Gross said.

———————

New Rescue. Keene's new rescue truck replaced the old international. Keene's equipment moved forward to meet the public's demand. Photo by: Dave Symonds.

Keene's New E1 and E2 (pictured), identical E-1 Pumpers out of Florida, were purchased moving the fleet forward to modernize its attack firefighting force. Photo by: Steve Goldsmith.

1993

As Reported by the *Keene Evening Sentinel* January 13th, 1993:

"FIRE"

Fire damages Keene house

A kitchen fire in a West Keene home was snuffed out Tuesday afternoon by neighbors using fire extinguishers.

The fire damaged the oven, cabinets and a wall in the kitchen of the home of Allan and Martha LaFleur at 89 Colonial Drive. Keene Fire Department officials said. Smoke damaged several other rooms in the house.

The fire was reported at 3:3 p.m.

The couple's 12-year-old son, Ross, had turned on the oven without realizing that plastic food containers were inside it, according to a fire department release. When the plastic ignited, he called police, who relayed the call to the Keene Fire Department.

————

As Reported by the *Keene Evening Sentinel* February 3rd, 1993:

"FIRE"

Teen saved from fire
From second-floor window, girl is rescued

A Keene teenager who was ready to jump out a second-floor window to escape a fire in her family's apartment Tuesday night was rescued by Keene firefighters instead.

Christina Hance, 15, suffered burns, as well as cuts from breaking the window with her hand. She was listed in stable condition at Cheshire Medical Center in Keene this morning.

No one else was hurt.

Hance, who lives with her mother and sister, was alone in the apartment, sleeping, when the fire broke out in a bedroom adjacent to hers. When she woke up, the fire blocked her escape down the stairs.

She called the fire department, then ran to a window and broke it so she could jump out.

But the breaking sound was heard by a neighbor, Dean Ericson, an off-duty firefighter who'd seen the fire and was helping to get the family living in the first floor out of the house.

"She was hanging out of the window from the waist up, "Ericson said. "I hollered to her to hang in there. She was a real trooper, a real tough kid. But at one point she said to me, "I'm really scared."

"She was pretty upset—as we all would be in that situation," said Keene Fire Chief William H. Pepler Jr.

Once fire trucks arrived, Lt. Thomas Loll and firefighter Arthur Johnson raised a ladder to the second floor and carried Hance to safety.

Pepler said the cause of the fire—believed to be accidental—is being investigated, but was unknown this morning.

Damage to the first-floor apartment was minimal, and Pepler said the family that lives there was able to sleep in the house Tuesday night.

The house is owned by Charles Dziengoski of St. Augustine, Fla. Fire officials declared the fire under control at 7:33 p.m., and all trucks left the scene by 8:57.

————

A Demon Called Fire

As Reported by the *Keene Evening Sentinel* March 5th, 1993:

"FIRE"

2,000 gallons of oil spill in restaurant parking lot

Portions of the 176 Main St. parking lot were glossed and slippery Thursday night, but it wasn't because of ice.

Cooking oil—2,000 slippery gallons of it—spilled Thursday night when a dumpster full of it turned over, Keene firefighters and public works employees has to clean up the yucky mess.

Keene Fire Chief William Pepler said about 1,000 gallons of the oil spilled into the city's storm drain before firefighters closed off the drain.

Public works employees dumped about a truck full of sand onto the oil, scooped it up and put it in the landfill, said Bruce Tatro, highway department superintendent.

City workers used a vacuum truck to clean oil out of the storm drain.

Pepler said the oil spilled when a disposal company was loading the restaurant's grease dumpster onto a truck. A cable broke, resulting in the spill, Pepler said.

As Reported by the *Keene Evening Sentinel* March 25th, 1993:

"FIRE"

Fire clears KSC dorm Students escape by ladder; 3 treated at hospital

Two students jumped from a second-floor window and 280 were driven from a Keene State College dormitory early this morning after fire broke out in one of the rooms.

About 280 residents of Carle Hall safely escaped the fire that completely destroyed room 210, shared by Ann P. Jackman of Holbrook, Mass., and Denyelle J. Potter of Nashua.

The women lost everything in the room, said Retha Lindsey, director of college relations.

Three students were treated at Cheshire Medical Center in Keene for smoke inhalation.

Cause of the fire is still under investigation, but is not considered to be suspicious, said Capt. Clayton R. Stalker Jr. of the Keene Fire Department.

The fire started at 3 a.m. and was declared under control just after 4:30. Fire damage was confined to room 210, though there was some additional smoke and water damage throughout the second floor.

Jackman and Potter are lucky they got out when they did, Stalker said.

The smoke first woke up Potter, who tried to extinguish the fire herself. When that didn't work, she woke Jackman—who was disoriented by the smoke and the early hour—and dragged her from the room, Stalker said.

Seven students on the third floor were trapped by the smoke. Four escaped down ladders from the fire department's ladders.

The fire shook dorm residents.

"I thought it was my alarm clock," Amy B. Lewis of Brookline said of the early morning alarm. "I kept trying to shut it off until I realized it was the fire alarm."

Lewis lives in Carle Hall and said she's a friend of Jackman and Potter.

It's scary," she said. "It kind of just makes you think. "What would you do if it was you?"

Most students, except those living in the wing where the fire occurred, were let back into their rooms at about 6 o'clock this morning.

Students living in the wing are being housed temporarily in other dormitories, Lindsey said. They will likely be let back in their rooms but this afternoon.

"It was different," freshman Joseph S. Malewicki of Monroe, Conn., said of his early morning wake-up call. "I thought it was a drill at first."

While many students were forced outside in their pajamas and bathrobes, the evacuation went smoothly, according to freshman Danielle M. Kukene of Haverhill, Mass.

"Everyone was cool about it," she said.

Most students had already gone to stay with friends in other residence halls by the time Carle Hall was reopened.

Lindsey said firefighters has just responded to a false alarm next door, at the Owl's Nest dormitory, when the Carle Hall alarm went off.

This is the second fire this school year in a Keene State residence hall. An earlier fire in Randall Hall on November 10, 1992, was considered to be suspicious and is still under investigation.

Keene firefighters were assisted by the Swanzey Fire Department, the Keene Police Department and DiLuzio Ambulance Service.

———

As Reported by the *Keene Evening Sentinel* March 29th, 1993:

"FIRE"

Fire damages garage

A Keene garage was damaged by fire Sunday morning after a motorcycle backfired and set fire to a wall.

Rick Lampher of 37 Fairbanks St. had tried to start the 1983 Honda motorcycle Saturday, but it flooded, according to Keene Fire Capt. Clayton R. Stalker.

On Sunday morning, while cleaning out the garage, Lampher tried starting the motorcycle again. It backfired, setting fire to the motorcycle and a wall behind it, Stalker said.

Lampher extinguished the motorcycle fire with a garden hose, but then realized the wall was on fire too.

When Keene firefighters arrived, heavy smoke and flames were coming out of the two-story building, but they were able to douse the fire and save most of the garage, Stalker said.

———

☙   *A Demon Called Fire*

As Reported by the *Keene Evening Sentinel* April 5th, 1993:

"STORY"

Treed coon cat finds savior in city firefighter

Lucky, the Maine coon cat stuck in a Keene tree for five days, is at home now, resting comfortably after a daring rescue.

Phillip "Butchy" Davis jr., a Keene firefighter, clambered up a 75 foot-tall pine tree early Saturday morning and carried Lucky down.

Since Tuesday, his owners had called, crooned and meowed, trying to lure their cat down the tree. No luck.

Davis to the rescue.

Davis, a part-time Keene firefighter and a tree-cutter, scurried up the tree in Tanglewood Estates, off Oriole Avenue, where the cat was marooned.

Friends say helping out is Davis' nature.

"Butch is that type of person," said Gary LaFreniere, a Keene firefighter. "Anybody needs help, he'll do it."

"It ain't nothing different from fighting fires," said Davis, 27. I've climbed worse trees than that this year."

Davis strapped spurs to his boots, tied safety straps to hold him to the tree, and spent about 20 minutes climbing up the tree, luring Lucky, and climbing back down.

Not that Lucky was interested in being rescued. As cats are inclined to do, the tree bound tabby climbed even higher—clear to the top of the tree—as Davis approached.

Lucky hissed and scratched, Davis said, but he was able to grab him anyway.

Even the cat's owner acknowledges that Lucky's not too smart. He suffered nerve damage as a young cat and walks with a tilted head, said Heather Collins.

But once in Davis' arms, the cat calmed down. Davis put Lucky in a backpack and brought him down to terrafirma.

Lucky was slightly dehydrated and had a fever, but he looked happy, happy to be down, said Collins, who works at Cheshire Animal Hospital.

"Hopefully, he won't go back up the tree. Hopefully, he's learned his lesson," she said.

The rescue was tricky. Lucky was way up the tree and seemed to have no idea how to get down.

Keene Tree Service figured initially that a rescue would cost $150, but then it backed off altogether.

What if Davis hadn't done his good deed?

"I think he would have died up there," Collins said.

———

As Reported by the *Keene Evening Sentinel* April 22nd, 1993:

"FIRE"

Minor fire hits KSC dorm

Students were evacuated from a Keene State College dormitory early this morning after someone set fire to a bulletin board, Keene police said.

A dormitory resident put out the fire with an extinguisher before firefighters arrived; no one was hurt, said Sgt. Frederick B. Parsells, a Keene police detective.

The fire was reported shortly before 1 a.m. on the third floor of Holloway Hall. Students were evacuated until it was certain the fire was out, Parsells said.

The dormitory's 252 residents waited outside for nearly an hour until firefighters allowed them to go into a meeting room, said Retha Lindsey, director of college relations.

"It's a very dangerous thing to do something like this," Lindsey said." "It doesn't make very much sense to set a fire in a residence hall where you're living. This is not really a rational act."

Parsells said police are investigating. The fire likely was started by a dormitory resident, said Parsells, who's part of the police arson investigation team.

"It was intentionally set, but was it arson? No," Parsells said. He described it as criminal mischief, the legal term for vandalism.

Parsells said the bulletin board was close to a lounge area. Papers on the board were lit and eventually the cork caught fire, he said.

Today's fire comes on the heels of a room fire in Carle Hall on March 25 that caused significant damage.

————

As Reported by the *Keene Evening Sentinel* April 24th, 1993:

"STORY"

Deputy fire chief is named

Clayton R. Stalker Jr. has been promoted to deputy chief of the Keene fire Department.

The deputy's job has been vacant since Paul E. Crowell retired last year.

Stalker has been a Keene firefighter for 16 years. For the four years before his promotion, he was the department's fire prevention officer. He holds a bachelor's degree from the University of Nee Hampshire and an associate degree to applied science from N.H.

Technical Institute. Now he's enrolled in the executive fire officer program at the National Fire Academy.

Stalker is a state-certified firefighter and a nationally registered emergency medical technician, and has received extensive training in fire and arson investigation at St. Anselm College and with the Boston Fire Department.

As deputy chief, Stalker will command the fire department's administration division, which handles fire prevention, education, investigation, training in firefighting and hazardous materials handling, fire alarm maintenance, emergency medical services and public relations.,

Stalker lives at 49 North Lincoln St. in Keene with his wife, Ellie, son Joseph and daughter Rachel. He has been active in many community activities, including the Keene Area Kiwanis Club, Keene Youth Baseball, and the Keene School District safety committee.

————

As Reported by the *Keene Evening Sentinel* May 3rd, 1993:

"FIRE"

Factory damaged by fire; firefighter injured in fall

A sprinkler system kept an electrical fire from spreading beyond a Keene factory's boiler room Saturday night until firefighters arrived and doused it.

Damage was minimal to Whitney Brother, a woodworking plant at 93 Railroad St. that makes children's furniture and toys, said Clayton Stalker, deputy Keene fire chief.

One firefighter was slightly injured, Lt Robert Crowell fell off a 4-foot dropoff to the boiler room onto his shoulder. He was examined at Cheshire Medical Center in Keene but suffered only bruises, Stalker said.

The fire was confined to the boiler room, but did not involve the boiler. It began in an electrical panel on one wall and spread to some conduit wire on the ceiling, Stalker said.

The building's sprinkler was activated at 5:01 p.m., which rang an automatic alarm at the Keene Fire Department.

————

As Reported by the *Keene Evening Sentinel* May 21st, 1993:

"FIRE"

Keene fire wrecks car

A fire that started in a car's engine compartment spread to the clapboards of a house at 115 North St., Keene, but was doused quickly by firefighters Thursday night.

The car was demolished.

Tanya Lowe told firefighters that she started the car at about 8:10 p.m., and heard a crackling sound and saw sparks coming from the engine area. The car was parked about 3 feet from the house, owned by Lowe's father, Bruce Hilow, and the flames started licking the house clapboards.

Firefighters raced to North Street and doused the flames before the interior of the house was damaged.

No injuries were reported.

————

As Reported by the *Keene Evening Sentinel* June 28th, 1993:

"FIRE"

Fire doused in Keene

A fire that started inside an electric rate meter at a Marlboro Street laundry caused minor damage to the building, but no in juries, early Sunday evening.

The fire, which was reported at about 6 p.m., spread to the back wall of the Wash House at 170 Marlboro St.

Part of Marlboro Street was closed while firefighters doused the flames.

Witnesses reported smelling something burning after power at the building went out, according to Deputy Fire Chief Clayton Stalker.

When firefighters arrived, they discovered smoke coming from the roof and a fire burning in the wall at the rear end of the furnace room, Stalker said.

————

As Reported by the *Keene Evening Sentinel* July 20th, 1993:

"STORY"

City's fire-alarm ordinance will force Keene State College to pay up

Keene State College will have to pay about $3,000 a year if it wants to be connected to a citywide fire alarm system, according to an ordinance passed last week by the city council.

The college owes the city about $30,000 for false fire alarms, responded to by the Keene Fiore Department. And while the ordinance won't make KSC pay that debt, it will ensure that the college will help pay for services in the future.

The ordinance requires all businesses that have master fire alarm boxes connected to the city's system to pay $150 for each box. Keene State, with about 20 fire alarm boxes, is the largest single user of the system, Fire Chief William H. Pepler Jr. said.

Pepler proposed the ordinance as a way to help maintain the aging fire alarm system. The money raised—about $45,000—will be placed in a fund that can be spent only on running and maintaining the fire alarm system.

As with the city's parking, sewer and water funds, the fire alarm fund is a user fee: Those who use the system pay for it.

"It's not on the taxpayer's back," Pepler said.

Pepler said establishing the annual fee is a way to make sure the college helps pay for the service it receives.

"I think the way the ordinance is written is fair, and applied evenly," he said.

The system: Keene's fire alarm system is about 100 years old. When it was installed, horses pulled hand-pumped water trucks to the scene. Today, ladder trucks and fire engines are used to fight fires, but the alarm system is the same.

When an alarm sounds, the signal travels through a low voltage wire to the station, where the department dispatches its trucks. All this happens almost instantly, giving the fire department a jump on the call.

If businesses or the college choose not to pay the annual fee, they won't be connected directly to the fire department. Instead, they would be forced to go through a private dispatching company, which can often add to the response time.

If a private dispatcher is used, the fire alarm signal is sent to another location. From there, the dispatcher calls the Keene Fire Department and firefighters respond. That takes time, Pepler said.

"In a fire situation, (that) can make all the difference," he said.

The city council approved $170,000 last year to update the system; money from the fire alarm fund will be used to maintain the system.

Though the college has refused to pay for the numerous false fire alarms at the college each year, Pepler said he's spoken with Keene State officials about the new ordinance. They have indicated a willingness to pay, he said.

Retha Lindsey, Keene State's director of college relations, said she hasn't heard about the new ordinance. She said the college is pleased with the fire department's response to two fires on campus last year.

Jay V. Kahn, the college's vice president for finance and planning, who usually deals with city-college issues, was on vacation and not available for comment.

———

As Reported by the *Keene Evening Sentinel* July 26th, 1993;

"STORY"

Emergency 911 still 2 years away Calling system puts information at finger tips of fire, police dispatchers

Taking the call- Phil Tirrell of Southewestern N.H. Fire and Mutual Aid takes a call at the Keene headquarters located in the Keene Fire Department building on Vernon Street,. In the background is Tom Redin. The local mutual aid does not have the 911 emergency system in place yet. Photo by Michael Moore.

When a police or fire dispatcher picks up the telephone and gets silence, a kind of queasy feeling sets in.

Sure, it could be a wrong number, with the caller rudely deciding to hang up.

But there's all sorts of reasons why someone calling for help can't talk: a man clutches his chest and gasps for air, an abuser rips the telephone off the wall and attacks his wife. Or, as happened in Claremont last year, a woman is choking and can't speak.

Recognizing those fears, the N.H. Legislature last year endorsed a system that will automatically identify the telephone call's origin and link it to the nearest fire, police and ambulance units.

People will have to remember just three numbers—911—to get help anywhere in the state.

That's compared to places such as Keene, where two seven-digit emergency numbers are in use: one for police, another for fire and ambulance.

But despite the Legislature's support, the high-tech system won't be operating statewide until July 1, 1995—and only than if all goes well.

"It's got a long way to go," said Bruce G. Cheney, a former Laconia police chief and director of the N.H. Bureau of Emergency Communication, which is setting up the enhanced 911 system.

The system will combine the high technology elements of caller identification, call forwarding and fact, data-base computing to put knowledge where it's needed the most: at the finger tops of people answering emergency calls.

"As a local chief, enhanced 911 makes all the sense in the world and should have been done years ago," said Chesterfield Police Chief Eric S. Sargent.

Currently, New Hampshire has a hodgepodge system in place for answering about 680,000 emergency calls each year.

In some remote areas, so-called "red networks" still exist, an emergency telephone rings in the homes of several people—most of them volunteer firefighters—with the hope that someone's around to pick up the p[hone.

Most of the state's larger cities use 911, but regionally, only Peterborough uses 911.

In most Monadnock Region cities and town, politics, long-distance networks and local control make for some awkward situations.

For example, local area firefighters and ambulance personnel are dispatched through Southwestern N.H. Fire Mutual Aid, set up in a small room off the Keene Fire Department building on Vernon Street. People needing emergency help call 352-1100.

But that's where continuity ends.

Keene and N.H. State Police have their own round-the-clock dispatchers. Many medium-sized police forces use secretaries to dispatch emergency calls during business hours Monday through Friday.

All local police departments have their different numbers.

Things get sloppy when someone dials 911 from a town that doesn't offer the service. That call can be answered as far away as Massachusetts, where an operator has to determine where to send the call.

Enhanced 911 would clear that up.

Wrong perception: But making things simple for dialers has complicated matters for dispatchers.

"The benefit is the public's perception of 911. It's been highly marketed by the telephone companies," said John S. Marechal, director of Southwestern N.H. Fire Mutual Aid.

"We've made it easy for the public to remember. We've made it hard for the public agency to receive it," he said.

That's because of the considerable time and money it will cost to get the enhanced portion of the system—the data retrieval part—up and operating.

Officials are about ready to seek bids on the data-base development and entry portion of the projects. It will be an 18-month task matching the state's 600,000 telephone numbers to a subscriber, street address and applicable police, fire and ambulance agencies.

"We're going to have access to the bowels of the phone company's data base," Cheney said.

According to specifications changes must be entered within 24 hours. Officials expect the contract will cost $3.2 million.

All calls will go into a central point—or Public Safety Answering Point—located somewhere near the middle of the state.

There, an operator will answer the telephone, and get an instant call up of the data that's entered.

Once the nature of the emergency is determined, the call will be forwarded to the appropriate dispatch center—such as mutual aid or the Keene Police dispatcher.

"This operation will be nothing more than a hand off," Cheney said.

Officials acknowledge another link is added to a chain, and someone needing help will have to talk to two people before help is summoned.

But they give several justifications for the system:

Having only one system with one data base, one set of equipment and one crew is three times less expensive than having one per county, Cheney said.

While talking to two people may add 20 seconds to an average emergency call, not having to look up a telephone number can save an average of 90 seconds, Cheney said.

Regional dispatchers are familiar with the local roads. Dispatchers at a statewide center would not be.

Tracing a call instantly is invaluable, according to emergency dispatchers.

Bonnie Johnson, a dispatcher with Southwestern N.H. Fire Mutual Aid, said she got a call a couple weeks ago from a woman in Swanzey. "Need some help," the woman said, and then the line went dead.

Luckily, the dispatch center has a simple form of enhanced 911—Caller ID, available through the phone company. Johnson recorded the number, traced it in the city directory and summoned police to the Swanzey address.

It turned out to be a domestic dispute.

"If there was no Caller ID, there's nothing you can do. You hope they call back," Johnson said.

Another dispatcher, Neal Collier, got a call from a child who said he lived on Base Hill Road. Someone was having a heart attack and the child said he had forgotten his last name. Collier traced the call and sent an ambulance. It was a prank.

While Caller ID worked in those cases, it is not perfect. People can have their number blocked, Caller ID cannot cross state lines and if a person's telephone number isn't published, dispatchers can't trace it.

"They're good as a resource," Marechal said about Caller ID, "but they're not the ultimate."

In Claremont last year, a woman who was choking called 911. Though the city has 911, it does not have Caller ID.

By the time dispatchers traced the call through the telephone company, the woman was dead, Cheney said.

"That's the most basic reason this enhanced system is going into place—to save lives," Marechal said. "Someone's choking, they can dial 911, they're going to automatically have their address identified."

With a request for bids on the data base about ready to go out, Cheney said the next step will be to organize street names and addresses in communities across New Hampshire.

That will require a big effort by city and town officials, Cheney said.

Unnumbered houses will have to get an address, and non-sequential addresses will have to be changed.

Also, roads with the same names will have to be renamed, he said.

————

As Reported by the *Keene Evening Sentinel* July 27th, 1993:

"STORY"

Contract talks stall between firefighters' supervisors, city

A mediator has been called in to help jump start stalled negotiations between the Keene city government and the union representing 10 fire department supervisors.

The two sides declared an impasse Monday and agreed to bring in mediator Richard Higgins to help move the process along.

Assistant City Manager Laurence R. Shaffer said this morning that Higgins is familiar with the issues being discussed between the two sides. He helped mediate contract negotiations in 1991 before a fact-finder was called in.

Fire Capt. Thomas L. Loll jr., president of the local union, said he didn't want to comment on issues separating the two sides until he spoke with the union's lawyer.

Mediation is the first step after impasse is declared. If the mediator cannot bring the two sides together, a fact-finder is called in to listen to the arguments from both sides and recommend a non-binding contract settlement.

Firefighters and their supervisors formed unions three years ago after City Manager J. Patrick MacQueen proposed reorganizing city government, and putting a public service director in charge of the fire, police, and code enforcement departments. Firefighters opposed the setup, and it was never enacted.

The supervisors' union and the city council agreed to a contract in June 1992. Under that contract, they received 5 percent raises—1 percent as a retroactive one-time payment. That contract expired in June.

Loll and Shaffer declined to comment on the specific issues separating the two sides.

"Suffice it to say, we're at impasse…and we hope to resolve some of the outstanding issues," Shaffer said.

No date has been set to meet with the mediator.

The supervisors' union is one of the five contracts with city employee unions that expired in June. The police supervisors' union also declared impasse after the city government proposed a 5 percent pay cut, a cap on health-insurance benefits, and a reduction in sick days and holiday time.

———

As Reported by the *Keene Evening Sentinel* August 12th, 1993:

"FIRE"

Woman burned in Keene

A coffeepot left on a stove apparently caused a fire at about 5:30 this morning in an apartment at 411 Washington St.

The apartment's occupant, Harriette Rau, received minor burns on one hand and her feet when she tried to douse the flames with a fire extinguisher, said Deputy Chief Clayton R. Stalker of the Keene Fire Department. She was treated at home.

Stalker said the fire was reported by neighbors who heard Ray calling for help. When firefighters arrived, smoke was coming out of the building, and the stove and a nearby wall was on fire. The flames were doused quickly, he said.

Fire officials were headed back to the apartment later today, Stalker said, because the apartment did not have the smoke detectors it's supposed to have.

———

As Reported by the *Keene Evening Sentinel* August 17th, 1993:

Fire department inspection finds Keene bar to be overcrowded

A Keene bar was "grossly overloaded" during a surprise inspection last week, and fire officials issued a warning to the owner to stay within his legal limit or face fines or a liquor license suspension.

Keene Deputy Fire Chief Clayton Stalker declined to name the establishment that was given a warning because no written citation was issued. However, he said the place has a maximum occupancy of 59, and was grossly over loaded with 110 people.

Four bars and restaurants—Penuche's Ale House, the Hon Dynasty, the Ashuelot River Yacht Club and the Sports Corner—were visited in surprise inspections Thursday night, he said.

According to city records, Penuche's, the smallest of the four establishments, has a maximum occupancy of 59. The maximum occupancy for the three restaurants: Ashuelot River Yacht Club, 150; Hon Dynasty, 138; and Sports Corner, 75.

When inspectors entered the establishment that was overcrowded, they asked the bartender to call the owner immediately. He arrived and kicked out about half the patrons, Stalker said.

Stalker and Fire Prevention Officer Brad Payne were accompanied by a police officer during the inspections, Stalker said. They checked for overcrowding, blocked exits and other possible fire code violations.

Officials did the surprise inspections after several complaints were made about overcrowding, Stalker said. The inspections are the second since William H. Pepler Jr. took over as fire chief last summer.

"We're going to do it on a periodic, unscheduled basis," Stalker said.

Initially, owners are given a warding. On subsequent offenses, they can be fined for violating city ordinances or the city can contact the N.H. Liquor Commission and ask that their license be suspended.

If violations continue, this city can ask the N.H. Fire Marshal's office to close the place down.

———

As Reported by the *Keene Evening Sentinel* August 24th, 1993:

"FIRE"

Gas leaks from grill, explodes; man is injured

A Keene man was slightly burned Monday night when gas leaked from his gas grill and exploded in his face when he hit the starter button, according to Keene fire officials.

John J. Desilets of 194 Pako Ave. suffered minor burns on his face, arms and head, but declined to go to the hospital for treatment, said Clayton Stalker, Keene's deputy fire chief.

Fire officials say a hose connecting the tank with the grill had loosened, and enough gas leaked out to cause a minor explosion.

"It doesn't burn; it flashes," Stalker said. "The flash is enough to cause a serious burn."

Firefighters used a fog spray to disperse the gas, and also cleared gas out of the Desilets house, Stalker said.

Firefighters are seeing more such problems, as gas grills and tanks start to wear over the years, Stalker said. He encouraged people to replace old tanks, clean their grills, and not light them on a porch, because the building could catch fire if gas leaked out.

———

Burn victim still critical

The man who was injured Tuesday in an explosion at Davis Oil Co. In Keene remains in critical condition in the burn unit of Massachusetts General Hospital in Boston.

Kevin Leblond, 29, of Brewer, Maine, suffered burns on 53 percent of his body Tuesday during an explosion inside an oil tank. He was taken first to the Cheshire Medical Center in Keene, then airlifted Tuesday afternoon to the Boston hospital.

According to fire officials, Leblond was painting the inside of an empty oil tank at the David Oil Co. when the explosion occurred. An electric light used to illuminate the inside of the tank is being blamed fort the explosion.

Officials from the federal Occupational Safety and Health Administration are expected to investigate the accident.

Leblond received second and third-degree burns on his arms, legs, back and hands.

———

As Reported by the *Keene Evening Sentinel* September 7th, 1993:

"STORY"

Federal agency investigating blast

Federal safety officials are investigating an explosion August 31 that severely burned a man while he was painting the interior of an oil-storage tank in Keene.

An investigator from the federal Occupational Safety and Health Administration visited Davis Oil Co. the day after the noontime explosion in which Kevin Leblond, 29, was injured.

Leblond was in fair condition this morning in the burn unit at Massachusetts General Hospital in Boston. Burns cover more than half of his body.

Keene Fire Department officials have criticized the safety practices of the contractor hired to paint the tank, National Service Group Inc. of Kittery Point, Maine.

The company president has said the company has good safety practices, but acknowledged some procedures were not being followed when Leblond was hurt.

———

As Reported by the *Keene Evening Sentinel* September 10th, 1993:

"FIRE"

Fire damages home

A dropped kerosene lantern is being blamed for a fire that severely damaged the kitchen of a mobile home at Tanglewood Estates in Keene on Thursday.

The fire at the home of Shirley Desrosier of 47 Oriole Ave. started shortly after 6 p.m., according to the Keene Fire Department.

Desrosier was cooking in the kitchen when she tried to remove a kerosene lamp from a cabinet, according to fire officials. The lamp slipped and broke on the counter next to the stove, igniting the fuel.

Heavy smoke was billowing from the kitchen when firefighters arrived. They were able to confine the blaze to the kitchen.

Kitchen cabinets, the stove and floor were damaged. There were no injuries.

Firefighters used fans to remove as much smoke as possible. Although the mobile home remains habitable, Desrosier probably will have to hire professional cleaners.

———

As Reported by the *Keene Evening Sentinel* September 12th, 1993:

"STORY"

KSC dorm is evacuated

Much of a Keene State College dormitory had to be evacuated Friday at about 10 p.m. after students complained of a strange smell in the building.

Several students from Randall Hall on Winchester Street were taken to Cheshire Medical Center in Keene as a precaution after some kind of gas was detected on the second floor of the building.

Though it was uncertain just what went on late Friday night, fire officials said it's possible that smokeless tear gas had been set off in the building.

One student said the odor at first was like a powerful incense. Students sitting in an ambulance on Winchester Street did not appear ill and chatted among themselves about the experience.

No further details were available when The Sentinel went to press.

————

As Reported by the *Keene Evening Sentinel* September 20th, 1993:

"STORY"

911 chief: Groundwork is a constant juggling act

New Hampshire is moving steadily toward a high tech emergency response system, but its organizers first must make their way through a logistical minefield of technology and tradition.

The Enhanced 911 system will allow people anywhere in the state to dial 911 and be connected in seconds to the police, fire or rescue dispatcher they need.

It also will let emergency dispatchers know the address, even if the caller can't speak, doesn't know where he or she is or if someone slams the phone down before the caller can yell for help.

The target date is July 1, 1995.

By then, Bruce Cheney, who is directing the conversion, will have driven tens of thousands of miles to every N.H. town.

"I spend most of my time traveling around the state telling people how I'm not trying to ruin their lives," said Cheney, retired chief of the Laconia Police Department.

One main misconception is that the 911 operation will be a super dispatch center.

Instead, the dispatcher will be able to read the address when the telephone gets answered and know which police or fire department to route the call to, said Keene Police Chief Thomas F. Powers 3rd, vice chairman of the commission.

Here's how Enhanced 911 would work.

Suppose someone in a car being driven by a motorist unfamiliar with the area has a heart attack.

The motorist stops at a telephone booth and dials 911.

An operator asks; "What is the nature of your emergency?"

As the caller explains what has happened, the telephone number is displayed for the operator, who says, "Stay on the line, we'll give you to the EMT's.

The operator hits a red, blue or green button on the console, to determine which fire or police department or rescue squad should be notified.

The computer determines the location of the telephone and the appropriate dispatcher, and the operator makes the connection.

The dispatcher asks for the caller's location, if the caller doesn't know, or gives an inaccurate location, the 911 operator provides the information.

The 911 operator hangs up and the local dispatcher sends help.

If the caller cannot speak English, the 911 operator hits a button and reaches a bank of interpreters.

As Reported by the *Keene Evening Sentinel* October 1st, 1993:

"FIRE"

Early morning fire reported at MPB plant in Keene

Lubricant caught on fire early this morning in a piece of machinery at an MPB Corp. plant in Keene, causing what officials estimate to be $3,000 worth of damage.

The fire started at about 6 a.m. in a turret lathe at the MPB Corp. plant No. 4 at 160 Emerald St., according to Clayton R. Stalker, deputy chief of the Keene Fire Department.

The fire burned an exhaust hose, and a sprinkler system was set off, Stalker said.

As Reported by the *Keene Evening Sentinel* November 8th, 1993:

"FIRE"

Fire damages Keene apartment; 5 treated

Five people suffered smoke inhalation and two cats were killed Saturday morning when a fire broke out in a third-floor apartment at 215 Church St in Keene.

Treated for smoke inhalation were Cindy Sue Royea, 26; Samantha Royea, 6; Warren Royea, 4; and David Guilhault, 36, all of 215 Church St., and Thomas Chase, 46, of 168 Washington St., Keene.

Firefighters helped a second-floor resident out of the building; she had been trying to rescue her cat. Her cat was saved, but two cats living in the third-floor apartment died, said Fire Chief William H. Pepler Jr.

The rescue unit from the Meadowood County Are Fire Department in Fitzwilliam helped the Keene Fire Department deal with the injured people.

The fire started in the apartment's kitchen; what caused it is still being investigated, said Deputy Keene Fire Chief Clayton R. Stalker Jr. Damage was estimated at $20,000, Stalker said. The third-floor kitchen was charred and the rest of that apartment received extensive heart and smoke damage. A second-floor apartment received minor water damage.

Even so, people who lived on the first and second floors were able to go back into their homes.

Smoke was billowing out the third-floor windows and smoke alarms were sounding when firefighters reached the building at about 8:30 Saturday morning.

Firefighters were able to douse the flames quickly, before they burned through the building's walls. The flames were out in about 15 minutes, but firefighters spent about two more hours checking for hidden embers, salvaging personal belongings, and pumping water out of the building.

As Reported by the *Keene Evening Sentinel* November 8th, 1993:

"FIRE"

2 hurt at KSC

Two students had breathing problems, and one needed hospital treatment after another student set off a fire extinguisher in a Keene State College dormitory at about 1 o'clock this morning.

There was no fire.

About 30 students, in a section of Carle Hall had to clear out of their rooms after the dry chemical fire extinguisher was emptied in a hallway.

Keene paramedic administered oxygen to two students who were having trouble breathing, and one of them, who has asthma, was taken to Cheshire Medical Center for more extensive treatment, said Deputy Fire Chief Clayton R. Stalker Jr.

The chemical in the fire extinguisher is not toxic, Stalker said, but can cause choking.

It's an irritant, along the lines of breathing in baby powder," he said.

Students had to spend about two hours in the college gymnasium while a cleaning crew cleared the chemical out of the hallway. Students were allowed to return to their rooms at about 5 this morning.

The student believed responsible for the incident may face penalties from the college and Keene police. "The college considers this kind of thing as a very serious infraction of the rules," said Retha Lindsy, head of KSC's information office. However, Lindsey would not release the student's name.

————

As Reported by the *Keene Evening Sentinel* November 22nd, 1993:

"STORY"

Intrepid reporter says, 'Pass the Ben-Gay'
Firefighters' strength test is 18 minutes of hell

I should have known I was in trouble when I was tying my sneakers Saturday morning, and I thought, "I knew I'd wear these someday."

Waiting for me was the Keene firefighters' physical ability test—the test all Keene firefighters will have to pass next year.

Full-time and o n-call, volunteer firefighters are encouraged to try the test this year as part of a fitness plan that Keene Fire Chief William H. Pepler Jr. established when he came to Keene 1 ½ years ago.

When Pepler worked for the Exeter Fire Department, a captain there had a heart attack while fighting a fire. Heart failure is the leading cause of on-the-job deaths for U.S. firefighters, according to national statistics.

I wasn't worried about my heart, though, as I drove up to the fire department's training center near Dillant-Hopkins Airport in North Swanzey. Still, I didn't expect I'd pass the test. I'm no hulk of a woman.

But I didn't expect to fail miserably. I was a gymnast, after all, and I could do more chin-ups than any of the boys in gym class. And in the summers, when I wasn't competing, I did 1,000 sit-ups per workout. My sisters teased me for looking like a man whenever I wore a bikini.

But that was then.

Fire Capt. Bruce W. Pollock was waiting for me Saturday morning, along with a handful of fire department volunteers and a couple of prospective full-timers. Only one other woman was there; she had bronchitis and was just going to watch.

Three women have taken the test and failed, though many were more physically fit than the men, said Deputy Fire Chief Clayton R. Stalker Jr.

It's upper-body strength, and that's one of the areas where women historically are weaker than men," said Stalker, explaining why no women have passed.

The Keene Fire Department has no women on staff.

Pollock walked us through the course. It looks simple, but not necessarily if you're wearing a firefighting helmet and jacket, a 26-pound air tank that fits like a backpack, and 5-pound weights on each ankle to simulate the weight of a firefighter's gear.

You're timed through the whole test, but there's no time limit (amen for that). You're also allowed one 45-second break—hallelujah. Most finished in 10 to 12 minutes. I did it in, um, 18.

Here's a look at the test:

Ladders: Pick up one end of a 24-foot ladder that's laying on the ground and walk forward, pushing it up until it's standing straight.

The ladder weighs 60 pounds. I discovered muscles stretching across my chest with at one.

Next, pick up a 14-foot long ladder, hanging horizontally on a rack, in the center, balance it on your shoulder, and carry it 20 feet around an orange cone. If you drop the ladder, you fail.

I didn't fail, because I didn't actually drop it. However, a couple of nervous onlookers interfered when they thought I was losing my balance.

Dummy: To simulate removing an unconscious person from a fire, drag a 140 pound dummy 120 feet while walking backward. This was one of the easier tasks, even though the dummy weighed more than I do. The hard parts were keeping your grip, and holding down your breakfast.

Pulleys: Using a rope-pulley apparatus, hoist the fly section of a 35-foot extension ladder, hand over hand.

The pulley system must have needed oil or something. I could have hung on that rope and the ladder wouldn't have budged an inch.

Next, also using a pulley and rope, pull up a 350foot-long, 2 ½-inch-diameter hose until it extends about two stories high. I got about halfway.

Hammering: Strike an 8-pound sledgehammer 50 times into a log, raising the hammer at least 24 inches on every strike. That simulates taking a pickax to a roof.

No sweat, I even gave the log an extra strike to boost my ailing ego.

Hose: Sling a fire hose over your shoulder and pull it 200 feet.

Easy enough—until I got 100 feet, I looked back to see which wise guy was standing on the hose, only to find nobody there.

Crawling: An attic level of a house is propped a few feet off the ground. You have to crawl through the rafters in a space about 2 feet high. If you step or fall through the beams, you're disqualified.

The black-and-blue marks on my shins show I met the challenge.

Last job: The final test is to lift a 50-foot, rolled-up fire hose and carry it around the airport parking lot, about 1,500 feet.

Here, I learned the true meaning of oxygen deprivation. Same with Eddie Lamoureaux, captain for the volunteer fire squad, who smokes a pack and a half of cigarettes a day.

A sort of bonus to the day was climbing a 100-foot truck-mounted ladder that's suspended in midair. This is required of job applicants.

I took it one rung at a time, 76 in all, before I reached the top. Normally, you fasten a hook to a rung and let go to prove you've got guts, as if climbing above the tree line doesn't show that.

I kind of got a real high being up there (pun intended), but I couldn't get the darn clip to open, so I could hang free.

The volunteer firefighters climb the ladder all the time, so they got to skip that part on Saturday. They all passed everything else. I didn't. But all acknowledged that the day was agony.

It is definitely a physical job.

Though Keene firefighters may sit around during much of their work shifts drinking coffee, when they fight a fire, they face the challenges of the test, and then some.

Twenty minutes of fighting a fire can be as stressful and physically demanding as an eight-hour laborer's job, said Pepler, citing national studies on the hazards of firefighting.

Fighting fires and saving lives takes brute strength as well as coordination, determination and some firefighters say—foolishness. You also need a chemistry background to handle hazardous spills, and the medical know how to save a person with a failing heart or a broken back.

Keene residents won't have to worry about me coming to their rescue. I'm sticking with my day job, and I'm buying stock in Ben-Gay.

————

As Reported by the *Keene Evening Sentinel* November 23rd, 1993:

"FIRE"

Fire destroys storage building

Shannon L. Kittredge of Keene was walking her dog Monday afternoon through the Woodland Cemetery in Keene when she saw a huge black cloud billowing above the trees near Washington Street.

The black cloud turned bright orange and then a drab gray, she said.

"To tell you the truth, it was actually pretty," she said.

It wasn't so pretty for Keene firefighters. The clouds were produced by a relentless fire at a storage building at 525 Washington St.

When firefighters arrived at 3:59 p.m., the old wood and brick building, tucked next to the southeast corner of the David Edwin Inc. business supply store, was engulfed in flames.

The cause of the fire is not yet clear, but it appears suspicious and is being investigated, said Keene Deputy Fire Chief Clayton R. Stalker Jr.

No one was injured in the fire, Stalker said.

A number of boys watching the fire, ages 10 to 13, said they'd been inside the building or knew of other neighborhood boys who'd set up a fort in there to hang out and occasionally smoke cigarettes.

Bruce T. DiCastro, assistant manager of David-Edwin Inc., said he has found the door to the old building ajar a few times. He dialed 911 Monday when someone reported smoke coming from the building.

But, because Keene has no 911 emergency service, it took awhile to make contact with Southwestern N.H. Fire Mutual Aid, the region's emergency communications center. He said it took about 15 minutes after his call before firefighters arrived.

Stalker said the fire department received the call at 3:55 p.m. When the firefighters realized the blaze had spread through the building, they called in two more trucks.

The fire roared for about an hour before it was put out because of an assortment of flammable items such as mattresses, office supplies and some type of combustible liquids, like kerosene, Stalker said.

"There was a lot of brush and stuff around it and trees," Stalker said. "It sat down in a gully, too, so it was difficult to get to."

Firefighters needed to get at the fire from the inside, but it was too involved to send anyone inside the building, he said.

————

As Reported by the *Keene Evening Sentinel* December 2nd, 1993:

"STORY"

Firefighters question proposal's legality

Opponents of a plan to consolidate the police and fire departments in Keene under one supervisor say the plan is illegal.

The city council is expected to discuss tonight a proposal to streamline the local government bureaucracy by consolidating 16 departments into four divisions.

Each division head would report to the city manager and be responsible for several departments.

According to the proposal from the city government's mission committee, the police and fire departments would be bunched together. The code enforcement department would become part of the fire department. The whole group would become the public safety department.

Supporters, namely the council's finance committee, say the change will make city government more efficient, and therefore save money.

But critics, including councilor-elect Robert Meagher, a former firefighter, Councilor Jacquelyn Hill, and fire Lt. Scott Collier, say the proposed structure is vague, and goes against state law.

Maegher said state law gives ultimate authority at a fire or emergency scene to the fire chief or highest ranking firefighter.

Under the city's plan, if the designated public safety director were not qualified as a firefighter, he could still take charge of the scene.

The proposal is similar to a 1989 consolidation plan proposed by City Manager J. Patrick MacQueen. Under that plan, 13 departments were to be consolidated into eight divisions. That plan, also opposed by firefighters, was eventually dropped.

Collier said public outcry about the 1989 proposal, including letters from business leaders and residents, should have been enough to tell the council that people don't want the two departments combined.

"People don't want police consolidated with fire in any way, shape or form whatsoever," he said.

Councilor Cynthia C. Georgina, a member of the mission committee that supported the reorganization, said the move will save money in the long run.

State law always takes precedence over local," she said. "Just as Pat MacQueen won't go take over a fire scene…a group head would not be permitted to take command at a fire scene any more than the city manager. We're not changing anything except who the department heads reports to."

Collier said the reorganization just won't work.

————

As Reported by the *Keene Evening Sentinel* December 24th, 1993:

"STORY"

Free video teaches safety

Keene area residents can learn how to react to a fire or refresh their memory on the issue with "Plan to Get Out Alive, a fire safety video provided by the New Hampshire Department of Safety's Division of Fire Service and the Keene Fire Department.

The free rental video is available throughout the holiday season at Keene City Video on West Street and Video Headquarters at West Street Plaza. Each store has five copies.

The fire safety video was created to alert families to the seriousness of fires in houses and to show them how to react in the case of a fire at home.

In 1992, 2 million fires in the United States claimed 4,730 lives and injured 28,700 people, according to the state Division of Fire Service. Of those deaths and injuries 78 percent were house fires.

The Keene Fire Department recommends that children under 10 years shouldn't watch the video without parental guidance, because of the dramatic nature of the fires in the video.

"It's helpful to have an adult around to answer the questions that children might be wondering," Clayton R. Stalker Jr. Said.

————

As Reported by the *Keene Evening Sentinel* December 30th, 1993:

"FIRE"

Shed catches fire Wednesday in Keene

Keene Fire Department officials believe discarded cigarettes may have caused a fire Wednesday afternoon that burned down half of a shed behind a Cheshire Housing Opportunity rooming house at 32 Emerald St.

Keene firefighters were called to the fire at 5:59 p.m., said Deputy Fire Chief Clayton R. Stalker Jr.

The 12-foot by 16-foot shed was in full blaze when firefighters arrived. The fire was extinguished within 30 minutes and half of the shed saved, Stalker said.

The shed is used in part to store trash, Stalker said.

"It looks like maybe some discarded smoking materials in the trash started the fire," Stalker said.

The cause of the fire was still being investigated this morning.

1994

As Reported by the *Keene Evening Sentinel* January 10th, 1994:

"STORY"

2nd fire station proposed for Keene

A branch fire station in West Keene. Scanners tabulating election results. A classroom at the Keene landfill.

That's what Keene residents could expect in 2000 if a capital improvement program being proposed by City Manager J. Patrick MacQueen is adopted.

The city council's finance committee and the Keene Planning Board will begin reviewing MacQueen's recommendations tonight.

The program schedules expensive construction project and big ticket purchases through 2000.

Among the other recommendations included in the capital improvement program: A new police station, a new fire station.

As Reported by the *Keene Evening Sentinel* January 17th, 1994:

"FIRE"

Hazardous chemicals found after fire

A small fire in a room at Ashbrook Apartments on Key Road in Keene Sunday afternoon could have been worse if it touched off a store of volatile chemicals in a closet, Keene police reported this morning.

An automatic alarm alerted Keene firefighters to a fire at the apartment rented to Douglas Bascom, 39. After extinguishing a small fire in the living room caused by a burning cigarette, firefighters found more than 200 chemicals.

They did not evacuate the building because the fire was small and was extinguished quickly.

Bascom was not home when the fire started. He returned to his apartment Sunday night and allowed police to search it, said police Cpl. Joseph J. Collins. After clearing out the smoke, authorities found the chemicals.

Bascom's collection of chemicals, Collins said, "appears to be a full-blown chemistry lab. It's his hobby," Collins said.

Some of the chemicals, including nitroglycerin, are volatile. They were being stored inside the apartment in glass jugs and vials.

A team from Keene Fire Department's Hazardous Response Team and a chemical specialist from Markem Corp., Thomas Lewis, investigated the chemicals and removed them.

No charges have been filed, Collins said. Police will continue to investigate.

————————

As Reported by the *Keene Evening Sentinel* January 18th, 1994:

"FIRE"

A worker using toxic substances to reseal a shower area in Carle Hall at Keene State College has been charged with disorderly conduct and resisting arrest after fumes from the work sent 13 students to the hospital.

It was a rude homecoming for students who returned from winter break on Monday to a dormitory filled with noxious fumes.

Thirteen students were treated at Cheshire Medical Center for difficulty breathing and dizziness. Another 12 students were treated by Keene firefighters at the dormitory.

Firefighters said a worker using noxious chemicals in a fourth floor bathroom was responsible. David M. Horton, 24, of Washington Street, Keene was using a combination of alcohol, ketones and xylene to reseal a shower in Carle Hall as students returned to the dorm. Horton works for Bob's Maintenance Plus of Winchester, a contractor for Keene State. Robert Berube owns the company. He was not available for comment today.

The use of such chemicals is extremely dangerous, Keene Fire Chief William H. Pepler Jr. said, and shouldn't have been done while the dorm was occupied. "You're supposed to have good ventilation and the person using the chemical is supposed to wear a respirator," Pepler said. Neither precaution had been taken, he said.

Mark Doyon of the college's physical plan office said the contractor did not have permission to do the resealing job while students were in the dorm. The work was supposed to be completed while students were away on winter break.

When questioned about the work he was doing, Horton was uncooperative, Pepler said. He was arrested by Keene police and charged with disorderly conduct and resisting arrest.

Meanwhile, 23 students complained of dizziness and nausea. "Two girls said they felt tingling in their arms," Pepler said. Rescue workers gave some students oxygen and took others to the hospital.

"Everybody who was here yesterday is back in the dorm and seems to be okay," said James Rowell, Carle Hall residence director.

Firefighters cleared the fourth floor of the dormitory until about 5 p.m. and ventilated the area.

Pepler said the incident could have been much worse. Despite warning labels on the chemicals he was using, Horton set up a heater in the fourth floor bathroom. "Those chemicals are highly flammable," Pepler said. "He could have blown up that entire area.

————————

As Reported by the *Keene Evening Sentinel* January 28th, 1994:

"FIRE"

Flames doused at Keene drugstore

Brooks Pharmacy in Keene was expected to open this afternoon, despite a fire early this morning in its stockroom.

The fire, reported just after midnight, burned documents and some merchandise at the rear of the store. Merchandise at the front of the store was damaged by smoke.

Though the cause of the fire was not immediately apparent, authorities do not believe it was set, said Clayton R. Stalker, deputy Keene fire chief.

Store officials declined to comment on the fire, but said the store should be open for business sometime this afternoon.

Stalker said a volunteer firefighter, who was doing some late night shopping next door at Shaw's supermarket, heard the Brooks Pharmacy sprinkler alarm sounding and called the fire department.

Water from the sprinklers prevented the fire from spreading, and firefighters quickly doused the flames.

The sprinklers and the firefighters "probably saved the plaza," he said. Shaw's and Bradlees department store are in the same building.

————

As Reported by the *Keene Evening Sentinel* February 8th, 1994:

"FIRE"

One dead after Keene house fire

Fatal Fire — Keene firefighters break a hole in the roof of a house on Cross Street, Keene as flames shoot out to their left. A Keene woman who was rescued from the house later died. Photo by Steve Hooper.

A deadly Keene house fire remained under investigation today, although it appears to have started accidentally.

Esther Cashman, 50, of 88 Cross St. was pronounced dead Monday night at Cheshire Medical Center after firefighters and hospital personnel made several attempts to revive her.

Cashman was rescued alive from the house, suffering from smoke inhalation. Despite feverish efforts by rescue workers, she succumbed at the hospital. The precise cause of death was not available this morning. The fire was under control within an hour, but not before two Keene firefighters were injured slightly. One slipped on ice and hurt his back; the other sprained a leg, said Clayton R. Stalker Jr. deputy fire chief of the Keene Fire Department.

Cashman's daughter spotted the fire just after 9 p.m. As she was driving down Cross Street, she saw flames shooting through the front door of her parents' two-story house, Stalker said.

After leaning Cashman was still in the house, firefighters raced through the first floor's flames and found her collapsed on a bathroom floor at the rear of the house, Stalker said.

She was alone when the fire broke out, he said.

Though what caused the fire to start in the living room was still unknown this morning. It didn't appear suspicious, Stalker said.

Investigators from the N.H. Fire Marshal's Office, Keene Police Department and Keene Fire Department are looking into the cause.

Although flames spread quickly through the walls and out through the front door, the exterior of the house appeared unscathed. The first floor received heavy fire damage, the second floor was damaged mostly by heat and smoke. Stalker said.

The house is salvageable, Stalker said.

Icy conditions and narrow streets hampered firefighting efforts. A hydrant and some hose lines froze up in the cold, and snow banks along the street made the travel lanes narrower that normal, so it was difficult to get fire equipment close to the house, Stalker said.

————

As Reported by the *Keene Evening Sentinel*:

Fatal Keene fire blamed on smoking; alarm had no battery

Careless smoking probably caused a house fire Monday that killed a 50-year-old Keene woman, fire officials said. And a smoke detector that might have sounded a warning was useless, because it had no battery.

Esther Cashman of 76 Cross St died of smoke inhalation at Cheshire Medical Center in Keene.

She was alive when firefighters pulled her from the burning housed, but could not be revived.

Clayton R. Stalker Jr., deputy Keene fire chief, said the fire started in Cashman's living-room couch, likely sparked by a lit cigarette and fueled by paper and couch material.

"It's total speculation as to whether the smoke detector would have alerted her sooner to the presence of fire. We suspect it would have," Stalker said. "Whether she would have been able to get out or not, it would be difficult to say."

The fire was reported at about 9 p.m. Monday. Just before firefighters arrived, flames engulfed the living room and began shooting through the front door, Stalker said.

Firefighters burst into the house and found Cashman on the floor in a back bathroom. They pulled her from the house and started cardiopulmonary resuscitation. However, she was pronounced dead at the hospital.

Many people fail to maintain the smoke alarms in their homes, Stalker said.

Since 1984, state law has required that all new single-family homes, apartment buildings, apartments and some businesses have smoke detectors that are powered by electricity, not batteries, Stalker said.

Newer detectors also have battery backups in case the electricity goes off, he said.

However, private homes built before 1984 are not required to have smoke detectors.

Stalker said battery0operated smoke detectors can be difficult to maintain and can be a nuisance, especially near kitchens, where a cooking mistake can set them off.

————

As Reported by the *Keene Evening Sentinel* February 12th, 1994:

"STORY"

Trucks, rescuers get full workout

Ambulances and fire trucks in Keene regularly zoomed all over the place in 1993, more than they did in previous years.

In 1993, the number of emergency calls to the Keene Fire Department was up 13.7 percent from 1992.

Fire Chief William H. Pepler Jr., said he doesn't see any trends to explain the increase.

"The way the population is down one – half percent but we're still a major hub area," he said. "We still have a lot of people coming through the city and working in the city."

Keene firefighters responded to 2,699 emergency calls, including 1,798 medical emergencies and 901 fire and hazardous materials emergencies, according to the department's records.

About one-quarter of the time, the fire engines and ambulances were headed out of the city. Of the 1,798 medical emergencies, 73 percent were in Keene, 15 percent in Swanzey, and the rest were—in descending order—in Chesterfield, Westmoreland, Sullivan, Nelson,

Surry and Roxbury. Of these emergencies, 290 were motor vehicle accidents.

Some of the year's significant incidents: the rescue of a young girl from a fire on Giffin Street; the rescue of seven Keene State College students from Carle Hall dormitory fire; an oil tank explosion at Davis Oil on Lower Main Street; the intentional spraying of an irritating gas in Randall Hall dormitory at KSC that sent 14 students to the hospital; and an apartment fire on Church Street that injured five people.

Firefighters responded to 25 fires, five of which required help from the entire department, Pepler said.

There were 37 motor-vehicle fires, 32 brush fires, 87 hazardous leaks or spills, 32 electrical problems and 43 false alarms set intentionally, according to department records.

––––––––––

As Reported by the *Keene Evening Sentinel* February 14th, 1994:

"FIRE"

Electrical fire at Papa Gino's

An electrical fire in a storeroom damaged Papa Gino's Restaurant at 333 Winchester St. in Keene early Saturday morning.

M. Joseph Tenters, the restaurant's general manager, spotted smoke coming from the storeroom at 1:38 a.m., as he was closing for the night. Tenters tried to douse the flames with a fire extinguisher, but the fire was too hot for that.

The restaurant building was evacuated, and Tenters called the fire department from a neighboring business.

Firefighters said the fire started in the ceiling above the storeroom, and damage was confined to the storeroom. The restaurant is expected to reopen by Thursday.

Initially firefighting efforts were hampered when a fire hydrant on Winchester St. had to be dug out of a snow bank before it could be connected.

––––––––––

As Reported by the *Keene Evening Sentinel:*

Papa Gino's still recovering from fire

Papa Gino's restaurant in Keene will be closed longer than expected—until the middle of next week—because of an electrical fire in the storeroom Saturday morning.

Joseph Tenters, general manager of the restaurant on Winchester Street, had hoped to reopen by today, but more work is needed before the restaurant is ready for customers.

After spotting smoke coming from the storeroom at 1:38 Saturday morning, as he was closing for the night, Tenters tried to douse the flames with a fire extinguisher, but couldn't. He had to call the fire department from a neighboring business.

––––––––––

As Reported by the *Keene Evening Sentinel* February 17th, 1994:

"STORY"

Future of Keene ladder truck up in the air
Chief William H. Pepler Jr.

The Keene Fire Department's Ladder 1 sits deep into the fire station, the cover of its engine compartment gaping open. Inside is…not much. Nothing you'd call an engine. Greasy parts are spread across the truck's chrome front bumper.

Fire Chief William H. Pepler Jr. stands alongside the aging fire truck—it's 22 years old—and says, "It's getting tired. It's served the city a long time."

Band-aid won't fix this. Keene Fire Chief William Pepler Jr., sits in the driver's seat of an ailing ladder truck that broke January after a fire at Riverside Plaza. Photo by Steve Hooper.

Ladder 1 saw its last action January 26, helping to halt a fire at Riverside Plaza on Winchester Street.

But when the flames were extinguished, the truck's engine died. It had to be towed back to the fire station on Vernon Street. It's still there. A sign, attached to the cap with a Band-Aid, notes that the truck is "out of service. Keene had planned to replace the ladder truck next year, at a cost somewhere between $375,000 and $650,000.

Since the truck's engine died, Pepler and the city council's finance committee have been talking about what do. A new truck costs so much, city officials are loath to move up the purchase.

Pepler has suggested buying a new gasoline-powered engine for $1,200, to keep the truck on the road until it can be replaced.

But City Councilor Michael E.J. Blastos thinks it might make more sense to pay a little more, buy a new diesel engine, and delay the need to replace the ladder truck altogether.

Under that plan, "we could avoid buying a new truck next year," Blastos said, "if this thing works, we'd get three to five more years out of it."

But it's also important to have a reliable second ladder truck. "These things don't go out often," Blastos said, "but when they go out, you want them to work.

Another possibility is rebuilding the engine that dies. Deputy Chief George H. Shepard Jr. and representatives of a Middleboro, Mass. company went through the engine on Wednesday, trying to estimate the cost of an overhaul. Pepler hopes to have a price in a couple of weeks.

But the engine is not the ladder truck's only problem. The mechanism that cranks out the ladder is wearing out, and parts for 22-year-old machinery are hard to scare up.

Why two: Keene has another ladder truck, but Pepler says one is not enough to protect the city.

"Because of the building in the city, and the heights of the buildings, we need ladders of significant heights," Pepler said.

Most ground ladders can't reach the upper floors of many downtown buildings. Pepler said; the 60-footers that might are unstable and unsafe. And they lack the mobility of a truck-mounted ladder, from which firefighters can pour water on a fire from above.

"Because of the hazards we face in the city with the buildings we have, we easily use two ladder trucks," Pepler said. "We can use it for a number of different types of emergencies."

"We've had occasions to use them both at the same time at different fires," the chief said.

And, at some Keene fires, truck-mounted ladders provided the only escape from burning buildings.

One example occurred last March at Keene State College dormitory. Smoke and fire had trapped seven students on the third floor of Carle Hall. The ladder trucks saved them.

A number of nearby fire departments—Brattleboro, Meadowood in Fitzwilliam, Peterborough and Walpole—have ladder trucks that Keene could call on, but that's not like having your own, Pepler said.

"With a ladder truck, if you need it, you need it quickly," Pepler said. Waiting 40 minutes or more for the truck to arrive defeats the purpose, he said.

Aging equipment: Keene's two ladder trucks were both built in 1972. Both show their age.

Keene brought ladder 1 new in 1972. Shepard said he couldn't begin to estimate how many fires it's been used at. The truck odometer reads more than 6,000 miles, but it's not the mileage that counts, Shepard said. The truck engine runs constantly at a fire. Twenty years' worth of firefighting has taken its toll.

"When we purchase a ladder, it's a 20-year investment," Pepler said.

The city bought Ladder 2 in 1990. Though it, too, is a 1972 truck, it was refurbished when the city government bought it from the fire department in Glendale, Calif., to replace a 1947 ladder truck.

Ladder 2 has more than 50,000 miles on it, "a tremendous amount of miles for a ladder truck," Pepler said.

And, like its counterpart, Ladder 2 has had engine troubles. A new engine was installed in November for $6,500.

Keene ladder truck may get a new engine

The Keene Fire Department ladder truck that's been out of service for nearly a month could be back helping to fight fires in about a month.

The truck has been out of service since the engine died while at a fire at Riverside Plaza in Keene.

Fire Chief William H. Pepler Jr. had proposed spending about $1,200 to replace the engine. The truck is scheduled to be replaced in 1995 and the new engine would help the truck last until then.

But members of the finance committee said they wanted to know how much a complete overhaul of the truck would cost and possibly delay having to buy a new truck.

But when the costs came in, committee members went with Pepler's original proposal.

It would have cost between $38,000 and $70,000 to install a new diesel engine and a new transmission. And even then, the truck and ladders might not have passed a national inspection.

A new ladder truck could cost between $350,000 and $750,000. Both Keene ladder trucks are more than 20 years old.

————

As Reported by the *Keene Evening Sentinel* February 21st, 1994:

"FIRE"

Fire damages Keene home

Grease in a pan ignited a fire Saturday morning at the H. Lee Burger residence in Keene.

Fire damaged the kitchen and dining room of the house at 267 Gilsum St., Keene fire officials said, but no one was injured.

Fire officials said Burger set the pan on the stove to heat, went downstairs to check on his cat, and found the area near the stove on fire when he returned to the kitchen.

Burger tried to contain the flames with a fire extinguisher, but couldn't. He woke his son, the only other person in the house at the time, and they got out safely.

Firefighters were called at 8:56 a.m., and they quickly halted the spread of the flames. They also rescued the cat.

————

As Reported by the *Keene Evening Sentinel* February 28th, 1994:

"STORY"

Fire supervisors ask council to reject 1% raises

The union representing Keene's firefight supervisors is rejecting recommendations from a fact-finder that could end a contract stalemate.

The union wants the city council to do the same.

In a statement released this morning, union representatives said recommendations of fact-finder Richard Higgins are scant.

The union is asking for a 4 percent pay raise. But city government negotiators want supervisors to accept a 5 percent pay cut and pay more for their health insurance.

Higgins has recommended a 1 percent raise.

Laurence R. Shaffer, Keene's assistant city manager who is negotiating for the city, had little to day about the union's stance.

Shaffer declined comment until the council meets on the fact-finder's report.

It just doesn't make a lot of sense" to talk about the rep[ort now, he said.

In the statement, Fire Lt. Thomas Loll said the pay cut and benefit changes would cost un ion members about $3,000 each.

Loll said the city's negotiating team is not negotiating in good faith. "We are serious about working with the city in what it claims to be hard times," the union said. "But in exchange, we want to be treated fairly."

The supervisors' contract expired on June 30, 1993.

_____

As Reported by the *Keene Evening Sentinel* March 11th, 1994:

"STORY"

Clinton-Keene visit: It's a go

President Clinton visited Keene and Members of the Keene Fire department were able to meet with him. Members from left to right Capt. Tom Chase, Lt. Ron Leslie and Capt. Jeff Morel. Photo by: Whitehouse photos.

President Clinton is coming to Keene Tuesday; just what he'll do when he gets here is the question.

Keene police are gearing up security; area democrats are readying to welcome their man; and Keene State College officials are keeping their fingers crossed they'll get a visit.

But no word from the White House about the president's schedule; just when he'll arrive in Keene and what he'll do when he's here is anybody's guess.

Clinton visit mostly closed

But president's schedule leaves some open time. People hoping to catch a glimpse of President Bill Clinton Tuesday will have their best chance at the Dillant-Hopkins Airport in North Swanzey. But, even that could be iffy.

The president's arrival at 11:40 a.m. is closed to the public; his departure at 3 p.m. will be open, however.

Spectators would be at the airport by 2 p.m. Swanzey Police "Chief Larss A. Ogren said parking at the airport will be limited, so be prepared to walk. Parking will be along the airport access road toward Keene's sewage treatment plant.

During his 3 ½ hour visit to Keene on Tuesday, Clinton will tour Markem Corp. and meet with employees.

————

As Reported by the *Keene Evening Sentinel*:

When the president's around, Secret Service agents are, too

He stepped onto Main Street from a limousine bearing the presidential seal.

The salt-and-pepper hair, the sharp suit, the big presence.

The crowd started to cheer but just as quickly stopped.

This man wasn't the president, but a dead-ringer, an apparent decoy for Bill Clinton; someone to catch the attention of would-be attackers. He scanned the crowd, an earphone stuck in his ear.

A minute later, Clinton himself emerged from another limousine and the dozens of Secret Service agents and state and local police on hand started their full-court press.

As Clinton made his way along a thick line of well-wishers toward Central Square, the double stood next to him, eyeing the hands in the crowd. From the back, with their hair styled the same, it was nearly impossible to tell the two men apart.

Another agent was a few feet further up the line, cheerfully asking that everyone raise their hands where they could be seen. He wiggled his own hands in a somewhat un-Secret Service-like manner to demonstrate.

"Have them up and ready" (to be shaken), he joked.

Agents were everywhere.
Just how many agents guard the president is a secret. But whether it was at the Dillant-Hopkins Airport in North Swanzey, Markem Corp. in Keene, or Main Street, their presences were felt.

The agents were just part of a huge contingent of security assigned to guard the president on his trip.

Long before Air Force One touched down at the Keene airport, security was tight. In addition to the delegation of local and N.H. state police assigned around the airport, there were uniformed and plain-clothed Secret Service agents.

Everyone venturing onto the tarmac was frisked and walked through a metal detector. An explosives-sniffing dog scoured the building and tarmac area.

Well-connected supporters wore label pins giving them direct access to the president. Keene City Councilor Patricia T. Russell sported a radio and sleeve microphone similar to those carried by the Secret Service agents.

There were dark-clothed commando-style lookouts perched atop the roof of the airport's terminal building. They canvassed the horizon as Air Force One roared down the runway.

At about the same time, a small van-load of commandos zoomed down the runway, trailing the jet.

When the plane touched down, the white van was there, racing behind it. It trailed the jet as it journeyed toward the terminal.

Inside the van, about eight commandos dressed in black, with thick bulletproof vests, sat armed with some serious fire power. Spectators caught glimpses of M-16s, and Uzi type weapons.

The presidential motorcade included N.H. state police cruisers and a black armored van equipped with communications equipment and a gun turret.

At the airport, as Air Force One flew out of sight, one tired-looking agent pulled the earpiece from his ear and, no doubt for the first time that day, turned his back to the crowd and walked away.

As Reported by the *Keene Evening Sentinel* March 14th, 1994:

"STORY"

Keene firefighters trained in disasters

Earthquakes and floods might seem like a California phenomenon but even Keene is susceptible to Mother Nature's whimsy.

Capt. Brad Payne and Lt. Robert S. Crowell of the Keene Fire Department recently attended a two-week course at the National Fire Academy on evacuation and command procedures for catastrophic disasters.

The course covered emergency response techniques to natural disasters such as, hurricanes, earthquakes and flooding. Keene might not have felt a tremble in years, but the Earth's fault lines aren't just in India and California.

Clayton R. Stalker r., deputy Keene fire chief, completed the second part of a four-year program on fire department command tactics and strategies. Stalker said the course addressed managing crews that are fighting large-scale fires, such as lumberyard or high-rise fires.

Capt. Steven W. Goldsmith completed a course on commanding emergency incidents and fire safety and survival. Lt. Scott Taylor completed a course on the chemistry of hazardous materials.

These intensive, two-week courses are held at the National Fire Academy, near Washington, D.C., and are paid for by the federal government.

As Reported by the *Keene Evening Sentinel* March 25th, 1994:

"STORY"

Smokey Bear still hot after 50 years Fear of attack during World War II prompted government promotion of fire safety

Most everyone is familiar with Smokey Bear. Whether you learned about him in school, through Scouting, on television or somewhere else, you could probably pick Smokey Bear out of a crowd. In fact, Smokey is the second most recognized character in the United States, between Santa Clause and Mickey Mouse. Worldwide, Smokey's image is second only to the Coca Cola logo.

If you don't believe it, just ask Alfred E. Grimes of Madbury. Grimes is a retired state forest ranger and a foremost authority on the big bear. In addition, for more than 20 years, he and his wife Sylvia have been collecting Smokey Bear memorabilia and have amassed thousands of items. A small portion of the collection (about 400pieces) was displayed last Saturday afternoon at the Colon y Mill Marketplace during the Smokey Bear 50th birthday party.

Many families that attended not only went away with comic books and balloons, but also a sense of responsibility for the great outdoors. They also learned about the role firefighters play while protecting people and property.

Forest Ranger Robert E. Steward explained, "The Cheshire County Forest Fire Wardens Association (did) this because we want to help publicize Smokey's birthday and to bring awareness to the people on the importance of fire safety."

If you missed the great gala, let's trace Smokey's roots from the beginning.

The year was 1942. The United States was embroiled in World War II, and many Americans feared enemy attack or sabotage could destroy the forests. After all, wood products were in high demand because timber was a primary commodity for battleships, gun stocks, and military packing crates.

As a result of this concern, the United States Department of Agriculture (USDA) Forest Service established the Cooperative Forest Fire Prevention (CFFP) program to encourage citizens to make a concerted, personal effort to prevent careless forest fires. The War Advertising Council, made up of advertising volunteers who donated their time and resources to the cause, got into the act and began a promotion to educate people on how to assist the war effort by practicing fire-safety techniques.

By early 1944, the War Advertising Council produced its first campaign poster. Walt Disney had generously loaned the Bambi character to the first fire prevention posters. Bambi, accompanied by Thumper the bunny and Flower the skunk, was a natural choice since he had escaped a deadly forest fire himself. Although Bambi was very popular, the Council decided to develop a more powerful member of the animal kingdom to relay the message.

Renowned animal illustrator Albert Stachle went to work creating an "appealing brown bear with an intelligent, slightly quizzical expression." In August of 1944, Smokey Bear was born, complete with the traditional ranger's hat and denim jeans.

Then, according to *Smokey Bear—The First 50 Years,* an historical booklet published by the USDA Forest Service: A significant chapter in Smokey's long history began early in 1950, when a burned bear cub survived a fire in the Lincoln National Forest near Captain, N.M.

This bear survived a terrible forest fire and won the love and imagination of the American public. After being nursed back to health, Smokey came to live at the National Zoo in Washington, D.C. as the living symbol of Smokey Bear. Little Smokey's recuperation and journey to the zoo was supported by citizens all across the country who donated money they raised through bake sales and other community events.

When Smokey was introduced in the 40's, the words on the first poster read: "Smokey says: Care will prevent 9 out of 10 forest fires."

Al has a copy of that poster. In fact, because of its age and historical significance, it is among the most treasured pieces in his collection. It is also a treasure to the U.S. government. In 1992, the government contacted Al and asked if they could come north to photograph many of his posters because the artwork needed to reproduce the posters in Washington had suffered water damage. Al not only agreed to share his collection, he packed the posters in the trailer and hit the road for the nation's capitol. Today, many of the poster reproductions used in government publications are courtesy of the Grimes.

Just as their collection has snowballed, so has their national involvement. Al and Sylvia now have a one-year Individual Services Agreement with the USDA Forest Service to travel around the country with their Smokey collection in honor of the 50th anniversary. And beyond that, when Al and Sylvia retire, their memorabilia will be preserved at the National Agricultural Library Special Collection Division in Washington.

But Smokey Bear is not to be taken lightly—and not just because he wears a pair of jeans with a 61-inch waist.

For 50 years he has been the guardian of our forests and there are strict rules and guidelines to be followed while portraying *the* bear. For example, Smokey may not speak and he must conduct himself in a most respectable manner at all times. After all, Smokey is and has been a positive role model for generations.

————

As Reported by the *Keene Evening Sentinel* April 4th, 1994:

"STORY"
Keene firefighters honored for their courage, service

Above firefighters and others received metals for acts above and beyond the call of duty. Call Capt. Lamoureaux, Call Lt. Rocheleau,(not pictured), Capt. Goldsmith, Call Lt. Mullet, Call firefigher Hackler and Acting Lt. Morel. Photos by Steve Hooper.

Like something out of the television show "Rescue 911". That's how William H. Pepler, Keene fire chief, describes the scene at 3 a.m. on March 25.

Fire in a second-floor dormitory room at Keene State College sent hundreds of students fleeing into the cold. As students stood around outside the building, sleepy-eyed and stunned, firefighters counted heads, not knowing if everyone had escaped.

Then the call came from Southwestern N.H. Fire Mutual Aid: Two students were trapped in a room above the fire. They had awakened to a hallway full of black, acrid smoke. One of them called the fire department, the other, an asthmatic began to panic.

The adrenaline started going—we knew we'd have to find them and bring them out," said Capt. Edward Lamoureaux of the Keene Fire Department. Lamoureaux and Lt. Michael Rocheleau did just that. They entered the burning building, hunting for the room. The smoke was so heavy, "you couldn't see anything. Even if you were crawling on the floor, you couldn't see," Lamoureaux said. He and Rocheleau felt their way to each dormitory room, checking to see if anyone was still inside.

Finally, they found the two students.

"We wrapped towels around their faces and began leading them out," Lamoureaux said. The student with asthma was breathing heavily, partly because of his condition, partly because he was so excited. "He was panicking," Lamoureaux said. "That's just what happens to some people in situations like that."

Paralyzed by fear, the asthmatic student didn't want to come with the firefighters, "so we had to be forceful. I grabbed him around the waist and just hauled him out," Lamoureaux said.

It was all in the line of duty, according to Lamoureaux and Rocheleau. But it was worthy of high praise just the same, their colleagues said Saturday, during an awards banquet for Keene firefighters.

Lamoureaux and Rocheleau were two of eight Keene firefighters honored for saving lives—although the promise of praise and a medal wasn't what motivated them.

"During everything you can do to try and save someone's life is part of the job," said Capt. Steven Goldsmith, another award winner. Once the job is done, the knowledge that a firefighter has just given someone more time in this world is "the best reward."

Lt. John Mullet and firefighter Don Hackler were also honored for lifesaving actions during the Keene State fire. They rescued two students who'd been wandering in a smoke-filled hallway.

Goldsmith, firefighters Chris Cram, Wayne Spofford and Michael Driscoll, and Capt. Thomas Chase, director of the department's emergency management services, received a teamwork award for reviving a 47 year old heart attack victim last May.

T. Jeffrey Morel won a citation for exceptional service—the cardiopulmonary resuscitation training he leads helped to save at least one life last year. An elderly Keene woman remembered Morel's instructions, gave herself the Heimlich maneuver, and avoided choking to death.

How does it feel to save a life? "I don't think the dictionary covers it," Goldsmith said. "It's just an unbelievably positive feeling. It makes you understand why you go through all the training we do."

One test of that training came after a car accident on West Street in Keene last May. Goldsmith and four other rescue workers found Thomas Mongeluzzi, 47, of Manchester City, Vt. Slumped over his car's steering wheel. He had suffered a heart attack and wasn't breathing. "Clinically, he was dead," Goldsmith remembered.

"The first thing you think in a situation like that is that you have between four and six minutes to bring him back before he's got brain damage," Goldsmith said. "And we weren't sure whether he had the heart attack after the accident, which would give us more time, or whether the accident was caused by the heart attack."

The team worked quickly, administering CPR and then electric shocks to restart his heart. Before the ambulance arrived, they could feel a slight pulse from their patient. By the time he reached an emergency room physician at Cheshire Medical Center, Mongeluzzi was breathing on his own.

He walked out of the hospital five days later.

"That kind of thing really makes you feel great," Goldsmith said. Several months after the session, Marge Grumbly was hurrying through her house, packing for a move, and popped a couple of miniature candy bars into her mouth. She began to choke.

Alone in the house and losing consciousness, Grumbly recalled what Morel had said about the Heimlich maneuver—you can give it to yourself, as well as to others. She pressed her abdomen against the nearest stable object—a metal shelf on a utility closet. That forced the candy bars out, and she could breathe again.

Morel says he keeps his teaching style simple. "I try to explain things in a way that a young child would understand and remember," he said. "You always wonder whether what you're teaching people is working, whether they will recall what they need to in an emergency situation. It's good to know it worked in that situation."

Longtime fire department members were also honored: Deputy Chief Wesley Peets, 40 years; retired deputy chief William Olmstead, 30 years, retired captain Harry Johnson 25 years, Capt. David Osgood, Lt. Wayne Crowell and Lt. Raymond Hadley, 20 years each and David Symonds, 15 years.

Hadley and firefighter Charles Harris received community service awards for raising more than $2,400 in an annual drive for the Muscular Dystrophy fund.

Receiving chief's citations of appreciation: Lamoureaux, Capt Bruce Pollock, Capt. Alex Matson jr. and firefighter Edward Hodgdon for fire-station work; firefighter James Dubriske for maintaining the fire department's fleet; acting Lt. Gary Lamoureaux for his actions at the firehouse; and to Lt. Robert Crowell for maintaining department records.

Service awards were also presented to Ladies Auxiliary members Shirley Peets, 40 years service, Esther Amadon 30 years and Tina Thompson, Rindy Hackler and Lori LaBriske, five years each.

———

As Reported by the *Keene Evening Sentinel* April 9th, 1994:

"STORY"

Keene City Council rejects contract recommendations

The Keene City Council has rejected a mediator's recommendations on a new firefighters' contract.

Gary Lamoureaux of the firefighters union said the council's decision Thursday night "probably means we go back to square one."

The city and the firefighters have been far apart in their negotiations. Now, firefighters are working under a contract that expired June 30, 1993.

The firefighters initially asked for a one-year contract with a 4 percent raise. The city government wanted a three-year contract that included a 5 percent pay cut the first year, and a salary freeze in the second and third years.

Allan S. McCausland, the mediator, proposed a two-year contract with 3 percent across-the-board raises each year. His decision is not binding, however.

Firefighters favor McCausland's recommendations.

The city government also wants a limit on how much it pays for firefighters' health insurance, and wants a cap on dental insurance premiums. McCausland disagreed with that.

————

As Reported by the *Keene Evening Sentinel* April 25th, 1994:

"FIRE"

Laundry room fire out fast

An overheated fluorescent light is the suspected cause of a fire early Saturday morning that scorched the ceiling at the Speed-Wash coin operated laundry in Keene.

Luckily for building owner George Streeter Jr., firefighters quickly reached and doused the fire; Speed-Wash is next door to the Keene fire station on Vernon Street.

Streeter, who lives in the building with his son, reported being awakened by smoke detectors shortly before 4 a.m.

Keene firefighters said the single alarm system in the three-story brick building was key to an early warning of the fire. The system alerted the eight tenants in apartments upstairs, and they quickly left the building, Streeter said.

Firefighters found a fire in the ceiling, over a row of washing machines. The fire reached into the second floor through the walls. Little damage was done.

We're very fortunate that we were able to clean everything up and get back in operation," Streeter said. "The fire department did a very good job."

The fire started from a malfunctioning fluorescent light fixture in the ceiling. The heat ignited the hanging ceiling.

Fire officials said customers had reported an odor in the building earlier in the day. The odor was probably from a smoldering fire, which broke out hours later.

————

As Reported by the *Keene Evening Sentinel* April 28th, 1994:

"STORY"

Keene fire union raising money

When Keene firefighters aren't out dousing flames, they're often answering questions about fire safety, said Gary LaFreniere, vice-president of the Keene Professional Firefighters Local 3265.

To deal with some of the more frequent queries, the Keene firefighters union is raising money to publish a fire safety handbook.

The group's goal is to print up to 10,000 handbooks and distribute them to local schools during fire prevention week in October. The handbooks will also be distributed at events such as the city's annual street fair, he said.

"One of the biggest jobs of a firefighter is protecting lives and property and one of the best tools is fire prevention and educating the public," LaFreniere said.

The union is in its second week of a fund-raising drive; about 70 percent of the money raised will go to prepare and publish the magazine-sized handbook, LaFreniere said. The other 30 percent goes to the union which sponsors fire safety events and represents firefighters' employment interests.

RGL Inc., a Connecticut company, will publish the handbook and solicit donations over the telephone from businesses and residences in Keene.

The phone calls have caused some confusion, said Clayton R. Stalker Jr., deputy fire chief. The fund-raiser is not from the Keene Fire Department and the people calling to solicit money are not firefighters.

"The (fire) chief isn't either for or against their efforts," said Stalker, as a department administrator, is not a union member.

In 1991, the union also published and distributed an emergency book on basic first aid. This year's handbook will focus on fire maintenance, how to use a fire extinguisher, preventing chimney fires and the safe use of charcoal and gas grills, among other safety tips.

————

As Reported by the *Keene Evening Sentinel* May 5th, 1994:

"STORY"

Smoke detector reminder issued

Keene landlords are being reminded to comply with the city's fire safety codes and state law.

The Keene Fire Department has sent out more than 500 notices to the owners and occupants of rental homes and multiple family dwellings, reminding them that smoke detectors are required for every floor, including basements and stairways.

The smoke detectors must run off electricity; battery-powered detectors are unacceptable.

Similar notices were sent in 1992, but fire officials didn't feel all landlords were aware of the law. Also, it's difficult to enforce the regulation because there are few inspectors. The notice is meant to increase awareness.

"This is a life safety thing," said Clayton R. Stalker Jr., deputy fire chief. "The majority of people (who) die in fires in Keene either die in apartment buildings or boarding houses."

Smoke detectors found in common areas of apartment buildings must be inter-connected, and all smoke detectors must be connected to the building's power source.

Smoke detectors can be installed only with a permit; landlords are responsible for installing and maintaining the smoke alarms.

Violators will receive one warning and, if they fail to comply, they can be fined $500 a day until they are up to code.

————

As Reported by the *Keene Evening Sentinel* May 5th, 1994:

"STORY"

Private or public?
Keene ambulance service will stay as it is for now

Whenever there's a serious car accident in Keene, the fire department's rescue truck responds along with the ambulance.

When there is a house fire, the ambulance responds along with the fire engines.

And when there is a serious hazardous material spill, the ambulance responds with the "hazmat" unit.

That's why it doesn't make much sense to Keene Fire Chief William H. Pepler Jr. to take the ambulance service away from the fire department and turn it over to a private contractor.

Even as a subcommittee of the Keene City Council has put on ho9ld plans to explore turning Keene's ambulance service over to a private company to run; privatization is still the trend among city governments trying to stretch tax dollars further.

But the ambulance service, at least, brings in money for city government—$263,347 last year, about $150 for a trip to the hospital. That's not enough to make the ambulance service profitable, but it goes a long way toward paying the bills.

Yet, there are some who say the city shouldn't be in the ambulance business—or water and sewer business for that matter—that private contractors can provide cheaper, more efficient service without the headaches—and costs—accompanying a city bureaucracy.

It's an idea that's caught on around the country and one that's been kicked around in Keene for several years. Some councilors say the time has come to jump into the privatization mix.

So, councilors and department heads have been kicking around the idea, trying to decide if privatization is worth investigating.

It may be a good idea for some departments, but it doesn't make sense for the ambulance service, Pepler said.

A subcommittee of the Keene council agrees. On July 1, it put on hold the idea of turning the ambulance service over to a private company, but reserved the right to resurrect the idea when budgets are squeezed again.

In the next two days, The Sentinel will take a look at the issue of privatizing the ambulance service" how it would work, the costs and how it's worked in other cities.

The costs: Last year, it cost $444,511 to run the ambulance division of the Keene Fire Department; income from ambulance runs, plus standby fees from the seven towns that use Keene's ambulance service, was about $263,647.

That's enough to pay salaries and benefits for seven firefighters/EMT's, their uniforms, oxygen and other first-aid supplies, insurance, training and ambulance payments.

That means taxpayers had to pay $187,864 last year to operate the ambulance service—about a third, of the total cost. While that's not cheap, it's doubtful any private contractor could match the low price while providing the same service, Pepler said.

But, Councilor Douglas E. Lovejoy, who supports privatization, said he's not convinced a private company couldn't offer the same quality service at a lower cost.

"I still believe, because it's so close to being self-supporting, that's where we should be starting (privatization)" Lovejoy said.

Two for one: The Keene Fire Department has provided ambulance service in Keene since 1977. That first year, it answered 861 calls.

In 1993, 1,798—65 percent—of the fire department's 2,699 calls were for the ambulance. That's almost a 14 percent increase from 1992—and a 140 percent increase since 1977.

Photo by Tom Powers.

"Even before we had the ambulance, we needed these people for fire protection," Pepler said.

Deputy Fire Chief Clayton R. Stalker was one of the six original emergency medical technicians hired by the city to run the ambulance service. Before that, he worked for Robert J. DiLuzio's Ambulance Service, which served Keene.

Although these six EMT's worked for the fire department, they worked solely on ambulance calls; money to pay their salaries came from user fees.

But when the city government and firefighters negotiated a new contract, part of the agreement was that firefighters would train to become EMT's and EMT's would train to become firefighters.

"It's most cost effective to take one person and have them do several jobs," Stalker said.

Now, every member of the fire department is trained as an emergency medical technician. But revenue from the ambulance service still pays the salaries of seven firefighters.

"That's why the fire department (budget) is so low is because we're able to fund these firefighters through the ambulance," Pepler said. "It's cost-effective because we provide two services. We need these people to be firefighters. They just happen to be EMT's. That's where the savings are."

City Councilor Robert Meagher, who retired last year after 16 ½ years as a firefighter, said the fire department needs at least eight firefighters on duty per shift.

"Whether you have the ambulance or not, you still need these eight firefighters to man the (fire) equipment, Meagher said.

That's why privatizing the ambulance might not work, said Councilor Cynthia C. Georgina.

"We need these people as firefighters," Georgina said. "The fact that they're ambulance attendants is a big plus. It's like getting double duty."

Georgina is chairman of the human services, health, and safety committee, which will ultimately make a recommendation to the city council about privatizing the ambulance.

"When you're talking about the ambulance, quality of care has got to be the top consideration," she said.

Quality would not suffer if the ambulance service were turned over to a private company, at least not DiLuzio's, said Robert J. DiLuzio, company president.

Though DiLuzio said his company will submit a proposal if the city council decides to privatize the ambulance, he doesn't think that's the way to go.

"In Keene, New Hampshire, I do not think (ambulance service) should be private," DiLuzio said. "We have a good system now. It's economical."

DiLuzio's has three ambulances; the fire department has two. If DiLuzio's is busy, then the fire department backs it up. And if the fire department is busy, then DiLuzio's provides back up.

DiLuzio's doesn't charge for being the city's backup. So in essence, the city is "getting five ambulances for the price of two," DiLuzio said.

About 80 percent of DiLuzio's business is transfers, taking patients from nursing homes to the hospital, or from hospitals to homes.

Quality of service: The privatization debate isn't just about money. It's about quality and patient care.

Turning the ambulance over to a private contractor means the city loses control over it, Stalker said.

Now, when the Keene ambulance rolls, there are three emergency medical technicians on board—two firefighters and an officer. One drives, the other takes care of patients, the third floats, either watching for traffic or helping with patient care.

That's not something that most ambulances services do, Stalker said. But it's reflected in the quality, he said.

"It's something we do here that very few, if any others, do" he said. "It's a three-person job."

"All the private ambulance services run with two men, and the problem with that is if you get a severe case, there's no way one man in the back of an ambulance can do it by himself," Meagher said.

It's doubtful that a private contractor will agree to have three EMT's on board each ambulance, Stalker said. "Nobody is going to run a business in Keene unless there is money in it."

The fire department doesn't have to constantly be thinking about the bottom line, Stalker said; that allows it to operate with three technicians on each call and a back-up ambulance.

You'd be hard pressed to find a private ambulance company that will agree to operate two ambulances, with three EMT's on each, 24 hours a day, Stalker said.

"You get what you pay for," he said.

DiLuzio said his ambulance rolls with three attendants sometimes. It's the exception, though, not the rule.

Lovejoy isn't worried about the quality of care suffering if a private company runs the ambulance service. "A private company is not going to be in business very long if people are dying," he said.

As a rule, private ambulances pay less and have more staff turnover than a city-run department, Stalker said.

And, high turnover hurts service, he said.

DiLuzio said his company, at least, has more training than the fire departments. All the city's firefighters are emergency medical technicians. Four of DiLuzio's attendants are intermediate-level EMT's, and one is an EMT-RN, which require more training than standard EMT's.

The city council has already approved spending $15,000 on a program to have eight firefighters trained at EMT intermediates starting this year.

Because the fire department already has at least eight firefighters on duty during each shift, it's able to staff two ambulances with three EMT's on each.

Those firefighters are already in the station, standing by in case of emergency, Pepler said.

"The beauty of it all is you have eight men on a shift, and you're providing two services," Meagher said. "If you privatize, you'll still need the eight men and you're going to have only one service.

If the ambulance service is taken out of the fire department, the department's call volume will shrink, so there will be less need for firefighters, Lovejoy said.

"I wonder if they need to be there anyway. I've never bought that," he said. "I'm not convinced you'd need the full complement there if the ambulance was run somewhere else."

To really save any money by privatizing the ambulance service, the city government would have to lay off seven firefighters whose salaries are paid through ambulance revenue, Stalker said.

"They cannot do that without compromising fire protection in the city, he said.

And even then, the fire department would still be responding to many of the same calls, Stalker said. Accidents, fires, and hazardous material spills require both an ambulance and the fire department, he said.

"I'd need to be shown they would need people hanging around anyway," Lovejoy said. The city could rely more on the call force in the event of a fire or other emergency, he said.

Paying for the seven jobs using taxpayer money would cost about $142,000 a year, according to fire department figures.

Not quite breaking even: Keene's ambulance isn't profitable. It costs more to run than it collects in user fees.

In October, the city council approved upping the ambulance rates from $120 to $150 per run, a 20 percent increase. The goal, fire officials say, is to make the ambulance service more self supporting.

Dover and Portsmouth charge $100 for an ambulance run; Salem $150 and Laconia $1390. Fees for advanced life support services vary. Health insurance usually pays for the ride.

"To be completely self supporting is an attainable goal," Stalker said. "It may not happen over night."

Fire officials expect the new rates to help the ambulance service to cover about 75 percent of its costs.

But the issue is more than just money, Stalker and Pepler said. It's about what Keene residents want.

"It is a very big mistake for a municipality that runs a quality service to give it up," Stalker said. "We don't see the need to change it."

———

As Reported by the *Keene Evening Sentinel* August 25th, 1994:

"STORY"

KSC building cleared after acid is found

At least 20 people were evacuated from the Keene State College Science Center late this morning after an explosive substance was discovered in one of the labs.

Keene firefighters called in the state bomb squad.

N.H. State Police bomb squad detonated a batch of perchloric acid behind public works department in Keene. Photo by: Michael Moore.

Perchloric acid is an unstable chemical that can explode if it comes into contact with any plant or animal matter, said Clayton R. Stalker, Keene deputy fire chief.

If the chemical is old, it can crystallize and explode easily, said Keene Fire Chief William H. Pepler Jr.; that's why the bomb squad was called in.

Faculty member Patrick Eggleston found the chemical—some of which had spilled from a box—Wednesday night; he got a hold of officials this morning.

"It's one of those things that, if left over a period of time, can be explosive," said Patrick Eggleston, a biology professor. He discovered the acid in one of the labs Wednesday night; no one know where it came from or how long it had been there, he said.

"This is a problem at colleges and universities across the country," Pepler said.

"(The faculty) buy things, and the staff turns over and these substances end up at the back of closets.

When Eggleston called the fire department this morning, he was told to get out of the building.

"When the guys tell you to get out of the building, you go," Eggleston said.

Firefighters wore oxygen masks as they entered the building to investigate the substance and evacuate the building. Emergency workers were expected to be working on the site through the day.

————

As Reported by the *Keene Evening Sentinel*:

A big bang
Acid detonated after discovery at Keene State

If four bottles of perchloric acid hadn't been discovered Thursday, they could have blown up an entire third-floor laboratory in the Keene State College science center, said Sgt. John W. McMaster, a bomb expert with N.H, State Police.

Acid in one of the jugs had crystallized, and it could have exploded if a cabinet door had simply been slammed. McMaster said.

Instead, the acid was detonated safely Thursday afternoon in an isolated area the Keene Public Works Department, sending black smoke 100 feet into the air.

Perchloric acid is a high explosive if it comes into contact with any organic matter, living or dead, things such as leaves, insects, or people, said Keene Fire Chief William H. Pepler Jr.

The acid also tends to crystallize as it ages, and becomes unstable, so that it will explode at any sudden shock.

————

As Reported by the *Keene Evening Sentinel* September 22nd, 1994:

"FIRE"

Five escape porch fire without injury in Keene

Five people, including two children under age 6, escaped a fire that engulfed a porch attached to their Keene home early this morning.

Damage to the interior of the house at 31 Rockwood Road was minimal, fire officials said. The family will be able to move back in later today.

Heather Thomas told firefighters that the sound of crackling flames outside the house woke her up at about 4:15 a.m. this morning.

Thomas got her two children, ages 2 and 5, her mother, Caroline Thomas, and a family friend out of the house safely.

A raised porch attached to the rear of the house was ablaze, and when firefighters arrived, they found that propane gas inside a barbecue grill's tank had also ignited, and was sending flames high into the air above the house.

Deputy Fire Chief Clayton R. Stalker Jr. said the cause of the fire is being investigated.

————

As Reported by the *Keene Evening Sentinel* September 27th, 1994:

"STORY"

Firefighters want talks to start over again

How to end a yearlong contract dispute with Keene firefighters? Start from scratch, says the firefighters' union.

Labor and management have been trying since early 1993 to negotiate a new contract to replace one that expired in June, 1993.

Last winter, both sides rejected recommendations from a fact-finder. And that's about the only thing they've agreed on since.

The firefighters' union president, Gary Lamoureaux, said the city government's insistence on a cap on health-insurance premiums has held up a settlement. Firefighters now pay 15 percent of their health-insurance costs.

The union representing firefighters and the firefighters' supervisors union are negotiating together.

Nor will city officials consider any proposal that contains a retroactive pay raise, dating back to when the last contract expired, Lamoureaux said.

Lamoureaux said firefighters will make a new offer—he declined to offer specifics—in an effort to bring the two sides together and raise sagging morale within the fire department.

Until now, firefighters have been seeking a 4 percent pay raise; city officials have pushed for 5 percent pay cut.

Alfred H. Merrifield, assistant city manager and the city's chief negotiator, could not be reached for comment this morning.

Firefighters are not the only union local unable to negotiate a new pact with the Keene city government.

Keene police are also concerned about morale after more than a year of unresolved contract talks.

Labor and management have been at impasse since last winter, when the Keene City Council rejected an independent fact-finder's recommendation for a two-year police contract, with pay raises of 3 percent each year.

—————

As Reported by the *Keene Evening Sentinel* September 29th, 1994:

"STORY"

Firefighters drop lawsuit

The union for Keene Fire Department supervisors has dropped its lawsuit against the city government.

The union sued in June, seeking six years' worth of back overtime pay it claims the city owes eight employees. The suit contends the city incorrectly calculated their overtime pay rate between April 1986 and March 1992.

Now, union members have decided to drop the suit because, if they lost the case, they could be liable for legal fees they can't afford.

Two fire department unions, representing supervisors and firefighters, are trying to negotiate a new contract. Their last contract expired more than a year ago.

This week, union representative Gary Lamoureaux announced a new proposal for settling the contract dispute, but would not disclose details.

—————

As Reported by the *Keene Evening Sentinel:*

Firefighters reach tentative contract

The Keene firefighters' union and the city government have reached tentative agreement on a new contract.

Terms of the agreement won't be disclosed unless it's ratified by members of the firefighters and the firefighters' supervisors union, and by the Keene City Council.

Laurence R. Shaffer, an assistant city manager who led the city's negotiating team, said the agreement was reached Wednesday.

Lt. Thomas Loll, a union negotiator, said union members will probably vote within two weeks on whether to ratify the agreement. Then, the city council will vote.

"I think it's a feeling of relief, if nothing else," Loll said. "At least we have something in hand."

Fire fighters and firefighter supervisors have been working without a contract since June 1993.

This week, union President Gary Lamoureaux said the city's demand for a cap on its contribution to health insurance.

Lamoureaux said firefighters were prepared to make a new proposal to the city, in hopes of reaching an agreement and quelling a growing morale problem within the fire department.

"We came around from a different point of view," Loll said of the fresh approach.

Shaffer said the new approach to the one sticking point helped the two sides reach an agreement during a six-hour negotiating session Wednesday.

———

As Reported by the *Keene Evening Sentinel* November 15th, 1994:

"STORY"

City shuts down Hundreds watch filming

Tuesday was the animal chase scene without the animals.

Fifty extras scrambled and raced throughout Central Square in Keene, carrying stereo equipment, plates, and even a satellite dish, as they pretended to loot stores and run from wild animals in the streets for the filming of "Jumanji."

The "Jumanji" screenplay, written by Jonathan Hansligh, is based on the award-winning children's book by Chris Van Allsburg. It stars Robin Williams and actress Kirsten Dunst ("Interview With the Vampire"), and is directed by Joe Johnston ("Honey, I Shrunk the Kids"). It's due out by Christmas 1995.

Parrish Shoes was painted on the corner of West Street and Central Square in Keene, New Hampshire for the movie "Jumanji." The city downtown was closed and all fire trucks and ambulances had to be rerouted within the downtown area while filming. Picture remains to remind people of the movie "Jumanji."

No *real* animals are actually used, said producer Scott Kroopf. They'll be added via special effects.

Between 500 to 1,000 people watched the filming Tuesday in downtown Keene, said Keene police Cpl. Joseph J. Collins. "The city is dead. Everyone's down here watching the movie."

Most of the people have cooperated with police and movie personnel, who are keeping the crowd behind yellow police lines and urging people to keep quiet and not to use flash photography during filming.

Williams has two doubles—one who is the stunt double, who dodged motorcycles and cars in traffic Tuesday afternoon, and Adam Bryant of New York City, who has been his stand-in for six years.

Bryant walks through each scene before Williams leaves his trailer. The director uses him to check lighting and camera angles. Bryant puts on his own makeup and he will wear clothes with colors similar to Williams' costume so the directors can get the lighting right.

———

As Reported by the *Keene Evening Sentinel* November 18th, 1994:

"FIRE"

No one hurt in fire in Beaver Brook Apts.

No one was injured when fire broke out in an apartment at the Beaver Brook Apartments on Washington Street in Keene at about 9 p.m. Thursday.

Cause of the fire in a first-floor apartment rented by Sharlene Blanchard is under investigation but is not considered suspicious. Blanchard was not home when the fire started.

Residents of the building, owned by S&S Realty of Keene, got out safely when the fire alarm sounded. The building's sprinkler system kept the fire contained to Blanchard's apartment, said Deputy Fire Chief Clayton R. Stalker.

Firefighters spent fewer than 30 minutes dousing the blaze then spent another hour testing the air quality inside the building.

————

As Reported by the *Keene Evening Sentinel*:

Report: Fire caused by cigarettes

A fire in a Keene apartment building Thursday was caused by careless handling of cigarettes, fire officials have ruled.

The fire started at about 9 p.m. at the Beaver Brook Apartments on Washington Street in the apartment rented by Sharlene Blanchard.

According to Deputy Fire Chief Clayton R. Stalker, Blanchard's teenage son and his friends were smoking cigarettes in an apartment bedroom. A short time after they left, Blanchard noticed smoke and fire coming from the bedroom. She tried to extinguish the flames herself, but gave up and called the fire department.

Stalker said the fire started on the corner of the bed.

Firefighters spend fewer than 30 minutes extinguishing the fire, which had been contained to Blanchard's apartment by the building's sprinkler system.

"That would have been an awful mess if not for the sprinkler," Stalker said.

The building is owned by S&S Realty of Keene. No one was injured in the fire.

————

As Reported by the *Keene Evening Sentinel* December 14th, 1994:

"STORY"

Firefighters seek help with contract

Frustrated by failed attempts to negotiate a new contract, Keene's firefighters want city councilors to step in.

Union President Gary P. Lamoureaux said his union has received little cooperation from the city government since negotiations began in March 1993. He wants residents to "contact those elected officials that we placed in office and urge them to intervene."

The firefighters and supervisors have been working without a contract for more than a year.

The union's negotiating team reached a tentative agreement with the city in September, but firefighters rejected the offer a month later because pay raises were too small.

The city had initially asked firefighters to take a 5 percent pay cut, but had tentatively agreed to maintain current salaries, with raises promised for the future.

Firefighters want 1.5 percent pay increases retroactive to June 1993, when their contract expired.

"We want to let the city councilors know that they're spending a lot of money on these negotiations," said Gary R. LaFreniere, vice president of the union.

"We think it would be better to settle it now rather than let it drag on. The firefighters are just looking for the pay raises the rest of the city got. We just want to get is resolved and go on,." LaFreniere said.

City officials have said the 1.5 percent increase for non-union employees was a one-time bonus.

Laurence R. Shaffer, the assistant city manager who's heading up negotiations for the city, said he regrets that no settlement has been reached yet, but he is still willing to work with the unions. "We're ready, willing and able to negotiate anytime, anywhere," Shaffer said.

No date for future talks has been set.

———————

As Reported by the *Keene Evening Sentinel* December 17th, 1994:

"STORY"

Keene's deputy fire chief answered bell for 32 years

Sitting in his office on the second floor of Keene's fire station, Deputy Chief George H. Shepard Jr. is surrounded by firefighting memorabilia.

Behind him is an olive-colored helmet, like the ones worn by soldiers in World War 1. Painted on the helmet is the white logo for the city's auxiliary fire department.

Nearby, an old brass hose nozzle stands, years removed from fighting fires. Hanging on the wall nearby are pictures of fire engines, including Engine No. 2, the department's newest.

Deputy Chief, George H. Shepard Jr. Photo by: Steve Hooper.

Piles of papers and manila folders are stacked neatly on his desk. His turnout gear is piled in the corner.

"Why some of us didn't get killed, I don't know, "he says, almost matter-of-factly, about the early days of his 32 ½ years as a Keene firefighter. "We were taught by on-the-job training, or the school of hard knocks."

Shepard's career as a Keene firefighter has spanned four decades and countless fires, disaster, and accidents. He's retiring in two weeks, reluctantly, as the department's deputy chief for operations.

Shepard had planned on retiring in 1997, after 35 years. But at his doctor's urging, and his wife Claudette's support, Shepard decided now was the time.

"I feel a little, I don't know if I want to say guilty, but I'm leaving in the middle of a lot of projects," Shepard says.

Like a lot of firefighters before him, Shepard, 54, wasn't the first in his family to enter the fire service. His father was a volunteer member of the Deluge Hose Co., one of three volunteer companies.

Shepard signed on as a volunteer firefighter in 1962. Seven months later, Chief Walter Messer called.

"He said "do you want to be a fireman?" Shepard says.

The fire department has changed considerably during the last 32 ½ years, Shepard says. Firefighters are more qualified, equipment is more sophisticated and the hazards more perilous.

But the basic tenor of the job—helping people—hasn't, Shepard says.

"It's something you do because you want to," he says. "It may be the thrill of getting in to fight a fire and testing yourself, I don't know.

Joining the team

Engine No. 2 is Keene's newest fire truck. It weight 32,660 pounds, and cost about $220,000. As deputy chief, Shepard headed the committee of firefighters that chose the engine and equipment.

"I think it's typical of the fire department," he says. "We're a team. Everything is done as teamwork. No one individual runs the show or calls all the shots."

The new engine is a far cry from the open-cab fire truck Shepard rode on to his first fire.

In those days, the fire truck was basically a convertible. There was no roof to protect firefighters during snow, rain or thunderstorms.

"In the winter, you rode in a convertible and hung off the tail board," he says.

Firefighters stood on the back of the truck, hanging on to rails as the fire truck zoomed to the scene. Shepard remembers his first call.

He was a volunteer firefighter then, and was at a training session when the fire bell rang.

There was a report of a kitchen fire at Pete's restaurant on Winchester Street—near where McDonald's now is.

"I had just enough room to hang on." He said of the ride. The fire, as it turned out, was minor.

Changing times

Like soldiers who have returned from battle, firefighters stockpile war stories—tales of past fires.

Shepard shares the stories, but doesn't glorify them. The dates and specifics are understandably fuzzy after 32 ½ years.

"There's an awful list of them, they just get foggy after awhile," he says.

His first big fire was at the old Carey Chair Mfg. Corp. plant on Victoria Street. It was a cold December night in 1962. Shepard drove one of the nine fire engines that responded to the fire that night.

"As we came through the square, we could see the flames," he says. "My foot kept going up and down, I was real nervous."

Firefighters battled the flames in below-zero temperatures for more than three hours. When it was over, the fire caused $50,000 damage, forced 35 workers out of a job, and injured one Keene firefighter.

The fires and accidents since then number far too many to remember. There are a few that stick out, though.

Like a trailer fire at the Cheshire County fairgrounds, Swanzey's fire department had knocked down the flames; Keene firefighters responded to provide assistance.

Two large snakes had escaped from the trailer, and were slithering around the fire scene. The hose leading from the fire engine to the scene, called the booster hose, snaked around the scene too.

Dazed, the snakes followed the hose to where Shepard was stationed. He saw the snakes heading his way, and wasn't too pleased.

"I didn't know what the heck they were," he says, laughing. "They thought the booster hose was another snake."

The fire that destroyed the former Eagle Hotel on Main Street, where Bagel Works is located now, is memorable—not for the fire as much as the date—November 11, 1968. It was Shepard's 28th birthday.

The blaze destroyed the building, which housed the Sport Shop, Benny and Frenchy's Barber Shop, and the Fletcher Pain Store. It caused about $500,000 in damage.

Through the ranks

Shepard was working as an electrician in 1962 when he got the call from Chief Messer offering him a full-time job as a firefighter., Although his father was a firefighter, Shepard wasn't sure he wanted to follow in those footsteps.

He was just starting a career as an electrician, and was ambivalent when Messer called.

The chief invited Shepard to his Spofford Lake cottage to talk about the job. They talked for several hours, and when it was over, Shepard was a firefighter.

"Here I am today," he says.

From 1962 until 1971, Shepard worked an average 72 hours a week. In those days, firefighters worked 240hour shifts, followed by 24 hours off.

There were no ambulance calls then. "Everything was fire," Shepard says. It wasn't until the mid 1970's that the department began providing ambulance service to the city.

With the arrival of the ambulance service, the department began providing ambulance service to the city.

With the arrival of the ambulance service, the department became increasingly busy. Technology, including sprinkler systems, fire alarms, and better construction standards have helped decrease the number of fires.

In 1971, Shepard was named the department's training officer. Two years later, he was promoted to lieutenant. In 1976, he was named captain of A-shift, where he remained until 1981. He's served as deputy chief since 1981.

"He was one of the guys you never hesitated following," said Lt. A. Scott Collier, who, with 22 ½ years experience, is the third most experienced firefighter in the city.

"You always trusted his judgment 110 percent. It's something that comes with years of experience," he said.

Even with Shepard's retirement, there's still a firefighter tin the family. His son Brian, 27, is a member of D-shift.

Shepard plans on working part time as a master electrician, and welcoming a new grandchild. Brian's wife, Dottie, is expecting the couple's first child any day now. Shepard's other son, Glenn, lives in Washington, D.C.

Losing part of the team

Fire Chief William H. Pepler Jr. was hired after Shepard had been with the department for 30 years. Pepler said Shepard remains one of the most progressive members of the department.

"He's a firefighter of the '90's who happens to have 30 years experience," Pepler said. "George is a walking encyclopedia, particularly of what's happened in the department, in the city, for the last 33 years.,"

Collier said Shepard's departure is a blow to the department Collier worked with Shepard for 22 of the 32 years.

Like Pepler, Collier said Shepard was successful because he changed with the times.

"To this day, he is still learning," Collier said. "He seems to adapt to be very receptive to change."

When Shepard retires, Lt. Thomas Loll will become the longest serving member of the fire department. He'll pick up the charge of being the veteran. It's a responsibility that Shepard met well, Loll said.

"He always led by doing it himself," Loll said. "He doesn't ask anyone to do anything he hasn't done or would be willing to do."

So Shepard's departure is bittersweet, he said.

"I'm really glad for him," Loll said last week from the fire station. "He's had a great career and has done a lot for the fire department. He's had a great career and has done a lot for the fire department. He's my friend. I'm going to miss him."

Although firefighting isn't like it was when Shepard started, he isn't complaining.

"It was a primitive fire department, but I have a lot of respect for those days," Shepard says. "(Now) it's a new ball game altogether."

Shepard says today's firefighters are expected to know more than just how to douse flames.

"There's a whole new set of rules," he says. "As I came up through the ranks, I thought I knew all the answers. Then they changed the questions on me."

1995

As Reported by the *Keene Evening Sentinel* January 3rd, 1995:

"FIRE"

Keene house damaged by a suspicious fire

Fire heavily damaged a house in Keene Monday afternoon, and investigators believe it was the result of arson.

The vacant house at 138 Howard St. is owned by Clayton Beauchemin of Brattleboro.

Capt. Goldsmith ordered a 2 floor simultaneous attack which made quick stop of the fire spreading to both floors. Photo by: Michael Moore.

On Monday night, Thomas M. Norton, an investigator from the N.H. Fire Marshal's Office, searched the charred shell of the house, accompanied by Cinder, a black Labrador retriever that can sniff out fire accelerants, such as gasoline. This morning, Norton said the dog found evidence in the house, but declined to elaborate.

Beauchemin was apparently in the building shortly before the fire started, police said, and they are interviewing him to see what he knows.

Police said Beauchemin had not been staying at the Keene house, although some of his belongings were destroyed in the fire.

At about 1 p.m. Monday, flames in the house could be seen from the street, police said.

The fire appears to have started in two different spots on the first floor of the unoccupied house, said Steven C. Tenney, a Keene detective.

The fire gutted the first floor of the house and part of the second, said Capt. Steven Goldsmith of the Keene Fire Department.

No one was injured.

Dozens of neighbors watched Monday afternoon as firefighters worked the smoky blaze. Dense, gray smoke billowed out of the doorway and a second-floor window.

When firefighters arrived, the smoke was so heavy that they could barely see the house.

It took just over an hour to bring the fire under control, Goldsmith said.

An investigative team from the Keene Fire Department was at the house until 8:30 Monday night.

As Reported by the *Keene Evening Sentinel*:

Arson tests in Keene fire

Arson tests are being done on a Keene house heavily damaged by fire January 2.

The tests should determine whether the fire at a vacant house at 138 Howard St. was set, police said. The fire gutted the first floor and part of the second. No one was injured.

The fire appears to have started in two different spots on the building's first floor. Hours after firefighters extinguished the blaze an investigator from the N.H. Fire Marshal's Office searched the house, using a dog trained to sniff out fire accelerants, such as gasoline.

The evidence the dog found is being tested at the state laboratory in Concord.

As Reported by the *Keene Evening Sentinel* January 4th, 1995:

"STORY"

Manager set to step down
Keene's MacQueen plans to resign after 16 years

Keene's low-key city manager stayed true to form, even as he was announcing his resignation.

J. Patrick MacQueen, the city government's chief executive for more than 16 years, quietly announced Tuesday that he will leave the job July 1.

The city manager works directly for the Keene City Council, which will hire a replacement. Mayor William F. Lynch said Tuesday he's not sure yet how the process will go; MacQueen has offered his assistance.

MacQueen handled all his duties during his 16 ½ year tenure as Keene's city manager leading by example, delving deeply into the smallest aspects of city government, yet asking no credit for himself.

Yet, for others, MacQueen was a ruthless negotiator who drove city workers to unionize and, who councilors sometimes complained, wasn't always forthcoming with information.

When the unions representing Keene's police and firefighters began negotiating with the city government for a new contract, the city's proposal was brutal: a 5 percent pay cut, and a freeze on city contributions to health insurance. It was classic MacQueen.

MacQueen announced Tuesday that he would be resigning on July 1, the start of the new fiscal year.

Still, MacQueen is an enigma of sorts. Even critics acknowledged he worked 65 hours a week, and cared deeply about the city. Former mayor Richard P. Peloquin was acting city manager when MacQueen was hired in 1978. He said MacQueen stood "head-and-shoulders" above the other 62 candidates for the job.

"He came here with a couple of years experience as an assistant city manager," Peloquin said. "He really cut his teeth here. He did a tremendous job. Certainly, no one is going to fault his work ethic."

Keene witnessed tremendous growth and change during MacQueen's tenure, Peloq1uin said. The railroad stopped running through Keene, the city's Main Street was refurbished, and the city hall renovated.

Overseeing those changes will be MacQueen's legacy, City Councilor Jacqueline D. Hill said.

"He's been here through some very, very significant changes to the city," Hill said.

But first-term Councilor Robert Meagher said MacQueen's legacy will be less pleasant. "He's a city manager that turned this city into a city of unions," said Meagher, a former firefighter.

Meagher said MacQueen had a heavy-handed negotiating style that drove firefighters, firefighter supervisors, public works employees, and police supervisors to unionize. The guys figured to protect themselves (they) had to go union," he said.

———————

As Reported by the *Keene Evening Sentinel* January 10th, 1995:

"STORY"

Trash pickup turns noxious

The Keene Fire Department's hazardous materials team responded Monday to the Keene landfill, where potentially toxic material was believed to be in the garbage truck. Above, Keene firefighter Mark Howard, dressed in protective gear, looks through trash for the suspected material. Photo by: Michael Moore.

Trash haulers inadvertently picked up some noxious cargo Monday morning while collecting garbage from a neighborhood near Keene High School.

This morning, the Keene Fire Department's hazardous materials team was still trying to determine what the substance was.

Two workers from Venture Sanitation of Keene were collecting trash on Worcester Street at about 9:30 a.m. when they noticed fumes coming from the back of their five-ton truck, firefighters said. When the workers doused the substance with water, white fumes began pouring out of the truck and the material began reacting with the metal inside the hauler.

Later, when lime was put on the substance, it stopped fuming.

The fumes irritated the workers' throats and skin. They were treated by firefighters, who went to the city landfill to handle the hazardous material. Both workers declined hospital treatment.

Firefighters dressed in protective suits and using self-contained breathing tanks examined the truck after it was driven to a remote area of the landfill.

"From the reports we received it appears to have been an acid-type substance. We found nothing that indicated it was hazardous when we got to it. The lime may have worked to neutralize whatever it was," Fire Captain Bruce Pollock said.

The two workers told investigators that the substance must have come from one of the residences where they picked up trash Monday morning. They had covered Robbins Court, Robbins Street and Worcester Street when they noticed the fumes.

Authorities said they planned to call neighborhood residents to determine where the substance came from.

———————

As Reported by the *Keene Evening Sentinel* January 11th, 1995:

"FIRE"

Fire in dryer forces evacuation

Residents of Brookside Apartments in Keene were forced out into the cold at about 4:45 p.m. Tuesday when a fire in a dryer set off smoke detectors.

Smoke drifted throughout the three-story apartment building. Keene Fire Chief William H. Pepler Jr. said. There were no injuries and residents living in the 24 apartments were allowed back into their homes shortly after the fire was extinguished.

———————

As Reported by the *Keene Evening Sentinel* January 13th, 1995:

"STORY"

Bad air sickens three emergency dispatchers

When the three emergency dispatchers started feeling sick Thursday night at Southwestern N.H. Fire Mutual Aid, they didn't have to go far for help.

The dispatchers recognized their symptoms—nausea, headaches, fatigue—as early signs of carbon monoxide poisoning.

They summoned Keene firefighters, on duty next door at the Keene fire station.

The firefighters hooked up the dispatchers to oxygen masks and took them to Cheshire Medical Center for treatment. They also ventilated the dispatch center, the emergency communications center for 76 communities in New Hampshire, Vermont and Massachusetts, and checked for carbon monoxide elsewhere in the building.

The problem turned out to be a clogged burner in the furnace that heats the dispatch center; it caused incomplete combustion of the gas.

Keene Fire Chief William H. Pepler Jr. said the incident shows that carbon monoxide poisoning is a serious problem.

"It could happen anywhere," Pepler said. "It could happen in anyone's home, or anyone's business."

The three dispatchers: Supervisor David Carter, 42, of Dublin; David Whipple, 30, of West Swanzey; and James Young, 38, of Gilsum. All three were treated at the Keene hospital and released.

Pepler said two other dispatchers were called in to cover the emergency communications center, and one Keene firefighter assisted. Service was never affected.

———————

As Reported by the *Keene Evening Sentinel* January 16th, 1995:

"FIRE"

Keene man hurt in fire

A Keene man suffered second-degree burns on his hands during a fire at his home Saturday night, and a downtown Hinsdale building was damaged in a weekend fire.

In Keene, Robert E. Kerbaugh of 30 Royal Ave. was burned when he tried to extinguish flames at his home Saturday night.

The house received minor damage.

Keene Fire Chief William H. Pepler Jr. said Barbara E. Kerbaugh had been cleaning with linseed oil on Friday, and had placed oil-soaked rags in a plastic bag in the pantry of the house, planning to dispose of them later.

However, linseed oil is notorious for spontaneous combustion, and a fire started inside the bag, Pepler said.

The flames were extinguished quickly, Pepler said, thanks in part to an off-duty Keene firefighter, Ronald Leslie, and Keene police Sgt. Edwin F. Bourassa, who were first to arrive at the fire and tried to extinguish the flames.

According to Pepler, the Kerbaughs had just gone to bed when Mrs. Kerbaugh spotted smoke.

"Luckily, they were home and noticed it," Pepler said.

————

As Reported by the *Keene Evening Sentinel* January 19th, 1995:

"STORY"

Keene and firefighters' unions reach agreement; deadlock ends

A long and testy contract dispute between Keene's firefighters and the city government may be over.

A six-hour bargaining session that ended early this morning may end a contentious 18-month battle between the city government and the unions representing firefighters and firefighter supervisors.

Neither labor nor management would provide details of the tentative agreement today, because union members and the Keene City Council have not yet voted on whether to approve it.

Members of the two unions have been working without a contract since mid 1993.

On Wednesday night, the two sides staked their ground inside Keene City Hall: Union representatives and their attorneys, from the Cook and Mollan law firm of Concord, set up shop in the second-floor city council chambers.

City negotiators—led by Assistant City Manager Laurence R. Shaffer, and with nine of the 15 city councilors in tow—headed for the third floor.

Richard G. Higgins, a state-certified mediator from Londonderry, hustled between the floors, shuttling proposals and counterproposals.

Finally, at about 1:20 this morning, all roadblocks had been cleared, and a tentative agreement was signed.

Union President Gary Lamoureaux said today he was relieved, but wary, about the agreement.

Union negotiators also reached a tentative agreement in October, but union members rejected it by a wide margin.

Lamoureaux said talks have been stalled for to long, and both sides wanted to reach a settlement.

"The public was starting to express its opinion. With the city council being involved, there were more heads put together. I think everybody decided to bend a little more," he said.

Councilor Randy L. Filiault, who attended Wednesday's session, agreed.

"It was tenacious" Filiault said of the negotiations. "It was about as much fun as having a root canal. But it's well worth it."

Though city officials have declined comment, union representatives have said pay raises were the main sticking point.

Initially, the city wanted the union members to take a t percent pay cut, then offered a contract with no first-year raises.

Apparently, the city came up with an offer that firefighters and their supervisors could accept.

There may also be some movement in the negotiations with the unions representing Keene's police supervisors and patrol officers whose last contract, also signed mid-1993.

————

As Reported by the *Keene Evening Sentinel* January 21st, 1995:

"STORY"

Union okay's deal; Firefighters accept city's offer

Unless Keene's city council says no, 34 firefighters and their supervisors will soon have a new three-year contract.

On Friday, the two city unions unanimously ratified the contract hammered out before dawn on Thursday.

The vote, reached in a one-hour meeting, ends a contentious, 18-month battle between city government and the unions representing the firefighters and firefighters' supervisors.

The new contract contains pay raises for all firefighters and supervisors, and an adjustment in their health insurance plan. Union officials declined to provide details of the contract until it's approved by the city council.

The council could vote at its regular meeting in two weeks or schedule a special meeting before then.

Wednesday evening, union representatives, Assistant City Manager Laurence R. Shaffer, nine city councilors and mediator Richard G. Higgins hammered out the agreement in a six-hour session.

Not one of the city councilors left the negotiating session until it ended at 1:20 Thursday morning.

"Just seeing them there made a difference," said negotiator John Beckta. "They all came and showed their commitment."

Pay raises had been the main sticking point. "The wages issue has been resolved to our satisfaction," said Beckta. "Now, we just want to resolve this and get on with our jobs."

There may also be some action in the negotiations with the unions representing the city's police supervisors and patrol officers, whose last contract expired in mid-1993. The city has called for a negotiating session next Tuesday.

————

As Reported by the *Keene Evening Sentinel* February 4th, 1995:

"FIRE"

Injured student recovering

Rescue workers attend to Derek A. Connary, 20 of Nashua a Keene State student, after he was struck by pickup truck on Winchester Street in Keene. Connary suffered a broken leg and internal injuries, and was taken by an ambulance to Cheshire Medical Center in Keene. Rescue workers from left to right, Lt. Chris Cram, Lt. Gary Lamourex, Lt. Mike Burke, Capt. Steve Goldsmith and Firefighter Mike Driscoll. Photo by: Michael Moore.

A Keene State College sophomore was continuing to recover this morning from injuries suffered when he was struck Friday by a pickup truck on Winchester Street in Keene.

Derek A. Connary, 20, of Nashua suffered a broken left thigh bone and kidney bruises in the accident. He underwent surgery Friday night at Cheshire Medical Center; initially he was listed in guarded condition, but was upgraded to good condition today.

Connary stepped out from behind a tree near the corner of Blake Street and into the path of a pickup driven by Robert E. Davis of Westmoreland, who was driving west at 25 to 30 mph late Friday afternoon. Davis said

he didn't see Connary until it was too late to avoid him.

————

As Reported by the *Keene Evening Sentinel* February 17th, 1995:

"FIRE"

Two fires hit Keene; one ruled suspicious

Two small fires within two hours of each other made for a busy Thursday night for Keene firefighters.

The first fire, at 32 Water St., was caused by French fries left cooking in a pan of oil. The second fire, in a Keene State College dormitory, is considered suspicious, and is being investigated by Keene police.

Deputy Fire Chief Clayton R. Stalker said both fires were extinguished quickly, and caused no injuries.

At about 9:57 p.m., firefighters were called to the Keene Housing Authority shelter on Water Street. When they arrived, smoke was coming out the door and windows, Stalker said. An unattended pan of grease on the stove top was burning.

Stalker said the flames were doused with a dry chemical extinguisher. The fire damaged the stove, and caused smoke and heat damage throughout the kitchen.

Firefighters cleared the scene at about 10:50 p.m. About one hour later, they were called to Monadnock Hall on Winchester Street.

Inside a bathroom on the second floor, a stuffed chair was smoldering. The chair had been cut open and set on fire, but the flames were doused before firefighters arrived.

Stalker said the students were evacuated as firefighters soaked the smoldering chair.

"Someone set it on fire for whatever reason," he said. "It was a really stupid thing to do."

The fire caused no damage to the dormitory. Keene police are investigating how the fire started.

———

As Reported by the *Keene Evening Sentinel* February 18th, 1995:

"FIRE"

Home damaged, 2 firemen hurt

Investigators are searching for the cause of a stubborn fire Friday night that heavily damaged a Keene house and injured two firefighters.

The fire began at about 6:05 p.m. in the basement of the house at 10 Marshall St. owned by Paul and Regina Perham. Smoke billowed from the house, and flames shot from the basement windows while firefighters worked to reach the fire.

Keene Fire Chief William H. Pepler Jr. said firefighters had a tough time reaching the flames because of partitions dividing the basement. The fire was declared under control at 7 p.m., less than an hour after the alarm sounded.

Pepler said the Perhams were home when the fire started. A smoke detector went off while Paul Perham was lighting a wood stove; he tried to douse the flames with a fire extinguisher, but was forced back.

"It was a very stubborn fire," Pepler said.

Firefighter Ronald Dunn was burned on the back of the neck during their initial attack on the fire. Another firefighter, Mike Gianferrari, cut his hand while taking out a window. Both were treated at the scene.

Most of the fire damage was limited to the basement, but there was smoke and water damage throughout the house. One family cat was taken from the house; another was missing.

The Marlborough Fire Department covered the Keene station during the fire.

———

As Reported by the *Keene Evening Sentinel* February 20th, 1995:

"FIRE"

Fire damages house in Keene

Firefighters in Keene had to tear through the walls of a Grant Street house Saturday night to reach a chimney fire that had spread into the walls.

Keene Fire Chief William H. Pepler said the fire caused minor smoke and fire damage to the house at 66 Grant St. Most of the damage was caused when firefighters had to cut through the walls to reach the flames.

The homeowner, Timothy Gallagher, called emergency dispatchers at about 20:20 p.m. after smoke started pouring out of electrical outlets on the wall.

"Luckily, the guy noticed it before he went to bed," Pepler said. "If not, it would have been a major fire."

It took firefighters three hours to make sure the fire hadn't spread any more, Pepler said.

Also this weekend:

The state fire marshal's office began searching for the cause of a fire that damaged a house on Marshall Street Friday night.

Pepler said the fire is not believed to be suspicious. It started in the basement of the house, and was probably accidental or electrical, he said.

Two firefighters received minor injuries fighting the fire, which caused heavy smoke and water damage in the house.

The fire marshal is also investigating a fire Sunday at Keene State College that damaged a dormitory elevator.

Pepler said the control panel of the elevator in Pondside Hall was melted by the fire, which was detected by the elevator's alarm.

Last week, firefighters were called to Monadnock Hall on Winchester Street to extinguish a chair fire in one of the bathrooms. Pepler said it was unclear whether the two incidents were related.

————

As Reported by the *Keene Evening Sentinel:*

Cause of fire still mystery

Investigators know that an electrical problem started a fire on Marshall Street in Keene Friday night. But the exact cause may never be known.

Deputy Fire Chief Clayton R. Stalker said the state fire marshal's office agreed with Keene's fire investigators that the fire was "of an electrical origin."

The fire, which damaged Paul and Regina Perham's home at 210 Marshall St., burned for almost an hour before firefighters declared it under control. The fire started in a storage area in the basement, and sent smoke throughout the house.

Two firefighters, Ronald Dunn and Michael Gianferrari, received minor injuries while fighting the fire.

————

As Reported by the *Keene Evening Sentinel* February 28th, 1995:

"STORY"

Firefighters sign pact, but not without grumbling

Keene's firefighters and supervisors signed a three-year deal with the city government Monday.

But, even at the last moment, the two sides found something to argue about.

The unions, whose members had been working without contracts since June 1993, reached a tentative contract agreement with the city last month.

As part of the agreement, the city is to pay each firefighter $750 for switching from a traditional health plan to a health maintenance organization, and for accepting a cap on the city's contribution to health-care costs—a move that will save money for the city.

Union President Gary P. Lamoureaux said city negotiators promised to have the checks ready at the signing.

When they found out that the checks won't be sent until Friday, March 3, some union members wanted to back out of the deal.

"We held up our side of the agreement, and they didn't, and that kind of bothered the guys," Lamoureaux said.

But, after a closed-door meeting to work out the dispute, union negotiators and City Manager J. Patrick MacQueen signed the contract.

The three-year contract gives no pay raise in the first year of the contract—which ended last June—a 2 percent raise in the current fiscal year, and 2.5 percent in the last year of the contract, which begins July 1.

That means a firefighter with six months' experience in the department will make $24,967 this fiscal year, while a firefighter with 5 ½ years' experience or more will make $30,368. This summer, the base pay will increase to $25,591, and the top salary will rise to $31,127.

For the supervisors, the salaries this year range from $27,696 to $35,505 for lieutenants, and from $31,605 to $40,516 for captains. In the next fiscal year, the ranges will increase to between $28,388 and $36,393 for lieutenants, and between $32,395 and $41,529 for captains.

However, the actual take-home pay could change for members of both unions. Negotiators decided the city would contribute up to $43.57 a week in health-care premiums for each member, $88.97 for a couple, and $121.41 for a family.

Every year, that figure will be revised, depending on how much health-care costs change. If premiums increase more than 10 percent, union members will have to make up the difference, up to the amount of his or her pay increase for that year.

———————

As Reported by the *Keene Evening Sentinel* February 28th, 1995:

"FIRE"

Smokey vat sends 15 to hospital from Markem

Smoke and fumes from a heating vat that caught fire inside Markem Corp. in Keene drove about 400 people outdoors Monday afternoon and sent 15 workers to the hospital.

Company officials are investigating why a new heating unit, about the size of a crockpot, caught fire Monday at about 3:30 p.m. at the company's plant on Congress Street.

The unit heats plastic resin that's used to coat cutting tools. The fire produced thick smoke and fumes in the machine shop, forcing the evacuation of the entire building.

The man working at the heating unit when it caught fire suffered first-degree burns on his hands and had difficulty breathing. He and other workers carried the vat outside the building after it caught on fire.

In all, 15 employees were given oxygen and taken to Cheshire Medical Center, where they were treated and released.

Using huge ceiling fans in the building and portable fans, Keene firefighters were able to clear the machine shop of fumes and smoke in minutes, Deputy Fire Chief Clayton R. Stalker Jr. said this morning.

Employees were allowed back inside the building after about 10 minutes, said David C. Hill, manager of Markem's human resources division.

———————

As Reported by the *Keene Evening Sentinel* April 1st, 1995:

"STORY"

Firefighters train, get new deputy chief

Some Keene firefighters are better prepared after completing an advanced course for emergency medical technicians, or EMT's.

Ten firefighters have completed more than 100 hours of training at Cheshire Medical Center in Keene to get their intermediate certification. The training focused on better assessment and treatment of various injuries, especially shock. EMT's with intermediate certification are trained to administer fluids intravenously to combat shock.

Deputy Chief Clayton R. Stalker Jr. said the training cost about $5,000, plus overtime and administrative costs for the 10 firefighters. Six more firefighters are set to start the training this year.

The goal is to train enough members of the department so half the firefighters on any given shift will be certified, Stalker said.

In other news from Vernon Street: the fire department holds one of its two yearly dinners tonight at 6:30 at the fire station. At the dinner, Chief William H. Pepler Jr. will announce the new deputy chief of operations, to replace George H. Shepard Jr., who retired earlier this year. Four captains from the department are in the running. They'll meet with Pepler this morning to find out who got the job.

The deputy chief of operations is responsible overseeing the day-to-day operations of the station.

New deputy

Bradley B. Payne was named the Keene Fire Department's new deputy chief of operations at the department's annual dinner Saturday night in the fire station. He replaces George H. Shepard Jr., who retired after more than 30 years. Payne has been on the force since 1976. He was promoted to shift lieutenant in 1984, shift captain in 1988, and fire prevention officer in 1993.Payne will be responsible for overseeing the eight shift officers, and the general day-to-day operations of the department. He lives in East Swanzey with his wife, Andrea, and daughter, Hannah.

As Reported by Elizabeth Crowley in *Keene Evening Sentinel* April 17th, 1995:

"STORY"

New 911 system will mean renaming some roads

What street do you live on? In this region, that simple question sometimes produces con fusing answers.

For example, if you live in Winchester and your answer is Main Street, you've got some explaining to do. Which Main Street? The one in Winchester proper, or the one in Ashuelot village?

And you'll have to do better if your answer is Scofield Mountain Road, because there are two unconnected roads in Winchester that bear that name.

Dispatchers at Southwestern N.H. Fire Mutual Aid in Keene can tell the difference between Main Street in Winchester and Main Street in Ashuelot—they've had plenty of practice.

But someone unfamiliar with the traditional, if not official, names of the streets, roads, avenues and highways of the Monadnock Region would struggle.

For example, would an out-of-towner know Route 78 by its informal name, the Old Warwick Road?

An enhanced emergency response system will try to take the guesswork out of identifying roads.

By July 5, emergency-response operators in Concord will begin routing calls through a statewide Enhanced 911 system. The system is called enhanced because it includes technology that lets emergency operators trace where the call is coming from, even if the person calling doesn't know or can't say. The seven=-digit number of the calling phone will automatically appear on a computer monitor in front of the Enhanced 911 operator receiving the call.

With regular 911, the caller would have to accurately identify where he or she is calling from for the system to work properly.

With the new system, people will be able to reach emergency help simply by punching 911 on their telephones. Either through the caller or by the seven-digit number on the computer screen, the emergency operator will determine where the call is coming from and relay it to the appropriate local police, fire or rescue department.

To avoid confusion, it's best if operators can trace the call to a specific street name and house number. They can only do that if houses are accurately numbered and if each roadway in each city and town has one, and only one, name, with no duplicates, said John S. Marechal, chief coordinator of Southwestern N.H. Fire Mutual Aid.

The system will work like this: A person dials 911 from, for example, a home in Acworth. The call goes to a bank of operators in Concord. The operator asks, "What is the nature of your emergency?"

Meanwhile, the caller's telephone number pops up on a computer monitor in front of the Enhanced 911 operator. In this case, it will be an Acworth number.

After the Acworth person gives an address—if he or she can—and says what kind of emergency is occurring (fire, rescue or police), the Enhanced 911 operator will connect the call to dispatchers at Southwestern N.H. Fire Mutual Aid in Keene, which handles emergency communications in the Acworth area.

The mutual aid dispatchers will know where to send help, and what king of help to send.

———

As Reported by the *Keene Evening Sentinel* May 3rd, 1995:

"FIRE"

Fire damages Keene house

Two people were treated for smoke inhalation after a fire Tuesday night at a house on Carroll Street in Keene.

Felix Beatty and Betty Castor, two of what officials believe may be as many as 14 residents of the house at 198 Carroll St., were released after treatment at Cheshire Medical Center Tuesday night.

Fire officials believe children playing with a cigarette lighter started the fire in a hallway near a bedroom in the rear of the house.

The fire began in a pile of mattresses and children's clothes and toys in the hallway and filled the two-story house with smoke. Daniel Hope, his wife and the couple's six children live in the house along with Beatty and Castor

and possibly others, Keene Deputy Fire Chief Clayton R. Stalker Jr. said.

Firefighters were called to the house at 9:15 p.m. and had put out the fire by 10:30. Residents were allowed back into the house after the fire was completely put out.

The house is owned by Norman Saunders of Weston, Mass.

———

As Reported by the *Keene Evening Sentinel* May 16th, 1995:

"STORY"

Ruined home a classroom for Keene fire department

Keene Firefighter Mike Gianferrari peers into a tunnel that firefighters were building as a safe passageway into a collapsed building on Appleton Street. Photo by: Michael Moore.

Lights and rescue trucks broke the mid-spring quiet on Appleton Street Monday afternoon, as Keene firefighters struggled to find survivors in a two-story house that had collapsed.

The scene was horrifying, but wasn't the real thing.

It was the first in a series of training sessions aimed at preparing the department for the real thing.

The session seems all the more timely in the wake of the bombing of the Alfred P. Murrah building in Oklahoma City. The session had been planned long before the bomb exploded, killing 167 people.

Oklahoma City rescue workers had to deal with massive concrete walls and floors blown apart, but Keene firefighters would have to dig through shattered wooden frame buildings, said Keene Deputy Fire Chief Clayton R. Stalker Jr.

The training covered every aspect of a house collapse, from the first emergency call all the way to the search for a rescue of victims.

One on the scene, firefighters would immediately shut off the electricity, gas and water lines to the collapsed building. They'd find out how many people were in the building.

Then they'd need absolute silence.

"You go around the building, you holler in, and you listen, Stalker said. "You listen for scratching, for banging, for (someone) calling."

Keene firefighters trained for that possibility Monday, on a building owned by Keene State College. The college plans to build a dormitory there in the future.

The second floor of the house on Appleton Street sat just a few feet off the ground; the first floor had slumped into the cellar at a 45-degree angle. Often, houses will shift and collapse that way during a tornado or earthquake, Stalker said.

Outside the house on a soggy Monday afternoon, firefighters were cutting up boards and making wooden frames to support the tunnel.

The opening of the tunnel was two feet high—just wide enough to allow firefighters through with their gear, and to pull out survivors. Long boards were slid over the tops of the frames to keep debris from falling onto the firefighters, which could injure them and block them inside the tunnel.

One firefighter crawled through the opening on his belly. Broken boards, ceiling tiles, and smashed glass drew closer the farther he went inside. Another firefighter slid in directly behind him. A third man crouched beside the opening, skinning a light inside so the two firefighters could find their way through.

What they saw was daunting. Straight ahead was a mess of crumbling plaster, split boards and broken glass that firefighters had to maneuver through. They moved the fallen boards aside carefully, but some boards wouldn't budge. The firefighters wiggled the boards to see if they could be cut without bringing the rest of the house down.

On the other side of the house, another crew tunneled down through the cellar, past mattresses that teetered on the first floor. As part of the training exercise, the firefighters were working through the house to connect their tunnels in the middle.

Then, they hit the brick chimney that had collapsed into the cellar. It stalled their progress, at least for the moment. There was a mountain of brick and cement blocks that the firefighters needed to get through, using crowbars and sledgehammers to open up the tunnel.

All of Keene's full-time firefighters had a chance to burrow into the collapsed house. Eventually, the Keene Fire Department, will develop a specialized team to rescue people from collapsed buildings, Stalker said.

On Wednesday, the firefighters will practice rescuing people from caved-in trenches. The rescue workers will spend Thursday and Friday training how to pull people out of man-holes and culverts.

It shows we don't just put out building fires anymore," said instructor David Joke. Joke and Shawn Allison, both Merrimack firefighters, taught the course.

As Reported by the *Keene Evening Sentinel* May 19th, 1995:

"FIRE"

Keene barn fire doused

A person playing with matches may have started a fire that destroyed a barn on Elm Street in Keene Thursday night.

Keene police are still investigating what caused the fire, which firefighters were able to knock down before it spread to an adjacent house.

Harold Farrington of West Milford, N.J., owns the house and barn, which are rented by Robert Tedford and Charles Guptill and their families. No one was injured in the fire.

The barn fire was reported at about 9:30 p.m., and firefighters spent about 2 ½ hours extinguishing the flames and cooling the charred shell of the barn.

Damage to the adjacent house was minimal, Deputy Fire Chief Clayton R. Stalker Jr. said.

———

As Reported by the *Keene Evening Sentinel* June 6th, 1995:

"STORY"

Tanker crashes off Route 9; Wreck spills about 500 gallons of gas, closes road 15 hours

A tanker truck hauling about 8,500 gallons of gasoline toppled off Route 9 in Keene Monday afternoon, spilling about 500 gallons of its cargo into Grimes Brook and closing the road for about 15 hours.

Sentinel photo by MICHAEL MOOR

Sentinel photos by STEVE HOOPE

STEP BY STEP — Keene firefighter George W. Shepard, at top, looks up from where a gasoline tanker came to rest at the bottom of an embankment off Route 9 in Keene. Above, foam is sprayed on the tanker before firefighters begin their work. At left, Keene fire and public works personnel, using hay and dirt, block the fuel from going into a culvert.

The driver of the truck, David Hale, 50, of Shelburne Falls, Mass., was treated for minor scrapes and bruises and released from Cheshire Medical Center.

Route 9 from Glebe Road in Spofford to Base Hill Road in Keene was closed from about 1:15 p.m. Monday until 5:30 this morning.

Hale told investigators that the truck stalled and apparently lost its power steering as he was driving down Chesterfield Hill toward downtown Keene. The tractor trailer went off the side of the road near the intersection of Old Chesterfield Road and into a 50-foot gully. It hit a tree, jackknifed and flipped onto its side, Keene Fire Chief William H. Pepler Jr. said.

Several hatches atop the tanker began leaking gasoline. Firefighters used huge clamps to stem the flow.

In all, Pepler said, at least 500 gallons of gasoline escaped into the brook.

That's an enormous amount, he said, "considering we send out hazardous materials team when someone spills just two gallons.

Hale was driving was hauling fuel for Rice Oil Company in Greenfield, Mass. Rice Oil supplies several gas stations in the Keene area.

Firefighters quickly build dams on the brook that empties into the Ashuelot River near the athletic fields at Keene State College.

"We were able to get ahead of the spill pretty quickly," Pepler said, although some fish were immediately killed by the gasoline.

Environmental cleanup workers were back at the scene this morning, testing soil and water wells for contamination .

In addition to the long-term danger posed by contamination, rescue workers had to contend with the threat of fire.

"There was a high level of gas vapors in the air," Pepler said. "Even a small spark could have started a flash fire that would have set the whole tanker off."

Three houses on Old Chesterfield Road were evacuated and their gas supplies and electricity shut off to guard against explosion, he said.

And firefighters covered the truck with flame-resistant foam.

The truck, emptied of its cargo, was towed to the Department of Public Works in Keene, where it was impounded by the N.H. Department of Safety. Highway Enforcement Division investigators will inspect the truck, trying to learn why it stalled and crashed.

————

As Reported by the *Keene Evening Sentinel* June 12th, 1995:

"FIRE"

Early-morning fire in Keene is suspicious

It took firefighters almost 2 ½ hours to contain a fire at the Monadnock Cutlery building early this morning, a fire that investigators believe was set.

"It appears the fire started on the outside of the building,." Fire Chief William H. Pepler Jr. said this morning. "That makes it very suspicious."

No one was injured as firefighters battled the blaze at the 100-year-old building on Railroad Street in Keene from about 3:20 until about 6 this morning. Sprinklers inside the building kept the fire from spreading, Pepler said.

Earlier in the morning, at about 1:30, firefighters doused a fire in a trash container near the cutlery building.

Keene police and the N.H. Fire Marshal's office are investigating the cause of both fires.

————

As Reported by the *Keene Evening Sentinel* June 12th, 1995:

"STORY"
A grand farewell to Keene manager

J. Patrick MacQueen

After hundreds of city council and committee debates, staff meetings, and interviews Keene City Manager J. Patrick MacQueen finally let his guard down.

About 220 people paid $22.50 per ticket for a dinner at the new Lloyd P. Young Student Center at Keene State College Tuesday night to honor MacQueen, 47, who's resigning June 30 after nearly 17 years as the Keene city government's top administrator.

The list of guests and speakers was a who's who of Keene politics, with present and former city councilors and mayors, presidents of community boards and committees, and other local and state officials praising MacQueen's accomplishments and leadership.

But it was MacQueen himself, in contrast to his usual reserve, who stole the show with a rambling, emotional, and at times profane, 20-minute speech.

[*Compiler's Note:* MacQueen was a good City Mgr Honest and tried to do the right thing for the tax payers of Keene, as did City Mgr Cheney before him.]

As Reported by the *Keene Evening Sentinel* June 26th, 1995:

"STORY"
Statewide switch to enhanced 911 to begin next month

New Hampshire's statewide emergency telephone system is ready to begin operating next month.

On July 5, technicians at the communications center in Concord will begin switching some of the state's larger dispatch centers over to the Enhanced 911 system.

"We will begin cutting over, every hour, central offices around the state," said Bruce Cheney, executive director of the Bureau of Emergency Communications.

By the middle of July, anyone in the state will be able to dial 911and reach a dispatcher who will know the caller's location, even if the caller doesn't.

Cheney said the switches are being thrown gradually, so technicians will be able to pinpoint problems more quickly than if the entire state were switched to the system at once.

"We do not anticipate any problems," he said.

The equipment has been running for about three weeks, and last week operators began dress rehearsals, taking test calls from around the state on a special number not 911) and checking address and phone number information from the database that will enable them to pinpoint a caller's location.

The system is designed to allow people anywhere in the state to dial 911 and be connected to the communications center, where the call will be routed in seconds to the police, fire or rescue dispatcher they need.

As Reported by the *Keene Evening Sentinel* June 28th, 1995:

"STORY"

Keene offers manager's job

MacLean invited to sign

The choice has been made, the contract details settled. All John A. MacLean has to do is sign his name, and Keene will have its first new city manager since 1978.

The Keene City Council voted unanimously Tuesday night to hire MacLean, after a closed-door meeting to nail down the fine points of the contract.

Those details won't be disclosed until MacLean signs, but the pay range for the job is $65,000 to $77,514.

————

As Reported by the *Keene Evening Sentinel* August 21st, 1995:

"FIRE"

Blaze: Is it arson?
Latest in rash of Keene fires

A suspicious fire early this morning gutted half of a historic railroad building off Cypress Street in Keene.

Keene firefighters were notified of the fire at 4:22 a.m. It engulfed half of the old Boston & Maine freight house, scarring the brick walls and reducing the roof to burned wooden timbers.

"When I arrived, the flames were going through the roof," Fire Chief William H. Pepler, Jr. said this morning. About 25 firefighters took almost an hour to get the fire under control, then spent the early-morning hours hosing down the embers.

The freight building had no electricity or heat, aiding this morning's blaze to the list of suspicious smaller fires and vandalism that have plagued the city-owned building.

Pepler said that a second, much smaller fire was apparently set about an hour before in a dumpster behind Paragon Cable, on Eagle Court near the freight house. Pepler guessed that both fires were set by the same person or group, though the investigation is continuing.

The suspected arson is the latest in a series that have plagued the area around the old railroad corridor in Keene, Pepler said, though he added that he wasn't sure all had been set by the same suspects.

The fire is a blow to plans to renovate the 19th-century railroad building that city officials and community activists have kicked around for years. In the late 1980's and early '90's, the city council was considering tearing the building down, but backed off at the urging of Paul F. Pietz, a partner with Pietz & Michal Architects in Keene.

Pietz wanted to renovate the building, relocate the Greater Keene Chamber of Commerce offices there, and turn it into a visitor's center and museum celebrating Keene's history and the history of railroads in the area.

"I thought this was a significant piece of railroad history," Pietz said this morning. "It was sort of a jewel just sitting there."

But the plan languished as other projects sprouted up for the railroad land, including a hotel and conference center, a baseball park and a nursing home.

It's sort of been sitting in limbo," Pietz said.

Today, engineers will visit the building to decide whether it needs to be torn down, Deputy Fire Chief Clayton R. Stalker said this morning.

The Keene police and fire departments will investigate the cause of the blaze, Stalker said.

————

As Reported by Elizabeth Crowley in *Keene Evening Sentinel* August 22nd, 1995:

"FIRE"

Arson caused Keene blaze Building will be torn down; investigators studying tape

The charred remains of the old Boston & Maine freight house in Keene will soon meet the wrecking ball.

That's the verdict from a structural engineer who studied what was left of the city-owned building hours after fire swept through it Monday morning—a fire police officials say was set.

"My understanding is that it is coming down," Deputy Fire Chief Clayton R. Stalker Jr. said this morning.

The job shouldn't be too difficult, he said. All that remains of the 144-year-old landmark are its crumbling brick walls.

"One of the things that was holding those walls together was the roof and that's gone now," Stalker said.

Police say the fire that engulfed the building at about 4:30 Monday morning was arson. The evidence includes images from a security camera at nearby CFX Bank that was filming when the fire began.

The lead investigator on the case, Keene Cpl. Joseph J. Collins, wouldn't say what's on the tape but called it valuable information. Police are questioning several people about the fire, he said. "We've got a lot of good leads."

Some of those leads tie in with other recent fires in and around the railroad property off Cypress Street, Collins said, including a dumpster fire on Dunbar Street that was reported about an hour before the railroad building burned. The area has long been a hangout for teenagers.

Reports that three youngsters were seen running from the railroad building with gasoline cans in hand Sunday afternoon are only partially correct, Collins said.

"Three individuals were in the building Sunday and they've been checked out," he said, "but it's untrue they were carrying gas cans."

City officials are expected to decide by this afternoon whether to hire someone to raze the building and cart it away or if city workers can handle the job.

"We're also in the process of working up some figures on the cost," Assistant City Manager Alfred H. Merrifield said this morning.

If the cost of demolishing the building is less than $10,000, the city officials won't have to accept bids from contractors, Merrifield said. That means the city manager can choose a company to do the job within the week.

"We expect the project will fall within (a range of) $3,000 to $10,000" Merrifield said.

The city has about $400,000 left in what is called the railroad land project account. That account was opened to buy the land on which the B&M building sits and the building itself. The demolition costs will be paid for with some of that money, Merrifield said.

Monday's fire wiped out plans to renovate the historic building and turn it into an office center, a visitors' center and-or museum.

Anyone with additional information about the fire Monday morning is asked to contact Keene police at 357-9815.

————

As Reported by Diane Riley in *Keene Evening Sentinel* September 2nd, 1995:

"FIRE"

Keene man pulls another from fire

A Keene man went out for a jaunt in his new car Friday night and ended up becoming a hero.

David Bishop, 34, of Woodbury Street, Keene, had just cleaned his car and asked his girlfriend, Jane Gambill, 44, also of Keene, out for a ride. While driving up Water Street, near the Keene water tower, Bishop saw that he thought was a bonfire.

"But Jane said it was a car burning," Bishop recalled. "I hit the brakes, pulled off the side of the road and ran to the car.

"It was cooking pretty good," he said.

The car, a 1967 Ford Galaxy, had hit a utility pole and burst into flames, according to Lt. Robert L. Crowell of the Keene Fire Department.

The car was being driven by Ronald Reinbult, 32, of 88 Roxbury Court, Keene, said Sgt. Wallace G. Riddle of the Keene Police Department.

Because of the smoke, Bishop said he couldn't tell if anyone was in the car. The car's back seat was engulfed in flames, he said.

"I yelled, "is anyone in there? Is anyone in there?" But I didn't see anything. Then I saw a little bit of movement and heard a groan."

Bishop said he can't explain what drove him to do it, but "I grabbed his arm. I thought (the car) was going to blow. The flames were white hot. I just thought I had to get him out."

As Bishop struggled to get Reinbult out of the car, Reinbult fought his rescue attempts. Reinbult's arms were burned, Bishop said.

"He was saying, "No leave me alone." I think it was because he was hurt," Bishop said. "I just ignored him."

As Bishop dragged Reinbult out the driver's side door, flames started coming through the front seat and Reinbult's pant legs caught fire, Bishop said. He used his own shirt to put out the pant fire, then dragged Reinbult along the pavement for about 10 to 15 feet.

Two other men were involved in the rescue, Bishop and Crowell both said.

However, neither Bishop nor Crowell knew their names.

Bishop asked one man to call 911, the statewide emergency number. "He took off like a bolt of lightning and got help," Bishop said.

Another man helped Bishop drag Reinbult farther from the fire. "We each grabbed an arm and got him on the cool grass."

The accident was called in shortly before 8 p.m., and Keene police and fire departments responded, Crowell said. Public Service of New Hampshire was also called in to replace a broken utility pole.

Reinbult was brought to Cheshire Medical Center in Keene, treated and released, Riddle said. Reinbult was arrested and charged with driving while intoxicated, Riddle said.

————

As Reported by Kenneth Arron in *Keene Evening Sentinel* September 18th, 1995:

"FIRE"

Keene blaze more arson? Another empty building damaged on Railroad St.

Fire damaged a building on Railroad Street in Keene Saturday afternoon, the latest in a string of arson fires that have plagued that section of the city.

The building was locked and empty when the fire broke out; damage was confined to the building's exterior and one outside stairway and no one was hurt.

The Keene Fire Department reached the 115 Railroad St. fire three minutes after it was reported at 12:19 p.m. By 12:49 p.m., 15 firefighters had the fire under control.

Fire department officials said that Saturday's fire might be part of the string of the six other suspicious fires in the area.

"We suspect that they may be related," said Deputy Fire Chief Clayton Stalker Jr. this morning.

Still, Stalker was hesitant to say that here was a serial arsonist in the area.

"They don't appear to us to be attempts to burn buildings flat," he said.

If the fires continue, though, he said somebody could get hurt.

Though lab results were not back yet, Stalker said that department officials suspect an accelerant, such as gasoline, was used to fuel the flames.

Accelerants were apparently, used in the other fires, also.

The building's owner, Ronald Farina of Keene, is no stranger to the fires; an adjacent building also owned by him, Monadnock Cutlery, was damaged by a suspicious fire in June.

He didn't expect to be struck again especially in daylight.

"Good God, how do you know when anybody is going to do anything?' he asked on Monday.

The former Boston & Maine freight house near Cypress Street was destroyed by an arsonist on Aug 21. That building had to be demolished because structural damage from the fire made it unsafe to leave standing.

Like most of the other blazes, Saturday's fire was set on the building's outside Stalker said that the building sustained a "couple of thousand " dollars with of damage mostly to its siding and a set of steps leading up to a loading dock.

Farina said that the building, which was being used to store steel, was largely empty in the part that was burned.

———

Reported by Elizabeth Crowley in *Keene Evening Sentinel* September 21st, 1995:

"FIRE"

Fire guts porch

Investigators want to question a man seen sitting on the first-floor porch of a three-apartment building in Keene shortly before it caught fire Wednesday evening.

The fire destroyed the two-story, enclosed porch at the front of the building on Grove Street.

The fire gutted the porch but firefighters managed to contain it before it reached into the house. The fire was reported at 6:18 p.m. and was under control by about 6:40 p.m. The house is owned by Elizabeth and Theodore Chabott.

David and Kimberly Gamache, who live in the building's rear apartment, were the only tenants home when fire broke out. They left their apartment safely. The second-story tenant, Susan Sousie, and the first-floor tenant, Mildred E. Dearden, were not home.

Keene's deputy fire chief, Clayton R. Stalker Jr., said the fire apparently started in the first-floor porch. He said a man was seen on the porch shortly before the flames were detected. Investigators know who the man is, and plan to question him.

"We're trying to determine whether it was intentional or accidental," Stalker said. He said the man on the porch is a cigarette smoker.

Stalker said that investigators don't believe the fire on Grove Street was in anyway connected with a weekend blaze at a building on Railroad Street.

Firefighter Jeffrey Chickering was taken to Cheshire Medical Center after wrenching his knee while he fought the fire. He was treated for torn cartilage in his right knee and released Wednesday night.

While investigators are still determining whether Wednesday's fire was suspicious, they know several other fires recently were set.

Keene has been hit by a rash of suspicious fires in the Railroad Street area. Last weekend, firefighters responded to a sixth suspicious fire on or near Railroad Street.

————

As Reported by the *Keene Evening Sentinel* November 20th, 1995:

"FIRE"

Short-circuit causes fire

A short-circuiting heater caused a smoky fire Sunday morning at Netherlands Insurance Companies, 62 Maple Ave., Keene.

When firefighters arrived at about 11:30, smoke was pouring out of the ductwork. Firefighters cut electrical power to the heater, the smoke was blown out of the building with a fan, and no other area of the building was damaged.

————

As Reported by Erin Caddell in *Keene Evening Sentinel* December 9th, 1995:

"STORY"

A firefighter's lot isn't easy, Keene city councilors discover

Five city councilors now have a different perspective on the fire department they oversee.

Councilors Peter D. Bradshaw, Dana A. Edwards,, Mitchell H. Greenwald and councilor-elect Christopher C. Coates—along with Cynthia Messer of Paragon Cable's Local Edition and this writer, Erin Caddell,—braved the cold and wind last Saturday to take the Keene Fire Department's physical test. Mayor elect Patricia T. Russell and councilor-elect Nancy M. Wilkinson showed up to cheer.

New recruits must pass the test before they can join and either full or part-time firefighters, and pass it again each year they're on the force.

The test requires walking through an obstacle course firefighters have set up on city-owned land near the Dillant-Hopkins Airport in North Swanzey.

The councilors made their way through the course's nine parts, including lifting ladders, carrying hose and wriggling through a crawl space—all while wearing a heavy firefighter's jacket, helmet, a heavy air pack and ankle weights to simulate the weight of a fire-proof uniform.

"It was fun. If you got tired, someone would be there to cheer you on," Bradshaw said. "But it really gives you an idea of what these guys go through."

Bradshaw topped the field of councilors and reporters by cruising through the course in 9 minutes, 9 seconds—just a minute and change off the department's record of 7:59.

————

1996

As Reported by the *Keene Evening Sentinel* January 18th, 1996:

"FIRE"

Fire's source traced

A 43-year-old homeless woman has told authorities she caused a fire at a Keene apartment building Monday.

The woman told police that she fell asleep while smoking a cigarette inside the James C. Cleveland Building, a six-story apartment building for elderly people.

The cigarette set a couch on fire on the building's first floor, but alarm and sprinkler systems worked and no one was injured.

The woman had been asked earlier to leave the building, but managed to get back inside and find a couch to sleep on, said Clayton P. Stalker Jr., Keene's deputy fire chief.

She told police that when she woke up the couch was on fire, and she couldn't extinguish the flames so she got out of the building, Stalker said.

The building's automatic fire alarm sounded Monday at 12:39 a.m., and a sprinkler above the couch apparently doused the flames.

Stalker said the woman will not be charged.

————

As Reported by the *Keene Evening Sentinel* February 29th, 1996:

"FIRE"

Employees control fire at MPB plant in Keene

No injuries resulted when a drilling machine caught fire Wednesday night at an MPB Corp. plant on Optical Avenue in Keene, fire officials said this morning.

Deputy Fire Chief Clayton R. Stalker Jr. said the drilling machine overheated and ignited lubricating oil inside the building at 59 Optical Ave., called MPB Plant 3. It's manufacturing facility for MPB, which makes ball bearings.

Two MPB workers had extinguished much of the fire by the time Keene police and fire crews arrived just before 10 p.m.

Stalker said the fire damaged some of the machine's wiring and exhaust tube, and smoke had filled the building. Firefighters used fans to clear smoke out of the building, then tested air quality before letting employees back inside. The crew also examined the two workers who doused the blaze.

————

As Reported by the *Keene Evening Sentinel* March 11th, 1996:

"FIRE"

Keene fire is suspicious

A small fire, which began under a desk, caused little damage Saturday to a Keene real-estate office, but city officials are calling it suspicious.

The fire was in Christopher J. Tasoulas' office at 103 Winchester St. No one was injured, and firefighters quickly extinguished the flames before they could spread inside the building, which Tasoulas owns.

Tenants in an apartment above the office spotted smoke Saturday at about 4:25 p.m. and called for help. No one was inside the ground-floor office when firefighters arrived.

Authorities don't know how the fire began, but consider it suspicious. The M.H. State Fire Marshal's Office is also investigating.

————

As Reported by the *Keene Evening Sentinel* March 12th, 1996:

"FIRE"

After-school snack sparks fire in Keene

A 12-year-old girl whose after-school snack went up in flames was treated for smoke inhalation Monday at Cheshire Medical Center.

Crystal Carro was cooking on the electric stove in her family's Court Street condominium in Keene at about 2:30 p.m., according to fire officials. She apparently left the kitchen for a minute and, when she returned, a burner on the stovetop had caught fire. She tried to extinguish the flames with a small rug, but it caught fire; she tried to throw the rug out the back door into the snow, but the flaming rug set some curtains on fire.

There wasn't a lot of fire, but there was a good amount of smoke," Deputy Fire Chief Clayton R. Stalker Jr. said this morning. "And (Crystal) took a lot of that smoke in."

Stalker said the girl was lucky she was not burned. She was treated at Cheshire Medical Center and released Monday.

––––––––

As Reported by Erin Caddell in *Keene Evening Sentinel* March 21st, 1996:

"STORY"

Fire union negotiations first test of city manager's bartering skills

Keene's two firefighter unions are negotiating again with city management, and both sides hope the talks go more smoothly than last time.

Union representatives for firefighters and their supervisors met Wednesday with City Manager John A. MacLean and other city negotiators, union President Gary P. Lamoureaux said.

The union hopes to reach a contract agreement by June 30, when its current pact expires.

Neither labor nor management would disclose their initial offers, or whether they're shooting for a one-year or multi-year contract. Under state law, details of union negotiations can be kept secret.

Firefighters signed a three-year contract just over a year ago, but it will expire in three months because the union worked without a contract for more than a year and a half, while labor and management fought over pay, health insurance and other issues.

The final deal gave no pay raises in the first year of the contract, and raises of 2 percent in the second and 2.5 percent in this fiscal year.

The city also paid each firefighter $750 for switching from a traditional health plan to a health-maintenance organization, and for accepting a cap on the city's contribution to health-care costs. If premiums increase more than 10 percent a year, union members must cover the difference, up to the amount of their pay raises for that year.

These are MacLean's first union negotiations since he became Keene's city manager last August. When MacLean was appointed, some city councilors said they hoped he would be able to smooth out sometimes rocky relationships with the city's fire, police and public works unions.

––––––––

As Reported by Erin Caddell in *Keene Evening Sentinel* March 23rd, 1996:

"STORY"

Keene fire department honors own

The Keene Fire Department handed out its annual awards at a banquet last Saturday.

Chief William H. Pepler Jr. presented the following awards at the American Legion Hall on Court Street.

Ten years of service: Charles Harris.

Citation: Stephen McKenna, for helping an Antrim ambulance squad rescue a patient in shock.

Chief's appreciation award: Lt. Donald Hackler, who organized several fire department activities.

Lifesaving award: Lt. Ronald J. Leslie and Mark Howard, who helped rescue six people who fell from a boat in Wilson Pond in North Swanzey.

Teamwork awards: two shifts for resuscitating several heart-attack patients.

Pepler also recognized members of the fire investigation team, responsible for determining the cause of all fires: deputy chiefs Clayton R. Stalker Jr. and Bradley B. Payne, Capt. Robert S. Crowell, Lt. Gary R. Lefreniere, acting lieutenants Ronald Leslie and Gary P. Lamoureaux, and firefighters David E. Symonds and Brian M. Shepard.

————

As Reported by the *Keene Evening Sentinel* March 26th, 1996:

"FIRE"

Fire destroys kitchen in Keene; $30,000 damage

A candle fell onto a hot stove Monday night, starting a fire that caused about $30,000 damage to a house on Liberty Lane in Keene.

No one was injured.

Tracy Summers told fire officials she was cooking on the kitchen stove when a candle, burning on a shelf above the stove, fell onto a burner, splattering hot wax and setting the kitchen aflame.

Summers tried to douse the flames, but couldn't; she then got her two children out of the house, and called for help at about 6:30 p.m., fire officials said.

The fire destroyed the kitchen area, but Keene firefighters were able to bring the fire under control within about 25 minutes and save the rest of the structure.

————

As Reported by the *Keene Evening Sentinel* March 29th, 1996:

"FIRE"

Families escape Keene fire

Smoke detectors that went off shortly before 2 a.m. Thursday in an apartment house at 52 Marlboro St. allowed several families to escape a fire without injury, Keene fire officials said.

The fire was blamed on a cigarette smoker who fell asleep on a couch on the building's first floor. That person's name was not available.

The fire didn't spread very far but the smoldering couch sent smoke throughout the house. Residents were allowed back into their apartments early Thursday morning.

The number of people evacuated wasn't available this morning.

Charles Tousley of Keene owns the building.

————

As Reported by the *Keene Evening Sentinel* April 9th, 1996:

"FIRE"

Keene fire burns house, but doesn't hurt anyone

D-Shift battled blaze Tuesday Morning on Liberty Lane in Keene. Photo by: Steve Hooper.

Fire damaged a house on Liberty Lane in Keene this morning, but police reported no injuries.

Donald McConchie, who owns the house at 33 Liberty Lane, wasn't home when the fire was reported, but he arrived soon after, watching as firefighters quickly brought the blaze under control.

The fire was reported by Clesson Jones, who lives across the street. Jones said he saw flames shooting from the kitchen door and speculated that the fire started in the kitchen. He said no one was home when the fire broke out.

Few other details were available this morning, including information on the fire's origin and the extent of damage. McConchie declined comment.

————

As Reported by Robert Rand in *Keene Evening Sentinel* April 10th, 1996:

"FIRE"

Keene fire leaves 4 homeless

A firefighter suffered minor burns Tuesday in a fire that severely damaged a house on Liberty Lane in Keene.

An electrical problem most likely started the fire at the Donald McConchie home at 33 Liberty Lane, fire officials say though they hadn't yet pinned down the details.

Keene firefighter Mark Boynton was treated for minor burns at Cheshire Medical Center and released.

A neighbor, Clesson Jones, spotted the fire and called the fire department just after 9:15 a.m.

But by that time, Keene officials say, the fire had a good head start. When they arrived, flames were showing from the front door and window. The fire was kept mainly to the kitchen, although it did try to sneak up a partition into a second-floor bedroom.

Firefighters were able to save some of the McConchies' belongings, but the house isn't habitable, said Deputy Fire Chief Clayton RT. Stalker Jr.

McConchie, his wife, Susan, and their teenage sons, Trevor and Chip, are staying elsewhere.

————

As Reported by the *Keene Evening Sentinel* April 16th, 1996:

"FIRE"

Fire guts Keene house; 89-year-old man not hurt

A house on Branch Road in Keene went up in flames this morning. The sole occupant of the house, an 89-year-old man, was not injured.

Southwestern N.H. Fire Mutual Aid did not release the man's name this morning.

Smoke was pouring out broken windows of the house as firefighters streamed jets of water inside it. A witness, Anthony G. Dionne, said that it did not take long for the smoke to completely engulf the building. The fire was reported to authorities shortly after 10 this morning.

It appeared that the fire started toward the back of the house, where the charring was the greatest. A porch like structure there was destroyed by the flames.

Firefighters from Swanzey, among other towns, assisted Keene firefighters in battling the flames.

————

As Reported by Kenneth Arron in *Keene Evening Sentinel* April 17th, 1996:

"FIRE"

Keene fire starts on stove

Racing to the Rescue – Keene firefighters dash toward a house at 19 Branch Road on Tuesday, trying to quell the flames; homeowner Edwin C. Thresher, 89 watches the effort. Photo by Michael Moore.

An 89-year-old Keene man escaped his burning house unharmed Tuesday, but lost all his possessions in the fire.

Edwin C. Thresher of 19 Branch Road said he put milk on the stove, then went downstairs to do laundry.

Investigators believe the fire started on the stove while Thrasher was downstairs. When he heard noises in the kitchen, he went upstairs and saw the flames. He tried to call the fire department, but had to leave.

Thresher, who had lived in the house for 30 years, stood in a downpour as fire crews from Keene, Marlborough, Swanzey and Meadowood Area County Fire Department tried to douse the thick smoke pouring from the windows.

He said that he wasn't physically hurt. "It hurt my feelings a little," he said, wearing a yellow slicker, watching heat melt the yellow siding off his home.

The fire, reported by a neighbor at 10:11 a.m., was declared under control at 11:32 a.m.

A bucket of highly combustible magnesium on the porch complicated matters for the firefighters.

The building may not be able to be saved, fire department officials said this morning.

Thresher said that he has family in the area and will be able to stay with them.

As Reported by Erin Caddell in *Keene Evening Sentinel* April 19th, 1996:

"STORY"

A breakthrough in contract talks? Keene, fire supervisors settle quickly

Ten Keene fire supervisors have a new contract, and City Manager John A. MacLean has passed the first test of his union negotiating skills.

A three-year contract with fire supervisors was approved unanimously Thursday by the Keene City Council.

The contract will raise the fire supervisors' pay more than 10 percent in the next three years, MacLean said this morning: 2 percent July 2, when the contract takes effect; 2 percent January 1, 1997; 3 percent July 1, 1997; and 3.25 percent July 1, 1998.

"It's a good package for them and for us," MacLean said.

Capt. Bruce W. Pollock, a member of the supervisors' negotiating team, referred questions this morning to union President Gary P. Lamoureaux, who could not be reached for comment.

MacLean is still negotiating with another fire union, the one representing line firefighters, and declined to say if he expects a settlement soon. Under state law, details of union negotiations can be kept secret.

MacLean and the supervisors union reached agreement in less than a month, a far cry from the last round of talks, which dragged on from 1993 until early 1995.

That standoff—and similar contract disputes with unions for firefighters, police officers and police supervisors—caused a lot of grumbling among employees.

Several councilors said a big reason they hired MacLean last summer was his strong record on union negotiations. One councilor characterized MacLean's approach as a break from the past, when the city's negotiating stance was tough, and not always immediately productive.

"The hard-line negotiating style says, "It's us against you, and we're going to stock this out until somebody wins," said Councilor Roger T. Zerba. "The win-win school that John comes from says, "Let's get together and get something done."

In addition to the pay raises, the contract increases each fire supervisor's allowance for cleaning uniforms from $350 to $400 a year.

It retains a requirement that supervisors be paid at least one hour of overtime if asked to work more than 40 hours a week. But the contract will halve the increments in which supervisors are paid overtime, from 30 minutes to 15 minutes. So, if a supervisor works 2 hours and 10 minutes of overtime, he or she will be paid for 2 ¼ hours, rather than 2 ½ hours, as is now the case.

The contract also reduces the city's cap on absorbing higher costs for health insurance. Now, the city covers annual cost increases of up to 10 percent: the new cap is 6 percent a year and supervisors will have to cover any increases beyond that.

———

As Reported by the *Keene Evening Sentinel* May 13th, 1996:

"STORY"

Longtime Keene fire Chief Walter R. Messer dies

Pictured is Walter Messer shortly before he died in 1996. Photo by Michael Moore and Steve Hooper.

Walter R. Messer, Keene's fire chief from 1946 until 1971, died Saturday at Cheshire Medical Center in Keene. He was 90.

Messer's legacy includes Southwestern N.H. Fire Mutual Aid, the regional emergency communications and aid-response that helps to coordinate firefighting, police and ambulance calls in more than 60 communities.

The mutual aid agency was established at his urging, and with his help, in 1953. At its core are comprehensive firefighting plans for buildings around the region, with the capability of systematic dispatching of fire departments from a number of communities to help deal with an emergency.

But, Mr. Messer said in a Sentinel interview last year, the achievement he most cherished was earning the respect of Keene's firefighters.

Mr. Messer was born in Keene to a firefighting family, and never strayed far from those roots. His father, Arthur, who died when Mr. Messer was 4, was a volunteer firefighter. His stepfather, Fred W. Towne, was Keene's fire chief for almost 10 years.

Mr. Messer became a volunteer firefighter while still a student at Keene High School, and continued to volunteer after taking a job as an auto mechanic at the F.J. Bennett Co. on Washington Street. He lived in a room at the firehouse on Vernon Street so he could respond to night calls at a moment's notice.

After a brief stint in the Navy and three years in business in Glen Cove, N.Y., Mr. Messer returned to Keene in 1934 with his wife, Elsa, and their son, Bruce, to rejoin the fire department. He was named a permanent firefighter in 1941 and became chief in 1947.

Mr. Messer jokingly referred to his retirement in 1971 as "the time they kicked me out." "Even after more than two decades away from the firehouse, Mr. Messer's instincts remained sharp. On a windy, chilly spring day last year, he predicted there would be trouble. When a voice on the emergency scanner that was always on in his Sweeney Road home announced a possible chimney fire, he said, "I knew it."

Almost 25 years after his retirement, Mr. Messer continued to attend fire organization meetings and kept up with the latest firefighting techniques and trends.

His other love was his family. He and his wife were married for 62 years. She died in 1993. He spoke proudly of the woman dubbed by firefighters as Keene's "first lady of the firehouse."

He and his wife lent their volunteer support to their church and a number of firefighter organizations. Walter R. Messer, 90, of 25 Sweeney Road, Keene, former chief of Keene Fire Department, died Saturday at Cheshire Medical Center in Keene.

He was born in Keene, April 27, 1906, son of Arthur and Martha (Randall) Messer, attended Keene schools and was a graduate of Keene High School.

During World War II, he served in the U.S. Navy.

Chief Messer joined the Keene Fire Department and was assigned to the Steam Fire Engine and Hose Company on May 27, 1926. In 1935, he transferred to the Deluge Hose Company and served there until he was appointed a permanent firefighter on April 1, 1941.

He was promoted to fire chief on January 5, 1946, and served as chief for 25 years, retiring on May 1, 1971.

Chief Messer was instrumental in helping to organize the Southwestern N.H. Fire Mutual Aid System in 1953, one of the first mutual aid systems in the country.

He was president of the Keene Firemen's Relief Association from 1947-1971 and was president of the N.H. State Firemen's Association in 1969. He was past president of the New England Fire Chiefs Association and was a life member of the N.H. Association of Fire Chiefs. He was a member of the Cheshire County Fire Wardens Association and the International Association of Fire Chiefs.

Chief Messer was a member of the Tri-State Mutual Aid Association and was a member and former chairman of the N.H. State Board of Fire Control. He was also a member of the International Association of

Chiefs of Police, the Fire Chiefs Association of Massachusetts, and was a life member of the International Municipal Safety Association.

He was a member of the United Church of Christ and served on several church committees. He was a member of the Jerusalem Lodge 104 Masonic Order.

His wife, Elsa E. Messer, died April 29, 1993.

Survivors include a son, Bruce Messer of Swanzey, several nieces and nephews.

The funeral, with full departmental honors, is Wednesday at 11 a.m. at United Church of Christ, 23 Central Square, Keene. Burial will be in Monadnock View Cemetery, West Keene.

————

As Reported by Elizabeth Crowley in *Keene Evening Sentinel* May 16th, 1996:

"FIRE"

Fire wrecks Keene cars
No one is hurt; damage may exceed $300,000

Fire-damaged cars and trucks remain in the Westwood Apartments carport on Park Avenue, Keene. The fire on May 15th destroyed 13 cars and damaged six others.

Fire roared through an 18-bay carport at Westwood Apartments in Keene Wednesday night, destroying 13 cars, damaging six others and threatening nearby buildings.

No one was injured in the fire; fire officials say the damage could exceed $300,000.

Firefighters don't know what started the blaze but haven't found any signs of foul play, Chief William H. Pepler Jr. said this morning. They continue to investigate.

The fire quickly spread from one end of the 140-foot-lon g wooden carport to the other, consuming cars, gas grills and everything else in its path. The heat was intense, Pepler said. "Some of the firefighters described it as like being in a microwave."

Six minutes after the first call for help, the first fire truck arrived. The flames were so high and the smoke so thick, Pepler said, it wasn't immediately clear what was on fire.

Flames licked the top of large pine trees growing in back of the carport but firefighters managed to prevent them from spreading to nearby apartments. As a precaution, the residents of the apartment building closest to the blaze were asked to leave their rooms at about 10:30 p.m. They were allowed back in after the fire was extinguished, about an hour later.

The heat from the fire melted the back ends of six cars parked in another car port about 30 yards away. "The fire was so involved when we got here that we concentrated on stopping it from spreading to the other carport and to apartments," Pepler said.

Mark Ericson, who lost a pickup truck and a motorcycle in the blaze, said he was awakened by the sound of what he thought were gunshots outside his apartment.

"I heard several loud pops and then one really loud one. That's when I looked out my window and saw the fire," he said this morning. What Ericson thought were gunshots may actually have been barbecue grills'

propane tanks exploding, or automobile tires bursting from the heat.

Ericson said he couldn't tell at first whether another apartment building was on fire or if it was the carport. "The fire was huge," he said.

"I tried to get to my truck but two spots over there was a car on fire. The smoke was pouring toward me," Ericson said. Two car owners did get their vehicles out. All that remains of 13 other vehicles are charred shells.

Keene firefighter John Bates lives at the apartment building and prevented several people from trying to get their vehicles out of the burning carport. "Good thing he did, too," Chief William H. Pepler Jr. said. "We could have had some serious injuries otherwise.

Flames from the fire were visible from several streets away a Sweeney Road resident said. It looked like the whole street was on fire," Stanley Chickering said.

As Reported by the *Keene Evening Sentinel:*

Charcoal grill blamed in $300,000 Keene fire

A charcoal grill that looked cool, but wasn't, is being blamed for the fire that caused more than $300,000 damage Wednesday night at Westwood Apartments on Summit Road in Keene.

After completing an investigation, officials "feel certain that the fire was accidental," Keene Fire Chief William H. Pepler Jr. said this morning.

The fire destroyed 13 cars parked in a wooden 18-bay carport, and damaged six others.

The heat from the flames was so intense that it melted the taillights of vehicles parked nearby.

Pepler said a resident of the apartment complex placed his charcoal grill on a lawn chair in the carport, thinking the coals were all out. The resident, Tom McKenney, could not be reached for comment this morning. His wife refused to talk about the incident.

However, heat from the still-hot coals ignited the chair, which in turn ignited a bag of charcoal lying against the back wall of the carport, Pepler said.

"The fire spread up the back wall, and that was it," he said. "Just about the entire structure was in flames when the first fire truck arrived."

The grill owner also lost a vehicle in the fire.

———

As Reported by the *Keene Evening Sentinel:*

Owners of burned cars file claims in aftermath of savage Keene fire

Owners of 13 cars destroyed last Wednesday in a Keene fire are dealing with their insurance companies in efforts to cover their losses.

It's between them and their insurance carriers," said Donald H. Roloff Jr., manager of Westwood Apartments on Summit Road in Keene.

The fire destroyed 13 cars and damaged six others that were parked in or near an 18-bay carport at the apartment complex.

Preliminary estimates are that damage could exceed $300,000.

Heat from the flames was so intense that it melted the taillights of vehicles parked 20 feet away.

According to Keene fire investigators, the blaze began when an apartment resident placed his charcoal grill on a lawn chair in the carport, thinking the coals were all out.

However, heat from the still-hot coals ignited the chair, which in turn ignited a bag of charcoal lying against the back wall of the carport, Keene fire officials said.

The resident, Thomas McKenney, was among those who lost a fir in the fire.

Fire quickly spread from one end of the 140-foot-long wooden carport to the other end.

While they fought the blaze, firefighters asked residents of the apartment building nearest the carport to leave their apartments as a safety precaution.

———

As Reported by the *Keene Evening Sentinel* June 1st, 1996:

"STORY"

City searching for answers to emergency building woes $25,000 study will examine needs of fire and police

Keene's fire station is old, cramped and expensive to heat. And Keene's police station, although nicely planted in the heart of downtown, simply won't fit the department's needs for the future, officials there say.

Both departments are looking at ways to fix the problems; they have each set aside $12,500 for a study investigating the needs of the city's emergency services.

City officials have known about problems at the fire station since November. A report found that the building doesn't even meet fire and safety codes.

The departments have set aside $12,500 each for the project

City officials have said that significant repairs to the 110-year-old fire station will be too expensive. Right now, the bay doors aren't big enough to accommodate newer equipment and the building's layout and other hazards—such as asbestos—make renovation a tricky proposition.

Over the past few years, the fire department has received a new emergency generator, new bay doors and major electrical upgrades. Further repairs, including repairing floors and upgrading the fire alarm system, will cost an estimated $250,000.

One possibility is that the police and fire stations will share a new home; regardless, the study will outline the requirements of each department in terms of site location, building design and cost.

As Reported by Ellen Grimm in *Keene Evening Sentinel* June 14th, 1996:

"FIRE"

Wild lightning hits the region Keene family escapes fire

A lightening storm crackled through the region Thursday, badly damaging a Keene house, washing out roads near Bellows Falls, and kayoing power in many communities.

The family dog died in the Keene blaze, and firefighter Charles Harris needed treatment for a minor cut.

Today, the Vermont National Guard was mobilizing cleanup crews to help people in Grafton, Vt., just west of Bellows Falls, where half a foot of rain caused widespread flooding and washouts.

David S. Kyle of Keene knew there was trouble Thursday just before 4:30, when he heard an ominous crack outside his house on Avalon Place, a short, dead-end street off Marlboro Street in Keene.

In a heartbeat, lightning had hit a tree, jumped to a house at 8 Avalon Place, snapped down an inside wall, and set a rear bedroom ablaze.

Kyle called 911, but the lightning had given the fire a big head start. When the Deputy Fire Chief Clayton Stalker arrived, smoke was pouring from the eaves and some windows of the home owned by William and Marion O'Donnell.

"It was raining real hard so the smoke hung really low in the street…It was difficult to see the house," Stalker said. "It took half an hour to get it under control, but they had it knocked down in the first 15 minutes."

The O'Donnell's had been in the house with their son Patrick when the lightning struck; they were safely outside when firefighters arrived. They told firefighters that the lightning strike sounded like an explosion inside their house.'

Their two cats were rescued from the cellar, but a dog—which apparently was in the rear bedroom—perished.

"They were very wise," Stalker said, "in that they got out of the house without taking the time to look for the pets. They could have compromised their own safety. They were in danger. That was no question. That was a pretty fast moving fire."

The O'Donnell's stayed Thursday night at a neighbor's home; their house will need extensive repairs to deal with fire and smoke damage. The family declined comment.

Power failures were widespread.

As Reported by the *Keene Evening Sentinel* June 20th, 1996:

"FIRE"

Fire rouses residents

A fire inside a Marlboro Street house in Keene chased residents out of their beds this morning, but didn't hurt anyone.

Firefighters contained the flames to a first-floor room in the two-story wood-frame house. They arrived at about 6:30 a.m., shortly after a woman telephoned from the house for help.

Plaster fell on a Keene firefighter. He wasn't hurt, but was sent to Cheshire Medical Center to be checked out. He was released and returned to work.

"We're not yet sure who owns the house, because the residents evacuated right after calling for help," Keene Fire Chief William H. Pepler Jr. said this morning. The cause of the fire is being investigated.

"The house is definitely salvageable," Pepler said. "Fire damage was confined to the one room and there's some smoke damage, but it's not too bad."

————————

As Reported by Elizabeth Crowley in *Keene Evening Sentinel* June 27th, 1996:

"FIRE"

Keene fire kills one
Woman had just moved in

A 41-year-old woman was killed early today when fire swept through her apartment at Harper Acres off Castle Street in Keene.

Annette Layman had just moved into the public-housing complex on Friday, a Keene Housing Authority official said today.

"I don't think too many people knew her well," said Mary Angela Toms of the housing authority.

Eight apartments for elderly and handicapped people were in the two-story building where the fire broke out; no one else was hurt.

Investigators aren't yet sure what killed Laymon. Flame and smoke engulfed her living room, but did not spread beyond her second-floor apartment.

Firefighters who charged into the smoky building found Layman lying in a hallway of her apartment, between the living room and a bedroom. They could not revive her.

She was rushed to Cheshire Medical Center, but could not be revived there either. Keene Fire Chief William H. Pepler Jr. said, and was pronounced dead.

An investigator from the N.H. Fire Marshal's Office sifted through the charred remains of the apartment this morning, looking for clues to what happened. Keene detectives are also on the case.

Reports that Laymon had had a guest in her apartment Wednesday night turned out to be false, Pepler said. She lived alone.

Aside from the blackened outline of two second-story windows, the Keene Housing Authority building looks undamaged. The building still has electricity. But smoke and water damage will prevent residents from moving back in today, Toms said.

"We will try to get the apartments ready as soon as possible," she said.

Residents of the building were taken to the Valley Green Motel on West Street at about 3 this morning. Several of them declined comment about the fire, which broke out at about 12:45 this morning.

Toms was allowed to enter the building this morning to gather residents' medications, Pepler said.

Fire alarms inside the apartment building are connected to the Keene Fire Department on Vernon Street. Pepler said firefighters were on Castle Street moments after the alarm sounded and found smoke wafting out of second-story windows.,

While police helped residents—some in wheelchairs—get out of the building, firefighters soaked the woman's apartment with water, extinguishing the flames before they could spread to other apartments.

This morning's fire was the first fatal blaze in Keene in more than two years. In February 1994, Esther Cashman, 50, died of smoke inhalation inside her house on Cross Street. While Cashman was taking a shower, smoldering cigarettes and newspapers on a living room couch ignited a fire. Toxic gases and extreme heat met Cashman when she opened the bathroom door.

————————

As Reported by the *Keene Evening Sentinel*:

Fire probe continues

Smoke and flames killed the woman who died in an apartment-house fire Thursday morning, an autopsy has revealed.

The N.H. State Fire Marshal's Office is investigating the cause of the fire that killed Annette L. Lamon, 41, officials said this morning.

Keene firefighters found Lamon's body shortly before 1 a.m. Thursday as they attacked a fire in her Harper Acres apartment off Castle Street. Fire damage was confined to Lamon's second-story apartment. Eight other residents of the Keene Housing Authority apartments escaped uninjured.

The N.H. Medical Examiner's Office has listed Lamon's cause of death as smoke inhalation and burns. She had just moved into the public housing complex on Castle Street last Friday.

Building residents driven out of their apartments by the fire will be able to move back in late tonight or early Saturday, said Mary Angela Toms of the housing authority.

Volunteers from N.H. West chapter of American Red Cross helped residents find a place to sleep Thursday morning, paying for rooms at the Valley Green Motel on West Street. The RedCross also provided meals and items such as toothbrushes and soap to stranded Harper Acres residents.

A few residents have been staying with relatives while the others have been staying at the motel.

As Reported by the *Keene Evening Sentinel*:

Fire officials: Smoking caused fatal fire

Fire officials have concluded that careless smoking caused a fire in June that killed a Keene woman in her apartment.

Annette L. Lamon, 41, died from a combination of smoke inhalation and burns. The cause of the fatal fire¨ a cigarette that fell on Lamon's couch and set it on fire.

Last week, we were able to duplicate what happened that caused the fire," Thomas M. Norton, an investigator with the N.H. State Fire Marshal's Office,, said Tuesday.

Investigators believe Lamon was smoking on the couch and fell asleep. A burning cigarette fell out of her hand and onto the couch. Lamon apparently awoke, got up from the couch, then collapsed in the hallway of her Castle Street apartment, Norton said. That's where firefighters found her.

No one else in the apartment complex, owned by the Keene Housing Authority, was injured.

As Reported by the *Keene Evening Sentinel* June 28th, 1996:

"FIRE"

Suspicious fire burns shingles at Keene store

Arson is strongly suspected in a fire that destroyed a stack of roofing shingles outside Perking Home Center in Keene early this morning.

No one was injured in the blaze, which was reported shortly after midnight at the Ralston Street building supply store. The fire charred about a dozen 4-foot-square blocks of shingles and singed the outside of a storage room at the rear of the building.

Sprinklers in the storage room stopped the flames from spreading, Keene fire officials said this morning. But merchandise such as carpets, doors and windows were damaged by the soaking.

Perkins owner Fred Dill of Walpole was meeting with insurance adjusters this morning and could not be reached for comment.

The presence of a sprinkler system in this building was the major reason damage was limited to a small area," said Keene Fire Chief William H. Pepler Jr. The fire never made it inside the main store.

Fire and police investigators will work together to find the cause of the blaze. It's considered "very suspicious," according to a press release from the fire department.

————

As Reported by the *Keene Evening Sentinel* July 6th, 1996;

"FIRE"

Fire in Keene Friday is being investigated

Keene firefighters were investigating the cause of a fire Friday night that damaged part of an apartment house on Beech Street in Keene.

The fire apparently started at about 5:45 p.m. in a first-floor workshop on the back end of 54 Beech St. The blaze was quickly doused, but parts of the building had smoke and water damage.

Keene firefighters initially had reports that a woman was trapped on the second floor of the apartment house. The woman, whose identity was unknown Friday night, managed to get out of the smoky apartment on her own.

————

As Reported by Kenneth Arron in *Keene Evening Sentinel* July 19th, 1996:

"STORY"

City, workers strike a deal
New fire contract signals labor relations on the mend

Keene firefighters have a new contract, in a deal approved unanimously Thursday by the Keene City Council. The three-year pact means a pay increase totaling 10 percent over the next three years.

City Manager John A. MacLean said the contract mirrors the one signed by the department's supervisors earlier this month.

The relatively swift crafting of the contracts is a break from the past; in recent years the city's relations with its unionized workers were characterized by rancor over often long and drawn-out contract talks.

The new contract delivers a 2 percent raise retroactive to July 1; another 2 percent increase on January 1, 1997; a 3 percent raise July 1, 1997; and a final 3.25 percent pay hike July 1, 1998.

Firefighters have already approved the contract. Now both sides have to sign it: That date has not been scheduled yet. MacLean said that he is "very happy" with the agreement.

Councilors, in turn, say they are very happy with MacLean who was hired partly because of his expertise in union negotiations. The contract process generated far less heat than the last time around, when the deal-making process dragged on and on.

————

As Reported by the *Keene Evening Sentinel* July 22nd, 1996:

"FIRE"

Series of arson fires sweeps through Keene

Here we go again: That's what police and fire investigators said Sunday morning, after three deliberately set fires were doused.

They were remembering a series of suspicious fires last summer.

"There's no question we've got a big problem here," Deputy Fire Chief Clayton R. Stalker Jr. said this morning. "We had a lot of fires off Railroad Street last summer, and it's starting again."

The most serious of this weekend's fires was set next to a trailer full of auto parts at Walier Chevrolet Oldsmobile Geo on Winchester Street, and destroyed about $25,000 worth of merchandise. However, it didn't spread to the car dealership's building.

The other two fires were set in trash containers off Railroad Street.

All three fires were reported within about 40 minutes, beginning at about 5:10 Sunday morning. No one was injured.

Police say the fire at Walier's was very similar to one set last month outside Perkins Home Center on Ralston Street, around the corner from Walier's. Police are still investigating the Perkins fire.

Stalker said police and fire investigators are working closely together on the case.

————

As Reported by the *Keene Evening Sentinel* August 16th, 1996:

"FIRE"

Keene fire caused by kids with lighter

A house fire in Keene Thursday afternoon is being blamed on two girls playing with a cigarette lighter.

The fire began in a second-floor bedroom at David Bergeron's house at 139 Old Walpole Road. Firefighters had it under control in less than 30 minutes. No one was injured.

Fire officials estimated the damage at $10,000. The ages of the children involved were not available.

The fire was confined to the one bedroom; smoke damaged other rooms on the second floor of the house.

————

As Reported by the *Keene Evening Sentinel* October 4th, 1996:

"FIRE"

Trailer fire contained

No one was injured when the underside of a mobile home in Tanglewood Estates caught fire Thursday night.

Brian and Shelia Colburn escaped unharmed from their mobile home at 35 Oriole Drive. They called for help shortly before 8 p.m. as smoke filled their home.

Fire investigators said the fire was probably caused by a faulty heating tape used to wrap pipes under the trailer. Keene Deputy Fire Chief Clayton E. Stalker Jr. said the fire was confined to the underside of the mobile home. Firefighters spend about three hours making sure all the flames were extinguished.

The Colburn's will be allowed back into their home after an electrician repairs the wiring.

————

As Reported by Elizabeth Crowley in *Keene Evening Sentinel* October 9th, 1996:

"FIRE"

Reluctant rescue in Keene Woman pulled from house, but she didn't want to go

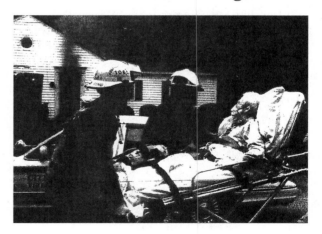

She's safe – Keene firefighter Jeff Chickering, left and Lt Ron Leslie wheel Marion Whitney, 97 away from her burning house Tuesday afternoon on Highland Avenue, Keene. Photo by: Steve Hooper.

Firefighters rescued a Keene woman who didn't want to leave her burning house Tuesday afternoon.

Marion Whitney, 97, was treated at Cheshire Medical Center in Keene for smoke inhalation and released.

Fire officials blamed the fire in her 11 Highland Ave. house on an overloaded electrical outlet.

Whitney called for help from her home in the residential neighborhood on her Lifeline medical emergency system at about 12:40.

She told the person who answered at Cheshire Medical Center that her house was on fire and she couldn't get out. But when firefighters arrived, Whitney didn't want to leave, Capt. Thomas L. Loll Jr. said. "She thought just a rug was on fire," he said.

One of the first firefighters to arrive, Brian Shepard, found Whitney huddled in the corner of her breezeway and dragged her to the door, Loll said. "Then I went in and bodily grabbed her and carried her across the street," he said.

'Pretty feisty'

It was the second time in recent years that Loll has helped rescue a Keene resident from a burning house.

He also helped rescue a 15-year-old girl trapped in a Keene house fire on Griffin Street about four years ago, Fire Chief William H. Pepler Jr. said this morning.

Whitney was conscious when firefighters reached her, Pepler said. "She was pretty feisty, actually," Loll said.

"There were definitely some tense moments for us," Pepler said. "Whenever you have to go into a house to look for someone inside, it's a risky situation."

Loll, a 25-year veteran of the fire department, said any fire is scary but especially those in which a person is involved. "You just do what you have to do and hopefully you don't even think about it, you just react," he said.

The overheated electrical outlet ignited a rug and the flames spread quickly in the house, Pepler said.

The heat of the fire was so intense it melted the Plexiglas window on the front door of the house. Firefighters quickly struck a second alarm after arriving at the scene.

Fire damaged the living room and a hallway and smoke damaged other rooms in the house but fire officials said the house can be repaired.

Firefighters extinguished the flames and had the situation under control by about 1:15 in the afternoon.

———

As Reported by the *Keene Evening Sentinel* October 11th, 1996:

"FIRE"

Fire forces evacuation at Keene State College

A bulletin board set ablaze inside Randall Hall at Keene State College sent dozens of sleepy students out onto the sidewalk at about 3 a.m. today.

No one was injured. The dormitory was evacuated after smoke alarms on the third floor went off. When Keene firefighters arrived, the fire was out.

Keene police are investigating what appears to be a case of arson.

"It's a fairly serious problem to have someone set something like that on fire," said Bradley B. Payne, Keene deputy fire chief.

———

As Reported by the *Keene Evening Sentinel* November 2nd, 1996:

"FIRE"

Fire put out quickly

Keene firefighters quickly extinguished what could have been a major fire at the state liquor store on Ralston Street Friday afternoon.

The fire started shortly before 1 p.m. near a ceiling-mounted oil furnace in a storage space next to the store's retail area. Combustible ceiling materials may have been too close to the flue stack and caught fire, Capt. Bruce W. Pollock said.

Store manager Thomas Jagel and an employee used a portable extinguisher to contain the fire until firefighters arrived. There was little damage to the store. However, had the fire spread to the cases of alcohol, which is highly combustible, a major fire could have resulted, Pollock said.

No injuries were reported.

Ralston Street was closed for about a half hour as firefighters placed a 4-inch hose across the roadway.

————

As Reported by the *Keene Evening Sentinel* November 20th, 1996:

"FIRE"

Keene man burned in fire

The owner of a Keene house that caught fire Tuesday night was treated for burns on his arms and for smoke inhalation.

Deud Hourd managed to put the fire out in his house at 624 Marlboro St., but had to be taken to Cheshire Medical Center, where he was treated and released.

No one else was injured.

Fire officials said the insulation melted off an overloaded extension cord, igniting a fire in an upstairs bedroom closet.

A box heater was connected to the cord, and its power draw probably overloaded the cord, said Keene Deputy Fire Chief Clayton R. Stalker Jr.

Hourd, his wife and two children were home when the fire began, and they smelled smoke.

Hourd used water to douse the flames, which had spread to sheetrock that formed the closet walls.

Firefighters spent about 45 minutes at the house, making sure the fire was extinguished.

————

As Reported by the *Keene Evening Sentinel* November 20th, 1996:

"STORY"

Keene sniffs out options for W. Keene fire station

Back before many of today's Keene firefighters were born, then fire chief Walter Messer had a notion that a fire station in West Keene might be possible, even desirable.

On June 17, 1952, The Sentinel wrote, "Messer…could picture a West Keene fire station at the intersection of Arch Street and Park Avenue, but he added, "I have nothing definite as yet."

Well, nobody still has anything definite, but Keene officials say the need for a substation is still there, and the National Guard Armory at 110 Hastings Ave. looks like a decent place to put it.

Current Fire Chief William H. Pepler Jr. said the building is an inexpensive, long-term solution to long response times on that side of town.

"We're excited about it and we think it's a project that's long overdue," Pepler said. Tuesday.

National Guard officials in Concord say it's too early to talk about fire trucks at the armory. "There's so many things in the air," said Leslie P. Mason, a business manager for the Guard.

He couldn't say whether Keene may lease part or all of the location, or how fire trucks might affect armory operations.

It's at the discussion phase right now," Mason said.

Keene City Manager, John a MacLean said leasing the armory may be a good idea.

"It's an opportunity that needs to be investigated, and that's what the fire chief is doing," he said this morning. "It could be a wonderful opportunity for the city."

Today, the Keene Fire Department has one location on Vernon Street.

In an emergency, that's a long way from West Keene. Response times to West Keene—in the range of eight to 10 minutes—are unacceptable, Pepler said. A person unconscious for more than four minutes may face brain damage.

"What starts as a small fire may be a big fire" by the time emergency crews arrive, he said.

Other pressures to get a second fire station are growing, along with Keene itself. With new industrial development in the Black Brook corporate park, off Route 12, and new residential zoning in the area, Pepler said the need for a substation becomes obvious.

Renting a building is cheaper and quicker than building a new one, Pepler said—especially considering that the armory needs almost no renovation for use as a firehouse.

The armory has indoor parking for 20 vehicles; the fire department needs space for only two. The building also has a kitchen, classroom, offices and showers.

"We could almost move in overnight," Pepler said.

Crews can be siphoned from the department's headquarters to staff a second location, Pepler said. Just one additional firefighter per shift—there are four shifts a day—would have to be hired.

Other than a telephone and a radio, he said, the department already owns enough equipment to keep the station running.

The only other option the fire department is mulling is building a new substation, and MacLean said that's not on the horizon.

A new station will cost far more than the $125,000 a year it may cost to run a leased station. That figure is included in MacLean's recently released list of major projects between fiscal 1998—which starts next summer—and 2003.

Keene already faces a multimillion-dollar tab for building a new police and fire station, to replace the outmoded quarters each department now occupies. Design for a new building big enough for both departments is scheduled for 1999, with construction starting in the summer of 2000.

————

Chief Officers L to R: Deputy Bradley Payne, Chief William Pepler, Deputy Clayton Stalker.

Staff Officers L to R: Lieutenant Gary Lafreniere - Fire Prevention, Captain Bruce Pollock - Training (Fire), Captain Thomas Chase - Training (EMS), Lieutenant John Beckta - Fire Alarm.

A Shift Back Row L to R: 2nd Lieutenant Ron Leslie, Captain Alex Matson Jr., Lieutenent Scott Collier, Firefighter David Wagstaff. Front Row L to R: Firefighter Jeff Chickering, Firefighter Tim Read, Firefighter Chris Cram. Missing: Firefighter Mick Discoll. Photos by Firefighter David Symonds.

B Shift Back Row L to R: Firefighter David Gaillardetz, Lieutenant Art Johnson, Captian Robert Crowell, Firefighter Chris Simino. Front Row L to R: Firefighter Wayne Spofford, Firefighter Edwin Hodgdon, 2nd Lieutenant Mark Boynton, Firefighter Hank Memmesheimer.

C Shift Back Row L to R: 2nd Lieutenant Gary Lamoureux, Captain Steven Goldsmith, Lieutenant Dean Ericson, Firefighter Harry Nelson. Front Row L to R: Firefighter Mike Gianferrari, Firefighter Mike Burke, Firefighter Mike Abbott, Firefighter Mark Howard.

D shift Back row L to R: Firefighter Jim Dubrske, Captain Tom Loll, Lieutenant Scott Taylor, Firefighter Ron Dunn. Front Row L to R: Firefighter Steve McKenna, Firefighter Brian Shepard, Firefighter David Symonds, 2nd Lieutenant Jeff Morel. Photos by Firefighter David Symonds.

1997

As Reported by the *Keene Evening Sentinel* January 4th, 1997:

"STORY"

Calendar needs correcting; Keene fire calls are up

It's not a statistic anybody wants to be a part of, but it broke records nonetheless: the Keene Fire Department responded to a record number of emergencies last year.

Chief William H. Pepler Jr. said that the 3,377 responses is an 8.5 percent increase from 1995.

"Every year, the population gets a little older," Pepler said Friday.

Of those calls, 2,328 were for medical emergencies and 1,049 were for fires or hazardous material problems.

Included in those year-end figures were a number of big blazes: A woman died in a Castle Street apartment fire. Two firefighters rescued a 97-year-old woman from a Highland Avenue scorcher, Kmart, the N.H. Liquor Store, Perkins Lumber and Walier Chevrolet all had minor fires; the latter two were allegedly set.

Ambulance service was up about 11.5 percent last year, as officials responded to 240 more calls than 1995.

Since 1977, when the fire department took over ambulance service, the number of responses has gone from 861 to 2,328, a 170 percent increase.

While some of those calls went out-of-ton—ambulances went to 338 calls in Swanzey, 75 in Chesterfield and 58 in Westmoreland, for example—the bulk were to Keene.

"Keene is a hub for everybody who basically shops, works or goes to school in the county," Pepler said to explain the increase. "They have to come through Keene."

As Reported by the *Keene Evening Sentinel* February 10th, 1997:

"FIRE"

Accidental fire extinguished in Keene

A Keene woman was scorched as she tried to extinguish a fire Sunday afternoon at her home at 147 Main St., Keene.

Yvonne Sherrick, 22, burned her hands and the right side of her face. She was taken to Cheshire Medical Center, treated and released. Her young daughter, also in the apartment, was not hurt, fire officials said.

Keene fire officials say the fire started accidentally when a stove burner was turned on, causing a candle on the stove to melt and light at about 2:30 p.m. The fire was confined to the stove and sink.

As Reported by the *Keene Evening Sentinel* February 20th, 1997:

"FIRE"

Two buildings evacuated in Keene this morning

People were evacuated from two downtown Keene buildings at about 2:30 this morning, because of a carbon-monoxide problem.

People who live in the Carriage House condominiums and the Cracker Factory building, both on Church Street, were roused from their beds this morning. They were allowed back in at about 5 a.m., after firefighters aired out the buildings and tested the air again.

A mechanical problem at the Keene Gas Corp. plant had caused the wrong mixture of propane and air to be sent through gas lines, causing higher-than-safe levels of carbon monoxide in both buildings.

"We evacuated the buildings as a precaution," Keene Deputy Fire Chief Clayton

R. Stalker Jr. said. "No one had to be taken to the hospital."

Stalker wasn't sure how many people live in the two buildings.

This morning, Keene Gas Corp. was answering calls from other downtown businesses and residents, reporting problems.

The problem resulted when a steam boiler malfunctioned and failed to do its job: turn liquid propane to vapor. Some liquid propane got into the two main gas lines leading from the company's Emerald Street plant, according to plant operator John DiBernardo. The liquid propane is much more concentrated than propane gas, DiBernardo explained.

Gas company workers fixed the problem early this morning but some of the highly concentrated gas made its way to downtown businesses and homes, DiBernardo said.

———————

As Reported by the *Keene Evening Sentinel* April 5th, 1997:

"STORY"

City firefighters honored

Veterans of the Keene Fire Department got their due last Saturday night, when the department held its annual awards banquet at the American Legion Hall on Court St.

Capt. Thomas Loll and firefighter Brian Shepard captured the department's lifesaving award for their rescue of an elderly woman from a burning house on Highland Avenue last October.

Second Lt. Jeffrey Morel won an award for promoting fire education in schools and the community. Capt. Robert Crowell, Second Lt. Ronald Leslie and firefighters Ronald Dunn and Shepard were rewarded for their participation in the city's fire investigation team.

Also acknowledged were the following for service to the city:

Serving 25 years: Capt. Thomas Loll, Capt. Bruce Pollock and Capt. Robert Crowell.

Serving 15 years: Second Lt. Ronald Leslie.

Serving 10 years: Lt. John Mullett.

Serving five years: Firefighter Bruce Crowell.

———————

As Reported by Kenneth Arron in *Keene Evening Sentinel* April 19th, 1997:

"STORY"

Fire department drills

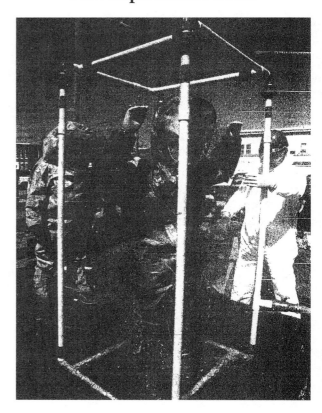

Just Practicing – A Keene firefighter goes through the decontamination process during a training session in the handling of hazardous materials Tuesday. Photo by: Michael Moore.

If there's ever a chemical spill or poison-gas leak in Keene, the city is in good hands.

That's because members of the Keene police and fire department's hazardous materials team took a 16-hour refresher course earlier this week on how to handle such a disaster.

The annual course is a requirement of the federal Occupational Safety and Health Administration.

Fire Chief William Pepler said that in addition to reviewing terminology and chemistry, the crew practiced handling a simulated chlorine leak.

The crew also tackled responses to terrorist acts, such as bombs and chemical gases. Keene may not be a big city, Pepler said, but "we're also not naïve enough to think that nothing could ever happen here in Keene."

If a major disaster such as the sarin gas attack in Tokyo is ever unleashed here, Pepler said that the department has the proper equipment to help deal with it.

The city doesn't plan for one, but Pepler said equipment necessary to handle potential industrial accidents here matches what's needed for a gas attack.

Both the police and fire departments will handle any incidents should anything happen. That's odd, Pepler said.

"We're probably one of the few hazmat teams in the country that are comprised of police and firefighters," he said.

In other places, competition between the two branches is often too gre3at for them to work together. But in Keene, he said both departments just want to serve the public.

"Probably the most important thing is we each now have a good understanding of the other department's needs, tactics and procedures," he said.

———

As Reported by the *Keene Evening Sentinel* May 2nd, 1997:

"FIRE"

Child, dog, house all saved in Keene fire; garage burns

Firefighters saved a house on Route 101 in Keene Thursday night, after two passers-by had already rescued a child from his bedroom.

The house, a 1 1/2 –story cape at 878 Marlborough Road—Route 101—is just east of the Rocky Brook Motel. Kate and Richard Corliss rented the house from its owner, Euripides Ioannou of Keene.

Two men, whom fire officials didn't identify this morning, spotted the fire at about 10:45 p.m.

Kate Corliss had already gotten out of the house with her baby, but an older child was still inside, Keene Fire Chief William H. Pepler Jr. said. The men managed to open the child's unlocked bedroom window and let him out. Pepler did not know the child's age or name.

Richard Corliss was fishing in Harrisville when the fire broke out.

Earlier, other drivers had seen the fire, alerted Kate Corliss, then raced to a neighbor's house to call the fire department.

The fire started in a two-car garage attached to the house. Richard Corliss used the garage for small engine repairs, Pepler said.

The fire razed the garage, which had "quite a fuel load," Pepler said. A propane heater and some chemicals were inside the garage, and the gasoline in a 1988 Chevrolet Blazer ignited, too.

Investigators were at the house this morning, trying to determine how the fire started.

Firefighters went into the house, fighting the flames from the inside and managing to keep them confined to the garage, Pepler said. As firefighters worked, Kate Corliss and her children watched from inside a fire-department vehicle, huddles in blankets on the chilly night.

A Keene firefighter, Harry Nelson , went upstairs to save the family's pet collie.

"It was in the upstairs hallway and then ran into a bedroom," Nelson said. "I checked the other rooms first, then picked up the collie."

Nelson said he didn't know the dog's name. "I'd call him Lucky, I guess," he said.

No one was injured. The fire was declared under control an hour after firefighters arrived.

Because the house is outside Keene's fire-hydrant system, tanker trucks were called in from other area fire departments to haul water to the fire. Firefighters came from the Marlborough, Meadowood County Area, Swanzey and Troy departments.

Route 101 was closed to traffic for more than an hour.

————————

As Reported by Shawna Sevigny in *Keene Evening Sentinel* May 6th, 1997:

"FIRE"

Hero faces fire
KSC student rescued boy

A Hero – Eric Koski, at work Monday at the Best Western in Keene, helped save a child from a burning house last week in Keene. Photo by: Steve Hooper.

Some call Eric Koski a hero. But the 23-year-old Keene State College student from Jaffrey says he was just trying to repay a debt.

Last Thursday night, Koski helped save a handicapped child from a burning house on Route 101 in Keene.

Koski was driving home at 10:45 p.m. from the Best Western Sovereign Hotel in Keene, where he works as a waiter. He saw smoke and a fire at the house, but no fire trucks. When he slowed to get a better look, he saw a woman in the window.

"I wasn't sure if she knew there was a fire," he said. "I got out of the car and went over just as the woman came out screaming."

Kate Corliss and her 2-year-old daughter, Brittany, had managed to get out of the house, but Corliss said a foster child staying with the family was still inside. The boy, Evan Fatley, is handicapped and can't walk.

Koski and another passer-by, Hans Schule of White River Junction, Vt., decided they couldn't wait for the firefighters. There was too much smoke and fire near the front door.

So, they went around to an unlocked bedroom window. Koski boosted Schule through the window, and Shule handed the child down to Koski.

"He certainly deserves credit," said Koski's mother, Pamela. "But this is about people helping people and giving back to the community."

Koski says he was just trying to repay the kindness of strangers who help him after a car accident a year ago.

In April 1996, he was driving home from work in a freak snowstorm when his car slid off Route 101 in Marlborough, and bounced into some trees and a ditch. The impact shattered his car's windshield, and he needed several stitches in both is hands. Had Koski not been wearing his seat belt or put his banks in front of his face, the cuts in his face could have been much worse, he said.

A stranger who saw Koski crash stopped and called for help. He stayed with Koski until paramedics arrived.

Koski praised the volunteer firefighters and paramedics in Marlborough for their expert medical care and for calming his nerves.

"They were great to me," Koski said. "It's great when people can help each other."

The Corlisses have contacted Koski and have been trying to arrange a reunion. Though the fire destroyed a garage and the vehicle inside, their rented house was saved, and it's being repaired so it is livable again.

The cause of the fire is still undetermined.

————

As Reported by Shawna Sevigny in *Keene Evening Sentinel* May 6th, 1997:

"STORY"

KSC student accused of causing $50,000 damage

A Keene State student may be in a heap of trouble: He's accused of setting off a dormitory sprinkler and causing $50,000 in water damage.

Seven students in Owls Nest 3, a residence hall, had to move out after their rooms were flooded early Sunday.

The flooding couldn't have come at a worse time for students. Today's the first of a full week of final exams at Keene State.

"The information seems to indicate it was done purposely and not accidentally," Andrew Robinson, associate dean of student affairs, said this morning, while refusing to identify the student at this point.

An administrative hearing will be held today to discuss whether the student tampered with the sprinkler. If so, he could be suspended, or his on-campus housing could be revoked for the next school year. He may also have to pay for damages to students and school property.

Keene police are also investigating, but have not filed charges.

The Keene Fire Department responded to the building on Butler Court at 12:40 a.m. Sunday, when the sprinkler tripped the fire alarm.

About 45 residents were evacuated for two hours while the fire department investigated. Most students were wearing just their pajamas, and they camped out with blankets and pillows in nearby Holloway Hall.

According to Deputy Keene Fire Chief Clayton R. Stalker Jr., the sprinkler in the second d-floor room sent 50 gallons of water per minute pouring into the dormitory. The water seeped through the floors and leaked into a six-person apartment below.

The student accused of setting the sprinkler was visiting a friend in the second-floor dorm room. He is a Keene State student, and lives in another dorm on campus.

Firefighters spend several hours Sunday trying to vacuum up some of the water.

Total damage could exceed $50,000, and new ceilings, walls, and carpets need to be installed before either the upstairs or downstairs apartment is livable again, said Anne Miller, director of residential life at the college. The students lost everything—from computers to clothing and all their books and homework.

All the displaced students—six women and one man—are being housed at other dorms. They are also trying to get extensions or incomplete grades on their exams, Robinson said.

"It's not only the property loss," Miller said this morning.

"You can imagine the emotional damage."

————

As Reported by Kenneth Arron in *Keene Evening Sentinel* May 21st, 1997:

"STORY"

Fire chief: Now's the time for West Keene station

A West Keene branch for the Keene Fire Department isn't in the 1997-98 city budget proposal, but Fire Chief William Pepler Jr. is doing his best to drum up support for one.

For 50 years, the fire department has hoped for a satellite station on the west side of the city. Now, the city has one fire station; it's on Vernon Street, a block north of Central Square.

Pepler faces a scrape trying to get a West Keene station this year, but says a building is now available for rent, more money will come from higher ambulance fees, and it's time to get the thing done.

"I think it's the right year because of all the projects that are going on" in West Keene, Pepler told city councilors Tuesday night, referring to construction of an apartment complex and development of a major industrial park.

Also at the second night of hearings on City Manager John A. MacLean's $26.1 million proposal, councilors heard from Keene Public Library officials who want to start a $3.5 million renovation-expansion of the Winter Street building.

The library's plans have been reviewed with councilors several times and have faced little resistance so far.

But Pepler might have a harder battle on his hands.

Councilors were asked Tuesday to confine their comments to questions, and keep any real debate to the final budget-review session tonight. And there promises to be some.

MacLean cautioned councilors that a West Keene fire station would cost about $240,000 a year to run, and would raise the property-tax rate in future years.

Leasing space at the National Guard armory on Hastings Avenue would cost only $1,500 a year, but paying firefighters and buying extra equipment push up the overall expense.

A new fire station may not affect taxes this year, MacLean said, because a budget surplus can limit the impact. But there aren't surpluses every year, and property owners will eventually have to pay the freight.

That's not to say Pepler's proposal isn't valid, MacLean said. Someday soon, Keene will have to consider a West Keene station.

The fire chief thinks now is the time. Pepler wants to take all the extra income from a proposed increase in ambulance rates and use it for the West Keene station. The fire department operates the ambulances.

City ambulance rates are slated to rise to $200 per call, up from $150 now. That should boost income by about $178,000 a year—cutting the next cost of the West Keene fire station to about $60,000

MacLean doesn't think it's such a good idea to plow all the extra ambulance revenue into the West Keene station.

Councilors are split on the issue.

"There will be a very strong effort in favor of this West Keene station," said Councilor Mitchell H. Greenwald, not only from the council, but from residents whom the station would protect.

It takes seven to 12 minutes, depending on traffic, for fire trucks and ambulances from the downtown station to reach homes and businesses in West Keene. Optimum response time should be three to five minutes; once a person stops breathing, for example, it takes only four minutes before permanent brain damage occurs. With major projects continuing to sprout in the city's western half, fire officials contend better service is needed.

Councilor William A. Beauregard wants to study the situation before making any commitments. Keene has a long history of effective planning, he said, and more is needed on the fire station issue.

West Keene fire station still to come

A debate over whether to pay for a West Keene fire station was pushed back until Wednesday, when department officials will present more information and options for city councilors to mull.

———

As Reported by Elizabeth Crowley in *Keene Evening Sentinel* May 27th, 1997:

"STORY"

Waiting to save lives
A tense weekend for Keene ambulance crew

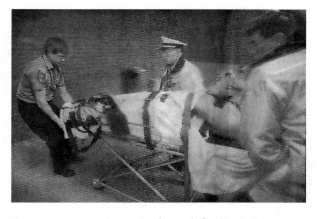

Emergency — Harry Nelson, left, Capt. Steve Goldsmith and Mike Gianferrari, all members of the Keene Emergency Medical Service, rush a Swanzey motorcycle accident victim into the emergency room Saturday at Cheshire Medical Center in Keene. The victim is holding tight to his father's hand. Photo by Steve Hooper.

It's Sunday night, the middle of the Memorial Day weekend.

Keene firefighters—about 98 percent of whom are certified as emergency medical technicians—are standing by for holiday emergencies.

Except for a motorcycle accident Saturday evening, it's been relatively quiet so far.

Bust, as Sunday night approaches, the sense of tension is heightened.

Seared into memory:

Ask anyone who works on an ambulance, and he'll say the same thing: Most runs blend into one another, and become indistinguishable only a few days after they occur.

But not all.

Some calls—car accidents or other medical emergencies—aren't so easily forgotten. They sear even the most trivial detail into the minds of the ambulance crews who race to offer help.

"Some calls I've gone on, I can still remember the time out and the time back in," Said Gary Lamoureaux, a 2nd Lieutenant in the Keene Fire Department who works on the city ambulance service. "You remember every single detail of some of them.

The ones that stick come in two varieties: the odd and the emotional, firefighters say.

Some bizarre ambulance runs in Keene are worthy of Ripley's "Believe It or Not." Like the time the 14-year-old boy threw a 16-inch-long lawn dart at his grandmother.

"All we knew on the ride there was that we had a domestic situation," Capt. Steven Goldsmith said. "When we get there, there's a woman down on her knees, leaning against a fence, with one hand to her head."

Firefighters had trouble believing what they were seeing: The lawn dart had pierced the woman's face and was lodged between her eyes. It was deeply embedded in her nasal cavity.

"We had all we could do to keep her from pulling it out," Goldsmith said. "If she had moved it, she probably would have died, because it was just about touching her brain.

"Even the doctors couldn't believe that one," he said. "They had someone take photographs before they took her to surgery."

Then there are calls that can't be erased from the mental record, because they touch too close to home.

At least seven people were injured in weekend traffic accidents around the Monadnock Region.

In Keene, a woman was hurt slightly in a three-car pileup at Routes 9 and 12 Sunday morning.

Mary E. Smith, 82, of Saratoga Springs, NY, was taken to Cheshire Medical Center to be checked.

Police said she was riding in a car with her husband, Robert D. Smith, 80, when the accident happened at about 10:30 a.m. According to police, Smith's 1997 Ford Tempo hit the back of a car driven by Timothy D. Douglas, 37, of Peter borough. Douglas had stopped at the traffic light when Smith's car hit his.

Douglas' 1987 Dodge Dakota was pushed forward into the 1993 Volvo ahead of him at the light; that drive Gerald W. Zwaga, 51, of North Swanzey, wasn't injured.

Ellin M. Moore, 35, and Catherine Moore, 75, both from New York City, were injured Monday when their car flipped atop Chesterfield Hill, near the point where the Keene, Chesterfield and Westmoreland boundaries intersect.

Ellin Moore, the driver, was treated for minor injuries and released; Catherine Moore was in stable condition this morning at the Keene hospital.

Police said their 1997 Fort hit the rocks along Route 9 and flipped at about 2:50 p.m., after the driver was distracted.

———

As Reported by Kenneth Arron in *Keene Evening Sentinel* May 27th, 1997:

"STORY"

2nd fire station, 3 hours per day Keene hoping to cure time lag

It's 5 p.m. somebody's had a heart attack on Base Hill Road. Keene rescue crews are suited up, in their ambulances, blaring their sirens, and facing a 13-minute trip to get there. They've got to thread through heavy traffic on West Street.

That's trouble Keene Fire Chief William H. Pepler Jr. wants to prevent, and it's the

Photo by Steve Goldsmith.

reason a Keene City Council committee voted Wednesday night to endorse $67,000 for a part-time fire station in West Keene.

The station would operate three hours a day, five days a week, during peak traffic hours.

That idea is much cheaper than Pepler's first plan, an all-day, all-week operation.

"It's a good attempt to start the process," he said Wednesday night.

The cheaper option was unveiled at a meeting of the finance and organization committee, and approved 4-0 with little discussion.

If the 15-member council approves the plan, Keene will rent space at the National Guard armory on Hastings Avenue and keep an ambulance crew there from 3 to 6 p.m., Monday through Friday.

That setup will cost $73,000 a year. But because it wouldn't open until August, the net cost for the fiscal year starting July 1 would be about $67,000. The full-time choice would cost $247,000.

A full-time squad in West Keene would require another fire engine and new firefighters. The part-time deal can be staffed with firefighters already on the city's force, working overtime.

For decades, fire officials have wanted an extra station in West Keene. New development is mushrooming there.

Now, Keene's only fire station is on Vernon Street, a block north of the Central Square rotary downtown,

"The fire station downtown was perfectly located in 1885," Pepler said.

But with tremendous housing development over the years in West Keene, the recent advent of the Black Brook Corporate Park, and other construction, city officials say it takes ages—in emergency response time— to get places.

A trip from the fire station on Vernon Street to Base Hill Road can take 13 minutes. From the station to Maple Avenue, 8 minutes.

Considering it only takes 4 minutes or so for permanent brain damage to set in, officials worry.

During the next year, city officials will go over past response times, evaluate how the West Keene station works, and study how much extra service is needed.

Something definitely needs to be done, said City Manager John A. MacLean.

"Our run times appear to be unacceptable," he said.

Some communities do just fine without extra—or any—stations, countered Councilor William A. Beauregard. In fact, he said, they do just fine with volunteer emergency crews.

"I think talking about response times is a bit of a straw man when compared to surrounding towns, Beauregard said. He wants a study before the city spends money on the project.

Keene has more residents than any town in the region, MacLean replied, and so bears more risk.

As for a study, MacLean said Keene has enough information to know that something should be done in the meantime.

"If we save one life, it's obviously worth the cost of the experiment," he said.

Property taxes will not rise to cover the fire station;' the city government's share of the property tax rate is expected to stay flat in the next year.

Including the part-time West Keene station, the city budget proposal needs $9.4 million from property taxes for fiscal 1998— $79,128 more than MacLean called for when he got the budget process started.

Some neighbors have told city officials they're worried about the safety of ambulances whizzing through their quiet neighborhoods. But MacLean sought to placate those fears, saying that the drivers will act responsibly.

Otherwise, councilors said the residents they've spoken to seem happy with the fire station proposal—though they are looking for more comment.

Another option, to provide 12 hours of service per day at the West Keene station, was rejected. It actually costs more than the full-time station, because the workers would be on overtime.

————————

As Reported by Kenneth Arron in *Keene Evening Sentinel* June 6th, 1997:

"STORY"

Idea passes review
Neighbors like W. Keene plan

Susan A. Doyle lives beyond Keene's Central Square, beyond the blinking radio tower in an empty cornfield, beyond the flashing yellow light on Route 9, and beyond a distant mobile-home park on Base Hill Road.

She lives in Farmste4ad Commons, a condominium complex the Keene Fire Department considers one of the toughest to get to during peak traffic hours.

And she says opening a West Keene fire station is a heck of an idea.

"To get from downtown to here is a pain in the neck," Doyle said Thursday afternoon.

She's not the only person in favor of putting a second fire station into the National Guard armory on Hastings Avenue. Several neighbors were nearly unanimous in their support.

Call it the YIMBY syndrome—Yes, In My Back Yard.

Though some Keene officials had braced for complaints about noise and traffic, residents backed the idea of having an ambulance in the neighborhood, and maybe a fire truck—aside from a few people asking that the department go easy on the sirens.

Only one person contacted Thursday was against the idea.

"I think we can be very good neighbors," Fire Chief William H. Pepler Jr. said this morning.

Hastings Avenue is not a street welcoming to big trucks. The street is narrow enough for neighbors to talk across, front yard to front yard. Basketball hoops with flaking paint hang from some homes, their junior players long grown up and gone: in nearby developments, new fiberglass backboards have been planted and young families have moved in.

That new construction has attracted the fire department's eye. In addition to housing construction over the years, companies will be moving into the Black Brook Corporate Park in short order, 120 apartments are under construction at the former Winding Brook Lodge now.

All that development so far from the department's only station on Vernon Street, could be trouble, Pepler says.

It only takes four or five minutes before a person whose heart stops suffers permanent brain damage. It takes 13 minutes to get to some parts of West Keene when traffic is heaviest.

While most neighborhood residents said that they feel pretty safe now, a little extra protection never hurts.

Noise is a potential sticking point for some. "I'm not real happy about it, because of the sirens," said Rachel Elkins, who lives on Evans Lane.

If firefighters don't use their noisemakers until they leave the neighborhood, that will make things easier to take, she said.

The department won't use air horns or traffic sirens, Pepler said, and the trucks will stay silent as long as nobody's on the roads.

"We don't need them, we don't use them," he said of the fire department's approach to sirens.

Emergency crews at the station will be reminded of neighborhood concerns and how to work around them, Pepler said.

The second station will run three hours a day, five days a week, if approved. It will cost Keene $73,000 per year, well below the $247,000 annual budget for a full-time station.

City officials plan to keep an ambulance at the West Keene outpost initially, but no fire trucks; after a year or so, they'll take another look.

Robert E. Martineau, who lives on Trowbridge Road, thinks the city ought to just go at it headfirst.,

"If you have it, you might as well have it," he said.

The biggest fire in the neighborhood last year destroyed a carport at a Summit Road apartment complex, and destroyed several vehicles. Having a fire truck at the West Keene station wouldn't have been a factor. That fire happened in the middle of the night, and the part-time station would run only from 3 to 6 p.m., when traffic is heavy.

Most neighborhood residents weren't too worried that the fire station would mean extra traffic. Hastings Avenue already has plenty of it, they said.

What will be necessary, one woman said, is for the city to fix the awkward, five-spoked intersection at the street's north end.

"It is dangerous now," said Delores L. Parker. Courtesy may be enough to get drivers through the tricky intersection now, but big fire trucks barreling through might pose a problem.

————

As Reported by the *Keene Evening Sentinel* June 6th, 1997:

"FIRE"

Keene apartment fire causes heavy damage

A burning candle, left unattended, started an apartment fire in Keene Thursday night, but firefighters contained the flames and no one was injured.

The fire at the five-apartment building at 47 Colorado St. owned by city Councilor William A. Beauregard, started at about 8 p.m.

When the woman who reported the fire said she was trapped in the building, a second alarm was sounded, but the woman was able to get out on her own.

"There were a few tense moments," Fire Chief William H. Pepler Jr. said this morning.

The fire began in the living room of an apartment rented by Colby Campbell, Travis Moulton and Julie Porter, who were not in the building when the fire started.

Firefighters had the fire under control in about 20 minutes.

Smoke and water damage also left another apartment uninhabitable, but the tenants were able to return to the other three apartments in the building. Damage was estimated at $30,000.

In a bad news-good news note, Beauregard had recently renovated the building—but the new wall materials helped contain the fire, Pepler said.

————

As Reported by Robert Rand in *Keene Evening Sentinel* June 11th, 1997:

"STORY"

Spill clears factory

An ammonia spill at a Keene jewelry manufacturer sent five employees to the hospital Tuesday afternoon and forced the building's evacuation.

Keene firefighters treated the spill at Findings Inc. at Carpenter and Water streets on Keene's east side, as a hazardous material accident. They closed part of Water Street, from Valley Street to Grove Street, for 3 ½ hours, effectively shutting down the entire thoroughfare. Most of Carpenter Street was also closed to traffic.

Firefighters launched a full-scale hazardous-materials operation, setting up decontamination areas and donning protective gear.

About 125 Findings employees tried to stay cool in the 90-degree heat outside while firefighters checked out the spill. A few neighboring buildings were also evacuated.

The five employees all inhaled small amounts of ammonia fumes. They were checked at Cheshire Medical Center in Keene and released.

This morning, company President James A. Craig said, all five were back at work.

At 1:30 p.m., 20 gallons of a low concentration of ammonia spilled, Keene Fire Chief William H. Pepler Jr. estimated.

A truck was delivering ammonia to the company's 1,000-gallon outdoor tank when the hose came off the truck's tank, spilling the ammonia on the ground.

The ammonia is used to create a "pure atmosphere" in the plants solder ovens, Craig said.

Ammonia is considered a corrosive, nonflammable liquid, and a respiratory irritant if inhaled, Pepler said. The five workers who went to the hospital complained of some mild symptoms: nausea, headaches and scratchy throats.

A higher concentration of ammo0nia could have caused more serious injuries, Pepler said.

In dealing with the spill, four firefighters put on spacesuit-like, white plastic suits, under which they wore oxygen tanks and ice vests to keep cool. By the time they checked out the spill, the ammonia had vaporized on the hot, breezy day and there was nothing to clean up.

With the middle stretch of Water Street closed, there were some minor traffic tie-ups on the city's east side. Elementary school students in the Water Street neighborhood attend Wheelock School and some had a long walk home Tuesday.

By 5 p.m., workers had returned to the building and the streets were reopened to traffic.

About 25 firefighters went to the accident, which cost between $3,000 to $4,000 for overtime pay, equipment and supplies, Pepler said. The city will bill the delivery company, Tanner Industries of Philadelphia; that's routine practice, he said.

Findings make fashion accessories, including earring posts, ring settings and finished jewelry for discount stores such as Wal-Mart.

At about 6:05 p.m., firefighters went to Webber Energy Co's fuel tanks at 164 Martell Court, where a 500-gallon propane storage tank was releasing gas.

Firefighters cooled the tank with water; a relief valve shut down, stopping the propane release.

Company officials removed some of the propane from the tank; they determined it had been filled too much to allow for expansion of the gas in hot weather.

————

As Reported by Kenneth Aaron in *Keene Evening Sentinel* July 2nd, 1997:

"STORY"

FAA urged to require firefighters at Keene airport

If the Federal Aviation Administration puts up the money, the Keene Fire Department may soon have three times as many stations as it does now.

The National Transportation Safety Board recommended Tuesday that the FAA find ways to pay for fire and rescue protection at small airports—including Keene's Dillant-Hopkins Airport in North Swanzey.

The suggestion stems from a commuter-plane collision in which most passengers survived the impact, but died in a subsequent fire.

FAA rules do not require firefighter protection for aircraft with fewer than 30 seats the board recommended that the FAA find ways to pay for that protection. The Colgan Air commuter planes serving the Keene airport have about 20 seats.

Kathryn Creedy, an FAA spokeswoman, said the agency is considering a comprehensive fire and rescue rule and is expecting a proposal by the end of the year.

Keene now has a crash truck at the airport, but no firefighters are stationed there.

Should the FAA order service, Keene Fire Chief William H. Pepler Jr. said the fire department will need at least three crew members at the airport, with the total depending on what they'll have to do, whether airport fire protection is a full-time requirement, and how often flights arrive.

"I think the good news is the FAA considered paying for this, he said this morning.

Though the Keene department knew an order might eventually come, the city has budgeted no money for an airport fire station in the fiscal year that began Tuesday.

The budget does include money to put an ambulance in a second, part-time fire station on Hastings Avenue in West Keene, something that city fire officials have wanted for years.

Adding an airport fire station could cost thousands of dollars for overtime pay or for hiring new firefighters, Pepler said.

When larger planes served the Keene airport some years ago, firefighters were on duty for landings. Today, though, if disaster struck, they would respond from the department's Vernon Street station.

The National Transportation Safety Board said a United Express Beechcraft 1900 collided last November 19 with a private twin engine Beechcraft King Air at Quincy, Illinois, because the King Air pilot failed to monitor a common radio frequency on which the United Express pilot repeatedly reported her position and intention to land.

Fourteen people were killed when the commuter plane landed in the dusk just at the King Air began taking off on an intersecting runway. The Quincy airport is one of hundreds nationwide that have no tower and no regular fire and rescue protection. Seventy of those airports, including Keene's, have scheduled commuter service.

––––––––

As Reported by Karen Tolkkinen in *Keene Evening Sentinel* July 29th, 1997:

"FIRE"

Early-morning fire wakes tenants; no one is injured

Sleepy tenants safely evacuated an aging Keene apartment building early this morning after one of them felt an unusually hot wall on the third floor.

When Keene firefighters arrived at about 1:40 a.m., smoke was curling from under the eaves at the Minerva Apartments at 347 Court St; Faulty electric wiring apparently started the blaze, Deputy Chief Clayton R. Stalker Jr. said this morning.

"The wiring is very old," Stalker said. "It's not in good condition." The fire department has responded to minor fires there in the past, he said.

Landscaper Gordon Martin, 27, had just moved into the building—a beehive of nine small apartments and rooms—a week ago from Massachusetts.

He woke up in his second-floor apartment after hearing a commotion on the floor above him. When he went upstairs to investigate he found tenants pressing their palms against the back wall of the hallway, near the electric-power boxes.

One of the tenants looked back at him.

He said, "That's not right. Walls don't get hot like that," Martin said this morning.

Martin shrugged. He couldn't smell or see any smoke, so he went back to sleep.

But his slumber was interrupted again when firefighters arrived and evacuated the building which houses 10 tenants.

He spent a couple of hours in his shorts in the windy night before being allowed to go back in, retrieve a change of clothing, and go to the Valley Green Motel for the night.

Smoke alarms did sound, and firefighters found the attic full of smoke, with a small fire burning in the building's rear walls. They tore out two walls and doused the blaze.

Nobody was hurt.

The building's owner, John Byrnes of Keene, was truing to fix the electrical problems this morning and restore power to the building, Stalker said. Damage was estimated at between $2,000 to $5,000. Byrnes described the damage as minimal, thanks to "exceptionally good" work by the fire department.

"The potential was there for a fire," he said. Byrnes said people were moving back in today.

———

As Reported by Lindsay Cobb in *Keene Evening Sentinel* August 2nd, 1997:

"STORY"

Cool in fire's face Bruce Pollock shares his knowledge of firefighting and its intricacies

Capt. Bruce Pollock. Photo by Robert Diluzio Sr.

Bruce Pollock remembers the fire at the old MacKenzie Dairy in Keene for one reason—his leather helmet finally saw some action.

Pollock, 46, had special ordered the leather helmet, with the ornately tooled brim and the tailored headband, to uphold a time-honored tradition of the fire service.

"You go to Boston , New York, even some of the major departments in New Hampshire, and talk to them about leather helmets; they'll tell you it's the only way to go. With 23 years of service on the Keene Fire Department including 12 years as training officer, Pollock knows his traditions, and he has seen his share of fires and medical emergencies. In 1975, his first year, the department answered

330 calls. By the time Pollock retired in June, the station averaged 3,700 calls a year.

That's a lot of fires. But for months after buying his helmet in 1980, Pollock had no opportunity to wear it. Then came the fire at Mackenzie's.

It was early August 5:30 p.m. in the morning. Pollock went straight from his apartment to the fire, in full gear, his leather helmet firmly on his head. On the second floor of the main building, he was breaking some windows for ventilation with a tool, when his arm slipped; he cut his wrist on a shard of glass. He required 18 stitches, and had to leave the fire.

The next day, he retired the helmet.

It hasn't been on my head since," he says now from his house in Keene. "I figured if it was going to take a fire like that to get me hurt, then the leather helmet needed to say on the wall. It's seen a fire, and it can tell a story."

Today, the helmet hangs in his basement office at home, where he lives with his wife, Deb Buckley and their son Jay, who is 12. Pollock also has two daughters, Kristen, 22, and Kellie, 19, both of whom attend the University of Delaware.

The helmet is only one of many prized mementos from a fulfilling career. And if each memento can tell a story, Pollock himself can tell dozens more.

In his role as training officer, Pollock established an orientation program by which he trained all new firefighters in the city, as well as numerous fire departments around Cheshire County. He is also an adjunct faculty member at Keene State College, where he teaches introduction to fire science, and transportation of hazardous materials.

But Pollock remains a modest man, preferring to talk about the teamwork and friendships he's seen over the years. His friends and colleagues are more than willing to heap praise on him.

Information to life:

Brad Payne, the department's deputy chief of operations, says that Pollock was "one of our better training officers. He related to the guys really well."

Vicky Farer-Feld, who teaches industrial technology and safety at the college, was originally a student of Pollock's. She is impressed with Pollock's presentation of the material and his rapport with the students.

"Bruce brings the information to life," says Farer-Feld. "I see how the students react to him—they love him. He'

S got the4 whole dog-and-pony show."

Born in 1951, Pollock hails from a long line of Keene firefighters. His grandfather was a call deputy chief, his father was a call lieutenant firefighter, and his uncle was one of Keene's first full-time firefighters.

But it took Pollock a few years before he joined his elders. After graduating from Keene High School in 1970, Pollock attended Keene State College to study architectural drafting.

After one year, he couldn't stand the thought of spending the rest of his life sitting at a board and drawing. "That's not in my genes," he says.

So he left college and went to work for Kingsbury Machine Tool, first as a machine assembler, then as a computer programmer for purchasing and payroll.

On weekends during the winter, Pollock and his father volunteered for the Gopher Ski Patrol, a local chapter of the National Ski Patrol, taking care of injured skiers at Timber Ridge and Roundtop Mountain in Vermont.

Pollock enjoyed his work on the ski patrol even more than computer programming. "We had the jackets with the big gold crosses on the backs, and the first aid kits. We had a ball.

A nightmarish night:

Early in 1974, Pollock's best friend, Bruce Boucher, went to work for the Keene Police

Department; he got Pollock involved as a special officer, a part-time job.

Pollock patrolled on Friday nights or in case the department was shorthanded. Pollock fell in love with the work, and when the opportunity soon came to go full-time, Pollock jumped at it.

"You never knew what was next," Pollock recalls. "No two calls were ever alike. Each one was a different person, and a different situation." Pollock greatly preferred this kind of work to sitting at a desk.

One night in Late November of that year, Pollock and Boucher headed for a police benevolent association meeting at the station and stopped at the fire department to see Pollock's father. His mother was at the Grand Union; his father was going to pick her up in a while. Pollock told his dad he'd call him later, to discuss their Thanksgiving plans.

As the meeting ended, cruisers were being dispatched to a car accident on Maple Avenue. "The calls were coming in that this thing was really bad," Pollock says. As Pollock and Boucher seemed not to be needed immediately, Boucher suggested they go back to his apartment and follow it on his scanner.

While there, they were visited by their supervisor, Sgt. Hugh McLellan, and given the news: It was Pollock's parents. Their car had been hit by a drunken driver, and both were killed.

When Pollock recalls that night, his voice lowers to a whisper. "That was nightmarish. You just can't imagine." There was the funeral to get through, and then, later, the trial of the driver. In the meantime, McLellan put Pollock on the desk, until he could get over the shock.

"At that point, Hugh almost became my replacement father," says Pollock. "There was a lot of stuff that came out."

It was some months before McLellan let Pollock drive a cruiser again—and then, only after Pollock could drive past where the accident happened.

"Even then, says Pollock, "it just wasn't the same." Every time he stopped a car, he wondered if the driver was drinking. Every time he made a DWI arrest, people said he had a vendetta.

But his luck turned in the middle of 1975, when he got a job at the fire department. "It was the best move I ever made." He says now. "It kind of put everything behind me.

"The two guys who were doing the training were good, but it was all OJT— on-the-job training. Here's your helmet, here's your coat, when that bell rings get on the truck and they'll tell you what to do.

Then again, some situations just weren't covered in training programs. Pollock particularly remembers the night Blaisdell's Sport-o-Rama, a concrete building on Roxbury Street, burned.

"With that amount of fire and heat, it was like walking into an oven," Pollock recalls. "You can't imagine the heat." Dragging a 2 ½ inch nozzle, Pollock had to crawl through falling clothes racks with his colleagues, while ammunition in the gun shop section, kept exploding.

"But," Pollock says, "it's still standing."

Becoming a teacher:
Pollock got his first taste of teaching in 1978, when the National Fire Protection Association selected Keene to be a pilot city to test a new fire safety course.

Pollock was asked by then chief Robert Guyette to be the liaison between KFD and the Keene public schools.

"That was one of the most fun things I've ever done in my career," Pollock says. "I liked working with the people, being up in front of the kids and doing stuff."

For awhile after that, Pollock traveled across the country teaching courses.

By now, Pollock realized how much he enjoyed teaching. When the fire department's training officer's job opened in the mid-1980's, Pollock applied.

Keene's new Fire Alarm Bucket Truck replaces the old International Fire Alarm Bucket Truck. Photo by Steve Goldsmith.

It wasn't easy. He had to first take tests to be promoted to lieutenant, then pass courses in emergency medical training in order to be promoted to captain.

That accomplished, he got the job. Pollock's education, however, did not end there. In 1992, he received a degree in safety studies from KSC.

Pollock likes to tell the story of using a defibrillator a few years ago, on a man in Central Square who was in full cardiac arrest. Pollock and two other technicians answered the call, the rest of the company having been sent to answer a fire alarm at the high school.

The defibrillator checked the heart and administered a shock, which got the heart beating again, so that Pollock and his colleagues could get the man to the hospital.

Pollock thought that was the end of it, until a few weeks later, when the man showed up at the station with a cake.

"He said, "I was the guy on Central Square, and I just want to thank you guys, and he handed us the cake."

Pollock beams to recall his patient's gratitude. "Man, that's okay," he says. "That's dynamite."

And that's what means the most to Bruce Pollock: a job well done, and someone who is still alive to be thankful.

———————

Firefighter/EMT-P Karen Fleury, Keene's first permanent female firefighter/paramedic. Assigned to D Shift.

August 6th, 1997. Fire Department Photo.
Keene's new ladder truck replaces a 1973
Maxium ladder.

As Reported by *Keene Evening Sentinel* August 21st, 1997:

"FIRE"

Smoke detectors save two Keene families

Fire officials say smoke detectors saved the lives of two Keene families—twice within the same night.

According to officials, Brian Goodell of 22 Bellevue St. reported the first fire just before 3 a.m. Saturday. A small fire was extinguished in the cellar of that house, and fire crews set up fans to blow the smoke out of the building.

No injuries were reported from that incident, and emergency crews returned to the fire station by 4 a.m.

But just before 7 a.m., firefighters were sent to the building again for a bigger fire in the cellar.

Fire officials said the second blaze caused heavy fire damage to the entire cellar and smoke damage to the rest of the building.

The Goodell family lost its cat in the fire, but no other injuries were reported. Officials said they are investigating the fires, and consider them both to be suspicious.

The building is owned by Lenny and Barbara MacDonald of Marlborough. Smoke detectors alerted the two families living in the building both times, officials said.

As Reported by *Keene Evening Sentinel* October 6th, 1997:

"STORY"

It's Fire Prevention week

Captain Steven Goldsmith participates in a fire prevention demonstration, demonstrating to Symonds school students how firefighters go from one floor to the apparatus floor to jump the trucks quickly.

A parade down Main Street in Keene Sunday afternoon kicked off a busy Fire Prevention Week for the Keene Fire Department.

More than 50 fire departments across New Hampshire were represented in the parade, as well as marching bands from Keene High School, Monadnock Regional School in Swanzey Center and Gordon Bissell American Legion Post 4 of Keene.

Afterward, there was an open house at the firestation, where firefighters demonstrated the department's new ladder truck, how to use fire extinguishers and what children should do in a fire.

"It was a perfect day and very well attended," said

William H. Pepler Jr., Keene's fire chief. Several departments took out their antique equipment for the parade.

————————

As Reported by *Keene Evening Sentinel* October 7th, 1997:

"STORY"

New fire station opens

If you live in West Keene, try to keep your emergencies between the hours of 3 and 6 p.m.

That's when the city will staff the National Guard armory building on Hastings Avenue with a fire engine and ambulance with crew. The crews will respond to emergencies in West Keene from 3 to 6 p.m.

Officials say the experiment will help them determine the need for shorter response times in West Keene and examine which times of day are busiest.

Afternoon rush-hour traffic on West Street, sometimes slows down emergency service vehicles heading to West Keene.

With residential and commercial growth anticipated for the city, officials believe a West Keene emergency substation may be needed sooner rather than later.

A tentative joint-use agreement has been reached between the city government and the National Guard; it will come before the city council in the near future, say fire officials.

————————

1998

As Reported by the *Keene Evening Sentinel* February 2nd, 1998:

"FIRE"

Chimney fire forces woman from house

A chimney fire forced an elderly Keene woman from her smoke filled house Sunday morning.

Josephine Lagerberg of 179 Gilsum Road called 911 at about 11:27 a.m. after her house started filling with smoke. Capt. Goldsmith led Lagerberg to a waiting ambulance, she had inhaled some smoke, from the house, said a Keene Fire Department spokesman.

Lagerberg, who's in her late 70's heated her house with wood, and the fire apparently started after creosote in her chimney ignited, officials said. The fire was under control by 12:30 p.m. Damage was minimal.

Firefighters encourage residents with wood stoves to clean their chimneys annually.

Lagerberg is now staying with a daughter.

––––––––

As Reported by the *Keene Evening Sentinel* February 16th, 1998:

"FIRE"

In a day's work for fire crews

A pipe in the Keene State College Science Center burst Sunday afternoon, flooding two rooms with hot water and filling them with steam.

Keene firefighters were called to the building on Appian Way at 2:50 p.m. A second-floor chemistry-equipment room and a vacant first-floor room were damaged.

Clayton R. Stalker Jr., deputy chief of the Keene Fire Department, said the rooms were monitored to make sure the chemicals used in laboratories were contained.

It took the fire department and college work crews more than an hour to clean up the water and debris.

Bertha Lindsey Fielding, public relations director for Keene State, said today that ceiling tiles had to be replaced in both rooms and some equipment was damaged. She did not know the cost of repairs. Both rooms are open today.

"It's all been mopped up and we're back in business," Fielding said.

Chemical spill cleaned

A chemical spill at Markem Corp. Brought Keene firefighters to the plant of Optical Avenue this morning, but employees cleaned it up and there were no in juries.

Sometime during the night Sunday, a catalyst hardener spilled into a 6-by-8-foot section of floor in a work room, said Clayton R. Stalker Jr., Keene's deputy fire chief. The chemical is not toxic but it can irritate skin and the respiratory system, he said.

The fire department was called to the Congress Street building at 6:30 a.m. and its hazardous materials team was put on alert.

After almost an hour researching the chemical, Markem officials determined they had personnel certified to clean up the spill, the workers isolated the area and handled the spill appropriately, Stalker said.

Stalker said the cause of the spill is under investigation.

––––––––

Susan Reed became the first full time secretary for the Keene Fire Department. Photo by: Dave Symonds.

[*Compiler's Note*: When Chief Pepler became chief, secretary Hellen Hope was shared by DPW and the Keene Fire Department. Soon, more became required by the fire department secretary and Susan Reed was hired. She later became the first full-time secretary. Prior to secretaries, the Deputy Chiefs completed the required duties.]

———————

As Reported by the *Keene Evening Sentinel* March 30th, 1998:

"FIRE"

Pre-dawn blaze guts Keene house

A loud ruckus from their house across the street woke Marilyn Braley of Keene just after 4:30 a.m. Sunday.

"Somebody was blowing on the horn and pounding on the house hollering," she said.

When she looked out her window, she saw flames eating the yellow clapboard home with the black shutters at 83 Rule St. where her neighbor, Norris Cashman lived alone. He was away in Atlantic City, N.J. for the weekend, and a man on his way to work had

seen the fire and stopped, not knowing if anyone was still inside.

He said it was so hot he couldn't get close enough to break the window," Braley said this morning.

Nobody was injured in the fire but Clayton R. Stalker, Keene deputy fire chief said it caused at least $100,000 in damage.

Investigators say they don't know what started the fire, which gutted the top story, shattered windows and made the roof cave in.

"It makes finding the exact point of origin very difficult when there's that much damage. Stalker said. At this point, arson isn't suspected, but has not been ruled out, he said.

The fire apparently started in the rear of the house, near the patio. Firefighters had to contend with "drop fire"—burning chunks falling from upper levels that can ignite new fires. They focused their efforts on saving what they could, had the fire mostly out within a half-hour, and stayed for more than four hours, Stalker said.

By this morning, the upper story windows were already boarded up and boards bearing the words, "Danger" and "Keep out" covered holes in the outer walls. Yellow police tape surrounded the house. On the front lawn were a blackened mattress and box spring, a television set and a plastic laundry basked full of ashes.

Neighbor Gerald C. Carey said he turned on his police scanner when he heard sirens, then looked out the window at a series of flashing lights and smoke. It wads still dark out, but warm, and he went to watch from Braley's driveway.

"There were flames at least 30 feet high," he said. "It was really bad because I know the devastation Cashman is going through."

Keene fire caused by faulty refrigerator

A compressor motor in a 24-year-old refrigerator let to a fire that gutted a house in Keene early Sunday morning.

Keene fire officials made that determination this morning, in conjunction with Keene police and the N.H. Fire Marshal's Office.

The fire started in the lower back of the refrigerator at the home at 83 Rule St, it spread to a paneled wall. No one was hurt in the fire which fire officials said caused $100,000 in damage to the home.

The man who lives in the house, Norris Cashman, was away in Atlantic City, N.J., when the fire hit.

———————

As Reported by the *Keene Evening Sentinel* April 20th, 1998:

"STORY"

Keene hero to be honored

A Keene man is being hailed as a hero for rescuing a child from a burning house last year.

Eric Koski, of Maple Avenue will be among the honorees Tuesday at the 1998 Hero Awards Dinner in Manchester. The event is sponsored by The Union Leader N.H. Sunday News.

The award comes nearly a year to the day after Koski and a Vermont man charged into the home of Richard and Kate Corliss at 878 Marlboro Road—Route 101—and rescued their foster son from his bedroom as fire raged in the attached garage.

It was about 10:45 p.m. on May 1 as fire burned through the two-car garage, Koski and Hans Schule noticed smoke as they passed by the house. Kate Corliss and her 2-year-old daughter managed to escape as the fire began, but smoke and heat kept Corliss from returning in the house for the foster child. Richard Corliss was away from the house at the time. Koski and Schule entered the house, found the boy in a rear bedroom and brought him to safety.

Thanks to Koski and Schule—and firefighters who managed to save the house and the family's pet collie—a potential disaster was limited to a burned garage.

———————

As Reported by the *Keene Evening Sentinel* May 20th, 1998:

"STORY"

Ambulance proposal causes concern for councilors

A proposal to upgrade emergency workers' training plunged Keene city councilors into a philosophical debate Tuesday, as they worried about the impact it might have on an established private ambulance service.

Chief William H. Pepler Jr. of the Keene Fire Department wants $172,500 over the next two years to upgrade 13 emergency medical technicians to paramedics.

"Most metro units have paramedics on staff. What we're trying to do is trying to bring that standard of care to the city," Pepler said during a council committee discussion of the city government's 1998-99 budget proposal.

Councilors' worries were twofold: They worried about spending the money when such service is already provided by DiLuzio Ambulance Service; but they also worried about the effect on that business.

"We're not copying," Pepler said. "We want direct control. I want to know them and have control to ensure quality service.

"Why should the city be competing with private enterprises?" Councilor Angelo D. DiBernardo asked Pepler.

"We're not competing," Pepler responded.

"The city should interfere with private enterprises only in a time of need." Councilor Joseph W. Bendzinski said.

Councilors wanted to know if Keene really needs more paramedics.

Councilor Nancy M. Wilkinson asked Pepler if he had any statistics that showed how many times having a paramedic would have helped prevent or lessen a serious injury. Pepler said he didn't have figures.

Councilor Michael E.J. Blastos was concerned with the bottom line, but City Manager John A. MacLean said the city would bill for the added level of service: the extra money from the billing would pay for the training over three years.

West Keene fire station: It's not yet officially in the budget proposal, but Pepler wants councilors to add money to staff a full-time fire station in West Keene.

He estimated it will cost $168,838 to convert the National Guard Armory on Hastings Avenue, up $100,000 from this year's estimated cost of running the part-time station.

The bottom line is response time, Pepler said. If the West Keene fire station reduces response time to an emergency, then Keene should staff it full-time, he said.

On the average, fire department personnel get to an emergency in West Keene 3 1/2 minutes faster from the West Keene spot than from the fire station downtown.

Downtown tidbits: Councilors also discussed whether the city government should continue holding on to the bus station on Gilbo Avenue. The city takes in $10,000 in rent a year from center tenants, but it spends $22,000 per year.

Mayor Patricia T. Russell said having public bathrooms downtown was worth the cost.

As Reported by the *Keene Evening Sentinel* May 29th, 1998:

"STORY"

A part-time fire station Branch in West Keene may not go to full-time

The West Keene branch of the Keene Fire Department is open only a few hours a day, but since it opened in October it's already helped save property and perhaps a life, says the city's fire chief.

To William H. Pepler Jr.'s disappointment, however, the substation probably won't be expanded.

The Keene City Council's finance committee recommended Thursday against operating the station full-time.

Since October, the fire department has operated a part-time substation at the National Guard armory on Hastings Avenue. The station operated weekdays, from 3 to 6 p.m., when traffic is at its peak and it's difficult for ambulances and fire trucks to move quickly throughout the city.

Pepler told the committee the West Keene arrangement works well, and he'd like to expand it.

Pepler said that, because of the West Keene assignment, his crews were able to save two buildings that were on fire and to revive a resident whose heart had stopped.

Keene is spending $106,000 this year to operate the West Keene station three hours a day.

It would cost an additional $168,838 to keep it open around the clock. No new equipment would be needed, but four more employees would be.

For decades, fire officials have wanted a station in West Keene. Hundreds of houses have been built in that part of the city in the last 35 years, and it can take ages—in emergency response time—for firefighters and ambulance crews to get from the downtown fire station to that part of the city.

It takes only about four-minutes before a person whose heart stops suffers permanent brain damage, Pepler told the committee; it can take 13 minutes to get to some parts of West Keene from downtown when traffic is heaviest.

On average, it takes firefighters 7 ½ minutes to get to West Keene from downtown, Pepler said. The substation cuts 3 ½ minutes off that response time.

But councilors said Thursday they wanted more information—and a closer look at the future of the current fire station—before spending extra money on the substation.

A study committee has recommended replacing Keene's 110-year-old fire station and 100-year0old police station with a $4 million headquarters, housing both police and fire operations. Long-range city plans call for designing the building in 2000 and starting construction in 2001.

"We're jumping the gun with this until we know about the joint facility." Councilor William A. Beauregard said of Pepler's West Keene request. And time is short, since the 1998-99 city budget will be adopted next month.

Some councilors blanched at doubling the budget for the West Keene station. The $168,838 increase would bump the city government's share of the property tax rate from $10.16 per $1,000 of assessed value to $10.34, according to an analysis of the upcoming budget. But that would still be less than the 1997 tax rate, $10.78.

Councilor Randy L. Filault pushed to open the West Keene station full-time. He said he has gone on several calls with emergency crews, including one in which a person's heart had stopped. The person died and Filault wondered if that life would have been saved if rescue workers had gotten there sooner.

Pepler said the extra personnel would be helpful, even if the West Keene station were to close someday. He said emergency calls have increased from 381 in 1971 to 3,384 in 1997, while the number of emergency personnel in duty has dropped from 11 in 1971 to eight in 1997, Pepler said the extra employees would spread the workload.

Mayor Patricia A. Russell and several councilors were concerned about expanding the West Keene operation without holding a public hearing.

Although there have been few complaints from neighbors since the West Keene station opened, making it full-time could raise concerns about noise and traffic.

Pepler and Cynthia C. Georgina, who chairs the finance committee, said residents have been circulating a petition in favor of the full-time West Keene station.

In the end, the finance committee gave itself six months to reach conclusions about emergency services in West Keene. The discussion will include a location for the new police-fire headquarters, and public hearings are likely.

But Filault said he's not giving up the fight. Before the council adopts the 1998-99 budget, Filault plans to ask that at least half of Pepler's $168,838 request be added to the package.

———

As Reported by the *Keene Evening Sentinel* June 3rd, 1998:

"STORY"

It was only a drill

The bleachers had collapsed at Keene's Alumni Field, the report said, and disaster teams from Keene, Marlborough, Troy and Brattleboro converged Tuesday to help the victims. In truth, it was a drill to test the readiness of fire and ambulance crews to deal with a major disaster. Above, Capt. Steve Goldsmith of the Keene Fire Department is tugged at by a "distraught mother," played by Pam Lepkowski of the Keene Police Department. At right, firefighter Michael Gianferrari of Keene checks on injured "victim."

As Reported by the *Keene Evening Sentinel* June 4th, 1998:

"STORY"

Fire station may expand Councilors reconsider plan for West Keene operation

Back from the dead—for the time being, anyway—is the idea of a full-time West Keene fire substation.

Last week, city councilors all but killed off the idea, saying its cost—an extra $168,838 a year—was not justified by the evidence.

But now, Ward 2 Councilor Randy L. Filault says eight of the 15 councilors are lined up to approve the project.

"I feel this will go through on (budget) adoption night," Filault said. The council will enact a city budget June 18.

A fight is still likely, though. At-large Councilor Michael E.J. Blastos and Ward 1 Councilor William A. Beauregard say the fire station proposal didn't get the review normally given to such ideas, and many questions about the project still lack answers.

Keene Fire Chief William H. Pepler persuaded the council last year to put an ambulance and fire truck in West Keene three hours a day—from 3 to 6 p.m. weekdays, when traffic is heaviest. That's when it takes the longest for emergency vehicles to reach West Keene from the city's only fire station, a block off Central Square.

The substation opened in October in the National Guard armory on Hastings Avenue, and Pepler said it's proved its worth. Hew asked for money to make it a full-time operation in the fiscal year that begins July 1.

But the council's finance committee thought Pepler was premature, that the facts didn't justify the costs.

Pepler said the West Keene substation shaves three to four minutes off the arrival time for an ambulance and fire truck, and minutes are crucial to save people stricken with heart attacks and other afflictions.

The 168,838 would pay four new firefighters and cover minor modifications at the armory.

"This is really a no-brainer," Filault said. "Every six to eight weeks I alternate between riding with the fire department and police. You immediately see the need.

"You can't decide on this based on black and white—can't get a feel in an air-conditioned room. You get a sense of the importance of three or four minutes. Any councilor would have to agree, if they went."

But, why did Filault go along with the committee's recommendation to study the substation for up to six more months? Pragmatism, Filault said. Rather than risk have the substation voted down, he voted for the wait-and-see option.,

Now, he said, he feels comfortable with taking the $1689,838 proposal to the council later this month.

Similarly, committee member Cynthia C. Georgina, an at-large councilor, said she, too, voted for more study because she didn't want the substation voted down. She said she will side with Filault when the budget comes up for a vote.

Two West Keene councilors—Joseph W. Bendzinski of Ward 5 and Philip M. Jones of Ward 4—said they favor the full-time substation. Bendzinski, generally a hold-the-line guy on spending, said West Keene needs it.

Filault said At-large Councilors Mitchell Greenwald and Dale E. Thompson favor the substation, and so-do- Karen R. Fitzpatrick of Ward 3, Dana A. Edwards of Ward 4 and Christopher C. Coates of Ward 2.

Filault said a dozen people have called him, urging approval of the full-time substation and members of the Meadow View Knolls condominium association in West Keene are circulating a petition, asking that the part-time substation stay in operation until a real West Keene fire station can be built.

The substation still faces sharp questions from councilors who say its worth remains unclear.

"No one has done an in-depth study," Blastos said. He, Beauregard and Ward 5 Councilor Peter D. Bradshaw say not enough is known about the project.

Blastos wants to know if the $106,000 in overtime now budgeted for the part-time substation is in addition to the $168,838 for the full-time substation. He has heard that staffing the station full-time would cost $178,000 a year. If that's the case, he said, he would probably support the full-time station.

He doesn't like having the substation in the armory, smack in the middle of a residential area.

"I hate to spend big bucks at that location," Blastos said.

As for the procedural issues, the chief chose the wrong path, Blastos said. Had the proposal been raised months ago, it would have gone through extensive reviews by council committees, Blastos said, and the remaining questions would already have answers. Instead, he said, it came up late, as part of the budget proposal.

Beauregard agreed, saying $168,838 is serious money and decisions shouldn't be made lightly or too quickly.

"We didn't drop the ball," replied City Manager John A. MacLean. Councilors have known about the West Keene proposal for six months, he said.

And there may be other irons in the fire, Beauregard said. For instance, a study committee is due to report later this month on the idea of a new headquarters housing both fire and police operations. If it's proposed for a West Keene location, why put money into the armory?

And, if the four extra firefighters aren't needed once the new joint headquarters is build, what happens to them," Beauregard asked. It wouldn't be fair to let them go, he said.

So far, all the substation information has come from the fire department, Beauregard said. Now, the city manager needs to compare Keene's setup with those in other cities and analyze the need for better and faster service.

That's what Keene did with its landfill, sewer plant, and other big projects. "All of these have been analyzed discussed and debated," Beauregard said.

Beauregard and Blastos said they won't support Filault's push to add the $168,838 to the budget. Bradshaw said he is still undecided;' he still has many questions.

"I wish we had brought it up sooner," Bradshaw said.

————

As Reported by the *Keene Evening Sentinel* June 9th, 1998:

"ACCIDENT"

Sadness in the street
Keene boy, 10, dies after being hit by car

A 10-year-old boy was killed when he ran into traffic on Court Street in Keene Monday afternoon.

Mark A. Tellier of 183 Armory St., Keene, was a 4th-grade student at Fuller School on Elm Street in Keene. His teachers and classmates are grieving today.

"He was very much loved by his family, friends and the staff here," said Fuller School Principal Joseph M. Cunningham. "He'll really be missed."

Mark died when he was hit by two cars on Court Street near the Westview Street intersection, Keene police said. The accident occurred at 4:30 p.m. about 50 yards from Cheshire Medical Center.

Mark was pronounced dead at the accident by Dr. Barry Stern, Cheshire County Medical Examiner.

Witnesses told police the boy had run into the busy roadway while playing with friends.

There, a northbound car driven by Pauline Roby Howard, 73, of Turners Falls, Mass. struck the boy, throwing him into the southbound lane, where he was struck by a car driven by Earl Thomas Larrabee, 88, of Keene.

No charges have been filed against either driver, police said. It took rescue workers more than an hour to free the boy's body from beneath one of the cars.

Cunningham, the Fuller principal, said this morning he was still in shock. He heard about the tragedy from a friend who witnessed the accident and called him on her cellular phone.

Cunningham and other school officials spent Monday evening calling teachers and staff members who work in the school, which is for students in kindergarten through grade 5. The staff members then called the parents of all 72 4th-graders at Fuller, to tell them personally of Mark's death.

Cunningham said Mark was well-known and well-liked, in and out of school. Mark was a member of the Pirates baseball team in the Keene Bambino Junior League, was on the Keene Dolphins swim team, and enjoyed skiing with his family.,

"This has touched every classroom in the school," Cunningham said." In one way or another, he touched every class. This will be going on for several days."

Counselors from all over the Keene School District are at Fuller School today, speaking with entire classrooms and with individual students, to help the youngsters deal with their grief, Cunningham said.

Students in 4th grade are very impressionable, said Burt G. Hollenbeck Jr., a Keene psychologist. They are just starting to understand the permanency and impact of death, he said, and they are looking to adults for ways to respond.

It's important not to stifle any expression of grief, Hollenbeck said. Children should be allowed to ask questions and talk about the accident and the loss.

"It's important to give them permission for a range of feelings," Hollenbeck said.

Fuller School has had its share of grief. Sunday was the one-year anniversary of the death of another well-known Fuller School student, Matthew Swett, who died of leukemia last June 7. Matt was 11.

The shock at Mark's death took hold immediately Monday. At the accident, dozens of neighbors and other onlookers stood nearby. They were silent, some with their hands over their mouths, others with their heads bowed.

One woman, who saw the accident, was shaking and crying.

"I've never seen anything like it before," another witness said as she was led off by police.

A child's shoe lay several feet in front of the first car that struck the boy.

Rescue workers did whatever they could to help out. They consoled drivers, witnesses and each other. It took police several hours to locate Mark's parents, Kevin and Claudette Tellier.

Emergency workers draped a large white sheet and a blue tarpaulin over the hood of the southbound car to shield the body's body from view. They surrounded the area with yellow crime-scene tape, and ordered people away.

"There are going to be things they think they can handle, but they really don't want to see," Keene Fire Chief William H. Pepler Jr. said.

Car accidents involving pedestrians are fairly common in Keene, but it's rarely as serious at this," Pepler said.

Although it carries a lot of traffic, that section of Court Street isn't usually a trouble spot for accidents, Pepler said. Yet, three people have died there in less than six months. Just a block from Monday's accident, two men were killed in January in a head-on collision near Court and Elm streets.

Court Street was blocked off to traffic for more than two hours Monday evening.

————

As Reported by the *Keene Evening Sentinel* June 17th, 1998:

"STORY"

Keene boosts budget Fire station, paramedics, nonprofits win

The alarm goes off. Doors fly open. The fire truck screams out of the fire station off Keene's Central Square; in four to seven minutes, firefighters will be in West Keene.

Too long, some say.

That will change September 1, when the city government expects to have firefighters stationed full-time at the National Guard armory on Hastings Avenue. It's now a three-hour-a-day substation.

Six weeks of lobbying by West Keene residents won the day Tuesday, when the Keene City Council added $168,838 to the 1998-99 budget to pay for the fire-station upgrade. A council committee had recommended delaying the move.

Councilors also approved a $33.3 million budget for the fiscal year that begins July 1, and made winners out of most groups that asked for money. Councilors restored cuts in aid to no0nprofit groups, an annual bone of contention.

But the fire station vote was more emotional.

"I'm delighted. I feel it's needed because this area is growing so fast," said West Keene resident Roger U. Day, who circulated a petition for a full-time substation. Keeping a fire truck and ambulance on Hastings Avenue full-time will save lives, because emergency workers can serve the neighborhood far more quickly than firefighters at the downtown station.

Councilor William A. Beauregard proposed the substation remain part-time for six more months, while the pros and cons of a full-time substation got more study. Councilors Angelo D. DiBernardo and Nancy M. Wilkinson voted against adding the money.

Councilor Randy Filault said the council had plenty of information and time about the substation. The issue wasn't money, but saving lives by reducing response time in an emergency, he said.

The $168,838 will add $21 to the property-tax bill for a $100,000 house. Overall, though, the budget adopted Tuesday night will need less money than last year from property taxes. The city government's share of the tax rate is expected to drop 44 cents, to $10.34 per $1,000 of assessed value. School and county taxes come on top of that.

DiBernardo, Wilkinson, Dale E. Thompson and Joseph W. Bendzinski voted against the $33,373,750 budget, which was $184,337 more than City Manager John A. MacLean had proposed.

DiBernardo said the budget process was fair, but he wanted more discussion about spending.

Paramedic training: Councilors approved $172,500 to train 13 firefighters to be paramedics, although they also said they want to work with a private ambulance service.

Keene Fire Chief William H. Pepler Jr. wants trained paramedics on his ambulance staff—now, emergency-medical technicians run the ambulances—but needed the $172,500 for training between now and December 1999.

DiLuzio Ambulance Service of Keene already has trained paramedics on its staff, and some councilors were concerned about competition, and duplication of services. Robert J. DiLuzio, who owns the service, had offered to have one of his paramedics standing by who could be sent to accidents and other serious medical emergencies for a $50 fee.

Paramedics can handle much more complex medical treatment than EMT's

DiLuzio said his offer would avoid the upfront training cost of $172,500, and Pepler could phase in paramedics as he replaced EMT's who resigned or took different assignments.

"We thought we would save taxpayers a few dollars," DiLuzio said.

Wilkinson wanted the council to study DiLuzio's proposal and delay approving the $172,500.

In the end, councilors voted to do both.

————

As Reported by the *Keene Evening Sentinel* June 22nd, 1998:

"STORY"

Red light special
Towns spurn city ambulance

Saying they got a better deal, Swanzey officials say they'll contract with a private ambulance service after month's end instead of re-signing with the city of Keene's ambulance.

Starting in July, a private competitor will take some business away from the city. DiLuzio Ambulance Service of Keene is working on contracts to provide emergency ambulance services for the towns of Swanzey and Roxbury.

Robert A. Beauregard, a Swanzey selectman, said the town is currently negotiating with owner Robert J. DiLuzio for services. The town's three-year contract with Keene ambulance expires June 30.

Beauregard said there aren't any complaints about Keene's ambulance service; DiLuzio offered more options at a better price, he said. Roxbury officials were unavailable for comment this morning.

Keene's ambulance service handles calls in Chesterfield, Keene, Nelson, Roxbury, Spofford, Sullivan and Swanzey. All the contracts are for three years and expire June 30.

Keene Fire Chief William H. Pepler Jr. said it's too early to say how his department will be affected by the switch.

Pepler expects most of the towns to stick with the city's service, but the contracts haven't been signed yet.

Swanzey accounts for 14 percent of all ambulance calls the city ambulance makes, Pepler said.

DiLuzio was started in 1951 and provided emergency care until 1977, when the Keene ambulance took over. Now, the private company does all the non-emergency business for the city and provides backup emergency service to Keene and other area ambulances.

DiLuzio said he is ready for the increased business. He has hired extra employees and recently bought a fourth ambulance—and he's submitted proposals for service to other towns, too.

Beauregard said there are several reasons selectmen want to switch to DiLuzio. A big plus, he said, was training offered.

Three of DiLuzio's paramedics are also certified instructors and will offer Swanzey firefighters free training. DiLuzio also promised to bring the company's paramedics,

and its full-time nurse, into the community for blood-pressure tests and free education.

But Pepler said his proposal was less expensive than the current contract and also included training for firefighters.

"I think we matched what (selectmen) were looking for," Pepler said.

Another appealing part about DiLuzio's is the stable fee structure, selectmen said.

Keene's flat fee for service, about $22,000 a year, is similar to what DiLuzio charges. Beauregard said. But towns using the Keene ambulance also have to settle bills their town residents can't pay. Those yearly bills can be as much as $10,000. In 1997, a total of about $34,000 of Swanzey's budget went toward ambulance service.

DiLuzio charges a flat rate and doesn't hold the town responsible for any payments. He said his company has a private billing and collection agency and handles all unpaid bills.

"That's a big plus for a lot of people," DiLuzio said this morning.

DiLuzio also has trained paramedics on its staff. Paramedics have the highest level of training offered, and DiLuzio said five of his employees have two years of college medical training.

Now emergency-medical technicians run the ambulances in Keene, but that will also change in time. The Keene City Council recently approved spending $172,500 to train 13 Keene firefighters to be paramedics. The council also approved opening a second full-time fire station in West Keene and hiring four new emergency workers to staff it.

Pepler said Keene's ambulance service has lots more to offer. City ambulances go to calls with three attendants, compared to the two that go on DiLuzio's emergency calls. Keene personnel are also trained in firefighting, rescue, extrication and hazardous materials, not just medical care.

Beauregard said selectmen aren't worried about decreasing the quality of care.

He thinks DiLuzio provides similar service and has a good backup system. DiLuzio and the city have an agreement that if one is busy and needs help, the other will assist.

————

As Reported by the *Keene Evening Sentinel* June 24th, 1998:

"STORY"

Fire, police under 1 roof? Keene committee proposes one big station for both

Keene's police and fire stations need to be retired from service, a committee says, and it proposes building a new, combined facility in West Keene.

The 1 1/2 –year-old Emergency Services Facilities Committee formed to study whether the fire and police departments needed new stations, and if yes, where.

The nine-member committee unanimously agreed that a joint station would be cheapest, costing between $8 million and $7 million. It also recommended that it be build on city-owned land, to save money.

The only spot suitable for that, the committee said, is at 521 Park Ave., near Monadnock View Cemetery in West Keene.

City Manager John A. MacLean cautioned that the report is only a departure point for more discussion. Nothing has been decided about a location or even a joint station. For example, the fire department might have a building built for it first and then a police station added later, he said.

A big question that will remain is what to do with the recently upgraded fire substation on Hastings Avenue, just down the road from where the proposed new station would go. Councilors approved spending $232,000 to convert the former National Guard Armory to a full-time station.

The existing fire and police stations won't go away; the committee suggested converting most of the police station on Washington Street for city government use, while maintaining a small "storefront" police presence.

Committee members suggest using the fire station on Vernon Street as a substation, with remaining space used as a museum or public meeting rooms.

There just isn't enough land to build the proposed combined building downtown, the committee said. The former railroad land off Main Street doesn't have enough access to main roads; other land is privately owned and would be too expensive to buy, the committee said.

The Center at Keene land was deemed excellent, as was the Granite Bank or CFX Bank branches on West Street, but the committee said their cost ruled them out.

In the end, the cost of suitable land and the inability to find that ideal 4 to 5 acre plot downtown led to the West Keene proposal.

Committee member and City Councilor Michael E. J. Blastos said the most important issue is where any building will go. Blastos has his own ideas: He'd like to use the land behind the city's public works garage on Lower Main Street, and build an access road to Route 101. Council committees will be looking at locations for the joint station this week.

Although Blastos voted in favor of the report, he questions why fire and police have to share one station. Taken separately, Blastos said city government might be able to find a big enough chunk of land for one or the other.

"I would really have to be convinced that his is good," Blastos said.

Fire Chief William H. Pepler Jr., Police Chief Thomas F. Powers 3rd and Parks and Recreation Director Brian A. Mattson were on the committee, along with Vernon L. Baisden, who was the chairman, Roger U. Day, Alan LaFleur, Joyce B. Lehman, Blastos and Virginia Vidaver.

The committee toured joint fire and police stations in White River Junction, Vt., Hanover, Lebanon and Hudson, giving it the idea to include community rooms.

Pepler said firefighters and police officers have a "good-natured" rivalry, but they also work closely together—and well. "I don't see that as a negative," he said.

————

As Reported by the *Keene Evening Sentinel*:

More towns mull ambulance switch Westmoreland, Chesterfield thinking

Seeing an opening to expand his ambulance business in the region, Robert J. DiLuzio has been pitching his private—and he says better trained—service to Cheshire County towns that now contract with the city of Keene.

DiLuzio Ambulance Service of Keene has taken a bite out of Keene's municipal ambulance service's customer base: the towns of Swanzey and Roxbury have already switched to the private medical emergency carrier, and Westmoreland and Chesterfield are considering it.

"DiLuzio's been up and talked to us. There are good points to both proposals," said Linn J. Starkey Jr., a Westmoreland selectman. "Now we are going to check with Keene to see what is best for the town."

Keene has yet to submit a contract to Westmoreland selectmen, but Starkey said Keene's advantage is that it keeps a full-time ambulance in Westmoreland. Keene officials are meeting with Westmoreland selectman today.

Keene's ambulance service handles calls in Chesterfield, Keene, Nelson, Roxbury, Spofford, Westmoreland, Sullivan and Swanzey. All the contracts are for three years and expire June 30.

Like Swanzey Selectman Robert Beauregard, Starkey said DiLuzio's big plus is that it offers a flat rate and doesn't hold the town responsible for any delinquent payments.

DiLuzio said his company has a private billing and collection agency and handles all unpaid bills. That would save Westmoreland $2,000 a year, Starkey said.

Keene's ambulance service holds the towns' responsible for their residents' unpaid bills. That cost Swanzey $10,000 last year in addition to its $24,000 Keene bill.

Keene Fire Chief William H. Pepler Jr. said it's too early to say how his department will be affected by the switches, though Swanzey accounted for 14 percent of its business last year. Keene City Manager John A. MacLean said city staff will be looking into it.

Roxbury paid Keene $543 for ambulance service in 1997, Westmoreland $6,360, Chesterfield $13,200—which includes payments to Rescue Inc. in Brattleboro—and Swanzey about $24,000.

Pepler expects most of the towns to stick with the city's service, but the contracts haven't been signed yet. Nelson Selectman Michael W. French said his town is sticking with Keene. And Pepler said Sullivan will also continue with Keene.

Pepler said he didn't know if this was the first time DiLuzio had solicited business from nearby towns that contracted with the city. DiLuzio was unavailable for comment this morning.

Asked if this would hurt the working relationship between DiLuzio and the fire department, Pepler said he's making an effort to ensure it doesn't, and hopes to keep a close working relationship with DiLuzio.

DiLuzio and the city have an agreement that if one service is busy and needs help, the other will assist.

DiLuzio's service started in 1951 and provided emergency care until 1977, when the Keene municipal ambulance took over.

Now, the private company does all the non-emergency business for the city and provides backup emergency service to Keene and other area ambulances.

DiLuzio said he is ready for the increased business. He has hired extra employees and recently bought a fourth ambulance, hired paramedics—they have the highest level of emergency medical training—and offered paramedic service to Keene. Earlier this month, city councilors welcomed DiLuzio's paramedic service.

DiLuzio Ambulance Service has a paramedic in each ambulance. In July it will start a less expensive intercept service in which paramedics will respond to medical emergencies in a car and won't transport patients.

DiLuzio offered to contract with the city of Keene for $50 per patient, which would be collected by DiLuzio. MacLean is considering that proposal, though he has yet to meet with DiLuzio. MacLean said he couldn't comment on how DiLuzio's contracts with Swanzey and other towns would effect negotiations with city government.

Currently Keene and nearby towns do not have paramedic services. Paramedics are better trained and are allowed to perform more complicated lifesaving medical techniques than emergency medical technicians.

DiLuzio said this could save city government from training 13 firefighters to be paramedics, having $172,500. Instead the city could hire firefighters with paramedic training as attrition allows, he said.

"We thought we would save taxpayers a few dollars. We already have the service," DiLuzio said. "We are just offering the service at $50 a use fee without the city going into a training program."

But Pepler still says the Keene Fire Department needs to have paramedics on its staff. He requested $172,500 over the next two years to train 13 emergency medical technicians to be paramedics. The paramedic training wo0uld be completed in December 1999, Pepler said.

However, MacLean said if paramedic firefighters are hired, some of the $172,500 for training could be saved.

Councilors voted to include the $172,500 in the 1998-99 budget, but also said city government should look at contracting with DiLuzio until 1999 so the city would have paramedic service while the firefighters were being trained.

————

As Reported by the *Keene Evening Sentinel* June 27th, 1998:

"FIRE"

Five injured in Keene house fire

Photo by Jill Gnade.

Careless smoking sparked a three-alarm house fire on Court Street in Keene Sunday morning in which three firefighters and two residents were slightly injured.

Keene firefighters were called to 195-197 Court St. shortly after 6 a.m. and found a large fire on the first floor of the 2 ½ story duplex. After the fire was upgraded to three alarms, firefighters from four other departments—Marlborough, Swanzey Center, West Swanzey and Meadowood County—were helping out.

Because of heavy smoke, the first firefighters didn't know if the building was empty and they split their efforts between controlling the fire and searching for anyone who might be inside.

A second crew went into the building from the back and other firefighters pulled down ceilings and opened walls, checking to see if the fire was spreading and dousing pockets of flames.

The fire was declared under control around 7:40 a.m., but crews stayed for another two hours, putting out hot spots and checking the area.

Keene firefighter Ronald Dunn received minor injuries when he fell into an open stairwell. He was treated at Cheshire Medical Center in Keene and released. Firefighters Michael Driscoll and William Greenwood were treated at the scene for minor injuries.

Kevin D. Konsella, 24, and Jonathan J. Gorman, 23, of 197 Court St. escaped with minor injuries that were treated at the scene; two other residents, David Meyers and Jason Alexander, who lived there were not home at the time. The other half of the duplex was unoccupied. The residents, who lost all of their possessions in the fire, stayed with friends Sunday night.

The house is owned by Steve and Peter Walsh of Keene.

Damage is estimated at $80,000. The 197 side of the building was gutted; 195 Court St sustained extensive smoke damage and there was substantial damage to the back of the building.

Officials ruled the fire accidental, caused by smoking materials left near a living room couch. Smoke detectors apparently didn't work, officials said.

Peter Walsh said this morning that the smoke detectors in the house were hard-wired and not battery-powered, and he does not know why the alarms did not go off.

————

As Reported by the *Keene Evening Sentinel* July 30th, 1998:

"FIRE"

Fire disrupts work day

An electrical fire Wednesday at Peerless Insurance Co. on Maple Avenue in Keene forced the company to evacuate employees from the building. Above, Keene firemen haul lights and fans into the building.

————

As Reported by the *Keene Evening Sentinel* September 3rd, 1998:

"STORY"

West Keene's fire station now a full-time setup

Keene opened a satellite fire station full-time Wednesday morning.

Housed in the National Guard Armory on Hastings Avenue, the substation complements Keene's main fire station on Vernon Street and will end a time lag in getting fire trucks and ambulances into heavily populated West Keene, Fire Chief William H. Pepler Jr. said.

The substation cuts rush-hour arrival at a West Keene emergency from eight minutes to three, Pepler said, and that will save lives.

One fire truck, one ambulance and three firefighters will be at the substation at all times.

A trial run for the substation began last year. It was open week in West Keene occurred before 3 p.m.

Still, housing development in the past 30 years, plus the growth of Black Brook Corporate Park, have added to the need for a second Keene fire station, Pepler said.

The Keene City Council approved $168,000 in June to add four full-time firefighters to the city force, enough to staff the substation. Several councilors thought more studies were needed before the city committed to a full-time West Keene station.

———

As Reported by the *Keene Evening Sentinel* September 11th, 1998:

"STORY"

Plaque reported stolen from fire station

A $5 plaque has been reported stolen from the Keene fire station on Vernon Street, and Keene police are investigating.

The plaque was apparently left behind several years ago, when a firefighter left the department, said Fire Chief William H. Pepler Jr. Another firefighter took it when he left, and was believed authorized to do so, Pepler said. Now, a third firefighter has reported it stolen.

Pepler would not discuss the significance of the plaque—why it might be the source of disagreement among firefighters, or why someone would report it missing.

"We know where it is; we know who has it," he said. "The person who has it feels he has it legitimately, and was authorized to take it."

He said he was surprised to hear about the report—which he learned of two weeks ago, though it just appeared in the Keene police log this week.

"My reaction was either someone doesn't understand the whole story or maybe I didn't," he said.

Pepler declined further comment.

———

As Reported by the *Keene Evening Sentinel* October 26th, 1998:

"FIRE"

Two-alarm fire guts Keene barn

As fire gutted a barn in Keene early Sunday, but firefighters were able to control the blaze before it could reach a nearby house and garage.

The two-alarm fire gutted a 2 ½ story barn at Court and North streets, owned by Gary and Susan Murata.

By the time firefighters arrived at about 3 a.m., the building was engulfed in flames. The barn and a motorcycle inside it were destroyed; a vehicle parked in front of the building was damaged.

A house and a garage about 15 feet away sustained minor heat damage, including cracked windows. Fire officials don't know how the fire started, but said it didn't appear suspicious.

Keene firefighters also doused two smaller fires this weekend.

South Street blaze under investigation

Police say a juvenile is to blame for a two-alarm fire that destroyed a garage behind a Keene house Friday. But they haven't yet labeled it intentional or an accident.

The detached garage was set back from the house at 23 South St., and though it did not spread to the house, it did generate enough heat to melt some siding, according to Deputy Chief Bradley B. Payne of the Keene Fire Department. Payne said the garage did not have any cars in it and appeared to be used for storage.

The blaze started shortly before 11 a.m. and sent smoke billowing high into the air. But firefighters made quick work of extinguishing the flames and there was no danger that it would spread to neighboring lots or to Wheelock School, which backs up to the property.

Police blocked off the street and part of Marlborough Street for a short time while firefighters put out the flames.

The incident is still under police investigation.

————

As Reported by the *Keene Evening Sentinel* November 18th, 1998:

"FIRE"

Vandals burn cars in Keene

Arson tore through Keene early this morning as six cars, some of them stolen, were set ablaze.

Several other vehicles were vandalized, with slashed tires and other damage.

Police and fire investigators were still investigating the incidents late this morning. While all the incidents appear related, police said they could establish no apparent link among the owners of the damaged vehicles.

One of the fires spread from a car parked at the Westwood Apartments complex on Summit Road to a nearby carport. Firefighters worked to save both the car and structure there.

In all, Keene fire officials said the blazes may have caused $100,000 in damage.

For now, police said, it appears the rampage was just senseless vandalism.

According to Keene police Capt. Barry E. Wante, the today's day shift had to be called in at 5 a.m., and additional investigators were brought in to handle the barrage of calls between 3 and 5 a.m.

The first report came in shortly after 3 a.m. A car that had been stolen was set on fire near Findings Inc. on Water Street. AS few minutes later, another apparently stolen car was set ablaze in the Cheshire Medical Center parking lot on Court Street.

Just after 4 a.m., police were notified of another car fire in a parking lot at the Brookside Apartments on Maple Avenue. That fire damaged two other vehicles parked nearby, according to fire officials.

That fire left a parking place charred where the targeted car was burned. Pieces of melted plastic and metal, along with scraps of car molding and shattered glass lay in the fire's wake.

Then at 4:42 a.m., another car was lit up at the Parkwood Apartments on Park Avenue. Just after 5 a.m., firefighters doused another car at The Pines at Keene on Maple Avenue.

Keene Fire Chief William H. Pepler Jr. said he's never seen multiple calls involving car fires like this before.

"At one point we had units at three separate emergencies," he said.

But firefighters' biggest concern was the blaze at Westwood. Pepler said firefighters battled a carport fire at the same address last year; that blaze burned 17 different vehicles, he said.

"That was just across the alley last year," he said.

Most of the fires were started inside the cars, and then spread to involve the entire vehicle, Pepler said. Most, aside from the Westwood fire, were knocked down in short order, he said.

Pepler said preliminary investigations showed the incidents to all be arson. That makes the investigation a police matter now, he said.

It's pretty obvious all the fires were started by one group or person, Pepler said.

"They started downtown and went up Court Street," he said. "Then to the hospital, Maple Avenue, then Summit Road."

Wante said the car fires are apparently also connected to incidents of slashed tires and broken windows in several cars around town.

A tally of cars damaged but not burned wasn't available this morning.

Police will release more information later today as investigations continue, Wante said.

Tally is now 20 cars

The tally after a 2 ½-hour rampage early Wednesday morning, in which cars were torched and damaged from downtown to West Keene, is staggering.

In all, about 20 cars were burned, vandalized or stolen. Or a combination of the three.

Investigators say they have a few leads, but aren't expecting any arrests soon.

Another car fire in Swanzey may be related to the Keene arsons, police say.

Police and fire investigators combed the path of destruction Wednesday afternoon, discovering that, along with eight burned cars from Court Street to Summit Road, another dozen or so had slashed tires or broken windows or had items such as radios stolen from them.

In West Swanzey, a car owned by a Springfield, Vt., man was also burned up in a field off Christian Hill Road. The car, a 1987 Volkswagen Golf, had been stolen earlier that night from a residence on South Winchester Street in West Swanzey.

The same time Keene's first blaze was reported Wednesday at about 3 a.m. A Volkswagen Jetta, found near the residence from which it had just been stolen, was set on fire near Findings Inc. on Water Street. A few minutes later, another apparently stolen car was set ablaze in the Cheshire Medical Center parking lot on Court Street.

Just after 4 a.m., police were notified of another car fire in a parking lot at Brookside Apartments on Maple Avenue. That fire damaged two other vehicles parked nearby, fire officials said.

Then, at 4:42 a.m., another car was lit up at Parkwood Apartments off Maple Avenue. Just after 5 a.m., firefighters doused another car at The Pines, an apartment complex just to the north on Maple Avenue, at Court Street.

Police are trying to piece together what patter, if any, was used by the arsonists to target the cars. One trend they're looking at is the proximity of some of the fires to apartment buildings.

In all, four complexes were the site of car fires Wednesday: Park Place, Westwood, Brookside and Parkwood. Keene fire officials said managers of those complexes are cooperating to deal with the damage, and working to prevent future fires from happening.

The incidents also brought Robert B. Farley, a state fire investigator, to Keene to work with local po0lice and fire officials. On Wednesday, Farley and other investigators were trying to determine, among other things, whether an accelerant, such as gasoline, was used in any of the blazes.

Farley couldn't be reached for comment this morning.

Because of the seeming randomness of the crimes, police are urging residents to report anything suspicious quickly. Police also advise that car owners lock their vehicles and leave nothing valuable in them.

Two of the cars set ablaze Wednesday still had their keys in the ignitions, making them an easy steal.

Keene police are offering a reward for anyone with useful information on the arson binge. Investigators believe at least two people are responsible for the fires.

Victims wonder, what's happening?

A string of car fires and vandalism has left its victims frightened and wondering what is happening to their community.

About 24 cars, some of them stolen, were burned or vandalized two weeks ago. Most of the vehicles were near downtown or in West Keene. Another car theft and arson in Swanzey at the same time was linked to the Keene incidents.

Police speculate a group of people are committing the crimes, which have now grown to include two deliberately set brush fires in Swanzey Monday night, a stolen Saab burned in Montague, Mass, and possibly a U.S. Post Office box break in Swanzey.

The fires also fit with vandalism that occurred at Monadnock Regional High School earlier this month, when someone threw concrete statues through the school's plate-glass windows and a fire extinguisher through a car windshield.

Earlier this week, Detective Joseph J. Collins said the crimes appear to be random, with the vandals hitting several cars in one apartment complex or one street, such as Summit Road in West Keene. The vandals apparently followed a route from Water Street to Summit Road in West Keene the night of the spree.

But one of the victims, who asked that his name not be used because he fears retribution from the vandals, disagreed. He thinks he was targeted by a gang of out of town teenagers.

"I'm not so sure it was random. It's just funny to have problems with a couple of kids and then they (the vandals) hit us," he said. Gangs are a reality in Keene that the police department is ignoring, the Keene man continued.

"We're fresh pickings," he said of Keene.

"Everybody here is very, very attuned to this," Sgt. Kelvin J. Macie responded. Police still believe the acts of vandalism are random because a number of victims and half-hazard way in which they were committed.

Still, police aren't dismissing any theory.

"Every arrest you make you're asking have you heard anything," he said, but still nothing has turned up.

Collins said he may try and get the insurance companies to put up some reward money to encourage people to come forward.

"The police are doing everything they can," Germaine Y. Lambert said. Her car was one of those vandalized. That attack has left her feeling more insecure.

Perl Dahl, a West Keene victim, went along with Lambert. Yet, he doesn't think much about it, he said, just that it was a bunch of teenagers.

Another victim, Joanne F. Hall, said sadly she feels less safe because of the vandalism. She had to buy a new car because of damage caused by the vandals.

"It's surprising to have something like this happen in Keene," she continued. "It's kind of disillusioning. I wasn't angry, I was just really annoyed."

Despite the vandalism, Hall has managed to find some good. People are looking out for one another more now in her neighborhood.

"It may help bring the community closer together," she said, and hopes a crime watch group can be started.

Victim Beulah S. Dennis isn't going to do anything differently because her car tire was slashed that Wednesday night two weeks ago. The randomness of the crime bothers her, and like the others, it makes her feel more vulnerable to crime.

"It makes you wonder, after they did that," Dennis said of those that committed the crimes.

Police are seeking the public's help in solving these crimes. The Cheshire County Crimestoppers line can be called anonymously at 357-6600.

———

As Reported by the *Keene Evening Sentinel* December 12th, 1998:

"STORY"

West Keene fire station has pollution problem

The full-time fire station in West Keene is having growing pains, including a pollution problem.

The station, which has been operating full-time out of the National Guard Armory on

Hastings Avenue since August, is generating more truck activity and more diesel exhaust in the station than was originally expected.

"That's not a healthy situation," Fire Chief William H. Pepler Jr. told the city council's finance committee Thursday night.

The solution? A system than can pull exhaust directly from a truck's tailpipe and spit it out through a ventilating fan. The system, estimated at about $30,000 would be paid out of the fire department's emergency repair account. That would significantly add to the $15,000 city government was expecting to spend transforming the armory into a fire station.

Councilors had expressed reservations about spending too much money on the armory because of plans to bui8ld a new joint fire and police station which, they said, would likely be located in West Keene.

City Manager John A. MacLean said he and other city staffers have just begun to review the joint fire station. And in an interview last week he said it was too early to say where the station would go. Councilors had hoped the station would go downtown, but that might be too expensive.

Councilors decided at the end of June to open the West Keene station in the armory on Hastings Avenue to cut the time it took to get to emergencies in West Keene. Opening the station full-time cost the city an extra $168,838 on top of what the city already spend on the West Keene station when it was opening part-time last year.

Fire department officials have said they've used the substation more than expected.

Some councilors were concerned about sending the exhaust into the neighborhood, but Pepler said studies show that the systems work at dispersing fumes in the air.

The West Keene station also has fire officials juggling staff so that both that station and the Vernon Street station downtown have supervisors on duty. Union rules allow a supervisor and an acting supervisor to take simultaneous days off.

When that happens—as it did six times in November—the department is left with only one supervisor for two stations and overtime has to be paid to fill the second spot. Pepler wants to eliminate the acting officer slot by promoting four firefighters to lieutenant.

After the West Keene station opened the department hired four new firefighters.

For a total of about $9,000 a year in additional salaries, the department can cut down on overtime, Pepler said. Questions about the amount of overtime involved and union rules led to a closed-door session.

In the end, the committee voted unanimously to recommend the council approve both requests. The council will meet Thursday at 7:30 p.m.

————

As Reported by the *Keene Evening Sentinel* December 14th, 1998:

"FIRE"

KSC dormitory fire caused by cigarette

A misplaced cigarette led to a chilly morning for students in a Keene State College dormitory today.

The cigarette started a fire in a utility-room trash barrel on the third floor of Holloway Hall shortly after midnight. Students were evacuated while the fire was doused; they had to say out of the building for 10 or 15 minutes, Keene Fire Department officials said.

About 250 students live in Holloway Hall. College officials said the students were able to wait inside the dining commons and Carle Hall, another dormitory.

Sprinklers extinguished the fire, but caused minor water damage to a common area. No student rooms were damaged.

When students apply to live in a residence hall, they are asked whether they smoke, college officials said. If they do, they are allowed to smoke in their rooms, but not in any common areas of the dorm.

————

As Reported by the *Keene Evening Sentinel* December 16th, 1998:

"STORY"

2 men face charges in arson wave

For Keene residents, the fear is over.

That fear began November 18, when a string of fires and vandalism destroyed 20 cars in neighborhoods of Keene, and Elm City residents' feelings of security.

For police, there is relief in knowing they've caught two men suspected in the arson wave, and the framework for their prosecution is being laid out.

Steven A. Sullivan, 18, and William W. Lee Jr., 20, both of Winchester, were to be arraigned today in Keene District Court before Judge Richard J. Talbot.

Sullivan is charged with one count of arson. Lee is charged with conspiracy to commit arson.

Both charges are felonies; convictions can bring state prison sentences, Capt. Hal G. Brown, head of the Keene Police Department's investigation division, said more charges may be in the works.

Sullivan was unable to post $10,000 cash bail. Both Sullivan and Lee were held at "randomly committed acts of violence, with no particular pattern, victim or purpose of retribution in mind."

Which is exactly why the streak of arson-related fires, which began with the 3:11 a.m. burning of Court Street resident Christopher Ahern's 1997 Jeep Wrangler last month, was so troubling.

The property destruction , which included vehicles stolen or vandalized in addition to being torched, occurred over a 2 ½-hour period along Court Street and ranging west to Summit Road. Vehicles' tires were slashed and windows broken.

Meanwhile, other area fires, including one in Swanzey, may be related to the charges facing Sullivan and Lee. Cheshire County Attorney Edward J. Burke who will prosecute the case.

Investigators prepared 16 pages of court documents, supporting the issuance of a warrant for Sullivan's arrest.

Sullivan was arrested on the arson charge at a residence in Winchester. Lee was arrested on the conspiracy charge on the evening of December 11 by Keene police detectives, assisted directly by the Winchester Police Department, police said.

But it wasn't the arson charge that netted Sullivan. It was other charges connected with the case, according to police.

A warrant had already been issued for his arrest because he failed to appear in Keene District Court for a hearing in another case. Sullivan also faces charges of illegal conduct after an accident—driving away from a hit-and-run accident in Swanzey on the night of the arsons. He also is charged with two motor vehicle violations.

Lee also faces other charges. He's wanted by police in Northfield, Mass., on a charge of larceny, and Greenfield, Mass. District Court issued a fugitive warrant for him.

The men's arrest caps an investigation by four local police departments, N.H. State Police, and the Montague, Mass. police department.

Brown credited cooperation and assistance from the public and other local and state agencies with developing information that led to Sullivan's and Lee's arrests.

Two Keene arson suspects arraigned

The second of two suspects charged in a wave of car thefts and arsons in Keene last month was to be arraigned today in Keene District Court.

William W. Lee Jr., 20, of Winchester has been charged with conspiracy to commit arson , a felony. His attorney; in addition to the conspiracy charge, Lee faces a charge of being a fugitive from justice. He is wanted by police in Northfield, Mass., on a charge of larceny exceeding $250, and a warrant for Lee's arrest has been issued by Greenfield, Mass District Court.

Steven A. Sullivan, 18, of Winchester was arraigned Wednesday in Keene District Court, facing one charge of arson. Paul G. Schweizer is his attorney.

Sullivan told Judge Richard J. Talbot he was waiving the right to a probable cause hearing, at which the court evaluates the evidence. Instead, his case will be considered directly by a Cheshire County Superior Court grand jury, which will decide whether the prosecution has amassed enough evidence to warrant a trial.

Both Sullivan and Lee are being held at the Cheshire County Jail in Westmoreland.

They are the first people to be charged in the property destruction November 18, in which vehicles were stolen, vandalized and torched on a 2 ½ hour pulling the destructive wave ran along Court Street and ranged west to Summit Road.

In addition, other area fires, including one in Swanzey, may be related to the charges facing Sullivan and Lee.

Cheshire County Attorney Edward J. Burke is prosecuting the case.

Court documents say an 18-year-old woman told Keene police Cpl. Joseph Collins that Sullivan had told her that he had started the car fires in Keene. In all, police filed 16 pages of documents with the court to support an arrest warrant for Sullivan.

1999

As Reported by the *Keene Evening Sentinel* January 8th, 1999:

"FIRE"

Close call at oil depot in Keene

About a dozen Keene firefighters succeed this morning in containing a fire inside a garage where an oil-delivery truck was being filled. The garage is off Swanzey Factory Road. Photo by Steve Hooper.

A fire at an oil-filling depot rocked nearby houses and belched a pillar of black smoke that could be seen for miles this morning, but about a dozen firefighters were able to keep the blaze from reaching the oil tanks.

Jack M. Tenofsky of Keene was about to start filling his oil-delivery truck at the Patnode Oil garage, off Swanzey Factory Road near Route 101 at about 9:30 this morning when a fire broke out near a space heater in the garage, officials said.

The fire spread to the truck engine and throughout the truck, but the 100 gallons of home heating oil in the truck's 2,000-gallon tank didn't ignite.

However, the fire spread throughout the building in which there were a couple of small canisters of oil. Tenofsky, part-owner of the building, called the fire department.

There were three explosions," said a neighbor, Belinda Fennell, who lives on Depot Road, which leads off Swanzey Factory Road. Her home is right below the oil tanks, and "it felt like the house was hit," she said.

Flames reached above the tree line, Fennell said."

Firefighters used metal cutters to get into the tin-sided building.

They were able to keep the fire from reaching the oil-storage tanks adjacent to the building: those tanks hold 50,000 gallons of fuel.

Firefighters had the blaze under control in about half an hour, then installed dikes to control any oil-tainted water runoff.

The Swanzey and Marlborough fire departments covered the Keene station during the fire.

———————

As Reported by the *Keene Evening Sentinel* January 14th, 1999:

"STORY"

Fire chief sees 'collision course'

Sharing command of the Keene Fire Department's traffic-control system could put 25-ton fire trucks on a "collision course" with ambulances, as both vehicles charge into intersections on their way to emergencies.

That's the worst-case scenario Fire Chief William H. Pepler Jr. painted Wednesday for a Keene City Council committee, in person and in a strongly worded three-page memo.

At the very least, Pepler said, Keene fire trucks and ambulances would be delayed as they tried to respond to emergencies.

Pepler makes no bones about his feelings toward a proposal by Councilor Michael E.J. Blastos to allow other emergency services to override traffic signals; only the fire department can do it now.

Blastos was not at the meeting and could not be reached this morning for comment.

"It's an accident waiting to happen," Pepler told the committee, and he worries about liability of a private ambulance company were to use the city-owned system.

"The bottom line ism, this proposal is a bad idea," he wrote in the memo.

Every time a Keene fire truck or ambulance heads for an emergency, the Opticom Traffic Control System kicks into gear. Since 1995, the system allows the fire department to turn traffic lights green in the direction that a fire truck or ambulance is traveling, so the driver can get there in a hurry, but safely.

The system is maintained by the Keene Police Department, but only fire department vehicles are equipped to operate it. That way, Pepler said, his department knows who and where all the users are, and when they're using the system.

"We can control our own people," Pepler said.

But Councilor Angelo D. DiBernardo Jr. wasn't convinced that private ambulances, and ambulances from nearby communities, can't safely share the system.

"I don't understand the reluctance to share a piece of equipment that can help save lives," DiBernardo said. "Costs don't outweigh the benefits."

But Pepler stressed that the system was intended only to get Keene fire trucks and ambulances to emergencies faster and more safely.

The idea that private services would "compete" for the system, "in my mind, that's just not acceptable," Pepler reiterated this morning.

Pepler's colleagues in some of New Hampshire's other cities seem to agree.

More agencies on the system mean more problems, Nashua Fire Chief Richard J. Navaroli said in telephone interview

Wednesday, "especially when you look at intersections. If you have competing agencies speeding to the emergency kind of thing the other agency could hold up the progress of the people who are primarily responsible."

Navaroli said Nashua has used Opticom for 20 years or so. Other agencies have inquired about sharing the system, but it remains for the exclusive use of the city fire department.

"We didn't want to have other people involved competing for the intersection," Navaroli said. "That's where the accidents occur."

In Concord, the 18 towns in the area's mutual aid system do have access to the city's Opticom system. But Donald Peloquin, the city's fire alarm and traffic superintendent said the question of control keeps private agencies out of the system.

Because all the municipal agencies are on a single radio frequency," dispatchers know where everybody is and know how to respond," Peloquin said by telephone Wednesday.

In Keene, Pepler's concern is a targeted primarily at private services. But he said that, for their own good, ambulances traveling to Keene's Cheshire Medical Center from nearby towns shouldn't use the system.

Pepler and other emergency officials said they want to encourage those ambulances to stay off Keene streets when transporting patients. They said it's faster and safer for all concerned if they stick to the highway bypass system and the hospital's emergency access road.

As for the private agencies, Pepler said he doesn't know of any that are behind the request to open the system. He said he spoke to Robert J. DiLuzio of Keene, owner of the area's largest private ambulance service, and he has no interest in using the system.

"I want you to know the Opticom this is not my issue," Pepler quoted DiLuzio as

saying. "I'm not interested in it and I don't want it."

DiLuzio was not available this morning for comment.

The committee voted 4-1 to accept Pepler's recommendation that Opticom's use remain limited to his department. DiBernardo was the lone dissenter. The issue now heads to the 15-member council for consideration.

————

As Reported by the *Keene Evening Sentinel* January 22nd, 1999:

"STORY"

Keene City Council responds to Emergency Ambulance Service

It was as though the subject was near and dear to his heart—a little too near, in fact.

At Thursday night's Keene City Council meeting as Councilor Michael E. J. Blastos discussed whether private ambulances should be allowed to control traffic lights, he revealed he was kept alive by recent heart surgery.

A little over a week ago, Blastos told a hushed city council and a stunned Mayor Patricia T. Russell, he had triple-bypass surgery to improve blood flow to his heart.

The irony was evident discussion of a medical issue in relation to the city's concerns for rushing ambulances through intersections.

The city fire trucks and ambulances make their way through those clogged intersections because they have a device that lets them control the traffic lights.

Councilors have discussed letting private ambulances use the system, too, to speed their response time, but Keene Fire Chief William H. Pepler Jr. warned councilors that that might cause collisions between private and municipal ambulances, and most seemed to agree.

At least 18 private services could apply for use of the system, called Opticom. No municipalities in the region allow private services to control traffic lights.

Blastos, appearing well Thursday night, asked the council to refer the issue back to a committee for one last look.

Councilor Dana A. Edwards objected to further study. Revisiting the issue was akin to beating a dead horse.

Why are we spending so much time? He asked. Allowing private ambulances to change the traffic lights would be "unsafe to people in the ambulances and to pedestrians on Main Street."

The best route for ambulances to get to Cheshire Medical Center would be by the highway bypass, not cruising down Keene's streets, he said.

_____

As Reported by the *Keene Evening Sentinel* January 25th, 1999:

"STORY"

Arson dominates indictment cases

Two men have been indicted for their alleged roles in a car-looting and burning spree that terrorized Keene residents last fall.

William W. Lee Jr., 20, is currently incarcerated in the Cheshire County Jail on a reckless conduct charge unrelated to the arson charges.

Lee, of Winchester, is charged with two Class A felonies. If convicted of those charges, he could face up to 30 years in the state prison. The indictments by the Cheshire County grand jury, made public Friday, allege that Lee possessed an "infernal machine" and that he was not a law-enforcement officer acting in the line of duty. An "infernal machine" is a device for setting fires.

Lee is also charged with being an accomplice to a theft. He allegedly tried to help Steven A. Sullivan, also a suspect in last fall's arson spree, by driving Sullivan to parking lots of various apartment complexes. Either Lee or Sullivan, the indictment reads, stole a CD player, a cell phone, a Keene State College soccer coat, a purse, sneakers, radios and other items.

The grand jury, which met January 8, also released information about two Class A misdemeanors Lee allegedly committed: two counts of hindering apprehension.

Lee allegedly gave Sullivan a ride from the parking lot of Cheshire Medical Center after Sullivan allegedly started a fire in a Jeep. Lee also allegedly gave Sullivan a ride from the area of Christian Hill Road in Swanzey after Sullivan started a fire in a Volkswagen Golf, court documents allege.

Sullivan, 18, also of Winchester, was indicted on three counts of Class B arson. If he is convicted of each charge, he could face up to 21 years in N.H. State Prison. The indictments allege Sullivan knowingly started a fire in a 1986 Volkswagen Jetta, a 1997 Jeep Wrangler and a 1998 Nissan Sentra., Damage to each car was estimated at over $1,000.

Sullivan also is charged, in misdemeanor complaints, submitted by William M. Albrecht 4th, Cheshire County assistant attorney, Suyllivan allegedly received stolen property an Adidas sweatshirt, a Keene State College jacket and a Nokia cell phone.

As of this morning, Sullivan was not incarcerated at the Cheshire County Jail.

Arson charges account for quite a few of this month's grand jury indictments. An indictment is not an indication of guilt or innocence; rather it is a judgment by the grand jury that prosecutors have amassed enough evidence to warrant a trial.

_____

As Reported by the *Keene Evening Sentinel* February 6th, 1999:

"STORY"

Keene unveils city wish list

New fire trucks and ambulances and a new emergency services building in which to park them, are all part of the Keene city government's plans for the next six years.

The city's list of major construction projects and purchases was outlined at a public hearing Thursday night, but there wasn't so much as a peep from anyone on the plan.

The plan details the investments that Keene officials want to make in roads, bridges, the water system, parks and other areas by mid-2005.

In the year that begins this July 1, the plan calls for more than $20 million in projects. Of that about $2.8 million is already in hand or expected soon; the remaining $17.7 million would come from loans, state and federal grants, and other sources.

No property tax increases are tied to the first-year projects, nor are any increases ion sewer or water rates planned to finance the work.

Highlights of the plan include:

Emergency building: Design of a $6 million public-safety building to house the police and fire departments, with money for construction set aside in the following year. The current police station in City Hall would become a new city records center.

Fire training: A new Keen Fire Department training center behind the public works yard off Lower Main Street. The current training site is at the city-owned airport in North Swanzey. The fire department is also due for a new generator and new fire equipment.

———

As Reported by the *Keene Evening Sentinel* February 11th, 1999:

"STORY"

Keene sets criteria for new police, fire station

The need to build a new police and fire station in Keene is there, and so is the will. Now the only question is, where?

City officials discussed criteria Wednesday night, to guide their hunt for a location fort the recommended 50,000-square-foot building.

They know they need about 5 acres, but that could be a single parcel, or a combination of smaller lots. It could be land the city government already owns, or land it would have to buy.

A committee of city staff members came up with these criteria to keep in mind.

Proximity to downtown. This point prompted the most debate.

The assumption is that the Keene Fire Department will need to maintain two fire stations. With so many buildings, elderly people, apartments and Keene State College in the downtown area, one of the stations will certainly be there.

So Councilor Angelo D. DiBernardo Jr. suggested limiting the search for the new site to downtown.

But, while every official who expressed a preference was keen on downtown, most felt it best not to limit the search so early in the game.

"I think you keep all of your options open if you look citywide," City Manager John A. MacLean told the committee. "What harm is done by looking at all potential sites and considering all your options?"

Response times and travel distances
Convenience, and easy access to city hall.
At least 5 acres.

Ease and cost of site development, such as availability of utilities.

Compatibility with the neighborhood.

The property's price.

Direct access to adequate streets, avoiding heavy traffic, preferably on a corner lot.

The city staff will look at all of Keene, apply the criteria, and deliver a list of matches—in no particular order—to the Keene City Council, probably within a few months.

The search is starting from scratch.

"I can honestly say we don't have a site in mind or a group of sites in mind," MacLean said.

————

As Reported by the *Keene Evening Sentinel* February 21st, 1999:

"STORY"

Another call to Keene State College Alarming statistics on the decline at Keene State

Fire Department photo.

Where there's smoke, there's fire; but where there's the ringing of a fire alarm, there is often just a malicious prankster.

Just as co-ed dorms, late-night study sessions and a diet of pizza and candy bars are staples of many a college freshman's initiation to college life, so too is the piercing scream of the fire alarm, pulled not because the building is burning down but because sending hundreds of fellow students from the comfort of their beds into the cold night is some people's idea of a good laugh.

But while fire alarms may always prove a tempting target for bored college students, the instances in which Keene firefighters have had to suit up and head down Main Street to Keene State College, sirens blaring, only to find another false alarm, have declined considerably, according to Keene Fire Chief William H. Pepler Jr.

Fire officials distinguish between false alarms triggered accidentally and those pulled intentionally. Recent numbers suggest that the extent of the problem of willfully triggered false alarms is unpredictable, with next to none one year and an average of more than one a month the next.

But fire and college officials agree that the situation is far better than it was in the early 1990's, when it was a big strain on town grown relations. "We had a serious problem with false alarms at the college," Pepler said of that time.

At one point the college had racked up about $307,000 worth of $250 fines owed to the city for its response to pulled alarms. The college was fining the students it caught yanking the alarms, but it said those penalties were a matter of internal discipline and would not be turned over to the city.

The city has since lowered the fine to $100 and relations over the issue have mellowed. The fine doesn't just apply to the college, though in the past one of its complaints has been that it was being signaled out for penalties.

Other schools and businesses whose fire alarms are wired directly to the Keene Fire Department have the same responsibilities to guard against false alarms, and face the same penalties if they fail to do so.

"The college has since taken actions that have reduced false alarms dramatically," Pepler said.

Those steps included upgrading the colleges alarm system to minimize other sources of false alarms and stressing the penalties at student orientation.

Upgrades include installation of what's called an addressable alarm system, which lets firefighters pinpoint the exact location from where an alarm is triggered, regardless of the cause. In addition, an electrician responds to false alarms, along with the fire department, Keene police and campus security, to make sure that if a technical problem is to blame, it's immediately fixed.

"Students are spoken to during orientation about how serious this is and I think for the most part students respect that," says Frank Mazzola, director of physical plant at the college.

For those students who don't, there are physical deterrents on many of the alarms. Some are covered with lids that have to be flipped before the alarm can be pulled. When the lids are lifted, a loud screech echoes through the building.

Other times, firefighters stand at dorm entrances as students head back in after a false alarm and scan their fingers with ultraviolet light in search of telltale markings from a substance put on some alarms.

Looking just at false alarms that were pulled intentionally, there were just two in 1995, but the number jumped to 17 in 1996. It dropped to nine in 1997, but went up again last year to 15.

And the trend is up again. "We've had an awful problem last year leading up to this year," said Lt. John Beckta, who manages fire alarms systems for the Keene Fire Department. But he added that "in general, overall, in the last four years, we have reduced our runs down there."

Beckta said the problem usually flares up around Halloween and either gains momentum or trails off from there, depending on the year.

Pepler said that said.

False alarms this semester have been limited to one or two, but the college has been back in session only the fall semester did see a jump in the number of prank false alarms, but the problem has since leveled off. "We're back to the status quo," he since the end of January.

What progress has been made, Pepler credits to increased cooperation and understanding between the city and the college. Among officials that meet regularly to discuss common concerns are representatives of both the city fire department and Keene State safety department.

College officials say they drill home the seriousness of playing with fire alarms every chance they get. Aside from being an issue at student orientation, frustrated residence directors take the opportunity of having everyone gathered together while firefighters search their dorm and issue not-so-subtle reminders to their charges that the nonsense has to stop.

Students are encouraged to tip off college officials if they know who's behind a false alarm.

Students found to be responsible for pulling a false alarm face a loss of their college housing without refund, possible suspension from the school and prosecution by the Keene Police Department on criminal charges, according to Andrew P. Robinson, associate dean of student affairs.

When officials can't put their finger on the culprit, dorm residents get to share in fines of up to $500 and more, depending on the incident.

Of course, no one is suggesting that the problem will ever go away completely. With the large number of buildings and the large number of students living in a concentrated area, Pepler says "it's reasonable to expect a few false alarms."

———————

As Reported by the *Keene Evening Sentinel* March 8th, 1999:

"FIRE"

Small fire set in KSC dormitory

"Start the year off right." Perhaps someone was not having a good year when he put a match to a paper banner bearing those words in a Keene State College dormitory early Sunday morning, causing minor damage.

Police say the fire was started shortly after 4 a.m. on the second floor of Monadnock Hall on Winchester Street. The fire was out by the time firefighters got there. No sprinklers were activated. A match was found on the floor nearby.

The letters "...ear...right," were all that was left of the banner. Other papers hanging nearby on the wall also caught fire and there were scorch marks on the wall. Police say they have some leads, but are still investigating the fire.

———————

As Reported by the *Keene Evening Sentinel* April 24th, 1999:

"STORY"

Pepler heeds a new call

Chief William H. Pepler Jr.

It's almost last call for Keene Fire Chief William H. Pepler Jr.

Pepler announced his resignation late Friday afternoon, swaying he was taking a job as chief of the Merrimack Fire Department. He cited both personal and professional reasons for leaving the job he's held for the last seven years.

"All of my family and the vast majority of my friends are on the other side of the state," said Pepler, who came to Keene in 1992 from Exeter. "This was an opportunity to get back to everyone I want to be with and I see Merrimack as a challenge."

Challenges in Keene were what attracted Pepler seven years ago. And with departure on his mind, he said the department had several accomplishments he was proud of, including upgrading equipment and opening a station in West Keene last year.

Pepler also said he was proud of the expansion of the department's paramedic program, which will train another 12 paramedics in conjunction with Cheshire Medical Center. At present the department has five paramedic/firefighters. An agreement with the hospital to allow paramedics to use their advanced training in the field should be finalized next month.

"A lot of the credit needs to go to the firefighters because this has been a cooperative effort for the past seven years," Pepler said of the changes. "I feel very good leaving the department in the condition it is in—probably the best in the state training-wise, apparatus-wise, and personnel-wise.

"You work so hard and accomplish so much that you almost feel like you are a parent," he added. "It's hard to leave this place, but it is the right time in my life and my career,"

Pepler's style, considered progressive by many, includes an emphasis on education. It's a quality some firefighters say they will miss.

"He brought a lot of new equipment and technology, and he was for educating everyone," said firefighter/EMT Brian M. Shepard.

Pepler has been a fire chief since 1986, first in Exeter, then Keene. He graduated from the National Fire Academy in Maryland in 1993 and now teaches there, as well as at the N.H. Fire Academy in Concord. Pepler has also taught part time at Keene State since 1993 in the technology, design and safety Department. Pepler called teaching his "love in life" and said he hopes eventually to go back to school for a doctorate in education.

Pepler begins his new job in Merrimack June 7, replacing retiring Chief Charles Hall. Last year he earned $67,270 in Keene;' Merrimack's salary range for fire chief is between $49,682 and $71,655. What kind of salary Pepler will be paid was not available Friday night.

Pepler said an interim fire chief will have to be appointed while a search for a permanent successor gets under way. By charter, the hire will be City Manager John A. MacLean's to make: he was not available for comment Friday afternoon.

————

As Reported by the *Keene Evening Sentinel* April 25th, 1999:

"STORY"

Ready, willing and waiting
Red tape stops the paramedics

It was a cold morning in January and Kevin M. Holdredge and several other Keene firefighters raced to the Best Western to try to save a dying man.

Their patient that day had been eating breakfast at the Keene hotel when he suffered a heart attack. By the time the ambulance arrived, he was in cardiac arrest. Holdredge, trained as a firefighter and paramedic, attached the ambulance's automatic defibrillator, which delivered a jolt of electricity to the man's chest three or four times.

If this was television, Holdredge's training and quick work would have brought the man back to life. But this was real: the man was pronounced dead at Cheshire Medical Center a few minutes later.

Had the man been stricken in Concord, Francestown or just about anywhere else in the country, the situation might have been different. The man still might have died, but Holdredge would have been able to do more to save him.

He might have administered a drug such as epinephrine to make the man's heart more susceptible to the defibrillator's jolts. He might have turned off the machine's automatic function and used a 12-lead electrocardiogram to get a better picture of the man's chest. He might have inserted a special tube into the victim's lungs to let him breathe while protecting against aspiration.

But while Holdredge was trained to do all of these things, he wasn't allowed to do any of them. Cheshire Medical Center hadn't given the authorization for local paramedics to provide advanced life-saving services. And that, says Holdredge and others in emergency medicine, endangered lives.

It's not clear whether paramedic treatment would have saved the life of the man at the Keene hotel, but without question, those being rushed to Cheshire Medical Center by ambulance have not been getting the best available care en route.

But this may change: Friday, it was reported that Keene City Manager John A. MacLean, Robert J. DiLuzio Jr., the owner of a private ambulance service, and hospital administrators had ironed out their differences. According to DiLuzio, hospital officials said paramedics could be in service within a month. But details of Thursday's meetings could not be confirmed and not all were optimistic.

"This isn't the first time that we've heard this," Holdredge said, after hearing about the potential deal. "But we're certainly excited if it turns out to be true."

Knowing he can do more

Even if there are no more snags, Keene remains an anomaly, an extremely late bloomer. Most Americans have been receiving immediate care from paramedics since the 1970's, and about 80 percent of the state's citizens receive it now, according to the N.H. Emergency Medical Services Medical Control Board.

So why the delay in Keene? Ask Dr. Franz Reichsman, medical director of Cheshire Medical Center's emergency room. He alone has the power to allow or prohibit the use of emergency procedures by paramedics in Keene and more than a dozen surrounding towns for whom Cheshire Medical Center is the closest hospital. The state licenses all emergency care providers, but it's left to the local medical directors to sign off on what level of care and kinds of procedures ambulance crews can provide in the field.

Without written protocols from Reichsman, Holdredge and the 14 other paramedics in Keene—as well as paramedics in the surrounding towns—remain handcuffed, unable to provide the care they've been trained to give.

Reichsman says the process of developing policies for in-the-field care takes time. There are risks to racing through it, particularly if there aren't enough calls to maintain a safe level of training.

Still, it's been two years since the 177-bed hospital first agreed to move from intermediate emergency care to the paramedic level. Reichsman initially estimated that the permission process would take weeks and, with that in mind, Keene allocated more than $150,000 in the 1998 budget to train

about a dozen of its firefighters to become paramedics. The fire department also hired five paramedics with a combined 84 years of experience.

The Robert J. DiLuzio Ambulance Service, which handles calls in Swanzey and backs up the ambulances, did the same. The private Keene-based company now has 10 paramedics on its payroll. That means that at any given time, there are at least two paramedics available, but neither of them can do their job.

And according to the N.H, EMS Control Board, paramedic care is appropriate in 20 percent of all emergency calls. Looking at the data, that means that in the past two years, more than 1,000 people who were taken to Cheshire's emergency room in an ambulance didn't receive the degree of care they needed.

DiLuzio said he has documented four cases of people in the past two years who needed paramedic care but didn't get it. Capt. Dean Ericson of the Keene Fire Department said his shift has seen about the same number, including his father-in-law, who survived a heart attack only because he lived near the hospital.

And along with these stories of potentially fatal situations are the tales of men and women who could have received on-the-spot, IV pain medication: the man who fell from his attic; the old woman who was trapped between her bed and the wall. Both could have had their pain alleviated by a drug such as morphine, allowing Ericson and others to move them with ease and transport them more quickly to the hospital. Instead, both patients suffered longer than they needed to, possibly lengthening their recovery, Ericson says. The ambulances that sped them to the hospital didn't even carry the drugs that might have helped.

For Holdredge, who joined the city department in September after leaving a department outside Washington, D.C., that answers more calls in a year than Keene has in a decade, the real frustration comes from knowing he could do more.

"Sometimes we have a hard time stopping ourselves,: he said of his fellow paramedics, all of whom still practice in other towns to keep up their skills: "you want to do A, B, C, D, and E, but you can barely do A."

People in the Monadnock Region don't know what they're missing, said Karen Fleury, a paramedic with 10 years of experience who was also hired by Keene ion September.

Ericson, who is not a paramedic, agreed. "We're not trying to reinvent the wheel," he said. "This is care most towns have had since the 70's."

Ant it's care the firefighters are especially worried about. More than nearly anybody else, they run a high risk of needing what they themselves aren't allowed to give.

"We always say that if we needed a medic—if something serious happened— we'd rather be out of town," Ericson said.

War and peace

Paramedic care found its start in battle, says Susan D, McHenry, an emergency medical service specialist for the National Highway Traffic Safety Administration.

Surgeons from the Korean and Vietnam wars saw that soldiers were getting better pre-hospital care than people at home, so upon their return they worked to end the inequality. Inspired by their stories, the National Academy of Sciences issued a report in 1966 calling accidental death and disability "the neglected disease of modern society." The white paper made more than 20 recommendations for emergency care. Speed of care was considered so vital that one of these recommendations entailed developing pilot programs of physician-staffed ambulances.

That never happened, but over time the level of care available on the expanded. In the 1970's the first federal curriculum for paramedics and EMT's was established, while

the television show "Emergency" heightened public awareness.

"Gage and DeSoto (the two lead characters) changed the public's expectation because many people didn't know anything about EMS units and what they could do," McHenry said.

Since then, almost every city and town across the country has made emergency care available, most at a paramedic level. Even the 67-bed Monadnock Community Hospital in Peterborough has signed off on paramedic care, though it is generally used only to bring patients from Monadnock to other hospitals.

Below that level of care are three other emergency care providers: first responders, basic EMT's and Intermediate EMT's. It's important to note that regardless of the level, no one in the field does a doctor's duty. They are essentially registered nurses, but with "10 times" more assessment skills, all of them focused specifically on emergency medicine, says David Tauber of the Advanced Life Support Systems Institute, which is employed to train Keene's paramedics. Ultimately, procedural decisions lie with the local medical director.

But training does not. In New Hampshire, paramedics must train for about 1,000 hours while EMT intermediates study for about a tenth of that time. People in both categories must also take yearly refresher courses to maintain their skills.

Generally, that extra training lets paramedics administer five times more medications, manage defibrillators without the auto-pilot function and use breathing devices that protect against aspiration and do a better job getting oxygen to the brain and body.

Cardiac patients could use all three of these extra procedures. Several drugs prepare the heart for a defibrillator's jolt, improving its chances of working: the machine itself can help in other ways too—but only if paramedics are allowed to control it. The pacemaker and 12-view electrocardiogram functions cannot be used by EMT intermediates.

Keene paid more than $15,000 each for its two high-end machines, but when paramedics aren't allowed to use such manual functions, the city is only receiving about a fifth of its investment, Holdredge says.

"It's like going out and buying the most expensive car in the world and not being allowed to open the power windows or listen to the radio," he said.

Those with difficulty breathing—a common category of patient that ends up in Cheshire's ER—also stand to benefit. Drugs such as Lasix could help reduce fluid in the lungs and other drugs ameliorate allergies and asthmas, two ailments soon to strike with force as the weather warms.

In severe cases, paramedics could also do a better job keeping a patient's airway open. At present, Keene's EMT intermediates use a tube pushed into the esophagus. Most communities no longer use it, according to Krohmer. Holdredge calls the process ancient. The device's main problem is that it does not go directly into the lungs, thus allowing for a greater chance of aspiration, or choking on one's own vomit.

Paramedics can employ several other options. In some states, intermediates arte even allowed to use a combi-tube, a tool which also goes into the lungs. Reichsman agreed that the combi-tube was a better option, but said that it would require special state approval to be used by EMT intermediates.

————

As Reported by the *Keene Evening Sentinel* July 18th, 1999:

"FIRE"

Quick response limited damage

Smoke billows from the attic area of a house on West Street on Thursday as two firefighters, Capt. Goldsmith (top) firefighter Chris Cram (bottom) advance line to attack fire. Firefighters brought the blaze under control in 20 minutes. Photo by: Steve Hooper.

An electrical short circuit started a fire that gutted the attic of a single-family house in Keene late Thursday morning.

Smoke and flames were billowing and shooting from Susan J. and James T. Pettapiece's house at 677 West St., near the Keene

Country Club, shortly after 11 a.m. Firefighters arrived shortly and had the blaze under control in about 20 minutes.

No one was injured. Fire damage was confined to the attic, but water damaged the second floor.

A faulty electric heater-fanlight unit in the second-floor bathroom sparked the fire, according to the Keene fire officials.

The Pettapieces returned home from an appointment shortly after the fire erupted.

"I just came home and it was up in smoke," Susan Pettapiece said. "I pulled up and there were all these people in my yard."

Among the crowd were George Shuffleton and Michelle Martin, who, with another man, had searched the house before firefighters arrived.

Shuffleton and Martin were driving by when they saw smoke coming from the attic. They stopped, knocked on the door and, after no one answered, entered through a side door searched for someone who might have been asleep or trapped. They found no one.

———————

As Reported by the *Keene Evening Sentinel* September 1st, 1999:

"STORY"

Someone's idea of a prank almost put the city's hazardous materials team on alert Tuesday.

Emergency officials were called to the parking lot near the Toy Works toy store on Key Road Tuesday morning for a hazardous materials barrel that had been tipped over near a storm drain. The plastic barrel didn't appear to have anything in it, but fire officials treated the situation as dangerous when they first arrive, according to Keene Fire Chief Bradley B. Payne.

Payne said several similar barrels are stored behind the store as part of an environmental cleanup from about a year ago.

"They pulled an underground fuel tank out of the ground a year ago over there and there was some contamination," he said. A local environmental company is taking care of the long-term job of pumping the contamination out of the ground, he said.

The contaminated waste is put in barrels stored behind the toy store until they are picked up by the company. Someone must have taken one of the empty barrels and placed it next to the storm drain to make it appear as though corrosive material had gone down the drain, Payne said.

The N.H. Department of Environmental Services knows about the contamination from a year ago and about Tuesday's incident, Payne said.

"And

They'll put a fence around the barrels now so kids or whoever can't get at them," he said. "But everything's all under control over there, it's being monitored."

———————

As Reported by the *Keene Evening Sentinel* September 3rd, 1999:

"STORY"

Payne named city fire chief
Local man earns the top job

Keene has a new fire chief—native son Bradley B. Payne.

Payne, 53, has been the department's acting chief since William H. Pepler Jr. resigned to become head of the Merrimack Fire Department June 5. Pepler had been Keene's chief for seven years.

City Manager John A. MacLean announced the appointment at Thursday night's Keene City Council.

While all of Payne's professional experience has been local, MacLean said, its breadth and depth make him an ideal man to run the department, which includes 42 permanent firefighters and officers, 30 call firefighters and officers, and stations in downtown Keene, West Keene and Dillant-Hopkins Airport in North Swanzey.

The appointment took effect Monday.

Payne, who has worked for 30 years as a firefighter—24 of them full-time—graduated Keene High School in 1964, and served in the U.S. Army Airborne Division in Vietnam.

Through the years, Payne worked his way up the ranks. He was promoted to shift lieutenant in 1984, to shift captain in 1988, to fire prevention officer in 1993, to deputy fire chief of operation in 1995, to deputy fire chief of administration in 1998, and then became acting fire chief after Pepler resigned.

Payne lives in Swanzey with the wife, Andrea, and 8-year-old daughter, Hannah.

Payne takes over during a busy season for the department. It's new paramedic program is expanding from four paramedics to 16. A dozen firefighters are now training to be paramedics, so they can staff the city ambulance service. Paramedics are able to perform more treatment on emergency patients than emergency medical technicians can. They will complete that training in less than a year.

In addition, the department is preparing its equipment and computers to deal with any potential Y2K problems.

"We're in pretty good shape," said Payne, who has worked on the project for several months. "We don't anticipate any major problems with our emergency program."

Just in case, Keene's main fire station on Vernon Street will get a larger emergency generator, the old one will be installed at the West Keene station.

Also the department is busy preparing for The Sentinel's bicentennial parade on September 19 and Keene's annual Pumpkin Festival October 23. Each is expected to draw a huge crowd.'

"We have a lot going on," Payne said, "but the existing projects are not a surprise to me—we've been working on them for a while now."

Reported by Steven Goldsmith, Deputy Chief, September 17th, 1999:

"STORY"

When Chief Pepler took the helm of the Keene Fire Department the training was dramatically increased for all personnel. Members of the department were encouraged to increase their own level training. Officers were encouraged to attend the National Fire Academy in Emmetsburg, MD.

The National Fire Academy has one course which is a 4 year program, called the Executive Fire Officer Program. The course is a 4 year program with each student enrolling and being selected out of a large group of fire officers throughout the United States.

Each fire officer enrolling in this program must have a college degree and be in a position where he or she makes command decisions during their daily tasks and functions performing the duties assigned.

Each year a handful of students are selected to enter the elect four year program and be willing to complete one applied research project for each year of the four year course.

The reports are sent to the National Fire Academy within 6 months of the completed course. A project must be evaluated as acceptable in order for the student to continue in the Executive Fire Officer Program. To be an acceptable project, a project must receive a grade of "C" or higher to move on to the next course. Course papers are graded by the Gettysburg College and each student can receive 3 credit hours as recommended by the American Council on Education.

Only at present 4 members of the Keene Fire Department have graduated and achieved this prestigious award the title of an Executive Fire Officer. These members are Chief William Pepler Sr. and Deputy Chief .Clayton Stalker and Deputy Chief Stevens Goldsmith and Deputy Chief Mark Boynton.

————

As Reported by the *Keene Evening Sentinel* October 6th, 1999:

"STORY"

Keene firefighters strike new contract with city

After three months of give and take, Keene firefighters and city officials signed a three-year contract Tuesday.

Both sides say the new deal is fair to both the firefighters and taxpayers.

"The firefighters are tough negotiators and they did a good job bargaining," said City Manager John A. MacLean.

MacLean also thanked them for their dedication to the city. "You never lost sight of your primary purpose, which is to serve and protect the community," MacLean said. "And that is something you do extremely well."

National Fire Academy

In the end, about 40 full-time firefighters, lieutenants and captains received a 13.1 percent wage increase over the three-year contract, an added vacation day paid at time and a half, and the latitude to bill 60 more days of sick leave after 20 years of service.

"It's nice-to-know that we don't have to worry about this for another three years," said Mark Howard, president of Local International Association of Firefighters 3265.

The old contract expired June 30.

Under the new contract, valid from July 1, 1999, until June 30, 2002, firefighters and supervisors will receive no cost-of-living increase this year. However, on January 1, all will receive a 4-percent raise, followed by 2-percent raises on July 1, 2000, January 1, 2001, and July 1, 2001. On January 1, 2002, all will receive a 2.5-percent raise.

This means a firefighter starting at the lowest pay scale now earning $28,315, will earn $32,032 by the time the contract expires. Similarly, a new captain now earning $35,843 will earn $40,548 by the contract's end.

Firefighters and supervisors will continue to be paid holiday pay, which is regular pay for 8.4 hours for 11 holidays a year, whether they work those holidays or not. If a firefighter works Christmas or Thanksgiving, that pay is increased in time and a half.

The new contract includes Labor Day as the third holiday pad at time and a half.

Hours for firefighters and supervisors remain the same under the new contract. A firefighter works an average of 42 hours a week, with number of hours not exceeding 168 in a 28-day cycle.

In addition, the cap on 120 sick days for at least 20 years of service is raised to 180 days, under the new contract.

Keene's two deputy chiefs and Chief Bradley B. Payne is not part of the union, and therefore are not affected by the union negotiations. Their annual salaries this fiscal year are about $53,000 and 69,000 respectively.

The union made one major concession; an extension of the probationary period from six to 12 months, just like other city positions. Until now, new firefighters have been covered by the union after six months, now they will have to wait a year before they can start earning $28,315 a year.

Payne said negotiations between the city and firefighter's union "have come a long way since I was involved in the negotiations."

————

As Reported by the *Keene Evening Sentinel* December 2nd, 1999:

"FIRE"

Gas leak evacuates Keene High School

About 100 students were evacuated from Keene High School late Wednesday afternoon after a bulldozer sheared the top off a 100-gallon propane tank.

The accident happened at about 4:30 p.m. as workers were installing an underground oil tank at the back of the school, which is right next to the propane tank.

The bulldozer hit a pipe leading from the top of the propane tank, breaking it off, and both liquid propane and propane gas began leaking rapidly.

The stench of propane quickly filled the air.

An estimated 100 gallons of propane leaked from the tank, according to Gary M. Patnofde, general manager of Keene Gas. The tank is owned by the company, and its workers came to the scene to help with the leak, he said.

The 1,000-gallon tank was about 60 percent full when the accident occurred and was about 50 percent full when checked later, Patnode said.

Propane is highly explosive, and Keene firefighters acted quickly to keep the gas from igniting. They used 2,500 gallons of water to drown the propane tank and the area near it, trying to dissipate gas vapors and so reduce the risk of an explosion.

Meanwhile, school officials and teachers herded students quickly out Keene High's front door, on the side of the building opposite the gas leak. Keene police sealed off both ends of Arch Street, which runs past the school, to minimize traffic.

Fans were used to vent the school, and Keene Fire Chief Bradley B. Payne declared the incident under control at 6 p.m.

The tank installation is part of a two-year, $17.5 million expansion-renovation project at Keene High.

Most Keene High students had already left for the day when the gas leak occurred, but the leak forced cancellation of all after school activities, and night classes.

Sarah L. Larocca, 18, and Rebecca T. Wood, 14, were at cross-country ski practice when they were told to leave the school.

"We could smell the gas in the locker room before practice," Larocca said.

School officials and teachers evacuated students through the front of the building. Some kids waited on Arch Street to be picked up—one in shorts in the freezing cold—and others went into a separate steel building that's part of the high-school complex.

Paul Roy, the Keene High football coach, was scheduled to pick up his son Brad Ray, 18, from basketball practice at 4:30.

But 15 minutes before that, students were told to evacuate.

"I'm just trying to get them home," Paul Roy said in the bitter-cold night, as three teenagers climbed into his car.

Beverly R. Seymour, who has lived next to the high school for four years, watched what was happening from her living room.

"I could see the police lights from the porch window," Seymour said. "Nothing like this has ever happened here before."

Seymour didn't want to leave home, but was considering going to her daughter's house on Island Street if she had to evacuate.

Her granddaughter, Jenni-Lee Allen, 14, was at cheerleading practice when the gas leak began.

"The kids weren't scared," she said. "It was sort of exciting. Some were hoping we won't have school tomorrow."

But they did; the school opened as usual this morning.

The accident shouldn't delay the construction project, said Deane B. Haskell, assistant school superintendent for business.

"I think we will still be on schedule," he said.

————

As Reported by the *Keene Evening Sentinel* December 8th, 1999:

"STORY"

Police-fire station on Keene priority list

Booked for 2002 is a joint fire-police station, replacing the 100-year-old police station next to city hall and the 110-year-old fire station on Vernon Street. The cost is estimated at $6 million; about $500,000 of that has already gone into site selection, planning and designs. The fire department also wants a new location for its training center, with construction starting in 2002. The department now trains in Swanzey; it would prefer a Keene location, so crews are still inside the city if an emergency occurs. A new training center would cost $211,900, with a building that could be burned repeatedly in firefighting drills, plus a ladder tower and other equipment.

The new fire-police headquarters could also be a boon to city record-keeping. Now, city records are stored all over the place, including basements, closets and file cabinets. Some of those spots are prone to mildew and mold. Once police move out of the current station, that could be a great place for centralized records-storage center, City Clerk Patricia A. Little said. The location is good, the building has a loading area and a strong floor, and a lack of windows in the back minimizes the effect of light and weather on documents.

A modest increase in the city government's portion of the property tax rate will probably be needed to help pay for next year's projects, said Martha L. Mattson, city finance director—in the order of 2.7 percent. That would add about 28 cents to the city government's property tax rate; this year, the city government is getting $10.26 of the overall rate of $32.87 per $1,000 of assessed value.

———————

2000

As Reported by the *Keene Evening Sentinel* January 19th, 2000:

"FIRE"

Frozen sprinklers fail at Center at Keene

Frigid temperatures are being blamed for two water main breaks at the Center at Keene shopping center Tuesday.

A sprinkler head in a kitchen closet at Imperial China restaurant froze up and ruptured at about 2:30 p.m. Keene firefighters were able to divert the water out a side door to the parking lot.

Keene fire Capt. Dean Ericson said several hundred gallons of water flowed from the broken sprinkler before the water could be turned off.

At 8:30 p.m., Keene firefighters were called to a second sprinkler head break, this time on the second floor of the building.

That sprinkler was located in a crawl space between the two floors and dumped

between 800 and 1,000 gallons, said Keene fire Deputy Steven Goldsmith.

Crews spend nearly two hours cleaning the mess, using wet/dry vacuums, portable pumps and pails, he said.

"The water was 4 inches deep in some places," Goldsmith said.

Sheri Lorette, general manager of the Center at Keene, said the fast response by the Keene Fire Department prevented more damage.

"They were fantastic," she said. "They were here right away and cleaned up the mess. They did a great job."

Still, some businesses were damaged. The Herb Shop did not open today because of the water damage, Lorette said.

Renee Gembarowski, owner of the Herb Shop, could not be reached for comment this morning.

Goldsmith also said Toy City received some damage but was expected to open.

The Center at Keene uses a wet sprinkler system, in which water is always in the system. When the temperature drops, the water freezes and pipes can burst.

Lorette said she is encouraging businesses to keep their heat on to prevent further problems.

———————

As Reported by the *Keene Evening Sentinel* January 28th, 2000:

"FIRE"

Porch fire doused at fraternity house

A blazing pillow on a porch set off the fire alarm early today at a Keene State College fraternity house, alerting the Keene Fire Department and residents sleeping in the house.

About a dozen members of fraternity Phi Mu Delta, who live in the house at 57

Winchester St., piled out into the cold at about 5 a.m. and doused the small fire that was beginning to take hold of the first-floor side door.

The fire was out before time firefighters arrived, Capt. Gary R. LaFreniere said. LaFreniere is investigating the cause of the fire.

Keene police are also investigating. Officers responded to a disturbance call at the house hours earlier.

————————

As Reported by the *Keene Evening Sentinel* March 3rd, 2000:

"STORY"

On-call firefighters get raise

On call firefighters—termed call company personnel—have been paid a flat rate ranging from $450 to $1,000 annually, based on experience, said Keene Fire Chief Bradley B. Payne. The new range is $625 to $1,500. Unchanged is a stipend based on the number of calls they go on, up to a maximum of $500.

Call company personnel are not city government employees; they are extra sets of hands that can help at large fires or with special details.

————————

As Reported by Steven Goldsmith, Deputy Chief Operations March 7th, 2000:

"STORY"

On March 7, 2000 The Keene Fire Department held one of the largest promotional badge-pinning ceremonies in its history.

9 Key positions were filled from Chief to 3 Deputy Chief positions and 4 Captains and one Lieutenant.

The ceremony consisted with the open remarks from Chief Payne and turned the

evening over to the Mayor Michael Blastos and other city officials.

Those honorees with the badge pinning presentation was Chief Bradley Payne, Deputy Chief Gary Lamoureaux, of administration, Deputy Chief Stevens Goldsmith, operations, Call Deputy Paul Szoc, Captain Gary LaFreniere, fire prevention, Captain John Beckta of fire alarm and Captain Mark Boynton of the Training Div., Captain Arthur Johnson, operations and Lieutenant Jeffrey Checkering, operations.

————————

As Reported by the *Keene Evening Sentinel* March 12th, 2000:

"FIRE"

Practice makes perfect

Keene firefighters carry hose around the side of a burning home on Mathews Road Saturday toward the end of a training session designed to help the department respond better to real-life emergencies. The house was burned to the ground to make way for new construction planned for the site. [*see photo next page*]

————————

As Reported by the *Keene Evening Sentinel* April 8th, 2000:

"STORY"

Keene thanks those who helped prepare for Y2K

Keene experienced virtually no Y2K computer problems when 1999 became 2000.

On Thursday night, the city government thanked 102 city employees and two Southwestern N.H. Fire Mutual Aid employees for their contributions to a seamless transition.

About half of the honored employees briefly attended the city council meeting, and they received a standing ovation from Mayor Michael E.J. Blastos, City Manager John A. MacLean, the 15 member city council, and the audience.

The success is owed to "a lot of hard work by a lot of people," MacLean said Friday morning. "We tried to thank as many people as we could and all of them deserve a lot of credit."

As Reported by the *Keene Evening Sentinel* April 9th, 2000:

"STORY"

Fire alarm spoils Sadie Hawking Day

A couple hundred Keene Middle School students experienced a damp and early end to their Sadie Hawkins Day dance Friday night.

Training Burn, From left to right front row: FF/EMT-I David Wagstaff, Deputy Chief Gary Lamoureaux, Capt Mark Boynton, Deputy Chief Stevens Goldsmith, Call Lt. Phillip Davis Jr., Call Capt. Raymond Hadley, FF Kevin Brindle, FF/EMT-I Eric Mattson, FF/EMT-I William Greenwood. 2nd row left to right: FF/EMT-I David Gaillardetz, Capt. Fire Alarm John Beckta, Capt/EMT-I EMS Coordinator Jeffery Morel, Chief Bradley Pauyne, Call FF Eden Vinyarsky, FF/EMT-P Karen Fleury, Call FF Steve Dunchee, Call Capt. Robert Spicher. 3rd row and back from left to right: Call Lt. Charles Harris, Capt. Mike Burke, Lt. Mark Howard, Capt Dean Ericson, Lt. Jeffery Chickering, Call Deputy Paul Scoz, Call FF Mike Reed, Capt Arthur Johnson, FF/EMT-I Michael Abbott, FF/EMT-I Timothy Read, Lt/EMT-I Ronald Leslie, FF/EMT Brian Shepard. FF/EMT-I Ronald Clace, Call FF Sherry Davis, Call FF Michael Rocheleau, FF/EMT-P Timothy Clark, FF/EMT-P Robert DiLuzio Jr., FF/EMT-I Michael Gianferrari, Capt. Scott Taylor.

At about 9:34 p.m., foggers blowing on the dance floor set off a fire alarm. The students evacuated the building as Keene firefighters secured the building.

Students milled in the front yard of the school, as a fire engine's red lights flashed and raindrops splattered dresses and jackets. Central Square and Washington Street filled with cars as parents arrived to pick up their children. Students were allowed back in the building in small groups to collect their belongings.

————

As Reported by the *Keene Evening Sentinel* April 13th, 2000:

"STORY"

City council eyes fire-police station

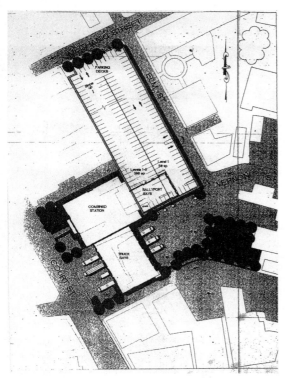

Keene officials are proposing a large new joint fire-police station downtown, adjacent to a new three story parking garage on Elm Street.

The proposal, which could cost as much as $15 million, would address two concerns that have simmered in recent years, as street traffic has increased, particularly in the downtown area.

Keene City Manager John A. MacLean says the 53,000-square-foot facility is targeted for across the street from the current fire station on Vernon Street, between Washington and Court streets.

If approved by the city council, the project will take about four years to complete. Adoption of the plan, which still awaits considerable detail and public discussion, would lay to rest a series of efforts to establish a large fire station elsewhere in the city.

Under the proposal, which MacLean spelled out at a municipal services committee meeting Wednesday. Vernon Street would become one-way, with an entrance on Washington Street, with all traffic flowing into Elm Street. The new combined station and fire truck bays would be built right across the Court Street end of Vernon Street. Fire trucks would be able to drive onto Court Street and Elm Street.

The plan would also provide more parking in an area already squeezed for parking. The existing Elm Street parking lot would expand, becoming a three deck parking garage with 400 spaces. The current lot has 157 spaces and has a waiting list.

Talk of an Elm Street parking garage began surfacing informally last year as officials discussed a collection of alternative parking garage ideas for a spot near the Cheshire County Superior Court house. The largest of such plans called for building a five-story facility on Winter Street in a neighborhood that, because it is still largely a two-story environment, was generally considered to be the wrong places for such a parking solution.

The new police-fire station concept would require buying and demolishing four properties: the existing fire station, the former law offices of Wrigley, Weeks and Martin at 39 Vernon St., and two properties owned by the United Church of Christ on Central Square: the Elsie Priest Memorial Park, named after a Chinese missionary, and a parking lot on Vernon Street.

The preliminary plan keeps the police and fire stations downtown—something city councilors said they support, especially for the fire department. The West Keene fire station became a full-time operation about 1 ½ years ago, covering that part of the city, and since then councilors have said keeping a fire station downtown is a priority.

The proposed Vernon Street site, while smaller the 5 acres, has many advantages, MacLean said.

First, the city owns some of the land that would be taken, potentially saving millions of dollars in acquisition costs.

Second, MacLean said, the neighborhood is accustomed to the fire station and the sirens and traffic associated with it.

Third, the plan keeps the police and fire stations downtown. Councilors have said they think this is important, especially for the fire department.

―――――――

Fire Department News Release By Steven Goldsmith April 14th, 2000:

"FIRE"

Haz-Mat Incident at Sims Production Ave. Keene

Keene firefighters from Station 2 West Keene and units from Central Station responded at 3:30 pm to a reported chemical spill within the Sims complex on Production Ave. Keene. Units were advised while in route that a chemical of Sulfuric Acid and Ethylene Glycol, which is used in their production process, was spilled due to a broken fitting. Sims personnel were able to control the leak and vent the area

until fire department personnel arrived on scene. Members of the Keene Haz-Mat Team suited in level B entry suits gained access to the area and monitored the air quality and made the area safe for entry and disposal of the chemical. At no time was the public or Sims personnel in the building in any danger during this Haz-Mat incident. The incident was brought under control at 5:17 pm and all Keene equipment was back in stations at 6:00 pm.

―――――――

Fire Department News Release By Steven Goldsmith April 14th, 2000:

"FIRE"

Dryer Fire

Dryer fires are a common cause of home and building fires.

Keene firefighters from station 2 West Keene responded at 12:56 pm to reported unknown smoke at 447 Park Ave. Upon arrival of engine 2 Lt. Leslie up graded to a first alarm with smoke showing from the front side of the building. Central station from downtown Keene responded with additional engine and ladder and fire attack operations began to make an interior attack on the fire, which had started in the middle of the building in the laundry room area. Upon arrival Deputy Chief Goldsmith assumed command and called for a 2nd alarm at 1:07 pm when fire and heavy smoke extended to the upper floors with possible extension of the fire. Upon arrival of the first units it was reported that it was possible that an elderly female might be trapped on the upper floor of the building due to her not being accounted for. When additional units arrived divisions were set up to search upper floors for possible trapped people in the apts. on 2nd and 3rd floors. The fire was brought under control and investigation began by the Keene Fire Department Fire Prevention and the Keene Police Department. There was damage to all three floors due to heavy smoke and limited water damage on the first floor. 12 people were placed throughout the complex or with friends while work is being completed to let the residence back into their apts. It was determined that a dryer was the cause of the fire. All units were back in stations at 3:15 pm.

As Reported by the *Keene Evening Sentinel* April 26th, 2000:

"STORY"

Dateline NBC News Keene Fire story on dryer fires

Dateline NBC visited the Keene Fire Department on Tuesday, "Dateline" interviewed Deputy Chief Steven Goldsmith (top) in the morning and Donald P. Bliss (bottom) in the afternoon. Bliss pictured, director of the National Association of State Fire Marshals, Cameraman David Zapatka puts a little makeup on Bliss before the interview. Camera crews rode with Deputy Chief Goldsmith and filmed while responding to a fire within the city. Photo by: Steve Hooper.

As Reported by the *Keene Evening Sentinel* April 26th, 2000:

"STORY"

Police-fire station plan raises concerns

Several Keene businesses and organizations could be affected by a $15 million plan to build a new police-fire station, plus parking at Vernon and Elm streets.

But so far, few of them know the details of the plan.

City Manager John A. MacLean proposed the joint station two weeks ago, to solve problems with cramped and outmoded facilities at both the police and fire stations.

However, he emphasized this week that the plan is just a concept, and so far just one idea for the location has been explored.

"I think there's real potential for the Elm Street location, but it might well look totally different from the idea we presented," MacLean said.

Keene's main fire station is now on Vernon Street, but is old and cramped, and built for a time when fire trucks were much smaller.

The plan outlined by MacLean would turn Vernon Street into a one-way street, with traffic entering from Washington Street and turning north onto Elm Street. The new combined police-fire station would block Vernon Street on the Court Street end. Fire trucks could leave the station by either Court Street or Elm Street.

There's now a municipal parking lot on Elm Street; it would be turned into a three-story parking garage with 400 spaces—about 250 more spaces than the lot now has.

A lack of parking has long been a problem to the neighborhood.

Supporters of the plan like the central location, especially desirable for a fire station; the fact that with the fire station already on Vernon Street, the area is already used to the noise and activity associated with fire departments; and savings to the city's taxpayers, as the city government already owns much of the land.

But other people aren't sure they like the idea.

The United Church of Christ of Keene, for example, would be affected by the joint station. A small church-owned park at Court and Vernon streets would have to be moved east, next to where the current fire station stands. The church would also lose some parking spaces at the rear of its building, but MacLean said church members could park in the new parking deck.

Rev. Charles J. "Woody" Shook, associate minister of the church, questions whether church members will favor the change.

———

As Reported by the *Keene Evening Sentinel* June 22nd, 2000:

"STORY"

New station plans shift in Keene; Church park would stay put

The latest idea for a joint police-fire station and parking garage in downtown Keene may satisfy three hard-to-please groups; city officials, taxpayers, and neighbors of the new facility.

The revised plan was outlined Wednesday night by City Manager John A. MacLean. The building would face Mechanic Street, between Washington and Court streets, and avoiding altogether the United Church of Christ's Elsie Priest Memorial Park.

The current fire station would remain intact, and the city government could decide what to do with it.

MacLean said the revised concept disturbs the neighborhood the least, while keeping the fire station downtown, which is a priority. The proposal also costs less than a previous version, because the city owns more of the land involved.

In addition, the project would add 379 badly needed downtown parking spaces, with a three-level garage facing Court Street.

Four properties needed to be bought: a law office at 39 Vernon St., a small parking area owned by Bell Atlantic, and two apartment office buildings on Mechanic Street.

"We'd try not to overpower the neighborhood; we'd blend in," MacLean said.

An earlier plan to orient the facility on Vernon Street, entailed razing the current fire station and other building—N&K Printing's building at 32 Washington St., next to the fire station, and the law office on Vernon— and moving the church park. It would have provided 400 parking spaces, with Vernon Street becoming one-way.

That plan had a $15 million price tag. The new idea, MacLean said, may cost only $11 million.

Neighbors, especially the church, objected strongly to the first plan, and the city government promised to look at alternatives that wouldn't involve taking church property.

The new plan, "at first glance, makes sense for the church." Said Rev. Charles J. "Woody" Shook, Jr. the church's associate pastor, Wednesday night.

"We came in with a concept that wasn't acceptable to our neighbor, and we understand that," MacLean said of the first idea. If the city council commits to the Mechanic Street site, MacLean said, "We'll still have a lot of work to do." We'll still have a lot of work to do." Still, he said, architectural planning could begin.

While city officials haven't yet spoken with all neighbors of the project, one doesn't seem to mind. MacLean said Robert J. DiLuzio, who owns Foley Funeral Home and the DiLuzio Ambulance Service at 49 Court St., supports it.

MacLean presented five ideas to the city council's municipal services committee Wednesday. Besides the original plan and the one he recommended, there were three options, but MacLean said all three had safety, cost or parking problems.

The committee voted 4:1 to endorse the Mechanic Street orientation.

Councilor Angelo D. DiBernardo Jr. objected, saying he wanted more cost information before supporting the plan.

MacLean said these facts will come later. Right now, he needs to know if the council likes the site itself, so architectural planning and cost estimating can move forward.

————

As Reported by the *Keene Evening Sentinel* July 7th, 2000:

"STORY"

City endorses police-fire site Next, cost estimates and designs for safety headquarters

A joint fire and police station, plus a parking garage, in the Mechanic-Elm-Vernon Street area was endorsed 11-0 Thursday night by the Keene City Council.

Two councilors, Karen R. Fitzpatrick and Michael H. Greenwald, abstained from voting because they have a connection to the location; two others, Christopher C. Coates and Charles Redfern, were absent.

City Manager John A. MacLean has been pushing the council to endorse a specific location, so cost estimates and architectural plans can be prepared. Without that commitment, MacLean said, the investments wouldn't make sense.

"Without approval of this site, we don't have enough information to do anything," agreed Councilor Robert H. Farrar. "We need (the approval) to go ahead."

MacLean said the city staff favors the location for three reasons: The city government already owns properties there, including the city's main fire station, which avoids some property-acquisition costs, almost everyone agrees the main fire station should stay downtown, and the plan provides not only a new safety headquarters, but also more downtown parking.

Some councilors were leery of endorsing a site without knowing how much the project will cost—a Catch-22, in MacLean's view.

"There are too many questions left unanswered," said Councilor Angelo D. DiBernardo Jr. "The council would be wise to keep its options open."

MacLean agreed, but said zeroing in on a site will allow some of those questions to be answered.

The proposal orients the building toward Mechanic Street, at the northern end of the city's Elm Street parking lot. A three-deck, 379-car parking garage behind the new building would face Vernon Street.

Vernon Street would remain as is, so would the existing fire station, although it would be used in some other capacity.

MacLean said last month the project might cost about $11 million.

———

As Reported by the *Keene Evening Sentinel* August 17th, 2000:

"FIRE"

Officials: Fire at Bradlees was arson

A fire in the men's bathroom at Bradlees department store was deliberately set Wednesday afternoon, by lighting a box of toilet paper, investigators say.

Store employees said no fire alarm or sprinklers went off. They saw smoke, but no flames, coming from the men's room.

Customers were asked to leave the store because of an electrical problem.

"At this point we are treating it as arson," said Keene police Sgt. Joseph Collins. "It was intentionally set."

Steven Goldsmith, Keene's deputy fire chief, estimated damage at less than $5,000, not including smoke damage throughout the store.

Collins said investigators are examining video surveillance footage, they also think the fire may be linked to one Saturday afternoon at the Bradlees store in Concord. That fire started in the curtain department and extensively damaged that section of the store.

Harold E. Abbott, assistant manager of the Concord store, said he thinks that fire was also set. The fire alarm didn't sound at his store, either.

Keene police ask anyone with information about the fire to call them at 357-0813, or Crime stoppers at 357-6600.

———

Fire Department News Release By Steven Goldsmith August 17th, 2000:

"FIRE"

Kitchen Fire on Church Street

The Keene Fire Department was dispatched this afternoon at 5:44 pm to a reported kitchen fire at 241 Church Street Keene upon arrival, Lt Mark Howard assumed command and ordered crews into the kitchen area to battle the fire. Upon arrival command requested an ambulance crew to the scene to assist with a male patient who had suffered smoke inhalation. The fire was confined to the stove area and was declared completely under control at 5:50 pm. Additional overhaul was required to completely remove extensive smoke, which had filled the house.

The house is owned by the Pollock family of Bedford N.H. Damage was confined to the kitchen-stove area and smoke throughout the house and hall ways. One resident was taken to Cheshire Medical Center for treatment of smoke inanition. His injuries were minor and he was treated and released a short time later. The fire was determined to be accidental. Marlboro Fire Company covered the Keene Station while Keene units were at the fire. All Keene units were back in station at 6:15 pm.

As Reported by the *Keene Evening Sentinel* September 8th, 2000:

"STORY"

Firemen start your engines Keene okay's new fire truck

The Keene Fire Department got the okay from city councilors Thursday night to waive the normal bidding process and buy a new fire engine to replace two older trucks.

The need for a new truck isn't a surprise, either for the department or the council. The fire department mapped out a truck-replacement schedule in 1998.

But problems have cropped yup with one truck, which made time of the essence in getting a new truck, said Keene Fire Chief Bradley B. Payne. That's why the council was asked to waive bidding requirements.

On August 2, the fire department discovered a leak in the motor of a 1982 American LaFrance pumper truck, which is used as a backup. It would cost up to $25,000 to replace the motor. Also, the pump that sends water gushing through fire hoses is outdated, Payne said, and even if replaced wouldn't meet state firefighting standards.

Keene also needs to replace a 1972 ladder truck, also made by American LaFrance, which the city acquired in the early 1990's.

"I feel it's imperative to get the vehicle as soon as possible," Payne told councilors Thursday night. "And it takes eight to 10 months once it's ordered."

Deputy Chief Steven Goldsmith said the department will compare prices at as many companies as possible that supply the kind of truck Keene needs. He said the department hasn't selected a supplier yet, but is looking at trucks at several New England companies; Blanchard Fire Apparatus, Greenwood Motors and American LaFrance Freightliner.

"We have several vendors and are looking at various trucks," Goldsmith said. "The city manager and chief will make the decision about which truck to buy."

Goldsmith said factors in the purchase include pump power, ladder length, and emergency equipment.

Payne expects the new truck to cost about $500,000.

The last truck Keene bought in 1999, cost $473,000, Payne said. The city government wants a five-year lease-purchase deal on the new truck, and the first payment will be made after the next fiscal year begins, on July 1, 1001, City Manager John A. MacLean said. The annual payments are estimated at $118,000.

One truck being considered can carry six firefighters, has a 75-foot-long aerial ladder, and has a pump that can shoot 1,500 gallons of water per minute.

As Reported by the *Keene Evening Sentinel* October 24th, 2000:

"FIRE"

Teacher puts out fire at Keene High School

A small fire in the boys bathroom at the Cheshire Vocational Center at Keene High School Monday was put out quickly by a teacher and did little damage.

The fire was suspicious and is being investigated by both the Keene police and fire departments.

Students told police they could smell something burning around 12:15 p.m. and told teacher William Mattson. Mattson used a fire extinguisher to put out a burning plastic soap dispenser.

The fire department responded, but the fire had already been extinguished.

Police say they have spoken to witnesses but do not have any suspects.

––––––––

As Reported by the *Keene Evening Sentinel* October 25th, 2000:

"FIRE"

Keene man hurt in mobile-home fire

A Keene man was burned slightly when a two-alarm fire gutted his mobile home in Tanglewood Estates Tuesday night.

Firefighters arrived at 5 Thrasher Lane shortly after 10 p.m. to find half of the home engulfed in flames, said Keene fire officials, who called in Surry firefighters to help.

Even before the first of about 30 firefighters arrived, Charles McDonald drove to Cheshire Medical Center for treatment of first and second-degree burns to his hands, feet and head.

Fire Chief Bradley Payne said investigators are spending the day at the house, trying to figure out what sparked the fire.

A resident told police the fire may have started after the home filled with propane gas and a woman lit a cigarette.

"It was fast, whatever happened," said Payne, who called it an accident.

The fire also damaged the awning of Robert and Edna Croft's home at 3 Thrasher Lane. While the fire raged, the Crofts removed their belongings, including several cats, from their home.

––––––––

As Reported by the *Keene Evening Sentinel* October 27th, 2000:

"FIRE"

Fire at Markem causes little damage

A small fire this morning at Markem Corp. in Keene sent two employees to the hospital for treatment of smoke inhalation, but caused little damage to the building.

The fire started shortly after 6 a.m. in the dust-collection system of a grinding machine at the Congress Street plant. The fire was noticed in the plant's paint room, said Keene Fire Chief Bradley Payne.

Before firefighters arrived, two employees had already put out the fire with a dry chemical extinguisher, Payne said. The workers, whom Payne did not identify, suffered a reaction to the chemical and inhaled smoke; they were examined at Cheshire Medical Center and released.

The building was evacuated when firefighters arrived, but production was barely interrupted, said company spokesmen Roderick Sipe.

Payne said firefighters—about 20 of them—worked to get a considerable amount of smoke out of the building. By 7:30 a.m. air quality in the plant returned to acceptable levels, Payne said, and employees could return to work.

––––––––

As Reported by the *Keene Evening Sentinel* November 2nd, 2000:

"FIRE"

Family plucked off roof

A Keene family was rescued from a porch roof at their burning home at 9 Monadnock St. early this morning.

Michael and Susanna Woods were asleep when a fire broke out in the basement of their apartment building at about 2 a.m.

The Woods and their two children were awakened by the smoke, and tried to leave the home, but could not escape down the stairs. They then went out a second-floor window onto the roof of their porch, according to Keene fire officials.

Firefighters used a ladder to rescue the four, who were not hurt.

Flames damaged the basement and outside wall; the rest of the house had water and smoke damage. Damages are estimated at $15,000.

The fire was put out about 20 minutes after it was reported.

The building is owned by Paul and Nancy Vincent of Keene.

Officials are investigating the cause, but say it does not appear suspicious.

A West Swanzey fire crew manned the Keene station during the fire.

As Reported by the *Keene Evening Sentinel* December 4th, 2000:

"STORY"

Keene offers new police-fire option

A new option has surfaced for providing more space for the Keene police and fire departments, and more parking.

As in a concept outlined in June, this one calls for a new building and parking garage in the Mechanic-Elm Street area. But the new building would house only the fire department, not both agencies; instead, what's now the fire station would be gutted and renovated for the police department.

In the earlier plan, the fire station would be vacated, and perhaps sold or turned into a museum.

The new proposal would "not dominate and would be less offensive to neighbors" then the earlier proposal, City Manager John A. MacLean told the five-member Keene City Council municipal services committee Wednesday night. The meeting was heavily attended by other councilors and city staff members.

"it fits in with the neighborhood, reuses the existing structure, and opens up room for more space" in city hall, where the police department's now located, MacLean said.

If the police station moves, its space can be used to alleviate cramped conditions for other city agencies, and for storage of documents.

Details are not yet available on the size of the new fire station, or the parking garage, or how either would fit on the land, MacLean said.

The new fire station would have training facilities that both fire and police departments could use.

First, though, "we have to find out if it's even feasible to use the old fire building," MacLean said.

The answer hinges on costs, and whether the building can be adapted to police needs.

City councilors hope to decide on a plan by next October.

The option continued in June entails building a 28,900 square-foot building, shared by the police and fire departments, with a four-level, 379 space parking garage. The structures would be in a rectangle formed by Mechanic, Elm, Vernon and Court streets.

The city government has already bought a law firm's office at 39 Vernon St. for the project.

MacLean pinned up a timetable for design and construction of both options. City councilors gave the city manager a green light to begin pursuing both possibilities.

MacLean will convene a steering committee of department heads and city councilors to examine all aspects of both options, from engineering to architecture.

Meanwhile, a design committee will also be formed, including police and fire representatives, a system that worked well for renovation of the Keene Public Library, MacLean said.

Both committees will report to the city council by August, aiming for a decision in October.'

The city government has earmarked more than $9 million for the police-fire plans in its capital improvement schedule. Both stations are more than 100 years old; neither is designed for current emergency service needs or federal disability act standards.

"I have no plans to revisit any other sites," MacLean said. During a two-year search, city officials looked at a number of locations for a police-fire station: the Tire Warehouse retail store on Lower Main Street; a lot bounded by School and Emerald streets and Gilbo Avenue; the former drive-in theater off Optical Avenue; and former railroad property just east of Main Street.

The Elm-Mechanic Street area is favored for several reasons.

First, the city owns some of the land needed for the project, potentially saving millions of dollars in acquisition costs. Second, the neighborhood is accustomed to the fire station and the sirens and traffic associated with it.

Third, it keeps the police and fire stations downtown, which city councilors say is important.

"Most of what we've heard has been positive" bout the Elm-Mechanic location, MacLean said. "But, I know there are other ideas out there."

————

December 6th, 2000 Fire Department News Release By Steven Goldsmith:

"FIRE"

Possible Chemical Spill Markem Corporation

The Keene Fire Department was dispatched this afternoon at 12:13 to a box alarm at Markem Corporation 150 Congress Street. Upon arrival, Lt. David Symonds assumed command and was met by Markem Corporation personnel and was advised that the plant had a possible chemical spill.

Upon arrival of additional equipment the building was still being evacuated. Deputy Chief Stevens Goldsmith was given command and with Captain Scott Taylor Keene's Haz-Mat Coordinator an operational plan was set into motion.

Along with Markem Corporation personnel it was determined that possible a chemical was spilled. A ventilation attack was set up and the air was monitored with fire department meters. All crews entered the building with self-contained breathing apparatus and the entire building was checked. It was determined that it was an overheated ink machine along with some cleaning fluids.

Keene Fire Department ambulance transported three Markem personnel to Cheshire Hospital for evaluation

The incident was under control in about 40 minutes and all equipment was back in station by 2:00 pm..

————

December 6th, 2000 Fire Department News Release By Steven Goldsmith:

"FIRE"

Building Fire 52 Matthews Road

Photo on top approaching house from street side rear, upon arrival. Bottom picture front of house and barn fully involved extending to the house. Photo by: Cindy Boynton.

The Keene Fire Department was dispatched this afternoon at 12:18 to a reported barn fire at 52 Mathews Road Keene. A passerby called in the fire and alerted the owner Phillip LaReviere who was asleep at the time of the fire. While en route a large column of smoke could be seen from Main Street by responding units. Captain Matson requested additional equipment while en route to the fire. Upon arrival Deputy Chief Goldsmith assumed command and called for a 2nd alarm, with heavy fire showing. Prior to arrival of the 1st fire units the Swanzey Chief reported that the barn was fully involved and the fire had extended into the structure of the house, which was connected to the barn. The fire crews concentrated on saving the main house from involvement due to the spread of fire. The fire had extended into the main house and was stopped by venting the structure and an aggressive interior fire attack by fire crews to the fire in check. The main house was saved and extensive overhaul was done to complete the extinguishment. A backhoe was called to the scene to remove the post and beam barn debris from the floor when fire was still burning. The Keene Fire Investigation Team headed by Fire Prevention Officer Captain LaFreniere and along with the Keene Police Department will try to determine the cause of the fire. The Marlborough Fire Company and Swanzey Fire Units were called direct to the scene to assist Keene. Spofford Fire Department was called to cover the Keene station while units were at the fire scene. The fire was declared under control at 1:23 pm. And units still remain on the scene this evening.

The damage was estimated at $145,000.

LaRiviere has made arrangements through his work for a place to stay.

Firefighters also managed to save a cat. The cat, Samantha, was being treated at the Cheshire Animal Hospital and was listed in stable condition Friday evening.

_____

As Reported by the *Keene Evening Sentinel*:

Retirement

Firefighter Wayne Spofford.

When firefighter retire they receive a ride home in an engine and just seem to be hosed down. As Wayne Spofford the picture shows. FF Spofford was hosed down in front of his home when left off and the good buys are said. All Members who retire receive a fire bugle that represents the fire service. Sadly not all receive their bugles, due to unknown reasons or receive there just due. It's a little sad tthat when a member retires with 25 or 30 years serving their community that some is and some are not but I guess that's politics. Good luck to all who retire.

2001

As Reported by Robert Koch of the *Keene Evening Sentinel* January 3rd, 2001:

"FIRE"

Two Keene teenagers escape burning garage

Two teenagers ran out of a garage in Keene Tuesday afternoon just before flames engulfed it.

The garage fire at 130 George St. began when a drop light fell and broke, igniting gasoline, Deputy Fire Chief Steven Goldsmith said.

Jamie R. Walters, 16, who lives in the hose to which the garage belonged, said he tripped while sliding a 10 to 20 gallon fuel container on a sled. That started a spill, which made its way to an extension cord and light.

Troy S. Webster, 17, was helping Walters.

They saw the problem developing and "we were out before it hit the (gasoline)," said Webster, who immediately ran into the house in search of a fire extinguisher.

The fire "wasn't" that big when it started, "he said.

"But by the time I ran in and got the fire extinguisher, I came out and the whole thing was up in flames."

Walters and Webster said they were moving the container while cleaning the garage floor.

Keene Fire Chief Bradley B. Payne said about 30 fire fighters was able to contain the garage fire before the flames could spread to the adjacent house.

"When we got here (at 4:42 p.m.), it was free burning, "he said. "They got the water on it before it got to the roof."

Firefighters declared the blaze under control by 4:59 p.m. By then, the garage door had burned away the wooden building smoldered and smoke poured from the eaves.

But the walls stood and some snow remained on the roof."

The fire scorched a pickup truck parked in front of the garage, but two vans parked behind the building weren't damaged, Payne said.

Some neighbors reported hearing what they thought was a vehicle's gas tank exploding.

Kenneth R. Lawrence who lives on nearby Knight Street, said his cousin came over at about 4:15 and told something was burning Lawrence grabbed a camera and began videotaping the fire.

Jamie's mother Carrel J. Walters and two renters living at the house were not home when the fire started.

Marlborough Fire Department crews covered the Keene department during the fire.

————

As Reported by Teal Krech of the *Keene Evening Sentinel* January 22nd, 2001:

"FIRE"

Cold, fuel costs blamed for fires

A spate of local fires including one at a Keene Homeless shelter is being blamed on the combination of plummeting temperatures and high fuel prices.

"If you get three or four cold days when it's below zero, you see an increase in fires, "Keene Fire Chief Bradley B. Payne said. "With fuel (prices) being so high, a lot of people are trying to find ways to heat their houses as cheap as possible."

On Sunday at 12:35 p.m., firefighters were called to 32 Water Street, one of Keene's homeless shelters, when a clothes dryer in the kitchen caught fire. Two of the eight residents were inside the shelter at the time; no one was hurt. The residents were moved to another homeless shelter.

Deputy Keene Chief Gary Lamoureux said the fire is still being investigated. However, he said dryer fires are typically caused by dirty lint traps and clogged heat vents. Lamoureux estimated damage to the building at $8,000 to $10,000.

An hour after firefighters returned from the dryer on Water Street, they were called out to a washer fire in the basement of an apartment building at 4 Chapman Road.

Firefighters arrived at 2:37 Lamoureux said the washer had filled with smoke. The building was evacuated until 3 p.m.; damage was minimal, and residents were allowed back into their apartments.

In Keene Saturday night, a mattress accidentally caught fire when two youngsters were playing with matches, Lamoureux said.

It took firefighters two hours from 10:45 p.m. to 12:45 a.m. to get the fire under control at 3:43 Elm Street.

Ronald Prime and his wife and two children were displaced for the night, Lamoureux said. He said smoke and water damaged the building's second floor.

————

Keene's new Quint E1 replaced the 19 M1 American LaFrance engine and replaced Ladder 2 and Americal LaFrance. Photo by: Dave Symonds.

As Reported by Deputy Fire Chief Steven Goldsmith January 2001:

"STORY"

Engine 1 Keene's American LaFrance had engine problems and was down and Ladder 2 had issues with rust and a ladder that may not pass inspection.

Chief Payne was forces to evaluate what was the course of action to do for the city and the department.

Chief Payne directed Deputy Goldsmith to take pictures of the ladder and determine the cost of repair via a report and Chief had Engine 1 evaluated to have the engine redone.

The cost was considerable, and the engine and ladder were aged seemed the only course to do was to draw up a proposal and present it to The City Manager to have the City Council to authorize an emergency replacement for the two pieces of equipment.

Deputy Goldsmith was tasked to retrieve estimates to replace the two pieces of equipment. It was determined by Chief Payne that a Quint would be the best piece of equipment and the least expensive to the tax payer.

Chief Payne and Deputy Goldsmith and Deputy Lameroux made the proposal to the City Manager to propose the to the council the emergency purchase. The council and the city manager approved the purchase of replacement not to exceed $500,000 dollars.

The purchase was to be a 75 foot Quint that would be available for immediate delivery.

Chief Payne and Deputy Chief Goldsmith flew to St. Lewis and looked and test drove and operated an American LaFrance 75 foot Quint.

American LaFrance also demonstrated 2 75 foot Ladders at the Central Fire Station in Keene and one was purchased by the Leominster Fire Department.

Blanchard Fire Apparatus who deals with Pierce Fire Equipment also demonstrated a new 75 Foot Quint at the Central Station.

Prices ranged for $447,000 to $489,000 dollars. Ultimately Keene decided to purchase E-One.

Keene during Chief Peplers tenure two E-Ones were purchased and that was the factor. Keene had two and had little problem and was a good pumpers and Ladder.

The Quinnt was purchase for station 2 and served as an Engine, Pumper, and Ladder for the West Keene Tax payers.

As Reported by Robert Koch in the *Keene Evening Sentinel* April 9th, 2001:

"STORY"

Six cars, one engine land in the water; no one hurt; fuel leaks

Walpole—A freight train derailed this morning, dumping six cars—plus a locomotive—into the Connecticut River just before 6 a.m.

In all, 13 cars and two locomotives went off the tracks in Westminister, Vt.

Two people operating the lead locomotive of the northbound train were not hurt; that engine stayed on the tracks. The other locomotives were unmanned.

It appeared no one else was hurt, either.

However, the spring-swollen river quickly swept diesel fuel downstream.

Vermont State Police said the derailment involved nine cars, two slurry cars and two locomotives. The entire train had more than 80 cars.

At midmorning, one train engine lay in the river, and another rested perpendicular near the track against a washed-out embankment. A third engine was still on the track. Each engine can carry 7,000 gallons of diesel fuel, Vermont State Police say.

Six salt-laden cars also lay in the river; seven boxcars formed a mangled mess alongside the embankment, their wheels ripped off and salt spilling from them.

The train derailed after thawing snow softened the ground underneath part of the track, said Christopher r. Brown, an engineer for New England Central Railroad, the company that runs the line.

"It's a bad one," Brown said, "the type of derailment that happens once every couple of years."

Police and firefighters used chain saws this morning to remove downed trees around the derailed cars still on dry ground; the trees were smashed down when the cars ran into them.

The train derailed east of downtown Westminister, in an area just north of Grout Avenue which runs down a steep hill to the railroad tracks. Rescue crews are using the street to reach the wreckage.

————

As Reported by the *Keene Evening Sentinel* April 14th, 2001:

"STORY"

Fire department joins product recall effort

It's spring. It's the weekend. It's time to hit garage sales and flea markets. What's better than finding that perfect steal—a toaster, looks like new, for half of what you would have paid off the shelf?

Well, hold on. Put the toaster down.

The Keene Fire Department wants you to know that some of these steals may have been banned by the consumer product police recalled because of the hazards they pose to you and your family. April 17 is recall round-up day, a federal state and local effort to get dangerous products out of your home.

The list is five pages. Lighters that aren't child-proofed take the cake on page one. Grenade, alligator, and telephone-shaped lighters, lighters shaped as lamps, flying saucers, motorcycles, guns, pagers, miniature scuba or propane tanks, and, to top it off, Godzilla.

Most were sold between 1997 and 1999. They were designed by Kikkerland Designs, C and H Trading, ZNY Enterprises or Prometheus International Inc.

Other fire hazards include children's decorative lamps called "Little Ones," sold at Kmart from 1992 to 2000. "Power Drivers" or "Buddy L"—battery-powered children's riding vehicles made by Empire Industries. Black and Decker horizontal toaster ovens, halogen floor lamps.

"What it's doing is getting any unsafe products that could start a fire out of the home and off the market and properly disposed of," Capt. Gary R. LaFreniere said. LaFreniere said the list of bad products will be broadcasted on Channel 9 on April 17. Residents should bring any bad products to the Keene fire department.

Questions? Call the US Consumer Products Safety Commission at

1-800-638-2772, or visit the web side at www.cpac.gov.

————

Fire Department News release April 16th, 2001:

"STORY"

Walpole driver plucked quickly from river

Photo by: Gary LaFrenier.

The Keene Fire Department was dispatched to a Motor Vehicle Accident involving a motor vehicle that left the roadway and was submerged into the Branch River on April 16th, at 11:25 a.m.

City of Keene Fire Department's A Shift responded with Heavy Rescue I, Ambulance 1 and Chief-3.

Upon arrival C-3 Deputy Chief Steven Goldsmith evaluated the scene, and ordered additional equipment from Keene bringing Engine Co. 2, Ladder 1 and Ambulance 2 to the scene.

A 1997 Dodge pickup truck was heading south on Optical Ave. as it approached the Route 101 T-intersection, the driver passed out and busted through the guard rail at a very high rate of speed. The pick-up became airborne as it left the tarmac and struck an embankment, than launched a second time and continued its flight into the Branch River.

The nose of the pickup landed in the river and the vehicle did a single rollover and came to rest on its wheels. The vehicle was occupied by a single male occupant, who was wearing his seat belt which kept him in the vehicle. The damaged truck had trapped the driver in his seat from under the steering wheel.

The driver was awake but disoriented upon arrival of 1st due units. The truck was taking on water, up to the occupants waist, and he was very cold. The Branch River had a fast moving current due to the spring thaw. The water was estimated to be 7 ft. deep in this location. The current was estimated at 15 mph.

Firefighter John Bates and Firefighter Bill Greenwood donned cold water rescue suits and made numerous attempts to reach the victim. On some of the attempts, both firefighters were swept downstream by the rapid current submerged at length.

Firefighter Bates was able to make contact with the occupant who was identified as Mr. Bezanson as the Engine and Ladder Company lowered a 24 ft. ground ladder from shore to the hood of the truck.

Firefighters Bates and Greenwood assisted with extricating the driver's legs out from underneath the steering wheel, by pushing down on the seat cushions. The driver then assisted the rescuers with extrication through the front windshield.

Once out onto the hood/dashboard, rescuers secured a lifejacket, rescue harness and ultimately removed the victim via a stokes basket. The victim was brought to shore across the ladder which was lowered to the vehicle via stokes.

He was taken by Keene Fire Department via ambulance to Cheshire Medical Center, treated for bruises and cuts, and was released Monday night.

Route 101 in Keene was shut down between Optical Avenue and Main Street for about two hours after the accident

––––––––

As Reported by the *Keene Evening Sentinel:*

Not all is what you see

Fire units from Central Statvion and Station 2 responded to this single motor vehicle accident with entrapment. Amazingly, once on the scene, the driver was pinned and extricated by the fire units with no injuries. Photo by Steve Goldsmith.

––––––––

As Reported by the *Keene Evening Sentinel* April 20th, 2001:

"STORY"

Keene firefighters on 'Dateline NBC'

"Dateline NBC" will air a story about clothes dryer safety tonight that will feature members of the Keene Fire Department.

The story, on the broadcast at 8 p.m., was taped in Keene last summer. It will include information about appliance safety, with specifics on the dangers of dryers.

Reporters interviewed Keene firefighters after several dryer fires in the city.

The show will remind people about the dangers of leaving dryers on when they leave the house, according to an NBC producer.

———

As Reported by the *Keene Evening Sentinel* May 9th, 2001:

"FIRE"

Fire leaves Keene State students homeless

Fire Department Photo.

A fire gutted part of a former Keene State College fraternity home Tuesday night, sending three residents scrambling for safety.

Three dozen firefighters rushed to prevent the blaze from spreading to adjacent homes.

The fire, which officials call suspicious, started at about 9:30 p.m. in a barn attached to the back of a two-story house at 107 Davis St., according to one of the residents, Gary W. Burke, a Keene State College senior.

"We were upstairs and smoke alarms started going off," Burke said. "I went to the downstairs kitchen and opened the barn door and there were flames. I saw a ball (of fire) inside. A small section of the barn fell right next to me.

Burke said he ran back into the house, grabbed a fire extinguisher, alerted his roommates and called 911. By the time the residents were safely outside, police and firefighters were beginning to arrive, he said.

Neither Burke nor Keene Deputy Fire Chief Steven W. Goldsmith knew this morning what ignited the fire in the barn, which the students sometimes used as a party room. Burke said the section where flames erupted had no electrical outlets.

Goldsmith said the first firefighters to arrive spotted smoke and flames as they turned the corner from Main Street and immediately called for a second alarm.

"When I got here, there was still heavy fire showing in the rear of the building," Goldsmith said.

"Eventually, officials dispatched two ladder trucks, two other engines and rescue crews. Firefighters tapped water from a hydrant at Davis and Blake streets as a tanker truck arrived to battle a brush fire behind the barn. The Marlborough Fire Department covered for Keene during the fire.

By 11:15, Keene firefighters were busy putting out flames inside the walls, Goldsmith said. Others stood atop ladders and picked at second-floor walls with axes; windows on all sides had been smashed out.

"The rear is structurally unsound. It's uninhabitable right now," said Goldsmith, who estimated the fire destroyed the back third of the house, from the basement up through second floor and into the attic.

Traffic crews blocked off Davis Street at Wilson Street. Dozens of people, including many students, looked on from the south side of Davis Street.

Among the onlookers was Elliott H., Mazzola, who said he saw a "big reddish cloud of smoke" from his house near Ashuelot River Park—about a half-mile away.

"When I got there, about 10 p.m., there was just smoke coming out of those windows, but the back porch was still on fire," he said.

Watching from across the street was landlord Todd Tousley, who said he bought the house at a foreclosure sale in August and since had met with fire department officials three times to update its wiring and install fire doors,.

"It's so ironic I did everything they wanted me to do and then there's a fire," he said. "I hope my insurance covers it."

Tousley said up to eight students lived in the house before classes wrapped up at Keene State College last week.

Toward midnight, Burke continued to look on reminiscing about his three years living in the house. "I'm going to be sad. There are a lot of memories in there," he said. The Keene State student said he plans to stay with a friend down the street.

The house was once home to Kappa Delta Phi, now an interactive fraternity, according to college officials.

The fire also spoiled plans by Andrew W. Wilson and two other Keene State students, who said they had hoped to move into the house this fall. "It's one less place on our agenda," said Wilson, as he watched firefighters finish up.

———

As Reported by the *Keene Evening Sentinel* June 1st, 2001:

"FIRE"

Keene fire quelled quickly Two escape second floor unharmed

An elderly woman and her grandchild escaped injury Thursday night when a two-alarm fire broke out in their Keene home.

Fire crews arrived at 74 Knight St. shortly after 10:30 and reported flames on the second floor and stairway of the house. They knocked down the fire within several minutes, and busted second-floor windows to ventilate the building. They brought the fire under control by 10:57, Deputy Chief Gary P. Lamoureaux said.

Meanwhile, an ambulance crew checked Alice C. Sharkey and her adult grandchild for smoke inhalation. The grandchild's name was not available at press time.

Investigators said faulty extension cords sparked the fire, which damaged the second floor, and resulted in smoke and water damage in the rest of the house. They estimated damage at $10,000 to $15,000.

Afterward, insulation littered the staircase as neighbors watched from afar.

It's an old house. It wouldn't take that much for it to go up in flames," one neighbor said.

Lamoureaux said the NH West Chapter of the American Red Cross in Keene will find housing for the Sharkey family, adding the house may be razed for Habitat for Humanity to rebuild.

Nearly 30 firefighters arrived at the scene with two engines, a ladder truck, rescue unit and ambulance. One firefighter received finger cuts from broken glass. The Marlborough Fire Department covered the Keene central station.

———

As Reported by the *Keene Evening Sentinel* June 13th, 2001:

"FIRE"

Fire closes Imperial China

A grease fire got out of control Tuesday morning, forcing a Keene restaurant to close its doors, temporarily.

The fire started at 11:49 in a deep fryer at Imperial China Restaurant at the Center at Keene, 149 Emerald St., said Keene Fire Chief Bradley Payne. No injuries were reported.

Employers threw water on the fire, trying to dose it, but that only made the blaze worse, Payne said. The fire spread behind the hood of a stove, though sprinklers had yet to go off. Firefighters sprayed the fire with foam, and it was out within 30 minutes.

The NH Department of Health closed the restaurant until damage from the smoke and fire is cleaned up, Payne said. No one from Imperial China could be reached for comment this morning.

As Reported by the *Keene Evening Sentinel*:

Keene restaurant open after fire

Imperial China restaurant at the Center of Keene is open again following a kitchen fire a week ago. The restaurant was closed by the N.H. Board of Health after a grease fire got out of hand June 11.

But the mess was cleaned yup within a day, and the restaurant has been open since. Still, customers have continued to call, thinking the business was still shut down, manager Eva Wu said Tuesday.

As Reported by the *Keene Evening Sentinel* July 17th, 2001:

"STORY"

Keene Fire Department goes thermal

Deputy Fire Chief Steven Goldsmith uses new Thermal Imaging camera during fire department burn. Photo by: Dave Symonds.

The Keene Fire Department put on a smoke-and-mirrors show Monday evening for an audience of politicians, insurance executives and local residents.

It involved some expensive gadgets—new thermal imaging equipment that has just been donated to the fire department.

Two thermal-imaging cameras and a monitor for the cameras, will allow firefighters to "see" in smoke-filled rooms. The cameras can detect heat differences among objects and create "a blurred vision of a room," said Gary Lamoureaux, deputy fire chief.

The equipment gives firefighters several advantages they don't have now.

For starters, they'll be able to detect the hottest parts of a room—the places where flames are smoldering behind a partition or under a floorboard. That way, they can attack the problem before it bursts into the air and really takes off.

In addition, the equipment improves the ability to rescue people—children overcome by smoke inhalation and lying on the floor, or firefighters whose breathing tanks have gone empty and they can't find their way out.

Outlines of people appear distinctly on the monitor that reads the camera images.

The equipment "is going to make for a much safer situation for firefighters and cut loss of property and life," Lamoureaux said.

The equipment didn't cost the city government a dime. In February, a retired Keene police officer, John J Byrnes, asked city officials for permission to raise money for two cameras and a portable monitor to supplement the single camera and an immobilized monitor the city already owns.

Byrnes jokes that he collected a city paycheck for more than 20 years on the police force, and helping the fire department was "a way to pay back the city for being so good to me."

Byrnes found a supplier, and lined up a demonstration for Michael R. Christiansen, president of Peerless Insurance Co. in Keene. Christiansen was impressed and Peerless agreed to donate $18,500 for one thermal-imaging camera.

Similarly, Byrnes approached National Grange Mutual Insurance Co., which is also headquartered in Keene, and it pledged the money for the second camera.

Finally, State Farm Insurance Co. wrote a check for $9,000 to buy the monitor for the system.

In a brief ceremony Monday, sandwiched between demonstrations of the new equipment, the three donors and Byrnes were honored. Mayor Michael E.J. Blastos said the insurance companies through their community support, "truly do exemplify all that Keene is about."

City Manager John MacLean called the donations "the gift that keeps on giving," as it will help make firefighters, residents and business people safer.

Demand for thermal imaging technology has grown significantly in the past few years, said Bill Ricker, president of R&R Safety of Maine, the company that sold the units to Keene. Ricker estimates that 50 or more such units are already in service in New Hampshire.

However, few are located in the Monadnock region because the price is pretty high for a small-town fire department, Lamoureaux said.

————

As Reported by the *Keene Evening Sentinel* July 25th, 2001:

"STORY"

Keene moves ahead with fire, police station plans

A local engineering company will prepare preliminary design plans for a joint police-fire station, a renovated fire station, and a parking garage in downtown Keene.

Two basic plans are competing for 6 acres bounded by Court, Vernon, Mechanic and Elm streets. Both have been picked as ways to help space-crunched police, firefighters and downtown workers.

On Tuesday night, City Manager John A. MacLean and city councilors met at the Keene Police Library to review a contract with Clough, Harbour & Associates, the design consultants.

That contract—not to exceed $16,000—calls for the Keene firm to prepare by November preliminary design plans for two basic options.

A new 30,000 square-foot fire station, with renovation of the existing Vernon Street fire station for police use.

A new 52,500 square-foot joint police-fire station that does not use the existing fire station.

"The final report will come out in early November. If one idea falls out or if one takes precedent, we'll wait to go to the council immediately," MacLean said.

Councilor Dale E. Thompson disagreed. He preferred councilors and engineers to study renovation of the fire station. "I think you ought to concentrate on the fire station and see whether renovation is feasible."

Keene Police Chief Barry Wante wouldn't weigh in on either option, but praised the dual approach.

Keene Fire Chief Bradley B. Payne did not attend the workshop and was unavailable fore comment by press time this morning.

But Deputy Fire Chief Steven W. Goldsmith said today, the department is prepared to back which ever plan the city endorses, whether that's building a joint station or renovating the fire station for the police department; the fire station was build in 1885.

"We've got to do what's best for the taxpayers. If it's cheaper to go jointly, I suppose that's the way to go," most of the people in the fire department are in favor of whatever the city recommends.

———————

Fire Department News Release July 30th, 2001:

"FIRE"

Fire Damages Apartment Building 15 Damon Court

Keene Firefighters responded to a reported building fire at 9:58 a.m. that was reported to be at 15 Damon Ct. in a vacant apt. Keene units responded on a 1st alarm and arrived on scene at 9:59 a.m. Deputy Chief Stevens Goldsmith reported fire visible on the 1st floor upon arrival of Captain Arthur Johnson and crews made entry to the apt with an inch and three/quarter attack line. The fire was extinguished quickly and confined to the kitchen area. Throughout the apt was heavy smoke damage and moderate smoke damage to the remaining apts.

The caller reported smoke coming through the ceiling with no smoke detectors working within the residence upon arrival of the fire department.

The Thermal Imaging Camera was used to check for extension within the ceilings and walls and the upper floor area. Fans were set up to remove smoke from the structure.

Captain Gary LaFreniere Fire Prevention Officer and the Keene Fire Department Investigation team, along with the Keene Police Department are jointly working together, to determine the cause of the fire. At this time the fire appears to be accidental.

All unites were back in quarters at 11:03 a.m.

The owner of the building is Mr. Todd Tousley of Keene.

———————

As Reported by the *Keene Evening Sentinel* August 30th, 2001:

"FIRE"

Keene Off-duty firefighters rescue woman in crash

Quick action by Mark Howard and Timothy Clark rescued Martha Healey, 51 from burning car. Fire Department Photo.

A Keene woman s luck to be alive, thanks to quick action by two off-duty firefighters, according to Keene's fire department.

According to Deputy Chief Steven Goldsmith, Martha Healey, 51, was headed south on Hurricane Road Tuesday night when her 1995 Chrysler Concorded left the road and struck a utility pole. The accident happened at about 7 p.m.

"She hit the pole and the engine compartment of her vehicle burst into flames," Goldsmith said. "But two of our firefighters happened to live in that neighborhood and they responded right away."

Mark Howard and Timothy Clark raced to the scene and tried to extinguish the fire, "but the driver was screaming to get out," Goldsmith said. "They got her out of the burning vehicle. If they hadn't been there, there most likely would have been a fatality. By the time the fire department responded the vehicle was fully involved. Their quick action saved her life."

Healey was taken to Cheshire Medical center, where she was treated for a broken ankle. She was listed in fair condition. Police are investigating the cause.

————

As Reported by the *Keene Evening Sentinel:*

New Hampshire Fire Service Committee of Merit

Keene Fire Deputy Chief Steven Goldsmith put fire fighters Mark Howard and Timothy Clark in for recognition of their act on August 30, 2001 of the life saving moves during the crash of Martha Healey on Hurricane Road.

The State of New Hampshire invited The Keene Fire Department and Mark Howard and Timothy Clark to receive an award.

Deputy Chief Goldsmith Represented the Keene Fire Department and had the honor of presenting the medal to Mark Howard and Timothy Clark. They both received Unit Citations for their bravery.

The Ceremony was conducted at the Capitol Center for the Arts in Concord New Hampshire for the entire fire service throughout the state.

————

As Reported by the *Keene Evening Sentinel* September 11th, 2001:

"STORY"

U. S. under attack; nation takes cover Bush pledges to hunt down the terrorists behind horror

New York—In a horrific sequence of destruction, terrorists crashed two planes into the World Trade Center, and both of the towers collapsed this morning, raining debris onto the street below.

A witness said he saw bodies falling from the 110-story towers and people jumping out.

The fate of the 50,000 people who work in those buildings was not immediately known. Authorities had been trying to evacuate people from the towers, but many were thought to be trapped.

Explosions also rocked the Pentagon and the /State Department and spread fear across the nation.

President Bush ordered a full-scale investigation to "hunt down the folks who committed this act," which he called an apparent terrorist attack.

Within the hour an aircraft crashed at the Pentagon as well, and officials evacuated the White House and other major government buildings.

Authorities went on alert from coast to coast, halting all air traffic, evacuating high-profile buildings and tightening security at strategic installations.

Evacuations were ordered at the United Nations in New York and at the Sears Tower in Chicago. Los Angeles mobilized its anti-terrorism division, and security was intensified around the naval facilities in Hampton Roads, VA.

One of the planes that crashed into the Trade Center was American Airlines Flight 41, hijacked after takeoff from Boston en route to Los Angeles, American Airlines said.

The second plane may have flown out of Newark, N.J.

The spate of attacks fed into a rumor mill that kept growing as each new horror was revealed. Live television coverage riveted the nation, as people watched scenes of destruction that seemed beyond belief.

First one tower, then the other: The planes that slammed into the Trade Center blasted fiery, gaping holes in the upper floors of the twin towers. The southern tower collapsed with a roar about an hour later. With a huge cloud of smoke' the other tower fell about a half-hour after that.

Firefighters trapped in the rubble radioed for help.

Downtown New York turned into a crumbling, smoking nightmare.

"I just saw the building I work in come down," said businessman Gabriel Ioan, shaking in shock outside City Hall, a cloud of smoke and ash from the World Trade Center behind him. "I just saw the top of Trade Two come down."

Nearby, a crowd mobbed a man on a pay phone, screaming at him to get off the phone so that they could call relatives.

Dust and dirt flew everywhere. Ash was 2 to 3 inches deep in places. People wandered dazed and terrified.

Today we've had a national tragedy: The twin disaster at the World Trade Center happened shortly before 9 a.m. and then right around 9 a.m.

Heavy, black smoke billowed into the sky above the gaping holes in the side of the twin towers, one of New York City's most famous landmark, and debris rained down upon the street, one of the city's busiest work areas.

When the second plane hit, a fireball of flames and smoke erupted, leaving a huge hole in the glass and steel tower.

Wall Street shut down this morning, as did much of the downtown district, including the nearby Financial Center. It was difficult to make phone calls to the downtown business district and throughout Manhatten.

September 11

Let us take some comfort from this fact. The people responsible for yesterday's mind-numbing events in New York and Washington were no doubt hoping to further some cause, and whatever that cause may be, it is now lost. By the magnitude of their atrocity, these fanatics have assured that there will be no forgive and forget.

Tuesday began with Americans normally preoccupied with their own lives and their differing interests. But the worst terrorist attack in history has swept those differences away for a time. The country is united. There will be retribution. And if our leaders, and the leaders of the rest of the civilized world, behave rationally and cooperatively, it will be effective.

Not since Pearl Harbor has the United States experiences on its own territory the kind of devastation we witnessed yesterday. Out vulnerability is now evident—unfortunately, too late for the thousands of victims. Our self-confidence is shaken, but we can rebuild self confidence. We'd done it before.

September 11, 2001, takes it place alongside December 7, 1941, as a day that will be permanently engraved in the country's history. Sixty years ago, the United States knew who the enemy was and immediately set about to protect itself and even the score. Today's enemy is not yet clear, but, the determination of Americans is every bit as strong as it was then—perhaps even stronger, as we were all able to see this assault played

Photo by IAFF 9-11.

out in real time on our television screens. This was more than a political or military event; this was personal, something we felt in our chests and in our hearts.

Soon the shock and fear turned to anger. Yet, if our wisdom is as deep as our wounds, we will not meet hate and fanaticism with still more hate and fanaticism. We have learned that fighting indiscriminate violence with indiscriminate violence is a self-defeating proposition. One recalls commentator Eric Sevareid's bitter remark at the height of the bombing campaign in Vietnam that American policy seemed predicated on the assumption that Asia would eventually run out of Asians.

What's needed now is to meet insanity with intelligence, tempered as always by the very American values that are under attack. The United States possesses the world's most powerful military, which will be needed. But it also possesses extraordinary economic, intellectual and political-resources, all with unprecedented international reach. In the long run, those weapons, mangled with great resolve and the cooperation of allies, could prove most effective at isolating evil.

First, we need to identify friends and economics and work with the former to incapacitate the latter. As President Bush said last night, there must be no refuge for co-conspirators, whether they are nations, organizations or individuals. This is a time for choosing up sides, and then for choosing the right targets and the proper tools for the task ahead. Our goal must be not to create more martyrs, but to create conditions in which martyrdom losses its appeal.

The United States will prevail. The country has met greater challenges than this, because it has had sound leadership and a resilient people. If we keep our heads while we have our weapons, we will emerge from this crisis stronger and more secure.

Local officials placed on alert

Fire and Police departments were in heightened alert in Keene and the Monadnock Region Tuesday after the terrorist attacks in New York and Washington.

In part the alerts were a precaution in case the terrorist's attacks spread through the country; in part, they were reassurance to the citizens that law and order would prevail.

The State of NH Fire Standards and Training notified each fire department to build a recourse list if manpower and equipment was needed for New York. Deputy Fire Chief Steven Goldsmith notified that the list was

already established for Keene and the whole department was ready. Keene placed on the list an Engine Company one Chief and car in case it was needed at a moment's notice.

————

As Reported by the *Keene Evening Sentinel:*

Anthrax: Nation on edge

Keene Fire Department responded to nurmous Anthrax scares during 9-11. Photo by: Steven Goldsmith.

The discovery of a fourth anthrax case and warnings about additional terror attacks sent a riptide of anxiety through the nation Friday, creating a communal case of physical and psychological jitters.

News organizations, the targets in all the anthrax cases confirmed so far, responded to fresh incidents Friday at NBC and the New

York Times by intensifying their scrutiny of mail and packages, as did package-delivery companies. Keene was no different as the area received numerous calls for Anthrax scares throughout the city.

————

As Reported by the *Keene Evening Sentinel* September 29th, 2001:

"STORY"

Firefighting's in his blood Alexander Matson Jr. is retiring, in a way

Captain/EMT Alex Matson Jr.

When Keene firefighter Alexander W. Matson Jr. and his shift answered a call Tuesday night at Markem Corp., his career path came full circle.

Twenty-five years earlier, Matson worked two jobs, one with the printing division of Markem Corp., the other as a call firefighter for the Deluge Hose Co. It was then that the Keene Fire Department asked him to come aboard full-time.

For Matson, it was an easy decision.

"I wanted to go with the fire service. At the time, the fire service had its hooks in me," recalled Matson son of a Keene firefighter and father of two firefighters in training. I was able to be at the right place at the right time.

So, while Tuesday night's call was unremarkable—a sounding fire alarm—it made an ironic end to a quarter century with the department. On Tuesday, Capt. Matson retired from the department to take his passion for firefighting to other forums.

Firefighting domination Matson's past, his present and his future.

He calls it an opportunity to help others, saving everything from chairs to family photo albums to people's lives. He also likes being around firefighters whom he calls his brothers and sisters. At the department, Manson is known as "Buddy".

Born in Fitzwilliam and raised in Keene, Matson got his first taste of fire departments as a child. After Monday night Boy Scout meetings, he'd stop by the Keene fire station to visit his father and other firefighters. He remembers the trucks, the gear and the camaraderie of men who'd soon teach him the trade.

But things were different then. Firefighters worked longer hours and earned less money than now. In 1976, the department had 10 full-time firefighters, who worked 56 hours a week in three day shifts, three night shifts, with three days off, Matson earned $8,100 his first year.

Matson's wife, Nancy, earned more at her 35-hour-a-week job at National Grange Mutual Insurance Co.

Where money lacked, enthusiasm—often comical—didn't. As a new firefighter, Matson once rushed off out of uniform—really out of uniform. Matson would have arrived pant less at the emergency, were it not for a senior firefighter who passed him in the station.

"Where you going," asked the firefighter.

"Well, I guess I'm going to get my clothes," answered Matson, realizing his error. "I was so excited I forgot my bunker pants."

No matter, Matson learned his trade, largely by watching the older firefighters.

They showed him how to fight structural fires and to use a breathing apparatus. They paired up with him as he entered blazing buildings.

And there were plenty of opportunities to learn. Of the thousands of calls Matson answered over the ye4ars, most were traffic accidents or medical emergencies; others were blazing infernos that required skill and luck.

During a Water Street fire, to which his father also responded, Matson climbed atop a burning building and began to cut a hole when he suddenly sensed danger.

"I was cutting a whole in the roof and I could feel the roof giving way. I threw the saw at the chief and said," It's time to leave," Matson said.

Still not one firefighter fell in the line of duty during Matson's time with the department. He attributes that to skill and ever improving technology. For example, the department recently received thermal-imaging equipment that allows firefighters to sense temperature differences and rescue trapped people faster.

These days, Keene firefighters work 42 hours a week. That's two 11-hour day shifts, followed by a day off, then two 13-hour night shifts, followed by three days off.

If it seems as if firefighting dominates Matson's life, it's true. It has engaged his family, from his sons' career choices to his wife's free time, to everyone's dinner schedule.

Son Alexander 3rd, 19, is on the department's call force. Craig, 17, is with the department's Explorer group.

For Nancy Matson, it's meant being "shift mom" for a firefighting family, doing bookkeeping for her husband's entrepreneurial ventures, such as selling fire extinguishers, and a strange relationship between dinner time and fires.

"You'd prepare a big dinner and it would mean we'd have a fire," Alexander Matson said.

Most work-related family problems have been mundane. For example, Matson never seemed to lose the smell of smoke, no matter how many times he showered. It lingered for days, Nancy Matson said.

Odors, anxieties and disrupted dinners aside, firefighting has made for a memorable 25 years. The couple sits at their kitchen table, pouring over photographs of firefighting trips to Western states. Worn and dirtied duffel bags rest nearby, full of firefighting gear, ready to go at a moment's notice.

Matson spends his vacations battling blazes and training other firefighters. He's been to Idaho, Nevada, Oregon, Alabama, Minnesota and elsewhere. Several photos show fire crews posed before a helicopter.

"This is how he relaxes," said Nancy, pointing at the photographs.

Other images have brought shock to the Matsons'. On Sept. `11, they watched in horror as terrorists destroyed the World Trade Center towers in New York, killing thousands. Among the dead were several hundred firefighters, who had rushed to their deaths to save others as the towers collapsed.

"I could never fathom two 110-story buildings coming down, to lose that many firefighters, the planes, the people within the structures and the businesses," Alexander Matson said." Hopefully we'll never see this again."

Still, Matson hasn't seen his last fire.

His departure from the fire department is not a retirement in the traditional sense. Rather, he's devoting his energies toward teaching and training. As a representative of Minnesota-based Hypro Corp., Matson will instruct dealers and firefighters how to install and use the company's FoamPro line.

The devices calibrate and feed firefighting foam into fire engines' waterlines.

Matson's garage is now his office. Promotional brochures sit piled high, bound for 11 states from Maine to Delaware. And his firefighting gear stands ready in the kitchen ready for the next trip out West.

I get to play with fire trucks and still get to be with fire department personnel and train people. I'm basically a teacher now," Matson said.

Deputy Chief Steven W. Goldsmith predicts Matson will do well—and good—but added it's sad to see firefighters move on. Goldsmith said the department is losing a good firefighter, one whom he wishes the best of luck.

That said, Keene firefighters couldn't let Matson go without a memorable send-off. On Wednesday, they gave him a ride home in a fire engine, siren screaming, light flashing, water wet.

"That's somewhat of a tradition. They hose you down. You get wet whether you want to or not," Goldsmith said.

————

As Reported by the *Keene Evening Sentinel* September 30th, 2001:

"FIRE"

Small fire at Sims Portex

Smoke coming from a stack on the roof of a Keene business on Saturday drew three fire departments to the area.

At 5 p.m., crews from the Keene Fire Department responded to a fire in a room off the warehouse area at Sims Portex, Inc., 10 Bowan Drive, Keene.

The fire, in the room's dryer unit, was under control by 6 p.m., with smoke and minor water damage to the warehouse area.

There were no injuries. The cause is still unknown.

Keene Fire Department was assisted by crews from Marlborough and West Swanzey.

————

As Reported by the *Keene Evening Sentinel* October 11th, 2001:

"FIRE"

Keene business loses part of roof

Firefighters had to rip open part of the roof at People's Linen Rental in Keene Wednesday afternoon to get at flames.

Employees at the business, located at 9 Giffin St., tried to contain the fire with dry chemical extinguishers, but that didn't do the job, and firefighters had to tear out a 6-by-20 foot roof section to reach the fire.

The fire was confined to one area of the building, the Keene Fire Department said. The cause is still being investigated; damage estimates are unknown.

Keene firefighters were assisted by Swanzey, Marlborough and Brattleboro fire departments.

————

As Reported by Robert Koch in *Keene Evening Sentinel* October 24th, 2001:

"STORY"

Pumpkin Festival Keene readies for a plethora of pumpkins

Keene police and Pumpkin Festival organizers have stepped up security for this year's event.

More police, jersey barriers and other—unspecified—measures will ensure a safe Pumpkin Festival in Keene this weekend, police say.

The increased security measures are in response to the 'Sept. 11 terrorist attacks, said Keene Police Chief Barry E. Wante.

"There's an increased expectation of security and certainly, we're responding to that," Wante said. However, he emphasized that police have not received any threats of violence for this weekend.

More uniformed police officers, both Keene and N.H. State Police, will be present. Concrete jersey barriers will block off parts of Main, Washington, West, Court and Roxbury streets. In prior years, wooden barricades were used to block streets.

"If someone tries to drive around a barrier, that's not going to be taken lightly." Wante said.

For example, the Keene police and fire departments will again manage as emergency operations center. There, police and fire officials can communicate with officers around Keene, give directions or watch lost children until their parents are found.

"We want a good event, and people have the right to feel safe," Wante said.

Emergency rolls change due to 9/11

The pumpkin Festival throughout the years has grown in size and demand on the safety service. 9/11 brought changes.

Nancy Sporborg in 1991 created the event and was known as the Harvest Festival.

Each year the event population grew due to the most lit pumpkins in the world when Keene entered the Guinness Book of World Records.

Due to the tragic events of 9/11 this year our rolls became more complicated and our role of emergency services changed the way we do business.

Dealing with more than 65,000 people together in an area of Central Square and Main Street area created special attention on the safety of the event.

Deputy Fire Chief Steven Goldsmith contacted the Military Support Administration to assist with the security and safety of the Pumpkin Festival.

The military team with its special equipment could gather information that would assist our departments both police and fire which involved 3 states, NH, Maine and Mass.

The information gathered and equipment used improved our readiness and assisted our department for future events.

————

As Reported by Gref Coffey in *Keene Evening Sentinel* November 9th, 2001:

"STORY"

Scare closes Keene FedEx Clinic threat link possible

A suspicious package filled with white powder shut down the Federal Express packaging center at Black Brook Corporate Park in Keene Thursday.

Around the country Thursday, letters with threats of death by anthrax poisoning arrived at the offices of 132 Planned Parenthood and about 200 other abortion clinics.

Five letters were addressed to clinics in New Hampshire, one to a Maine clinic and three to Massachusetts clinics, said Gail Marcinkiewicz, a spokesman for the Federal Bureau of Investigation in Boston.

Federal Express delivered packages that turned out to contain a white powder and a threatening message Thursday to Planned Parenthood in Derry, the Portsmouth Feminist Health Care Center in Greenland, and the Concord Feminist Health Center.

After a nationwide alert about items addressed to women's clinics, Federal Express workers intercepted packages in Keene and Lebanon before they were delivered. Both cities have Planned Parenthood offices.

It's not yet clear if the package found in Keene is related to the packages that arrived at Planned Parenthood offices.

Shortly before 11 a.m. Thursday, workers at Federal Express in Keene found the suspicious package. They opened it carefully, and found it was filled with white powder and had a threatening note in it.

Federal Express workers who are trained to deal with hazardous materials wrapped up the package and put in a container, while the Keene fire and Police departments were called, said Ed. A. Coleman, a Federal Express spokesman.

Only a few people at the facility handled the package. Keene Police Chief Barry E. Wante said.

The building was blocked off for about three hours while the Keene Police and Fire department hazardous materials team searched the area, making sure that everything suspicious had been collected, Wante said.

The package was sent to the state forensic laboratory in Concord. Testing should be completed in four to six days, Marcinkiewicz said.

The incident is being investigated by the Federal Bureau of Investigation's Boston office.

The envelopes carried the return address of Ann Glazier. Planned Parenthood's security director, Wagner said. Inside the envelopes were notes from a group calling itself the Army of God, an extreme anti-abortion group that has claimed responsibility for bombing clinics and killing doctors who perform abortions.

Parts of the letter said, "this contains anthrax. You're going to die," and, "don't take this home to your children," Wagner said.

The agency's national offices in New York City, received one of the letters this morning, so there may be more letters that have not been discovered, Wagner said.

"This isn't simple harassment; this is terrorism, pure and simple," Wagner said.

The directors of Planned Parenthood, the National Abortion Federation and the Feminist Majority asked Thursday for a meeting with U.S. Attorney General John Ashcroft and Homeland Security Director Thomas Ridge.

"Anthrax threats are clearly designed to scare reproductive health-care providers," said Vicky Jaffe, a spokeswoman for Planned Parenthood of Northern New England.

———

November 10th, 2001 event sponsored by Keene State College:

"STORY"

The Night of Broken Glass

Fire Department personnel are requested at local events to assist agencies in presenting messages of remembrance.

On the night of November 9 &10th a program was orchestrated throughout Germany and Austria by the third Reich's Propaganda Ministry and the SA (Sturmabteilung or Storm Troops) 91 Jews were killed in addition 815 shops, 29 department stores, 171 residences and 267 Synagogues were burned or otherwise destroyed.

The shattered panes of beveled plate glass that littered sidewalks, most of it coming from shop windows of Jewish stores, gave the program its long-standing name. Kristallnacht or "Night of Broken Glass."

Chief officers of police and Fire had the privilege to be part of this program. Deputy Chief Steven Goldsmith represented the Keene Fire Department as the voice of Iman Vahidin Omanovich and Chief Barry Wante represented the Keene Police Department and his voice of Rabbi Micah Becker-Klein.

———

As Reported by the *Keene Evening Sentinel* November 19th, 2001:

"FIRE"

Fire guts Portland Street home

Fire Department Photo.

A fire gutted part of a Keene home Sunday afternoon as the homeowner performed in an operetta.

The fire broke out at 42 Portland St., sending flames shooting through the roof of the single-family home by the time firefighters arrived shortly before 5 p.m., firefighters said.

Homeowners Peter B. and Martha L. Wright were away when the fire broke out. Peter Wright was performing in the chorus of the matinee performance of "The Yeoman of the Guard" at the Colonial Theater.

"The family lost their dog in the fire and was relocated due to the extent of the fire damage," said Deputy Fire Chief Steven W. Goldsmith.

The blaze heavily damaged the rear third of the home and caused extensive heat and smoke damage to the front and upper portions of the home, Goldsmith said.

Arriving at the scene, Keene Fire Department Capt. Arthur Johnson found "heavy fire in the rear with fire through the roof in the first section. The crews stopped the fire at the one third part," Goldsmith said.

Albert H. Weeks, judge of Cheshire County Probate Court who lives near the Wrights, spotted the fire as he rushed to finish raking leaves before the sun set.

"I heard this pinging sound—probably breaking glass—and looked up and saw flames shooting up above one of my neighbors' garage." Weeks said. "I ran over there and saw my neighbor's house on fire and sprinted back to my own house and dialed 911.

"I happened to be outside when it started, thankfully," Weeks said.

Firefighters used the department's new thermal-imaging camera to see whether the fire had extended into the walls and ceiling of the upper floors. Crews set up fans to remove heat and smoke as they fought the blaze.

Fire crews from both of Keene's fire stations helped battle the fire; the Marlborough and Brattleboro fire departments helped cover for the Keene

firefighters in case any other emergencies occurred.

The American Red Cross was called out for assistance, and the Wrights reportedly spend the night with neighbors.

"The actual structure of the house is salvageable. They did a good job stopping the fire, because it was going," Goldsmith said.

———

As Reported by the *Keene Evening Sentinel* December 6th, 2001:

"FIRE"

Two Keene fires called suspicious

Two suspicious fires that broke out late Wednesday night and early this morning in Keene are being investigated.

The first fire, Wednesday at about 11:30 p.m., burned most of a grass hut outside the Millennium Club on Gilbo Avenue, Keene police said.

The sound fire was in a storage building at the Island Mills complex on Island Street, police said. The complex is home to many businesses.

No further information about the fires was available this morning.

As Reported by the *Keene Evening Sentinel* December 7th, 2001:

"STORY"

Police, fire site eyed in Keene

A new contender has emerged in Keene's long search for new police and fire headquarters; what used to be the Supervalu food-distribution warehouse at 350 Marlboro St.

Now, the police station is part of Keene City Hall, and the fire station is around the corner on Vernon Street. Both are cramped.

For several years, Keene officials have been studying what to do. The fire department has dealt with some of its logistical problems by opening a branch station in the National Guard armory on Hastings Avenue, getting around downtown traffic problems that can interfere with fire trucks and ambulances speeding to an emergency.

The latest contender has been a joint police-fire station at Elm and Vernon streets, incorporating a big overhaul of the Elm Street parking lot. However, it's been a hard sell, for multiple reasons—security, parking and costs among them. Project estimates were in the $16 million range.

The sprawling Supervalu building became available when the Minneapolis-based company closed its Keene distribution center at the end of August, consolidating its operation elsewhere.

About 130 people worked at the 200,000 square-foot warehouse, which was a distribution center for about 130 Big Kmart Pantry stores in New England. The closing announcement came 15 months after the company said it would keep the Keene warehouse open for several more years. Supervalu is one of the nation's largest grocery distributors and 10th-largest supermarket retailer.

At 200,000 square feet, the building is big enough to handle trucks, staff quarters and offices for the fire department, and the offices, detention and booking facilities, and conference areas that police need.

The location is outside the city center, but close to downtown. And the state's planned Keene by pass overhaul would make Marlboro Street a major entry point for traffic headed downtown.

The Supervalu building could also solve another headache for Keene: good records storage. Now, many of the city's records are jammed into a vault and other spaces at City Hall; preserving deteriorating records has become a major effort in the city clerk's office.

The idea surfaced Thursday night, when the Keene City Council authorized City Manager John *MacLean to negotiate, and execute, a contract with Supervalu.*

As Reported by the *Keene Evening Sentinel* December 9th, 2001:

"STORY"

Officials like what they see

The vacated Keene warehouse has ample space to play football in, drive fire trucks and snow plows through—or simply get lost walking around in.

And for about $15 million, the former Supervalu food-distribution center at 350 Marlboro St. also could become home to the city's space-crunched police, fire and public works departments.

On Saturday morning, two dozen city officials glimpsed the warehouse during the two-hour 2001 capital improvement program tour, which surveyed past, present and future projects throughout the city.

Clearly, the warehouse was the highlight.

The warehouse emerged suddenly this week at the prime contender in Keene's long search for new police and fire headquarters. The police station is now part of Keene City Hall; the fire station is around the corner on Vernon Street.

City Manager John A. MacLean pitched the Marlboro Street property at a cost-saving alternative to a joint police-fire station at Elm and Vernon Streets. For that plan, land purchases, building construction, a 400-space parking deck and other related improvement could cost $25 million, he said.

By contrast, the Marlboro Street location "would be $15 million to do all that work

—a $10 million savings immediately. It would be a significant shot in the arm for the city if this location can work for us," MacLean said.

MacLean said New York based Eastern Development is selling the property for $3.7 million; an additional $10 million renovation would reconfigure the warehouse to department needs and replace 25 percent of the building's roof.

Department heads seemed impressed. Fire Chief Bradley B. Payne called the building

and location excellent, but added firefighters have yet to tour the warehouse. Police Chief Barry E. Wante called the building a "fresh canvas" and said his department would no longer be constrained by limited space.

————

As Reported by the *Keene Evening Sentinel* December 20th, 2001:

"FIRE"

Keene fire traced to lamp

A heat lamp probably caused the fire that destroyed a manufactured home in Keene Monday.

Peter Scott and his family lost their home at 30 Starling St. after a heat lamp was knocked over, setting the fire, Keene firefighters said. The lamp was being used to warm reptiles the family kept as pets.

The reptiles and a cat and dog died, killed in the fire. No members of the family were home when the heat lamp was knocked over, and the fire may have burned for a little while before it was reported.

————

As Reported by the *Keene Evening Sentinel* December 23rd, 2001:

"FIRE"

Fire forces families out of building on Pine Street

Four days before Christmas, Hugh Brown and his four children were forced to find shelter when fire destroyed their home Friday.

In all, three households were forced into the cold when fire destroyed a three-story house at 55 Pine St. at 10:40 p.m.

Photo by: Robert J. Diluzio Sr.

Upon arrival of the first fire units the call went to a second alarm and as chief officers arrived on scene the fire was upgraded to a third alarm with additional pumper and ladder.

According to Keene Fire officials, the fire was first visible on the first floor and spread throughout the building. Before extinguishing the fire; Keene Deputy Fire Chief Stevens Goldsmith was fire scene safety officer and while checking the building ordered all emergency personnel out of the building as the roof was about to collapse.

Deputy Goldsmith called South Western Mutual Aid and advised to put a mayday tone out to Keene radios for a building evacuation due to a possible roof collapse.

The tone went out and air horns started blowing. As Captain Dean Ericson, last to leave the building evacuated the chimney went over bringing the roof in and bricks and roof material chased the captain to the street.

There were no injuries. However, the three apartments in the building were deemed unlivable. The fire department is still investigating the cause.

The other two households found shelter with friends.

Contributions can be sent to the American Red Cross Local Disaster Relief Fund, 83 Court St., Keene 03431, or call 352-3210. Pine Street resident Joan Ryder is also accepting donated clothing. She can be reached at 357-1713.

———————

2002

January 3rd, 2002 Fire Department News Release By Steven Goldsmith:

"FIRE"

Fire Damages Mobile Home at 19 Blue Jay Court Tanglewood Ests.

Keene firefighters responded to a reported fire in a mobile home at 19 Blue jay Court at 12:45 pm. Thursday afternoon. While Keene fire units were en route to this fire Keene Mutual Aid Dispatch Center received calls that the fire was through the roof. Lt harry Nelson from Station 2 arrived on scene and gave a report that they had heavy fire and the fire was through the roof in the middle of the mobile home. Crews from Station 2 and Central made an interior attack that kept the fire to the back third of the home.

The Thermal Imaging Camera was used for search and rescue and also used to check for extension of fire within the home. The camera was also used to safe a cat's life which was discovered in the kitchen by call Firefighter Davis. The cat was handed to FF. Gianferrari along with Capt Boynton who placed oxygen to the cat. Keene Police transported the cat to Court Street Veterinary Hospital where the cat is doing fine.

Deputy Chief Steven Goldsmith declared the fire under control at 1:05 pm.

Capt Gary LaFreniere Fire Prevention Officer and the Keene Fire Department Investigation team are working to determine the cause of the fire. At this time the fire appears to be accidental.

Fire units remain on scene during press release. There were no reported injuries during the fire.

While at the scene units from Surry and Swanzey were called to the scene for tankers and Marlborough, NH. Fire Department covered the central station.

————

As Reported by Greg Coffey in *Keene Evening Sentinel* January 30th, 2002:

"STORY"

Keene firefighters train in darkened maze

Trailer simulates real condition

Two Keene firefighters, cladding in fire suits, helmets, masks and air tanks, climb up a ladder and down a hatch into total darkness.

About 10 minutes later, the two emerged, unscathed. That's because they weren't fighting a fire, but were conducting a training exercise inside a 26 foot long trailer, on loan from the N.H. department of safety.

Inside the trailer ate two levels and a maze of cages, tubes, hatches and hurdles that must be negotiated by two firefighters at a time.

Firefighters start the course by climbing through a hatch in the top of the trailer, and finish by exiting a door on the other end. Loud music or fire-like noises can be blasted into the trailer so firefightrers can't hear each other, forcing the pair to keep in direct contact with each other.

The idea is to allow firefighters to experience conditions the inability to see or hear each other or to see where they are going, they might encounter during a real fire.

"Other than the heat and the smoke, it's very realistic," said Lt. Mark Howard.

The safety department bought the trailer in 1997 for $95,000 and it's loaned to fire departments around the state at no cost.

The Keene Fire Department had the trailer for about 10 days, and finished up Tuesday.

From start to finish, the maze can take anywhere from 10 to 30 minutes, said Capt. Mark Boynton, head of training for the Keene fire Department.

At times, firefighters must climb over walls or through tubes. Some of the larger firefighters couldn't fit into a 24 inch tube with their air tanks on. They are forced to take their tanks off and slide them in front of them to fit through.

"It tests your limit to see if you're claustrophobic or not. It makes you stop and think," said Firefighter Eric Matson.

The trailer has two rooms, one is the maze, which takes up most of the space, and the other is a control room, which is about 3 feet wide. Firefighters can be heard banging around inside as they pass the control room.

Inside the control room, firefighters are monitored by three infrared cameras, which are in the maze room. The cameras relay images of the firefighters as they weave their way through the maze. Several microphones allow observers to talk to the firefighters or to hear what they are saying.

The cages, tubes and hatches inside the trailer can be switched around so firefighters see a different maze each time they go through.

"Sometimes we send them in from where they finished the first time, and they swear you've changes it around, "Boynton said."

Sometimes, a firefighter might be forced to turn around and go back to where they started, he said. "It doesn't mean that they failed. That's all part of the training; realizing what you're capable of and what you're not."

While most Keene firefighters agreed the trailer is good training it doesn't match up to the real thing, said Lt. Harry Nelson.

You know there's nothing in there that's going to hurt you. You know you're safe he said."

————

As Reported by *Keene Evening Sentinel* February 2nd, 2002:

"STORY"

Crews Clean up Keene Spill

Photos by Steven Goldsmith.

A maintenance crew pumped an unidentified yellow liquid out of the ground electric volt and onto Central Square are in Keene Friday morning.

At 8:30 a.m. Public Service of New Hampshire maintenance crews was pumping water from an underground transformer vault. They halted the routine maintenance whet her realized they were not pumping water but yellow liquid into the street said Deputy Fire Chief Steven Goldsmith of the Keene Fire Department.

The liquid flowed into the street and onto the snow around Central Square. Something was in the vault that they were unaware of

Goldsmith said. We really don't know what it is, that's why were taking all the precautions.

The maintenance crew called a PSNH emergency response worker to clean up the mess. They placed white absorbent booms into the puddleing of the yellow substance in the hope that the booms would contain the liquid.

The underground transformer is located in front of city hall and traffic was still able to move downtown.

At 11 p.m. workers with Mass based Clean Harbors Inc. an emergency response clean up company, were still working on cleaning up the area. Cleaning crew members said it may take two or three days to clean up the area and identify the liquid.

———

Keene Fire Department Deputy Goldsmith March 6th, 2002:

"STORY"

Paramedic Honorees and Promotions

On March 6th, a Paramedic and Promotion Ceremony were held at the Central Fire Station on Vernon Street in Keene.

10 members of the Keene Department were honored for completing a long and durable course which at times was wonder if it would ever end or c complete the intense study and clinical time at major hospital trauma units. Those members that were honored were Capt. Jeffrey Morel, Lieut. Jeffrey Chickering, Lieut. Mark Howard, Lieut. Stephen McKenna, Lieut. Christopher Simino, Firefighters Michael Abbott, FF Michael Bailey, FF John Bates, FF Michael Gianferrari and FF Timothy Read.

Officers that were promoted were Lieut. Jeffery Morel to Captain, Lieut. Michael Burke to Captain, Firefighters Stephen McKenna to Lieut. And FF Christopher Simino to Lieut.

———

As Reported by Dan Gearino in *Keene Evening Sentinel* May 2nd, 2002:

"STORY"

Debts nudge Keene budget higher

Loan payments are the major factor behind a small hike in the Keene city government's budget.

That's according to City Manager John A. MacLean's 2002-03 budget proposal, issued Wednesday afternoon.

The $32,149,555 proposal is up 3.8 percent from current spending, and would boost the city government's portion of the property-tax rate by roughly 2 percent, to $10.40. That would add $20 to the tax bill on a $100,000 house.

The Keene City Council will review MacLean's proposal and adopt a budget before the next fiscal year begins July 1.

The tax-rate estimate assumes that the value of Keene's taxable property will increase about 5.6 percent to about $1.2 billion, partly from new construction and partly from growth in property values.

The higher cost of debt stems from big purchases, most notably the $4.7 million spent to buy the former Supervalu food warehouse at 350 Marlboro St. which the city plans to convert into a police-fire-public works headquarters.

"We have been able to accommodate some of the large projects, while maintaining a low tax increase," MacLean said this morning.

He is requesting about $2.5 million for debt payments, up from $2 million in the current year budget by far the largest increase in the budget.

MacLean proposes little, if any increase in city department budgets, with no major increases in staffing or programs.

However, he wants to promote the leader of city's community services departments to the rand of assistance city manager. Those departments include police, fire, youth services, library, parks recreation facilities and human resources. The change likely means that an existing city employee will get the new title and pay raises making a total of three assistant city managers in city government.

————

As Reported by Robert Koch in *Keene Evening Sentinel* June 7th, 2002:

"STORY"

Keene raising its ambulance fees

The council approved raising the city's ambulance fees 10 percent higher than the prevailing Medicare payments for many common services.

Medicare, the federal health-insurance program for people 65 and older, revamped its ambulance rates April 1. Now Medicare reimburses Keene $163.89 for each case of advanced life support service, such as treatment for heart attacks. That rate is targeted to climb $478.59 by 2006.

————

As Reported by Robert Koch in *Keene Evening Sentinel* August 17th, 2002:

"STORY"

Fund-raiser aids local firefighters

After last September's terrorist attacks, Martha C. Hongisto and other Keene choir leaders wanted to do something patriotic.

Keene Chorale Inc., the Keene Pops Choir and the Chamber Singers of Keene-more than 200 singers-threw one grand concert at Keene Middle School in February and donated $2,770 in ticket sales to local firefighters.

"We wanted to do something patriotic and do something locally, as opposed to sending our money off to New York," said Hongisto, Keene Chorale president.

A half-year later, Keene firefighters are seeing the results of the singers' generosity; four lifesaving inflatable air bags that they will use to free victims in the worst car wrecks.

"We'd been working to get new airbags," said Keene fire Capt. Michael A. Burke, who's president of firefighters union Local 3265. "They don't get used that often, but it's one of those tools: When you need it, you have it."

The Hurst air bags-made by the manufacture of the Jaws of Life, the hydraulic tools that can peel back automobile roofs or doors to free people trapped in wreckage-resemble heavy duty black rubber doormats. Air lines attach to their corners inflating the bags with enough pressure to lift up to 26 tons.

That force can also spell the difference between life and death. Firefighters will slip the 1 inch thick rectangular mat under a leverage point on your overturned vehicle inflate it and you'll have overcome the first hurdle in surviving a wreck.

Burke said the department's old air bags date to the 1970s. The new ones, he said, are better because they're quieter. That means rescuers can talk to trapped victims as they work, instead of being drowned out by a noisy compressed air hose.

Truth be told, the new air bags and their accompanying control box cost $5,000-$2,230 more than the singers raised.

"We were hoping we'd come up with $5,000, but we were a little under," said Jean P. Nelson, conductor of the Keene Pops and Chamber Singers.

The concert drew more than 500 people to the middle school, Dressed in red white and blue attire, the singers sang, among other songs, "god Bless the USA," "Let There Be Peace on Earth" and "Battle Hymn of the Republic."

Several firefighters carried the American flag as the national anthem was sung.

Firefighters will demonstrate their new air bags Tuesday at 3:30 p.m. at the Central fire station 32 Vernon Street.

————

As Reported by the *Keene Evening Sentinel* September 5th, 2002:

"FIRE"

Transformer fire causes blackout

A power line transformer fire on Old Walpole Road knocked power out to most of western Keene early this morning.

Details on what caused the fire weren't available this morning. A report of a transformer on fire was called in to Southwestern N.H. Fire Mutual Aid at 12:07 a.m. Keene fire officials responded and quickly had the blaze under control, an emergency dispatcher said this morning.

Although the fire didn't cause any major damage, it knocked out power for several hours.

Officials from Public Service Co. of New Hampshire couldn't be reached this morning for details about the number of homes affected.

————

As Reported by the *Keene Evening Sentinel* September 6th, 2002:

"FIRE"

Fire doused at Keene factory

A small fire was found in ductwork at Timken Super Precision Bearing (MPB) on Optical Avenue, Keene, at about 3 this morning.

The Keene Fire Department found the fire while investigating what caused smoke in the building. No details were available this morning.

The building was evacuated and the fire was extinguished.

Robert Rooney, director of organizational advancement at Timken said there were about 60 employees in the building at the time. One employee was taken to the hospital, released and returned later to complete his shift, Rooney said.

––––––––

As Reported by the *Keene Evening Sentinel* September 11th, 2002:

"FIRE"

Smoke detectors save family

Smoke detectors saved a family from a fire late Tuesday night on Schult Street in Keene.

Firefighters were called to 29 Schult St., part of a mobile-home park off Base Hill Road, shortly after 10 p.m. The fire was reported under control about 20 minutes later.

Smoke alarms awoke the family of four and allowed them to escape serious injury, according to the Keene Fire Department.

Amanda Loder was taken to Cheshire Medical Center for treatment of minor smoke inhalation. Her three children, whose ages weren't available, were uninjured, Deputy Fire Chief Gary P. Lamoureaux said this morning. He said the home sustained minor smoke damage.

––––––––

As Reported by Robert Koch in *Keene Evening Sentinel* September 11th, 2002:

Photo by: Robert J. Diluzio Sr.

Photo by: Robert J. Diluzio Sr.

"STORY"

Bitter memories haven't faded Tragedy's victims and heroes are honored

Hundreds packed Keene's Central Square Wednesday morning to remember the thousands killed in last September's terrorist attacks.

Tear-filled eyes, bowed heads and solemn faces spoke louder than words at the one-year anniversary of the attacks that killed more than 3,000 people in New York City, Washington D.C., and Pennsylvania.

Rev. Robert C. Hamm of United Church of Christ in Keene called the ceremony an opportunity to remember the lives of those lost, and thank firefighters, police officers and others who protect public safety.

"It's a day to remember, to grieve, to thank all those who functioned and did their duty," said Hamm, who's the Keene Fire Department chaplain.

Mayor Michael E.J. Blastos, city and Cheshire County officials, and uniformed police officers and firefighters shouldering rifles and axes stood by silently as Keene police Officer Darryl Madden marched to the gazebo, playing "Going Home" on a bagpipe.

At 10:30, a.m. the Keene Fire Department whistle at 32 Vernon St. sounded "5-5-5," recognized by firefighters nationwide as a signal that firefighters have fallen.

"It's a day to remember to grieve, to… thank all those who functioned and did their duty,"—Rev. Robert C. Hamm Fire Dept. Chaplain.

After a minute of silence for the attacks' victims, Keene police and fire department color guards lowered their flags, and Madden played "Amazing Grace."

From the gazebo, firefighter William Shea read the "Fireman's Prayer":

"Guard my every neighbor and protect his property…and if, according to my fate, I am to lose my life, please bless with your protective hand my children and my wife."

Keene police Cpl. Eliezer Rivera followed with the Policeman's Prayer":

"Oh Almighty God…protect these brave men. Grant them Your almighty protection. Unite them safely with their families after duty has ended."

After a closing prayer, Madden played "Grand O'le Flag," and people consoled one another and reflected on the tragedy.

Alyse G. Bettinger, who moved to Keene from New York City several years ago, pondered how New York has changed since the attacks. She said it's been difficult hearing relatives recall the smell of dirt and dust from the collapsed World Trade Center towers, as military jets patrolled the skies.

"They lost their lives for no real reason—they were just living and being free," Bettinger said of the victims.

Jeremey J. Barcomb, an Army reservist from Keene, took the day off from working at Wal-Mart in Keene. He put on his olive-drab uniform and came to the American-flag-ringed square because "I thought this was more important.

"I'm just out here to pay tribute like everyone else," Barcomb said.

The remembrance followed a 24-hour vigil on the square by M.H. Peace Action. The Concord-based group also held vigils in Concord, Dover, Durham, Franklin, Hanover, Laconia,Peterborough and Portsmouth. The vigils mourned the victims of the attacks, and lives lost in Afghanistan, Iraq, Israel, Palestine, Columbia and elsewhere to terrorism and warfare.

———

As Reported by Benjamin Yelle in *Keene Evening Sentinel* October 5th, 2002:

"FIRE"

Fire damages wooden shed on Dunbar Street

Firefighters from several area departments quickly knocked down a fire at an abandoned shed next to the N.G. Gurnsey Building on Dunbar Street in Keene Friday night.

No one was injured, said Keene Fire Chief Bradley B. Payne. The cause of the fire was still undetermined at press time. The area, a collection of warehouse buildings surrounded by woods, is a known party spot for teenagers.

"We've had a lot of homeless people back here," said Dunbar Street resident Helena Landis, who was walking her dog when she noticed the fire engines lining her street shortly after 10 p.m.

"As I came down Dunbar Street, I could see the smoke way up in the air, and I thought it was my apartment," she said.

Dozens of firefighters from Keene, Swanzey, Marlborough and the Meadowood Area Community Fire Department in Fitzwilliam responded to the fire.

Flames shot several feet into the sky, drawing onlookers to the parking lot next to the buildings. Firefighters had the flames extinguished within seconds of their arrival, but spend about 45 minutes dousing the charred remains of the building and making sure the fire hadn't spread.

The Gurnsey Building, a brick structure, is used as warehouse space, Landis said. The wood structure that caught fire was next to the building.

"It was strictly outside," Payne said, of the fire. "They had it under control quickly."

Fire explorers entered the two-story structure to make sure the fire hadn't spread into the warehouse, and that no one was inside.

Witnesses said a young man told them his friend was homeless and living in the dilapidated structure.

Several firefighters from the Keene department showed up at the fire in suits, with their wives. Payne, who was wearing his dress uniform, said the department was in the middle of a firemen's ball when they were called to the warehouse.

———

As Reported by Benjamin Yelle in *Keene Evening Sentinel* October 10th, 2002:

"STORY"

Firefighters honored for heroism

Whether they were rescuing people from frigid water or burning cars, Keene rescue personnel were up to the challenge last year.

On Wednesday, four members of the Keene Fire Department were recognized for their heroism at a ceremony in Concord.

Lt. Mark Howard, firefighter William M. Greenwood, and paramedics Timothy Clark and John Bates were recognized by the N.H. Fire Service Committee of Merit for heroic rescues in 2001.

Bates and Greenwood were awarded Class 2 medals of honor for rescuing Edward S. Bezanson, 31, of Walpole, whose pickup truck crashed into the Branch River, off Route 101 near Optical Avenue in Keene, on April 16, 2001.

Bezanson suffered a seizure and lost control of his pickup, which became airborne before crashing into the river. Bates and Greenwood used dive gear and ladders to reach the truck, which had partially filled with water, and remove Bezanson.

The Class 2 medals were awarded to 10 rescue workers across the state.

Howard and Clark received unit citation bars for rescuing a woman from a car that crashed into a telephone pole and burst into flames August 29, 2001. The bars are similar to military decorations and can be affixed to their uniforms.

"If it wasn't for them being on the scene, she would have probably lost her life," said Deputy Keene Chief Steven W. Goldsmith. "It's extraordinary we have individuals willing to risk their lives."

A panel of 13 rescue officials from across the state chose the award winners.

The awards program was started in 1987 and is funded entirely through donations.

———

By Steven Goldsmith October 21st, 2002:

"STORY"

We must do our best

Now that Sept. 11 has come and gone, it is only fitting that we as safety service personnel say thank you.

I had the privilege to be asked to speak as a representative of Keene and area firefighters along with Sheriff Dick Foote of the Cheshire County Sheriff's Department, at an evening service held at Sturtevant Chapel on Washington Avenue in Keene on Sept 11. Many memorial services were held throughout the city and the country that evening.

As we deeply honored the murdered victims following our first year of a lifetime of mourning, the losses of the civilians, police officers and especially our brother firefighters in the N.Y. Fire Department, keep in mind the importance of our freedoms and what we stand for.

A year has passed and we remember those who have given the ultimate sacrifice.

Not only fire and police, but also those so many whose only thought was to go to work and do an honest day's work and then return home. As firefighters, we know that each call we respond to may be different and may not be a routine call. Today, you just don't know what to except, as our lives have been forever changed.

We as a community and a nation can let what happened a year ago defeat us or strengthen us. We must choose the latter. We must dedicate ourselves to helping others in their honor. We must make our professional lives a testimonial to honoring those victims by doing only the best all the time.

We as firefighters must carry on their heroic work in ways both small and large when people are looking, and most importantly when no one has a chance of noticing-just as they would have done.

It is our privilege to serve the members of our community. For the opportunity to serve, I thank you, and God bless all of you. Take care of each other and be safe.

Steven Goldsmith Keene Fire Department

As Reported by the *Keene Evening Sentinel* November 25th, 2002:

"FIRE"

Basement fire doused quickly

Keene firefighters put out a fire in a basement Saturday night that was likely kindled by a clothes dryer.

Smoke was showing outside 98 Woodburn St. at about 7:30 p.m. when firefighters arrived. After the crews entered the basement, they found flames had gone up a wall and into a space between the basement ceiling and the floor of the home's first story.

Laurie Jean Baker was home with her child when the fire started. There were no injuries or significant damage.

The fire started somewhere near the dryer, said Deputy Gary Lamoureux of the Keene Fire Department, which is still investigating.

2003

As Reported by Robert Koch in *Keene Evening Sentinel* January 18th, 2003:

"STORY"

Keene gets new decontamination trailer

Photo by Steve Goldsmith.

Doff your duds, step under the shower, scrub behind your ears, leave the water running and move along to let the next radioactive person step into Keene's new decontamination shower trailer.

What sort of trailer was that?

It's a white 8-by-28 foot trailer with six swing out shower heads outside, two show stalls inside, a hot-water heater, and a 2,000 gallon holding tank to cleanse 800 people per hour who have been sprinkled with radioactive fallout, or with dangerous chemical and biological goop.

On Wednesday, Keene Deputy Fire Chief Steven W. Goldsmith and Capt. Scott Taylor, coordinator of the fire department's hazardous materials team, picked up the $75,000 trailer. The trailers are made by Advanced Containment Systems, Inc. of Houston. The NH Office ofEmergency Management landed a dozen of them, using federal grant money, Goldsmith said.

"It's another step toward the reality of what our future brings," Goldsmith said grimly. "Let's hope we never have to use it except in training.

True enough.

But with the Sept. 11, 2001, terrorist attacks, the looming prospect of war with Iraq, and ever-increasing talk of "weapons of mass destruction," state-of-the-art emergency trailers have taken on new importance.

That Keene got a decontamination trailer is no fluke.

The Vermont Yankee nuclear power plant lies across the Connecticut River in Vernon, Vt, Goldsmith said winds probably wouldn't carry radioactive releases to Keene, but they could send several thousand Chesterfield, Hinsdale and Swanzey residnets rushing to the trailer that's now parked at the West Keene fire station.

In the event of a chemical or biological attack, Goldsmith envisions the trailer being used to scrub up to 70,000 people.

If you should ever be one of those 70,000, stay tuned to your radio or television to find out where to find the decontamination trailer.

Goldsmith said firefighters would likely tow the trailer—using a 1-ton pickup—to Keene State College, or perhaps Brattleboro,

or wherever N.H. emergency management officials decide it can best be used.

Once you find it, strip down, and step either inside a shower stall or underneath an outside showerhead. If you're the modest type, there are privacy curtains.

The 70-degree water is mixed with whatever sort of soap the particular emergency demands.

"When you walk out of that (after) being decontaminated, you're clean" Goldsmith said.

———

As Reported by Robert Koch in *Keene Evening Sentinel* February 14th, 2003:

"STORY"

Ambulance, fire truck still in plan

Keene Fire Department has placed into service at the West Keene Fire Station, a new brush truck. It is a 2002 Ford F350 with a Lighting 15,000-lb. winch and accessories installed by City of Keene Fleet Service. Its radio was installed by the SWNHDFMA Radio Shop. The lettering was sone by Mac Mackenzie. The truck will have a new slide-in bruch unit with a 150-gal.poly tank, hose reel, Scotty foam system and high pressure pump.

A new ambulance and fire department tanker truck are still part of the Keene city government's plans in coming years, but just barely.

Those purchases—totaling $490,000—are part of Keene's capital improvement plan for 2008-09, a six-year schedule for financing major projects such as roads, bridges, sewers and big-ticket purchases. The city uses the plan to minimize the financial impact of any particular project, while consistently reviewing priorities for what Keene needs.

On Thursday night the Keene City Council's finance committee recommended approving the $106.8 million package, which is 6.3 percent lower than last year's version of $114 million.

The panel recommended a one-year delay in spending $685,746 to build a parking lot and rebuild several intersections. That drops the first-year cost of the plan to $13.9 million.

The 15-member council may amend the plan further before adopting it next week.

The Keene Taxpayers Association had hoped to delay purchase of the $115,000 ambulance and $375,000 Engine Pumper tanker truck.

That didn't happen. After 90 minutes of debate among councilors, taxpayers and firefighters, the ambulance and tanker truck remained on the schedule for 2004.

The committee split 2-2 on both purchases, which left the plan intact. Voting to postpone the purchases were Robert M. Farrar and Nancy Stout voted to buy the vehicles by next year.

Christopher C. Coates was absent for both votes; he's in the chorus of the Keene Lions Club production of "South Pacific," a major charity fund-raiser that opened a three-day run Thursday night.

The combination tanker-pumper truck could carry 1,800 gallons of water, five firefighters and their gear. It would replace a a987 two-man tanker that carries 1,000 gallons, but has little room for equipment.

"Houses are being built where there are no fire hydrants. We've reached a point where a larger tanker is needed," said Keene Fire Chief Bradley B. Payne, citing a half-dozen neighborhoods on Keene's outskirts.

Taxpayers and two councilors didn't dispute the needs, but said the existing vehicles are diesel powered and should last longer than the city's replacement schedule envisions. They said the department can wait at least a year.

Olivo Road resident Pasquale R. DiNardo—a former Pennsylvania firefighter—said the tanker should be replaced, but asked the department to shop for a less-expensive version.

The $115,000 ambulance would replace one of three ambulances. Payne said Keene keeps its ambulances six years, buying one new ambulance every two years. For comparison, Derry keeps its ambulances three years; Exeter and Lebanon keep their ambulances five years. In Bow, ambulances last eight to 10 years, Payne said.

Judith W. Bright, Keene Taxpayers acting chairman, said private ambulance companies, such as DiLuzio Ambulance of Keene, run their ambulances much longer than municipal services do.

Said Farrar: The ambulance to be replaced "has 37,000 miles on it…I don't see any reason under the sun to buy a new ambulance."

Committee Chairman Randy L. Filiault said the city's vehicle-replacement plan may need review, but should not be abandoned without study. He recalled when the city had no such plan and ambulances and fire trucks broke down.

"We're not talking about a dump truck, a and truck or a pickup truck," Filiault said." "We're being penny-wise and pound-foolish by putting this off another year."

————

As Reported by Robert Koch in *Keene Evening Sentinel* February 27th, 2003:

"STORY"

Helping hearts to beat again Defibrillators are becoming commonplace in region

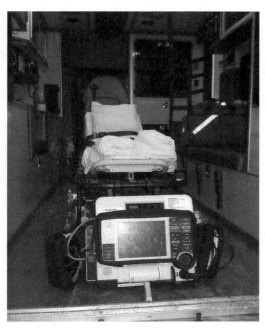

Sixteen years ago, the Keene Lions Club helped raise $10,000 to buy city firefighters their first heart defibrillator.

Keene Fire Capt. Jeffrey W. Morel remembers a heavy, suitcase-size machine that nevertheless did its job; save heart-attack victims by shocking their stopped or irregularly beating hearts back into normal action.

"It was state-of-the-art and we were very fortunate to have it, but now it's like a boat anchor" compared to the compact, automated defibrillators available today, said Morel, the fire department's coordinator for emergency medical services.

Automated defibrillators "are going to be everywhere, which us really exciting, because lay people are going to be saving lives," Morel added.

A Sentinel survey suggests that Morel's prediction is slowly becoming reality, as automated external defibrillators, sometimes called AED's, are popping up in police cruisers, schools, businesses and even general stores in the Monadnock Region. In fact, defibrillators are even being marketed for home use.

In several decades, the life-saving devices have evolved from emergency room novelties to standard equipment for paramedics, firefighters and police. Modern defibrillators walk their users through the heart-shocking process with voice commands, and the increasing availability of the devices can spell the difference between life and death for millions more heart-attack victims.

Lifesaving minutes:

On Jan 9, Keene resident Larry E. Ruest suffered a heart attack at his home on Eastview Road. As paramedics arrived and readied Ruest for the ride to Cheshire Medical Center, his heart stopped. That's when paramedics jolted his heart back into motion with a defibrillator.

If it were not for that defibrillator on that ambulance, my husband would be dead," said his wife, Angie Ruest who is The Sentinel's executive secretary.

Larry Ruest is now recovering, but he easily could have become one of more than 250,000 Americans who die each year from sudden cardiac arrest. Only 5 percent of those stricken survive a full cardiac arrest—8 percent in New Hampshire—according to the American Heart Association.

Cardiac-arrest victims will die in 10 minutes if they can't be revived. In rural New Hampshire, where hospital emergency rooms and even ambulances are often a half-hour distant, that's a short window. Nor are simple cardiopulmonary resuscitation skills frequently enough to restart a stopped heart.

"For every minute that goes by from the point a person collapses, they have a 7 percent to 10 percent less chance of survival," said Nancy S. Pederzini, health initiatives director at the American Heart Association in Manchester. "We'd like to see defibrillation provided in three to five minutes.

Years ago, defibrillators were exclusively for trained hospital staff, who could read complex electrocardiograms and decide whether to shock a patient's failing heart. In the 1980's, automated defibrillators began to emerge, which could monitor heart rhythms and walk users through defibrillation when needed.

At Cheshire Medical Center in Keene, patients who arrive at the emergency room by ambulance are already hooked to the devices.

"That's absolutely good. The quicker you can get a defibrillator to a patient that has had sudden cardiac arrest, the greater their chances of survival are," said Mark T. Parker, Cheshire Medical emergency room director.

Typically, police and firefighters are first to arrive at medical emergencies. The Keene Fire Department has a dozen paramedics, who are trained to operate defibrillators and administer up to 60 drugs.

The department also has 18 intermediate emergency medical technicians, who can start intravenous lines and give some drugs. Even basic emergency technicians are trained to use automated defibrillators, perform CPR and stabilize patients.

Last year, the department answered 2,502 ambulance calls; some were paramedic intercepts, where crews met ambulance crews from surrounding communities. About two dozen calls involved cardiac arrests. In all, firefighters hooked up defibrillators 916 times but shocked only about three dozen patients.

Paramedics often use the devices simply for diagnosis. By evaluating a patient's heartbeat, as seen on a defibrillator's computerized screen, they can decide whether to shock the heart or treat the patient with oxygen, aspirin, morphine or nitroglycerin.

Keene paramedic John Bates steps inside a department ambulance, sets a defibrillator on the patient cot and turns the machine on. The screen lights up ready to display a patient's cardiac rhythms; electrode leads are ready to be attached to a victim's chest.

An automated defibrillator walks users step-by-step through defibrillation with voice prompts such as "connect electrodes," "charging" and "stand clear" to prevent users from being shocked themselves. The device reads heart rhythms and it doesn't allow patients with normal heart rhythms to be shocked.

During a cardiac arrest, a patient's heart stops beating. By contrast, a fibrillating heart beats so rapidly and irregularly that is fails to pump blood through the body. Both conditions can be deadly.

Keene paramedics also have three semiautomatic defibrillators that give them greater control but also require more skill to use. Those devices can spit out a hard copy of a patient's heart rhythm, ranging from normal spikes to the rapid fluctuations of a fibrillating heart. Doctors can later read the tape to better understand the patient's illness.

As Reported by the *Keene Evening Sentinel* March 7th, 2003:

"STORY"

Keene man helps nuclear planning

Stevens Goldsmith of Keene, a retired Keene deputy fire chief, has been hired to help towns in the Vernon, Vt. Area plan their emergency response to an accident at the Vermont Yankee nuclear power plant.

Vermont Emergency Management, an agency of the state public safety department, recently created the position.

Goldsmith said one of his priorities will be bringing local concerns to the attention of state and federal agencies responsible for safety of nuclear plants.

He will also help towns plan for other disasters, such as floods and ice storms.

Goldsmith has more than 20 years of experience in emergency services. He has a four-year degree from the U.S. Fire Administration National Fire Academy, is an emergency services instructor and is a hazardous-materials technician.

———

As Reported by Benjamin Yelle in *Keene Evening Sentinel* March 22nd, 2003:

"STORY"

Emergencies are a way of life

A building fell on Stevens W. Goldsmith on his first day as a Keene firefighter.

He wasn't even on duty February 23, 1975, when the Elm City Grain building on Railroad Street caught fire, but eagerly he joined the firefighting force.

Goldsmith said the way the building was laid out didn't allow for water to reach the source of the fire from outside, so he and Paul Symonds went inside, to run the hoses to the fire's source.

They were in about 200 feet when the building started to collapse around them.

"The whole second floor came down, no crack, no warning, nothing," Goldsmith said.

After about eight minutes trapped under a ceiling beam and surrounded by burning embers, other firefighters were able to free the men.

"We were covered with ash from head to toe," Goldsmith recalled.

He and Symonds escaped serious injury in the disaster, and even went back to the fire after being taken to Cheshire Hospital, now Cheshire Medical Center, to be examined.

"That was my first day on the job. I learned from that," Goldsmith said.

"Next time I'm going run faster," he told Fire Chief Robert N. Guyette, when he was asked about the collapse.

After 30 years in the Keene Fire Department, Goldsmith, 52, left his job as deputy chief in charge of operations Monday to become the local emergency planning one planner for the Vermont office of Emergency Management.

From his office in Brattleboro, he will be responsible for coordinating the evacuation plans of the five Vermont towns within 10 miles of the Vermont Yankee nuclear power plant. He will also be responsible for working other planners in New Hampshire and Massachusetts to evacuation efforts in case there is a disaster at the power plant.

This week, Goldsmith looked back o his time in the Keene department, and forward to his responsibility for keeping thousands of people in three states safe in an emergency.

A lifelong dream:

Goldsmith, who grew up in Keene and now lives in Surry, was inspired to become a firefighter when his 10-year-old cousin was hit by a car and killed while riding her bicycle in the mid-1960's.

At that time, firefighters weren't trained to provide medical aid beyond the most basic care, and interest in the field was minimal, he said. He remembers asking Robert DiLuzio, Sr., owner of DiLuzio Ambulance Inc., why there was so little interest in fire services, and was told "no pay and long hours."

When Goldsmith started, the job paid $6,800 a year for 63-hour work weeks, he said.

Goldsmith began his fire service career as a volunteer firefighter with the Keene auxiliary civil defense, a service that had been set up during World War II and is no longer in operation. He was a member of that organization for roughly two years, until he graduated from Keene High School and enlisted in the Marines in 1969.

Goldsmith was a jet mechanic in during the Vietnam War, than became a helicopter Crew Chief when he returned to the United States. He remained in the Marine Reserves until 1992, and activated for the Persian Gulf during Operation Desert Storm but his unit never made it to the Gulf.

Goldsmith supports the war in Iraq, which started Wednesday. He says Saddam Hussein needs to be deposed. He's aware of the increased possibility of terrorist attacks caused by the war, but says that's a risk the country has to take.

War "is one of those things people don't really understand," he said. "Hitler was a threat in World War II and nobody really understood that until we went to war."

Serving more people:

Goldsmith says he loves the Keene Fire Department, but the opportunity to serve so many more people persuaded him to make the move to Brattleboro.

He's planning for a drill in April, and seeing how the drills affect Keene—a major receiving area for people evacuated from the nuclear plant's emergency zone—will help him plan from the other side of the river.

"I understand Vermont Yankee, I understand how it works," he said.

Goldsmith said more than 40 people applied for the emergency management job, and the interview process was intense.

"I feel pretty pleased I was able to be one of the finalists, not only get the job," he said.

Goldsmith said Brattleboro Fire Chief David Emery urged him to apply for the job. Emery says Goldsmith's experience in Keene, will bring a new approach to emergency planning.

"I don't anticipate any major changes, but I think Steve will bring a fresh eye to evacuation planning," Emery said.

Emery said he's known Goldsmith for years and his dedication and knowledge would be helpful for his department.

He has a great deal of integrity," Emery said.

As the planning director, Goldsmith is responsible for overseeing the evacuation of residents in the Vermont towns of Brattleboro, Dummerston, Guilford, Halifax and Vernon.

He will also work with planners for the New Hampshire towns of Hinsdale, Chesterfield, Richmond, Winchester, and parts of Swanzey; and the Massachusettes towns of Bernardston, Colrain, Gill, Greenfield, Lyden, Northfield and Warwick.

Goldsmith's experience in the military and as a longtime firefighter should help in his new role, he said, adding that the terrorist attacks of September 11, 2001, brought to light many aspects of public safety that hadn't previously been given adequate attention.

One of the most alarming trends Goldsmith has seen, and which he says still hasn't been given enough attention, is terrorists' use of secondary explosives in bombings and arsons.

"It happens quite frequently and you don't hear about it," he said. "It's really become evident after September 11."

"Almost every single metropolitan area" has seen examples of terrorists planting explosive devices designed to go off after emergency personnel respond to a disaster, Goldsmith said.

"That's the whole key of terror—to create a panic in the community," he said, and killing firefighters is one way to achieve that goal.

"September 11 has changed the whole world and changed fire service the way we do business," Goldsmith said.

Now, instead of rushing headlong into a fire or other disaster, firefighters are careful to look for things that might seem out of place at disaster scenes, Goldsmith said.

From horses to helicopters:

"From shift changes to make the firefighters' hours more workable, to a greater emphasis on education—he was one of the first Keene firefighters to earn a degree in fire prevention—Goldsmith has watched the Keene department change with the times.

Medical training is "a major, major change" between firefighters now and those of 30 years ago, Goldsmith said. "The (emergency medical service) is now the life-blood of fire service."

Goldsmith said most of the calls the fire department responds to are for medical emergencies. He said the change in emphasis brought the department from the 20th century to the 21st.

But Goldsmith isn't content to just know about the 20th and 21st centuries; he's writing the history of the Keene Fire Department, dating back to 1750.

"I've always been sort of a history buff," he said.

So far, he's traced documents, reports from fire chiefs and newspaper articles from 1750 to about 1950.

"Thank God for the (Keene Public) library," he said. He said that local historical societies and the city clerk's office have helped with the project.

One of Goldsmith's favorite stories involves a Mr. Fish, who brought one of the fire department's horses when it switched to motor vehicles in the early 1900's. Fish was bringing a load of lumber and milk from Keene to Swanzey when the fire bell sounded. The well-trained horse galloped for the fire station—hauling Fish and his cargo.

"I guess there was wood flying everywhere," Goldsmith chuckled.

Other topics Goldsmith covers are mascots, memorial services for fallen firefighters, major disasters to hit Keene, and the fire department's response.

Goldsmith hoped to finish the book in about a year. He was inspired to write it after reading Keene police Capt. Hal G. Brown's history of the police department.

Goldsmith's other interests include flying and scuba diving, both activities he does for pleasure, but also ways he's helped save lives.

Goldsmith was still in the Marine reserves, stationed on Cape Cod, during the blizzard of 1978. He was part of a helicopter crew that pulled eight people out of the Atlantic Ocean after they were washed away by high winds, rain and snow. He explains, matter-of-factly, that his mission was to fly a helicopter close enough to the ruined homes to see if anyone was in them, and, if they were, to pull them out.

Goldsmith also worked with Brown as a member of the Connecticut Valley Underwater Rescue Team. In his first year in that program, Goldsmith said he helped pull three drowning victims out of lakes and rivers and get them medical attention.

But his love of fighting fires outshines everything else.

Goldsmith was promoted to a captain's rank in 1988. As a captain he was responsible for overseeing firefighters on the scene of a fire. One of his first command operations was a tragic blaze at a High Street apartment building that left four people dead.

"I learned a lot from that fire," he said. "Every officer has to know building construction."

Goldsmith compared that apartment building to a maze. He said some rooms only had one way in and, with the smoke and darkness, finding his way around was nearly impossible.

"It was zero visibility," he recalled, dead serious.

Thermal-imaging cameras have become almost necessary tools for most fire departments, but at the time the technology wasn't widely used. Goldsmith said the cameras probably wouldn't have saved the doomed family, but would've made him and other firefighters safer.

"It would've given us an idea of where to go," he said. "Once you get into a smoke filled room, you don't know what's up and what's down.

While Goldsmith is excited about his new job, the decision to leave the fire department wasn't easy.

"It's sad to leave something you've done for so long," he said.

The Keene Fire Department has been good to Goldsmith, he says. It's even how he met his wife, Laurie, an emergency-room nurse at Cheshire Medical Center. They have three daughters, Lindsay, 11, Courtney, 10, and Jaime, 19, a nursing student at Rivier College in Nashua.

Although Goldsmith will be working on the other side of the Connecticut River, he will continue to live in Surry and said he won't be a stranger at the Keene Fire Department.

"The fire station is my home," he said.

————

Permanent members of the Keene Fire Department as of 2003
Administration

Deputy/Administration
Gary Lamoureux

Chief
Bradley Payne

Deputy/ Operations
Stevens Goldsmith

Dept. Secretary
Susan Reed

Captain/EMT
Gary LaFreniere
Fire Prevention

Captain/EMT-I
Mark Boynton
Training Officer

Captain/EMT-I
Jeffrey Morel
EMS Coordinator

Captain/EMT
John Beckta
Fire Alarm

A Shift

Captain/EMT-I
Arthur Johnson

Lieutenant/EMT-I
Ronald Leslie

Lieutenant/EMT-I
Christopher Cram

Firefighter/EMT
Michael Driscoll

Firefighter/EMT-I
William Greenwood

Firefighter/EMT-P
Kevin Brindle

Firefighter/EMT-I
Ronald Clace

Firefighter/EMT-I
Timothy Read

Permanent members of the Keene Fire Department as of 2003
B Shift

Captain/EMT
Dean Ericson

Lieutenant/EMT-I
Michael Burke

Lieutenant/EMT-P
Stephen McKenna

Firefighter/EMT
Wayne Spofford

Firefighter/EMT
Edwin Hodgdon

Firefighter/EMT-I
Christopher Simino

Firefighter/EMT-I
David Gaillardetz

Firefighter/EMT-I
Jason Martin

Firefighter/EMT-P
Robert Diluzio Jr.

C Shift

Captain/EMT
Alex Matson Jr.

Lieutenant/EMT
Harry Nelson

Lieutenant/EMT-I
Mark Howard

Firefighter/EMT-I
Michael Gianferrari

Firefighter/EMT-I
Michael Abbott

Firefighter/EMT-I
Stephen Boutwell

Firefighter/EMT-I
Eric Mattson

Firefighter/EMT-P
Timothy Clark

Firefighter/EMT-I
William Shea

Permanent members of the Keene Fire Department as of 2003
D Shift

| Captain/EMT-I Scott Taylor | Lieutenant/EMT David Symonds | Lieutenant/EMT-I Jeffrey Chickering | Firefighter/EMT James Dubriske | Firefighter/EMT Ronald Dunn |

Firefighter/EMT-I Brian Shepard
Firefighter/EMT-I John Bates
Firefighter/EMT-I Michael Bailey
Firefighter/EMT-P Karen Fleury

Permanent members of the Keene Fire Department as of 2003

Front row from Left to Right: Call Capt. Robert Diluzio, Randy Beaton, Tim Read, Joe Amato, Bill Greenwood, Brian Shepard, Call Lt. Tim Mason, Ronald Clace. 2nd Row Left to Right: Steve Boutwell, John Bates, Capt. John Beckta, Capt. Gary LaFreniere, Capt. Art Johnson, Capt. Scott Taylor, Deputy Chief Stevens Goldsmith, Chief Bradley Payne, Deputy Chief Gary Lamoureux, Capt. Mike Burke, Capt. Dean Ericson, Capt. Mark Boynton, Dept. Sec. Susan Reed. 3rd Row From Left to Right: Jason Martin, Robert Diluzio Jr., Lt. Mark Howard, Call Lt. Phil Davis Jr., Call Capt. Robert Spicher, Call Lt. Donald Hackler, Call Lt. Chris Batchelaer, Lt. Harry Nelson, Lt. Dave Symonds, Lt. Ron Leslie, Lt. Chris Cram, Lt. Jeff Chickering, Lt. Chris Simino, Jim Dubriske, Bill Shea. Back Row Left to Right: Dan Nowill, Mike Abbott, Dave Garlardetz, Tim Clark, Arron Cooper, Call FF Geoff Davis, Call FF Charlie Konkowski, Call Lt. Mike Blanchard, Call FF Francis Markert, Call FF Hanz Dennie, Chris Staples, Call FF Jim Pearsail, Eric Matson, Ron Dunn, Call FF Randy Pillioult.

Fire Department
City of Keene
New Hampshire

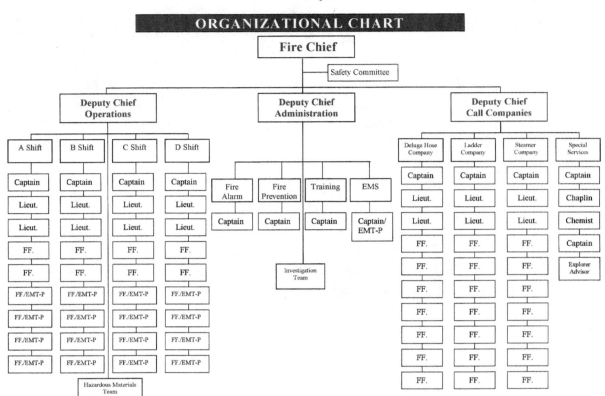

ORGANIZATIONAL CHART

Keene's organizational chart as it appears today.

The Roll of Honor has the list of names of those who have passed away over the years. The wall-mounted board was made by Ronald Amadon. Each year during the Memorial Service each name is read to honor those who have passed.

The wall-mounted bell with firefighter plate was made and donated to the fire department by Stevens Goldsmith. The bell is from Engine 4, the 1959 Ward LaFrance that Stevens Goldsmith owns. The firefighter plate which was used to make posters was found in the back shed on the rafters and was added to the bell wall-mounted board. It is used for attention to call and other special events.

Appendix A
Badges, Helmets, and Patches

BADGES

Keene's first official badges were not worn, but carried. In 1781 the Council and House of Representatives recognized that when Fires break out, "goods inevitably are exposed to plunder, some hardy and Evil minded persons taking advantage of the calamity to steal such goods, whereby the loss such suffers is increased."

An amended Fire Code was deemed necessary because the laws in the state had been found ineffectual.

Provision was made for the election of "any suitable number of Free Holders, persons of approved ability and fidelity, to be denominated Fire Wards." The distinguishing badge of office was a staff five feet long, painted red and headed with a bright brass spire six inches long. These Fire Wards were required, "upon a notice of the breaking out of fire, to take with them the badge of their office and immediately respond to the place where such fire may be, and vigorously exert themselves, and require and demand assistance of any inhabitants of the town, to extinguish and prevent the spreading of such fire and remove goods and effects out of any houses or places endangered thereby." The Fire Wards had power to appoint necessary guards to care for property thus removed.

This the first badge of the Keene Fire Department. It hangs in the Central Fire Station today. It was presented to the Department by Mrs. Hadley P. Muchmore whose husband was the Fire Chief form 1865-1870.

It wasn't until the mid to late 1800s that a badge to be worn on the breast of the uniform was made. It was supposed to be placed over the heart on the left side of the uniform. The Chief's badge displayed above was worn by the Fire Chief in the mid to late 1800s.

In the mid to late 1800s this badge was worn by the members of the Phoenix Hose Company of the Keene Fire Department. This badge shows the Phoenix Hose carriage in the center of the badge.

The Deluge Hose badge was worn during the mid to late 1800s by the members of the Deluge Hose Company. The Deluge Hose wagon is set in the middle of the badge.

The above badge was worn by the Members of the Steamer Hose Company in the mid to late 1800s. This badge shows the steam fire engine in the center of the badge.

This badge was worn by the members of the Steamer Company from the beginning to mid 1900s. This badge is still worn today by members of the company.

This badge was worn by the 2nd Lieutenants in the Call Company in the late 1800s to the mid 1900s.

When Louis A. Nims became Fire Chief, the Chief's Badge was changed to the pictured badge. This gold badge was worn on the dress uniform by each future chief; Eugene B. Riley, 1922-1946; Walter R. Messer, 1946-1971; and Robert N. Guyette, 1971-1992. The badge remains virtually the same, with little changes.

This badge was worn by the Deputy Chiefs of the Keene Fire Department from the 1900s to the present.

This Chaplain's badge is worn by the Fire Department Chaplains. This badge has remained unchanged for decades.

This badge was worn by the Clerk of the Washington Hook and Ladder Company. Each company - Ladder, Deluge, Neptune and Steamers, along with the Permanent Company, wore these. (All had "Clerks" for their Company name.)

This badge was worn by the members of the Washington Hook and Ladder Company. It dates from the late 1800s to mid 1900s.

This badge worn by the members of the Civil Defense was created during WWII. This badge was worn from its start in 1941 until 1987, when the Keene Fire Department Auxiliary was finally retired.

This Photographer's badge was worn by Captain Robert J. Deluzio, who was the Fire Department Photographer in the 1970s and 1980s.

This is the badge worn by the Captains of the Keene Fire Department from the 1900s to present day.

This is the badge worn by the Lieutenants of the Keene Fire Department from the 1900s to present day.

This badge was worn by the fire engine drivers. The badges of these firefighters have not changed much over the years. They have been used from the 1900s to the present, with some minor changes, such as updating the center of the badge.

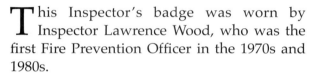

This Inspector's badge was worn by Inspector Lawrence Wood, who was the first Fire Prevention Officer in the 1970s and 1980s.

This is the badge worn by the Steamer Hose Company's Captain since the mid 1900s.

HAT BADGES WORN BY THE KEENE FIRE DEPARTMENT

This hat badge was designed for the driver of the Combination Wagons during the late 1800s and early 1900s.

This hat badge was worn in the early 1900s and was designed when Keene purchased its first motorized fire apparatus.

This badge was designed in the late 1900s and is still worn, to a degree, by today's members of the Keene Fire Department.

This badge was worn by the Assistant Engineer of the Fire Department, today called the Deputy Chief. The Chief's hat badge read "Chief Engineer."

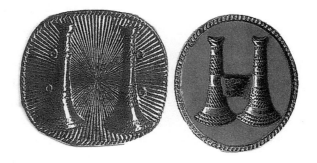

Hat badges for the officers were designed differently. The traditional designation for officers was that of a single bugle. Chief Officers and Captains previously used bugles to shout orders to firefighters during fires. As shown above, a single bugle designated the rank of Lieutenant.

As shown above, two bugles designated the rank of Captain. Prior to the 1990s, the hat badge shown had slightly raised silver bugles for both Lieutenants and Captains. After 1991, the round full color background of red and silver bugles were used on hats.

Chief officers such as Chief Engineer and Assistant Chief Engineer, or Deputy Chief, wore gold bugles. The number of bugles (three bugles for Deputy Chief and five for Chief) designated rank, as did color. After 1991, the background became red with gold bugles, as shown above.

KEENE'S FIRE HELMETS

Keene Fire Department traditionally has followed all fire service trends as far back as the late 1800s, especially in regards to fire helmets. Keene Fire Department first used helmets only as part of the parade uniforms, but the primary purpose of the helmets were to provide protection to the head against the effects of impact during fires.

Aluminum helmets were purchased due to the high cost of leather helmets. It was believed that the aluminum helmets gave a good resistance to impact and penetration but its tendency to deform and its high conductivity of heat and electrical energy were major drawbacks.

Fire helmets of the Chief Engineer and Engineers were painted black with white front pieces and a solid piece of black leather stitched behind it. Firefighter helmets were black leather with a black front. The helmet also had the company that the firefighter belonged to on it. There are no helmets of Keene firefighters from the late 1800s left except for the helmets of the Chief Engineers. Leather helmets lasted about three decades, from the late 1800s to the early 1900s.

The style of leather helmets offered protection from impact and penetration for the firefighters. Also, the brim sheds heated water, melted tar from roofs and embers from fires. Leather was becoming expensive and each helmet was handmade. At this point the department moved away from leather and purchased aluminum helmets.

The chief engineers changed helmets for a short time. This white leather helmet was worn during the change from leather to aluminium helmets.

As the Keene Fire Department moved into the mid 1900s, other styles and materials were used to make fire helmets other than leather and aluminum. Cost was a big factor for most fire departments and the national trend was to develop a material for fire service that was cheap. Other materials that were developed by manufacturers for making fire helmets were fiberglass, polycarbonate, and phenolic helmets.

For more than three decades Keene Fire Department firefighters wore the helmet pictured above.

In the mid 1970s the fire department instituted fire helmets in a more traditional style. Permanent members, along with Call Company firefighters and officers, were made to change their helmets. Chief officer's helmets remained white in color with a black helmet shield, and depiction of rank.

During World War II auxiliary firefighters and air raid watchers wore the style helmet shown above, a metal steel helmet, which was short lived due to its weight and the development of new helmets.

Firefighters and officers of the department were issued black helmets with a black helmet shield. Officers, Captains and Lieutenants both permanent and paid call, had a white strip on the top of the helmet to designate a fire officer. This made it easier to pick them out during fire operations.

In the mid 1980s the department changed from black helmets to yellow helmets with a black helmet shield, which designated the rank of the fire officer. The NFPA (National Fire Protection Association) had a lot to do with the changes in helmets. Safety and accountability became buzzwords throughout the fire service.

Departments across the country ran into the same problems with fire service helmets. For decades departments used leather fire helmets. Leather helmets had good impact and penetration resistance. The seams and reinforcing ridges on the crown of the helmet provided stiffness and, combined with the suspension cap, the helmet resisted the transmission of force and afforded excellent protection to the firefighter. The shift from leather fire helmets to other fire helmets was made because of budget costs. A leather helmet is expensive, as each helmet is handmade. As mentioned before, other material had been developed by manufacturers for fire helmets. Mainly aluminum, fiberglass, polycarbonate, and phenolic helmets.

Keene purchased polycarbonate helmets, but these did not last long due to problems with the helmets. The polycarbonate was popular; it offered high impact and penetration resistance, and was quite inexpensive. But polycarbonate has a low heat resistance. It will begin to soften around 250 degrees to 300 degrees Farenheit. One firefighter in Keene, during a training burn, had his polycarbonate helmet soften and begin to melt.

Keene also changed to fiberglass helmets, which had a good resistance to heat, flame, and chemicals. It is also self-extinguishing. To keep the same level of impact resistance as polycarbonate, the shell of the helmet must be made thicker, thus increasing the weight of the helmet substantially. The style matched the traditional style fire helmets and seemed to be good for the fire service. The helmet 1010 Cairns meet or exceeded the performance requirements of NFPA 1972 (1992 Edition), US-OSHA (NBSIR-1977), Cal OSHA and other known state OSHA requirements.

Fire helmets had the name of the fire fighter on the back of the helmet. As times changed and numbered shirts were given to the fire fighter officers, this number was added to the helmets as well.

The life span of the polycarbonate helmet was about five years (compared to leather's ten), because of its sensitivity to the sun's ultraviolet rays. It is also extremely susceptible to damage from detergents, gasoline and chlorinated hydrocarbons.

Keene followed the NFPA standards and changed its colors: white for Chief Officers, yellow or black designated firefighters, red designated Fire Officers, blue designated EMS. This made designation on the fire ground easier and safer for all emergency scenes throughout the fire service.

In the mid 1990s Keene changed helmets to a new style, N660C Metro, manufactured by Cairns & Brother. The color designation remained the same.

Today Keene firefighters and officers wear either the N660C as shown above, or a leather fire helmet.

KEENE'S FIRE HELMET SHIELDS

Keene Fire Department helmet shields date back to the late 1800s, as shown above. Helmet fronts were stitched with letters cut out of a white piece of leather with a solid piece of black leather stitched behind it. This style of helmet shield is used to this day.

The call firefighters, permanent fire fighters, and officers wore the helmet shield. This was their identification shield for more than three decades.

In the mid 1900s, as Keene changed helmets, the helmet shields changed with them. During World War II the helmet shield was a Civil Defense shield, as shown above. This was for the auxiliary firefighters and air raid watchers.

Figure #1

In the early to mid 1970s, as helmets once again changed, so did the helmet shields. The department moved to a traditional style. The shield was black with a red background behind the white lettering indicating Keene Fire Department as shown in figure #1. Chiefs and officers had the same background with their rank listed, as shown in figures #2 and #3.

Figure #2

Lieutenant's helmet shield with one bugle and a Captain's helmet shield with two bugles side by side.

Figure #3

Chief's helmet shield with five crossed bugles and the Deputy Chiefs will have three crossed bugles.

In the mid 1980s the department changed helmets to conform to the ever-growing NFPA helmet safety requirements. During the late 1980s, Lieutenant Stevens Goldsmith approached Chief Guyette and asked to change the helmet shields from black to white, as shown in figures #4 and #5. Chief Guyette approved the change in 1990 for all officers, both call and permanent. The firefighters retained the same black with red and white letters, and officers white with red background.

Figure #6

Figure #4

Figure #7

In the mid 1990s Chief Pepler changed the fire helmets and also made changes to the helmet shield, as shown in figures #6 and #7.

Figure #5

In 2000, Chief Payne changed the helmet options and the shields, as shown in figures #8 and #9.

Figure #8

Figure #9

KEENE'S UNIFORM PATCHES

It wasn't until the early 1970s that Keene Fire Department had its first uniform patch. Prior to the 1970s, breast badges identified Keene Fire Department members. Then a uniform change occurred. Permanent firefighters wore gray shirts with the words "Keene Fire Department" in red lettering on the back. Chief Guyette changed uniforms during the early 1970s, which brought forth a uniform patch to be worn on both Class A uniforms and work uniforms.

A group of permanent firefighters: Chester Dubriski, Emile DeRosier, Fred Beacchesne and others, presented to Chief Guyette the above patch, which was adopted in 1972.

On June 5th, 1965 the *Keene Evening Sentinel* published the article "Keene NH All American City." Keene became an All American City and the patch above was the first patch worn on uniforms of the Keene Fire Department. The patch was worn for the year that Keene was declared an "All American City." This brought forth the design of the patch, designed and adopted by the department in 1972.

The Keene Fire Department patches would remain the same for more than two decades. It wouldn't be changed until Chief William Pepler asked the department to come up with a new design in 1993. Members of the department designed a new patch, with the complete City Seal and other firefighting symbols. The Chief, department and members accepted the new patch and it is worn today on all uniforms.

Chief Pepler, along with call captain Raymond Hadley, also developed the patch that is worn by the Keene Fire Department Color Guard members during parades, funerals, and special events.

Another patch, which was also developed but never placed on uniforms, was the "Paramedic" patch, designed by Chief Pepler for the new paramedic program of the Keene Fire Department.

Members of the Keene Fire Department also wore two other patches. The first patch below was worn by the Keene Fire Department auxiliary firefighters, which was part of the Civil Defense Program. These members assisted at fires, picked up hose, assisted at the fire station, and later became members of one of the three call companies—Deluge, Ladder, or Steamers. The patch on the bottom, was authorized by Chief Guyette for the Fire Alarm Superintendent Lawrence Thompson to wear on his work uniforms.

The tradition of a "patch" identifying the department is carried on in Keene today and throughout our Nation. The Keene Fire Department has only had two patches throughout its long history to officially identify the department.

Appendix B: Chief Engineers

Nathan Bassett	1847 to 1849
Robert Wilson	1849 to 1850
Joshua Wyman	1951 to 1855
Arba Kidder	1855 to 1856
Daniel Buss	1856 to 1857
George W. Tilden	1857 to 1860
Robert Wilson	1860 to 1861
Joseph P. Wells	1861 to 1863
Francis A. Perry	1863 to 1863
H. P. Muchmore	1863 to 1866
George D. Dort	1866 to 1869
John Humphrey	1869 to 1871
John Proctor	1871 to 1872
Virgil Wright	1872 to 1875
Leonard A. Tuttle	1875 to 1876
Joseph E. Babbitt	1876 to 1878
A. O . Fisk	1878 to 1879
Virgil A. Wright	1879 to 1881
Freeman A. White	1881 to 1882
George D. Wheelock	1882 to 1886
John A. Batchelder	1886 to 1889
Henry H. Haines	1889 to 1891
Joseph E. Griffith (Act.)	1891 to 1892
Oscar P. Applin	1892 to 1895
Jerry P. Wellman	1895 to 1897
John A. Jones	1897 to 1900
Fred W. Towne	1900 to 1906
Louis A. Nims	1906 to 1919
Fred W. Towne	1919 to 1922
Eugene B. Riley - 1st full time chief	1922 to 1946
Walter R. Messer	1946 to 1971
Robert N. Guyette	1971 to 1992
William H. Pepler Jr	1992 to 1999
Bradley B. Payne	1999 to 2003

In 1847 the Board Of Engineers became the official title of the chief and assistants and what is now called Deputies of the Keene Fire Department. The Chief was called the Chief Engineer as is today, but the word Engineer has been left of his title and this position is called Chief.

It's worth to mention at this time on April 12th, 1856 the Board of Engineers adopted the tile Keene Fire Department and is the official title of the department today.

All Chiefs, Officers and Fire Fighters past and present members of the Keene Fire Department

R esearching the names was one of the most difficult tasks due to the writing and quality of the members as listed in historical documentation. It is my hope that this compiler transcribed all members past and present accurately. Please accept my apology if any names are mis-spelled or omitted.

Abbott, Charles
Abbott, E. L.
Abbott, Henry
Abbott, Michael J.
Abbott, Warren
Adams, Benjamin F.
Adams, Charles G.
Adams, Daniel
Adams, David G.
Adams, Grant
Ahern, John
Aiken, E.
Aiken, Enoch
Alber, John L.
Alden, L. P.
Aldrich, Darion M.
Aldrich, George E.
Aldrich, George R.
Aldrich, Harry N.
Aldrich, L. R.
Aldridge, E. R.
Alexander, Foster
Allen, Daniel
Allen, George W.
Allen, Warren P.
Allen, William
Amadon, Frank E.
Amadon, Ronald P.
Amato, Joseph
Ames, Thomas F.

Anderson, Clark E.
Anderson, Deoten
Anderson, Ray
Angell, John B.
Angier, Lilas
Appleton, Aaron
Applin, Elwin H.
Applin, Oscar P.
Ashcroft, H. H.
Atherton, G. A.
Atkins, Homer L.
Atwell, Geo W.
Auger, Edmund J.
Austin, Albert C.
Babbitt, John W.
Babbitt, Joseph
Babbitt, William H.
Bacon, George
Baham, Edward L.
Bahan, Edward J.
Bailey, Michael D.
Baker, George
Baker, H. C.
Baker, J. B.
Balch, Charles A.
Balch, George A.
Balcome, George
Baldvins, Jon O.
Baldwin, James
Baldwin, William

Balek, Charles A.
Balek, George A.
Ball, E. G.
Ball, Edward J.
Ball, Edwin F.
Ball, George M.
Ballon, W. D.
Ballou, Charles E.
Ballou, Charles M.
Ballou, Harry
Ballou, Harvey
Ballou, Lemeon
Bancroft, Amos
Banett, Abijah H.
Barden, Hiram
Barker, David
Barker, Eghar
Barker, Henry H.
Barker, Livi
Barker, Stephen
Barnard, John S.
Barnard, William L.
Barrett, A. H.
Barrett, Henry L.
Barrett, L. J.
Barrett, M. J.
Barrett, Philip A.
Barrett, Thomas
Barrett, William
Barrows, Ernest C.

Barrows, J. N.
Barry, John C.
Bartlett, Nelson
Basco, James
Bassett, Nathan
Bassett, Thomas F.
Batch, George A.
Batchelder, Christopher
Batchelder, John A.
Batchelder, Ken (Rev.)
Batchelor, Russell F.
Batchelor, Russell F., III
Bates, Albert
Bates, John
Beaton, Randy
Beauchesne, Frederick H.
Beauregard, James
Beckta, John M.
Bedard, Andre (Rev.)
Begin, Wilfred E., Sr.
Begin, Wilfred E., Jr.
Beigern, Paul
Belter, G. H.
Bemis, H. A.
Bemis, M. C.
Bemis, O. H.
Bennett, Frank J.
Bennett, John
Bennett, W. A.
Benoit, Paul
Bergeron, Gary E.
Bergeron, Paul J.
Bienvenu, Timothy
Bigelofsd, Fredrick
Bigelow, G. S.
Bignall, Charles P.
Bilio, William
Billings, Heleina
Billings, John A.

Billings, Zebina
Bingham, Donald
Bingham, Frederick S.
Bissell, Charles
Blake, Abel
Blake, C.
Blancato, Bernard N.
Blanchard, A. A.
Blanchard, Donald W.
Blanchard, Michael
Blodget, George
Blodgett, Sylvester
Bobgitt, William H.
Bocchiaro, Paul A.
Bohannon, Lawrence
Bolio, Joseph
Bolis, Theodore
Bolster, Joseph
Bond, Enoch
Bond, John, G.
Bond, William W.
Bond, Ebenezer
Bonenfant, Raymond
Bonston, G. L. (Rev.)
Booster, Joseph
Boriwejz, Charles A.
Borne, Warman
Bouier, Peter
Boulerisse, Norman R.
Bounier, Phillifed
Bourke, Ryane
Boutwell, Stephen R.
Bouviar, L. C.
Bouvier, Charles A.
Bouvier, E.
Bouvier, Joseph
Bouvier, Peter
Bouvier, Phillip
Bouvuae, C. A.

Bowen, Fred A.
Bowen, Herman
Bowier, J. E.
Boyle, William
Boynton, Mark R.
Bradford, A. T.
Bradford, Daniel
Bradford, George E.
Bradford, James H.
Breen, Michael
Brian, Austin O.
Brick, Jerome H.
Brick, Jerome S.
Bridge, Roy E.
Bridgeman, Charles
Briggs, Elijah, Jr.
Briggs, Eliphalet
Briggs, Eliphalet, Jr.
Briggs, Harry C.
Briggs, J. W.
Briggs, William F.
Brindle, Kevin C.
Brine, High
Brinsmoor, J.
Britt, L. W.
Britton, Charles
Britton, Elton P.
Britton, William H.
Brooks, George
Brooks, John
Brooks, Joshua
Brooks, M. H.
Brown, Amasa
Brown, George
Brown, James W.
Brown, Joseph
Brown, Lebanan
Brown, William
Brown, Yho

Bryant, Augustus
Buckminster, D. W.
Buffin, James
Buffum, George B.
Buffum, Samuel
Bufs, Daniel
Bundel, Alvin A.
Bundy, A. A.
Burbank, J. H.
Burchard, T.H.
Burdett, George L.
Burke, Michael A.
Burnham, F. R.
Burns, George W.
Burns, J. C.
Burns, James
Burns, John H.
Burns, Joseph A.
Burr, William
Burrell, Hubbard
Burril, Herbert F.
Burt, Lawrence A.
Bush, Joseph
Butler, C. H.
Butler, L. H.
Butler, L. M.
Butler, Parker
Butterfield, Charles
Button, George D.
Byron, James
Cady, Abel
Caldwell, Clarence F.
Calef, William
Calif, Benjamin B.
Califf, Jonathan
Callahan, Daniel
Callahan, Robert
Campbell, Alan B.
Campbell, Robert A.

Capen, Josiah
Capenter, E. R.
Capron, Curtis W.
Carey, Gilman
Carey, Michael J.
Carney, James
Carpenter, Albert
Carpenter, David
Carpenter, Hashell
Carpenter, O. C.
Carrier, Mark A.
Carrigan, Edward P.
Carrigan, Patrick
Carroll, George
Carroll, Henry
Carroll, J. L.
Carroll, Michael
Carter, Charles
Carter, Elijah
Carter, V.
Casjunter, Caleb
Cass, Lyman O.
Castaw, Alfred J.
Cepelak, Robert J.
Chadwick, Rushford
Chadwick, Samuel
Chafman, Charles W.
Chambeau, Joseph
Chamberlain, Albert
Chamberlain, E. W.
Chamberlain, Sivi
Chamberlin, George
Chandler, William
Chapin, Alba
Chapin, William P.
Chapman, Charles
Chapman, D. D.
Chapman, David W.
Chapman, Frank

Chapman, Sam
Chapman, Wyman
Chase, Alfred
Chase, Ithamar
Chase, John
Chase, R. M.
Chase, Sherman
Chase, Thomas
Cheeney, E.
Chickering, Jeffrey C.
Church, W. K.
Cibb, Samuel
Clace, Ronald E.
Clark, Augustin E.
Clark, David
Clark, Edgar
Clark, Franklin A.
Clark, Henry Clay
Clark, Martin V.B.
Clark, Timothy P.
Clarke, George
Cleary, William C.
Cleveland, Lance
Clough, Henry
Clough, W. R.
Cloutier, Bruce N.
Cloutier, Russell P.
Coates, D. C.
Coates, Stephen
Coffey, Daniel
Coffey, James
Coffey, John
Colburn, George N.
Colburn, H. W.
Colburn, Herman W.
Colburn, W. W.
Coleigh, E. E.
Collier, A. Scott
Collier, Allan O.

Collier, Carl S.
Collier, Neal F.
Collier, Randy
Collins, Michael
Colony, G. J.
Colony, Horatio
Colony, Josiah
Colony, Lewis
Comstock, D. M.
Comstock, S. D.
Conant, Kenneth G.
Cone, James
Cone, Robert L.
Confenter, David
Conley, William
Connell, G. J.
Conner, John
Conway, Patrick
Cook, Lewis
Cooke, Noah
Cooke, Phinchas
Cooke, Phineher
Cooke, R.
Coolidge, A. P.
Coolidge, Vinny
Cooper, Aaron
Cooper, George
Cooper, William H.
Corbit, John
Corey, L.
Cory, Sumner
Cote, Bernard
Cotta, A. R.
Craig, George
Craig, Thomas
Cram, Christopher
Craven, John
Cressey, J. A.
Crosfield, Charles

Crosfield, Min
Crosfield, William
Cross, A. E.
Crossfield, Kendall
Croteau, Robert P.
Crotto, Gregory H.
Crouley, William
Crowell, Bruce B.
Crowell, Felicity
Crowell, Paul E.
Crowell, Robert S.
Crowell, Wayne F.
Crowley, D. J.
Crown, Edward H.
Crozier, Nelson A.
Cuff, Thomas
Cummings, Charles M.
Cummings, Joseph W.
Cummings, L. N.
Cummings, Thomas
Cummings, W. P.
Cummings, William
Curnier, J. S.
Currell, George
Curtis, Linwood H.
Cutting, Franklin H.
Dackey, Joseph
Damon, Elmer R.
Daniels, Ebenezer
Daniels, Eleen
Daniels, Josiah
Darling, Dwight
Darling, G. N.
Darling, H. P.
Darling, S. D.
Darling, W. H.
Daroczi, Laszlo T.
Dart, A. G.
David, William

Davis, Aaron
Davis, Alfred
Davis, Charles
Davis, Edward
Davis, Elias
Davis, Frances
Davis, Frank
Davis, George
Davis, Gordon R.
Davis, Henry
Davis, John L.
Davis, Joseph
Davis, L. B.
Davis, Ostinelli
Davis, Phillip L., Jr.
Davis, Phillip L., Sr.
Davis, Robert E.
Davis, S. B.
Davis, Sherry
Davis, William
Day, Henry
Dayley, T.
Dean, Arthur
Dean, Clarence S.
Dean, H. A.
Dean, H. T.
Dean, Lewis H.
Dee, John
Deern, Arthur
Dengman, Peter
Dennie, Hans
Dennis, Jack
Dennis, John H.
Dennison, John A.
Denny, C. C.
DeRosier, Emile H.
Devgneau, Hector
Devior, Noah
Devoir, Joseph

Dickensen, Abbott
Dickenson, May
Dickerson, George
Dickinson, Abbott W.
Dill, Thomas M.
Dillon, James
DiLuzio, Robert J., Jr.
DiLuzio, Robert J., Sr.
Dinsmoor, Samuel
Dinsmoor, Samuel, Jr.
Dodge, Charles
Domina, Eli
Donavan, Francis R.
Donnall, A. J.
Donovan, Conrad
Donovan, James
Doolittle, Ernest
Door, Henry
Door, Joseph
Doretty, John
Dort, Eli
Dort, George D.
Dort, Gilman O.
Dort, William
Doyle, Jerry
Doyle, John
Drafer, J. A.
Drew, G. T.
Drimell, Marcus M.
Driscoll, D. B.
Driscoll, Francis J., Jr.
Driscoll, Francis J., Sr.
Driscoll, Michael J.
Driscoll, Robert F.
Driscoll, Robert R.
Driscoll, Russell J.
Drummer, John A.
Dubriske, Chester E.
Dubriske, James G.

Dudley, H. O.
Duinell, Marcus M.
Dulton, S. F.
Dunbar, Elijah
Dunbar, John P.
Dunchee, Steve
Dunn, Ronald R.
Dunn, William
Dutton, Ormond
Eames, George H.
Earl, Seymore
Eastabrook, Austin
Eastman, Abel
Eastman, George
Eastman, H.W.
Eaton, O. F.
Eaton, William
Edwards, Edward
Edwards, Thomas M.
Edwards, Willis C.
Elliot, Charles
Elliot, James B.
Elliot, John
Elliot, Samuel B.
Ellis, Ashley E.
Ellis, Calvin
Ellis, David B.
Ellis, Frank
Ellis, George L.
Ellis, I.
Ellis, John E.
Elwin, Applin H.
Emerson, William
Emmerson, Vann
Erickson, Wayne
Ericson, Dean L.
Erwin, George C.
Erwin, J. M.
Estui, L. E.

Esty, George W.
Esty, Jacob
Evans, Harvey W.
Evans, Jeremy
Evans, Nathanial
Every, Reese E., III
Ewards, Eward
Fairbanks, Asa
Fairgreene, C. R., IV
Fajsett, J. P.
Falgel, S. R., Jr.
Farley, Dallas P.
Farnsworth, Arthur
Farnsworth, Henry
Farnsworth, J. H.
Farnsworth, J. M.
Farnum, Henry
Farnum, Newell J.
Farr, Fred M.
Farrar, Edward
Fassett, T. W.
Fastey, John
Faubert, Robert R.
Faulkner, Charles
Faulkner, Francis
Faulkner, Grant
Fay, Oscar H.
Felder, G.
Felps, F. B.
Felt, Luther W.
Fifeld, Richard
Fifield, Sheldon, Jr.
Filt, Arther M.
Fish, A. E.
Fish, Abner
Fish, Albert O.
Fish, George E.
Fisher, G. W.
Fisher, Orlando L.

Fisk, Albert E.

Fisk, Albert O.

Fisk, G. A.

Fisk, Lewwill A.

Fiske, P.

Fitch, Leon M.

Fitzgerald, John B.

Flagg, Francis

Flagg, Gilmore

Flagg, Horace

Flagg, Merrill

Flarney, James G.

Fletcher, Frank

Fletcher, Isaac

Fleury, Karen

Fluton, Oliver

Foley, Dennis J.

Foley, Frank J.

Foley, Joseph

Foley, Timothy

Folley, Daniel J.

Forbes, George

Ford, Joel

Ford, Leonard

Foster, A. C.

Foster, Charlie E.

Foster, Edwin S.

Foster, Fred C.

Foster, Henry S.

Foster, Hosea

Francis, Inserra

Frasier, Augustus S.

French, Jason

French, Orren

French, Stillman

French, Whitecomb

French, William

Frink, Adam

Frink, S. W.

Froitehell, Amos

Frost, Lovin C.

Frost, S. L.

Fruman, Amos H.

Fruman, J. W.

Fuld, E.

Fuller, Eleard

Fred, A. Fuller

Fuller, J. W.

Fuller, Patrick

Fulton, Charles F.

Fyford, Jeremiah

Gaillardetz, David S.

Gale, John W.

Gallagher, James F.

Gallop, Joseph

Gallup, Paul E.

Gardner, Todd

Garfield, Kendall

Garfield, William A.

Gates, Albert C.

Gates, G. W.

Gates, Rufus

Gates, Samuel O.

Gay, Edward

Gearry, John

Gears, E.

Geddes, William H.

Gemmell, Fay (Rev.)

Gernsey, N. G.

Geronler, J. A.

Gerould, Allen

Gerould, Harvey

Gerould, S. A., Jr.

Gerould, Samuel A.

Gianferrari, Michael

Gibson, Stephen E.

Gifield, John

Gilbert, Elwyn E.

Gilbo, H.W.

Gilbo, Lawrence E.

Gillett, C. H.

Gilmore, Charles G.

Glasier, Walter W.

Gleason, Orren L.

Godfrey, Albert

Goldsmith, J. H.

Goldsmith, Stevens W.

Goodhue, George

Gosselin, John

Gould, Frank L.

Gowdy, James M.

Graham, Fred

Graham, George D.

Graves, Albert

Graves, H. P.

Graves, Oliver

Graves, Oliver C.

Gray, Charles

Greeley, Garrett J.

Greely, Harim

Green, Albert W.

Green, Jacob

Green, Thomas,

Greenway, George

Greenwood, Edward, Sr.

Greenwood, George

Greenwood, James

Greenwood, William

Greg, Charles

Griffin, Asa

Griffin, C. A.

Griffin, Frances

Griffith, Albert

Griffith, D. D.

Griffith, Edward L.

Griffith, Henry

Griffith, Irving J.

Griffith, John G.

Griffith, Joseph E.

Grimes, James H.

Grinman, George G.

Grory, Isaac

Grossejean, Annett

Grout, Fred

Grout, Henry

Guillemette, Roland H., Sr.

Guillow, Chester K.

Gupill, Beniah

Guyette, Robert, Jr.

Guyette, Robert N.

Guyette, Samuel J.

Guyette, Wayne F., Jr.

Hackler, Daniel J.

Hackler, David G.

Hackler, Donald

Hadley, A.

Hadley, Ethan, Jr.

Hadley, F. H.

Hadley, Raymond M.

Hadley, Raymond M., Jr.

Hadley, Raymond M., Sr.

Hagar, George

Haines, Henry H.

Hale, Fred

Hale, Samuel W.

Hall, Aaron

Hall, Edward E.

Hall, Elton A.

Hall, Hatch

Hall, Henry

Hall, Howard E.

Hall, Joseph

Hall, O. P.

Hall, Samuel E.

Hall, Timothy

Hamm, Robert C. (Rev.)

Hammond, Frank

Hammond, Harry F.

Hancock, Frank M.

Handerson, Henry L.

Handerson, Phinchus

Hanes, H.H.

Hannaaford, A. B.

Hannifin, Dannil

Hannon, James

Harding, Otis

Hardwood, C. F.

Hardy, Frank

Harkins, John

Harkniss, Albert L.

Harlow, Edward

Harmon, Frank

Harmon, Thomas L.

Harrington, Charles E.

Harrington, N. B.

Harrington, Stephen

Harris, James E.

Harris, Charles

Harris, Charles R.

Harris, George K.

Harris, James

Harris, Winslow

Hart, Henry H.

Hart, M.

Hart, Michael

Hartis, Charles E.

Hartnett, Edward

Hartnett, James

Hartwell, George E.

Harver, Barlow

Harver, James B.

Harvey, Bertrand G.

Harvey, H. W.

Harvey, James

Harvey, James G.

Haskell, Sylvester

Haskin, A.

Haskins, A. A.

Hastings, Emory

Hastings, J. W.

Hastings, Thomas

Hatch, Chauncy A.

Hatch, Dan W.

Hatch, Daniel D.

Hatch, John C.

Hathorn, Daniel E.

Hathorn, H. H.

Haughton, Albert

Haynes, Henry H.

Hays, Patrick

Hayward, Francis E.

Hayward, P. R.

Hayward, Rolph E.

Heaton, Oliver

Heilt, Nichols

Heminway, A. C.

Hemminway, Charlie

Henry, J. M.

Henry, J. W.

Henry, Robert, Jr.

Herls, R. J.

Hermon, Frank

Herriek, Jarib

Higgins, Charles R.

Hill, F. R.

Hill, Fred L.

Hill, Horace

Hill, Richard H.

Hill, William H.

Hills, C. B.

Hills, Joseph, Jr.

Hills, L. N.

Hilt, Nichols

Hitchcock, Albert E.

Hitchcock, R. P.
Hobbs, Albert
Hobson, Allison S.
Hodgdon, Edwin A.
Hodger, A.
Hodgkin, Jason
Hodgkins, A.
Hodgkins, Henry
Hogan, John
Hokanson, Jeffrey
Holbrook, Dan W.
Holbrook, E. L.
Holbrook, Wilder
Holden, Owen
Holden, Thresher
Holdredge, Kevin
Holey, James
Hollbrook, George H.
Holleren, M. A.
Holman, Oliver
Holman, S.
Holmes, George
Holmes, Lewis
Holt, Jedediah,
Holt, Ralph J.
Holton, Augustus W.
Holton, C. F.
Homes, George
Hood, John
Hoods, J. E.
Hooper, William H.
Hope, Helen (Sec.)
Horton, William H.
Hosmere, George W.
Hough, Dan
Houghton, Abel
Houghton, George
Houle, Dennis (Rev.)
Houston, Jarrod

Houston, Michael
Howard, A. E.
Howard, Ambrose W.
Howard, C. F.
Howard, J. N.
Howard, John B.
Howard, Lucian A.
Howard, Mark F.
Howard, S. E.
Howard, Samuel
Howard, William H.
Howas, W. C.
Howe, George F.
Howe, George W.
Howe, Grover
Howes, John H.
Howes, Warren T.
Howey, J. P.
Howland, A. P.
Howland, P.
Howrs, W. C.
Hoyt, James
Hubbard, Albert
Hudson, Walter
Hulett, E. D.
Hunnington, Stephen
Hunt, Elijah
Hunterant, Issac
Huntly, W. H.
Hurt, George L.
Hurt, Jeffrey A.
Huston, G. A.
Hutchins, B. G.
Hutchins, David
Hutchins, Edmund E.
Ingalls, James W.
Ingalls, Joseph
Irwin, Arthur D.
JacQues, Armand R.

Janes, Morman A. (Rev.)
Jardine, Daniel
Jennision, Edward S.
Jerould, T. A.
Jogereth, C. W.
Johnsen, Henry
Johnson, Arthur
Johnson, Barbara B.
Johnson, Carl W.
Johnson, Frank N.
Johnson, Fred A.
Johnson, Harry H., Jr.
Johnson, N. B.
Johnson, Sanford R.
Johnson, Stephen
Jolingtieuse, M. J.
Jolong, Timothy
Jones, Ashley
Jones, E. L.
Jones, Frank A.
Jones, J. L.
Jones, John E.
Jones, John Q.
Jones, Milan
Jones, Richard F.
Jones, Stephen
Joslin, Charles E.
Joslin, Horace
Joslyn, Tilman
Jotman, A. F.
Joyce, Maurice
Joyrith, Collins H.
Kafren, Josiah
Keandall, Stephen
Keating, Edward T.
Keating, Jeremiah J.
Keaton, Oliver
Keats, Almond A.
Kellogg, Chancy W.

Kellogg, James
Kellom, Barry
Kemp, Ezra A.
Kendall, M. M.
Kendall, W. D.
Kendall, Warren
Kennedy, Timothy
Kenney, L. M.
Kent, Herbert J.
Kent, Timothy
Keyer, Elbridge
Keyes, Charles
Keyes, F. N.
Keyes, Herbert H.
Keys, Frank E.
Kiblin, H. O.
Kiblin, Robert L.
Kidden, A.
Kidder, Arba
Kidder, Henry
Kimball, E.
Kimball, John A.
Kimball, Walter
King, John
Kingman, G. H.
Kingsbury, Adam
Kingsbury, Albert
Kingsbury, Aljah
Kingsbury, Chester L.
Kingsbury, John
Kingsbury, Willard
Kingsbury, William E.
Kinsman, G. H.
Kise, E.
Kise, Zebediah
Kitredge, S. G.
Knights, Jerome W.
Knowlton, William
Konkowski, Charles

Koski, Theresa
LaBounty, Edward P.
LaBounty, Edward P., II
Ladd, D. E.
Lafayette, Dean P.
Laffond, Frederick R.
LaFreniere, Gary R.
Lake, Joseph
Lamb, Freeman B.
Lamert, James
Lamoureux, Edward, Jr.
Lamoureux, Gary P.
Lamson, William
Landall, J. L.
Lane, Alexander
Lang, Daniel
Lans, L. M.
Lanzulls, Charles
LaPlante, Jeremy
Larson, Charles
Larson, William, Jr.
Lathrope, George M.
Laudall, Joseph E.
Laurent, Gregoire
Laurent, James W.
Lavage, Fred
Laverett, T.
Lavigne, Ryan
Laweans, Gustane
Lawler, Anno A.
Lawler, Henry
Lawler, T. C.
Lawyer, John W.
Leach, Charles
Leaky, John
Leamer, Frank
Leanard, S. F.
Learry, James
Leathrope, George

Lebouneau, Arron
Lemfill, Charles
Lenant, Ralph M.
Lenny, W. B., II
Leonard, Alvak Smit
Leonard, Byron J.
Leonard, Curtis
Leonard, George
Leonard, H. O.
Lepelok, Robert J.
Lerill, Scott
Leslie, Ronald J.
Levering, W. H.
Levering, W. S.
Lewis, Dean
Lewis, Edwin E.
Liberty, Joseph
Lidd, Sylvester J.
Lileston, C. K
Linch, F.
Linsley, D. W.
Little, Albert I.
Little, Earl W.
Little, Jessie O.
Little, John W.
Little, Prescott M.
Livermore, Charles
Lockheart, Willard, Jr.
Loll, Thomas L.
Long, J.
Looiselle, Max
Lottingham, C. H.
Lottingham, E.
Lovejoy, O.
Low, Roswell
Lundell, John
Lurian, Arthur D.
Lynch, F.
Mabery, George

Macintosh, W. E.

Mack, Patrick

Madden, Thomas

Magee, John

Magroverere, Thomas

Malone, Henry

Malone, Henry B.

Manning, C. R.

Mansfield, E. R.

Mansfield, Walter

Manwaring, William A

Marcey, S.

Marco, A.

Marcy, Herbert

Marechal, John S.

Maren, Columbus A.

Markert, Francis

Marquette, Francis

Marrison, W. J.

Marsh, Henry

Marsh, William,

Marstons, William W.

Martin, Jason A.

Martin, Mitchell

Martin, Moses

Martin, Peter

Martin, Saxton

Martin, William L.

Marvin, Aren

Masiello, Peter J.

Mason, Albert D.

Mason, Charles A.

Mason, Charles W.

Mason, Christopher

Mason, Columbus

Mason, Harry W.

Mason, Robert

Mason, Timothy

Mason, William C.

Matson, Alexander W., III

Matson, Alexander W., Jr.

Matson, Alexander W., Sr.

Matson, Graig

Matson, J.

Matthews, George M.

Mattson, Eric

Mattson, Eric A.

Maxham, J. A.

Maynard, Asu

McBride, John

McCarthy, Gerald, J.

McCurdy, James

McCurely, John M.

McDermontt, Patrick

McGerry, John

McGreene, Thomas

McKenna, Stephen J.

McLure, Manly

McNamara, Ryan

McQuade, Michael

Mead, David

Mead, Elias

Meade, Walter R., Jr.

Meagher, Robert

Mellen, Gilbert

Mells, Joseph

Melure, Hener, S.

Memmesheimer, Hank C.

Merrall, Ira

Merritt, Fred

Merry, Albert S.

Messer, Arthur T.

Messer, Walter

Metcalf, Abijah

Metcalf, Henry

Meury, Edward (Rev.)

Milikin, C.

Millard, David S.

Millard, James R.

Millard, Lockhart, Jr.

Miller, Able

Miller, Chad L.

Miller, Edgar G.

Miller, George M.

Miller, James

Mills, Merton H.

Mimbers, Henry

Mims, Oscar B.

Minor, A. B.

Mioh, John E.

Mitchell, Elijah

Montague, Richard

Montgomery, Raymond

Moon, John

Moon, Nathan

Moore, Mathew

Morand, Cleuphas

Morel, Jeffrey W.

Morisson, Robert

Morris, Joyce

Morse, Fred

Morse, George

Morse, J. H.

Morse, Worcester

Morton, Thomas R.

Muchmore, Hadley

Muchmore, N. P.

Muller, Eric

Mullett, John

Munroe, Edmund

Munsell, Thomas

Murphy, Daniel

Murray, Robert H.

Mymau, Joshua

Namm, James

Nash, David O.

Nash, Harold D.

Neil, Charles
Neil, Michael
Nelson, G. E.
Nelson, Harry E.
Nelson, Samuel
Nessle, John I.
Newcomb, Daniel
Newcomb, Emerson L.
Newcomb, Ruben H.
Newcomb, Seth
Newell, Ralph W., Jr.
Nichol, Chester
Nicholass, Amos
Nichols, Oscar H.
Nims, A. B.
Nims, Frank
Nims, George A.
Nims, Louis A.
Nims, Sannon
Nims, Seth
Noilson, James, Jr.
Nolela, Chad M.
Norman, James A. (Rev.)
Nowak, Brian
Nowill, Dan
Nutt, James
O'Connell, Timothy J.
O'Leary, James
O'Leary, Willie
O'Neil, Bruce W.
O'Neil, Jerry
O'Neil, John
O'Brian, W. D.
O'Brien, Austin
O'Brien, Daniel
O'Brien, Patrick
O'Donnell, Henry
O'Donnell, Michael
O'Dowed, H. J.

O'Grady, Martin
O'Leary, James,
O'Leary, Patrick
Oliver, David
Olmstead, David
Olmstead, William
Olson, Benjamin
O'Neil, Bruce W.
O'Neil, Charles H.
O'Neil, Jerry
O'Neil, John
O'Neil, Patrick
Osborn, Chas N.
Osborn, S. D.
Osgood, David
Osgood, Dauphin W.
Osgood, John
Osir, Corbet
Page, Chase
Page, Lewis
Paige, Calvin
Parish, David
Parker, A. L.
Parker, Clinton
Parker, David H.
Parker, Edward
Parker, Elijah
Parker, F. A.
Parker, Fedrich
Parker, H. H.
Parker, Isaac
Parker, James
Parker, Joel
Parker, Jonas
Parker, Neil (CD)
Parmela, Amos
Partridge, Jasper
Patnaude, Lawrence P.
Patria, Michael E.

Patrick, Gerald
Payne, Bradley B.
Pearsall, James
Pearson, Barry G.
Pearson, Fred
Peasley, Henry
Peck, George N.
Peets, Terry R.
Peets, Wesley J., Jr.
Peirce, Charles
Peirce, H. H.
Pelky, Wallace
Pemberton, Charles
Penock, Edward
Pepler, William H., Jr.
Pepler, William, III
Perhen, Elijah
Perkins, Abe
Perkins, Charles P.
Perley, Asa P.
Perry, Frank
Perry, Fred R.
Perry, Gilbert
Perry, Henry O.
Perry, Justus
Perry, O. R.
Pettergill, Asa
Pettingill, J. R.
Phelps, F. B.
Phelps, Heney A.
Phillips, Francis
Phillips, John
Phillips, John L.
Phillips, John N.
Phillips, Ray
Piche, Rudolph L.
Pick, Walter G.
Pickering, W. A.
Pickett, Laurence M.

Pickett, Thomas

Pierannuzi, Francis

Pierce, C. W.

Pierce, H.

Pierce, H., Jr.

Pierce, Wesley

Pierson, Frank

Pike, Jesse

Piper, George H.

Pishon, Melvin I.

Plaistia, Elisha

Plasted, E.

Plumb, John H.

Plummer, Chesley A.

Pollack, R. L.

Pollock, Bruce W.

Pollock, Richard E.

Pollock, Stephen W., Jr.

Pollock, Stephen W., Sr.

Pond, Albert

Pond, Amos

Pond, Henry

Pool, Edward

Porter, Charles E.

Porter, H. C.

Poster, Herbert

Poter, Charles E.

Potter, George

Powers, James

Powers, John

Powers, Michael

Powers, Reuben

Pratt, E. P.

Pratt, George B.

Pratt, Nelson E.

Pratt, O. D.

Preckle, William H.

Prentiss, E. A.

Prentiss, John

Presler, Christian

Pressey, Eugene E.

Priekle, Henry W.

Prindall, Charles F.

Prindell, John, F.

Prindle, J. F.

Procter, John

Proulx, Robert

Prue, Charles

Prutt, M.

Pugs, B.

Purell, Henry

Putman, J. M.

Putnam, E. L.

Putzel, Justin

Quinlin, Martin

Quinn, Fred

Raffam, Caleb

Ralston, Alexander

Randall, Edwin L.

Randall, G. L.

Randall, Stephen L.

Randall, W. H.

Rawson, Ralf S.

Raymond, G. W.

Raymond, George S.

Raymond, James

Raymond, Joseph W.

Raymond, Robert

Raymond, Robert W.

Raymond, S. W.

Rayn, Robert W.

Read, Timothy I.

Reason, Edward L.

Reason, Henry A.

Reason, James

Reason, Rupert A.

Reed, Michael K.

Reed, Daniel

Reed, Michael

Reed, Susan (Sec.)

Reed, Walter

Reid, Frank M.

Renouf, E. (Rev.)

Reymond, S.

Reynolds, J. W.

Reynolds, Morrin

Reyours, R. C.

Richard, G. H.

Richards, Jarcissus

Richards, William

Richardson, Alfred

Richardson, Frank F.

Richardson, George

Richardson, Josiah S.

Richardson, Justus

Riley, Eugene B.

Riley, James

Riley, Randall D.

Ripley, Barritt

Riscow, S.

Riseng, George

Roach, J. E.

Roach, Harry V.

Roach, Michael

Roberts, John E.

Robertson, George

Robitaille, David

Roche, Carl D.

Roche, F. E.

Roche, Harry N.

Roche, Thomas E.

Rocheleau, Michael

Rocheleau, Whitney

Rogers, Fred M.

Rogers, George A.

Rokes, Peter M.

Rositter, Herbert

Ross, R. C.
Ross, William W.
Rowell, Clark A.
Rowell, Clark F.
Rowell, L. F.
Royal, Walter
Royce, E. A.
Royce, James
Royce, Jonas
Royce, Lafayette
Ruby, George M.
Rudgers, Bryan
Rufrell, David
Rugg, Elias
Rushlow, Paul
Russell, Charles F.
Russell, Fred A.
Russell, George
Russell, Harry J.
Russell, J. W.
Russell, L. A.
Rust, Eugene
Ruwd, T. E.
Safford, Charles
Safford, F. G.
Safford, Ronald W.
Samson, B. G.
Samson, Charles
Sandal, J. E.
Sanders, James
Sanderson, H. William
Sanderson, Laurance
Sawler, Roswell
Sawtell, A. H.
Sawyer, Franklin
Sawyer, George
Scaner, Gardner H.
Seavey, Charles L.
Seavey, Eugene E.

Seavey, James
Selby, Ernest M
Sewall, John
Seward, Edgar
Seymore, L. C.
Sharkey, Fred W.
Shashun, George
Shaw, Elbridge A.
Shea, Patrick
Shea, William J.
Sheehan, J. F.
Sheldon, A. W.
Sheldon, G. W.
Sheller, Joseph
Sheller, Robert
Shelly, G. O.
Shelly, Joseph
Shelly, Nim O.
Shelly, Robert
Shepard, Brian M.
Shepard, George H., Jr.
Shepard, George H., Sr.
Shepard, George W.
Shepardson, Jennifer
Shephers, G. H.
Sheridan, Thomas
Shew, William
Shilly, W. O.
Shinson, William
Shirtiff, Ben
Shutliffe, Minoni
Silverman, Ezra
Simino, Christopher
Simino, Mark
Simonds, Eugene
Simonds, Everett W.
Simonds, George W.
Simpson, John H.
Simpson, Joseph (Rev.)

Skantzee, Norman
Skiff, Frank B.
Skiff, Frank B.
Skyard, George H.
Slown, W. W.
Small, John P.
Smith, Charles
Smith, Earl A.
Smith, Edmund
Smith, George H.
Smith, James
Smith, L. W.
Smith, Luther
Smith, Royal
Smith, Samuel
Smith, Walter E.
Smith, William L.
Smitte, Asa C.
Snow, John, Jr.
Sovering, Warren
Sovering, William
Sowe, R.
Spaneding, F. H.
Spargue, Edward
Sparhawk, Samuel
Spaulding, Alfred
Spaulding, Daniel
Spaulding, Dauphin
Spaulding, Edward
Spaulding, Harry H.
Speague, F. L.
Spencer, J. N.
Spicher, Greg
Spicher, Robert
Splaney, Jeremiah
Spoageu, Fadiah O., Jr.
Spofford, Charlie H.
Spofford, Wayne A.
Spooner, F. E.

Sprague, Adna W.

Sprague, Nathaniel

St. Johns, David

Stalker, Clayton

Stanford, Henry

Stanley, Warren J.

Staples, Christopher

Starkey, George L.

Starkey, Osen

Steams, George A.

Stearns, Charles C.

Stearns, E. S.

Stearns, Frank F.

Stearnski, George A.

Stebbins, Seth J.

Stebbins, Seth L.

Stebbins, Thomas

Steurns, Charles

Stevenson, William

Stewart, Alex H.

Stickls, William F.

Stiles, L. K.

Stinson, William

Stockwell, Edward F.

Stone, Asa J.

Stone, Ashell

Stone, Edwin H.

Stone, Henry A.

Stone, Henry S.

Stone, John T.

Stone, Warren W.

Stowell, J. W.

Stowits, William

Streeter, Frank W.

Streeter, Fred

Stromgren, William P.

Strong, C. D.

Stroover, Fran

Stubbins, J. S.

Sturnes, E. S.

Sturteuvant, George

Sturtevant, I.

Sturtevant, William W.

Stwell, George W.

Sullivan, Daniel

Sullivan, John

Sullivan, Michael J.

Sullivan, T. H. (Rev.)

Superba, Matthew J.

Superba, Thomas

Swan, Nermel

Swan, Reginold C.

Swan, Verne C.

Sway, Howard W

Sweeney, Daniel

Sweeney, Peter

Symonds, B. G.

Symonds, Bertrem

Symonds, Clare H.

Symonds, Cleon

Symonds, David

Symonds, Eugene

Symonds, George C.

Symonds, Paul E., Jr.

Symonds, Paul E., Sr.

Symonds, Robert A., Jr.

Symonds, Robert A., Sr.

Szoc, Paul

Taft, Hardy S.

Taft, Hollis

Tarmenter, J. E.

Tateum, Thomas

Taylor, J. D.

Taylor, John L.

Taylor, Scott B.

Tennes, James H.

Tenney, Henry H.

Tenney, William B.

Terry, J. H.

Thacher, John G.

Thatcher, Albert

Thatcher, Lucius

Thayer, O. H.

Thomas, Fordyce J.

Thompson, Bernard

Thompson, Charles E.

Thompson, H. A.

Thompson, Laurence E.

Thompson, Samuel I.

Thompson, Samuel V.

Thompson, Thomas

Thompson, W. N.

Tidd, Sylvester

Tie, John

Tiffeney, John

Tilden, Abiel S.

Tilden, George

Tilman, Joslyn

Tims, Daniel

Tinns, F. B.

Tinns, Givey G.

Tinsley, D. W.

Tolman, S. E.

Tower, George R.

Towers, Samuel

Town, A. D.

Town, Elton W.

Town, Leyman

Towne, Fred W.

Towne, Lyman A.

Towne, Othelo

Towns, Charles

Towns, Hosea

Towns, J.

Towns, Joshua A.

Towns, Samuel, II

Towns, William

Tracey, Martin
Trash, Augustus S.
Trask, Dan W.
Trask, Norman O.
Trask, Paul S.
Trask, William
Trombley, Herman H.
Trudell, Robert D.
Trumbull, L. W.
Trunk, Daniel
Tubbs, George W.
Tucker, J. S.
Tucker, William G.
Tucker, Y. S.
Tudell, John
Tufts, A. J.
Tufts, George F.
Turcott, John
Turner, Jonathan
Turner, Ralph H.
Tuthill, H. A.
Tuttle, Leonard J.
Twitchell, Amos
Twitchell, George A.
Udcoff, Eli
Underwood, Elmer
Valley, (Rev.)
Vinyarszky, Eden
Vonderhorst, Jarod
Vorce, George I.
Vorce, William H.
Vorse, Irving
Vose, Chad W.
Vose, Charles
Vose, Fred
Vose, George H.
Vose, George W.
Wagner, George
Wagstaff, David M.

Walbank, Thomas B.
Waldman, Steven
Waldo, Charles
Waldo, E. G.
Waling, Maurice G.
Walker, Thomas
Walkin, Alva
Wall, Sam E.
Wallbank, Thomas B.
Ward, Richard W.
Warden, J.
Warder, Josiah
Wardwell, George O.
Wardwell, Leo O.
Warkell, Sylvester
Warner, Anderson
Warner, Herbert
Warner, J. S.
Watson, Benn
Watson, Daniel
Webb, E. A.
Weeks, F. H.
Welch, Alan R.
Wellman, Jerry P.
Wells, James
Wells, Joseph P.
Welly, James
Wennington, J.
Weymouth, Edward
Wheeler, Daniel H.
Wheeler, Fred
Wheeler, Joseph
Wheeler, Salon
Wheeler, Sumner
Wheeler, T. C.
Wheelis, D. H
Wheelock, George A.
Wheelock, Leo D.
Wheelock, Thomas

Whiatker, Marshal
Whilder, Agustis
Whippie, George J.
Whitaker, Marshall
Whitcomb, Albert S.
Whitcomb, C. G.
Whitcomb, George
Whitcomb, J. P.
Whitcomb, Page J.
Whitcomb, William
White, Charles H.
White, Charles A.
White, Freeman A.
White, George
White, James F.
White, S.
Whitham, Elliot
Whitker, Marshall
Whitney, Edward
Whitney, Floyd Sam (CD)
Whitney, G. S.
Whitney, George A.
Whitney, George L.
Whittaker, Joseph W.
Whittemore, Edward
Whittle, A. L.
Whittle, C. L.
Wiber, James
Wilber, Westly
Wilcox, Bruce
Wilder, Abijah, Jr.
Wilder, Allen
Wilder, Azel
Wilder, Benjamin
Wilder, David
Wilder, Silas, Jr.
Wilder, Walter W.
Wilet, Samuel R.
Wiley, A.

Willard, David S.

Willard, Henry

Willard, James R.

Willard, Joseph

Willard, Josiah

Willberg, H. B.

Willett, Dennis

Willey, A. B.

Wilson, Ben

Wilson, George A.

Wilson, James

Wilson, James, Jr.

Wilson, Jordan

Wilson, Norman

Wilson, Robert

Wilson, Samuel

Wilson, Sidney

Wilson, William

Wilson, Wyman

Winch, Charles

Wing, Robert

Winn, Francis E.

Winn, Francis W.

Winn, Thomas

Winn, William T.

Wise, Jebadiah

Witham, C. E.

Witham, Charles

Witham, Elliot

Witman, C. E.

Wolhok, Gene B.

Wolman, Oliver

Wood, H. A.

Wood, John V.

Wood, John W.

Wood, Laurence V.

Wood, Mann

Wood, Matthew

Wood, Zeb

Woodbury, Chelson

Woodbury, Henry

Woodbury, William

Woodcock, A.

Woodcock, Charles

Woods, Charles, P.

Woods, G. W.

Woods, John, L.

Woods, John W.

Woodward, Cyrus

Woodward, E. J.

Woodward, F. Y.

Woodward, G. N.

Woodward, George

Woodward, J.

Woodward, N. L.

Worsely, George R.

Wright, Adolphus

Wright, Albert

Wright, Alvin

Wright, Caleb N.

Wright, Clarence A.

Wright, Douglas E.

Wright, Elijah

Wright, George

Wright, Murray V.

Wright, Salmon

Wright, Virgil A.

Wright, William E.

Wunt, John

Wyman, C.

Wyman, Joshua

Wyman, William

Yarley, Dallas J.

Young, H. O.

Acknowledgments

It gives me great pleasure to thank those who gave me the support, help and resources that made it possible to obtain, coordinate and put into printable format the data for this history book. It is my hope that this book will give future generations a snapshot of how the Keene Fire Department has progressed over the past 250+ years. It brought back a lot of memories for me and I hope it will create some for you.

William Dow, CRM, Records Manager/ Deputy City Clerk, Keene NH

Bill's dedication to the preserving and cataloging of pictures and artifacts belonging to the fire department was instrumental to this book. This provided me with the catalyst to compile and preserve these documents to give you, the reader, a look at some of this important historical documentation.

Anne-Marie Pasquarelli, AAI, Kapiloff Insurance Agency

Anne-Marie worked every week for a decade to scan, crop and insert all photos and assist with formatting of the manuscript. This was a long, tedious project. Without her help this project would have taken much longer than just one decade to complete.

Nancy M. Driscoll, Typist

Nancy assisted in typing many of the stories that dated from the years 1964 to 2003. This gave me the opportunity to continue to research as the typing progressed.

Staff of Peter E. Randall Publisher

For their support, guidance and suggestions to ensure the quality of the final product.

Ashley Correia, Peter E. Randall Publisher

Ashley spent many hours finalizing the formatting of the manuscript, which helped prepare it for the designer.

Historical Society of Cheshire County Alan Rumrill, Executive Director

Alan assisted by providing pictures from their collection, ensuring that the best photos were used for clarity and that they accurately represented the specific era in history.

Keene Evening Sentinel

For printing the news, stories and photos of Keene, NH from 1799 to present, making all of this research possible.

Keene Public Library

For the use of the facility, staff, and for the resources that made it possible to obtain much of the material.

Michael Kapiloff, President, Kapiloff Insurance Agency, Inc.

For the donation of resources at the office used to compile the material. The research and development of this book took a decade to complete and Michael helped provide the resources necessary to make this book a reality.

About the Author

Stevens W. Goldsmith, "Goldie" as he is known by many, is a retired Deputy Fire Chief for the city of Keene.

Stevens was born and raised in Keene, New Hampshire. He attended Keene schools and graduated from Keene High School, after which he entered the United States Marine Corps.

Stevens also found his calling as a firefighter. Interestingly enough, his first day on the job with the Keene Fire Department was almost his last. Stevens, along with fellow firefighter Paul Symonds, was responding to a call at Elm City Grain when the roof collapsed. Both men were trapped for several minutes in the burning debris before being pulled out and taken to the Cheshire County Hospital by ambulance.

As a Keene firefighter, Stevens Goldsmith made his way through the ranks, eventually achieving the position of Deputy Chief, Operations. His happiest times were serving as Operations Fire Captain, but even happy times come with some sadness. As a young Captain, one of his first fires was the loss of a family of four at 88 High Street. Losing not only one, but four people, provided young Deputy Chief Goldsmith with a learning experience that all the textbooks in the world could not convey. It also lent him a certain purpose when he responded to every fire thereafter.

Stevens had several highlights in his exemplary career as a public servant to Keene. He helped to implement the fire prevention program that granted Keene national recognition as it became a test center for the Learn Not To Burn Program. Stevens was also instrumental in changing the helmet shield of officers to the color white, and also changed hose loads from "Accordion A" to "Flat Loads." Deputy Chief Goldsmith, along with State Fire Marshall Donald Bliss, was interviewed for an NBC Dateline show as an advocate for a "bring safety" campaign in which both men talked about clothes dryer fires (a common cause of household fires) and how to prevent them.

Deputy Chief Goldsmith was the first Keene firefighter to graduate from University with an Associate's Degree in Science and the third graduate for the KFD to graduate from the National Fire Academy Course which is a four-year program earning him the title of Executive Fire Officer. He was also the first Keene firefighter to be trained as a SCUBA diver for the emerging rescue team (later known as the Connecticut River Valley Rescue Team). A few of his qualifications include: United States Department Course; Certified Instructor, Weapons of Mass Destruction in Biological Chemical Incidents; Department of Justice Hazardous Materials Technician; Emergency Medical Technician (EMT); Company Officer I, II and Firefighter I, II, III.

His military career spanned twenty-one years. He served four years active duty and seventeen years with the United States Marine Corps Reserve out of South Weymouth, Massachusetts Naval Air Station.

He completed "A Schools" during his four years of active service with the United States Marine Corps (1969-1973), which was during the Vietnam conflict. After 1973 Stevens was assigned to HML-771, a Marine Helicopter Squadron, as a Helo-Crew Chief. He received his wings crewing an UH-34 and was later assigned to an UH-1E which flew missions during the storm of 1978, serving as a rescue unit along the cape of Massachusetts.

In 1980, after completing college at New Hampshire Vo-Tec, he was assigned to a Marine Attack Squadron, VMA-322, out of South Weymouth, Massachusetts. While serving both active duty and reserve M.Sgt., Stevens was an instructor in Water Survival and CPR for pilots and crews assigned to the Naval Air Station in South Weymouth. He was assigned Line Chief, and after graduating from Aviation Physiology, flew back seat in the T-A4. In 1992, after Desert Storm, M.Sgt. Stevens Goldsmith retired from the United States Marine Corps with the decommissioning of VMA-322.